T0310784

Concepts, Technologies, Challenges, and the Future of Web 3

Pooja Lekhi
University Canada West, Canada

Guneet Kaur
University of Stirling, UK & Cointelegraph, USA

A volume in the Advances in Web Technologies and Engineering (AWTE) Book Series

Published in the United States of America by
    IGI Global
    Engineering Science Reference (an imprint of IGI Global)
    701 E. Chocolate Avenue
    Hershey PA, USA 17033
    Tel: 717-533-8845
    Fax: 717-533-8661
    E-mail: cust@igi-global.com
    Web site: http://www.igi-global.com

Copyright © 2023 by IGI Global. All rights reserved. No part of this publication may be reproduced, stored or distributed in any form or by any means, electronic or mechanical, including photocopying, without written permission from the publisher. Product or company names used in this set are for identification purposes only. Inclusion of the names of the products or companies does not indicate a claim of ownership by IGI Global of the trademark or registered trademark.

                        Library of Congress Cataloging-in-Publication Data

Names: Lekhi, Pooja, 1990- editor. | Kaur, Guneet, 1994- editor.
Title: Concepts, technologies, challenges, and the future of Web3 / edited
  by Pooja Lekhi, Guneet Kaur.
Description: Hershey, PA : Engineering Science Reference, [2023] | Includes
  bibliographical references and index. | Summary: ""The core building
  blocks of Web3: Concepts, Technologies, Challenges, Use-cases, and The
  Future" will explore the subject area of Web3, which refers to the third
  generation of the World Wide Web. Web3 is a decentralized internet
  architecture that uses blockchain technology, smart contracts, and other
  decentralized technologies to create a more secure and transparent
  internet"-- Provided by publisher.
Identifiers: LCCN 2023023852 (print) | LCCN 2023023853 (ebook) | ISBN
  9781668499191 (hardcover) | ISBN 9781668499207 (ebook)
Subjects: LCSH: Blockchains (Databases) | Metaverse. | World Wide
  Web--Technological innovations.
Classification: LCC QA76.9.B56 C666 2023 (print) | LCC QA76.9.B56 (ebook)
  | DDC 025.042--dc23/eng/20230725
LC record available at https://lccn.loc.gov/2023023852
LC ebook record available at https://lccn.loc.gov/2023023853

This book is published in the IGI Global book series Advances in Web Technologies and Engineering (AWTE) (ISSN: 2328-2762; eISSN: 2328-2754)

British Cataloguing in Publication Data
A Cataloguing in Publication record for this book is available from the British Library.

All work contributed to this book is new, previously-unpublished material. The views expressed in this book are those of the authors, but not necessarily of the publisher.

For electronic access to this publication, please contact: eresources@igi-global.com.

Advances in Web Technologies and Engineering (AWTE) Book Series

Ghazi I. Alkhatib
The Hashemite University, Jordan
David C. Rine
George Mason University, USA

ISSN:2328-2762
EISSN:2328-2754

MISSION

The **Advances in Web Technologies and Engineering (AWTE) Book Series** aims to provide a platform for research in the area of Information Technology (IT) concepts, tools, methodologies, and ethnography, in the contexts of global communication systems and Web engineered applications. Organizations are continuously overwhelmed by a variety of new information technologies, many are Web based. These new technologies are capitalizing on the widespread use of network and communication technologies for seamless integration of various issues in information and knowledge sharing within and among organizations. This emphasis on integrated approaches is unique to this book series and dictates cross platform and multidisciplinary strategy to research and practice.

The **Advances in Web Technologies and Engineering (AWTE) Book Series** seeks to create a stage where comprehensive publications are distributed for the objective of bettering and expanding the field of web systems, knowledge capture, and communication technologies. The series will provide researchers and practitioners with solutions for improving how technology is utilized for the purpose of a growing awareness of the importance of web applications and engineering.

COVERAGE

- Case studies validating Web-based IT solutions
- IT education and training
- Security, integrity, privacy, and policy issues
- Data and knowledge validation and verification
- Quality of service and service level agreement issues among integrated systems
- Web systems engineering design
- Software agent-based applications
- Mobile, location-aware, and ubiquitous computing
- Knowledge structure, classification, and search algorithms or engines
- Integrated user profile, provisioning, and context-based processing

IGI Global is currently accepting manuscripts for publication within this series. To submit a proposal for a volume in this series, please contact our Acquisition Editors at Acquisitions@igi-global.com or visit: http://www.igi-global.com/publish/.

The Advances in Web Technologies and Engineering (AWTE) Book Series (ISSN 2328-2762) is published by IGI Global, 701 E. Chocolate Avenue, Hershey, PA 17033-1240, USA, www.igi-global.com. This series is composed of titles available for purchase individually; each title is edited to be contextually exclusive from any other title within the series. For pricing and ordering information please visit http://www.igi-global.com/book-series/advances-web-technologies-engineering/37158. Postmaster: Send all address changes to above address. Copyright © 2023 IGI Global. All rights, including translation in other languages reserved by the publisher. No part of this series may be reproduced or used in any form or by any means – graphics, electronic, or mechanical, including photocopying, recording, taping, or information and retrieval systems – without written permission from the publisher, except for non commercial, educational use, including classroom teaching purposes. The views expressed in this series are those of the authors, but not necessarily of IGI Global.

Titles in this Series

For a list of additional titles in this series, please visit: www.igi-global.com/book-series

Perspectives on Social Welfare Applications' Optimization and Enhanced Computer Applications
Ponnusamy Sivaram (Department of Artificial Intelligence, G.H. Raisoni College of Engineering, Nagpur, India)
S. Senthilkumar (University College of Engineering, BIT Campus, Anna University, Tiruchirappalli, India) Lipika
Gupta (Department of Electronics and Communication Engineering, Chitkara University Institute of Engineering
and Technology, Chitkara University, India) and Nelligere S. Lokesh (Department of CSE-AIML, AMC Engineering College, Bengaluru, India)
Engineering Science Reference • © 2023 • 336pp • H/C (ISBN: 9781668483060) • US $270.00

Internet of Behaviors Implementation in Organizational Contexts
Luísa Cagica Carvalho (Instituto Politécnico de Setúbal, Portugal) Clara Silveira (Polytechnic Institute of Guarda,
Portugal) Leonilde Reis (Instituto Politecnico de Setubal, Portugal) and Nelson Russo (Universidade Aberta, Portugal)
Engineering Science Reference • © 2023 • 320pp • H/C (ISBN: 9781668490396) • US $270.00

Advancements in the New World of Web 3 A Look Toward the Decentralized Future
Jane Thomason (UCL London Blockchain Centre, UK) and Elizabeth Ivwurie (British Blockchain and Frontier
Technology Association, UK)
Engineering Science Reference • © 2023 • 323pp • H/C (ISBN: 9781668466582) • US $240.00

Supporting Technologies and the Impact of Blockchain on Organizations and Society
Luís Ferreira (Polytechnic Institute of Cávado and Ave, Portugal) Miguel Rosado Cruz (Polytechnic Institute of
Viana do Castelo, Portugal) Estrela Ferreira Cruz (Polytechnic Institute of Viana do Castelo, Portugal) Helder
Quintela (Polytechnic Institute of Cavado and Ave, Portugal) and Manuela Cruz Cunha (Polytechnic Institute of
Cavado and Ave, Portugal)
Engineering Science Reference • © 2023 • 310pp • H/C (ISBN: 9781668457474) • US $270.00

Architectural Framework for Web Development and Micro Distributed Applications
Guillermo Rodriguez (QuantiLogic, USA)
Engineering Science Reference • © 2023 • 268pp • H/C (ISBN: 9781668448496) • US $250.00

Trends, Applications, and Challenges of Chatbot Technology
Mohammad Amin Kuhail (Zayed University, UAE) Bayan Abu Shawar (Al-Ain University, UAE) and Rawad
Hammad (University of East London, UK)
Engineering Science Reference • © 2023 • 373pp • H/C (ISBN: 9781668462348) • US $270.00

701 East Chocolate Avenue, Hershey, PA 17033, USA
Tel: 717-533-8845 x100 • Fax: 717-533-8661
E-Mail: cust@igi-global.com • www.igi-global.com

Table of Contents

Detailed Table of Contents

This chapter delves into the core building blocks of Web3, the transformative phase of the internet characterized by decentralized and user-centric digital ecosystems. It explores the ethos of Web3, emphasizing openness, transparency, trustlessness, and user empowerment. The chapter examines blockchain technology for secure transactions, smart contracts revolutionizing agreements, and cryptocurrencies facilitating peer-to-peer value transfer. It discusses decentralized finance (DeFi) as a transformative building block and explores decentralized applications (DApps) and non-fungible tokens (NFTs) for creating user-centric platforms. The importance of interoperability along with governance mechanisms like decentralized autonomous organizations (DAOs) is highlighted. The chapter concludes by envisioning the interconnectedness between Web3 and the metaverse, where virtual and physical realities merge. Overall, it provides a comprehensive overview of Web3's emergence and its transformative impact on decentralization, transparency, and user empowerment.

The emergence of Web 3.0, or the decentralized web, has the potential to transform the finance industry. Web 3.0 introduces new technologies such as blockchain, decentralized apps, and smart contracts that enable secure, transparent, and decentralized financial transactions. This can reduce the need for intermediaries, decrease transaction costs, and enhance the speed and efficiency of financial processes. Additionally, Web 3.0 allows for the creation of new financial products and services that were previously impossible, such as decentralized exchanges, NFTs, peer-to-peer lending platforms, and decentralized autonomous organizations. These innovations could democratize access to financial services and provide new opportunities for individuals and businesses alike. However, Web 3.0 also poses challenges for regulators and financial institutions in terms of risk management, compliance, and adapting to new business models.

Chapter 3

Babita Jha, CHRIST University (Deemed), India
Pratibha Giri, CHRIST University (Deemed), India
Deepak Jha, CHRIST University (Deemed), India
Debora Dhanya, CHRIST University (Deemed), India

Web3 is a ground-breaking invention that has the ability to address the shortcomings of web1 and web2. The industry witnessing its major impact is the finance sector. A wave of innovation in traditional finance has been inspired by the introduction of Web3. It is also referred to as the decentralised web and is a developing movement that is upending conventional finance by providing a more open, safe, and decentralised substitute. Traditional banking should work to adopt the features that Web3 offers, including stability, scalability, interoperability, security, performance, extensibility, management, and openness. In order for TradFi to maintain its relevance and expertise in the face of the widespread adoption of digital financial modes, it is now necessary to embrace several Web3 capabilities. Keeping into consideration the relevance and importance of Web3 in finance, this chapter will basically focus on analysing the key features and characteristics of Web3 in comparison to traditional finance.

Chapter 4

Tanuj Surve, University of California, Berkeley, USA
Risha Khandelwal, JECRC University, India

This chapter explores the evolution of cryptography in blockchain technology, studying its significance, challenges, and implications. It analyzes the various cryptographic algorithms employed in blockchain systems, emphasizing their significance in ensuring transaction security and anonymity. The chapter looks at the challenges of using cryptography in blockchain, such as scalability, key management, and the arrival of quantum computing. It also looks at how cryptography has influenced the emergence of cryptocurrencies and smart contracts. It also examines current cryptographic trends and their possible impact on blockchain security, highlighting the importance of using best practices while implementing cryptography in blockchain systems. Overall, this chapter presents a detailed review of the critical role that cryptography plays in maintaining blockchain technology's integrity, privacy, and trustworthiness.

Chapter 5

S M Nazmuz Sakib, International MBA Institute, School of Business and Trade, Dhaka
International University, Bangladesh

This chapter explores the intersection of finance, art, and marketing in the new frontier of digital assets, specifically focusing on cryptocurrencies, NFTs, and the metaverse. The authors analyze the potential impact of these innovative technologies on traditional financial systems, art markets, and advertising strategies. Through a comprehensive examination of the concepts of blockchain, virtual reality, and decentralization, this chapter aims to provide insight into how these emerging digital assets can reshape the way people perceive and interact with financial, artistic, and marketing landscapes.

This chapter delves into the development of decentralized governance models for Web 3 ecosystems. It analyzes the shortcomings of traditional governance models and how decentralized models can overcome them. The chapter then investigates several decentralized governance models, such as reputation-based systems, liquid democracy, and decentralized autonomous organizations (DAOs), as well as their benefits and drawbacks. The challenges associated with establishing decentralized governance models are also explored. Lastly, the chapter explores potential future advancements as well as best practices for creating and implementing decentralized governance models in Web 3 ecosystems. All in all, the importance of decentralized governance models in encouraging openness, participation, and accountability in Web 3 ecosystems is highlighted in this chapter.

Chapter 7

In this chapter, the authors give a theoretical overview of the landscape of decentralized autonomous organizations (DAOs) as the native organizational structure of Web 3. The authors place this new formation in the existing theoretical framework of transaction cost economics and new institutional economics analyzing their governance from economic and legal perspectives. They argue that DAOs are so-called hybrid organizations, which embrace features from the free market and from hierarchical organizations. DAOs show characteristics of hybrids such as pooling resources, coordinating operations by contracts and facing competition in their coordination. However, their changing nature imposes challenges in their identification.

Chapter 8

This chapter delves into the burgeoning world of smart contracts and their critical role in powering decentralized autonomous organizations (DAOs). Beginning with an exploration of the logical foundations of smart contracts, it underscores the parallels between smart contract creation and traditional contract formulation, with a keen emphasis on the concept of conditional execution. It further elucidates the integral role of smart contracts in underpinning DAOs, illuminating how these automated, transparent, and immutable constructs facilitate the decentralization and autonomy of such organizations. A rigorous examination of the complex interplay between technology, law, and economy in DAO operations is also undertaken. The chapter additionally navigates the challenging regulatory landscape, drawing on international legal frameworks and proposed regulations. Throughout, it maintains a balanced perspective on the transformative potential of smart contracts and DAOs in reshaping societal structures, alongside the profound challenges their implementation presents.

Chapter 9

Airi Helen Schnauder, Frankfurt School of Finance and Management, Germany

The landscape of work is undergoing significant changes, and the advent of Web 3 technologies is poised to accelerate this transformation. The gig economy, which emphasizes short-term contracts and freelance work, has been subject to criticism for its lack of job security, limited worker protections, and heightened competition. However, the emergence of Web 3 technologies and decentralized autonomous organizations (DAOs) offers a potential solution to these problems, by providing greater worker autonomy, transparency, and democratic decision-making. DAOs can help to give workers greater control over their working environment, as well as offering them greater job security. These technologies can also create new opportunities for workers to work remotely and receive payment more quickly than traditional methods. This chapter aims to examine the potential opportunities and obstacles presented by Web 3 and DAOs for the future of work.

Chapter 10

Sasha Shilina, Lomonosov Moscow State University, Russia

This chapter explores the potential of the novel Web 3 phenomenon – decentralized social networks – to address the growing concerns over privacy, censorship, and user control on centralized social media platforms. Offering an alternative to traditional social media, decentralized social platforms utilize distributed ledger technologies like blockchain where data is stored on multiple nodes and controlled by the users, rather than a central authority. Such systems are designed to enable trust and transparency in online interactions, provide the ability to communicate without censorship or interference, and empower users with greater control over their personal data. This chapter discusses the benefits and challenges of blockchain-based social networks, as well as existing initiatives working towards a more decentralized, democratic, and user-centric model of social networking.

Chapter 11

Shailey Singh, BUK technology, USA & Symbiosis International University (Deemed), India
Himanshu Sisodia, GroCurv.com, India & University of Stirling, UK & SSBM Geneva, Switzerland

The term 'metaverse,' was first coined in Neal Stephenson's 1992 novel "Snow Crash," and has since been used to describe various types of virtual and augmented reality experiences. . The metaverse holds varying interpretations for different individuals. From its origins in science fiction literature to its recent rise to prominence in popular culture and the technology industry, the metaverse has captured the imagination of many. For some, it represents a virtual arena for socializing with friends, while others perceive it as a potential commercial arena for businesses and their clients. This chapter explores the concept of metaverse and its core building blocks. The chapter has three major sections: the first deals with an understanding of the emergence and concept of metaverse with a focus on virtual worlds, the second presents insight into the economy and commercial value generation by this new meta-era, and the third delves into the techniques and tools that enable the metaverse.

Non-fungible tokens (NFTs) revolutionize digital property rights and the representation of value. NFTs provide various digital assets with transparency, immutability, and traceability by leveraging blockchain technology and smart contracts. NFTs represent tangible assets digitally, bridging the gap between the physical and digital worlds. Luxury brands such as BMW, Balenciaga, Dolce & Gabbana, Louis Vuitton, and Gucci use NFTs in the metaverse to facilitate distinct brand experiences and expression. NFTs authenticate digital identities and property in virtual environments, thereby promoting self-expression and social interactions. They establish a new economic paradigm, facilitating the exchange of value across domains and the preservation of intellectual property. Scalability, sustainability, and legal issues present themselves, necessitating solutions such as layer-2 scaling and copyright protection. It is essential for platforms, creators, and regulators to collaborate in order to establish standards and frameworks.

Chapter 13

Transformative discoveries are available across several disciplines because of the convergence of integrated geospatial information management with the Metaverse. Through the study of geospatial data, integrated geospatial information management (GIM) offers useful insights that can support emergency response, transportation, and urban planning. Immersive encounters, virtual travel, brand activation, cultural preservation, education, healthcare, and entertainment can be possible by the metaverse. The Metaverse's integration of GIM can improves visualization, teamwork, decision-making, and data sharing. However, issues like interoperability, data accuracy, and data privacy require special consideration. Accepting the potential of GIM in the metaverse can opens doors for creative developments across many industries, promoting societal improvement and improving user experiences in virtual settings.

Chapter 14

This chapter explores the emerging trends in the web-based XR (Extended Reality) technology, which is expected to shape the next generation of the web. XR refers to the spectrum of technologies that extend the reality of the physical world by integrating virtual and augmented reality elements. The chapter discusses how web-based XR experiences can engage our senses by creating immersive and interactive environments that go beyond the traditional 2D screen. The authors argue that the current web technology stack is evolving to support more powerful and seamless XR experiences that can be accessed through standard web browsers. The chapter also examines the challenges and opportunities that arise from the integration of XR technology with the web, including issues related to privacy, security, and accessibility. Overall, this book chapter provides a comprehensive overview of the potential of web-based XR technology and its impact on the future of the web.

Chapter 15

    Kaveri Banerjee, Department of CSE, SOET, Adamas University, Kolkata, India & Nopany
        Institute of Management Studies, Kolkata, India
    Sajal Saha, Department of CSE, SOET, Adamas University, Kolkata, India

Smart contracts are altering traditional industries and business processes. Smart contracts, which are entrenched in blockchains, allow the contractual requirements of a contract to be enforced automatically without the participation of a trustworthy third party. As a significance, smart contracts can minimise administration and service costs, improve business process efficiency, and reduce risks. Although smart contracts have the potential to spark a new innovation wave in corporate operations, they face a number of complications. This chapter offers an overview of smart contracts. This chapter provides an overview of smart contracts. The authors initiate by discussing blockchains as well as smart contracts. The problems of smart contracts are then discussed, in addition to contemporary technological breakthroughs. In addition, the authors assess common smart contract platforms also to provide a classification of smart contract applications, together with some exemplary instances.

Chapter 16

    Senthil Kumar Arumugam, CHRIST University (Deemed), India
    Amit Kumar Tyagi, Department of Fashion Technology, National Institute of Fashion
        Technology, New Delhi, India

Gamification has become a popular approach to engage employees, customers, and other stakeholders in various industries. With the advent of Industry 5.0 and Society 5.0, the use of gamification is expected to increase, as companies and organizations look for innovative ways to enhance productivity, creativity, and collaboration. Industry 5.0 is the next phase of industrial development, characterized by the integration of advanced technologies, such as AI, IoT, and robotics, with human skills and creativity. Society 5.0, on the other hand, refers to a human-centered society that leverages technology to create solutions for social problems. This chapter explores the potential of gamification in the context of Industry 5.0 and Society 5.0. It discusses the various applications of gamification, including training, education, marketing, and sustainability. It also examines the benefits of gamification, such as increased engagement, motivation, and collaboration.

Chapter 17

    Moumita Sarkar, Brainware University, India
    Sandip Roy, JIS University, India
    Rajesh Bose, JIS University, India

The continuous development of interconnected devices is reconstructing livelihood and with the emergence of advanced technology yields growth in the usage of IoT devices. Though it is revolutionary and brings convenience, it faces different security challenges. The transition from traditional to smart in varieties of sectors makes the use of IoT technologies to become an integral part of lives which obviously requires a protection shield that can be offered by Blockchain. Blockchain's protected decentralization overcomes different hazards the IoT structure is facing. In this chapter, the authors have represented a detailed study on IoT, its layer and applications, a comparative analysis of different security threats, how an association with blockchain would mitigate different shortcomings of present IoT architecture, and the issues that exist in Blockchain-associated IoT.

Chapter 18

SzuTung Chen, University of Glasgow, UK

As customer demand and regulations drive the coffee industry towards greater traceability and sustainability, coffee farmers in producing countries continue to face challenges in capturing the intangible value-added in their products. This chapter examines the implementation of blockchain technology to address economic and social challenges faced by producers in the coffee industry. The findings demonstrate that blockchain implementation holds promise in reducing information asymmetry in the supply chain, establishing stronger customer-farmer connections, and generating various economic and social benefits for coffee farmers. However, blockchain-enabled third-party verification remains relatively uncommon in current practice. Several challenges must be effectively addressed to realize the full potential of blockchain and foster a more transparent, equitable, and sustainable coffee supply chain.

Chapter 19

Ratnakar Mann, University Canada West, Canada

Web 3.0 has revolutionized the internet with its salient features of decentralization, trustful and permissionless, artificial intelligence and machine learning, connectivity, and ubiquity. Although the idea of Web 3.0 gained much popularity in 2021, the term was coined in 2014 by Gavin Wood. The advent of Web 3.0 has ushered in a new era of blockchain technology, and this chapter is an attempt to unleash the tremendous potential of this technology with a prime focus in the education sector. Although the fields in which this technology has contributed are wide and diverse, the innovative potential of Web 3.0 in the education field is explored in this chapter and its future implications are assessed and analyzed. There has been a profound impact of Web 3.0 in education services and the amalgamation of Web 3.0 technologies has altogether transformed the education sector and its contribution to society is undeniably important. In adherence to this, this chapter unravels the transformations caused by Web 3.0 in the teaching-learning process.

Chapter 20

Himanshu Sisodia, SSBM Geneva, Switzerland

Web 3, or the decentralized web, uses blockchain technology and decentralised principles to revolutionize online interactions and commercial practises. It gives people authority, builds trust, and allows for peer-to-peer interactions. Blockchain is a decentralized and secure database that ensures transparent transactions without the need of middlemen. Web 3 is reshaping the financial, healthcare, supply chain, and entertainment industries. Cryptocurrencies provide safe and borderless transactions. It improves supply chain management, assures ethical sourcing, and gives content producers more influence. Decentralised identification systems overcome the problems associated with centralized identity. Scalability, interoperability, and performance are all difficult issues. The importance of interoperability and standardization cannot be overstated. Regulatory and legal problems must be consistent with the ideas of decentralized identity. Decentralized identification systems provide personalised and transparent experiences that foster trust and consumer loyalty.

Chapter 21
Jaspal Singh, University Canada West, Canada

With the initial development of Web 1.0 in 1989, the groundwork was laid out for radical and rapid transformation of an accounting industry which had been slowly evolving over thousands of years. In the late 1990s, with Web 2.0, simple websites and email were eclipsed by innovative accounting software and collaborative online tools. Accountants have taken advantage of these features as many of the lower-level functions are now replaced by value-adding analytics and ongoing communication. The newest version of the World Wide Web, Web 3.0, strives to progress business further with decentralized, blockchain-based applications. Distributed ledger technology, securely storing data in multiple locations with immutable transaction records, is increasing reliability of accounting functions. With smart contracts, business agreements can be executed via blockchain, adding another layer of security. However, the accounting industry is not without challenges as technology advances- it must stand with its ethical principles as the business world around it evolves with Web 3.0.

Chapter 22
Guneet Kaur, University of Stirling, UK

The development of digital banking and the introduction of cryptocurrencies have drawn considerable attention to central bank digital currencies (CBDCs) in the global financial system. Policymakers, economists, and business experts are debating the deployment of CBDCs and their effects on financial stability as central banks examine their potential. In order to investigate the possible risks and advantages of CBDCs for financial stability, this study presents a thorough narrative literature review that critically evaluates a wide range of academic publications, reports, and research studies. This study also highlights the necessity of a user-centric financial ecosystem that incorporates Web 3 concepts. It also explores the significance of carefully constructed CBDC frameworks by looking at the potential impacts of CBDC adoption on monetary policy, systemic risks, and banking intermediation.

Chapter 23
Alexandra Overgaag, Thrilld Labs, Italy

This chapter highlights the need for a systemic, multi-disciplinary approach to understanding Web3's development. By disaggregating Web3 into interrelated networks of actors that hold distinct interests and beliefs, this chapter aims to describe and map Web3 to advance a more systemic understanding of its order and functioning. While presenting Web3 as a black box, the work underscores the importance of considering both the inherent nature of the technology itself and the broader societal context in which it operates and interacts with. Employing a Science, Technology, and Society lens, the work combines industry insights with a holistic approach to conceptualize the values, interests, and risks associated with Web3. The research holds that systemic challenges flow from Web3's inherent socio-technical and early-stage nature, and that its development is neither solely technologically determined nor entirely reliant on social actors. Instead, Web3's trajectory results from a complex interplay of its technological nature, societal values, stakeholder interests, and external (f)actors.

Chapter 24

The novel use of distributed ledger technology (DLT) in the financial sector poses considerable regulatory challenges, such as anonymity, technology neutrality, interconnectedness within the market of virtual assets, as well as with the traditional financial system and new legal risks to regulators around the globe. At the same time, the novelty of DLT for financial uses embodies also significant potential benefits to the financial sector, like innovation, inclusion, and competition. This chapter analyses these challenges and opportunities in detail and subsequently reviews possible regulatory responses at the current stage of virtual asset revolution and financial services innovation. Given the ongoing rapid development in the DLT financial services sphere, the analysis identifies the risk-based regulatory approach as potentially the most universal approach for national/regional regulators with advantages of high flexibility and resource efficiency.

Chapter 25

This article examines the ways in which Web 3.0 technologies can be advanced through research and innovation across disciplines. To completely benefit from the semantic web, efforts must be made to establish semantic standards and compensate data providers. To ensure ethical AI in the Web 3.0 era, researchers in the field must fixate on creating systems that are both reliable and readily explicable. Enhanced scalability, usability, and governance models are among the objectives of developing decentralized technologies like blockchain. When decentralized and AI-enabled systems become the norm, security, privacy, and accountability research will become increasingly crucial. Multi Stakeholder engagement will be required to resolve governance concerns in order to maximize the benefits of Web 3.0 while minimizing the risks.

Preface

Welcome to *Concepts, Technologies, Challenges, and the Future of Web 3*, a comprehensive reference book edited by Pooja Lekhi and Guneet Kaur. In this volume, we embark on a journey to explore the exciting world of Web 3, the next generation of the internet that promises to revolutionize the way we interact with digital technology.

In a world where technology is always developing, the internet's evolution has been at the forefront of this transformation. The internet has gradually changed the way we interact, do business, and perceive the world, from the early static web pages to the modern dynamic and interconnected systems. With the arrival of Web 3.0, a new era is dawning as we stand at the intersection of innovation, promising to transform our digital world in unimaginable ways. This revolutionary paradigm change is thoroughly explored in the book. In the chapters that follow, various experts and thought leaders explore the fundamental ideas, technology, difficulties, and opportunities that Web 3.0 provides.

Web 3 is a decentralized and open-source network that leverages blockchain technology to facilitate secure, transparent, and trustless transactions. By removing the need for intermediaries, such as governments, banks, and corporations, Web 3 empowers individuals and communities to take control of their digital lives.

In this book, we delve into the fundamental principles of blockchain technology, smart contracts, decentralized applications (dApps), decentralized autonomous organizations (DAOs), and decentralized finance (DeFi). These core building blocks form the foundation of Web 3 and are essential to understanding its potential and limitations. The subsequent chapters navigate through the intricate intersections of Web 3.0 with various industries, delving into how blockchain and decentralized finance are disrupting the financial sector and how traditional models are being juxtaposed with the innovative potential of the third iteration of the internet.

One of the significant aspects we explore is how Web 3 addresses crucial societal issues, such as privacy, data ownership, and financial inclusion. We analyze how this new paradigm can pave the way for a more open, transparent, and equitable web, enabling new forms of collaboration, value exchange, and governance while supporting the development of more decentralized and democratic systems.

The book also provides valuable insights into the challenges and opportunities that come with Web 3. We highlight the importance of interoperability, the role of decentralized identity in data control, and the transformative impact of Non-Fungible Tokens (NFTs) on ownership and value creation in the metaverse.

Moreover, we investigate the potential of Web 3 in disrupting and revolutionizing social networks, work structures, and supply chain management. The integration of cryptography in blockchain technology is also examined, unraveling its role in safeguarding the decentralized landscape.

The book delves into the metaverse as the path unfolds, where blockchain, NFTs, and virtual worlds combine to reinvent ownership, value, and interaction. This new frontier's benefits and difficulties are examined, including everything from geospatial information management to the thrilling potential of interactive extended reality (XR) experiences.

The book decodes the subtleties of smart contracts, gamification, integrated geographic information management, blockchain-integrated IoT, and much more through meticulous comparison studies. It is investigated how these technologies affect society, from altering industrial paradigms to promoting social transformation and improving supply chain traceability.

Crucially, *Concepts, Technologies, Challenges, and the Future of Web 3* doesn't shy away from addressing the hurdles that accompany this transformative journey. Regulatory, systemic, and technological challenges are probed, along with a forward-looking roadmap for the decentralized web.

The *Concepts, Technologies, Challenges, and Future of Web 3* book targets a diverse audience, including researchers, academics, and students in computer science and related fields, developers, entrepreneurs, and businesses building Web 3 applications, policymakers, regulators, and legal professionals. The book provides insights into the fundamental building blocks, latest developments, technical and conceptual frameworks, challenges, and opportunities of Web 3. It also highlights the potential impact of Web 3 on governance, regulation, and law, and the need for new policy frameworks. This book can be used in academic courses, research programs, and training and educational programs for developers, entrepreneurs, and businesses in the Web 3 space.

We believe that *Concepts, Technologies, Challenges, and the Future of Web 3* will serve as a valuable resource for a diverse audience. Researchers, academics, and students in computer science and related fields can gain insights into the latest developments in Web 3, guiding their future research in this exciting domain. Developers, entrepreneurs, and businesses building applications in the decentralized web will find a clear understanding of the technical and conceptual frameworks, challenges, and opportunities that await them.

We hope this book serves as a valuable resource for academic courses, research programs, and training initiatives, sparks curiosity, inspires innovation, and fosters meaningful discussions about the immense potential of Web 3 to shape a more inclusive and decentralized digital future.

ORGANIZATION OF THE BOOK

The book is organized into 25 chapters. A brief description of each of the chapters follows:

Chapter 1 delves into Web 3's core principles, spotlighting its decentralized and user-centric nature. It explores values like openness, trustlessness, and peer-to-peer systems. Blockchain's secure transactions and smart contracts are dissected, alongside cryptocurrencies for peer-to-peer value exchange. DeFi's transformative potential in Web 3 is pivotal, while DApps and NFTs prioritize user experiences. Interoperability's role in integrating Web 3 components is discussed. Governance mechanisms like DAOs ensure decentralized ecosystem efficiency. The chapter envisions Web 3's linkage with the metaverse, merging virtual and physical realms. Overall, it offers a profound look into Web 3's impact on decentralization, transparency, and user empowerment, shaping the internet economy's future.

Chapter 2 delves into the profound implications of Web 3.0's emergence within the finance industry. As the decentralized web gains traction, a seismic shift is underway, redefining financial transactions through blockchain, decentralized applications (dApps), and smart contracts. This transformative trifecta promises heightened security, transparency, and efficiency, minimizing the reliance on traditional intermediaries. The chapter explores how this recalibration slashes transaction costs and expedites processes. Furthermore, the chapter unravels the canvas of innovation painted by Web 3.0, spotlighting decentralized exchanges, Non-Fungible Tokens (NFTs), peer-to-peer lending platforms, and Decentralized Autonomous Organizations (DAOs). These nascent financial frontiers democratize access, fostering financial inclusion for marginalized communities. Amid these transformative prospects, the chapter also probes the regulatory and adaptability challenges facing stakeholders. Ultimately, this exploration navigates the horizon where Web 3.0 reshapes financial paradigms, encapsulating both promise and prudence.

Chapter 3 explores the transformative potential of Web 3, a groundbreaking innovation poised to address the limitations of both web 1 and web 2. While its influence spans various sectors, it's particularly impactful in the finance industry. Web 3's introduction has sparked a wave of innovation within traditional finance, setting the stage for a radical shift. Often dubbed the decentralized web, Web 3 disrupts conventional financial norms, offering an open, secure, and decentralized alternative. This chapter delves into the vital realm of traditional finance embracing Web 3's attributes, such as stability, scalability, security, and more. To stay pertinent and proficient amidst the digital finance surge, traditional banking must integrate the capabilities Web 3 presents. In light of the profound relevance of Web 3 in the financial landscape, this chapter meticulously examines and contrasts its key features and attributes against those of traditional finance.

Chapter 4 embarks on a comprehensive journey into the symbiotic relationship between cryptography and blockchain technology. It unfolds the critical evolution of cryptography's role within this landscape, unraveling its significance, challenges, and far-reaching implications. The chapter meticulously examines the diverse cryptographic algorithms at play within blockchain systems, illuminating their pivotal contribution to transaction security and anonymity. It delves into the intricate challenges cryptography encounters in this context, including scalability, key management, and the impending quantum computing era. Moreover, the chapter sheds light on how cryptography has catalyzed the emergence of cryptocurrencies and the transformative potential of smart contracts. Current cryptographic trends are scrutinized, underscoring their potential impact on the security of blockchain systems. Ultimately, this chapter underscores cryptography's role as the guardian of blockchain's core tenets - integrity, privacy, and trustworthiness.

Chapter 5 delves into the convergence of finance, art, and marketing within the uncharted realm of digital assets, honing in on cryptocurrencies, NFTs, and the metaverse. The authors meticulously dissect the potential ramifications of these groundbreaking technologies on established financial structures, the art market, and advertising tactics. By conducting a comprehensive analysis of blockchain, virtual reality, and decentralization, this chapter seeks to shed light on how these nascent digital assets possess the capacity to reconfigure our engagement with financial, artistic, and marketing domains, redefining the very essence of these landscapes.

Chapter 6 delves comprehensively into the intricate realm of establishing decentralized governance models within the Web3 ecosystems. It systematically dissects the evolutionary journey from traditional governance structures, identifying their limitations and subsequently, how decentralized models triumph over these shortcomings. Through meticulous analysis, this chapter scrutinizes an array of decentralized governance paradigms, encompassing reputation-based systems, liquid democracy, and Decentralized Autonomous Organizations (DAOs), meticulously weighing their merits and demerits. The exploration further extends to encompass the hurdles entailed in implementing these decentralized governance frameworks. As the narrative unfurls, the chapter also contemplates future possibilities and advancements, alongside offering insightful best practices that underpin the creation and successful execution of decentralized governance models within the Web3 landscapes. Ultimately, this chapter accentuates the paramount significance of decentralized governance models as catalysts for engendering openness, participation, and accountability within the expansive realms of Web3 ecosystems.

Chapter 7 delves into the emergence of Decentralized Autonomous Organizations (DAOs) within Web 3, characterizing them as hybrid entities that blend technological innovation with traditional organizational principles. Situating DAOs within the Transaction Cost Economics framework, the chapter emphasizes their role as coordination mechanisms that minimize transaction costs, showcasing their capacity to pool resources, deploy contractual governance, and adopt democratic decision-making. These characteristics underscore DAOs' significance in the evolving economic landscape. However, their technological novelty, particularly flexible governance structures, presents challenges in legal classification and theoretical understanding. Despite meeting theoretical hybrid criteria, the nuanced legal positioning of DAOs remains intricate. Addressing the multifaceted aspects of DAOs and their implications on economic theory and regulatory frameworks necessitates comprehensive future exploration.

Chapter 8 offers insights into the burgeoning field of smart contracts and their transformative role in shaping Decentralized Autonomous Organizations (DAOs). Amidst the rapidly evolving digital landscape, the intricate interplay between these innovative constructs and blockchain technology is explored in detail. The authors, combining their expertise in law, finance, and computer science, provide an in-depth examination of the operational mechanisms, structural designs, and evolutionary progression of smart contracts. The role of smart contracts as the lifeblood of DAOs is also thoroughly analyzed, discussing how these digital contracts facilitate automated decision-making processes, foster transparency, and ensure rule immutability. The chapter addresses the delicate balance between the independence of these decentralized organizations from state control and the need for appropriate legal recognition, security measures, and governance structures. It further unpacks the challenges and risks intrinsic to this technology, such as trust issues, fairness, and the potential for manipulation. Drawing on current research and real-world case studies, the authors present a balanced and comprehensive view of this nascent organizational form, inspiring thought about the potential opportunities and implications for societal cooperation and economic models in a digital age.

Chapter 9 investigates the drastic changes in the workplace, and the potential of blockchain technology in the introduction of Web3 technology is expected to accelerate this development. The gig economy, which focuses on short-term contracts and freelance employment, has been chastised for its lack of job stability, restricted worker safeguards, and increased competition. However, the rise of Web3 technologies and decentralized autonomous organizations (DAOs) provides a potential answer to these issues by increasing worker autonomy, transparency, and democratic decision-making. DAOs can help workers have more influence over their working environment while also increasing job security. These technologies may also open up new chances for people to work remotely and receive compensation more promptly than in the past. This chapter examines the possible opportunities and challenges posed.

Chapter 10 delves into the potential of decentralized social networks to address the growing concerns surrounding privacy, censorship, and user control on centralized social platforms. Offering an alternative to traditional social media, decentralized social networks foster trust and transparency in online interactions by leveraging distributed ledger technologies like blockchain where data is stored across multiple nodes controlled by the users themselves. Decentralized networks utilize such systems to offer the means for privacy and communication without censorship or interference, empowering users with greater control over their personal data. Combining the exploration of decentralized social networks' fundamental features, analysis of advantages and challenges, and examination of real-world initiatives, this research aims to contribute to the understanding of this Web 3 phenomenon and its potential to reshape the social media landscape in a decentralized, democratic, and user-centric way.

Chapter 11 provides an in-depth exploration of Metaverse's evolution and significance. Originating from Neal Stephenson's "Snow Crash," the term now envelops diverse virtual experiences, gaining prominence with Ernest Cline's "Ready Player One" and Facebook's rebranding as Meta in 2021. Roblox, Decentraland, and others have ventured into Metaverse development, offering immersive user-generated environments. This chapter delves into the concept's evolution, economic potential, and technological foundations. It encompasses virtual worlds, the Metaverse's economic landscape, and vital tools. From virtual social spheres to commercial hubs, the Metaverse holds diverse interpretations. By analyzing its roots, applications, and infrastructure, this chapter presents the Metaverse as a compelling force shaping the digital future.

Chapter 12 is dedicated to exploring the intricate symbiosis between the Metaverse and NFTs, delving into their pivotal role in ownership, wealth creation, future potential, evolving trends, and the hurdles they face. By dissecting NFTs' transformative power in redefining ownership and wealth, this chapter aspires to offer a comprehensive comprehension of their integration into the Metaverse's fabric. In contributing to the dialogue on decentralized digital economies, it scrutinizes NFTs' historical trajectory, advantages, challenges, and prospective applications, all while shedding light on their profound effects on sectors like art, gaming, and real estate. In a landscape of heightened stakeholder interest, this chapter stands as a crucial resource, igniting deeper exploration and advancement of this revolutionary technology. Its evaluation of NFTs' capacity to revolutionize ownership and prosperity in the Metaverse holds significance for investors, developers, artists, and enthusiasts, catalyzing insights into the potential of blockchain-driven innovation.

Chapter 13 delves into the profound impact arising from the dynamic convergence of Integrated Geospatial Information Management (GIM) and the revolutionary Metaverse. This fusion sparks transformative advancements across disciplines, ushering in an era of innovation. GIM's exploration of geospatial data offers valuable insights for emergency response, transportation, and urban planning, while the Metaverse extends possibilities with immersive experiences, virtual travel, brand activation, education, healthcare, and entertainment. Seamlessly integrated, the Metaverse and GIM enhance visualization, collaboration, decision-making, and data sharing in virtual realms, promising enriched user experiences. However, critical factors such as interoperability, data accuracy, and privacy considerations require prudent attention amidst these transformative potentials.

Chapter 14 explores the emerging trends in the web-based XR (Extended Reality) technology, which is expected to shape the next generation of the web. XR refers to the spectrum of technologies that extends the reality of the physical world by integrating virtual and augmented reality elements. The chapter discusses how web-based XR experiences can engage our senses by creating immersive and interactive environments that go beyond the traditional 2D screen. The authors argue that the current web technology stack is evolving to support more powerful and seamless XR experiences that can be accessed through standard web browsers. The chapter also examines the challenges and opportunities that arise from the integration of XR technology with the web, including issues related to privacy, security, and accessibility. Overall, this chapter provides a comprehensive overview of the potential of web-based XR technology and its impact on the future of the web.

Chapter 15 unfolds the transformative impact of smart contracts on traditional industries and business processes comes into focus. Ingrained within blockchains, these contracts enable automatic enforcement of contractual obligations, eliminating the need for intermediaries. The consequential benefits include streamlined administration, reduced service costs, enhanced process efficiency, and risk mitigation. However, this promising innovation is not without challenges. The chapter commences with an exploration of blockchains and smart contracts, delves into their complexities, considers recent technological strides, evaluates common platforms, and categorizes applications, accompanied by real-world examples. In essence, the chapter crafts a narrative that traverses the evolution, intricacies, and potential implications of smart contracts, showcasing their capacity to revolutionize diverse domains.

Chapter 16 delves into the pervasive adoption of gamification as a strategic means to engage stakeholders across industries, gaining particular traction in the context of Industry 5.0 and Society 5.0. In Industry 5.0, the integration of advanced technologies with human creativity shapes the landscape, while Society 5.0 leverages technology to address societal challenges. The chapter navigates through gamification's applications in training, education, marketing, and sustainability, highlighting the benefits of heightened engagement, motivation, and collaboration. It presents concrete instances of gamification success across various sectors, while also addressing challenges such as design precision, ethical considerations, and potential addictive tendencies. Ultimately, the paper asserts that, when thoughtfully aligned with users' needs and goals, gamification emerges as a potent tool within Industry 5.0 and Society 5.0, fostering innovation in the face of complexity.

Chapter 17 presents the transformative landscape reshaped by the continual evolution of interconnected devices, catalyzing the pervasive integration of IoT technology into various facets of life. Despite its revolutionary potential and convenience, the proliferation of IoT devices raises substantial security concerns. As traditional systems transition to smart solutions across sectors, the indispensability of IoT technologies necessitates a safeguard, aptly provided by Blockchain. The fortified decentralization inherent in Blockchain offers a viable solution to counter the diverse challenges faced by the IoT ecosystem. The paper offers an in-depth exploration, encompassing the layers and applications of IoT, a comparative analysis of security threats, the potential of blockchain to rectify shortcomings within the present IoT architecture, and a comprehensive examination of challenges within the realm of Blockchain-associated IoT.

Chapter 18 examines the potential of blockchain technology in addressing economic and social challenges encountered by local producers in the coffee supply chain. Despite the Fairtrade initiatives and the growing demand for premium specialty coffee, farmers face difficulties in capturing the intangible value-added of their coffee and lack market knowledge. The study utilizes qualitative methods, including semi-structured interviews, to explore the benefits, opportunities, and challenges of blockchain integration in the coffee supply chain. The findings reveal that blockchain can enhance trust, transparency, and customer-farmer connections while reducing information asymmetry. By studying the ongoing project examples, this research provides valuable insights into how blockchain can empower coffee producers and contribute to a more transparent, equitable, and sustainable coffee supply chain.

Chapter 19 narrates the world of Web 3.0, unveiling its innovative potential and profound implications within the Education Sector. With its foundations of decentralization, trust, and the amalgamation of AI and Machine Learning, Web 3.0 has captured attention since its inception in 2014. This chapter intricately explores its transformative influence on education, spotlighting how it reshapes the learning landscape. Through meticulous analysis, it anticipates the future ramifications of Web 3.0, as its dynamic integration redefines educational paradigms, ultimately forging a new path towards interactive and immersive learning experiences that hold far-reaching societal implications.

Chapter 20 presents an exploration of the transformative role of decentralized identity (DID) within the context of Web 3.0 and blockchain technology. DID has revolutionized digital identification and its implications for marketing and consumer interaction. The chapter delves into the significance of DID in the modern digital landscape, highlighting its potential to empower individuals with greater control over their personal data. By securely storing information on the blockchain and allowing selective sharing with businesses, DID fosters transparency, trust, and personalized relationships. The chapter further elucidates how DID empowers marketers with consent-driven insights for tailored campaigns, enhancing engagement and conversions. It also streamlines authentication processes, offering seamless single sign-on experiences without compromising data security. While DID's potential benefits in marketing and consumer interaction are substantial, challenges such as interoperability and standardization must be addressed for widespread integration. The chapter underscores the importance of awareness and education to drive adoption, ultimately revealing how DID shapes a more secure, transparent, and user-centric digital economy within the transformative landscape of Web 3.0.

Chapter 21 reviews the evolutionary journey of the accounting industry alongside the development of the World Wide Web. The chapter explores that as Web 3.0 emerged as the next frontier, marked by decentralized, blockchain-based applications, distributed ledger technology, featuring secure data storage and immutable transaction records enhances the reliability of accounting processes. The integration of smart contracts on the blockchain adds another layer of security by enabling business agreements. Yet, amid these technological strides, the accounting industry must navigate challenges and uphold its ethical principles as it evolves alongside the business landscape shaped by Web 3.0.

Chapter 22 delves into the realm of Central Bank Digital Currencies (CBDCs), a topic gaining significant prominence due to the rise of digital banking and cryptocurrencies. The financial landscape is abuzz with discussions among policymakers, economists, and business experts regarding the deployment of CBDCs and their potential impact on financial stability. In this context, the chapter undertakes an in-depth narrative literature review, meticulously analyzing a wide array of academic publications, reports, and research studies to unravel the potential risks and benefits of CBDCs for financial stability. It also emphasizes the necessity of crafting a user-centric financial ecosystem in line with Web 3 concepts. The chapter delves into the intricacies of CBDC frameworks, probing their potential effects on monetary policy, systemic risks, and banking intermediation, highlighting the significance of a well-structured approach to CBDC adoption.

Chapter 23 emphasizes the necessity of a holistic, interdisciplinary approach to comprehend the development of Web 3. While presenting Web3 as a black box, the work underscores the importance of considering both the inherent nature of the technology itself and the broader societal context in which it operates and interacts with. Employing a Science, Technology, and Society lens, the work combines industry insights with a conceptual approach to grasp the values, interests, and risks associated with Web3. By disaggregating Web3 into interrelated networks of actors that hold distinct interests and beliefs, the research examines Web3 to advance a more systemic understanding of its order and functioning. The research concludes that various systemic challenges flow from Web3's inherent socio-technical and early-stage nature and that its very development is neither solely technologically determined nor entirely reliant on social actors. Instead, Web3's trajectory results from a complex interplay of its technological nature, societal values, stakeholder interests, and other external factors.

Chapter 24 focuses on the application of distributed ledger technology (DLT) in financial applications like virtual assets, with a deep dive into the regulatory challenges and opportunities it presents. DLT's decentralized nature promises faster, cheaper, and secure transactions, disrupting traditional intermediaries and fostering financial inclusion. However, this shift poses regulatory uncertainties impacting newcomers, regulators, and markets, leading to gaps and setbacks. The chapter examines regulatory complexities encompassing anonymity, technological neutrality, integration within virtual assets and traditional finance, and novel legal risks for global regulators. Simultaneously, it highlights potential benefits such as innovation and inclusivity. Despite decentralization's origin, many current applications involve intermediaries, invoking familiar regulatory approaches. The chapter identifies risk-based regulation as a flexible and resource-efficient strategy, while acknowledging the challenge of addressing decentralized features and virtual asset applications.

Chapter 25 delves into the realm of Web 3.0, exploring the potential for cross-disciplinary research and innovation to propel its development. The discussion highlights key areas demanding attention, including the implementation of semantic standards and equitable data provider compensation to maximize the semantic web's capabilities. Additionally, the chapter emphasizes the need for transparent, trustworthy technologies to ensure ethical AI deployment. Blockchain's role in improving scalability, usability, and governance is also scrutinized. Security, privacy, and accountability research take center stage, vital for navigating the evolving landscape of decentralized and AI-powered systems. To harmonize Web 3.0's advantages with its potential hazards, the chapter underscores the importance of multi-stakeholder engagement to address governance intricacies.

Pooja Lekhi
University Canada West, Canada

Guneet Kaur
University of Stirling, UK & Cointelegraph, USA

Acknowledgment

With a deep sense of humility and profound gratitude, we offer our sincere recognition, honoring all the individuals whose unwavering support and contributions have played a pivotal role in the extraordinary accomplishment of this project. Above all, we are thankful to the divine God, expressing our heartfelt gratitude for the blessings and guidance bestowed upon us. The grace and guidance of a higher power have formed the foundation on which this endeavor has flourished.

Moving forward, we wish to convey our sincere appreciation to the esteemed authors who have generously shared their valuable insights and expertise. Shailey Singh, Himanshu Sisodia, Alexandra Overgaag, Dr. Lisa-Marie Ross, Dr. Munir Ahmad, Dr. Asmat Ali, Tanuj Surve, Dr. Risha Khandelwal, Elenora Bassi, Margherita Bandirali, Benjamin Kenwright, Airi Helen Schnauzer, Kaveri Banerjee, Dr. Amit Kumar Tyagi, Moumita Sarkar, Dr. Sandip Roy, Dr. Rajesh Bose, Azadeh Eskandarzadeh, Sasha Shilina, Dr. Babita Jha, Dr. Deepak Jha, Dr. Pratibha Giri, Dr. Debora Dhaniya, SzuTung Chen, Ratnakar Mann, Aneta Napieralska, Przemysław Kępczyński, Jaspal Singh, and M Nazmuz Sakib – your unwavering dedication and diligent efforts have made an indelible impact on this initiative. Each of you brought forth a distinctive perspective and a wealth of knowledge, enhancing the content's depth and breadth. Your innovative ideas and groundbreaking contributions have significantly propelled the advancement of the subject matter. Collaborating with such a diverse group of interdisciplinary scholars has been a privilege we deeply cherish.

Our gratitude also extends to the cherished individuals, including close family members and friends, who stood by us throughout this journey. Your unwavering support has been the driving force behind our determination, and we are profoundly thankful for your unwavering presence.

Our sincere thanks go to Cointelegraph for their insightful contributions and expertise, enriching the content of this work. We would also like to express our appreciation to the University of Stirling and the University of Canada West for their support and resources that have been instrumental in shaping the ideas presented in this book.

A special acknowledgment goes to the IGI team, whose dedication and efforts have been pivotal in the successful compilation of this comprehensive reference book. Their expertise, guidance, and commitment have been an essential driving force throughout the entire process.

We are truly thankful for the collaborative spirit and contributions from all those involved, as this work aims to shed light on the intricate and evolving landscape of Web 3.0 and its multifaceted implications.

With sincere gratitude and deep appreciation.

Chapter 1
The Emergence of Web 3 and Its Core Building Blocks:
Understanding the Third Iteration of the Internet

Shailey Singh

BUK technology, USA & Symbiosis International University (Deemed), India

ABSTRACT

This chapter delves into the core building blocks of Web3, the transformative phase of the internet characterized by decentralized and user-centric digital ecosystems. It explores the ethos of Web3, emphasizing openness, transparency, trustlessness, and user empowerment. The chapter examines blockchain technology for secure transactions, smart contracts revolutionizing agreements, and cryptocurrencies facilitating peer-to-peer value transfer. It discusses decentralized finance (DeFi) as a transformative building block and explores decentralized applications (DApps) and non-fungible tokens (NFTs) for creating user-centric platforms. The importance of interoperability along with governance mechanisms like decentralized autonomous organizations (DAOs) is highlighted. The chapter concludes by envisioning the interconnectedness between Web3 and the metaverse, where virtual and physical realities merge. Overall, it provides a comprehensive overview of Web3's emergence and its transformative impact on decentralization, transparency, and user empowerment.

INTRODUCTION

The internet has undergone several transformative phases since its inception, revolutionizing the way we access information, connect with others, and participate in digital interactions. From its guarded beginnings as a tool exclusively available to governments and military projects, the internet has gradually transitioned into an accessible platform that empowers individuals across the globe. Today the web has become an indispensable resource in various aspects of our lives, ranging from education and employment to government services, commerce, healthcare, recreation, and beyond (Powell & Clarke, 2002). It

DOI: 10.4018/978-1-6684-9919-1.ch001

Copyright © 2023, IGI Global. Copying or distributing in print or electronic forms without written permission of IGI Global is prohibited.

serves as a vast network of interconnected hypertext documents that are accessed through the multiple devices. By utilizing a web browser, users can seamlessly explore web pages that feature diverse content, including text, images, videos, and other multimedia elements. With the incorporation of cutting-edge technology over the last three decades, the internet has redefined how humans utilize the internet to organize, communicate, and collaborate with one another (Musiał & Kazienko 2013).

With time, the internet has evolved creating new paradigm shifts. This chapter explores the emergence of web 3 and its core building blocks. The first section takes the reader through the journey of web evolution, examining the challenges of web 2 and how web 3 addresses these challenges. The later sections discuss the fundamental concepts of web 3, its guiding principles, and the technological enablers. This will help readers gain insights into the potential impact of web 3 on various aspects of our lives, economy, and the internet ecosystem as a whole. By the end of this chapter, readers will be equipped with a solid understanding of web 3, enabling them to navigate the evolving digital landscape and leverage its concepts for personal and professional pursuits.

THE EMERGENCE OF WEB 3

World Wide Web

Sir Tim Berners-Lee, invented the world wide web in 1989, at CERN (The European Organisation for Nuclear Research) in Geneva, Switzerland. While working at CERN, he was realized the hurdles which the scientists encountered in sharing, communicating and collaborating. Different computer systems and networks had their own isolated methods of storing and accessing data, making it difficult to share information across different platforms. Berners-Lee envisioned a solution that would enable seamless communication and information exchange across different computer systems. He proposed a system of interlinked documents that could be accessed through a network, creating a web of information that anyone could access and contribute to. This concept laid the foundation for the world wide web. Berners-Lee actively participated in directing the development of web standards (Bizner, Health & lee, 2011) including markup languages used to construct web pages. While in 1989, this work was intended to improve the CERN communication system and was intended for the usage of the scientific community, but Berners-Lee soon realized the idea could be applied globally and would benefit majority public at large. He open-sourced the web giving birth to the World Wide Web (Lee et.al, 2010).

Web 1

The initial phase of the internet, often referred to as web 1, introduced static web pages that provided limited user involvement. It was essentially a "read-only" web, where information was readily available, but interaction and participation were limited. Web 1 provided a gateway of access to vast amounts of information, revolutionizing the way we consumed knowledge and expanding the horizons of human potential (Jacksi & Abass, 2019). One of the most significant opportunities created by web 1 was the democratization of information. Prior to the widespread adoption of the internet, accessing knowledge often required significant resources and effort. Libraries, books, and physical archives were the primary sources of information, limiting access to a select few. However, with the advent of web 1, a wealth of information became available to anyone with an internet connection (Beniiche, et al., 2022).

Web 1 broke down the barriers to knowledge, significantly reducing the obstacles to obtaining information. It opened up new horizons for education, research, and personal growth. People could access vast amounts of information on a wide range of topics, expanding their understanding of the world and empowering them to pursue their interests and passions. Furthermore, web 1 provided opportunities for businesses and entrepreneurs to establish a global presence. Websites became a powerful tool for showcasing products, services, and ideas to a worldwide audience. The opportunities created by web 1 laid the foundation for the subsequent phases of the internet's evolution, setting the stage for the transformative changes to come in web 2 (Tanaka et al, 2010) and later in web 3.

Web 2

Web 2 emerged as a response to the static nature and limitations of web 1 and aimed to address the evolving needs and expectations of growing internet users. While web 1 revolutionized information access, it lacked interactivity and user participation, leaving room for further innovation. Web 2, also known as the "read and write" web, introduced a range of features and capabilities that transformed the online experience and gave rise to the digital era we are familiar with today (Nath, 2022).

One of the primary needs met by web 2 was the desire for increased user engagement and interaction. Web 1 primarily provided static content, limiting users to passive consumption. Web 2 introduced social media platforms, dynamic content, and interactive websites that enabled users to actively participate, share their thoughts, and contribute their own content. This shift from being mere consumers to active participants marked a significant leap in the evolution of the internet. Web 2 addressed the need for connectivity and collaboration by adding accessibility, and users found ways to connect and communicate with others across vast distances. Social networking platforms like Facebook, Twitter, and LinkedIn emerged, allowing individuals to build online networks, share updates, and engage in conversations.

With the advent of social media and dynamic content, the web transformed into a more interactive and participatory space. Web 2 enabled users to create and share content, connect with others, collaborate on projects, and experience a more social and engaging online environment. This phase propelled the rise of the digital economy and set the stage for a more user-centric internet experience. However, owing to growing user demands and breakthrough technological changes, the internet is on the brink of another paradigm shift - the emergence of web 3.

Web 3

Web 3, or the "decentralized web", refers to the next phase of the internet's evolution, characterized by a decentralized, user-centric, and trustless ecosystem. It represents a paradigm shift from web 2, where users are not only consumers but active participants, co-creators and owners of the digital landscape. Web 3 is seen as a holistic technological movement with profound cultural, social, and financial implications. It represents a transformative shift from the current centralized and siloed web architecture to a more open, inclusive, and secure digital ecosystem. At its core, web 3 is built on the principles of decentralization, transparency, and user ownership. It is powered by ground-breaking technologies such as blockchain, which enables secure and transparent record-keeping, and smart contracts, which automate participatory execution. Emphasis is on utilizing blockchain technology to enable decentralized protocols that empower users with more control over their digital identities, data, and online interactions. This involves concepts like self-sovereign identity, where individuals have ownership and control of their personal information, and decentralized applications (DApps) that run on blockchain networks rather than centralized servers.

Web 3 signifies a departure from the current centralized internet model and aims to reshape the way we interact with digital platforms. Overall, web 3 represents a vision of the internet that is more democratic, decentralized, and aligned with user interests, with the potential to revolutionize how we interact, transact, and communicate online.

Figure 1. Web1, web2, and web3 era

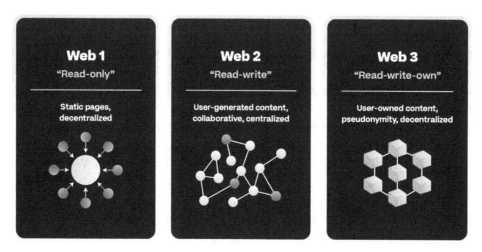

Why Does Web3 Matter?

There are several compelling reasons for web 3 to gain popularity. Some of the primary drivers for this shift include:

Decentralization and Trust

Web 2 ushered in the era of prominent tech giants such as Facebook, Google, and Amazon which brought in a massive digital economy. This created many jobs, entrepreneurs, Youtubers, influencers and gave small businesses a platform to showcase their products and run their shop (Ukpere et al., 2014). However, very soon these small number of major big tech companies exerted significant control over the vast amount of internet traffic and value generation, leveraging advertisement-driven revenue models, safeguarded algorithms, and yielding significant control other monetization strategies (Beuscart & Mellet, 2008). Consequently, they became formidable entities in terms of customer data acquisition.

In web 2, users have minimal control over their data or its storage. Most companies routinely track and retain cookies and cached data (Zhang et al., 2009). All the accumulated data remains the exclusive property of these companies, subject to sale to third parties and monetization by online sellers. Despite the belief that personal Facebook, Instagram, or Twitter accounts belong to their users, the irony lies in the fact that if one were to sever ties with Facebook, for instance, all posts, pictures, comments, and reactions from a decade's worth of social media presence would be irretrievably lost. The centralization of data control became abundantly clear with scandals and hacks as seen in the infamous Cambridge Analytica scandal amid rumours of election data vulnerabilities (Issak and Hanna, 2018). Furthermore, there has been abundant criticism of similarly centralized control exists for profit sharing, where industry giants like YouTube claim a significant portion of content creators' profits and wield the power to monetize or remove content at their discretion (Wang & Chan-Olmsted, 2020).

This concentration of control raises concerns about data privacy, censorship, and the potential for abuse of power. Web 3, on the other hand, aims to change this by establishing a decentralized internet architecture based on blockchain technology. By distributing control and decision-making authority among participants in the network, web 3 promotes greater transparency, autonomy, and trust. It allows individuals to have more ownership and control over their data, mitigating the risks associated with centralized control.

User Empowerment and Ownership

In web 2, users often lack control and ownership over the content they generate and the digital assets they accumulate. Establishing ownership amidst the vast sea of proliferating content becomes increasingly challenging. For instance, a music tune or a meme or even a photograph can go viral in numerous iterations, making it arduous to determine the original creator. Similarly, a piece of digital art may have countless replicas available online, complicating the task of proving ownership. Unless individuals resort to legal means of intellectual property (IP) protection or copyright regulations, it becomes difficult to ascertain true ownership. The prevalence of fake news (Figueira & Oliveira, 2017), fraudulent artists, and scams further exacerbates these challenges. Furthermore, social media platforms and online services retain ownership rights and can exert significant influence over user-generated content.

Web 3 seeks to empower individuals by enabling true ownership of digital assets through blockchain-based systems. It allows users to have verifiable ownership and control over their data, intellectual property, and other digital creations. At its core, web 3 uses blockchains, cryptocurrencies, and nonfungible tokens (NFTs) to give power back to the users in the form of ownership. This shift towards user-centric ownership enhances autonomy, fosters innovation, and enables new economic models.

Enhanced Privacy and Security

Web 2 platforms rely on centralized servers and databases. These centralized servers serve as the backbone of the internet, hosting and storing vast amounts of user data and content. Centralized controls have their set of challenges and limitations. With a centralized server architecture, there is a heightened risk of a single point of failure. If the central server experiences technical issues or is compromised, it can result in widespread disruptions, data loss, and service outages affecting a large number of users. Centralized servers become attractive targets for hackers and malicious actors. If a hacker gains unauthorized access to the central server, they can potentially exploit and compromise a significant amount of user data, leading to privacy breaches, identity theft, and other security concerns. Web 2 centralized servers require users to trust the service providers with their personal data. Users have limited control over how their data is handled, stored, and shared. This lack of control raises concerns about data privacy, as the service providers may have the ability to collect, analyze, and monetize user data without explicit consent. Additionally, with centralized control, service providers can exert significant influence over the content and information that users can access and share. They have the power to enforce content policies and remove or restrict certain types of content, leading to potential issues of censorship and limited freedom of expression.

Web 3 leverages decentralized technologies like blockchain to enhance privacy and security. Blockchain's cryptographic protocols provide robust encryption and data integrity, reducing the risk of data breaches and unauthorized manipulation. Additionally, web 3 introduces concepts like self-sovereign identity, where users have more control over their personal information and can selectively share it with trusted parties, thereby protecting privacy and reducing reliance on centralized systems.

Interoperability and Openness

Web 2 is characterized by siloed platforms and walled gardens, limiting data and asset interoperability between different services. This limited openness prevents easy integration and collaboration with external services. Users and developers encounter barriers when attempting to share data, access features, or build applications that span multiple platforms (Schrepel, 2023). Web 2 platforms typically offer proprietary application programming interfaces (APIs) that control access to their services and data. These APIs are often designed to serve the interests of the platform providers rather than fostering interoperability with external systems. It can be difficult for developers to integrate services from different platforms due to variations in API designs and restrictions. Moreover, Web 2 platforms often prioritize user lock-in by making it challenging to export or migrate user data to other services. Users have limited control over their data and face difficulties in transferring their profiles, connections, and content between platforms. This lack of data portability restricts user autonomy and limits their ability to switch between services.

Web 3, on the other hand, aims to establish open protocols and standards, facilitating seamless interaction and interoperability across various DApps and services. This interoperability fosters innovation, encourages collaboration, and allows for the creation of more comprehensive and integrated user experiences (Yu et.al., 2022). Web 3 leverages blockchain technology to enable cross-chain compatibility. Different blockchain networks can communicate and exchange assets and data through standardized protocols, enhancing interoperability between disparate blockchain ecosystems. This interoperability allows users and developers to leverage the unique features and capabilities of different blockchains. Developers can contribute to shared protocols, libraries, and toolkits, fostering innovation and interoperability across the ecosystem. Open-source projects encourage transparency, peer review, and community involvement, leading to the development of interoperable solutions that highlight the benefit of the entire web 3 ecosystem.

In response to these issues, web 3 emerges as an endeavor to address these concerns and envision a more refined and improved future for the internet.

Defining Features of Web3: Core Drivers and Ethos

The web 3 ethos and core drivers are presented in figure 2 and explained in the below section.

Figure 2. Web3 ethos and core drivers

Decentralization

Decentralization refers to the distribution of control and decision-making across a network rather than relying on a single central authority or entity. In web 3, decentralization is a core principle that aims to address the limitations and challenges associated with centralized systems. Web 3 employs decentralized consensus mechanisms, such as Proof of Stake (PoS) or Proof of Work (PoW), to achieve agreement and validation of transactions or information across the network. Consensus mechanisms ensure that decisions are collectively made by the network participants, maintaining the integrity and security of the system without requiring trust in a centralized authority (Lashkari & Musilek, 2021). Decentralized storage, governance, application, finance etc., are some of the major focus areas of web 3 growth. De-centralization has given birth to many popular use-cases like decentralized exchanges (DEX) - Uniswap or SushiSwap, which facilitate peer-to-peer cryptocurrency trading without the need for intermediaries.

Openness and Transparency

Applications and programmes in web 3 are created open-source. In essence, the community has access to the development code, which is a virtual resource, and the development process is maintained open. Web 3 embraces open-source development, where software code is freely available for anyone to view, modify, and distribute. Open-source projects encourage transparency and community collaboration, allowing developers to audit the code, identify vulnerabilities, and contribute to its improvement. This transparency builds trust and ensures that the software is accountable and free from hidden agendas or malicious intent. The new models of governance in web 3 include decentralized autonomous organizations (DAOs), where decision-making is transparent and community-driven. DAOs leverage blockchain technology to enable stakeholders to participate in voting, propose changes, and collectively shape the direction of a project or platform. Transparent governance ensures that decisions are made openly, fostering trust and accountability within the community (Voon, 2022).

Furthermore, web 3 leverages blockchain technology, which provides an auditable and immutable ledger for recording transactions and data. Every transaction and change are recorded on the blockchain, creating a transparent and tamper-proof record of events. This transparency allows users to verify the authenticity and integrity of data, ensuring trust in the system. Through open protocols, transparent governance, auditable data, and user control, web 3 ensures that the internet operates in a more transparent and trustworthy manner (Allen et al., 2023). These principles foster innovation, collaboration, and user empowerment while mitigating risks associated with centralized control and lack of transparency in web 2.

Trustless and Permissionless

In web 3, trustless refers to the ability to engage in transactions and interactions without relying on trust in a central authority or intermediary. Traditional systems, such as those in web 2, often require trust in centralized entities, like a bank, to facilitate and verify transactions. In contrast, web 3 leverages blockchain technology and smart contracts to establish trust through mathematical proofs and cryptographic mechanisms. Trust resides in the code and not in a third-party or intermediary.

Web 3 is also characterized as permissionless, meaning that anyone can participate and access the network without requiring explicit permission or approval from a centralized authority. This openness allows individuals, developers, and businesses to join the web 3 ecosystem, contribute to its growth, and utilize its services without facing barriers or gatekeepers. By combining trustless and permissionless qualities, web 3 strives to create a more inclusive and transparent internet ecosystem (Kim et al., 2022). It enables direct peer-to-peer interactions, eliminates the need for blind trust in intermediaries, and empowers individuals to participate in and shape the future of the internet without restrictive barriers or centralized control.

The ethos of web 3 reflects a collective effort to redefine the internet, prioritizing user empowerment, privacy, trust, and open collaboration. It strives to create a more equitable, resilient, and sustainable digital future, where individuals have greater control over their online experiences and can actively participate in shaping the evolution of the internet.

FUNDAMENTAL BUILDING BLOCKS OF WEB 3

Web 3 in 2023 is still in its nascent phase and is seeing new innovation and developments at a fast pace. The core building blocks of web 3 is not a single block but rather a confluence of technologies, tools, concepts and solutions which are helping create this third iteration of the internet. It is important to get into a know-how of all these different aspects and their intertwining nature to understand web 3. The core building blocks of web 3 are presented in Figure 3 and explained below.

Blockchain Technology

Blockchain is a foundational technology in web 3. It is a distributed ledger that maintains a decentralized record of transactions or information across a network of computers (nodes). Blockchains provide transparency, immutability, and security through cryptographic mechanisms (Politou et al., 2019). They

Figure 3. Building blocks of web3

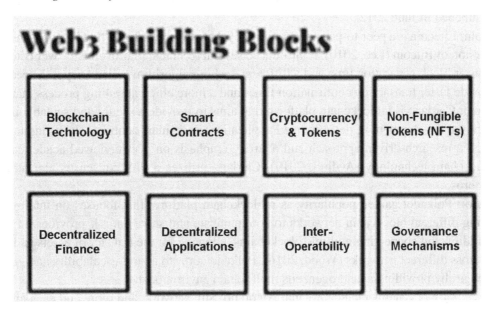

enable trustless interactions and eliminate the need for intermediaries in various applications, including digital currencies (like Bitcoin and Ethereum) and DApps. There are several major blockchains that have played significant roles in the development and adoption of blockchain technology. Some notable ones:

- Bitcoin: Bitcoin is the first and most well-known blockchain-based cryptocurrency. It was created by an anonymous person or group using the pseudonym Satoshi Nakamoto. The Bitcoin whitepaper, titled "Bitcoin: A Peer-to-Peer Electronic Cash System," was published by Satoshi Nakamoto in 2008, introducing the concept of blockchain and decentralized digital currency. The Bitcoin network launched in 2009, marked the beginning of the first operational blockchain where bitcoin was mined using Proof of Work (PoW) consensus mechanism.
- Ethereum: Ethereum is a blockchain platform that introduced the concept of smart contracts, which are self-executing agreements with predefined conditions coded on the blockchain. Ethereum's co-founder, Vitalik Buterin, published the Ethereum whitepaper in 2013, proposing a blockchain platform with smart contract functionality. Bitcoin blockchain was limited to Bitcoin cryptocurrency and payments. Ethereum expanded the capabilities of blockchain beyond simple transactions and enabled the development of DApps and decentralized finance (DeFi) protocols. The Ethereum blockchain was launched in 2015. Ethereum also introduced the ERC-20 token standard, which facilitated the creation of various tokens and contributed to the growth of the initial coin offering (ICO) trend (Cuffe, 2018).
- Ripple: Ripple is a blockchain-based payment protocol designed for fast and low-cost cross-border transactions. It aims to enable efficient global money transfers by providing real-time settlement and liquidity solutions. Ripple's blockchain, called the XRP Ledger, utilizes a consensus algorithm different from Bitcoin's PoW mechanism, known as the Ripple Protocol Consensus Algorithm (RPCA). Rather than use blockchain mining, Ripple uses a consensus mechanism, via

a group of bank-owned servers, to confirm transactions (Merteen et al., 2023). The XRP Ledger first launched in June 2012.

- Litecoin: Litecoin is a peer-to-peer cryptocurrency that was created as a "lite" (synonymous, lighter) version of Bitcoin (Lee, 2010). It introduced several technical improvements over Bitcoin, such as a faster block generation time and a different hashing algorithm called Scrypt. Litecoin aimed to provide faster transaction confirmation times and a more efficient mining process than Bitcoin.
- Cardano: Cardano is a blockchain platform that aims to provide a secure and scalable infrastructure for the development of decentralized applications and smart contracts. It distinguishes itself through a research-driven approach and a strong emphasis on peer-reviewed academic research in blockchain technology (Aydinli, 2019). Cardano utilizes a PoS consensus algorithm called Ouroboros.
- Polkadot: Polkadot gained popularity as a blockchain platform that focuses on interoperability, enabling different blockchain networks to communicate and share data. It provides a framework for building and connecting multiple blockchains, allowing for the transfer of assets and information across different networks (Wood, 2016). Polkadot aims to address scalability and governance challenges by providing a heterogeneous multi-chain environment.
- Other major blockchains include Solana, Algorand, Sui Network, and more and each aims to add value to the growing facets of web 3 evolution.

Layer One and Layer Two Blockchains

Layer 1 blockchains are the underlying main blockchain networks, such as Bitcoin and Ethereum, that serve as the foundation for decentralized applications and smart contracts. They provide the core functionality, consensus mechanisms, and security for the blockchain ecosystem. Layer 1 blockchains handle the processing and validation of all transactions and data directly on the main chain. However, one of the limitations of Layer 1 blockchains is scalability (Gangwal et al., 2023). Due to their design, they have inherent restrictions on the number of transactions they can process per second, leading to potential congestion and higher transaction fees (called gas fees) during periods of high network activity. Layer 1 solutions focus on improving the performance of the main chain itself. Examples of Layer 1 blockchain projects include Ethereum, Cardano, Polkadot, and Solana, which prioritize scalability, interoperability, and faster transaction processing times.

Layer 2 blockchains are secondary protocols or solutions built on top of Layer 1 blockchains. They aim to alleviate the scalability issues by taking some computational processes off the main chain, while still benefiting from the security and decentralization of their Layer 1 chain (Xu & Chen, 2022). Layer 2 solutions provide additional scalability, reduced transaction costs, and faster confirmations by processing transactions in a more efficient manner. Examples of Layer 2 blockchains include Polygon, Starknet, Optimism, Arbitrum, and more.

The Blockchain Trilemma

The blockchain trilemma is a fundamental concept in the world of blockchain technology that outlines the inherent trade-offs between three key attributes: decentralization, security, and scalability (Monte, et.al, 2020). This concept suggests that it is challenging to achieve all three of these attributes simultaneously in a blockchain system; improving one aspect often comes at the expense of the others.

- Decentralization: Decentralization refers to the distribution of authority and control across a network of nodes or participants. It ensures that no single entity has complete power over the network, enhancing transparency and reducing the risk of censorship. However, achieving high levels of decentralization can hinder scalability and require more computational resources, potentially impacting the overall efficiency of the network.
- Security: Security involves safeguarding the integrity of data and transactions on the blockchain. In a secure blockchain, data is immutable and resistant to tampering, ensuring trust in the system. A robust security architecture often involves mechanisms like cryptographic hashing, consensus algorithms, and network validation. Nevertheless, maintaining high security might limit scalability due to the computational overhead required to validate and secure transactions.
- Scalability: Scalability relates to a blockchain's ability to handle an increasing number of transactions and users without compromising its performance. As more participants join a blockchain network, the system must be capable of processing transactions efficiently and in a timely manner. However, achieving high scalability can lead to centralization, as more efficient processing often requires concentrating computational power or decision-making authority, which contradicts the principle of decentralization.

The blockchain trilemma signifies that blockchain systems need to carefully balance these three attributes according to their intended use cases and goals. Projects must make strategic choices when designing their networks, deciding which attribute to prioritize and to what extent (Monte et al., 2020). While advances in technology and innovative consensus mechanisms have aimed to address this trilemma, it remains a significant challenge for blockchain developers seeking to strike the right balance between decentralization, security, and scalability.

Smart Contracts

Smart contracts are self-executing programmable agreements coded on blockchain platforms. They automatically enforce predefined rules and conditions without the need for intermediaries. These contracts are coded in a programming language (such as Solidity for Ethereum) and reside on the blockchain, making them tamper-proof and transparent. Smart contracts eliminate the need for intermediaries or trusted third parties to enforce agreements, as the execution of the contract is automatic and verifiable (Khan, 2021). They enable trustless and transparent interactions by automating the execution of contractual obligations. Smart contracts find applications in areas such as DeFi, supply chain management, decentralized governance, and other web 3 use-cases.

Cryptocurrencies and Tokens

Cryptocurrencies play a crucial role in the web 3 ecosystem, serving as the native digital currencies that power decentralized networks and enable various functionalities within the decentralized economy. Cryptocurrencies, such as Bitcoin (BTC) and Ethereum (ETH), act as digital currencies that facilitate peer-to-peer transactions within the decentralized ecosystem. They enable individuals to transfer value directly, without the need for intermediaries like banks. Their hallmark is fast, borderless, and secure transactions, allowing for efficient cross-border payments and often reducing transaction costs compared to traditional financial systems (Singh, 2023).

Cryptocurrencies often serve as incentives for participants within decentralized networks. For example, in PoW blockchain networks like Bitcoin, miners validate transactions and secure the network by solving complex mathematical puzzles. In return, they are rewarded with newly minted bitcoins. This incentivization mechanism ensures the participation and security of the network by aligning the interests of network participants. Cryptocurrencies can also be used for decentralized governance within blockchain networks. Projects may introduce governance tokens that allow holders to participate in decision-making processes, such as proposing and voting on protocol upgrades, changes to network parameters, or allocation of resources (Liu & Wang, 2019). Holders of these tokens have a say in the future direction of the project, fostering a more democratic and community-driven approach to governance. Tokens and cryptocurrencies are essential for incentivization, community participation, and economic models within decentralized ecosystems.

Non-Fungible Tokens (NFTs)

NFTs have emerged as a significant component of web 3, revolutionizing digital ownership, creativity, and the concept of value. NFTs represent unique digital assets, such as artwork, collectibles, virtual real estate, music, videos, and more. Unlike cryptocurrencies like BTC or ETH, which are fungible and interchangeable, NFTs are indivisible and possess distinct characteristics that differentiate them from one another. Each NFT has a unique identifier stored on the blockchain, verifying its authenticity, ownership, and provenance (Voshmgir, 2020).

By tokenizing digital creations, NFTs provide a means to prove originality and authenticity in the digital realm, addressing the long-standing challenge of digital content duplication and plagiarism. Artists, musicians, writers, and other content creators can mint and sell NFTs representing their work, allowing them to retain ownership and control over their creations while monetizing their talent (Ross, et.al, 2019). While NFTs have gained significant attention in the art world, their utility extends far beyond the realm of art and artists. They have diverse applications and can be used in various sectors including, and not limited to:

- Gaming and Virtual Worlds: NFTs are widely used in the gaming industry and virtual worlds. They enable the ownership and trade of in-game assets, such as characters, weapons, skins, or virtual real estate (Steinkuehler and Williams, 2006). They provide players with true ownership and the ability to transfer or sell their assets both within and outside the game ecosystem. This enhances player engagement, fosters a player-driven economy, and enables cross-platform interoperability.
- Collectibles and Memorabilia: NFTs have revitalized the concept of digital collectibles, allowing people to own and trade unique virtual items. These can include sports memorabilia, trading cards, digital toys, or limited-edition items associated with celebrities, movies, or popular franchises. NFT-based collectibles tap into the nostalgia and passion of collectors, creating new opportunities for fan engagement and digital ownership.
- Music and Entertainment: NFTs are being used in the music industry to tokenize music rights, albums, concert tickets, or exclusive experiences. Musicians can release limited-edition NFTs as a form of merchandise or unique collectibles for their fans. This provides a direct connection between artists and their supporters, allowing fans to own a piece of their favorite artist's work or gain access to exclusive content.

- Intellectual Property and Licensing: NFTs have the potential to revolutionize intellectual property rights and licensing. Content creators can tokenize their work, establishing provable ownership and enabling secure digital licensing. NFTs can automate royalty payments and ensure artists receive fair compensation for the use of their intellectual property. This has implications for industries such as publishing, photography, film, and more.
- Supply Chain and Authenticity Verification: NFTs can be used to track and verify the authenticity and provenance of physical goods throughout the supply chain. By linking a unique NFT to a physical item, it becomes possible to ensure that the product is genuine, not counterfeit, and to trace its origin and ownership history. This has applications in luxury goods, art authentication, collectibles, and other industries where authenticity is crucial.
- Decentralized Finance (DeFi): NFTs are also being integrated into the DeFi space, where they can be used as collateral for loans, as a basis for lending and borrowing, or as liquidity providers in decentralized exchanges and yield farming platforms. NFTs representing rare or valuable assets can be leveraged to access additional financial opportunities and services within decentralized finance.

These examples demonstrate the versatility of NFTs and their potential to disrupt various industries. NFTs offer a new paradigm of ownership and value exchange in the digital realm, empowering creators, collectors, gamers, musicians, and businesses with unique opportunities for monetization, engagement, and interaction.

Decentralized Finance (DeFi)

DeFi serves as a catalyst for financial innovation, inclusivity, and empowerment within web 3 by creating programmable financial infrastructure. It provides the infrastructure and tools for individuals to access, manage, and create financial services in a decentralized, transparent, and permissionless manner. DeFi protocols are programmable, allowing developers to create complex financial applications and automate financial processes through smart contracts. DeFi protocols operate on public blockchains, ensuring transparency and auditability of financial transactions. This programmability enables the building of innovative financial products and services that can be tailored to specific needs (Harvey et al., 2021). Developers can leverage existing DeFi protocols and compose them to create new, more sophisticated financial systems, expanding the possibilities for users and driving further innovation. Smart contracts, the backbone of DeFi applications, are open-source and can be verified by anyone, ensuring that the rules and logic governing financial interactions are visible and tamper-resistant (Birrer,et al., 2023). This transparency fosters trust, as users can independently verify the integrity and security of the protocols they interact with.

The power of DeFi lies in the elimination of intermediaries. DeFi removes the need for intermediaries, such as banks or brokers, in financial transactions. By eliminating intermediaries, DeFi protocols reduce costs, increase efficiency, and minimize the risk of censorship or control by centralized entities. Users retain full ownership and control over their assets, and transactions occur directly between parties through the execution of smart contracts. This disintermediation revolutionizes traditional financial systems, empowering individuals and fostering a more peer-to-peer and user-centric financial ecosystem.

DeFi enables financial empowerment and ownership. It allows individuals to become active participants in the financial system rather than passive consumers. Users can lend their assets to earn interest, borrow against their collateral, provide liquidity to decentralized exchanges, participate in yield farming, and more. While DeFi has undoubtedly transformed the financial landscape, but it is not without its challenges. One primary concern is security, as the rapid development of DeFi projects can lead to vulnerabilities and smart contract exploits. Additionally, the lack of regulation can result in risks like fraud and scams, posing threats to investors and users. High transaction fees, a difficult user experience with protocol complexity and web 3 wallet usage, and network congestion on popular blockchain networks like Ethereum can impede accessibility and scalability. As the DeFi ecosystem evolves, addressing these issues is crucial to ensure its sustainable growth and wider acceptance in the traditional financial world. Overall, DeFi serves as a catalyst for financial innovation, inclusivity, and empowerment within web 3. By leveraging blockchain technology, smart contracts, and open protocols, DeFi transforms the traditional financial system into a more equitable, accessible, and user-centric ecosystem in the web 3 era.

Decentralized Applications (DApps)

DApps play a crucial role as building blocks in web 3, transforming the way applications are built, deployed, and operated. They leverage decentralized networks, typically blockchain or distributed ledger technology, as their underlying infrastructure. This decentralized infrastructure eliminates the reliance on central servers, making applications more resilient to failures, censorship-resistant, and less vulnerable to single points of control. DApps distribute data and computing power across a network of participants, ensuring a more robust and secure architecture (Antonopoulos & Wood, 2018). These web 3 applications operate on open protocols and standards, ensuring transparency and accessibility to their inner workings. The code of DApps is often open-source, allowing anyone to inspect, verify, and contribute to their development. This fosters trust, as users can independently review the code to ensure the absence of backdoors or malicious behavior. Openness and transparency promote collaboration, innovation, and community-driven development within the web 3 ecosystem.

However, while DApps offer innovative solutions, but they face several challenges. Scalability, fractured user experience and interface design pose hurdles to mass adoption. This is because DApps often demand a certain level of technical proficiency, limiting their accessibility to mainstream users.

Interoperability

Interoperability, as a key building block of web 3, refers to the ability of different blockchain networks, protocols, and applications to seamlessly communicate and interact with each other. It ensures that information, assets, and functionalities can be transferred and shared across diverse platforms, enhancing the overall efficiency and utility of the web 3 ecosystem. In simpler terms, interoperability ensures seamless connectivity and interaction between different blockchain networks and protocols. It enables users to move their assets seamlessly between different wallets, exchanges, and decentralized applications, enhancing liquidity and accessibility (Lafourcade & Lombard, 2020). Interoperability enables cross-protocol functionality, where applications built on different blockchain platforms can interact and utilize each other's services. For example, a decentralized lending application on one blockchain can access liquidity from a decentralized exchange on another blockchain, creating a more comprehensive and integrated user experience. Various interoperability solutions have emerged to bridge the gap between different blockchain networks. These include decentralized bridges, sidechains, relay protocols, and interoperability-focused projects that facilitate the seamless transfer of assets and data between different chains.

Governance Mechanisms

DAOs are at the forefront of web 3 governance, embodying the principles of decentralization and enabling collective decision-making. DAOs are autonomous entities that operate through smart contracts on the blockchain, allowing stakeholders to participate in the decision-making process. They provide a platform for stakeholders to vote on proposals, contribute to discussions, and shape the direction of the organization. DAOs distribute power and decision-making authority among participants, ensuring a more inclusive and democratic governance model. This decentralized decision-making process ensures that changes are made collectively, with the consensus of the community (Avellaneda, 2019).

Apart from this decentralized storage, identity, social networks are still evolving and will continue to play a pivotal role in the internet of tomorrow.

Challenges and Drawbacks

Web 3, with its decentralized and blockchain-based approach, certainly presents a promising vision of the future internet. However, it is not without its drawbacks and challenges. One of the primary concerns is the developmental phase of blockchain technology itself. Despite its potential, blockchain is still a relatively nascent technology, and as such, it faces various vulnerabilities like protocol hacks, smart contract flaws, and scalability issues (Kushwaha, 2022). These vulnerabilities can lead to significant security breaches and financial losses for users and businesses involved in the web 3 ecosystem.

Another significant challenge is the lack of regulation in the web 3 space. The absence of comprehensive legal frameworks and oversight limits the avenues for detecting potential abuses, frauds, and mitigating damages. As a result, users might find themselves exposed to higher risks and uncertainty, particularly when dealing with novel decentralized financial instruments and services.

Additionally, the user experience (UX) of decentralized solutions remains a significant obstacle. Web3 interfaces are often complex, technical, and challenging to navigate, especially for non-native users who might not be familiar with blockchain terminologies or concepts. This poor UX can deter mainstream adoption and hinder the seamless integration of Web3 technologies into everyday applications. Many organizations still rely on legacy systems built over the years. Integrating these outdated systems with cutting-edge Web3 technologies can be challenging due to differences in architecture, programming languages, and design principles.

In conclusion, while web 3 offers innovative solutions and exciting possibilities for the future of the internet, it must address these drawbacks and challenges to realize its full potential. Efforts to enhance blockchain technology's security, establish regulatory frameworks, and improve user experiences are crucial for the successful and widespread adoption of web 3 technologies. Only by addressing these issues can web 3 truly revolutionize the way we interact and transact online.

WEB 3 AND METAVERSE: THE INTERLINK

Web 3 and the metaverse are closely linked in the vision of a future digital landscape. The metaverse refers to a virtual universe, a collective space where users can interact with each other and digital content in a three-dimensional, immersive environment (Stephenson, 2003). Web 3, on the other hand, represents the evolution of the internet towards a more decentralized, user-centric, and interoperable paradigm. The two growing concepts share an interlinked infrastructure, technology and a vision for the digital future:

Decentralized Infrastructure

Web 3 decentralized infrastructure, often built on blockchain technology, is also laying the underlying foundation for popular evolving metaverses like Decentraland, Sandbox, and other new-age virtual metaverse environments. Blockchain enables secure and transparent transactions, ownership of digital assets, and verifiable identities. By utilizing decentralized networks, the metaverse can ensure that interactions and transactions within the virtual space are transparent, secure, and resistant to censorship or control by centralized authorities.

Digital Asset Ownership

Web 3 concept of digital asset ownership aligns with the idea of owning and trading assets within the metaverse. Through blockchain-based technologies, users can have true ownership of digital assets such as virtual land, avatars, collectibles, and in-game items. These assets in the metaverse need tokenization to allow for seamless transfer, provenance tracking, and interoperability across different metaverse platforms.

Interoperability and Portability

The web 3 emphasis on interoperability allows different components of the metaverse to connect and interact seamlessly. Users should be able to move their digital assets, identities, and experiences across various metaverse platforms without restrictions. web 3 protocols and standards facilitate this interoperability, enabling a unified and connected metaverse experience.

Decentralized Governance

Web 3 governance mechanisms, including DAOs, play a vital role in shaping the rules, policies, and development of the metaverse. Decentralized governance ensures that decisions about the metaverse's infrastructure, protocols, and experiences are made collectively and transparently. It allows participants to have a say in the evolution and direction of the metaverse, fostering a more inclusive and democratic environment.

Token Economies

Web 3 native token economies can be integrated into the metaverse, providing incentives, rewards, and economic systems within the virtual space. Cryptocurrencies and tokens enable new monetization models, digital commerce, and value creation within the metaverse. They can be used for in-world transactions, governance participation, and rewarding content creators, fostering a vibrant and sustainable ecosystem.

Immersive Experiences and User Agency

Web 3 technologies can enhance the immersive experiences and user agency within the metaverse. With advancements in virtual reality (VR), augmented reality (AR), and spatial computing, users can have more engaging and interactive experiences in the metaverse. web 3's focus on user empowerment, data privacy, and control over personal information aligns with the goal of providing users with agency and autonomy within the virtual space.

EMERGING DEVELOPMENTS AND FUTURE OUTLOOKS OF WEB 3

As the landscape of web 3 continues to evolve, emerging developments and the future outlook for this transformative paradigm looks promising. A prominent challenge facing many blockchain networks is scalability. To address this concern, Layer 2 solutions have emerged as a beacon of hope. These solutions enable off-chain transactions and computations, alleviating the burden on the underlying blockchain while preserving its security guarantees. Protocols like Lightning Network for Bitcoin and state channels like Polygon, Optimism for Ethereum exemplify how Layer 2 solutions enhance transaction throughput and lower fees, paving the way for more efficient and user-friendly DApps.

Cross-chain interoperability is a crucial area of innovation that bridges the gap between siloed ecosystems. With the proliferation of diverse blockchain networks, achieving seamless interaction between different chains has become imperative. Projects like Polkadot, Cosmos, and Avalanche are pioneering cross-chain technologies, enabling assets and data to move fluidly between disparate blockchains. This fosters collaboration, enabling users to harness the strengths of multiple chains and broadening the potential applications of web 3.

Advancements in Consensus Mechanisms lie at the heart of blockchain technology and networks, influencing their security, scalability, and energy efficiency. While PoW and PoS are well-known, ongoing research is exploring novel consensus mechanisms like proof-of-space, proof-of-history, and delegated proof-of-stake. These advancements are shaping the landscape of web 3 by addressing the limitations of traditional mechanisms and enhancing network performance and sustainability.

LIMITATIONS OF THE STUDY

While this chapter aims to provide a comprehensive overview of the emergence of web 3 and its core building blocks, there are certain limitations that should be acknowledged. Firstly, the rapidly evolving nature of technology means that some of the information presented in this chapter may become outdated relatively quickly. New developments in web 3 and related technologies could arise after the publication of this chapter, potentially altering the landscape and implications discussed herein. Additionally, the depth of coverage for each core building block might vary due to space constraints, potentially leaving some readers desiring more detailed insights into specific concepts. Furthermore, this chapter may not delve extensively into the potential ethical, legal, and regulatory challenges that web 3 could introduce, as these issues are complex and multifaceted, deserving of more in-depth exploration.

CONTRIBUTIONS OF THE STUDY

This chapter makes several contributions to the understanding of web 3 and its transformative potential. Firstly, it provides a comprehensive and accessible overview of the evolution from web 1 to web 3, highlighting the shortcomings of the current web 2 paradigm and explaining how web 3 addresses these limitations. The chapter elucidates the foundational concepts of web 3, such as blockchain technology, tokenization, DApps, and smart contracts. By doing so, it equips readers with a solid understanding of these concepts, fostering greater awareness of their implications for various sectors and industries. The exploration of decentralized governance models, particularly DAOs, offers readers insights into the democratization of decision-making processes. Moreover, the discussion on the interplay between web 3 and the metaverse illustrates the potential of these core building blocks to reshape the digital experiences of tomorrow. Overall, this chapter contributes to a deeper understanding of web 3's emergence, its foundational elements, and its potential impact on reshaping the digital landscape and our interactions within it.

CONCLUSION

In conclusion, the emergence of web 3 represents a transformative phase in the evolution of the internet. This chapter has explored the core building blocks that underpin web 3 and shape its development. From blockchain technology to decentralized applications, smart contracts, tokenization, and governance mechanisms, each building block plays a vital role in creating a more decentralized, user-centric, and innovative digital ecosystem.

web 3's foundation lies in blockchain technology, which enables trust, transparency, and security through decentralized consensus and smart contracts. It paves the way for the tokenization of assets, allowing for the seamless transfer and ownership of digital assets within a decentralized framework. This, in turn, opens up new possibilities for economic models, value creation, and participation in the digital realm.

Decentralized applications (DApps) drive the user experience in web 3, offering a wide range of services and functionalities that are not controlled by a single entity. These DApps harness the power of blockchain, peer-to-peer networks, and decentralized storage to provide users with greater control, privacy, and autonomy over their data and digital interactions.

Smart contracts, powered by blockchain technology, enable self-executing agreements and automate the enforcement of contractual conditions. They facilitate trustless interactions and eliminate the need for intermediaries, revolutionizing how business and financial transactions are conducted.

Tokenization, another key building block, allows for the representation and ownership of both tangible and intangible assets in the form of digital tokens. This concept has not only disrupted the world of finance but has also expanded into areas such as art, collectibles, and intellectual property rights, unlocking new opportunities for creators, investors, and users.

Furthermore, governance mechanisms in web 3 promote decentralization, transparency, and community participation in decision-making. Decentralized Autonomous Organizations (DAOs) empower stakeholders to collectively shape the future of protocols, applications, and the overall ecosystem. This inclusive governance model ensures that decisions are made by the community and align with the interests of its members.

As web 3 continues to evolve, it brings us closer to the realization of the metaverse—a virtual universe where users can interact, create, and transact in a seamless and immersive manner. The metaverse represents the ultimate convergence of web 3's building blocks, offering a decentralized, interconnected, and user-centric digital experience.

In conclusion, the emergence of web 3 and its core building blocks heralds a new era of decentralized, open, and inclusive internet. By leveraging blockchain technology, tokenization, DApps, smart contracts, and decentralized governance, web 3 lays the foundation for a digital landscape that empowers individuals, fosters innovation, and transforms the way we interact with information, assets, and each other.

REFERENCES

Allen, D. W., & Potts, J. (2023). Web3 toolkits: A user innovation theory of crypto development. *Journal of Open Innovation*, *9*(2), 100050. doi:10.1016/j.joitmc.2023.100050

Antonopoulos, A. M., & Wood, G. (2018). *Mastering ethereum: building smart contracts and dapps*. O'reilly Media.

Avellaneda, O., Bachmann, A., Barbir, A., Brenan, J., Dingle, P., Duffy, K. H., & Sporny, M. (2019). Decentralized identity: Where did it come from and where is it going? *IEEE Communications Standards Magazine*, *3*(4), 10–13. doi:10.1109/MCOMSTD.2019.9031542

Aydinli, K. (2019). Performance Assessment of Cardano. *Independent Study–Communication Systems Group*, 1-39.

Belchior, R., Vasconcelos, A., Guerreiro, S., & Correia, M. (2021). A survey on blockchain interoperability: Past, present, and future trends. [CSUR]. *ACM Computing Surveys*, *54*(8), 1–41. doi:10.1145/3471140

Beniiche, A., Rostami, S., & Maier, M. (2022). Society 5.0: Internet as if people mattered. *IEEE Wireless Communications*, *29*(6), 160–168. doi:10.1109/MWC.009.2100570

Berners-Lee, T., Cailliau, R., Groff, J. F., & Pollermann, B. (2010). World-wide web: The information universe. *Internet Research*, *20*(4), 461–471. doi:10.1108/10662241011059471

Beuscart, J. S., & Mellet, K. (2008). Business models of the web 2.0: Advertising or the tale of two stories. [special issue]. *Communications & Stratégies*.

Birrer, T.K., Amstutz, D., & Wenger, P. (2023). Decentralized Finance: From Core Concepts to DeFi Protocols for Financial Transactions (*Vol. 1*, pp. 39). *Financial Innovation and Technology* (FIT). Springer Wiesbaden.

Bizer, C., Heath, T., & Berners-Lee, T. (2011). Linked data: The story so far. In *Semantic services, interoperability and web applications: emerging concepts* (pp. 205–227). IGI global. doi:10.4018/978-1-60960-593-3.ch008

Cuffe, P. (2018). *The role of the erc-20 token standard in a financial revolution: the case of initial coin offerings.*

D'Amato, C., Bernstein, A., & Tresp, V. (2011). *Induction on the Semantic Web1.*

Figueira, Á., & Oliveira, L. (2017). The current state of fake news: Challenges and opportunities. *Procedia Computer Science*, *121*, 817–825. doi:10.1016/j.procs.2017.11.106

Gangwal, A., Gangavalli, H. R., & Thirupathi, A. (2023). A survey of Layer-two blockchain protocols. *Journal of Network and Computer Applications*, *209*, 103539. doi:10.1016/j.jnca.2022.103539

Harvey, C. R., Ramachandran, A., & Santoro, J. (2021). *DeFi and the Future of Finance*. John Wiley & Sons.

Isaak, J., & Hanna, M. J. (2018). User data privacy: Facebook, Cambridge Analytica, and privacy protection. *Computer*, *51*(8), 56–59. doi:10.1109/MC.2018.3191268

Jacksi, K., & Abass, S. M. (2019). Development history of the world wide web. *Int. J. Sci. Technol. Res*, *8*(9), 75–79.

Khan, S. N., Loukil, F., Ghedira-Guegan, C., Benkhelifa, E., & Bani-Hani, A. (2021). Blockchain smart contracts: Applications, challenges, and future trends. *Peer-to-Peer Networking and Applications*, *14*(5), 2901–2925. doi:10.100712083-021-01127-0 PMID:33897937

KimH. M.TanaS.LaskowskiM.ZhongC.JainA. (2022). Overcoming the Balkanization of Blockchain Research: Web3 is about Tokens AND Protocols AND Online Communities. *Available at* SSRN 4248958. doi:10.2139/ssrn.4248958

Lafourcade, P., & Lombard-Platet, M. (2020). About blockchain interoperability. *Information Processing Letters*, *161*, 105976. doi:10.1016/j.ipl.2020.105976

Lashkari, B., & Musilek, P. (2021). A comprehensive review of blockchain consensus mechanisms. *IEEE Access : Practical Innovations, Open Solutions*, *9*, 43620–43652. doi:10.1109/ACCESS.2021.3065880

Lee, C. (2011). Litecoin whitepaper. *Litecoin White Paper*.

Liu, C., & Wang, H. (2019). Crypto tokens and token offerings: an introduction. *Cryptofinance and mechanisms of exchange: The making of virtual currency*, 125-144.

Monte, G. D., Pennino, D., & Pizzonia, M. (2020, September). Scaling blockchains without giving up decentralization and security: A solution to the blockchain scalability trilemma. In *Proceedings of the 3rd Workshop on Cryptocurrencies and Blockchains for Distributed Systems* (pp. 71-76). ACM. 10.1145/3410699.3413800

Musiał, K., & Kazienko, P. (2013). Social networks on the Internet. *World Wide Web (Bussum)*, *16*(1), 31–72. doi:10.100711280-011-0155-z

Nakamoto, S. (2008). Re: Bitcoin P2P e-cash paper. *The Cryptography Mailing List*, 1-2.

Nath, K. (2022). *Evolution of the internet from web 1.0 to metaverse: The good, the bad and the ugly.*

Politou, E., Casino, F., Alepis, E., & Patsakis, C. (2019). Blockchain mutability: Challenges and proposed solutions. *IEEE Transactions on Emerging Topics in Computing*, *9*(4), 1972–1986. doi:10.1109/TETC.2019.2949510

Poon, J., & Buterin, V. (2017). Plasma: Scalable autonomous smart contracts. *White paper*, 1-47.

Powell, J., & Clarke, A. (2002). The WWW of the World Wide Web: Who, what, and why? *Journal of Medical Internet Research*, *4*(1), e4. doi:10.2196/jmir.4.1.e4 PMID:11956036

RossO.JensenJ. R.AsheimT. 2019. Assets under Tokenization. *Available at* SSRN 3488344.

Schrepel, T. (2023). The Complex Relationship between Web2 Giants and web 3 Projects. *Amsterdam Law & Technology Institute Working Paper*, 1-2023.

Singh, S. (2023, April 14). What are cross-border payments, and how do they work? *Cointelegraph*. https://cointelegraph.com/explained/what-are-cross-border-payments-and-how-do-they-work

Steinkuehler, C. A., & Williams, D. (2006). Where everybody knows your (screen) name: Online games as "third places". *Journal of Computer-Mediated Communication*, *11*(4), 885–909. doi:10.1111/j.1083-6101.2006.00300.x

Stephenson, N. (2003). *Snow crash: A novel*. Spectra.

Tanaka, K., Nakamura, S., Ohshima, H., Yamamoto, Y., Yanbe, Y., & Kato, M. P. (2010). Improving Search and Information Credibility Analysis from Interaction between Web1. 0 and Web2. 0 Content. *Journal of Software*, *5*(2), 154–159. doi:10.4304/jsw.5.2.154-159

Ukpere, C. L., Slabbert, A. D., & Ukpere, W. (2014). A relationship between social media platforms and the financial success of modern African entrepreneurs. *Mediterranean Journal of Social Sciences*, *5*(4), 479. doi:10.5901/mjss.2014.v5n4p479

van Meerten, M., Ozkan, B. K., & Panichella, A. (2023, May). Evolutionary Approach for Concurrency Testing of Ripple Blockchain Consensus Algorithm. *In 2023 IEEE/ACM 45th International Conference on Software Engineering: Software Engineering in Practice (ICSE-SEIP)* (pp. 36-47). IEEE.

Voon Kiong, L. (2022). *Web3 Made Easy: A Comprehensive Guide to Web3: Everything you need to know about Web3, Blockchain, DeFi, Metaverse, NFT and GameFi*. Xiang Xiang Liew.

Voshmgir, S. (2020). *Token Economy: How the Web3 reinvents the Internet* (Vol. 2). Token Kitchen.

Wang, R., & Chan-Olmsted, S. (2020). Content marketing strategy of branded YouTube channels. *Journal of Media Business Studies*, *17*(3-4), 294–316. doi:10.1080/16522354.2020.1783130

Wood, G. (2016). Polkadot: Vision for a heterogeneous multi-chain framework. *White paper, 21*(2327), 4662.

Xu, Z., & Chen, L. (2022). L2chain: Towards High-performance, Confidential and Secure Layer-2 Blockchain Solution for Decentralized Applications. *Proceedings of the VLDB Endowment International Conference on Very Large Data Bases*, *16*(4), 986–999. doi:10.14778/3574245.3574278

Yu, G., Wang, X., Wang, Q., Bi, T., Dong, Y., Liu, R. P., & Reeves, A. (2022). Towards web 3 applications: Easing the access and transition. arXiv preprint arXiv:2210.05903.

Zhang, L., Xu, H., & Hu, H. (2009, December). Design and Implementation of Web2. 0-Based XCU2. 0. In *2009 International Conference on Computational Intelligence and Software Engineering* (pp. 1-4). IEEE.

Chapter 2
Web 3.0 Revolution in the Finance Industry:
Exploring Blockchain and Decentralized Finance

Pooja Lekhi
University Canada West, Canada

ABSTRACT

The emergence of Web 3.0, or the decentralized web, has the potential to transform the finance industry. Web 3.0 introduces new technologies such as blockchain, decentralized apps, and smart contracts that enable secure, transparent, and decentralized financial transactions. This can reduce the need for intermediaries, decrease transaction costs, and enhance the speed and efficiency of financial processes. Additionally, Web 3.0 allows for the creation of new financial products and services that were previously impossible, such as decentralized exchanges, NFTs, peer-to-peer lending platforms, and decentralized autonomous organizations. These innovations could democratize access to financial services and provide new opportunities for individuals and businesses alike. However, Web 3.0 also poses challenges for regulators and financial institutions in terms of risk management, compliance, and adapting to new business models.

INTRODUCTION

Web 3.0 has led to several recent developments in the finance industry. One significant development is the emergence of decentralized finance (DeFi) platforms that enable users to access financial services without the need for intermediaries (Bohme et al., 2015). These platforms are built on blockchain technology and smart contracts and offer services such as lending, borrowing, and trading of digital assets. DeFi has grown rapidly in recent years, with the total value locked in DeFi protocols surpassing $100 billion in mid-2021 (DeFi Pulse). Another development is the use of non-fungible tokens (NFTs) in the finance industry. NFTs are unique digital assets that are stored on a blockchain and cannot be replicated.

DOI: 10.4018/978-1-6684-9919-1.ch002

Copyright © 2023, IGI Global. Copying or distributing in print or electronic forms without written permission of IGI Global is prohibited.

They have been used in the art world to create digital art that can be bought and sold, but they are also being used in the finance industry to represent ownership of assets such as real estate, fine wines, and even tweets (Hagerty, 2021). Web 3.0 has also led to the development of decentralized exchanges (DEXs), which enable peer-to-peer trading of digital assets without the need for intermediaries (Changelly). DEXs use smart contracts to execute trades and are often more secure and transparent than traditional centralized exchanges. Overall, the impact of Web 3.0 on the finance industry has been significant, with the emergence of new business models, products, and services. However, there are also challenges to be addressed, such as regulatory compliance and risk management in these new decentralized financial systems (Böhme et al., 2015).

The Emergence of Decentralized Finance (DeFi): Advantages, Risks, and Challenges

Decentralized finance (DeFi) is an emerging area of the blockchain industry that leverages decentralized technology to offer traditional financial services. DeFi platforms use blockchain technology and smart contracts to create a transparent, secure, and decentralized system for lending, borrowing, and trading digital assets. These platforms remove intermediaries and offer a more efficient, cost-effective, and accessible way of accessing financial services compared to traditional finance

According to DeFi Pulse, the total value locked in DeFi protocols has surpassed $150 billion as of March 2023, a significant increase from $1 billion in June 2020 (DeFi Pulse, 2023). The growth of DeFi can be attributed to its ability to provide services such as lending, borrowing, and trading of digital assets without intermediaries, enabling more people to access financial services worldwide (Consensys, 2022).

The use of smart contracts is one of the most significant advantages of DeFi, as it ensures transactions are secure, and funds are locked until certain conditions are met (Swan, 2021). The transparency of DeFi platforms is also due to their open-source nature, which allows anyone to review the code, identify vulnerabilities, and suggest improvements (The Block, 2021).

Benefits of Smart Contracts

Smart contracts offer a fast, efficient, and accurate way to execute agreements. As soon as the conditions specified in the contract are met, the contract is automatically executed without the need for any human intervention. Unlike traditional contracts that require a lot of paperwork and manual processing, smart contracts are completely digital and automated. This eliminates the potential for errors that can arise from manual data entry, saving time and resources in the process. Overall, smart contracts provide a reliable and streamlined approach to executing agreements that can benefit various industries and use cases (IBM.com).

The use of blockchain technology in recording transactions ensures a high level of security due to the encryption of the records, making it extremely difficult for hackers to gain unauthorized access. Additionally, the records are linked to each other on a distributed ledger, so if a hacker attempts to modify one record, they would need to alter the entire chain, making it even more challenging to tamper with the records. (Kohli, A., Lekhi, P., & Hafez, G. A. A. (2023).

Smart contracts eliminate the need for intermediaries in facilitating transactions, which results in cost and time savings. By cutting out the middlemen, the transaction fees and delays associated with their involvement are removed, allowing for a more streamlined and efficient process (IBM.com).

Non-Fungible Tokens

NFTs, or non-fungible tokens, are unique digital assets that are stored on a blockchain. Each NFT is one-of-a-kind and cannot be replicated, making it valuable and unique. NFTs can represent various types of digital content, such as artwork, music, videos, and even tweets. They are bought and sold like traditional assets, but their value is based on their uniqueness and rarity. NFTs have gained popularity in recent years, with some selling for millions of dollars in high-profile auctions. They are seen as a new way for creators to monetize their digital content and for investors to own and trade unique digital assets

NFT Statistics in 2023

The NFT market has been making headlines lately, with a worth of over $22 billion and a staggering growth of 220x since 2021. Last year alone, NFT sales reached a total of $25 billion. It is predicted that the NFT market will continue to boom, and will be worth an impressive $80 billion by 2025.

However, it's not all smooth sailing for the NFT market. Sales have dropped significantly by over 90% since September 2021, and some experts are speculating that this may be due to the market becoming saturated with too many NFT offerings.

Despite this setback, there are still some noteworthy sales happening in the NFT world. For example, the most expensive collection of NFTs to date was sold for a jaw-dropping $91.8 million.

On average, NFT sales generate approximately $1.8 billion in revenue every month. It's worth noting that while some NFTs fetch millions of dollars, half of all NFT sales cost less than $200.

Overall, the NFT market has experienced significant growth and generated substantial revenue. However, with sales dropping and the market becoming more crowded, it remains to be seen how sustainable the NFT boom will be in the long run (Katatikarn J, 2023)

Figure 1. The top ten countries with the greatest number of NFT users
Source: Composed by Author, data retrieved from <u>demandsage.com</u>

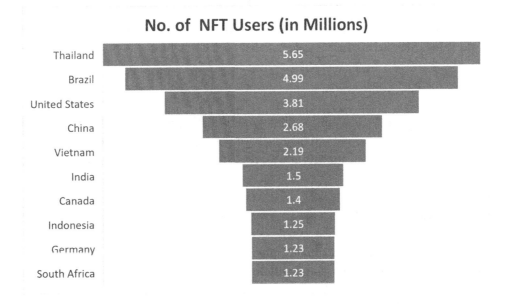

No. of NFT Users (in Millions)

Thailand	5.65
Brazil	4.99
United States	3.81
China	2.68
Vietnam	2.19
India	1.5
Canada	1.4
Indonesia	1.25
Germany	1.23
South Africa	1.23

Figure 1 elucidates, With a user base of 5.65 million, Thailand currently boasts the highest number of NFT users globally. Brazil and the United States come in second and third place, with 4.99 million and 3.81 million NFT users, respectively.

Role of NFTs in Finance Industry

Non-Fungible Tokens (NFTs) have gained significant attention within the finance industry due to their unique properties and potential applications. As stated, NFTs are digital assets that represent ownership of a specific item or piece of content, often using blockchain technology to ensure provenance, authenticity, and scarcity. Their role in the finance industry is multifaceted and can be understood through several key aspects.

1.   Digital Ownership and Asset Tokenization:

NFTs enable the tokenization of real-world and digital assets, allowing individuals to represent ownership and transfer value digitally. This concept has the potential to revolutionize the way various financial assets are managed and traded. For example, real estate properties, art pieces, collectibles, and intellectual property rights can be tokenized as NFTs, facilitating fractional ownership and liquidity. This has the potential to democratize access to traditionally illiquid assets. Katatikarn (2023)

2.   Investment and Speculation:

NFTs have also become a subject of investment and speculation. Collectors and investors purchase NFTs with the expectation of their value appreciating over time. However, this aspect of NFTs has raised concerns about the potential for market bubbles and volatility.

3.   Gaming and Virtual Economies:

NFTs are integrated into various blockchain-based games and virtual worlds. Players can own, trade, and use NFTs within these environments. This has given rise to virtual economies where in-game items have real-world value. Messari (2021)

4.   Risk Management and Insurance:

NFTs can be used to represent insurance policies and risk-sharing agreements. These digital contracts could automate claims processing and settlements based on predefined conditions. Additionally, NFTs could enable peer-to-peer insurance models and increase transparency in the insurance industry. Lekhi, P. (2023)

5.   Supply Chain and Trade Finance:

NFTs can enhance transparency and traceability in supply chain management. They can represent unique product identifiers, certificates of authenticity, and ownership records. This has implications for trade finance, as NFTs can streamline verification processes, reduce fraud, and improve efficiency in cross-border transactions. (Kohli, A., Lekhi, P., & Hafez, G. A. A. (2023)

Blockchain's Revolution in the Financial Services Industry

The financial services industry is on the brink of a revolution, thanks to the transformative power of blockchain technology. (Lekhi, P, 2023). This technology has the potential to streamline processes, reduce costs, and increase efficiency, thus transforming the industry in multiple areas. From capital markets and asset management to payments and remittances, banking and lending, trade finance, and even insurance, blockchain can change the way we do business. In this article, we will delve into how blockchain is transforming various sectors of the financial services industry, highlighting the potential benefits that this technology can bring.

- Blockchain Transforms Capital Markets

Blockchain technology can revolutionize capital markets by reducing costs, increasing efficiency, and increasing transparency and security. This technology eliminates intermediaries, such as brokers, by digitizing workflows and assets, thus making capital markets more accessible and efficient. With the ability to tokenize assets, they become programmable, more manageable, tradeable, and fractionalized, resulting in increased liquidity and decreased cost of capital.

Smart contracts, which are self-executing contracts with the terms directly written into code, automate and enforce the transactional processes, resulting in faster and more accurate settlements.

Transparency and security are inherent features of blockchain technology. The distributed ledger system ensures that all participants have access to the same information, creating a transparent and auditable record of transactions. This transparency reduces the risk of fraud, as any attempt to tamper with the data would be immediately noticeable to all participants. Additionally, the use of cryptographic algorithms ensures the security and integrity of the data, making it highly resistant to hacking or unauthorized modifications (Lekhi P,2023).

Also, Tokenization allows assets to be divided into smaller fractions, enabling fractional ownership. This can open up new investment opportunities, as investors can own a portion of high-value assets without the need for large upfront investments.

Traditional assets like real estate or private equity can be illiquid and challenging to sell quickly. Tokenization can unlock liquidity by facilitating secondary markets where token holders can buy and sell their fractional ownership stakes easily.

- Revolutionizing Asset and Stakeholder Management with Blockchain

Blockchain technology provides a solution for streamlining asset and stakeholder management for venture capital firms, private equity firms, real estate funds, and specialty markets. With blockchain, firms can launch funds automatically, digitize their portfolios and holdings for wider market access, liquidity, and fractionalization. Customizable privacy settings ensure transaction confidentiality, and digital assets can be programmed with voting and other shareholder rights and obligations to reduce the risks of human error.

With blockchain, firms can automate the launch of funds through smart contracts. This reduces manual intervention and speeds up the fund creation process, allowing firms to establish new investment vehicles and onboard investors quickly.

Blockchain technology allows for the digitization of portfolios and holdings, making them easily accessible to a wider market. This digitization facilitates secondary market trading and fractionalization, enabling greater liquidity and the ability to divide ownership stakes into smaller units.

- Revolutionizing Global Payments with Blockchain

Blockchain technology can revolutionize global payments and remittance systems by streamlining processes, reducing settlement times, and minimizing costs. With blockchain, it is possible to achieve rapid and secure domestic and cross-border payments, digitized KYC/AML data and transaction history, and automated regulatory oversight and auditing. Multiple forms of payment, including tokenized fiat, stablecoin, and cryptocurrency, are possible with blockchain, eliminating the need for multiple intermediaries that charge hefty fees.

Blockchain offers robust security features that protect sensitive customer data. By leveraging encryption and consensus algorithms, blockchain ensures that KYC/AML data is stored in an immutable and tamper-proof manner. This reduces the risk of data breaches and unauthorized access, providing a higher level of security compared to traditional centralized databases.

With blockchain, KYC/AML data can be stored on the distributed ledger, allowing different parties, such as financial institutions and regulators, to access and verify the data more efficiently. This eliminates the need for repetitive verification processes, as the data can be shared securely and instantly among authorized entities, reducing duplication of effort and saving time.

Traditional KYC/AML processes often involve manual paperwork, back-and-forth communication between parties, and lengthy verification timelines. By digitizing KYC/AML data on the blockchain, the onboarding process can be accelerated. Users can provide consent for sharing their verified data across multiple service providers, simplifying the onboarding process for new accounts or services.

- Transforming Traditional Banking: How Blockchain Streamlines Lending and Transaction Services

Blockchain technology can streamline banking and lending services, reducing risk, and decreasing issuance and settlement times. Blockchain benefits include verified documentation, streamlined credit scoring and prediction, automated underwriting and disbursement of funds, and facilitated collateralization of assets. This technology results in a faster, more secure, and more efficient banking system for all (Lekhi, P,2023).

Blockchain technology allows for the secure storage and verification of financial documents, such as loan agreements, identity documents, and property titles. This reduces the risk of fraudulent activities and provides a transparent and auditable trail of documentation. According to a survey by Accenture, 77% of banking executives believe that blockchain technology can help eliminate the need for physical documents within the next five years.

Blockchain can enhance credit scoring processes by leveraging a decentralized and transparent ledger of financial data. This enables more accurate and reliable credit assessments, as it provides a comprehensive view of an individual's financial history. According to a study by the World Economic Forum, blockchain-based credit scoring systems have the potential to expand credit access for up to 1.7 billion unbanked individuals worldwide.

Blockchain technology can automate the underwriting process by using smart contracts. Smart contracts can automatically evaluate loan applications based on predefined criteria, eliminating manual interventions and reducing processing times. For example, a study by Deloitte found that blockchain-based lending platforms can reduce the time for loan origination and disbursement from weeks to just a few hours.

- Transforming Trade Finance with Blockchain: Revolutionizing Supply Chain Processes

Blockchain technology can streamline and digitize the entire trade finance process, increasing security and efficiency, and eliminating the cumbersome and outdated practice of negotiating independent finance vehicles for each stage of the trade. Blockchain enables digitizing and authenticating documentation, asset digitization for faster settlement times, and creating a consistent financing vehicle for the entire trade lifecycle, which results in a more streamlined and cohesive trade finance process.

- Blockchain's Impact on the Insurance Sector

Blockchain technology can revolutionize the insurance industry by providing secure data verification and smart contract automation, streamlining claims processing and disbursement, and creating more efficient and transparent systems. Parameterized contracts and tokenized reinsurance markets can create more efficient, and transparent systems, thereby reducing fraudulent claims and slow processing times.

- Blockchain Streamlining Compliance and Regulation

Blockchain technology is revolutionizing regulatory compliance by providing unique governance and compliance attributes programmed into digital assets. Blockchain offers streamlined processes that automate data verification and reporting, facilitate regulatory oversight, and eliminate errors associated with manual auditing. In addition, blockchain enables the creation and enforcement of incentive structures to improve network governance, reducing operational friction and ensuring compliance with applicable laws and regulations in real-time.

Risks, Challenges in DeFi Ecosystem

DeFi is a rapidly growing sector within the cryptocurrency and blockchain space, offering users the ability to access financial services in a decentralized manner. While there are numerous benefits to DeFi, such as increased accessibility, transparency, and security, there are also several challenges that the industry must address.

The DeFi ecosystem still faces scalability issues, as the blockchain technology it relies on has limitations in terms of transaction throughput and speed (CoinDesk, 2022). Despite these challenges, the DeFi ecosystem's potential for innovation and disruption in the traditional finance sector remains significant, offering more accessible, efficient, and cost-effective financial services to users worldwide (Consensys, 2022). DeFi still poses several challenges, including regulatory compliance, security, and scalability.

Regulators worldwide are still grappling with how to regulate DeFi protocols, and there have been several cases of hacks and scams, leading to significant losses for users (CNBC, 2021).

Security concerns: DeFi hacks have resulted in the loss of millions of dollars. One of the most notable examples is the hack of the Poly Network in August 2021, which resulted in the loss of over $600 million worth of cryptocurrency. Another example is the hack of the decentralized lending platform, bZx, in February 2020, which resulted in a loss of $350,000. (Coindesk - Poly Network Hack,2021)

Regulatory challenges: The lack of clear regulations around DeFi has been a topic of concern. The US Securities and Exchange Commission (SEC) has indicated that some DeFi projects could be classified as securities and may fall under their jurisdiction. The European Union has also proposed new regulations that would apply to cryptocurrency-related services, including DeFi. (Bloomberg - DeFi Faces Regulatory Crackdown,2021)

Scalability concerns: The growth of DeFi has also highlighted scalability issues, as some networks struggle to handle the increasing demand for transactions. Ethereum, which is the most widely used blockchain platform for DeFi, has experienced congestion and high transaction fees during periods of high demand. (Cointelegraph, 2021)

User experience challenges: DeFi is still relatively new and can be complex for new users to navigate. Users must understand the risks associated with using DeFi platforms and the potential consequences of making mistakes such as sending funds to the wrong address. Additionally, the user interfaces of many DeFi platforms can be confusing and difficult to navigate for beginners. (Decrypt - DeFi's UX Problem: Why Decentralization Is Not User-Friendly, 2021)

While DeFi offers significant potential benefits, it also faces various challenges and concerns that must be addressed to ensure its continued growth and success

CONCLUSION

The emergence of Web 3.0 has brought significant developments in the finance industry, including decentralized finance (DeFi) platforms, non-fungible tokens (NFTs), and decentralized exchanges (DEXs). DeFi platforms leverage blockchain technology and smart contracts to offer traditional financial services without intermediaries, resulting in more accessible and efficient financial services. NFTs represent unique digital assets that cannot be replicated, and their popularity has grown as creators and investors seek to monetize and own digital content. the DeFi ecosystem has witnessed significant growth and development in recent years, offering more accessible, efficient, and cost-effective financial services to users worldwide. Despite the challenges, the DeFi ecosystem's potential for innovation and disruption in the traditional finance sector remains significant.

However, the full potential of Web 3.0 in finance has yet to be realized. The technology is still in its early stages of development, and there are still significant challenges to overcome, such as scalability, security, and user adoption. Nevertheless, with continued innovation and investment, Web 3.0 has the potential to revolutionize the finance industry, making it more efficient, secure, and accessible to everyone.

REFERENCES

Accenture. (2021). Banking on AI: Unlocking Value. *Accenture*. https://www.accenture.com/_acnmedia/PDF-56/Accenture-Banking-on-AI-Unlocking-Value.pdf

Bloomberg. (2021, February 10). DeFi Faces Regulatory Crackdown in European Union's Latest Crypto Proposal. *Bloomberg*. https://www.bloomberg.com/news/articles/2021-02-10/defi-faces-regulatory-crackdown-in-european-union-s-latest-crypto-proposal

Böhme, R., Christin, N., Edelman, B., & Moore, T. (2015). Bitcoin: Economics, technology, and governance. *The Journal of Economic Perspectives*, 29(2), 213–238. doi:10.1257/jep.29.2.213

Changelly. (n.d.). What is a Decentralized Exchange (DEX)? *Changelly*. https://changelly.com/blog/what-is-decentralized-exchange-dex/

CNBC. (2021). *DeFi has a money laundering problem, but experts say it can be fixed*. CNBC. https://www.cnbc.com/2021/08/31/defi-has-a-money-laundering-problem-but-experts-say-it-can-be-fixed.html

CoinDesk. (2022). Scalability. *Coindesk*. https://www.coindesk.com/scalability

Coindesk. (2021, August 10). Poly Network Hack: $600M in Stolen Crypto Has Been Returned So Far. *Coindesk*. https://www.coindesk.com/poly-network-hack-600m-in-stolen-crypto-returned-so-far

Cointelegraph. (2021, May 15). Ethereum's DeFi ecosystem faces its biggest challenge so far. *Cointelegraph*. https://cointelegraph.com/news/ethereum-s-defi-ecosystem-faces-its-biggest-challenge-so-far

Consensys. (2022). Decentralized Finance (DeFi). *Consensys*. https://consensys.net/decentralized-finance-defi/

Decrypt. (2021, May 21). DeFi's UX Problem: Why Decentralization Is Not User-Friendly. *Decrypt*. https://decrypt.com/72033/defis-ux-problem-why-decentralization-is-not-user-friendly

DeFi Pulse. (2023). Home. *DeFi Pulse*. https://defipulse.com/

DeFi Pulse. (n.d.). Decentralized Finance (DeFi) - Total Value Locked (TVL) in USD. *DeFi Pulse*. https://defipulse.com/

Deloitte. (2022). *Real estate prediction 2022*. Deloitte. https://www2.deloitte.com/content/dam/Deloitte/nl/Documents/real-estate/deloitte-nl-fsi-real-estate-predictions-2022.pdf

Hagerty, J. R. (2021, March 11). Non-Fungible Tokens 101: A Primer On NFTs For Brands And Business Professionals. *Forbes*. https://www.forbes.com/sites/jonathanhagerty/2021/03/11/non-fungible-tokens-101-a-primer-on-nfts-for-brands-and-business-professionals/

IBM.com. (2020). *What are smart contracts on blockchain?* IBM. https://www.ibm.com/topics/smart-contracts#:~:text=Smart%20contracts%20are%20simply%20programs,intermediary's%20involvement%20or%20time%20loss

Katatikarn, J. (2023). *NFT Statistics 2023: Market Size and Trends*. Academy of Animated Art. https://academyofanimatedart.com/nft-statistics/

Kohli, A., Lekhi, P., & Hafez, G. A. A. (2023). Blockchain Tech-Enabled Supply Chain Traceability: A Meta-Synthesis. In *Financial Technologies and DeFi: A Revisit to the Digital Finance Revolution* (pp. 99–107). Springer International Publishing. doi:10.1007/978-3-031-17998-3_7

Lekhi, P. (2023). Currency and Payment Tech: Cryptocurrencies Transforming the Face of Finance. In *Financial Technologies and DeFi: A Revisit to the Digital Finance Revolution* (pp. 57–66). Springer International Publishing. doi:10.1007/978-3-031-17998-3_4

Messari. (2021). *Non-fungible tokens (NFTs)*. Messari. https://messari.io/resource/non-fungible-tokens

Non-Fungible Tokens (NFTs) Market Size Worth $2.7 Billion by 2027 | CAGR: 48.4%: Grand View Research, Inc. (2021, September 1). PR Newswire. https://www.prnewswire.com/news-releases/non-fungible-tokens-nfts-market-size-worth-2-7-billion-by-2027--cagr-48-4-grand-view-research-inc-301367259.html

NonFungible.com. (2021). *NFT Market Report Q1 2021*. NonFungible. https://nonfungible.com/blog/nft-market-report-q1-2021

NonFungible.com. (2021). *NFT Market Report Q2 2021*. NonFungible. https://nonfungible.com/blog/nft-market-report-q2-2021

NonFungible.com. (2021). *NFT Market Report Q3 2021*. NonFungible. https://nonfungible.com/blog/nft-market-report-q3-2021

Swan, M. (2021). *What is Decentralized Finance (DeFi)?* CoinMarketCap. https://coinmarketcap.com/alexandria/article/what-is-decentralized-finance-defi

Chapter 3
Traditional Finance vs. Web 3:
A Comparative Analysis of Key Features and Characteristics for Better Readability Purposes

Babita Jha

https://orcid.org/0000-0001-8586-0250
CHRIST University (Deemed), India

Pratibha Giri

https://orcid.org/0000-0002-9700-4918
CHRIST University (Deemed), India

Deepak Jha

CHRIST University (Deemed), India

Debora Dhanya

CHRIST University (Deemed), India

ABSTRACT

Web3 is a ground-breaking invention that has the ability to address the shortcomings of web1 and web2. The industry witnessing its major impact is the finance sector. A wave of innovation in traditional finance has been inspired by the introduction of Web3. It is also referred to as the decentralised web and is a developing movement that is upending conventional finance by providing a more open, safe, and decentralised substitute. Traditional banking should work to adopt the features that Web3 offers, including stability, scalability, interoperability, security, performance, extensibility, management, and openness. In order for TradFi to maintain its relevance and expertise in the face of the widespread adoption of digital financial modes, it is now necessary to embrace several Web3 capabilities. Keeping into consideration the relevance and importance of Web3 in finance, this chapter will basically focus on analysing the key features and characteristics of Web3 in comparison to traditional finance.

DOI: 10.4018/978-1-6684-9919-1.ch003

Copyright © 2023, IGI Global. Copying or distributing in print or electronic forms without written permission of IGI Global is prohibited.

INTRODUCTION

The internet has become such a vital part of everyday life for so long that its evolution may be divided into several separate stages. These stages define technical progress, how we engage using digital technology, and the impact that interaction has on society as a whole and the economy. The initial consumer-ready form of the internet was available in the mid-1990s. web 1 is the name given to this phase. web 1 enabled the development of basic websites (Nath, 2014) as well as internet applications, which influenced both the social and financial systems. The dot-com surge and its concomitant exemplified in this era.

Then came web 2, which brought an improved user-focused, responsive internet (Wan et al.,2023) that enabled more effective and equitable data sharing that wasn't previously feasible. This internet era encompasses everything from Wikipedia to apps for mobile devices to online banking, and it continues to influence much of today's internet experience. However, many people argue that the web 2 internet is faulty because of its reliance on centralized architecture and rent-seeking business structures. web 3, which is mostly based on blockchain, has gained more traction in recent years, promising decentralization, more egalitarian access, and more democratized economic models. Defi has played a crucial role in the expansion of the blockchain technology known as Ethereum as well as web 3. The advent of the blockchain platform Ethereum and related smart contract capability in 2015 established the basis for the far-reaching growth of web 3. Many people believe that web 3 is enabling the establishment of a new internet that will eliminate the inefficiencies that have plagued web 1 and web 2. Web 3 makes use of decentralized computer networks, distributed apps, and smart contracts by incorporating blockchain technology (Cao, 2022). The network of Ethereum contributed to the creation of many protocols aimed at facilitating accessibility to a more transparent, unrestricted and accessible financial system.

The development of web 3 technology has created a plethora of new options across the financial services sector. web 3 is gaining popularity in traditional finance because the fundamental technology of web 3 has the potential to change the face of trading. The world of money is undergoing a huge transition, and the way that we conduct financial transactions is changing. web 3's emergence has spawned an upsurge of innovation in traditional finance. The decentralized web, as it is often known, is a developing phenomenon that poses a challenge to traditional finance by providing a more transparent, safer, and decentralized alternative.

THEORETICAL BACKGROUND

In recent years, internet has witnessed remarkable transformation. Infrastructural support for operating enterprises and delivering services is also becoming increasingly important. The Semantic web serves as the backbone of web 3, a new Internet architecture that makes the internet far more stable, resilient, and practical (Suryono et al., 2020). A decentralized, unrestricted blockchain-based economy, new types of information architecture, and new forms of worldwide social interaction are all allegedly part of web 3. Due to its distinctive decentralized features, Web 3.0 has gained a lot of attention (Chen et al.,2022).

Using the Internet, new financial systems have proven more unified, efficient, and trustworthy. web 3 is a term used to describe an era of financial systems that has the potential to disrupt the present financial system as a result of the Internet's development. This term is widely used in the banking industry to describe solutions that function as a digital medium for the exchange of value as well as instruments for managing and trading value. For digital wallets, the cost of acquiring a customer is about $20, compared to about $1,000 for traditional financial institutions (Friedrich, 2020; Agarwal & Zhang, 2020). While Square's Cash App and PayPal's Venmo took less than ten years to accomplish this milestone, JPMorgan Chase took more than 30 years and multiple acquisitions to get there (Friedrich, 2020). With 360 million users and a market valuation of $330 billion as of February 2021, PayPal has more clients than any other bank outside JPMorgan Chase (Clifford, 2021). PayPal only attracted 16 million new customers in the fourth quarter of 2020. New opportunities to deliver financial activities are opened up by technologies like artificial intelligence, machine learning, and blockchain.

The modern commercial activities have transformed as a result of new information technologies, particularly the Internet (Zhao et al., 2016; Gu et al., 2016). The rise of e-finance, along with technology advancements, offers significant advantages to customers all over the world (Claessen et al., 2000; Vučinić, 2020). The spillover and growth of technical knowledge are the sources of supply-side technology innovation, particularly financial technology innovation (Kauffman et al., 2014). (Lerner & Tufano, 2011; Lyytinen & Rose, 2003) in their study pointed out that innovation in technology has made life more convenient, which encourages demand-side financial innovation.

The use of web 3 in finance is perfectly demonstrated by Decentralized finance (Defi). DeFi represents a new financial system based on securely distributed ledgers similar to those used by cryptocurrencies (cryptocurrencies (Chu et al., 2023; Meegan & Koens, 2021). The new financial system abolishes the authority that financial institutions, especially banking institutions, hold over money, financial commodities, and financial services. It has the potential to make financial markets more accessible, wide, and equitable to anybody with a web connection. Decentralized finance eliminates middlemen by allowing people, organizations, and merchants to conduct financial transactions using innovative technology ((Aquilina et a., 2023). Peer integrates these platforms into peer financial networks by utilizing proper connectivity and computer software data security standards. Money can be lent, borrowed, and transacted employing technology that logs and verifies monetary transactions in decentralized database systems from anywhere using an internet connection (Ozili, 2023; Yavin & Reardon, 2021).

REVIEW OF LITERATURE

The "Semantic Web" is another name for web 3.0. According to Naik & Lingaiah (2008), the term "web 3.0" was coined to characterize the interaction between the growth of web usage and the transformation of the web into a database. Web 3.0 allows computers to define what a search query implies and what the user's intentions and wants are (Miranda et al., 2014). Ian these settings, the software tools find the data, evaluate it, and then transform it into useful information that can be transmitted.

With its decentralized and open architecture, the web 3 ecosystem is the ideal environment for DeFi to grow (Aquilina et al., 2023). The possibility of lowering the cost and increasing the efficacy of financial transactions, as well as the creation of a more equitable and inclusive financial system is enabled with DeFi (Sahani, 2022; Lara et al., 2007). A blockchain-based financial infrastructure (Murray & Combs, 2023) called decentralized finance (DeFi) has recently experienced significant growth. According to Buterin (2013), the word DeFi typically refers to a protocol stack that is open, permissionless, and highly interoperable and is constructed on open smart contract platforms like the Ethereum blockchain. It mimics current financial services in a more transparent and open manner. DeFi, in particular, does not depend on middlemen or centralized organizations. A decentralized blockchain-based smart contract platform was proposed by Buterin (2013) to address any concerns with the execution environment's level of trust and to enable secure global states. The contracts on this platform can also communicate with one another and build upon one another (Kumar et al., 2020).

Innovations in finance are not a recent occurrence; they have always gone hand in hand with technical advancements (Michalopoulos et.al., 2009). It is well-known that technological and financial advances are intertwined and develop over time. Wood (2015) further formalized the idea, which was then put into practice as Ethereum. Ethereum is the most popular smart contract platform in terms of market value, applications offered, and development activity, despite the fact that there are numerous competitors Szabo (1997) claimed that many contracts may be embedded in the hardware and software we deal with. Compared with conventional financial institutions, fintech companies are frequently nimbler and provide greater customer service and convenience at considerably lower costs (Browne, 2021; Egan, 2020).

TRADITIONAL FINANCE

Traditional finance refers to the techniques applied over time. It encompasses financial practices like obtaining loans, overdrafts, and opening accounts at traditional brick-and-mortar banks. Walking into a bank to obtain an advance or using a check to withdraw money from a bank are examples of traditional finance (Bagrecha et al., 2020).. Investors in traditional finance frequently make thoughtful, logical decisions under uncertain circumstances. Additionally, conventional finance fits the definition of normative because everyone abides by the predetermined laws and guidelines. But because these guidelines are purely fact-based and unaffected by personal judgement or emotion, many individuals refer to this sort of finance as objective (De Filippi, & Mauro, 2014).

The foundation of traditional finance comprises a centralized authority that manages all of the funds that clients provide. The various financial organizations such as investment banks, commercial banks, brokerage houses, and insurance companies act as an intermediary. Each of these institutions charges a certain portion of their commission rate or fee on their assistance, which includes acting as third parties to facilitate the movement of money (Sims, 2019). Traditional finance is a centralized financial system that uses custodial accounts. Any transaction is handled by the central authority, and money is held in trust by the bank with the assurance that they would be released whenever you make a claim (Martino, 2019).

In conventional finance, the fundamental tenet of the system is that you must have faith in the business that you're working with, the bureaucracy in charge of handling your money, and the individuals who work there. Money management is not entirely under your control. Public administration, financial authorities, legislation, and financial institution licenses are the sources of confidence. In other words, people are trusted more than math and code. If you don't follow their rules, they'll be able to undo your transactions.

Key Features of Traditional Finance

a) **Regulated financial institutions:** Conventional finance is distinguished by the existence of financial institutions that are regulated, which include credit unions, banking institutions, insurance organizations, and investment firms. According to the Basel Committee (2010), financial institutions are subject to a variety of national and international rules designed to promote financial stability, protect customers, and deter money-related crime (Basel Committee, 2010).

b)   **Standardized financial instruments:** Traditional finance provides a wide range of standardized financial services, including deposits, mortgages, credit, insurance plans, and investment vehicles. These solutions meet clients' different financial needs while also facilitating economic progress (Mishkin, 2012).

c)   **Risk management techniques:** To assess, monitor, and mitigate different financial risks, like market risk, credit risk, and operational risk, traditional financial institutions use stringent risk management techniques. These procedures safeguard the interests of clients while preserving the soundness of the monetary system (Alexander, 2008).

d)   **Financial intermediation:** Financial intermediation, which includes transferring money from savers to borrowers, is one of the main functions of traditional finance. This procedure makes it possible to allocate resources effectively, fostering growth and development in the economy (Mishkin, 2012).

e)   **Centralized and hierarchical structure:** Financial institutions serve as mediators between savers and borrowers in traditional finance, which is characterized by a centralized and hierarchical structure. This structure gives the financial system stability and effectiveness, but it may also stifle creativity and adaptability (Berger, 2003).

Advantages

Traditional Finance involves centralized organizations that administer resources and money on behalf of users. All financial categories, including loan, borrowing, and trading, in this kind of system, need for a borrower or receiver, lender, and a financial middleman who handles all such financial transactions. Traditional Finance has the following advantages:

a)   **Stability and safety:** As there are less chance of theft or fraud in a centralized system, it is more stable and safer than a decentralized one.

b)   **Traceability:** In a centralized system, transactions are easy to track, making it quicker to identify and fix any glitches that may develop.

c)   **Improved control:** A centralized authority can oversee all of an organization's financial processes in one location.

d)   **Cost-efficiency:** Transaction prices and speed are significantly greater as compared to cefi and defi.

e)   **Ready-made infrastructure:** a large range of financial services from various corporations and institutions

Disadvantages

TradFi lacks accountability, is opaque, and has little to no transparency. Following are some of the disadvantages associated with Traditional Finance:

a)   **Less transparent:** A centralized authority maintains greater influence on the transmission of information, making other sections of the structure less aware of what happens within the organization.

b)   **Susceptible to corruption:** People in power may prioritize their own interests over ensuring that all members of the system benefit fairly from financial services.

c) **Less democratic**: Traditional finance favors larger institutions and organizations, which end up with greater advantages than other competitors in the financial market, such as less-favored SMEs or startups.

WEB 3 IN FINANCE

The Internet has dramatically revolutionized the way in which we communicate and manage business, nonetheless it remains fundamentally an analogue system. Before many banks began to understand web 2, web 3 had already begun to emerge in the finance industry. Financial technology has grown alongside the Internet, resulting in the establishment of new businesses. In order to capitalize on these technical advancements that could change how money, payments, as well as and digital assets are used in the future, it is more important than ever to reinvent services and business models. As a decentralized network, web 3 does not need authorization from centralized authorities, who are no longer able to control who can access what services. Financial systems that enable the exchange of money include banks, insurance firms, and stock exchanges. web 3 has developed novel financial systems that are more connected, effective, and safe because the financial system as a whole is always evolving.

Web 3, being an innovative technology, has the ability to address the limitations associated with web 2 in banking. Its main purpose is to provide solutions to these archaic problems by providing decentralized alternatives, resulting in a better financial reality. Web 3 has opened the door for a new wave of financial technology that could eventually take over the present financial system. It also safeguards user privacy, which was not feasible with its predecessors, enabling virtual transactions to take place between two or more people without the intrusion of an intermediary. Cryptocurrencies may replace fiat money in the financial sector thanks to web 3.

Web 3 has being utilized to construct novel financial systems which are better connected to one another, efficient, and secure than the present financial system. DeFi has totally taken over the financial sector. It is the most accessible, transparent, and creative alternative to traditional finance. Decentralized Finance (Defi), the financial layer of the web 3 ecosystem, alters the layout of the entire financial infrastructure. DeFi makes financial products available to the general public that were previously restricted to institutions, seasoned traders, and business experts. Decentralized exchanges as well as peer-to-peer borrowing protocols are examples of services that provide accessible and potentially profitable financial alternatives.

Some of the examples below demonstrate how web 3 may revolutionize or redefine financial services.

a) **Stablecoins:** Cryptocurrencies known as stablecoins have a value based on another currency. They are accessible to everyone since they run on blockchain technology and are administered by decentralized autonomous organizations. Stablecoins are valuable in the financial world because they process more quickly than fiat money. In order to address the problem of price volatility, stablecoins were developed. Stablecoins have minimal swings because they are backed by local currencies. Stablecoins are used to pay for meals, tickets, and utility costs.

b) **Decentralized Trading:** Users have limited control over their assets on a centralized exchange, which might put them in jeopardy if the network is hacked. However, decentralized exchanges have the ability to reduce the problem associated with users relinquishing control of their assets. Decentralized exchanges are built with open-source software, enabling anyone with an interest to observe how they work. Transaction details in a decentralized exchange are recorded in the block-chain instead of in a database, as in a centralized exchange.

c) **Borrowing and Lending:** Systems such as banks believe that if a client has a good credit rating and appropriate collateral, they are trustworthy and have the ability to repay the loan, allowing underserved individuals to obtain loans while leaving the legitimate ones behind.

web 3 in finance eliminates such lending and borrowing obstacles. It is still a method to produce a return on assets while participating in lending pools and safeguarding digital assets to receive loans. It enables financial operations like borrowing and lending to be carried out without the need for an account with a bank.

d) **Derivatives:** Derivatives are rapidly gaining popularity in the world of web 3 finance, and every growing financial sector creates new prospects for them. The creation and use of Defi derivatives are motivated by the need for leverage, the desire to profit from speculation, or the need to protect against price risk associated with exposure to a digital asset. Decentralized derivatives, however, can be created freely, without authorization, and without any limitations.

e) **Management of Funds:** DeFi encourages numerous new investors to enter and study the markets. It is very advantageous to asset or fund administrators, as they have access to many more potential customers than they could have obtained through conventional finance. Users are able to manage their money and make the best investments for them. Fund management comprises keeping a close watch on your assets, particularly cash flow management, in order to secure a profitable return on your investment. Active fund management entails constant buying and selling in order to outperform a given benchmark, while passively fund management just duplicates a specified benchmark to equal its performance. web 3 level of transparency in finance helps individuals know how their wealth is being spent.

f) **Insurance:** Web 3 in finance transforms the business, benefiting both insurance companies and policyholders. Users of Defi can purchase insurance services to protect their investment funds against a number of threats, such as smart contract hacks, issues involving multi-sig wallets, and attacks on Defi protocols. In Defi, rather than relying on policyholder claims, parametric insurance settles when the criteria stated in the policy are met because the tool used to create parametric insurance comprises a smart contract. The fact that everything is specified in the smart contract, including the amount of the payout and other insurance terms, simplifies the procedure by allowing it to be completed more quickly and effectively. Because insurance depends on smart contracts, policyholders are protected from fraudulent claims.

g) **Governance:** The most important aspect of web 3 in banking that cannot be disregarded is decentralized autonomous organizations. To encourage democratic decision-making in autonomous groups and streamline cryptographic governance, DAOs were developed. They are in favor of power sharing within a group, coordinating the interests of participants, and suppressing self-interest on the part of any group or person. Users are able to vote and participate in shaping the future of the protocol using governance tokens offered by DAOs. Decentralized apps, along with additional tools, have also been developed to support effective governance.

Characteristics of web3 in Finance

A decentralized financial ecosystem is being actively developed by web 3 development companies using blockchain and smart contract technology. The following are some of web 3's finance system features:

a) **Open and without restrictions:** Web 3 cryptography projects aim to be equal, open, and without restrictions. Users can access the network without seeking authorization from a central authority, which is known as permissionless. Anyone can engage in open, public blockchain networks, which is what the web 3 name is designed to signify. With the help of this functionality, users may easily access their cryptocurrency wallet and other network-specific infrastructures from their laptop or smartphone.

b) **Decentralized:** In the context of blockchain, decentralization refers to the network's independence from a centralized middleman. This is typically demonstrated by the globally dispersed network of servers that aid in the network's operation.

c) **Interoperable:** Interoperability is the capacity of multiple blockchain networks and DeFi applications to seamlessly communicate technology, information, and tokenized assets with each other.

d) **Non-custodial:** non-custodial refers to the fact that a bank or other financial service provider does not hold the funds belonging to users. Users can leverage a variety of financial products (lending, borrowing funds, staking, etc.) in their own terms rather than relying on centralized mechanisms. Users can withdraw their money whenever they choose thanks to this, without needing a bank's permission or custodianship.

e) **Programmability:** It is the capacity of software developers to create network infrastructure that can carry out an almost infinite number of use-case-specific iterations. Smart contracts, which enable users to do particular actions in real time without the need for a middleman, are often used to achieve this. These activities include carrying out preset contractual obligations, exchanging value and data, and using other on-chain processes.

f) **Immutable and cryptographically verifiable:** DeFi networks and blockchain systems are also invulnerable to tampering and irreversible because of robust cryptography, thus rendering it nearly hard to alter, reverse, or fabricate records on-chain. DeFi crypto systems can be made more private, safe, and transparent with the aid of immutability, which is essential for the industry's long-term survival.

g) **Tokenization:** Web 3 use economic and governance frameworks based on tokenization of assets and decentralization. Many blockchain and decentralized finance platforms are built on Proof-of-Stake (PoS) architecture, enabling network participants to influence these networks to evolve over time.

Advantages of web3 in Finance

a) **Accessible:** Anyone with a wallet connected to a DeFi wallet is able to use its services. Users are not required to complete time-consuming paperwork or open accounts. Even those without having a bank account can carry out financial transactions at any moment using it. Everyone can use Defi, and there are no intermediaries meddling with users' financial issues. web 3 in finance has the potential to be effective in resolving centralized finance-related concerns like problems with microtransactions, high brokerage fees, security weaknesses, and delayed fund transfers.

b) **Identify protection:** You don't have to reveal your true identify because DeFi platforms don't ask for information like your email id, full name etc. Using web 3, anyone can gain access to financial services regardless of their place of residence or identification. By granting customers more influence over their financial resources, Defi ensures that its products and services are adapted to their needs and requirements.

c) **Flexible:** Since transfers of funds can be done without a permit, transferring funds from a particular account to another is simple.

d) **Interoperability:** Web 3 in banking paves the way for interoperability opportunities. The user can save time, money, and effort by using interoperable payment options.

e) **Transparency:** Since everyone has access to the transaction records, there is an extremely high degree of transparency that is not feasible in a centralized financial system. Being open and honest with its bank customers allows Defi to provide them with the financial data they require to make wise decisions. It is helpful to keep tabs on whether they are getting loans at a reasonable interest rate.

f) **Corruption-free:** Corruption has decreased as a result of eliminating middlemen. Users can choose the course of action that is beneficial to them as well as their community, thanks to decentralized governance. Additionally, it prevents those driven by monetary gain from influencing organizational decisions for their own benefit.

BENEFICIAL CHARACTERISTIC OF WEB3 IN COMPARISON TO TRADITIONAL FINANCE

By delivering a more secure, effective, and transparent financial ecosystem, web 3 development has the potential to revolutionize the financial industry. The important characteristics web 3 in finance over traditional finance includes:

a) **Decentralized Control**

DeFi services are mainly accessed through dApps, which provide customers with personal cryptocurrency wallets to give them more control over their money. Without the need for a centralized financial system, everyone can access financial services independent of location or identity thanks to web 3. Additionally, DeFi platforms enable trade and other services catered to the demands and wants of customers.

b) **Easy Accessibility**

Worldwide, there are billions of people who lack access to a bank account, making it very challenging for them to engage in financial transactions. For them, doing financial transactions without putting their money at danger is nearly difficult. For them, even large-scale trading is just a fabrication of their mind. One of the main causes of people turning to payday loans to deal with their liquidity needs is a lack of access to a well-established financial system. Even having a bank account does not ensure that money is available right away. A financial institution might not be keen to lend the modest sum that a startup business requires. In the financial industry, web 3 is quite helpful. DeFi is available to everyone, and there is no middleman interfering with users' financial affairs.

c) **Control over Inefficiencies**

The centralized financial system has numerous flaws. Credit card exchange rates and fees for remittance are excessively exorbitant, and payment settlement times are excessively long. Microtransaction difficulties, excessive brokerage costs, security risks, and delayed transfers of funds are among the other inefficiencies. And, because centralized financial institutions, such as banks, must cover themselves brick-and-mortar costs, they maintain loan rates high while keeping deposit interest rates low. All of this makes the centralized financial system inefficient in comparison to web 3 finance. DeFi fills such obvious gaps in the centralized financial arrangement, making web 3 finance and banking the preferred option for many.

d) **Interoperability**

The existing financial system is isolated and lacks interactivity and interoperability. Furthermore, the switching costs are substantial. Even shifting money across institutions is a complicated and time-consuming operation. A wire transfer, for example, can take up to three days to settle. web 3 in banking, on the other hand, brings new interoperability possibilities within the DeFi ecosystem. Interoperability between payment systems minimizes the user's work, time, and monetary expenses.

e) **Transparency**

Transparency is lacking in the existing financial system. Bank consumers do not have enough financial information at their disposal to make wise financial decisions. They also struggle to determine whether the interest rate on the loans they are provided is reasonable. Financial technology companies that can discover the "lowest" rate have advanced in the consumer insurance sector, but the loan market remains splintered. Furthermore, even the lowest pricing reflects the substantial back-office expenditures and brick-and-mortar costs of traditional financial institutions. As a result, everyone suffers from the system's inefficiencies, both lenders and borrowers.

f) **Corruption**

The likelihood of corruption is reduced by doing away with middlemen and sharing records. Additionally, distributed ledgers are more secure than centralized financial record systems since they cannot be changed. Bankers and brokers are not seeking a profit or an unfair advantage. What's next? Users may make decisions that are best for them and their community thanks to decentralized governance. This stops those who are motivated by money from influencing decisions within their organization for their own gain.

CHALLENGES AND WAY AHEAD

Web 3 is anticipated to have a huge impact on the internet's future. Greater security, privacy, and control of data are just a few benefits that decentralized infrastructure offers over conventional centralized systems. Additionally, a new generation of decentralized applications that will enable a more open and egalitarian internet are anticipated to be brought about by the development of web 3 technology. web 3 has started to take off in a number of industries, particularly finance. It can deliver the banking sector efficiency that has never before been achievable thanks to its innovative technologies.

DeFi has several advantages over the traditional finance, still it has several barriers in its adoption. One of the most significant obstacles to decentralized finance replacing traditional finance systems is the requirement for consumers to trust unregulated open-source technology. Because anyone has access to the source code that powers a decentralized finance system, anyone can gain access to a smart contract and obtain all the keys, potentially causing people to lose large sums of money. The technology underlying the decentralized finance application is currently undeveloped and unpleasant, and it will always be vulnerable to weaknesses that could harm the technology's image.

Web 3-based Defi has a bright future, according to recent studies. There is no doubt that Defi will create new markets and business models in the future that will help those who participate in the financial system. By replacing the present financial system, web 3 has been utilized to establish new financial systems which are more connected, effective, and secure. Companies must now take the necessary action to reorganize their business operations and deal with these developments head-on.

CONCLUSION

While the usage of digital ledger technologies in the worldwide financial system is still in its early stages, one cannot deny this technology's eventual potential. Traditional finance may increase the efficacy, safety, availability, reliability, and visibility of its services by implementing web 3 insights and technologies. As more and more individuals turn to the internet for their financial requirements, traditional banking must accept the advances in technology and adjust to the changing landscape.

REFERENCES

Agarwal, S., & Zhang, J. (2020). FinTech, lending and payment innovation: A review. *Asia-Pacific Journal of Financial Studies*, *49*(3), 353–367. doi:10.1111/ajfs.12294

AquilinaM.FrostJ.SchrimpfA. (2023). Decentralised finance (DeFi): a functional approach. Available at SSRN 4325095.

Bagrecha, N. R., Polishwala, I. M., Mehrotra, P. A., Sharma, R., & Thakare, B. S. (2020). Decentralised blockchain technology: Application in banking sector. In *2020 International Conference for Emerging Technology (INCET)*. IEEE. 10.1109/INCET49848.2020.9154115

Basel Committee on Banking Supervision. (2010). *Basel III: A global regulatory framework for more resilient banks and banking systems*. Bank for International Settlements.

Berger, A. N. (2003). The economic effects of technological progress: Evidence from the banking industry. *Journal of Money, Credit and Banking*, *35*(2), 141–176. doi:10.1353/mcb.2003.0009

Browne, R. (2021). *Forget Bitcoin–Fintech Is the "Real Covid-19 Story*. Jpmorgan Says.

Buterin, V. (2014). A next-generation smart contract and decentralized application platform. *white paper, 3*(37), 2-1.

Cao, L. (2022). Decentralized ai: Edge intelligence and smart blockchain, metaverse, web3, and desci. *IEEE Intelligent Systems, 37*(3), 6–19. doi:10.1109/MIS.2022.3181504

Chen, C., Zhang, L., Li, Y., Liao, T., Zhao, S., Zheng, Z., & Wu, J. (2022). *When digital economy meets web 3.0: Applications and challenges.* IEEE Open Journal of the Computer Society.

Chu, J., Chan, S., & Zhang, Y. (2023). An analysis of the return–volume relationship in decentralised finance (DeFi). *International Review of Economics & Finance, 85,* 236–254. doi:10.1016/j.iref.2023.01.006

Claessens, S., Glaessner, T., & Klingebiel, D. (2002). Electronic finance: Reshaping the financial landscape around the world. *Journal of Financial Services Research, 22*(1/2), 29–61. doi:10.1023/A:1016023528211

Clifford, T. (2021). *Paypal Cfo Says Company Is Unlikely to Invest Cash in Cryptocurrencies.* CNBC. https://www.cnbc.com/2021/02/11/paypal-cfo-says-company-is-unlikely-to-investcash-in-cryptocurrencies.html?__source5google%7Ceditorspicks%7C&par5google

De Filippi, P., & Mauro, R. (2014). Ethereum: the decentralised platform that might displace today's institutions. *Internet Policy Review, 25*(08).

Egan, M. (2020). *This Startup Is Taking on Big Banks. And It's Working.* CNN. https:// www.cnn.com/2020/10/05/business/chime-bank-startup/index.html

Friedrich, M. (2020). *Square Valuation Model: Cash App's Potential.* ARK Invgaurgaestment. https:// ark-invest.com/articles/analyst-research/square-valuation/

Gu, B., Jiang, W., & Tan, C. W. (2016). Theme: Embracing the Internet of Things to drive data-driven decisions. *Journal of Management Analytics, 3*(1), 112–113. doi:10.1080/23270012.2016.1140597

Kauffman, R. J., Liu, J., & Ma, D. (2015). Innovations in financial IS and technology ecosystems: High-frequency trading in the equity market. *Technological Forecasting and Social Change, 99,* 339–354. doi:10.1016/j.techfore.2014.12.001

Kumar, M., Nikhil, N., & Singh, R. (2020). Decentralising finance using decentralised blockchain oracles. In *2020 International Conference for Emerging Technology (INCET) IEEE,* (pp. 1-4). IEEE. 10.1109/INCET49848.2020.9154123

Lara, R., Cantador, I., & Castells, P. (2007). Semantic web technologies for the financial domain. In *The Semantic Web: Real-World Applications from Industry* (pp. 41–74). Springer US. doi:10.1007/978-0-387-48531-7_3

Lerner, J., & Tufano, P. (2011). The consequences of financial innovation: A counterfactual research agenda. *Annual Review of Financial Economics, 3*(1), 41–85. doi:10.1146/annurev.financial.050808.114326

Lyytinen, K., & Rose, G. M. (2003). The disruptive nature of information technology innovations: The case of internet computing in systems development organizations. *Management Information Systems Quarterly, 27*(4), 557–596. doi:10.2307/30036549

Martino, P. (2019). Blockchain technology: Challenges and opportunities for banks. *International Journal of Financial Innovation in Banking*, 2(4), 314–333. doi:10.1504/IJFIB.2019.104535

Meegan, X., & Koens, T. (2021). *Lessons learned from decentralised finance (DeFi)*. ING. https://new. ingwb. com/binaries/content/assets/insights/themes/distributed-ledger-technology/defi_white_paper_v2. 0. pdf.

Michalopoulos, S., Leaven, L., & Levine, R. (2009). Financial Innovation and Endogenous Growth. National Bureau of Economic Research. (*Working Paper 15356*). Cambridge.

Miranda, P., Isaias, P., & Costa, C. J. (2014). E-Learning and web generations: Towards Web 3.0 and E-Learning 3.0. *International Proceedings of Economics Development and Research*, *81*, 92.

Mishkin, F. S. (2007). *The economics of money, banking, and financial markets*. Pearson education.

Murray, A., Kim, D., & Combs, J. (2023). The promise of a decentralized internet: What is Web3 and how can firms prepare? *Business Horizons*, *66*(2), 191–202. doi:10.1016/j.bushor.2022.06.002

Nath, K., Dhar, S., & Basishtha, S. (2014, February). Web 1.0 to Web 3.0-Evolution of the Web and its various challenges. In *2014 International Conference on Reliability Optimization and Information Technology (ICROIT)* (pp. 86-89). IEEE. 10.1109/ICROIT.2014.6798297

Ozili, P. K. (2023). Digital finance research and developments around the World: A literature review. *International Journal of Business Forecasting and Marketing Intelligence*, *8*(1), 35–51. doi:10.1504/ IJBFMI.2023.127698

Sahani, A. R. (2022). The Potential Applications and Implications of Decentralized Finance. *NOLEGEIN-Journal of Information Technology & Management*, *5*(2), 22–28.

Shivalingaiah, D., & Naik, U. (2008). *Comparative study of web 1.0, web 2.0 and web 3.0*.

Sims, A. (2019). *Blockchain and decentralised autonomous organisations (DAOs): the evolution of companies?*

Suryono, R. R., Budi, I., & Purwandari, B. (2020). Challenges and trends of financial technology (Fintech): A systematic literature review. *Information (Basel)*, *11*(12), 590. doi:10.3390/info11120590

Szabo, N. (1997). Formalizing and securing relationships on public networks. *First Monday*, *2*(9). doi:10.5210/fm.v2i9.548

Trivedi, S., Mehta, K., & Sharma, R. (2021). Systematic literature review on application of blockchain technology in E-finance and financial services. *Journal of Technology Management & Innovation*, *16*(3), 89–102. doi:10.4067/S0718-27242021000300089

Vučinić, M. (2020). Fintech and financial stability potential influence of FinTech on financial stability, risks and benefits. *Journal of Central Banking Theory and Practice*, *9*(2), 43–66. doi:10.2478/ jcbtp-2020-0013

Wan, S., Lin, H., Gan, W., Chen, J., & Yu, P. S. (2023). Web3: The Next Internet Revolution. arXiv preprint arXiv:2304.06111.

Wood, G. (2014). Ethereum: A secure decentralised generalised transaction ledger. *Ethereum project yellow paper, 151*(2014), 1-32.

Yavin, O., & Reardon, A. J. (2021). What digital banks can learn from decentralised finance. *Journal of Digital Banking, 5*(3), 255–263.

Zhao, Q., Li, Y., & Xue, J. (2016). *Research on influence factors of the internet financial product consumption based on innovation diffusion theory.* CORE.

Chapter 4
The Emergence of Cryptography in Blockchain Technology

Tanuj Surve

iD https://orcid.org/0009-0009-6495-6232
University of California, Berkeley, USA

Risha Khandelwal
JECRC University, India

ABSTRACT

This chapter explores the evolution of cryptography in blockchain technology, studying its significance, challenges, and implications. It analyzes the various cryptographic algorithms employed in blockchain systems, emphasizing their significance in ensuring transaction security and anonymity. The chapter looks at the challenges of using cryptography in blockchain, such as scalability, key management, and the arrival of quantum computing. It also looks at how cryptography has influenced the emergence of cryptocurrencies and smart contracts. It also examines current cryptographic trends and their possible impact on blockchain security, highlighting the importance of using best practices while implementing cryptography in blockchain systems. Overall, this chapter presents a detailed review of the critical role that cryptography plays in maintaining blockchain technology's integrity, privacy, and trustworthiness.

INTRODUCTION

Blockchain technology has emerged as a revolutionary force, transforming industries across sectors such as finance and supply chain management to healthcare and voting systems (Kumar, Lim, Sivarajah, & Kaur, 2022). Cryptography, a discipline of study concerned with secure communication and data protection, is at the heart of this technological breakthrough (Guegan., 2017). Cryptography is essential for assuring the security, integrity, and anonymity of transactions in blockchain networks.

This chapter investigates the origins of cryptography in blockchain technology and its importance in providing security and anonymity. Its objective is to look into the various cryptographic methodologies used in blockchain systems, the challenges observed when using cryptography, and the significance of

DOI: 10.4018/978-1-6684-9919-1.ch004

Copyright © 2023, IGI Global. Copying or distributing in print or electronic forms without written permission of IGI Global is prohibited.

cryptography in the evolution of cryptocurrencies and smart contracts. Furthermore, the chapter investigates current cryptographic trends and their potential consequences for blockchain system security in the future. Lastly, it defines best practices for implementing cryptography in blockchain technology.

To begin with, a brief introduction to blockchain technology and its significance lays the groundwork for understanding the importance of cryptography in this context. Blockchain's decentralized and distributed nature, combined with its capacity to give trust and transparency without intermediaries, has positioned it as a game-changing technology with far-reaching consequences across multiple industries.

With an eye to the future, the chapter investigates current cryptographic trends and their potential consequences for blockchain security. The chapter delves into topics like homomorphic encryption, multiparty computation, and post-quantum cryptography, offering insight into how developing cryptographic techniques can improve the security and privacy of blockchain systems.

This chapter seeks to provide a full understanding of how cryptographic approaches contribute to the security, anonymity, and integrity of blockchain transactions by unraveling the close relationship between cryptography and blockchain technology. It is a valuable resource for anyone fascinated by blockchain technology and its underlying cryptographic principles.

A Brief Introduction of Blockchain Technology and its Importance

Blockchain technology has evolved as a game-changing concept with far-reaching consequences in a variety of businesses (Shalender, Singla, & Sharma, 2023). A blockchain, at its heart, is a decentralized and distributed ledger that secures and transparently records transactions (Kakavand, Sevres, & Chilton, 2017). Blockchain was first introduced as the underlying technology behind Bitcoin, the world's first decentralized cryptocurrency, but it has since developed to embrace a wide range of applications beyond digital currencies (Mathis, 2016).

Blockchain's relevance stems from its capacity to deliver trust, security, and transparency without the use of intermediaries. Blockchain technology provides safe transactions and data storage that are resistant to tampering and fraud by utilizing a decentralized network of participants (Bhushan, Sinha, Sagayam, & J, 2020). Blockchain's decentralized structure makes it particularly appealing for applications involving several stakeholders who may not fully trust one another.

Introduction to the Role of Cryptography in Ensuring Security and Anonymity

Cryptography is critical to the confidentiality and anonymity of transactions within a blockchain network (Junejo, et al., 2022). Cryptographic techniques are used to protect the integrity and secrecy of data, validate the identity of participants, and enable secure communication and computation inside the blockchain ecosystem.

Encryption is a fundamental cryptographic technique used in blockchain technology. Using an encryption key, data can be changed into an unreadable format, rendering it indecipherable to unauthorized parties. Encryption is used in a blockchain setting for safeguarding the privacy of sensitive information such as transaction data and user identities (Zyskind, Nathan, & Pentland, 2015).

The digital signature is another important cryptographic tool utilized in blockchain technology. Digital signatures allow you to validate the validity and integrity of digital data (Maulani, Gunawan, Leli, Nabila, & Sar, 2021). Digital signatures are used in blockchain transactions to prove asset ownership, check the integrity of transaction records, and ensure that transactions are not tampered with while being transmitted through the network.

Another key cryptographic building block used in blockchain technology is hash functions. A hash function takes an input and returns a fixed-size output, which is typically referred to as a hash or digest (Swathi, Vivek, & Rani, 2016). Hash functions are important for the integrity of blockchain data. When a block's hash that includes the transactions contained inside it is computed, any change to the data results in a new hash value, alerting the network to any tampering attempts.

In blockchain systems, cryptographic techniques like zero-knowledge proofs and ring signatures are used to improve privacy and anonymity. Zero-knowledge proofs allow one person (the prover) to demonstrate the correctness of a statement to another party (the verifier) without revealing any extra information (Wu, Zheng, Chiesa, Popa, & Stoica, 2018). This enables private transactions and verifications within a blockchain network. Ring signatures, on the other hand, allow a participant to sign a transaction on behalf of a group without revealing the identity of the real signer, improving transaction anonymity.

We can get insights into the mechanisms that underpin the security and privacy guarantees of blockchain systems by digging into the complexities of cryptography in blockchain technology. This knowledge is vital for individuals and organizations trying to maximize the benefits of blockchain technology while minimizing security concerns. This knowledge enables us to confidently navigate the complicated environment of blockchain implementation, making educated decisions about cryptography approaches, protocol architecture, and best practices. Furthermore, as the field of cryptography evolves, staying on top of the latest developments and their implications for blockchain security is important for remaining one step ahead of potential attackers. We can foresee and prepare for future issues and assure the long-term security and sustainability of blockchain ecosystems by studying the present state of cryptographic developments and their potential impact on the blockchain. This chapter will provide readers with the information and tools they need to harness the power of cryptography in the context of blockchain technology, allowing them to construct resilient, secure, and privacy-enhancing blockchain applications.

BLOCKCHAIN TECHNOLOGY CRYPTOGRAPHIC SECURITY MEASURES

Cryptographic security measures play a major role in preserving the integrity, privacy, and security of blockchain transactions and data. Blockchain systems can build trust, prohibit unauthorized access, and enable safe interactions among members by utilizing various cryptographic algorithms. This section goes into the most important cryptographic security mechanisms used in blockchain technology.

Public Key Cryptography

A core cryptographic approach used in blockchain technology is public key cryptography, often known as asymmetric cryptography (Aydar, Cetin, Ayvaz, & Aygun, 2020). It is based on the usage of two cryptographic keys: a public key and a private key. The public key is freely distributed; allowing anybody to encrypt messages or verify digital signatures, but the private key is kept secret and is used for decryption or digital signature generation.

Public key cryptography facilitates secure and private communication between blockchain participants (Das, Tao, & Cheng, 2020). Each participant has their own set of keys, and the public key is linked to their identity. When starting a transaction, the sender encrypts the transaction data with the recipient's public key. Only the recipient, who possesses the associated private key, can decrypt and access the data. This procedure ensures the transaction's confidentiality and integrity.

Public key cryptography also enables digital signatures, which are critical for confirming the validity and integrity of blockchain transactions (Thompson, 2017). To generate a digital signature, the sender encrypts a hash of the transaction data with their private key. The recipient, or any other participant, can then use the sender's public key to validate the signature. If the signature is authentic, it ensures that the transaction came from the expected sender and was not tampered with.

Hash Functions and Merkle Trees

In blockchain technology, hash functions are critical for protecting data integrity. A hash function takes an input, such as a data block, and generates a fixed-size output known as a hash value or digest (AlAhmad & Alshaikhli, 2013). Hash functions have the properties of determinism, which means that the same input will always return the same hash value, and pre-image resistance, which means that determining the input purely on the hash value is computationally infeasible.

Hash functions are used in a variety of ways in blockchain systems. They are first used to generate a unique identifier for each block in the blockchain. When a new block is formed, the hash function is applied to the block's data, yielding a hash value that serves as the block's digital fingerprint. Any alteration to the contents within the block would result in a different hash value, making tampering attempts easier to identify.

Hash functions also allow for the creation of Merkle trees, often known as hash trees, which organize and validate the integrity of transactions within a block. Each transaction in a Merkle tree is hashed individually, and pairs of hashes are joined and hashed recursively until a single root hash, known as the Merkle root, is achieved. The Merkle root is provided in the block's header and represents all of the transactions in the block in a simple manner. Participants can guarantee that all transactions within the block are intact and have not been altered by checking the Merkle root.

Zero-Knowledge Proofs

Zero-knowledge proofs are cryptographic protocols that allow one person, the prover, to prove the correctness of a statement to another party, the verifier, without exposing any extra information. Zero-knowledge proofs can improve privacy and security in the context of blockchain technology by verifying a statement's validity without revealing the underlying sensitive information.

A zk-SNARK (Zero-Knowledge Succinct Non-Interactive Argument of Knowledge) is one type of zero-knowledge proof used in blockchain. Zk-SNARKs allow for efficient computation verification without revealing the algorithm's input, output, or intermediate steps (Wu, Zheng, Chiesa, Popa, & Stoica, 2018). This method enables parties to validate transactions and smart contracts without disclosing sensitive information such as transaction amounts or contract logic.

Blockchain systems can provide privacy-enhancing capabilities such as secret transactions and anonymous identity verification by exploiting zero-knowledge proofs. Zero-knowledge proofs help blockchain technology's overall security and privacy aims by allowing participants to maintain confidentiality while maintaining the integrity and correctness of transactions and computations.

Multi-Factor Authentication

Multi-factor authentication (MFA) is a security approach that combines many independent elements to validate a user's identity (Dasgupta, Roy, & Nag, 2017). In the context of blockchain technology, MFA can improve the security of user accounts, wallets, and other access points to prevent unauthorized access and protect digital assets.

MFA often entails the use of two or more factors, such as something the user knows (e.g., a password or PIN), something the user has (e.g., a hardware token or mobile device), or something the user is (e.g., biometric data such as fingerprints or facial recognition). MFA adds an extra layer of security to a single password or key by combining these factors.

MFA can be used in blockchain systems to safeguard user wallets or access to blockchain networks. To access their funds, a user may be required to give a password, sign transactions with a hardware wallet, and undergo biometric authentication. This multi-layered strategy improves security and reduces the danger of unauthorized access, shielding user accounts and digital assets from potential threats.

Hence, cryptographic security measures are critical to the operation and security of blockchain technology. While hash functions and Merkle trees protect data integrity within blocks, public key cryptography assures safe communication and transaction integrity. Zero-knowledge proofs improve privacy and confidentiality, while multi-factor authentication adds an additional degree of security. Blockchain systems can create trust, protect data, and provide a secure environment for decentralized transactions and interactions among members by utilizing various cryptographic approaches.

CHALLENGES IN APPLYING CRYPTOGRAPHY TO BLOCKCHAIN TECHNOLOGY

While cryptography is the backbone of blockchain security, its use is not without challenges and limitations. As blockchain systems expand and scale, various problems arise in efficiently implementing cryptographic approaches. This section looks at the issues of cryptographic implementations in blockchain technology, with a focus on scalability, key management, and the possible threats posed by quantum computing.

Scalability Challenges

Scalability is a key factor in blockchain technology since it defines the system's ability to accommodate an increasing number of transactions and participants. Scalability issues arise when cryptographic techniques are used within blockchain systems due to the processing complexity associated with these approaches (Tsai, Blower, Zhu, & Yu, 2016).

Cryptographic operations are conducted for each transaction in typical blockchain structures to validate signatures and assure data integrity. The computational expense of cryptographic processes becomes a bottleneck as the network extends and transaction volume increases, resulting in slower transaction processing times and less scalability.

The scalability issue in blockchain is caused by the fact that cryptographic techniques often involve sophisticated mathematical computations, particularly in the case of public key cryptography. Verifying digital signatures, encrypting and decrypting data, and conducting hash computations can all necessitate a substantial amount of computer power.

Various strategies have been proposed to address these scaling issues. One approach is to use off-chain transactions, in which certain transactions are carried out outside of the main blockchain. Off-chain transactions enable parties to conduct high-frequency or low-value transactions without putting undue strain on the main network. Off-chain transactions relieve the scalability issue and improve overall system performance by lowering the number of on-chain cryptographic procedures.

The concept of sharding is another solution to scalability issues. Sharding is the process of separating the blockchain network into smaller subsets known as shards, each of which handles a percentage of the total transactions. This approach to parallel processing allows several shards to execute cryptographic operations concurrently, dramatically boosting transaction throughput and scalability. Sharding poses new cryptographic issues, such as ensuring cross-shard transaction integrity, but also has the potential to improve blockchain system scalability.

Moreover, optimizing consensus algorithms can help with scalability. Consensus methods, like Proof of Work (PoW) or Proof of Stake (PoS), are critical to the security and integrity of blockchain networks. These techniques, however, frequently involve intensive computational computations or resource requirements, which can limit scalability. The focus of the research is on optimizing consensus methods to reduce computational complexity while maintaining essential security assurances. Blockchain systems can achieve faster transaction throughput and scalability by expediting the consensus process.

It should be noted that scalability issues in blockchain technology are not confined to cryptographic activities. Network bandwidth, storage capacity, and transaction validation all have an impact on overall system scalability. Addressing these issues needs a comprehensive approach that takes into account numerous aspects of blockchain architecture and design, including cryptographic approaches.

Key Management Complexity

Effective key management is essential for the secure operation of cryptographic algorithms in blockchain systems. Key management encompasses the secure development, storage, distribution, and revocation of cryptographic keys used for encryption, decryption, and digital signatures (Tian, Wang, Xiong, & Ma, 2020).

Key management presents notable challenges in the context of blockchain technology because of the network's decentralized and distributed structure. Unlike traditional centralized systems, where a trusted institution manages and safeguards keys, blockchain participants are responsible for creating and managing their keys.

The secure generation of cryptographic keys is one key management challenge. To ensure the security of cryptographic methods, strong and random keys must be generated. Weak or predictable keys can make cryptographic operations susceptible to attacks, jeopardizing blockchain system security. Participants must produce cryptographic keys with appropriate entropy using reliable methods such as safe random number generators.

A further problem is the safe storing of keys. Private keys, in particular, must be kept private and safeguarded against unauthorized access. It is critical to secure private keys to avoid theft or unauthorized use. However, striking a balance between security and convenience is difficult. While storing keys offline or in hardware security modules (HSMs) can improve security, it can also bring operational difficulties and possible sources of failure. Key storage in software wallets or mobile devices, on the other hand, can improve accessibility but may increase the danger of key compromise.

Another challenging aspect of key management in blockchain systems is key distribution. Participants must safely disclose public keys to enable secure communication and digital signature verification. To prevent impersonation or man-in-the-middle attacks, key distribution techniques must verify that the correct public keys are connected with the corresponding entities. Secure and trusted channels, such as secure messaging protocols or decentralized identity management systems, can help participants distribute public keys securely.

Key rotation and revocation present further challenges. In order to minimize the impact of key compromise, it is recommended that cryptographic keys be rotated on a regular basis. However, key rotation in a decentralized blockchain system necessitates cooperation among participants to enable a smooth transition and compliance with existing blockchain data. It is also essential to revoke compromised keys to prevent unauthorized access. Revocation procedures must be effectively implemented to ensure that compromised keys are invalidated and no longer useable, ensuring blockchain system security.

The blockchain community is actively investigating solutions to key management complexity. Hardware security modules (HSMs) or secure enclaves protect cryptographic keys by providing tamper-resistant storage and execution environments. Multi-signature schemes require many keys to authorize transactions, which distributes confidence and reduces the danger of a single-key compromise. Decentralized identity management systems also seek to simplify key management and provide safe procedures for key generation, storage, and verification. These systems use decentralized technologies like blockchain or distributed ledger technology to generate self-sovereign identities in which individuals own their keys and personal information.

Quantum Computing Risks

Quantum computing might put at risk the security of cryptographic techniques employed in blockchain technology (Kappert, Karger, & Kureljusic, 2021). Traditional cryptographic techniques, such as RSA and elliptic curve cryptography (ECC), rely on the computational complexity of specific mathematical problems to ensure their security. However, quantum computers have the ability to utilize the computing benefits provided by quantum principles and break these methods.

Quantum computers use quantum mechanics' unique features, such as superposition and entanglement, to conduct calculations in a fundamentally different way than conventional computers. This enables quantum computers to perform some mathematical problems significantly more effectively than classical computers, such as huge number factorization and discrete logarithm issues. These issues underpin the security of many frequently used cryptographic techniques.

The security of blockchain systems that rely on existing cryptographic algorithms may be jeopardized if quantum computers grow powerful enough to breach them. Transactions and data that were previously thought to be secure may now be subject to unauthorized access and alteration. This puts the integrity, secrecy, and validity of blockchain-based transactions and smart contracts at risk.

To address these quantum computing risks researchers are working on quantum-resistant cryptographic algorithms, often known as post-quantum cryptography. Even in the presence of powerful quantum computers, post-quantum cryptography strives to give security guarantees. These algorithms are meant to survive attacks from both classical and quantum computers, ensuring blockchain systems' long-term security.

Several post-quantum cryptographic methods, including lattice-based cryptography, code-based cryptography, multivariate cryptography, and hash-based cryptography, have been proposed. These algorithms are based on mathematical issues that are thought to be resistant to quantum algorithms, maintaining their security even as quantum computing advances.

The shift to post-quantum cryptography is fraught with challenges. Upgrading old systems and ensuring compliance with future quantum-resistant standards requires careful preparation and coordination among the blockchain community. Cryptographic agility, or the capacity to fluidly transition to new algorithms, is critical for adapting to the shifting landscape of quantum computing while maintaining the security of blockchain systems

The adoption of quantum-resistant cryptographic protocols, such as quantum-resistant digital signatures and quantum-resistant key exchange protocols is another strategy for minimizing quantum computing issues. In the presence of powerful quantum computers, these protocols use quantum-resistant algorithms or quantum-resistant features to offer secure communication and authentication. Using these protocols, blockchain systems can preserve their security even in the presence of quantum computers in the future.

Continuous research and collaboration between the blockchain and cryptography communities are required to adequately address quantum computing concerns. This includes assessing the vulnerability of existing blockchain systems to quantum assaults, inventing and standardizing post-quantum cryptographic algorithms, and incorporating quantum-resistant protocols into blockchain architectures.

ROLE OF CRYPTOGRAPHY IN CRYPTOCURRENCIES

Cryptocurrencies have altered our perceptions of and relationships with established financial institutions. The unique use of cryptography at the heart of these digital currencies offers the security and integrity required for their operation. In this section, we will look at how cryptography is used in cryptocurrencies and explain the cryptographic algorithms used by popular cryptocurrencies such as Bitcoin and Ethereum.

The Security and Integrity of Cryptocurrencies

A key component of cryptocurrencies is ensuring transaction security and integrity. Traditional financial systems rely on trusted middlemen to confirm and protect transactions, such as banks or payment processors. Cryptocurrencies, on the other hand, function in a decentralized environment in which individuals communicate directly without the use of intermediaries. Cryptography is critical in ensuring the security and integrity of these transactions.

Transaction privacy is a major concern in the digital environment. Cryptocurrencies address this concern by utilizing cryptographic techniques that allow users to communicate confidentially. To achieve transaction privacy, public key cryptography is commonly used. Each participant in this method has a pair of cryptographic keys: a public key and a private key. The public key is widely distributed and acts as the recipient's address, whereas the private key is kept private and is used for decryption or the creation of digital signatures.

Aside from privacy, preserving transaction integrity is critical for the trustworthiness of cryptocurrencies. The application of cryptographic hash functions maintains the integrity of transactions in blockchain technology, which underpins most cryptocurrencies. Hash functions take an input, such as transaction data, and return a fixed-size result known as a hash value or digest. Hash functions are distinguished by the fact that even little changes in the input result in a completely different output.

In the context of cryptocurrencies, a transaction's hash value is calculated and included in the next block of the blockchain. Each block holds a reference to the previous block's hash value, forming a chain of blocks. This chaining approach assures that any change or tampering with a transaction will change its hash value, rendering it invalid. Participants can confirm the integrity and tamper-proof nature of transactions by checking the consistency of hash values across the network.

Authentication is another key component of cryptocurrencies, making sure that participants can prove that they are owners of digital assets and authenticate their identities during transactions. To meet this requirement, public key cryptography is once again used. When a participant wants to start a transaction, they use their private key to establish a digital signature. The digital signature is attached to the transaction as confirmation of its legitimacy and integrity.

When other participants receive a transaction, they can use the sender's public key to validate the digital signature. They can detect whether the signature is legitimate and whether the transaction has been tampered with by executing a mathematical verification process. This authentication process ensures that the transaction came from the rightful owner and was not altered during transmission.

Cryptography's security and integrity in cryptocurrencies enable trustless transactions in a decentralized system. Through safe authentication techniques, participants can deal directly with one another without the use of intermediaries, while guaranteeing privacy, ensuring integrity, and demonstrating ownership.

It is important to remember, however, that the security of cryptocurrencies is not simply dependent on cryptography. Other factors that contribute to the overall security of cryptocurrencies include secure key management, secure network protocols, and secure implementation of cryptographic algorithms. To identify and mitigate potential vulnerabilities, best practices, and frequent security audits must be implemented.

Cryptographic Algorithms in Popular Cryptocurrencies

To protect the security and integrity of their operations, popular cryptocurrencies such as Bitcoin and Ethereum rely on specialized cryptographic algorithms. These algorithms are deliberately chosen to provide a strong defense against various cryptographic threats. This section will look at the cryptography algorithms employed in these popular coins.

Bitcoin, the first cryptocurrency, is built around multiple cryptographic algorithms. One of the key cryptographic functions used by Bitcoin is the Secure Hash Algorithm 256-bit (SHA-256). SHA-256 is a well-known cryptographic hash method that generates a 256-bit fixed-size output. It is widely used in the Bitcoin protocol to generate unique hash values for transactions, blocks, and other data structures. The safe and collision-resistant characteristic of SHA-256 maintains the Bitcoin blockchain's integrity and immutability.

Digital signatures are essential for verifying the validity and integrity of Bitcoin transactions. The Elliptic Curve Digital Signature technique (ECDSA) is the cryptographic technique used in Bitcoin transactions to generate and validate digital signatures. ECDSA is a secure and efficient mechanism for digital signature generation and verification that is based on elliptic curve cryptography (ECC). The use of ECDSA by Bitcoin maintains transaction integrity while keeping processing costs low in comparison to other cryptographic methods.

Another popular cryptocurrency, Ethereum, uses a distinct set of cryptography methods. Ethereum's cryptographic procedures rely heavily on the Keccak-256 hash function, better known as SHA-3. Keccak-256 has similar security features as SHA-256 but is built on a different foundation. The adoption of Keccak-256 ensures the blockchain's cryptographic integrity, ensuring that transactions and blocks stay tamper-proof.

Ethereum, like Bitcoin, uses the Elliptic Curve Digital Signature Algorithm (ECDSA) to generate and validate digital signatures. However, Ethereum's elliptic curve parameters differ from those of Bitcoin. Ethereum employs the secp256k1 elliptic curve, which provides a good blend of security and efficiency. The secp256k1 curve is well-suited for blockchain applications because it provides a strong foundation for authentication and ownership verification in Ethereum transactions.

CRYPTOGRAPHY'S ROLE IN SMART CONTRACTS

Smart contracts use cryptography to enable secure execution and to enforce the terms and circumstances of blockchain agreements. Cryptographic approaches play an instrumental part in assuring the integrity and security of smart contracts by providing verifiability, authentication, and contract enforcement mechanisms.

Verifiability is an important characteristic of smart contracts since it enables participants to independently verify the correctness and integrity of contract execution. To ensure verifiability, cryptographic hash functions are used. Hash functions provide distinct hash values for contract content, which operate as digital fingerprints. Participants can confirm the integrity of the contract's content by comparing the computed hash value of the contract's content to the stored hash value on the blockchain. Hash function verification ensures that the contract has not been altered since its deployment.

Contract enforcement is a vital aspect of smart contracts, allowing for the automatic fulfillment of predefined requirements without the use of intermediaries. Through the use of conditional expressions and cryptographic primitives, cryptography promotes contract enforcement. Smart contracts can use cryptographic protocols to enforce complicated requirements while protecting the privacy and confidentiality of sensitive data, such as zero-knowledge proofs or secure multi-party computing. These cryptographic techniques enable users to engage securely, collaborate on computations, and enforce contractual conditions without revealing sensitive information.

Furthermore, cryptography allows for secure key management in smart contracts. To maintain the cryptographic keys required for contract authentication and encryption, public key infrastructure (PKI) systems are often used. PKI assures that the public keys used for verification are genuine and that they belong to the intended participants. Private keys are protected from unauthorized access and modification by secure key management practices such as the usage of hardware security modules (HSMs) or secure enclaves. Robust key management is essential for smart contract security and integrity.

Cryptography is needed for the secure execution of smart contracts. Cryptography provides the integrity, authenticity, and privacy of smart contracts on the blockchain through processes such as verifiability, authentication, and contract enforcement. Smart contracts provide parties with a secure and trustless environment for executing agreements by employing cryptographic algorithms and secure key management practices. As smart contracts become more popular, continued research and developments in cryptography will improve the security and effectiveness of these novel digital agreements.

CURRENT CRYPTOGRAPHIC TRENDS IN BLOCKCHAIN

Blockchain technology is quickly evolving as a result of continual advances in cryptography. Cryptographic techniques are the core of blockchain security, providing transactions and data stored on the blockchain with privacy, integrity, and validity. In this section, we will examine recent cryptographic trends in blockchain technology, concentrating on major advancements and developing strategies that improve blockchain system security and functionality. We will also explore Secure Multi-Party Computation in Blockchain.

Analysis of Recent Advancements and Emerging Cryptographic Trends

Significant advances in cryptography approaches have occurred in recent years, revolutionizing the field of blockchain technology. These developing trends are solving significant difficulties and improving blockchain systems' security, privacy, and functionality. The development and deployment of zero-knowledge proofs (ZKPs) is an important cryptography trend. Zero-knowledge proofs allow a party to demonstrate the accuracy of a proposition without exposing any extra information. This characteristic allows for private transactions and verifiability in blockchain systems. ZKPs have the potential to transform the way blockchain transactions are done by allowing transactions to be validated without exposing sensitive data. Within blockchain networks, this cryptographic trend has cleared the way for privacy-focused applications such as anonymous transactions and identity management systems.

An additional significant accomplishment is the implementation of secure multi-party computation (MPC) protocols. Multiple participants can use MPC to jointly compute a function over their private inputs without disclosing individual inputs to other parties. This method protects the privacy and confidentiality of computations involving several stakeholders. MPC supports secure and decentralized computations within smart contracts in the context of blockchain, enabling complicated actions involving several parties without revealing sensitive data. Blockchain systems can attain a higher level of security, anonymity, and trust among participating parties by using MPC.

Due to the potential threat posed by quantum computers to existing cryptographic techniques, post-quantum cryptography (PQC) has emerged as a critical field of attention. Many commonly used public-key encryption and digital signature algorithms can be broken by quantum computers, thereby jeopardizing the security of blockchain networks. PQC's goal is to create cryptographic algorithms that are immune to quantum computer attacks, ensuring the long-term security of blockchain-based applications. Researchers are currently investigating and creating post-quantum cryptographic techniques to safeguard the integrity and confidentiality of blockchain transactions and data in the face of a quantum attack.

Homomorphic encryption is another significant innovation in cryptography that bears potential for blockchain technology. Homomorphic encryption allows computations on encrypted data to be conducted without disclosing the plaintext, retaining privacy and confidentiality. This trait has enormous potential in blockchain applications, where sensitive data can be stored and handled securely. Homomorphic encryption allows for secure data sharing and collaborative analysis while maintaining privacy, making it an appealing solution for blockchain-based applications. Blockchain networks can enable new options for privacy-preserving apps and safe data processing by utilizing homomorphic encryption.

Secure hardware integration into blockchain systems is gaining popularity. HSMs and trusted execution environments (TEEs) enable secure enclaves for performing sensitive activities and storing cryptographic keys. These hardware-based solutions improve blockchain system security by shielding important assets from physical and software-based threats. Blockchain networks may protect the secrecy and integrity of cryptographic operations and key management by exploiting the capabilities of HSMs and TEEs, lowering the risk of compromise.

Secure Multi-Party Computation in Blockchain

Blockchain technology is much more than just decentralized transactions; it is also about executing smart contracts and calculations that involve numerous participants. Secure multi-party computation (MPC) approaches play an essential role in these circumstances for maintaining privacy, integrity, and trust.

Secure multi-party computation allows many participants to compute a function over their private inputs while maintaining their confidentiality. MPC allows the execution of complicated processes involving several parties in the context of blockchain without revealing sensitive data. This method protects the confidentiality of individual inputs while producing a verified outcome.

MPC has numerous applications in blockchain, including decentralized finance (DeFi) and supply chain management. Multiple participants may donate assets or engage in lending and borrowing methods in DeFi apps. Interest rates, collateral management, and profit distributions can be computed safely and without revealing individual financial data by employing secure multi-party computation.

MPC is also gaining popularity in supply chain management. In supply chain networks, multiple entities and stakeholders collaborate, each giving data while retaining privacy. By allowing computations to be done on the combined data without disclosing the separate inputs, secure multi-party computation promotes trust and verifiability. This improves supply chain transparency, reduces the danger of data loss, and allows for more secure decision-making.

Blockchain networks can obtain higher privacy assurances by utilizing MPC. Participants retain control of their personal information, and the calculation can be carried out without risking the privacy of individual inputs. This method offers a practical answer to the problem of performing secure and privacy-preserving calculations in decentralized systems.

Various cryptographic techniques are applied to achieve secure multi-party computing in the blockchain. Techniques like secret sharing, secure function evaluation, and secure two-party computing are examples of this. Each of these protocols addresses a distinct component of secure computation and adds to the overarching aim of blockchain privacy and trust.

While secure multi-party computation holds enormous potential for privacy and security in blockchain, there are multiple challenges to consider. Some of the primary areas of concern are computation efficiency, scalability, and the possibility of collusion among members. Ongoing research and development are aimed at improving the performance of MPC protocols and addressing these issues in order to make secure multi-party computation more feasible and scalable for wider use in blockchain applications.

IMPLICATIONS OF CRYPTOGRAPHIC TRENDS ON BLOCKCHAIN SECURITY

Emerging cryptographic trends have the potential to drastically alter the security of blockchain systems as blockchain technology evolves. In this part, we will examine the potential effects of these developing cryptographic trends on the security of blockchain networks.

Evaluation of Potential Impacts of Emerging Cryptographic Trends on the Security of Blockchain Systems

Enhancing the privacy and secrecy of blockchain transactions and data is one of the primary areas where developing cryptographic trends can have a significant influence. Techniques such as zero-knowledge proofs (ZKPs) and homomorphic encryption can help to improve privacy requirements. Zero-knowledge proofs enable the verification of a statement without disclosing any additional information, ensuring that sensitive transactional details stay private while yet guaranteeing verifiability. Homomorphic encryption allows computations to be conducted on encrypted data while protecting sensitive information's privacy. Blockchain systems can increase the security and privacy of user data by using various cryptographic protocols, ensuring that sensitive information is shielded from unauthorized access.

Furthermore, developing cryptographic trends have the potential to improve blockchain system authentication and identity management. With the rise of decentralized applications and blockchain-based ecosystems, robust identity management solutions are becoming increasingly important. New cryptographic approaches, such as decentralized identity systems and self-sovereign identification, provide novel alternatives for improving authentication and identity verification in blockchain networks. These approaches provide consumers control over their identities and allow them to build trust without relying on centralized authorities. Blockchain solutions can enable safe and tamper-resistant identity management by employing cryptographic techniques, lowering the risks of identity theft, fraud, and unauthorized access.

A key area of impact on blockchain security is the introduction of post-quantum cryptography (PQC). Traditional encryption techniques such as RSA and ECC may become vulnerable to quantum attacks as quantum computers improve. Post-quantum cryptography algorithms strive to create new approaches that can withstand quantum computer attacks, ensuring the long-term security of blockchain systems. Blockchain networks can proactively handle the emerging threat of quantum computing by using post-quantum cryptography, ensuring the integrity and confidentiality of transactions and data.

Incorporating these emerging cryptographic patterns into blockchain systems may pose additional security concerns and obstacles. While new cryptographic approaches can improve security, it is critical to thoroughly assess their possible weaknesses and ensure that adequate security measures are in place. Thorough security audits, peer review mechanisms, and continual evaluation of cryptographic implementations are required to mitigate potential threats and keep blockchain systems secure.

It is important to highlight that the successful implementation of developing cryptographic trends in blockchain systems necessitates collaboration and coordination across a variety of stakeholders, including cryptographic specialists, developers, researchers, and industry participants. Participating in open and transparent debates, sharing knowledge, and encouraging innovation can result in the identification of best practices and the development of robust cryptographic protocols and algorithms that address the particular security requirements of blockchain technology.

Consideration of Challenges and Opportunities in Adopting New Cryptographic Approaches

Although emerging cryptographic trends provide multiple opportunities to improve blockchain security, their implementation also presents certain challenges. To maximize the benefits of new cryptographic systems, it is important to carefully analyze these problems and identify appropriate solutions.

The need for robust implementation and testing of new cryptographic algorithms and protocols is a key challenge. Creating secure cryptographic systems takes careful planning, implementation, and thorough peer review. Inadequate implementation or incorrect ideas can create vulnerabilities in blockchain systems, compromising their security. To mitigate this danger, professionals must be involved in the creation and evaluation of new cryptographic techniques, as well as extensive security audits and open and transparent peer review processes.

A second challenge is balancing security and performance. Some advanced cryptographic approaches, such as zero-knowledge proofs and safe multi-party computation, need a significant amount of computer power. The resources needed to carry out these cryptographic processes can have an impact on the performance and scalability of blockchain networks. It is critical to find a balance between security and performance to ensure that the adoption of new cryptographic algorithms does not impair the efficiency and usability of blockchain systems. Ongoing research and development efforts are aimed at improving the performance of these cryptographic approaches to make them more practical and scalable for usage in real-world blockchain applications.

Interoperability and standardization are two further issues to consider. As new blockchain platforms and networks arise, it is crucial to ensure the interoperability and smooth integration of cryptographic techniques across disparate systems. Establishing cryptographic standards and protocols can help with interoperability, allowing different blockchain networks to securely connect and share data. Collaboration among industry players, standardization organizations, and cryptography specialists can aid in addressing these issues and encouraging the widespread adoption of secure cryptographic approaches in blockchain systems. Emerging cryptographic trends have the potential to drastically impact blockchain system security. Blockchain networks can make informed judgments about adopting new cryptographic approaches by examining the potential implications and considering the accompanying difficulties and opportunities.

BEST PRACTICES FOR CRYPTOGRAPHY IN BLOCKCHAIN SYSTEMS

Effective cryptography implementation is essential for assuring the security and integrity of blockchain systems. This section will provide an overview of best practices for implementing cryptography in blockchain technology, with a focus on key elements for secure key management, algorithm selection, and cryptographic protocol design.

Secure key management is a significant best practice. Cryptographic keys are the backbone of blockchain networks' secure communication and transactions. To safeguard keys from unauthorized access and potential compromises, it is important to use strong key management practices. Best practices for key access include generating strong random keys, securely storing keys in hardware security modules (HSMs) or secure enclaves, rotating keys regularly, and adopting multi-factor authentication. Furthermore, the adoption of multi-signature methods can spread confidence among numerous parties and reduce the chance of a single key compromise.

Algorithm selection is another key part of integrating cryptography in blockchain systems. It is vital to select well-established cryptographic algorithms that have been subjected to considerable peer review and study. Algorithms commonly employed include symmetric encryption algorithms such as AES, asymmetric encryption algorithms such as RSA and elliptic curve cryptography (ECC), and secure hash functions such as SHA-256. Algorithms should be chosen with security, performance, and compatibility with current systems in mind. It is also essential to examine and update algorithms on a regular basis to ensure that they are in line with industry best practices and security standards.

The design of cryptographic protocols is critical to assuring the security and durability of blockchain systems. It is of the utmost significance to observe the concept of least privilege while building cryptographic protocols, ensuring that protocols give only the capability required to achieve their intended goal. Protocols should be built to withstand potential attacks and vulnerabilities such as replay attacks, man-in-the-middle attacks, and cryptographic flaws. During the design process, a thorough threat modeling and risk assessment should be performed to identify potential security issues and build effective countermeasures.

CONCLUSION

Cryptography plays an important part in assuring the security, privacy, and integrity of blockchain systems. Throughout this chapter, we've looked at the various cryptographic algorithms utilized in blockchain technology and how they provide security and anonymity to transactions. We also looked into the difficulties of using cryptography in blockchain, the significance of cryptography in the evolution of cryptocurrencies and smart contracts, and the potential implications of current cryptographic trends on blockchain security.

Blockchain systems can achieve a high level of security and trust by utilizing cryptographic techniques like symmetric and asymmetric encryption, digital signatures, hash functions, and zero-knowledge proofs. These cryptographic primitives provide secure transactions, data immutability, and information verifiability, all of which are critical for the development and adoption of blockchain technology.

As blockchain technology evolves, it is critical to remain on top of developing cryptographic developments. Homomorphic encryption, multi-party computation, and post-quantum cryptography are current research areas that have the potential to improve privacy, scalability, and resistance against quantum attacks.

Blockchain systems can pave the way for a secure and trustworthy digital future by adhering to best practices and embracing evolving cryptographic developments. Individuals, organizations, and businesses will be able to utilize the transformational potential of decentralized, transparent, and tamper-resistant systems while protecting data integrity, privacy, and trust in the digital environment if cryptography is successfully integrated into blockchain technology.

REFERENCES

AlAhmad, M. A., & Alshaikhli, I. F. (2013). Broad View of Cryptographic Hash Functions - ProQuest. [IJCSI]. *International Journal of Computer Science Issues*, *10*(4). https://www.proquest.com/openview /848b6a4f46a36abf1c97cf30c78acd2f/1?pq-origsite=gscholar&cbl=55228

Aydar, M., Cetin, S. C., Ayvaz, S., & Aygun, B. (2020). Private key encryption and recovery in blockchain. ArXiv:1907.04156 [Cs]. https://arxiv.org/abs/1907.04156

Bhushan, B., Sinha, P., Sagayam, K. M., & J, A. (2020). Untangling blockchain technology: A survey on state of the art, security threats, privacy services, applications and future research directions. *Computers & Electrical Engineering*, *90*, 106897. doi:10.1016/j.compeleceng.2020.106897

Das, M., Tao, X., & Cheng, J. C. P. (2020). A Secure and Distributed Construction Document Management System Using Blockchain. *Lecture Notes in Civil Engineering*, 850–862. doi:10.1007/978-3-030-51295-8_59

Dasgupta, D., Roy, A., & Nag, A. (2017). Multi-Factor Authentication. *Infosys Science Foundation Series*, 185–233. doi:10.1007/978-3-319-58808-7_5

Guegan, D. (2017). Public Blockchain versus Private blockhain. *Shs.hal.science*. https://shs.hal.science/halshs-01524440

Junejo, A., Hashmani, M., Alabdulatif, A., Memon, M. M., Jaffari, S. R., & Abdullah, M. Z. (2022). RZee: Cryptographic and statistical model for adversary detection and filtration to preserve blockchain privacy. *Journal of King Saud University - Computer and Information Sciences, 34*(10), 7885–7910. doi:10.1016/j.jksuci.2022.07.007

KakavandH.Kost De SevresN.ChiltonB. (2017, January 1). *The Blockchain Revolution: An Analysis of Regulation and Technology Related to Distributed Ledger Technologies*. SSRN. https://papers.ssrn.com/sol3/papers.cfm?abstract_id=2849251 doi:10.2139/ssrn.2849251

Kappert, N., Karger, E., & Kureljusic, M. (2021, June 24). *Quantum Computing - The Impending End for the Blockchain?* Social Science Research Network. https://papers.ssrn.com/sol3/papers.cfm?abstract_id=4075591

Kumar, S., Lim, W. M., Sivarajah, U., & Kaur, J. (2022). Artificial Intelligence and Blockchain Integration in Business: Trends from a Bibliometric-Content Analysis. *Information Systems Frontiers*. doi:10.100710796-022-10279-0 PMID:35431617

Mathis, T. (2016). Blockchain: A Guide To Blockchain, The Technology Behind Bitcoin, Ethereum And Other Cryptocurrency. Level Up Lifestyle Limited.

Maulani, G., Gunawan, Leli, Nabila, E., & Sari, W. (2021). Digital Certificate Authority with Blockchain Cybersecurity in Education. *International Journal of Cyber and IT Service Management, 1*, 5.

Shalender, K., Singla, B., & Sharma, S. (2023). *Emerging Technologies and Their Game-Changing Potential: Lessons from Corporate World*. Contemporary Studies of Risks in Emerging Technology.

Swathi, E., Vivek, G., & Rani, G. S. (2016). Role of Hash Function in Cryptography. *International Journal of Advanced Engineering Research and Science*. doi:10.22161/ijaers/si.3

Thompson, S. (2017). The preservation of digital signatures on the blockchain. *See Also, 3*. doi:10.14288a. v0i3.188841

Tian, Y., Wang, Z., Xiong, J., & Ma, J. (2020). A Blockchain-Based Secure Key Management Scheme With Trustworthiness in DWSNs. *IEEE Transactions on Industrial Informatics*, *16*(9), 6193–6202. doi:10.1109/TII.2020.2965975

Tsai, W.-T., Blower, R., Zhu, Y., & Yu, L. (2016, March 1). *A System View of Financial Blockchains*. IEEE Xplore. doi:10.1109/SOSE.2016.66

Wu, H., Zheng, W., Chiesa, A., & Popa, R. (2018). *DIZK: A Distributed Zero Knowledge Proof System Open access to the Proceedings of the 27th USENIX Security Symposium*. USENIX. . https://www. usenix.org/system/files/conference/usenixsecurity18/sec18-wu.pdf

Zyskind, G., Nathan, O., & Pentland, A. 'Sandy'. (2015). Decentralizing Privacy: Using Blockchain to Protect Personal Data. *2015 IEEE Security and Privacy Workshops*. doi:10.1109/SPW.2015.27

KEY TERMS AND DEFINITIONS

Asymmetric Encryption: A cryptographic approach that uses two keys, one for encryption and one for decryption, to provide secure communication and digital signatures.

Authentication: The process of confirming the identity of blockchain transaction participants to ensure that only authorized entities can access and interact with the system.

Blockchain Technology: A decentralized and distributed ledger system that securely records and validates transactions between numerous parties in an immutable and transparent manner.

Contract Enforcement: The use of cryptographic techniques to assure the secure and tamper-proof execution and fulfillment of smart contracts, hence establishing trust and reliability in blockchain-based agreements.

Cryptography: The practice of securing and protecting information using mathematical techniques to ensure secrecy, integrity, and validity.

Key Management: The process of securely producing, storing, and distributing cryptographic keys while maintaining their confidentiality and protecting them from unauthorized access or compromise.

Quantum Computing: An emerging field that uses quantum mechanics to do sophisticated calculations, potentially posing a challenge to standard encryption algorithms employed in blockchain systems.

Scalability: A blockchain system's ability to accommodate an increasing number of transactions or participants without sacrificing performance, speed, or security.

Symmetric Encryption: A cryptographic technique that uses the same key for both data encryption and decryption, assuring secrecy and integrity.

Verifiability: The ability to validate and authenticate the validity of blockchain transactions and data using cryptographic techniques, hence assuring system transparency and confidence.

Chapter 5
Navigating the New Frontier of Finance, Art, and Marketing:
A Look at Cryptocurrencies, NFTs, and Metaverse

S M Nazmuz Sakib

https://orcid.org/0000-0001-9310-3014

International MBA Institute, School of Business and Trade, Dhaka International University, Bangladesh

ABSTRACT

This chapter explores the intersection of finance, art, and marketing in the new frontier of digital assets, specifically focusing on cryptocurrencies, NFTs, and the metaverse. The authors analyze the potential impact of these innovative technologies on traditional financial systems, art markets, and advertising strategies. Through a comprehensive examination of the concepts of blockchain, virtual reality, and decentralization, this chapter aims to provide insight into how these emerging digital assets can reshape the way people perceive and interact with financial, artistic, and marketing landscapes.

INTRODUCTION

Cryptocurrency

A cryptocurrency is a form of digital money, not overseen by a central authority. Any data on transaction and ownership changes are stored in a digital ledger using distributed ledger technology (Han et al., 2019); Pestunov, 2020). The storage, transmission, and recording of bitcoin data to public ledgers involve sophisticated code. All payment transactions using this digital currency are verified via encryption. The goal of using encryption is to provide security and protection of transaction information, mostly from a third party. This type of technology enables anyone to send and receive payments without relying on banks for transaction verification. This distributed ledger technology, in the context of crypto, is referred to as blockchain technology (Albayati et al., 2020; Parino, Beiró, & Gauvin, 2018).

DOI: 10.4018/978-1-6684-9919-1.ch005

Copyright © 2023, IGI Global. Copying or distributing in print or electronic forms without written permission of IGI Global is prohibited.

Cryptocurrency can be obtained through purchasing coins or mining (Pastrana & Suarez-Tangil, (2019). It exists solely in a digital form and acts as a decentralized system of value exchange, with bitcoin being the most well-known cryptocurrency (Guides, 2021). The global cryptocurrency market capitalization was $2.21 trillion in December 2021, with bitcoin being the dominant player with a 38.88% share as of September 2022 (de Best, 2022a; CoinMarketCap, 2019; Mitic, 2022). The popularity of other cryptocurrencies like Ethereum and Tether has also increased over the years (CoinMarketCap, 2019).

NFTs

NFTs or non-fungible tokens are cryptographic assets that are distinguished from each other by unique identification codes and metadata (Sharma et al., 2022). An NFT can also be described as a token used to identify something unique in a blockchain. NFT s are used to represent lottery tickets, digital and non-digital collectables like digital art, pictures, video clips and even a digital trading card (Levy, 2022).

NFTs were first created by Anil Dash and Kevin McCoy on May 3, 2014, at the New Museum in New York City. Four years later, the ERC-721 standard, which is an Ethereum standard (Sharma et al., 2022) was the first standard used to mint an NFT. The ERC-721 smart contract, which was created by some of the individuals who had created the ERC-20 smart contract, outlines the minimal interface—ownership information, security, and metadata—needed for the trading and distribution of gaming tokens. Other NFT standards are ERC-998 and ERC-1155 (2021). The ERC-1155 standard builds on the idea of the ERC-721, by batching many non-fungible tokens into a single contract and lowering the transaction and storage costs necessary for NFTs (Wilson et al., 2021).

NFTS are distinguishable from cryptocurrency in that, they cannot be traded or exchanged at equivalency i.e. their value isn't identical and they can't, generally speaking, be used for commercial transactions (Sharma, 2021a). However, NFTs do have a bigger application as an investment opportunity, especially in the trading of digital artworks. Recent statistics have shown that the NFT digital art market has grown both in popularity and sales, almost rivalling the traditional art market. In a report on NFT statistics published by Chainalysis Inc., a blockchain analytics company, the NFT industry sales reached $41 billion in the year 2021, closing in on $50 billion in sales achieved in the traditional art market in 2020.

Meta-Verse

A metaverse is a networked online world with digitally permanent surroundings, which users may access as avatars via virtual reality, augmented reality, gaming consoles, mobile devices, or traditional PCs for real-time interactions and experiences (Bobrowsky & Needleman, 2022; Sharma, 2021b. In a metaverse, individuals can communicate and transact with each other, use currency to buy and sell land, buildings, avatars, and even identities, go on virtual adventures with their friends, and attend virtual events. According to Sharma (2021b) a metaverse can be described as the 'world's digital counterpart'.

The concept of metaverse technology was first developed for online video games like Fortnite (Bult, 2022). The success story of Fortnite, made huge technology companies like Microsoft and Facebook to try and implement the components of metaverse technology in other aspects of life like office meetings, online working, virtual concerts, etc. (Bobrowsky & Needleman, 2022). As of September 2022, some of the most well-known metaverse platforms are Meta Horizons (Facebook), Fortnite, Decentraland, Nvidia Omniverse, Roblox, The Sandbox, Otherside, and Pokemon Go (Abrol, 2022; Marr, 2022).

LITERATURE REVIEW

Some studies have been published on the acceptance ad adoption of cryptocurrency, NFTS and the metaverse among the general population. Most of the studies on cryptocurrencies have looked at its application for payment in different economic fields, studies for NFTS have mostly accessed its adoption as investment and the trading of digital art. Studies on the metaverse have majorly looked into its impact on social interactions and as an investment for large tech companies like Microsoft and Facebook. Most of the studies on the three topics also looked at the social and behavioural factors that impact the intention to adopt these technologies among people (Nam et al., 2019). One of the most recurring factors was the attitude towards these technologies and trust. They also looked at the potential outcomes of adopting these technologies, and the financial, economic and social effects on small and medium-sized enterprises and individuals.

To look at the potential outcome of using cryptocurrencies (Treiblmaier et al., 2020) looked at its present adoption in the tourism sector. Treiblmaier et al. (2020) reported that the adoption of cryptocurrency for payment in the tourism industry appears to be beneficial since it is universal and accrues minimal fees because there is no intermediary and it avoids foreign currency exchange costs. Tham and Sigala (2020) goes further to report that the benefits of using cryptocurrencies are not limited to efficient transactions, but crypto adoption may support the growth of sustainable tourism by decentralizing access to economic institutions and dispersing economic power. But these benefits as conditioned by are only to be enjoyed fully if the adoption of crypto payments is well adopted universally. Nam et al. (2019) studied the factors that affect crypto adoption. In their conceptual paper, Nam et al. (2019) stressed that the benefits offered by cryptocurrencies will be the main factor facilitating a higher degree of adoption in the tourist sector. In the same study, the researchers stress that the adoption of blockchain payment technology in the future is a behavioural issue that depends on consumers' attitudes and behaviours as well as the technological aspect. These factors on adoption appear to be similar for also NFTs and the metaverse (Ante, 2022; Bobrowsky & Needleman, 2022; Chalmers et al., 2022; Purdy, 2022; Smith, 2022). Smith (2022) proposed that another factor that may lead to the adoption of these technologies is curiosity, and the novelty they induce into people's lives. Not only people but also owners of small businesses are adapting these technologies due to curiosity about their potential benefits (Ante, 2022; Purdy, 2022; Smith, 2022). The report by Mitic (2022) seems to support this idea. The report found that over 32% of small businesses in the US accepted cryptocurrency payments, this acceptance may be due to the prospect of potential benefits or the fear of missing out on these potential benefits. Mitic (2022) also reported that 27% of Americans supported adopting Bitcoin as a legal tender. Fungibility is one of the attributes that make cryptocurrencies a viable option for digital trading and payments (Mitic, 2022; Sharma, 2021a, 2021b). One of the earliest fields in which cryptocurrency was used for payment was on NFTS, the most notable transaction was the selling of Beeple's First 5000 Days digital artwork for over 42,300 ETH in 2021 (de Best, 2021).

When the existence of crypto plus NFTs plus metaverse platforms is taken into consideration, it seems like a completely different financial world. One that is gaining popularity and operates differently compared to the traditional one (Albayati et al., 2020; Haar, 2021; Wu et al., 2022). The growth of these three technologies raises the question of how future interactions and transactions will be conducted. This paper examines how this "alternative financial living" may interfere with the existing way of living, with a special look at small businesses and individuals.

STUDY OBJECTIVES AND RESEARCH QUESTIONS

This paper looks at three existing technologies, cryptocurrency, NFTs and metaverse platforms, and their effect on SMEs (small and medium-sized enterprises) and entrepreneurs. This paper seeks to understand the existing and future relationship between these technologies and SMEs and individuals. It also looks at the dynamics, attributes; and effects of this relationship for the advancement of these technologies and the entrepreneurial space.

The specific research questions formulated for this paper are:

1. What is the adoption rate of cryptocurrency, NFTS and metaverse among individuals and SMEs?
2. If cryptocurrencies become adopted by SMEs as a payment method, how would that affect their success and will that attract more buyers?
3. What use can SMEs make of NFT / Crypto etc., and how can SMEs benefit?
4. How will cryptocurrencies and NFTs affect the future of SMEs and individuals?
5. How will NFTs change specific industries, e.g. art industry, and traditional art publishers?
6. What research area(s) does this fall into finance, resourcing, marketing, risk, etc.?

RESEARCH METHODOLOGY

This paper uses the research onion methodology proposed by Saunders et al. (2016) to examine the outcomes of adopting or failing to adopt cryptocurrencies, NFTs, and metaverse in everyday life and business transactions. A pragmatism research philosophy was adopted, and both quantitative and qualitative studies were considered eligible as data sources. The time horizon used for this paper adopted both the cross-sectional and longitudinal timeframes to study how the effects and acceptance of cryptocurrencies, NFTs, and metaverse have varied over a certain time (Melnikovas, 2018).

SEARCH METHODOLOGY

An extensive search for articles was done on Scopus, Taylor and Francis Online, Science Direct, Emerald Insight and Google Scholar. The reference lists of identified studies were also screened. The list of similar and related articles in database searches was also screened. No consideration was made for grey literature. Since technology is a quickly changing phenomenon, and academic studies on crypto, NFTs and metaverse, have only been published recently, the date range was limited to the past 5 years i.e from 1st January 2017.

The search string:

Table 1. Search strings

Database	Search String
Scopus, Taylor and Francis Online, Emerald Insight	(Cryptocurrencies OR "digital currency" OR "decentralized currency" OR "non-fungible token" OR NFT OR NFTs OR metaverse) AND ("small and medium - sized enterprise" OR enterprise OR entrepreneurship OR entrepreneur OR business)
Science Direct,	(Cryptocurrencies OR "decentralized currency" OR "non-fungible token" OR NFT OR metaverse) AND ("small and medium - sized enterprise" OR entrepreneur OR business)
Google Scholar	(cryptocurrency) AND (business OR "small and medium-sized enterprise") / (NFT) AND (business OR "small and medium-sized enterprise") / (metaverse) AND (business OR "small and medium-sized enterprise")

To identify and include only topic-relevant studies, a study selection process was employed. The following inclusion and exclusion criteria were used.

Inclusion Criteria

Studies with primary data, these are case studies, surveys and experimental studies, as mentioned earlier in the research methodology section. The articles had to be written in English. The topic of study had to be on cryptocurrency, NFTs and metaverse and any relationship to small businesses or entrepreneurship.

Exclusion Criteria

Articles that were published earlier than 2017 or written in another language, other than English, were excluded. Any study with secondary data, including systematic reviews, literature reviews, conference papers, comments of papers and letters to editors. Any articles that had a research topic irrelevant or dissimilar to the research of this paper.

REVIEW METHODOLOGY

Data Extraction

Certain study attributes were extracted into a study descriptor table. These attributes are author, year of publication, study design, study region, study aim, and area of study (cryptocurrency, NFTs, metaverse).

Data Synthesis

Thematic and narrative analysis was used to analyze and report included study findings, Consistent themes like adoption, effect, and applications across articles were reported.

RESULTS

Search Results

5,249 articles were identified from database search and 23 from the screening of reference lists. 593 articles from Scopus, 99 from Emerald Insight, 1,183 from Taylor and Francis online, 3,224 from Science Direct and 150 articles from Google Scholar. 2,314 duplicates were removed and the remaining 2,958 articles were subjected to title and abstract screening. 2,729 were excluded during this process mostly due to irrelevancy and wrong study design. The remaining 229 articles were read in full, and only 22 were accepted for analysis after satisfying all attributes in the inclusion criteria.

Figure 1. PRISMA flowchart diagram

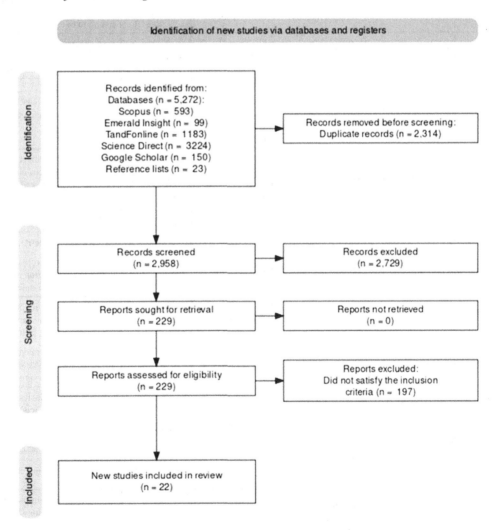

Data Extraction Results

Table 2. Data extraction

Author and Year	Study Design	Data Source	N	Study Region	Study Aim
Cryptocurrency					
(Leung & Dickinger, (2017)	Exploratory study	Survey	138 travellers	Europe	To examine the experience and intention to use of bitcoin users travelling to and from Europe
Alaeddin & Altounjy, (2018)	Observational study	Quantitative online questionnaires	230 university students	Malaysia	To investigate the factors affecting the use of cryptocurrency among Generation Z
(Albayati et al., (2020))	Descriptive study	online survey lasting 2 months	251 respondents (72% male)	Online	to investigate the behavioural factors that affect customers' intention to use cryptocurrency
Chen et al., (2022))	Observational study	Online survey questioning	295 respondents	Malaysia	To evaluate the factors that influence the adoption of cryptocurrency in the digital market
Daryaei et al., (2020)	Descriptive study	Professional interviews and a Delphi survey	8 professionals in the tourism sector, 16 Delphi panellists	–	To identify factors that lead to the acceptance of crypto payments in a tourism network
Guych et al., (2018)	Descriptive study	Questionnaire	101 respondents	Taiwan	to investigate the effect of individual and social characteristics on business adoption of cryptocurrency payments in hotels
Jonker, (2019)	Observational study	Online survey	768 online retailers	Netherlands	to investigate the factor that influences the adoption of crypto-payments by online-retailers
(Mendoza-Tello et al., (2018)	Descriptive study	Survey	125 respondents	Spain	To investigate the role of social media in the intention to use cryptocurrency for online payments
(Treiblmaier et al., (2020)	Exploratory study	Survey	161 travellers	Asia-Pacific region	To investigate the adoption of cryptocurrency payments in the travel and tourism sector
Wu et al., (2022)	Descriptive study	Online survey	211 respondents	Asia-Pacific region	To investigate the intention of online retailers in Asian and pacific regions to adopt crypto payments
Zubir et al., (2020)	Descriptive study	Survey	400 people (25% male)	Malaysia	to investigate if Malaysians are aware of cryptocurrency as a financial product, to determine how demographic factors affect the awareness and adoption of cryptocurrency
NFTs					
(Patrickson, (2021))	A research article, mixed methods study	Telephone interviews and online research	30 digital creative industries spokespersons	Scotland	To investigate the impact of blockchain technology on the producers of creative digital output or service

continues on follwoing page

Table 2. Continued

Author and Year	Study Design	Data Source	N	Study Region	Study Aim
Chalmers et al., (2022))	Research article	online research	–	–	to investigate the impact of NFTs on creative industry entrepreneurs
Christian et al., (2022)	Descriptive study	Questionnaire	53 respondents	Indonesia	to investigate how user-generated content, affects the intention to invest among investors
Hrenyak, (2022)	Observational study	Interviews	7 artists	–	to investigate the effect of NFTs on the work of online visual artists
Kanellopoulos et al., (2021)	Research article	Data from eBay sales + online research	–	–	To investigate if and how the prices of NFTs affect the price of physical card products
(Sahni, (2022))	Descriptive study	online research	–	–	To explore the effect of NFTs on the art market
(Schrader-Rank, (2021)	Research article	Interviews +online research	Unclear	–	To investigate the effect of NFTs on the art market and the environment, and why these effects occur.
Metaverse					
Bousba & Arya, (2022)	Descriptive cross-sectional study	online survey lasting 2 months	90 respondents	Online (9 countries)	To examine the impact of using metaverse marketing antecedents on a consumer's affective brand engagement.
(Bushell, (2022)	Descriptive cross-sectional study	Interviews + online research	–	–	
Kadry, (2022)	Research article	online research	–	–	To investigate the future impact of the metaverse on the way advertising is done
(Seth et al., (2022)	Descriptive study	Survey	82 respondents	–	To examine how the metaverse will affect the banking and financial businesses

Results of Included Studies: A Summary

This paper included a total of 22 articles, 11 articles on cryptocurrency (Leung & Dickinger, 2017; Alaeddin & Altounjy, 2018; Albayati et al., 2020; Chen et al., 2022; Daryaei et al., 2020; Guych et al., 2018; Jonker, 2019; Mendoza-Tello et al., 2018; Treiblmaier et al., 2020; Wu et al., 2022; Zubir et al., 2020), 7 articles on NFTs (Patrickson, 2021; Chalmers et al., 2022; Christian et al., 2022; Hrenyak, 2022; Kanellopoulos et al., 2021; Sahni, 2022; Schrader-Rank, 2021), and four on metaverse (Bousba & Arya, 2022; Bushell, 2022; Kadry, 2022; Seth et al., 2022). Most of the studies were descriptive and used data from surveys, interviews and online research. Among the studies with survey respondents or interviews, Zubir et al. (2020) had the largest number with 400 people and Hrenyak (2022) had the lowest number with 7 people. Also, the study regions were diverse, these included regions like Europe (Leung & Dickinger, 2017), Malaysia (Alaeddin & Altounjy, 2018; Chen et al., 2022; Zubir et al., 2020), Taiwan (Guych et al., 2018), Netherlands (Jonker, 2019), Spain (Mendoza-Tello et al., 2018), Asia-Pacific region (Treiblmaier et al., 2020; Wu et al., 2022), Scotland (Patrickson, 2021) and Indonesia (Christian et al., 2022).

Section 1: Cryptocurrency

Among papers that studied cryptocurrency, the data source, data collection method, data analysis method, study design and study aims were different. Some studies majored on the current adoption rate of crypto payments (Jonker, 2019; Leung & Dickinger, 2017; Treiblmaier et al., 2020; Zubir et al., 2020) and other that studied reasons for adopting or failing to adopt cryptocurrency among businesses and customers (Chen et al., 2022; Jonker, 2019; Leung & Dickinger, 2017; Treiblmaier et al., 2020; Zubir et al., 2020). All of the studies looked at factors that affect crypto adoption or intention to adopt (Alaeddin & Altounjy, 2018; Albayati et al., 2020; Chen et al., 2022; Daryaei et al., 2020; Guych et al., 2018; Jonker, 2019; Leung & Dickinger, 2017; Mendoza-Tello et al., 2018; Treiblmaier et al., 2020; Wu et al., 2022; Zubir et al., 2020). Daryaei et al. (2020), Leung and Dickinger (2017), and Treiblmaier et al. (2020) looked at the potential benefits for businesses and entrepreneurs for adopting crypto payments.

The Adoption Rate of Cryptocurrency

Jonker (2019) did a study among e-commerce retailers and found that only 2% (43 out of 768 e-retailers) of them accepted cryptocurrency payments, with 27 of them accepting bitcoin. Most of the retailers accepted iDEAL8 payments (79%), online credit transfers (61%), PayPal (46%), credit cards (43%), cash (21%), and debit card on delivery (10%). It was also interesting that 63% of the e-retailers who accepted cryptocurrency, would immediately exchange it for Euros (Jonker, 2019).

Treiblmaier et al. (2020) assessed the use rate of cryptocurrency among travellers in the Asia-pacific region. 50% of the respondents had previously used crypto payments for air tickets and accommodation. About 33% had used crypto to buy travel packages, and 41.6% had used crypto to buy tourism products and/or services.

In a survey done by Zubir et al. (2020) to assess the use of cryptocurrency in Malaysia. The study reported that 74.25% of the respondents had heard about cryptocurrency but 0% of them owned any crypto at the time of the survey. Also, none of the respondents had any preference for cryptocurrency payments. The most preferred modes of payment were debit cards (76%), credit cards (12.72%), and PayPal (11.25%).

Leung and Dickinger (2017), which evaluated crypto use among European travellers, found that only 35.5% of them had used Bitcoin. 73.5% of the users had used it for online shopping/ e-commerce and 59.2% had used it for travel-related expenses.

Reason for Cryptocurrency Acceptance Among Retailers (Expected Benefits)

In a survey done by Jonker (2019), the reasons for acceptance cited by e-commerce retailers were, to attract new customers (42%), because of customer recommendations/inquiries (23%), interest in new technology (21%) and because of low crypto transaction fees (7%).

Reason for Cryptocurrency Un-Acceptance Among Retailers (Expected Fears)

In a survey done by Jonker (2019), some of the reasons why e-retailers were not accepting cryptocurrency were, unfamiliarity (58%), lack of consumer demand (36%), not seeing any benefits for business (17%), lack of trust in crypto (16%), safety concerns (9%) and perceived difficulty in use (5%). Jonker (2019) also cited the risk of the perceived exchange rate between crypto and normal currencies as a barrier to crypto adoption among retailers.

Motivators for Cryptocurrency Acceptance Among Customers

In the study done by Treiblmaier et al. (2020), travellers in the Asia-pacific region were asked about their reasons for using crypto payments. In order of effect, the following reasons were given, universal usability, curiosity to use the new technology, lower transaction costs in cryptocurrency payment compared to other payment systems, disintermediation, user privacy and easy verification (no need for pin or signature). Among the survey respondents In Leung and Dickinger (2017), the most cited reasons were, security (by 45.7% of the respondents), universal usability (41.3%), lower transaction cost (33.3%) and ease of use (21.7%).

Inhibitors to Cryptocurrency Acceptance Among Customers

Zubir et al. (2020) report lack of understanding, lack of universal usability, lack of perceived usefulness, price volatility, and difficulty in use, as being reasons why 40%, 18.25%, 9.25%, 2.75% and 4.5% of the survey respondents did not adopt crypto payments. Some of these inhibitors were also present in Daryaei et al. (2020). In the interviews done by Daryaei et al. (2020), 92% of the blockchain experts agreed that the adoption of bitcoin hugely depended on awareness and knowledge about the mechanism surrounding bitcoin. Also, 87% of the experts agreed that volatility had a negative impact on the adoption of cryptocurrency payments. In the study by Leung and Dickinger (2017) the most cited inhibitors were lack of knowledge (60.1%), lack of crypto accepting-retailers (42.8%), volatility i.e high risk of loss of value (31.2%), and security/ lack of regulation (25.4%).

Factors Affecting Cryptocurrency Adoption Among Retailers

The most common factors are consumer demand (Jonker, 2019), the retailer's demographic characteristics (Jonker, 2019), net transactional benefits (Jonker, 2019; Daryaei et al., 2020), perceived ease of accessibility (Jonker, 2019; Daryaei et al., 2020; Wu et al., 2022), Technostress (Wu et al., 2022), and the type of service providers (Jonker, 2019).

1. Consumer demand

Jonker (2019) states that the most important indicator of whether a retailer will adopt crypto payments is customer demand. Using an ordered probit regression model the researchers found that a 1% increase in customer adoption of cryptocurrency increases the probability that a retailer will adopt cryptocurrency by 0.2%. This relationship is supported by the report that only 5% of payments made to retailers were through crypto, alongside the finding that the adoption rate among retailers was 2% (Jonker, 2019).

2. Retailer's demographic characteristics

Jonker (2019) reports that the retailer's age decreases the adoption rate by 1% for each increase of 1 year in age. The business age and size also had a negative effect on the adoption rate. Businesses older than 5 years were less likely to adopt crypto payments, and businesses with 5 to 19 employees were 1% less likely to adopt crypt0 payments compared to businesses with more than 20 employees.

3.   Net transactional benefits

Results from using an ordered probit regression model by Jonker (2019), showed that a 1% increase in favourable transaction cost ratio, increased the likelihood of adoption by 2.5%. Also benefits from the perceived reduction in labour cost, positively increased the probability of adoption. This was agreed on by Daryaei et al. (2020), where 86% of interviewed blockchain experts cited speed and the inexpensive nature of bitcoin transactions as one of the reasons for its adoption.

4.   Perceived ease of accessibility for accepting crypto-payments

Using an ordered probit regression model, Jonker (2019) found that a 1 point (1-7 scale) increase in "Perceived compatibility" increased the probability of adoption by 4.4%. This is seconded by Daryaei et al. (2020), where 83% of interviewed experts proposed that the integration of bitcoin payment with other payment systems, would increase its rate of adoption. According to Wu et al. (2022), retailers and customers are more likely to adopt crypto payments, if they have crypto efficacy and perceive crypto payments as highly convenient. Crypto efficacy is the ability to easily access and use crypto (Wu et al., 2022).

5.   Technostress

Among the included studies, only Wu et al. (2022) assessed the effect of technostress among retailers on the intention to adopt cryptocurrency. The researchers found that technostress had a negative impact on the behavioural intention to adopt crypto, with a beta value of $\beta = -0.35$ (Wu et al., 2022). Technostress was negatively affected by cryptocurrency efficacy and positively affected by technology involvement.

6.   Service providers

In their findings, Jonker (2019) reported that service providers and intermediaries, play an important role in deciding if retailers adopt crypto payments by directly influencing accessibility, competition, innovation and the process of transacting. In Jonker (2019) retailers who used PSP services were found to have a 7.3% less likelihood of adopting crypto payments.

Factors Affecting the Intention to Use Cryptocurrency Among Customers

The studies looked at behavioural elements such as trust (Alaeddin & Altounjy, 2018; Albayati et al., 2020; Daryaei et al., 2020; Mendoza-Tello et al., 2018; Treiblmaier et al., 2020; Zubir et al., 2020), attitude (Alaeddin & Altounjy, 2018; Albayati et al., 2020; Chen et al., 2022), perceived ease of use (Albayati et al., 2020; Daryaei et al., 2020; Guych et al., 2018; Jonker, 2019; Treiblmaier et al., 2020; Zubir et al., 2020), perceived usefulness (Albayati et al., 2020; Guych et al., 2018; Mendoza-Tello et al., 2018; Zubir et al., 2020), customer satisfaction (Alaeddin & Altounjy, 2018; Treiblmaier et al., 2020), social support (Chen et al., 2022; Mendoza-Tello et al., 2018; Treiblmaier et al., 2020). Studies also examined the effect of customer demographic characteristics (Zubir et al., 2020), transparency (Chen et al., 2022), price value (Chen et al., 2022), and traceability (Chen et al., 2022).

1. Customer demographic characteristics

Alaeddin and Altounjy (2018), Albayati et al. (2020), Jonker (2019), Leung and Dickinger, (2017), Zubir et al. (2020) all reported that the rate of adoption of cryptocurrency can be affected by other confounding factors not directly related to behavioural intention. These factors are average earnings (Zubir et al., 2020), level of education (Albayati et al., 2020), ethnicity (Zubir et al., 2020), gender (Jonker, 2019); Leung & Dickinger, 2017), and age Zubir et al., 2020). The above studies seemed to agree that people who are younger, employed and have a higher level of education are more willing to adopt cryptocurrency payments. The gender of the customers seemed to also influence the e-retailers' decision to adopt cryptocurrency. Jonker (2019) found that retailers with women as their main clientele are 4.1% and 9.6% less likely to adopt cryptocurrency compared to retailers with a missed clientele and those with a male clientele, respectively.

In Leung and Dickinger (2017), it was reported that among those who had adopted crypto, 69% of them were male, 65.5% of them had a high level of internet usage experience (9 years and above), and 65.5% had an online purchasing experience. Although the author did not directly state these as factors, it is upright to consider the effects of gender, internet use experience and online purchase experience, as predictors on whether a person will adopt crypto payments or not. For internet usage experience, this is later on ascertained in the study when correlation test analysis reveals a positive relationship between the likelihood of use and familiarity with the payment option (Leung & Dickinger, 2017).

2. Customer satisfaction

Alaeddin and Altounjy (2018) and Treiblmaier et al. (2020) proposed that customers with a higher level of satisfaction were more intent on adopting crypto payment. Treiblmaier et al. (2020) proposed that other than ease of use, attitude, and trust, other factors directly affect customer satisfaction; consequently affecting the behavioural intention to adopt. These other factors are novelty, safety and reliability of cryptocurrencies, hedonic aspects of cryptocurrencies, good usability, availability, and high performance of cryptocurrency. These all had a positive effect. Treiblmaier et al. (2020) additionally reports that crypto volatility and insecurity had a negative impact on the customer's level of satisfaction. In Alaeddin and Altounjy (2018), customer satisfaction was reported to have a positive effect on the intention to adopt cryptocurrency.

3. Trust

Alaeddin and Altounjy (2018), Albayati et al. (2020), Daryaei et al. (2020), Mendoza-Tello et al. (2018), and Treiblmaier et al. (2020) reported that trust had a significant positive effect on the intention to adopt cryptocurrency payment. In the study by Zubir et al. (2020), 25.25% of the respondents cited distrust; arising from privacy, lack of regulation and security concerns; as the main reason for not adopting crypto payments. In Daryaei et al. (2020), the source of distrust was a loss of or theft of Private Keys. In the study by Mendoza-Tello et al. (2018), which measured the magnitude of effect using a Structural Equation Model (SEM), trust was found to have an effect magnitude path = 0.209 (f2 = 0.029) on the intention to adopt cryptocurrency. Trust was influenced by regulatory support, customer experience (Albayati et al., 2020) and social commerce (Mendoza-Tello et al., 2018).

4. Attitude

Albayati et al. (2020) reported that attitude was responsible for 63.8% of the effect on behavioural intention. Alaeddin and Altounjy (2018) and Chen et al. (2022) reported that attitude had a positive effect on cryptocurrency adoption. In Alaeddin and Altounjy (2018), attitude was found to have an effect of technology awareness and trust.

5. Perceived usefulness

Albayati et al. (2020) reported that perceived usefulness was responsible for 57.6% of the effect on behavioural intention. The influence of perceived usefulness was also mentioned by Leung and Dickinger (2017), where 21.7% of the respondents cited perceived usefulness/ convenience as the main motivating factor for them to use bitcoin. Guych et al. (2018), Mendoza-Tello et al. (2018), and Zubir et al. (2020) concluded that perceived usefulness had a positive effect on behavioral intention.

In Mendoza-Tello et al. (2018), which measured the magnitude of effect using a Structural Equation Model (SEM), found that perceived usefulness had an effect magnitude of path = 0.332 (f2 = 0.167) on the intention to adopt cryptocurrency. In Guych et al. (2018), the perceived usefulness was significantly affected by trust (p value= 0.0000), other factors like financial risk, social risk, and technological risk were ruled out as having a statistically insignificant effect.

6. Perceived ease of use crypto payments

Albayati et al. (2020), Guych et al. (2018), and Zubir et al. (2020) reported that perceived ease of use had a positive effect on the intention to adopt cryptocurrency payments. In Albayati et al. (2020) perceived ease of use was responsible for 48.4% of the effect on behavioural intention. In Guych et al. (2018), perceived ease of use was significantly affected by convenience of cryptocurrency payment. In a survey done by Treiblmaier et al. (2020), the authors reported that universal usability was the biggest contributor to the adoption of crypto payments. Daryaei et al. (2020) looked at Technology Complexity (opposite to ease of use) and concluded that it had a negative effect on adoption/acceptance level.

Unlike other studies, Jonker (2019) found that perceived ease of use did not affect the customers' intention to adopt cryptocurrency adoption.

7. Social support

Using Structural Equation Models (SEM) based on variance, Mendoza-Tello et al. (2018) investigated how social commerce affected the intention to adopt cryptocurrency. The study findings showed that social support does not have any significant direct effect on the intention to adopt crypto. However, social commerce has a significant effect on perceived trust (path = 0.577, f2 = 0.515, using a partial least square analysis technique for an SEM) and perceived risk which in turn, affects the behavioural intention (Mendoza-Tello et al., 2018). In Mendoza-Tello et al. (2018) which used a Structural Equation Model (SEM), social support had an effect magnitude path of 0.177 (f2 = 0.031) on the intention to adopt cryptocurrency. The results from Mendoza-Tello et al. (2018) were collaborated by Chen et al. (2022) and Treiblmaier et al. (2020). Chen et al. (2022) concluded that social influence had a positive effect on customer satisfaction, which in turn had a positive effect on cryptocurrency adoption. Treiblmaier et al. (2020) reported that social media had a huge role to play in determining the trust and attitude towards adopting crypto payments.

8. Transparency

Chen et al. (2022) reported that the transparency of crypto had a positive effect on customer satisfaction, which in turn has a positive effect on cryptocurrency adoption.

9. Price Value

Chen et al. (2022) reported that cryptocurrency price value has a positive effect on cryptocurrency adoption.

10. Traceability

Chen et al, (2022) reported that traceability has a positive effect on customer satisfaction, which in turn has a positive effect on cryptocurrency adoption.

The Benefits to Businesses Using Cryptocurrency

In the study by Daryaei et al. (2020), 85% of the interviewed experts agreed that the universal usability of bitcoin made it possible for businesses using cryptocurrency to have a competitive edge, especially businesses in travel and tourism.

In studies carried out by Daryaei et al. (2020), Leung and Dickinger (2017), and Treiblmaier et al. (2020), most of the respondents who had used bitcoin considered it an advantage over the conventional means of payment like cash or centralized digital currency. This was true for both consumers and retailers. The most cited areas of application were purchasing travel packages (10.3% of bitcoin users in Leung & Dickinger, 2017, 33% of respondents in Treiblmaier et al., 2020), purchasing air tickets, Bitcoin (17.2% of bitcoin users in Leung and Dickinger, 2017, 50% of respondents in Treiblmaier et al., 2020), travel accommodation (20.7% of bitcoin users in Leung and Dickinger, 2017, about 50% of respondents in Treiblmaier et al., 2020), purchasing tourism products e.g. artefacts (41.6% of respondents in Treiblmaier et al., 2020), and purchasing food (31% of bitcoin users in Leung and Dickinger, 2017).

Daryaei et al. (2020), Leung and Dickinger (2017), and Treiblmaier et al. (2020) all seemed to drift towards the conclusion that there was an added leverage for businesses in the tourism sector that adopted crypto payments. Especially those in European and Asia-Pacific regions.

Section 2: NFTs

Factors That Lead to NFT Adoption

1.   User Generated Content

Christian et al. (2022) used a partial least square analysis technique for SEM developed from sample data. The article used R^2 values to establish the strength (strong = 0.75, moderate = 0.5, and weak = 0.25) of the effect of user-generated content on some of the factors that directly impact the intention to invest in NFTS among investors. The effect sizes were NFT Popularity ($R^2 = 0.275$), Tech Adoption ($R^2 = 0.235$) and on Intention to Invest ($R^2 = 0.609$). From this Christian et al. (2022) was able to conclude that User-Generated Social Media Content has a positive effect on NFT Popularity, which in turn has a positive effect on the intention to invest in NFTs (Christian et al., 2022).

2.   NFT popularity

After a PLS analysis, Christian et al. (2022) concluded that NFT popularity had a positive effect on investors' intention to invest in NFTs; using Tech Adoption as the mediating factor.

3.   Tech adoption

In Christian et al. (2022), tech adoption, meaning literacy in blockchain technology, was reported to have a positive effect on the intention to adopt/invest. This finding was true when tech adoption was used as a mediating factor and as a stand-alone factor (Christian et al., 2022).

Effects of NFTs on the Digital Creative Market

1.   Solving the problem of proof of ownership

According to Chalmers et al. (2022), the ownerability and verifiability aspect attributed to NTFs makes it easier to develop and promote original content. This is partly because theft is reduced (Chalmers et al., 2022).

2.   Solving the problem of digital scarcity

In a world where copying of digital code in pictures, files etc. is relatively easy to accomplish, the aspect of originality and uniqueness has taken quite a blow. Scarcity, which is established from uniqueness, is one of an artist's biggest pillars. According to a musician interviewed (Patrickson, 2021), the application of blockchain i.e NFT brings about digital scarcity by preventing duplication of work, this creates a range of new possibilities and markets.

3.   Popularity and Social growth among NFT artists

In Hrenyak (2022), one of the interviewed artists, states that her Twitter account massively gained support after she started creating and selling NFTs. The artist had also observed that despite NFTs creating a supportive social following, a social following is also a requirement for an artist's NFT art to be successful (Hrenyak, 2022). This may end up being a problem, where social participation begins to weigh more on NFT success that the artist's quality of work. Schrader-Rank (2021) discussed the involvement of celebrities in the NFT world. Even though their involvement creates awareness and participation, it also means that small digital artists producing quality art are often overlooked (Chalmers et al., 2022; Schrader-Rank, 2021; Samudra, 2022).

Hrenyak (2022) also mentioned the use of Discord, an online instant messaging app. This platform was cited by artists as one of the major reasons for their success. This success arose from engagement, empowerment and inspiration from other NFT artists.

4.   Democratization and removal of intermediaries

According to a blockchain expert interviewed in Patrickson (2021), blockchain technology greatly reduced the need for an intermediary person or institution and consequently increased the artist's profit margin by eliminating sales commission. This also helps to reduce supply disruption by connecting the artist directly to the customer (Patrickson, 2021). This attribute of NFT markets was referred to as democratization by Hrenyak (2022). Since NFT marketplaces are online, and not limited by geographical regions, they are more accessible than traditional art markets meaning anyone can create and sell NFT art (Hrenyak, 2022).

5.   Financial gains and new opportunities

According to Chalmers et al. (2022), Patrickson (2021), Schrader-Rank (2021), NFTs have made it possible to create new capital investment sources for businesses, individuals and digital creators. The growing NFT markets create a potentially innovative entry point for most digital SMEs, with uses ranging from gaming, and digital collectables, to e-sports (Patrickson, 2021). Hrenyak (2022) describes NFTs as a possible way for artists to attain financial freedom and democratization of arts. The artists who were interviewed in Hrenyak (2022) also stressed the difference in sales revenue between NFT and non-NFT art. One of the artists stated that she made more from selling an NFT collection in three hours than she had ever made from selling physical art in one year (Hrenyak, 2022). Another artist also stated that she was able to make 3 times by selling art as an NFT creator compared to what she would've made if she decided to sell it physically/online. Schrader-Rank (2021) reported that with the growth of the NFT market, artists are able to reach a wider audience.

According to Chalmers et al. (2022), the attribute of NFTs which are ownerability and verifiability, have the potential of creating novel revenue streams from previously non-monetizable outputs. And, according to the musician Brian Eno dryly, a way for artists to partake in and benefit from global capitalism (Chalmers et al., 2022). The benefit of resale royalties, which was reported by Chalmers et al. (2022) and Schrader-Rank (2021), was also mentioned by artists interviewed by Hrenyak (2022). NFTs that are minted on specialized marketplaces usually earn the artist/ digital creator 10% in royalties every time they are resold. The NFT artists regarded resale royalties as a positive change in the treatment and appreciation of digital artists (Hrenyak, 2022).

6.   Cross-fertilization/opening new market and customers

In their studies, Chalmers et al. (2022) and Sahni (2022) noted that there were collectors and buyers of NFTs, who had never had an interest in physical art. Apart from being investors, these collectors entail a new market that has been opened up to artists by the existence of NFTs. Chalmers et al. (2022) refer to this "new market" and its benefits as cross-fertilization.

NFTS Impact on Investors and Entrepreneur

Despite Chalmers et al. (2022) warning about the possibility of a market crash for NFTs, the article also talks of the possibility of a new form of investment among digital entrepreneurs. One of the possible futures of NFTs according to Chalmers et al. (2022) is the development and adoption of securitized NFTs. These are NFTs where smart contracts are used to create an ongoing revenue stream for investors and artists alike. Also when looking at the relationship between NFTs technology and the metaverse, Chalmers et al. (2022) reports that the role played by NFTs in the metaverse (property ownership etc.) is a call to digital market entrepreneurs to be vigilant and not to miss on the potential profit of the rapidly evolving blockchain market (Gillpatrick et al., 2022).

NFT Effect on Physical Markets/Card Collectables

Kanellopoulos et al. (2021) did a study to investigate how the prices of basketball trading card collectables were affected by the introduction of related NFT art. The study found that the introduction of NFT art meant that the value of the physical collectable decreased by 5% and the intention to buy physical cards reduced by 10%. Kanellopoulos et al. (2021) also reported that the sell volume for physical cards had reduced by 3.8%. When looking at the economic impact of the introduction of NFT cards, the study found that eBay's revenue from basketball trading cards had decreased by $35,801/day equivalent to a 22.5% reduction (Kanellopoulos et al., 2021). According to Chalmers et al. (2022), other ways in which the art sector may be positively disrupted by NFTs is from the benefits of community development and cultural affirmation.

Negative Effects of NFTs

1.   Possible market crash

The NFT market capitalization has been on the increase, gradually. Chalmers et al. (2022) raised a concern about the reason behind this "growth", warning art creators to not be dependent on revenue from the NFT marketplace in the long run. Chalmers et al. (2022) referred to the NFT purchases as a "gold rush", where most people and investors are buying due to market speculation and the fear of being left out. This was agreed on by Hrenyak (2022), where artists viewed the NFT marketplace as a place for primarily financial gain, and some artists were of the view that the interest in NFTs would fizzle out in the near future. Chalmers et al. (2022) also observed that major trades were of crypto collectables, which are majorly generated by standard algorithms. The authors conclude that NFTs have the potential to support digital art and creative patronage, but artists should be fearful of the loss of revenue in the event of a market crash or major market fraud. In the case where high volatility and fraud happen, most investors are likely to pull out and return to traditional ways of ownership and commercialization (Chandra, 2022; Chalmers et al., 2022).

2. Theft

Another concern that was raised by Hrenyak (2022) was the rampant theft of art, accompanied by a lack of preventive measures in NFT marketplaces. Interviewed artists complained of tokenization of their art without consultation.

3. Environmental impact

According to Chalmers et al. (2022), the minting of an NFT takes energy. This becomes even worse when online sites like Openseas, offered free NFT minting, leading to ridiculously high levels of minting and consequently high levels of energy consumption. This negative effect is also stated by Hrenyak (2022) and Schrader-Rank (2021).

Effect of NFTs on Related Technologies

Chalmers et al. (2022) looked at how the growth of NFTs had the potential of disrupting the development of the metaverse. The authors ended up concluding that NFTs open up the possibilities of developing practices surrounding commercial exchange, property ownership and advertising in virtual places in the metaverse.

Section 3: Metaverse

Applications for Businesses

1. Marketing and branding

Bushell (2022) did a survey on the potential use and benefits of the metaverse for marketing. The majority of the respondents in this survey, supported the idea that using metaverse for advertisement had potential benefits such as increased customer reach and engagement.

Bousba and Arya (2022) sought to understand the effect of a brand's marketing in the metaverse, on affective brand engagement. Brand Gamification Activities in Metaverse (BGAM) had a positive significant effect on Affective Brand Engagement in Metaverse (ABEM) with β value $= 0.56$ (Bousba & Arya, 2022). In turn, Affective Brand Engagement in Metaverse (ABEM) had a positive significant impact on Anticipated Brand Advocacy in Metaverse with a β-value $= 0.39$ (Bousba & Arya, 2022). This meant that clear branding and advertising in the metaverse meant better advocacy for the brand. In the study, novelty, inter-activity and vividness were evaluated for their effect on brand gamification effects. Novelty, Interactivity, and Vividness all had a positive significant effect on Brand Gamification Activities in Metaverse (BGAM) with β-values of 0.42, 0.24 and 0.35 respectively. This means that the inclusion of novelty, inter-activity and vividness when creating brand advertisements in the metaverse, significantly impacts the brand gamification activity which in turn impacts the brand's advocacy.

Kadry (2022) looked at the attributes that would make metaverse a better adverting platform compared to today's digital advertising.

(i) **Inclusivity:** In fashion and cloth advertising, it is possible for the user to not just see the product but to experience it as well (Kadry, 2022). According to Kadry (2022), this would make the user the star of the show (Kirjavainen, 2022).

(ii) **New ways of advertising:** According to Kadry (2022), metaverse makes it possible for advertisers to be able to track their advertisements and invest diligently. The use of in-game advertising has been made possible by metaverse technology. In their study, Kadry (2022) found that in-game advertising increased the player's intention to buy the product by 12%. Apart from in-game advertising, advergames were also discussed in the study (Kadry, 2022).

(iii) **Interactive live performances:** Kadry (2022) gives an example of when Fortnite collaborated with the artist Travis Scott, to hold a virtual concert where the promotion of the Jordan Sneakers was the goal.

2. Reaching potential customers

The users of the virtual world are potential customers for many brands, entrepreneurs and businesses. The growth of the metaverse offers the possibility of reaching this vast audience through virtual advertising (Bousba & Arya, 2022; Bushell, 2022). If done correctly, the effect of virtual advertising will be brand advocacy and popularity in the real ad online world (Bousba & Arya, 2022). In the survey done by Seth et al. (2022), among the respondents, 19.51% strongly agreed and 43.9% agreed that the use of the metaverse would attract new markets, especially young people.

3. Virtual payments in the banking industry

Among the respondents in Seth et al. (2022), 40.24% of them strongly agreed and 23.17% of them agreed that the metaverse had the potential of improving payments, by making them virtual. This will in turn go ahead to enhance customer experience. Another benefit mentioned by Seth et al. (2022) was about linked payments. The metaverse technology enables the identification of the sender and recipient quickly, effectively promoting better services and reducing waiting times.

4. Improve existing functionality in the banking industry

Seth et al. (2022) reported that 46.34% of respondents strongly agreed and 28.05% agreed that the adoption of the metaverse would create better functionality through 3D interaction.

DISCUSSION

This research paper selectively identified 22 relevant articles, intending to answer the research questions formulated earlier on in this paper. These questions are answered based on collected data, while at the same time trying to bridge some knowledge gaps, identifying repetitive themes and giving possible explanations for contradicting results among studies. The research questions and findings relevant to each, are detailed below.

1. What is the adoption rate of cryptocurrency, NFTS and metaverse among individuals and SMEs?

Only four studies looked at the adoption rate of crypto payments. Jonker (2019) did a study among e-commerce retailers, Treiblmaier et al. (2020) among Asia-Pacific travellers, Zubir et al. (2020) among the Malaysian general public, and Leung and Dickinger (2017) among travellers in the European region. The adoption rates were 2% in Jonker (2019), 50% in Treiblmaier et al. (2020), 0% in Zubir et al. (2020), and 35.5% in Leung and Dickinger (2017). The rates differed mostly due to the region and study population. In the studies done in European countries, there seemed to be a higher awareness of the existence and usability of cryptocurrency. The study population seems to affect the adoption rate, since Treiblmaier et al. (2020) and Leung and Dickinger (2017), which had the biggest adoption rate were done among travellers and Zubir et al. (2020) which had the lowest rate was done among random people in the general population. Only Jonker (2019) looked at SMEs and found a relatively low adoption rate among e-commerce retailers. One reason for this low rate, as mentioned by the authors, was due to the lack of consumer demand and lack of acceptance among customers.

Unfortunately, no study looked at the adoption rate for NFTs and metaverse technology, either among SMEs or among individuals. It can be argued that in Hrenyak (2022) the adoption rate is 57.1% since it included 3 non-NFT artists and 4 NFT artists. However, it should also be considered that Hrenyak (2022) did not aim to study NFT adoption, also the study did not include a large enough sample size. Hence any conclusion on the adoption rate based from Hrenyak (2022) is purely assumption and not based on data.

2. If cryptocurrencies become adopted by SMEs as a payment method, how would that affect their success and will that attract more buyers?

According to Jonker (2019), the reason why most retailers (42%) adopted crypto payments was to attract new customers, it is also prudent to notice that only 2% of the e-retailers had adopted cryptocurrency. This then raises the question of why the adoption rate is low despite crypto having been in existence for a time. This may be due to a lack of awareness or mistrust, but it might also be because crypto payments haven't become impactful enough to affect the financial dynamics in many SMEs, and are considered of no consequence among many small entrepreneurs. When the findings from Jonker (2019) are examined alongside those from Treiblmaier et al. (2020), Leung and Dickinger (2017), and Zubir et al. (2020), looking at the reasons for adoption, business success was not one of them. It can hence be concluded that the adoption of cryptocurrency has no significantly huge effect on the success of the business.

In the question of attracting more customers, Daryaei et al. (2020), Leung and Dickinger (2017), and Treiblmaier et al. (2020) all seemed to agree that the adoption of crypto payments gave the business a competitive edge, especially those businesses in the tourism/travel sector (Marco et al., 2020). It should, however, be noted that none of the studies stated or concluded that the adoption of cryptocurrency will attract more customers.

1.   What use can SMEs make of NFT/Crypto, etc., and how can SMEs benefit?

Among the 11 studies that looked at cryptocurrency and 7 that looked at NFTs, none of them specifically studied the potential benefits for a business that adopted these technologies. From data analysis and synthesis, this paper was able to identify the following benefits.

Cryptocurrency

The only mentioned use of cryptocurrency for SMEs was payment transactions. From this use, the SMEs may benefit from the following.

i.   Secure payments (Chen et al., 2022; Daryaei et al., 2020; Jonker, 2019; Mendoza-Tello et al., 2018)
ii.   Faster payments due to lack of intermediaries (Alaeddin & Altounjy, 2018; Albayati et al., 2020; Guych et al., 2018; Jonker, 2019; Treiblmaier et al., 2020)
iii. Low crypto transaction fees for retailers (Daryaei et al., 2020; Jonker, 2019; Leung & Dickinger, 2017; Treiblmaier et al., 2020)
iv.   Gain a slight competitive edge among other businesses that have not adopted cryptocurrency (Daryaei et al., 2020). This benefit is highly dependent on the business sector and the type of customers the business has.

NFTs

Some of the benefits of NFTs in the art industry are, creating new opportunities, improving an artist's financial gains, removal of intermediaries, solving the problem of proof of ownership, and solving the problem of digital scarcity (Chalmers et al., 2022; Hrenyak, 2022; Patrickson, 2021; Sahni, 2022; Schrader-Rank, 2021).

2.   How will cryptocurrencies and NFTs affect the future of SMEs and individuals?

Articles included in this paper, all seemed to agree that cryptocurrency and NFTs would play a huge role among businesses in the near future. The conclusion that can be pooled from these studies is that SMEs need to adopt these technologies, for them to be relevant in the coming future. By adopting these technologies they stand to benefit a lot in the new era of decentralized payments and digital encrypted ownership.

3.   How will NFTs change specific industries, e.g art industry, and traditional art publishers?

The adoption of NFTs has been reported to have benefits like reaching a wider market and increased financial gain (Chalmers et al., 2022; Hrenyak, 2022; Patrickson, 2021; Sahni, 2022; Schrader-Rank, 2021; de Haro, 2022). However, these are benefits that are only afforded to those artists that adopt NFTs. In the study by Kanellopoulos et al. (2021) NFTs seem to have a negative effect on physical art collectables. The presence of NFT counterparts meant that the value of the collectables was reduced by

5% and the intention among consumers to buy them decreased by 10% (Kanellopoulos et al., 2021). The introduction of NFTs has also brought about NFT theft art, where an artist's work is tokenized without approval (Hrenyak, 2022).

4. What research area(s) does this fall into finance, resourcing, marketing, risk, etc?

The topic of NFTs, cryptocurrency and the metaverse is so broad, such that it becomes impossible to narrow it all down to one specific research area (Ananya Babu & Mohan, 2022). But, according to the studies included in this paper, the most studied areas were, marketing, finance, economics, and social science.

CONCLUSION

Since their introduction, cryptocurrency, NFTs and metaverse technologies, have not only disrupted the technological world but also the financial world, including small and medium-sized businesses. The adoption intention, adoption rate and acceptance of these technologies vary, mostly depending on the behavioural characteristics of the individual (consumer or retailer), business goals, and business sector. These technologies have brought about benefits to those who have adopted them but have also negatively disrupted how some of the related business was earlier run. From the paper, it is clear that NFTs have been beneficial to artists who have adopted them, but they have also reduced the sales of physical arts and collectables. Cryptocurrency on the other hand seems to have made transactions universal, cheaper and faster. However, due to the low adoption rate and the small number of studies, it is difficult to establish if they are beneficial to SMEs and small businesses. The metaverse technology, which is still in its infant years, seems to have the potential to vigorously shake up the advertising and marketing businesses. This new technology seems to offer a novel way of advertising that is more vivid, clear and interactive, compared to traditional digital marketing. According to experts, this will be a game changer.

RECOMMENDATION

The data on the adoption rate of cryptocurrency was low and data on the adoption of NFTs among artists was non-existent. One possible reason for this is due to the novel nature of these technologies. This paper calls for more research to be done on crypto adoption and for new studies specifically looking at the adoption of NFTs.

IMPLICATION OF STUDY

The results of this study help to understand the world of blockchain technologies (cryptocurrency, NFTs and metaverse), looking at their adoption, uses, benefits and impacts on the entrepreneurial and business space.

REFERENCES

Abrol, A. (2022). *Decentraland Metaverse: A Complete Guide*. Blockchain Council. Available at: https://www.blockchain-council.org/metaverse/decentraland-metaverse/

Alaeddin, O., & Altounjy, R. (2018). Trust, Technology Awareness and Satisfaction Effect into the Intention to Use Cryptocurrency among Generation Z in Malaysia. *International Journal of Engineering and Technology*, *7*(4.29), 8–10. doi:. doi:10.14419/ijet.v7i4.29.21588

Albayati, H., Kim, S. K., & Rho, J. J. (2020). Acceptance of financial transactions using blockchain technology and cryptocurrency: A customer perspective approach. *Technology in Society*, *62*, 101320. doi:10.1016/j.techsoc.2020.101320

Ananya Babu, M. U., & Mohan, P. (2022). Impact of the Metaverse on the Digital Future: People's Perspective. IEEExplore. doi:10.1109/ICCES54183.2022.9835951

Ante, L. (2022). Non-fungible token (NFT) markets on the Ethereum blockchain: Temporal development, cointegration and interrelations. *Economics of Innovation and New Technology*, 1–19. doi:10.1080/10438599.2022.2119564

Antier. (2021). *An In-depth Insight into ERC-721 and Other NFT Standards*. Antier Solutions. https://www.antiersolutions.com/an-in-depth-insight-into-erc-721-and-other-nft-standards/#:~:text=ERC-721%20is%20an%20Ethereum%20standard%20used%20in%20non

Bobrowsky, M., & Needleman, S. E. (2022). *What Is the Metaverse? The Future Vision for the Internet*. WSJ. https://www.wsj.com/story/what-is-the-metaverse-the-future-vision-for-the-internet-ca97bd98

Bousba, Y., & Arya, V. (2022). Let's Connect in Metaverse. Brand's New Destination to Increase Consumer's Affective Brand Engagement & their Satisfaction and Advocacy. *Journal of Content. Community & Communication*, *15*(8), 276–293. doi:10.31620/JCCC.06.22/19

Bult, T. (2022). The implications of non-fungible tokens in video games from the perspective of the stakeholder capitalism theory. *USA Today*.

Bushell, C. (2022). The Impact of Metaverse on Branding and Marketing - A Study of How Individuals and Celebrities Use Metaverse as a Brand Extension, and the Implications for Marketing. SSRN *Electronic Journal*. doi:10.2139/ssrn.4144688

Chalmers, D., Fisch, C., Matthews, R., Quinn, W., & Recker, J. (2022). Beyond the bubble: Will NFTs and digital proof of ownership empower creative industry entrepreneurs? *Journal of Business Venturing Insights*, *17*, e00309. doi:10.1016/j.jbvi.2022.e00309

Chandra, Y. (2022). Non-fungible token-enabled entrepreneurship: A conceptual framework. *Journal of Business Venturing Insights*, *18*, e00323. doi:10.1016/j.jbvi.2022.e00323

Chen, X., Miraz, M.H., Gazi, A.I., Rahaman, A., Habib, M. & Hossain, A.I. (2022). Factors affecting cryptocurrency adoption in digital business transactions: The mediating role of customer satisfaction. *Technology in Society*, *70*. . doi:10.1016/j.techsoc.2022.102059

Christian, R., Luois Cenisius, V., Darmawan, M., Ferrero, J., & Yansen, E. (2022). Impact of User-Generated Content on Intentions to Invest in NFTs. *Budapest International Research and Critics Institute (BIRCI-Journal). Humanities (Washington), 5*(2). doi:10.33258/birci.v5i2.5642

CoinMarketCap. (2019). *Global Charts | CoinMarketCap*. CoinMarketCap. https://coinmarketcap.com/charts/

Daryaei, M., Jassbi, J., Radfar, R., & Khamseh, A. (2020). Bitcoin Adoption as a New Technology for Payment Mechanism in a Tourism Collaborative Network. Boosting Collaborative Networks 4.0, 167–176. doi:10.1007/978-3-030-62412-5_14

de Best, R. (2021). *Topic: Cryptocurrency adoption among businesses*. Statista. https://www.statista.com/topics/7712/cryptocurrency-adoption-among-businesses/#topicHeader__wrapper

de Best, R. (2022a). *Cryptocurrencies - statistics & facts*. Statista. https://www.statista.com/topics/4495/cryptocurrencies/#topicHeader__wrapper

de Best, R. (2022b). *NFT - statistics & facts*. Statista. https://www.statista.com/topics/8513/nft/#topicHeader__wrapper

de Haro, I. D. (2022). *How NFTs Are Driving the Latest Evolution of Art from Physical to Digital in a Pandemic Age*. Proquest. https://www.proquest.com/openview/7d11aa8708c36a3081171854dea8cab8/1?cbl=18750&diss=y&parentSessionId=HU7qElwYw9pMEjgn5sfhiRy82ePOolb69cXoyHpVJNQ%3D&pq-origsite=gscholar&parentSessionId=GTdHpKNqLM%2FmmU065Eipn82vv%2F6AtczufDrsmsAHYck%3D

Haileyesus, S. (2022). How to Make Money with Cryptocurrency. *Small Business Trends*. https://smallbiztrends.com/2022/06/how-to-make-money-with-cryptocurrency.html#:~:text=There%20are%20three%20ways%20to%20acquire%20cryptocurrency%3A%20you

Forra. (2018). *Methods and ways to obtain cryptocurrency*. Forra. https://forra.io/obtaining-cryptocurrency/

Gillpatrick, T., Boğa, S., & Aldanmaz, O. (2022). How Can Blockchain Contribute to Developing Country Economies? A Literature Review on Application Areas. *ECONOMICS, 10*(1), 105–128. doi:10.2478/eoik-2022-0009

GlobalData. (2022). *Bitcoin's Market Capitalization History (May 1, 2013 – September 4, 2022, $ Billion)*. GlobalData. https://www.globaldata.com/data-insights/cards-amp-payments/bitcoins-market-capitalization-history/

Guides, C. (2021). *Why was Cryptocurrency Created, was there a reason?* Crypto Set Go. https://cryptosetgo.com/why-was-cryptocurrency-created-was-there-a-reason/ .

Guych, N., Anastasia, S., & Jennet, A. (2018). *Munich Personal RePEc Archive Factors influencing the intention to use cryptocurrency payments: An examination of blockchain economy*. MPRA. https://mpra.ub.uni-muenchen.de/99159/1/MPRA_paper_99159.pdf

Haar, R. (2021). The Future of Cryptocurrency: 5 Experts' Predictions After a 'Breakthrough' 2021. *Time*. https://time.com/nextadvisor/investing/cryptocurrency/future-of-cryptocurrency/

Han, R., Foutris, N., & Kotselidis, C. (2019). Demystifying Crypto-Mining: Analysis and Optimizations of Memory-Hard PoW Algorithms. In *2019 IEEE International Symposium on Performance Analysis of Systems and Software (ISPASS)*. IEEE. 10.1109/ISPASS.2019.00011

Hrenyak, A. (2022). *Implications of Non-Fungible Tokens for the Online Artist* [Theses within Digital Humanities, Uppsala University]. Digitala Vetenskapliga Arkivet. https://www.diva-portal.org/smash/record.jsf?pid=diva2%3A1675820&dswid=-1340

Jonker, N. (2019). What drives the adoption of crypto-payments by online retailers? *Electronic Commerce Research and Applications*, *35*, 100848. doi:10.1016/j.elerap.2019.100848

Kadry, A. (2022). The Metaverse Revolution and Its Impact on the Future of Advertising Industry. *Journal of Design Sciences and Applied Arts*, *3*(2), 347–358. doi:10.21608/jdsaa.2022.129876.1171

Kanellopoulos, I. F., Gutt, D., & Li, T. (2021). Do Non-Fungible Tokens (Nfts) Affect Prices of Physical Products? Evidence from Trading Card Collectibles. SSRN *Electronic Journal*. [online] doi:10.2139/ssrn.3918256

Kaspersky. (2019). *What is Cryptocurrency? Cryptocurrency Security: 4 Tips to Safely Invest in Cryptocurrency*. Kasperksy. https://www.kaspersky.com/resource-center/definitions/what-is-cryptocurrency

Kirjavainen, E. (2022). *The future of luxury fashion brands through NFTs*. Aaltodoc. https://aaltodoc.aalto.fi/handle/123456789/114089

Leung, D., & Dickinger, A. (2017). Use of Bitcoin in Online Travel Product Shopping: The European Perspective. *Information and Communication Technologies in Tourism*, *2017*, 741–754. doi:10.1007/978-3-319-51168-9_53

Levy, A. (2022). *Digital Collectibles: What They Are and How to Get Started*. The Motley Fool. https://www.fool.com/investing/stock-market/market-sectors/financials/non-fungible-tokens/digital-collectibles/

Marco, V., Cinzia, D. A., Rosario, F., & Elmo, G. C. (2020). *About on Organizational Impact on the Adoption of New Technologies in Tourism*. Cultural and Tourism Innovation in the Digital Era. doi:10.1007/978-3-030-36342-0_20

Marr, B. (2022). The 10 Best Examples Of The Metaverse Everyone Should Know About. *Forbes*. https://www.forbes.com/sites/bernardmarr/2022/05/16/the-10-best-examples-of-the-metaverse-everyone-should-know-about/?sh=6afa4a3a3f5f

Melnikovas, A. (2018). Towards an Explicit Research Methodology: Adapting Research Onion Model for Futures Studies. *Journal of Futures Studies*. Advance online publication. doi:10.6531/JFS.201812_23(2).0003

Mendoza-Tello, J. C., Mora, H., Pujol-Lopez, F. A., & Lytras, M. D. (2018). Social Commerce as a Driver to Enhance Trust and Intention to Use Cryptocurrencies for Electronic Payments. IEEE Access, 50737–50751. doi:10.1109/ACCESS.2018.2869359

Mitic, I. (2022). *30 Cryptocurrency Statistics for 2022: A Modern-Day Gold Rush*. Fortunly | Statistics. https://fortunly.com/statistics/cryptocurrency-statistics/#:~:text=Here%20are%20the%20top%2010%20statistics%20on%20the

Nam, K., Dutt, C. S., Chathoth, P., & Khan, M. S. (2019). Blockchain technology for smart city and smart tourism: Latest trends and challenges. *Asia Pacific Journal of Tourism Research*, 1–15. doi:10.1 080/10941665.2019.1585376

NFTs Street. (2021). *History Of NFT or Non-Fungible-Tokens | How NFTs came into Existence?* NFT Street. https://www.nftsstreet.com/history-of-nft/#:~:text=NFT%20or%20Non-fungible-token%20 was%20first%20created%20by%20Kevin

Pastrana, S., & Suarez-Tangil, G. (2019). A First Look at the Crypto-Mining Malware Ecosystem. In *Proceedings of the Internet Measurement Conference*. ACM. 10.1145/3355369.3355576

Patrickson, B. (2021). What do blockchain technologies imply for digital creative industries? *Creativity and Innovation Management*, *30*(3), 585–595. doi:10.1111/caim.12456

Pestunov, A. I. (2020). Cryptocurrencies and Blockchain: Potential Applications in Government and Business. *Problems of Economic Transition*, *62*(4-6), 286–297. doi:10.1080/10611991.2020.1968751

Purdy, M. (2022). *How the Metaverse Could Change Work*. Harvard Business Review. https://hbr. org/2022/04/how-the-metaverse-could-change-work

Sahni, S. (2022). How are NFTs affecting the art market? *International Journal of Mechanical Engineering*, *7*(5).

Samudra, A. (2022). Non-Fungible Tokens (NFTs): New Renaissance for the Artists. SSRN *Electronic Journal*. doi:10.2139/ssrn.4112932

Saunders, M. N. K., Lewis, P., & Thornhill, A. (2016). *Research Methods For Business Students*. Pearson Education Limited.

Schrader-Rank, A. (2021). *How NFTs Influence Society: A Look at Scarcity Mindset*. Generational Gaps in Education, and the Impact on the Environment.

Seth, D., Gupta, M., & Singh, B. J. (2022). *A Study to Analyse the Impact of Using the Metaverse in the Banking Industry to Augment Performance in a Competitive Environment*. Advances in Marketing, Customer Relationship Management, and E-Services. doi:10.4018/978-1-6684-6133-4.ch002

Sharma, R. (2021a). *Non-Fungible Token Definition: Understanding NFTs*. Investopedia. https://www. investopedia.com/non-fungible-tokens-nft-5115211

Sharma, T., Zhou, Z., Huang, Y., & Wang, Y. (2022). *'It's A Blessing and A Curse': Unpacking Creators' Practices with Non-Fungible Tokens (NFTs) and Their Communities*. doi:10.48550/arXiv.2201.13233

Sharma, V. (2021b). *What is the Metaverse? Beginner's Guide*. Quytech Blog. https://www.quytech. com/blog/what-is-metaverse/

Sharma, V., & Halevi, T. (2022). A Survey on Research Directions in Blockchain Applications Usability. In *Proceedings of Seventh International Congress on Information and Communication Technology* (pp.727–738). Springer. 10.1007/978-981-19-1610-6_64

Smith, R. (2022). NPD with the Metaverse, NFTs, and Crypto. *Research Technology Management*, *65*(5), 54–56. doi:10.1080/08956308.2022.2090182

Tham, A., & Sigala, M. (2020). Road block(chain): bit(coin)s for tourism sustainable development goals? *Journal of Hospitality and Tourism Technology.* . doi:10.1108/JHTT-05-2019-0069

Treiblmaier, H., Leung, D., Kwok, A. O. J., & Tham, A. (2020). Cryptocurrency adoption in travel and tourism – an exploratory study of Asia Pacific travellers. *Current Issues in Tourism*, 1–17. doi:10.108 0/13683500.2020.1863928

Wilson, K. B., Karg, A., & Ghaderi, H. (2021). Prospecting non-fungible tokens in the digital economy: Stakeholders and ecosystem, risk and opportunity. *Business Horizons.* doi:10.1016/j.bushor.2021.10.007

Wu, R., Ishfaq, K., Hussain, S., Asmi, F., Siddiquei, A. N., & Anwar, M. A. (2022). Investigating e-Retailers' Intentions to Adopt Cryptocurrency Considering the Mediation of Technostress and Technology Involvement. *Sustainability*, *14*(2), 641. doi:10.3390u14020641

Zubir, D., Aishah, D. N., Ali, D. A., Mokhlis, D. S., & Sulong, D. F. (2020). Doing Business using Cryptocurrency in Malaysia. *International Journal of Management and Humanities*, *4*(9), 148–157. doi:10.35940/ijmh.I0899.054920

Chapter 6
The Development of Decentralized Governance Models for Web 3 Ecosystems

Tanuj Surve

https://orcid.org/0009-0009-6495-6232
University of California, Berkeley, USA

Risha Khandelwal
JECRC University, India

ABSTRACT

This chapter delves into the development of decentralized governance models for Web 3 ecosystems. It analyzes the shortcomings of traditional governance models and how decentralized models can overcome them. The chapter then investigates several decentralized governance models, such as reputation-based systems, liquid democracy, and decentralized autonomous organizations (DAOs), as well as their benefits and drawbacks. The challenges associated with establishing decentralized governance models are also explored. Lastly, the chapter explores potential future advancements as well as best practices for creating and implementing decentralized governance models in Web 3 ecosystems. All in all, the importance of decentralized governance models in encouraging openness, participation, and accountability in Web 3 ecosystems is highlighted in this chapter.

INTRODUCTION: WHAT ARE DECENTRALIZED GOVERNANCE MODELS AND WHY ARE THEY IMPORTANT FOR WEB 3 ECOSYSTEMS?

The rapid development of blockchain technology has resulted in the creation of web 3 ecosystems. Unlike Web2 ecosystems, which are dominated by centralized entities, web 3 ecosystems are meant to be decentralized, transparent, and democratic (Voshmgir, 2020). web 3 proponents envision an Internet in which trust is built without the use of centralized entities (Madhwal & Pouwelse, 2023). Decentralized governance models are an important component of web 3 ecosystems. Decentralized governance models

DOI: 10.4018/978-1-6684-9919-1.ch006

Copyright © 2023, IGI Global. Copying or distributing in print or electronic forms without written permission of IGI Global is prohibited.

distribute decision-making throughout society, resulting in a more democratic, efficient, and resilient structure. This chapter delves into the concept of decentralized governance models, their importance in web 3 ecosystems, and how they work.

web 3 ecosystems have been created to be decentralized, which means that no single entity has control over them (Murray, Kim, & Combs, 2023). This provides for more equitable power and decision-making authority allocation. web 3 ecosystems use decentralized governance models to disseminate decision-making throughout a network of stakeholders, rather than depending on centralized authorities to make choices.

Blockchain technology enables decentralized governance models by providing a safe and transparent means for tracking choices and verifying that they are made in accordance with set standards (Centobelli, Cerchione, Vecchio, Oropallo, & Secundo, 2022). Compared to traditional centralized governance models, these models have several advantages. For one thing, they enable better transparency and accountability. This is because all stakeholders can observe and participate in the decision-making process.

What Are Decentralized Governance Models?

Decentralized governance models offer a unique way to make decisions. Decentralized governance models distribute decision-making among a network of users, who frequently possess tokens or voting rights on a platform (Jnr., 2022). Smart contracts, which enable automated decision-making, are important to decentralized governance models. All stakeholders have a say in how a platform runs in a decentralized governance model. This comprises platform developers, users, investors, and any other parties with an interest in the platform.

Decentralized governance models are built on the ideas of decentralization and the blockchain technology that supports web 3 ecosystems. Decentralization is the process of transferring power and decision-making authority from a single entity to a network of stakeholders (Karjalainen, 2020). Blockchain technology allows for the establishment of tamper-proof and transparent smart contracts that can automate platform decision-making. Smart contracts are used in decentralized governance models to allow stakeholders to participate in decision-making and ensure that decisions are transparent and democratic. There are several types of decentralized governance models. These will be discussed further in the chapter.

Why Are Decentralized Governance Models Important For web 3 Ecosystems?

Decentralized governance models are consistent with the principles of and are important to the advancement of web 3 ecosystems. The following are some of the reasons why decentralized governance methods are vital for web 3 ecosystems:

Transparency: Decentralized governance models ensure transparency in decision-making. All stakeholders can observe and participate in the decision-making process (Mabel & Onwukwe, 2022). This promotes accountability and openness, both of which are critical for the success of web 3 ecosystems. Transparency is especially critical in web 3 ecosystems since they are decentralized and lack a centralized authority. Decentralized governance models give the transparency and accountability tools required to ensure stakeholder trust in the decision-making process.

Democratic: Decentralized government models are democratic in nature (Atzori, 2015). They make sure that all stakeholders have a voice in decision-making, resulting in a more egalitarian system. Decisions are made based on consensus rather than a single entity's interests. This is critical in web 3 ecosystems because they are intended to be community-driven. Decentralized governance models ensure that the community has a voice in decision-making and that choices are made in the best interests of the entire community.

Efficiency: Decentralized governance models have been designed to be efficient. Smart contracts enable decisions to be made swiftly and without the need for a central authority (Peters & Panayi, 2016). This allows web 3 ecosystems to move faster and respond to community requirements more quickly. Decentralized governance models also allow stakeholders to participate in decision-making without the need for intermediaries or gatekeepers, lowering the time and resources required to make choices.

Community-driven: Decentralized governance models are community-driven, which means that choices are made based on the requirements of the community. This promotes a more collaborative atmosphere in which stakeholders interact to achieve common goals. Decentralized governance models allow stakeholders to engage in decision-making and provide input, which can aid in the identification of community needs and priorities.

Resilient: Decentralized governance models outperform traditional centralized governance models in terms of resilience. Because decision-making is not based on a single point of failure, decentralized governance models enable web 3 ecosystems to resist attacks and failures. This is especially true in web 3 ecosystems, which have been designed to be decentralized and resistant to censorship and control.

Innovation: Decentralized governance models foster innovation by allowing for more flexible and adaptable decision-making processes. This is due to the fact that stakeholders can suggest and implement improvements without the involvement of intermediaries or gatekeepers. Decentralized governance models also encourage experimentation and iteration by allowing stakeholders to test and enhance ideas in a more collaborative and transparent setting. The advantages of decentralized governance models extend beyond the operation of web 3 ecosystems. Decentralized governance models also comply with the increasingly crucial principles of decentralization, transparency, and democracy in today's society. Decentralized governance models can also foster innovation by allowing a broad range of stakeholders to engage in decision-making.

Decentralized governance models have evolved as critical components of web 3 ecosystems. They allow decision-making to be shared across the community, resulting in a system that is transparent, democratic, efficient, community-driven, and resilient. Decentralized governance models are compatible with web 3 ecosystem principles and allow them to thrive. In the parts that follow, we will look at the many sorts of decentralized governance models that exist in web 3 ecosystems, as well as the challenges and constraints that come with them.

HISTORICAL CONTEXT: HOW HAVE GOVERNANCE MODELS IN PRIOR TECHNOLOGIES INSPIRED THE CREATION OF DECENTRALIZED GOVERNANCE MODELS IN WEB 3 ECOSYSTEMS?

The evolution of decentralized governance models in web 3 ecosystems did not occur in a vacuum; rather, it was influenced by prior technologies' governance models. This section will look at the historical context that led to the emergence of decentralized governance models in web 3 ecosystems, as well as how prior governance models influenced their evolution.

Early Internet Governance Models

Early internet governance models were characterized by decentralization, with no centralized body governing the network. The early days of the internet were focused on creating a network that could connect computers and ease communication between them. This decentralized concept allows anyone with an internet connection to engage in the network without the requirement for permission or approval from a central authority.

However, as the Internet's popularity and significance expanded, the decentralized governance model began to fail. It became clear that a centralized authority was required to oversee the domain name system (DNS) and coordinate internet protocol (IP) address allocation. To fill this duty, the Internet Corporation for Assigned Names and Numbers (ICANN) was established in the mid-1990s.

The establishment of ICANN signaled a transition toward a more centralized Internet governance approach. ICANN is a non-profit organization that is overseen by the US Department of Commerce. Its mission is to oversee the development and management of top-level domains (TLDs) and also to administer DNS and IP address allocation.

The governance model of ICANN has been criticized for its apparent lack of transparency and accountability, as well as its US-centric orientation. Some claim that ICANN's governance mechanism does not effectively represent the global internet community and that a more decentralized and transparent governance model is required.

This history has affected the development of web 3 ecosystems, as the requirement for decentralized governance models became apparent to avoid the dangers of centralization and censorship that had emerged in the previous period of Internet administration. Blockchain technology's decentralized nature makes it a natural fit for decentralized governance models since it allows stakeholders to participate in decision-making without the need for a central authority.

Decentralized governance models that are transparent, accountable, and community-driven have arisen during the web 3 era. To enable stakeholders to engage in decision-making, these models rely on blockchain-based smart contracts and token-based voting systems.

Open-Source Governance Models

Open-source governance models have had a significant impact on the development of decentralized governance models in web 3 ecosystems. Open-source software is software that is licensed under an open-source license, permitting users to freely use, modify, and distribute the software. Open-source software is created by a community of contributors who collaborate to enhance and add new features to the software. This collaborative development methodology involves a transparent, inclusive, and community-driven governance mechanism.

The Linux operating system employs one of the first and most well-known open-source governance models (Ljungberg, 2021). The Linux Foundation, a non-profit organization that controls Linux kernel development, is administered by a board of directors elected by the Linux community. The board is in charge of determining the Linux Foundation's strategic direction as well as managing the development of the Linux kernel and other associated projects. The governance model of the Linux Foundation is intended to be transparent and inclusive, with a focus on community-driven decision-making. The board of directors is made up of a mix of individuals and businesses to represent the needs of both the community and the industry.

Other open-source projects have created their own governance structures, emphasizing transparency, inclusivity, and community-driven decision-making. The Apache Software Foundation, for example, is a non-profit organization that manages the development of the Apache web server and other open-source projects. The Apache Software Foundation is controlled by an elected board of directors from the Apache community. The board is in charge of determining the organization's strategic direction as well as managing the development of the Apache web server and other related projects.

Open-source governance methods in web 3 ecosystems have been developed to include blockchain-based smart contracts and token-based voting mechanisms. Without the requirement for a centralized authority, these decentralized governance models allow stakeholders to engage in decision-making.

The Ethereum community, for example, has created a decentralized governance model. Anyone can make improvements to the Ethereum protocol through the Ethereum Improvement Proposal (EIP) process, which is subsequently evaluated and discussed by the community. If a proposal has enough support, it can be implemented using a smart contract. The governance model of the Ethereum community is built on a token-based voting system in which token holders can vote on proposals with their tokens. This mechanism is intended to encourage stakeholders to engage in decision-making by giving those with more tokens a greater influence in the protocol's development.

DAOs and Token-Based Governance Models

Decentralized Autonomous Organizations (DAOs) were created in 2016 as a significant step forward for decentralized governance models. DAOs are organizations that function on a blockchain using smart contracts, with decision-making power divided among token holders. This methodology gives stakeholders a direct say in decision-making and provides for transparent and unchangeable decision-making.

DAOs have been used for several reasons, including project finance and management, and their success has led to the development of token-based governance models in web 3 ecosystems. Token-based governance models express voting power with blockchain-based tokens, allowing for more granular and flexible decision-making.

MakerDAO, a DeFi protocol that allows users to borrow and lend cryptocurrencies using collateralized debt positions (CDPs), is one of the most well-known examples of a DAO. MakerDAO's governance mechanism is based on token-based voting, with decisions determined by the MKR token holders' community. Changes to the protocol's parameters, such as the collateralization ratio or the stability cost, can be proposed by MKR token holders.

Lessons From Cryptocurrency Governance Models

Cryptocurrencies like Bitcoin and Ethereum have also aided in the creation of decentralized governance models (Scott, Loonam, & Kumar, 2017). Consensus mechanisms, such as proof of work or proof of stake, control these cryptocurrencies, ensuring that decision-making authority is dispersed among stakeholders.

However, cryptocurrency governance models have faced their own set of issues, such as the potential of centralization through mining pools or stake concentration. These concerns have prompted the development of new consensus methods and governance models aimed at addressing these issues.

The historical backdrop of past governance models has had a considerable impact on the development of decentralized governance models in web 3 ecosystems. The necessity for decentralization and transparency, as well as the lessons learned from earlier governance models, have resulted in the development of novel and effective governance models that show tremendous promise for the future of web 3.

TYPES OF GOVERNANCE MODELS: WHAT TYPES OF DECENTRALIZED GOVERNANCE MODELS EXIST IN WEB 3 ECOSYSTEMS, AND HOW DO THEY DIFFER?

Decentralized governance models are critical to the operation of web 3 ecosystems. As web 3 systems are distributed and decentralized, choices concerning the network's development, protocols, and incentives must be made in a way that guarantees all players have a say and power is not concentrated in a single entity or group.

There are various sorts of decentralized governance models, each with its set of advantages and disadvantages. In web 3 ecosystems, the following are some of the most frequent types of decentralized governance models:

Reputation-Based Governance Models

Reputation-based governance models are a sort of decentralized governance mechanism that is becoming increasingly prevalent in web 3 ecosystems. Participants in this model receive reputation points for their contributions to the ecosystem, such as creating valuable material, giving technical expertise, or assisting others (Qin, et al., 2022). These reputation points can then be utilized to influence policy decisions.

The platform Stack Exchange, which manages a network of question-and-answer websites on diverse themes, is one example of a reputation-based governance model. Users gain reputation points by asking and answering questions, and these points are used to assess their level of authority and influence on the platform. Users with more reputation points have more privileges, such as being able to monitor content or access particular features.

The project Aragon is another example of a reputation-based governance model. It provides tools for forming and administering decentralized organizations. Participants in the Aragon network acquire reputation points by holding and staking the project's native token, ANT, and these points are put to use to vote on proposals and make governance decisions. The more reputation points a participant possesses, the greater impact they have in the decision-making process.

There are various advantages to reputation-based governance models over other forms of governance models. Firstly, they promote active engagement and contributions to the ecosystem by incentivizing individuals to acquire reputation points by adding value to the community. Secondly, they provide a fair and merit-based method of allocating influence and decision-making power, as opposed to models in which influence is entirely dependent on token ownership or wealth. Lastly, because players with high reputation points are scattered around the ecosystem rather than concentrated in a few wealthy or important individuals, they can assist in preventing centralization and promoting decentralization.

However, there are several barriers and constraints to reputation-based governance approaches. One problem is identifying how to effectively assess and quantify ecosystem contributions, as different sorts of contributions might be difficult to compare or evaluate. Furthermore, reputation-based governance models may be susceptible to manipulation or gaming, as members may attempt to obtain reputation points through deceptive or immoral ways. Reputation-based governance models may not be appropriate for all ecosystems or communities because some may require more direct or formal decision-making procedures.

Liquid Democracy Governance Models

Liquid democracy, also known as delegative democracy, is a form of governance that combines features of direct and representative democracy (Kashyap & Jeyasekar, 2020). Individuals in this model have the option of voting directly on an issue or delegating their vote to someone else. Delegation can take several forms, including delegating to a trusted friend, a community leader, or a subject matter expert. This enables people to participate in decision-making even if they lack the time or competence to make informed decisions on every subject.

Liquid democracy governance models have been implemented in a number of web 3 ecosystems, including the platform Democracy Earth. Participants in Democracy Earth can delegate their voting authority to representatives or experts on a certain issue, or they can vote directly on a single issue.

The fact that liquid democracy governance models integrate the benefits of both direct and representative democracy is one of their main advantages. They enable direct participation in decision-making while also allowing for delegation to someone with better knowledge or skill on a specific subject. As a result, more informed and nuanced decisions can be made. A further advantage of liquid democracy governance models is that they can assist in preventing power from being concentrated in the hands of a few affluent or prominent individuals. Individuals who do not have great wealth or influence can nevertheless have a say in decision-making by permitting delegation.

However, there are several limitations and obstacles to liquid democracy governing models. The main challenge is ensuring that delegated votes are not exploited or used in ways that are detrimental to the delegator's interests. Another problem is choosing how to handle circumstances when delegates disagree or delegates and direct voters disagree.

Quadratic Voting Governance Models

Quadratic voting is a governance model that tries to make decision-making more democratic and equitable. Individuals in this model have a fixed number of voting credits that they can use to vote on an issue. However, the cost of each consecutive vote increases quadratically, so the first vote costs one, the second vote costs four, the third vote costs nine, and so on.

The purpose of this model is to provide people who care profoundly about an issue more voting power while reducing the impact of those who are less involved or have less at risk. Quadratic voting is used in many web 3 ecosystems, including the Quadratic Diplomacy platform, which uses this approach to ease decision-making in decentralized organizations.

The Ethereum Community Sponsor (ECF) is an example of a quadratic voting governance model. ECF members were given a set quantity of tokens to vote for the projects they wanted to support. Each token was worth one vote, but the cost of each extra token climbed quadratically, making allocating numerous tokens to a single project more expensive.

Quadratic voting governance models have the advantage of preventing majority tyranny by giving more voting power to those who care the most about an issue. This has the potential to result in more equal and representative decision-making.

The allocation of voting credits in a fair and transparent manner is a challenge for Quadratic Voting Governance Models. Quadratic voting may not be appropriate for all types of decisions or ecosystems since it may be difficult to establish how to allocate costs to specific concerns or how to quantify the level of investment or interest of individuals. Quadratic voting also requires a lot of time from voters (Thompson, et al., 2022).

Futarchy Governance Models

Futarchy governance concepts are built on the concept of prediction markets (Groos, 2020). Individuals in this model wager on the outcome of a proposed decision. The outcome with the most bets is then executed. The notion is that people will put their money where their opinions are, and the market will determine the best decision. Futarchy has been used in a few web 3 ecosystems; however, its implementation is still in the early stages.

Futarchy is divided into two stages: prediction and decision markets. Participants in the prediction market phase can purchase and sell shares in the various outcomes of a given choice. The real decision is taken in the decision market phase based on the outcome with the greatest market price.

The use of prediction markets to forecast political elections is one real-world example of Futarchy in action. Prediction markets such as PredictIt and Betfair have been used in the United States to accurately forecast the outcomes of presidential elections, congressional races, and other political contests.

The main benefit of futarchy is that it allows for more accurate and fair decision-making by utilizing the market's collective intelligence. Futarchy also incentivizes people to make correct predictions. Participants who correctly guess the outcome of a decision stand to profit.

However, it raises questions regarding whether decisions should be taken based on monetary incentives and whether or not certain groups may be excluded from the market due to a shortage of resources.

Hybrid Governance Models

Hybrid governance models combine many governance models to create a more customized decision-making strategy. A web 3 ecosystem, for example, may employ a hybrid of token-based and reputation-based governance to balance the influence of token holders with those who have contributed the most to the ecosystem. The purpose of hybrid governance models is to make decision-making more efficient and adaptive.

MakerDAO is an example of a hybrid governance model in which aspects of representative democracy are combined with market principles (Axelsen, Jensen, & Ross, 2023). Participants can borrow and lend money using Dai, the platform's native cryptocurrency, while MKR token holders can vote on proposals that affect the ecosystem. This system offers stability and efficiency through market mechanisms, but it has disadvantages such as complexity and vulnerability to manipulation or fraud.

An advantage of hybrid governance models is that they can combine the best features of many governance models while minimizing their shortcomings. They promote increased participation and transparency while also ensuring that decisions are made efficiently and with a clear sense of accountability.

They are, however, more complex and difficult to implement than single governance models. In addition, they need careful consideration of how the various models will interact and how decision-making power will be distributed. Despite these obstacles, hybrid governance models provide a viable approach to decision-making in web 3 ecosystems by combining the strengths of several governance models while limiting their flaws.

To summarize, different governance models provide different benefits, and selecting the optimal model is dependent on the network's unique characteristics and the needs of the participants.

GOVERNANCE TOKENS: WHAT ARE GOVERNANCE TOKENS AND WHAT ROLE DO THEY PLAY IN DECENTRALIZED GOVERNANCE MODELS?

To enable decision-making in web 3 ecosystems, decentralized governance models employ a variety of mechanisms. One such mechanism is the use of governance tokens, which play an essential role in enabling decentralized decision-making. Governance tokens are a kind of cryptocurrency that allows holders to take part in the decision-making process of a protocol or platform (Burda, Locca, & Staykova, 2022). In this part, we will define governance tokens, explain how they work, and examine their advantages and disadvantages in decentralized governance models.

What Are Governance Tokens?

Governance tokens are digital assets that reflect the right to vote in a protocol or platform's decision-making process. They are typically distributed to network participants as a reward for contributing to the ecosystem or as an investment in the platform's future growth. Governance tokens are frequently constructed on blockchain technology and are decentralized, which implies that decisions are made by the community rather than a central authority.

How Do Governance Tokens Function?

Holders of governance tokens have the authority to propose, vote on, and implement changes to the protocol or platform. Token holders can use their tokens to propose changes or enhancements to the platform. After submitting a suggestion, other holders can vote on it. If the proposal wins enough votes, it is then implemented. Depending on the protocol or platform, the number of votes required to pass a proposal can vary.

The allocation of governance tokens is an essential part of how they work. Governance tokens are frequently granted to project early adopters or investors, as well as individuals that contribute to the platform's development or upkeep. This token distribution ensures that people with a vested stake in the platform's success have a role in its governance.

Benefits of Governance Tokens in Decentralized Governance Models

Governance tokens have a number of advantages in decentralized governance models. For starters, they give a way for community members to have a say in platform decision-making. This ensures that when significant choices are made, the needs and interests of the community are considered. Secondly, governance tokens can be used to incentivize ecosystem engagement and contribution. Users are encouraged to join and assist grow the ecosystem by awarding governance tokens as a reward for contributing to the platform. This can lead to increased platform innovation and growth.

Transparency is another advantage of governance tokens. Governance choices are transparent and publicly observable because they are made on-chain and recorded on a blockchain. This ensures that all decisions are made fairly and openly and that the governance process is not dominated by a single entity.

Governance tokens can also help to align incentives and avoid conflicts of interest. In a decentralized exchange, for example, the governance token can be used to reward liquidity providers with a percentage of the trading costs to encourage them to contribute to the platform. This aligns their interests with the platform, as they have a vested interest in its success.

Challenges of Governance Tokens in Decentralized Governance Models

Despite the benefits of governance tokens, there are also drawbacks to using them in decentralized governance models. If a small number of individuals or companies hold governance tokens, they can be exposed to centralization. This can lead to a concentration of power and influence in decision-making, which is contrary to the ideas of decentralized government.

An additional problem is voter indifference. The number of voters in many decentralized governance models is generally minimal, which can lead to a lack of variety in decision-making and a concentration of power in the hands of a small group of persons. This can make reaching a consensus and making good decisions challenging. Furthermore, governance tokens can be manipulated and used to buy votes.

To reduce these concerns, several projects have incorporated mechanisms such as vote weighting based on how long a user has held the token or imposing a restriction on the number of tokens a single user can retain.

All in all, governance tokens play an important role in decentralized governance models by allowing users a voice in decision-making and aligning incentives to encourage the ecosystem's growth and success. However, it is critical to carefully assess their application and associated hazards in order to preserve the ecosystem's long-term health and sustainability.

DECENTRALIZED AUTONOMOUS ORGANIZATIONS (DAOS): WHAT ARE DAOS AND HOW DO THEY FUNCTION AS DECENTRALIZED GOVERNANCE MODELS?

In web 3 ecosystems, Decentralized Autonomous Organizations (DAOs) emerged as a prominent decentralized governance model. DAOs are organizations that use smart contracts on a blockchain to make decisions that are decentralized and democratic (Staff, 2021).

What Are DAOs?

DAOs are a new type of organization that enables people to collaborate and coordinate in a decentralized and autonomous manner. They use smart contracts to automate decision-making processes and are driven by blockchain technology. Members of a DAO can use governance tokens to vote on proposals and decisions, and the results are executed automatically by the smart contract.

DAOs are managed by their members, who vote on issues like resource distribution, investment, and governance. DAOs, unlike traditional organizations, do not have a single owner or CEO. They instead divide authority among all members in a transparent and democratic manner.

DAOs are transparent and immutable in addition to being autonomous and decentralized, which means that all transactions and decisions made inside the organization are recorded on the blockchain and can be read by everyone. This level of transparency and accountability is a fundamental premise of DAOs and is critical in fostering confidence among members and the broader community.

DAOs are not confined to a single industry or use case and can be used for anything from managing digital assets and investment funds to decentralized social networks and marketplaces. Despite being relatively new, DAOs have already piqued the interest of investors and the wider blockchain community, with multiple high-profile initiatives such as MakerDAO and Uniswap now running as DAOs.

How do Daos Function?

DAOs, or Decentralized Autonomous Organizations, run on a set of rules and regulations written in a smart contract on a blockchain. These regulations are enforced automatically by software, and decision-making processes are decentralized, which means they are determined by a group of persons who own tokens or shares in the organization.

DAOs operate through a proposal and voting process. Anyone with an interest in the organization can propose a rule change or a new project, which is subsequently voted on by token holders. Voting is typically weighted based on the number of tokens or shares held by each participant, allowing individuals with a higher investment in the organization a stronger say in decision-making.

When a proposal is approved, the smart contract performs the change or project automatically. This means that decisions are made openly, and everyone in the organization can see what is going on at any given time. The smart contract also ensures that the rules are obeyed and that no individual or group can manipulate the system to their advantage.

DAOs can be used in a variety of industries and applications, ranging from banking and investing to art and culture. They provide a decentralized mechanism for individuals to collaborate and work towards a common objective, with decision-making power divided evenly among all stakeholders. Furthermore, DAOs provide a level of openness and accountability that traditional organizations frequently lack, because every action made by the organization is recorded on the blockchain and easily audited by anybody.

Examples of DAOs

There are numerous sorts of DAOs, each with its own structure and function. MakerDAO, a decentralized lending platform, and MolochDAO, a funding platform for Ethereum projects, are two popular examples of DAOs. Furthermore, the DAO is a well-known example of a DAO that collected considerable funds via an initial coin offering (ICO) but ultimately collapsed due to a critical smart contract flaw.

Advantages and Challenges of DAOs

DAOs have various benefits over traditional organizations, including improved transparency, accountability, and decentralization. Since decision-making is decentralized and democratic, there is less chance for a central authority to influence or manipulate. Moreover, as DAOs are powered by smart contracts, there is no need for intermediaries. This reduces costs and increases efficiency.

Despite its benefits, DAOs face some challenges including the complexity of smart contracts and the difficulty of making decentralized choices. There is also the potential for smart contract flaws or faults, which could result in severe losses for DAO participants. Additionally, because DAOs are still a relatively new idea, there is a lack of legislative clarity which can cause participants to be hesitant.

DAOs are an interesting new development in web 3 ecosystem decentralized governance models. They have several advantages over traditional organizations, but they also face major challenges. It will be interesting to see how DAOs and other decentralized governance models impact the future of organizational governance as the technological and regulatory landscape evolves.

CHALLENGES AND LIMITATIONS: WHAT ARE THE CHALLENGES AND LIMITATIONS OF DECENTRALIZED GOVERNANCE MODELS IN WEB 3 ECOSYSTEMS?

Decentralized governance models have been heralded as a game-changing approach to controlling web 3 ecosystems, with the potential to promote openness, accountability, and community participation. These models confront a number of challenges and limitations that must be addressed. Scalability, interoperability, regulatory compliance, and energy usage are all significant challenges for decentralized governance models in web 3 (Ray, 2023). In this section, we will take a look at some of these challenges and limitations.

Participation and Engagement: Decentralized governance models rely significantly on community members' active participation and engagement. However, attaining high levels of participation and engagement can be difficult, particularly in big and complex ecosystems. Moreover, there may be voter apathy or disengagement concerns, in which a small group of highly motivated individuals ends up dominating the decision-making process.

Imbalances in Power: Decentralized governance models seek to disseminate power and decision-making authority among members of society. Power inequalities can still occur within these structures though because certain persons or organizations may have more influence or resources than others. This can result in decisions that are not indicative of the interests of the larger community.

Technical Complexity: The technical complexity required in establishing and executing decentralized governance models is one of the key obstacles. Decentralized governance models need significant technological expertise and resources, which can be unbearably costly for smaller communities and organizations.

Governance Attack Vectors: Decentralized governance models are vulnerable to a variety of attack vectors, such as Sybil attacks, in which a single person generates many fake identities in order to influence decision-making. Malicious actors can also conduct additional attacks, such as vote-buying, bribery, or collaboration, to influence the outcome of governance decisions.

Lack of Legal Frameworks: Decentralized governance models operate in a legal grey area, with few established legal frameworks for their functioning. This lack of legal clarity might make it difficult for decentralized governance models to acquire widespread adoption, as well as create regulatory ambiguity.

Forking and Fragmentation: Decentralized governance models are susceptible to forking and fragmentation which can lead to a loss of community cohesion and deterioration in the effectiveness of governance procedures. Forking and fragmentation can occur if the community becomes divided on fundamental governance issues, resulting in the formation of many competing networks.

Lack of Scalability: Decentralized governance models can be difficult to scale, especially as the community expands in size. As more members of the community participate in decision-making, the number of proposals and conversations can become overwhelming, resulting in a lack of focus and effectiveness.

Power Concentration: Despite the objective of decentralization, there is a risk that power will become concentrated in the hands of a few individuals or entities. This can happen if particular individuals or entities own a disproportionate amount of governance tokens or can to influence the voting process.

Voter Apathy: Although decentralized governance models rely on community participation, voter apathy is a prevalent issue. Many users may be uninterested in or lack the time to participate in the governance process, resulting in poor voter turnout and community involvement.

Governance Token Distribution: Governance tokens are an important component of decentralized governance models, but distributing them can be difficult. Governance token allocation should be fair and equitable. However, this might be challenging to do in practice. Early adopters may wind up with a disproportionate amount of governance tokens in some situations, which can lead to a concentration of power.

Therefore, while decentralized governance models present a possible substitute for established centralized governance models, they also have substantial drawbacks. To build an environment that supports the growth and development of decentralized governance models in web 3 ecosystems, it will be necessary for developers, community members, and regulators to work together to address these issues.

BEST PRACTICES: WHAT ARE SOME BEST PRACTICES FOR DEVELOPING DECENTRALIZED GOVERNANCE MODELS AND IMPLEMENTING THEM IN WEB 3 ECOSYSTEMS?

As discussed above, there are different kinds of governance models, and each has benefits and drawbacks. A successful decentralized governance model must be designed and put into place, which is a difficult process. It involves meticulous preparation, implementation, and assessment. The best practices for creating and implementing decentralized governance models in web 3 ecosystems will be covered in this section.

Transparency: In decentralized governance models, transparency is crucial. Every choice the governance model makes ought to be open to the public. This covers choices made in connection with voting, proposal submission, and other decision-making procedures. Transparency guarantees that all stakeholders have access to the same information and fosters confidence between the community and the governing model.

Community Participation: Decentralized governance models should encourage active community participation. This entails making methods available for members of the community to make proposals, vote on proposals, and participate in decision-making processes. It is critical to ensure that the governance model represents the community's interests, and the best method to do so is through active community participation.

Flexibility: Decentralized governance models should be adaptable and versatile. The governance model should be developed so that it may change over time to meet the changing needs of the community. This includes procedures for amending governance rules, adjusting voting systems, and introducing new decision-making processes.

Security: Security is an important factor in developing and implementing decentralized governance models. The governance model should be intended to be resistant to attacks and manipulation. This includes maintaining the security of voting processes, protecting against Sybil attacks, and putting in place safeguards to prevent 51% of attacks.

Clear Governance Framework: Decentralized governance models should have a clear governance framework that explains all stakeholders' roles and duties. The governance structure should be built such that stakeholders can easily understand and participate in the governance process.

Building Consensus: Decentralized governance solutions should prioritize building consensus. This involves guaranteeing that choices are made through a consensus-based process in which all stakeholders are given the opportunity to express their ideas and opinions. Consensus building promotes community trust in the governance model and ensures that choices are made in the best interests of the community.

Regular Assessment: Regular assessment is required to guarantee that the governance model is working properly. This includes analyzing the effectiveness of decision-making procedures, reviewing governance norms, and evaluating levels of community participation. Regular review assists in identifying areas for improvement and ensuring that the governance model is still meeting the needs of the community.

web 3 ecosystems may create resilient and efficient decentralized governance models that encourage community involvement and trust by adhering to these best practices.

FUTURE DIRECTIONS: WHAT ARE SOME EXPECTED POTENTIAL ADVANCEMENTS IN WEB 3 ECOSYSTEM DECENTRALIZED GOVERNANCE MODELS?

Since their origin, decentralized governance models have come a long way, but there is still much space for growth and progress in this domain. As the web 3 ecosystem evolves, there are various potential future options for decentralized governance models. The following are some potential future developments in web 3 ecosystem decentralized governance models:

Cross-Chain Governance: As blockchain technology becomes more widely used, it is expected that more blockchains will develop. As a result, cross-chain governance mechanisms will be required to ensure the interoperability and coordination of these various blockchains. Cross-chain governance solutions could enable more efficient and effective collaboration by allowing for seamless integration between different blockchain ecosystems.

Dynamic Governance Models: Traditional governance models are rigid and inflexible, with hard-to-change rules and processes. However, in web 3 ecosystems where technology is continually changing, more dynamic governance models may be required. Dynamic governance models may allow communities to quickly adjust to changing conditions and make decisions in a more flexible and responsive manner.

AI-Based Governance: As artificial intelligence (AI) improves, it may be able to integrate AI-based governance processes into web 3 ecosystems. Machine learning algorithms could be used in AI-based governance models to analyze data and make more informed judgments. This could lead to more efficient and effective decision-making while decreasing the possibility of human bias.

Decentralized Identity: Decentralized identity solutions, such as self-sovereign identification (SSI) systems, could play an important role in decentralized governance models. These systems could allow individuals to own and control their own digital identities, which could subsequently be used to authenticate their involvement in decentralized governance processes. Decentralized identity could also aid in the prevention of fraud and the integrity of governance decisions.

Decentralized Dispute Resolution: Disputes are an unavoidable component of every governance system, and decentralized governance models are no exception. Traditional dispute resolution processes, such as courts and arbitration, may not be well-suited to decentralized ecosystems. Decentralized dispute resolution mechanisms, such as decentralized autonomous arbitration systems, may provide a more efficient and effective approach to resolving issues in web 3 ecosystems.

Decentralized Finance (Defi): DeFi is one of the most significant advancements in the web 3 ecosystem, and decentralized governance models are critical to its operation. In the future, we should expect more complicated and novel DeFi applications that will call for enhanced governance models to handle complex financial systems.

CONCLUSION

In web 3 ecosystems, decentralized governance models have the potential to revolutionize how we govern and make decisions. This chapter has looked at the various sorts of decentralized governance models available, including reputation-based, liquid democracy, quadratic voting, futarchy, and hybrid models. We've also discussed how governance tokens and decentralized autonomous organizations (DAOs) fit into these schemes.

Despite the potential benefits of decentralized governance models, a number of challenges and limitations must be addressed. These include voter apathy, collusion, and a lack of accountability. These issues, however, can be minimized by introducing best practices such as openness, inclusivity, and security.

Looking ahead, we can anticipate significant advancements in decentralized governance models. The use of artificial intelligence (AI) and machine learning algorithms to optimize decision-making processes and decrease human bias is one possible area for growth. Integration of decentralized governance models with other developing technologies such as blockchain-based identity management systems and decentralized finance (DeFi) platforms provides another area of research.

Decentralized governance models have significant implications for the future of web 3 ecosystems. These models can lead to more egalitarian and transparent government by decentralizing decision-making processes, allowing for greater participation and representation. This can aid in the resolution of issues like inequality, corruption, and a lack of faith in centralized institutions. Decentralized governance models can also facilitate more efficient and effective decision-making processes, resulting in faster innovation and development in web 3 ecosystems.

Decentralized governance models have the ability to transform how we govern and make decisions in web 3 ecosystems. We can ensure that these models are effective and equitable by following best practices and addressing obstacles and constraints.

REFERENCES

Anthony, B. Jnr. (2022). Investigating the Decentralized Governance of Distributed Ledger Infrastructure Implementation in Extended Enterprises. *Journal of the Knowledge Economy*. doi:10.100713132-022-01079-7

Atzori, M. (2015). Blockchain Technology and Decentralized Governance: Is the State Still Necessary? SSRN *Electronic Journal*. doi:10.2139/ssrn.2709713

Axelsen, H., Jensen, J. R., & Ross, O. (2022). When is a DAO Decentralized? *Complex Systems Informatics and Modeling Quarterly*, *31*(31), 51–75. doi:10.7250/csimq.2022-31.04

Burda, M., Locca, M., & Staykova, K. (2022, February 28). *Decision rights decentralization in DeFi platforms*. Wrap. warwick.ac.uk

Centobelli, P., Cerchione, R., Vecchio, P. D., Oropallo, E., & Secundo, G. (2022). Blockchain technology for bridging trust, traceability and transparency in circular supply chain. *Information & Management*, *59*(7), 103508. doi:10.1016/j.im.2021.103508

Cryptopedia Staff. (2021, December 1). *What Is a DAO's Role in Decentralized Governance?* Gemini. https://www.gemini.com/cryptopedia/dao-crypto-decentralized-governance-blockchain-governance#section-what-is-a-dao

Groos, J. (2020). *Crypto Politics: Notes on Sociotechnical Imaginaries of Governance in Blockchain Based Technologies*. Semantic Scholar. https://pdfs.semanticscholar.org/4809/ea5ae690a4b332dad0660a-5834e2706182eb.pdf

KarjalainenR. (2020, May 21). *Governance in Decentralized Networks*. Papers.ssrn.com. https://papers.ssrn.com/sol3/papers.cfm?abstract_id=3551099 doi:10.2139/ssrn.3551099

Kashyap, S., & Jeyasekar, A. (2020, September 1). *A Competent and Accurate BlockChain based E-Voting System on Liquid Democracy*. IEEE Xplore. doi:10.1109/BRAINS49436.2020.9223308

Ljungberg, J. (2000). Open source movements as a model for organising. *European Journal of Information Systems*, *9*(4), 208–216. doi:10.1057/palgrave.ejis.3000373

Madhwal, R., & Pouwelse, J. (2023). The Universal Trust Machine: A survey on the web 3 path towards enabling long term digital cooperation through decentralised trust. ArXiv:2301.06938 [Cs]. https://arxiv.org/abs/2301.06938

Murray, A., Kim, D., & Combs, J. (2023). The promise of a decentralized Internet: What is web 3.0 and HOW can firms prepare? *Business Horizons*, *66*(2), 191–202. doi:10.1016/j.bushor.2022.06.002

OnwukweA.AdeniranI. (2022, December 31). *Proposing Policy Formulation for Web 3.0*. Papers.ssrn.com. https://papers.ssrn.com/sol3/papers.cfm?abstract_id=4315626 doi:10.2139/ssrn.4315626

Patel ThompsonA.WinnE.OatesG.EsberJ.JinL.KanterM.MannanM.PouxP.HubbardS.MooreS.DeleveauxS.ScholzT. R.HumQ. Z. (2022, December 14). *Toward A More Cooperative web 3*. https://papers.ssrn.com/sol3/papers.cfm?abstract_id=4302681 doi:10.2139/ssrn.4302681

Peters, G. W., & Panayi, E. (2016). Understanding Modern Banking Ledgers Through Blockchain Technologies: Future of Transaction Processing and Smart Contracts on the Internet of Money. In Banking Beyond Banks and Money (pp. 239–278). doi:10.1007/978-3-319-42448-4_13

Qin, R., Ding, W., Li, J., Guan, S., Wang, G., Ren, Y., & Qu, Z. (2022). web 3-Based Decentralized Autonomous Organizations and Operations: Architectures, Models, and Mechanisms. *IEEE Transactions on Systems, Man, and Cybernetics*, *53*(4), 2073–2082. doi:10.1109/TSMC.2022.3228530

Ray, P. P. (2023). web 3: A comprehensive review on background, technologies, applications, zero-trust architectures, challenges and future directions. *Internet of Things and Cyber-Physical Systems*, *3*, 213–248. Advance online publication. doi:10.1016/j.iotcps.2023.05.003

Scott, B., Loonam, J., & Kumar, V. (2017). Exploring the rise of blockchain technology: Towards distributed collaborative organizations. *Strategic Change*, *26*(5), 423–428. doi:10.1002/jsc.2142

Voshmgir, S. (2020). Token Economy: How the web 3 reinvents the Internet. *Token Kitchen.* https://books.google.com.pk/books?hl=en&lr=&id=vWo-EAAAQBAJ&oi=fnd&pg=PT6&dq=Unlike+Web2+ecosystems

KEY TERMS AND DEFINITIONS

Consensus Mechanism: The process through which a decentralized network obtains unanimous agreement on the state of the system.

Dao: Decentralized Autonomous Organizations that run on a blockchain and are managed by smart contracts that enforce the organization's rules and regulations.

Decentralization: Distribution of power and decision-making over a network of nodes rather than a centralized authority.

Decentralized Governance: A decision-making system that allows a network of stakeholders to participate in decision-making without relying on a centralized authority.

Forking: The process of forming a new blockchain network by breaking away from an existing one, usually owing to conflicts about governance or other causes.

Governance Tokens: Tokens that provide holders the right to participate in the decision-making process of a network or organization.

Immutable: data that is permanently stored on a blockchain and cannot be changed or removed.

Smart Contracts: Self-executing contracts in which the conditions of the buyer-seller agreement are directly written into code.

Sybil Attack: A sort of attack in which a single user generates numerous false identities in an attempt to gain influence or control in a decentralized network.

Transparency: The practice of making all choices and activities inside a decentralized network that is open and available to all participants.

Web 3 Ecosystems: Refers to the internet's third generation, in which blockchain and decentralized technologies are utilized to develop and operate digital systems and applications that enable peer-to-peer interactions without the use of intermediaries.

Chapter 7
The Evolution of Web 3 and Decentralized Governance

Eleonóra Bassi

Zurich University of Applied Sciences, Switzerland & DAO Suisse, Switzerland

Margherita Bandirali

DAO Suisse, Switzerland

ABSTRACT

In this chapter, the authors give a theoretical overview of the landscape of decentralized autonomous organizations (DAOs) as the native organizational structure of Web 3. The authors place this new formation in the existing theoretical framework of transaction cost economics and new institutional economics analyzing their governance from economic and legal perspectives. They argue that DAOs are so-called hybrid organizations, which embrace features from the free market and from hierarchical organizations. DAOs show characteristics of hybrids such as pooling resources, coordinating operations by contracts and facing competition in their coordination. However, their changing nature imposes challenges in their identification.

INTRODUCTION - WEB 3 AND THEIR NATIVE ORGANIZATIONS THE DAOS

In our chapter, we analyze the latest developments in Web 3-native governance, aiming to understand how the initial motivations of the movements that led to the emergence of this system have impacted the new application of democracy and economic freedom, thereby posing new challenges to the concept of governance.

The Web has undergone significant development over the years, through the Web 1, Web 2, and Web 3 stages[1], evolving from a simple collection of static pages to a dynamic platform that enables rich multimedia experiences, social networking and e-commerce, to the point of representing a new model of expression of individual power in an economic and idealistic sense. The term "Web 3" refers to a fresh rendition of the World Wide Web that encompasses principles of decentralization, blockchain technologies, and token-based economics. Coined by Gavin Wood, co-founder of Ethereum in 2014, which is the

DOI: 10.4018/978-1-6684-9919-1.ch007

Copyright © 2023, IGI Global. Copying or distributing in print or electronic forms without written permission of IGI Global is prohibited.

preferred platform for developing decentralized applications that are the foundations of Web 3. As the Ethereum website describes, Web 3 services can be completely dependent on algorithmic settings and peer-to-peer transactions, creating an ecosystem where all participants serve some form of contribution to the overall experience[2] and participation occurs in a completely horizontal and distributed manner.

The technological innovation was never merely a development that affected computer science but it was embedded within social ideology. Decentralization, in conjunction with cryptography, assumes a pivotal role within the "Cypherpunk movement"[3], a collective of activists advocating for privacy, security, and anonymity. Anderson (2022) Emerging in the 1990s, this movement comprised academics, researchers, and hackers who aimed to subvert government surveillance and advance the utilization of cryptography to safeguard individual privacy. Within the framework of system operability's initial layer, users engage directly with the smart contracts[4] of a protocol, engendering actions that possess equivalent attributes of censorship resistance, permissionless, and decentralization as the underlying protocol itself. This decentralized paradigm hinges upon the implementation of resilient encryption systems to reconfigure prevailing social, political, or economic disparities, as analyzed by Ramiro and Queiroz (2022). In this context, we can identify the importance of the concept of DAO as a form of relationship management capable of eliminating several of the problems manifested by ordinary legal structures of corporations or associations. As argued by Berg, Davidson and Potts (2019), blockchain technology is primarily an institutional innovation, rather than solely or merely technological.

A DAO operates on the principles of blockchain technology, utilizing predetermined rules and criteria facilitated by the permanent notarization of information. The DAO represents a significant manifestation of decentralization, arising from the foundational principles established by the Cypherpunks and the technological advancements in blockchain that paved the way for the development of Web 3. In contrast to traditional systems that rely on a central authority to record transactions, a DAO functions autonomously, eliminating the need for a manager or leader. Instead, decision-making authority rests within the community, embodying the essence of decentralized decision-making. Furthermore, a DAO can be formulated with diverse objectives, encompassing a collective of investors seeking collaboration, an endeavor focused on providing financial support to a specific entity, or even initiatives involved in cultural exploration or multimedia dissemination. Essentially, it encompasses any form of undertaking characterized by the pursuit of various projects, distinguished by their detachment from a centralized decision-making structure.

While DAOs embody numerous technological and organizational innovations, we argue that the social and organizational principles on which they are based are deeply rooted in broader economic and legal traditions. Accordingly, they can and need to be integrated into existing organizational structures. Why is it beneficial for DAOs and regulators to position the organization on a classical theoretic framework? For DAOs, it helps in selecting the most suitable governance method for their specific institutional structure. For regulators, it serves as an indicative signal that the organizational ecosystem is quite complex, and oversimplified or misinterpreted regulation may lead to market anomalies. The institutional responses observed in the United States vividly illustrate the impact of the differences in interpretation on society and the economy.

However, it remains a question as to what extent legally unregulated and socially undefined entities, which are constantly changing in terms of their number and form, can be categorized and identified. We believe that placing them within a broader interpretative framework and identifying certain characteristics that make them similar to one or another type of organization will overcome the pitfall of creating schematic systems "too early" that cannot be applied to the new or forming elements of a transforming group.

THE LANDSCAPE OF DAOS

A Short History of The Concept

The DAO's theoretical foundation is based on a concept or rather thought experiment of Dan Larimer, Stan Larimer and Vitalik Buterin. In 2013 Dan Larimer introduced the term Decentralized Autonomous Corporation (DAC) in his blog post which described cryptocurrencies as DAC, where the code can be seen as a bylaw and token holders are shareholders. Stan Larimer further elaborated on the idea by pointing to Bitcoin. He described DAC, or as he named it "unmanned company", as a metaphor for Bitcoin. (Larimer, 2013) Dan Larimer applied his theory in the form of a company, called BitShare, which he founded in 2013. Vitalik Buterin reflected on the concept of DAC in subsequent blog posts. Presumably, these thoughts served as inspiration for the concept of DAO, which is first mentioned in the Ethereum Whitepaper.

In the Whitepaper, Buterin (2014) considered DACs as a subcategory of DAOs, referring to them as profit-oriented organizations, while he described DAOs as non-profit organizations that can still generate profit for participants. (Riva, 2020) The two different concepts, or rather their merging, are clearly noticeable in the discourses surrounding DAOs. Some analysts argue that the original concept of a DAO can be traced back to systems based on autonomous, decentralized technology, considering them as ideal types. (Delphi Labs, 2023) Meanwhile, other interpretations consider decentralized decision-making as the essential element of DAOs, which can be freely applied in various areas regardless of organizational form and envision a broader effect than transforming business organizations. (Atzori, 2017; Saito & Rose, 2023)

Santana and Albareda (2022) offer a great variety of definitions, based on scientific literature, and among this variety, our definition of DAO aligns most closely with the interpretations of Hassan and De Filippi: "A DAO is a blockchain-based system that enables people to coordinate and govern themselves mediated by a set of self-executing rules deployed on a public blockchain, and whose governance is decentralized (i.e., independent from central control)." (2021, p. 2)

Although the concept of decentralized technology empowering decentralized governance was born in the 90s, it took two decades until the vision became a reality on Ethereum. Ethereum is a blockchain platform that allows developers to build decentralized applications and smart contracts on top of their network. The birth of technology was shortly followed by the birth of a new organizational structure. Strongly reflecting Buterin's vision, the first DAO was created in 2016 by a group of developers who called themselves "The DAO". Its main goal was to operate as a decentralized venture capital fund, allowing members to vote on investment decisions and receive dividends based on the fund's profits. The DAO was able to raise over $150 million in Ether during its crowdfunding campaign, making it one of the largest crowdfunding projects in history at the time. In June 2016, a vulnerability in The DAO's smart contract was exploited, resulting in a hack that allowed an attacker to steal a significant portion of the fund's assets, which led to a hard fork[5] of the Ethereum blockchain. Despite its controversial ending, The DAO represented an exciting experiment in decentralized governance and remains an important milestone in the history of blockchain and DAOs. Not only because it showed the great potential and pitfalls of the new organization but also clearly showed the "human factor" cannot be ignored. The role and significance of The DAO are well discussed by DuPont (2017) and Wang et al. (2019).

Capturing and Counting DAOs

Since the first DAO came into life, many others followed, and they moved on to an extensive variety of levels of decentralization, and autonomy. They have gained significant attention and adoption in recent years, particularly within the cryptocurrency and blockchain communities. Analyzing their landscape is a rather complex methodological task. Although the individual operation of the organizations is transparent and accessible by nature, the lack of institutional registration makes it difficult to give an up-to-date aggregated number of the existing DAOs. At the present stage of scientific analysis, most of the authors are rather trying to identify relevant attributes regarding how they can be captured instead of giving a comprehensive overview. Wright (2021) for example offers a rather theoretic categorization in the form of "algorithmic DAOs" and "participatory DAOs". In the empirical research-based taxonomy of Ziegler and Welpe (2022) four attributes are named as inadmissible characteristics for DAOs: their treasury is controlled by smart contract; the treasury is public; the DAO has governance voting process; and it has a governance token. Harder to identify DAOs, which are in the stage of formation but didn't move or only partly moved their operation to the blockchain.

Most of the statistical reviews are based on platform-related data, which are supporting the creation and operation of DAOs, such as DAOStack, Colony and Aragon or from platforms providing analytics regarding DAOs like DeepDAO or DAOMaster. Based on the data of given platforms the ecosystem of DAOs is diverse and dynamic, with a wide range of DAOs currently in operation across various sectors and industries. In theory, any blockchain that supports smart contracts can host a DAO, but the vast majority of them are built on Ethereum. Based on the data of Cointelegraph's report (2022), 83 out of the top 100 governance tokens are built on Ethereum. By market capitalization and by user base, Ethereum is the second largest blockchain and the first supporting smart contracts, which gives a competitive advantage over other solutions. A common feature of their categorization is the field of their operation, which is rather practical than a scientific categorization. The most well-known and financially successful DAOs are decentralized finance (DeFi) protocols that allow users to initiate financial transactions in cryptocurrencies in a trustless and decentralized manner. They are also being used for various other purposes, such as infrastructure building, community-driven decision-making, crowdfunding, and art curation.

Following the scientific approach in the categorization, the sample-based clustering of Ziegler and Welpe (2022) identified five categories: *off-chain product and service DAOs with community focus*; *on-chain product and service DAOs*; *investment-focused DAOs*; *networking-focused community DAOs*; and *off-chain product and service DAOs with investor focus*. However, the sample-based classification doesn't offer an indication regarding the size of each category within the population.

A frequently cited source for DAO statistics is DeepDAO. It's platform aggregates information related to DAOs, including token, treasury, governance, and membership data. According to the company's data, there are 2,363 registered DAOs on the website. However, for further analysis, the company utilizes data from 12,745 organizations. Based on the information available on the dashboard at the time of our analysis[6], the aggregated treasury size of the listed DAOs was approximately 19,5 billion USD. Roughly 7 percent of the organizations have a treasury larger than 1 million USD, 3,4 percent have a treasury larger than 10 million USD, and 0,8 percent have a treasury exceeding 100 million USD. In terms of treasury size, Arbitrum One, Optimism Collective, Uniswap, and BitDAO hold the largest treasuries, each exceeding 1 billion USD.

When considering the number of token holders, Polkadot stands out with 1,3 million token holders. However, it's important to note that this information can be misleading because Polkadot is a layer one blockchain itself, while the other organizations are protocols built on specific chains. Two exceptions are Arbitrum One and Polygon, both of which are layer two blockchains built on Ethereum. Out of the top 20 DAOs, fourteen are built on the Ethereum chain, and eleven focus on financial services.

DAOs Most Challenging Aspect, Governance

DAOs are a new form of organization that does not have an established guideline to structure their operations. Most of them are experimenting with different solutions, based on the needs of the project and the community. In DAOs, just in classical organizations decision-making power is distributed among its participants, but the rules governing the organization's operations are enforced by smart contracts. There are certain elements of DAO governance, which are not known in other organizations, because they appeared with the technological invention, such as on-chain voting. The governance of a DAOs typically involves a combination of on-chain and off-chain decision-making[7] processes. Even the DAOs, which execute their voting on-chain use different channels off-chain for the preparation of the decision-making which involves discussions around the given subject.[8]

Another specific element of DAO governance is the cost of participation. Every on-chain transaction, including voting or voting delegation, infers a small amount of transaction fee. In the case of Ethereum, the amount depends on the actual gas price, which is the fee paid by users for including a transaction in a new block. The individual costs of participation are small, but the more complex the on-chain voting system the more transactions are required, and it can add up on the level of the organization. Based on the calculation of Feichtinger and his colleagues (2023) the cost of on-chain governance can reach millions of dollars.[9]

Since the invention of the DAOs there are two main voting solutions which represent in our understanding two different organizational settings and by choosing one of them the DAO gives a signal regarding its position. As mentioned before, we cannot present valid statistics regarding the number of DAOs and even less about their governance solutions. However, the first and most well-known DAOs implemented a token-based voting system, where each token counts as one vote. The token-based voting method was used by "The DAO". The principle of token-based voting clearly resembles shareholder voting in corporations, where voting power is proportional to the number of shares held. Hence, we can conclude that the first DAOs introduced firm-like governance systems. Another typical form of decision-making system is wallet-based voting, where each wallet has one vote, independently from the amount of the token the given wallet holds. It clearly mimics the one-member one-vote system of hybrid organizations e.g. cooperatives.

DAOs need to make compromises on the distribution of decision-making power not only due to the driving principle but because of certain technological challenges. The token-based voting system ties voting to the financial power of the participants and protects the organization from so-called "sybil attacks". Sybil attack potentially appears in the case of wallet-based voting if individuals are using multiple wallets for gaining fraudulent extra voting power. Token-based voting however holds the danger of plutocracy, where participants with big token shares can move decisions while ignoring the interest of participants with small token shares. Token-based voting is also sensitive to voting manipulations, where tokens are purchased short-term with the purpose of influencing decision-making. Wallet-based voting offers equal say to each participant, but it is sensitive to sybil attacks. Pure wallet-based voting is rare between established DAOs; Governor DAO uses this solution with the combination of "Proof of Existence" token, which can be obtained only after a biometric enrollment. (Hellström, 2022) Besides the two dominant models, there are several mixed solutions. The field of operation, the degree of maturity and the size of the community are all decisive factors and even if DAOs are starting with one solution the changing nature of the project or community might require modifications in the decision-making. Often dominant token holders, low participation or efficiency motivate the modification of the existing governance model.

Token-Based Voting Methods

One of the common solutions to change the status quo without interfering with the whole governance system is modifying the calculation of each vote. There is a group of voting systems, where weighted voting is applied. In different literature, the meaning and explanation of "weighted voting" deviates. In some sources, weighted voting is simply the synonym for token-based voting. However, it also includes multiple-choice methods where voters have the opportunity to express their degree of preference by putting weight on their choices. It means that the token holder can split the vote between more options and put weight on each choice.

A modified version of weighted voting is quadratic voting, a popular choice between DAOs. In quadratic voting, participants are not only able to express the degree of their preference, but the calculation helps to flatten the differences between small and big token holders. The method makes every single vote more costly for the voter, in the way that after the first vote every extra vote "cost" a squared amount.

It was originally proposed for decision-making about financing public goods. The method can be taken as truly democratic if the size of the token shares is equal, however, in DAO governance it only helps to decrease differences. The system is also sensitive to sybil attacks because token holders can split their token shares between accounts and manipulate the weighting. (Buterin, Hitzig, & Weyl, 2019)

Moving away from token-based voting DAOs introduced methods which allow to build-up of the voting system around the person and around participation instead of the wealth of the token holder. The logic of reputation-based voting is similar to the proof of existence solution. However, the voting rights are given based on earned reputation in the DAO instead of pure verification of personhood. DAOs issue a reputation token which is a non-transferable token, and it provides voting rights in the organization based on the level of active participation. DAOStack introduced the solution on its platform in 2019. (Levi, 2019) The concept is recognized as a potential tool for non-profit organizations to incentivize participation with the help of blockchain. (Saito & Rose, 2023)

Incentivization Through Staking

The concept of knowledge-extractable voting also aims to rely on the participants' expertise and participation. In the method of knowledge-extractable voting system contributors, who propose winning proposals or vote for a winning proposal are earning knowledge tokens which are non-refundable and non-transferable. They are used in every vote to weigh the choice of the given participant. (Gajek, 2018) Although knowledge-extractable voting incentivizes educated decision-making, it also expects participants to stake their tokens, which brings some market-like/speculative aspects into the method. Another interesting voting mechanism takes time into account, as a sign of strong conviction. In conviction voting participants can stake their tokens on different proposals and the longer they keep their token staked, the higher weight their vote has. The method has the disadvantage of being a slow decision-making process.

DAOstack introduced the mechanism of holographic consensus to create a voting system which supports resilience and scalability. The Alchemy platform implemented it first in its operation. Holographic consensus involves some market-like/ functions in the life circle of the proposals. In certain decisions, the method enables a relative majority with the help of "boosting". Boosting a proposal means that voters can spend tokens to promote the given proposal until either an agreed threshold is reached or the boosting period ends. Voters can bet and stake the acceptance or refusal of certain proposals. After the vote of the DAO members, promoters can earn or lose their tokens depending on the outcome of the vote. (Faqir-Rhazoui et al., 2021)

Delegation

Solving the problem of inefficient decision making, some DAOs recalled solutions which were invented long before the introduction of DAOs. Liquid democracy is one of those solutions, which is based on liquid delegation. In this system the token holders can decide whether they want to delegate their decision-making power to another member of the DAO, or they want to participate themselves. This solution helps to overcome the problem of inefficiency and low participation in the cases where token holders don't want to participate in the decision-making due to the lack of interest or competence. Liquid democracies follow similar logic as representative democracies and hold similar pitfalls. Frequently mentioned challenge, that it moves the organization towards a centralized entity, and introduces classical principal-agent dilemmas.

Multisig is an increasingly employed voting method where the execution of community decisions falls within the authority of a narrower group. Community decisions are not automatically executed by the smart contract. A group of members possess signing rights while the entire community participates in signaling votes. Multisig voting faces similar challenges to other delegation-based methods regarding potential centralization and principal-agent problems.

Despite strong missions and new solutions, the ecosystem continues to struggle with tendencies towards centralization. *"Emergent empirical analysis of existing DAOs reveals that they do not always involve real decentralized practices and lack of hierarchy; by contrast, DAOs are less rigid hierarchically than other organizations, though some actors, such as the founders or developers, have a powerful influence on the peer community (DuPont, 2019; Hsieh et al., 2018, Hsieh et al., 2018a). This imbalance in power can generate tensions in DAOs, for example, with off-chain human or community governance and novel types of emerging hierarchies..." (Santana & Albareda, 2022, p. 5)*

The latest empirical studies show signs of centralization even in the case of organizations, which are the most often quoted examples of established DAO governance. Feichtinger and his colleagues (2023) analyzed 21 DAOs' governance activity on the Ethereum chain, using the data acquired through GraphQL API. Based on the findings of the research, the given DAO's governance system is highly centralized considering the distribution of power (governance token and voting power). In seventeen out of twenty-one DAOs, the majority of voting power is controlled by less than 10 participants, in half of the DAOs it's not more than three people. The study also showed very high transaction costs fueling the delegation and voting system. Costs were particularly high for organizations, where delegation is mandatory.

Legal Perspective on DAOs

The present economic landscape, shaped by centuries of regulatory and economic developments, has perfected diverse legal, social, and economic structures primarily based on the principles of the free market, the protection of vulnerable parties, and the preservation of trust, which the market must maintain. It is legitimate to question whether these principles can (or should) also apply to DAOs.

Traditional legal entities acquire legal personality when they are entered into the commercial register, while DAOs are forms of commercial organizations that have not yet been fully accounted for in a legal sense. They often lack a clear legal identity, making it difficult to hold them accountable for actions or to determine a fair liability to their members. Traditional organizations possess a recognized legal status and are subject to specific regulations and legal frameworks governing their operations. For example, compliance with corporate governance standards, registration with relevant government authorities, and adherence to taxation are mandatory for corporations. Conversely, DAOs often operate as decentralized networks, giving rise to complexities in establishing their legal status and accountability. One of the challenges faced by DAOs is their inability to meet the requirements for legal identity, such as providing a unique name, a physical office address, and the name of at least one director.

Often, DeFi DAOs do not set up any legal entity and try to create a fully decentralized structure. However, this does not mean that DAOs without a registered legal entity can ignore the law and the DAO can still have unlimited liability, like judicial liability, tax liability, or financial liability. (Østbye, 2022). Additionally, an unregistered DAO might be recognized in some jurisdictions as a general partnership. Regarding the special conditions of the token holder in a DAO (which is considered a general partnership), the personal liability of every participant is a relevant topic. (Mienert, 2021) In general partnerships, each member has unlimited legal liability for all activities conducted by the organization. This improves the risk of imputed ownership by governance token holders of the DAO's holdings responsibilities.

Although some jurisdictions have begun recognizing DAOs legally, comprehensive regulatory frameworks governing their governance and operations are still in a nascent stage of development. In the United States, the State of Vermont the legislator determined that the autonomous quality of DAOs needs greater protection than those of a traditional business entity and accounted for the extension of the numerus clausus of corporation forms through the creation of a new entity type, namely a blockchain-based limited liability company (BBLLC). Differently, the State of Wyoming introduced in the DAO Bill the concept of an algorithmically managed DAO (looking at the impact of AI in the DAO governance), in order to include the possibility that not-human DAOs may be developed without involving the matter of legal personhood at all, and still giving the chance of incorporation. (Schuppli & Jafari, 2023)

In Malta, the legislator introduced through the Malta Digital Innovation Authority Act a DAO-based corporate scheme. The legislator allows in this way the registration of Innovative Technology Agreements. Whilst this does not grant legal personality, it does allow some assurance about approval and recognition. What characterizes these Technology Arrangements is that they might all have a degree of autonomy whereby, when interacting with human counterparts, they might produce damages or losses of various kinds. The question of the responsibility for suffering losses or damages caused by DAOs remains. (Ganado & Tendon, 2018)

Hence, if a DAO interacts with the external economic environment, it must consider the economic and legal conditions in which it operates and determine how it can integrate into the factual reality. (Bridg esmith et al., 2022) When a DAO ventures into an economic context outside the Web 3 space, such as acquiring assets, distributing capital gains, or taking on credits, the question arises as to what recognized legal identity it can operate under. This inquiry becomes even more intriguing as DAOs increasingly assume functions unique to traditional business organizations. This means that at this point a DAO has to adopt a legal structure in order to continue. In Switzerland, the most usual legal wrappers are the Foundation (Dubnevych, 2023), the Association and the Private International Act (PILA). (Riva, 2020) Another new form was elaborated by the "MME" Swiss Law Firm in a collective project concerning the Swiss Fintech Industry, structuring the shape of a Decentralized Autonomous Association (DAA), improving the model of Swiss association for DAO's specific purposes. (Glarer et al., 2020)

DAOs employ governance structures to facilitate decision-making processes, although their approaches differ significantly from classical business organizations. In contrast to traditional legal entities, DAOs operate autonomously and deterministically, relying on algorithms and smart contracts to govern their operations. The encoded rules and conditions within these algorithms dictate the functioning of DAOs, while the law governs the operations of traditional economic entities. When specific conditions are met, DAOs act independently and execute actions as outlined in the smart contract.

Smart contracts can implement contractual obligations as well as business logic rules, and most management and administrative functions could be automated, so that the consequences of these proceedings would be distributed among virtual stakeholders automatically. However, the independence to perform actions does not mean that the performed action itself is rather independent from the decision-making process. A DAO is still bound by the governance and decision-making rules encoded in a smart contract, and the decision needs to pass through a designated algorithmic consensus mechanism, designed by a developer. (Schuppli & Jafari, 2023)

The governance structure of a traditional company is determined by legal requirements, leaving limited room for adaptation unless the company incorporates in a different jurisdiction. (Bruno et al., 2007) DAOs, on the other hand, operate on a fundamentally different concept, emphasizing the ability to dismantle control mechanisms. This enables DAOs to achieve a complete self-management, eliminating the need of oversight and administration. Unlike traditional companies, DAOs offer significant flexibility in establishing governance, allowing founders to determine alternative models and balance structures. This flexibility is made possible by ensuring at the same time discouraging opportunistic behavior and enabling more efficient modifications to governance structures and rules, through token holder voting and smart contract updates. (Han et al., 2023) DAOs also generally demonstrate a greater level of transparency compared to traditional companies. Operating on public blockchain networks, DAOs record their transactions and decision-making processes on the blockchain, making them accessible to all participants. This transparency fosters trust and allows stakeholders to closely examine the organization's activities.

THEORETICAL FRAMEWORK, DAOS AS HYBRID ORGANIZATIONS

For understanding the mutually overlapping and dependent nature of business organizations, we use the Transition Cost Economics theory (TCE) and new institutional economics (NIE) as an explanatory frame, and we follow deductive logic. TCE gives a comprehensive understanding of the existence of economic organizations, based on the work of Coase (1937) and Williamson (1975), who formalized the framework of TCE. After describing the core of the theory and placing DAOs in the category of hybrid organizations, we show its parallels with another hybrid form, cooperatives. We have chosen cooperatives as the basis of our comparison because they share a strong common element with DAOs, namely collective actions as a guiding principle. It is important to emphasize the distinction between principle and practice. While collective action is an important element in the operation of DAOs, empirical evidence shows that many functioning DAOs treat the shared principle as a means rather than an end, with its manifestation primarily observed in decision-making mechanisms.

Figure 1. Theoretical framework of the authors' argumentation

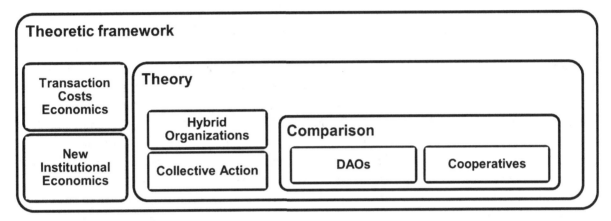

Based on TCE, organizing transactions holds uncertainty, which comes from the opportunistic behavior of the agents and their bounded rationality. To overcome this uncertainty, agents implement governance structures: the market, which is regulated by price and the firm or hierarchy, which is regulated by authority. (Williamson,1975) As a dominant theoretical frame of economics, the different aspects of blockchain technology and DAO as a business organization were evaluated by using the TCE theoretic framework by several authors. (Ahluwalia et al., 2020; Meunier and Zhao-Meunier, 2019, Berg et al., 2019)

Williamson (1991) later also added a third form of governance structure, the hybrid organizations, which included market-like and firm-like features. Hybrid organizations as a category got more attention due to the growing number of organizational structures in the 90s which didn't fit in the traditional classification frame of TCE, such as social enterprises. However, it served as a good opportunity for long-standing organizational forms such as cooperatives, joint ventures or strategic alliances to be incorporated into TCE. (Ménard, 2004)

These new organizational structures have given rise to an entirely new branch in economics, namely the new institutional economics (NIE), with its first mention also attributed to Williamson (1975). The new approach not only broadened the scope of analyzed institutions but also expanded the interpretative frames, incorporating, for instance, Ostrom's (1990) theory, which focused on collective actions and brought a completely new perspective to the understanding of organizational decision-making, "legitimizing" decentralized decision-making mechanisms alongside hierarchies. Several authors refer to NIE as interpretative theories to understand the importance of DAOs or blockchain as a technology (Davidson et al., 2017; Howell and Potgieter, 2019). We follow the recommendation of Santana and Albareda (2022) and place DAOs at the intersection of TCE and collective actions theory.

Hybrid Organizations

Hybrid organizations and their economics is well discussed by Ménard (2004, 2018, 2021), whose interpretation relied on Williamson's (1991) discrete alignment principle. According to the principle, an agent chooses the organizational structure where the agent can minimize transaction costs related to the given type of exchange. *"More precisely, my interpretation is based on the discrete alignment principle (Williamson (1991)): hybrid organizations and the specific forms they adopt are selected through efforts made by agents to reduce transaction costs by aligning governance structures with exchange attributes."* (Ménard, 2004, p. 10)

Williamson (1991) and Ménard (2004) pointed to two relevant attributes in this optimization, the specificity of assets and the costs of governance. The more complex the assets are, the higher the governance cost is, and the agents tend to organize transactions with hierarchic governance. Ménard gave the definition of hybrid organizations as the following: "... *legally autonomous entities doing business together, mutually adjusting with little help from the price system, and sharing or exchanging technologies, capital, products, and services, but without a unified ownership. These characteristics are likely the minimum required to encapsulate the variety of hybrids."* (Ménard, 2004, p. 4)

The group of hybrids include a great variety of cooperative arrangements, however, based on empirical regularities, Ménard (2004, pp. 6-9) described the following key features as recurring elements of hybrid structures: pooling, contracting, and competing. We argue that DAOs match well the criteria of hybrid organizations. A common feature of hybrids is pooling sources where coordination and cooperation emerge due to the perceived limitations of markets in efficiency. One of the central challenges for hybrid organizations lies in achieving low-cost coordination while preserving the benefits of decentralized decision-making. We contend DAOs fit well the given requirement since their core element is the pooling of different resources in the shape of capital, work or technology. They also consequently point out the limitations and inefficiency of the given market where they operate. Also, one of their essential challenges is their governance and coordination.

The hybrid arrangements use contracts as a means of regulating relations among participants and creating transactional reciprocity. The aim of the contracts is to ensure risk minimization in the cooperation. However, hybrids often face limitations regarding their contractual relations in the form of simplified, incorrect, or incomplete contracts. We argue that the contracting element is an essential point of DAO's existence, especially if we think about the advantages and challenges regarding smart contracts. They are also meant to regulate the circumstances of cooperation and coordination and the modification of those conditions can carry high costs.

Hybrid arrangements maintain competition as a central characteristic, inherited from the market. Participants within an agreement can compete against each other, either through overlapping activities or by cooperating on some aspects while competing on others. Competing hybrids emerge in highly competitive markets, where pooling resources is seen as a means of dealing with uncertainties and surviving. The environment of DAOs can be well described as competitive, where creating the right incentives to minimize the risk of freeriding or fraudulent behavior (voting manipulation, attacks, etc.) is a challenging task.

Ménard also identified another common feature in hybrids, which differentiates them from classical hierarchies, their governance. He pointed to a democratic decision-making system, which helps to coordinate collective action. However, he didn't elaborate on the given element.

Collective Action

The collective action theory provides a complementary perspective to understand the operation of DAOs. Ostrom's (1990) theory underscores how groups can collaboratively manage shared resources, in the absence of explicit government or private sector oversight, by self-organizing and establishing shared norms and rules. The significance of Ostrom's work lies in her presentation of alternatives for resolving "the tragedy of the commons". The theory of "the tragedy of the commons" was introduced by Hardin (1968). The concept refers to a situation in which multiple individuals, acting independently and rationally, deplete a shared and limited resource, which ultimately leads to its degradation. Hardin argued that the attempts to manage the commons through voluntary cooperation alone were often ineffective. He proposed that the solution to avoid "the tragedy of the commons" lies in either privatizing the resource or implementing some form of centralized regulation and control. Ostrom challenged Hardin's theory and showed that under certain conditions, communities can successfully manage common-pool resources without resorting to privatization or state regulation. Her work highlighted the importance of local, community-based governance systems and the role of collective action and cooperation in resource management.

Olstrom (1990, p. 90) identified eight principles along which collective actions can be managed:

1. Clearly defined boundaries
2. Congruence between appropriation and provision rules and local conditions
3. Collective-choice arrangements
4. Monitoring
5. Graduated sanctions
6. Conflict-resolution mechanisms
7. Minimal recognition of rights to organize
8. Nested enterprises

DAOs essentially symbolize this concept, as they are self-organizing entities where participants agree on protocols and rules, leveraging the technology for enforcement, hence mitigating "the tragedy of the commons" scenarios. Rozas and his colleagues (2021) give a detailed overview of how blockchain technology meets the principles of Ostrom's theory and they analyze six technological elements[10] which have the potential to support common governance. The authors argue that blockchain can support overcoming challenges, which are faced by communities following commons-based peer production, such as coordination, scaling common governance or exchange between communities.

Applying Ostrom's principles, the framework proposed by van Vulpen and Jansen (2023) offers explicit requirements for DAOs to achieve collective action and unite communities towards their common purposes. The authors apply the definitional framework of Rozas and colleagues (2021), which describes the fulfillment of each principle in the case of DAOs. These are utilized for their secondary analysis regarding DAO governance. They focus on three essential governance areas for DAOs to create collective action: the governance structure; enabling technology and community governance.

We contend that in the context of collective actions, emphasizing the decentralized nature is of great importance. This not only implies immunity from external influences but also presupposes relatively equal power dynamics within the community. In cases where power is heavily centralized within organizations, community members might contribute to the direction of processes, yet lack substantive decision-making rights. In scenarios characterized by the latter structures, alternative governance principles and incentivization systems are likely to yield greater success.

Ostrom worked on resolving a theoretical dilemma and analyzed case studies to identify patterns, among which local cooperatives played a significant role. It is no coincidence that her work greatly contributed to the revitalization of the cooperative form, which we will discuss in detail in the next section of our chapter. We believe that among institutionalized (important criteria) organizations, these are the ones closest to DAOs, and comparing them contributes to a better understanding of the new organizational form.

BETWEEN MARKETS, HYBRIDS, AND HIERARCHIES

After giving a short overview of the theoretic frame of our analysis, we would like to place DAOs on the spectrum of hybrids between markets and hierarchic organizations. We follow Ménard's (2007) reasoning that he applied in his work regarding placing cooperatives on the hybrid scale. Not only because they are categorized as hybrids themself, but they also show several similarities with DAOs, one of the crucial elements between them is the importance of collective action in their operation. The similarities in their constructive principle, historic development, governance and challenges they face are well discussed in several articles. (Langley, 2021a; Langley, 2021b; Davila, 2021; Nambiampurath, 2022; Gurkov, 2022)

Cooperatives' most exciting feature from our perspective is their ability to incorporate collective action in their very divergent governance structures. From the early formation of cooperatives, they were seen as unusual organizations, which were meant to correct market anomalies, and they were the first business organizations holding a unique attribute, the democratic governance, or one-person, one-vote system. (Pereira, 2016) They share another similar feature, obstacles related to growth have motivated the transformation of the cooperative form, and the emergence of the divided-cooperative. Just as challenges regarding community growth often motivate the modification of governance models in the case of DAOs. (Gurkov, 2022)

In their placement on the hybrid scale, Ménard (2007) argued that in terms of resource pooling, contracts, and competition - although they fulfill criteria to different extents - in most cases one can identify the common regularities of hybrids, just as we can identify the given elements in the case of DAOs. However, besides the two central elements of the theory (asset specificity and governance costs), there is a feature, which gives them very different positions on the hybrid spectrum, placing one closer to the market and another closer to hierarchies. This special feature is the separation or combination of property rights and decision-making rights. Ménard handled the application of democratic governance in hybrids as the most common solution, we argue that it also contributes to the different positions of DAOs on the hybrid spectrum. We also suggest the consideration of one additional characteristic, namely that the position of individual DAOs is not stable in the range. It can change due to modification of their governing structures, which creates an extremely challenging situation in their evaluation.

Based on Ménard's (2007) evaluation, cooperatives move on a huge variety of the spectrum regarding their separation of property rights and decision-making rights. There are organizations where the two are separated from each other and the transactions are organized between quasi-market conditions, hence they are close to the market on the hybrid spectrum. As examples, we can mention DAOs, which offer certain services for community members but don't require coordination of transactions due to smart contract solutions.

On the other hand, organizations which combine property rights with decision-making rights are closer to hierarchies on the same hybrid spectrum. The more decentralized and democratic their decision-making process is, the closer they are to hybrids, such as traditional cooperatives. The more centralized the share of the decision-making power, the closer they get to firms, such as divided-cooperatives or corporations. Most of the DAOs offer some sort of decision-making right to the members of the community. However, the quality of those rights greatly differs, and it would be also important to discuss which level of involvement implies decision-making rights. For example, can a signaling vote be seen as decision-making, where the outcome of a community decision does not have direct consequences? Important distinctions between hybrids and DAOs are that many DAOs follow some version of token-based voting, which further pushes those organizations toward hierarchic organizations.

Considering the given features, we created a hybrid categorization of DAOs, as a combination of their characteristics. Following the concept of Ménard's original theory, those are not a distinct group of DAOs but rather a spectrum of organizations.

Figure 2. Relevant features influencing the position of DAOs on the hybrid spectrum

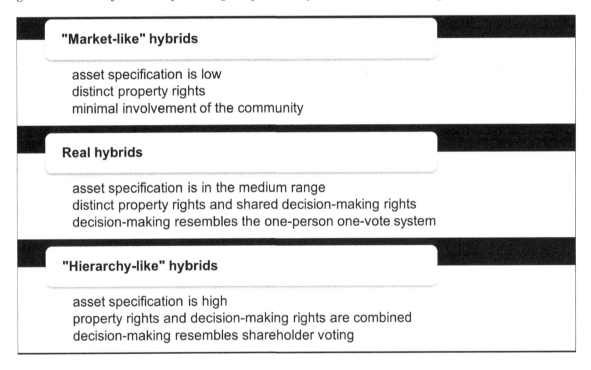

"Market-like" hybrids

asset specification is low
distinct property rights
minimal involvement of the community

Real hybrids

asset specification is in the medium range
distinct property rights and shared decision-making rights
decision-making resembles the one-person one-vote system

"Hierarchy-like" hybrids

asset specification is high
property rights and decision-making rights are combined
decision-making resembles shareholder voting

According to the principle of TCE, market-like DAOs emerge in cases of low asset specification, where the nature of the asset allows for low transaction costs, enabling peer-to-peer exchanges without external coordination. Trading platforms can be mentioned as examples, where transactions do not require human intervention due to smart contracts. Their hybrid nature stems from the fact that, unlike traditional markets, community members can have a say in the operation of DAOs - for instance, they can make decisions about protocol modifications. While there are initiatives that aim to eliminate human intervention from their operation, such as the concept of Delphi Labs (2023).

In the case of real hybrid DAOs, the asset specification is moderate, necessitating coordination around transactions. In these cases, property rights and decision-making rights are only partially intertwined, and the extent of influence is not determined by token shares. The decision-making mechanism resembles the one-person, one-vote system. An example could be a community of creators of open-source software. The cooperative form and the parallelism between cooperatives and DAOs are most pronounced in this type. Furthermore, we argue that the application of Ostrom's principles of collective action is likely to be most successful within this context. This stems from the fact that the community members can make decisions on acceptable rules on an equal footing.

Lastly, hierarchy-like DAOs emerge in the case of specific assets that require significant coordination. Based on the theory of TCE, the shift towards hierarchy is a rational consequence of containing transaction costs. In the case of hierarchy-like DAOs, decision-making rights and property rights are intertwined, and the decision-making process resembles shareholder voting. We argue that these processes can be identified in larger DAOs where the protocol's original function extends or evolves and operating democratic decision-making processes becomes increasingly costly and complex. This becomes particularly challenging in cases where the ownership structure is heavily centralized, and the participation of smaller token holders is symbolic yet costly. Presumably, similar processes motivated the establishment of divided-cooperatives.

FINDING DAOS PLACE ON THE HYBRID SPECTRUM BY THE LAW

Although we find the theoretical framework of TCE very useful in placing DAOs in the interpretative frame of economics we also agree with Hodgson (2002) regarding his critics about the blurry legal definition of firms and hybrids in TCE. Hence besides our theoretic argumentation, we offer a comparison regarding the differences between DAOs and legally defined business organizations. We mostly focus on cooperatives as another hybrid type, but we refer to the differences where features of DAOs are rather close to corporations. As with any similar attempt, this generalization can only scratch the surface of the question due to the nature and differences between the two disciplines.

Separation of Rights in DAOs

The legal form of cooperatives enables members to jointly achieve economic goals and benefit from the advantages of a collective business structure, and while shareholders or stockholders are often owned by other corporations, cooperatives are owned by their members or the individuals who utilize the cooperative's services. Additionally, certain cooperatives may have an ownership structure where the employees themselves are the owners. This shows more similarities between DAOs and cooperatives than between DAOs and corporations. However, a similarity can also be identified between DAOs and shareholder corporations, they feature stakeholders who hold ownership in the respective organizations, although ownership in corporations is typically represented through shares of stock, while in DAOs, it is derived from token ownership.

Although the literature differentiates cooperatives from a corporation it is important to note that by law the cooperative business structure can be seen, as a type of corporation. Although they have some peculiarities and a specific legal form. (Deller et al. 2009) In Swiss law, for example, cooperatives are founded by a group of persons who pursue a common economic interest (according to Art. 828 I Swiss-

CO). In contrast to joint-stock companies or limited liability companies, where the capital is divided into shares, the basic principle of a cooperative is that the members manage the company jointly and are the owners. (Holmstrom,1999) This aspect of direct contribution to the running of the organization and the possibility of being the owner at the same time creates a clear parallel between cooperatives and DAOs. We can find a similarity also in the purpose of sharing economic resources. However, typically, the tokens that give access to the DAO also constitute the participation share. Therefore, it is possible to hold more participation tokens to the DAO itself, when for example, the intent is to invest in a project that is considered worthy, and that would increase the participation fee to the DAO based on the number of tokens held. Hence, it can be argued that the token is an incorporation of a property right and not just a legitimation of participation. In this sense cooperative and DAO differ.

Decision-Making in the DAOs

As a rule, the purpose of a cooperative is to maximize the economic benefit for its members. Members have both co-determination rights and the right to share in profits based on their participation in the enterprise. Decision-making is often democratic, with each member having a vote, regardless of the amount of their contribution or financial interest. As we discussed before, the voting system of DAOs shows a huge variety, whereas the wallet-based voting system resembles the principle of cooperative governance. However, there is a relevant difference between participation in DAOs and cooperatives. Many participants in DAOs operate on the basis of pseudonymity, which further complicates the issue. (Ruane & McAfee, 2022) Especially, in the case of cooperatives, the identity of the members is an essential requirement for being able to become part of the organization and the related data is recorded and confirmed in the members' books[11]. It is therefore impossible to participate in a cooperative (pseudo-) anonymously.

In contrast, corporations typically adopt a centralized structure, concentrating decision-making authority within a hierarchical framework that includes a board of directors and executive management. DAOs operate differently on a decentralized model, distributing decision-making authority among token holders, thereby enabling a more democratized decision-making process. Token holders can actively participate in decision-making through voting mechanisms, and their decisions are enforced through self-executing smart contracts. This decentralized and automated approach distinguishes DAOs from conventional legal firms. (Hassan & De Filippi, 2021)

A further difference between DAOs and cooperatives is the restriction regarding members. A cooperative must involve often a minimum number of members in the foundation[12] and where the number of members subsequently drops below the minimum number, the provisions of the law on companies limited by shares on defects in the organization of a company apply mutatis mutandis. In a DAO the membership can change to a high extent. It is easy to enter or leave the organization because formally the only legitimacy needed is the availability of the token. While on and out boarding in a DAO just follow the token ownership, the process of welcoming new members into the cooperative and managing their transition out of the cooperative is more articulate in terms of entitlement while it is important for maintaining the integrity and functionality of the cooperative and ensuring a positive experience for all members. (Ménard, 2007)

From the analysis conducted, it is possible to show that corporations or cooperatives and DAOs have several points of similarity but a great many differences and that they are organizational models that cannot be equated. (Liu et al., 2021) Therefore we can argue that DAOs represent a novel paradigm for organizational structure and governance. While various existing organizations and governance models can be identified in the operations of DAOs, none of them aligns perfectly with all DAOs. However, establishing parallels with traditional organizations from a legal perspective is challenging due to the diverse nature of both sides. Therefore, the focus lies in determining which types of DAOs exhibit similarities with specific organizational structures.

CONCLUSION

In our chapter, we introduced DAOs as a new organizational formation, which provides insights into the native governance structure of Web 3. Although DAOs include several technological innovations in their operation, they also resemble structures and principles which were known and chased before their existence. Hence, we argued that they can be placed in a classical framework of business organizations. We gave a theoretical overview of the position of DAOs based on the framework of TCE, which expects agents to find optimal coordination mechanisms for organizing their transactions while minimizing their transaction costs.

In our understanding, DAOs can be seen as hybrid organizations, which include market-like and firm-like elements in their operation. DAOs embody important characteristics of hybrids: they are based on resource pooling; their operation is governed by contracts; and their participants cooperate on certain elements of transactions while competing on others. Albeit to varying degrees, they also embrace democratic governance, which is often associated with hybrids. We propose that placing DAOs on the hybrid spectrum contributes to understanding their relationship with classical economic organizations, supporting not only their orientation but also the navigation of potential regulators. Based on our conclusions, although they fulfill the theoretical requirements of hybrids, they also hold several new (technology-enabled) features, which makes understanding their legal positioning very challenging. Among those, their flexible or modifiable governance structures pose a challenge not only from a legal but also from a theoretical standpoint.

REFERENCES

Ahluwalia, A., Mahto, R. V., & Guerrero, M. (2020). Blockchain technology and startup financing: A transaction cost economics perspective. *Technological Forecasting and Social Change, 151*, 119854. Advance online publication. doi:10.1016/j.techfore.2019.119854

Anderson, P. (2022). Of cypherpunks and sousveillance. *Surveillance & Society, 20*(1), 1–17. doi:10.24908s.v20i1.14322

Atzori, M. (2017). Blockchain technology and decentralized governance: Is the state still necessary? *Journal of Government & Regulation, 6*(1), 45–62. doi:10.22495/jgr_v6_i1_p5

Berg, C., Davidson, S., & Potts, J. (2019). *Understanding the blockchain economy: An introduction to institutional cryptoeconomics*. Edward Elgar. doi:10.4337/9781788975001

Bridgesmith, L., Elmessiry, A., & Marei, M. (2022). Legal service delivery and support for the DAO ecosystem. In S. Chen, R. K. Shyamasundar, & L. J. Zhang (Eds.), Lecture Notes in Computer Science: Vol. 13733. *Blockchain – ICBC 2022* (pp. 18–28). Springer. doi:10.1007/978-3-031-23495-8_2

Buterin, V. (2014). *Ethereum: A next-generation smart contract and decentralized application platform [White paper]*. Ethereum. https://ethereum.org/669c9e2e2027310b6b3cdce6e1c52962/EthereumWhite-paper_-_Buterin_2014.pdf

Buterin, V., Hitzig, Z., & Weyl, E. G. (2019). A flexible design for funding public goods. *Management Science, 65*(11), 4951–5448. doi:10.1287/mnsc.2019.3337

Coase, R. (1937). The nature of the firm. *Economica, 2*(1), 386–405. doi:10.1111/j.1468-0335.1937.tb00002.x

Cointelegraph Research. (2022, October). *DAO: The evolution of organization*. Cointelegraph Research. https://research.cointelegraph.com/reports/detail/dao-the-evolution-of-organization

Cornforth, C. (2004). The governance of cooperatives and mutual associations: A paradox perspective. *Annals of Public and Cooperative Economics, 75*(1), 11–32. doi:10.1111/j.1467-8292.2004.00241.x

Cyberpunk manifesto. (n.d.). Nakamoto Institute. https://nakamotoinstitute.org/static/docs/cypherpunk-manifesto.txt

Davila, J. (2021, May 27). Decentralisation at work: Cooperatives on the blockchain. *General format.* https://www.dgen.org/blog/decentralisation-at-work-cooperatives-on-blockchain

Deller, S., Hoyt, A., Hueth, B., & Sundaram-Stukel, R. (2009). *Research on the economic impact of cooperatives*. University of Wisconsin Center for Cooperatives Projecthttps://resources.uwcc.wisc.edu/Research/REIC_FINAL.pdf

Delphi Labs. (2023). Assimilating the BORG: A New Framework for CryptoLaw Entities. *Medium.* https://delphilabs.medium.com/assimilating-the-borg-a-new-cryptolegal-framework-for-dao-adjacent-entities-569e54a43f83

Dubnevych, N. (2023). Three key functions of a DAO foundation. *Legal nodes.* https://legalnodes.com/article/dao-foundation-functions

DuPont, Q. (2017). Experiments in algorithmic governance: a history and ethnography of the DAO, a failed decentralized autonomous organization. In M. Campbell-Verduyn (Ed.), *Bitcoin and Beyond: Cryptocurrencies, Blockchains and Global Governance* (pp. 157–177). Routledge. doi:10.4324/9781315211909-8

Faqir-Rhazoui, Y. Arroyo, & J., Hassan, S. (Eds). (2021). A scalable voting system: Validation of holographic consensus in DAOstack. In *Proceedings of the 54th Hawaii International Conference on System Sciences*. Scholar Space. http://hdl.handle.net/10125/71296

Feichtinger, R., Fritsch, R., Vonlanthen, V., & Wattenhofer, R. (2023). *The hidden shortcomings of (D) AOs—An empirical study of on-chain governance*. doi:10.48550/arXiv.2302.12125

Gajek, S. (2018). Knowledge extractable voting for blockchain & distributed governance. *Hacker Noon*. https://hackernoon.com/knowledge-extractable-voting-for-blockchain-distributed-governance-radically-new-mechanisms-ed2ca47f065f

Ganado, M., & Tendon, S. (2018). Malta: Legal personality for Blockchains, DAOs and Smart Contracts. *MonDaq.*. https://www.mondaq.com/fin-tech/707696/legal-personality-for-blockchains-daos-and-smart-contracts

Glarer, A., Linder, T., Müller, L., & Mesero, S. D. (2020, May 4). Decentralized Autonomous Assotiation (DAA). *MME*. https://www.mme.ch/en/magazine/articles/decentralized-autonomous-association-daa

Gurkov, A. (2022). Alignment of a traditional cooperative identity to the design of Decentralised Autonomous Organisations. In *Nottingham Insolvency and Business Law E-Journal, 10* (9). http://hdl.handle.net/10138/351666

HanJ.LeeJ.LiT. (2023). *DAO governance*. SSRN. doi:10.2139/ssrn.4346581

Hardin, G. (1968). The Tragedy of the Commons. *Science, 162*(3859), 1243–1248. https://pages.mtu.edu/~asmayer/rural_sustain/governance/Hardin%201968.pdf. doi:10.1126cience.162.3859.1243 PMID:5699198

Hassan, S., & De Filippi, P. (2021). Decentralized autonomous organization. *Internet Policy Review: Journal on Internet Regulation, 10*(2), 1–10. doi:10.14763/2021.2.1556

Hellström, E. (2022). *Fair Voting System for Permissionless Decentralized Autonomous Organizations*. [(UPTEC IT, ISSN 1401-5749; 22005) [Independent thesis, Uppsala University]. https://uu.diva-portal.org/smash/record.jsf?pid=diva2%3A1671220&dswid=-508

Hiremath, B. K., & Kenchakkanavar, A. Y. (2016). An alteration of the Web 1.0, Web 2.0 and Web 3.0: A comparative study. Imperial Journal of Interdisciplinary Research, 2(4), 705–710.https://www.academia.edu/download/51816194/327-660-1-SM.pdf

Hodgson, G. M. (2002). The legal nature of the firm and the myth of the firm-market hybrid. *International Journal of the Economics of Business, 9*(1), 37–60. doi:10.1080/13571510110102967

Holmstrom, B. (1999). Future of cooperatives: A corporate perspective. *Liiketaloudellinen aikakauskirja LTA - The Finnish Journal of Business Economics, (*4), 404–417.

Langley, K. (2021a). Distributed Autonomous Organizations, A primer. *Insight*. https://insight.openexo.com/distributed-autonomous-organizations-daos-getting-started/

Langley, K. (2021b). DAO's are novel but not new. *Insight*. https://insight.openexo.com/daos-are-novel-but-not-new/

Larimer, S. (2013). Bitcoin and the three laws of robotics. *Insight*. https://steemit.com/bitshares/@stan/bitcoin-and-the-three-laws-of-robotics

Levi, A. (2019). Reputation vs Tokens. *Medium*. https://medium.com/daostack/reputation-vs-tokens-6d7642c7a538

Liu, L., Zhou, S., Huang, H., & Zheng, Z. (2021). From technology to society: An Overview of blockchain-based DAO. *IEEE Open Journal of the Computer Society, 2*, 204–215. doi:10.1109/OJCS.2021.3072661

Ménard, C. (2004). The economics of hybrid organizations. *Journal of Institutional and Theoretical Economics, 160*(3), 345–376. doi:10.1628/0932456041960605

Ménard, C. (2007). Cooperatives: Hierarchies or hybrids? In K. Kostas & N. Jerker (Eds.), *Vertical Markets and Cooperative Hierarchies* (pp. 1–18). Springer. doi:10.1007/1-4020-5543-0_1

Ménard, C. (2018). Research frontiers of new institutional economics. *RAUSP Management Journal, 53*(1), 3–10. doi:10.1016/j.rauspm.2017.12.002

Ménard, C. (2021). Hybrids: Where are we? *Journal of Institutional Economics, 18*(2), 297–312. doi:10.1017/S1744137421000230

MeunierS.Zhao-MeunierD. (2019). Bitcoin, Distributed Ledgers and the Theory of the Firm. doi:10.2139/ssrn.3327971

Mienert, B. (2021). How can a decentralized autonomous organization (DAO) be legally structured? *E-zeitschrift für Wirtschaftsrecht und Digitalisierung, 336.* https://www.lrz.legal/2021Rn336

Nambiampurath, R. (2022). What is a DAO? *The Defiant.* https://thedefiant.io/what-are-daos

ØstbyeP. (2022). Exploring The Role of Law in The Governance of Cryptocurrency Systems and Why Limited Liability DAOs might be a Bad Idea. doi:10.2139/ssrn.4007547

Ostrom, E. (1990). *Governing the Commons: The Evolution of Institutions for Collective Action.* Cambridge University Press. doi:10.1017/CBO9780511807763

Pereira, J. R. (2016). Producer Cooperatives: A Transaction Cost Economic Approach. In F. Taisch, A. Jungmeister, & H. Gernet (Eds.), *Cooperative Identity and Growth: Conference Proceedings of ICCS 2016 in Lucerne* (pp. 528–536). Verlag Raiffeisen Schweiz.

Ramiro, A., & de Queiroz, R. (2022). Cypherpunk. *Internet Policy Review, 11*(2). doi:10.14763/2022.2.1664

Riva, S. (2020). Decentralized Autonomous Organizations (Daos) In the swiss legal order. In A. Bonomi & G. P. Romano (Eds.), *Yearbook of Private International Law, 21,* 601-638. Verlag Dr. Otto Schmidt & Swiss Institute of Comparative Law, Germany. https://www.unine.ch/files/live/sites/florence.guillaume/files/Publications/Riva%20DAO%20in%20Swiss%20legal%20order.pdf

Rozas, D., Tenorio Fornés, A., Díaz Molina, S., & Hassan, S. (2021). When Ostrom meets Blockchain: Exploring the potentials of blockchain for commons governance. *SAGE Open, 11*(1), 1–14. doi:10.1177/21582440211002526

Ruane, Y., & McAfee, A. (2022, May 10). What a DAO Can—and Can't—Do. *Harvard Business Review.* https://hbr.org/2022/05/what-a-dao-can-and-cant-do

Saito, Y., & Rose, J. A. (2022). Reputation-based Decentralized Autonomous Organization for the non-profit sector: Leveraging blockchain to enhance good governance. *Frontiers in Blockchain, 5*(1083647), 1083647. doi:10.3389/fbloc.2022.1083647

Santana, C., & Albareda, L. (2022). Blockchain and the emergence of Decentralized Autonomous Organizations (DAOs): An integrative model and research agenda. *Technological Forecasting and Social Change, 182*, 121806. Advance online publication. doi:10.1016/j.techfore.2022.121806

Schuppli, B., & Jafari, G. A., (2023). Piercing the Digital Veil: A Case Study for a DAO legal framework under Swiss Law. *Journal of Intellectual Property, Information Technology and E-Commerce Law* (JIPITEC), *12* (331).

Van VulpenP.JansenS. (2023). Decentralized Autonomous Organization Design for the Commons and the Common Good. doi:10.2139/ssrn.4418782

Wang, S., Ding, W., Li, Y., Ouyang, L., & Wang, F. (2019). Decentralized autonomous organizations: Concept, model, and applications. *Institute of Electrical and Electronics Engineers (IEEE). Transactions on Computational Social Systems, 6*(5), 870–878. doi:10.1109/TCSS.2019.2938190

WilliamsonO. E. (1975). Markets and hierarchies: Analysis and antitrust implications: A study in the economics of internal organisation. SSRN https://ssrn.com/abstract=1496220

Williamson, O. E. (1991). Comparative economic organization: The Analysis of discrete structural alternatives. *Administrative Science Quarterly, 36*(2), 269–296. doi:10.2307/2393356

Wright, A. (2021). The Rise of Decentralized Autonomous Organizations: Opportunities and Challenges. *Stanford Journal of Blockchain Law & Policy.* https://stanford-jblp.pubpub.org/pub/rise-of-daos/release/1

Ziegler, C., & Welpe, I. (2022). A Taxonomy of Decentralized Autonomous Organizations. In *ICIS 2022 Proceedings*, 1, AISeL. https://aisel.aisnet.org/icis2022/blockchain/blockchain/1/

ENDNOTES

[1] In accordance with the analysis of Hiremath and Kenchakkanavar (2016), Web 1 is a static and read-only web with limited interactivity. Web 2 is an interactive and participative web with social media and user-generated content, while Web 3 is the decentralized web with blockchain, NFTs, and user control over data.

[2] https://ethereum.org/en/web3.

[3] Cyberpunk Manifesto: https://nakamotoinstitute.org/static/docs/cypherpunk-manifesto.txt

[4] A smart contract is a computer program or transaction protocol that is designed to automatically execute, control, or document events and actions according to the terms of a contract or agreement. It is a self-executing program that automates the actions required in an agreement or contract. (Hiremath & Kenchakkanavar, 2016)

[5] The definition of hard fork: "A permanent divergence in the blockchain; also known as a hard-forking change. One commonly occurs when nonupgraded nodes can't validate blocks created by upgraded nodes that follow newer consensus rules." https://ethereum.org/en/glossary/#hard-fork

[6] July 7, 2023

[7] On-chain decision-making refers to decisions that are made directly on the blockchain. While off-chain decision-making mostly happens on some form of social media or chat platforms.

8   However, there are new infrastructure providers, which are working on solutions to move those phases of preparation at least partly on the chain, as a useful and valued way of participation. Not incidentally thereby increasing the incentives for participation, which are often divided among the participants of the discussions.

9   Due to the difficult-to-understand and costly nature of advanced voting systems, some DAOs are moving away from complex solutions, creating a decision-making system more efficient, cheaper and in general more accessible for DAO participants. https://www.coindesk.com/web3/2022/12/21/uniswap-dao-community-members-vote-in-favor-of-new-governance-process/

10   The analyzed elements are: tokenization, self-enforcement and formalization of rules, autonomous automatization, decentralization of power over the infrastructure, increasing transparency, and codification of trust.

11   Art. 837 I Swiss-CO.

12   Art 831 I Swiss-CO.

Chapter 8
Smart Contracts and Web 3:
From Automated Transactions to DAOs

Aneta Napieralska
https://orcid.org/0009-0004-0463-3646
Humanitas University, Poland

Przemysław Kępczyński
https://orcid.org/0009-0006-8427-3162
Humanitas University, Poland

ABSTRACT

This chapter delves into the burgeoning world of smart contracts and their critical role in powering decentralized autonomous organizations (DAOs). Beginning with an exploration of the logical foundations of smart contracts, it underscores the parallels between smart contract creation and traditional contract formulation, with a keen emphasis on the concept of conditional execution. It further elucidates the integral role of smart contracts in underpinning DAOs, illuminating how these automated, transparent, and immutable constructs facilitate the decentralization and autonomy of such organizations. A rigorous examination of the complex interplay between technology, law, and economy in DAO operations is also undertaken. The chapter additionally navigates the challenging regulatory landscape, drawing on international legal frameworks and proposed regulations. Throughout, it maintains a balanced perspective on the transformative potential of smart contracts and DAOs in reshaping societal structures, alongside the profound challenges their implementation presents.

INTRODUCTION

Throughout the course of human history, societies have established various organizational forms to govern societal life. The evolution of these structures, influenced by factors such as population growth, industrial revolutions, and technological advancements, has transitioned societies from autocratic regimes to diverse democratic systems. Presently, the continuous development of technology introduces a transformative influence on society, affecting governance, economic, and labor organization. Widespread

DOI: 10.4018/978-1-6684-9919-1.ch008

Copyright © 2023, IGI Global. Copying or distributing in print or electronic forms without written permission of IGI Global is prohibited.

access to information, combined with the capacity for instantaneous, long-distance communication, provides new opportunities for societal cooperation and grassroots formation, independent of state control. However, for these organizations to function effectively, they need a set of privileges and operational rules. Without such rules, their activities could be confined to expressing demands, or they could be susceptible to control by a select group of individuals or a single authority.

In recent years, the emergence of blockchain technology has introduced a novel organizational form: the Decentralized Autonomous Organization (DAO). Enabled by smart contracts—computer programs that autonomously execute transactions upon predefined conditions—DAOs offer a structure where decision-making processes are automated, and rules are both transparent and immutable (Mougayar, 2016). DAOs signify a radical shift in organizational structures, echoing the transition from autocracies to democracies but now within a digital context. Considering the exponential growth of blockchain technology—evidenced by a transaction value nearing 1.4 trillion U.S. dollars in 2021 alone (Statista, 2022)—the implications of DAOs are far-reaching.

This chapter aims to present a comprehensive understanding of smart contracts and their pivotal role in the construction and operation of DAOs. Additionally, we explore the degree of autonomy these decentralized structures have from state control, a pertinent topic in an increasingly digital world. Operating on the peripheries of traditional governmental regulation, DAOs present unique challenges, including issues of legal recognition, security, governance, and user trust. Simultaneously, they provide opportunities for the reformation of societal cooperation and economic models.

By examining real-world examples and current research, we endeavor to offer a balanced perspective on DAOs and their enabling technology: smart contracts. Our goal is to promote critical thinking about the opportunities and challenges inherent to these emerging organizational forms. Such understanding is crucial in guiding the evolution of DAOs to maximize their potential, overcome challenges, and contribute positively to society. In sum, this exploration into the symbiotic relationship between smart contracts and DAOs seeks to enhance comprehension of their history, potential obstacles, and their capacity to reshape societal structures in the digital age. Such knowledge is increasingly important in a world where technology, law, economics, and sociology converge, and effectively navigating these intersections is vital for societal advancement.

SMART CONTRACTS

Smart Contract: General Information

The rise of blockchain technology has ushered in a new class of contracts, referred to as "smart contracts." These contracts are known for their inherent features of irreversibility and automation. Once activated, these contracts adhere to predetermined outcomes and resist any modifications or premature terminations, except under certain predefined conditions (Tapscott, 2016).

This section intends to outline the progressive evolution, structural design, and operational mechanisms of smart contracts. It aims to shed light on how these digital contracts interact synergistically with blockchain technology, an advanced record-keeping system that stores transactions in individual blocks (Mougayar, 2016b).

An in-depth examination of smart contracts includes exploring their practical applications across various sectors, insurance being a prime example. The implementation of blockchain technology and smart contracts has introduced solutions for multiple complex processes, such as insurance placement, data sharing, Know Your Customer (KYC) compliance, Anti-Money Laundering (AML) procedures, fraud prevention measures, claim processing, and exhaustive record-keeping. However, the introduction of smart contracts also brings with it challenges. This section aims to shed light on the main difficulties associated with the integration of these digital contracts, which encapsulate technical, regulatory, and societal issues.

Smart Contract: Evolution History

The history and evolution of smart contracts are intricately intertwined with the trajectory of digital and cryptographic technologies. Cryptographer Nick Szabo first conceptualized the term "smart contract" in 1994, defining it as a digital protocol allowing parties to fulfill their agreements (Szabo, 1996).

However, the potential of smart contracts could only be practically realized with the advent of blockchain technology. Initially, Bitcoin's underlying technology, though revolutionary, was not suitable for executing complex smart contracts due to its lack of Turing-completeness (Nakamoto, 2008). It wasn't until the rise of Ethereum in 2015, boasting a Turing-complete system, that smart contracts found an environment conducive to widespread adoption and evolution (Buterin, A Next-Generation Smart Contract and Decentralized Application Platform, 2014). Like Bitcoin, Ethereum is built on blockchain technology, has a distributed ledger, and utilizes a decentralized peer-to-peer network. Unlike Bitcoin, Ethereum is designed for building DApps (decentralized applications) and implementing smart contracts. Ethereum's design, which uses a Turing-complete language, allows anyone to write smart contracts and DApps with their own rules for ownership, transaction formats, and state transition functions (Buterin, A Next-Generation Smart Contract and Decentralized Application Platform. Ethereum White Paper, 2014).

Recent enhancements to the Ethereum network, known as Ethereum 2.0 or "Eth2", bring significant improvements in scalability, security, and sustainability. These modifications are expected to directly impact the functionality and capabilities of smart contracts on the Ethereum platform (Ethereum Foundation, 2020). A notable aspect of Eth2 is the transition from a Proof of Work (PoW) consensus mechanism to a Proof of Stake (PoS) consensus mechanism, which provides a faster and more energy-efficient network, contributing directly to the efficiency of smart contracts (Zamfir & Rush, 2020). Moreover, the introduction of shard chains – smaller chains running parallel to the main Ethereum chain – significantly expands Ethereum's capacity to process transactions and smart contracts (Zamfir & Rush, 2020). These advancements make the Ethereum blockchain more cost-effective and environmentally friendly, thereby expanding the potential application of smart contracts.

While the evolution of smart contracts is undoubtedly promising, ongoing vigilance is needed to address their unique challenges. As Ethereum continues to develop, the environment in which these smart contracts operate will also change, necessitating continuous study and understanding.

Types of Smart Contracts

While the concept of smart contracts is universal, they can take on various forms and serve diverse functions depending on the specific requirements of a use case. The term "smart contract" encompasses a wide array of contracts with varying levels of complexity and autonomy. These contracts can be classified based on several dimensions. In reference to the Ethereum whitepaper (Buterin, 2014), several types of smart contracts can be identified.

Firstly, there exist "fully self-contained" contracts that store all necessary data and do not require any communication with other contracts. They function independently and autonomously. An example of such contracts could be a basic token contract that keeps track of all the token holders' balances.

Secondly, "inter-contract" smart contracts are identifiable. These contracts rely on communication with other contracts, and their function cannot be achieved without this interaction. For instance, a decentralized exchange contract that needs to interact with various token contracts to execute a trade falls under this category.

Thirdly, there are "oracle-based" contracts that rely on external data fed to them via oracles. These contracts are commonly utilized when the execution of the contract depends on real-world data, such as stock prices or weather conditions.

Lastly, "hybrid" smart contracts combine the features of the previously mentioned types. For instance, a prediction market contract may store data (partially self-contained), require communication with other contracts (inter-contract aspect), and depend on real-world data provided by oracles (oracle-based aspect).

It is crucial to emphasize that the above classification is neither exhaustive nor rigid. It primarily serves to demonstrate the diversity of smart contract applications and the extensive range of functionalities they can provide. As the field of smart contracts continues to develop, it is expected that more complex and sophisticated types will emerge, potentially blurring the boundaries between the categories mentioned above.

Smart contracts, as key components of blockchain technology, can take many forms and perform a wide array of tasks, each varying significantly in their inherent functionalities and their mode of communication with the external world and users. These variations not only present superficial differences but significantly impact the scope and nature of potential applications for these smart contracts, shaping the landscape of potential solutions within this domain.

As we delve deeper into the world of decentralized organizations, the complexity of smart contract structures begins to unfold. Building such organizations requires a complex structure of interconnected smart contracts, underpinned by suitable logical connections. These connections ensure that the resulting framework can effectively cater to the requirements of a given organization or proposed solution, validating the fundamental premise of decentralized organizations. Current developments in this field are largely driven by market demand. As these demands evolve, blockchain technology continues to respond by facilitating the creation of tailor-made solutions. Therefore, the versatility of smart contract technology is not limited to its current range of applications. Instead, it paves the way for emerging solutions that align with the changing contours of market needs, highlighting its role as a dynamic and adaptable tool in the ever-evolving landscape of blockchain technology.

How Smart Contracts Are Built

A smart contract, in its essence, is a programmable contract that self-executes when certain predefined conditions are met. This conditioned are specified by the parties of agreement and could be different depending on type of commitment relationship. The creation of smart contracts bears significant similarity to the drafting of traditional contracts. Both foresee a response to the occurrence of specific conditions, whether in the form of a reward or the imposition of a penalty. Thus, the construction of each smart contract is based on the principles of logical reasoning, often taking the form: "If event X occurs, then Y will happen". This contract is written in code and is stored and replicated on a distributed ledger, which is a key feature of a blockchain (Knottenbelt, 2019). The smart contract code facilitates, verifies, and enforces the negotiation or performance of an agreement, allowing reliable transactions without the need for third-party intermediaries (llul, 2020).

A majority of smart contracts today are developed on the Ethereum platform, primarily using the Solidity programming language. Alternatively, to Solidity some of smart contract uses Vyper language. These languages are specifically designed for expressing smart contracts, focusing on security, simplicity, and auditability (Devetsikiotis, 2016).

Continuing with the football wager example, the smart contract's structure can be dissected further. The contract begins with the declaration of the parties involved and the establishment of the oracle. The 'constructor' function initiates the contract and the 'resolveBet' function carries out the contract's purpose based on the oracle's input.

```
contract FootballBet {
    address payable public gambler1;
    address payable public gambler2;
    bool public team1Won;
    Oracle public oracle;
    ...
```

The 'address payable' lines represent Ethereum addresses of the parties involved in the bet. The 'bool' is a boolean[1] value that indicates the outcome of the match, as provided by the oracle. The 'Oracle' line refers to the oracle's address, where it would send match outcome data.

```
    constructor(address payable _gambler2, address _oracle) public payable {
        gambler1 = msg.sender;
        gambler2 = _gambler2;
        oracle = Oracle(_oracle);
    }
    ...
```

The 'constructor' function is executed once when the contract is first created. 'msg.sender' is a special variable that refers to the sender of the message (i.e., the contract creator). '_gambler2' and '_oracle' are arguments passed into the constructor upon the contract's creation.

```
    function resolveBet() public {
        team1Won = oracle.didTeam1Win();
        if(team1Won) {
            gambler1.transfer(address(this).balance);
        } else {
            gambler2.transfer(address(this).balance);
        }
    }
}
```

The 'resolveBet' function is the heart of the contract. It first fetches the match's result from the oracle ('oracle.didTeam1Win()') and then transfers the contract's entire balance to the winning gambler based on the result.

```solidity
pragma solidity ^0.5.16;
contract Betting {
    address payable public teamA;
    address payable public teamB;
    address public oracle;

    enum Team { A, B }
    Team public winningTeam;

    mapping(address => uint256) public bets;
    bool public bettingActive;
    constructor(address _teamA, address _teamB, address _oracle) public {
        teamA = _teamA;
        teamB = _teamB;
        oracle = _oracle;
        bettingActive = true;
    }
    function placeBet(Team _team) public payable {
        require(bettingActive, "Betting no longer active");
        require(msg.value > 0, "Must send ETH to place bet");
        // Record bet for team
        bets[_team] += msg.value;
    }

    function closeBetting() public {
        require(msg.sender == oracle, "Only oracle can close betting");
        bettingActive = false;
    }

    function setWinningTeam(Team _winningTeam) public {
        require(msg.sender == oracle, "Only oracle can set the winning team");
        require(!bettingActive, "Betting must be closed to set winner");

        winningTeam = _winningTeam;

        // Payout winners
        if (_winningTeam == Team.A) {
            teamA.transfer(address(this).balance);
        } else {
            teamB.transfer(address(this).balance);
```

```
        }
    }
}
}
```

ORACLES: CRUCIAL MEDIATORS FOR INFORMATION TRANSFER

Oracles play an indispensable role in actualizing the potential of smart contracts. Owing to the deterministic and isolated nature of blockchains, they lack the capacity to independently interact with or fetch data from external sources, thereby necessitating the intervention of oracles (Al-Bassam, 2019; Zamyatin, 2019). An oracle can be conceptualized as a bridge, enabling a smart contract to traverse the boundary separating the blockchain from the broader digital world. Acting as intermediaries, they retrieve and translate pertinent external information into a format that can be interpreted and utilized by smart contracts. The scope of data oracles handle is vast, ranging from financial metrics and weather reports to sports outcomes and various forms of real-time data (Ellul, 2020; Popov, 2016).

Classification of Oracles: A Spectrum of Functionalities

Oracles are a heterogeneous group, characterized by the diversity of data sources they interact with and the verification methods they employ. A generalized classification can categorize oracles into software, hardware, and consensus oracles based on their data sources, and into inbound and outbound oracles according to their data verification location. Software oracles primarily interact with online sources to extract data, while hardware oracles collect real-world data from physical devices. Consensus oracles are employed when a single, reliable data source is unavailable, and a consensus amongst multiple data sources is required. Inbound oracles fetch data from external sources to the blockchain, while outbound oracles perform the reverse operation, transmitting data from the smart contract to external entities (Ellul, 2020; Popov, 2016).

The Oracle Problem: A Bottleneck in Blockchain's Efficacy

The use of oracles, however, presents a critical predicament known as the "oracle problem". This term encapsulates the challenge faced by smart contracts due to their dependence on oracles for fetching external data. Despite the deterministic and decentralized nature of blockchains, oracles are often centralized and non-deterministic, which opens a gateway for manipulation and undermines the trustless ethos intrinsic to blockchains (Elliptic, 2020; Knottenbelt, 2019). The quest to solve this paradox remains a significant focal point in the realm of blockchain research, with solutions like decentralized oracle networks, including Chainlink, being proposed (Chainlink, 2020). Yet, these solutions, while promising, are not devoid of challenges, including achieving swift consensus and ensuring the reliability of participating oracles. Consequently, the pursuit of a robust solution to the "oracle problem" persists as an ongoing venture within the field of blockchain technology.

DECENTRALIZED AUTONOMOUS ORGANIZATIONS: TOWARDS A NEW PARADIGM OF ORGANIZATIONAL STRUCTURE

The previous section offered a comprehensive examination of smart contracts, their characteristics, benefits, and challenges. In doing so, we have established a foundation for understanding the technological basis of Decentralized Autonomous Organizations (DAOs). Now, we pivot towards DAOs as an emerging application of these digital contracts. This section aims to explore the genesis of DAOs, their typologies, and their significance within traditional and non-traditional organizational structures. Further, we aim to discuss the evolution of DAOs and their growing legal recognition worldwide, setting the stage for subsequent sections that delve deeper into the intricacies of DAOs, their mechanics, and legal and regulatory challenges.

Having explored the underpinnings of smart contracts, we now turn our attention to a profound application of these digital arrangements - Decentralized Autonomous Organizations (DAOs). These innovative entities offer a fresh lens through which to examine organizational structures, reflecting the ideals of decentralization, transparency, and autonomy underpinning blockchain technology (Norta, 2015). Unlike traditional organizations that are centralized and hierarchical, DAOs distribute decision-making powers among their members, a process facilitated by smart contracts. This shift from conventional models is motivated by numerous factors, including greater transparency, more equitable participation in decision-making processes, and the potential to mitigate corruption and inefficiencies endemic to centralized systems (Aztori, 2015).

The Rise of DAOs

DAOs reflect a groundbreaking shift in conceptualizing and operating organizations, championing autonomy, transparency, and decentralization. First proposed within the cryptocurrency community, these digital entities function without central authority by leveraging consensus mechanisms inherent to blockchain technology (Mougayar, 2016).

"The DAO," the inaugural significant application of a DAO, was launched on Ethereum's platform in 2016. Despite its downfall due to a severe security breach, it spotlighted the potential of blockchain-based organizations and spurred subsequent developments (DuPont, 2017). It garnered an unprecedented $150 million in crowdfunding, indicating the profound interest and potential of these decentralized entities (Siegel, 2016). Since then, DAOs have rapidly evolved, encompassing an array of complex structures and objectives.

DAOs' typologies extend beyond mere participation from members or their specific purposes. Some DAOs function as participatory organizations requiring active involvement from all members, while others may incorporate more hierarchical structures with defined roles and responsibilities. They can vary in focus areas, encompassing financial applications or addressing governance, social, or environmental issues (Beck, 2018).

It is vital to note that the scope of DAOs isn't confined to the digital realm or metaverse. They introduce a novel organizational approach applicable to various traditional economic and social structures, including cooperatives, nonprofits, and for-profit businesses. The inherent features of transparency, immutability, and collective decision-making offer a unique governance blend that can be tailored to suit organizational needs (Othman, 2020).

DAO CLASSIFICATIONS

In the ever-evolving blockchain technology landscape, diverse types of decentralized organizations catering to unique use-cases and sectors have surfaced. Here, we identify and discuss three key types: Decentralized Finance (DeFi) platforms, Decentralized Applications (DApps), and other forms of DAOs that do not fall within the earlier categories (Tapscott, 2016).

- Decentralized Finance (DeFi): DeFi is a groundbreaking sector where DAOs have significant operations. With the aim to replace conventional financial systems like lending, borrowing, and trading, DeFi proposes decentralized alternatives that function without intermediaries (Mougayar, 2016b). Uniswap, MakerDAO, and Compound are some DeFi protocols regulated by DAOs (Zetzsche, 2019). As of 2023, the total value in DeFi protocols exceeded $150 billion, demonstrating a substantial market presence and future growth potential (DeFi Pulse).
- Decentralized Applications (DApps): DApps refer to applications that function on a P2P network of computers rather than one (Mougayar, 2016b). These applications interface with the blockchain to facilitate transactions. While all DeFi platforms are considered DApps, the reverse isn't true. DApps encompass other sectors like gaming (Axie Infinity, CryptoKitties), decentralized exchanges (DEXs), and NFT marketplaces (OpenSea) (DappRadar, 2023).
- Other DAOs: Beyond DeFi and DApps, DAOs find applications in areas like content creation, data storage, and collective investment ventures. For example, the LAO and Flamingo DAO are investment groups that pool resources for investing in blockchain and NFT projects respectively. Meanwhile, platforms like Aragon and DAOstack offer users the opportunity to create and manage their own DAOs.

Decentralized Finance (DeFi): A New Approach Towards Financial Systems

In recent years, the rise of Decentralized Finance (DeFi) has provided significant opportunities for Decentralized Autonomous Organizations (DAOs) to alter traditional financial structures. DeFi platforms such as Uniswap, Compound, and Aave have adopted DAO structures to decentralize control and to widen the distribution of profits. Often functioning as decentralized exchanges (DEXs), these platforms offer an alternative to traditional centralized exchanges (CEXs) by eliminating the need for intermediaries in facilitating trades.

Understanding DeFi Exchanges: DEXs vs. CEXs

CEXs bear a resemblance to conventional banking systems where users deposit funds and the exchange assumes the custody of these funds. In this setup, the exchange maintains order books and oversees transactions, subsequently charging fees for their services. Conversely, DEXs operate via smart contracts on blockchain platforms. Here, users maintain control of their assets, and trades are directly conducted between participants. The replacement of order books with liquidity pools is another notable attribute of DEXs.

Despite DEXs providing more transparency, lower costs, and greater privacy than their centralized counterparts, they also bring challenges. These include slower transaction speeds, lower trading volumes, and potential vulnerability to smart contract breaches. Consequently, the choice between using a DEX or CEX often hinges on individual requirements and risk tolerance.

DECENTRALIZED AUTONOMOUS ORGANIZATIONS (DAOS): STRUCTURE AND OPERATIONS

This section unpacks the fundamental mechanics and design principles that shape Decentralized Autonomous Organizations (DAOs). DAOs, as a paradigm shift in organizational structure, harness blockchain technology to foster transparency, autonomy, and potential efficiency.

Understanding DAOs: The Technical Bedrock

At the core of DAOs are smart contracts, blockchain technology, and distributed governance. To truly grasp DAOs, one must first understand these foundational components.

The creation of a DAO usually involves a group of individuals drafting a set of smart contracts on a blockchain platform. These contracts serve as the DNA of the DAO; they outline its structure and dictate its operations. The architectural blueprint of a DAO is layered, drawing inspiration from the principles of layered architecture observed in smart contracts.

The foundational layer, akin to the protocol layer in smart contracts, is composed of the blockchain platform. This platform provides the necessary infrastructure for executing smart contracts and recording transactions. Complementing this protocol layer is the governance layer, which spells out the rules and mechanisms for decision-making within the DAO. The governance layer, implemented via smart contracts, encompasses various functions including voting rights, proposal submission, and resource allocation.

Many DAOs employ a token model, which assigns voting rights to members. The quantity of native tokens held by a member translates into their voting power, aligning the interests of the members with the broader objectives of the DAO. Blockchain networks, particularly Ethereum due to its ability to execute complex smart contracts, offer an ideal environment for DAO operations, enabling transparent and immutable record-keeping.

Treasury Management in DAOs: A Critical Component

The design of a DAO can be programmed to fulfill various objectives, but the basic blueprint typically encompasses token governance and treasury management.

Treasury management, a fundamental mechanism for the operational funding of a DAO, can be fuelled by member contributions, an Initial Coin Offering (ICO), or other forms of fundraising. It plays a critical role in ensuring the financial and operational stability of a DAO (Tapscott, 2016). The treasury of a DAO is a collective pool of resources, often tokens, held by the community (Wright, 2015). These resources are utilized to finance activities of the DAO, ranging from software development to community initiative funding. DAO treasuries can be financed through various avenues, including initial coin offerings (ICOs), membership fees, or revenues generated from the DAO's operations (Zetzsche, 2018).

Managing these resources calls for transparency and democratic principles, with every decision related to spending or investing the treasury's funds being put to a community vote (Norta, 2015). Achieving a consensus amongst community members and making timely decisions requires a delicate balancing act. Moreover, the DAO's treasury, typically denominated in cryptocurrencies, is susceptible to market volatility. This necessitates the deployment of risk management strategies to mitigate significant losses and ensure the DAO's longevity (Mougayar, 2016b). Consequently, several DAOs adopt treasury management strategies that encompass asset diversification, hedging strategies, and engaging external providers for treasury management services (Chen, 2018).

In conclusion, treasury management in DAOs, though complex, is a crucial process. It demands careful planning, transparent governance, and active risk management. The sustainability of a DAO hinges significantly on the effective management of its treasury.

Governance in DAOs: the role of tokens

Governance tokens, representing a distinct type of digital tokens, empower owners with participation rights in the decision-making processes of decentralized protocols or a decentralized autonomous organization (DAO) (Aztori, 2015). As a central operational instrument in DAOs, these tokens embody the core principles of community-driven governance and decentralization (Azouvi, 2020).

In essence, governance tokens act as digital voting rights within a network (Mougayar, 2016). Token holders can introduce modifications, vote on proposals, or even delegate their voting power. The influence a token holder wields in decision-making typically correlates with the quantity of their tokens, which is known as "token-based governance" or "liquid democracy" (Swan, 2015). Governance tokens, significantly different from other tokens like utility or security tokens, primarily serve as a decision-making tool and offer no particular utility or claim on assets (Werbach, 2018).

However, governance tokens can align interests towards DAO success and growth by acting as an incentive mechanism (Catalini, 2021). Contributors to a DAO could receive these tokens as rewards, thereby fostering active participation and contribution to the community (Schär, 2021). On the flip side, governance tokens carry the risk of centralization where a small group holding substantial tokens could exert undue influence, underlining the need for fair distribution strategies and checks and balances in DAO structures (Zetzsche, 2019).

Participation in DAOs

Active engagement in a Decentralized Autonomous Organization (DAO) generally necessitates the acquisition of the organization's governance tokens. This can be achieved through either direct purchase from a cryptocurrency exchange or by active contribution to the DAO's objectives and activities. The spectrum of involvement can vary significantly, extending from simply voting on organizational decisions to a more proactive role in shaping the DAO's development and strategies. The anticipated rewards for such participation can be both tangible, in the form of financial gains from successful DAO initiatives, and intangible, such as the fulfillment derived from being an active member of a community-driven project.

CHALLENGES IN THE REALM OF DECENTRALIZED AUTONOMOUS ORGANIZATIONS

Decentralized Autonomous Organizations (DAOs) represent an avant-garde approach to reimagining governance, decision-making, and organizational structures in the digital age. Drawing upon the principles of decentralization, transparency, and cryptographic security offered by blockchain technology, DAOs promise a paradigm shift from traditional centralized entities to more democratic and inclusive models of organization (Nakamoto, 2008; Tapscott & Tapscott, 2016). As with any innovative technological framework, the ascent of DAOs is accompanied by a series of challenges, complexities, and concerns. A thorough comprehension of these challenges is imperative, not only for the academic community but also for stakeholders and practitioners vested in the DAO ecosystem. In the forthcoming section, we will delve deeper into the potential hurdles and challenges DAOs face amidst their growing influence and prominence.

Governance Mechanisms: An In-depth Examination

Theoretical Foundations: The concept of governance in DAOs is deeply rooted in the broader study of organizational governance. In conventional organizations, governance relates to decision-making structures, including the mechanisms, processes, and relations by which corporations are controlled and directed. DAOs extend this paradigm by attempting to democratize governance through blockchain technology, emphasizing transparency, inclusivity, and decentralized decision-making (Hirst, 2010).

Plutocratic Tendencies: One of the primary challenges within DAOs' governance is the emergence of plutocratic tendencies, where decision-making power becomes concentrated among a few affluent token holders. This phenomenon finds its parallel in classical organizational studies where shareholders with substantial equity stakes can disproportionately influence corporate decisions (Aztori, 2015). Such accumulation of power not only undermines the decentralized ethos of DAOs but also raises concerns about the equitable distribution of influence and potential conflicts of interest.

Alternative Voting Mechanisms: To address the challenges posed by plutocracy, the DAO community has been exploring alternative voting mechanisms. Quadratic voting, for instance, is a method where individuals allocate a pool of votes to issues based on their preferences. This approach can potentially ensure that the influence is balanced and not overly dominated by large token holders (Buterin, 2019).

Technical Vulnerabilities: Beyond the Infamous DAO Hack

Smart Contracts and Their Limitations: Central to the functionality of DAOs are smart contracts. These self-executing contracts with the terms of agreement directly written into code lines are revolutionary but are susceptible to technical flaws. In the broader software development paradigm, bugs are commonplace. However, when transposed to the immutable realm of blockchains, these errors can have irreversible consequences (Daian, 2020).

The DAO Hack – A Case Study: The 2016 DAO hack stands as a testament to the gravity of technical vulnerabilities in DAOs. While the event itself resulted in the loss of millions, it served as a watershed moment, prompting rigorous scrutiny of smart contract designs and stimulating discussions on enhancing security protocols (Siegel, 2016).

Security Enhancements: Post the DAO hack, there's been a heightened emphasis on improving the security of smart contracts. Robust auditing, formal verification of contracts, and bug bounty programs are some measures being implemented to safeguard against potential vulnerabilities (Daian, 2020).

Oracles and Information Manipulation: The Lifeline and Its Challenges

Role of Oracles: In the nexus between the physical world and blockchain ecosystems, oracles act as bridges, relaying external data to smart contracts. Their pivotal role ensures that smart contracts can interact dynamically with real-world data (Teutsch, 2021).

Potential Fallibilities: Oracles, however, are not infallible. Since they serve as intermediaries, their compromise or malfunction can lead to cascading errors, affecting the outcome of smart contracts. This is especially crucial in sectors like Decentralized Finance (DeFi) where accurate, real-time data is quintessential (Harz, 2020).

Countermeasures: The challenge posed by oracle vulnerabilities has led to the exploration of various solutions. Decentralized oracle networks, where multiple oracles corroborate data before it's fed to a smart contract, and the usage of multiple data aggregators to cross-verify information, are among the proposed solutions (Elliptic, 2020).

Regulatory Compliance and Jurisdictional Challenges

DAOs operate on a global scale, often transcending national borders. This brings forth challenges related to jurisdiction and regulatory compliance. Which laws apply to a DAO that has members from multiple countries? How can national regulators ensure compliance from an entity that doesn't have a physical presence or centralized decision-making body?

International law scholar Anne-Marie Slaughter's concept of "disaggregated world order" becomes pertinent here. In a world where non-state actors play increasingly vital roles in global governance, understanding and designing regulatory frameworks that accommodate entities like DAOs becomes imperative. Future regulatory advancements might require multi-jurisdictional collaborations and the crafting of international treaties or guidelines tailored for decentralized entities.

Historically, legal systems have primarily operated within the confines of nation-states, each with its distinct set of regulations. The rise of DAOs, inherently borderless entities, presents new challenges in determining applicable jurisdiction and enforcement. Since DAOs operate on a decentralized global network, it's difficult to pinpoint a singular location for them. This can create ambiguities in jurisdiction. For example, if a dispute arises between DAO members from different countries, it remains unclear which country's laws should apply and how judgements could be enforced. As DAOs become more prevalent, there's a potential need for the development of international legal frameworks or treaties that specifically address DAO operations. Alternatively, the incorporation of self-executing smart contracts could provide solutions, minimizing disputes by ensuring predefined outcomes based on coded agreements.

Smart Contracts: Immutable but Fallible

Smart contracts are the bedrock of DAO operations. Their self-executing and immutable nature ensures the unbiased implementation of stipulated conditions. However, code, as any legal document, can be fallible. In instances of code vulnerabilities or unforeseen scenarios, rigid adherence to the smart contract might lead to unjust outcomes. The famous DAO hack of 2016, where a loophole in the DAO's smart contract was exploited, leading to the loss of millions of dollars, serves as a cautionary tale.

From a legal standpoint, the challenge is to strike a balance between the immutability of smart contracts and the flexibility to rectify errors or injustices. This might entail the integration of off-chain governance mechanisms or introducing legal provisions that recognize and remedy the fallibilities of code.

In summation, while DAOs promise transformative shifts in organizational structures and operations, they also pose complex legal challenges. Integrating DAOs into our current legal frameworks necessitates both a rethinking of traditional legal norms and the innovative crafting of new regulations that align with the decentralized and global nature of DAOs.

OPPORTUNITIES

As we traverse the evolving landscape of Decentralized Autonomous Organizations (DAOs) and the broader world of blockchain technology, it becomes imperative to recognize the vast potential these innovations present. While the challenges associated with DAOs and smart contracts are evident, they are accompanied by a myriad of opportunities that can catalyze transformative change in various sectors of society. This section delves into the promising prospects DAOs offer, from fostering decentralized governance and transparent decision-making processes to revolutionizing economic models and societal cooperation in the digital era. By understanding these potential benefits, stakeholders can harness the power of blockchain technology to craft a more equitable, transparent, and efficient future.

Economic Opportunities and Future Concepts of DAOs

Decentralized Autonomous Organizations (DAOs) stand at the nexus of innovative technological advancement and emergent economic paradigms. Their genesis and evolution not only echo the perennial shifts in economic theories but also respond proactively to the changing contours of the global economic landscape. From the intricate dance of Game Theory and incentive alignment to the promise of market efficiency realized through decentralization, DAOs offer a vantage point to envision a new economic order. Furthermore, undergirded by the robust framework of blockchain and its manifestation through smart contracts, DAOs promise a level of security and integrity hitherto unseen in traditional systems. This section seeks to explore the profound economic ramifications of DAOs, examining their present functionalities and projecting their transformative potential in shaping the future economic paradigms.

Game Theory and Incentive Structures in DAOs

Decentralized Autonomous Organizations (DAOs) employ a profound alignment with the principles of Game Theory, a branch of mathematics developed by John Nash, which examines decision-making among independent and interdependent actors.

In the context of DAOs, this theory is operationalized through voting mechanisms and incentive structures. Take, for example, the DAO Compound. Within this platform, members who vote on interest rate adjustments must consider both individual short-term gains and the long-term health of the entire ecosystem. By prioritizing the well-being of the collective, DAOs ensure that the Nash Equilibrium is achieved, where individual strategy outcomes are optimal in the context of the strategies chosen by others.

As the digital economy evolves, DAOs could potentially harness more sophisticated game theoretical models, ensuring that the balance between individual and collective welfare remains equitable. Moreover, as DAOs span across national boundaries, they might also help in eradicating economic disparities stemming from individual-centric models prevalent in traditional systems.

Decentralization and Market Efficiency

Central to the economic prowess of DAOs is the principle of decentralization. Drawing insights from Friedrich Hayek's postulation on the role of decentralized information in markets, DAOs present a distinct advantage over traditional hierarchical entities.

Traditional centralized organizations often suffer from inefficiencies owing to informational bottlenecks. DAOs, however, capitalize on collective intelligence. Platforms such as Yearn.finance are testament to this phenomenon. By aggregating insights from a global user base, they can refine strategies, thereby promoting a more efficient market operation.

Looking ahead, the inherent decentralization of DAOs can redefine global economic structures. As more sectors embrace DAOs, markets could become more efficient, resilient, and inclusive. Furthermore, the universality of DAOs, functioning independent of geographic constraints, may pave the way for a borderless economic landscape.

Security and Integrity Through Smart Contracts

One of the foundational elements of DAOs is the utilization of blockchain technology and, by extension, smart contracts. These are self-executing contracts with the terms of the agreement being directly written into code.

Smart contracts ensure the integrity and functionality of DAOs. By automating processes and minimizing human intervention, they guarantee that predefined conditions are met before transactions are executed. This automation not only reduces operational friction but also enhances trust among members, given the transparent and tamper-proof nature of blockchain. As cyber threats become increasingly sophisticated, the immutable and secure nature of smart contracts could be the bulwark that defends DAOs. Moreover, as global commerce increasingly shifts online, the role of smart contracts in standardizing and securing international transactions will likely become indispensable.

Societal Implications of DAOs

In the intricate tapestry of human societies, the threads of collective cooperation, shared values, and power dynamics have played pivotal roles in shaping civilizational narratives. DAOs, emerging as the vanguard of technological and social convergence, hold the potential to not only reweave but also redefine these threads in novel and profound ways. Drawing upon foundational sociological theories, DAOs offer glimpses of a future where collective action transcends geographical boundaries, where decentralized ownership bolsters social capital, and where traditional power hierarchies are upended in favor of egalitarian networks. This section delves deep into the societal ramifications of DAOs, tracing their current impact and elucidating their transformative promise in sculpting the socio-cultural contours of tomorrow.

Evolution of Collective Governance

DAOs signify a paradigm shift in how we conceptualize and execute governance on a collective scale. Historically, hierarchical organizations—where power is concentrated at the top and decisions trickle down—have been the norm. DAOs, however, propose a more horizontal structure, leveraging the collective intelligence of its members.

Research in sociology has long discussed the potency of collective intelligence and wisdom. James Surowiecki's "The Wisdom of Crowds" provides an argument that large groups of people are often smarter than an elite few, especially when it comes to solving complex problems, fostering innovation, and coming to wise decisions.

Within a DAO, decision-making processes aren't limited to a board of directors or a CEO; instead, they become democratized, with each member having a say proportional to their stake or reputation within the organization. This can lead to decisions that better reflect the interests and values of the entire group, as opposed to a select few.

Empowerment of Marginalized Communities

DAOs could play a pivotal role in empowering marginalized communities. Traditional systems of governance and finance often exclude or hinder participation from those who don't fit the established norms or lack the necessary resources. By offering a decentralized model that doesn't rely on intermediaries or gatekeepers, DAOs offer a more inclusive platform for collaboration and value creation. The sociological concept of "social capital"—the networks, norms, and trust that enable participants to act together more effectively to pursue shared objectives—finds a practical application here. DAOs can function as tools to enhance social capital by connecting individuals and communities in cooperative endeavors, irrespective of their socio-economic background or geographical location.

Reconfiguring Trust Mechanisms

The idea of trust has been central to sociological debates, particularly in how societies establish and maintain it. DAOs introduce a shift from trust in people or institutions to trust in code and protocols. Smart contracts that power DAOs are transparent and immutable. This means that once rules are established, they can't be easily altered, ensuring that operations are executed as intended. This has a profound implication for societal trust mechanisms. While institutions and intermediaries might lose their monopoly over trust, DAOs promote a form of "algorithmic trust." While this does raise concerns about over-reliance on technology, it also paves the way for more transparent and accountable systems of governance and cooperation.

DAOs as the Future Of Collective Cooperation

The conceptual roots of DAOs resonate deeply with the sociological theories of collective action and cooperation. Decades before the advent of DAOs, sociologists had postulated the power of decentralized networks in enhancing group cohesion and mutual trust.

DAOs have the potential to redefine how individuals perceive and engage in collective action. They don't simply represent a novel approach to governance; they symbolize a societal shift where individuals globally can collaborate without intermediaries. This breaks the barriers of national boundaries and promotes a truly global cooperation. Take the example of the MolochDAO, dedicated to funding Ethereum projects. It showcases how passionate individuals can come together, pool resources, and make collective decisions for shared goals.

As societies become increasingly digitized and networked, the role of DAOs in fostering international collaborations can expand beyond technology projects to areas like global health, environment, and education. By doing so, DAOs can help in transcending parochial national interests for global good.

Enhancing Social Capital through Decentralized Ownership

Social capital, a concept popularized by sociologists like Pierre Bourdieu and Robert Putnam, speaks to the benefits derived from social networks and shared values. DAOs, by their very design, contribute to this notion. The democratic and transparent structure of DAOs ensures that each member has a stake and voice in decision-making. This engenders a sense of ownership and mutual trust. With platforms like DAOstack, even large groups can operate efficiently, ensuring that individual members feel their contribution is valued and their identity recognized. In a world where organizational alienation is often a concern, DAOs can become a beacon of participatory governance, fostering deeper trust and collaboration. They might also help in combating the decline of communal values in urban settings, providing a digital platform for community engagement.

Legal Implications of DAOs

As the digital frontier expands, integrating advanced decentralized systems like DAOs, it inevitably collides with the established bulwarks of legal conventions and frameworks. These traditions, built over centuries, find themselves grappling with the fluid, borderless, and highly autonomous nature of DAOs. From the intricacies of jurisdictional challenges to the transformative promise and potential pitfalls of smart contracts, the legal landscape faces a profound need for introspection and evolution. Simultaneously, as we stand on the precipice of this legal paradigm shift, there emerges a synergy between the old and new, manifested in innovative concepts like Decentralized Liability Entities (DLEs). This section will navigate the multifaceted legal intricacies of DAOs, dissecting current challenges and forecasting the legal metamorphosis on the horizon.

Legal Status and Recognition

Historically, legal systems have evolved around the premise of centralized entities and individuals. Within these frameworks, corporations, partnerships, and other organizational structures have clear legal definitions and responsibilities. DAOs, being decentralized and operating autonomously via smart contracts, challenge these traditional legal norms.

One of the critical debates surrounding DAOs is their legal classification. Are they akin to partnerships, where all members share liabilities? Or should they be seen as corporations with distinct legal personalities? The Wyoming DAO law, for instance, took an innovative step by recognizing DAOs as a new form of limited liability companies (LLCs), termed Decentralized Autonomous Organizations LLCs (DAO LLCs). Such recognitions pave the way for DAOs to interact with traditional systems, especially in matters of contractual obligations and dispute resolutions. An inherent trait of DAOs is the absence of a central authority. While this fosters autonomy and decentralization, it raises concerns about accountability and liability. If a DAO's operation harms an individual or another entity, who is held responsible? The emergence of Decentralized Liability Entities (DLEs) is a significant stride towards addressing this concern. DLEs propose a fusion of traditional corporate liability norms with the decentralized ethos of DAOs. By doing so, they aim to provide clearer paths for redress and dispute resolution while maintaining the decentralized and autonomous operations of DAOs.

The Evolution of Contract Law With Smart Contracts

Traditional contract law operates on the principles of mutual assent, offer, acceptance, and consideration. With DAOs, smart contracts—self-executing contracts with the agreement directly written into code—challenge these principles.Smart contracts, the backbone of many DAOs, automate the execution of an agreement, ensuring it's carried out to the letter. This reduces the ambiguity inherent in traditional contract interpretation. However, issues arise when there are bugs in the code or unintended consequences, as seen in the DAO hack of 2016. There might be a shift towards a hybrid model of contracts in the future, combining traditional legal language with coded provisions. Legal professionals may need to acquire skills in blockchain and coding, and there could be an emergence of a new niche: smart contract auditing.

Liability and Governance in Decentralized Entities

One of the cornerstones of modern corporate law is the concept of limited liability, which protects individuals behind corporations. In the context of DAOs, which lack a centralized governance structure, questions arise about liability in cases of malfeasance or negligence. Who bears responsibility in a DAO? Without a central governing body or clearly identified leaders, it's challenging to pinpoint liability. If a DAO's actions or its smart contract negatively impacts individuals or other entities, the pathway for recourse remains ambiguous.

There's potential for innovative legal structures that merge aspects of traditional corporate entities with DAO features. One such example could be the creation of "Decentralized Liability Entities" (DLEs) which provide clearer frameworks for accountability while retaining the decentralized ethos of DAOs.

Decentralized Liability Entities (DLEs): A New Paradigm in Organizational Structures

As the decentralized digital landscape burgeons, the challenge remains: how do we reconcile the borderless and autonomous nature of Decentralized Autonomous Organizations (DAOs) with established legal frameworks? Enter Decentralized Liability Entities (DLEs) – a proposal that seeks to bridge traditional and decentralized entities. DLEs emerged from the recognized need to provide a legal foundation for DAOs. Traditional organizations possess identifiable jurisdictions and regulations, ensuring protections for stakeholders and providing avenues for conflict resolution. DAOs, by their nature, defy these conventions, operating in a digital, decentralized manner with no fixed jurisdiction or governing law. DLEs, thus, represent an attempt to hybridize these two models.

Distinctive Features of DLEs:

Legal Recognition and Jurisdictional Flexibility: DLEs aim for compatibility with traditional legal frameworks, without compromising the decentralized ethos. This means they would be registered and recognized under a particular jurisdiction but would maintain operations decentralized across borders.

Accountability Protocols: The decentralized and anonymous nature of DAOs presents accountability challenges. DLEs propose systems like reputation metrics and collateral deposits to ensure participant responsibility and provide mechanisms for addressing malfeasance.

Smart Contract Integration: Smart contracts serve as the backbone of DLE operations. These programmable contracts help automate decision-making processes, ensuring consistency and reducing administrative overhead.

The Broader Implications:

Towards a Global Business Environment: With DLEs, businesses could potentially operate in a truly global manner, enjoying both the flexibility of decentralized operations and the stability of legal recognition.

Dispute Resolution in the Digital Age: By providing clear frameworks for accountability and jurisdiction, DLEs could revolutionize how contractual disputes are handled in the increasingly digital business environment.

Anticipated Challenges and Criticisms:

Uniformity vs. Diversity: While the goal is to establish a universally adaptable DLE structure, the diversity of legal systems worldwide might require unique configurations, potentially complicating widespread adoption. Balancing the open nature of DAOs with the regulated structure of DLEs may raise concerns. Critics might argue that too much regulation could stifle innovation, while too little could lead to misuse and fraud.

DLEs are more than just a conceptual exercise. They represent the evolving face of organizational structures in a digital age, reflecting the need to innovate while ensuring accountability. As they transition from theory to practice, DLEs could pave the way for a new era of global, decentralized business practices.

LIMITATIONS AND CONTRIBUTIONS

Limitations

While this chapter endeavors to provide a comprehensive examination of smart contracts and their role in the formation and operation of Decentralized Autonomous Organizations (DAOs), there are some limitations that readers should be cognizant of:

Scope of Research: The chapter primarily focuses on the foundational principles and functional aspects of DAOs and smart contracts, with less emphasis on the in-depth technical intricacies of blockchain technologies.

Dynamic Landscape: The world of blockchain and DAOs is rapidly evolving. Although the chapter captures the state of affairs up to the current year, advancements post-publication might introduce new aspects not covered herein.

Diversity of DAOs: While some prominent examples of DAOs are explored, the sheer diversity and multitude of DAOs in existence mean that not all specific use cases or models are addressed in detail.

Legal and Regulatory Frameworks: The chapter briefly touches upon the regulatory challenges surrounding DAOs. However, legal frameworks differ globally, and a comprehensive analysis of each jurisdiction's stance on DAOs is beyond the scope of this work.

Contributions

This chapter brings forth several notable contributions to the literature on blockchain technology and its societal implications:

Holistic Overview: By intertwining the history, functionality, and implications of smart contracts and DAOs, the chapter provides readers with a holistic perspective, filling a gap in the existing literature that often segregates these interconnected domains.

Real-World Applicability: Through the exploration of real-world examples, the chapter transcends mere theoretical discussions, offering readers insights into the practical applications and challenges of DAOs.

Societal Implications: Going beyond the technical and operational aspects, the chapter delves into the broader societal implications of DAOs, sparking critical discourse on how these decentralized structures can reshape governance, economy, and societal cooperation in the digital age.

Foundation for Further Research: By presenting both the opportunities and challenges of DAOs and smart contracts, the chapter serves as a foundational reference for researchers, policymakers, and enthusiasts seeking to further delve into the complexities of decentralized organizational structures.

SUMMARY

This research delves into the multifaceted relationship between smart contracts and Decentralized Autonomous Organizations (DAOs), unveiling the complex interplay of technological, legal, economic, and sociological dimensions they encompass. Rooted deeply in blockchain technology, DAOs' transformative potential derives significantly from smart contracts—immutable, self-executing digital agreements that form the bedrock of DAO operations.

Smart contracts' adaptability underpins the diverse incarnations of DAOs, facilitating a broad spectrum of functionalities across myriad sectors. Such versatility not only establishes DAOs as formidable entities but accentuates the need to interpret them as confluences of interrelated domains, rather than isolated phenomena. This intricate mesh of technology, law, economics, and sociology calls for a holistic approach, emphasizing the intrinsic relationship between DAOs' opportunities and challenges and the attributes of smart contracts.

While smart contracts introduce unprecedented efficiency by negating intermediaries, they also bring forth challenges—predominantly stemming from the 'code is law' tenet, which could engender issues surrounding error rectification and dispute resolution. Legal considerations, hence, become paramount. Existing legal architectures, tailored for centralized entities, face the arduous task of adapting to the decentralized ethos of DAOs. Crafting regulations that resonate with DAOs' principles of decentralization and autonomy, without inhibiting their innovative potential, is a daunting yet essential endeavor.

As DAOs burgeon, propelled by the sturdy foundation of smart contracts, there's an imperative for a comprehensive grasp of this technological marvel. Representing both an uncharted territory and an immense responsibility, DAOs epitomize human ingenuity's quest for a decentralized, just, and collaborative future. Navigating this technological renaissance, it's pivotal to acknowledge the potency of DAOs and smart contracts and judiciously harness them, ensuring they align with society's greater good.

REFERENCES

Al-Bassam, M., Sonnino, A., & Bano, S. (2019). Fraud Proofs: Maximising Light Client Security and Scaling Blockchains with Dishonest Majorities. arXiv preprint arXiv:1809.09044.

Amsden, R., & Schweizer, D. (2021). Are blockchain crowdfunds the future of finance? Initial coin offerings (ICOs) as an alternative financing method. *European Journal of Finance*, 1–25.

Azouvi, S., Maller, M., & Meiklejohn, S. (2020). Egalitarian Society or Benevolent Dictatorship: The State of Cryptocurrency Governance. In *International Conference on Financial Cryptography and Data Security* (pp. 127-146). Springer, Cham.

Aztori, M. (2015). Blockchain technology and decentralized governance: Is the state still necessary? SSRN Electronic Journal.

Beck, A. R., Avital, M., Rossi, M., & Thatcher, J. B. (2017). Blockchain technology in business and information systems research. *Business & Information Systems Engineering*, *59*(6), 381–384. doi:10.100712599-017-0505-1

Beck, R., Avital, M., Rossi, M., & Thatcher, J. B. (2018). Blockchain technology in business and information systems research. *Business & Information Systems Engineering*, *59*(6), 381–384. doi:10.100712599-017-0505-1

Beck, R., Czepluch, J. S., Lollike, N., & Malone, S. (2016). Blockchain-the gateway to trust-free cryptographic transactions. In ECIS.

Buccafurri, L. N. (2023). Blockchain-based Metaverses: Challenges and Opportunities. *Frontiers in Blockchain*.

Buterin, V. (2014). A Next-Generation Smart Contract and Decentralized Application Platform. *Ethereum*. https://ethereum.org/en/whitepaper/

Buterin, V. (2014). DAOs, DACs, DAs and More: An Incomplete Terminology Guide. *Ethereum Blog*. Vitalik. https://vitalik.ca/general/2019/04/03/collusion.html

Buterin, V., & Griffith, V. (2017). Casper the Friendly Finality Gadget.

Catalini, C., & Gans, J. S. (2021). The Tokenization of Assets and Blockchain Technology. *The University of Chicago Law Review. University of Chicago. Law School*, *88*(4), 1569–1604.

Chainlink. (2020). *What is the Oracle Problem?* Chainlink. https://chain.link/blog/what-is-the-oracle-problem.

Chen, Z., Xu, Y., & Lim, E. T. (2018). Towards decentralised governance: Blockchain and the question of technology-based power. *Information Systems Frontiers*, *22*(3), 501–515.

Christidis, K., & Devetsikiotis, M. (2016). Blockchains and Smart Contracts for the Internet of Things. *IEEE Access: Practical Innovations, Open Solutions*, *4*, 2292–2303. doi:10.1109/ACCESS.2016.2566339

Cong, L. W., Li, Y., & Wang, N. (2020). Tokenomics: Dynamic Adoption and Valuation. *Review of Financial Studies*, *34*(5), 2258–2300.

Croman, K., Decker, C., Eyal, I., Gencer, A. E., Juels, A., Kosba, A., & Wattenhofer, R. (2016). On scaling decentralized blockchains. In *International Conference on Financial Cryptography and Data Security* (pp. 106-125). Springer, Berlin, Heidelberg.

Daian, P., Goldfeder, S., Kell, T., Li, Y., Zhao, X., Bentov, I., Breidenbach, L., & Juels, A. (2020). Flash Boys 2.0: Frontrunning, Transaction Reordering, and Consensus Instability in Decentralized Exchanges. *IEEE Symposium on Security and Privacy*. IEEE.

DappRadar. (2023). *All Dapp rankings*. Dappar Radar. https://dappradar.com/rankings

De Filippi, L. (2016). *The invisible politics of Bitcoin: governance crisis of a decentralized infrastructure*. Internet Policy Review.

De Filippi, W. (2018). *Blockchain and the Law: The Rule of Code*. Harvard University Press.

DeFi Pulse. (2023). *Total Value Locked in DeFi*. DeFi Pulse. https://defipulse.com/

DuPont, Q. (2017). Experiments in algorithmic governance: A history and ethnography of "The DAO," a failed Decentralized Autonomous Organization. In Bitcoin and Beyond (pp. 157-177). Routledge.

Elliptic. (2020). *The Importance of Oracles in DeFi*. Elliptic. https://www.elliptic.co/blog/the-importance-of-oracles-in-defi

Elliptic. (2020). *The Oracle Problem: How Can Smart Contracts Reach Out to the Real World?* Elliptic. https://www.elliptic.co/blog/the-oracle-problem-how-can-smart-contracts-reach-out-to-the-real-world

Ethereum Foundation. (2020). *Ethereum 2.0 Overview*. Ethereum Foundation.

German Federal Government. (2020). Blockchain Strategy of the German Federal Government.

Hacker. (2018). *Smart contracts: A smart way to automate performance*. Georgia Law Review.

Harz, D., Gudgeon, L., Gervais, A., & Knottenbelt, W. (2020). Balance: Dynamic Adjustment of Cryptocurrency Deposits. *Workshop on Trusted Smart Contracts*.

Hofmann, S. B. (2019). Digital supply chain management agenda for the automotive supplier industry. *Journal of Business Logistics*.

Hsiao, J., Chung, T. M., & Liang, C. (2021). On design issues and architectural styles for blockchain-driven IoT services. *Computers & Electrical Engineering*, *87*, 106781.

Huckle, S., Bhattacharya, R., White, M., & Beloff, N. (2016). Internet of things, blockchain and shared economy applications. *Procedia Computer Science*, *98*, 461–466. doi:10.1016/j.procs.2016.09.074

Ilul, J., & Pace, G. J. (2020). The Blockchain 2.0 Factor in The Internet of Things. *IEEE Consumer Electronics Magazine*, *9*(4), 35–40.

Knottenbelt, Z. & [Second Author Needed]. (2019). XCLAIM: Trustless, Interoperable Cryptocurrency-Backed Assets. *IEEE Symposium on Security and Privacy*. IEEE.

Kuo, T. T., Kim, H. E., & Ohno-Machado, L. (2017). Blockchain distributed ledger technologies for biomedical and health care applications. *Journal of the American Medical Informatics Association : JAMIA, 24*(6), 1211–1220. doi:10.1093/jamia/ocx068 PMID:29016974

Lessig, L. (1999). *Code and Other Laws of Cyberspace*. Basic Books.

Long, C. (2021). *Wyoming's DAO law: What it means and how it came to be*. CoinDesk.

Lucking, L. (2020). *Decentraland: A virtual world owned by its users*. TechCrunch.

Luu, L., Chu, D. H., Olickel, H., Saxena, P., & Hobor, A. (2016). Making smart contracts smarter. In *Proceedings of the 2016 ACM SIGSAC Conference on Computer and Communications Security* (pp. 254-269). ACM. 10.1145/2976749.2978309

Marx, D., & Chli, M. (2018). *On the Security of Oracles for Smart Contracts*. In *UK Workshop on Cyber Security (UKWCS)*. UK.

MiCA. (2023). *Regulation of The European Parliament and of The Council on Markets in Crypto-assets, and amending Directive (EU) 2019/1937*. European Commission.

Mougayar, W. (2016). *The Business Blockchain: Promise, Practice, and Application of the Next Internet Technology*. John Wiley & Sons.

Nakamoto, S. (2008). *Bitcoin: A Peer-to-Peer Electronic Cash System*.

Norta, A. (2015). Creation of smart-contracting collaborations for decentralized autonomous organizations. In *International Conference on Business Informatics Research* (pp. 3-17). Springer, Cham. 10.1007/978-3-319-21915-8_1

O'Dwyer, R. (2017). The Revolution Will (Not) Be Decentralized: Blockchains. In *Proceedings of the 8th International Conference on Social Media & Society* (pp. 1-5). ACM.

Othman, A. (2020). The Application of Decentralized Autonomous Organizations for Sustainable Management and Operations: A Case Study Approach. *International Journal of Advanced Computer Science and Applications, 11*(5).

Popov, S. (2016). *The Tangle*. IOTA Whitepaper. https://assets.ctfassets.net/r1dr6vzfxhev/2t4uxvsIqk0 EUau6g2sw0g/45eae33637ca92f85dd9f4a3a218e1ec/iota1_4_3.pdf

Poskitt, Z. (2019). Annotated bibliography: Decentralized autonomous organization. SSRN Electronic Journal.

Raskin, M. (2017). The Law and Legality of Smart Contracts. *Georgetown Law Technology Review, 1*(2).

Schär, F. (2021). Decentralized Finance: On Blockchain-and Smart Contract-Based Financial Markets. *Review - Federal Reserve Bank of St. Louis, 103*(1), 153–176.

Schmid, J. J., & Amsler, T. (2021). The Emergence of Local Government Blockchain Applications: A Swiss Case Study. In *Handbook of Blockchain and Sustainable Finance* (pp. 267–280). Springer.

Scholz, T. (2016). *Platform cooperativism. Challenging the corporate sharing economy. Rosa Luxemburg Stiftung*. New York Office.

Schweizer, D., Amsden, R., & Morkunas, V. J. (2021). A Blockchain Perspective on Process Inefficiencies in the Life Cycle of a Corporate Bond. *Journal of Alternative Investments*, *23*(4), 9–24.

Siegel, D. (2016). *Understanding The DAO Attack*. CoinDesk.

Statista. (2022). Total Value of Blockchain Transactions Worldwide from 2017 to 2021. Statista. https://www.statista.com/statistics/647231/worldwide-blockchain-transactions/

Swan, M. (2015). *Blockchain: Blueprint for a New Economy*. O'Reilly Media, Inc.

Szabo, N. (1996). Smart contracts: Building blocks for digital markets. EXTROPY. *The Journal of Transhumanist Thought*, *16*, 18–26.

Tapscott, D., & Tapscott, A. (2016). *Blockchain revolution: how the technology behind bitcoin is changing money, business, and the world*. Penguin.

Tapscott, [First Name Needed]. (2020). Financial services: Building blockchain one block at a time. *Financial Times*.

Teutsch, J., & Masmej, A. (2021). *Oracles: The State of the Art and Future Directions*. Chainlink. Retrieved from https://research.chain.link/whitepaper-v2.pdf.

Werbach, K. (2018). *The Blockchain and the New Architecture of Trust*. MIT Press. doi:10.7551/mitpress/11449.001.0001

Werbach, K., & Cornell, N. (2017). Contracts Ex Machina. *Duke Law Journal*, *67*(2), 313–382.

Wood, G. (2014). Ethereum: A secure decentralised generalised transaction ledger. *Ethereum project yellow paper*, 151, 1-32.

WrightA.De FilippiP. (2015). Decentralized Blockchain Technology and the Rise of Lex Cryptographia. Available at SSRN 2580664. doi:10.2139/ssrn.2580664

Yaga, D., Mell, P., Roby, N., & Scarfone, K. (2019). Blockchain technology overview. arXiv preprint arXiv:1906.11078.

Zamfir, V., Rush, A., & Asgaonkar, A. (2020). *Ethereum 2.0: A Complete Guide [Complete Source Needed]*. Ethereum.

Zamyatin, A., Harz, D., Lind, J., Panayiotou, P., Gervais, A., & Knottenbelt, W. J. (2019). XCLAIM: Trustless, *Interoperable Cryptocurrency-Backed Assets. IEEE Symposium on Security and Privacy (SP)*, (pp. 193-210). IEEE.

Zetzsche, B. A. (2018). The ICO Gold Rush: It's a Scam, It's a Bubble, It's a Super Challenge for Regulators. *University of Luxembourg Law Working Paper*.

Zetzsche, D. A., Buckley, R. P., Arner, D. W., & Föhr, L. (2018). The ICO Gold Rush: It's a Scam, It's a Bubble, It's a Super Challenge for Regulators. *University of Luxembourg Law Working Paper No. 11/2017*.

Zhang, K., & Poskitt, C. J. (2019). Annotated bibliography: Decentralized autonomous organization. SSRN Electronic Journal.

Zhang, Y., Wen, J., & Qian, Y. (2020). DeFi: Blockchain and the rise of decentralized financial market. *Frontiers of Computer Science*, *15*, 1–24.

Zheng, Z., Xie, S., Dai, H., Chen, X., & Wang, H. (2018). An overview of blockchain technology: Architecture, consensus, and future trends. In *2018 IEEE International Congress on Big Data (BigData Congress)* (pp. 557-564). IEEE.

Zupan, M. (2020). *Moloch DAO: a new era of collaboration*. Cryptonews.

Zyskind, G., Nathan, O., & Pentland, A. S. (2015, June). Decentralizing privacy: Using blockchain to protect personal data. In *Proceedings of the 2015 IEEE Security and Privacy Workshops* (pp. 180-184). IEEE. 10.1109/SPW.2015.27

ENDNOTE

[1]   Boolean means a binary variable, having two possible values called "true" and "false."

Chapter 9
Web 3 and the Future of Work:
From Gig Economy to DAOs

Airi Helen Schnauder

ⓘ https://orcid.org/0009-0006-6664-9381

Frankfurt School of Finance and Management, Germany

ABSTRACT

The landscape of work is undergoing significant changes, and the advent of Web 3 technologies is poised to accelerate this transformation. The gig economy, which emphasizes short-term contracts and freelance work, has been subject to criticism for its lack of job security, limited worker protections, and heightened competition. However, the emergence of Web 3 technologies and decentralized autonomous organizations (DAOs) offers a potential solution to these problems, by providing greater worker autonomy, transparency, and democratic decision-making. DAOs can help to give workers greater control over their working environment, as well as offering them greater job security. These technologies can also create new opportunities for workers to work remotely and receive payment more quickly than traditional methods. This chapter aims to examine the potential opportunities and obstacles presented by Web 3 and DAOs for the future of work.

INTRODUCTION

The area of law is being disrupted by the Fourth Industrial Revolution, or Industry 4.0, as indicated by the presence of controversies around data ownership and privacy, legal responsibility for Artificial Intelligence (AI), and litigation surrounding the classification of gig economy workers. The individual in question might be classified as either an independent contractor or an employee. (Sulkowski, 2019, p. 1) The founder of the World Economic Forum, Klaus Schwab, has expressed criticism towards the area of law, asserting that it is entrenched within the epoch of the Second Industrial Revolution. In light of the quick and extensive effects of the Fourth Industrial Revolution, lawmakers and regulatory bodies are facing an unprecedented level of difficulty, sometimes unable to effectively respond. (Schwab, 2016)

DOI: 10.4018/978-1-6684-9919-1.ch009

Copyright © 2023, IGI Global. Copying or distributing in print or electronic forms without written permission of IGI Global is prohibited.

This chapter presents food for thought to engage in action, so promoting the pursuit of more inquiry and investigation. Policy-making should strive to at least align with, if not preempt and proactively prepare for, emerging developments becoming reality. This chapter is an integral component of a broader discourse that is the emergence of fresh legal controversies leads to an inevitable process of evolution.

This chapter's opening segment will describe the gig economy and its limitations, examining both the advantages and disadvantages of this model for workers and employers. Critiques of the gig economy, including issues such as exploitation, job insecurity, and limited worker protections, will be explored. Recent developments in the utilization of DAOs have increased the need to introduce the concept of DAOs and analyze the characteristics of this organizational model. The emergence of decentralized autonomous organizations and Web 3 technologies is a major development for the future of work. These technologies offer increased worker autonomy, transparency and democratic decision-making, providing a potential solution to the issues that the traditional labor market has.The benefits and drawbacks of DAOs for workers and employers will be evaluated. (Nabben, 2023)

In the last few years, there has been increasing interest in the transition from the gig economy to DAOs, including the driving forces behind this shift and its potential impact on the overall workforce. The differences between centralized control in the gig economy and decentralized control in DAOs will be scrutinized, and the potential advantages and disadvantages of this change will be explored. Another part will be the assessment of challenges and opportunities of implementing DAOs, including governance and decision-making challenges, regulatory hurdles and the effect on the workforce. (Brummer & Seira, 2022)

A comparison between Web 3 and traditional centralized work models will be conducted, emphasizing the potential benefits of Web 3 for workers. It will examine how Web 3 can affect workers' rights and protections, including potential challenges for workers in the DAO model. DAOs can create an environment in which workers have increased autonomy over their work, as well as improved job security. This could lead to a shift in the labor market, in which workers are empowered to make decisions about their own career paths and are less dependent on the traditional employer-employee relationship. Web 3 technologies have the potential to provide improved access to digital services and resources. This could lead to greater access to jobs, as well as the ability to easily find and apply for jobs. Furthermore, these technologies could provide access to financial services that are not available through traditional banking, potentially eliminating the need for workers to rely on difficult and expensive traditional banking services. (Filipčić, 2022, p. 1278)

The conclusion summarizes the key points covered in the chapter, including the ramifications of the shift to DAOs for the future of work. The potential of Web 3 to transform the work landscape will be assessed, highlighting the potential for increased worker autonomy, transparency, and democratic decision-making. (Atherton, Bratanova & Markey-Towler, 2020)

THE GIG ECONOMY AND ITS CRITICISMS

In recent years, the gig economy has gained prominence as a new way of working, offering flexibility and convenience for both workers and employers. The gig economy is rapidly expanding, leading to significant changes in work relations and human resource management (HRM) for a large number of workers. (Brewster, Dowling & Holland, 2022, p. 63)

In the sharing economy with the promotion of the gig economy, where the company's function could be fulfilled by an open community of platform entrepreneurs, they would be responsible for network maintenance. A set of smart contracts would define the governance and distribution of token interests on the platform. This example demonstrates how blockchain systems can decentralize and evolve the existing system. (Rocas-Royo, 2019, p. 220).

Because of developments in technology over the last decade, these services may now be available not just in the local marketplace, but also in the worldwide marketplace, a workplace of freelancing issues in a gig economy. The term "gig economy" is defined as the end of the job and the future of work and also indicates that labor protection and employment regulation are not automatically enforced. (Green, McCann, Vu, Lopez & Ouattara, 2018, p. 282)

In the United Kingdom, the number of people engaged in gig work on a platform has tripled in just 6 years, from 2.3 million in 2016 to 7.25 million in 2022. However, empirical research has difficulty keeping up with this rapid growth and the complex implications it brings for workers and HRM. (Fennell, 2022) This lack of research has resulted in limited understanding of the working conditions faced by gig workers and the ethical concerns related to their treatment and HRM practices. (Rubery & Johnson, 2018, p. 408) The current literature highlights the need for further investigation to address these critical issues. (Sundararajan, 2016, p. 35)

As this model has evolved, its limitations have become increasingly apparent. Exploitation, job insecurity, and limited worker protections have raised concerns about the sustainability and fairness of the gig economy. (Naughtin, Hajkowicz, Schleiger, Bratanova, Cameron, Zamin, & Dutta, 2022, p. 31) In response to these challenges, the emergence of decentralized autonomous organizations (DAOs) and Web 3 technologies has ushered in a new era. This chapter delves into the disadvantages of the gig economy and explores how DAOs offer potential solutions to these issues.

The gig economy has garnered praise for its advantages, such as providing individuals with the freedom to work on their own terms. Workers can choose when and where they work, allowing for a flexible work-life balance. This model has also created opportunities for income generation by leveraging underutilized assets or skills. Gig workers can monetize their time and resources, tapping into a wide range of platforms and services in the sharing economy. (Sundararajan, 2016, p. 25)

These advantages come at a cost as exploitation is a critical concern within the gig economy. Many gig workers lack the benefits and protections traditionally associated with employment. They often face challenges in accessing health insurance, retirement plans, and paid leave. As independent contractors, they are excluded from essential worker protections, such as minimum wage guarantees, protection against unfair termination, and the right to unionize. This vulnerability exposes gig workers to potential exploitation by employers, who may exploit their lack of legal protections and bargaining power. (Nabben, Puspasari, Kelleher, Sanjay, 2021)

Job insecurity is another significant disadvantage of the gig economy. Gig workers face unpredictable work opportunities and income fluctuations. They navigate an uncertain landscape, with no guarantees of stable employment or career progression. Without a safety net or employer-provided benefits, they bear the full burden of financial instability during periods of illness, injury, or economic downturns. This lack of stability hinders their ability to plan for the future and achieve long-term financial security.

Additionally, the gig economy perpetuates a lack of social cohesion and collective bargaining power among workers. With no centralized representation or formal channels for negotiation, gig workers find it challenging to advocate for their rights and improve their working conditions. The fragmented nature of gig work and the absence of collective action diminish their ability to address systemic issues and negotiate fairer terms with platform operators. One analysis from 2023 highlights the influence of ownership structures on sharing within gig firms. It reveals that gig economies relying on investor ownership exhibit a greater degree of sharing with investors, but also tend to exploit workers. On the other hand, platforms based on collaborative ownership foster more equitable peer-to-peer sharing, leading to improved work relations and human resource management. Ultimately, these findings underscore the impact of ownership structures on the nature of sharing and its consequences in the gig economy. (Le Brocq, Hughes & Donnelly, 2023)

In response to the limitations of the gig economy, the emergence of DAOs and Web 3 technologies presents a transformative alternative.

DECENTRALIZED AUTONOMOUS ORGANIZATIONS (DAOS)

Decentralized autonomous organizations (DAOs) are a new organizational model that leverages blockchain technology to enable decentralized decision-making and governance. DAOs are typically governed by smart contracts that execute pre-determined rules and processes, eliminating the need for central authorities or intermediaries. This section will provide a detailed explanation of DAOs, including their advantages and disadvantages for workers and employers. The inherent autonomy and code-based control mechanisms of DAOs make them an ideal fit for decentralized applications, especially those in the DeFi space that involve the management and processing of digital assets. Additionally, DAOs offer significant advantages for coordinating groups of individuals, such as networks of collectors or donors seeking to raise funds for charitable causes, due to their efficiency and flexibility. These attributes are increasingly recognized as critical, regardless of the specific use case. (Mienert, 2022, p. 34)

Figure 1. Traditional organization versus DAOs
(Adapted from Schecter, 2021)

	Traditional Organization	**DAO**
Decision making	Centralized	Collective
Ownership	Permissioned	Permissionless
Structure	Hierarchical	Flat / distributed
Information Flows	Private and gated	Transparent and public
IP	Closed-source	Open-source

Vitalik Buterin first framed new forms of organization and autonomy in the Ethereum white paper and defined DAOs as a "virtual entity that has a certain set of members or shareholders which have the right to spend the entity's funds and modify its code". (Buterin, 2014a) DAOs were first thought of as a new form of corporate governance that utilize tokenized tradable shares to provide dividends to shareholders. These businesses were described as "incorruptible," with no human involvement and publicly auditable bylaws delivered as open-source software across their stakeholders' computers. Anyone can be a stakeholder in a DAO by purchasing stock or receiving it as payment for services rendered, according to this definition. As a result, DAO stockholders are qualified for a part of profits, growth participation and a voting right in how the company is managed. (Hassan & De Filippi, 2021, p. 2)

A team of Ethereum developers started in 2016 a project called "TheDAO" which famously failed technically due to an error in the code. (Glatz, 2023) There are multiple types of DAOs e.g. investment (theLAO), social (Radicle), collector, media, service or protocol DAOs, such as Uniswap, Compound, MakerDAO or Gitcoin. (Filipčić, 2022, p. 1282) For the many variations of DAOs and the question which governance infrastructure is to be applied, please also note relevant chapters in this book about DAOs.

Figure 2. Breakdown of types of DAOs based on technology and deployment type
(Adapted from Rikken, Janssen & Kwee, 2023, p. 7)

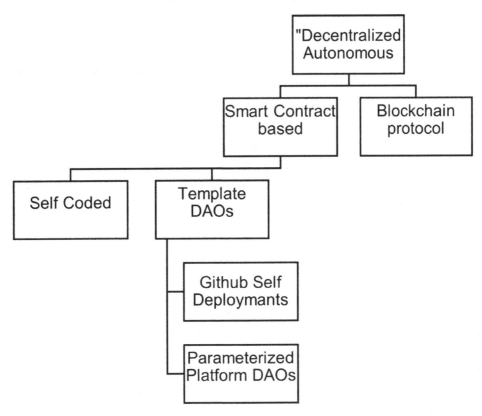

The potential use cases of DAOs are numerous. To accurately evaluate DAOs and their taxonomy, it is crucial to distinguish between DAO categories. However, classifying DAOs is difficult. All DAOs operate on the basis of digital assets, which may be desirable for their monetary value, but not all DAOs are designed to make money; some are even intended to give it away. (World Economic Forum, 2022, p. 13) Technically there are self-coded or platform-based DAOs. (Faqir-Rhazoui, Arroyo & Hassan, 2020, p. 4; Rikken, Heukelom-Verhage, Naves & Terpoorten, 2018) The Dash project team suggested that blockchains can be viewed as DAOs as such themselves. As blockchain is the platform on which DAOs are built, this would not result in any distinguishing characteristics.

DAOs are organizations that operate through rules encoded as computer programs on a blockchain. They are decentralized, meaning that they don't rely on a central authority to make decisions or manage resources. Instead, decisions are made collectively by the members, who can vote and influence the organization's direction through a transparent and democratic process. This innovative approach to organizational management has the potential to revolutionize the gig economy and traditional employment models. (Pries & Quakernack, 2023, p. 83)

- Decentralization: DAOs are built on blockchain technology, removing the need for a central authority to make decisions or manage resources.
- Democratized decision-making: Members of a DAO can vote on proposals and collectively decide the organization's direction.
- Transparency: All transactions and decisions within a DAO are recorded on a public blockchain, ensuring full transparency and accountability.
- Smart contracts: DAOs utilize smart contracts to automate processes, enforce rules, and manage resources.
- Token-based governance: DAO members often use tokens to represent their stake in the organization, giving them voting power and a share of profits.

DAOs make other assumptions than traditional corporations, legal entities or industry associations. They are governed by democratic or strongly participatory procedures or algorithms, alternately to boards or managers. They aim to have a global reach, bringing together thousands or even hundreds of thousands of members from diverse backgrounds. DAOs often avoid written agreements or other legal formalities, preferring to govern their affairs using software and the rule of code. (Wright, 2021, p. 2)

THE SHIFT FROM THE GIG ECONOMY TO DAOS

One could argue that DAOs (Decentralized Autonomous Organizations) represent the next stage in the development of human organizational systems, offering a fresh perspective on how we perceive work. By dismantling the hierarchical nature of conventional corporate setups and empowering participants with complete responsibility, DAOs introduce innovative means to engage and apply individual skills for the benefit of the overall ecosystem. If you have a strong belief in a particular concept, a DAO could serve as the ideal platform to launch your endeavors. (Nabben, 2022, p. 74)

One of the most significant benefits of DAOs for gig workers is the increased autonomy and control they can have over their work conditions. Since DAOs are inherently decentralized, gig workers can participate in decision-making processes and have a say in project development, resource allocation, and other critical aspects of their work. DAOs operate on a global scale, allowing gig workers to access opportunities from around the world without the need for intermediaries or geographic limitations. This expanded access can help gig workers find projects that align with their skills, interests, and values, as well as expose them to diverse perspectives and experiences. Traditional gig workers often face income instability and a lack of long-term financial benefits. DAOs have the potential to change this by offering profit-sharing and token-based incentives. Gig workers who contribute to the success of a DAO may receive tokens that represent a stake in the organization, granting them a share of future profits and a sense of ownership. This model could provide gig workers with more stable income streams and long-term financial benefits, fostering a greater sense of financial security and well-being. Although gig platform-based work shares certain similarities, such as for example feedback processes, there is significant difference across platforms and workers. Therefore, it is essential to exercise caution when applying theories of work and workers behavior to the gig economy. (Kuhn & Galloway, 2019, p. 189).

Transparency is a core principle of DAOs, as transactions and decision-making processes are recorded on a public blockchain. This level of transparency can benefit gig workers by providing clear information about their earnings, work expectations, and performance metrics. Additionally, the community-driven nature of DAOs encourages collaboration and knowledge-sharing among gig workers, fostering a supportive environment where individuals can learn from one another and work together to achieve common goals. Higher education certificates can be stored on blockchain zero-knowledge EVM (Ethereum virtual machine) in a cost sensitive and non-bureaucratic manner. (Fekete & Kiss, 2023, p. 189)

Although DAOs aim to democratize decision-making and empower individuals, they can still be susceptible to exploitation and power imbalances. For example, a small group of token holders with significant influence may make decisions that disproportionately benefit themselves, at the expense of other gig workers. Additionally, gig workers who lack the technical skills or resources to participate in DAO governance may find themselves marginalized and excluded from decision-making processes. Employers have the capability to utilize algorithmic systems of dominance in order to control a more flexible work force. (Muldoon & Raekstad, 2022, p. 17)

The DAO ecosystem relies heavily on technology, which can exacerbate existing digital divides and create new barriers for gig workers. Those who lack access to the necessary tools, infrastructure, or education may find it difficult to participate in DAOs and take advantage of the opportunities they offer. Furthermore, the rapidly evolving nature of blockchain technology and smart contracts may require gig workers to continually update their skills, which can be both time-consuming and costly. The growth of the DAO gig economy has the potential to significantly reshape traditional employment models. After its creation, a DAO has the potential to draw in additional investors in order to expand its operations in networks with other DAOs. (Mehdi, Sbai, Mazlin & Azghiou, 2022, p. 2)

Figure 3. DAO activation to networks
(Adapted from Stroh, 2023)

As technology progresses, we are embarking on a journey, to create a collaborative environment focused on taking action and enabling seamless connections with other DAOs. This interconnectedness gives rise to expansive ecosystems where autonomous entities collaborate harmoniously. (Wright, 2021) It will be essential for gig workers to stay up-to-date with the latest trends and developments, ensuring they can fully harness the potential of the DAO ecosystem and thrive in the gig economy's future landscape. Some predictions for the future of the DAO gig economy include:

- An increasingly borderless job market
- The rise of decentralized worker cooperatives
- The development of more sophisticated tools and platforms for decentralized gig work
- A growing emphasis on education and upskilling within the DAO job market
- The integration of neutral network technologies into the DAO ecosystem
- The increasing prominence of DAOs in the gig economy as a viable and sustainable long-term career option

DAOs hold immense potential to revolutionize the gig economy and traditional employment models, offering gig workers increased autonomy, global access, and profit-sharing opportunities. "In the future, people will earn income in non-traditional ways by taking actions such as playing games, learning new skills, creating art, or curating content." (Schecter, 2021) As DAOs continue to evolve, they may become an integral part of a broader movement toward a more sustainable and socially responsible gig economy, where the well-being and empowerment of gig workers are central to its success. "We show that the share of gig workers among all workers has risen substantially between 2005 and 2016 and some of the increase coincided with the introduction and proliferation of online platforms." (Jeon, Liu & Ostrovsky, 2022) The World Economic Forum points out in a 2022 publication that the next evolution might be virtual work in the metaverse with avatars to socialize and work. (Jesuthasan & Zarkadis, 2022)

CHALLENGES OF IMPLEMENTING DAOS

Governance and decision-making, regulatory hurdles and the impact on the workforce need to be discussed when organizations are embracing technological developments, particularly blockchain technology, as part of Industry 4.0. (Ellul, 2021, p. 10) Blockchain technology allows for decentralized autonomous organizations (DAOs) which utilize smart contracts to make sure that rules are adhered to without third-party interference and costs. DAOs have been shown to increase organizational efficiency, strengthen data ownership, improve privacy, reduce transaction costs, improve security, assure reliability and resilience, and improve financial benefits. Large corporations such as Visa, JPMorgan Chase, MasterCard, Walmart, and Tesco have adopted DAOs to improve their competitive advantage. However, DAOs are still in their early stages of rollout and may pose significant issues when due diligence is not maintained by all users. More should be done to consider whether DAOs can be brought into traditional models in order to benefit from both styles of operational construct. (Saurabh, Rani & Upadhyay, 2023, p. 28)

However, DAO gig economy challenges must be addressed for this new model to succeed. One of the primary DAO gig economy challenges is the token-based governance system. Token holders are responsible for making decisions and voting on proposals. This can lead to a concentration of power in the hands of a few token holders, which can undermine the decentralized nature of the organization. DAOs often have fluid membership, with participants entering and exiting the network as they please. This can create difficulties in decision-making, as there is no clear authority or hierarchy to enforce decisions. This fluidity can also lead to an unaccountability and nontransparency in the organization. (Buterin, 2016)

Dispute resolution is another challenge faced by DAOs. Traditional gig economy platforms have centralized dispute resolution mechanisms, while DAOs lack a centralized authority to resolve conflicts. This can lead to unresolved disputes and dissatisfaction among workers and clients. Regrettably, the very features that render DAOs attractive also present significant challenges for them in bankruptcy proceedings. The growth of DAO ecosystems raises concerns about how disputes arising from DAO functions and smart contracts will be addressed. While self-governance and automated smart contracts may reduce disputes, it is unlikely that all disputes will be eliminated through technology. This is particularly concerning given the significant economic value of assets managed by many DAOs. Dispute resolution mechanisms for members and associates within the DAO may not be sufficient for those outside the organization with whom the DAO reaches agreements. Traditional dispute resolution options such as courts, tribunals, industry schemes, mediation, arbitration, and online processes may not adequately address the complexities of DAO formation, operation, and functionality. The resolution of disputes involving smart contracts, decentralized organizations, blockchain, NFTs, and cryptocurrency requires exceptional expertise and experience possessed by only a small group of people. (Bridgesmith & ElMessiry & Marei, 2022, p. 25)

Although the future of the DAO economy remains uncertain, it is inevitable that some DAOs will encounter failure. In such instances, bankruptcy professionals must be prepared to confront the obstacles that arise in the context of DAO bankruptcies. (Rosenberg, 2022, p. 51)

DAOs face unclear legal status, as they do not fit neatly into existing legal frameworks for corporations, nonprofits, or partnerships. This ambiguity can make it difficult for DAOs to operate legally and navigate regulatory requirements. Tax implications are another challenge faced by DAOs. Since DAOs are decentralized and operate on a global scale, it can be difficult to determine the appropriate tax jurisdiction and tax treatment for the organization and its participants. Employment law is another area where DAOs face challenges. As DAOs do not have traditional employer-employee relationships, it can be unclear how labor laws and worker protections apply to participants in the DAO gig economy. (Brummer & Seira, 2022, p. 1)

The decentralized nature of DAOs can create uncertainty for workers regarding job security and stability. Without a clear employer, workers may face inconsistent income and lack job benefits like health insurance and retirement plans. Another challenge faced by workers in the DAO gig economy is the potential lack of skill development and career advancement opportunities. As tasks are automated and decentralized, workers may struggle to develop new skills and advance within the organization. Legal wrappers can help address some of the challenges faced by DAOs. By wrapping established legal forms around DAOs, organizations can mitigate frictions and enhance legal compliance. Legal wrappers can include corporate structures, partnerships, and nonprofit organizations. Thoughtful legal engineering can help optimize tax treatment for DAOs and their participants. By choosing the appropriate legal wrapper and jurisdiction, DAOs can minimize tax liabilities and ensure compliance with tax regulations. Limited Liability Companies (LLCs) are legal structures that provide the same level of liability protection as corporations, while also offering the flexibility and tax advantages typically associated with partnerships. A well-designed legal wrapper can mitigate liability for DAO participants. By establishing a clear legal structure, DAOs can limit the exposure of their participants to unlimited liability and potential financial losses. (Brummer & Seira, 2022, p. 9)

The question of whether a DAO can be considered a separate legal entity from the human actors who operate it has sparked discussions in both the blockchain and legal fields. There is a debate on whether a DAO should be recognized as a legal person or only when identified as such by the law. However, the prevailing understanding is that the autonomous nature of a DAO is incompatible with the concept of legal personhood, which requires identified actors to be responsible for the entity's actions. This discussion has significant implications for the legal field, as it determines the extent to which a DAO can be viewed as a separate legal entity from its human actors, and how much these actors can be protected from the liabilities of the DAO. (Hassan & De Filippi, 2021, p. 7)

Besides a legal partnership, other organizational structures could apply for DAOs such as in the US (Bridgesmith & ElMessiry & Marei, 2022, p. 22):

- Unincorporated DAOs
- Corporation
- Limited Liability Company
- DAO LLC
- Nonprofit
- Private Foundations and Public Charities
- Political Nonprofit
- Social Clubs
- Unincorporated Nonprofit Association
- Limited Cooperative Associations

There can be identified a number of taxation, entity formation, and operational issues regarding Decentralized Autonomous Organizations ("DAOs") and to propose a type of legal entity suited to handling these issues, including filing and paying U.S. taxes, opening a bank account, signing legal contracts, and restricting the liability of DAO members. Determining whether a DAO is for-profit or not-for-profit is a prerequisite for identifying the most appropriate domestic entity structure for it. (Jennings, Kerr, 2022) Not-for-profit is not synonymous with tax-exempt, and while very few DAOs will qualify as tax-exempt organizations, many may satisfy the requirements of not-for-profit organizations under state law. DAOs that satisfy the requirements should therefore consider registering as unincorporated nonprofit associations ("UNA") in states that recognize this entity form. (A16zcrypto, 2022)

DAOs need to engage in off-chain transactions to interact with the traditional economy. Legal wrappers can enable DAOs to enter into contracts, hire employees, and engage in other off-chain transactions with third parties. Legal wrappers can also help DAOs comply with regulatory expectations. By selecting the appropriate legal structure and jurisdiction, DAOs can better navigate complex regulatory environments and protect their participants. The state of Wyoming implemented the Wyoming DAO Supplement in mid-2021, which includes provisions that classify a DAO as a limited liability company. (Wyo. Stat. Ann. § 17-31-101) In addition to this, the supplement outlines other relevant details. Following this, Tennessee also adopted its own DAO-specific statutes, known as the "Tennessee DAO Statutes," in April 2022. (Tenn. Code Ann. § 48-250)

The case of U.S. Commodity Futures Trading Commission (CFTC) vs. Ooki DAO was decided in June 2023, with the ruling indicating that the DAO had been functioning as an unregistered derivatives exchange. The recent ruling has established a significant legal precedent that prohibits DAOs from offering financial services without obtaining an appropriate license or conducting KYC procedures, which are expected to be challenging to obtain. Consequently, it can be inferred that all DAOs will now fall under the jurisdiction of the United States, given that every DAO is expected to have some members who are US citizens. (CFDC vs. Ooki DAO, U.S. District Court for the Northern District of California, June 9th 2023)

The court's verdict regards each DAO as an unincorporated association and, as such, it is recognized as a legal entity and can be subject to legal proceedings. It should be noted that all tokenholders within a DAO are considered members and can be held personally accountable for any debts or obligations. While the rise of DAOs presents significant opportunities for the gig economy, the DAO gig economy challenges must be addressed for this new model to succeed. By navigating governance and decision-making challenges, regulatory hurdles, and workforce impacts, DAOs can revolutionize the future of work in the digital age. Legal wrappers, tax optimization, and compliance strategies will play a crucial role in addressing these challenges and ensuring the success of the DAO gig economy. (Brummer & Seira, 2022, p. 31)

WEB 3 AND TRADITIONAL CENTRALIZED WORK MODELS

The rise of Web 3 and DAOs has led to a shift in work models, with potential implications for gig economy workers. To better understand these implications, it's essential to compare Web 3 work models with traditional centralized work models.

In traditional centralized work models, decision-making and governance are often concentrated in the hands of a select few individuals or entities. In contrast, Web 3 models, such as DAOs, prioritize decentralization and consensus-driven decision-making, empowering gig economy workers to have a greater say in the organization's direction. The decision-making process is decentralized through token holders and autonomous from the founders or a central group. The DAO governance can differentiate between numerous voting scenarios. (Faqir-Rhazoui, Arroyo & Hassan, 2021)

Web 3 work models often provide greater flexibility and autonomy for gig economy workers compared to centralized models. DAOs enable workers to choose their projects, working hours, and compensation structures, resulting in a more personalized work experience. Blockchain technology, which underpins Web 3 and DAOs, is inherently transparent and tamper-proof. This ensures greater transparency and accountability in work models compared to centralized systems, where information may be more easily manipulated or concealed. Web 3 technologies offer several potential benefits for gig economy workers, addressing some challenges faced in traditional work models. Web 3 technologies can facilitate financial inclusion and empowerment for gig economy workers by enabling access to decentralized financial services and cryptocurrencies. This can help workers overcome limitations associated with traditional financial systems, such as cross-border transactions and banking restrictions.

Blockchain-based systems can help establish and maintain a worker's reputation and trust in the gig economy. Through decentralized identity solutions and verifiable credentials, workers can demonstrate their skills, expertise, and past performance, increasing their credibility in the marketplace. DAOs often utilize tokens and other incentive mechanisms to motivate and reward gig economy workers for their contributions. This can create a more equitable work environment, where workers are recognized and compensated based on their value and contributions.

Legal wrappers are essential for DAO gig economy workers as they offer protection from unlimited liability, optimize tax treatment, and enable compliance with regulatory requirements. As DAOs continue to evolve, legal engineering is crucial for mitigating frictions between established legal forms and DAO operations. (Mienert, 2021, p. 347)

Navigating tax implications and regulatory compliance can be particularly challenging for DAO gig economy workers. Understanding the tax treatment of cryptocurrencies and decentralized work models, along with complying with relevant regulations, is essential for workers participating in DAOs. (Sims, 2021, p. 27)

As DAOs and Web 3 technologies continue to mature, their impact on the gig economy will likely become more pronounced. Embracing these technologies and addressing the associated challenges can pave the way for a more equitable, decentralized, and efficient gig economy.

LIMITATIONS OF THE STUDY

Due to the rapidly evolving nature of Web3 technologies and the future of work, the study's scope may be limited to a specific time period. As a result, the findings may not capture long-term trends or changes that could occur beyond the study's timeframe. External factors that could influence the future of work, such as global economic trends, regulatory changes, or unforeseen technological advancements, might not be adequately controlled for in the study. Consequently, attributing all observed changes solely to Web3 technologies and DAOs may be challenging. As the current available data is insufficient for the intended study, it is crucial to undertake data collection efforts to acquire a more comprehensive and refined dataset.

CONTRIBUTIONS BY THE STUDY

The study provides valuable insights into the transformative impact of Web3 technologies and decentralized autonomous organizations (DAOs) on the future of work. By examining emerging trends, it offers a glimpse into potential shifts in work arrangements and organizational structures. The study sheds light on the concept of DAOs and decentralized governance models, illustrating their potential role in reshaping how work is organized and coordinated. It contributes to a better understanding of the principles underpinning these novel organizational structures. The study identifies both opportunities and challenges associated with the adoption of Web3 technologies and DAOs in the future of work. It highlights potential benefits, such as increased autonomy and efficiency, as well as challenges, such as regulatory uncertainty and potential socio-economic disparities. Based on its findings, the study offers valuable policy recommendations for governments, businesses, and stakeholders involved in shaping the future of work. These recommendations aim to foster a more inclusive and sustainable transition to Web3-based work arrangements.

CONCLUSION

According to LinkedIn, blockchain skills are predicted to be the most in-demand skill in 2020. However, what exactly does a blockchain employee need to be skilled in? To explore this topic, Australian labor market data was analyzed to determine the skills that are in demand among blockchain workers. The findings show that in addition to "hard" software engineering abilities like proficiency in programming languages and computer science, blockchain-related careers also necessitate "soft" skills like ingenuity, effective communication and adept leadership. To achieve mass adoption of blockchain, the industry will require employees with both hard and soft skills, and blockchain and community leaders will need to gain "blockchain literacy" to coordinate expectations between developers and users. The skilled workforce may determine the success or failure of blockchain technology, as overcoming challenges related to strategic management, usability, and marketability is crucial for mass adoption. (Atherton, Bratanova & Markey-Towler, 2020, p. 10)

To advance this research, there is a need to gather more and better data, as suitable data does not exist yet. The existing data has methodological drawbacks and does not represent the average experience of DAO members. There is a need for a strong DAO survey and measurement method to gather reliable data specific to the DAO economy. (Ilyushina & MacDonald, 2022, p. 52)

Emerging DAOs have the potential to improve the transparency, autonomy, and decentralization of large-scale infrastructure operations. (Wright, 2023, p. 4) Issues like trust, governance, privacy or cybersecurity need to be resolved. As digital platforms and algorithms become more prominent in our professional and personal interactions, it is crucial to investigate the ways in which they can both empower and constrain our freedom. This ongoing exploration is essential to understand the impact of these technologies on our lives.

The future of work will be different. Within structured patterns of economic cooperation, the emerging canon of DAO-related literature emphasizes minimizing agency costs. In lieu of centralized enterprises, the political economy of the future will be a "bazaar economy" comprised of nominally independent Law, Economics, and Decentralized Governance contractors. The decentralization of software production that we have witnessed thus far is only the beginning. (Allen, 2021, p. 3) These trends have led to four significant changes that will impact the future of work in software development. These changes include: a transition towards scalable technologies, a heightened focus on data, the merging of IT and non-IT industries, and the dominance of cloud computing as the prevailing computing paradigm. (Laato, Mäntymäki & Islam, 2022). The term "Metaverse" encompasses the collective conceptualization of technology entrepreneurs about a virtual realm that exists in three dimensions, whereby the internet is embodied and involves both people and elements of the physical world. The Metaverse is believed to enhance the scope of human activity by surpassing the limitations imposed by nature, including geographical, temporal, and resource-related limits. The technical framework of the Metaverse, often referred to as Web3, encompasses blockchain technology, smart contracts, and Non-Fungible Tokens (NFTs). (Momtaz, 2022) These components serve to minimize transaction and agency expenses while facilitating trustless social and economic engagements via decentralized consensus processes. The emergence of the Metaverse has the potential to facilitate the development of novel goods and services, provide new employment opportunities, and establish innovative economic frameworks.

The subsequent significant generational evolution of the web: Web 3 is already having a profound impact on numerous industries. As each of these platforms improves and comes together to make Web 3 apps, it becomes more important to talk about how to get ready for this future. (Park, Wilson, Robson, Demetis & Kietzmann, 2023, p. 529) It is necessary to discuss what specific talents will be required to effectively address and minimize the potential hazards associated with Web3 technologies, while also maximizing the potential benefits for enhanced socioeconomic outcomes.

REFERENCES

Allen, J. (2021). Bodies without Organs: Law, Economics, and Decentralised Governance. *Stanford Journal of Blockchain Law & Policy*. https://stanford-jblp.pubpub.org/pub/law-econ-decentralised-governance

Atherton, J., Bratanova, A., & Markey-Towler, B. (2020). Who is the Blockchain employee? Exploring skills in demand using observations from the Australian labour market and Behavioural Institutional Cryptoeconomics. *The Journal of the British Blockchain Association*, *3*(2), 1–12. doi:10.31585/jbba-3-2-(4)2020

Brewster, C., Dowling, P., & Holland, P. (2022). HRM and the smart and dark side of technology. *Asia Pacific Journal of Human Resources*, *60*(1), 62–78. doi:10.1111/1744-7941.12319

Bridgesmith, L., ElMessiry, A., & Marei, M. (2022). Legal Service Delivery and Support for the DAO Ecosystem. *Springer, Blockchain – ICBC 2022*. 18-28.

BrummerC. J.SeiraR. (2022). Legal Wrappers and DAOs. Available at SSRN: doi:10.2139/ssrn.4123737

Buterin, V. (2014a). Ethereum: A Next-Generation Smart Contract and Decentralized Application Platform. *Ethereum (blog)*. https://ethereum.org/669c9e2e2027310b6b3cdce6e1c52962/Ethereum_Whitepaper_-_Buterin_2014.pdf

Buterin, V. (2014b) DAOs, DACs, DAs and More: An Incomplete Terminology Guide. *Ethereum (blog)*. https://blog.ethereum.org/2014/05/06/daos-dacs-das-and-more-an-incomplete-terminology-guide/

Buterin, V. (2016) DAOs as a concept existed long before Ethereum. *Medium (blog)*. https://medium.com/@VitalikButerin/i-invented-the-term-in-2013-and-daniel-larimer-came-up-with-dacs-s-organization-corporation-a-ef86db1524d5

CFDC vs. Ooki DAO, U.S. District Court for the Northern District of California, June 9th 2023. https://storage.courtlistener.com/recap/gov.uscourts.cand.400807/gov.uscourts.cand.400807.76.0.pdf

EllulJ. (2021). Blockchain is dead! Long live Blockchain! *The Journal of The British Blockchain Association*. SSRN. https://ssrn.com/abstract=3813872

Faqir-Rhazoui, Y., Arroyo, J., & Hassan, S. (2020). An overview of decentralized autonomous organizations on the blockchain. pp. 1-8. *Proceedings of the 16th International Symposium on Open Collaboration*. UCM. https://eprints.ucm.es/id/eprint/62273/1/os20-paper-a11-el-faqir.pdf

Faqir-Rhazoui, Y., Arroyo, J., & Hassan, S. (2021). A Comparative Analysis of the Adoption of Decentralized Governance in the Blockchain Through DAOs. doi:10.21203/rs.3.rs-166470/v1

Fekete, D. L., & Kiss, A. (2023). Toward Building Smart Contract-Based Higher Education Systems Using Zero-Knowledge Ethereum Virtual Machine. *Electronics (Basel)*, *12*(3), 664. doi:10.3390/electronics12030664

Fennel, A. (2022). Gig economy statistics UK. *Standout CV*. https://standout-cv.com/gig-economy-statistics-uk

Filipčić, S. (2022). Web 3 & DAOs: an overview of the development and possibilities for the implementation in research and education. *45th Jubilee International Convention on Information, Communication and Electronic Technology (MIPRO)*, Croatia. 10.23919/MIPRO55190.2022.9803324

Glatz, F. (2023). DAOs are Dead! Long live DAOs! *Hecker Hut*. https://heckerhut.medium.com/daos-are-dead-long-live-daos-50de94e8ee1e

Green, D., McCann, J., Vu, T., Lopez, N., & Ouattara, S. (2018). Gig economy and the future of work. A Fiverr.com case study. *Management and Economics Research Journal, 4*(2), 281–288. doi:10.18639/MERJ.2018.04.734348

Hassan, S., & De Filippi, P. (2021). Decentralized Autonomous Organization. *Internet Policy Review, 10*(2), 1–10. doi:10.14763/2021.2.1556

Ilyushina, N., & MacDonald, T. (2022). Decentralised Autonomous Organisations: A New Research Agenda for Labour Economics. *The Journal of the British Blockchain Association, 1*(5), 50–53.

Jennings, M., & Kerr, D. (2022). How to pick a DAO legal entity. *A16ZCrypto.* https://a16zcrypto.com/posts/article/dao-legal-entity-how-to-pick/

Jeon, S., Liu, H., & Ostrovsky, Y. (2022). Measuring the gig economy in Canada using administrative data. *The Canadian Journal of Economics. Revue Canadienne d'Economique.*

Jesuthasan, R., & Zarkadis, G. (2022). How will Web 3 impact the future of work? World Economic Forum. https://www.weforum.org/agenda/2022/07/web-3-change-the-future-of-work-decentralized-autonomous-organizations/

Johnson, M., & Rubery, J. (2019). HRM in crisis. In D. Collings & G. Wood (Eds.), *Human Resource Management: A Critical Approach* (pp. 396–411). Routledge. doi:10.4324/9781315299556-20

Kuhn, K., & Galloway, T. (2019). Expanding perspectives on gig work and gig workers. *Journal of Managerial Psychology, 34*(4), 186–191. doi:10.1108/JMP-05-2019-507

Laato, S., Mäntymäki, M., Islam, A., Hyrynsalmi, S., & Birkstedt, T. (2022). Trends and Trajectories in the Software Industry: Implications for the future of work. *Information Systems Frontiers, 25,* 929–944. doi:10.100710796-022-10267-4

Le Brocq, S., Hughes, E., & Donnelly, R. (2023). Sharing in the gig economy: From equitable work relations to exploitative HRM. *Personnel Review, 52*(3), 454–469. doi:10.1108/PR-04-2019-0219

Mehdi, I., Sbai, M., Mazlin, M., & Azghiou, K. (2022). Data Centric DAO: When blockchain reigns over the Cloud. *IEEE International IOT, Electronics and Mechatronics Conference (IEMTRONICS),* (pp. 1-7). IEEE. 10.1109/IEMTRONICS55184.2022.9795753

MienertB. (2021). How Can a Decentralized Autonomous Organization (DAO) Be Legally Structured? *Legal Revolutionary Journal LRZ 2021.* SSRN. doi:10.2139/ssrn.3992329

Mienert, B. (2022). Dezentrale autonome Organisationen (DAOs) als alternative Organisationsstruktur der Zukunft. *Rethinking Law., 04,* 2022.

Momtaz, P. (2022). Some Very Simple Economics of Web3 and the Metaverse. FinTech. *MDPI AG, 1*(3), 225–234. doi:10.3390/fintech1030018

Muldoon, J., & Raekstad, P. (2022). Algorithmic Domination in the Gig Economy. *European Journal of Political Theory, 0*(0), 1–21. doi:10.1177/14748851221082078

Nabben, K. (2022). The Ethnography of a 'Decentralized Autonomous Organization' (DAO): Demystifying Algorithmic Systems. *EPIC,* (1), 74–97.

Nabben, K. (2023). "Governance by Algorithms, Governance of Algorithms: Human-Machine Politics in Decentralised Autonomous Organisations (DAOs)", *puntOorg. International Journal (Toronto, Ont.)*, *8*(1), 36–54. doi:10.19245/25.05.pij.8.1.3

Nabben K. Puspasari N. Kelleher M. Sanjay S. (2021). Grounding Decentralised Technologies in Cooperative Principles: What Can 'Decentralised Autonomous Organisations' (DAOs) and Platform Cooperatives Learn from Each Other? doi:10.2139/ssrn.3979223

Naughtin, C., Hajkowicz, S., Schleiger, E., Bratanova, A., Cameron, A., Zamin, T., & Dutta, A. (2022). *Our Future World: Global megatrends impacting the way we live over coming decades*. MPRA.

Park, A., Wilson, M., Robson, K., Demetis, D., & Kietzmann, J. (2023). Interoperability: Our exciting and terrifying Web3 future. *Business Horizons, Volume*, *4*(66), 529–541. doi:10.1016/j.bushor.2022.10.005

Pries, J., & Quakernack, N. (2023). Decentralized Autonomous Organization. *Organisationsentwicklung*, (2), 81–83.

Rikken, O., Janssen, M., Kwee, Z. (2023). The ins and outs of decentralized autonomous organizations (DAOs) unraveling the definitions, characteristics, and emerging developments of DAOs. *Blockchain: Research and Applications* . doi:10.1016/j.bcra.2023.100143

Rikken, O., van Heukelom-Verhage, S., Naves, J., & Terpoorten, H. (2018). *Smart Contracts as Specific Application of Blockchain Technology*. Dutch Blockchain Coalition. https://dutchdigitaldelta.nl/uploads/pdf/Smart-Contracts-ENG-report.pdf

Rocas-Royo, M. (2019). Decentralization as a new framework for the sharing economy. Handbook of the Sharing Economy, pp. 218-228.

Rosenberg, A. (2022). Getting down with DAOs: Decentralized autonomous organizations in bankruptcy. *American Bankruptcy Institute. Journal Issue*, *41*(7), 12–51.

Saurabh, K., Rani, N., & Upadhyay, P. (2023). Towards blockchain led decentralized autonomous organization (DAO) business model innovations. *International Journal (Toronto, Ont.)*, *30*(2), 475–502. doi:10.1108/BIJ-10-2021-0606

Schecter, B. (2021). The Future of Work is Not Corporate — It's DAOs and Crypto Networks. *A16ZCrypto*. https://a16zcrypto.com/posts/article/the-future-of-work-daos-crypto-networks/#section--3

Schwab, K. (2016) The Fourth Industrial Revolution: What It Means, How to Respond. *World Economic Forum*. https://www.weforum.org/agenda/2016/01/the-fourth-industrialrevolution-what-it-means-and-how-to-respond

Sims A. (2021). Decentralised Autonomous Organisations: Governance, Dispute Resolution and Regulation. SSRN. doi:10.2139/ssrn.3971228

Stroh, J. (2023). *DAOs, Web 3, Decentralization, Governance. Blockchance 2023 Hamburg*. Conference Keynote.

Sulkowski, A. (2019). Industry 4.0 Industry 4.0 era technology (AI, big data, blockchain, DAO): Why the law needs new memes. *Kan. JL & Pub. Pol'y*, *29*, 1.

Sundararajan, A. (2016). *The Sharing Economy: The End of Employment and the Rise of Crowd-Based Capitalism*. MIT Press.

World Economic Forum. (2022). *Decentralized Autonomous Organizations: Beyond the Hype*. White paper, pp. 1-24. https://www3.weforum.org/docs/WEF_Decentralized_Autonomous_Organizations_Beyond_the_Hype_2022.pdf

Wright, A. (2021). The Rise of Decentralized Autonomous Organizations: Opportunities and Challenges. *Stanford Journal of Blockchain Law & Policy*. https://stanford-jblp.pubpub.org/pub/rise-of-daos

Wright, A. (2023). DAOs & ADSs. IEEE 15th International Symposium on Autonomous Decentralized System (ISADS), (pp. 1-6). IEEE. 10.1109/ISADS56919.2023.10091973

Chapter 10
The Promise of Blockchain–Based Decentralized Social Networks:
Enabling Privacy, Censorship Resistance, and User Control

Sasha Shilina

(iD) https://orcid.org/0000-0003-4696-0739

Lomonosov Moscow State University, Russia

ABSTRACT

This chapter explores the potential of the novel Web 3 phenomenon – decentralized social networks – to address the growing concerns over privacy, censorship, and user control on centralized social media platforms. Offering an alternative to traditional social media, decentralized social platforms utilize distributed ledger technologies like blockchain where data is stored on multiple nodes and controlled by the users, rather than a central authority. Such systems are designed to enable trust and transparency in online interactions, provide the ability to communicate without censorship or interference, and empower users with greater control over their personal data. This chapter discusses the benefits and challenges of blockchain-based social networks, as well as existing initiatives working towards a more decentralized, democratic, and user-centric model of social networking.

INTRODUCTION

The term "social" in the context of social media implies that these platforms are designed to prioritize user engagement and foster communal activity. In recent years, social media platforms have undergone a transformative revolution in the way people communicate, share information, and connect with others globally (Dijck, 2013). These platforms have become instrumental in shaping public discourse, mobilizing social movements, and fostering online communities (Hwang and Kim, 2015; Kidd and McIntosh,

DOI: 10.4018/978-1-6684-9919-1.ch010

Copyright © 2023, IGI Global. Copying or distributing in print or electronic forms without written permission of IGI Global is prohibited.

2016; Pouwels et al., 2022). Major social networks serve as hubs for interaction, communication, and entertainment (Ahn and Shin, 2013; Kuem et al., 2017; Yurder and Akdol, 2020), while also playing a crucial role in the dissemination of information and news (Vosoughi et al., 2018), not necessarily true or relevant (Shu et al., 2020). Enabling individuals to generate and share false information quickly and anonymously (Del Vicario et al., 2016), social media has accelerated misinformation dissemination, particularly fake news (Di Domenico et al., 2021; Pennycook & Rand, 2021).

The boundless adoption of social networks is evident in the growing number of users worldwide. According to DataReportal, in April 2023, there were 4.80 billion social media users around the world, equating to nearly 60 percent of the total global population, with projections estimating this number to surpass six billion by 2027 (Dixon, 2023). The influence of social media extends beyond online activities, affecting offline behaviors and overall life experiences. Presently, social media usage ranks among the most popular online activities, with internet users globally spending approximately 147 minutes per day on social media as of 2022, a slight increase from 145 minutes in 2021 (Dixon, 2022).

However, the growing dominance of major industry players such as Meta and X (formerly Twitter) has raised concerns about privacy, as personal information is vulnerable to data breaches and misuse (Li, 2015; McHatton, 2023; Senthil Kumar, 2016; Smith, 2012; Trepte, 2021), and centralized control over users' content and interactions, leading to debates about censorship and the suppression of diverse viewpoints (Benson et al, 2015; Bradshaw and Howard, 2019; Gunitsky, 2015). Moreover, the centralization of power in a few entities raises questions about accountability and the potential for undue influence over public discourse.

Given the concerns surrounding centralized social networks, this chapter aims to explore the landscape of blockchain-based decentralized social networks, highlighting their advantages over traditional social networks and examining the current state-of-the-art initiatives. By harnessing the power of blockchain technology, these networks enhance privacy, enable users to have greater control over their personal data, ensure resistance against censorship, and foster a more inclusive and democratic online environment.

The chapter begins by tracing the evolution of social networks, from their inception to their widespread adoption. It then delves into the fundamental differences between decentralized social networks and their centralized counterparts, emphasizing the need for a paradigm shift in how we conceptualize and interact with social media. Furthermore, the chapter explores the emergence of the first peer-to-peer (P2P) social networks and the subsequent introduction of blockchain technology, which has revolutionized the concept of decentralization. By leveraging blockchain's inherent features such as immutability, transparency, and consensus mechanisms, a new generation of decentralized social media has emerged, promising greater privacy, security, and user control. To provide an overview, the chapter examines notable blockchain-based social media initiatives, focusing on Ethereum-based decentralized social media platforms. It also highlights noteworthy blockchain social media platforms on other chains. However, the integration of blockchain technology into social networks is not without its challenges. The chapter addresses these issues, such as scalability, user experience, content moderation, competition from established centralized networks, interoperability, regulatory compliance, and the impact of market volatility on monetization models. By understanding and addressing these challenges, blockchain-based decentralized social networks can strive to deliver on their promises and offer a compelling alternative to centralized platforms.

Combining the exploration of decentralized social networks' fundamental features, analysis of advantages and challenges, and examination of real-world initiatives, this research aims to contribute to the understanding of this phenomenon and its potential to reshape the social media landscape. Ultimately, our goal is to pave the way for a more user-centric, democratic, and empowering online environment.

SOCIAL NETWORKS: FROM BIRTH TO SPREAD

Tim Berners-Lee's integration of hypertext software with the Internet in 1991 paved the way for the creation of the World Wide Web (Berners-Lee, 1992), ushering in a new era of networked communication. This technological breakthrough not only enabled the formation of online communities but also provided support for offline groups through weblogs, list servers, and email services. As the online landscape continued to evolve, the concept of online services expanded beyond mere channels for communication. With the emergence of Web 2 (DiNucci, 1999), these services transformed into interactive platforms for networked social interaction (Dijck, 2013).

Pioneering social media started in the mid-1990s with the advent of platforms like GeoCities, Classmates.com, and SixDegrees.com (Ngak, 2011). The first formal definition is from 1996 and uses "computer-supported social networks" or "CSSNs" (Wellman, 1996) although the term social media was coined about two years earlier (Aichner et al., 2021). Later, researchers used different terms such as "virtual communities" (Balasubramanian & Mahajan, 2001; Hagel, 1999; Ridings et al., 2002; Romm et al., 1997), "social networks" (Garton et al., 1997), "social networking services" (Marwick, 2005), "online social network" (Acquisti & Gross, 2006), "social network sites" (Boyd & Ellison, 2007; Sledgianowski & Kulviwat, 2009) and "social media" (Carr & Hayes, 2015; Kaplan & Haenlein, 2010; Kapoor et al., 2018; Kietzmann et al., 2011).

During the early 2000s, social media platforms experienced a surge in popularity, with platforms like Friendster and Myspace leading the way (Boyd & Ellison, 2007). While Friendster gained traction in the Pacific Islands, MySpace attracted the majority of media attention in the U.S. and abroad, social networks were proliferating and growing in popularity worldwide. Thus, Orkut became the premier social network in Brazil before growing rapidly in India (Madhavan, 2007), Mixi attained widespread adoption in Japan, LunarStorm took off in Sweden, Dutch users embraced Hyves, Grono captured Poland, Hi5 was adopted in smaller countries in Latin America, South America, and Europe, and Bebo became very popular in the United Kingdom, New Zealand, and Australia. Additionally, previously popular communication and community services began implementing social network features. The Chinese QQ instant messaging solution added profiles and made friends visible (McLeod, 2006), while the forum tool Cyworld cornered the Korean market by introducing homepages and buddies (Ewers, 2006).

In the mid-2010s, these platforms were quickly followed by the emergence of giants such as Facebook, YouTube, and X (formerly Twitter), among others. According to Statista, Facebook, the market leader in social networking, was the first to achieve a significant milestone by surpassing one billion registered accounts and currently boasts over 2.9 billion monthly active users. Today, Meta Platforms, the parent company of Facebook, holds ownership of four of the largest social media platforms, each with over one billion monthly active users. These platforms include Facebook, WhatsApp, Facebook Messenger, and Instagram. Other popular social networks, with more than 100 million registered users, include WeChat, ShareChat, Instagram, QZone, Weibo, VK, Tumblr, Baidu Tieba, and LinkedIn. Despite the widespread popularity and provision of these sites, their centralized nature has introduced imbalances in the ecosystem of the Internet. The current landscape of mainstream social networking is characterized by a consolidated infrastructure hosted on the cloud, controlled solely by a single authority. This means that platforms like Facebook have complete control over thousands of servers, including user-generated content. The authority in control can assert ownership rights over the user's content to some extent and exploit it for their own business purposes, which has raised questions about user privacy and data security (De Salve et al., 2023; Jain et al., 2021; Qamar et al., 2016; Rathore et al., 2017;). Dominant social networks collect vast amounts of personal information from their users, including demographic details, interests, and online behavior, which are frequently attacked by hackers. In 2020, database breaches within social networks such as X (ex-Twitter) and Facebook accounted for approximately 25% of leaked records. However, the situation has worsened since then, with the numbers soaring to about 41% in 2022, indicating a significant increase in data leaks and theft from social media platforms (Muhammad, 2022).

The monopoly held by major social platforms poses another significant challenge (Ranttila, 2020), as a small number of dominant platforms, such as Facebook, and Instagram, attract the majority of users, leaving limited room for competition and innovation in the social media landscape. This concentration of power can hinder diversity, limit user choice, and inhibit the development of alternative platforms that may offer different features, values, or privacy protections.

DECENTRALIZED SOCIAL NETWORKS VS. TRADITIONAL SOCIAL NETWORKS

A number of research efforts have been motivated by the limitations posed by the centralized architecture of the current social networks (Marcon et al., 2011). Such alternative proposals shared a common objective of granting users greater autonomy in terms of storing and controlling access rights to their content (Rahman, 2020; Modi, 2023). They emerged striving to decentralize storage and control in social networks (Qamar et al., 2016), and creating decentralized architectures (Chowdhury et al., 2015; Paul et al., 2014).

In this work, we define a decentralized social network as an online social media platform that operates in a distributed environment, where the architecture is based on a peer-to-peer (P2P) model, and users directly interact with each other without relying on a central authority or server. They are characterized by decentralized, open-source, ad-free, and community-owned nature (Chowdhury et al., 2015). Decentralized networks prioritize user ownership and control over their data and interactions, allowing individuals to have greater agency in managing their personal information. Privacy is a key focus here, with minimized data collection, encryption techniques, and selective data sharing to enhance user experience. Moreover, decentralized networks strive to resist censorship by employing distributed content storage, community-driven moderation, and anti-censorship tools. Content in decentralized networks is less susceptible to removal or suppression, promoting freedom of expression.

Both traditional and decentralized social networks come with their own advantages and challenges. Decentralized networks put first privacy, user autonomy, resistance to censorship and resilience to single points of failure. On the other hand, traditional centralized networks often provide convenience, a large user base, and a seamless user experience. Their comparative features are presented in Table 1.

FIRST PEER-TO-PEER (P2P) SOCIAL NETWORKS

Early alternative proposals to traditional social networking predominantly advocated for a decentralized P2P architecture, where a platform infrastructure is formed through the collaboration of autonomous users, aiming to empower them to have more control over the storage and access of their content. In 2011, an early proposal suggested a decentralized architecture to federate centralized social media services as a starting point for addressing these challenges (Yeung et al., 2011). At the same time, researchers

Table 1. Comparative features of centralized and decentralized social networks

Centralized Social Networks vs Decentralized Social Networks		
Aspect	**Centralized Social Networks**	**Decentralized Social Networks**
Architecture	Centralized architecture	Peer-to-peer (P2P) or decentralized architecture
Data storage	Stored on centralized servers	Distributed across multiple servers
Data control	Platform provider retains control and ownership over user data and content	Users have more control over their data and content
Privacy	Privacy may vary, dependent on platform policies	Prioritizes user privacy and data protection
Censorship resistance	More susceptible to censorship and content control	More resistant to censorship
User experience	Well-established user interfaces and feature-rich experiences	Developing stages, may have limitations in features
Network effects	Large user base, extensive network effects	Still developing, may have limited user base
Revenue model	Advertising, sponsored content, premium subscriptions	Crowdfunding, donations, token economy, premium features

conducted measurement studies to demonstrate the feasibility of sharing social content directly from users' homes (Marcon et al., 2011).

In 2009, the first complete architecture for a P2P online social network called PeerSon was proposed (Buchegger, 2009). SafeBook (Cutillo et al.; 2009), PrPl (Seong et al., 2010), Cachet (Nilizadeh et al., 2012), and Decent (Jahid et al., 2012) were among other notable proposals for decentralized media platforms, primarily concentrating on aspects such as system design, communication protocols, consistency, encryption schemes, and profile dissemination within the network. Basically, the decentralization in these systems was a consequence of their P2P nature.

Researchers distinguish three main categories of P2P architectures for social networks (Schwittmann et al., 2014). First is federated architecture consisting of independent servers. Mastodon (Zignani et al., 2018) is a noteworthy example of an open-source federated social media platform. Unlike traditional social media platforms, Mastodon operates as interoperable code deployed across multiple websites. It allows developers to create and manage their own servers, known as "instances," within the Mastodon network. Each instance is owned, operated, and moderated by its respective creators. Many instances are funded by the community, devoid of advertisements, and collectively owned. The decentralized nature of Mastodon has sparked interest in studying how it influences the dynamics of the resulting social network. Recent research has revealed that this federated structure creates a unique social network with distinct patterns of social interactions (Zulli et al., 2020; La Cava et al., 2021). Two other notable examples of federated systems are OneSocialWeb and Diaspora (Bielenberg et al., 2012). Another category of systems utilized end-to-end client-side data encryption to ensure the privacy of data content, with examples including Persona (Baden et al., 2009), Vegas, and SoNet (Nepali et al., 2013). The third class of systems, namely PeerSoN, Safebook, Cachet, and LifeSocial (Graffi et al., 2011), opt for a distributed hash table (DHT) instead of relying on federated servers. By utilizing a DHT, these networks achieve scalability, as they can easily accommodate a growing number of users and their social connections.

In the late 2000s and early 2010s, numerous other proposals emerged, each offering different levels of decentralization and addressing specific aspects of deployment (Asthana et al., 2013; Famulari et al., 2013; Pouwelse et al., 2008; Shakimov et al., 2011; Sharma & Datta, 2012).

On top of that, scholars argue that the dynamic P2P nature of decentralized social networks necessitates the use of distributed and lightweight access control techniques (De Salve et al., 2017; Bodriagov et al., 2013). However, guaranteeing data availability, defining privacy-preserving access control algorithms, and developing suitable information diffusion algorithms in a distributed environment are ongoing challenges in this field. Various proposed architectures for social media emphasized encryption to ensure privacy (Buchegger, 2009; Guidi et al., 2019; Wang & Vassileva, 2007), some architectures incorporated the concept of trust to safeguard privacy (Conti et al., 2014; Rahman et al., 2020). Techniques such as Attribute-based Access Control (ABAC) (Shakimov et al., 2011), role-based access control (RBAC) (Maesa et al., 2017), and rule-based access control have been proposed to enhance privacy and provide better control over data (Datta et al., 2020; De Salve et al., 2015; Jain et al., 2021; Nasim & Buchegger, 2014). Nonetheless, these techniques faced scalability and efficiency issues when it comes to meeting the security requirements of decentralized social networks, given the current usage of social media. The distributed nature of decentralized social networks presents challenges related to managing private user data, ensuring its availability, and implementing access control mechanisms.

In addition to architectural proposals, significant research efforts have been dedicated to addressing particular issues relevant to decentralized social networks, including privacy, security, scalability, and data management (Aiello et al, 2012; Bodriagov et al, 2013; Forsyth & Daudjee, 2013; Han et al., 2012; Shahriar et al., 2013).

BLOCKCHAIN-BASED: A NEW GENERATION OF DECENTRALIZED SOCIAL NETWORKS

In recent years, significant advancements in internet technology (IT) have brought about the transformation in Web2 and the emergence of Web3, an innovative vision for the future evolution of the World Wide Web and a paradigm shift towards a more decentralized and user-empowered internet ecosystem (Nath et al., 2014). By leveraging distributed ledger technologies like blockchain, Web3 aims to empower individuals, enhance data privacy and security, and foster peer-to-peer interactions. Additionally, Web3 explores the integration of token economies, enabling new models of value exchange and incentivizing user participation.

A number of research efforts are exploring a new generation of decentralized social networks with the integration of blockchain technology, to address the flaws of centralized and early P2P social networks, and enhance their security and privacy aspects (Ba et al., 2022; Ciriello et al., 2018; Cong & He, 2019; Guidi, 2020; Guidi, 2021; Jiang & Zhang, 2019; Rahman, 2020; Wang et al., 2023; Zeng et al, 2019).

Blockchain technology plays a crucial role in powering decentralized applications by providing a robust infrastructure for the network. At the heart of the blockchain is a distributed and immutable ledger that records all transactions and interactions within the network. Unlike traditional centralized database technologies, blockchain has a unique data structure consisting of a series of blocks, storing data across multiple nodes or computers. The initial block, known as the genesis block, undergoes a hash algorithm to convert its information into a fixed-length hash value. This hash value is then stored in the subsequent block. This process continues as each new block is generated, with each block's information, including the hash value of the preceding block, producing a fixed-length hash value for storage in the subsequent block. In this way, the blocks are linked together, and any modifications to a block will result in changes to all subsequent blocks. Consequently, the original blockchain is resistant to tampering, ensuring that recorded data remains unalterable once it is stored on the blockchain (Nakamoto, 2008).

In addition to its data structure, a blockchain incorporates encryption and consensus mechanisms to maintain synchronicity among network nodes and to ensure transparency and trust among network participants. When a user initiates a transaction, the transaction data is encrypted using the user's private key. Nodes within the network then verify the encrypted transaction and proceed to establish consensus among themselves using a specific algorithm. For instance, Bitcoin employs the Proof-of-Work (PoW) algorithm to achieve consensus, while Ethereum employs Proof-of-Stake (PoS) (Buterin, 2013). Once consensus is reached, the new block, containing the new transactions, is shared with other nodes and added to the blockchain. Through these methods, the network remains synchronized across thousands of nodes without relying on a centralized authority. Consensus mechanisms can provide a democratic and decentralized approach to decision-making within the network, preventing malicious activities and maintaining the integrity of the ecosystem.

As a result, blockchain-based decentralized social networks operate on a fundamentally different architecture compared to traditional platforms. Unlike centralized platforms that rely on a central server or authority to facilitate communication and data storage, blockchain networks distribute these functions across a network of interconnected nodes. Each node in the network acts as both a client and a server, allowing direct communication between users without relying on a central intermediary. Such architecture offers several advantages. Firstly, it enhances privacy by minimizing the need for third-party intermediaries that have access to users' personal data. Secondly, it improves resilience and availability, as there is no single point of failure that can disrupt the entire network. Lastly, it promotes collaboration and community-driven interactions, empowering users to have more control over their network experience.

The concept of user-owned data and identity is a fundamental principle of decentralized social networks. In contrast to centralized platforms where users often relinquish control of their data to the platform, decentralized networks empower users to retain ownership and control over their personal information. Decentralized identity systems enable users to manage their digital identities independently, using cryptographic techniques to verify and authenticate their online presence (Avellaneda et al., 2019; Dib & Toumi, 2020). End-to-end encryption ensures that only the intended recipients can access the content, safeguarding against eavesdropping and unauthorized surveillance. This encryption is often implemented at the protocol level, enhancing privacy by default for all network participants. The system enables users to selectively share their personal information, granting them greater control over their privacy and minimizing the risk of unauthorized access or data misuse.

Furthermore, blockchain technology provides censorship resistance mechanisms in decentralized social networks. Unlike centralized platforms that can censor or moderate content based on their policies, blockchain-based social networks allow users to create and share content freely without the fear of censorship. Once the content is recorded on the blockchain, it becomes immutable and cannot be altered or removed by any central authority. This promotes freedom of expression and empowers users to have full control over their own data and content.

Blockchain-based decentralized social networks often adopt a community-driven approach to content filtering and moderation. Instead of relying on a centralized authority to dictate acceptable content, such networks enable users to participate in the moderation process. This distributed moderation approach reduces the potential for censorship by preventing a single entity from having unilateral control over content decisions. It promotes a diverse range of viewpoints and encourages user empowerment in shaping the platform's content ecosystem. Also, to ensure censorship resistance networks employ distributed content storage mechanisms, making it difficult for any individual or authority to censor or remove specific content from the network.

On top of that, blockchain's smart contracts can play a crucial role in powering decentralized social media. These contracts contain the backend code that defines the logic and operations of these networks and enables transparent and trustless interactions among users (Kaur & Dabas, 2023). Smart contracts facilitate communication by automating and enforcing predefined rules and conditions. For example, when users engage in social interactions like following, liking, or sharing content, smart contracts can be programmed to execute these actions based on predefined conditions, ensuring transparency and eliminating the need for intermediaries.

Additionally, blockchain-based decentralized social networks often incorporate token economies, where digital currencies or tokens are used to incentivize participation, reward content creators, and facilitate economic transactions within the network. These tokens can be earned through active engagement, content creation, or other desired actions. Token economies incentivize users to contribute to the network, fostering a vibrant and engaged ecosystem.

Moreover, blockchain provides mechanisms for decentralized decision-making (Chao et al., 2022). Community governance empowers network participants to have a say in the decision-making processes of the social network. Through DAOs, users can collectively make decisions on platform upgrades, feature implementations, content policies, and other important matters. This decentralized approach ensures that decisions are made transparently, inclusively, and according to the consensus of the community.

The list of advantages of blockchain for decentralized social networks is provided in Table 2.

Table 2. Advantages of blockchain for decentralized social networks

Advantages of Blockchain for Decentralized Social Networks	
Advantage	**Description**
Increased security and immutable records	The distributed nature of blockchain and cryptography techniques ensures enhanced security and tamper-resistant records of interactions.
Enhanced privacy and data control	Users have greater control over their personal data, and censorship-resistant features protect privacy.
Transparency and trust	Blockchain technology and smart contracts ensure automation, transparent and verifiable interactions, promoting trust among users.
Resistance to censorship and data manipulation	Blockchain-based social networks are less susceptible to censorship and data manipulation by central authorities.
Monetization opportunities	Users can directly monetize their content through tokenization, NFTs, and cryptocurrency rewards.
Community governance	Decentralized networks allow for community-driven decision-making processes and decentralized governance models.
Secure user authentication	Users are identified and authenticated through a secure public key infrastructure, where cryptographic techniques are used to verify user identities without relying on a central authority.
Interoperability and cross-platform integration	Blockchain protocols can be multichain enabling seamless integration with other decentralized applications and platforms.
Resilience and availability	Distributed architectures enhance resilience and availability. There is no single point of failure, making it difficult for the network to be taken down or disrupted.
Innovation and diversity	Decentralized networks foster innovation by allowing developers to create dApps and services that interact with the network through open protocols and APIs, encouraging diversity and competition, and resulting in a more vibrant ecosystem.

BLOCKCHAIN-BASED SOCIAL MEDIA INITIATIVES: STATE-OF-THE-ART

Blockchain-based social media platforms have been the subject of research and exploration in recent years (Ba et al., 2022; Bhattacharya et al., 2021; Guidi, 2020; Guidi, 2021; Pfeiffer et al., 2020; Poongodi et al., 2020). Each blockchain-based social media platform brings its own unique features and characteristics depending on factors such as the underlying blockchain technology, platform purpose, target audience, and more. Different projects offer varying degrees of decentralization and tackle different subsets of issues related to the practical implementation of decentralized social networks.

Ethereum-Based Decentralized Social Media

Ethereum is the platform of choice for developers seeking to build decentralized social media networks, largely due to its smart contracts feature, widespread adoption, the universality and popularity of its token standards, such as ERC-20 and ERC-721. While Ethereum is widely recognized for its extensive ecosystem, as well as its significant contributions to decentralized finance (DeFi) and the non-fungible token (NFT) space, it has also provided a foundation for 50+ social media platforms, each on the different stages of development. The comparison of noteworthy Ethereum-based social media is presented in Table 3.

Peepeth

Created in 2018, Peepeth is an open-source smart contract-based microblogging platform similar to X (formerly Twitter), which operates on the Ethereum blockchain and utilizes The InterPlanetary File System (IPFS) for storing user data (Benet, 2014). Peepeth aims to provide a more secure, private, and censorship-resistant social media experience as an alternative to X. It allows users to send immutable short messages called "Peeps" that cannot be deleted or altered. One of its unique features is the ability to collect tips or tip other users on the platform in Ether (ETH) cryptocurrency. While using Peepeth incurs a modest cost in Ether, the platform ensures transparency by disclosing expenses to users. The platform encourages high-quality content and engagement by allowing users only one daily "Ensō" (similar to a "like").

Minds

Launched in 2015, Minds is a blockchain-based decentralized social network that offers a comparable experience to Facebook, with millions of users already onboard. It operates on Ethereum and employs its native ERC-20 token, MIND, for various transactions within the platform. The project offers open-source code and algorithms, along with transparent content moderation and spam policies. The primary objective of Minds is to establish a more transparent and open social media platform that upholds the principles of free speech and digital rights. Users have the freedom to express themselves without censorship and enjoy enhanced privacy protections. Furthermore, they can earn MIND tokens by publishing quality content, contributing to the platform's ecosystem, and referring others to join. Uses IPFS for data storage.

Mirror

Mirror is a blockchain-based writing platform that embraces the principles of Web3 and strives to be decentralized and user-owned. By connecting their wallets, users can enjoy the freedom to read and write on Mirror without any cost. When users publish their posts on Mirror, they are stored permanently on Arweave, a decentralized storage platform. These posts can also be transformed into collectible NFTs called 'Writing NFTs'. On top of that, Mirror empowers writers to monetize their work through crypto subscription payments, allowing them to directly benefit from their creative endeavors. The project facilitates the establishment of decentralized autonomous organizations (DAOs), enabling communities to collectively govern and shape the future of the platform. By embracing Web3 principles, Mirror sets a new standard for the media industry and paves the way for a more inclusive and equitable publishing landscape.

Sapien

Sapien is an Ethereum-based social news platform that offers adaptability and a democratic approach. As a Web3 social network, it addresses the issue of fake news while providing incentives to content creators. The platform's focus is on giving users ownership of their data and content. By sharing content that the community collectively determines as accurate or engaging with other members, Sapien creators can earn SPN tokens. These tokens can then be utilized within the platform and marketplace, providing users with opportunities for engagement and participation. Furthermore, on Sapien, users can participate by staking SPN tokens, allowing them to receive tokenized rewards for activities such as making comments, voting on posts, and generating content. The platform uses external storage.

CyberConnect

CyberConnect is a decentralized social network that operates on the CyberConnect protocol. The primary objective of CyberConnect is to provide a platform for mass adoption and network effects while maintaining identity sovereignty. It accomplishes this by allowing users to create profiles on EVM-compatible blockchains, serving as the foundation for their decentralized identities. One of the advantages of CyberConnect is that it grants users ownership over their social graph, content, monetization channels, and social data. This means that users have full control and ownership of their information, enabling them to seamlessly navigate across various dApps without the need to recreate their network on each new platform.

Status

Status is a secure messaging dApp that prioritizes user privacy. It utilizes an open-source, peer-to-peer protocol and employs end-to-end encryption to safeguard users' messages from unauthorized access by third parties. By leveraging decentralized technologies, Status ensures that user communications remain confidential and protected. The dApp's peer-to-peer architecture eliminates the need for a central authority, reducing the risk of data breaches or surveillance. Furthermore, the implementation of end to end encryption ensures that only the intended recipients can decrypt and read the messages, guaranteeing user privacy. SNT is the Status Network Token, an ERC20 token, used to power the Status Network.

Farcaster

Farcaster is a decentralized social network that operates as an open protocol, comparable to mailboxes. It provides support for multiple clients, allowing users to freely migrate their social identities between different applications. Additionally, developers have the freedom to build new applications on the Farcaster network, incorporating innovative features and functionalities. One of the key features of Farcaster is the ability to send short text message broadcasts that are linked to users' Ethereum addresses. Farcaster's decentralized nature ensures that users have full control over their social interactions and data. Farcaster is currently built on the Goerli Ethereum testnet with plans to migrate to Ethereum Mainnet sometime this year. Currently, Farcaster is invite only.

Indorse

Another notable project, Indorse, can be described as a decentralized version of LinkedIn with elements reminiscent of Instagram. Powered by its ERC-20 token called Indorse (IND), the platform aims to provide more accurate credentialing and skills verification through its "indorsements" system. The platform aims to provide IND staking and gradually decentralize governance through the Indorse Decentralized Autonomous Organization (DAO). (Pfeiffer, 2020).

Paragraph

Paragraph is a decentralized publishing analog of Substack that empowers writers, DAOs (Decentralized Autonomous Organizations), and NFT communities to monetize their content through its newsletter service. With Paragraph, users can create Web3-powered newsletters, offering the ability to token-gate their content and unlock new monetization opportunities. It provides a platform for users to grow their audience, and foster a vibrant community around their work. Moreover, developers have the flexibility to build on Paragraph, catering to specific needs and requirements.

Table 3. Ethereum-based decentralized social media

Ethereum-based Decentralized Social Media			
Network	**Blockchain**	**Key Features**	**Token**
Peepeth	Ethereum	Secure, private, and censorship-resistant microblogging platform	ETH
Minds	Ethereum	Transparent, open-source social network emphasizing free speech	MIND
Mirror	Ethereum	Decentralized writing platform with NFT integration	ETH
Sapien	Ethereum	Social news platform with content creator incentives	SPN
CyberConnect	CyberConnect	Identity sovereignty and ownership of social data	CYBER
Status	Ethereum	Secure messaging app with end-to-end encryption	SNT
Farcaster	Ethereum	Decentralized social network supporting multiple clients	Ethereum testnet
Indorse	Ethereum	Decentralized credentialing platform	IND
Paragraph	Ethereum	Decentralized publishing platform for newsletters	ERC20 / ERC721

Web2 Social Media on Ethereum

Web3 native social platforms are not the only ones trying to incorporate blockchain technology. Admitting their benefits, several major Web2 platforms are aiming to integrate Web3 features into their infrastructure, namely Ethereum ones.

Thus, Reddit has introduced Community Points, which are ERC-20 tokens that users can earn by posting quality content and contributing to online communities (subreddits). These tokens, such as "Moons" on the r/CryptoCurrency subreddit, are independent of Reddit and can not be taken away. Reddit is working with Arbitrum, a layer 2 rollup solution, to scale Ethereum transactions and make Community Points more efficient and scalable.

In 2022, X's premium subscription service, Twitter Blue, has added support for non-fungible tokens (NFTs). Users can connect their wallets and display NFTs as their profile pictures. Additionally, X has announced plans to create a decentralized social network in the future, although specific details are yet to be revealed. Moreover, Instagram has announced support for NFTs on Ethereum and Polygon. Its users can connect their Ethereum crypto wallets and post NFTs directly on their Instagram profiles, allowing them to showcase and share their digital collectibles with their followers.

These centralized platforms integrate crypto and blockchain technology to offer users new features, incentives, enhanced digital ownership, and a more decentralized and transparent experience in their online social interactions.

Notable Blockchain Social Media Platforms on Other Chains / Multichain

The crypto space has witnessed the emergence of several noteworthy decentralized social media platforms operating on various blockchains, demonstrating the abundance of diversity and innovation in this space. These platforms have harnessed the capabilities of their respective blockchain infrastructures to build robust social media ecosystem. Table 4 highlights some of the notable platforms that have made significant strides in this domain.

The Lens Protocol Ecosystem

Launched in 2022 by the experienced team behind Aave, Lens Protocol stands out as a promising decentralized social media network. It introduces Lens, a fully composable and decentralized social graph that empowers users with complete control over their social profile and its usage. With Lens Protocol, users have the ability to mint a Lens handle as a non-fungible token (NFT) to their crypto wallet. These Lens NFTs are compatible with various decentralized applications (dApps) and smart contracts within the expanding LensVerse ecosystem. Operating on the Polygon network/EVM, Lens Protocol provides users with the advantage of low gas fees and fast transactions, enhancing the overall user experience. In terms of functionality, Lens Protocol serves as a viable alternative to traditional social media platforms such as Facebook and Medium. It allows creators to assert ownership over their content and offers the necessary tools for users to build their own social media platforms using Web3 technology.

As for ecosystem projects, Lenster is a feature-rich, decentralized social media web application with similarities to X in terms of layout and execution, Lenster stands out by supporting a wide range of NFT types and enabling composability with other Web3 applications built on the Lens Protocol.

Powered by the Lens Protocol, Lenstube is a decentralized social video-sharing platform that offers an alternative to traditional platforms like YouTube. In addition to content discovery and short-form videos, Lenstube integrates blockchain to offer unique functionalities. Users can tip their favorite creators using MATIC coins, a cryptocurrency based on the Polygon network. This provides a direct and transparent way for content consumers to show their appreciation and support to the creators they enjoy. Furthermore, Lenstube the curation of videos as NFTs, meaning that videos can be tokenized and traded as unique digital assets, potentially providing additional revenue streams and opportunities for creators.

The Steem Universe

Steem, known as the "social blockchain," is a notable blockchain for decentralized social media platforms (Guidi et al., 2020; Ba et al., 2022). It has its own native coin called STEEM which powers various social networks built on its native blockchain.

First, Steemit, one of the oldest and most prominent blockchain-based social media platforms, combines elements of blockchain, social media, and cryptocurrency, offering functionality similar to Facebook and Reddit. The platform fosters user engagement by providing incentives in the form of STEEM tokens. Users who actively contribute to the community by sharing content, commenting, and upvoting other users' posts receive higher rates of STEEM rewards.

Second is D.tube, a blockchain-based social media video platform. Initially built on Steem and IPFS, it rewarded users in STEEM. It has since transitioned to its own blockchain called Avalon and now utilizes its native coin, DTUBE.

Third in the Steem ecosystem is Dlive which focuses on livestreaming. It has undergone ownership changes and switched chains, initially moving to the Lino blockchain and later to the TRON network. The Dlive system leverages three basic tokens: Lemon, BTT, and BTT Stake.

Hive-Based

Hive is a decentralized social media platform that emerged as a fork from the Steem blockchain. It was initiated by a community of users from Steem who desired increased decentralization and governance within the platform. Hive operates using its own native token called HIVE. The primary goal of Hive is to offer a social media experience that is more community-driven and resistant to censorship. By leveraging blockchain technology, Hive aims to provide a secure and transparent environment where users have greater control over their data and content.

Polkadot-Based

Subsocial is a popular decentralized social media platform that operates on the Polkadot network and utilizes the InterPlanetary File System (IPFS) for decentralized storage. It offers various features to enable crypto monetization within the platform, including tipping, smart contracts, and advertisements. As a decentralized platform, Subsocial allows users to maintain control over their data and engage in censorship-resistant communication. The platform has garnered support from the Web3 Foundation, which has provided grants, and it has also received backing from the Substrate Builders Program.

Cosmos Network-Based

Desmos Network, a blockchain built on the Cosmos SDK, is specifically designed for social networking applications and projects. The main goal of Desmos is to address the issues faced by social media users, such as censorship and privacy breaches, by prioritizing user interests and decentralizing the business models of social networks (Franco, 2021). By leveraging game theory and on-chain governance, Desmos aims to create a decentralized ecosystem where developers can build social media applications while taking responsibility for handling issues like fake news or criminal activity. The DSM asset, which is the native asset of Desmos, plays a role in governance and other network functions. The Desmos Chain serves as a protocol that allows for the development of various applications on top of it.

Solana-Based

First, Only1 is a decentralized social media protocol that operates on the Solana blockchain. It offers content creators a platform to establish a stronger connection with their audience. By adopting a subscription-based model similar to Patreon and OnlyFans, Only1 leverages NFTs and its native token, LIKE, to power its ecosystem.

Second, Dialect is a smart messaging protocol with broad compatibility across Solana, Ethereum Virtual Machine (EVM), and Aptos. All of its tooling is open source and freely available for developers to utilize. The messaging protocol provided by Dialect will operate both on-chain and off-chain and will include the multi-chain messaging protocol which allows communication across different blockchain networks. One of the standout features of Dialect is its concept of Smart Messaging, due to which developers can embed smart contracts directly into messages. This means that users can interact with the embedded transactions and execute them directly from the message itself.

Binance Smart Chain-Based

Torum is a decentralized social media network that aims to create a social media platform that caters specifically to the crypto community, incorporating features like NFTs, a mining game, crypto news, and crypto-themed emotes. The use of the XTM utility token further enhances the platform's functionality and provides compatibility with the Ethereum network.

Bitcoin SV-Based

Twetch is a social media application designed for various platforms, built on the Bitcoin SV blockchain. It leverages blockchain to prioritize data privacy, decentralization, and transparency within its ecosystem. One key aspect of Twetch is its commitment to on-chain operations. Each Twetch account functions as a cryptocurrency wallet, ensuring that every user's data and interactions are stored directly on the blockchain. This approach enhances security and provides a permanent and auditable record of all user activity. In addition to its focus on privacy and decentralization, Twetch incorporates a native NFT marketplace, providing opportunities for creators to monetize their content and for users to collect and trade digital collectibles directly within the ecosystem.

Bitcoin Cash-Based

Bitcoin Cash has fostered the development of various decentralized social media networks within its ecosystem. These platforms leverage the blockchain's capabilities and integrate BCH as a native currency. They are Read.cash, a blogging platform, where BCH is used to upvote articles; Memo.cash, a decentralized social network that enables users to post visual content and messages, where each Memo.cash account is associated with a crypto wallet address, and all posts are visible to anyone on the blockchain.

Dfinity-Based

DSCVR is a blockchain-based social network built on Dfinity's Internet Computer protocol. By leveraging the capabilities of this protocol, DSCVR aims to address the challenges of scalability and provide a robust infrastructure for a decentralized social platform. The platform aims to offer users greater control over their data and privacy while fostering a community-driven and censorship-resistant social media experience.

Table 4. Non-ethereum-based social media platforms

Non-Ethereum-based Social Media Platforms			
Blockchain	**Platform**	**Notable Features**	**Token**
Polygon/EVM	Lens Protocol	Composable social graph, ownership of content	Lens NFT
Polygon/EVM	Lenster	X-like layout, NFT support	MATIC
Polygon/EVM	Lenstube	Video-sharing, tipping with crypto, NFT curation	MATIC
Steem	Steemit	Facebook/Reddit-like functionality, STEEM rewards	STEEM
Avalon	D.tube	Blockchain video platform, DTUBE rewards	DTUBE
TRON	Dlive	Live streaming, crypto rewards	Lemon, BTT, and BTT Stake
Hive	Hive	Community-driven, resistance to censorship	HIVE
Polkadot	Subsocial	Monetization, censorship-resistant communication	SUB
Cosmos Network	Desmos Network	Game theory, decentralized social ecosystem	DSM
Solana	Only1	Subscription-based model, NFTs, LIKE token	LIKE
Solana, EVM, Aptos	Dialect	Messaging protocol, multi-chain communication	-
Binance Smart Chain (BSC)	Torum	Crypto-focused, NFTs, mining game	XTM
Bitcoin SV	Twetch	Privacy, decentralization, NFT marketplace	BSV
Bitcoin Cash	Read.cash	Blogging platform, BCH upvotes	BCH
Bitcoin Cash	Memo.cash	Decentralized social network, accounts associated with crypto wallets	BCH
Dfinity (Internet Computer)	DSCVR	Data control, censorship resistance	DSCVR (soon)

The popularity of blockchain-based social networks is increasing, with dozens of projects in the cryptocurrency space attracting millions of users. As technology continues to advance, we can anticipate the emergence of the decentralized social network landscape full of initiatives each presenting unique features and expanding capabilities. With the growing interest and ongoing development in this space, we can expect decentralized social networks to diversify further, offering users a wider range of options and functionalities to choose from.

CHALLENGES OF BLOCKCHAIN-BASED DECENTRALIZED SOCIAL NETWORKS

Blockchain-based social networks face a range of challenges that are mainly inherent in the very nature of the blockchain (Zheng et al., 2018). They need to be carefully addressed to ensure their widespread adoption and long-term success. Table 5 presents an overview of issues highlighting the complexities and considerations involved in building and operating social media platforms on blockchain.

Table 5. Challenges of blockchain-based decentralized social networks

Challenges of Blockchain-based Decentralized Social Networks	
Challenge	**Description**
Scalability	Decentralized social networks need to address scalability issues to accommodate a growing user base and handle a large volume of transactions and data effectively.
User experience	Providing a seamless and intuitive user experience is crucial for decentralized social networks to attract and retain users. The interface and functionality should be user-friendly and accessible.
Content moderation	Ensuring appropriate content moderation presents a challenge for decentralized social networks. Implementing mechanisms to filter and moderate content while respecting freedom of expression is vital.
Tough competition	Major centralized social media like Facebook and Instagram have monopolized the market, making it difficult to attract new users to alternative solutions.
Adoption and network effects	Gaining widespread adoption and creating strong network effects are key challenges. Encouraging users to join and engage with the network, and attracting content creators and communities, are critical for success.
Interoperability	Interoperability among different decentralized social networks and blockchain platforms is crucial for seamless communication and the exchange of data and assets between different networks.
Data storage	The decentralization of content presents a challenge when utilizing a blockchain as a storage solution due to the potential size limitations. To address this issue, various existing proposals appeared (IPFS, Arweave).
Regulatory and legal hurdles	Addressing regulatory and legal challenges, such as compliance with data privacy regulations and navigating jurisdictional complexities, is important for decentralized social networks to operate within the law.
Market volatility	Because many platforms are tied to supporting cryptocurrencies, bear markets and crypto market fluctuations can devalue a network's monetization offerings.

Building network effects and attracting users away from well-established centralized platforms pose significant challenges. Decentralized social media need to offer compelling incentives and value propositions to entice users to migrate and actively participate in the network. Creating a vibrant and engaged user community is crucial for the success of decentralized networks, as network effects play a pivotal role in driving adoption and increasing the network's utility and value. Although, these networks face tough competition from dominant centralized platforms that have amassed large user bases and offer a wide range of features and functionalities.

The value proposition of blockchain-based decentralized social networks is often tied to the support and integration of cryptocurrencies. However, one of the issues faced by these networks is the potential impact of bear markets and fluctuations in the cryptocurrency market. When the market experiences a downturn or significant price volatility, the value of the cryptocurrencies used within the network can decrease. This can have implications for the monetization offerings and incentives provided by the network, as users may be less inclined to participate or engage if the value of the tokens or rewards they receive is diminished. Therefore, decentralized social networks need to consider strategies to mitigate the effects of market fluctuations and ensure the sustainability of their monetization models, potentially by diversifying their offerings or implementing mechanisms to stabilize token value.

Also, scalability is a critical challenge for blockchains (Chauhan et al., 2018; Xie et al., 2019). As blockchain-based decentralized social media expand and attract more users, they must effectively handle the increasing volume of data and transactions. It becomes crucial to ensure scalability while maintaining efficiency and decentralization. Still, achieving this balance is a complex task that requires innovative solutions such as layer 2 protocols or sharding (Zhou et al., 2020). These approaches help alleviate the strain on the network infrastructure and enable decentralized networks to handle the growing demands placed upon them.

Interoperability is another important challenge (Belchior et al., 2021) that needs to be addressed in decentralized social networks. Users should be able to interact and share content seamlessly across different networks without encountering barriers or friction. Achieving interoperability requires the development of standardized protocols and bridges between different networks, enabling the exchange of data and transactions. This fosters a more interconnected and collaborative environment, enhancing the overall user experience and expanding the possibilities within decentralized social networks.

The decentralization of content presents a challenge when utilizing a blockchain as a storage solution due to the potential size limitations. To address this issue, various existing proposals such as IPFS or Arweave appeared. This approach resembles previous methods like DHT.

User experience is also a challenge (Na & Ye, 2021). As many blockchain-based social media platforms are still in their early stages of development, their user interfaces and overall experience may not be as refined as those of well-established centralized platforms. To attract and retain users, it is vital to improve the user experience and provide seamless and intuitive interactions. Decentralized social networks need to invest in developing user-friendly interfaces and features that rival or surpass what users are accustomed to on centralized platforms.

Moreover, content moderation is an ongoing issue in blockchain-based social networks. Ironically, free speech is a double-edged sword. Without content moderation, they can become breeding grounds for unrestrained hate speech and cyberbullying. Striking the right balance between freedom of speech and preventing the spread of harmful or illegal content is a complex task. It requires careful consideration and innovative approaches to develop effective moderation mechanisms that maintain the network's integrity while upholding user rights and safety.

As a new phenomenon, blockchain and crypto still face regulatory and legal challenges (Yadav et al., Yeoh, 2017). The regulatory landscape surrounding them continues to evolve, requiring blockchain-based social platforms to navigate complex compliance requirements while upholding privacy and security principles. Ensuring regulatory compliance without compromising the core principles of decentralization pose an ongoing challenge that necessitates close collaboration with regulatory authorities and the development of innovative solutions.

Addressing the aforementioned challenges necessitates continuous research, technological advancements, and collaboration within the community. Overcoming them is crucial for blockchain-based decentralized social networks to realize their potential as a more inclusive, transparent, and user-centric alternative to centralized platforms.

CONCLUSION

Blockchain-based decentralized social networks have the potential to address the limitations and concerns of traditional centralized social platforms. Through the utilization of blockchain's inherent properties such as transparency, immutability, and decentralization, these networks offer enhanced privacy, censorship resistance, and increased user control over personal data.

As these media platforms continue to gain popularity, individuals will experience a newfound level of users' autonomy and power to protect their privacy and utilization of their data. This shift towards freedom of speech, and democratized content creation can cultivate a diverse range of perspectives, challenge the dominance of mainstream media, and provide a platform for emerging voices and narratives to thrive, enabling them to freely express and share their ideas, creativity, and knowledge.

Nonetheless, it is important to acknowledge the challenges that blockchain-based decentralized social networks face so far. Scalability, user experience, content moderation, tough competition with major platforms, interoperability, regulatory compliance, and market volatility are hurdles that must be overcome to realize the full potential of these networks. Collaboration, research, and technological advancements are crucial in addressing these obstacles and finding innovative solutions. Technological advancements, particularly in DLT, hold promise for enhancing the scalability, efficiency, and interoperability of decentralized social media. Policymakers and regulatory bodies will need to adapt and develop frameworks that balance innovation, user rights, and societal concerns. The development and implementation of effective content moderation techniques will be crucial for decentralized social networks to maintain a healthy and safe online environment. Additionally, raising awareness among the general public and educating users about the benefits and advantages of decentralized media, are needed to accelerate adoption and overcome competition.

To date, notable blockchain-based social media initiatives have emerged, with Ethereum serving as a prominent platform for decentralized social applications. The integration of Web2 social media on top of blockchain technology and the presence of other blockchain social media platforms on various chains further expand the possibilities and choices available to users.

To conclude, the future prospects of decentralized social networks seem promising, with the potential to empower individuals, foster digital inclusion, and reshape the online landscape. As technology continues to advance and user awareness grows, decentralized social networks have the opportunity to play a crucial role in creating a more user-centric, private, and democratic online environment.

REFERENCES

Ahn, D., & Shin, D.-H. (2013). Is the social use of media for seeking connectedness or for avoiding social isolation? Mechanisms underlying media use and subjective well-being. *Computers in Human Behavior*, *29*(6), 2453–2462. doi:10.1016/j.chb.2012.12.022

Aichner, T., Grünfelder, M., Maurer, O., & Jegeni, D. (2021). Twenty-Five Years of Social Media: A Review of Social Media Applications and Definitions from 1994 to 2019. *Cyberpsychology, Behavior, and Social Networking*, *24*(4), 215–222. doi:10.1089/cyber.2020.0134 PMID:33847527

Aiello, L. M., & Ruffo, G. (2012). Lotusnet: Tunable privacy for distributed online social network services. *Computer Communications*, *35*(1), 75–88. doi:10.1016/j.comcom.2010.12.006

Asthana, H., & Cox, I. J. (2013) A framework for peer-to-peer micro-blogging. In: *5th International workshop on peer-to-peer systems and online social networks, (HotPOST 2013)*. IEEE. 10.1109/ICDCSW.2013.63

Avellaneda, O., Bachmann, A., Barbir, A., Brenan, J., Dingle, P., Duffy, K. H., & Sporny, M. (2019). Decentralized identity: Where did it come from and where is it going? *IEEE Communications Standards Magazine*, *3*(4), 10–13. doi:10.1109/MCOMSTD.2019.9031542

Ba, C., Zignani, M., & Gaito, S. (2022). The role of cryptocurrency in the dynamics of blockchain-based social networks: The case of Steemit. *PLoS One*, *17*(6), e0267612. doi:10.1371/journal.pone.0267612 PMID:35709197

Baden, Randy & Bender, Adam & Spring, Neil & Bhattacharjee, Bobby & Starin, Daniel. (2009). Persona: An Online Social Network with User-Defined Privacy. *Computer Communication Review – CCR, 39*, 135-146. . doi:10.1145/1594977.1592585

Belchior, R., Vasconcelos, A., Guerreiro, S., & Correia, M. (2021). A survey on blockchain interoperability: Past, present, and future trends. [CSUR]. *ACM Computing Surveys*, *54*(8), 1–41. doi:10.1145/3471140

Benet, J. (2014). *IPFS - Content Addressed, Versioned, P2P File System*. ArXiv. /abs/1407.3561.

Benson, V., Saridakis, G., & Tennakoon, H. (2015). Information disclosure of social media users: Does control over personal information, user awareness and security notices matter? *Information Technology & People*, *28*(3), 426–441. doi:10.1108/ITP-10-2014-0232

Berners-Lee, T., Cailliau, R., Groff, J.-F., & Pollermann, B. (1992). World-Wide Web: The Information Universe. *Electron. Netw. Res. Appl. Policy.*, *2*(1), 52–58. doi:10.1108/eb047254

Bhattacharya, R., White, M., & Beloff, N. (2021). An Exploration of Blockchain in Social Networking Applications. In K. Arai (Ed.), *Intelligent Computing. Lecture Notes in Networks and Systems* (Vol. 284). Springer. doi:10.1007/978-3-030-80126-7_60

Bielenberg, A., Helm, L., Gentilucci, A., Stefanescu, D., & Zhang, H. (2012). *The growth of Diaspora - A decentralized online social network in the wild*. In 2012 Proceedings IEEE INFOCOM Workshops (pp. 13-18). Orlando, FL. 10.1109/INFCOMW.2012.6193476

Bodriagov, O., & Buchegger, S. (2013). Encryption for peer-to-peer social networks. In *Security and privacy in social networks* (pp. 47–65). Springer. doi:10.1007/978-1-4614-4139-7_4

Boyd, D. M., & Ellison, N. B. (2007). Social Network Sites: Definition, History, and Scholarship. *Journal of Computer-Mediated Communication, 13*(1), 210–230. doi:10.1111/j.1083-6101.2007.00393.x

Bradshaw, S., & Howard, P. N. (2019). *The Global Disinformation Order: 2019 Global Inventory of Organised Social Media Manipulation.* University of Nebraska - Lincoln. https://digitalcommons.unl.edu/scholcom/207

Buchegger, S., Schi̇oberg D, Vu L-H, Datta A (2009) Peerson: P2Psocial networking: early experiences and insights. In: Proceedings of the second ACM EuroSys workshop on social network systems, SNS '09, (pp. 46–52). ACM. 10.1145/1578002.1578010

Buterin, V. (2013). *A Next Generation Smart Contract & Decentralized Application Platform.* Ethereum White Paper.

Chao, C. H., Ting, I. H., Tseng, Y. J., Wang, B. W., Wang, S. H., Wang, Y. Q., & Chen, M. C. (2022). The Study of Decentralized Autonomous Organization (DAO) in Social Network. In *Proceedings of the 9th Multidisciplinary International Social Networks Conference* (pp. 59-65). 10.1145/3561278.3561293

Chauhan, A., Malviya, O. P., Verma, M., & Mor, T. S. (2018). *Blockchain and Scalability.* In 2018 IEEE International Conference on Software Quality, Reliability and Security Companion (QRS-C) (pp. 122-128). Lisbon, Portugal. 10.1109/QRS-C.2018.00034

Chowdhury, S. R., Roy, A. R., Shaikh, M., & Daudjee, K. (2015). A taxonomy of decentralized online social networks. *Peer-to-Peer Networking and Applications, 8*(3), 367–383. doi:10.100712083-014-0258-2

Chu, J., Labonte, K., & Levine, B. N. (2002). Availability and locality measurements of peer-to-peer file systems. In Proceedings of ITCom.

Ciriello, R., Beck, R., & Thatcher, J. (2018). The Paradoxical Effects of Blockchain Technology on Social Networking Practices. *Conference: International Conference on Information Systems (ICIS 2018).* 10.2139srn.3920002

Cong, L. W., & He, Z. (2019). Blockchain disruption and smart contracts. *Review of Financial Studies, 32*(5), 1754–1797. doi:10.1093/rfs/hhz007

Cutillo, L., Molva, R., & Strufe, T. (2009). Safebook: A privacy-preserving online social network leveraging on real-life trust. *Commun Mag IEEE, 47*(12), 94–101. doi:10.1109/MCOM.2009.5350374

Datta, A., Buchegger, S., Vu, L.-H., Strufe, T., & Rzadca, K. (2010). Decentralized online social networks. In *Handbook of Social Network Technologies and Applications* (pp. 349–378). Springer. doi:10.1007/978-1-4419-7142-5_17

De Salve, A., Mori, P., & Ricci, L. (2018). A survey on privacy in decentralized online social networks. *Computer Science Review, 27*, 154–176. doi:10.1016/j.cosrev.2018.01.001

De Salve, A., Mori, P., Ricci, L., & Di Pietro, R. (2023). Content privacy enforcement models in decentralized online social networks: State of play, solutions, limitations, and future directions. *Computer Communications, 203*, 199–225. doi:10.1016/j.comcom.2023.02.023

Dhawan, S., Hegelich, S., Sindermann, C., & Montag, C. (2022). Re-start social media, but how? *Telematics and Informatics Reports, 8*, 100017. doi:10.1016/j.teler.2022.100017

Di Domenico, G., Sit, A., & Ishizaka, D. (2021). Fake news, social media and marketing: A systematic review. *Journamedia, Business Research, 124*, 329-341. ISSN 0148-2963. doi:10.1016/j.jbusres.2020.11.037

Dib, O., & Toumi, K. (2020). Decentralized identity systems: Architecture, challenges, solutions and future directions. *Annals of Emerging Technologies in Computing (AETiC)*.

DiNucci, D. (1999). *Fragmented Future., 53*(4), 32.

Dixon, S. (2022). Average daily time spent on social media worldwide 2012-2022. Statista. Retrieved June 18, 2023, from.

Dixon, S. (2023). *Daily time spent on social networking by internet users worldwide from 2012 to 2022*. Statista.

Douceur, J. R., & Wattenhofer, R. P. (2001). Large-scale simulation of replica placement algorithms for a serverless distributed file system. In *Proceedings of MASCOTS*. IEEE. 10.1109/MASCOT.2001.948882

Famulari, A., & Hecker, A. (2013). Mantle: a novel dosn leveraging free storage and local software. In *Advanced Infocomm Technology* (pp. 213–224). Springer. doi:10.1007/978-3-642-38227-7_24

Forsyth, S., & Daudjee, K. (2013). Update management in decentralized online social networks. In *5th International workshop on peer-to-peer systems and online social networks (HotPOST 2013)22*.

Franco, A. (2021). *How Blockchain Technology Can Help Rearchitect Social Networks: An Analysis of Desmos Network*. Università Ca' Foscari Venezia. http://dspace.unive.it/handle/10579/19800

Global Social Media Statistics. (2023). DataReportal – Global Digital Insights. GSMS.

Graffi, K., Gross, C., Stingl, D., Hartung, D., Kovacevic, A., & Steinmetz, R. (2011). *LifeSocial. KOM: A Secure and P2P-based Solution for Online Social Networks*. IEEE. . doi:10.1109/CCNC.2011.5766541

Guidi, B. (2020). When Blockchain meets Online Social Networks. *Pervasive and Mobile Computing, 62*, 101131. doi:10.1016/j.pmcj.2020.101131

Guidi, B. (2021). An Overview of Blockchain Online Social Media from the Technical Point of View. *Applied Sciences (Basel, Switzerland), 11*(21), 9880. doi:10.3390/app11219880

Guidi, B., Michienzi, A., & Ricci, L. (2020). Steem Blockchain: Mining the Inner Structure of the Graph. *IEEE Access : Practical Innovations, Open Solutions, 8*, 210251–210266. doi:10.1109/ACCESS.2020.3038550

Gunitsky, S. (2015). Corrupting the Cyber-Commons: Social Media as a Tool of Autocratic Stability. *Perspectives on Politics, 13*(1), 42–54. doi:10.1017/S1537592714003120

Han, L., Nath, B., Iftode, L., & Muthukrishnan, S. (2011). Social butterfly: social caches for distributed social networks. In: Proceedings of SocialCom/PASSAT, (pp. 81–8623). PASSAT. doi:10.1109/PASSAT/SocialCom.2011.105

Han, L., Punceva, M., Nath, B., Muthukrishnan, S. M., & Iftode, L. (2012) SocialCDN: caching techniques for distributed social networks. In: *2012 IEEE International conference on peer-to-peer computing*. IEEE. 10.1109/P2P.2012.6335799

Hwang, H., & Kim, O. (2015). Social media as a tool for social movements: The effect of social media use and social capital on intention to participate in social movements. *International Journal of Consumer Studies*, 39(5), 478–488. doi:10.1111/ijcs.12221

Jahid, S., Nilizadeh, S., Mittal, P., Borisov, N., & Kapadia, A. (2012). Decent: A decentralized architecture for enforcing privacy in online social networks. In *Pervasive Computing and Communications Workshops, 2012 IEEE International Conference on* (pp. 326-332). IEEE. 10.1109/PerComW.2012.6197504

Jain, A. K., Sahoo, S. R., & Kaubiyal, J. (2021). Online social networks security and privacy: Comprehensive review and analysis. *Complex Intell. Syst.*, 7(5), 2157–2177. doi:10.100740747-021-00409-7

Jemielniak, D. (2020). Researching Social Networks: Opportunities and Challenges. *Frontiers in Human Dynamics*, 2, 528336. doi:10.3389/fhumd.2020.00001

Jiang, L., & Zhang, X. (2019). Bcosn: A blockchain-based decentralized online social network. *IEEE Transactions on Computational Social Systems*, 6(6), 1454–1466. doi:10.1109/TCSS.2019.2941650

Jing, T. W., & Murugesan, R. K. (2019). A theoretical framework to build trust and prevent fake news in social media using blockchain. In *Recent trends in data science and soft computing: Proceedings of the 3rd international conference of reliable information and communication technology (IRICT 2018)* (pp. 955-962). Springer International Publishing. 10.1007/978-3-319-99007-1_88

Kaur, J., & Dabas, D. (2023). *Literature Review of Smart Contracts Using Blockchain Technology*. New Approaches for Multidimensional Signal Processing. doi:10.1007/978-981-19-7842-5_16

Kidd, D., & McIntosh, K. (2016). Social Media and Social Movements. *Sociology Compass*, 10(9), 785–794. doi:10.1111oc4.12399

Kuem, J., Ray, S., Siponen, M., & Kim, S. S. (2017). What leads to prosocial behaviors on social networking services: A tripartite model. *Journal of Management Information Systems*, 34(1), 40–70. doi:10.1080/07421222.2017.1296744

La Cava, L., Greco, S., & Tagarelli, A. (2021). Understanding the growth of the Fediverse through the lens of Mastodon. *Applied Network Science*, 6(1), 1–35. doi:10.100741109-021-00392-5

Li, Y., Li, Y., Yan, Q., & Deng, R. H. (2015). Privacy leakage analysis in online social networks. *Computers & Security*, 49, 239–254. doi:10.1016/j.cose.2014.10.012

Liu, N., & Ye, Z. (2021). Empirical research on the blockchain adoption – based on TAM. *Applied Economics*, 53(37), 4263–4275. doi:10.1080/00036846.2021.1898535

Liu, Z., Li, Y., Min, Q., & Chang, M. (2022). User incentive mechanism in blockchain-based online community: An empirical study of Steemit. *Information & Management*, *59*(7), 103596. doi:10.1016/j.im.2022.103596

Madhavan, N. (2007, July 6). India gets more Net Cool. *Hindustan Times*. http://www.hindustantimes.com/StoryPage/StoryPage.aspx?id=f2565bb8-663e-48c1-94ee-d99567577bdd

Maesa, D. D. F., Mori, P., & Ricci, L. (2017). Blockchain-based access control. In *IFIP International Conference on Distributed Applications and Interoperable Systems* (pp. 206-220). Springer.

Mannell, K., & Smith, E. T. (2022). Alternative Social Media and the Complexities of a More Participatory Culture: A View From Scuttlebutt. *Social Media + Society*, *8*(3). Advance online publication. doi:10.1177/20563051221122448

Marcon, M., Viswanath, B., Cha, M., & Gummadi, K. P. (2011). Sharing social content from home: A measurement-driven feasibility study. In *Proceedings of NOSSDAV '11* (pp. 45-50). ACM. 10.1145/1989240.1989253

McHatton, J., & Ghazinour, K. (2023) Mitigating Social Media Privacy Concerns - A Comprehensive Study. In *Proceedings of the 9th ACM International Workshop on Security and Privacy Analytics (IWSPA '23)*. Association for Computing Machinery, New York, NY, USA. 10.1145/3579987.3586565

Modi, N. (2023). Comparative Analysis of Different Blockchain Technology to Improve the Security in Social Network. In V. E. Balas, V. B. Semwal, & A. Khandare (Eds.), *Intelligent Computing and Networking. Lecture Notes in Networks and Systems* (Vol. 632). Springer. doi:10.1007/978-981-99-0071-8_7

Nakamoto, S. (2008). *Bitcoin: A Peer-to-Peer Electronic Cash System*. Bitcoin. https://bitcoin.org/bitcoin.pdf

Nasim, R., & Buchegger, S. (2014). Xacml-based access control for decentralized online social networks. In *2014 IEEE/ACM 7th International Conference on Utility and Cloud Computing* (pp. 671-676). IEEE. 10.1109/UCC.2014.108

Nath, K., Dhar, S., & Basishtha, S. (2014). Web 1.0 to Web 3.0 - Evolution of the Web and its various challenges. In *2014 International Conference on Reliability Optimization and Information Technology (ICROIT)* (pp. 86-89). Faridabad, India. 10.1109/ICROIT.2014.6798297

Nepali, R. & Wang, Y. (2013). SONET: A SOcial NETwork model for privacy monitoring and ranking, (pp. 162-166). IEEE. . doi:10.1109/ICDCSW.2013.49

Ngak, C. (2011) Then and now: a history of social networking sites. *CBS news*.

Nilizadeh, S., Jahid, S., Mittal, P., Borisov, N., & Kapadia, A. (2012). Cachet: A decentralized architecture for privacy preserving social networking with caching. In *Proceedings of the 8th CoNEXT* (pp. 337-348). ACM. 10.1145/2413176.2413215

Paul, T., Famulari, A., & Strufe, T. (2014). A survey on decentralized Online Social Networks. *Computer Networks*, *75*, 437–452. doi:10.1016/j.comnet.2014.10.005

Pennycook, G., McPhetres, J., Zhang, Y., Lu, J. G., & Rand, D. G. (2020). Fighting COVID-19 misinformation on social media: Experimental evidence for a scalable accuracy-nudge intervention. *Psychological Science*, *31*(7), 770–780. doi:10.1177/0956797620939054 PMID:32603243

Pfeiffer, A., Kriglstein, S., Wernbacher, T., & Bezzina, S. (2020). Blockchain technologies and social media: A snapshot. In *ECSM 2020 8th European Conference on Social Media* (p. 196). Academic Conferences and publishing limited.

Pouwels, J. L., Keijsers, L., & Odgers, C. (2022). Who benefits most from using social media, the socially rich or the socially poor? *Current Opinion in Psychology*, *47*, 101351. doi:10.1016/j.copsyc.2022.101351 PMID:35662060

Pouwelse, J. A., Garbacki, P., Wang, J., Bakker, A., Yang, J., Iosup, A., Epema, D. H., Reinders, M., Van Steen, M. R., & Sips, H. J. (2008). Tri-bler: A social-based peer-to-peer system. *Concurr Comput PractExperience*, *20*(2), 127–138. doi:10.1002/cpe.1189

Qamar, M., Malik, M., Batool, S., Mehmood, S., Malik, A. W., & Rahman, A. (2016). Centralized to decentralized social networks: Factors that matter (pp. 37-54).

Ranttila, K. (2020). *Social Media and Monopoly. Ohio NUL Rev.*, *46*, 161.

Rathore, S., Sharma, P. K., Loia, V., Jeong, Y., & Park, J. H. (2017). Social network security: Issues, challenges, threats, and solutions. *Information Sciences*, *421*, 43–69. doi:10.1016/j.ins.2017.08.063

Schwittmann, L., Wander, M., Boelmann, C., & Weis, T. (2014). Privacy Preservation in Decentralized Online Social Networks. *IEEE Internet Computing*, *18*(2), 16–23. doi:10.1109/MIC.2013.131

Senthil Kumar, N., Saravanakumar, K., & Deepa, K. (2016). On Privacy and Security in Social Media – A Comprehensive Study. *Procedia Computer Science*, *78*, 114–119. doi:10.1016/j.procs.2016.02.019

Seong, S.-W., Seo, J., Nasielski, M., Sengupta, D., Hangal, S., Teh, S. K., Chu, R., Dodson, B., & Lam, M. S. (2010). Prpl: A decentralized social networking infrastructure. In *Proceedings of the 1st ACM Workshop on Mobile Cloud Computing & Services: Social Networks and Beyond* (pp. 8:1-8:8). ACM.

Shahriar, N., Chowdhury, S. R., Sharmin, M., Ahmed, R., Boutaba, R., & Mathieu, B. (2013) Ensuring β-Availability in P2P Social Networks. In: *5th International workshop on peer-to-peer systems and online social networks (HotPOST 2013)*. IEEE. 10.1109/ICDCSW.2013.91

Shahriar, N., Sharmin, M., Ahmed, R., Rahman, M., Boutaba, R., & Mathieu, B. (2012). Diurnal availability for peer-to-peer systems. In *Proceedings of CCNC*, Las Vegas, Nevada, USA.

Shakimov, A., Lim, H., Caceres, R., Cox, L. P., Li, K. A., Liu, D., & Varshavsky, A. (2011). Vis-`a-vis: privacy-preserving online social networking via virtual individual servers. In: *Proceedings of COMS-NETS*, (pp. pp 1–10). IEEE.

Sharma, R., & Datta, A. (2012) Supernova: super-peers based architecture for decentralized online social networks. In: Proceedings ofCOMSNETS, (pp. 1–10). IEEE. doi:10.1109/COMSNETS.2012.6151349

Shilina, S. (2022). *A comprehensive study on Non-Fungible Tokens (NFTs): Use cases, ecosystem, benefits & challenges*. Research Gate. . doi:10.13140/RG.2.2.15324.67206

Shu, K., Bhattacharjee, A., Alatawi, F., Nazer, T. H., Ding, K., Karami, M., & Liu, H. (2020). Combating disinformation in a social media age. *Wiley Interdisciplinary Reviews. Data Mining and Knowledge Discovery*, *10*(6), e1385. doi:10.1002/widm.1385

Smith, M., Szongott, C., Henne, B., & von Voigt, G. (2012). Big data privacy issues in public social media. In *2012 6th IEEE International Conference on Digital Ecosystems and Technologies (DEST)* (pp. 1-6). Campione d'Italia, Italy. 10.1109/DEST.2012.6227909

Stutzbach, D., & Rejaie, R. (2006). Understanding churn in peer-to-peer networks. In *Proceedings of IMC* (pp. 189-202). ACM. 10.1145/1177080.1177105

Trepte, S. (2021). The Social Media Privacy Model: Privacy and Communication in the Light of Social Media Affordances. *Communication Theory*, *31*(4), 549–570. doi:10.1093/ct/qtz035

Ur. Rahman, M., Guidi, B., & Baiardi, F. (2020). Blockchain-based access control management for Decentralized Online Social Networks. *Journal of Parallel and Distributed Computing*, *144*, 41–54. doi:10.1016/j.jpdc.2020.05.011

van Dijck, J. (2013). *The Culture of Connectivity: A Critical History of Social Media*. Oxford University Press. doi:10.1093/acprof:oso/9780199970773.001.0001

Vosoughi, S., Roy, D., & Aral, S. (2018). The spread of true and false news online. *Science*, *359*(6380), 1146–1151. doi:10.1126cience.aap9559 PMID:29590045

Wang, P., Zhu, J., & Ma, Q. (2023). Private Data Protection in Social Networks Based on Blockchain. *International Journal of Advanced Networking and Applications.*, *14*(04), 5549–5555. doi:10.35444/IJANA.2023.14407

Wellman, B., Salaff, J., Dimitrova, D., Garton, L., Gulia, M., & Haythornthwaite, C. (1996). Computer networks as social networks: Collaborative work, telework, and virtual community. *Annual Review of Sociology*, *293*(1), 2031–2034. doi:10.1146/annurev.soc.22.1.213

Xie, J., Yu, F. R., Huang, T., Xie, R., Liu, J., & Liu, Y. (2019). A Survey on the Scalability of Blockchain Systems. *IEEE Network*, *33*(5), 166–173. doi:10.1109/MNET.001.1800290

Yadav, S. P., Agrawal, K. K., Bhati, B. S., Al-Turjman, F., & Mostarda, L. (2022). Blockchain-Based Cryptocurrency Regulation: An Overview. *Computational Economics*, *59*(4), 1659–1675. doi:10.100710614-020-10050-0

Yen, N. Y., Zhang, C., Waluyo, A. B., & Park, J. J. (2015). Social Media Services and Technologies Towards Web 3.0. *Multimedia Tools and Applications*, *74*(14), 5007–5013. doi:10.100711042-015-2461-4

Yeoh, P. (2017). Regulatory issues in blockchain technology. *Journal of Financial Regulation and Compliance*, *25*(2), 196–208. doi:10.1108/JFRC-08-2016-0068

Yeung, C., Liccardi, I., Lu, K., Seneviratne, O., & Berners-Lee, T. (2011). Decentralization: The Future of Online Social Networking (2nd ed.). Research Gate.

Yurder, Y., & Akdol, B. (2020). Social Media as a Communication Channel. In A. Özbebek Tunç & P. Aslan (Eds.), *Business Management and Communication Perspectives in Industry 4.0* (pp. 115–131). IGI Global. doi:10.4018/978-1-5225-9416-1.ch007

Zheng, Z., Xie, S., Dai, H. N., Chen, X., & Wang, H. (2018). Blockchain challenges and opportunities: A survey. *International Journal of Web and Grid Services*, *14*(4), 352–375. doi:10.1504/IJWGS.2018.095647

Zhou, Q., Huang, H., Zheng, Z., & Bian, J. (2020). Solutions to Scalability of Blockchain: A Survey. *IEEE Access : Practical Innovations, Open Solutions*, *8*, 16440–16455. doi:10.1109/ACCESS.2020.2967218

Zignani, M., Gaito, S., & Rossi, G. P. (2018). Follow the "Mastodon": Structure and Evolution of a Decentralized Online Social Network. *Proceedings of the International AAAI Conference on Web and Social Media, 12*(1), 541-550. 10.1609/icwsm.v12i1.14988

Zulli, D., Liu, M., & Gehl, R. (2020). Rethinking the "social" in "social media": Insights into topology, abstraction, and scale on the Mastodon social network. *New Media & Society*, *22*(7), 1188–1205. doi:10.1177/1461444820912533

Chapter 11
Building Blocks for the Metaverse:
Virtual Worlds, Marketplaces, and Tools

Shailey Singh

BUK technology, USA & Symbiosis International University (Deemed), India

Himanshu Sisodia

(iD) https://orcid.org/0009-0003-1550-0884

GroCurv.com, India & University of Stirling, UK & SSBM Geneva, Switzerland

ABSTRACT

The term 'metaverse,' was first coined in Neal Stephenson's 1992 novel "Snow Crash," and has since been used to describe various types of virtual and augmented reality experiences. . The metaverse holds varying interpretations for different individuals. From its origins in science fiction literature to its recent rise to prominence in popular culture and the technology industry, the metaverse has captured the imagination of many. For some, it represents a virtual arena for socializing with friends, while others perceive it as a potential commercial arena for businesses and their clients. This chapter explores the concept of metaverse and its core building blocks. The chapter has three major sections: the first deals with an understanding of the emergence and concept of metaverse with a focus on virtual worlds, the second presents insight into the economy and commercial value generation by this new meta-era, and the third delves into the techniques and tools that enable the metaverse.

INTRODUCTION

The term "Metaverse", was first coined in Neal Stephenson's 1992 novel "Snow Crash" and has since been used to describe various types of virtual and augmented reality experiences. Over the course of the next two decades, the term was sparingly used, and mostly by sci-fi evangelists. But the concept once again rose to discussion in 2011 when Ernest Cline published his futuristic and best-seller novel - *Ready*

DOI: 10.4018/978-1-6684-9919-1.ch011

Copyright © 2023, IGI Global. Copying or distributing in print or electronic forms without written permission of IGI Global is prohibited.

Player One, where the protagonist goes on a search for an easter egg in a worldwide virtual reality game. The best-seller novel later led to a box-office hit movie and a popular game title.

This set the pace for the next decade where many video game companies explored what the metaverse really is. Roblox offered immersive user-generated games, and Decentraland tried creating new virtual experiences, but the term "Metaverse" gained widespread recognition when Facebook renamed itself to Meta in October 2021 and unveiled its intentions to allocate a minimum of $10 billion towards the development of this concept.

The Metaverse holds varying interpretations for different individuals. From its origins in science fiction literature to its recent rise to prominence in popular culture and the technology industry, the Metaverse has captured the imagination of many. For some, it represents a virtual arena for socializing with friends, while others perceive it as a potential commercial arena for businesses and their clients. This chapter explores the concept of metaverse and its core building blocks. The chapter has three major sections: the first deals with an understanding of the emergence and concept of Metaverse with a focus on virtual worlds, the second presents insight into the economy and commercial value generation by this new meta-era, and the third delves into the techniques and tools that enable the metaverse.

VIRTUAL WORLDS

Understanding the Potential of the Metaverse

The emergence of virtual worlds as a central component of the metaverse provides a glimpse of the transformative potential of immersive digital environments. Virtual worlds, which are defined as explorable and interactive online simulations, have become increasingly influential in shaping the future of the internet (Ball, 2020). Virtual worlds serve as dynamic platforms that transcend physical boundaries in the metaverse, allowing users to engage with digital realms in a highly immersive manner (Stephenson, 2020). These virtual environments allow users to construct, investigate, and interact within a variety of fabricated environments, and are frequently accessible via a variety of devices including computers, mobile phones, and virtual reality headgear. The ability to establish a virtual identity and interact with other users bolsters the significance of virtual environments in the metaverse (Dionisio et al, 2013).

The transformative power of virtual environments in the metaverse resides in their capacity to break down barriers and provide unparalleled immersion. By leveraging technologies like virtual reality (VR), augmented reality (AR), and mixed reality (MR), users can transcend physical limitations and immerse themselves in digital worlds that obscure the line between the real and the virtual (Gartner, 2023). Users can engage in previously inconceivable experiences by transcending the limitations of physical space afforded by virtual environments' immersion. The impact of virtual worlds is not limited to individual users; it extends to multiple industries, such as education, healthcare, and entertainment, revolutionising how we learn, rehabilitate, and interact with media (Dionisio et al, 2013). Particularly, virtual reality offers users a completely immersive and interactive experience, transporting them to simulated environments that can imitate real-world settings or offer wholly fantastical landscapes (Schuemie et al., 2001). Utilising specialised headsets, controllers, and haptic feedback devices, which enhance the sense of presence and immersion, users can interact with virtual environments. Augmented reality, on the other hand, augments users' perception and interaction with their physical surroundings by superimposing digital information onto the actual world (Milgram et al., 1995). Augmented reality allows users to experience virtual elements within the context of their physical surroundings by fusing the digital and physical worlds. Mixed reality integrates virtual reality and augmented reality, allowing users to interact with virtual objects and environments while maintaining a connection with the real world (Blanchard et al, 2022). The differences between Augmented Reality (AR), Virtual Reality (VR), and Mixed Reality (MR) are depicted in Figure 1.

Figure 1. VR, AR, & MR

Differences

VR
(Virtual Reality)

Virtual Reality (VR) involves virtual environments which are digital with a complete cut from the physical environment. These environments can be used in games, training, and demonstration. There are several digital agencies which provide customized training solutions based on business needs. The VR example involves police training, sports training, live broadcast.

In the VR scenario, the user gets completely involved in the digital environment without the involvement of the physical environment. The user is expected to have access to a suitable system and compatible VR device (VR headset) to get involved in the applications or games having support for VR. The popular VR devices include Oculus Rift, HTC Vive, and Google Cardboard. The gaming agencies target their games specific to these devices having their control mechanism.

AR
(Augmented Reality)

Augmented Reality (AR) involves real environments with the addition of digital elements. The live view can be captured using the camera. The digital elements will be added on top of the live view. Similar to VR, AR can also be used in games, training, and demonstration. The most popular example of AR is the game Pokemon Go.

Users can engage in AR-based application even with their smartphones having a camera. In most of the cases, there is no need for high-end systems to experience AR. The applications or games just add digital elements on top of live capture to engage the user.

MR
(Mixed Reality)

Mixed Reality (MR) involves a mix of aspects from both virtual and real environments with the involvement of digital elements. The virtual objects can be mapped to the physical environment. It differs with AR where the virtual objects are placed on a separate layer on top of the physical world. Mixed Reality can be much more useful in AI-based training involving the mapping or interaction of digital elements with the physical world.

In the case of MR, the user can experience the involvement of virtual objects with the real world or physical view. The user needs a headset capable of MR. The HoloLens device from Microsoft can provide such an experience.

TECHNOLUSH
www.technolush.com

Analysing the impact of virtual worlds on the future of the Internet exposes the profound impact they can have on numerous facets of online life. Virtual environments facilitate social connections, allowing users to develop meaningful relationships, collaborate on projects, and participate in shared experiences. Furthermore, these immersive environments can stimulate economic activity by establishing new marketplaces and virtual commerce opportunities. In an article Hendaoui et al (2008) highlighted the potential for virtual worlds to facilitate novel forms of economic exchange, including virtual real estate and in-game economies.

Through the use of avatars – digital representations of oneself within the virtual environment – virtual worlds also provide an avenue for creative expression and customization. Avatars are capable of communicating with other users, displaying emotions, and engaging in a variety of activities, allowing users to transcend the limitations of corporeal embodiment. This feature of virtual worlds provides users with a sense of anonymity, which can be advantageous in situations such as online gaming or social networking, allowing individuals to freely express themselves and investigate various aspects of their identities.

Virtual environments play a crucial role in releasing the metaverse's potential. These immersive digital environments provide transformative experiences, redefine conventional online interactions, and create new opportunities for social engagement, economic activity, and innovation. As virtual worlds continue to evolve and influence the future of the Internet, it is crucial for businesses, policymakers, and researchers to comprehend their significance and effectively navigate this emerging landscape.

Increasing Participation in Virtual Worlds

In the domain of virtual worlds, user engagement is essential for the development of immersive experiences that captivate and involve individuals within digital realms. The various facets of enhancing user engagement in virtual environments, with an emphasis on the breaching of boundaries in digital realms through the use of immersive technologies. It explores the domains of virtual reality (VR), augmented reality (AR), and mixed reality (MR), highlighting how these technologies can be used to generate unparalleled user immersion.

Immersive experiences are at the vanguard of virtual worlds, expanding the possibilities of digital domains. By utilising technologies such as VR, AR, and MR, users are transported to completely new dimensions, distorting the boundaries between the physical and digital worlds (Jung et al, 2020). Particularly, virtual reality provides a fully immersive experience by positioning users in a simulated environment where they can interact with objects and interact with other users in a realistic manner (Mollet et al., 2009). Augmented reality enriches users' perception of reality by superimposing digital information, imagery, and interactive elements on the real-world environment (Azuma, 1997). Mixed reality incorporates elements of both virtual reality and augmented reality, allowing users to simultaneously interact with virtual and real-world objects (Milgram & Kishino, 1994).

Adoption of immersive technologies has revolutionised virtual world user engagement. These technologies facilitate unprecedented levels of interaction and presence by immersing users in a virtual environment (Bailenson, 2018). Users are able to investigate and manipulate virtual objects, collaborate with others, and experience "being there" in the digital world (Slater, 2009).

In recent years, the expansion and adoption of immersive technologies have been remarkable. The global VR and AR market is expected to reach $859.35 billion by 2030, according to statistics (Rossi et al, 2023). Increasing affordability of VR headsets, advances in AR-enabled smartphones, and the development of MR devices have all contributed to the pervasive adoption of these technologies (Alam et al, 2021). This exponential growth demonstrates the increasing interest and demand for immersive virtual world experiences.

Utilising immersive technologies is essential for developing virtual environments with unparalleled user immersion. By incorporating cutting-edge hardware, software, and interactive design principles, developers can transport users to entirely new dimensions (Bowman & McMahan, 2007).

Immersive technologies facilitate a sense of presence and realism, allowing users to interact with virtual objects and engage in natural interactions with other users (Lanier, 2017). As user immersion increases, they are more likely to invest time, attention, and resources in virtual environments.

The ability to create customised and individualised experiences is a significant advantage of immersive technologies in virtual environments. According to Dede (2009), users can customise their virtual environment to suit their preferences and requirements, creating a unique and immersive space.

Integration of immersive technologies into virtual environments is not limited to the entertainment and gaming industries. (Korkut and Surer, 2023) It has implications in various fields, including education, healthcare, architecture, and training. Immersive experiences in education allow students to investigate historical events, scientific concepts, and complex environments in a hands-on and engaging way (Herrington, 2006). Virtual environments have been utilised in the healthcare industry for simulation training, surgical planning, and therapeutic interventions (Gee, 2013).

Social Interactions and Teamwork in Virtual Worlds

Virtual worlds offer unprecedented opportunities for social interactions and collaboration, allowing users to connect and collaborate in digital spaces. Within these virtual environments, users are able to construct avatars, which serve as their virtual identities. (Ducheneaut et al., 2007) Avatars serve as a means for users to convey their identity and interact with others. In addition, users can communicate with others in a variety of ways, including text-based messaging, vocal chat, and non-verbal signals such as their avatars' gestures and movements. (Ducheneaut et al., 2007) These communication channels allow for complex and nuanced interactions, allowing users to articulate themselves and partake in meaningful conversations. The elimination of geographical barriers is one of the most remarkable features of socialisation in virtual environments. Users from different regions of the globe can interact in a virtual environment, transcending geographical and cultural distances. This global connectivity fosters a diverse and inclusive community in which individuals from various backgrounds and points of view can interact and collaborate (Steinkuehler & Williams, 2006). In virtual environments, virtual gatherings, events, and conferences have become increasingly prevalent. These events provide opportunities for users to engage in collaborative activities, attend presentations and seminars, and network with peers (Minocha and Roberts, 2008). Furthermore, numerous communities centred on shared interests, activities, or professional affiliations have emerged in virtual environments. (Steinkuehler & Williams, 2006) These communities provide spaces for individuals to gather, establish relationships, and collaborate on initiatives.

Social Interaction and Community Development

Socialisation and community building are essential aspects of virtual environments, as they provide a venue for individuals with shared interests to interact and form relationships. Within virtual environments, users can join and actively participate in virtual communities centred on specific topics, interests, or shared objectives. These communities serve as centres for social interactions, knowledge sharing, and collaboration, nurturing a sense of community and belonging among their members (Resnik et al., 2021). Virtual worlds feature numerous communities that appeal to a variety of interests and inclinations. Whether it's a community dedicated to art and creativity, gaming enthusiasts, or professionals from various industries, virtual worlds provide a space for individuals to engage in meaningful interactions with others who share their pursuits. These communities serve as a support system where users can seek guidance, share their experiences, and collaborate on initiatives (Resnik et al., 2021). In addition, virtual environments allow users to transcend physical limitations and interact with people from diverse cultural and geographical contexts. This global reach and diversity enhance the socialisation experience within virtual communities, as users are exposed to diverse viewpoints and engage in cross-cultural exchanges (Steinkuehler & Williams, 2006). Users engage in a vast array of social activities within virtual communities. They can engage in group discussions, attend virtual events, collaborate on projects, and even form virtual enterprises. Through shared experiences and interactions, virtual communities become a place where enduring friendships, mentorship opportunities, and connections are forged (Resnik et al., 2021). Moreover, virtual worlds provide a secure and inclusive environment for individuals to freely and authentically express themselves. Through customization options, users are able to construct avatars that reflect their identities and indulge in self-expression. This capacity to exhibit uniqueness and originality fosters a sense of self-assurance and acceptability within virtual communities (Steinkuehler & Williams, 2006).

The Development of Virtual Events, Congregations, and Conferences

There has been an extraordinary increase in the prevalence of virtual events, conferences, and gatherings. This trend has been propelled by technological advancements and the rising global demand for remote connectivity. Virtual worlds have emerged as a compelling alternative to conventional physical events, providing immersive and interactive experiences that transcend geographic boundaries (Tussyadiah & Pesonen, 2016). Virtual events enable users to attend presentations, seminars, and workshops without having to physically travel. Participants can access live or pre-recorded content, interact with presenters, and engage in discussions with other attendees via virtual platforms (Alcañiz et al., 2019). Networking is one of the most significant advantages of virtual events. Users can connect with like-minded individuals, industry professionals, and potential international partners. The networking capabilities of virtual worlds allow for the interchange of contact information, private dialogues, and the development of relationships that may lead to future collaborations or business opportunities (Alcañiz et al., 2019). Virtual exhibitions and demonstrations are an additional essential element of virtual events. Participants can investigate virtual spaces showcasing products, services, and innovations at these exhibitions. Users are able to interact with virtual representations of physical products, view product demonstrations, and even make virtual purchases (Alcañiz et al., 2019). In addition, virtual events provide an inclusive and accessible platform for individuals who encounter obstacles in attending physical events, such as financial constraints, limited mobility, or geographical distances. (Tussadiah & Pesonen, 2016). Virtual events have also demonstrated their resilience and adaptability during difficult periods, such as the global pandemic of COVID-19. When physical events became impracticable or restricted, virtual events provided organisations with a viable alternative to continue engaging their audiences and delivering valuable content. (Tussadiah & Pesonen, 2016).

Magnum's Museum in the Metaverse: A Case Study

In June 2022, Magnum, a renowned ice cream brand, created a virtual exhibition within the metaverse in order to engage with a tech-savvy audience. Magnum invited delegates to the MET AMS metaverse festival in Amsterdam to visit the Magnum Pleasure Museum hosted in Decentraland. Magnum's collaborations with renowned painters, designers, and sculptors yielded a breathtaking collection of original artwork on display in this virtual museum. Guests were captivated by the comprehensive gallery experience, which allowed them to appreciate the beauty and originality of Magnum's artistic collaborations. However, the experience extended beyond the domain of sight. Magnum deftly fused the metaverse with real-world experiences by allowing visitors to purchase Magnum ice cream from a vending machine within the virtual exhibition. This futuristic method presented a view into the possible future of food procurement, demonstrating how ice creams could be obtained easily in the metaverse. Using the existing partnership between Unilever and Deliveroo, the guests' ice cream orders were delivered in the real world, bridging the divide between the virtual and the actual. This novel idea not only enthralled the participants, but it also demonstrated the ultra-futuristic potential of food purchasing. Magnum's Marketing Manager, Matteo Trichilo, emphasised the company's commitment to delivering happiness to people's lives. This insight underscores the brand's recognition of the unique value of physical sensory experiences, even in the rapidly evolving digital landscape. Federico Russo, Global eCommerce Lead at Magnum, emphasised the potential for innovative creativity and transformative consumer interactions in the metaverse. He highlighted the strategic significance of Magnum's entrance into the metaverse, aligning the brand's extensive history of art collaborations with the future consumer journey. By immersing participants in a virtual exploration of Magnum's creative history and concluding with the consumption of a real Magnum ice cream, the brand successfully integrated the past, present, and future into a single experience. Magnum's foray into the metaverse via the establishment of the Magnum Pleasure Museum exemplifies the brand's pioneering character and desire to inspire other businesses and industry leaders. The virtual exhibition effectively demonstrated Magnum's dedication to art, delight, and innovation, while also demonstrating the potential of virtual environments to redefine consumer engagement and brand experiences. This case study illustrates how Magnum utilised the metaverse to engage a tech-savvy audience, deliver immersive brand experiences, and bridge the divide between the virtual and physical domains. Magnum has positioned itself at the vanguard of technological innovation by adopting the metaverse, paving the way for other brands to investigate the infinite possibilities of this emergent space.

Opportunities for Economic Growth and Innovation in Virtual Worlds

In addition to being spaces for social interaction and engagement, virtual worlds also provide immense economic opportunities and avenues for innovation. The emergence of virtual currencies and their effect on virtual economies are analysed, and the economic potential of virtual worlds is highlighted.

1) Revolutionising Commerce in the Metaverse: Virtual Economies: The emergence of virtual economies within virtual environments has revolutionised conventional notions of commerce. Within these immersive digital environments, users engage in a variety of economic activities, including the purchase and sale of virtual products, services, and even virtual property. These transactions are made possible by virtual currencies, which are the sustenance of virtual economies (Castronova, 2019). Virtual economies are distinguished by their ability to transcend geographical and traditional

Figure 2. Magnum in the metaverse

boundaries. In the metaverse, users from all over the world can seamlessly trade products and services in a unified virtual marketplace. This global connectivity enables entrepreneurs, innovators, and content creators to demonstrate their abilities, products, and services to a large and diverse audience (Lehdonvirta, 2020). Within virtual economies, the concept of virtual proprietorship and virtual property has acquired significant traction. Users can acquire and trade virtual assets with value in the virtual world, such as virtual real estate, virtual vehicles, and virtual collectibles (Castronova, 2019). As users realise the potential value and scarcity of these virtual assets, this creates new opportunities for investment, conjecture, and economic growth. In addition, virtual economies have spawned novel business models and monetization techniques. Within virtual environments, content creators can generate revenue by selling their creations or providing virtual services. For instance, users can purchase virtual apparel, accessories, and digital works of art created by talented designers and artists (Lehdonvirta, 2020). The influence of virtual economies extends beyond consumers and enterprises. Virtual transactions and the circulation of virtual currencies may have repercussions for the global economy as a whole. As these virtual economies continue to develop and mature, they may influence real-world monetary policies, taxation, and regulation (Castronova, 2019).

2) Market Trend Analysis and the Economic Potential of Virtual Worlds: Not only have virtual worlds experienced phenomenal growth, but they have also developed into flourishing economic ecosystems. The tremendous economic potential of these digital domains can be better understood by analysing market trends within them. The market for virtual products within virtual environments has experienced a significant increase, transforming into a billion-dollar industry (Apostu et al, 2022). Virtual products include apparel, accoutrements, in-game objects, and even virtual real estate. The rising demand for these virtual items reflects the changing preferences of consumers and the users' propensity to invest in enhancing their virtual experiences. Non-fungible tokens

(NFTs) have emerged as a revolutionary innovation in virtual environments, expanding the economic landscape. NFTs are one-of-a-kind digital assets that can represent ownership of a variety of objects, including art, music, and collectibles (Singer, 2021). Notable artists, personalities, and brands are monetizing their digital creations through NFT marketplaces, which have experienced unprecedented sales and investments. The economic potential of virtual environments is not limited to the sale of virtual products and non-fungible tokens (NFTs). Virtual events, exhibitions, and experiences have also become an important revenue source. Global audiences are attracted to virtual conferences, concerts, and exhibitions, creating opportunities for businesses, artists, and content creators to monetize their offerings (Minocha and Roberts, 2008). Virtual event platforms have witnessed a rise in registrations and ticket sales, which has contributed to the expansion of the virtual economy. In addition, virtual worlds have spawned novel monetization models, including virtual advertising and sponsorships. Brands are promoting their products and services to a highly engaged audience by utilising the immersive nature of virtual environments (Minocha and Roberts, 2008). This creates new revenue streams for virtual world operators and content creators, as well as a unique platform for brands to connect with their target demographic. Increasing integration of financial systems from the real world augments the economic potential of virtual environments. With its decentralised and secure nature, blockchain technology has enabled the seamless exchange of virtual currencies and assets (Singer, 2021). Integration of virtual economies with real-world financial systems not only increases user confidence, but also paves the way for cross-platform transactions and interoperability.

3) OpenSea - Revolutionising NFT Trading: A Case Study: OpenSea, founded in 2017, has become the largest and most popular NFT marketplace, offering individuals a global platform to purchase, trade, and research digital assets. OpenSea has experienced significant growth and adoption in recent years due to its extensive selection of non-fungible tokens, which spans art, music, virtual property, and collectibles. This case study examines the factors that led to OpenSea's success, including its revenue generation strategies, key features, obstacles encountered, and commitment to security and user education. Several factors contributed to OpenSea's success. The platform's intuitive and user-friendly interface makes it accessible to both seasoned traders and novices in the NFT space. In addition, OpenSea provides comprehensive filtering and search capabilities, allowing users to discover NFTs that align with their interests and preferences. The community features of the platform, such as forums and social interactions, promote user engagement and knowledge sharing. OpenSea generates income via multiple channels. OpenSea levies a 2.5% fee for each transaction conducted on the platform, providing a sustainable revenue stream. In addition, OpenSea provides users with paid services, such as featured listings, sponsored search results, and partnerships with NFT creators, developers, and blockchain-related businesses. These premium services offer enhanced visibility and promotional opportunities for users seeking greater exposure for their non-fungible tokens. OpenSea's extensive feature set contributes to its popularity and user satisfaction. Advanced search and filtering capabilities enable users to efficiently navigate the extensive collection of NFTs, ensuring a seamless browsing experience. Community features, including user forums and social profiles, foster a sense of belonging and facilitate connections between NFT enthusiasts. OpenSea also offers comprehensive transaction administration tools, ensuring customers' and merchants' transactions are secure and transparent. In addition, the availability of a mobile application for iOS and Android allows users to access OpenSea's services on their favoured devices.

MARKETPLACES

The Development of Metaverse Markets

Marketplaces: Driving the Economy of the Metaverse

In the metaverse, marketplaces drive the flow of transactions and shape the economy as a whole. Utilising the opportunities presented by the metaverse, virtual marketplaces provide a lively location where users can engage in trade. Users have the ability to purchase, sell, and trade a variety of products, such as virtual real estate, digital assets, virtual currencies, and in-game objects. These marketplaces allow individuals to monetize their creations, capitalising on the immense economic development potential of the metaverse (Oláh and Nica, 2022).

Analysing market dynamics and trends within virtual marketplaces reveals that these platforms are undergoing rapid evolution. Virtual marketplaces are experiencing a surge in user engagement and activity, with a growing number of users actively engaging in commerce and trade within virtual worlds. The market landscape is ever-changing, with new trends and patterns arising as users acclimatise to and investigate the metaverse's possibilities (Valaskova, 2022). According to ResearchAndMarkets, the global virtual and augmented reality market, which includes the metaverse, will surpass $125 billion by 2026. This expansion is fueled by the expansion of virtual marketplaces and the growing adoption of immersive technologies (ResearchAndMarkets, 2020). In the metaverse, marketplaces serve as crucial economic agents, facilitating transactions and influencing the economy as a whole. Analysis of market dynamics and trends reveals the active participation of consumers in shaping the market environment. Statistical evidence bolsters the economic potential of virtual marketplaces by illustrating their projected revenue and the considerable impact they can have on the economy of the metaverse.

Unlocking Virtual Environments for Trade and Exchange

Entrepreneurs and businesses have found success in virtual marketplaces by capitalising on the unique opportunities offered by these digital platforms. Virtual marketplaces have become fertile ground for innovation and entrepreneurship, from independent artists selling their digital artwork to virtual fashion designers designing and selling virtual apparel (Jones, 2023). A virtual fashion brand that began its voyage in a metaverse marketplace is an example of a noteworthy success story. Through their innovative designs and marketing strategies, they attracted a devoted customer base and generated substantial revenue from online apparel sales. They successfully capitalised on the increasing demand for virtual fashion by utilising their expertise to design distinct and desirable virtual apparel (Taylor, 2022). Moreover, virtual marketplaces have enabled small businesses and independent creators to reach a global audience and compete on a level playing field with larger, more established businesses. Through these platforms, enterprises can exhibit their products and services to a large number of consumers, regardless of their location or financial resources (Miller, 2021). In addition to fostering a sense of community and collaboration, virtual marketplaces contribute to their development and success. Users collaborate to share knowledge, give and receive feedback, and support one another's endeavours, thereby establishing a dynamic and supportive ecosystem (Garcia, 2023). Virtual marketplaces feature a vast selection of goods and services, affording consumers diverse trading opportunities. The emergence of decentralised marketplaces and blockchain technology has revolutionised the virtual economy, bringing with it increased security and transparency. Utilising the distinct opportunities and reaching a global audience, entrepreneurs and businesses have flourished in virtual marketplaces. Within virtual marketplaces, the sense of community and collaboration contributes to their expansion and success.

Decentraland - Virtual Marketplace: A Case Study

Decentraland is a revolutionary decentralised virtual reality platform that enables users to investigate, interact, and trade in the Metaverse, a virtual world. This case study investigates the distinctive characteristics and impact of Decentraland as a marketplace for virtual land, focusing on its decentralised nature, the concept of digital land ownership, and the economic opportunities it provides to users. Decentraland was established in 2017 with the intention of establishing a virtual world that is completely owned and governed by its users. Built on blockchain technology, specifically Ethereum, Decentraland enables users to purchase, sell, and trade non-fungible tokens (NFTs) known as LAND to acquire virtual land. In the virtual world, each LAND token represents a unique piece of digital real estate. Decentraland introduces an innovative concept of digital land ownership, enabling users to claim ownership of virtual parcels and create and monetize their own virtual experiences. The significance of digital land ownership, highlighting the active role of users in creating and moulding the virtual landscape. On their land, users are free to design and construct structures such as art galleries, virtual enterprises, gaming experiences, and social spaces.

The marketplace on Decentraland is a bustling trading centre for virtual property parcels. A decentralised and peer-to-peer marketplace in which users can peruse, discover, and purchase LAND parcels directly from other users. This marketplace's decentralised nature eliminates intermediaries, giving users direct control over their transactions and nurturing a sense of ownership and independence. Through its virtual land marketplace, Decentraland offers consumers diverse economic opportunities. Users can create and monetize virtual stores, art galleries, and entertainment venues. They can generate income by selling virtual products and services, leasing or renting out their land, or hosting events and experiences on their virtual properties. Additionally, the marketplace facilitates the exchange of virtual assets and collectibles, thereby enhancing Decentraland's economic potential. Unique digital assets, such as artwork, accessories, and virtual currencies, can be acquired and traded by users, fostering a flourishing ecosystem of digital commerce. With ongoing development, partnerships, and community engagement, Decentraland continues to evolve and expand in the future. Decentraland is at the forefront of this emergent industry, influencing the future of virtual land ownership and commerce as virtual reality and the Metaverse receive mainstream attention.

Legal and Regulatory Obstacles to Virtual Market Adoption

The pervasive proliferation of virtual marketplaces in the metaverse presents a number of challenges that must be addressed in order to establish trust and guarantee a secure environment for virtual transactions. Trust and security challenges in virtual marketplaces, including cybersecurity concerns and the role of blockchain in securing transactions. In addition, legal considerations pertaining to virtual marketplaces, such as intellectual property rights, licencing, and emergent legal challenges.

Building Confidence in Virtual Transactions on the Foundation of Trust and Security

1) Cybersecurity Preoccupations and Risk Mitigation: Cybersecurity is one of the greatest challenges confronting virtual marketplaces. The landscape of the virtual marketplace is described to emphasise the potential risks and obstacles. As with any online platform, virtual environments are susceptible to cyber threats such as hacking, identity theft, and fraud (Chalmers et al, 2021). Virtual marketplaces must prioritise the implementation of comprehensive security measures to mitigate cybersecurity risks. Multi-factor authentication can add another layer of security to user accounts (Johnson, 2022). Regular security audits should be performed to identify and rectify vulnerabilities in the infrastructure of the virtual marketplace. In addition, educating users on cybersecurity best practises is crucial for preserving a secure virtual marketplace environment. Virtual marketplaces can empower users to defend themselves from potential cyber threats by providing educational resources and guidelines on topics such as password hygiene, phishing awareness, and secure browsing behaviours (Moro-Viscont, 2022). Cybersecurity is a formidable obstacle for online marketplaces, necessitating proactive measures to mitigate risks. Implementing stringent security measures, undertaking regular audits, and educating users about cybersecurity best practises are essential steps for assuring the safety and reliability of online marketplaces.

2) Blockchain's Role in Securing Virtual Transactions: Blockchain technology has emerged as a promising solution for bolstering the trustworthiness and safety of online marketplaces. Using distributed ledger technology, blockchain provides virtual transactions with transparency, immutability, and traceability (Ross et al, 2019). One of the primary benefits of blockchain technology is its capacity for decentralised and secure recordkeeping. Blockchain eliminates the need for a central authority by leveraging a network of decentralised nodes, thereby reducing the risk of data manipulation or unauthorised access (Spathoulas et al, 2021). Each transaction recorded on the blockchain is cryptographically secured and linked to previous transactions, thereby creating an auditable and tamper-proof audit trail. In addition, blockchain technology can facilitate the use of smart contracts on online marketplaces. Smart contracts are agreements that implement predefined actions autonomously when certain conditions are met. The blockchain stores these contracts, ensuring their transparency and immutability. Smart contracts enable virtual marketplaces to establish trust and enforce agreements without the need for intermediaries, thereby reducing transaction costs and expediting business processes. By providing virtual transactions with transparency, immutability, and traceability, blockchain technology offers a revolutionary solution to trust issues. The decentralised nature of blockchain, in conjunction with the use of smart contracts, enables secure and automated transactions on virtual marketplaces. As blockchain technology evolves, it has the potential to revolutionise the way transactions are conducted, nurturing a more secure and dependable ecosystem for the virtual marketplace.

3) Intellectual Property Rights and Licencing Analysis in Virtual Environments: Intellectual property rights (IPR) and licencing are crucial factors that must be carefully considered in the virtual marketplace. Virtual marketplaces serve as platforms for a diverse array of digital content, including virtual products, artwork, and music, which may all be subject to copyright, trademark, and patent laws. Understanding and abiding by these legal limits is crucial for both content creators and marketplace administrators (Hopkins, 2022). Within virtual marketplaces, intellectual property rights and licencing play a crucial role in preserving the interests of content creators. These rights guarantee that creators have control over how their digital assets are used and distributed. By understanding

and abiding by copyright, trademark, and patent laws, market participants can foster a just and ethical environment in which the rights of creators are protected (Hopkins, 2022). To establish a legally compliant environment, proprietors of virtual marketplaces must take proactive steps. Developing precise guidelines and policies regarding intellectual property rights and licencing is a crucial step. By establishing transparent and well-defined guidelines, marketplace administrators can plainly outline the rights and responsibilities of creators and users. These guidelines serve as a foundation for fostering trust and confidence among content creators, thereby encouraging their participation in the market (Levi et al, 2021). Collaboration with legal professionals is another essential aspect of traversing the legal terrain of virtual marketplaces. Intellectual property laws are in a constant state of evolution; therefore, it is essential to keep abreast of the most recent regulations and legal developments. By retaining legal counsel, marketplace administrators can ensure ongoing compliance with intellectual property laws and resolve any emerging issues (Oláh and Nica, 2022). In virtual marketplaces, technological solutions play an important role in protecting intellectual property rights. Digital watermarking and encryption technologies, for instance, can be used to safeguard the authenticity and integrity of digital assets. These technologies offer additional security elements and aid in preventing the unauthorised use and distribution of content. By implementing such technological solutions, marketplace administrators demonstrate their dedication to safeguarding the rights of content creators and preserving a level playing field (Patil et al, 2022). In addition to establishing guidelines, proprietors of virtual marketplaces can collaborate with legal professionals to ensure ongoing compliance with intellectual property laws (Oláh and Nica, 2022). In virtual marketplaces, technological solutions can also play a significant role in protecting intellectual property rights. For instance, digital watermarking and encryption technologies can be used to safeguard the authenticity and integrity of digital assets.

4) Legal Frameworks for Understanding Virtual Currencies and Digital Assets: The rise of virtual currencies and digital assets in virtual marketplaces has created a unique set of legal issues that must be addressed with caution. The legal complexities associated with these assets and to emphasise the need for a thorough comprehension of the applicable regulations (Macedo et al, 2022). Due to their decentralised nature and possible implications for classification, taxation, and money laundering risks, virtual currencies such as cryptocurrencies have attracted regulatory scrutiny. Complying with extant regulatory frameworks and comprehending the legal complexities surrounding virtual currencies is essential for ensuring compliance and safeguarding the interests of all market participants (Macedo et al, 2022). Digital assets, such as non-fungible tokens (NFTs), have added new dimensions to the landscape of the virtual marketplace. These assets pose ownership, licencing, and resale rights concerns that may not have been as prevalent in conventional markets. The necessity of comprehending and abiding by the legal requirements associated with NFTs is highlighted by the necessity of navigating these legal obstacles. Clear licencing agreements and mechanisms for safeguarding the rights of both creators and purchasers are necessary for establishing a fair and ethical marketplace (Macedo et al, 2021). To effectively address these legal challenges, it is of the utmost importance to remain abreast of evolving regulations and engage legal professionals. The administrators of virtual marketplaces, legal experts, and regulatory authorities can establish guidelines and frameworks that promote transparency, consumer protection, and compliance with applicable laws through collaboration. By cooperating, they can guarantee that virtual marketplaces operate within the law while fostering innovation and economic development (Oláh and Nica, 2022). Implementing Know Your Customer (KYC) and Anti-Money Laundering (AML) proce-

dures and policies is a proactive measure to mitigate the risks associated with virtual currencies. These measures aid in verifying the identities of market participants and detecting any suspicious activity, thereby ensuring the integrity of virtual transactions and safeguarding the market from potential fraudulent activity. By incorporating KYC procedures and AML policies, administrators of virtual marketplaces demonstrate their dedication to maintaining a secure and trustworthy environment for all stakeholders (Kenney and Zysman, 2019). It is crucial to acknowledge that the legal landscape encompassing virtual currencies and digital assets is swiftly evolving. Regulatory frameworks are continuously updated to accommodate the evolving digital environment. Therefore, market participants must maintain vigilance and keep abreast of the most recent developments in order to comply with regulations and mitigate potential risks.

The Metaverse's Markets: An Economic Engine

Economic Potential: Market Projection and Effects on the Metaverse

The metaverse industry possesses substantial economic potential, with virtual marketplaces serving as key producers of the emerging digital economy. Extensive market research and projections reveal encouraging indicators of robust growth and substantial revenue opportunities within the ecosystem of the metaverse. These projections highlight the active role of virtual marketplaces in evaluating the economic impact of the metaverse and influencing its future (Oláh and Nica, 2022). Virtual marketplaces in the metaverse provide users with a variety of revenue streams and monetization models, enabling them to generate income through the sale of virtual products, services, and immersive experiences. Individuals can transmute their creative endeavours into viable sources of income and establish themselves as entrepreneurs in the metaverse by capitalising on these opportunities (Kenney and Zysman, 2019). The participation of these revenue streams demonstrates the economic potential of virtual marketplaces. These revenue streams include the sale of digital art, virtual clothing and accoutrements, virtual real estate, collectibles, gaming assets, and virtual services such as design, development, and consulting. Entrepreneurs, artists, developers, and content creators can monetize their creations and establish their own businesses and brands within the metaverse by leveraging their unique skills. These individuals contribute to the vibrancy and economic vitality of this digital realm by actively engaging in virtual marketplaces (Kenney and Zysman, 2019). In addition, virtual marketplaces in the metaverse are not restricted to individual vendors and makers. The value of establishing a presence in the metaverse is actively acknowledged by well-known brands, corporations, and organisations. By extending their reach into this digital landscape, these entities can engage with a new generation of consumers, investigate novel revenue streams, and develop distinctive brand experiences. This demonstrates the transformative potential of virtual marketplaces to reshape traditional business models and stimulate economic development (Oláh and Nica, 2022). As the metaverse continues to evolve and expand, virtual marketplaces will play an increasingly important role in generating economic development and sustaining this digital domain. By grasping the opportunities presented by metaverse marketplaces, participants actively contribute to the transformation of this landscape while reaping the economic benefits it offers. The active participation of individuals, businesses, and brands in virtual marketplaces highlights their pivotal role in influencing the metaverse economy and capitalising on its immense revenue generating and innovative potential (Kenney and Zysman, 2019). Virtual marketplaces have enormous potential to develop into flourishing innovation and collaboration centres within the metaverse. By providing a dynamic environment for creators and entrepreneurs, these marketplaces can cultivate interdisciplinary collaboration, incubate new ideas, products, and experiences, and stretch the limits of the metaverse ecosystem. The active role of virtual marketplaces in nurturing innovation and serving as catalysts for creative collaboration highlights their importance as key drivers of economic growth and development.

Encouraging Innovation and Creative Expression

Virtual marketplaces empower entrepreneurs and creators by providing them with distinct opportunities to monetize their digital works and convey their creativity. These marketplaces provide a venue for content creators, such as artists, designers, and musicians, to exhibit and sell their digital works to a global audience, thereby extending their reach and transforming their passion into a viable source of income (Moro-Viscont, 2022). Virtual marketplaces' accessibility and visibility enable creators to establish a presence in the digital landscape and communicate with potential consumers and admirers of their artistic endeavours. In the future, virtual marketplaces could serve as flourishing innovation and collaboration centres within the metaverse. They can serve as dynamic incubators for new ideas, products, and experiences, going beyond their function as simple marketplaces. These marketplaces provide a fertile environment for creative minds to congregate, experiment, and stretch the limits of what is possible in the digital domain (Chen, 2022). The ability of virtual marketplaces to facilitate inter-disciplinary collaboration is one of their primary benefits. Within these marketplaces, creators from various disciplines can collaborate and co-create innovative digital experiences. For instance, artists and developers can collaborate to create immersive virtual environments that combine visual art with interactive elements.

Collaboration between musicians and game designers can result in captivating soundtracks that enhance the gaming experience. Fashion designers can collaborate with specialists in virtual reality to create immersive virtual fashion experiences that enable users to investigate and interact with fashion in novel and engaging ways. These collaborations not only improve the quality of digital creations but also offer up new creative expression possibilities (Chen, 2022). By actively engaging the opportunities provided by virtual marketplaces, participants contribute to the development of this transformative digital landscape while unleashing its economic and creative potentials. These marketplaces serve as entrepreneurial catalysts, allowing individuals to develop their identities, launch businesses, and generate income from their digital creations. The availability of virtual marketplaces enables creators to communicate with a global audience, transcending geographical barriers and reaching consumers with a genuine interest in their work. In addition to financial success, creators gain audience recognition, feedback, and support, nurturing a sense of community and appreciation for their talents (Moro-Viscont, 2022). Virtual marketplaces provide emerging artists and creators with a level playing field, allowing them to demonstrate their work alongside established industry professionals. This democratisation of the creative landscape increases the variety of artistic voices and promotes inclusiveness in the metaverse. Thus, virtual marketplaces contribute to an ecosystem where creativity and innovation prosper.

METAVERSE TOOLS

Techniques and Tools Enabling the Metaverse: The Metaverse represents a vision of a fully immersive and interconnected digital universe, where users can engage in various activities, socialize, and explore virtual worlds. Achieving such a complex and expansive virtual realm requires the utilization of a wide array of techniques and tools. In this section, we will delve into the key components and technologies that enable the development and operation of the Metaverse.

Virtual and Augmented Reality Hardware and Software

VR and AR technologies play pivotal roles in creating immersive experiences within the Metaverse. VR technology allows users to immerse themselves in a digital environment, typically through the use of a headset or other devices. By blocking out the physical world and replacing it with a virtual one, users can engage with digital objects and interact within virtual spaces. AR, on the other hand, integrates digital information into the physical world, overlaying virtual objects onto the real environment. This technology enhances the user's perception and interaction with their surroundings, blending the real and virtual seamlessly. AR can be experienced through mobile devices, smart glasses, or heads-up displays. Advancements in VR and AR hardware have contributed to the growth and potential of the Metaverse. Head-mounted displays (HMDs), motion tracking systems, and haptic feedback devices have become more sophisticated, offering users a more immersive and realistic experience. These technologies continue to evolve, providing higher resolution graphics, wider field of view, reduced latency, and more natural user interactions. Moreover, VR and AR software development kits (SDKs) and platforms have emerged, providing developers with the necessary tools and frameworks to create compelling virtual experiences. These tools enable the creation of interactive environments, realistic simulations, and seamless integration of virtual objects into the user's perception of reality.

Modeling and Design Software

The creation of digital objects and environments within the Metaverse relies heavily on 3D modeling and design software. These tools allow developers and users to design, build, and manipulate virtual assets, shaping the virtual worlds and objects that populate the Metaverse.

Powerful 3D modeling software, such as Autodesk Maya, Blender, or SketchUp, provide artists and designers with the means to create intricate and realistic 3D models. These models can range from characters and creatures to buildings, vehicles, and landscapes. Through the use of sculpting, texturing, and animation tools, artists can breathe life into their creations, making them visually appealing and interactive. Design software specifically tailored for the Metaverse often includes features that streamline the process of creating and importing assets into virtual environments. These tools may offer simplified workflows, compatibility with various virtual platforms, and optimization techniques to ensure efficient performance within the Metaverse.

One notable use case is the creation of virtual showrooms or galleries for architectural firms. Using 3D modeling software, architects can digitally recreate their designs and showcase them within a virtual space. Users can navigate these virtual environments, exploring various architectural styles, materials, and spatial configurations. They can interact with virtual objects, such as opening doors, changing lighting, or even experiencing simulations of different weather conditions. This use case not only provides a unique experience for clients but also offers architects an opportunity to receive immediate feedback on their designs. Clients can immerse themselves in the virtual spaces, gaining a better understanding of the scale, proportions, and aesthetics of the proposed architectural projects. This interactive and immersive experience enables more effective communication between architects and clients, facilitating collaborative decision-making and reducing the risk of misunderstandings. Examples include:

- The Louvre Museum Virtual Tour: The Louvre Museum in Paris, France, offers a virtual tour that allows visitors to explore its iconic galleries and view famous artworks. The virtual tour utilizes 3D modeling to recreate the museum's interior spaces, enabling users to navigate through the exhibits and admire the artworks virtually.
- Volkswagen Virtual Showroom: Volkswagen created a virtual showroom to showcase their latest car models. The virtual showroom employs 3D modeling to create detailed virtual representations of the cars, allowing users to explore the vehicles from different angles, customize features, and even take virtual test drives.
- IKEA Virtual Home Planning: IKEA offers a virtual home planning tool that utilizes 3D modeling. Users can design and visualize their ideal rooms, incorporating IKEA furniture and accessories into the virtual spaces. The tool enables users to experiment with different layouts, styles, and furniture combinations before making any physical purchases.
- Christie's Virtual Auction Room: Christie's, the renowned auction house, has embraced virtual technology to host virtual auction rooms. Utilizing 3D modeling, they recreate the atmosphere and experience of a live auction, allowing bidders to participate remotely and view detailed 3D representations of the auction items.

User-friendly interfaces and intuitive controls make 3D modeling and design software accessible to a broader audience, empowering individuals to contribute their creativity and shape the digital universe. As the Metaverse continues to evolve, these tools are expected to become even more user-friendly, enabling a wider range of users to participate in the creation of virtual content.

Cloud Computing

The realization of the Metaverse poses significant challenges in terms of computational power and storage requirements. Processing vast amounts of data and maintaining a seamless experience for millions of users simultaneously demands a robust and scalable infrastructure. Cloud computing emerges as a crucial technology to address these challenges.

Cloud computing provides the Metaverse with the necessary computing resources, including processing power, storage capacity, and networking capabilities, delivered over the internet. The scalability of cloud services allows for on-demand allocation of resources, ensuring that the Metaverse can handle fluctuating user demand without compromising performance. By leveraging cloud-based infrastructure, virtual environments within the Metaverse can be hosted and distributed across a network of servers, minimizing latency and providing a consistent experience for users regardless of their geographical location. Cloud computing also facilitates collaborative development, enabling distributed teams to work together seamlessly on the creation and maintenance of the Metaverse. Furthermore, cloud-based machine learning and AI services can be utilized within the Metaverse to enhance user experiences, personalize content, and optimize resource allocation. AI algorithms can analyze user behavior, generate dynamic content, and provide intelligent recommendations, enhancing the realism and engagement of the virtual environment.

Case Study: Scalable Virtual Worlds With Cloud Computing

Cloud computing plays a critical role in enabling the creation and operation of scalable virtual worlds within the Metaverse. The ability to handle massive amounts of data and provide seamless user experiences for millions of users simultaneously is a significant challenge, and cloud computing offers a robust solution. One prominent example is the virtual world platform Second Life. Second Life utilizes cloud computing to host its virtual world, where users can create avatars, interact with each other, and explore user-generated content. The platform leverages cloud-based infrastructure to handle the computational and networking requirements of its vast and dynamic virtual environment. By using cloud computing, Second Life can scale its resources based on user demand. During peak times, such as large-scale events or gatherings, the platform can allocate additional computing power and bandwidth to ensure a smooth and uninterrupted experience for users. Cloud-based scalability enables virtual worlds like Second Life to accommodate a growing user base and handle the ever-increasing complexity of interactive virtual environments.

Gaming Within the Metaverse

Massive multiplayer online games (MMOs) often require robust computational resources to support large numbers of players interacting in a shared virtual world. Cloud computing provides the necessary infrastructure to handle the real-time processing, networking, and storage demands of these games. Cloud-based gaming platforms, such as Google Stadia or Microsoft Azure PlayFab, leverage cloud computing to offer seamless and responsive gaming experiences. By offloading the computational load to the cloud, these platforms can deliver high-quality graphics, low latency, and consistent performance to players, regardless of the device they are using. Cloud computing enables gamers to access their favorite games from various devices and eliminates the need for expensive gaming hardware, making gaming more accessible and convenient within the Metaverse.

Cloud computing enables the scalability, performance, and flexibility required to build and operate large-scale virtual worlds within the Metaverse. It provides the necessary computational power, storage capacity, and networking capabilities to handle the vast amounts of data and user interactions. Through cloud computing, virtual worlds can seamlessly scale resources, deliver immersive experiences, and leverage AI-powered features, making the vision of the Metaverse a reality.

Spatial Computing

Spatial computing is a technology that merges the physical and virtual worlds, allowing users to interact with virtual objects and information as if they were part of the real environment. It enables the Metaverse to extend beyond the confines of screens and headsets, seamlessly integrating digital information into our physical surroundings. Spatial computing relies on a combination of sensors, cameras, and advanced tracking technologies to understand the user's physical position and movements. By accurately mapping the real-world environment, virtual objects can be anchored and manipulated within that space. This technology opens up new possibilities for immersive interactions and user interfaces within the Metaverse. Devices such as smartphones, tablets, smart glasses, and heads-up displays can serve as windows into the spatial computing experience. By leveraging the capabilities of these devices, users can view and interact with virtual objects in their immediate surroundings, enhancing their perception of the Metaverse. Spatial computing also enables multi-user interactions within the Metaverse. Users can see and interact with each other's avatars or virtual representations, fostering social connections and collaboration. This technology has the potential to revolutionize various industries, from entertainment and gaming to education, architecture, and retail. Some use-case examples of organizations working to develop spatial computing include:

- Unity MARS: Unity MARS (Mixed and Augmented Reality Studio) is a spatial computing software developed by Unity Technologies. It enables the integration of virtual content into the physical world, allowing for interactive and immersive experiences. Organizations like Volkswagen have utilized Unity MARS for creating virtual showrooms that enable customers to explore and customize virtual car models in real-world environments.
- ARCore by Google: ARCore is a software development kit (SDK) provided by Google for building augmented reality (AR) experiences on Android devices. It enables developers to create AR applications that incorporate digital information and objects into the real world. Organizations like IKEA have utilized ARCore to develop applications that allow customers to virtually place and visualize furniture in their own homes.Apple ARKit: ARKit is a software framework provided by Apple for building AR experiences on iOS devices. It provides developers with tools and resources to create interactive and immersive AR applications. Organizations such as Pokemon Go, an augmented reality mobile game, have used Apple ARKit to enable players to interact with virtual characters and objects in the real world.
- Microsoft HoloLens: Microsoft HoloLens is an augmented reality headset that combines virtual content with the user's physical surroundings. It incorporates spatial computing technology to allow users to interact with holograms and digital information in a natural and intuitive manner. Organizations like Trimble, a company specializing in spatial computing solutions, have utilized Microsoft HoloLens for applications in industries such as architecture, construction, and engineering.
- Magic Leap One: Magic Leap One is another spatial computing headset that enables users to experience mixed reality (MR), blending virtual and physical elements seamlessly. It offers spatial computing capabilities, allowing for realistic and interactive digital content within real-world environments. Organizations like Wayfair, an online furniture retailer, have used Magic Leap One to create MR applications that allow customers to visualize furniture in their own spaces.

These spatial computing software and technologies are used to create interactive and immersive experiences within the Metaverse. From virtual showrooms and furniture visualization to gaming and industrial applications, spatial computing plays a crucial role in bridging the gap between the physical and virtual worlds.

Blockchain and NFTs for Securing Digital Assets

In the Metaverse, the creation, ownership, and exchange of digital assets become crucial aspects of the user experience. Blockchain technology and Non-Fungible Tokens (NFTs) play a vital role in securing and managing these digital assets, ensuring authenticity, ownership, and scarcity. Blockchain, a decentralized and transparent ledger system, provides a secure and tamper-proof mechanism for recording transactions and verifying ownership. Within the Metaverse, blockchain technology can be utilized to establish a trusted and transparent ecosystem for buying, selling, and trading digital assets. Smart contracts, powered by blockchain, automate the execution of agreements and ensure that ownership rights and royalties are properly enforced. NFTs, built on blockchain, represent unique digital assets, such as virtual land, artwork, or in-game items, with verifiable ownership and scarcity. These tokens enable users to prove ownership of digital assets within the Metaverse and trade them securely on decentralized marketplaces. NFTs also provide creators with a means to monetize their digital creations, establishing a new economy within the Metaverse. Several blockchain-based platforms and marketplaces have emerged, facilitating the creation, discovery, and exchange of NFTs within the Metaverse. These platforms offer users a way to showcase their digital assets, participate in auctions, and engage in peer-to-peer transactions.

As the Metaverse evolves, these discussed tools and techniques will play an integral role. They demonstrate how virtual and augmented reality, 3D modeling and design software, cloud computing, spatial computing, and blockchain technology contribute to the creation of immersive experiences, user-generated content, secure asset management, and economic opportunities within the Metaverse. Embracing and leveraging these tools will be essential in unlocking the full potential of the Metaverse and shaping the future of digital interactions and experiences.

LIMITATIONS OF THE STUDY

In the exploration of the Metaverse and its multifaceted dimensions, it is crucial to acknowledge the inherent limitations that might influence the depth of this study. The Metaverse is a dynamic concept shaped by rapid technological advancements, and as this chapter is being crafted, there might be new breakthroughs that surpass the content covered herein. Cultural and ethical considerations also play a significant role in the Metaverse's development, with impacts on privacy, data security, and digital addiction potentially extending beyond the scope of this chapter. Moreover, ensuring accessibility and inclusivity for all individuals, including those with physical disabilities or limited access to advanced technologies, remains an ongoing challenge that demands recognition.

FUTURE OUTLOOK OF THE METAVERSE

As we delve into the Metaverse's current manifestations and its potential implications, it iss imperative to cast a gaze toward the trajectory it may follow in the years ahead. The evolution of the Metaverse is likely to be shaped by a multitude of factors, potentially revolutionizing various facets of our lives. An essential aspect of this trajectory is the envisioned integration of distinct virtual worlds and platforms, creating an intricate web of interconnected digital experiences. This metamorphosis could seamlessly merge various virtual interactions, blurring the lines between recreational activities, social engagements, educational pursuits, and commercial ventures.

Societal embrace of the Metaverse hinges on its capacity to address real-world challenges and offer meaningful contributions to individuals and communities. The extent of its success will depend on the enrichment it provides across both personal and collective dimensions of human existence. At the same time, the economic implications of the Metaverse are poised to be substantial. Beyond its role in gaming and entertainment, the Metaverse could emerge as a dynamic marketplace, exerting its influence over industries as diverse as real estate, fashion, art, and more. This shift in the economic landscape could foster the emergence of novel job roles and innovative business models, potentially reshaping global economic dynamics.

As the Metaverse assumes a more central role in society, ethical and legal frameworks will become increasingly pivotal. Issues surrounding data privacy, intellectual property rights, digital ethics, and online behavioral norms will necessitate comprehensive and adaptable frameworks to foster a secure and equitable digital environment. Meanwhile, ongoing technological advancements are inevitable, promising to enhance immersive experiences further. Innovations in immersive technologies could lead to even more realistic and captivating virtual encounters, potentially broadening the Metaverse's adoption across various demographic segments.

CONCLUSION

In this chapter, we have explored the concept of the Metaverse and its core building blocks, the emergence and concept, the economy and commercial value generation, and the techniques and tools that enable its development. The Metaverse represents a paradigm shift in how we interact, collaborate, and engage with digital spaces. It opens up new possibilities for social connections, creativity, commerce, and entertainment. By understanding and embracing the core building blocks of the Metaverse, we can unlock its full potential and shape the future of digital experiences in this transformative era.

As the Metaverse continues to evolve, these building blocks will undergo further innovation and refinement. We can anticipate more advanced technologies, increased accessibility, and broader participation from individuals and organizations alike.

REFERENCES

Alam, S. S., Susmit, S., Lin, C. Y., Masukujjaman, M., & Ho, Y. H. (2021). Factors affecting augmented reality adoption in the retail industry. *Journal of Open Innovation*, *7*(2), 142. doi:10.3390/joitmc7020142

Alcañiz, M., Bigné, E., & Guixeres, J. (2019). Virtual reality in marketing: A framework, review, and research agenda. *Frontiers in Psychology*, *10*, 1530. doi:10.3389/fpsyg.2019.01530 PMID:31333548

Apostu, S. A., Panait, M., Vasa, L., Mihaescu, C., & Dobrowolski, Z. (2022). NFTs and Cryptocurrencies—The Metamorphosis of the Economy under the Sign of Blockchain: A Time Series Approach. *Mathematics*, *10*(17), 3218. doi:10.3390/math10173218

Azuma, R. T. (1997). A survey of augmented reality. *Presence (Cambridge, Mass.)*, *6*(4), 355–385. doi:10.1162/pres.1997.6.4.355

Bailenson, J. (2018). *Experience on demand: What virtual reality is, how it works, and what it can do.* WW Norton & Company.

Ball, M., 2020. The Metaverse: What It Is. *Where to Find It, Who Will Build It, and Fortnite, 13.*

Blanchard, J., Koshal, S., Morley, S., & McGurk, M. (2022). The use of mixed reality in dentistry. *British Dental Journal*, *233*(4), 261–265. doi:10.103841415-022-4451-z PMID:36028682

Boll, K. (2021). OpenSea: The world's largest NFT marketplace. *Opensea.* https://opensea.io/

Boll, K. (2021). Decentraland: A virtual world powered by Ethereum. *Decentraland.* https://decentraland.org/

Bowman, D. A., & McMahan, R. P. (2007). Virtual reality: How much immersion is enough? *Computer, 40*(7), 36–43. doi:10.1109/MC.2007.257

Castronova, E. (2019). *Synthetic worlds: The business and culture of online games.* University of Chicago press.

Chalmers, D., Fisch, C., Matthews, R., Quinn, W., & Recker, J. (2022). Beyond the bubble: Will NFTs and digital proof of ownership empower creative industry entrepreneurs? *Journal of Business Venturing Insights, 17,* e00309. doi:10.1016/j.jbvi.2022.e00309

Chen, Y. 2022, November. Research on the Communication of Sports Events in the Context of Metaverse. In *2022 International Conference on Sport Science, Education and Social Development (SSESD 2022)* (pp. 369-383). Atlantis Press.

Dede, C. (2009). Immersive interfaces for engagement and learning. *Science, 323*(5910), 66-69.

Dionisio, J.D.N., III, W.G.B. & Gilbert, R. (2013). 3D virtual worlds and the metaverse: Current status and future possibilities. *ACM Computing Surveys (CSUR), 45*(3), 1-38.

Ducheneaut, N., Yee, N., Nickell, E., & Moore, R. J. 2006, April. "Alone together?" Exploring the social dynamics of massively multiplayer online games. In *Proceedings of the SIGCHI conference on Human Factors in computing systems* (pp. 407-416). ACM. 10.1145/1124772.1124834

Ducheneaut, N., Yee, N., Nickell, E., & Moore, R. J. 2007, April. The life and death of online gaming communities: a look at guilds in world of warcraft. In *Proceedings of the SIGCHI conference on Human factors in computing systems* (pp. 839-848). ACM. 10.1145/1240624.1240750

Gartner. (2022). *Emerging Technology Analysis: Virtual Worlds.* Gartner. [www.gartner.com/en/information-technology]

Gee, J.P. (2013). *Digital media and learning: A prospective retrospective.* ACM.

Hendaoui, A., Limayem, M., & Thompson, C. W. (2008). 3D social virtual worlds: Research issues and challenges. *IEEE Internet Computing, 12*(1), 88–92. doi:10.1109/MIC.2008.1

Herrington, J. (2006). Authentic e-learning in higher education: Design principles for authentic learning environments and tasks. In *E-Learn: World Conference on E-Learning in Corporate, Government, Healthcare, and Higher Education* (pp. 3164-3173). Association for the Advancement of Computing in Education (AACE).

Hopkins, E. (2022). Virtual Commerce in a Decentralized Blockchain-based Metaverse: Immersive Technologies, Computer Vision Algorithms, and Retail Business Analytics. *Linguistic and Philosophical Investigations,* (21), 203–218.

Jung, T., tom Dieck, M. C., & Rauschnabel, P. A. (Eds.). (2020). *Augmented reality and virtual reality: Changing realities in a dynamic world.* Springer. doi:10.1007/978-3-030-37869-1

Kenney, M., & Zysman, J. (2019). Work and value creation in the platform economy. In *Work and labor in the digital age* (Vol. 33, pp. 13–41). Emerald Publishing Limited.

Korkut, E. H., & Surer, E. (2023). Visualization in virtual reality: A systematic review. *Virtual Reality (Waltham Cross)*, *27*(2), 1–34. doi:10.100710055-023-00753-8

Lanier, J. (2017). *Dawn of the new everything: Encounters with reality and virtual reality*. Henry Holt and Company.

Levi, S., Fisch, E., Drylewski, A., Skadden, A., Slate, M., & Flom, L. L. P. (2021). *Legal considerations in the minting, marketing and selling of NFTs*. Global Legal Insights.

Macedo, C. R., Miro, D. A., & Hart, T. (2022). The Metaverse: From Science Fiction to Commercial Reality—Protecting Intellectual Property in the Virtual Landscape. *NYSBA Bright Ideas*, *31*(1), 216.

Milgram, P., & Kishino, F. (1994). A taxonomy of mixed reality visual displays. *IEICE Transactions on Information and Systems*, *77*(12), 1321–1329.

Milgram, P., Takemura, H., Utsumi, A., & Kishino, F. 1995, December. Augmented reality: A class of displays on the reality-virtuality continuum. In Telemanipulator and telepresence technologies (Vol. 2351, pp. 282-292).

Minocha, S., & Roberts, D. (2008). Laying the groundwork for socialisation and knowledge construction within 3D virtual worlds. *ALT-J*, *16*(3), 181–196. doi:10.3402/rlt.v16i3.10897

Mollet, N., Chellali, R., & Brayda, L. (2009). Virtual and augmented reality tools for teleoperation: improving distant immersion and perception. Transactions on edutainment II, 135-159.

Moro-Visconti, R. (2022). The Valuation of Digital Platforms and Virtual Marketplaces. In *The Valuation of Digital Intangibles: Technology, Marketing, and the Metaverse* (pp. 591–612). Springer International Publishing. doi:10.1007/978-3-031-09237-4_20

Oláh, J., & Nica, E. (2022). Biometric Sensor Technologies, Virtual Marketplace Dynamics Data, and Computer Vision and Deep Learning Algorithms in the Metaverse Interactive Environment. *Journal of Self-Governance & Management Economics*, *10*(3).

PatilA.ShindeA.PanigrahiA.AroraA.RavirajaD. S.BabuR. 2022. The role of blockchain technology in decentralized real estate marketplace: recent findings. *Available at* SSRN 4096395. doi:10.2139/ssrn.4096395

ResearchAndMarkets. (2020). *Global virtual and augmented reality market - Growth, trends, and forecast*. Research and Markets.

Resnik, F., & Bellmore, A. (2021). Is Peer Victimization Associated With Adolescents' Social Media Use, Engagement, Behavior, and Content? *Merrill-Palmer Quarterly*, *67*(2), 175–202. doi:10.13110/merrpalmquar1982.67.2.0175

RossO.JensenJ. R.AsheimT. 2019. Assets under Tokenization. SSRN 3488344.

Rossi, S., Guedes, A., & Toni, L. (2023). Streaming and user behavior in omnidirectional videos. In *Immersive Video Technologies* (pp. 49–83). Academic Press. doi:10.1016/B978-0-32-391755-1.00009-2

Schuemie, M. J., Van Der Straaten, P., Krijn, M., & Van Der Mast, C. A. (2001). Research on presence in virtual reality: A survey. *Cyberpsychology & Behavior*, *4*(2), 183–201. doi:10.1089/109493101300117884 PMID:11710246

Slater, M. (2009). Place illusion and plausibility can lead to realistic behaviour in immersive virtual environments. *Philosophical Transactions of the Royal Society of London. Series B, Biological Sciences*, *364*(1535), 3549–3557. doi:10.1098/rstb.2009.0138 PMID:19884149

Spathoulas, G., Negka, L., Pandey, P., & Katsikas, S. (2021). Can Blockchain Technology Enhance Security and Privacy in the Internet of Things? Advances in Core Computer Science-Based Technologies: Papers in Honor of Professor Nikolaos Alexandris.

Steinkuehler, C. A., & Williams, D. (2006). Where everybody knows your (screen) name: Online games as "third places". *Journal of Computer-Mediated Communication*, *11*(4), 885–909. doi:10.1111/j.1083-6101.2006.00300.x

Turk, A. (2021). Decentraland: A virtual world powered by Ethereum. *Decentraland*. https://decentraland.org/

Tussyadiah, I. P., & Pesonen, J. (2016). Impacts of peer-to-peer accommodation use on travel patterns. *Journal of Travel Research*, *55*(8), 1022–1040. doi:10.1177/0047287515608505

Valaskova, K., Machova, V., & Lewis, E. (2022). Virtual Marketplace Dynamics Data, Spatial Analytics, and Customer Engagement Tools in a Real-Time Interoperable Decentralized Metaverse. *Linguistic and Philosophical Investigations*, *21*(0), 105–120. doi:10.22381/lpi2120227

Chapter 12
NFTs Enabling Ownership and Value in the Metaverse

Himanshu Sisodia

iD https://orcid.org/0009-0003-1550-0884

SSBM Geneva, Switzerland

ABSTRACT

Non-fungible tokens (NFTs) revolutionize digital property rights and the representation of value. NFTs provide various digital assets with transparency, immutability, and traceability by leveraging blockchain technology and smart contracts. NFTs represent tangible assets digitally, bridging the gap between the physical and digital worlds. Luxury brands such as BMW, Balenciaga, Dolce & Gabbana, Louis Vuitton, and Gucci use NFTs in the metaverse to facilitate distinct brand experiences and expression. NFTs authenticate digital identities and property in virtual environments, thereby promoting self-expression and social interactions. They establish a new economic paradigm, facilitating the exchange of value across domains and the preservation of intellectual property. Scalability, sustainability, and legal issues present themselves, necessitating solutions such as layer-2 scaling and copyright protection. It is essential for platforms, creators, and regulators to collaborate in order to establish standards and frameworks.

INTRODUCTION

Non-fungible tokens (NFTs) have arisen as a game-changing concept in the quickly growing digital ecosystem, redefining concepts of ownership and value. The core of NFTs is their capacity to create unique representations of ownership, which has far-reaching ramifications in the digital environment. NFTs, a term coined by Buterin in 2015, are digital assets that resist division and one-to-one exchange, distinguishing them from traditional currencies and even cryptocurrencies such as Bitcoin and Ethereum. NFTs, unlike interchangeable tokens, have essentially unique and irreplaceable characteristics, owing to the underpinning technology of blockchain (Idelberger & Mezey, 2022).

The fundamental basis of NFTs differs from that of traditional tokens such as Bitcoin and Ethereum, which are easily convertible. This unique feature of NFTs, which resulted from the union of blockchain technology and innovation, has led to their use as vehicles for reflecting ownership across diverse types

DOI: 10.4018/978-1-6684-9919-1.ch012

Copyright © 2023, IGI Global. Copying or distributing in print or electronic forms without written permission of IGI Global is prohibited.

of digital material. NFTs have gained global interest, establishing themselves at the vanguard of digital ownership, from artworks and antiques to music, films, virtual real estate, and even digital identities. The value of any non-fungible token is determined by criteria such as scarcity, legitimacy, and demand for the underlying digital asset. To achieve complete transparency, immutability, and provenance, these tokens are typically built on blockchain networks that make use of smart contract features, such as Ethereum's ERC-721 and ERC-1155 standards (Buterin, 2015).

NFTs have quickly invaded the digital arena as a way of monetizing creative works, providing a transformative path for artists, musicians, innovators, and developers. Artists may now retain ownership rights, issue limited editions, and earn royalties via secondary sales, all thanks to the tokenization of their artworks as NFTs. This direct creator-to-consumer engagement has the potential to disrupt traditional art markets by giving artists a greater sense of power over their products (Buterin, 2015). The market for NFTs has seen an unparalleled parabolic rise, propelled by high-profile transactions and celebrity endorsements. The selling of artworks, virtual real estate, and antiques for exorbitant prices has unmistakably shown the perceived worth and financial potential of NFTs. As with any emerging technology, it is critical to recognize that the NFT market is still in its infancy and subject to the ebbs and flows of volatility (Idelberger & Mezei, 2022).

NFTs are fundamentally endowed with the notion of verifiability and ownership validation, which is a cornerstone of their relevance. Each NFT has a unique identity, information, and a cryptographic signature, resulting in convincing proof of authenticity and ownership, removing the threat of forgery and increasing confidence in the digital world. The decentralized nature of blockchain technology preserves the purity of NFT ownership records, making them impenetrable to manipulation and change and therefore reinforcing the concept of digital ownership (Buterin, 2015; Idelberger & Mezes, 2022).

In recent years, similar to the NFTs there has been a growing interest with the notion of the metaverse, a visionary world of immersive digital landscapes. The metaverse is essentially a seamlessly linked virtual reality (VR) or augmented reality (AR) expanse, an interconnected matrix of digital environments where real-time interactions and engagements with both digital entities and fellow persons flourish (Gilbert, 2022). This expansive view of the metaverse seeks to blur the lines between the digital and the physical, beginning on a mission to unite two allegedly separate realms.

Users travel and explore a myriad of virtual environments, engaging in social interactions, economic pursuits, and digital content consumption. The DNA of the metaverse is underpinned by a confluence of virtual reality, augmented reality, blockchain, artificial intelligence, and the Internet of Things, resulting in a digital tapestry interlaced with interconnectivity. It solidifies into a vast digital vista that resembles the rich fabric of the actual world (Gilbert, 2022).

The celebration of user agency and customization, a symphony of individual invention, is central to the metaverse's fabric. Users have the ability to create and personalize their virtual identities, known colloquially as avatars, as well as the worlds they occupy. This customization extends to virtual goods like as digital art, clothing, accessories, and even virtual real estate, all of which serve as an embodiment of self-expression in a digital environment (Gilbert, 2022; Lanier, 2011).

The metaverse develops as a fertile field for economic aspirations and opportunities, coordinating a wide range of commercial enterprises. The metaverse acts as a marketplace for virtual goods, virtual services, immersive events, and one-of-a-kind digital experiences. It also provides a platform for content producers, artists, and entrepreneurs to sell their digital assets, therefore contributing to the metaverse's expanding ecosystem (Lanier, 2011; Gilbert, 2022). However, in its infancy, the metaverse's developing story necessitates attention. Its technological underpinnings, standards, and interoperability are constantly evolving toward complete realization. To create an inclusive and safe metaverse experience, privacy, security, and ethical issues must be coordinated harmoniously (Gilbert, 2022; Steuer, 1995).

Enter the nexus between Non-Fungible Tokens (NFTs) and the metaverse, a meeting point that reveals a plethora of chances and benefits inside this immersive digital universe. The ecosystem of NFTs adds a new layer of ownership, value representation, and economic opportunities. NFTs provide a safe, verifiable, and transparent ownership story for digital assets within this symbiotic relationship, sustaining trust in a decentralized domain.

The importance of NFTs in authenticating and establishing ownership has repercussions throughout the metaverse's growth. NFTs emerge as the core of authenticity and originality in this wide area where digital material, artwork, and keepsakes flourish (Christodoulou et al., 2022). NFTs, which are based on blockchain technology, provide an immutable ownership record, extinguishing the flames of fraudulent copying and unlawful transmission. This characteristic is of exceptional importance in the metaverse, where the entire basis of virtual assets is the certainty of ownership.

NFTs, on the other hand, weave the metaverse's tapestry of value representation. These tokens transform become valuable digital assets as a result of scarcity and exclusivity. The metaverse, a domain where digital art, virtual fashion, property, and identities are very valuable, transforms into a stage for the portrayal and trading of these priceless commodities (Christodoulou et al., 2022). Users may discover a level of value contained by scarcity, demand, and the entity's digital nature via NFTs. NFTs offer up new perspectives on value representation, beginning on an expedition that welcomes creative artists, inventors, and investors alike.

NFTs go beyond basic value and ownership to reshape the metaverse's economic landscape. Artists and creators are embracing NFTs to commercialize their digital initiatives, bypassing conventional middlemen and forging a direct link with their audience (Christodoulou et al., 2022). NFTs enable artists to value limited editions, earn royalties from secondary sales, and enjoy direct support from collectors and enthusiasts. This tectonic change expands the creative industry's metaverse panorama, supporting a digital artistic renaissance.

Individual ownership and value representation are not the only consequences of NFTs in the metaverse. These tokens foster a culture of involvement, cooperation, and community-building. NFT markets are growing in popularity as hubs for artists, collectors, and connoisseurs, allowing for chance meetings with new digital material and immersive experiences (Christodoulou et al., 2022). NFT communities sprout within shared passions and interests, supporting an ecology rich in cooperation, social relationships, and idea cross-pollination.

The intersection of NFTs and the metaverse demonstrates the confluence of two revolutionary ideas. A symphony of blockchain-enabled ownership and value representation harmonizes with the immersive canvas of the metaverse, ushering in an age of flourishing digital kingdoms. As this chapter goes further into the complexities of Non-Fungible Tokens in the metaverse, it will unravel the many threads intertwined in this transforming tapestry, providing insights into the symphony that redefines our digital horizons.

THE CONCEPT OF NFTS

Characteristics and Definition of NFTs

Non-fungible Tokens (NFTs) have emerged as a revolutionary and disruptive phenomenon in the digital ecosystem, successfully distinguishing themselves from traditional digital assets due to their special characteristics. These NFTs, which are effectively digital tokens, serve to represent ownership or testify to the legitimacy of a given digital object or commodity. Unlike fungible equivalents, such as cryptocurrencies, which are easily replaceable in one-to-one transactions, each NFT has a distinct and indivisible personality (Buterin, 2015). The unrivalled uniqueness of NFTs is its distinguishing feature. Every NFT is a physical representation of a specific digital item or asset, whether it be artwork, collectibles, sounds, films, virtual real estate, or even digital identities (Idelberger & Mezei, 2022). This uniqueness is intricately woven into the production, storage, and trade of NFTs via the complex fabric of blockchain technology. Each NFT, which uses blockchain as its base, has a unique identification, metadata, and cryptographic signature, providing convincing proof of its legitimacy and allowing users to authenticate ownership (Buterin, 2015; Idelberger & Mezei, 2022). Another distinguishing feature of NFTs is the idea of indivisibility. NFTs, unlike traditional digital assets, are not susceptible to division or one-to-one exchange. Instead, they are full and comprehensive pieces that include a whole digital entity (Idelberger & Mezei, 2021). This indivisibility emerges as a defining feature, ensuring the digital entity's integrity and uniqueness. NFTs thrive on keeping the entity's totality, as opposed to partial ownership or fragmented pieces.

NFTs provide a higher degree of validity and ownership authentication. The use of blockchain technology creates a landscape of tamper-proof and transparent ownership records. Each non-fungible token has a unique identification and information that is securely maintained on the blockchain, allowing for seamless validation of its legality and ownership (Buterin, 2015). This increased verifiability builds trust in the digital environment, essentially removing the threat of forgery and illegal copying. NFTs often include linked metadata, which is an extension of the digital property or object they represent. This metadata serves as a storehouse for extra information on the item's origin, history, provenance, and other notable traits or characteristics (Chandra, 2022). The addition of information enhances the value and context of the digital entity, providing collectors and enthusiasts with a more comprehensive understanding.

Non-Fungible Tokens (NFTs) are built with a number of essential components, each of which contributes to their particular character and functioning in the digital domain. These pieces include metadata, token standards, and smart contracts, and together they shape the NFT environment.

Metadata emerges as a key component of NFTs, encompassing the context and complexities of the digital object or value that the token represents (Wang et al., 2020). Attributes such as the creator's name, description, genesis date, provenance, and other relevant qualities may be found inside metadata. The information may be natively contained inside the token or act as a bridge to other sources, allowing users to access and comprehend connected insights with ease.

Token standards, such as Ethereum's ERC-721 and ERC-1155, play an important role in establishing the criteria and requirements for NFT creation and integration (Buterin, 2015). These standards provide a unified framework that ensures the interoperability and harmonious interaction of various NFTs and platforms. These standards define the structural blueprint of an NFT, which includes a unique identification, transferability, metadata structure, and auxiliary functionality. Token standards enable the easy cross-pollination of diverse NFT initiatives and platforms, supporting a thriving and linked ecosystem.

Smart contracts, which are embedded as the foundation of NFTs, contribute to the automation and execution of a wide range of activities and functions. Smart contracts, which are embedded directly into the contract's code, work as self-executing agents, describing the logic and rules that govern NFTs. This encapsulation encompasses aspects like ownership transfer, royalty distribution, and other NFT-specific characteristics (Wang et al., 2021). Smart contracts enable transparency, immutability, and dependability in the NFT ecosystem, strengthening the enforcement of rights and conditions, including artists' claim to royalties from secondary sales. Furthermore, the underlying infrastructure for NFTs is the backbone of blockchain technology. NFTs are created, stored, and transferred inside blockchain networks, which provide the trifecta of decentralization, security, and immutability (Wang et al., 2021). This decentralized design protects NFT ownership records against manipulation and change, enhancing their validity and trustworthiness. Furthermore, the blockchain architecture enables visible and traceable transaction histories, ushering in provenance and safeguarding the NFT ecosystem's integrity.

Differences Between NFTs and Traditional Digital Assets

Non-Fungible Tokens (NFTs) have ushered in a new paradigm in the domain of digital assets, distinguishing themselves from traditional digital assets through their unique characteristics. Understanding these distinctions is crucial for appreciating the transformative potential of non-fungible tokens in the digital landscape. NFTs are distinguished from conventional digital assets by their uniqueness and indivisible nature. Each NFT represents a unique and non-divisible digital item or asset (Yousaf & Yarovaya, 2022). Traditional digital assets, on the other hand, can be duplicated, shared, and divided without differentiating between instances of the same asset.

The ownership and verifiability of NFTs is an additional significant distinction. The blockchain technology underlying NFTs makes ownership records transparent and tamper-proof (Buterin, 2015). Each NFT includes a unique identifier and metadata, which are stored on the blockchain and serve as proof of authenticity and ownership validation, respectively. In contrast, traditional digital assets frequently lack a transparent and immutable system for authenticating ownership, which can lead to problems with unauthorised duplication, piracy, and establishing the asset's provenance.

NFTs differ from conventional digital assets in the manner in which their value is represented. NFTs derive their value from their inherent uniqueness and the digital content or item they represent (Yousaf & Yarovaya, 2021). The scarcity and veracity of NFTs contribute to their perceived value, resulting in frequently high prices for desirable digital assets within the NFT ecosystem. In addition, NFTs provide enhanced opportunities for creators to monetize their digital works. NFTs enable creators to establish direct connections with consumers, sell limited editions, and receive royalties on secondary sales (Yousaf & Yarovaya, 2021). In contrast to traditional digital assets, where creators frequently face difficulties in retaining control and earning fair compensation for their work, NFTs enable creators to establish direct connections with consumers, sell limited editions, and receive royalties on secondary sales. This paradigm shift affords artists, musicians, and creators new opportunities to assert their rights and profit financially from their digital works.

Examples of NFT Initiatives and Platforms

- Axie Infinity: Axie Infinity is a prominent NFT game that functions as an Ethereum-based virtual universe. Axies, which are NFTs, are distinctive digital creatures that users can own and propagate. Using the native token $AXS, these Axies are tradable on the Axie Infinity Marketplace. The platform also includes a play-to-earn (P2E) element that enables users to compete with their Axies to earn rewards, such as the $SLP token, which can be traded on major cryptocurrency exchanges. The initiative has attracted considerable interest due to its combination of financial opportunities and immersive gaming experiences.

- Invisible Friends is an NFT initiative created by the Swedish animator Markus Magnusson and the Random Character Collective. The collection consists of 5,000 animated, invisible figures, each uniquely outfitted with apparel, sporting equipment, and scientific instruments. On the first day of trading, a floor price of 12 ETH was established for the initiative, which sparked significant interest. There are currently 4,008 token holders out of a total of 5,000, and the initiative has amassed a significant following on social media platforms such as Twitter and Discord.

- SuperRare: SuperRare is a digital art marketplace built on Ethereum. It enables creators to distribute authenticated and collectible limited-edition digital artworks, such as videos, GIFs, static photographs, and 3D artworks. Each work of art is produced by a network participant and tokenized on the blockchain. There are currently 6,846 SuperRare proprietors, with a total token supply of 32,036, demonstrating the platform's prominence among artists and aficionados.

- Azuki is a collection of 10,000 2D anime-style characters that grant access to "The Garden," a space designed to integrate the real and virtual worlds. Each character in the collection has distinctive facial characteristics, attire, and accessories, and they all face left. Azuki utilises its characters and partnerships to facilitate collaborations with streetwear brands, upcoming NFT releases, and prospective live events. Currently, 5,149 people possess the 10,000 Azuki tokens. The project has investigated inventive initiatives, such as the release of Bobu the Bean Farmer, in which token holders can influence the character's future in the Azuki universe.

- Otherside is a forthcoming metaverse project affiliated with the Bored Ape Yacht Club (BAYC). It intends to develop a Massively Multiplayer Online-Role-Playing Game (MMORPG) that incorporates non-fungible tokens (NFTs) from multiple platforms, such as Cool Cats, CrypToadz, and World of Women (WoW). The incorporation of these NFT collections will enable players to interact with interactive NFTs in-game. Otherside demonstrates promise as an MMORPG set in the BAYC metaverse, expanding the possibilities of NFTs in gaming environments despite still being in development.

NFTS AS A VALUE STORE

Traditional Value Storage Methods and Their Limitations

Traditional techniques of value storage have long served as the foundation of economic institutions; and the digital era has highlighted their inherent limitations. These traditional methods, which include real cash, bank accounts, and centralized databases, have unquestionably played an important part in the preservation and diffusion of wealth. As the digital world advances at a fast pace, these established systems face constraints that hinder their efficacy and flexibility. Traditional value storage systems are limited by their reliance on physical infrastructure. Tangible media, such as coins and banknotes, are prone to loss, theft, and deterioration since they need physical storage and transit (Swan, 2015). Similarly, conventional banking systems are vulnerable to cyberattacks, fraud, and system failures owing to their dependence on centralized institutions and infrastructure. The physical aspect of these old techniques limits their efficiency, accessibility, and scalability in an environment marked by increased digital interconnection.

Traditional techniques of value storage can include complex and time-consuming transaction and transfer procedures. Traditional banking systems include middlemen, multi-party engagement, and manual validation processes, which result in delays, inefficiencies, and additional expenses (Swan, 2015). Similarly, worldwide transactions may devolve into complicated endeavours that need a slew of middlemen and incur significant expenses. These constraints, particularly in a multinational, digitally connected economy, inhibit the smooth, efficient interchange of value.

Lack of transparency and deteriorating trust are two further chains that constrain conventional asset storage techniques. The basis upon which these systems operate is trust in the dependability and security of centralized enterprises such as banks and financial institutions. Throughout history, financial crises, disputes, and administrative blunders have eroded public confidence (Swan, 2015). The inability of traditional value storage methods to build trust and confidence might be hampered by a lack of openness and agency over one's assets. Conventional value storing techniques may have accessibility and inclusiveness restrictions. Access to traditional banking services remains a challenge for many people, particularly those from underserved or unbanked communities. Physical presence, minimum balance standards, and demanding verification procedures, for example, might effectively remove underprivileged groups from the official economic fold (Swan, 2015). This restriction exacerbates economic inequities and impedes financial inclusion.

Despite being the foundation of economic frameworks, conventional value storage techniques are already exhibiting flaws in the digital era. In a rapidly changing digital world, dependency on physical infrastructure, cumbersome transactional procedures, opacity, and limited accessibility seem as barriers. Exploring ground-breaking solutions such as decentralized digital currencies and value storage systems based on blockchain technology can alleviate these constraints and usher in novel opportunities for efficient, transparent, and inclusive value archiving and exchange in an era marked by increased interconnectivity and digitization.

NFTs As Distinct Digital Assets with Inherent Value

Non-Fungible Tokens (NFTs) have emerged as an innovative concept in the digital landscape, providing digital assets with intrinsic value. In contrast to fungible tokens such as cryptocurrencies, NFTs represent unique digital objects that cannot be duplicated or traded one-for-one. NFTs derive their intrinsic value from their inherent uniqueness, scarcity, and the digital content they represent.

Uniqueness is a crucial aspect of NFTs that contributes to their intrinsic value. Each NFT denotes a particular digital asset or object, such as artwork, music, videos, virtual real estate, or even virtual identities. Utilising blockchain technology, each NFT is given a unique identifier and its ownership is recorded on the blockchain (Ali & Bagui, 2021). This verifiable uniqueness increases the desirability and value of NFTs, as collectors and enthusiasts look to acquire these unique digital assets. Scarcity contributes to the intrinsic value of non-fungible tokens. Numerous NFTs are created in limited quantities or with unique characteristics, making them scarce in the digital domain. The scarcity of non-fungible tokens can be determined by factors such as the number of editions produced, the rarity of particular attributes, or the exclusivity of the associated digital content (Liu et al., 2021). In the NFT ecosystem, the limited supply and high demand for these finite digital assets contribute to their perceived value.

The digital content associated with NFTs contributes significantly to their intrinsic value. NFTs serve as a portal for accessing and displaying distinct digital creations, such as artworks, music albums, virtual fashion, and virtual real estate. The digital content associated with an NFT can range from the tangible to the intangible, capturing the creators' creativity, talent, and individuality (Ali & Bagui, 2021). This association between the NFT and its digital content increases the value of the NFT, as individuals seek to acquire and appreciate these digital works.

The ability to demonstrate proprietorship and authenticity of NFTs increases their inherent value. NFTs employ blockchain technology to establish a transparent and immutable record of ownership, allowing individuals to assert ownership rights and demonstrate the authenticity of the digital asset. The verifiability and provable ownership of NFTs eliminate concerns regarding counterfeiting or unauthorised duplication, thereby enhancing confidence in the value of these digital assets (Buterin, 2015). This characteristic is especially important in the digital sphere, where issues of ownership and authenticity have been enduring obstacles. Due to their inherent uniqueness, scarcity, associated digital content, and provable ownership, NFTs possess intrinsic value. Uniqueness, scarcity, and the desirability of the digital content associated with NFTs all contribute to their intrinsic value within the NFT ecosystem. The ability to verify ownership and authenticity through blockchain technology increases the perceived value and credibility of non-fiat currencies. As the digital landscape continues to evolve, NFTs provide new opportunities for digital ownership, appreciation, and value representation.

Aspects Affecting the Value of NFTs

Non-Fungible Tokens (NFTs) in the digital environment are influenced by a variety of factors that contribute to their perceived value. These elements include scarcity, desirability, reputation, origin, and cultural significance. Understanding these influences is essential to comprehending the dynamics of the NFT market and the factors that contribute to the value of these one-of-a-kind digital assets.

Scarcity is a foundational factor influencing the value of non-fungible tokens. The limited supply or rarity of non-fungible tokens can substantially increase their perceived value (Andringa, 2022). Within the NFT ecosystem, NFTs that are issued in limited editions or possess distinct characteristics, such as uncommon attributes or specific properties, are frequently deemed more valuable. As collectors and devotees seek to acquire unique and exclusive NFTs, the inherent scarcity of these digital assets is consistent with the laws of supply and demand. Additionally influential in determining the value of NFTs is desirability. The appeal and attractiveness of associated digital content play a significant role in increasing the value of NFTs (Liu et al., 2020). High-quality works of art, iconic artefacts, or immersive virtual experiences can generate a strong demand among collectors and devotees, resulting in a rise in market value. The subjectivity of desirability renders it a variable factor, as trends, cultural preferences, and individual preferences influence the perceived value of NFTs.

Reputation and creators' reputations also contribute to the value of non-fungible tokens. Due to their established reputation and track record, non-fungible tokens created by renowned artists, musicians, or well-established entities often bear a higher market value (Chen et al., 2021). The creator's reputation influences the perception of quality, authenticity, and investment potential, thereby affecting the value ascribed to NFTs associated with them. Collectors and investors tend to assign greater value to non-tradable tokens whose creators are credible and well-known.

Another factor that affects the value of non-fungible tokens is their provenance, or history of ownership and authenticity. The ability to trace an NFT's ownership history and verify its authenticity increases trust and confidence, thereby increasing its value (Buterin, 2015). NFTs with a transparent and verifiable provenance provide collectors and investors with assurance, mitigating their concerns regarding forgery, unauthorised duplication, and ownership disputes. Establishing provenance mechanisms within the NFT ecosystem increases the worth of these digital assets.

Cultural significance can considerably affect the value of non-fungible tokens, especially in the realms of digital art and virtual experiences. Culturally significant NFTs that depict cultural moments, social commentary, or historical events can convey immense value (Andringa, 2022). These NFTs become artefacts representing a particular time period or capturing a specific cultural expression, resonating with individuals and communities. The cultural context and significance of NFTs increase their perceived value, as they transcend their status as mere digital assets to become symbolic representations of shared experiences and collective identity.

METAVERSE NFTS AND DIGITAL IDENTITIES

Importance of Digital Identity Within Virtual Environments

Digital identity is significant in virtual environments because of its function in establishing a sense of personal presence and representation. Individuals are able to interact, communicate, and partake in virtual communities by creating and projecting their digital identities (Peachey & Childset, 2011). These identities can include various components, such as usernames, avatars, profiles, and metadata. By embodying a digital identity, individuals establish a link between their real-world selves and their virtual representations, enabling a personalised and immersive experience in virtual environments.

Digital identity is a means of identification and authentication within virtual spaces. Users are frequently required to establish and verify their digital identities in order to access specific virtual platforms or engage in specific activities. This process contributes to security and trust by ensuring that individuals are accountable for their actions and behaviours in the virtual domain (Peachey & Childset, 2011). Digital identity verification mechanisms, such as two-factor authentication or biometric authentication, improve the security of virtual environments by decreasing the likelihood of impersonation, deception, and unauthorised access. Digital identity also plays a crucial role in facilitating personalised interactions and experiences within virtual environments. Using digital identities, virtual platforms can collect and analyse user data, preferences, and behaviour patterns, allowing for personalised recommendations, content suggestions, and social connections (Peachey & Childset, 2011). Within virtual environments, this personalised approach improves user engagement, satisfaction, and the overall user experience.

The significance of digital identity is determined by its effect on reputation and social capital in virtual spaces. Individuals' digital identities acquire a reputation based on their actions, contributions, and interactions as they interact, collaborate, and conduct business within virtual communities (Koosel, 2013). This reputation, which is frequently reflected in ratings, evaluations, and endorsements, influences how others perceive and interact with individuals in virtual environments. Developing a positive digital identity and reputation can result in increased opportunities, social connections, and confidence in the virtual community.

Digital identity acts as a link between the virtual and actual worlds. (Wachsmuth et al., 2018) Individuals frequently maintain consistent digital identities across different virtual platforms, allowing for a coherent representation of themselves in various virtual spaces. This continuity allows for the establishment and maintenance of long-term relationships, networks, and communities that extend beyond a singular virtual environment. Digital identity facilitates the transmission of trust, reputation, and relationships between virtual and physical contexts.

NFTs' Function in Representing and Verifying Digital Identities

Non-Fungible Tokens (NFTs) represent and authenticate digital identities within virtual environments. NFTs provide a unique and potent mechanism for establishing, verifying, and representing digital identities as individuals participate in online interactions and virtual communities. NFTs' capacity to serve as a unique and verifiable representation of a person in the virtual domain is one of their most important functions in digital identities. NFTs can be utilised to construct and associate digital personas or profiles with particular attributes, characteristics, or personal data (Eltuhami et al., 2021). By associating a non-fungible token (NFT) with a digital identity, users can establish a distinct and recognisable presence in virtual environments. Enabled by blockchain technology, the uniqueness and immutability of NFTs provide a reliable means of representing digital identities, thereby reducing the risk of impersonation or identity fraud.

NFTs facilitate the authentication of digital identities in virtual spaces. NFTs can be used to establish trust and verify the identity of individuals by associating them with real-world or verified information (Liu et al., 2020). Individuals can demonstrate their qualifications, accomplishments, and membership in specific communities by affixing digital certificates or credentials to an NFT. These verifiable digital identities can increase trust, credibility, and reputation in virtual environments, allowing for more meaningful interactions and collaborations. NFTs also facilitate the establishment of possession and authority over digital identities. Individuals can assert ownership rights over their digital identities represented by NFTs using blockchain technology (Buterin, 2015). This ownership grants individuals control over the use, transmission, and administration of their digital identities in virtual environments. Individuals acquire autonomy and sovereignty over their digital identities through the ability to prove ownership using the unique identifier and blockchain records associated with an NFT.

Moreover, NFTs enable the preservation and monetization of digital identities. Individuals are able to capture and preserve their digital personas, avatars, and profiles as valuable digital assets using NFTs (Eltuhami et al., 2021). These digital identities can be purchased, sold, and traded, allowing individuals to profit from their virtual presence and creativity. NFTs offer a means of assigning value and establishing a market for unique digital identities, enabling individuals to investigate new avenues of economic participation and expression within virtual environments.

In virtual environments, NFTs play a crucial role in representing and authenticating digital identities. Individuals can establish unique and verifiable representations of their digital personas or profiles by utilising NFTs. NFTs facilitate the authentication of digital identities, thereby fostering trust, credibility, and repute within virtual communities. Individuals are able to assert autonomy and sovereignty over their digital identities as a result of the ownership and control enabled by NFTs. In addition, NFTs enable the preservation, monetization, and exchange of digital identities as valuable digital assets. As virtual environments continue to evolve, non-fungible tokens will continue to shape and redefine the landscape of digital identities, unleashing new opportunities for expression, interaction, and economic participation.

Avatars and Virtual Possessions Based on NFT

Non-Fungible Tokens (NFTs) have introduced new possibilities in the domain of digital avatars and virtual possessions. Avatars and virtual possessions founded on NFT represent a paradigm shift in how people interact, personalise, and express themselves in virtual spaces. By utilising NFT technology, individuals can establish unique and valuable digital identities, personalise their virtual representations, and acquire virtual assets with both personal and economic value.

Momtaz et al. (2022) mentions NFT-based avatars allow users to construct and customise distinctive virtual personas that signify their digital identities. Users can assert the proprietorship, uniqueness, and authenticity of their virtual personas through the association of an NFT with an avatar. The use of NFTs assures the scarcity and provenance of these avatars, thereby increasing their collectibility and value within the virtual environment. By customising and possessing NFT-based avatars, individuals can establish a stronger connection with their virtual presence and interact with others in the digital domain in a more meaningful manner. Avatars based on NFT allow users to monetize their virtual identities and creativity. By assigning value to NFT-based avatars, users are able to purchase, sell, and trade these digital representations, thereby creating a market for distinctive and desirable avatars (Momtaz et al., 2022). Individuals are afforded the opportunity to derive value from their virtual identities and convey their originality by virtue of this economic dimension. Avatars founded on non-fungible tokens serve as a bridge between the virtual and real economies, enabling users to partake in the emerging digital marketplace and potentially generate income from their virtual possessions.

NFTs also revolutionise the concept of virtual possessions within digital environments, in addition to avatars. NFT-based virtual possessions can include a vast array of digital assets, including virtual apparel, accoutrements, virtual real estate, and even virtual pets (Liu et al., 2021). Within virtual ecosystems, the unique characteristics, scarcity, and provable ownership of these digital assets make them desirable and valuable. Individuals can personalise their virtual spaces, demonstrate their taste and style, and engage in virtual commerce using NFT-based virtual possessions.

The significance of NFT-based avatars and virtual property extends beyond individual expression and economic opportunities. They also have cultural and social significance, influencing how individuals interact, collaborate, and form virtual communities. Individuals are able to align themselves with particular virtual communities or subcultures through the use of NFT-based avatars and possessions (Liu et al., 2021). Individuals are able to establish connections, affiliations, and shared experiences through the incorporation of these digital representations into their social interactions.

Avatars and virtual property based on NFT have revolutionised how individuals interact with and convey themselves in digital environments. Individuals can establish and customise their virtual personas, assert ownership and authenticity, and partake in the emerging virtual economy with the help of these distinctive digital assets. Avatars and virtual possessions founded on NFT provide opportunities for customization, monetization, and artistic expression. In addition, they facilitate social connections, cultural ties, and shared experiences within virtual communities. As the digital landscape continues to evolve, NFT-based avatars and virtual possessions will continue to influence how individuals navigate and interact within virtual spaces.

Implications for Self-Expression and Interpersonal Relationships

Non-Fungible Tokens (NFTs) have profound implications for virtual environments' self-expression and social interactions. They offer unprecedented opportunities for individuals to express their identities, exhibit their creativity, and engage in meaningful interactions. Individuals can shape their virtual experiences, nurture connections, and navigate digital domains in novel and transformative ways by leveraging the distinctive characteristics and properties of NFTs. The ability to construct and customise distinct digital assets that reflect one's identity and values is a significant implication of NFTs for self-expression (Sung et al., 2011). Through the ownership of NFT-based avatars, artworks, or virtual possessions, individuals can authentically represent themselves within virtual environments and communicate their interests, preferences, and affiliations. Individuals are able to transcend the limitations of corporeal existence and investigate new dimensions of identity and creativity by expressing themselves through NFTs. Additionally, NFTs enable individuals to engage in social interactions within virtual communities, nurturing relationships and shared experiences. NFT-based virtual possessions, such as virtual fashion or collectibles, can serve as conversation starters, allowing individuals to form alliances and share common interests (Liu et al., 2021). The ownership and display of NFTs become a form of social currency, enabling interactions, collaborations, and the formation of communities based on a shared appreciation for digital assets. NFTs foster a sense of community and empower users to traverse virtual environments with a sense of purpose and social engagement.

NFTs improve the social dynamics of virtual spaces by allowing users to actively support and interact with creators (Sung et al., 2011). Individuals can directly support artists and creators by purchasing and possessing NFTs representing digital artworks, audio, and other forms of creative content. This direct link between creators and consumers fosters a sense of community, gratitude, and mutual support. Individuals can convey their admiration for the work of creators and establish a direct relationship with them through NFTs, thereby dissolving the lines between artist and audience. They have the potential to democratise the creation and distribution of digital content, allowing people from disparate origins to partake in the creative process (Liu et al., 2021). By involving their audience in the production and possession of NFTs through crowdfunding or tokenization, creators can foster a more inclusive and collaborative creative economy. This democratisation of content creation enables people to express themselves, share their experiences, and contribute to the cultural fabric of virtual environments.

NFTs have extensive ramifications for self-expression and social interactions in virtual environments. Individuals are able to convey their identities, exhibit their creativity, and engage in meaningful interactions through the use of these distinctive digital assets. NFTs enable personalization, creativity, and the formation of communities centred on the appreciation of digital assets and shared interests. The direct connection facilitated by NFTs between creators and consumers fosters a sense of belonging, support, and engagement. In addition, the democratisation of content creation made possible by NFTs enables individuals from disparate backgrounds to participate in the creative process. As the digital landscape evolves, NFTs will influence how individuals express themselves, interact with others, and navigate virtual spaces.

NFTS AND PROPERTY RIGHTS IN THE METAVERSE

Nfts' Contribution to Establishing Verifiable Proprietorship

Non-Fungible Tokens (NFTs) are essential in demonstrating indisputable ownership of digital assets. NFTs provide transparent and secure means of establishing ownership over digital items by using their unique characteristics and underlying technology, successfully solving persisting issues in the digital domain.

The use of blockchain technology to create immutable ownership records is at the heart of NFTs. Every NFT has a unique identification and information that are securely recorded on the blockchain, creating a transparent and immutable basis (Solouki & Bamakan, 2022). The potential of counterfeit ownership claims or illegal reproduction is eliminated by this decentralized and tamper-proof blockchain system, offering a trustworthy foundation for certifying ownership. Cryptographic signatures encoded in NFTs provide an additional degree of reliability and validity. These digital signatures serve as separate indicators, ensuring the uniqueness of each NFT and its rightful owner (Solouki & Bamakan, 2022). The verification of these cryptographic signatures enables users to confirm the NFT's legitimacy and integrity, essentially preventing any unauthorized edits or interventions.

NFTs allow for the thorough tracing of ownership history and origin. Because blockchain technology is immutable, it provides for the documenting and tracking of ownership transactions throughout the life of an NFT. This lineage data generates a verifiable and auditable record of the asset's journey (Buterin, 2015). This is especially important for items of historical, cultural, or aesthetic value, where confirming provenance is critical. The ability to attach information to NFTs improves ownership verification. Metadata includes information such as the name of the author, the description of the item, and supplemental qualities (Solouki & Bamakan, 2022). This metadata gives a comprehensive view of the item, allowing users to confirm its legitimacy and ownership by depending on the accompanying information. By providing contextual information and value to the NFT, metadata increases the believability of ownership statements.

Non-fungible tokens play an important role in creating authentic ownership that extends beyond the digital domain. NFTs provide as a link between the virtual and physical worlds by allowing the ownership of tangible goods to be represented digitally. NFTs, for example, might represent tangible artworks or real estate ownership, with the digital token functioning as solid evidence of validity and ownership (Solouki & Bamakan, 2022). The combination of digital and physical ownership increases the verifiability and reliability of asset ownership.

Difficulties Posed by Digital Proprietorship in The Metaverse

While the metaverse offers thrilling opportunities for digital ownership, it also presents unique challenges that must be addressed to ensure a secure and trustworthy environment. These difficulties are a result of the metaverse's character as a virtual space where digital assets are created, traded, and consumed. The risk of counterfeiting and unauthorised duplication is one of the greatest obstacles to digital ownership in the metaverse. As the value and prominence of virtual assets increase, there is a possibility that counterfeit versions of valuable digital items will be created, resulting in a loss of trust and confidence in the authenticity of these assets (Hurst et al., 2023). Verifying the authenticity and verifiability of digital assets within the metaverse is essential for preserving the ecosystem's integrity.

The issue of intellectual property rights and copyright infringement is another obstacle. The metaverse facilitates the vast creation and distribution of digital content, which raises concerns regarding the protection of creators' and artists' rights. Unauthorised use, reproduction, or distribution of copyrighted materials can diminish the value and exclusivity of digital assets, possibly discouraging creators from participating in the metaverse or resulting in legal disputes (Hurst et al., 2023). Establishing robust mechanisms to safeguard intellectual property rights and enforce copyright regulations is crucial for promoting a sustainable and ethical metaverse. In addition to scalability and sustainability, digital proprietorship in the metaverse faces additional obstacles in terms of scalability and longevity. As the metaverse grows and attracts an increasing number of users, the underlying technical infrastructure must be able to accommodate the escalating demands for storage, processing, and transaction capabilities. To ensure a seamless user experience, scaling blockchain networks to accommodate a large number of NFTs and users in a seamless and efficient manner is essential (Hurst et al., 2023). Furthermore, the energy consumption associated with blockchain technology raises sustainability concerns. The carbon footprint of blockchain networks may have environmental repercussions that must be addressed in order to establish a more sustainable metaverse ecosystem.

Interoperability and standardisation are obstacles that must be surmounted in order to facilitate seamless ownership and transmission of digital assets within the metaverse. Currently, there is a lack of uniformity and compatibility between various NFT platforms and token standards, which impedes the fluid movement and interaction of assets across platforms (Hurst et al., 2023). Establishing common standards and protocols that facilitate interoperability and cross-platform compatibility is essential for guaranteeing a cohesive and inclusive metaverse experience.

Examples of Non-Fungible Tokens That Enable Ownership in the Metaverse

- BMW: BMW has created a metaverse dubbed Joytopia to enhance the brand's communication initiatives. Joytopia is comprised of three virtual environments, Re:THINK, Re:IMAGINE, and Re:BIRTH, that align with BMW's fundamental strategies, including circular economy, electric mobility, and urban sustainability. Re:THINK allows users to investigate the concepts of the circular economy, while Re:IMAGINE functions as a platform for essential presentations and communications. Re:BIRTH provides insight into individual urban mobility options. Within Joytopia, users can run, fly, and leap using customizable avatars to navigate these environments. They can also construct their own spaces for public events, capture photographs, and upload them to social media. On the day of its debut, Joytopia received more than 150,000 visits from 30 countries, with an average duration of 13 minutes per visit.
- Balenciaga collaborated with the popular gaming metaverse platform Fortnite to issue an exclusive collection of apparel and accoutrements. The collaboration involved outfitting four of Fortnite's most popular characters in Balenciaga costumes that could be purchased with V-Bucks, the game's virtual currency. In addition, Balenciaga made the ensembles accessible for purchase in their online and brick-and-mortar stores. This strategic partnership capitalises on Fortnite's large user base of over 350 million players who invest considerable time in the creative mode.
- Dolce & Gabbana: At Metaverse Fashion Week in Decentraland, Dolce & Gabbana made an impact in the metaverse by presenting a custom collection of 20 metaverse garments. The brand also entered the realm of Non-Fungible Tokens (NFTs) by partnering with luxury NFT platform UNXD to release a collection dubbed "Collezione Genesi." This NFT collection, designed by

Domenico Dolce and Stefano Gabbana, sold for nearly $6 million. Notably, the Doge Crown, the most expensive NFT, sold for 423.5 ETH. Some of the NFT champions also received tangible objects as prizes. Dolce & Gabbana continues to investigate the metaverse and has recently launched the DGFamily NFT, which offers holders exclusive benefits and collaborations.

- Louis Vuitton: To commemorate the 200th birth anniversary of its progenitor, Louis Vuitton has published a mobile app game with 30 integrated NFTs, including contributions by renowned digital artist Michael Joseph Winkelman. The objective of the virtual adventure is to assist the protagonist acquire 200 candles, which will activate mementos detailing Louis Vuitton's life. These envelopes are designed to resemble NFTs. The game has surpassed two million downloads since its release in August 2021, providing users with an immersive experience that combines gaming and NFT collectibles.

- Gucci: Gucci was among the first luxury brands to implement NFTs. The brand auctioned a one-of-a-kind artwork from the Gucci Aria campaign film on Christie's, donating the proceeds to UNICEF USA. The artwork sold for $25,000, demonstrating the increasing demand for Gucci's NFT offerings. Gucci also collaborated with Superplastic, a manufacturer of animated celebrities, vinyl toys, and digital collectibles, to issue a series of limited-edition and uncommon NFTs. This partnership increases Gucci's digital presence and capitalises on the expanding market for digital collectibles and artwork.

These examples illustrate how luxury brands such as BMW, Balenciaga, Dolce & Gabbana, Louis Vuitton, and Gucci have adopted the metaverse and NFTs to engage with their audiences, offer unique experiences, and create new channels for brand expression and ownership. By investigating the potential of the metaverse and digital assets, these brands demonstrate their dedication to innovation and their desire to remain at the vanguard of the rapidly evolving digital landscape.

METAVERSE ECONOMIC OPPORTUNITIES FOR NFTS

Metaverse NFTs as a New Economic Paradigm

Non-Fungible Tokens (NFTs) have emerged as a new economic paradigm in the metaverse, redefining how value is created, exchanged, and experienced in virtual environments. NFTs have created unprecedented opportunities for economic participation, creativity, and proprietorship in the metaverse by leveraging blockchain technology and distinct digital assets.

The ability to represent and monetize distinct digital assets is one of the distinguishing characteristics of NFTs as a new economic paradigm (Hackl et al., 2022). Individuals can create, own, and trade digital assets such as artworks, virtual real estate, virtual apparel, and even virtual identities using non-fiat currencies. The value of these digital assets derives from their uniqueness, scarcity, and cultural significance. By creating a market for these digital assets, NFTs facilitate economic transactions and the exchange of value within the metaverse.

NFTs enable individuals to participate as creators, collectors, and investors in the emerging digital economy. By creating and selling NFT-based digital assets, creators can monetize their skills, talents, and creativity while circumventing traditional intermediaries and gatekeepers (Liu et al., 2021). This enables creators to engage directly with their audience, establish their own economic models, and profit from their digital works. In addition, collectors and investors can partake in the market by purchasing and trading NFTs, thereby capitalising on the potential for price appreciation and diversification within the metaverse. Additionally, NFTs redefine the notions of ownership and value representation. NFTs provide a transparent and verifiable record of ownership in the metaverse, ensuring that individuals have provable control over their digital assets (Buterin, 2015). This shift towards digital ownership affords new opportunities for value representation and transfer. NFTs enable individuals to assign value to ethereal digital assets, nurturing a new conception of ownership and value in the digital domain.

NFTs facilitate the development of novel business models and revenue streams within the metaverse. Through fractional ownership and incorporated royalties in NFTs, creators can receive recurring income and benefits from the use and resale of their digital assets (Liu et al., 2021). This creates a more equitable and sustainable ecosystem in which creators can continue to earn income after the initial sale of their NFTs. In addition, NFTs enable the development of virtual marketplaces, platforms, and services that accommodate to the requirements and preferences of the metaverse community, thereby promoting economic activity and innovation.

As a new economic paradigm, the influence of NFTs extends beyond the metaverse itself. The incorporation of non-fungible tokens (NFTs) with real-world assets, such as tangible artworks or real estate, enables cross-domain value exchange and interoperability (Hackl et al., 2022). NFTs can serve as a bridge between the physical and digital worlds, facilitating tokenization and value transfer across domains. This interconnectedness between the metaverse and the physical world creates opportunities for economic integration and the blurring of the lines between the real and virtual economies.

In the metaverse, NFTs have ushered in a new economic paradigm, offering unprecedented opportunities for economic participation, creativity, and ownership. NFTs empower creators, collectors, and investors by allowing the representation and monetization of distinct digital assets. The transparent and verifiable nature of NFTs revolutionises the concept of digital property ownership and value representation. In the metaverse, NFTs also foster new business models, revenue streams, and marketplaces. In addition, the integration of NFTs with physical assets bridges the divide between the physical and digital economies. NFTs will influence the future of economic transactions, creativity, and proprietorship in virtual environments as the metaverse continues to evolve.

Models of Monetization for NFT Creators and Artists

Non-Fungible Tokens (NFTs) have introduced innovative monetization models for creators and artists, giving them new ways to generate income and derive value from their digital creations. The monetization models enable creators to engage directly with their audience, establish their own economic frameworks, and open up new revenue sources within the domain of NFTs.

Direct sale of digital creations as NFTs is a prominent method for NFT creators and artists to generate revenue. Creators can monetize their artworks, music, virtual fashion, and other forms of digital content by minting and selling NFTs (Rutskiy et al., 2022). This model enables creators to disseminate their work directly to collectors and enthusiasts, bypassing traditional middlemen. The direct sale of NFTs allows creators to set their own prices, retain a greater portion of the proceeds, and have a more direct relationship with their audience. Creators can add royalties to the NFTs they sell, thereby generating a recurring revenue stream. Creators can integrate a percentage of future sales or utilisation of their NFTs as royalties using smart contracts (Liu et al., 2021). This model ensures that creators continue to profit from the continued success and esteem of their digital works, even after the initial sale. Royalties provide creators with a more sustainable income model, aligning their incentives with the long-term value of their NFTs and nurturing a sense of partnership between creators and collectors.

Fractional ownership and tokenization of their digital assets is a second method for NFT creators to generate revenue. By partitioning an NFT's ownership into fractions, creators can sell fractional ownership to multiple investors (Rutskiy et al., 2022). This permits creators to raise funds while maintaining partial ownership and control over their works. Fractional ownership enables collectors and investors to participate in the prospective value appreciation of the NFT, thereby establishing a shared ownership model that is advantageous for both creators and investors. This model allows creators to gain access to capital, cultivate communities around their work, and increase the liquidity of their digital assets. Creators can leverage NFTs to offer additional services or experiences, thereby generating additional revenue streams. For instance, artists may offer limited edition prints or merchandise in conjunction with their NFTs (Liu et al., 2021). Creators may also grant NFT holders access to exclusive events, collaborations, or behind-the-scenes content. These additional offerings augment the NFTs' value proposition and provide creators with additional revenue streams beyond the initial sale.

NFT creators can generate income through collaborations and partnerships with brands, platforms, or other creators. Collaborative NFT initiatives enable creators to combine their skills and fan bases, thereby expanding their reach and earning potential (Rutskiy et al., 2022). By utilising the fame and renown of multiple creators, these collaborations can attract more collectors and enthusiasts, thereby increasing the demand for and value of the NFTs. Moreover, creators can collaborate with brands or platforms to produce branded NFT collections, promotional campaigns, and sponsored content, thereby generating revenue for both parties.

NFTs have introduced a variety of monetization models for creators and artists, allowing them to generate income and derive value from their digital works. Direct sales of NFTs, royalties, fractional ownership, additional services, and collaborations provide opportunities for creators to monetize their work and engage with their audience in novel ways. These models enable creators to control their economic destinies, establish direct connections with their audience, and profit from the continued success of their digital assets. As the NFT ecosystem continues to evolve, creators will continue exploring and refining monetization models, thereby influencing the future of economic participation and creativity within the NFT domain.

Markets, Auctions, and Secondary Transactions of Non-Fungible Tokens

Non-Fungible Tokens (NFTs) have spawned a thriving ecosystem of marketplaces, auctions, and secondary transactions where individuals can purchase, sell, and trade these unique digital assets. These platforms have become indispensable for collectors, creators, and devotees, serving as a marketplace for NFT transactions and nurturing liquidity within the NFT economy.

NFT-specific marketplaces have emerged as crucial facilitators for the purchase and sale of NFTs. These platforms provide a centralised marketplace where creators can list their NFTs for sale and purchasers can discover and acquire digital assets that correspond to their interests (Du et al., 2022). To enhance the user experience and facilitate transactions, marketplaces provide a number of features and tools, including search filters, categorization, and reputation systems. These platforms link creators with a larger audience, providing them with exposure and access to potential purchasers. Moreover, marketplaces frequently manage the technical aspects of NFT transactions, such as the storage, transmission, and verification of NFT ownership, thereby ensuring secure and reliable transactions.

For the sale of non-fungible tokens, auctions have gained popularity, providing a thrilling and dynamic environment for collectors and investors. Individuals can bid on digital assets at NFT auctions, contending with others to acquire highly coveted items (Du et al., 2022). Auctions generate a feeling of scarcity, exclusivity, and exhilaration, thereby increasing the value and demand for non-fungible tokens. They create a market in which the true value of an NFT is determined by competitive bargaining, fostering a transparent and efficient price discovery procedure. Auctions have become a venue for high-profile sales and record-breaking transactions, attracting attention to the NFT sector and captivating the curiosity of collectors and the general public alike.

In addition to primary sales, secondary markets have emerged as significant venues for the resale and trading of non-traditional securities. Individuals are able to purchase and sell previously possessed NFTs on these secondary markets, establishing a prospering ecosystem of secondary sales and exchanges (White et al., 2022). Secondary markets provide NFT holders with liquidity, allowing them to realise the value of their digital assets by locating new purchasers who may have missed the initial transaction. These platforms also facilitate the discovery and acquisition of NFTs that have increased in value or are no longer available through primary sales. Secondary markets contribute to the continued vitality of the NFT ecosystem, enabling the continued trading and investment in digital assets.

The emergence of decentralised marketplaces based on blockchain technology has expanded the scope of NFT transactions. (White et al., 2022) Decentralised marketplaces operate on blockchain networks, facilitating peer-to-peer transactions without the need for intermediaries. These platforms provide NFT transactions with enhanced security, immutability, and transparency, thereby eradicating the need for centralised authorities. Decentralised marketplaces conform to the principles of decentralisation and open access, granting individuals greater control over their NFTs and promoting a more democratic and inclusive NFT economy.

The NFT ecosystem has incorporated marketplaces, auctions, and secondary markets. These platforms provide opportunities for creators to exhibit and monetize their digital creations, as well as for purchasers to discover and acquire exclusive digital assets. Marketplaces provide a centralised location for non-fiat currency transactions, assuring secure and trustworthy exchanges. Auctions generate a dynamic environment for price discovery and competitive bargaining. Secondary markets promote liquidity and continuous trading in the NFT market. Decentralised marketplaces expand the scope of peer-to-peer transactions and are consistent with decentralisation principles. Together, these platforms constitute the infrastructure that facilitates the purchasing, selling, and trading of NFTs, thereby contributing to the vitality and expansion of the NFT economy.

Intellectual Property Rights and Royalties

Non-Fungible Tokens (NFTs) have emerged as a revolutionary instrument for creators and artists to establish and secure their intellectual property rights and royalties in the digital sphere. NFTs provide a mechanism for creators to assert ownership, establish authenticity, and enforce their rights over their digital creations, while also facilitating the seamless monitoring and distribution of royalties.

The ability to establish ownership and provenance of digital assets is one of the main benefits of NFTs for intellectual property (IP) rights. Creators can link their digital works to a unique and verifiable token on the blockchain by minting an NFT (Macedo et al., 2022). This blockchain-based record functions as a digital certificate of authenticity, allowing creators to demonstrate ownership and establish a trustworthy record of the asset's creation and history. The blockchain's immutability and transparency provide a tamper-proof and trustworthy mechanism for protecting and asserting intellectual property rights.

NFTs enable creators to incorporate royalty mechanisms directly into the smart contracts that govern NFTs. Through the use of smart contracts, creators can autonomously distribute a portion of each subsequent sale or use of the NFT as royalties to the original creator (Macedo et al., 2022). This royalty feature ensures that creators continue to profit from the commercial success and increased value of their digital works. The automation of royalty payments enabled by NFTs simplifies the process and reduces the need for middlemen, allowing creators to receive their fair share in a transparent and efficient manner. NFTs grant creators greater control over the utilisation and distribution of their digital assets. Using smart contracts, creators can enforce particular terms and conditions regarding the use, reproduction, or display of their digital works (Macedo et al., 2022). These contractual agreements may stipulate limitations, licencing conditions, or even restrictions on how the NFT may be utilised or transferred. By attaching these conditions to the NFT, creators can exert a greater degree of control over the dissemination and commercialization of their intellectual property, ensuring that their creative works are utilised in accordance with their intentions. NFTs allow creators to experiment with novel business models and revenue streams associated with their intellectual property. Creators can tokenize various aspects of their intellectual property, including characters, narratives, and even virtual experiences, enabling the development of NFT-based franchises or ecosystems (Macedo et al., 2022). Using NFTs, creators can monetize their intellectual property through the sale of digital assets, licencing agreements, and partnerships with other artists and brands. NFTs' adaptability and programmability afford creators the freedom to experiment with novel methods of IP monetization and revenue generation.

In the digital domain, NFTs have emerged as a potent mechanism for intellectual property rights and royalties. NFTs allow creators to establish ownership, demonstrate authenticity, and safeguard digital works. The incorporation of royalty mechanisms through smart contracts guarantees that creators receive their fair share of future sales and uses. Additionally, NFTs provide creators with greater control over the utilisation and distribution of their intellectual property. In addition, NFTs provide new opportunities for IP monetization and revenue streams, allowing creators to experiment with novel business models pertaining to their digital assets. As the NFT ecosystem continues to evolve, NFTs will play a greater role in influencing the landscape of intellectual property rights and royalties in the digital age.

CHALLENGES FOR NFTS IN THE METAVERSE

Scalability and Longevity of NFTs

Non-fungible tokens (NFTs) have garnered significant attention and popularity, but their pervasive adoption and long-term viability within the digital ecosystem raises concerns about scalability and sustainability. As the demand for NFTs continues to rise, it becomes crucial to resolve these issues in order to ensure their efficient operation and minimal environmental impact.

Scalability is a major concern in the context of non-fungible tokens, especially with regard to blockchain technology. The majority of NFTs are based on public blockchains such as Ethereum, which may encounter scalability issues due to limited transaction processing capabilities (Ante, 2022). As more users conduct NFT transactions, network congestion worsens, resulting in increased fees and delayed transaction speeds. This can impede the accessibility and efficacy of NFTs, particularly for creators and collectors attempting to navigate an ecosystem that is seamless and efficient. To address scalability issues, developers are examining various solutions, including layer-2 scaling solutions, sidechains, and alternative blockchains that can manage higher transaction volumes without compromising security or decentralisation.

The environmental sustainability of NFTs is an additional significant concern, particularly in terms of energy consumption and carbon footprint. Blockchain networks, such as Ethereum, rely on a consensus mechanism known as Proof of Work (PoW), which requires substantial computational capacity and energy consumption (Ante, 2022). The energy-intensive nature of PoW-based blockchains has raised concerns regarding their environmental impact, particularly in relation to prominent NFT events and the minting of large quantities of NFTs. There is a growing interest in transitioning to more sustainable consensus mechanisms, such as Proof of Stake (PoS), which consumes substantially less energy, in order to mitigate these concerns. PoS-based blockchains offer a promising alternative that can mitigate the negative environmental impact of NFTs.

There are also concerns regarding the carbon footprint associated with the creation and storage of NFTs, particularly those containing multimedia content. The process of minting and storing NFTs consumes computing resources and produces greenhouse gas emissions (Ante, 2022). As the market for NFTs expands and more digital assets are tokenized, it becomes essential to investigate sustainable storage solutions and evaluate the environmental effects of the NFT lifecycle. Various initiatives to mitigate the carbon footprint of NFTs or advocate carbon-neutral practises within the NFT ecosystem have emerged. However, ongoing efforts are required to ensure the long-term viability of NFTs. Moreover, as the prevalence of NFTs rises, the issue of digital waste becomes more prominent. NFTs are retained indefinitely on the blockchain, and while they may hold value and significance for their proprietors, they may also contribute to the growth of digital detritus (Ante, 2022). The indefinite storage of non-fungible tokens, particularly those with limited ongoing utilisation or demand, raises concerns regarding the long-term effects of this digital accumulation. Striking a balance between preserving the authenticity and integrity of non-fungible tokens (NFTs) and managing the potential digital waste they may generate is a difficult task that requires careful consideration.

Concerns regarding scalability and sustainability hinder the extensive adoption and long-term viability of NFTs. To ensure the seamless and efficient operation of NFT ecosystems, it is essential to address scalability issues by investigating alternative blockchain solutions or scaling mechanisms to accommodate rising transaction volumes. In terms of blockchain consensus mechanisms and the lifecycle of digital assets, it is necessary to reduce the energy consumption and carbon footprint associated with NFTs. In addition, the management of digital detritus and the long-term consequences of perpetual storage of NFTs merit consideration. As the NFT ecosystem evolves, it is crucial to prioritise the development of scalable and long-lasting frameworks to support the sustained growth and responsible use of NFTs.

Possibility of Fraud, Piracy, and IP Infringement

Non-Fungible Tokens (NFTs) have introduced intriguing opportunities for creators, collectors, and investors, but they also raise concerns regarding the potential for digital fraud, piracy, and copyright infringement. The decentralised and transnational nature of NFTs, coupled with the simplicity of duplicating and distributing digital content, presents challenges that must be addressed to maintain creators' rights and maintain trust.

The possibility of fraud within the NFT market is a major concern. Due to the relative novelty and complexity of NFTs, fraudulent activities, such as the sale of counterfeit or unauthorised NFTs, are possible (Yalabik, 2023). Fraudulent actors may attempt to misrepresent ownership or authenticity, causing unsuspecting customers to purchase NFTs that are not authentic or have questionable legal standing. These fraudulent activities can erode confidence in the NFT ecosystem and cause damage to both creators and purchasers. To mitigate this risk, it is crucial to establish defined standards, verification procedures, and reputation systems within NFT marketplaces to ensure the legitimacy and authenticity of NFTs.

Another concern related to the digital character of NFTs is piracy. While NFTs provide a mechanism for establishing ownership and provenance, the underlying digital content associated with NFTs can still be copied and distributed without authorization. The ease of duplicating and sharing digital files increases the risk of piracy, as individuals can create unauthorised copies of NFTs and distribute the associated content without authorization (Yalabik, 2023). This undermines the value and exclusivity of NFTs, as illegal copies can saturate the market and dilute the market value of legitimate NFTs. Implementing comprehensive digital rights management systems, watermarking techniques, or encryption mechanisms can help reduce the risk of piracy and safeguard creators' rights.

Infringement of intellectual property rights is another concern that arises in relation to NFTs. NFTs permit the tokenization and trading of digital assets, such as works of art, music, and other copyrighted materials. Copyright infringement can result from the unauthorised tokenization or sale of copyrighted content without the permission of the copyright holder (Yalabik, 2023). The blockchain-based nature of NFTs can make it difficult to regulate and enforce copyright laws, raising legal and ethical concerns. Collaboration between NFT platforms, creators, and copyright holders is essential for establishing explicit licencing mechanisms, ensuring appropriate attribution, and protecting content creators' rights. In addition, the issue of stolen or improperly appropriated content being tokenized as NFTs has received increased attention. Individuals have tokenized and sold artworks or other digital assets without the permission or knowledge of the original creators (Yalabik, 2023). This raises concerns regarding the ethical implications of profiting without permission from the labour of others. Developing mechanisms to verify the ownership and authenticity of digital assets associated with NFTs, as well as promoting ethical practises and respect for intellectual property rights, can assist in mitigating these challenges.

Within the NFT ecosystem, the possibility of fraud, piracy, and copyright infringement presents significant obstacles. Establishing trust, ensuring the authenticity of NFTs, and protecting creators' rights are crucial factors. Implementing rigorous verification processes, digital rights management systems, and stakeholder collaboration can mitigate fraud and piracy-related risks. In addition, cultivating a culture of ethical conduct and respect for intellectual property rights is crucial for addressing concerns regarding copyright infringement. As the NFT market continues to evolve, it is essential to resolve these challenges in order to preserve the ecosystem's integrity, trustworthiness, and long-term viability.

Laws and Regulations in the Metaverse

The concept of the metaverse evolves and gains prominence, it raises a variety of legal and regulatory concerns that must be addressed. The metaverse, a virtual environment in which users interact with each other and digital assets, raises concerns pertaining to jurisdiction, intellectual property rights, data privacy, and online governance. These factors are essential for guaranteeing ethical, equitable, and secure participation in the metaverse.

Jurisdiction and the applicability of extant laws are two of the most important legal considerations in the metaverse. As the metaverse transcends physical boundaries, it can be difficult to determine the jurisdiction where activities occur and legal disputes arise (Kasiyanto & Kilinc, 2022). Existing legal frameworks may find it difficult to keep up with the rapid advancements in technology and the unique challenges presented by the metaverse. It is essential to develop exhaustive legal frameworks capable of addressing the unique characteristics of the metaverse while protecting the rights and interests of individuals and entities involved.

Legal considerations in the metaverse also include the importance of intellectual property rights. The metaverse enables the creation, distribution, and consumption of digital assets such as works of art, virtual clothing, and virtual real estate. It is essential to ensure adequate protection of intellectual property rights within the metaverse in order to encourage creativity, promote equitable competition, and safeguard the interests of creators (Kasiyanto & Kilinc, 2021). Determining the ownership, licencing, and enforcement mechanisms for digital assets in the metaverse presents difficulties that necessitate legal solutions and cooperation between creators, platforms, and regulators.

In the metaverse, where immense quantities of personal information can be collected, stored, and processed, data privacy and protection are of the utmost importance. Within the metaverse, users engage in a variety of activities, and their personal information and interactions may be captured and used for a variety of purposes. Maintaining stringent data privacy regulations and ensuring user consent, transparency, and security is crucial (Kasiyanto & Kilinc, 2021). To safeguard the rights of individuals and promote responsible data practises in the metaverse, robust data protection frameworks must be implemented. Online governance is an important factor in the metaverse. As the metaverse evolves into a complex digital society, issues such as online harassment, deception, and conflicts demand efficient governance mechanisms. Establishing codes of conduct, moderation policies, and dispute resolution mechanisms is essential for sustaining a safe and inclusive metaverse environment (Kasiyanto & Kilinc, 2022). Platform operators, developers, users, and regulators must collaborate to define standards and frameworks that promote responsible behaviour, safeguard user rights, and guarantee a fair and equitable metaverse experience.

Taxation and economic regulations in the metaverse must be carefully considered. The metaverse has the potential to generate substantial economic activity, including sales of non-fungible tokens, virtual commerce, and digital services. Regulators face difficulties in determining tax obligations, enforcing economic regulations, and preventing illegal activities in the metaverse (Rosenberg, 2022). The development of appropriate taxation frameworks and economic regulations that strike a balance between the requirements of participants, encourage innovation, and prevent abuses is essential for the metaverse's sustainable growth.

The emergence of the metaverse necessitates thorough consideration of a variety of legal and regulatory issues. It is essential to address issues pertaining to jurisdiction, intellectual property rights, data privacy, online governance, and economic regulations in order to foster a just, secure, and ethical metaverse ecosystem. Collaboration between stakeholders, including creators, platforms, regulators, and users, is required to develop legal frameworks capable of adapting to the unique challenges and opportunities presented by the metaverse. By proactively resolving these factors, the metaverse can prosper as a thriving and accountable digital ecosystem.

Governance of NFT Ecosystems

Non-Fungible Tokens (NFTs) have spawned thriving and dynamic ecosystems that are significantly dependent on community participation and governance. These ecosystems consist of creators, collectors, investors, developers, and platform administrators, all of whom contribute to the development and sustainability of the NFT market. Nevertheless, the dynamic nature of these ecosystems raises a number of community and governance issues that necessitate attention and collaboration to ensure equity, inclusivity, and responsible practises.

In NFT ecosystems, the possibility of exclusion and elitism is a significant community concern. As the prevalence of non-fungible tokens (NFTs) has increased, there have been concerns that certain communities or individuals will be marginalised or excluded from the ecosystem (Ali et al., 2023). Access to resources, technical knowledge, and existing networks can function as barriers to entry, preventing a greater number of people from participating. Fostering inclusivity through education, outreach programmes, and initiatives that support underrepresented communities can help promote diversity and equal opportunity within the NFT ecosystem in order to address this issue. Transparency and accountability are crucial governance issues. Given the decentralised and frequently pseudonymous nature of blockchain-based platforms, it is essential to ensure transparency in the operations of NFT marketplaces and the behaviour of participants (Ali et al., 2023). Lack of transparency can lead to concerns regarding discriminatory practises, market manipulation, or illegal activities. Within the NFT ecosystem, implementing transparent governance mechanisms, disclosure requirements, and reputation systems can aid in establishing trust and ensuring responsible behaviour.

The issue of intellectual property and copyright infringement is another major concern surrounding NFT communities. Due to the simplicity of tokenizing and trading digital assets, there is a risk that individuals will mint NFTs containing copyrighted content without the necessary authorization (Macedo et al., 2022). In addition to undermining the rights of content creators, this creates legal and ethical issues within the NFT ecosystem. Creators, platforms, and regulators must work together to establish clear guidelines, verification procedures, and licencing mechanisms to safeguard intellectual property rights and encourage responsible tokenization practises.

Scams and fraudulent activities also present difficulties for NFT communities. The increasing prominence and monetary value of NFTs have attracted malicious actors seeking to exploit unaware participants (Macedo et al., 2021). This includes the sale of counterfeit NFTs, phishing schemes, and the impersonation of well-known creators. Establishing rigorous security measures, educating participants about potential risks, and encouraging prudence can help prevent community members from falling prey to schemes. In addition, the development of reporting mechanisms and enforcement procedures on NFT platforms can aid in the identification and mitigation of fraudulent activities.

The issue of environmental sustainability has received increased attention in NFT communities. The energy consumption and carbon footprint associated with blockchain networks that support NFTs, especially those utilising Proof of Work (PoW) consensus mechanisms, have raised concerns regarding the ecological influence of NFT ecosystems (Majer, 2022). Adopting sustainable practises, such as switching to energy-efficient consensus mechanisms or supporting carbon offset initiatives, can contribute to the long-term viability and responsible development of NFT communities.

Diverse communities actively participate and collaborate to influence NFT ecosystems. To ensure fairness, inclusion, and responsible practises within these ecosystems, it is essential to address community and governance issues. A vibrant and diverse NFT community can be fostered by promoting inclusiveness, transparency, and accountability. Protecting intellectual property rights and preventing frauds and fraudulent activities are crucial for sustaining the ecosystem's credibility and trustworthiness. Moreover, addressing environmental sustainability issues contributes to the responsible development and long-term viability of NFT communities. NFT ecosystems can flourish as ethical, equitable, and sustainable digital environments by proactively addressing these issues.

CONCLUSION

In conclusion, the complex panorama of issues surrounding NFTs in the metaverse emphasizes the need of a comprehensive and coordinated approach. The multidimensional nature of these difficulties necessitates an integrated solution that combines technical breakthroughs, legislative changes, and community participation. From scalability issues to environmental sustainability, the field of NFTs need creative solutions that may handle their growing popularity while reducing their environmental effect. A key move toward energy-efficient consensus methods, together with attentive research of alternative blockchain technology, may pave the way for a more sustainable future.

The issue of fraud, piracy, and intellectual property infringement needs the implementation of severe verification procedures, powerful copyright enforcement, and partnerships between platforms, artists, and regulatory agencies. These safeguards protect the rights of artists, foster trust, and maintain the uniqueness of NFTs.

Legal and regulatory elements emerge as key aspects of the metaverse, necessitating the development of adaptive frameworks capable of balancing jurisdiction, data privacy, and intellectual property protection. Such frameworks should take into account the metaverse's transcendent character while also assuring equal participation, ethical behavior, and safe interactions.

Despite these issues, the administration of NFT ecosystems is critical to cultivating inclusion, openness, and ethical conduct. Cultivating a community that emphasizes responsible behavior and collaboration may help to reduce possible exclusion, increase trustworthiness, and deter fraudulent behavior.

As producers, collectors, platforms, regulators, and users come together, their collaborative efforts will be critical in determining the metaverse's development of NFTs. The metaverse has the potential to blossom into a dynamic, transformative digital space that enriches the experiences and livelihoods of all participants by collectively addressing scalability issues, championing environmental responsibility, upholding intellectual property rights, and establishing adaptive legal frameworks. The present issues may eventually drive the formation of a metaverse that is not just imaginative but also sustainable, secure, and really effective via proactive involvement and cooperation.

REFERENCES

Ali, M., & Bagui, S. (2021). Introduction to NFTs: The future of digital collectibles. *International Journal of Advanced Computer Science and Applications*, *12*(10), 50–56. doi:10.14569/IJACSA.2021.0121007

Ali, O., Momin, M., Shrestha, A., Das, R., Alhajj, F., & Dwivedi, Y. K. (2023). A review of the key challenges of non-fungible tokens. *Technological Forecasting and Social Change*, *187*, 122248. doi:10.1016/j. techfore.2022.122248

Andringa, C. (2022). *Property of the future-A research into factors influencing the value of virtual land* [Doctoral dissertation, Groningen University].

Ante, L. (2022). Non-fungible token (NFT) markets on the Ethereum blockchain: Temporal development, cointegration and interrelations. *Economics of Innovation and New Technology*, 1–19. doi:10.10 80/10438599.2022.2119564

Buterin, V. (2015). Ethereum: A Next-Generation Smart Contract and Decentralized Application Platform. *Ethereum.* https://ethereum.org/whitepaper/

Chandra, Y. (2022). Non-fungible token-enabled entrepreneurship: A conceptual framework. *Journal of Business Venturing Insights*, *18*, e00323. doi:10.1016/j.jbvi.2022.e00323

Christodoulou, K., Katelaris, L., Themistocleous, M., Christodoulou, P., & Iosif, E. (2022). NFTs and the metaverse revolution: Research perspectives and open challenges. *Blockchains and the Token Economy. Theory into Practice*, 139–178.

Du, L., Kim, M., & Lee, J. (2022). The Art NFTs and Their Marketplaces. arXiv preprint arXiv:2210.14942

Eltuhami, M., Abdullah, M., & Talip, B. A. (2022, November). Identity Verification and Document Traceability in Digital Identity Systems using Non-Transferable Non-Fungible Tokens. In *2022 International Visualization, Informatics and Technology Conference (IVIT)* (pp. 136-142). IEEE. 10.1109/IVIT55443.2022.10033362

Gilbert, S. (2022). *Crypto, web3, and the Metaverse. Bennett Institute for Public Policy.* Policy Brief.

Hackl, C., Lueth, D., & Di Bartolo, T. (2022). *Navigating the metaverse: A guide to limitless possibilities in a Web 3.0 world.* John Wiley & Sons.

Hurst, W., Spyrou, O., Tekinerdogan, B., & Krampe, C. (2023). Digital Art and the Metaverse: Benefits and Challenges. *Future Internet*, *15*(6), 188. doi:10.3390/fi15060188

Idelberger, F., & Mezei, P. (2022). Non-fungible tokens. *Internet Policy Review, 11*(2).

Kasiyanto, S., & Kilinc, M. R. (2022). The legal conundrums of the metaverse. *Journal of Central Banking Law and Institutions*, *1*(2), 299–322. doi:10.21098/jcli.v1i2.25

Koosel, S. M. (2013). *Exploring digital identity: Beyond the private public paradox. The digital turn: Users' practices and cultural transformations.* Peter Lang.

Lanier, J. (2011). *You are not a gadget: A manifesto.* Vintage.

Liu, H., Li, X., Xu, K., & Jiang, F. (2021). NFT and Its Application in Virtual Asset Economy. In *2021 IEEE International Conference on Blockchains and Cryptocurrencies (IEEE ICBC)* (pp. 141-148). IEEE.

Macedo, C. R., Miro, D. A., & Hart, T. (2022). The Metaverse: From Science Fiction to Commercial Reality—Protecting Intellectual Property in the Virtual Landscape. *NYSBA Bright Ideas*, *31*(1), 216.

Magazzeni, D., McBurney, P., & Nash, W. (2017). Validation and verification of smart contracts: A research agenda. *Computer*, *50*(9), 50–57. doi:10.1109/MC.2017.3571045

Majer, A. (2022). *The Carbon Footprint of NFTs.* The Linux Foundation.

Momtaz, P. P. (2022). Some very simple economics of web3 and the metaverse. *FinTech*, *1*(3), 225–234. doi:10.3390/fintech1030018

Peachey, A., & Childs, M. (Eds.). (2011). *Reinventing ourselves: Contemporary concepts of identity in virtual worlds*. Springer Science & Business Media. doi:10.1007/978-0-85729-361-9

Rosenberg, L. (2022, March). Regulation of the Metaverse: A Roadmap: The risks and regulatory solutions for largescale consumer platforms. In *Proceedings of the 6th international conference on virtual and augmented reality simulations* (pp. 21-26). ACM. 10.1145/3546607.3546611

Rutskiy, V., Allam, S., Elkin, S., Beknazarov, Z., Semina, E., Ikonnikov, O., & Tsarev, R. (2022). Non-fungible Tokens: Value for Digital Arts and Pricing Factors. In *Proceedings of the Computational Methods in Systems and Software* (pp. 805-816). Cham: Springer International Publishing.

Solouki, M., & Bamakan, S. M. H. (2022). An in-depth insight at digital ownership through dynamic NFTs. *Procedia Computer Science*, *214*, 875–882. doi:10.1016/j.procs.2022.11.254

Steuer, J. (1995). Defining Virtual Reality: Dimensions Determining Telepresence. *Journal of Communication*, *42*(4), 73–93. doi:10.1111/j.1460-2466.1992.tb00812.x

Sung, Y., Moon, J., & Lin, J. S. (2011). Actual self vs. avatar self: The effect of online social situation on self-expression. *Journal of Virtual Worlds Research*, *4*(1). doi:10.4101/jvwr.v4i1.1927

Swan, M. (2015). *Blockchain: Blueprint for a New Economy*. O'Reilly Media.

Wang, Q., Li, R., Wang, Q., & Chen, S. (2021). Non-fungible token (NFT): Overview, evaluation, opportunities and challenges. arXiv preprint arXiv:2105.07447.

White, B., Mahanti, A., & Passi, K. (2022, April). Characterizing the OpenSea NFT marketplace. In *Companion Proceedings of the Web Conference 2022* (pp. 488-496). 10.1145/3487553.3524629

Xiong, W., & Xiong, L. (2019). Smart contract based data trading mode using blockchain and machine learning. *IEEE Access : Practical Innovations, Open Solutions*, *7*, 102331–102344. doi:10.1109/AC-CESS.2019.2928325

Xiong, W., & Xiong, L. (2019). Smart contract based data trading mode using blockchain and machine learning. *IEEE Access : Practical Innovations, Open Solutions*, *7*, 102331–102344. doi:10.1109/AC-CESS.2019.2928325

Yousaf, I., & Yarovaya, L. (2022). Static and dynamic connectedness between NFTs, Defi and other assets: Portfolio implication. *Global Finance Journal*, *53*, 100719. doi:10.1016/j.gfj.2022.100719

Chapter 13
Integrated Geospatial Information Management in the World of Metaverse:
Challenges and Opportunities

Munir Ahmad

ⓘD https://orcid.org/0000-0003-4836-6151

Survey of Pakistan, Pakistan

Asmat Ali

ⓘD https://orcid.org/0000-0002-8804-2285

Survey of Pakistan, Pakistan

ABSTRACT

Transformative discoveries are available across several disciplines because of the convergence of integrated geospatial information management with the Metaverse. Through the study of geospatial data, integrated geospatial information management (GIM) offers useful insights that can support emergency response, transportation, and urban planning. Immersive encounters, virtual travel, brand activation, cultural preservation, education, healthcare, and entertainment can be possible by the metaverse. The Metaverse's integration of GIM can improves visualization, teamwork, decision-making, and data sharing. However, issues like interoperability, data accuracy, and data privacy require special consideration. Accepting the potential of GIM in the metaverse can opens doors for creative developments across many industries, promoting societal improvement and improving user experiences in virtual settings.

INTRODUCTION

The concept of the Metaverse has garnered significant interest across industries, society, and scientific communities alike. However, there is currently a lack of a universally accepted scientific definition for this concept (Weinberger, 2022). According to Davis et al., (2009), a virtual environment that incorporates

DOI: 10.4018/978-1-6684-9919-1.ch013

Copyright © 2023, IGI Global. Copying or distributing in print or electronic forms without written permission of IGI Global is prohibited.

aspects of the actual world with immersive digital experiences is called the Metaverse. Using avatars and holograms, it allows users to move between the real world and the virtual world with ease. The idea of the Metaverse has received a lot of attention and is predicted to revolutionize several industries, including marketing, tourism, gaming, entertainment, and education. Users can take part in a variety of activities, including social interactions, virtual travel, and the building of virtual worlds. According to statistics from Google Trends, the phrase "Metaverse" is becoming more popular across several nations. The search volume index is shown in Figure 1 and illustrates the amount of interest in various geographic areas. The numbers show that there is a large volume of searches in particular nations, with China leading the pack with 100, followed by Singapore with 82, the United Arab Emirates with 70, Turkey with 65, and Hong Kong with 65. These figures show how widely the idea of the Metaverse is being discussed and how much interest there is in it.

Figure 1. Metaverse interest by region
(own diagram based on data from Google Trends)

The gathering, processing, and visualization of geographical data are the main objectives of integrated geographic information management. This calls for the employment of tools like satellite photography, remote sensing, and geographic information systems (GIS). Geospatial information offers useful insights into the features and spatial relationships of the Earth's surface, including its topography, built environment, and natural resources.

For many different businesses and areas, the integration of GIM into the Metaverse has enormous promise. Real-world geospatial data and virtual environments can be used to create immersive experiences, improve decision-making, and revolutionize industries including entertainment, urban planning, tourism, and crisis management. This integration offers strong justification for investigating the connections between GIM and the Metaverse and comprehending their future ramifications. It is crucial to dynamically generate interactive virtual reality environments that accurately represent real-world settings to enable immersive visualization, exploration, and analysis of spatial data within a geographical information system. Users should be able to engage physically with the data in these settings, which will enhance the realism and interest of the encounter (Abdalla & Esmail, 2019).

The overall objective of this chapter is to investigate how geographic information management may be used in the Metaverse. This chapter will examine the interaction between geospatial data management and virtual worlds, emphasizing how geospatial data can be used in the immersive settings of the Metaverse.

To achieve the objective, the rest of the chapter is organized as follows. Section 2 defines geospatial information management and discusses its significance in many fields, including transportation, emergency response, and urban planning. Methods and tools used for collecting, analyzing, and displaying geographic data are also discussed. The concept of the Metaverse is covered in Section 3. Possible advantages in fields including virtual travel, urban design, and disaster relief that might result from the Metaverse's incorporation of geographic information management are endorsed in section 4. The difficulties in incorporating geographical data into the Metaverse such as data interoperability, accuracy, and privacy are covered in section 5. Section 6 is elaborated on mitigation strategies to handle the challenges. The chapter's main conclusions are summed up in the last part, along with suggestions for further study.

INTEGRATED GEOSPATIAL INFORMATION MANAGEMENT

The procedure of gathering, arranging, analyzing, and visualizing data with a geographic component is referred to as geospatial information management. Maps, satellite images, aerial photos, terrain models, and attribute data are all examples of geospatial data, which also include information about the Earth's surface (Breunig et al., 2020).

GIM's Historical Development

Geographic Information Management has a lengthy history that spans several decades. It has changed as a result of technological breakthroughs, shifting societal demands, and the expanding significance of geospatial data. The roots of GIM can be traced back to the 1960s when the first geographic information systems (GIS) were conceptualized. The "Canada Geographic Information System," created by Roger Tomlinson in the 1960s, is one of the pioneering works on this subject. The Canadian government commissioned this system intending to manage and analyze massive amounts of geographic data for resource management and land-use planning (Tomlinson, 1969). Tomlinson's work created the groundwork for contemporary GIS and paved the way for the development of GIM historically.

GIS technology developed throughout the 1970s and 1980s, and its use grew to encompass several industries, such as transportation management, urban planning, and environmental monitoring. Additional expansion in the industry was sparked by the development of robust computing systems and enhanced data processing capabilities (Longley, 2005). With the incorporation of remote sensing data and the introduction of web-based mapping applications, GIM underwent a substantial transformation in the 1990s. The study of satellite imagery and other sensor data was made possible by the merging of GIS and remote sensing data, resulting in more accurate and recent geospatial information (Foody, 2002). Additionally, the development of web-based mapping tools like Google Maps and MapQuest made geographic data more freely available to the general public and democratized access to it (Goodchild, 2007).

Spatial data constitutes a fundamental element within the entirety of information retrieval processes geared toward facilitating effective decision-making. The procurement of spatial data necessitates substantial financial investments and time commitments. The Integrated Geospatial Information Framework (IGIF) serves as a foundational and instructive tool for the advancement, amalgamation, fortification, and optimal utilization of geospatial information management and its associated assets on a global scale. In response to this imperative, governments across the globe are initiating the establishment of spatial data infrastructures (SDIs) (Ahmad et al., 2022; Ali et al., 2021; Ali & Imran, 2020). The essential physical and organizational framework necessary to facilitate the efficient and proficient utilization of spatial data is encapsulated within the concept of spatial data infrastructure (SDI) as outlined by Rajabifard et al.,

(2006). Ahmad et al., (2023) underscored that fog computing can amplify the effectiveness and productivity of SDI through its provisions for instantaneous geospatial data processing, expedited geospatial data analysis, fortified data security and privacy measures, heightened availability and ease of access to geospatial data, along with the capability to expand computing resources as needed.

With the advent of location-based services (LBS) and the spread of GPS-enabled devices in the early 2000s, GIM continued to develop. These innovations completely changed the way location data was gathered and used, paving the way for the broad adoption of location-based applications across a range of sectors, including social networking, retail, and transportation (Haklay, 2010). With current research concentrating on topics like spatial data mining, geographic data visualization, and the integration of real-time data streams into decision-making processes, the future of GIM offers enormous promise. GIM is anticipated to play a significant role in influencing smart cities, sustainable development, and informed policy-making in the years to come with the arrival of 5G and the continuous development of AI.

GIM's Applications

Urban planning, transportation, and emergency response are just a few of the areas where geospatial information management is crucial. It offers useful insights into spatial linkages, patterns, and trends, allowing decision-makers to make thoughtful decisions and create successful strategies.

Urban Planning

By enabling a thorough understanding of the spatial features and dynamics of cities, geospatial information management plays a crucial role in urban planning (Zhou, 2013). It entails utilizing GIS technology to create spatial data models, combining data from several sources, and granting access to many application systems for collaborative planning and information sharing (Chen et al., 2021). Urban planners can examine land use trends, transit systems, and infrastructure development by using geospatial data. Making informed judgments on zoning laws, managing urban growth, and resource allocation for the best possible city development is made easier with the use of this knowledge. Urban planners can be assisted by geospatial analytic tools in assessing the possible effects of planned modifications on the urban environment through scenario modeling and simulation (Batty et al., 2012; Long & Liu, 2016). Spatial analytical methods can be utilized to examine crime, safety, and human mobility patterns in metropolitan regions to analyze and plan for urban safety (Ceccato, 2013).

Transportation

Integrated Geospatial information management plays a crucial role in transportation systems. It involves the use of information systems to support efficient transportation planning and management. These systems integrate inputs from various data sources, including national or local data repositories, to provide a comprehensive view of transportation systems. The integration of data from different transportation fields allows policymakers to consider strategic elements that influence transportation decisions (Borzacchiello et al., 2009). It helps in the planning of effective transportation networks, route optimization, and traffic pattern analysis. Transportation planners can identify areas with high transportation demand, plan for new infrastructure projects, and optimize existing transportation systems by integrating geospatial data with other pertinent information, such as population density, demographic data, and land use information. The development of intelligent transport systems, detecting areas of high traffic congestion, and enhancing road safety are also aided by geospatial analytic approaches (Sobral et al., 2019).

Emergency Response

To effectively respond to emergencies, integrated geospatial information management is essential. It allows a broader, quicker, and more efficient use of geospatial data throughout the disaster management phases, such as mitigation, preparation, response, and recovery. Mapping susceptible regions, evacuation routes, and evaluating how disasters affect vital infrastructure may all be done with the use of geospatial data. Using geospatial data responders can more easily pinpoint impacted locations, distribute resources, and plan rescue and relief operations. However, geospatial data must be made available promptly so that decisions can be made that save lives and protect citizens (Zlatanova, 2010). To help with disaster preparation and response, several tools and systems have been created. One such system is the Integrated Disaster Management Information System (IEMIS), which offers interactive communications, map editing and display, evacuation modeling, and many other information databases (Yang et al., 2012). In emergency responses, real-time situational awareness is supported by geospatial analysis and visualization technologies, which speed up decision-making and increase reaction effectiveness.

Techniques and Technologies in Spatial Information Management

Geospatial information management involves various techniques and technologies for capturing, analyzing, visualizing, and sharing spatial data.

Geospatial Data Collection

Technologies and methods for acquiring geospatial data have made tremendous strides in recent years. These developments are meant to increase the spatial data's accuracy and effectiveness of use. Collecting geospatial data entails acquiring information on the characteristics and surface of the Earth. Techniques can use unmanned aerial vehicles (UAVs), airborne sensors, or satellites for remote sensing. While aerial photographs and UAVs deliver high-resolution data for limited regions, satellite imagery offers worldwide coverage. Furthermore, geographical data may be gathered through on-the-ground surveys, GPS receivers, and mobile mapping technologies (Lu & Liu, 2012).

Spatial data fusion is also a technique to collect geospatial data that includes combining and integrating data from several sources. This can be accomplished via vector data fusion, which combines coordinates unification, semantic information fusion, and data model fusion (Yu et al., 2013). Another approach is the employment of protected spatiotemporal data-collecting systems, such as moving devices placed on vehicles [2]. Additionally, data collecting via robotic total stations, 3D laser scanning, and image processing sensors has been transformed by the introduction of new geodetic tools and laser scanning technologies (Milinković et al., 2014).

Analysis of Geospatial Data

The process of obtaining useful information from geographical datasets is known as geospatial data analysis. Techniques include attribute analysis, which looks at the qualities and attributes connected to geographic features, and spatial analysis, which looks at geographical correlations and patterns. Spatial interpolation, proximity analysis, overlay analysis, and network analysis are a few examples of spatial analysis approaches. To find patterns and connections in the data, attribute analysis uses statistical analysis, data mining, and modeling. Analysis of geographical data using deep learning algorithms has shown promise, outperforming traditional methods in tasks like object detection and image categorization (Kiwelekar et al., 2020).

Visualization of Geospatial Data

Visualization of geospatial data involves understanding and creating information about people and physical contexts at geographical scales of measurement. The goal of geographic data visualization is to make geospatial information aesthetically pleasing and understandable. It uses methods including interactive maps, 3D visualization, and theme mapping. Decision-making processes are aided by the effective interpretation and communication of geographical data made possible by visualization technologies (Slocum et al., 2008). It combines classical cartography with scientific visualization techniques and can be used in different phases of data processing, spatial data mining, and knowledge creation (Kim, 2009). Instead of just showing maps, the primary goal of geographic visualizations is to offer insight. The handling of enormous volumes of complicated geospatial data is now possible because of advancements in visualization technology (Zou et al., 2018). Additionally, there is growing acceptance that the representation of spatial data should take other sensory modalities including sound, smell, and touch into account in addition to visual and topographic characteristics (Eve & Graham, 2020). This multi-sensory method of visualization can deepen our comprehension of the past and enthuse the public as well as researchers in novel and emotive ways.

Sharing Geospatial Data

Geospatial data sharing is essential for its efficient utilization in different applications like urban planning, disaster management, transportation, and so on. To ensure that data is used and updated by various people without causing any disruptions, authorization, and access are required. Threats like data theft and unauthorized access must be taken into account while developing solutions. For the conflict-free exchange of geospatial data, integration of encryption, computer security, database management, and computer networking is required (Frank, 2014). Geospatial fundamental data may be effectively shared using blockchain-based techniques, maximizing the utilization of data resources while maintaining data security (Cedeno Jimenez et al., 2022). Distributed geospatial data can be shared via grid technology, which offers a sizable infrastructure to easily integrate and retrieve the data (Wei et al., 2009).

METAVERSE

The term "Metaverse" is formed by combining the words "meta" and "universe." It signifies a virtual world existing in three dimensions, where avatars actively participate in political, economic, social, and cultural pursuits. This concept commonly represents a virtual realm that reflects aspects of our daily lives, where the boundaries between reality and imagination merge seamlessly (Wiki, 2023). The notion of "Metaverse" was initially coined by Neil Stevenson in his science fiction novel Snow Crash in

1992. In the book, it describes a world where virtual and physical realities intertwine, resulting in the creation of value through diverse social interactions (Stephenson, 1992). The Metaverse initially placed a lot of emphasis on the architecture of the virtual world, like gaming settings. However, there has been a change in how it is portrayed recently, with more emphasis placed on its function as a platform that encourages the sharing of interests and social interactions centered around content (Park & Kim, 2022).

The metaverse has the power to extend the boundaries of the physical world using augmented and virtual reality technology, allowing people to easily engage and interact in both real and simulated worlds. People may easily navigate and take part in experiences that integrate aspects from the actual and virtual environments by using avatars and holograms (Dwivedi, Hughes, Baabdullah, et al., 2022). Through the use of hand gestures and body language, the Metaverse enables users to express themselves more fully in their communication. Because it offers a stronger sense of presence and bridges the gap between on-line interactions and real-world experiences, it is frequently referred to as an embodied Internet (Clegg, 2022). It is projected that the metaverse would bring forth several advances and disruptions in a variety of spheres of existence. As a result, technology has a big impact on society and culture. technology also offers new opportunities and challenges for communities and markets around the world (Dwivedi, Hughes, Wang, et al., 2022).

According to McKinsey, the Metaverse is projected to emerge as a major industry in the upcoming years. It is estimated that by 2030, the Metaverse has the potential to generate a value of up to 5 trillion US dollars (Elmasry et al., 2022). This highlights the significant economic prospects associated with the widespread adoption and development of the Metaverse. The Metaverse is being used in a variety of ways and for diverse purposes. Social media, healthcare, education, and manufacturing are just a few of the industries that have recently seen an increase in interest in the metaverse. It functions as a gaming platform, providing realistic simulations. Additionally, it is used for marketing simulations and social phenomenon studies.

Since the creation of the Metaverse, people have had access to immersive virtual worlds where they can buy, sell, and possess virtual land. This creates opportunities for people to build virtual residences, take part in a thriving virtual economy, and produce and exchange virtual experiences inside these virtual land marketplaces. The Metaverse encourages a dynamic and interactive digital environment by enabling users to explore, invest in, and shape their virtual worlds. Table 1 presents the comparison of different metaverse platforms that dealt with virtual land.

Table 1 showcased various platforms that offer different features and integration within the Metaverse. These platforms include Decentraland, which enables decentralized virtual environments for trading and building virtual land using Ethereum blockchain and non-fungible tokens (NFTs), and The Sandbox, which allows users to purchase and possess virtual land for creating and marketing virtual experiences and games. Somnium Space provides an open, social virtual reality platform where users can acquire and hold virtual property, exploring and customizing an immersive virtual environment. Axie Infinity is a blockchain-based online environment focused on collecting and breeding virtual animals, while Voxels offers a digital environment on the Ethereum blockchain for buying virtual land, constructing buildings, and creating interactive experiences. Other platforms like VRChat, SuperWorld, Upland, Earth 2, and Next Earth also offer unique features and integration within the metaverse, allowing users to design avatars and worlds, explore and construct virtual properties, and trade virtual assets using blockchain technology. Figure 2 and Figure 3 depicted NextEarth and Earth2 platforms respectively showing the purchase of land in the virtual world of the metaverse.

Table 1. Comparison of virtual land platforms in the metaverse

Platform	Description	Blockchain Integration	Virtual Reality Support
Decentraland (https://decentraland.org/)	A decentralized virtual environment where people may trade and build virtual land using Ethereum blockchain non-fungible tokens (NFTs).	Yes	Yes
The Sandbox (https://www.sandbox.game/)	A platform for user-generated content that offers the ability to buy and possess virtual land called "LAND." On this platform, users can produce virtual experiences and games that they can then market.	Yes	Yes
Somnium Space (https://somniumspace.com/)	A platform for open, social virtual reality where users can acquire and hold virtual property. It provides users with access to an immersive, permanent virtual environment that they may explore and customize.	Yes	Yes
Axie Infinity (https://axieinfinity.com/)	A blockchain-based online environment where users can amass, breed, and exchange virtual animals known as "Axies." Within the game, players can own and develop virtual land.	Yes	No
Voxels (https://www.voxels.com/)	A digital environment created on the Ethereum blockchain. Blockchain technology allows users to buy virtual land, construct buildings, and create interactive experiences.	Yes	No
OVRLand (www.overthereality.ai)	It allows users to purchase digital land that is a replica of the actual world, giving them the unique opportunity to design and alter these digital plots following their analogous physical ones.	Yes	No
VRChat (https://vrchat.com/)	a social virtual reality application that enables users to make their avatars and worlds. On the site, users can design and create their locations.	No	Yes
SuperWorld (https://www.superworldapp.com/)	The virtual world now resembles the real world thanks to SuperWorld.	Yes	No
Upland (https://www.upland.me/)	A blockchain-based metaverse where users may trade, purchase, and sell virtual assets using physical addresses. In a digital recreation of actual cities, users can explore and construct virtual properties.	Yes	No
Earth 2 (https://earth2.io/)	A platform that allows users to buy, sell, and possess virtual pieces of land that correspond to actual places on Earth.	No	Yes
Next Earth (https://nextearth.io/)	It is a blockchain-based metaverse community where users can purchase and sell real estate in the form of virtual land.	Yes	No

Figure 2. Next earth platform
(https://nextearth.io/)

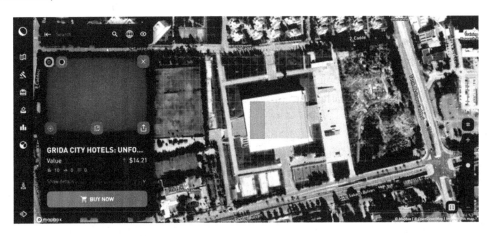

Figure 3. Earth 2 platform
(https://earth2.io/)

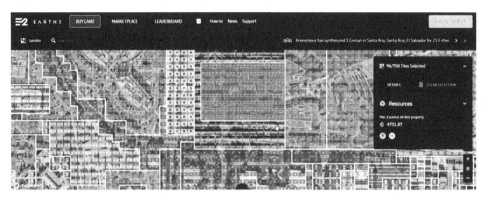

OPPORTUNITIES

Geospatial information management (GIM) the world of Metaverse has several opportunities and benefits for a variety of domains. In this section, a concise overview of how spatial data can support Metaverse is provided, as summarized and depicted in Figure 4.

Tourism

According to (Tatavarti, 2022) the tourism industry is recognized as one of the key sectors that stands to gain significant benefits from the implementation of the Metaverse. The Metaverse uses immersive technologies to produce a sample of the location, allowing travelers to digitally experience and study tourism sites and organizations before physically visiting them (Buhalis, Lin, et al., 2023). It is anticipated that the Metaverse would completely alter management and marketing strategies in the travel and tourist industry. Through the use of digital twins, it provides destination awareness, positioning, branding, and coordination. The Metaverse promotes interaction, engagement, and trip planning, changing consumer behaviour. Virtual visits and connection with destinations are anticipated to encourage and drive actual travel rather than replace it. This essay offers a vision for how the Metaverse may revolutionize traveler experiences and alter tourism administration and marketing (Buhalis, Leung, et al., 2023).

The "extensible metaverse" an open metaverse platform is advocated in (Suanpang et al., 2022) to promote adaptability, user pleasure, and improved tourism experiences in smart places. GIM's interaction with the Metaverse makes it possible to have high-fidelity virtual travel experiences that replicate actual sites. From the comfort of their homes, users may go to exotic locations, well-known landmarks, and historical locations. Realistic depictions of landscapes, cityscapes, and culturally significant locations are possible because of the spatial data provided by GIM integration.

Marketing

The "metaverse" is a seamless network of interconnected virtual worlds that has the power to revolutionize consumer interactions, brand engagement, and commercial transactions. The fast growth of this idea is being driven by the rising trend of consumers interacting with and transacting in virtual environments, as well as significant expenditures by businesses in technology relevant to the metaverse (Giang Barrera & Shah, 2023). The Metaverse is becoming more and more popular, especially among well-known international corporations. The real innovation is anticipated to happen when regional and local brands start utilizing the Metaverse, though. Metaverse functions as a digital depiction of the real world and allows users to communicate using custom avatars. This game-changing technology will have a big impact on how businesses approach marketing and how people interact in the future. The study (Hollensen et al., 2022) highlighted the potential of the Metaverse as a platform for brand activation in a 3D interactive digital environment. Tommy Hilfiger made an interesting revelation regarding its participation in the inaugural Decentraland Metaverse Fashion Week (PVH, 2022). This news signaled a major advancement in the field of online fashion shows. From March 24 to March 28, 2022, Decentraland, a user-owned virtual environment, sponsored a virtual event. The fashion industry was anticipating and buzzing as Tommy Hilfiger debuted its Spring 2022 collections on the occasion (PVH, 2022).

In order to facilitate brand interaction and business transactions within the metaverse, spatial data management is also essential. Businesses can target particular localities or geographic areas by utilizing geospatial data, which allows them to adjust their marketing plans and initiatives accordingly. This makes it possible for regional and local brands to use the metaverse as a platform for promoting their brands and engaging with consumers.

Education

The metaverse is viewed as a brand-new learning environment that offers improved freedom for creativity and sharing as well as immersive experiences through virtualization Distance learning could be considerably improved by improving the immersive experience for students at all academic levels, from elementary school to university specializations (Hirsh-Pasek et al., 2022). The four different forms of the metaverse such as augmented reality, lifelogging, mirror worlds, and virtual reality are briefly described in relation to educational applications in the study (Kye et al., 2021). According to the study, creative methods like an augmented reality T-shirt, for instance, augmented reality can be used in medical education to let students examine the human body in an anatomy lab. The study (Wu & Ho, 2023) emphasized the numerous ways that augmented reality (AR) and virtual reality (VR) can be incorporated into classroom instruction and clinical practice.

Utilizing geospatial data management, AR, or VR may be utilized to develop cutting-edge learning resources and experiences. This improves the realism and efficacy of such instructional apps by enabling the precise mapping and alignment of virtual elements with the things of the actual world.

Heritage

The Metaverse has the potential to explicitly examined cultural assets. The Metaverse can be used in the fields of education and museum visits, offering engaging and instructive experiences, due to its simulation benefits (Maharg & Owen, 2007). The study (Zhang et al., 2022) proposed a framework to examine five different dimensions linearity, planarity, space, time, and context, to better understand the dimensional patterns of the cultural heritage metaverse. The framework was proposed to create a cultural heritage metaverse using a methodical methodology that may provide better options for tourism advice, site upkeep, historic object conservation, and other related uses. The important components and the mapping between the real and virtual worlds of cultural assets are highlighted in the proposed framework for the cultural heritage metaverse.

Spatial data can be used to accurately represent and mimic cultural assets in the metaverse, giving people engaging, immersive experiences with history. In order to ensure proper depiction and alignment of virtual elements with their physical equivalents, spatial data makes it easier to map between the actual and virtual worlds of cultural assets.

Health

The Metaverse incorporates several enabling technologies, including robots, quantum computing, artificial intelligence, virtual reality, augmented reality, and the internet of medical devices. New avenues for providing high-quality healthcare services and treatments are made possible by these technologies. Patients and medical professionals can both have realistic experiences made possible by the metaverse, resulting in individualized and immersive care. It lowers barriers between patients and healthcare professionals by utilizing adaptable intelligent technologies (Chengoden et al., 2023). The study (Lee, 2022) looked into how the metaverse service is functioning and how it might be used in the healthcare sector by focusing on the metaverse service as a business model.

Spatial data can support telemedicine and remote consultations, allowing patients to consult with medical specialists from any location in the world. Healthcare practitioners may evaluate patients' ailments, make diagnoses, and provide individualized therapy by using realistic simulations and visualizations, improving the patient experience overall.

Urban Planning

Urban Planning may benefit from GIM integration in the Metaverse because it offers a platform for visualizing and analyzing design ideas before execution. Geospatial information like topography, land use, and transportation networks may be included in virtual models of cities and urban areas created by urban planners and architects. This makes it possible for interested parties to evaluate how design choices affect livability, sustainability, and the urban environment. GIM integration improves public involvement in influencing the built environment and streamlines collaborative design processes (Axford et al., 2007).

Disaster Relief

In terms of disaster relief activities, GIM and the Metaverse work well together. Emergency responders may more efficiently visualize disaster-affected regions, evaluate damage, and organize relief activities by combining real-time geospatial data. GIM integration makes it possible to simulate disaster scenarios, facilitating training, readiness, and cooperation amongst many authorities. The immersive environment of the Metaverse can also help to increase public awareness and encourage catastrophe resilience. Sermet & Demir, (2022) conducted a case study to examine flood dynamics, evaluate prospective losses, and make wise choices to lessen the effects of flooding. The study examined data layers including stream gauges, rain gauges, hydro stations for groundwater and soil moisture data, estimated flood damages for current or anticipated flood scenarios, and traffic congestion.

Entertainment and Gaming

The inclusion of GIM in the Metaverse improves the realism and immersion of these activities. Geospatial information may be incorporated into virtual worlds to create dynamic and engaging gaming scenarios based on actual places. Users may have distinctive and interesting experiences thanks to the gamification of geographical data, which promotes exploration, social engagement, and storytelling inside the Metaverse. The Fortnite Travis Scott concert was a remarkable and pioneering occurrence within the gaming realm, showcasing the immense potential of Fortnite to establish a virtual world or "Metaverse" where individuals can socialize and even inhabit (Tassi, 2020).

Transportation

In the realm of traffic management and monitoring transportation-related accidents and hazards, virtual reality-powered systems have become well-known instruments. This application field acknowledges the potential of virtual reality to deliver practical solutions for traffic monitoring, locating and minimizing accidents, and identifying possible risks (Li et al., 2016). Sermet & Demir, (2022) conducted a case study in the context of transportation using data layers like voltage detectors, radiation spills, construction zones, accident reports, and traffic congestion were looked at. With the help of data analysis, this study attempted to understand the current state of the transport network, spot any prospective problems or dangers to improve traffic flow, and protect the general public.

Real Estate

The concept of real estate in virtual worlds has become a tangible reality, users now have the option to buy and sell finished homes as well as virtual lots of land. With this novel strategy, people may make money off their assets in a variety of ways, like by renting out their virtual houses or taking on additional management responsibilities. This expanding tendency and its ramifications for virtual economies and user experiences are further explored in the study by Nakavachara & Saengchote, (2022). The incorporation of GIM into the Metaverse opens up new possibilities for the real estate sector. Potential buyers may take immersive tours of homes through virtual property displays, allowing them to evaluate features, measurements, and locations realistically. To make well-informed decisions, geospatial data integration enables specific property information, such as proximity to amenities, transit systems, and environmental considerations (Nieradka, 2019).

Benefits of GIM in the Metaverse

The creation and implementation of the metaverse depend heavily on spatial data management. The demand for effective geographic data management is growing as the metaverse develops and grows. The creation and upkeep of perfectly connected virtual worlds is one component of managing spatial data in the metaverse.

It is crucial to develop strong data infrastructure and systems that can handle the enormous volumes of spatial information generated within the metaverse in order to maintain a realistic relationship with spatial data management. This covers the archiving, cataloguing, and retrieval of spatial data pertaining to avatars, virtual worlds, and user interactions.

Figure 4. Opportunities for metaverse

Spatial data management also makes it possible to accurately map and represent the real world in the metaverse. Businesses and individuals can construct virtual representations of actual locations by combining geospatial data with geolocation technologies. This enables more immersive experiences and accurate spatial interactions.

The inclusion of GIM in the Metaverse offers numerous options to improve virtual environments with geospatial data, as listed below.

1. By incorporating GIM into the Metaverse, virtual settings can be enhanced with accurate geospatial information, such as topography, structures, landmarks, and other geographical elements. Through this connection, users will enjoy a more immersive environment where virtual representations closely resemble the real world.
2. Geospatial data visualization is facilized by GIM inclusion within the Metaverse. Users can investigate interactive maps, satellite photos, and other geospatial layers to learn more about the virtual world and get insightful knowledge.
3. By integrating GIM, users are given access to precise and up-to-date geographic information within the Metaverse, allowing them to make correct judgments regarding a variety of applications. Urban planners, for instance, can model and assess the effects of proposed developments, while emergency management professionals can identify possible threats and design efficient response plans.
4. By making it easier to share and analyze geographic data, GIM integration fosters cooperation within the Metaverse. Users can collaborate in real-time while using geospatial data to solve issues, make choices, and develop original solutions.

5. The integration of GIM into the Metaverse can help with the planning and administration of smart cities. Urban planners and policymakers may simulate and optimize urban systems, keep track of environmental conditions, and enhance the functionality of entire cities by using real-time geospatial data.

CHALLENGES

To provide a seamless and useful user experience, there are several issues associated with integrating geographic data into the Metaverse. The main issues of bringing geographical data into the Metaverse are covered in this section.

Data Privacy and Security Challenges in GIM Integration

Integrating geographic data into the ever-evolving Metaverse presents significant issues in terms of data security and privacy protection. GIM involves handling sensitive location-based data, including personal information, confidential company information, or classified government data. These data necessitate the strictest security precautions and the strongest privacy controls to prevent unauthorized access, breaches, or abuse.

Location-based data can provide important insights into a person's personality, preferences, and way of life (Chorley et al., 2015). As a result, adhering to privacy regulations and preserving anonymity becomes crucial. Additionally, protecting company data during integration is also essential, particularly when integrating confidential geographic datasets from several sources (Chaturvedi et al., 2019). Similarly, strict security protocols must be adhered to when integrating classified government data into the Metaverse in order to protect sensitive data from adversaries and prevent national security from being jeopardized.

Accuracy of Geospatial Data in the Metaverse

For the Metaverse to offer users a realistic and immersive experience, geospatial data must be ensured to be accurate and quality oriented. A fundamental difficulty, though, is how to integrate data from several sources with variable levels of accuracy, reliability, and currency (Ahmad et al., 2022). There are issues with data quality assurance, data validation, and spatial alignment when integrating and aligning geographic data with the Metaverse's virtual environment. When incorporating geographic data into the virtual world, spatial alignment is an important factor to take into account. Users can move between the real world and the virtual world with ease because of accurate alignment with physical locales.

Interoperability

Interoperability of spatial data in the context of the Metaverse refers to the smooth and efficient integration and exchange of geographic data among diverse virtual environments and platforms. However, achieving interoperability poses challenges due to the lack of standardization and compatibility across multiple Metaverse systems and geospatial data standards. The Metaverse is a vast collection of immersive environments, augmented reality settings, and virtual worlds that are all based on various technical pillars (Venugopal et al., 2023). These platforms might consequently use certain ontologies, spatial reference systems, and data formats. As a result, attempts to communicate or integrate geographic data between these disparate systems may encounter problems with data conversion, format incompatibilities, and semantic inconsistencies.

Data Governance and Ownership

Integrating geographic data into the dynamic Metaverse requires establishing clear ownership rights and implementing good data governance, both of which are essential but difficult tasks. When it comes to the use, sharing, and monetization of geospatial data, different stakeholders that are involved in its generation, collection, and use may have different interests and reservations (Ali, A., Ahmad, 2013). Finding out who owns which data in the Metaverse is one of the main issues. Many different stakeholders, including governments, businesses, and individual users, contribute geospatial data. Determining ownership rights can therefore very complicated.

Data Synchronization and Timeliness

Geospatial data must be kept up to date in the Metaverse since the real world is continually changing. Geographical information is impacted by ongoing changes in the actual world, such as new building projects, infrastructure improvements, and natural disasters. Therefore, it is crucial to maintain the accuracy and relevance of geospatial data in the Metaverse. Updates that are delayed might cause inconsistencies and misrepresentations in the virtual world. Applications for navigation and mapping in the Metaverse provide a practical illustration of this issue. Users rely on these apps to virtually explore real-world areas. However, old geospatial information may result in inaccurate directions or misrepresentations of the environment.

Data Bias and Representation

Spatial data biases can exert profound effects within the digital ecosystem, significantly influencing the comprehension and utilization of geographic data across diverse spheres of daily existence (Mark Graham, 2015). Without addressing these biases, integrating such data into the Metaverse may result in biased or unfair representations in the virtual world. For instance, information predominantly drawn from wealthy places may result in an unfair picture of other populations in the virtual setting. It is essential to identify and reduce biases in geographical data in order to combat data bias and guarantee a more inclusive virtual experience.

Scalability and Performance

Supporting a greater user base and managing enormous volumes of data becomes increasingly important as the Metaverse continues to grow. To give customers a seamless and immersive virtual experience, scaling and high-performance need to be maintained. There are a number of difficulties that need to be overcome when scaling the integration of geospatial data to satisfy the expanding requirements of a large-scale virtual environment.

Training and Education

The lack of knowledge and experience among developers and users is a significant obstacle to the integration of geographical data within the Metaverse. Many people might not be equipped with the knowledge and abilities needed to manage geographic data in an efficient manner, which restricts their capacity to contribute data and make the best use of it.

MITIGATION STRATEGIES AND FUTURE WORK

Mitigation Strategies

This section delves into the various mitigation strategies that can be used to address certain challenges mentioned in the above section.

Data Privacy and Security

It is essential to use methods like data aggregation, data anonymization, and differential privacy to ensure that persons cannot be recognized from the integrated geospatial data. Similarly, encryption, access restrictions, and secure data transmission methods need to be implemented to stop unauthorized data leaks (Romansky & Noninska, 2020). Moreover, to stop prospective cyberattacks and data breaches, multilayered security frameworks, safe network architecture, and ongoing monitoring are required.

Accuracy of Geospatial Data

To find and fix discrepancies, flaws, or inaccuracies in geographic data, data quality assurance is essential for GIM integration. To find and fix errors, automated tools, artificial intelligence, and machine learning algorithms can be used, improving the correctness of the data as a whole. Integrating validation procedures, such as cross-referencing with reliable sources, can help in confirming the accuracy of geographical data (Haklay et al., 2014). Precise spatial alignment can be accomplished using sophisticated georeferencing methods and algorithms.

Interoperability

The creation and adoption of standardized geographic data formats and open APIs are necessary to address interoperability issues. The development of common geospatial standards can be facilitated by initiatives like the Open Geospatial Consortium (Chaturvedi et al., 2019), which encourages smooth data exchange between various Metaverse platforms.

Data Governance and Ownership

The issue of who owns the crowdsourced data and how it might be used equitably emerges in the case of crowdsourced mapping data. Open data governance approaches, such as those specified by the Open Geospatial Data Framework, can be used to address this issue by outlining ownership and usage rights.

It is also becomes crucial to provide thorough frameworks for data governance that promote openness, confidence, and collaboration among stakeholders while addressing any ownership disputes.

Data Synchronization and Timeliness

Data suppliers and Metaverse platforms can set up reliable data synchronization procedures to maintain the information currency and pertinent in order to overcome the challenges of data synchronization and timeliness.

Data Bias and Representation

Inherent biases can be lessened by using a variety of data collection techniques and incorporating a wide range of stakeholders. A more accurate depiction of reality can also be achieved by working in conjunction with regional communities and taking historical context into account when gathering data.

Scalability and Performance

It is crucial to create dependable and scalable architectures for data integration in order to avoid performance bottlenecks and guarantee a positive user experience. For the ever-growing volume of geographic data, this necessitates optimizing data storage, retrieval, and processing processes. Real-time data synchronization is also necessary since the Metaverse includes dynamic modifications based on user actions and real-time interactions. For instance, users may modify the environment in virtual city simulations by adding structures or changing the topography. Geospatial data needs to be synchronized in real time throughout the virtual environment to preserve accuracy and responsiveness.

Training and Education

Promoting educational programmes and training initiatives can help to create a more skilled and knowledgeable community of Metaverse participants. Developers and data contributors can learn about the best methods for gathering, analyzing, and integrating geographic data from training programmes. Their knowledge of coordinate systems, data formats, and geographical analysis methods can help to increase the precision and caliber of the data they offer.

Future Work

To further enhance the progress in this field, future investigations could delve into strategies aimed at promoting harmonious integration and streamlined data sharing. This could involve exploring approaches to bolster interoperability among diverse Metaverse platforms and established geospatial data standards. For instance, researchers might explore the development of universally accepted data exchange formats, the refinement of metadata standards for consistent information representation, and the establishment of universally recognized spatial reference systems.

CONCLUSION

Numerous opportunities and advantages are provided by Integrated Geospatial Information Management and the Metaverse in several different fields. By offering insightful information about spatial linkages, patterns, and trends, GIM plays a crucial role in urban planning, transportation, emergency response, and other sectors. It provides well-informed choices, effective tactics, and better resource management.

On the other side, the Metaverse is a virtual environment that blurs the lines between reality and fantasy. Through avatars and holograms, it enables users to participate and interact in both real and artificial settings. Immersive experiences, improved communication, and the possibility of creative industry upheavals are all provided by the metaverse.

The Metaverse offers tourism potential, allowing people to virtually travel to destinations before making a physical trip there. Through brand activation in the 3D interactive digital environment, marketing experiences can be changed. The Metaverse has the potential to be a learning environment that encourages innovation and immersive experiences, which helps education. Immersive Metaverse simulations can be used to promote and conserve cultural artifacts. The Metaverse can be used by the healthcare industry to provide customized care and immersive patient experiences.

GIM's incorporation into the Metaverse improves the virtual world by supplying precise geospatial data, visualization tools, and access to current geographic data. It promotes teamwork and enables defensible decision-making. But issues like data security and privacy, accuracy, and compatibility with different Metaverse platforms and geospatial data standards must be resolved.

The Metaverse offers fascinating possibilities for a variety of industries, such as tourism, marketing, education, cultural preservation, healthcare, urban planning, transportation, and emergency response. The Metaverse can produce realistic and immersive experiences, improve decision-making, and promote collaboration by utilizing geospatial data. Realizing the full potential of GIM in the Metaverse will depend on overcoming the difficulties posed by integrating spatial data.

REFERENCES

Abdalla, R., & Esmail, M. (2019). Immersive Environments for Disaster and Emergency Management. In *Advances in Science*. Technology and Innovation. doi:10.1007/978-3-030-03828-1_8

Ahmad, M., Ali, A., & Khiyal, M. S. H. (2023). Fog Computing for Spatial Data Infrastructure: Challenges and Opportunities (pp. 152–178). doi:10.4018/978-1-6684-4466-5.ch008

Ahmad, M., Khayal, M. S. H., & Tahir, A. (2022). Analysis of Factors Affecting Adoption of Volunteered Geographic Information in the Context of National Spatial Data Infrastructure. *ISPRS International Journal of Geo-Information*, *11*(2), 120. doi:10.3390/ijgi11020120

Ali, A., & Ahmad, M. (2013). *Geospatial Data Sharing in Pakistan: Possibilities and Problems*. Spatial Enablement in Support of Economic Development and Poverty Reduction.

Ali, A., & Imran, M. (2020). The Evolution of National Spatial Data Infrastructure in Pakistan-Implementation Challenges and the Way Forward. *International Journal of Spatial Data Infrastructures Research*, *15*(0).

Ali, A., Imran, M., Jabeen, M., Ali, Z., & Mahmood, S. A. (2021). Factors influencing integrated information management: Spatial data infrastructure in Pakistan. *Information Development*. doi:10.1177/02666669211048483

Axford, S., Keltie, G., & Wallis, C. (2007). Virtual reality in urban planning and design. *Multimedia Cartography*, 283–294.

Batty, M., Axhausen, K. W., Giannotti, F., Pozdnoukhov, A., Bazzani, A., Wachowicz, M., Ouzounis, G., & Portugali, Y. (2012). Smart cities of the future. *The European Physical Journal. Special Topics*, *214*(1), 481–518. doi:10.1140/epjst/e2012-01703-3

Borzacchiello, M. T., Torrieri, V., & Nijkamp, P. (2009). An operational information systems architecture for assessing sustainable transportation planning: Principles and design. *Evaluation and Program Planning*, *32*(4), 381–389. doi:10.1016/j.evalprogplan.2009.06.012 PMID:19631382

Breunig, M., Bradley, P. E., Jahn, M., Kuper, P., Mazroob, N., Rösch, N., Al-Doori, M., Stefanakis, E., & Jadidi, M. (2020). Geospatial data management research: Progress and future directions. *ISPRS International Journal of Geo-Information*, *9*(2), 95. doi:10.3390/ijgi9020095

Buhalis, D., Leung, D., & Lin, M. (2023). Metaverse as a disruptive technology revolutionising tourism management and marketing. In Tourism Management (Vol. 97). doi:10.1016/j.tourman.2023.104724

Buhalis, D., Lin, M. S., & Leung, D. (2023). Metaverse as a driver for customer experience and value co-creation: Implications for hospitality and tourism management and marketing. *International Journal of Contemporary Hospitality Management*, *35*(2), 701–716. Advance online publication. doi:10.1108/IJCHM-05-2022-0631

Ceccato, V. (2013). Integrating geographical information into urban safety research and planning. In *Proceedings of the Institution of Civil Engineers: Urban Design and Planning* (*Vol. 166*, Issue 1). 10.1680/udap.11.00038

Cedeno Jimenez, J. R., Zhao, P., Mansourian, A., & Brovelli, M. A. (2022). Geospatial Blockchain: Review of decentralized geospatial data sharing systems. *AGILE: GIScience Series*, *3*, 1–6. doi:10.5194/agile-giss-3-29-2022

Chaturvedi, K., Matheus, A., Nguyen, S. H., & Kolbe, T. H. (2019). Securing Spatial Data Infrastructures for Distributed Smart City applications and services. *Future Generation Computer Systems*, *101*, 723–736. doi:10.1016/j.future.2019.07.002

Chen, Z., Chen, R., & Chen, S. (2021). Intelligent management information system of urban planning based on GIS. *Journal of Intelligent & Fuzzy Systems*, *40*(4), 6007–6016. doi:10.3233/JIFS-189440

Chengoden, R., Victor, N., Huynh-The, T., Yenduri, G., Jhaveri, R. H., Alazab, M., Bhattacharya, S., Hegde, P., Maddikunta, P. K. R., & Gadekallu, T. R. (2023). Metaverse for Healthcare: A Survey on Potential Applications, Challenges and Future Directions. *IEEE Access : Practical Innovations, Open Solutions*, *11*, 12765–12795. doi:10.1109/ACCESS.2023.3241628

Chorley, M. J., Whitaker, R. M., & Allen, S. M. (2015). Personality and location-based social networks. *Computers in Human Behavior*, *46*, 45–56. doi:10.1016/j.chb.2014.12.038

Clegg, N. (2022). *Making the Metaverse: What it is, how it will be built, and why it matters.* Medium.

Davis, A., Murphy, J., Owens, D., Khazanchi, D., & Zigurs, I. (2009). Avatars, people, and virtual worlds: Foundations for research in metaverses. *Journal of the Association for Information Systems, 10*(2), 90–117. doi:10.17705/1jais.00183

Dwivedi, Y. K., Hughes, L., Baabdullah, A. M., Ribeiro-Navarrete, S., Giannakis, M., Al-Debei, M. M., Dennehy, D., Metri, B., Buhalis, D., Cheung, C. M. K., Conboy, K., Doyle, R., Dubey, R., Dutot, V., Felix, R., Goyal, D. P., Gustafsson, A., Hinsch, C., Jebabli, I., & Wamba, S. F. (2022). Metaverse beyond the hype: Multidisciplinary perspectives on emerging challenges, opportunities, and agenda for research, practice and policy. *International Journal of Information Management, 66,* 102542. doi:10.1016/j.ijinfomgt.2022.102542

Dwivedi, Y. K., Hughes, L., Wang, Y., Alalwan, A. A., Ahn, S. J., Balakrishnan, J., Barta, S., Belk, R., Buhalis, D., Dutot, V., & ... (2022). How metaverse will change the future of marketing: Implications for research and practice. *Psychology and Marketing.*

Elmasry, T. K., Hazan, E., Khan, H., Kelly, G., Srivastava, S., Yee, L., & Zemmel, R. W. (2022). *Value creation in the metaverse: The real business of the virtual world.* McKinsey & Company.

Eve, S., & Graham, S. (2020). Spatial Data Visualisation and Beyond. In Archaeological Spatial Analysis. doi:10.4324/9781351243858-24

Foody, G. M. (2002). Status of land cover classification accuracy assessment. In Remote Sensing of Environment (Vol. 80, Issue 1). doi:10.1016/S0034-4257(01)00295-4

Frank, A. U. (2014). Sharing Geographic Data: How to Update Distributed or Replicated Data. *REAL CORP 2014–PLAN IT SMART! Clever Solutions for Smart Cities. Proceedings of 19th International Conference on Urban Planning, Regional Development and Information Society,* (pp. 959–966). ACM.

Giang Barrera, K., & Shah, D. (2023). Marketing in the Metaverse: Conceptual understanding, framework, and research agenda. *Journal of Business Research, 155,* 113420. doi:10.1016/j.jbusres.2022.113420

Goodchild, M. F. (2007). Citizens as sensors: The world of volunteered geography. In GeoJournal. doi:10.100710708-007-9111-y

Haklay, M. (2010). How good is volunteered geographical information? A comparative study of Open-StreetMap and ordnance survey datasets. *Environment and Planning. B, Planning & Design, 37*(4), 682–703. doi:10.1068/b35097

Haklay, M., Antoniou, V., Basiouka, S., Soden, R., & Mooney, P. (2014). *Crowdsourced geographic information use in government.* World Bank Publications.

Hirsh-Pasek, K., Zosh, J. M., Hadani, H. S., Golinkoff, R. M., Clark, K., Donohue, C., & Wartella, E. (2022). A whole new world: Education meets the metaverse. *Center for Universal Education, February.*

Hollensen, S., Kotler, P., & Opresnik, M. O. (2022). Metaverse – the new marketing universe. *The Journal of Business Strategy.* doi:10.1108/JBS-01-2022-0014

Kim, C. (2009). Spatial Data Mining, Geovisualization. In International Encyclopedia of Human Geography. doi:10.1016/B978-008044910-4.00526-5

Kiwelekar, A. W., Mahamunkar, G. S., Netak, L. D., & Nikam, V. B. (2020). *Deep Learning Techniques for Geospatial Data Analysis.* doi:10.1007/978-3-030-49724-8_3

Kye, B., Han, N., Kim, E., Park, Y., & Jo, S. (2021). Educational applications of metaverse: Possibilities and limitations. In Journal of Educational Evaluation for Health Professions (Vol. 18). doi:10.3352/jeehp.2021.18.32

Lee, C. W. (2022). Application of Metaverse Service to Healthcare Industry: A Strategic Perspective. *International Journal of Environmental Research and Public Health*, *19*(20), 13038. doi:10.3390/ijerph192013038 PMID:36293609

Li, X., Lv, Z., Wang, W., Zhang, B., Hu, J., Yin, L., & Feng, S. (2016). WebVRGIS based traffic analysis and visualization system. *Advances in Engineering Software*, *93*, 1–8. doi:10.1016/j.advengsoft.2015.11.003

Long, Y., & Liu, L. (2016). Transformations of urban studies and planning in the big/open data era: a review. In International Journal of Image and Data Fusion, 7(4). doi:10.1080/19479832.2016.1215355

Longley, P. (2005). *Geographic information systems and science*. John Wiley & Sons.

Lu, Y., & Liu, Y. (2012). Pervasive location acquisition technologies: Opportunities and challenges for geospatial studies. *Computers, Environment and Urban Systems*, *36*(2), 105–108. doi:10.1016/j.compenvurbsys.2012.02.002

Maharg, P., & Owen, M. (2007). Simulations, learning and the metaverse: changing cultures in legal education. *Journal of Information, Law and Technology, 1*(May 2014).

Mark Graham. (2015). The hidden biases of Geodata. *The Guardian.* https://www.theguardian.com/news/datablog/2015/apr/28/the-hidden-biases-of-geodata

Milinković, A., Ristić, K., & Tucikešić, S. (2014). Modern technologies of collecting and presenting of geospatial data. *Geonauka*, *02*(02), 19–27. doi:10.14438/gn.2014.12

Nakavachara, V., & Saengchote, K. (2022). Is Metaverse LAND a good investment? It depends on your unit of account! SSRN *Electronic Journal.* doi:10.2139/ssrn.4028587

Nieradka, P. (2019). Using virtual reality technologies in the real estate sector. *Annales Universitatis Mariae Curie-Skłodowska, Sectio H – Oeconomia*, *53*(2), 45. doi:10.17951/h.2019.53.2.45-53

Park, S. M., & Kim, Y. G. (2022). A Metaverse: Taxonomy, Components, Applications, and Open Challenges. *IEEE Access : Practical Innovations, Open Solutions*, *10*, 4209–4251. doi:10.1109/ACCESS.2021.3140175

PVH. (2022). *Tommy Hilfiger Joins the First-Ever Decentraland Metaverse Fashion Week.* PVH. https://www.pvh.com/news/tommy-hilfiger-metaverse-fashion-week-2022

Rajabifard, A., Binns, A., Masser, I., & Williamson, I. (2006). The role of sub-national government and the private sector in future spatial data infrastructures. *International Journal of Geographical Information Science*, *20*(7), 727–741. doi:10.1080/13658810500432224

Romansky, R. P., & Noninska, I. S. (2020). Challenges of the digital age for privacy and personal data protection. *Mathematical Biosciences and Engineering, 17*(5). doi:10.3934/mbe.2020286 PMID:33120553

Sermet, Y., & Demir, I. (2022). GeospatialVR: A web-based virtual reality framework for collaborative environmental simulations. *Computers & Geosciences, 159*, 105010. doi:10.1016/j.cageo.2021.105010

Slocum, T. A., McMaster, R. M., Kessler, F. C., Howard, H. H., & Mc Master, R. B. (2008). *Thematic cartography and geographic visualization*.

Sobral, T., Galvão, T., & Borges, J. (2019). Visualization of urban mobility data from intelligent transportation systems. In Sensors (Switzerland), 19(2). doi:10.339019020332

Stephenson, N. (1992). *Snow Crash*. Bantam Books.

Suanpang, P., Niamsorn, C., Pothipassa, P., Chunhapataragul, T., Netwong, T., & Jermsittiparsert, K. (2022). Extensible Metaverse Implication for a Smart Tourism City. *Sustainability (Switzerland), 14*(21), 14027. Advance online publication. doi:10.3390u142114027

Tassi, P. (2020). Fortnite's Travis Scott Concert Was a Stunning Spectacle and a Glimpse at the Metaverse. *Forbes*. https://www.forbes.com/sites/paultassi/2020/04/23/fortnites-travis-scott-concert-was-a-stunning-spectacle-and-a-glimpse-at-the-metaverse/?sh=b07798a2e1f5

Tatavarti, S. (2022). How the metaverse can be a force for good in an uncertain world. *World Economic Forum*.

Tomlinson, R. F. (1969). A Geographic Information System for Regional Planning. [Chigaku Zasshi]. *The Journal of Geography, 78*(1), 45–48. doi:10.5026/jgeography.78.45

Venugopal, J. P., Subramanian, A. A. V., & Peatchimuthu, J. (2023). The realm of metaverse: A survey. *Computer Animation and Virtual Worlds*, e2150. doi:10.1002/cav.2150

Wei, Y., Di, L., Liao, G., Zhao, B., Chen, A., & Bai, Y. (2009). Sharing of distributed geospatial data through grid technology. In Handbook of Research on Geoinformatics. doi:10.4018/978-1-59140-995-3.ch028

Weinberger, M. (2022). What Is Metaverse?—A Definition Based on Qualitative Meta-Synthesis. *Future Internet, 14*(11), 310. doi:10.3390/fi14110310

Wiki. (2023). *Metaverse*. https://en.wikipedia.org/wiki/Metaverse

Wu, T. C., & Ho, C. T. B. (2023). A scoping review of metaverse in emergency medicine. In Australasian Emergency Care (Vol. 26, Issue 1). doi:10.1016/j.auec.2022.08.002

Yang, L., Su, G., & Yuan, H. (2012). Design principles of integrated information platform for emergency responses: The case of 2008 Beijing Olympic Games. *Information Systems Research, 23*(3 PART 1), 761–786. doi:10.1287/isre.1110.0387

Yu, H., Guo, J., Cheng, Y., & Lou, Q. (2013). Techniques and Methods of Spatial Data Fusion. *Applied Mechanics and Materials, 263–266*(PART 1), 3274–3278. doi:10.4028/WWW.SCIENTIFIC.NET/AMM.263-266.3274

Zhang, X., Yang, D., Yow, C. H., Huang, L., Wu, X., Huang, X., Guo, J., Zhou, S., & Cai, Y. (2022). Metaverse for Cultural Heritages. *Electronics (Switzerland)*, *11*(22), 3730. doi:10.3390/electronics11223730

Zhou, Z. M. (2013). The role of the integrated management of spatial data in urban management. *Applied Mechanics and Materials*, *241*, 3063–3066.

Zlatanova, S. (2010). Geospatial Information Technology for Emergency Response. *Disaster Prevention and Management: An International Journal*, *19*(2), 275–276. doi:10.1108/dpm.2010.19.2.275.4

Zou, T., Li, W., Liu, P., Su, X., Huang, H., Han, Y., & Guo, X. (2018). An Overview of Geospatial Information Visualization. *Proceedings of the 2018 IEEE International Conference on Progress in Informatics and Computing, PIC 2018*. IEEE. 10.1109/PIC.2018.8706332

Chapter 14
Next Generation of the Web Will Engage Your Senses:
Unleashing Interactive Web-Based XR Experiences

Benjamin Kenwright

Zhejiang Normal University, China

ABSTRACT

This chapter explores the emerging trends in the web-based XR (Extended Reality) technology, which is expected to shape the next generation of the web. XR refers to the spectrum of technologies that extend the reality of the physical world by integrating virtual and augmented reality elements. The chapter discusses how web-based XR experiences can engage our senses by creating immersive and interactive environments that go beyond the traditional 2D screen. The authors argue that the current web technology stack is evolving to support more powerful and seamless XR experiences that can be accessed through standard web browsers. The chapter also examines the challenges and opportunities that arise from the integration of XR technology with the web, including issues related to privacy, security, and accessibility. Overall, this book chapter provides a comprehensive overview of the potential of web-based XR technology and its impact on the future of the web.

INTRODUCTION

Evolving Web Technologies

In the ever-changing digital landscape, the evolution of interactive technologies has been a driving force behind the transformative experiences we encounter on the internet. From the early days of static web pages to the dynamic and interactive web applications we have today, the continuous advancement of web technologies has not only shaped how we connect, communicate, and conduct business online but has also revolutionized the way we interact and engage with digital content using our senses (Sheridan et al., 2022).

DOI: 10.4018/978-1-6684-9919-1.ch014

Copyright © 2023, IGI Global. Copying or distributing in print or electronic forms without written permission of IGI Global is prohibited.

We are seeing many technological advancements, such as quantum computing, 3D-printing, flexible transparent screens and artificial intelligence. These innovations and advancements are changing how we use and interact with technologies online. Leading to new interaction paradigms, emotional data-driven design, and designs that employ 'no interfaces' that explore new human experiences. Experiences that transform our digital interactions into immersive and multisensory journeys (Kenwright, 2018).

One significant catalyst for change in recent years has been the advent of Web 3, a concept that represents the next phase in the evolution of the internet, emphasizing user-centric experiences and pushing the boundaries of sensory engagement. This has included decentralized crowdsourcing platforms for collecting and visualizing 3D models (Lin et al., 2023). Not to mention, the metaverse, which has gained a lot of attention recently (Kshetri, 2022; Purcarea et al., 2022). A particular area of interest, touched on by Jin and Parrott (Jin & Parrott, 2021) was content generation and distribution in the era of web 3 technologies, especially with the advancements of artificial intelligence and machine learning models (Guzdial et al., 2022; Ravichandran & Ilango, 2023).

Today's current Web 2 evolved out of the rise of social media, e-commerce, and cloud-based applications, while Web 3 introduces a paradigm shift that promises to redefine the internet as we know it, placing **emphasis on the integration of multisensory experiences to create truly immersive and engaging digital worlds**.

So, what exactly is Web 3, and how will it reinvent the internet in terms of interaction and userexperience? Web 3 can be understood as a decentralized and user-centric standard for the web, built on emerging technologies such as blockchain, decentralized networks, and cryptocurrencies. Unlike Web 2, which primarily focused on information sharing and limited user interaction, Web 3 envisions a future where our digital experiences will engage multiple senses, blurring the boundaries between the physical and virtual worlds (Yu et al., 2022; Aria et al., 2023).

As we explore the distinctions between Web 2 and Web 3, we will delve into the key principles and architectural concepts that underpin the new standard, emphasizing how they contribute to **enhanced interactivity, intuitive user-interfaces, and sensory stimulation**. We will examine the decentralized nature of Web 3 and its potential to foster a more personalized, engaging, and immersive online environment, where users can interact with digital content through touch, sight, sound, and beyond.

The Rise of Extended Reality (XR)

XR, or extended reality, is a game-changing technology that holds immense potential to reshape how we interact with the digital world. Blending the physical and virtual realms, XR transcends the limitations of traditional interfaces, offering immersive and interactive experiences that engage our senses and push the boundaries of what is possible. Whether it's virtual reality (VR), augmented reality (AR), or mixed reality (MR), XR opens up a realm of endless possibilities across industries, from education and healthcare to entertainment and beyond (Figure 2). It enables us to explore new frontiers, connect with others in unprecedented ways, and unlock innovative solutions to real-world challenges. XR has the power to revolutionize how we learn, work, play, and experience the world, bringing us closer to a future where the digital and physical seamlessly coexist, enhancing our lives and expanding the realms of human imagination. As XR continues to evolve and gain momentum, the integration of Web 3 and its associated APIs becomes increasingly important, unlocking new possibilities and enhancing the capabilities of XR experiences (Kenwright, 2020a, 2019).

Figure 1. Web 3 is inevitable, since it is driven by the inherent advantages of blockchain technologies offering enhanced security, privacy and data ownership, while promoting interoperability among different platforms and fosters collaboration, innovation, and inclusivity

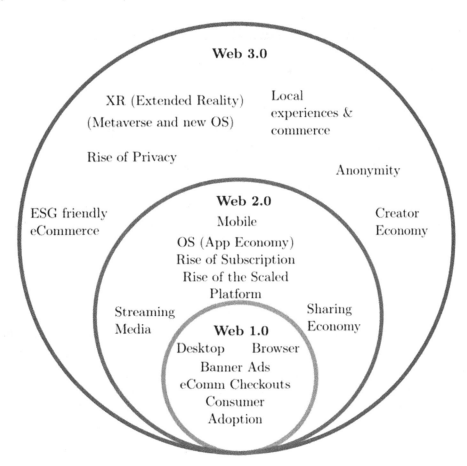

One crucial reason why Web 3 is important for XR lies in its ability to enhance interaction, userexperience, and sensory engagement. XR aims to provide immersive and interactive experiences that closely mimic real-world interactions, allowing users to engage with digital content in a natural and intuitive manner. Web 3, with its focus on user-centric design and multisensory engagement, aligns perfectly with these objectives, enabling XR developers to create richer and more immersive experiences (Kenwright, 2020b).

The WebXR API stands as a cornerstone of this convergence between Web 3 and XR. The WebXR API provides a standardized way for developers to create XR experiences that can be accessed through web browsers on various devices. Leveraging the capabilities of the WebXR API, developers can seamlessly integrate virtual and augmented elements into web-based XR applications, enabling users to access XR content without the need for additional installations or specialized hardware (Kenwright, 2021).

Web 3's emphasis on decentralization and user ownership also holds tremendous significance for XR. As XR applications become more prevalent and widespread, the decentralized nature of Web 3 provides a means to ensure data privacy, security, and user control. Leveraging blockchain technology and decentralized networks, XR experiences can offer users greater control over their personal data and digital identities, fostering trust and empowering individuals within the XR ecosystem.

UNDERSTANDING INTERACTIVE WEB-BASED XR EXPERIENCES

Defining Interactive Web-Based XR

Today standalone application based products and services that require you to step outside your normal web browsing experience is a big barrier. Interactive web-based XR combines the power of extended reality (XR) technologies, such as virtual reality (VR), augmented reality (AR), and mixed reality (MR), with web technologies to create immersive and interactive experiences accessible through web browsers. Eliminating the need for software installations (like plugsin) or specialized hardware, allowing users to engage with XR content on various devices. Web technologies like HTML5, JavaScript, and WebGPU/GL, users can access virtual environments, interact with virtual objects, and experience digital content seamlessly within their browsers, making XR experiences more accessible and widely available. Figure 3 provides a visualization of the research themes of XR (motor theme diagram).

Exploring the Potential of XR Technologies

The potential for XR technologies is tremendous. XR is expected to revolutionize various industries and human experiences as it will offer immersive and interactive environments that go beyond traditional screens, enabling users to engage with digital content in unprecedented ways. In fields like education, XR can enhance learning by providing realistic simulations, interactive visualizations, and immersive storytelling. In healthcare, XR applications can aid in surgical training, patient rehabilitation, and mental health treatments. The entertainment industry can leverage XR to create captivating virtual worlds and immersive gaming experiences. Additionally, XR has the potential to transform industries like architecture, engineering, and manufacturing by enabling virtual prototyping, remote collaboration, and spatial design visualization. With continuous advancements, the potential of XR technologies extends to areas like tourism, retail, marketing, and beyond, offering limitless possibilities for enhancing engagement, creativity, productivity, and human interaction.

Benefits of Web-Based XR Experiences

Web-based XR experiences offer numerous benefits that contribute to their increasing popularity and adoption. Firstly, accessibility is a key advantage, as users can access XR content directly from their web browsers without the need for additional installations or hardware. This eliminates barriers to entry and allows a wider audience to enjoy XR experiences. Secondly, web-based XR is platform-agnostic, meaning it can be accessed across various devices, including smartphones, tablets, and desktop computers, regardless of the operating system. This versatility ensures a broader reach and increases the potential user base. Moreover, web-based XR experiences are easily shareable and distributable through URLs, facilitating seamless sharing and collaboration. They also benefit from the constant evolution of web technologies, allowing for continuous updates and improvements without requiring users to download updates. Lastly, web-based XR opens up opportunities for innovative applications and use cases. For example, web-based AR experiences can be used for virtual try-on of products, virtual tours of real estate properties, or interactive educational content accessible to students worldwide. These benefits collectively make webbased XR experiences more inclusive, convenient, and adaptable, fostering wider adoption and exploration of XR technologies.

Figure 2. Extended Reality (XR) landscape encompasses the convergence of virtual, augmented, and mixed realities, creating immersive experiences that blur the boundaries between the physical and digital worlds

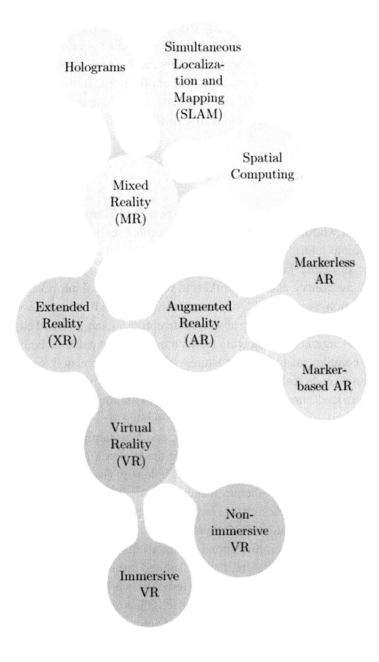

THE ROLE OF SENSORY ENGAGEMENT IN WEB-BASED XR

Immersive Audio: Amplifying the Experience

Sounds is more than just noise (Kenwright, 2020b). Audio is a powerful component that enhances and amplifies the overall experience of virtual and augmented reality environments. Providing spatial sound, immersive audio creates a realistic and engaging auditory environment that complements the visual elements. Through the use of advanced audio techniques, such as binaural rendering and positional audio, sound can be perceived as coming from specific directions and distances, creating a sense of presence and immersion. This adds a new dimension to XR experiences by enabling users to accurately locate and interact with audio sources within the virtual or augmented space. For example, in a VR game, immersive audio can create a lifelike soundscape where users can hear footsteps approaching from behind or the reverberation of their voice as they speak. In AR applications, immersive audio can be used to provide audio cues or guidance in real-world environments. Immersive audio, XR experiences become more captivating, realistic, and emotionally impactful, further blurring the line between the virtual and physical worlds.

Visual Augmentation: Enhancing Perception

Visual augmentation refers to the enhancement of human perception through the overlay of digital visual elements onto the physical world, often facilitated by augmented reality (AR) technology. Augmenting what we see with additional information, visuals, or context, visual augmentation expands our understanding and perception of reality. For instance, in industrial settings, AR can overlay real-time sensor data or instructions onto machinery, enabling workers to visualize critical information and perform tasks more efficiently. In education, visual augmentation can bring static textbook images to life by overlaying interactive 3D models or animations, making abstract concepts more tangible and engaging for students. In healthcare, AR can aid surgeons by projecting medical images onto patients' bodies during surgeries, helping them navigate complex anatomical structures with greater precision. Similarly, in navigation and exploration, AR can provide real-time directional cues, points of interest, or historical information overlaid onto a live camera feed, enriching our understanding of unfamiliar environments. Through visual augmentation, we can perceive and interact with our surroundings in new and enhanced ways, unlocking opportunities for improved learning, productivity, safety, and entertainment.

Motor themes are well developed and important for the research area and have strong centrality (well-developed external ties with other themes) and high density (welldeveloped internal ties, within its thematic network). Therefore, motor themes make a major contribution to the research area. Basic themes are important themes for the research area but are not well developed in terms of their internal ties within their thematic networks. Therefore, basic themes make an important but not focused contribution to the research area. Specialized themes correspond to themes that are internally well developed but are isolated from the other themes and, therefore, make a limited but focused contribution to the research area. Themes with a poorly developed internal and external network represent emerging themes in the research area. The sphere size can represent bibliometric indicators, such as the document number or number of citations by documents in the theme and in its internal network, thus adding an additional analytical dimension.

Figure 3. Themes

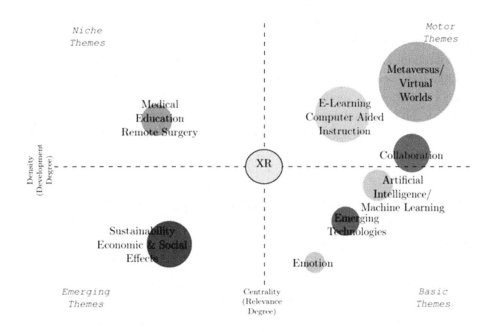

Haptic Feedback: Touching the Virtual World

The ability to **physically interact** with the visual world is important. Haptic feedback refers to the technology that allows users to physically interact and feel sensations for this, creating a sense of touch and enhancing the overall immersion of virtual reality (VR) experiences. Through the use of specialized haptic devices, such as gloves, controllers, or vests, users can receive tactile feedback in response to their actions or interactions. For example, in a VR game, haptic feedback can simulate the sensation of objects by providing vibrations or pressure when the user touches or interacts with virtual objects. In medical simulations, haptic feedback can replicate the sense of touch during procedures, allowing trainees to practice realistic surgical techniques. In architectural design, haptic feedback can enable users to feel the texture and resistance of virtual materials, aiding in the creation of accurate and immersive virtual environments. Incorporating haptic feedback, VR experiences become more realistic, engaging, and multisensory, bridging the gap between the physical and virtual realms and enabling a deeper level of interaction and presence within the virtual world (De Jesus Jr et al., 2022).

Beyond the Visual and Auditory: Feeling

Looking at XR through a dystopian lens, we can be sure that it will connect us in new and deeper ways. Feelings have the power to ignite the spark of connection, transform mere moments into cherished memories, and breathe life into the canvas of our existence. Beyond the visual and auditory senses, the sense of touch or haptic feedback plays a crucial role in enriching our experiences and interactions with technology. Virtual reality (VR) and augmented reality (AR) applications are increasingly incorporating haptic feedback to provide a more immersive and realistic user experience. For instance, in VR gaming, haptic gloves can simulate the sensation of objects or surfaces, allowing players to feel the impact of virtual punches or the texture of virtual objects they interact with. In the field of medicine, haptic feedback devices can provide tactile sensations during surgical simulations, helping trainees develop a sense of touch and improve their skills. In the automotive industry, haptic feedback in driving simulators can replicate the vibrations and resistance of different terrains, enhancing the realism and training value. Even beyond technology, wearable devices like haptic wearables or vibrating smartwatches use haptic feedback to provide notifications, alerts, or even navigation cues through touch. Incorporating haptic feedback, technology can transcend visual and auditory limitations, creating multisensory experiences that deepen our connection and engagement with the digital world (Schutte & Stilinovi´c, 2017; Flavi´an et al., 2021; Kenwright, 2023).

WEB TECHNOLOGIES POWERING INTERACTIVE XR EXPERIENCES

WebXR: Enabling Cross-Platform XR Development

WebXR with web 3, the integration of extended reality (XR) technologies with web-based blockchain platforms, offers significant advantages in enabling cross-platform development. The decentralized nature and accessibility of web technologies, WebXR with web 3 allows developers to create XR experiences that can be accessed and shared seamlessly across different platforms and devices. For example, a web-based XR application built on web 3 can be experienced on a desktop computer, a mobile device, or even within a virtual reality headset, providing a consistent user experience regardless of the platform. Additionally, web 3's decentralized infrastructure ensures interoperability, enabling XR content and assets to be stored, shared, and accessed across various blockchain networks, promoting collaboration and community-driven development. Furthermore, the integration of blockchain technology facilitates the secure and transparent exchange of digital assets, enabling unique virtual items, experiences, or currencies to be seamlessly utilized and traded across different XR platforms. This cross-platform compatibility and interoperability offered by WebXR with web 3 not only expands the potential user base but also fosters a more inclusive and collaborative ecosystem for XR development.

WebGL to WebGPU: Real-Time 3D Graphics on the Web

The transition from WebGL to WebGPU represents a significant advancement in enabling realtime 3D graphics on the web. While WebGL has been widely used to render interactive 3D graphics in web browsers, WebGPU takes it a step further by providing a lower-level, more efficient, and modern graphics API. With WebGPU, developers can harness the power of modern GPUs for accelerated rendering, allowing for complex and visually stunning 3D experiences on the web. For example, games and interactive simulations can benefit from improved performance and more realistic graphics, pushing the boundaries of what is achievable within a browser environment. Additionally, WebGPU's design facilitates cross-platform compatibility, making it easier for developers to create consistent experiences across different devices and operating systems. This transition also unlocks new possibilities for creative applications, such as 3D modeling and visualization, architectural design, virtual reality experiences, and scientific simulations, all accessible directly through web browsers. Ultimately, the shift from WebGL to WebGPU represents a significant leap forward in bringing high-fidelity, real-time 3D graphics to the web, opening doors to a new era of immersive and visually captivating web experiences (Kenwright, 2022b,a).

Web Audio API: Creating Immersive Soundscapes

Sound, the invisible brush that paints emotions and colors our experiences, holds the power to transcend barriers, ignite memories, and create a symphony of connection in our lives. The Web Audio API is one of the tools for creating immersive soundscapes on the web, enhancing the overall user experience and adding depth to web-based applications. With the Web Audio API, developers can dynamically generate, manipulate, and spatialize audio, allowing for the creation of realistic and interactive sound environments. For instance, in a virtual reality (VR) experience, the Web Audio API can be used to position audio sources in 3D space, giving users a sense of directionality and immersion. Imagine exploring a virtual forest where the chirping of birds comes from above and the rustling of leaves surrounds you as you move. In gaming, the Web Audio API enables the design of realistic sound effects, such as the echoes of footsteps bouncing off virtual walls or the distinct sounds of different environments. In music production, the API can be utilized to build interactive web-based synthesizers or audio visualizers, allowing users to create and manipulate sounds in real-time. Furthermore, the Web Audio API supports advanced audio effects and signal processing, enabling the development of interactive audio filters, spatial reverberation, or dynamic equalization for a truly immersive auditory experience. The capabilities of the Web Audio API, developers can push the boundaries of web-based audio, creating rich and captivating soundscapes that complement the visual elements and transport users to new digital realms (Kenwright, 2020b).

Web-Based Haptics: Simulating Touch in XR

Not just about seeing, but also feeling. Web-based haptics, enabling touch simulation in XR, is a dynamic field of research with potential future advancements. One area of interest is the development of more sophisticated haptic devices and technologies that offer finer control and a wider range of tactile sensations. For instance, researchers are exploring advancements in flexible haptic displays, shape-changing materials, and force feedback mechanisms to enhance the realism of touch sensations in web-based XR environments (Zhang et al., 2020). Additionally, there is ongoing research into optimizing haptic rendering algorithms and compression techniques to reduce latency and bandwidth requirements for web-based haptic communication (Adams & Hannaford, 1999). Future studies may focus on designing novel haptic interaction paradigms for web-based XR applications, investigating the perceptual and cognitive effects of haptic feedback in various scenarios, and exploring the integration of haptics with other sensory modalities for multisensory immersion (De Jesus Jr et al., 2022). These research efforts aim to push the boundaries of webbased haptics, enabling more realistic and engaging touch experiences in XR and paving the way for transformative applications across fields such as education, healthcare, and entertainment (Vi et al., 2017).

DESIGNING INTERACTIVE WEB-BASED XR EXPERIENCES

User-Centered Design Principles

User-centered design principles play a crucial role in creating meaningful and immersive experiences in the context of extended reality (XR). Prioritizing the needs, preferences, and capabilities of users, designers can ensure that XR and web 3 applications are intuitive, accessible, and engaging. User-centered design principles such as simplicity, consistency, and feedback are particularly relevant in this context (Figure 4). For example, simplicity entails designing XR and web 3 interfaces that are easy to understand and navigate, minimizing cognitive load for users. Consistency ensures that interactions and interfaces across different XR experiences follow established patterns and conventions, enhancing usability and reducing learning curves. Feedback mechanisms, such as visual cues or haptic responses, provide users with real-time information about their actions and help them understand the consequences of their interactions. Furthermore, personalization and customization are key considerations, allowing users to tailor their XR and web 3 experiences to their individual preferences and needs. Adhering to user-centered design principles, designers can create XR and web 3 applications that empower users, foster engagement, and deliver immersive and inclusive experiences.

Figure 4. Designing and testing XR systems (evaluation strategies)

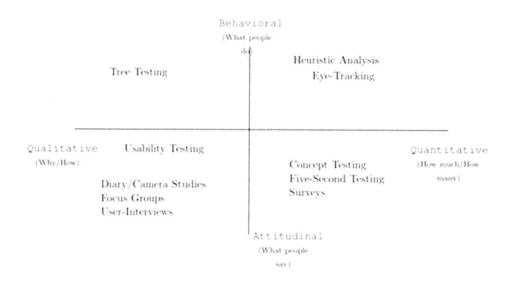

Crucial to ensure seamless and immersive user-experiences, mitigate potential risks and discomfort, optimize performance, and unlock the full potential of this transformative technology for various industries and applications.

Creating Intuitive User Interfaces

Creating intuitive user interfaces is essential to ensuring a seamless and user-friendly experience across various digital platforms. Through rigorous testing and evaluation, designers can gather valuable insights into the effectiveness and intuitiveness of their interfaces. Behavioral testing involves observing users' interactions with the interface and analyzing their actions, task completion rates, and navigation patterns to identify any usability issues. Attitudinal testing, on the other hand, focuses on gathering user feedback, opinions, and preferences through surveys, interviews, or questionnaires to understand users' subjective experiences and perceptions. Quantitative factors such as task completion times, error rates, and click-through rates provide measurable data for evaluating interface performance. Qualitative factors, including user feedback, comments, and suggestions, offer deeper insights into user preferences, pain points, and areas for improvement.

Combining behavioral, attitudinal, quantitative, and qualitative factors in the testing process, designers can gain a comprehensive understanding of user needs and preferences, enabling them to refine and iterate their interfaces to create intuitive user experiences that align with user expectations.

Navigating Challenges of Web-Based XR Design

Navigating the challenges of web-based XR design requires careful consideration of various factors to ensure a seamless and immersive user experience. One challenge is optimizing performance and minimizing latency, especially when delivering high-quality 3D graphics and immersive interactions through web browsers. Designers must strike a balance between visual fidelity and efficient rendering to ensure smooth and responsive XR experiences. Another challenge involves crossdevice compatibility and responsiveness, as web-based XR applications should adapt seamlessly to different screen sizes, resolutions, and input methods. Additionally, ensuring accessibility for users with disabilities is crucial, considering factors like providing alternative text for XR content, supporting screen readers, and accommodating users with different interaction capabilities. Designers also need to address privacy and security concerns, particularly when handling sensitive user data or integrating web 3 technologies. Addressing these challenges requires a combination of technical expertise, user research, and iterative design processes to create web-based XR experiences that are performance, accessible, secure, and enjoyable across a range of devices and user needs (Raybourn et al., 2019).

BUILDING INTERACTIVE WEB-BASED XR APPLICATIONS

XR Development Frameworks and Tools

Building interactive web-based XR applications requires leveraging XR development frameworks and tools that provide the necessary capabilities and functionalities. One popular framework is AFrame, an open-source web framework for building VR experiences using HTML and JavaScript. A-Frame simplifies the creation of 3D scenes, object manipulation, and user interactions through its declarative markup language. Another powerful tool is Three.js, a JavaScript library that enables the creation of 3D graphics and animations, making it ideal for building interactive webbased XR experiences. Babylon. js is another robust framework that supports both VR and AR development, providing a wide range of features like physics simulation, lighting effects, and animation support. Additionally, tools like WebXR Polyfill and WebXR Emulator aid in testing and debugging XR applications across various devices and browsers. These frameworks and tools streamline the development process, allowing developers to focus on creating immersive XR experiences without the need for extensive low-level programming. Utilizing these XR development frameworks and tools, developers can build compelling and interactive web-based XR applications that engage and captivate users.

WebXR API Integration: Code Examples

Getting started with the WebXR API has never been easier. We provide an overview of the key library components for initializing the API. The WebXR API enables developers to access and utilize XR capabilities within web browsers. This section provides code examples demonstrating the integration of the WebXR API for common XR interactions and functionalities.

1. **Initialization and Session Creation**: To start using the WebXR API, initialize the XR system and create an XR session. Here's an example using JavaScript (Listing 1):

Listing 1. Initialization and session creation

```
if ('xr' in navigator) { navigator.xr.requestSession('immersive-vr')
        .then((session) => {
           // XR session created, handle further interactions here
        })
        .catch((error) => {
           // Error handling
        });
} else {
    // XR not supported in the browser
}
```

2. **Render Loop and Frame Updates**: To provide a continuous and responsive XR experience, utilize a render loop to update the XR frames. Here's a code snippet showcasing the render loop using the 'XRSession' and 'XRFrame' objects (Listing 2):

Listing 2. Render loop and frame updates

```
function renderFrame(timestamp, frame) {
   // Perform necessary updates and rendering for each frame

   frame.session.requestAnimationFrame(renderFrame);
} session.requestAnimationFrame(renderFrame);
```

3. **XR Input and Interactions**: WebXR API enables capturing user input and interactions in XR. Here's an example of detecting button presses on a VR controller using the 'XRInputSource' object (Listing 3):

Listing 3. XR input and interactions

```
session.addEventListener('inputsourceschange', (event) => { const inputSources
=
    event.session.inputSources;

    inputSources.forEach((inputSource) => { inputSource.addEventListener('selec
tstart',
        (event) => {
            // Handle button press start event
        });

        inputSource.addEventListener('selectend', (event) => {
            // Handle button press end event
        });
    });
});
```

4. **Anchors and Augmented Reality**: In augmented reality (AR) experiences, anchors can be used to place virtual objects in the real world. Here's an example of creating an AR anchor using the 'XRAnchor' object (Listing 4):

Listing 4. Anchors and augmented reality

```
session.requestReferenceSpace('viewer')
    .then((referenceSpace) => { const anchorPosition = new Float32Array([0, 0,
-1]); // Example anchor position const anchor = new XRAnchor(anchorPosition,
referenceSpace);

    // Add the anchor to the XR session session.addAnchor(anchor); })
    .catch((error) => {
    // Error handling
    });
```

These code examples provide a starting point for integrating the WebXR API into web-based XR applications. Remember to Kenwright (Kenwright, 2021) for further examples and information.

Optimizing Performance for Web-Based XR

Optimizing webXR programs is crucial to deliver smooth, immersive experiences, reduce latency, enhance performance, and ensure broad accessibility across different devices, ultimately providing users with a seamless and enjoyable XR interaction. One effective approach is optimizing 3D assets, such as reducing polygon counts, using efficient textures, and employing level-of-detail (LOD) techniques to dynamically render objects at different levels of detail based on distance. Caching and preloading assets can minimize loading times and improve responsiveness. Additionally, leveraging techniques like occlusion culling and frustum culling helps eliminate rendering unnecessary objects outside the camera's view, optimizing GPU performance. Implementing efficient rendering strategies, like batch rendering and instancing, can reduce draw calls and improve overall rendering speed. Furthermore, optimizing JavaScript code by reducing unnecessary computations, utilizing requestAnimationFrame for rendering loops, and avoiding excessive memory usage is essential. Lastly, considering the performance impact of features like physics simulations, complex shaders, and dynamic lighting can help strike a balance between visual fidelity and performance. Employing these performance optimization techniques, web-based XR experiences can deliver seamless, responsive, and visually impressive interactions.

THE FUTURE OF INTERACTIVE WEB-BASED XR

Emerging Trends and Innovations

Web-based XR will revolutionize the way we perceive, interact, and connect, unleashing a realm of limitless possibilities and immersive experiences accessible directly through web browsers. The future of interactive web-based XR is filled with exciting possibilities, as emerging trends and innovations continue to shape the landscape. One trend is the increasing adoption of WebXR standards and APIs, enabling seamless and cross-platform XR experiences directly through web browsers, without the need for specialized applications. Another trend is the integration of artificial intelligence (AI) and machine learning (ML) techniques, allowing for more intelligent and personalized XR interactions, such as dynamic content generation, user behavior analysis, and adaptive user interfaces. Interestingly, it will not be any single industry that will embower XR. Blockchain is going to empower XR, and XR is going to be powered by AI technologies in the future. Additionally, the development of WebXR-based social platforms and collaborative environments is on the rise, enabling users to connect, communicate, and share XR experiences in real-time. Moreover, advancements in haptic feedback technologies are enhancing the sense of touch and tactile interactions in web-based XR applications, enabling users to feel and manipulate virtual objects with greater realism. Furthermore, the fusion of XR with other emerging technologies like 5G, edge computing, and Internet of Things (IoT) is opening up new possibilities for interconnected and immersive web-based XR experiences. The future holds immense potential for interactive web-based XR, where the boundaries between the digital and physical worlds continue to blur, revolutionizing industries such as education, entertainment, healthcare, and beyond.

Impact of Web-Based XR on Various Industries

The impact of web-based XR on various industries is supported by research and industry examples. For instance, in education, studies have shown the benefits of immersive XR experiences in improving learning outcomes and engagement. A study by Kenwright (Ibrahim & Kenwright, 2022) elaborates on the value of XR simulations for enhancing the students' understanding and motivation in science education. In healthcare, web-based XR applications have been utilized for surgical training and telemedicine. Research by Morimoto et al. (Morimoto et al., 2022) highlighted the effectiveness of XR simulations for surgical skills training. In the architecture industry, companies like Surgical Theater (https://surgicaltheater.com/) have developed webbased XR tools for design visualization and collaboration. The use of web-based XR for virtual experiences in retail is exemplified by companies like Apple and Meta, which are developing newt generations of XR technologies. These examples demonstrate the real-world impact of web-based XR across various industries, driving innovation, accessibility, and enhanced user experiences.

Ethical Considerations and User Privacy

Some of the biggest challenges and dangers area for XR are with the ethical and moral aspects (Kenwright, 2018, 2023). Ethical considerations and user privacy will continue to play a vital role in the development and deployment of web-based XR applications. However, it is crucial to prioritize the protection of user data and ensure transparent data practices. For example, when using web-based XR for healthcare applications, strict adherence to privacy regulations is essential to safeguard sensitive patient information. Additionally, addressing issues of consent and informed decision-making is critical, especially when capturing user data or implementing tracking technologies in XR experiences. Companies like Mozilla are actively advocating for user privacy in web-based XR through initiatives like Privacy Icons, which provide users with transparent information about data collection and sharing practices. Integrating privacy-bydesign principles, implementing robust security measures, and promoting informed user consent, web-based XR developers can create responsible and trustworthy experiences that respect user privacy and foster long-term user trust.

CONCLUSION AND DISCUSSION

Summary of Key Takeaways

Web-based XR is revolutionizing the accessibility and reach of extended reality experiences by leveraging web technologies, enabling users to access immersive XR content directly through web browsers. This eliminates the need for specialized hardware or applications, making XR experiences more widely available to a broader audience. The cross-platform compatibility of web-based XR ensures that users can access XR content seamlessly across different devices, including desktops, laptops, smartphones, and tablets. This democratizes the XR landscape and eliminates barriers to entry, as users can engage with XR experiences without the need for costly hardware investments or specific software installations. Moreover, web-based XR applications can be easily distributed and shared through URLs, allowing for convenient access and seamless collaboration. This accessibility and wide reach of web-based XR unlock opportunities for various industries, including education, healthcare, entertainment, architecture, and more, to leverage the transformative potential of XR and deliver engaging and immersive experiences directly through web browsers.

User-centered design principles are crucial for creating intuitive and engaging web-based XR applications that prioritize the needs and preferences of users. Applying principles such as simplicity, consistency, and feedback, designers can ensure that XR interfaces are easy to navigate and understand. Simplifying complex processes, minimizing cognitive load, and providing clear visual cues help users quickly grasp the functionality and purpose of different elements within the interface. Consistency in layout, terminology, and interaction patterns across the interface enhances familiarity and reduces confusion. Incorporating feedback mechanisms, such as visual cues or haptic responses, provides users with real-time information about their actions and helps them understand the consequences of their interactions. Continuous testing and iteration, encompassing both behavioral and attitudinal factors, are essential for optimizing the user experience and ensuring that web-based XR applications meet user needs and preferences. This iterative approach allows designers to refine and improve the interface based on user feedback and usability testing, resulting in more intuitive and user-friendly XR experiences.

Looking Ahead: The Exciting Possibilities of Web-Based XR

Looking ahead, the possibilities of web-based XR are nothing short of awe-inspiring, paving the way for a future where the lines between the virtual and physical worlds blur into an interconnected web of immersive experiences. Imagine a world where architects collaborate on building designs in real-time through web-based XR, walking through virtual blueprints and making instant modifications from different corners of the globe. Envision students embarking on educational quests that seamlessly blend virtual and real-world elements, exploring ancient civilizations or diving into the depths of the oceans, all from the comfort of their classrooms. Picture a world where doctors perform remote surgeries with the assistance of haptic feedback, feeling the texture of virtual tissues and collaborating with specialists worldwide to save lives. In the realm of entertainment, web-based XR takes us to mind-bending virtual concerts, where we dance alongside holographic superstars, or into immersive storytelling experiences where we become active participants in dynamic narratives, shaping the outcomes with our choices. These are just glimpses of the incredible possibilities that web-based XR holds, transforming industries, revolutionizing education, redefining entertainment, and connecting us in ways we never thought possible. As technology advances and the web-based XR ecosystem evolves, we can look forward to a future where the boundaries of what is real and what is virtual fade away, opening doors to a new era of imagination, connection, and exploration.

REFERENCES

Adams, R. J., & Hannaford, B. (1999). Stable haptic interaction with virtual environments. *IEEE Transactions on Robotics and Automation, 15*(3), 465–474. doi:10.1109/70.768179

Aria, R., Archer, N., Khanlari, M., & Shah, B. (2023). Influential factors in the design and development of a sustainable web3/metaverse and its applications. *Future Internet, 15*(4), 131. doi:10.3390/fi15040131

De Jesus, B. Jr, Lopes, M., Moinnereau, M.-A., Gougeh, R. A., Rosanne, O. M., Schubert, W., & Falk, T. H. (2022). Quantifying multisensory immersive experiences using wearables: Is (stimulating) more (senses) always merrier? In *Proceedings of the 2nd workshop on multisensory experiences-sensoryx'22.* 10.5753ensoryx.2022.20001

Flavi'an, C., Ib'an˜ez-S'anchez, S., & Oru's, C. (2021). Impacts of technological embodiment through virtual reality on potential guests' emotions and engagement. *Journal of Hospitality Marketing & Management, 30*(1), 1–20. doi:10.1080/19368623.2020.1770146

Guzdial, M., Snodgrass, S., & Summerville, A. J. (2022). *Procedural content generation via machine learning: An overview.* Springer. doi:10.1007/978-3-031-16719-5

Ibrahim, I. S., & Kenwright, B. (2022). Smart education: Higher education instruction and the internet of things (iot). arXiv preprint arXiv:2207.02585.

Jin, L., & Parrott, K. (2021). *The web3 renaissance: A golden age for content.* Online Communication Article.

Kenwright, B. (2018). Virtual reality: Ethical challenges and dangers. *IEEE Technology and Society Magazine, 37*(4), 20–25. doi:10.1109/MTS.2018.2876104

Kenwright, B. (2019). *Virtual reality: Where have we been? where are we now? and where are we going? Kenwright, B. (2020a). The future of extended reality (xr).* Communication Article. January.

Kenwright, B. (2020b). There's more to sound than meets the ear: Sound in interactive environments. *IEEE Computer Graphics and Applications, 40*(4), 62–70. doi:10.1109/MCG.2020.2996371 PMID:32540788

Kenwright, B. (2021). Introduction to webxr. In Acm special interest group on computer graphics and interactive techniques conference 2021.

Kenwright, B. (2022a). Introduction to computer graphics and ray-tracing using the webgpu api. In *15th acm siggraph conference and exhibition on computer graphics and interactive techniques in asia 2022.* ACM.

Kenwright, B. (2022b). Introduction to the webgpu api. In Acm siggraph 2022 courses (pp. 1–184). ACM. doi:10.1145/3532720.3535625

Kenwright, B. (2023). Impact of xr on mental health: Are we playing with fire? arXiv preprint arXiv:2304.01648.

Kshetri, N. (2022). Policy, ethical, social, and environmental considerations of web3 and the metaverse. *IT Professional, 24*(3), 4–8. doi:10.1109/MITP.2022.3178509

Lin, L., Duan, H., & Cai, W. (2023). Web3dp: A crowdsourcing platform for 3d models based on web3 infrastructure. In *Proceedings of the 14th conference on acm multimedia systems* (pp. 397–402). ACM. 10.1145/3587819.3592549

Morimoto, T., Kobayashi, T., Hirata, H., Otani, K., Sugimoto, M., Tsukamoto, M., Yoshihara, T., Ueno, M., & Mawatari, M. (2022). Xr (extended reality: virtual reality, augmented reality, mixed reality) technology in spine medicine: status quo and quo vadis. *Journal of Clinical Medicine*, *11*(2), 470. doi:10.3390/jcm11020470 PMID:35054164

Purcarea, I. M. (2022). Digital twins, web3, metaverse, value innovation and e-commerce retail. *Romanian Distribution Committee Magazine*, *13*(3), 41–47.

Ravichandran, K., & Ilango, S. K. (2023). A preliminary analysis of the quality of the content produced by ai bots using ai in content generation. *International Journal of Intelligent Systems and Applications in Engineering*, *11*(5s), 585–590.

Raybourn, E. M., Stubblefield, W. A., Trumbo, M., Jones, A., Whetzel, J., & Fabian, N. (2019). *Information design for xr immersive environments: Challenges and opportunities*. In Virtual, augmented and mixed reality. multimodal interaction. Orlando, Florida.

Schutte, N. S., & Stilinovi'c, E. J. (2017). Facilitating empathy through virtual reality. *Motivation and Emotion*, *41*(6), 708–712. doi:10.100711031-017-9641-7

Sheridan, D., Harris, J., Wear, F., Cowell, J., Jr., Wong, E., & Yazdinejad, A. (2022). Web3 challenges and opportunities for the market. arXiv preprint arXiv:2209.02446.

Vi, C. T., Ablart, D., Gatti, E., Velasco, C., & Obrist, M. (2017). Not just seeing, but also feeling art: Mid-air haptic experiences integrated in a multisensory art exhibition. *International Journal of Human-Computer Studies*, *108*, 1–14. doi:10.1016/j.ijhcs.2017.06.004

Yu, G., Wang, X., Wang, Q., Bi, T., Dong, Y., Liu, R. P., & Reeves, A. (2022). Towards web3 applications: Easing the access and transition. arXiv preprint arXiv:2210.05903.

Zhang, D., Huang, T., & Duan, L. (2020). Emerging self-emissive technologies for flexible displays. *Advanced Materials*, *32*(15), 1902391. doi:10.1002/adma.201902391 PMID:31595613

Chapter 15
A Comparative Study of Smart Contracts–Based Blockchain

Kaveri Banerjee

Department of CSE, SOET, Adamas University, Kolkata, India & Nopany Institute of Management Studies, Kolkata, India

Sajal Saha

Department of CSE, SOET, Adamas University, Kolkata, India

ABSTRACT

Smart contracts are altering traditional industries and business processes. Smart contracts, which are entrenched in blockchains, allow the contractual requirements of a contract to be enforced automatically without the participation of a trustworthy third party. As a significance, smart contracts can minimise administration and service costs, improve business process efficiency, and reduce risks. Although smart contracts have the potential to spark a new innovation wave in corporate operations, they face a number of complications. This chapter offers an overview of smart contracts. This chapter provides an overview of smart contracts. The authors initiate by discussing blockchains as well as smart contracts. The problems of smart contracts are then discussed, in addition to contemporary technological breakthroughs. In addition, the authors assess common smart contract platforms also to provide a classification of smart contract applications, together with some exemplary instances.

INTRODUCTION

Blockchain is the technology that has recently sparked widespread attention in academia and industry. Blockchain, a distributed software system, allows for the execution of transactions without the need for a trustworthy third party (Mohanta, Panda, & Jena, 2018). As a result, corporate operations can be accomplished in a cost-effective and timely manner. Moreover, blockchain immutability confirms distributed confidence as it is nearly difficult to modify with any transactions kept in blockchains as well as entirely past transactions are independently certifiable (Fauziah, Latifah, Omar, Khoirunisa, & Millah, 2020).

DOI: 10.4018/978-1-6684-9919-1.ch015

Copyright © 2023, IGI Global. Copying or distributing in print or electronic forms without written permission of IGI Global is prohibited.

Smart contracts, which were first proposed by Nick Szabo in the 1990s (Macrinici, Cartofeanu, & Gao, 2018), are made possible by blockchain technology. A smart contract's computer program-based clauses will take effect automatically when certain conditions are satisfied. Smart contracts made consisting of transactions are basically saved, copied, and modified in distributed blockchains. Traditional contracts, on the other hand, call for centralised fulfilment by a trusted third party, which adds time and cost to the execution process (Amir Latif et al., 2020). The notion of a "peer-to-peer market" will become a reality thanks to the integration of blockchain technology and smart contracts.

In fact, a key element of any blockchain-based application is the smart contract which refers to an agreement concluded between the numerous stakeholders engaged in the structured framework (Chang et al., 2019). A smart contract is a computer protocol that follows to predetermined rules, protocols, and boundaries set by all network users. For instance, the terms and limitations negotiated by each party involved in the process are all included in the smart contract covering banking transactions and financial reasons (Treleaven et al., 2017). Because traditional contracts are created through writing or other actions, they are generally believed to be time- and resource-consuming. On the other hand, smart contracts are digital programmes that run on computers and only self-execute when certain conditions are met. Medical systems make it possible for a range of stakeholders to collaborate effectively and extend medical services (Ahram et al., 2017). As a consequence, it will be crucial to establish appropriate rules for smart contracts in the healthcare industry, and the agreement of all relevant stakeholders will be necessary. The patient and other network stakeholders must provide personal information and sign a contract indicating their acceptance of the terms in the healthcare blockchain in order for the requirement to be established in the smart contract. For instance, which hospitals may store and exchange patient data, which physicians may access and edit the data, and what categories of data are accessible to both laboratories and pharmacies.

Figure 1 shows a smart contract application in a blockchain-based healthcare system with many service providers (Khatoon, 2020). The coding procedure of the smart contract begins by verifying the data contained in the transaction. It checks the appointment status, patient, healthcare provider, and pharmacy data. If all the data matches what is in the contract, then the contract is considered valid and the procedure continues.

Figure 1 depicts some of the essential features that smart contracts for healthcare may incorporate. The *address* identifies where the patient's data is stored in the database, and the address itself may be stored in blockchain. Using an *access code*, a patient can specify who has access to their information, including their doctor and any other parties like family and friends; *State* defines the system's variables or functions, and code specifies the agreement that stakeholders agreed to sign as well as additional tasks that must be carried out. After they have reached an agreement, the accounting records will be entered into the system and the other companies will be given access to the transaction data.

ETHEREUM SYSTEM DESIGN AND DEVELOPMENT

Smart contracts operate on their own. Human manipulation is not required, similar to the situation with paper contracts. There aren't any intermediates, and trust is not required because the blockchain executes the contract instantly whenever the terms are met. The blockchain smart contract framework for the healthcare sector has been created using Ethereum (Vujičić et al., 2018). With a lively community and a sizable public DApp repository, this open-source network is one of the current largest public blockchain

Figure 1. Healthcare applications of smart contracts

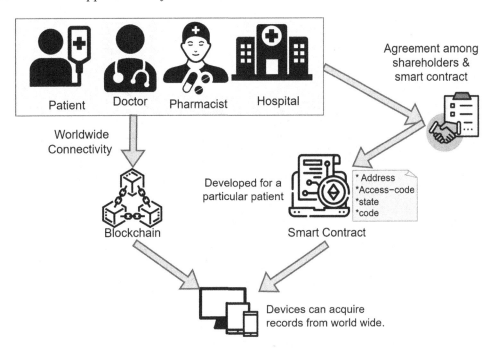

networks (Rupa et al., 2021).Despite plans to soon transfer to a proof-of-stake (PoS) scaling mechanism, the network now uses the Ethash proof-of-work consensus method. The finest consensus algorithms for building distributed networks are Delegated Proof-of-Stake (DPoS) and Practical Byzantine Fault Tolerance (PBFT) (Saingre et al., 2020) . The DApp would be able to identify abnormalities, unauthorised data insertions, and missing entities by comparing DFS contents with ledger records. A schedule for auditing is listed next to each level. The main elements of smart contracts, which were developed using the high-level programming language Solidity, are functions, triggers, local variables, and modifiers. Using the Remix and Kovan test networks, smart contracts have been placed on the testnet, and testnet ethers are being used to pay transaction fees (Fat & Candra, 2020).

A smart contract is produced using Solidity programming in three steps: authoring, compiling, and announcing. The bytecode is produced by the Solidity real-time compiler (Mukhopadhyay, 2018). Smart contracts have been added to the blockchain using Ethereum Wallet. Figure 2 illustrates how smart contracts using Ethereum work by omitting the mining phase for simplicity. The smart contract is machine-level compiled into byte code, where each byte represents a single operation. This byte code is then sent to the blockchain as just an EVM 1 transaction. It is picked up by a miner, who confirms Block 1. After a user submits a transaction through the web interface, the EVM 2 obtains the web-based information, incorporates it into Transaction (T), and distributes it to the blockchain. A status update for transaction (T) is made in Block 2. To witness the changes that T makes when inspecting the state that are later reflected in the contract, Node 3 must synchronise at least until Block 2.

Figure 2. Mechanism for Ethereum smart contracts

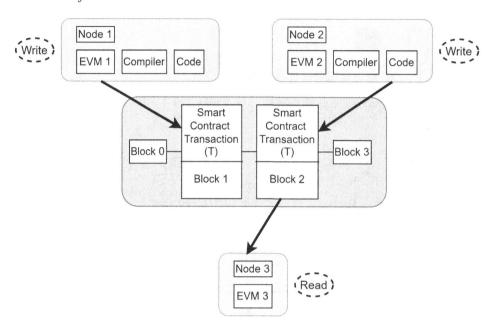

SMART CONTRACTS FOR HEALTHCARE ON THE BLOCKCHAIN

We construct intelligent representations of existing health records which are primarily kept on a network among individual nodes using Ethereum's smart contracts. Our contracts specify who owns records, who has access to them, and how to maintain data integrity. In our approach, management orders for these attributes are transmitted via blockchain transactions that contain cryptographic signatures (Sharma et al., 2020). The state-transition features of the contract impose data alteration only through legal transactions. As long as they can be represented computationally, these rules can be developed to enforce any set of limitations governing a particular health record.

Using blockchain smart contracts, we created a framework for intricate healthcare workflows. Smart contracts have been used to solve various health care workflows and the regulation of data access among various parties within the healthcare ecosystem (Pham et al., 2018). As seen in Figure 3, a blockchain-based smart contract can be constructed that satisfies all criteria, from controlling different permissions to accessing data. Furthermore, it is obvious that other parties are involved in this strategy and are carrying out various jobs. This will make it easier for patients and medical professionals to communicate more effectively. Data authorisation requirements are part of smart contracts. It can help in tracking every action connected to a specific ID, from its creation to its return. Smart contracts include several built-in features and processes, all of which have been meticulously described and supported by numerous scenarios. Smart contracts include several built-in features and processes, all of which have been meticulously described and supported by numerous scenarios. There won't be a requirement for a centralised organisation to supervise and approve the procedure because the smart contract can directly handle it. Because of this, the process's administrative costs will be significantly reduced. All medical record data is retained in local database storage to maintain performance and financial viability, and the hash of the data is used as the data element of each block that is added to the chain.

The data exchanges are signed using the owner's private key (patient or doctor). In such a peer-to-peer secure network, the system's block content represents the shared data ownership and viewing privileges of its users (Bozic et al., 2016). Blockchain technology supports smart contracts, which enables us to automate and track a certain system state. With the help of Ethereum blockchain smart contracts, we keep track of patient-provider interactions by connecting medical records to data retrieval instructions (essentially, information pointers) and viewing rights for external server execution. We also keep a hash function of the record on the blockchain, guaranteeing data integrity and preventing data modification.

Patients may provide their permission for their medical records to be shared amongst healthcare professionals, and healthcare professionals may add new records pertaining to a specific patient (Usman & Qamar, 2020). In both circumstances, the individual receiving the new data is notified automatically and has the option to evaluate the proposed records before the information is authorised or disapproved. The growth of their records results in participants becoming informed and involved. This system comprises a specified contract that aggregates references to each patient-provider relationship of a person in order to prioritise accessibility. This contract enables a single point of reference to verify for any changes to the

Figure 3. Workflow of the system with access control through smart contracts

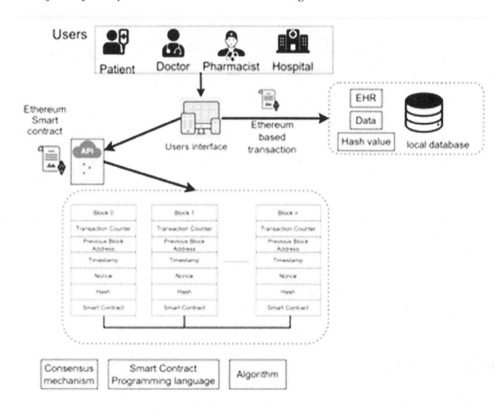

user's medical history. We use public key cryptography to implement identity verification and a DNS-like strategy to link a pre-existing and well-known form of identification, like a security number, with the user's Ethereum address (Storublevtcev, 2019). The "off-chain" data transfers between a provider database and a medical record are handled by a syncing mechanism that uses the blockchain to verify permissions through our database authentication server.

TAXONOMY OF SMART CONTRACT BASED BLOCKCHAIN

Figure 4. Blockchain-based smart contracts taxonomy

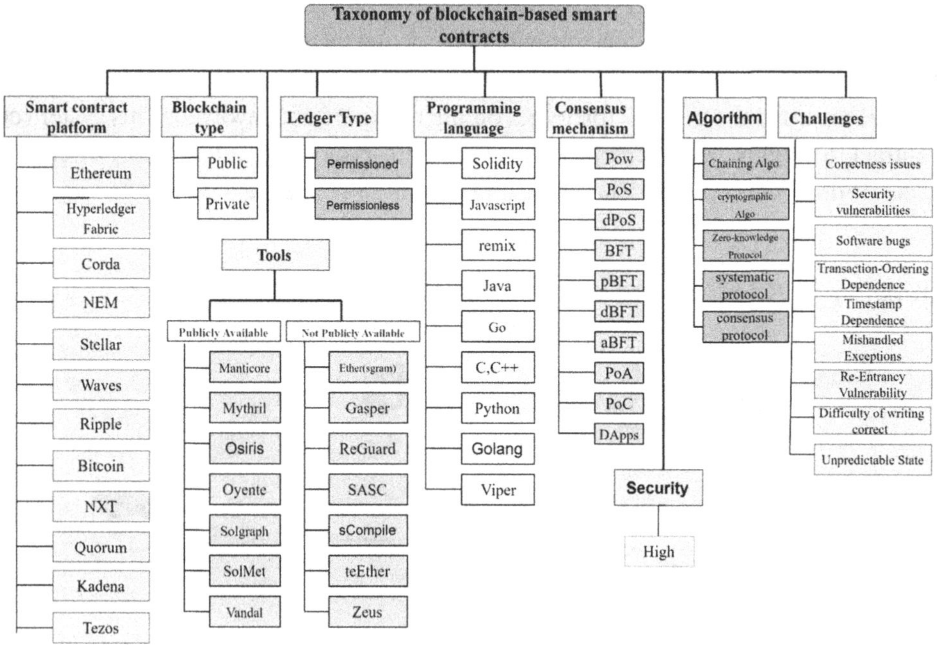

For the purpose of enabling blockchain applications, this section presents a thorough taxonomic treatment of fundamental topics. In-depth technical and practical study of blockchain-enabled smart contracts is provided in this work. Figure 4 shows a classification tree of previously published works that have been found in the literature and are categorised according to the following criteria: smart contract platform, blockchain type, ledger type, smart contract programming language, consensus mechanism, privacy, algorithm, and challenges. In this article, we present a design taxonomy that outlines dimensions and categories for classifying blockchains and the applications that use them ().

Smart Contract Platform

Several blockchain platforms allow for the creation and deployment of smart contracts. Platforms have different qualities. The most popular systems will be discussed in this part, including Ethereum and Hyperledger Fabric, NXT, NEM, Stellar, Waves, Corda, Bitcoin, Ripple, Quorum, Kadena, and Tezos (Zheng et al., 2020).

Ethereum

Ethereum is a decentralised blockchain platform that creates a peer-to-peer network for safely executing and confirmative smart contract application code. Participants can do business with one another using smart contracts without the need for the reliable central authority. Participants have complete ownership and visibility over transaction data since transaction records are irreversible, traceable, and reliably distributed across the network. Ethereum accounts that users have created both send and receive transactions (Bartoletti & Pompianu, 2017). As a cost of completing transactions on the network, a sender should sign transactions and use Ether, Ethereum's native coin. Ethereum deploys dApps, or decentralised apps, and executes smart contracts. The backend can be a smart contract in the Solidity platform and the front end can be implemented as a web application. Ethereum uses the ERC-20 and ERC-721 tokens to power smart contracts. The computation overheads in the execution of smart contracts are measured in gas. The amount of money that the user must spend in order to execute a smart contract is called the gas cost. The gas limit is the highest fee a user of a blockchain platform is prepared to pay for the execution of a smart contract.

Hyperledger Fabric

A permissioned blockchain framework built for business-grade use is called Hyperledger Fabric. For easy deployment, Hyperledger Fabric was adapted to the micro-services-based architecture. The no-sql CouchDB database served as the foundation for the ledger. Programming languages like Java, NodeJs, and GoLang can be used to create the smart contract known as Chain Code in Hyperledger terminology (Cachin, 2016). Through the use of remote procedure calls, they are connected. For the blockchain platform, Hyperledger offers a variety of specific versions and application tools. A notable example includes Hyperledger Fabric, Hyperledger Indy, and Hyperledger Sawtooth. Each version has evolved through context-specific specialisation.

NXT

A public blockchain network called NXT has pre-built smart contracts that can be used as templates. For the construction of smart contracts, NXT only supports those templates. However, because its programming language is not Turing-complete, it does not support customised smart contracts (Rhee, 2023).

NEM

The blockchain-based cryptocurrency platform NEM has a number of features that significantly increase its worth. NEM provides additional structures including document timestamping, identity verification, and custom digital asset generation (Dubey et al., 2022). If we compare the NEM to other cryptocurrencies, it has a significant potential for use in industrial applications. Beyond peer-to-peer value transfer, NEM has several potential use applications.

Stellar

A blockchain network called Stellar makes international financial transactions possible. When compared to other cryptocurrency platforms, the Stellar platform offers quicker transaction processing times. Lumen is the name of Stellar's native cryptocurrency (Yoo et al., 2019). The processing time for transactions involving the anchors notion is always under five seconds. The invention made use of the Ripple consensus algorithm-based Stellar consensus. The programming language for smart contracts is not Turing complete, but it may still be utilised to create multi-signature transactions as well as future executions.

The restriction on Turing completeness was introduced specifically to lessen the security risks associated with Turing complete programming languages.

Waves

An open-source blockchain platform for smart contracts called Waves is built on the Scala programming language. It enables users to start their own decentralised exchange and lets them establish their own cryptocurrency currency (DEX) (Dai, 2020). They have developed the idea of "custom application tokens," which are made specifically to meet the needs of the user. Users can quickly design, issue, transfer, and exchange bespoke tokens using the platform. A non-Turing complete smart contract language is used by the Waves platform. (Quasim et al., 2020).

Corda

A permissioned platform called R3 Corda can be used to install lawful contracts while protecting user privacy.The Corda platform's transactions were carried out in a way that was legally binding. Numerous industries, including finance, healthcare, and others use the platform. Flows, which are the series of actions contributing to a ledger update, specify the smart contract's execution routing. The R3 Corda platform's state serves as a representation of the smart contract that matches to actual contracts (Saraf & Sabadra, 2018).

Bitcoin

Although it has a very low computational capacity, the public blockchain platform known as Bitcoin can be utilised to handle bitcoin transactions. Bitcoin makes use of a stack-based bytecode scripting language. The ability to create complicated logic-based smart contracts using the Bitcoin programming language is extremely limited. In Bitcoin, it is feasible to use a straightforward logic that requires several signatures to confirm a single transaction just before payment is confirmed.

However, the restrictions of the Bitcoin programming language prevent building contracts with intricate logic (Macdonald et al., 2017). For instance, the scripting language for Bitcoin does not permit loops or withdrawal limitations. The only method to build a loop is to repeatedly repeat the code, which is ineffective.

Ripple

The Ripple Transaction Protocol (RTXP) or Ripple Protocol, which is constructed on a shared open network protocol consensus ledger and uses the cryptocurrency XRP, is used primarily enabling real-time gross settlement system trade and clearing. Ripple support tokens that stand in for fiat money, digital money, or any other valued asset. Depending upon a shared, public ledger that employs a consensus method, Ripple enables distributed trading, payments, and settlement (Benji & Sindhu, 2019). The Ripple website is referred to in the open-source protocol as a basic cross-bank transaction infrastructure technology. The Ripple protocol is incorporated into the systems of businesses in both the financial and non-financial sectors. A transaction must include two parties in it to take place. A licenced financial organisation that manages as well as handles money in the first instance on behalf of its clients; in the second, the market, which offers currency liquidity to aid in trading. A shared public ledger, the contents of which are decided by consensus, is the foundation of Ripple.

Quorum

Quorum implements Ethereum's permissioned ledger. Ethereum is a public, permissionless blockchain that may be used to develop decentralised applications in a range of domains.

It enables Turing-complete smart contracts, allowing for the development of general-purpose blockchain applications that cut across numerous industries. Because it is open and permissionless, its security is ensured by the Proof-of-Work (PoW) consensus algorithm and its internal token Ether. The PoW consensus mechanism on the Ethereum blockchain purposefully raises the level of cryptographic complexity. All use Ether, its cryptocurrency (Baliga et al., 2018).

Simulations on the Ethereum blockchain prevent spam and denial-of-service attacks. The Ethereum network's full nodes verify all transactions. The Ethereum platform's nodes all carry out smart contract execution. Every node uses the Ethereum Virtual Machine (EVM) to execute smart contracts in order to validate transactions that call the operations of the smart contract.

Kadena

Kadena is indeed a public blockchain platform aspires to be scalable and contains a brand-new smart contract language called Pact that has verification as well as upgradeable smart contracts. Additionally, Kadena employs a brand-new Proof-of-Work (PoW) technique called Chainweb, which consists of numerous concurrently operating, separately mined chains. Theoretically, this approach provides a large transaction throughput at the base layer without requiring any scalability or feature solutions at the second layer (Cachin, 2016).

The objective of Kadena is to create a scalable, developer-friendly public blockchain which offers security on par with Bitcoin. Kadena includes a revolutionary consensus technique, the Chainweb proof-of-work architecture, and the Pact smart contract language to fulfil this ambition. Without the aid of the any second layer scalability as well as functionality solutions, its goal is to optimise its base-layer for transaction throughput as well as developer adoption. A whole toolkit being offered on a single platform is meant to be much more developer-friendly because second layer solutions frequently make application development more difficult. The team further asserts that, based on internal tests, Kadena has no maximum limits on the number of transactions which can process each second.

Tezos

Tezos is a blockchain-based cryptocurrency and platform for building decentralised applications (dApps) with smart contracts. Tezos-smart contracts are created using Michelson language and liquidity high-level language. which is the language designed specifically for building smart contracts for the Tezos network (Allombert et al., 2019). Formal verification and security were taken into consideration when developing Tezos-smart contracts.

Blockchain Type

Decentralized applications, which have long been used in businesses to handle data, are the primary focus of blockchain technology. In addition, those who have recently become well-known and fascinating as a result of the dissemination of the concept via cryptocurrencies. Permissioned blockchains are a combination of public and private blockchains that anyone may access as long as they have permission from the administrators (Guegan, 2017). Public blockchains are accessible to everyone, private blockchains are only accessible to a select group of users.

Public Blockchain

The public blockchain is one in which that anybody is free to sign up and participate in the blockchain network's core activities. Anybody can read, write, as well as audit this same ongoing activity on a public blockchain network, that also contributes to the self-governed, decentralised nature that is frequently touted when discussing blockchain. A public network uses an incentive scheme to encourage new participants as well as maintain the system's agile (Irresberger et al., 2021). Public blockchain are an immensely useful solution for a truly decentralised, democratised, and authority-free operation.

Public blockchains are extremely valuable as they can serve as the foundation for almost any decentralised solution. Also, a secure public blockchain is shielded from data breaches, hacker attempts, and other cybersecurity problems by the enormous number of network users that join it. A blockchain is more secure the more participants it has.

Private Blockchain

Participants in private blockchain networks can only take part after being invited and having their identification or other necessary information vetted and verified. The validation is carried by by the network operator(s) or a precisely specified established protocol that the network implements using smart contracts and other automated approval techniques.

The ability to participate in the network is completely at the control of private blockchains. If the network is mining-capable, its privacy may restrict which users can operate the consensus mechanism that decides mining rights and rewards (Di Angelo & Salzer, 2019). Moreover, only particular people might have access to the shared ledger. The operator or owner has the authority to override, alter, or remove the required blockchain entries as necessary and as they deem appropriate.

Tools Used in Smart Contract

Based on their accessibility, we divide the tools for assessing smart contracts in this space into two groups:

Publicly Available

The tools focus on finding high-level bugs in smart contracts and produce a single report to highlight logic flaws including program re-entry, wrapping, as well as others. We're going to include another solidity evaluation method in this paper that executes smart contracts' symbols in detail. The publicly available tools are Remix-IDE, Manticore, Mythrill, Osiris, Oyente, Solgraph, SolMet, Vandal (Di Angelo & Salzer, 2019).

Not Publicly Available

The tools we are presenting here cannot be installed or tested since they have not been made publicly available. As the tools are not publicly available so we collect the name of the tools from different publications. The not publicly available tools are as follows, Ether(sgram), Gasper, ReGuard, SASC, sCompile, teEther, Zeus.

Types of Blockchain Ledger

The immutable structure of the Blockchain ledger and its capacity to ensure data transparency have forced an increasing number of industry verticals to research and implement it for their daily company operations. A network of interconnected blocks known as a blockchain is used to store digital data of any value (also known as a ledger). Although the public and private blockchain ledgers both have a decentralised, immutable structure, there are a few significant variations between them (Hamilton, 2020).

Public Blockchain Ledger

Everyone can join the blockchain because it is completely accessible to everyone. Every participant in the chain has complete access to read, write, and access transactions. Every node provides verification to approve each transaction because the system is decentralised and completely distributed. Once it is placed on the block, data cannot be changed or edited. Permissionless blockchains are another name for public blockchains. The most well-known examples include Bitcoin, Ethereum, etc.

Private Blockchain Ledger

It is also known as permissioned blockchains, and they have replicas of the network's users. Only the network initiator or a predetermined set of rules can allow access to a user. Once the user has given consent, they can carry out the same tasks as other users. Once more, the person who created the network decides the level of approvals. One of the major instances is Hyperledger.

Programming Languages Used to Develop Smart Contracts

As opposed to traditional software, which is developed using well-known general-purpose programming languages (like Python and Java), most smart contracts are generated using highly specialised programming languages (e.g., Solidity). The programming languages themselves were found to be a substantial barrier in our poll to the development of smart contracts. 39.7% of the participants in our survey (Parizi & Dehghantanha, 2018) indicated that this was one of their top 3 concerns. Solidity, Javascript, remix, Java, Go, C, C++, Python, Golang, Viper, and other specialised programming languages can all be used to create smart contracts.

Consensus Mechanism Used in Smart Contract

By facilitating transactions between diverse parties without the intermediaries ubiquitous in today's transactional systems, consensus is the method which allows blockchain's utopian feature. The users of the network must use a significant amount of processing effort to keep the blockchain current. Many consensus methods are in use, and more are constantly being created (Imteaj et al., 2021). The consensus mechanisms used in smart contracts are as follows: Proof of work (PoW), Proof of stake (PoS), Practical Byzantine fault tolerance (PBFT), Proof of elapsed time (PoET), Delegated proof of stake (dPoS), Delegated Byzantine Fault Tolerance (dBFT), aBFT, PoA, PoC, and DApps are examples of evidence-based techniques.

Figure 5. Challenges faced by Smart contract

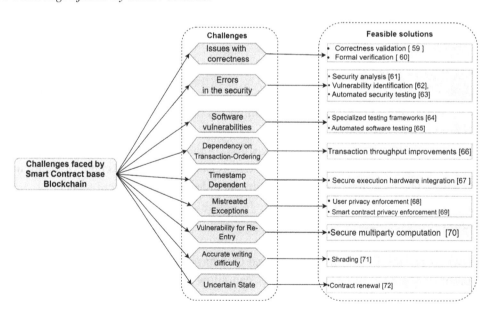

Algorithms Used in Smart Contract

To secure the smart contract, many cryptographic algorithms and chaining algorithms are used. The objective of this work was to develop an encryption algorithm using these fundamental technologies and future proven algorithms that secure real estate transactions (Xie et al., 2020).

Challenges Faced by Smart Contract

The smart contracts will ultimately be composed of computer programmes and algorithms. Smart contracts are subject to the same issues that apply to computer programmes and the traditional software development life cycle. The validation methods that are used to assess computer programmes and algorithms will also be used to validate smart contracts. Additionally, several substantial difficulties have been found that will result in functional gaps in the application (Zou et al., 2019). Figure 5 provides an overview of the problems and relevant solutions.

CONCLUSION

The paper provides a comprehensive examination of the applications for smart contacts based on blockchain. Smart contracts are notable for their importance because to their wide range of features, which include decentralisation, forging immunity, visibility, autonomous execution, and correctness. As a result, smart contracts created using blockchain technology are used in a variety of industries, including finance, healthcare, eGovernment, IoT, telephony, and many more. Ethereum, Hyperledger Fabric, Corda, NEM, Stellar, and Waves are just a handful of the blockchain platforms that can be leveraged to deliver smart contacts with special practical features into the market. Furthermore, it is projected that more platforms geared towards specialised application domains would emerge. But there are a few challenges that smart contracts must get through before widespread implementations. Some of these issues include scalability, data privacy, a lack of accountability, computational overheads, storage overheads, and network overheads. Future studies on smart contracts should focus on these challenges. The effectiveness of data consumption, transaction processing latency, and minimal memory overheads with very low latency can all be improved in the future.

REFERENCES

Ahram, T., Sargolzaei, A., Sargolzaei, S., Daniels, J., & Amaba, B. (2017, June). Blockchain technology innovations. In 2017 IEEE technology & engineering management conference (TEMSCON) (pp. 137-141). IEEE. doi:10.1109/TEMSCON.2017.7998367

Alharby, M., & Van Moorsel, A. (2017). Blockchain-based smart contracts: A systematic mapping study. arXiv preprint arXiv:1710.06372. doi:10.5121/csit.2017.71011

Allam, Z. (2018). On smart contracts and organisational performance: A review of smart contracts through the blockchain technology. *Review of Economic and Business Studies, 11*(2), 137–156. doi:10.1515/rebs-2018-0079

Allombert, V., Bourgoin, M., & Tesson, J. (2019, July). Introduction to the tezos blockchain. In *2019 International Conference on High Performance Computing & Simulation (HPCS)* (pp. 1-10). IEEE.

Amir Latif, R. M., Hussain, K., Jhanjhi, N. Z., Nayyar, A., & Rizwan, O. (2020). A remix IDE: Smart contract-based framework for the healthcare sector by using Blockchain technology. *Multimedia Tools and Applications*, 1–24.

Atzei, N., Bartoletti, M., & Cimoli, T. (2017, April). A survey of attacks on ethereum smart contracts (sok). In *International conference on principles of security and trust* (pp. 164-186). Springer, Berlin, Heidelberg. 10.1007/978-3-662-54455-6_8

Atzei, N., Bartoletti, M., & Cimoli, T. (2017). A survey of attacks on ethereum smart contracts (sok). *Principles of Security and Trust: 6th International Conference, POST 2017, Held as Part of the European Joint Conferences on Theory and Practice of Software, ETAPS 2017, Uppsala, Sweden, April 22-29, 2017 Proceedings*, 6, 164–186.

Baliga, A., Subhod, I., Kamat, P., & Chatterjee, S. (2018). Performance evaluation of the quorum blockchain platform. arXiv preprint arXiv:1809.03421.

Bartoletti, M., & Pompianu, L. (2017). An empirical analysis of smart contracts: platforms, applications, and design patterns. In Financial Cryptography and Data Security: FC 2017 International Workshops, WAHC, BITCOIN, VOTING, WTSC, and TA, Sliema, Malta, April 7, 2017, Revised Selected Papers 21 (pp. 494-509). Springer International Publishing. doi:10.1007/978-3-319-70278-0_31

Benji, M., & Sindhu, M. (2019). A study on the Corda and Ripple blockchain platforms. In *Advances in Big Data and Cloud Computing: Proceedings of ICBDCC18* (pp. 179-187). Springer Singapore. 10.1007/978-981-13-1882-5_16

Bez, M., Fornari, G., & Vardanega, T. (2019, April). The scalability challenge of ethereum: An initial quantitative analysis. In *2019 IEEE International Conference on Service-Oriented System Engineering (SOSE)* (pp. 167-176). IEEE. 10.1109/SOSE.2019.00031

Bhargavan, K., Delignat-Lavaud, A., Fournet, C., Gollamudi, A., Gonthier, G., Kobeissi, N., & Zanella-Béguelin, S. (2016, October). Formal verification of smart contracts: Short paper. In *Proceedings of the 2016 ACM workshop on programming languages and analysis for security* (pp. 91-96). ACM. 10.1145/2993600.2993611

Bigi, G., Bracciali, A., Meacci, G., & Tuosto, E. (2015). Validation of decentralised smart contracts through game theory and formal methods. *Programming Languages with Applications to Biology and Security: Essays Dedicated to Pierpaolo Degano on the Occasion of His 65th Birthday*, 142-161.

Bozic, N., Pujolle, G., & Secci, S. (2016). A tutorial on blockchain and applications to secure network control-planes. *2016 3rd Smart Cloud Networks & Systems (SCNS)*, 1-8.

Cachin, C. (2016, July). Architecture of the hyperledger blockchain fabric. In *Workshop on distributed cryptocurrencies and consensus ledgers* (Vol. 310, No. 4, pp. 1-4).

Chang, S. E., Chen, Y. C., & Lu, M. F. (2019). Supply chain re-engineering using blockchain technology: A case of smart contract based tracking process. *Technological Forecasting and Social Change*, *144*, 1–11. doi:10.1016/j.techfore.2019.03.015

Clack, C. D., Bakshi, V. A., & Braine, L. (2016). Smart contract templates: foundations, design landscape and research directions. arXiv preprint arXiv:1608.00771.

Cong, L. W., & He, Z. (2019). Blockchain disruption and smart contracts. *Review of Financial Studies*, *32*(5), 1754–1797. doi:10.1093/rfs/hhz007

Dai, C. (2020). DEX: A DApp for the decentralized marketplace. *Blockchain and Crypt Currency*, 95.

Di Angelo, M., & Salzer, G. (2019, April). A survey of tools for analyzing ethereum smart contracts. In *2019 IEEE International Conference on Decentralized Applications and Infrastructures (DAPPCON)* (pp. 69-78). IEEE. 10.1109/DAPPCON.2019.00018

Dubey, S., Subramanian, G., Shukla, V., Dwivedi, A., Puri, K., & Kamath, S. S. (2022). Blockchain technology: A solution to address the challenges faced by the international travellers. *OPSEARCH*, *59*(4), 1471–1488. doi:10.100712597-022-00597-x

Fat, J., & Candra, H. (2020, December). Blockchain Application in Internet of Things for Securing Transaction in Ethereum TestNet. *IOP Conference Series. Materials Science and Engineering*, *1007*(1), 012194. doi:10.1088/1757-899X/1007/1/012194

Fauziah, Z., Latifah, H., Omar, X., Khoirunisa, A., & Millah, S. (2020). Application of blockchain technology in smart contracts: A systematic literature review. *Aptisi Transactions on Technopreneurship*, *2*(2), 160–166. doi:10.34306/att.v2i2.97

Ferreira, J. F., Cruz, P., Durieux, T., & Abreu, R. (2020, December). Smartbugs: A framework to analyze solidity smart contracts. In *Proceedings of the 35th IEEE/ACM International Conference on Automated Software Engineering* (pp. 1349-1352). IEEE. 10.1145/3324884.3415298

Guegan, D. (2017). *Public blockchain versus private blockchain*. Academic Press.

Hamilton, M. (2020). Blockchain distributed ledger technology: An introduction and focus on smart contracts. *Journal of Corporate Accounting & Finance*, *31*(2), 7–12. doi:10.1002/jcaf.22421

Hewa, T., Ylianttila, M., & Liyanage, M. (2021). Survey on blockchain based smart contracts: Applications, opportunities and challenges. *Journal of Network and Computer Applications*, *177*, 102857. doi:10.1016/j.jnca.2020.102857

Hewa, T. M., Hu, Y., Liyanage, M., Kanhare, S. S., & Ylianttila, M. (2021). Survey on blockchain-based smart contracts: Technical aspects and future research. *IEEE Access : Practical Innovations, Open Solutions*, *9*, 87643–87662. doi:10.1109/ACCESS.2021.3068178

Imteaj, A., Amini, M. H., Pardalos, P. M., Imteaj, A., Hadi Amini, M., & Pardalos, P. M. (2021). Toward smart contract and consensus mechanisms of Blockchain. *Foundations of Blockchain: Theory and Applications*, 15-28.

Irresberger, F., John, K., Mueller, P., & Saleh, F. (2021). *The public blockchain ecosystem: An empirical analysis*. NYU Stern School of Business.

Khan, S. N., Loukil, F., Ghedira-Guegan, C., Benkhelifa, E., & Bani-Hani, A. (2021). Blockchain smart contracts: Applications, challenges, and future trends. *Peer-to-Peer Networking and Applications*, *14*(5), 2901–2925. doi:10.100712083-021-01127-0 PMID:33897937

Khatoon, A. (2020). A blockchain-based smart contract system for healthcare management. *Electronics (Basel)*, *9*(1), 94. doi:10.3390/electronics9010094

Kosba, A., Miller, A., Shi, E., Wen, Z., & Papamanthou, C. (2016, May). Hawk: The blockchain model of cryptography and privacy-preserving smart contracts. In 2016 IEEE symposium on security and privacy (SP) (pp. 839-858). IEEE.

Li, C., Palanisamy, B., & Xu, R. (2019, April). Scalable and privacy-preserving design of on/off-chain smart contracts. In *2019 IEEE 35th International Conference on Data Engineering Workshops (ICDEW)* (pp. 7-12). IEEE.

Liao, C. F., Cheng, C. J., Chen, K., Lai, C. H., Chiu, T., & Wu-Lee, C. (2017, November). Toward a service platform for developing smart contracts on blockchain in bdd and tdd styles. In *2017 IEEE 10th Conference on Service-Oriented Computing and Applications (SOCA)* (pp. 133-140). IEEE. 10.1109/SOCA.2017.26

Macdonald, M., Liu-Thorrold, L., & Julien, R. (2017). The blockchain: A comparison of platforms and their uses beyond bitcoin. *Work. Pap*, 1–18.

Macrinici, D., Cartofeanu, C., & Gao, S. (2018). Smart contract applications within blockchain technology: A systematic mapping study. *Telematics and Informatics*, *35*(8), 2337–2354. doi:10.1016/j.tele.2018.10.004

Mohanta, B. K., Panda, S. S., & Jena, D. (2018, July). An overview of smart contract and use cases in blockchain technology. In *2018 9th international conference on computing, communication and networking technologies (ICCCNT)* (pp. 1-4). IEEE. 10.1109/ICCCNT.2018.8494045

Mukhopadhyay, M. (2018). *Ethereum Smart Contract Development: Build blockchain-based decentralized applications using solidity*. Packt Publishing Ltd.

Parizi, R. M., & Dehghantanha, A. (2018). Smart contract programming languages on blockchains: An empirical evaluation of usability and security. *Blockchain–ICBC 2018: First International Conference, Held as Part of the Services Conference Federation, SCF 2018, Seattle, WA, USA, June 25-30, 2018 Proceedings*, *1*, 75–91.

Parizi, R. M., Dehghantanha, A., Choo, K. K. R., & Singh, A. (2018). Empirical vulnerability analysis of automated smart contracts security testing on blockchains. arXiv preprint arXiv:1809.02702.

Pham, H. L., Tran, T. H., & Nakashima, Y. (2018, December). A secure remote healthcare system for hospital using blockchain smart contract. In 2018 IEEE globecom workshops (GC Wkshps) (pp. 1-6). IEEE. doi:10.1109/GLOCOMW.2018.8644164

Pongnumkul, S., Siripanpornchana, C., & Thajchayapong, S. (2017, July). Performance analysis of private blockchain platforms in varying workloads. In *2017 26th International Conference on Computer Communication and Networks (ICCCN)* (pp. 1-6). IEEE. 10.1109/ICCCN.2017.8038517

Quasim, M. T., Khan, M. A., Algarni, F., Alharthy, A., & Alshmrani, G. M. M. (2020). Blockchain frameworks. *Decentralised Internet of Things: A Blockchain Perspective*, 75-89.

Raja, G., Manaswini, Y., Vivekanandan, G. D., Sampath, H., Dev, K., & Bashir, A. K. (2020, July). AI-powered blockchain-a decentralized secure multiparty computation protocol for IoV. In *IEEE INFOCOM 2020-IEEE Conference on Computer Communications Workshops (INFOCOM WKSHPS)* (pp. 865-870). IEEE. 10.1109/INFOCOMWKSHPS50562.2020.9162866

Rhee, E. (2023). Employment contract and wage payment using blockchain and smart contract. *International Journal of Internet Technology and Secured Transactions*, *13*(1), 1–10. doi:10.1504/IJITST.2023.127387

Rupa, C., Midhunchakkaravarthy, D., Hasan, M. K., Alhumyani, H., & Saeed, R. A. (2021). Industry 5.0: Ethereum blockchain technology based DApp smart contract. *Mathematical Biosciences and Engineering*, *18*(5), 7010–7027. doi:10.3934/mbe.2021349 PMID:34517569

Saingre, D., Ledoux, T., & Menaud, J. M. (2020, November). BCTMark: a framework for benchmarking blockchain technologies. In *2020 IEEE/ACS 17th International Conference on Computer Systems and Applications (AICCSA)* (pp. 1-8). IEEE. 10.1109/AICCSA50499.2020.9316536

Saraf, C., & Sabadra, S. (2018, May). Blockchain platforms: A compendium. In *2018 IEEE International Conference on Innovative Research and Development (ICIRD)* (pp. 1-6). IEEE.

Sergey, I., Kumar, A., & Hobor, A. (2018). Scilla: a smart contract intermediate-level language. arXiv preprint arXiv:1801.00687.

Sharifi, S., Parvizimosaed, A., Amyot, D., Logrippo, L., & Mylopoulos, J. (2020, August). Symboleo: Towards a specification language for legal contracts. In *2020 IEEE 28th international requirements engineering conference (RE)* (pp. 364-369). IEEE.

Sharma, A., Tomar, R., Chilamkurti, N., & Kim, B. G. (2020). Blockchain based smart contracts for internet of medical things in e-healthcare. *Electronics (Basel)*, *9*(10), 1609. doi:10.3390/electronics9101609

Singh, A., Parizi, R. M., Zhang, Q., Choo, K. K. R., & Dehghantanha, A. (2020). Blockchain smart contracts formalization: Approaches and challenges to address vulnerabilities. *Computers & Security*, *88*, 101654. doi:10.1016/j.cose.2019.101654

Sookhak, M., Jabbarpour, M. R., Safa, N. S., & Yu, F. R. (2021). Blockchain and smart contract for access control in healthcare: A survey, issues and challenges, and open issues. *Journal of Network and Computer Applications*, *178*, 102950. doi:10.1016/j.jnca.2020.102950

Storublevtcev, N. (2019). Cryptography in blockchain. In *Computational Science and Its Applications–ICCSA 2019: 19th International Conference, Saint Petersburg, Russia, July 1–4, 2019 Proceedings*, *19*(Part II), 495–508.

Treleaven, P., Brown, R. G., & Yang, D. (2017). Blockchain technology in finance. *Computer*, *50*(9), 14–17. doi:10.1109/MC.2017.3571047

Usman, M., & Qamar, U. (2020). Secure electronic medical records storage and sharing using blockchain technology. *Procedia Computer Science*, *174*, 321–327. doi:10.1016/j.procs.2020.06.093

Vardhini, B., Dass, S. N., Sahana, R., & Chinnaiyan, R. (2021, January). A blockchain based electronic medical health records framework using smart contracts. In *2021 International Conference on Computer Communication and Informatics (ICCCI)* (pp. 1-4). IEEE.

Vujičić, D., Jagodić, D., & Ranđić, S. (2018, March). Blockchain technology, bitcoin, and Ethereum: A brief overview. In *2018 17th international symposium infoteh-jahorina (infoteh)* (pp. 1-6). IEEE. 10.1109/INFOTEH.2018.8345547

Wang, S., Ouyang, L., Yuan, Y., Ni, X., Han, X., & Wang, F. Y. (2019). Blockchain-enabled smart contracts: Architecture, applications, and future trends. *IEEE Transactions on Systems, Man, and Cybernetics. Systems*, *49*(11), 2266–2277. doi:10.1109/TSMC.2019.2895123

Watanabe, H., Fujimura, S., Nakadaira, A., Miyazaki, Y., Akutsu, A., & Kishigami, J. (2016, January). Blockchain contract: Securing a blockchain applied to smart contracts. In 2016 IEEE international conference on consumer electronics (ICCE) (pp. 467-468). IEEE.

Xie, R., Wang, Y., Tan, M., Zhu, W., Yang, Z., Wu, J., & Jeon, G. (2020). Ethereum-blockchain-based technology of decentralized smart contract certificate system. *IEEE Internet of Things Magazine*, *3*(2), 44–50. doi:10.1109/IOTM.0001.1900094

Yoo, J., Jung, Y., Shin, D., Bae, M., & Jee, E. (2019, February). Formal modeling and verification of a federated byzantine agreement algorithm for blockchain platforms. In *2019 IEEE International Workshop on Blockchain Oriented Software Engineering (IWBOSE)* (pp. 11-21). IEEE. 10.1109/IWBOSE.2019.8666514

Zamani, M., Movahedi, M., & Raykova, M. (2018, October). Rapidchain: Scaling blockchain via full sharding. In *Proceedings of the 2018 ACM SIGSAC conference on computer and communications security* (pp. 931-948). ACM. 10.1145/3243734.3243853

Zheng, Z., Xie, S., Dai, H. N., Chen, W., Chen, X., Weng, J., & Imran, M. (2020). An overview on smart contracts: Challenges, advances and platforms. *Future Generation Computer Systems*, *105*, 475–491. doi:10.1016/j.future.2019.12.019

Zou, W., Lo, D., Kochhar, P. S., Le, X. B. D., Xia, X., Feng, Y., Chen, Z., & Xu, B. (2019). Smart contract development: Challenges and opportunities. *IEEE Transactions on Software Engineering*, *47*(10), 2084–2106. doi:10.1109/TSE.2019.2942301

Chapter 16
Gamification for Industry 5.0 at the Core of Society 5.0

Senthil Kumar Arumugam
https://orcid.org/0000-0002-5081-9183
CHRIST University (Deemed), India

Amit Kumar Tyagi
https://orcid.org/0000-0003-2657-8700
Department of Fashion Technology, National Institute of Fashion Technology, New Delhi, India

ABSTRACT

Gamification has become a popular approach to engage employees, customers, and other stakeholders in various industries. With the advent of Industry 5.0 and Society 5.0, the use of gamification is expected to increase, as companies and organizations look for innovative ways to enhance productivity, creativity, and collaboration. Industry 5.0 is the next phase of industrial development, characterized by the integration of advanced technologies, such as AI, IoT, and robotics, with human skills and creativity. Society 5.0, on the other hand, refers to a human-centered society that leverages technology to create solutions for social problems. This chapter explores the potential of gamification in the context of Industry 5.0 and Society 5.0. It discusses the various applications of gamification, including training, education, marketing, and sustainability. It also examines the benefits of gamification, such as increased engagement, motivation, and collaboration.

INTRODUCTION: AN OVERVIEW OF GAMIFICATION, INDUSTRY 5.0, AND SOCIETY 5.0

Industry 5.0 is the latest evolution of industrial production, where the focus is on merging human creativity and intelligence with advanced technologies such as artificial intelligence (AI), machine learning, and the internet of things (IoT). It emphasizes on the need to create a symbiotic relationship between humans and machines to optimize productivity while still emphasizing the importance of the human experience (Adel, 2022). On the other hand, Society 5.0 is a new concept that seeks to create a human-

DOI: 10.4018/978-1-6684-9919-1.ch016

Copyright © 2023, IGI Global. Copying or distributing in print or electronic forms without written permission of IGI Global is prohibited.

centered society that utilizes technology to solve social issues and improve the quality of life. Society 5.0 envisions a future where technology is utilized to enhance human well-being and happiness, and gamification is a tool that can be utilized to achieve this. The application of gamification in Industry 5.0 at the core of Society 5.0 can help to enhance productivity, creativity, and innovation while creating a positive human experience in the workplace. Gamification can motivate employees by providing feedback and recognition, creating a sense of achievement, and promoting collaboration and competition (Adel, 2022). Furthermore, gamification can also be utilized to solve social issues and improve the quality of life.

In summary, gamification has the potential to become a powerful tool in Industry 5.0 at the core of Society 5.0, helping to create a human-centered approach to work and social issues, while simultaneously leveraging technology for optimal productivity and well-being (Nahavandi, 2019). Now few of essential terms and components will be discussed here in details as:

- Gamification

Gamification is the process of using game mechanics and design elements in non-game contexts to engage and motivate people to achieve their goals(Narang et al., 2022). It is a technique used by businesses, educators, and organizations to create a more immersive and engaging experience for their users or customers. The concept of gamification is based on the idea that people enjoy playing games and are more likely to be engaged and motivated when they are given a sense of progress and accomplishment. It can be applied to various industries, such as marketing, education, health and wellness, employee training, and customer service. Some common gamification techniques include the use of points, badges, leaderboards, and rewards. Points can be awarded for completing tasks or achieving milestones, while badges can signify achievements or levels of progress. Leaderboards can encourage competition among users, and rewards can be given for reaching certain goals or milestones. Gamification has been shown to have a positive impact on engagement and motivation(Donnermann et al., 2021). It can increase participation and improve learning outcomes in education, increase customer engagement and loyalty in marketing, and improve productivity and performance in the workplace. However, gamification also has its limitations and challenges. It can be overused or poorly implemented, leading to disengagement or frustration among users. Additionally, some users may become too focused on the rewards rather than the underlying goals or objectives. In summary, gamification can be a powerful tool for engagement and motivation when used appropriately and with careful consideration of the user experience.

- Game elements

Game elements are the building blocks that make up a game, and can include mechanics, rules, objectives, challenges, feedback, narrative, aesthetics, and more(Díaz et al., 2022). Here's a brief overview of each:

- Mechanics: The rules and procedures that govern how the game is played. For example, movement, combat, or puzzle-solving mechanics.
- Rules: The guidelines and restrictions that define the boundaries of the game. For example, how players win or lose, how turns are taken, or how resources are acquired.
- Objectives: The goals that players must achieve in order to win the game. These can be short-term or long-term, and can range from collecting items to completing a story.

- Challenges: The obstacles or barriers that players must overcome to achieve their objectives. These can be both internal, such as difficult puzzles or opponents, or external, such as time limits or resource scarcity.
- Feedback: The responses that the game provides to the player's actions, such as visual, auditory, or tactile cues. Feedback can be positive or negative, and is often used to reinforce good play or discourage bad play.
- Narrative: The story or setting of the game. This can include characters, plot, world-building, and other elements that create a sense of immersion for the player.
- Aesthetics: The visual and auditory elements that give the game its distinctive look and feel. These can include graphics, sound effects, music, and other sensory inputs that contribute to the game's atmosphere.

- Game design techniques

Game design is a complex and multifaceted process, but here are some common game design techniques that designers use to create compelling, engaging, and fun games(Szczepanska et al., 2022):

- Prototyping: Prototyping is the process of creating a basic version of the game to test out gameplay mechanics, controls, and In summary game design. This can be done using paper and pen, digital tools such as Unity, or even physical materials.
- User-centered design: User-centered design involves designing the game around the needs, wants, and expectations of the player. This means taking into account the user experience (UX) and user interface (UI) design, as well as player feedback.
- Game mechanics: Game mechanics are the rules and systems that govern the behavior of the game. They can include things like scoring, player movement, combat, and puzzles.
- Storytelling: Storytelling is a key element in many games. It can include narrative elements such as plot, characters, and dialogue, as well as the visual and auditory components of the game.
- Playtesting: Playtesting involves having players test the game to identify any flaws, bugs, or areas that need improvement. This can be done in-house or by recruiting external playtesters.
- Balancing: Balancing involves tweaking the game mechanics, difficulty, and other factors to ensure that the game is challenging, but not too difficult or frustrating.
- Iteration: Iteration is the process of refining and improving the game based on feedback and testing. This can involve making small tweaks or major overhauls to the game design.
- Player motivation: Understanding what motivates players to play the game, such as achievement, exploration, socialization, or competition, can help designers create games that are more engaging and enjoyable.
- Game aesthetics: A game's aesthetics can include its visual design, sound effects, music, and other sensory elements that contribute to the game's In summary mood and atmosphere.
- Monetization: For games that are intended to generate revenue, monetization strategies must be considered, such as in-app purchases, subscriptions, or advertising.

- Industry 5.0

Industry 5.0 is a concept that has been proposed as the next phase of industrial development(Leng et al., 2022), following on from the previous phases of industry that include:

- Industry 1.0, which was characterized by the use of mechanization and water/steam power in the late 18th and early 19th centuries.
- Industry 2.0, which saw the development of mass production techniques using electricity and assembly lines in the early 20th century.
- Industry 3.0, which was marked by the introduction of computers and automation in the latter half of the 20th century.
- Industry 4.0, which involves the integration of digital technologies like the Internet of Things, artificial intelligence, and big data analytics into the manufacturing process.
- Industry 5.0 is seen as a human-centric approach to manufacturing, where machines and humans work collaboratively in the production process. This approach is thought to be necessary to address challenges like the aging workforce, growing demand for customization, and the need for sustainable production.

In Industry 5.0, robots and other automated machines are designed to work in close proximity with human workers, taking on tasks that are too dangerous, repetitive, or physically demanding for humans to perform(Maddikunta et al., 2022). Humans are then freed up to focus on more creative and complex tasks that require their cognitive skills. The goal of Industry 5.0 is to create a more harmonious and efficient relationship between humans and machines, where each can complement and enhance the capabilities of the other. It is also expected to enable greater customization and personalization in manufacturing, as machines can be programmed to produce small batches of highly individualized products.

- Society 5.0

Society 5.0 is a concept that has been proposed as a future society that would follow on from the previous four stages of societal development(Rojas et al., 2021), which are:

- Society 1.0, which was characterized by hunting and gathering.
- Society 2.0, which involved the development of agriculture and the creation of settled communities.
- Society 3.0, which was marked by the industrial revolution and the rise of mass production.
- Society 4.0, which is the current stage of societal development and is characterized by the widespread use of digital technologies and the internet.
- Society 5.0 is envisioned as a society that is based on a human-centric approach to technology, where cutting-edge technologies such as artificial intelligence, robotics, the Internet of Things, and big data are used to address the most pressing societal issues, such as aging populations, climate change, and urbanization.

In Society 5.0, technology is designed to enhance human well-being and empower individuals and communities to achieve their full potential. This is achieved by creating a seamless integration between the physical and digital worlds, where technologies are used to enhance social interaction, improve quality of life, and promote sustainability. One of the key features of Society 5.0 is the use of advanced data analytics to create a smart society that is capable of predicting and responding to societal challenges in real-time(Nair et al., 2021). For example, smart transportation systems can be used to reduce traffic congestion and improve air quality, while smart energy systems can be used to reduce carbon emissions and promote renewable energy. In summary, Society 5.0 represents a future society that is both technologically advanced and socially inclusive, where technology is used to enhance human well-being and solve some of the most pressing societal challenges of our time.

- Components of Industry 5.0 and Society 5.0

Industry 5.0 and Society 5.0 are both concepts that build upon the previous industrial and societal developments(Carayannis & Morawska-Jancelewicz, 2022). While Industry 4.0 focuses on the automation of production processes, Industry 5.0 incorporates the human factor into the manufacturing process to create a more collaborative and personalized approach to production. Society 5.0, on the other hand, aims to integrate technology and society to create a sustainable and inclusive society. The components of Industry 5.0 include:

- Human-machine collaboration: Industry 5.0 promotes collaboration between humans and machines to create a more efficient and productive manufacturing process.
- Customization and personalization: Industry 5.0 emphasizes the need for customization and personalization of products to meet the specific needs of consumers.
- Decentralization: Industry 5.0 advocates for decentralization of manufacturing, where production can take place on a smaller scale, closer to the end consumer.
- Sustainability: Industry 5.0 focuses on sustainable production practices that minimize waste and reduce the environmental impact of manufacturing.
- Artificial intelligence and automation: While Industry 5.0 emphasizes the human element in production, it still utilizes AI and automation to enhance productivity and efficiency.

The components of Society 5.0 include:

- Inclusivity: Society 5.0 aims to create an inclusive society that benefits everyone, regardless of their background or social status.
- Innovation: Society 5.0 encourages the development and adoption of innovative technologies to create new solutions to societal challenges.
- Digitalization: Society 5.0 promotes the use of digital technologies to create a more connected and efficient society.
- Sustainability: Like Industry 5.0, Society 5.0 emphasizes sustainability and the need for environmentally-friendly practices to ensure a better future for everyone.
- Human-centricity: Society 5.0 puts people at the center of its development, prioritizing their well-being and quality of life.

GAMIFICATION FOR INDUSTRY 5.0 AND SOCIETY 5.0

Gamification is the process of adding game-like elements to non-game contexts in order to increase user engagement and motivation (Triantafyllou & Georgiadis, 2022). It has been used in various industries to improve customer engagement, employee productivity, and education outcomes. With the advent of Industry 5.0 and Society 5.0, gamification has the potential to play an even greater role in transforming the way we work and live. Industry 5.0 is a concept that aims to combine the benefits of Industry 4.0 (automation and digitalization) with the human-centric approach of Industry 3.0. In Industry 5.0, human workers and machines work together in a collaborative and complementary way. Gamification can be used to incentivize workers to adopt new technologies and workflows, and to encourage collaboration and healthy competition among teams (Van der Heijden et al., 2020). For example, a manufacturing plant could use a gamified system to encourage workers to identify and report potential safety hazards or to optimize their workflow to reduce waste. Society 5.0, on the other hand, is a vision for a society that integrates cutting-edge technologies with human well-being and sustainability. Gamification can play a role in achieving these goals by encouraging behavior change and promoting social engagement (Wang, Gan, Wang et al, 2022). For example, a city could use a gamified system to incentivize citizens to reduce their energy consumption or to adopt sustainable transportation options. Gamification can also be used to promote health and wellness by encouraging physical activity and healthy habits.

In summary, gamification has the potential to be a powerful tool for driving positive change in both Industry 5.0 and Society 5.0. By leveraging game-like elements such as points, badges, and leaderboards, gamification can motivate people to adopt new behaviors, improve their skills, and work towards common goals. However, it's important to note that gamification should be designed carefully to avoid negative outcomes such as addiction, exploitation, and disengagement.

SCOPE OF GAMIFICATION FOR INDUSTRY 5.0 AND SOCIETY 5.0

Gamification can have a significant impact on Industry 5.0 and Society 5.0. Industry 5.0 refers to the integration of artificial intelligence, automation, and robotics into the manufacturing process, while Society 5.0 focuses on the use of technology to solve social issues and improve people's lives. In Industry 5.0, gamification can be used to motivate employees to learn new skills, improve their performance, and increase productivity. For example, companies can use gamified training programs to teach employees how to operate new machinery or perform complex tasks. By turning these learning experiences into games, employees may be more engaged and motivated to learn. Gamification can also be used to incentivize employees to meet productivity goals or other key performance indicators (Ana et al., 2020). By turning these goals into challenges or competitions, employees may be more likely to push themselves to perform better. In Society 5.0, gamification can be used to encourage people to participate in social and environmental causes. Overall, gamification has the potential to be a powerful tool in Industry 5.0 and Society 5.0, by motivating people to learn, work, and participate in positive social and environmental causes.

- Motivation/importance of Gamification for Industry 5.0 and Society 5.0

Gamification can play a significant role in driving positive outcomes in Industry 5.0 and Society 5.0 by motivating and engaging individuals, promoting collaboration, and driving behavior change(Tlili et al., 2023). Here are some of the key reasons why gamification is important for Industry 5.0 and Society 5.0:

- Motivating and engaging individuals: In Industry 5.0, human workers and machines work together in a complementary way. Gamification can motivate workers to adopt new technologies and work-flows and help them stay engaged with their work. In Society 5.0, gamification can encourage individuals to take action and work towards social and environmental goals.
- Promoting collaboration: In both Industry 5.0 and Society 5.0, collaboration is essential. Gamification can be used to promote healthy competition among teams, encourage knowledge sharing, and foster a sense of community among individuals working towards a common goal.
- Driving behavior change: One of the key goals of Society 5.0 is to promote sustainable behaviors and practices. Gamification can be used to encourage individuals to adopt sustainable practices such as reducing energy consumption, using public transportation, and recycling.
- Improving outcomes: By promoting motivation, collaboration, and behavior change, gamification can help organizations and communities achieve their goals more effectively. This can lead to improved outcomes in areas such as productivity, safety, environmental sustainability, and social justice.
- Enhancing learning: Gamification can be a powerful tool for education and training. By making learning more engaging and interactive, gamification can improve retention and skill develop-ment, leading to better outcomes in both Industry 5.0 and Society 5.0.

In summary, gamification can play a crucial role in driving positive outcomes in both Industry 5.0 and Society 5.0 by promoting motivation, collaboration, behavior change, and learning.

- Game mechanics

Game mechanics refer to the rules, systems, and interactions that govern how players engage with a game. These mechanics can include things like movement, combat, resource management, player abili-ties, and win/lose conditions. Game mechanics are the backbone of a game's design and are essential to creating a fun and engaging experience for players. Good game mechanics are designed to be intuitive and easy to learn, but also provide depth and complexity that allow for mastery over time (Fernandes, 2023). They should also be balanced and fair, so that players feel that their success or failure is determined by their own skill and strategy rather than luck or unfair advantages. Examples of game mechanics include:

- Health and damage systems in a combat-based game
- Movement and control in a platformer game
- Crafting and resource gathering in a survival game
- Dialogue and branching story paths in a narrative-driven game
- Point-based scoring and combo systems in an arcade-style game

- Need of Industry 5.0 and Society 5.0

Industry 5.0 and Society 5.0 are two related concepts that aim to address the challenges and opportunities presented by the Fourth Industrial Revolution (4IR). Here are some of the reasons why these concepts are needed:

- Advancing technology: The pace of technological change is accelerating, and Industry 5.0 and Society 5.0 provide frameworks for businesses and governments to manage this change and ensure that it benefits society as a whole.
- Economic competitiveness: Countries and companies that are able to leverage the benefits of the 4IR are likely to be more competitive in the global economy.
- Environmental sustainability: Industry 5.0 and Society 5.0 can help address environmental challenges by promoting the development of sustainable technologies and business practices.
- Social inclusion: These concepts aim to ensure that the benefits of technological change are shared across society, and that no one is left behind. This is particularly important in the context of rising income inequality and job displacement due to automation.
- Quality of life: Ultimately, the goal of Industry 5.0 and Society 5.0 is to improve the quality of life for individuals and communities. By promoting innovation and collaboration, these concepts can help create a more equitable, sustainable, and prosperous future.

- Design processes

Gamification can be a powerful tool to engage users, encourage desired behaviors, and promote positive outcomes (Sailer et al., 2017). The following are some design processes for gamification in Industry 5.0 and Society 5.0:

a. Identify Goals and Objectives: The first step in designing a gamification process is to identify the goals and objectives. In Industry 5.0, this could be improving productivity, increasing safety, reducing waste, or improving employee engagement. In Society 5.0, the goals could be to promote sustainable behaviors, increase civic engagement, or improve public health.
b. Define Target Audience: The next step is to define the target audience for the gamification process. This could be employees, customers, or the general public. Understanding the target audience's needs, preferences, and behaviors is crucial to designing an effective gamification process.
c. Determine Game Mechanics: The game mechanics are the rules and elements that make up the game. This includes points, badges, levels, challenges, and rewards. In Industry 5.0, game mechanics can be designed to incentivize desired behaviors, such as completing tasks, reporting safety incidents, or reducing waste. In Society 5.0, game mechanics can be designed to encourage sustainable behaviors, such as reducing energy consumption, recycling, or using public transportation.
d. Design Feedback Mechanisms: Feedback is essential to the success of a gamification process. Users need to know how they are progressing and how their actions are impacting the outcome. In Industry 5.0, feedback can be designed to provide real-time feedback on productivity, safety, or waste reduction. In Society 5.0, feedback can be designed to show users the impact of their actions on the environment, public health, or the community.

e. Test and Iterate: The final step is to test the gamification process and iterate based on feedback. It's important to monitor the effectiveness of the process and make changes as needed to improve engagement and outcomes. This could include adjusting game mechanics, feedback mechanisms, or the overall design of the process.

By following these design processes, gamification can be an effective tool to improve outcomes in Industry 5.0 and Society 5.0.

- Virtual economy

A virtual economy is a type of economic system that exists within a virtual environment, such as a video game or virtual reality world(). In a virtual economy, players or users engage in various economic activities, such as buying and selling virtual goods, earning virtual currency, and participating in virtual services. Virtual economies have become increasingly popular in recent years, particularly in online games such as World of Warcraft, Second Life, and Fortnite. In these games, players can earn virtual currency through a variety of activities, such as completing quests, selling virtual items, or participating in in-game events. Virtual economies can also have real-world implications, as some players are able to convert their virtual earnings into real money through online marketplaces and other platforms. Additionally, virtual economies can provide valuable insights into real-world economic phenomena, as researchers can study how users behave within the virtual environment and use that information to inform real-world economic policy. In summary, virtual economies represent an interesting and rapidly evolving area of study, with significant implications for both the virtual and real-world economies.

- Translational gamification

Translational gamification is the application of game design principles and mechanics to non-game contexts, such as education, health, or business. The goal of translational gamification is to use game elements to motivate and engage individuals in activities that might otherwise be perceived as dull, boring, or uninteresting. Translational gamification typically involves the use of game elements such as points, badges, leaderboards, and rewards to motivate individuals to engage in activities and to track and display their progress (Xu et al., 2022). For example, an educational app might use a game-based interface to teach math concepts, with the player earning points and unlocking new levels as they progress through the content. The use of translational gamification has become increasingly popular in a variety of fields, including education, healthcare, and marketing. In education, gamification has been used to enhance student engagement and motivation, as well as to improve learning outcomes. In healthcare, gamification has been used to encourage healthy behaviors and to improve patient adherence to treatment plans. In marketing, gamification has been used to increase customer engagement and loyalty. In summary, translational gamification represents a promising approach for motivating and engaging individuals in a variety of contexts, with the potential to improve outcomes and drive behavior change. However, it is important to ensure that game elements are used in a thoughtful and effective way, and that the underlying activity remains the primary focus.

- Gamification measurement and analytics

Gamification measurement and analytics refer to the process of assessing the effectiveness of a gamification strategy and analyzing the data collected from it to gain insights that can help improve the strategy. Gamification is the application of game design elements and mechanics to non-game contexts, such as education, marketing, or workplace training, to motivate and engage users (Siripipatthanakul & Siripipattanakul, 2023). The effectiveness of a gamification strategy can be measured using various metrics, such as user engagement, retention, completion rates, and satisfaction levels. Analytics tools are used to collect and analyze data from the gamification strategy. This data can include user behavior, game progress, user feedback, and other relevant information. By analyzing this data, gamification experts can identify areas where the strategy is successful and areas that need improvement. Gamification measurement and analytics can help organizations optimize their gamification strategies and improve user engagement and satisfaction. By understanding user behavior and preferences, organizations can make informed decisions about how to design and implement gamification strategies that are more effective in achieving their goals.

FUTURE ENABLING TECHNOLOGIES FOR GAMIFICATION

Gamification is the process of applying game-like mechanics and techniques to non-game contexts, such as education, marketing, and employee training, to motivate and engage people in achieving their goals. As technology advances, there are several emerging technologies that could have a significant impact on gamification in the future:

- Augmented Reality (AR): AR is an interactive experience that combines real-world environments with computer-generated content. It can enhance gamification experiences by creating immersive environments and interactions, allowing users to experience gamified activities in real-time.
- Virtual Reality (VR): VR is a simulated environment that can be similar or completely different from the real world. It provides a highly immersive experience that can be used to create gamified simulations for various applications, including education and training.
- Artificial Intelligence (AI): AI can enhance gamification by enabling personalized experiences and adapting to user behavior. By analyzing user data, AI algorithms can provide customized gamification experiences, providing more effective motivation and engagement.
- Blockchain: Blockchain technology can be used to create secure, decentralized platforms for gamification, providing transparency and accountability in gaming and reward systems.
- Internet of Things (IoT): IoT can be used to create intelligent and interactive environments that can enhance gamification experiences. By integrating sensors and devices, IoT can provide personalized and contextualized feedback, making gamification more engaging and effective.
- Wearables: Wearable technology, such as smartwatches and fitness trackers, can be used to create gamified experiences that promote healthy habits and behaviors. By tracking physical activity and providing feedback and rewards, wearables can provide a fun and engaging way to promote wellness.

In summary, the future of gamification will likely be shaped by these emerging technologies. By integrating these technologies into gamified experiences, we can create more personalized, immersive, and effective motivational tools that can help us achieve our goals.

- Wearable devices and systems

Wearable devices and systems refer to electronic devices that are worn on the body, typically on the wrist, fingers, head, or clothes, and are designed to collect and transmit data about the wearer's health, activity levels, and other relevant information (Vijayan et al., 2021). These devices can be used for various purposes, such as fitness tracking, monitoring vital signs, managing chronic conditions, and improving In summary health and wellness. Examples of wearable devices include smartwatches, fitness trackers, smart glasses, smart clothing, and health monitors. These devices often have sensors that measure biometric data such as heart rate, blood pressure, and sleep patterns, as well as other metrics like step count, calorie burn, and distance traveled. Wearable systems typically involve a combination of hardware, software, and data analytics. The hardware includes the wearable device itself, as well as any associated accessories or peripherals, such as chargers or syncing devices. The software may include mobile apps, web platforms, or other digital tools that enable users to view and analyze their data. Data analytics involves processing the data collected by the device and generating insights and recommendations for the user. Wearable devices and systems have become increasingly popular in recent years, as people have become more interested in tracking and improving their health and wellness. These devices have the potential to revolutionize healthcare by providing personalized, real-time data that can inform preventive care, disease management, and clinical decision-making.

- Emotion detection

Emotion detection refers to the use of technology to analyze a person's facial expressions, vocal tone, and other physiological cues to determine their emotional state (Wang, Song, Tao et al, 2022). This technology is often used in fields such as market research, advertising, and psychology, and is becoming increasingly popular in fields such as security, education, and healthcare. There are several approaches to emotion detection, including computer vision, speech recognition, and biometric sensors. Computer vision techniques involve analyzing images or video footage of a person's face to detect changes in facial expression, such as eyebrow movements, lip movements, and changes in skin color. Speech recognition techniques analyze the tone, pitch, and rhythm of a person's voice to detect changes in their emotional state. Biometric sensors, such as heart rate monitors and skin conductance sensors, can measure changes in physiological responses that are associated with emotional arousal. Emotion detection technology has a range of potential applications. For example, it can be used to monitor and improve customer service by identifying when customers are becoming frustrated or dissatisfied. In healthcare, it can be used to monitor patients' emotional state and provide personalized interventions to improve their mental health. In education, it can be used to identify students who may be struggling with emotional issues and provide them with appropriate support. However, there are also concerns about the accuracy and ethical implications of emotion detection technology. Some experts argue that the technology is not yet advanced enough to reliably detect complex emotions and that the data collected could be misused or used to discriminate against certain groups of people. As with any technology, it is important to carefully consider the potential benefits and risks before implementing emotion detection systems.

- Virtual and augmented reality

Virtual reality (VR) and augmented reality (AR) are two related but distinct technologies that offer users immersive and interactive experiences in digital environments (Kozinets, 2023). Virtual reality refers to a technology that allows users to experience and interact with a computer-generated 3D environment that feels like a real-world environment. VR typically requires the use of a headset or other specialized equipment that tracks the user's movements and adjusts the display accordingly, creating a sense of presence in the virtual environment. Augmented reality, on the other hand, overlays digital information or images onto the user's view of the real world. AR technology typically uses a camera or other sensors to track the user's location and orientation, and then adds digital content to the user's field of view in real-time. This can include things like virtual objects, text, or other visual elements.

Both VR and AR have a wide range of potential applications in areas like entertainment, education, training, and even healthcare. For example, VR can be used to create immersive gaming experiences, simulate dangerous or difficult-to-replicate training scenarios for firefighters or soldiers, or provide therapy for patients with anxiety or PTSD. AR, on the other hand, can be used to enhance the user's experience of the real world, such as by providing information about nearby landmarks or helping with navigation in unfamiliar environments.

- Virtual currencies

Virtual currencies, also known as cryptocurrencies or digital currencies, are digital assets that use cryptography to secure and verify transactions and to control the creation of new units (Yuniartik, 2023). These currencies operate independently of central banks and are decentralized, meaning they are not governed by a single authority. The most well-known virtual currency is Bitcoin, which was created in 2009. Since then, many other virtual currencies have emerged, such as Ethereum, Ripple, Litecoin, and Tether, among others. These currencies are usually traded on specialized digital platforms and can be used for a variety of purposes, including buying goods and services, investing, and speculating. Virtual currencies have several advantages, including fast and inexpensive transactions, increased privacy and security, and the potential for decentralization. However, they also face several challenges, such as regulatory issues, volatility, and the potential for fraud and hacking. As such, the use and regulation of virtual currencies are still a topic of ongoing debate and development.

- Big data intelligence and AI for gamification

Big data intelligence and AI (artificial intelligence) are powerful tools that can be used to enhance gamification (Pérez-Juárez et al., 2022). Gamification is the use of game-like mechanics, such as points, badges, and leaderboards, to motivate and engage users in non-game contexts, such as education, marketing, or health. Big data intelligence refers to the analysis of large and complex datasets to uncover patterns, trends, and insights. This can be applied to gamification by collecting and analyzing user data to better understand their behavior, preferences, and motivations. This information can then be used to tailor the gamification experience to the individual user, increasing their engagement and motivation.

AI can also be used in gamification to create more personalized and dynamic experiences. For example, AI algorithms can be used to analyze user behavior in real-time and adjust the game mechanics accordingly. This can create a more challenging and rewarding experience, as well as increase the sense of achievement and satisfaction for the user. In summary, big data intelligence and AI can help to make gamification more effective and engaging, by providing personalized and dynamic experiences that are tailored to the individual user.

- Cloud Computing for gamification

Cloud computing can be a useful tool for gamification because it provides a scalable and flexible platform for delivering and managing game-based applications (Hakak et al., 2019). Here are some ways that cloud computing can be used for gamification:

- Scalability: Cloud computing enables games to be scaled up or down as needed, without the need for additional hardware or infrastructure. This means that game developers can quickly and easily adjust the number of users, the size of the game, and the amount of data being processed to meet changing demand.
- Remote Access: Cloud computing allows games to be accessed from anywhere, anytime, on any device, as long as there is an internet connection. This means that players can access games from their smartphones, tablets, laptops, or desktops, and play at their own convenience.
- Data Management: Cloud computing can be used to store, manage, and process large amounts of game data, such as scores, user profiles, achievements, and game progress. This data can then be analyzed to gain insights into player behavior and preferences, which can be used to improve game design and user engagement.
- Collaboration: Cloud computing allows game developers to work collaboratively on game development projects, regardless of their location. This means that teams can share resources, collaborate on code, and work on different aspects of the game simultaneously.
- Cost Savings: Cloud computing can help to reduce the cost of game development by eliminating the need for expensive hardware and infrastructure. Instead, game developers can leverage cloud-based services and platforms to deliver their games more cost-effectively.

In summary, cloud computing can provide game developers with a powerful toolset for delivering engaging, interactive, and scalable game-based applications that can be accessed from anywhere, anytime, on any device.

- Blockchain Technology

Blockchain technology is a distributed database that allows multiple parties to have simultaneous access to a secure and tamper-proof ledger of transactions (Yang et al., 2020). It was originally developed for the digital currency, Bitcoin, but has since been applied to various industries and use cases. A blockchain consists of a series of blocks, each containing a list of transactions. Each block is linked to the previous block, forming a chain of blocks, hence the name "blockchain." This makes it very difficult to alter or delete any transaction without also changing all subsequent blocks in the chain, making it highly secure. One of the key features of blockchain technology is its decentralized nature. Rather than being controlled by a single entity, such as a bank or government, the blockchain is maintained by a network of computers around the world. This makes it difficult for any one party to manipulate the data on the blockchain, as any changes would need to be approved by a majority of the network. Blockchain technology has a wide range of potential applications, from financial services to supply chain management and beyond. It has the potential to revolutionize the way we store, transfer, and verify data, providing a more transparent, secure, and efficient system for many industries.

- Dew Computing

Dew computing is a new paradigm in the field of distributed computing that focuses on bringing computing resources closer to the data sources (Guberović et al., 2021). It is a concept that extends the cloud computing paradigm to the edge of the network, where data is generated, collected, and processed. Dew computing aims to address the limitations of cloud computing, such as high latency, bandwidth constraints, and security concerns. In dew computing, computing resources are distributed across the network, and the data processing and analysis are performed closer to the data source, reducing the need for data transfer to centralized data centers. Dew computing can be applied to a wide range of applications, including Internet of Things (IoT), smart cities, autonomous vehicles, and healthcare. It offers several benefits, such as improved data privacy and security, reduced network traffic, and faster processing and response times. However, it also presents new challenges, such as managing distributed computing resources, ensuring data consistency and integrity, and optimizing resource utilization.

APPLICATIONS OF GAMIFICATION

Gamification is the process of incorporating game mechanics and elements into non-game contexts to engage and motivate people to achieve their goals (Salah & Alzaghal, 2021). Here are some of the common applications of gamification:

- Education: Gamification has been widely used in education to make learning more fun and engaging. Gamification can be applied in various learning settings, from kindergarten to corporate training.
- Health and fitness: Gamification has been used in the health and fitness industry to motivate people to exercise and maintain a healthy lifestyle. Gamification elements, such as rewards and challenges, can be used to motivate people to reach their fitness goals.
- Marketing and advertising: Gamification can be used in marketing and advertising to increase customer engagement and brand loyalty. By incorporating game mechanics into marketing campaigns, companies can encourage customers to interact with their brand and products.
- Employee training and development: Gamification can be used to improve employee training and development programs. By incorporating game elements into training programs, companies can increase employee engagement and motivation, leading to better learning outcomes.
- Customer engagement: Gamification can be used to increase customer engagement and loyalty. By incorporating game mechanics into customer loyalty programs, companies can incentivize customers to engage with their brand and products more frequently.
- Product development: Gamification can be used to improve product development by providing designers and developers with feedback on how users interact with their products. By incorporating game elements into product testing and development, companies can gather valuable user data and insights.

- Social causes: Gamification can be used to raise awareness and support for social causes. By incorporating game elements into social campaigns, organizations can encourage people to get involved and take action to support social causes.

In summary, gamification can be applied to various contexts to increase engagement, motivation, and participation.

Now few of applications can be discussed in detail here as:

- Gamification in Entertainment

Gamification is the process of incorporating game-like elements into non-game contexts to increase engagement and motivate desired behaviors. In the entertainment industry, gamification is commonly used to enhance the user experience and keep consumers engaged. One popular example of gamification in entertainment is the use of loyalty programs. Many companies offer rewards programs that encourage customers to return and make more purchases, with rewards and perks being tied to certain actions or milestones. This creates a sense of achievement and progress, similar to what players experience in video games. Another example of gamification in entertainment is in mobile apps and online platforms. Many apps and websites incorporate game-like features such as points, badges, and leaderboards to keep users engaged and motivated. This can increase user retention and create a sense of competition among users, driving engagement and usage. Gamification can also be used in live events, such as concerts or festivals. By incorporating game-like elements, organizers can create more interactive experiences for attendees, increasing engagement and satisfaction. For example, some festivals have created scavenger hunts or other challenges that attendees can complete to win prizes or unlock special content. In summary, gamification is a powerful tool that can be used to increase engagement and motivation in a variety of entertainment contexts, from online platforms to live events. By incorporating game-like elements into these experiences, entertainment providers can create more immersive and engaging experiences for their customers.

- Gamification in Healthcare

Gamification is also being increasingly used in healthcare to motivate patients and promote positive health behaviors. By incorporating game-like elements into healthcare interventions, providers can make the experience more engaging and encourage patients to take an active role in managing their health. One example of gamification in healthcare is the use of health apps and wearables that track physical activity and other health metrics. These apps often use game-like features such as badges and rewards to encourage users to meet their fitness goals and make healthy lifestyle choices. Gamification is also used in patient education and adherence to treatment regimens. For example, patients with chronic diseases such as diabetes or heart disease may be given a game-like program to help them track their progress and manage their symptoms. These programs can be tailored to individual patients, making them more effective and engaging. Another application of gamification in healthcare is in medical training and education. Simulation games and virtual reality environments can be used to train medical professionals in a safe and controlled environment, allowing them to develop skills and experience without putting real patients at risk. In summary, gamification has the potential to improve patient engagement and outcomes by making healthcare interventions more engaging and motivating. By incorporating game-like elements into healthcare interventions, providers can promote positive health behaviors and help patients take an active role in managing their health.

- Gamification in Retail

Gamification is the use of game design elements and mechanics in non-game contexts to engage and motivate people to achieve their goals. Retail is one such context where gamification has been used to enhance customer engagement and drive sales. There are various ways in which gamification can be applied in retail. Some examples include:

- Loyalty Programs: Loyalty programs are a popular way to reward customers for their repeat business. Gamification can be used to enhance the experience of these programs by adding game-like elements such as points, badges, and leaderboards. Customers can earn points for making purchases, referring friends, and engaging with the brand on social media. These points can then be redeemed for discounts, free products, or other rewards.
- Interactive Displays: Retailers can use interactive displays to create a more engaging and immersive shopping experience for their customers. For example, they can use touchscreens to create games or challenges that are related to their products. These challenges can range from simple quizzes to more complex games that require problem-solving skills.
- Mobile Apps: Retailers can create mobile apps that use gamification to engage customers and drive sales. For example, they can create games that require customers to visit their stores and scan product barcodes to unlock rewards. They can also create apps that allow customers to compete with each other for prizes or discounts.
- Virtual Reality: Retailers can use virtual reality to create immersive shopping experiences that are both entertaining and informative. For example, they can create virtual reality experiences that allow customers to try on clothes, test out products, or explore different environments.

In summary, gamification can be a powerful tool for retailers to engage and motivate customers. By creating a more interactive and enjoyable shopping experience, retailers can build stronger relationships with their customers and drive sales in the process.

- Gamification in Tourisms

Gamification has become increasingly popular in the tourism industry as a way to enhance the visitor experience and increase engagement. Here are some examples of how gamification can be used in tourism:

- Scavenger Hunts: Scavenger hunts are a popular form of gamification in tourism. Visitors are given a set of clues or challenges to complete, often leading them to different locations or attractions. This encourages visitors to explore the destination and learn about its history and culture in a fun and interactive way.
- Geocaching: Geocaching is a modern treasure hunt that uses GPS technology to guide visitors to hidden caches or containers. Visitors use clues and coordinates to find the caches, which can contain small trinkets or messages left by other visitors. This encourages visitors to explore the destination and discover hidden gems.

- Virtual Tours: Virtual tours can be gamified by adding elements such as quizzes or challenges along the way. This allows visitors to engage with the content and test their knowledge while learning about the destination. .
- Mobile Apps: Mobile apps can be created to enhance the visitor experience by adding gamified elements such as scavenger hunts, quizzes, and challenges. These apps can also be used to provide visitors with personalized recommendations and to facilitate social sharing.
- Augmented Reality: Augmented reality can be used to gamify the visitor experience by overlaying digital elements onto the physical environment. For example, visitors can use their smartphone to scan a QR code or marker and reveal hidden information or interactive elements.

In summary, gamification in tourism can help to enhance the visitor experience and increase engagement. By adding fun and interactive elements, visitors are more likely to remember their experience and recommend it to others.

- Gamification in Education

Gamification is the application of game mechanics and design elements to non-game contexts, such as education, in order to increase engagement and motivation. In education, gamification can be used to enhance the learning experience by making it more interactive, immersive, and fun. Here are some ways gamification can be used in education:

- Points and badges: Students can earn points and badges for completing tasks and achieving milestones, which can serve as a source of motivation and recognition.
- Leaderboards: A leaderboard can be used to display student progress and rankings, which can create healthy competition and encourage students to work harder.
- Quests and challenges: Teachers can design quests and challenges that require students to complete tasks and solve problems in order to progress through a game-like environment.
- Simulations and role-playing: Students can participate in simulations and role-playing exercises to learn through immersive experiences that replicate real-life situations.
- Feedback and rewards: Instant feedback and rewards can be given to students for completing tasks or answering questions correctly, which can help reinforce learning and encourage continued engagement.

By using gamification in education, teachers can create a more engaging and motivating learning environment that encourages active participation and improves student outcomes. However, it is important to ensure that gamification is used in a way that supports learning objectives and is not simply a distraction from them.

- Gamification in Software Development

Gamification is also used in software development as a means to increase engagement and motivation among software developers. Here are some ways in which gamification is used in software development:

- Task completion: Developers can earn points or badges for completing tasks or achieving certain milestones. This can provide a sense of accomplishment and motivate developers to complete more tasks.
- Leaderboards: A leaderboard can be used to display the progress of different teams or individual developers. This can create healthy competition and motivate developers to work harder.
- Rewards: Developers can be rewarded with prizes or recognition for completing tasks or achieving certain goals. This can encourage developers to put in more effort and take on more challenging tasks.
- Learning and training: Gamification can be used in training programs to make learning more interactive and engaging. Developers can participate in simulations and role-playing exercises to learn new skills and improve their knowledge.
- Collaboration: Gamification can be used to encourage collaboration among developers. Teams can earn points or rewards for working together to complete tasks or solve problems.

In summary, gamification in software development can help create a more engaging and motivating work environment, which can lead to increased productivity, better quality software, and higher job satisfaction among developers. However, it is important to ensure that gamification is used in a way that supports the goals of the software development process and does not distract from them.

- Gamification in Science

Gamification is also used in science education as a means to increase engagement and motivation among students, as well as to make learning science more interactive and fun. Here are some ways in which gamification is used in science education:

- Virtual labs and simulations: Gamified virtual labs and simulations allow students to explore scientific concepts and conduct experiments in a safe, controlled environment. These tools can provide an immersive learning experience that engages students in the scientific process.
- Quests and challenges: Teachers can design quests and challenges that require students to apply scientific knowledge and solve problems in order to progress through a game-like environment. This can create a sense of achievement and motivation among students.
- Leaderboards and badges: Leaderboards and badges can be used to recognize and reward students for their achievements in science. This can foster a sense of competition and motivate students to learn more.
- Citizen science projects: Gamified citizen science projects allow students to participate in real scientific research projects and contribute to scientific knowledge. This can provide a sense of purpose and meaning to science education.
- Storytelling and role-playing: Gamified storytelling and role-playing exercises can be used to engage students in science concepts and create a memorable learning experience.

In summary, gamification in science education can help make learning science more interactive, engaging, and fun. It can also provide students with a sense of achievement and purpose, which can motivate them to continue learning about science. However, it is important to ensure that gamification is used in a way that supports learning objectives and is not simply a distraction from them.

- Gamification in agriculture

Gamification can be used in agriculture as a means to improve engagement, learning, and productivity. Here are some ways in which gamification is used in agriculture:

- Farm management games: Farm management games allow farmers and agricultural students to learn about farm management strategies in a fun and interactive way. These games can provide a safe environment to experiment with different techniques and strategies without the risk of real-world losses.
- Crop management simulations: Gamified simulations can allow farmers and agricultural students to explore different crop management scenarios and learn how different factors, such as weather, irrigation, and fertilizer, impact crop growth and yield.
- Rewards and recognition: Farmers can be recognized and rewarded for achieving certain milestones, such as improving crop yield or reducing water usage. This can encourage farmers to put in more effort and adopt more sustainable farming practices.
- Training and education: Gamified training and education programs can be used to teach farmers and agricultural students about new technologies, practices, and policies. These programs can be designed to be engaging and interactive, which can increase retention and understanding.
- Data collection and analysis: Gamification can be used to encourage farmers to collect and analyze data about their crops and farms. This data can be used to inform decision-making and improve farming practices.

In summary, gamification in agriculture can help improve engagement, learning, and productivity in the agricultural sector. It can also promote sustainability and innovation by encouraging the adoption of new technologies and practices. However, it is important to ensure that gamification is used in a way that supports the goals of sustainable and responsible farming practices.

- Gamification in any other Sectors like Military, etc.

Gamification has primarily been used in industries such as marketing, education, and healthcare, it has also been explored in military contexts. Gamification in the military is the use of virtual reality simulations for training purposes. Virtual reality simulations provide a safe and controlled environment where soldiers can practice scenarios that they may encounter in real-life combat situations. These simulations can also provide immediate feedback to soldiers, helping them to improve their skills and decision-making abilities.

Another example of gamification in the military is the use of game-based training programs. These programs use game elements such as points, badges, and leaderboards to motivate soldiers to engage with the training material. This approach has been shown to increase engagement and retention of training material, which can lead to improved performance on the battlefield. Gamification has also been explored in military recruitment efforts. For example, the US Army created a mobile game called "America's Army" to promote its recruitment efforts. The game allows players to experience the challenges and rewards of military service, and provides information about the various career opportunities available in the Army (Joy, 2017). While gamification has shown promise in military contexts, it is important to consider the ethical implications of using game elements in such contexts. For example, some have raised concerns about the potential for gamification to trivialize the serious and often life-threatening nature of military service. Additionally, there is a risk that gamification could be used to manipulate individuals into making decisions that are not in their best interests. As such, any use of gamification in military contexts should be carefully evaluated and monitored.

ISSUES AND CHALLENGES WITH GAMIFICATION FOR INDUSTRY 5.0 AND SOCIETY 5.0

Popular Issues with Gamification for Industry 5.0 and Society 5.0

Gamification is a powerful tool that has been used in various contexts to improve user engagement and motivation. However, in Industry 5.0 and Society 5.0, there are some popular issues that need to be addressed for gamification to be effective. One of the primary concerns is that gamification may lead to a short-term focus, where users are only interested in winning the game and not in achieving the long-term goals of the organization or society. Additionally, gamification may not be suitable for all types of tasks and may not be effective in motivating individuals who are not naturally inclined to play games. Another issue is that gamification can sometimes be too simplistic or may not take into account the complexities of the problem or task being addressed. Finally, gamification can be costly to implement, and the ROI may not be clear. Overall, gamification has the potential to be a powerful tool in Industry 5.0 and Society 5.0, but it is important to be mindful of these issues to ensure that it is used effectively (Rodrigues et al., 2019). Gamification, which involves the use of game design elements in non-game contexts, has gained widespread popularity in recent years for a wide range of applications, including in Industry 5.0 and Society 5.0 (Gil-Aciron, 2022). However, there are some issues associated with the use of gamification in these contexts. Here are some of the most popular ones:

- Lack of effectiveness: Gamification is not a panacea and there is little evidence to suggest that it is always effective in promoting desired behaviors or outcomes. In some cases, the use of gamification may even be counterproductive, leading to reduced motivation and engagement.
- Shallow engagement: Gamification can sometimes lead to shallow engagement, where users are primarily focused on earning points, badges, or other rewards rather than on the underlying behaviors or goals that the gamification is meant to promote.
- Over-reliance on extrinsic motivators: Gamification can sometimes rely too heavily on extrinsic motivators, such as rewards or punishments, rather than intrinsic motivators, such as a sense of purpose or mastery. This can lead to a focus on short-term goals at the expense of long-term engagement.
- Ethical concerns: There are also ethical concerns associated with the use of gamification, particularly when it comes to issues such as privacy, consent, and manipulation. For example, the use of gamification in healthcare or education could potentially lead to the exploitation of vulnerable populations.
- Cost: Gamification can also be expensive to develop and implement, particularly if it requires the creation of custom software or hardware. This can limit its accessibility to smaller organizations or communities.

- Cultural differences: Gamification may not always translate well across cultures, particularly if the game design elements are based on cultural norms or values that are unfamiliar to users in other parts of the world.
- Lack of sustainability: Gamification can also be difficult to sustain over the long term, particularly if users become bored or fatigued with the game design elements or if the underlying behaviors or goals are not meaningful or relevant to them.

In summary, while gamification can be a powerful tool for promoting engagement, motivation, and behavior change, it is important to be aware of these issues and to design gamification strategies that are grounded in research and ethics.

Challenges With Gamification for Industry 5.0 and Society 5.0

Gamification has the potential to bring about significant benefits for Industry 5.0 and Society 5.0, such as increased productivity, engagement, and social impact. However, there are also several challenges associated with gamification in these contexts. Here are some of the key challenges:

- Resistance to change: One of the primary challenges of gamification in Industry 5.0 and Society 5.0 is resistance to change. Many workers or individuals may be resistant to adopting new technologies or ways of working, particularly if they perceive the changes as threatening or unnecessary.
- Lack of alignment with organizational goals: Gamification strategies may not always be aligned with the broader goals of an organization or society, leading to a lack of effectiveness or even counterproductive outcomes.
- Limited impact on behavior change: While gamification can be effective at promoting short-term behavior change, it may not always lead to sustained or meaningful change over the long term.
- Accessibility barriers: Gamification strategies may not be accessible to all members of a given community or organization, particularly those who do not have access to the necessary technology or resources.
- Measurement and evaluation: Measuring the impact of gamification on productivity, engagement, and social impact can be challenging, particularly if the outcomes are difficult to quantify or if there are confounding factors that make it difficult to isolate the effects of gamification.
- Data privacy and security: Gamification often involves the collection and use of personal data, which can raise concerns around data privacy and security.
- Integration with existing systems: Integrating gamification strategies with existing systems or processes can be complex, particularly if the gamification requires significant changes to these systems or processes.

In summary, gamification has the potential to bring about significant benefits for Industry 5.0 and Society 5.0, but it is important to be aware of these challenges and to design gamification strategies that are grounded in research, ethics, and careful consideration of the specific context in which they will be implemented.

FUTURE OF GAMIFICATION

The future of gamification is likely to be shaped by a combination of technological advancements, evolving user preferences, and changing business needs. Here are some possible trends and developments that could define the future of gamification:

- Increased use of Virtual Reality (VR) and Augmented Reality (AR): VR and AR technologies have already made significant strides in recent years, and they are expected to become more sophisticated and widely adopted in the future. These technologies can provide immersive and interactive gaming experiences, allowing users to engage with digital environments in more realistic and engaging ways.
- More personalized and adaptive game mechanics: As data analytics and machine learning technologies continue to advance, gamification systems will be able to deliver more personalized experiences based on individual user preferences, behaviors, and performance. This could include adaptive game mechanics that adjust the difficulty level, pacing, or content of a game based on the user's performance.
- Greater integration with social media and online communities: Gamification systems will likely become more closely integrated with social media platforms and online communities, allowing users to share their achievements, compete with friends, and join online communities centered around specific games or activities.
- Expansion into new areas and industries: Gamification has already found applications in a wide range of industries, from education and healthcare to finance and retail. As the benefits of gamification become more widely recognized, it is likely that new applications and use cases will emerge, opening up new markets and opportunities for gamification developers and providers.
- Ethical considerations and responsible use: As gamification becomes more widespread and influential, there will be growing scrutiny and concern over its ethical implications and potential for exploitation. This could lead to increased regulation and oversight, as well as a greater emphasis on responsible and ethical use of gamification in business and other contexts.

Now the future of gamification with respect to business, technology, etc., perspective is explained as:

- Future of Gamification: Business Perspective

From a business perspective, the future of gamification is likely to be driven by several key trends and developments. Here are some possible ways in which gamification could evolve in the business world:

- Greater focus on employee engagement and productivity: As businesses continue to face challenges around employee engagement and productivity, gamification can offer a way to motivate and incentivize workers. In the future, we could see more companies using gamification to encourage collaboration, boost morale, and drive performance.
- Increased use of data analytics and machine learning: Data analytics and machine learning are already playing a significant role in gamification, allowing businesses to analyze user behavior, personalize experiences, and optimize game mechanics. In the future, we could see even more sophisticated use of these technologies to drive engagement and improve outcomes.

- Expansion into new markets and industries: Gamification has already been adopted by a wide range of industries, including healthcare, education, and finance. In the future, we could see even more diverse applications of gamification, as businesses seek to engage customers and employees in new and innovative ways.

- Integration with other technologies and platforms: Gamification is likely to become more closely integrated with other technologies and platforms, such as social media, virtual reality, and augmented reality. This could provide new opportunities for businesses to engage users in more immersive and interactive experiences.

- Greater emphasis on responsible and ethical use: As gamification becomes more widely adopted, there will be growing concerns about its ethical implications, particularly around issues such as privacy, data security, and addiction. In the future, we could see more emphasis on responsible and ethical use of gamification, as businesses seek to balance the benefits of engagement with the need to protect user rights and well-being.
  - Future of Gamification: Technology Perspective

From a technology perspective, the future of gamification is likely to be shaped by several key trends and developments. Here are some possible ways in which gamification could evolve from a technological standpoint:

- Continued growth in mobile and cloud computing: Mobile devices and cloud computing have already played a significant role in the growth of gamification, allowing users to access games and other gamified experiences from anywhere and on any device. In the future, we can expect even greater use of these technologies, as more users rely on mobile devices and cloud-based applications for their computing needs.

- Advancements in artificial intelligence and machine learning: Artificial intelligence (AI) and machine learning (ML) are already being used to personalize gamification experiences, optimize game mechanics, and analyze user behavior. In the future, we could see even greater use of these technologies to create more engaging and immersive gamification experiences.

- Greater use of virtual and augmented reality: Virtual and augmented reality technologies have the potential to revolutionize gamification, providing more immersive and interactive experiences. In the future, we can expect to see more gamification applications that leverage these technologies to create new and innovative experiences.

- Blockchain technology: Blockchain technology has the potential to create new opportunities for gamification, particularly around issues such as rewards and incentivization. In the future, we could see more gamification systems that rely on blockchain technology to provide secure, transparent, and decentralized reward systems.

- Integration with the Internet of Things (IoT): The Internet of Things (IoT) is already being used to create gamified experiences in areas such as fitness and health. In the future, we could see even greater use of IoT technologies to create gamification experiences that are more closely integrated with our daily lives and activities.

Overall, the future of gamification is likely to be driven by the continued evolution of technology, as well as the increasing recognition of the benefits that gamification can offer in a variety of industries and applications. As such, it is an exciting time for those interested in the field, and we can expect to see continued innovation and growth in the years to come (Koivisto & Hamari, 2019).

- Other Possible Future Directions for Industry 5.0 and Society 5.0

Industry 5.0 and Society 5.0 are concepts that aim to integrate advanced technologies into the economy and society in a way that benefits people and the environment. Here are some possible future directions for Industry 5.0 and Society 5.0:

- Increased emphasis on sustainability: As concerns about climate change and environmental degradation continue to grow, we could see Industry 5.0 and Society 5.0 placing a greater emphasis on sustainability. This could involve the development of new technologies and systems that minimize resource consumption, reduce waste, and promote sustainable lifestyles.
- Greater use of artificial intelligence and robotics: Artificial intelligence and robotics are already playing an increasingly important role in Industry 5.0, enabling automation and greater efficiency. In the future, we could see even more sophisticated use of these technologies, with AI and robotics playing a key role in areas such as healthcare, transportation, and manufacturing.
- Increased focus on social inclusion: Society 5.0 aims to create a more inclusive and equitable society, where everyone can benefit from technological advances. In the future, we could see more efforts to ensure that the benefits of Industry 5.0 are distributed more evenly, with a greater emphasis on addressing issues such as inequality and social exclusion.
- Development of new business models: Industry 5.0 could lead to the development of new business models that are more focused on collaboration, open innovation, and social impact. This could involve the creation of new platforms and ecosystems that enable businesses to work together to create value and address social and environmental challenges.
- Greater use of virtual and augmented reality: Virtual and augmented reality technologies could play a greater role in Industry 5.0 and Society 5.0, providing new opportunities for immersive and interactive experiences. This could include the use of VR and AR in areas such as education, entertainment, and healthcare.

Few of other importance opportunities are:

- Decentralized Economy

A decentralized economy refers to an economic system where the control and decision-making power are distributed among a network of participants, rather than being centralized in the hands of a few individuals or institutions (Bellavitis et al., 2022). In a decentralized economy, participants interact with each other through a peer-to-peer network, using blockchain technology or other decentralized systems. Transactions are verified and recorded on a distributed ledger, which is maintained by all network participants. This eliminates the need for intermediaries, such as banks or governments, to facilitate transactions and enforce rules. Decentralized economies are often associated with cryptocurrencies, such as Bitcoin, which operate independently of central banks and traditional financial institutions. However, decentralized economies can also include other types of decentralized applications, such as decentralized marketplaces, social networks, and governance systems. Agents/ people of decentralized economies argue that they offer greater transparency, security, and democratization compared to centralized systems. They also allow for greater innovation, as developers can build on top of existing decentralized infrastructure without needing permission from centralized authorities. However, decentralized economies also face challenges, such as scalability, regulatory uncertainty, and security risks.

- Decentralized Web

The decentralized web, also known as Web 3.0, is a vision for the future of the internet that aims to create a more open, secure, and user-centric web. Unlike the current centralized web, where data and services are controlled by a few powerful companies, the decentralized web is designed to give users greater control over their data and enable more peer-to-peer interactions. The decentralized web is built on a combination of technologies, including blockchain, peer-to-peer networking, and distributed computing. It allows users to interact directly with each other, without relying on centralized intermediaries such as social media platforms, search engines, or cloud storage providers. One of the main goals of the decentralized web is to enable users to control their own data and digital identity. This means that users would have the ability to choose where their data is stored and who has access to it, without relying on centralized platforms (Giordani et al., 2020). Additionally, the decentralized web aims to provide more privacy and security for users, by encrypting data and using decentralized authentication mechanisms. Other potential benefits of the decentralized web include greater resilience to censorship and network failures, as well as the ability to create more robust and open marketplaces for digital goods and services.

Note that while the decentralized web is still in its early stages of development, there are already a number of projects and platforms working towards this vision, such as IPFS, Ethereum, and Solid. However, there are also challenges to be overcome, such as scalability, usability, and interoperability, before the decentralized web can become a mainstream reality.

- Decentralized Cloud computing Services

Decentralized cloud computing services refer to the provision of cloud computing services through a decentralized network of computers, rather than relying on a centralized data center owned by a single company. In decentralized cloud computing, computing resources such as storage, processing power, and memory are distributed across a network of nodes, allowing users to access computing resources from multiple locations. One of the benefits of decentralized cloud computing is that it can be more cost-effective than traditional cloud computing, as it allows users to leverage computing resources that may otherwise be idle or underutilized. Additionally, decentralized cloud computing can be more secure, as data is distributed across multiple nodes, reducing the risk of a single point of failure. There are several decentralized cloud computing services available in the market, such as:

- Storj: Storj is a decentralized cloud storage platform that enables users to store their data across a network of nodes.
- Golem: Golem is a decentralized computing platform that enables users to rent out their unused computing resources to others on the network.
- Filecoin: Filecoin is a decentralized storage network that enables users to store and retrieve data across a network of nodes.

- MaidSafe: MaidSafe is a decentralized data storage and communications network that enables users to store and share data securely.

In summary, decentralized cloud computing services offer a promising alternative to traditional cloud computing, and are likely to play an increasingly important role in the future of computing.

- Evolution of 6G

6G is the sixth generation of wireless technology, which is still in the early stages of development (Giordani et al., 2020). While it is difficult to predict the exact evolution of 6G technology, it is expected to build on the advancements of 5G and bring even faster speeds, greater capacity, and lower latency. Here are some of the potential features and innovations that could be part of the evolution of 6G technology:

- Terahertz (THz) frequencies: 6G is expected to use higher frequency bands, including terahertz frequencies, to enable faster data transfer speeds.
- Artificial Intelligence (AI) and Machine Learning (ML): 6G is likely to incorporate AI and ML technologies to optimize network performance and enhance user experiences.
- Quantum Computing: The use of quantum computing could enhance the security of 6G networks, making them more resistant to cyberattacks.
- Integrated Satellite Networks: 6G could integrate satellite networks with terrestrial networks, enabling better coverage and connectivity, especially in remote areas.
- Holographic Communications: 6G may incorporate holographic technology to enable more immersive communications, such as holographic video calls.
- Wearable and Implantable Devices: 6G could facilitate the development of more advanced wearable and implantable devices, such as smart sensors, that rely on faster and more reliable connectivity.

In summary, the evolution of 6G technology is expected to bring significant improvements to wireless communications, enabling new applications and use cases that are not possible with current technology. However, it is important to note that the development and deployment of 6G technology will take several years and will require significant investments in research and development.

- Emergence of Digital Twin Technology

Digital twin technology is a relatively new concept that has emerged in the last decade. It refers to a virtual replica of a physical object or system, which can be used for simulation, analysis, and optimization. The idea of a digital twin was first introduced by Michael Grieves, a professor at the University of Michigan, in 2002. Since then, digital twin technology has evolved to include the use of real-time data and advanced analytics to create a digital representation of a physical object or system. This technology has been applied in various fields, including manufacturing, healthcare, and transportation, to improve efficiency, reduce costs, and enhance performance. The emergence of the Internet of Things (IoT) has also played a significant role in the development of digital twin technology. With the proliferation of sensors and connected devices, it has become easier to collect and analyze data from physical systems in real-time, making it possible to create accurate digital twins that can be used for predictive maintenance and other applications. In summary, digital twin technology has the potential to revolutionize the way we design, build, and operate complex systems, leading to greater efficiency, sustainability, and innovation in various industries.

- Emerging of AI- Blockchain-IoT based Smart Environment

AI-Blockchain-IoT based Smart Environment refers to the integration of Artificial Intelligence (AI), Blockchain, and the Internet of Things (IoT) to create a more efficient, sustainable, and secure environment. This technology is being developed to address the challenges of climate change, resource depletion, and environmental degradation. The AI component of the Smart Environment involves the use of machine learning algorithms to analyze and interpret data from sensors and other IoT devices. This data can be used to optimize energy consumption, reduce waste, and improve resource efficiency. The Blockchain component of the Smart Environment provides a secure and transparent way to store and share data between different stakeholders (Fang et al., 2022). Blockchain technology can be used to create a distributed ledger that records all the transactions and interactions between the various devices and entities in the Smart Environment. This creates a tamper-proof and immutable record that can be used to verify the authenticity and integrity of the data. The IoT component of the Smart Environment involves the use of sensors and other connected devices to collect data on various environmental parameters, such as air quality, water quality, and temperature. This data can be analyzed in real-time using AI algorithms, and actions can be taken to improve the environment based on the insights gained. In summary, the integration of AI, Blockchain, and IoT in a Smart Environment has the potential to transform the way we manage and protect our environment, leading to greater sustainability, efficiency, and innovation.

CONCLUSION

In conclusion, gamification has emerged as a promising approach to engage and motivate stakeholders in various industries, including education, healthcare, and manufacturing. With the advent of Industry 5.0 and Society 5.0, the use of gamification is expected to increase, as companies and organizations seek to leverage advanced technologies to create innovative solutions to complex challenges. This paper has explored the potential of gamification in the context of Industry 5.0 and Society 5.0, highlighting the various applications and benefits of this approach, as well as the challenges and limitations that need to be addressed. This paper has also provided examples of successful gamification initiatives and discussed the key factors that contribute to their effectiveness, such as careful design, alignment with user needs and goals, and ethical considerations. In summary, the paper suggests that gamification can play a significant role in enhancing productivity, creativity, and collaboration in Industry 5.0 and Society 5.0, but emphasizes the importance of a thoughtful and strategic approach to gamification, based on a deep understanding of user needs and behaviors, and aligned with the In summary goals and values of the organization. By adopting such an approach, companies and organizations can leverage gamification to drive innovation and positive social impact in a rapidly changing world.

REFERENCES

Adel, A. (2022). Future of industry 5.0 in society: Human-centric solutions, challenges and prospective research areas. *J Cloud Comp*, *11*(1), 40. doi:10.118613677-022-00314-5

Al-Gnbri M. (2022). Accounting and auditing in the metaverse world from a virtual reality perspective: A future research. *Journal of Metaverse*, *2*(1), 29–41.

Ana C., Junior, E., & Gewehr, B. B. (2020). Prospects for using gamification in Industry 4.0. *Thematic Section - Present and Future of Production*, *30*.

Bellavitis, C., Fisch, C., & Momtaz, P. P. (2022). The rise of decentralized autonomous organizations (DAOs): A first empirical glimpse. *Venture Capital*, 1–17.

Carayannis, E. G., & Morawska-Jancelewicz, J. (2022). The futures of Europe: Society 5.0 and Industry 5.0 as driving forces of future universities. *Journal of the Knowledge Economy*, *13*(4), 1–27. doi:10.100713132-021-00854-2

Díaz, R. L. S., Ruiz, G. R., Bouzouita, M., & Coninx, K. (2022). Building blocks for creating enjoyable games—A systematic literature review. *International Journal of Human-Computer Studies*, *159*, 102758. doi:10.1016/j.ijhcs.2021.102758

Donnermann, M., Lein, M., Messingschlager, T., Riedmann, A., Schaper, P., Steinhaeusser, S., & Lugrin, B. (2021). Social robots and gamification for technology supported learning: An empirical study on engagement and motivation. *Computers in Human Behavior*, *121*, 106792. doi:10.1016/j.chb.2021.106792

Fang, X., Wang, H., Liu, G., Tian, X., Ding, G., & Zhang, H. (2022). Industry application of digital twin: From concept to implementation. *International Journal of Advanced Manufacturing Technology*, *121*(7-8), 4289–4312. doi:10.100700170-022-09632-z

Fernandes, D. L. S. (2023). *Designing player agency experiences for environmental awareness gameplay* [PhD diss.]. UMA.

Gil-Aciron, L. A. (2022). The gamer psychology: A psychological perspective on game design and gamification. *Interactive Learning Environments*, 1–25. doi:10.1080/10494820.2022.2082489

Giordani, M., Polese, M., Mezzavilla, M., Rangan, S., & Zorzi, M. (2020). Toward 6G networks: Use cases and technologies. *IEEE Communications Magazine*, *58*(3), 55–61. doi:10.1109/MCOM.001.1900411

Guberović, E., Lipić, T., & Čavrak, I. (2021). Dew intelligence: Federated learning perspective. In *2021 IEEE 45th Annual Computers, Software, and Applications Conference (COMPSAC)*, (pp. 1819-1824). IEEE. 10.1109/COMPSAC51774.2021.00274

Hakak, S., Nurul, F. M. N., Ayub, M. N., Affal, H., Hussin, N., & Imran, M. (2019). Cloud-assisted gamification for education and learning–Recent advances and challenges. *Computers & Electrical Engineering*, *74*, 22–34. doi:10.1016/j.compeleceng.2019.01.002

Joy, M. (2017). An investigation into gamification as a tool for enhancing recruitment process. *Ideal Research An International Multidisciplinary e -Journal*, *3*(1).

Koivisto, J., & Hamari, J. (2019). The rise of motivational information systems: A review of gamification research. *International Journal of Information Management*, *45*, 191–210. doi:10.1016/j.ijinfomgt.2018.10.013

Kozinets, R. V. (2023). Immersive netnography: A novel method for service experience research in virtual reality, augmented reality and metaverse contexts. *Journal of Service Management*, *34*(1), 100–125. doi:10.1108/JOSM-12-2021-0481

Leng, J., Sha, W., Wang, B., Zheng, P., Zhuang, C., Liu, Q., Wuest, T., Mourtzis, D., & Wang, L. (2022). Industry 5.0: Prospect and retrospect. *Journal of Manufacturing Systems*, *65*, 279–295. doi:10.1016/j.jmsy.2022.09.017

Maddikunta, P. K. R., Pham, Q.-V., B, P., Deepa, N., Dev, K., Gadekallu, T. R., Ruby, R., & Liyanage, M. (2022). Industry 5.0: A survey on enabling technologies and potential applications. *Journal of Industrial Information Integration*, *26*, 100257. doi:10.1016/j.jii.2021.100257

Nahavandi, S. (2019). *Industry 5.0—A Human-Centric Solution*. Institute for Intelligent Systems Research and Innovation. doi:10.3390u11164371

Nair, M. M., Tyagi, A. K., & Sreenath, N. (2021). The future with industry 4.0 at the core of society 5.0: Open issues, future opportunities and challenges. In 2021 international conference on computer communication and informatics (ICCCI), (pp. 1-7). IEEE. doi:10.1109/ICCCI50826.2021.9402498

Narang, S., Bhardwaj, G., & Srivastava, A. P. (2022). Gamification in HRM: An Overview. *ECS Transactions*, *107*(1), 3573–3580. doi:10.1149/10701.3573ecst

Pérez-Juárez, M. A., Aguiar-Pérez, J. M., Alonso-Felipe, M., Del-Pozo-Velázquez, J., Rozada-Raneros, S., & Barrio-Conde, M. (2022). Exploring the Possibilities of Artificial Intelligence and Big Data Techniques to Enhance Gamified Financial Services. In Next-Generation Applications and Implementations of Gamification Systems, (pp. 187-204). IGI Global. doi:10.4018/978-1-7998-8089-9.ch010

Rodrigues, L. F., Oliveira, A., & Rodrigues, H. (2019). Main gamification concepts: A systematic mapping study. *Heliyon*, *5*(7), e01993. doi:10.1016/j.heliyon.2019.e01993 PMID:31360779

Rojas, N., Carolina, G. A. A. P., Diego, F. L. B., & Carlos, A. T. R. (2021). Society 5.0: A Japanese concept for a superintelligent society. *Sustainability*, *13*(12), 6567. doi:10.3390u13126567

Sailer, M., Hense, J. U., Mayr, S. K., & Mandl, H. (2017). How gamification motivates: An experimental study of the effects of specific game design elements on psychological need satisfaction. *Computers in Human Behavior*, *69*, 371–380. doi:10.1016/j.chb.2016.12.033

Salah, O. H., & Alzaghal, Q. K. (2021). A Conceptual Model for Implementing Gamification in Education and Its Impact on Academic Performance. In *Innovation of Businesses, and Digitalization during Covid-19 Pandemic: Proceedings of The International Conference on Business and Technology (ICBT 2021)*, (pp. 765-775). Cham: Springer International Publishing.

Siripipatthanakul, S., & Siripipattanakul, S. (2023). Gamification and Edutainment in 21st Century Learning. Multidisciplinary Approaches to Research, 2, 210-219.

Szczepanska, T., Antosz, P., Berndt, J. O., Borit, M., Chattoe-Brown, E., Mehryar, S., Meyer, R., Onggo, S., & Verhagen, H. (2022). GAM on! Six ways to explore social complexity by combining games and agent-based models. *International Journal of Social Research Methodology, 25*(4), 541–555. doi:10.1 080/13645579.2022.2050119

Tlili, A., Huang, R., & Kinshuk, X. (2023). Metaverse for climbing the ladder toward 'Industry 5.0' and 'Society 5.0'? *Service Industries Journal, 43*(3-4), 1–28. doi:10.1080/02642069.2023.2178644

Triantafyllou, S. A., & Georgiadis, C. K. (2022). Gamification Design Patterns for User Engagement. *Informatics in Education, 21*(4), 655–674. doi:10.15388/infedu.2022.27

Van der Heijden, B. I. J. M., Burgers, M. J., Kaan, A. M., Lamberts, B. F., & Koen Migchelbrink, R. C. P. M. (2020). Van den Ouweland, and T. Meijer. "Gamification in dutch businesses: An explorative case study. *SAGE Open, 10*(4), 2158244020972371. doi:10.1177/2158244020972371

Vijayan, V., Connolly, J. P., Condell, J., McKelvey, N., & Gardiner, P. (2021). Review of wearable devices and data collection considerations for connected health. *Sensors (Basel), 21*(16), 5589. doi:10.339021165589 PMID:34451032

Wang, W., Gan, H., Wang, X., Lu, H., & Huang, Y. (2022). Initiatives and challenges in using gamification in transportation: A systematic mapping. *European Transport Research Review, 14*(1), 1–19. doi:10.118612544-022-00567-w

Wang, Y., Song, W., Tao, W., Liotta, A., Yang, D., Li, X., Gao, S., Sun, Y., Ge, W., Zhang, W., & Zhang, W. (2022). A systematic review on affective computing: Emotion models, databases, and recent advances. *Information Fusion, 83-84*, 19–52. doi:10.1016/j.inffus.2022.03.009

Xu, L., Shi, H., Shen, M., Ni, Y., Zhang, X., Pang, Y., Yu, T., Lian, X., Yu, T., Yang, X., & Li, F. (2022). The effects of mHealth-based gamification interventions on participation in physical activity: Systematic review. *JMIR mHealth and uHealth, 10*(2), e27794. doi:10.2196/27794 PMID:35113034

Yang, J., Wen, J., Jiang, B., & Wang, H. (2020). Blockchain-based sharing and tamper-proof framework of big data networking. *IEEE Network, 34*(4), 62–67. doi:10.1109/MNET.011.1900374

Yuniartik, Y. (2023). Bitcoin Cryptocurrency Practices Sharia Maqashid Perspective. *International Journal of Humanities, Social Sciences And Business, 2*(1), 1–10.

Chapter 17
Study on Blockchain-Integrated IoT:
Reorientation With Amalgamation of Heterogenic Devices

Moumita Sarkar
Brainware University, India

Sandip Roy
https://orcid.org/0000-0002-5447-803X
JIS University, India

Rajesh Bose
JIS University, India

ABSTRACT

The continuous development of interconnected devices is reconstructing livelihood and with the emergence of advanced technology yields growth in the usage of IoT devices. Though it is revolutionary and brings convenience, it faces different security challenges. The transition from traditional to smart in varieties of sectors makes the use of IoT technologies to become an integral part of lives which obviously requires a protection shield that can be offered by Blockchain. Blockchain's protected decentralization overcomes different hazards the IoT structure is facing. In this chapter, the authors have represented a detailed study on IoT, its layer and applications, a comparative analysis of different security threats, how an association with blockchain would mitigate different shortcomings of present IoT architecture, and the issues that exist in Blockchain-associated IoT.

DOI: 10.4018/978-1-6684-9919-1.ch017

Copyright © 2023, IGI Global. Copying or distributing in print or electronic forms without written permission of IGI Global is prohibited.

INTRODUCTION

To understand the prospect of Blockchain-associated IoT, a clear understanding of both technologies is crucial. In the year 1999, the great computer scientist Kevin Ashton coined the term Internet of Things (IoT). He proposed attaching an RFID (Radio Frequency Identifier) tag to the object to track it online. IoT gained momentum as devices with embedded sensors and connectivity capabilities began to proliferate. The rapid growth of IoT may lead to the Internet of Everything. Blockchain's distributed nature offers a secure and transparent way to address IoT's challenges, enhancing trust and security in data sharing. This article aims to explore the dynamic relationship between Blockchain and IoT, the potential advantage of merging blockchain with IoT, exploring how this synergy can revolutionize industries, elevate data integrity, and cover the way for a more interconnected and secure world. Additionally, it seeks to shed light on the challenges and limitations that arise in implementing blockchain in IoT environments with a probable solution given by many researchers.

NEED FOR IOT IN THE CURRENT MARKET

IoT is a driving force in today's connected world, offering businesses and consumers opportunities for growth, efficiency, and innovation. Addressing key areas in the market is essential.

- **Enhanced Connectivity:** IoT enables seamless communication between devices, systems, and users, facilitating real-time data exchange and analysis.
- **Smart Automation:** IoT drives efficiency and cost reduction through intelligent device integration and process automation.
- **Data-Driven Insights:** IoT generates valuable data for informed decision-making and innovation.
- **Industry Transformation:** IoT revolutionizes healthcare, manufacturing, agriculture, and transportation with remote monitoring and predictive maintenance.
- **Improved Quality of Life:** IoT innovations enhance daily living through smart homes, wearables, and health monitoring, promoting convenience and safety.

The Internet of Things (IoT) is the arrangement of interconnected devices and sensing devices built into our daily lives. In 2005, the ITU officially recognized the IoT concept. McEwen et al. (2013) proposed an equation that describes vital components of the IoT:

IoT = Physical Object + Controller, Sensor, and Actuators + Internet (as shown in Figure 1).

The definition of IoT has been changed to the following equation by Atzori et al. (2017).

IoT = Sensors + Data + Services + Networks (as shown in Figure 2).

Earth is adapting to the rapidly embryonic technologies along with the interconnection of different heterogeneous devices and technologies, which is pushing us continuously toward the use of IoT. Figure 3 shows the advantages of IoT.

Figure 1. Constituents of the Internet of Things

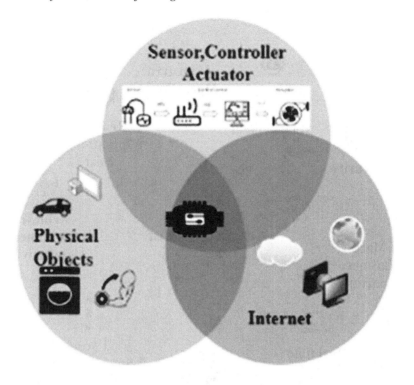

Figure 2. Modified constituents of the Internet of Things

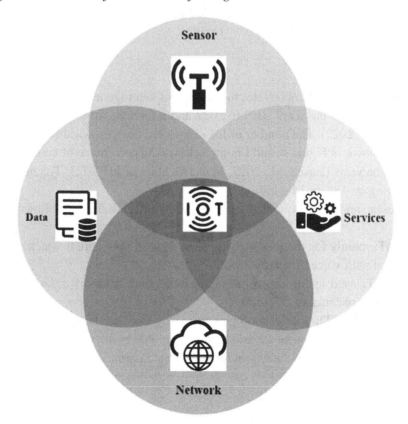

Figure 3. Advantages of IoT

The graphical representation demonstrates the number of heterogeneous devices connected to depict the "Internet of Things" over the years 2019 to 2022 and a forecast from 2023 to 2030 (Lionel Sujay Vailshery, November 22, 2022). The number of IoT-connected devices worldwide in 2019 - 2021, with forecasts to 2030, is shown in Figure 4, and Figure 5 shows the percentage of connected IoT devices of different types over the years (Hasan, M., 2022, May 18). State of IoT 2022: The number of connected IoT devices is growing by 18% to 14.4 billion globally.

Depending on usage and application, IoT devices are mainly classified as follows:

- **Consumer IoT:** mainly for the use of daily lives, for example, smart-watches and home appliances associated with voice or text control.
- **Commercial IoT:** used mainly in wellness apparatus and transport industries. Like regulation systems, and smart pacemaker systems.
- **Military Things (IoMT):** IoT technologies primarily used in the military domain include the robots used for surveillance purposes and human-wearable biometric systems.
- **Industrial IoT (IIoT):** mostly used in industry-oriented applications like industrial big data and Control systems.

- **Set-up IoT:** Principally deals with connectivity among smart cities. Here, we use devices like sensors.

Figure 4. Number of IoT-connected devices worldwide over the years

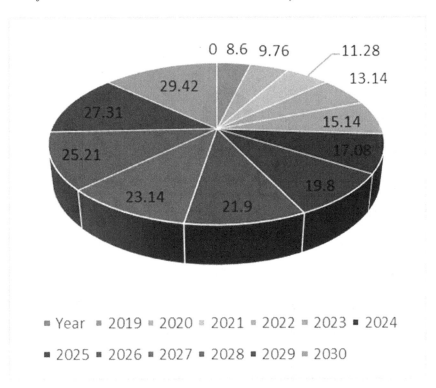

Figure 5. Global IoT market forecast

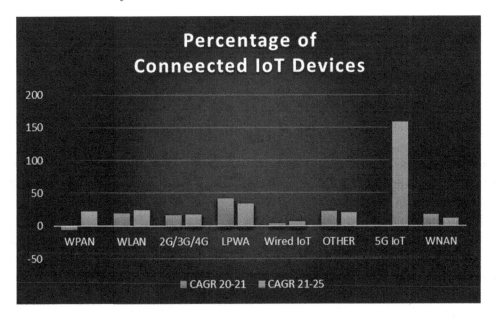

IOT APPLICATIONS

This increase in demand has led to the development of many IoT-based applications. Some major IoT applications are displayed in Figure 6.

Figure 6. Applications of IoT

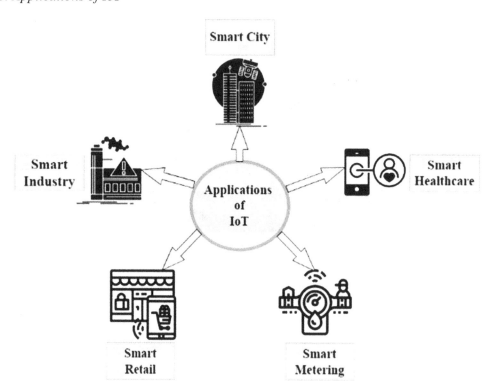

- **Smart City:** IoT solutions address traffic congestion, pollution, and energy efficiency issues with connected devices for better urban living (Gharaibeh et al., 2017). Smart cities aim to develop competent communication through technical aspects (Eckhoff et al., 2018), with government incentives supporting smart city applications.
- **Smart Industry:** Aimed toward providing Security-rich infrastructure for a sustainable solution, Geetanjali et al. (2021) noted the importance of intelligent decision-making for IoT-driven structures.
- **Smart Healthcare:** The rising population leads to more patients, necessitating challenging record-keeping and monitoring (Stephanie et al., 2027). IoT-driven healthcare is a research area.
- **Smart Metering:** According to Xia et al. (2017), this technology deals with electronic theft and the measurement of gas and water levels with the aim of reducing the wastage of any form of energy. The potential of IoT can be judged by different market players acquiring different services and providing various goods that meet several applications of IoT.
- **Smart Retail:** Smart retail combines traditional shopping with IoT-driven technologies, providing personalized and faster experiences (Sujana et al., 2020).

IOT SECURITY THREATS AND SECURITY ARCHITECTURE

Security threats in IoT have become a growing concern as the number of connected devices continues to proliferate. The interconnected nature of IoT devices, combined with the vast amounts of sensitive data they handle, makes them attractive targets for malicious actors. Below are some of the key security threats associated with IoT:

- **Weak Authentication and Authorization:** Weak authentication and authorization like default or easily guessable passwords, lack of two-factor authentication, and improper access control policies can expose devices to hackers, enabling them to compromise the entire IoT ecosystem.
- **Device Vulnerabilities:** Manufacturers may overlook essential security practices, leading to vulnerabilities in the firmware or software of the devices which can be exploited by hackers to gain control over the devices or to launch larger-scale attacks.
- **Inadequate Encryption:** Insufficient encryption of transmitting data can expose sensitive information to eavesdropping and interception.
- **Lack of Regular Updates and Patches:** Devices may not receive regular updates and security patches from manufacturers leaves devices exposed to known vulnerabilities that hackers can exploit over time.
- **Physical Security Concerns:** Physical tampering can also pose a significant threat.
- **Lack of Proper Privacy Controls:** If proper privacy controls are not implemented, the sensitive data may be mishandled or used for unauthorized purposes, compromising user privacy.
- **Supply Chain Vulnerabilities:** The IoT ecosystem involves multiple stakeholders, any weakness in them can introduce security vulnerabilities

Research is going on in IoT security architecture to achieve the parameters shown in Figure 7.

Figure 7. IoT security parameters

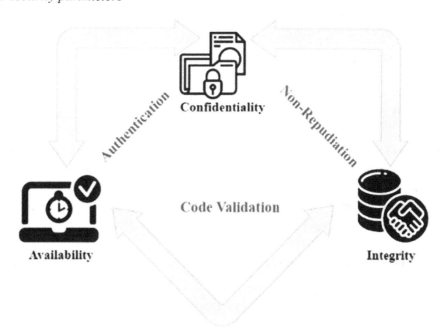

Figure 8 shows the layers in the layered IoT structure. Leian et al. (2007) have considered the overhead for managing the functionalities and interconnections between layers to be proportional to the number of layers. A comparative analysis of different IoT architectures is presented below

- **Three-Layered Architecture:** Three-layered IoT architecture includes the perception layer (sensors/devices), network layer (connectivity), and application layer (data processing and user interface). Advantages: Scalability, modularity, and easy device integration. Disadvantages: Security risks, complex management, and potential interoperability issues between different layers and devices.
- **Hierarchical Architecture:** Hierarchical IoT architecture with multiple tiers allows efficient data processing, reduced network traffic, and improved response time. However, it may have single points of failure and increased latency for critical decisions.
- **Flat Architecture:** Flat IoT architecture enables direct peer-to-peer communication, leading to simplified communication, reduced latency, and decentralized control. Scalability and security are concerns.
- **Mesh Architecture:** Mesh IoT architecture enables self-forming, self-healing networks with high reliability and extended coverage. However, it's complex to manage, consumes more energy, and may introduce latency with multiple hops.

Each IoT architecture has strengths and weaknesses. The three-layered architecture excels in security, making it ideal for large-scale IoT deployments. Figure 9 shows the layers and their applications in Three-layered IoT architecture.

- Perception Layer: The lowest layer of IoT architecture deals with gathering and processing information from sensory devices (Xu et al., 2013; Suo et al., 2012). Common security attacks in this Perception layer include node capture, playback attack, phony node attack, and timing attack (Bharathi et al., 2013; Puthal et al., 2016)
- Network and Transport Layer: Two types of Network and Transport layers: Wired enables upper layer processing, while Wireless allows data transmission.
- Application and Middleware Layer: This layer is responsible for allowing different devices to communicate and perform various actions using a bridge to amalgamate diversity.

Each layer addresses specific security concerns and collectively contributes to enhancing overall IoT security. Below are the reasons why the three-layered architecture is preferable for IoT security:

- **Segmentation of Security Concerns:** Addressing security challenges systematically at each level.
- **Enhanced Scalability:** Horizontal scaling to accommodate a growing number of interconnected devices securely.
- **Distributed Trust Model:** Trust established at each layer enhances overall security resilience.
- **Protection-in-Depth Strategy:** Multiple security layers to bolster resistance against attacks and breaches.
- **Device Authentication:** The perception layer focuses on device authentication and integrity verification.

Figure 8. Layered architecture

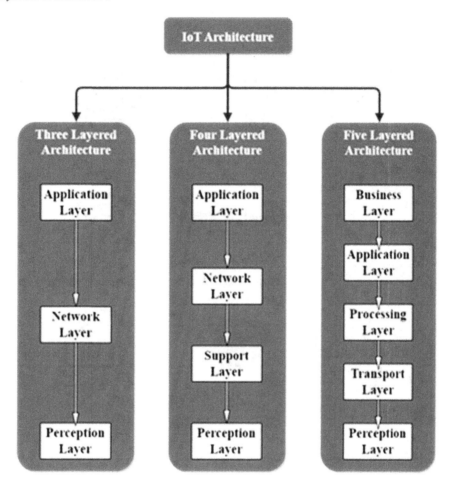

- **Data Encryption and Privacy:** The network layer ensures secure data transmission through data encryption.
- **Application Layer Security:** Access control and data processing prevent unauthorized access to sensitive data.
- **Flexibility and Interoperability:** Accommodates various devices and protocols with standardized security.
- **Centralized Management:** Distributes security functions across layers while allowing centralized monitoring and response.

The three-layered architecture provides a solid foundation for addressing IoT security challenges by segmenting concerns, distributing trust, and adopting a protection-in-depth approach.

Figure 9. Three-layered architecture and their applications

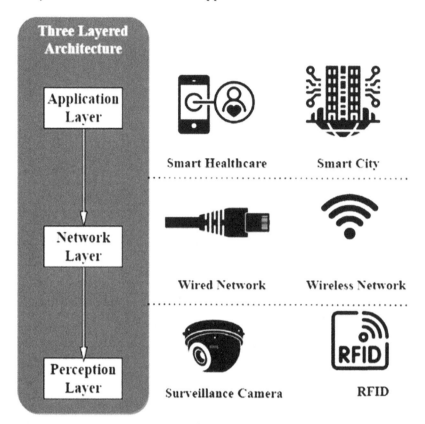

SECURITY CHALLENGES IN IOT

Security vulnerabilities pose serious challenges in the adoption of IoT devices globally.

- **Tag Cloning Attack:** A tag cloning attack in IoT involves duplicating a legitimate device's identification information, like RFID or NFC, for impersonation. Attackers use specialized equipment to clone the unique identifier, enabling the creation of counterfeit tags, risking unauthorized access, security breaches, and data compromise. Robust authentication and encryption are essential to mitigate such attacks (Yue et al., 2021; Hazalila et al., 2018, Figure 10). Figure 10 shows the tag cloning concept.

Lehtonen et al. (2009) present a radio frequency fingerprinting method to detect RFID tag cloning in IoT systems, analyzing differences in RF signals between authentic and cloned tags. Hazalila et al. (2018) highlight RFID's real-time data visibility but emphasize security concerns. Rixin et al. (2018), Jemal et al. (2013, 2015), and Guozhu et al. (2016) explore key collision detection using physical layer synchronization and route analysis. Various techniques, including authentication protocols, cryptography, and blockchain-based solutions, are proposed to enhance IoT tag security against cloning threats.

Figure 10. Tag cloning

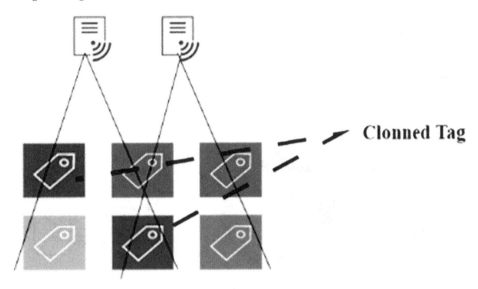

- **Sniffing Attack:** A sniffing attack in IoT involves intercepting data between devices and servers. Attackers eavesdrop on communication traffic to obtain sensitive information (Thorat et al., 2014; Rakesh et al., 2011). (Anu et al., 2017) analyzes sniffing attacks' techniques and implications on IoT system security, emphasizing strong encryption, secure protocols, and security audits as preventive measures. Figure 11 demonstrates the Sniffing attack.

Figure 11. Sniffing attack

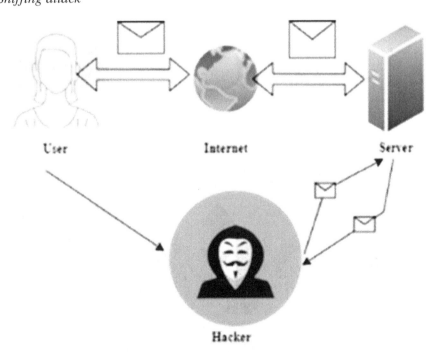

- **Brute force Attack:** Brute force attack in IoT involves automated and exhaustive attempts to access devices using all possible combinations (Rushabh et al., 2020). Strong passwords, account lockouts, and multi-factor authentication help prevent such attacks. Figure 12 demonstrates the Brute Force attack.

Figure 12. Brute force attack

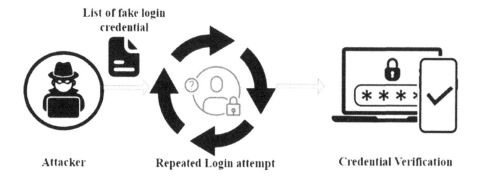

- **Routing Attack:** RPL is a widely used routing protocol for IoT networks (Wallgren et al., 2013; Winter et al., 2012). Routing attacks manipulate data packet flow, causing traffic misdirection and congestion, unauthorized access, and service disruptions. Implementing secure protocols, authentication, encryption, and monitoring are essential for mitigation (Rashmi et al., 2022). Figure 13 demonstrates the basics of a Routing attack.

Figure 13. Routing attack

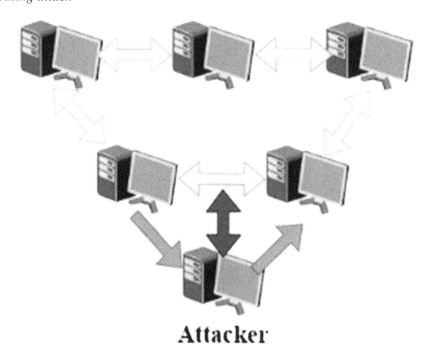

- **Reply Attack:** Reply attacks in IoT involve intercepting and replaying legitimate communication to deceive recipient devices. Implementing secure communication protocols, encryption, and message integrity checks prevent unauthorized access and data tampering, ensuring IoT network security. Figure 14 demonstrates the basics of a Routing attack.

Figure 14. Reply attack

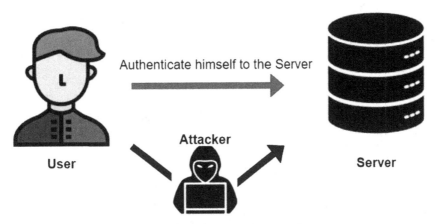

- **Wormhole Attack:** Wormhole attack in IoT creates shortcut tunnels for malicious nodes to disrupt communication. Mitigation requires secure routing, authentication, and monitoring.
- **Flooding Attack:** Flooding attack in IoT overwhelms devices with massive data or requests, causing service disruptions. Mitigation includes traffic filtering, rate limiting, and intrusion detection systems (IDS) for identifying abnormal patterns.
- **Sybil Attack:** Sybil attack in IoT involves creating multiple fake identities to deceive the network. Mitigation requires strong authentication, access control, and reputation-based schemes. Figure 15 shows the Sybil attack.
- **Sleep Deprivation Attack:** Sleep deprivation attack disrupts low-power modes, draining device batteries. Mitigation includes robust power management, hardware security, and monitoring.

Table 1 shows different attacks based on their consequences.

Not only these attacks, but IoT is suffering many other security challenges these days. Table 2 shows the Issues and Challenges in IoT.

Figure 15. Sybil attack

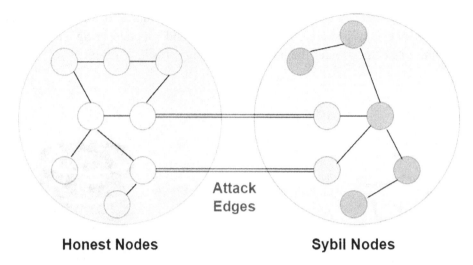

Table 1. Attacks in IoT infrastructure based on their consequences

Consequence	Security Threats	Security Countermeasures
Privacy violation	Tag Cloning	Concur OTP between the tag and the backend, Hash-based methods, tag isolation, and tag blocking (Khedr,2013)
	Brute Force Attack	Strong cryptographic techniques (Omar et al. 2020)
Man in the middle attack	Routing Attack	Authentication based on Signature, Distributed Hash table (Pongle et al.,2015)
	Sniffing	Mutual authentication, Preinstalled network key, and Tamper Detection (Mitrokotsa et al., 2010)
Denial of Service	Replay Attack	Fragments verification based on hash chain (Vidgren et al., 2013)
	Wormhole Attack	Measuring the signal strength, Management of- • Trust level • Key Geographic information binding and graph traversal (Weekly et al.,2012)
	Flooding Attack	Firewall implementation, Frequency change.
	Sybil Attack	Spamming, Unreliable Broadcast (Lu et al.,2014)
Energy Consumption	Sleep Deprivation Attack	Multi-layer-based intrusion detection targets IPv6 defense movement (Hummen et al., 2013)

BLOCKCHAIN

Blockchain is a decentralized and distributed ledger technology that records transactions across multiple computers (nodes) in a secure, transparent, and tamper-resistant manner. It allows participants in a network to maintain a shared database without the need for a central authority. The blockchain operates on the principles of cryptographic hashing, consensus mechanisms, and data linkage to create a secure and immutable chain of blocks.

Table 2. Issues and challenges in IoT

Issue	Concern	Challenges	Observation
Privacy	In the initial phase, it is actually very difficult for consumers to notice that their personal information is at stake. Devices in public spaces can gather data automatically.	Transparency.	Lack of multi-layer models to enforce transparency.
		Fairness in Information acquisition.	Lack of strict protocol against information acquisition and use.
		Protection.	Lack of data protection collected by many heterogeneous devices.
		Security expectation.	Lack of a systematic approach to gathering the security expectations of a wide range of users.
		Schematic design.	Lack of architectural designs to incorporate IoT devices with strong privacy protection principles.
Security	Intruders can get multiple entry points to get into an IoT network. Attackers always try to find vulnerabilities to gain access. Moreover, weak encryption and poor authentication standards make IoT devices face major security challenges.	Design Issue.	Lack of resources to deal with security aspects.
		Cost vs. Security skirmish.	Lack of Intelligent preference for cost-effective security benefits.
		Upgradation.	Lack of information on maintainability and upgradability.
		Standard and Regulation.	Lack of metrics to identify the standard and maintain the regulations.
		Shared responsibility.	Lack of information regarding the achievement of security in a collaborative manner.
		Device obsolesces.	Lack of information regarding replacing obsolete devices to mitigate security threats.
Interportability	The exponential growth of IoT technology gives rise to an amalgamation of heterogeneity in terms of Devices, Interfaces, Frameworks, Application Programming infrastructure, data formats, and standards, which in turn increase the overhead of Interportability.	Resources.	Lack of technical resources and investment.
		Risk.	Lack of awareness of Technical and Scheduled risks.
		Documentation.	Lack of proper documentation.
Legal and Regulatory Issues	Still, there is a lack of awareness and legal obligations regarding accessing IoT devices.	Interconnectivity of heterogeneous devices.	Lack of legal information about connectivity and regulation of several heterogeneous devices.
		Device liability.	Lack of awareness of the laws governing liability issues for IoT devices.
Standardization	To achieve universal acceptance among heterogeneity Standardization is much needed.	Standard and protocols.	Less effort is spent developing standards and protocols.
Economic and Developmental Concerns	Establishment of common and transparent goals among heterogeneity in the marketplace.	Investment.	Limited investment in IoT R&D activities.
		Infrastructure.	There are fewer activities involved in developing an effective IoT-bound communication infrastructure.

Integral Element of Blockchain Architecture

One integral element of Blockchain architecture is the "Block." A block is a fundamental component that contains a group of transactions and other relevant data. Blocks are sequentially linked together to form a chain, known as the "Blockchain." The core elements of Blockchain architecture are as follows:

- **Node**: Each participant either a user or computer can be considered a node. The individual device contains a local copy of the entire blockchain ledger.
- **Transaction**: Transaction can be viewed as the lowest finding block containing accounts of each operation.
- **Block**: It is an assembly of structure of data constructions depicting operations over distributed nodes.
- **Chain**: Sequential arrangement of blocks continued in a definite order
- **Miners**: Communicator nodes to approve and append genuine block into the existing blockchain structure
- **Consensus**: It consists of commands and organizations to function on blockchain processes.

Figure 16 shows the basic blockchain architecture.

Figure 16. Basic blockchain architecture

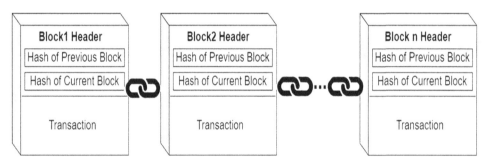

Functional Characteristics of Blockchain

- Decentralization: No central authority controls the blockchain network, providing a distributed and trustless environment.
- Immutability: Once data is recorded on the blockchain, it cannot be altered or deleted, ensuring a permanent and tamper-resistant ledger.
- Transparency: All participants can access the same version of the blockchain, promoting transparency and auditability of transactions.
- Security: Blockchain uses cryptographic techniques to ensure secure data storage and secure transaction validation.
- Consensus Mechanisms: Blockchain employs various consensus algorithms like Proof-of-Work (PoW) or Proof-of-Stake (PoS) to validate and agree on the state of the ledger.

- Smart Contracts: Blockchain supports self-executing smart contracts, enabling automated, trustless agreements and transactions.
- Interoperability: Blockchain can be integrated with various systems, allowing seamless data exchange and interoperability between different networks.

Emergent Characteristics of Blockchain

- Trustlessness: Participants can interact without the need for a central authority, relying on the blockchain's consensus mechanisms for trust.
- Interoperability: Blockchain can facilitate interoperability between different systems, enabling seamless data exchange and collaboration.
- Programmable Trust through Smart Contracts: The implementation of smart contracts enables programmable trust.
- Resilience and Redundancy: Due to its distributed nature, blockchain networks are highly resilient to failures and attacks. Even if some nodes fail or malicious actors attempt to disrupt the network, the majority of honest nodes can still maintain the network's integrity and functionality.

How Blockchain Works

- Transaction Initiation: A participant initiates a transaction in the blockchain network, such as financial transfers, data exchanges, or smart contract executions.
- Transaction Verification: Nodes in the network verify the transaction based on the consensus mechanism used. In PoW blockchains, miners solve mathematical puzzles, while PoS blockchains rely on validators staking cryptocurrency.
- Transaction Propagation: Validated transactions are broadcasted to the network to be included in the next block.
- Block Creation: Valid transactions are grouped into a block, with the block size determined by the blockchain protocol. Each block contains a header and a body.
- Block Header: The block header includes metadata like timestamp, previous block's hash, and a nonce (for PoW consensus).
- Block Body: The block body contains the validated transactions.
- Hashing: The block's data (header and body) undergoes a cryptographic hashing algorithm, generating a unique block hash.
- Proof of Work (Mining): In PoW blockchains, miners compete to find a nonce resulting in a hash that meets specific difficulty criteria.
- Adding the Block to the Blockchain: If a miner finds a valid block, it is broadcasted and validated by other nodes before being appended to the existing blockchain.
- Linkage: The new block's header references the hash of the previous block, ensuring chronological order and forming an unbroken chain.
- Consensus Agreement: All nodes reach a consensus on the validity of the new block, finalizing its addition to the blockchain.

Continuously growing blockchain with secure hashing and consensus mechanisms. Address scalability, interoperability, and privacy for successful IoT integration. Figure 17 shows the process of Block generation and appending to the existing chain.

Figure 17. Block generation and appending to the existing chain

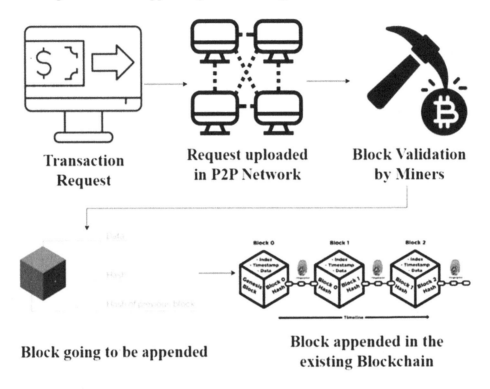

Consensus Protocols

Consensus protocol achieves secure, decentralized agreement on valid transactions, ensuring integrity, trustless applications, and scalability in the blockchain.

Types of consensus protocols: Some commonly used consensus protocols are:

- Proof of Work (PoW): Miners compete to solve puzzles, adding blocks. Resource-intensive, used in Bitcoin.
- Proof of Stake (PoS): Validators create blocks based on staking cryptocurrency. Energy-efficient, used in Ethereum 2.0.
- Delegated Proof of Stake (DPoS): Token holders vote for delegates to validate blocks. Used in EOS and Tron.
- Practical Byzantine Fault Tolerance (PBFT): A consensus algorithm for permissioned networks with trusted nodes. Used in Hyperledger Fabric.
- Proof of Authority (PoA): Blocks validated by approved validators. Used in private and consortium blockchains.

Consensus protocols have strengths and weaknesses and fit specific blockchain use cases (Salman et al., 2019). Blockchain enables decentralized data storage, addressing IoT security threats. The study explores Blockchain's role in the heterogeneous IoT ecosystem.

LITERATURE REVIEW ON BLOCKCHAIN-ASSISTED SCALABLE AND SECURE IOT

In the IoT era, blockchain is vital for data-intensive, decentralized applications, preserving privacy. It has various uses, including sensor data purchase (Worner et al., 2015), managing PKI (Axon et al., 2015; Fromknecth et al., 2014), goods purchase (Zhang et al., 2015), access control logs (Zyskind et al., 2015), access policies (Nathan et al., 2015), data loading (Vorick et al., 2014), document storage (Bocovich et al., 2015), metadata (Wilkinson et al.), voting systems (Matteis et al.), rating systems (Vandervort et al.), and lottery implementation (Bylica et al., 2015). Ongoing research explores the benefits of integrating blockchain with IoT. Table 3 shows the details.

Table 3. Data inserted into the Blockchain

Referred by	Data in the Blockchain
Worner et al.	Data purchased from the sensor
Axon et al.	Registration, update, and verification of the public key
Zhang et al.	Bitcoin exchange
Zyskind et al.	Data recovery
Nathan et al.	Access protocols
Vorick et al.	File contracts, storage proof
Bocovich et al.	Payment contract
Wilkinson et al.	Reference to data and metadata
Matteis et al.	Reference to published content
D. Vandervort	Information rating
Bylica et al.	Lottery contact
Wilson et al.	Verification address
Bartoletti et al.	Message metadata
Herbert et al.	License validation
Gipp et al.	Hash content would be timestamped
Fromknecth et al.	Registration information
Ateniese et al.	Transaction to safely deposit bitcoins

Various studies discuss the challenges and applications of blockchain in IoT. Feld et al. (2014) highlight P2P network limitations. J. A. Dev (2014) notes attackers' potential dominance. Selfish mining attacks are introduced by Eyal et al. (2013). Other works examine data exchange (Zhang et al., 2015; Worner et al., 2014) and data handling techniques (Zyskind et al., 2015). Blockchain's pseudonymity limitations are addressed in Axon et al. (2015), Barber et al. (2012), Valenta et al. (2015), Bissias et al. (2014), and Meiklejohn et al. (2015), with analysis of mixing protocols in Valenta et al. (2015), Bissias et al. (2014), and Meiklejohn et al. (2015).

BLOCKCHAIN IN SECURITY ENHANCEMENT OF IOT SYSTEM

The importance of blockchain in IoT lies in its ability to address critical challenges faced by IoT systems and unlock new possibilities for secure, reliable, and scalable deployments. Figure 18 shows the areas where Blockchain enhances the security of IoT.

Figure 18. Blockchain in security enhancement in IoT

Here are some key reasons why blockchain is crucial for IoT

Wide range of address space: Blockchain adopts a 160-bit ECC address space, supporting over 1500 IoT devices with GLI. Verification-free uniqueness checking and collision avoidance are feasible due to this ample address range.

Scalability: Blockchain eliminates centralized governance, benefiting IoT devices with computation and memory constraints. It offers better routing and address space, making it a scalable alternative. Dorri et al. (2017) proposed optimized storage to manage the blockchain size increase caused by IoT integration.

Ownership and Identity: Blockchain enables trustworthy identity registration, tenure track, and asset monitoring for IoT devices, addressing ownership challenges and ensuring reliable connections (Otte et al., 2017).

Authentication and Privacy: Blockchain provides separate authentication rules and with the in-build features of anonymity it also provides privacy for the data stored in different IoT devices. Privacy of data is achieved using a smart contract that actually applies a set of access rules.

Integrity and Security: In a Blockchain environment, data is encrypted and signed for data integrity. Sun et al. proposed a "double-chain" model merging "data blockchain" and "transaction blockchain" for IoT information-sharing security. Gero et al. introduced a proxy blockchain for communication and transaction control. Blockchain's distributed nature efficiently handles high-processing requests (Georgescu et al., 2015; Arif et al., 2020).

Trackability and Interoperability: Transactions kept in blocks provide trackability with the calculated hash number. Tomescu et al. proposed a trackable approach using Merkle trees. Cross-chain technology enables information sharing across heterogeneous structures and networks (Noura et al., 2019).

Secure Communication: Messaging protocols are crucial for secure IoT device communication. Fakhri et al. (2018) found Ethereum blockchain is more resilient to sniffing attacks than MQTT elementary Transport. Combining blockchain security with IoT can create robust and trustworthy systems across industries, revolutionizing various sectors as IoT expands.

POSSIBLE APPLICATIONS OF BLOCKCHAIN-BASED IOT

The amalgamation of Blockchain with IoT technology leads to secure, scalable, and efficient IoT solutions. There are numerous applications for Blockchain-based IoT, some major among which are shown in Figure 19.

Figure 19. Applicable areas for blockchain enhancement in IoT

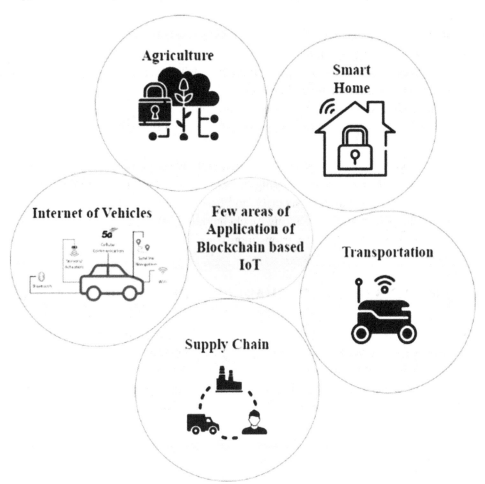

- **Blockchain-Based IoT in Agriculture:** IoT devices in agriculture can acquire field data for analysis and improving the agricultural sector.
- **Blockchain-based Smart Home:** Blockchain enhances smart homes with secure communication and high data secrecy and privacy.
- **Blockchain-based solution towards Automotive Transportation:** Blockchain-integrated solutions enhance automotive transportation, securing data against theft and crime in fuel payment, automatic driving, and smart parking.

- **Blockchain-based Supply chain Management:** Blockchain-based supply chain management ensures transparency, traceability, and automation for various business activities, enhancing efficiency and security.
- **Blockchain-based Internet of Vehicles**: Blockchain's distributed consensus is beneficial for vehicles in complex transportation, ensuring secure and decentralized applications.
- **Waste Management:** IoT smart bins monitor fill levels, and send data to blockchain for efficient waste collection and cost savings.
- **Water Management:** IoT and blockchain enable water data integrity and management for conservation efforts.
- **Asset Management and Tracking:** IoT-enabled asset tracking records movements and ownership of valuable assets on the blockchain.
- **Remote Monitoring and Maintenance:** Industrial IoT devices transmit real-time data to the blockchain for remote monitoring and predictive maintenance.
- **Identity and Access Management:** Blockchain enables secure and decentralized identity management for IoT devices, preventing unauthorized access and identity spoofing.

These applications demonstrate the transformative potential of combining blockchain and IoT technologies across various industries. By leveraging the strengths of both technologies, organizations can achieve greater efficiency, transparency, security, and trust in their operations and services. These applications showcase the potential of combining blockchain and IoT technologies to create more secure, efficient, and transparent systems across various industries.

SECURITY ANALYSIS ON BLOCKCHAIN-ASSOCIATED IOT PARADIGM

In today's world, IoT devices becoming a very essential part of people's lives. But due to the heterogeneous nature as well as lack of security monitoring people's personal data is at stake. Blockchain technology is associated with IoT technology to provide security on IoT devices.

Blockchain enhances the security of IoT in several ways, addressing critical security challenges that IoT devices and networks face. Here are some key ways blockchain improves IoT security:

- Immutable Data: Data recorded on the blockchain is tamper-resistant and immutable. Once data is added to the blockchain, it cannot be altered or deleted without the consensus of the majority of network participants.
- Decentralization: Blockchain operates on a decentralized network of nodes, eliminating the need for a central authority. This decentralized architecture makes it more difficult for attackers to compromise a single point of failure.
- Cryptographic Security: Blockchain uses cryptographic techniques to secure transactions and protect data.
- Data Encryption: IoT devices can encrypt data before transmitting it to the blockchain, ensuring that sensitive information remains confidential even if intercepted during transmission.
- Secure Identity Management: Each device can have a unique identity recorded on the blockchain, preventing unauthorized access and identity spoofing.

- Consensus Mechanism: Blockchain uses consensus mechanisms to validate and agree on the state of the ledger. This ensures that only valid and legitimate transactions are added to the blockchain, preventing unauthorized or malicious activities.
- Smart Contracts: Blockchain's smart contracts allow for self-executing agreements based on pre-defined conditions. These automated contracts can ensure that specific conditions are met before actions are taken, minimizing the risk of human error or manipulation.
- Distributed Ledger: The distributed nature of the blockchain ensures that each participant in the network holds a copy of the entire transaction history. This redundancy makes the network more resilient to attacks and data loss.
- Transparency and Auditability: All transactions on the blockchain are transparent and accessible to all participants. This transparency enables easy auditing and verification of data, making it a trustworthy source of truth.

Blockchain's security features address critical IoT concerns like data integrity, privacy, authentication, and access control. Various authentication methods are proposed, such as password-based (Renuka et al., 2019), anonymous (Abbasi et al., 2017), and password-based with scalability (Andrea et al., 2022). Consensus protocols like proof-of-concept anonymous verification (Abbasi et al., 2017) and proof-of-work (Dorriet al., 2017) are used. Cryptography, including parallel hashing, is crucial for blockchain architectures (Kravitz et al., 2017). Due to the widespread usage of IoT-enabled devices, the voluminous data generated as well as to be stored is a major concern. To manage the storage of such a bulky volume of data, the cloud is used which in turn raised two important issues

- How to handle data redundancy
- How to maintain data security

(Sarada et al., 2019) proposed an architecture with the double hashing approach where to deal with duplication before uploading each file will be checked with a tag. If the tag is present then the system would not allow the uploading of files by the user. To generate the tag, first, the hash of the file will be generated then again, the hash of this hash value will be generated to be used as a tag. To maintain security, the user having the file would encrypt it so strategically that the user having the identical file would verify the presence of it but the cloud server cannot. Figure 16 shows the areas where we still need to improve even in the case of Blockchain-associated IoT.

How Different Attacks on the IoT Paradigm Can Be Handled Through Association With Blockchain

- **Tag cloning Attack:**
  - Unique Identifiers: Assigning unique cryptographic identifiers to IoT tags ensures authenticity.
  - Immutable Records: Blockchain's tamper-resistant nature prevents alteration, identifying cloned tags without blockchain entries.
  - Smart Contracts: Enforcing access control and authentication allows only authorized tags to interact with the IoT network.
  - Decentralization: Distributing blockchain across nodes prevents data manipulation by attackers.

○ Traceability: Blockchain's transparency enables tracking the tag's history, identifying suspicious activities.

Figure 20. Challenges in blockchain-associated IoT

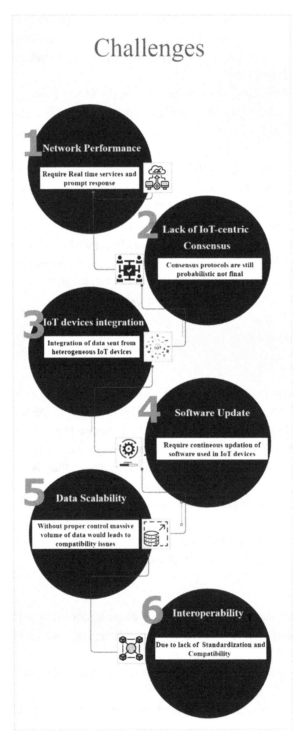

By leveraging these features, blockchain enhances IoT security and resilience, reducing tag cloning risks. Careful design, combined with other security measures, strengthens defense against attacks.

- **Brute force Attack:**
  - Multi-factor Authentication: Combining multiple authentication factors for IoT devices.
  - Rate Limiting: Limiting login attempts to prevent rapid brute force attacks.
  - Immutable Records: Recording authentication attempts on the blockchain for traceability and auditability.
  - Decentralization: Distributing blockchain to avoid single points of failure.
  - Reputation-Based Access Control: Using blockchain to assess IoT device behavior and detect potential malicious actors.

Leveraging blockchain's security features, the IoT association strengthens overall security and resilience. Careful design and implementation of blockchain infrastructure and smart contracts are crucial for optimal protection against threats.

- **Routing Attack:**
  - Secure Routing Protocols: Blockchain-based protocols ensure authenticated and tamper-resistant routing information.
  - Consensus Mechanisms: Blockchain's consensus validates and prevents unauthorized changes to routing data.
  - Distributed Ledger: Maintaining a distributed ledger enables decentralized access to routing information, reducing the risk of centralized attacks.
  - Anomaly Detection: Blockchain's transparency monitors and detects abnormal routing behavior, triggering alerts for potential attacks.
  - Immutable Records: Recording routing decisions on the blockchain prevents manipulation, establishing a trusted routing infrastructure.

By leveraging these features, blockchain enhances IoT security, reducing the risk of routing attacks. Careful design and implementation of blockchain infrastructure and smart contracts are essential for maximum protection. Combining blockchain with encryption, secure key exchange, and routing protocols strengthens IoT defense against attacks.

- **Sniffing Attack:**
  - Encrypted Communication: Blockchain-based encryption secures data transmission, preventing sniffers from intercepting and understanding data.
  - Private Key Management: Blockchain ensures secure distribution of private keys, allowing only authorized devices to decrypt data.
  - Public Key Infrastructure (PKI): Blockchain-based PKI validates device authenticity, preventing man-in-the-middle attacks.
  - Immutable Records: Data transactions on the blockchain provide an auditable trail, detecting unauthorized sniffing attempts.

    ○ Decentralization: Distributing the blockchain reduces single points of failure, enhancing IoT network security against sniffing attacks.

Leveraging these blockchain security features improves IoT security, but careful design and implementation are crucial for maximum protection. Combining blockchain with encryption, secure key exchange, and communication protocols strengthens the defense against sniffing attacks in the IoT ecosystem.

- **Reply Attack:**
  - Timestamping: Blockchain records data transactions' exact time, enabling identification and rejection of replayed messages.
  - Nonce Implementation: Blockchain-based nonces prevent acceptance of duplicate or replayed messages.
  - Smart Contracts: Validate data freshness using smart contracts to accept only current and valid data.
  - Consensus Mechanisms: Blockchain's consensus protocols detect and reject replayed messages.
  - Immutable Records: Blockchain's tamper-resistant ledger prevents manipulation or replaying of past messages.

By associating IoT with blockchain and implementing these mechanisms, data transmission integrity can be ensured, and reply attacks can be effectively mitigated. Continuous monitoring and updates remain essential to address emerging threats.

- **Wormhole Attack:**
  - Decentralization and Consensus: Blockchain's decentralized nature and consensus mechanisms prevent attackers from manipulating the network to create a wormhole.
  - Time Synchronization: Blockchain's timestamping ensures synchronized data, making it challenging for attackers to exploit time differences.
  - Smart Contracts Verification: Smart contracts can validate transactions for suspiciously distant locations, flagging potential wormholes.
  - Geo-Location Data: IoT devices' geolocation data verifies their physical location, detecting unrealistic communication ranges.
  - Identity and Access Management: Blockchain's PKI manages device identities, preventing impersonation and duplicate devices.
  - Secure Data Transmission: TLS and secure communication protocols protect data during transmission, making eavesdropping difficult.

By combining blockchain with other security practices, IoT systems can be more resilient against wormhole attacks and other threats.

- **Flooding Attack:**
  - Consensus Mechanisms: PoW or PoS in blockchain slows down malicious transactions, making flooding attacks harder to succeed.

- ○ Transaction Fees: Introducing fees prioritizes legitimate transactions over flooding attacks, deterring attackers.
- ○ Rate Limiting: IoT devices limit requests to prevent being overwhelmed during flooding attacks.
- ○ Dynamic Consensus Difficulty: Adjusting difficulty slows down malicious transactions in a flooding attack.
- ○ Blacklisting and Reputation Management: Identify and reject transactions from malicious nodes and assign reputation scores to prioritize well-behaving devices.
- ○ Decentralization and DDoS Protection: Distributing the network infrastructure prevents targeting centralized points of failure.
- ○ Smart Contracts Auditing: Auditing contracts identifies and addresses potential flooding attack vectors.

Blockchain should be integrated with other security measures for a robust defense against flooding attacks in IoT systems.

- **Sybil Attack:**
  - ○ Identity Verification: Blockchain stores and validates IoT device identities, preventing multiple fake identities.
  - ○ Proof of Stake (PoS): PoS consensus makes it hard for attackers to control the network with multiple identities.
  - ○ Reputation System: Blockchain tracks device behavior, identifying suspicious nodes based on reputation.
  - ○ Distributed Consensus: Decentralization reduces Sybil attack impact by distributing authority.
  - ○ Identity Attestation: Blockchain verifies device authenticity for trusted network participation.

By incorporating these mechanisms, IoT systems can effectively prevent Sybil attacks and maintain identity integrity. Regular monitoring and updates are crucial to address emerging threats.

- **Sleep Deprivation Attack:**
  - ○ Identity Verification: Blockchain validates IoT device identities, preventing attackers from creating fake identities.
  - ○ Proof of Stake (PoS): PoS consensus deters attackers from controlling the network with multiple identities.
  - ○ Reputation System: Blockchain tracks device behavior, identifying and isolating suspicious nodes.
  - ○ Distributed Consensus: Decentralization reduces Sybil attack impact.
  - ○ Identity Attestation: Blockchain verifies device authenticity for trusted network participation.

While blockchain enhances IoT resilience against sleep deprivation attacks, a comprehensive security strategy combining other measures, such as strong authentication and secure communication protocols, is crucial. Regular audits and monitoring are essential for a robust IoT environment.

LIMITATIONS

Having initially found success in cryptocurrencies, blockchain has now emerged as a promising and robust technology for IoT applications, offering significant security and privacy benefits (Rosenthal et al., 2018). At present, the substantial volumes of data generated by numerous IoT devices can create bottlenecks within the IoT system, leading to a decline in Quality of Service (QoS) (Panarello et al., 2018). A single point of failure denotes a system component whose failure can disrupt the entire network, hindering high availability and reliability, making it undesirable for any system (Huang et al., 2019). The P2P architecture of blockchain is seen as a potential remedy for issues related to single points of failure and bottlenecks. Embracing blockchain in IoT can effectively mitigate single points of failure and serve as a reliable method for secure and streamlined storage and processing of IoT data (Huang et al., 2019; Kong et al., 2019). The complexity of blockchain, encompassing elevated computational expenses and latency, poses a challenge in integrating blockchain with IoT, particularly for devices with limited power and storage capabilities (Özyılmaz et al., 2017). Following are a few areas where blockchain association still needs attention and research is going on these areas.

- **Scalability:** Scalability is a limitation of blockchain in IoT due to the increasing number of devices and transactions, overwhelming the network's efficiency. (Kyle, 2018) estimated that managing data for 1000 participants exchanging 2 MB images daily would require 730 GB of storage annually, posing a challenge for handling IoT data on the blockchain.
- **Interoperability:** Interoperability is a blockchain limitation in IoT, as diverse devices and networks with different implementations hinder seamless data exchange (Karafiloski et al., 2017).
- **Collaboration:** Collaboration is a blockchain limitation in IoT, requiring stakeholders to establish common standards and protocols.
- **Safety:** No matter the many safety advantages supplied with the aid of blockchain safety continues to be a crucial issue inside the context of shared structure.
- **Popularity:** Dappled reputations (e.g., Bitcoin's function in the dark net; IoT's safety vulnerabilities), prone to media propaganda and exaggeration, Disjointed market (employer carriers; across public versus private disbursed Ledger era; increase in sure industries), shared monetary and operational transactions are the areas nevertheless want to pay attention.
- **Challenges in maintaining transparent privacy:** Blockchain ensures transaction transparency, but in IoT systems like eHealth, it may compromise user confidentiality (Yu et al., 2019). Cost-effective access control mechanisms are essential.

The diverse security advantages offered by blockchain technology, such as decentralization, immutability, anonymity, and automation, hold promise for various IoT applications. However, the amalgamation of these features also introduces several novel regulatory challenges.

OBJECTIVE

The objective of writing this article on blockchain-associated IoT, its benefits, and challenges is to provide a comprehensive understanding of how the integration of blockchain technology with the Internet of Things can revolutionize various industries. This article discusses the integration of blockchain with IoT, exploring benefits such as enhanced security and transparency, while also highlighting challenges like scalability and resource constraints. (Ashraf et al., 2021, Calvaresi et al., 2018) suggested the adoption of blockchain technology in various IoT systems like smart cities, smart homes, healthcare, etc managed by autonomous agents driven by ML and AI who can perform actions as a substitute for the user. (Tom et al.,2020) proposed a smart energy distribution system based on an association of agents on the IoT Fog network. To solve the scalability matter in the blockchain-associated architecture (Qayumi et al., 2018) showed a multi-agent approach but the authors did not describe the roadmap for the achievement of such things. The section presents the issues and probable solutions in a tabular format.

Table 4 shows the challenges along with given solutions the blockchain-associated IoT is still facing as per the recent ongoing research.

Table 4. Challenges in blockchain-associated IoT

Challenges	Found by	Solution
Connectivity issues	(Click et al.,2020)	Mainchain or Sidechain hosted by Multi-access Edge Computing. On the Edge network, IoT devices using low bandwidth can interact with the sidechain.
Accommodation of voluminous data	(Andrew et al., 2020)	Data generated or consumed by distributed IoT across multiple storehouses which includes various repositories providing cloud service, native computers, and on-chain blockchain associations based on the features and miscellaneous circumstances.
High rate of bandwidth consumption	(Chen et al., 2019)	Sharding the process of dividing blockchain peer-to-peer networks into multiple clusters where each member is responsible for processing and verification of transactions. So, there is no question of transaction circulation across the whole network so bandwidth consumption can be reduced.
Resource constraint of IoT to lodge blockchain technology	(Gondal et al., 2020)	Introduction of smart agent to provide storage resources and performs computations. Another solution can be optimized blockchain algorithms.
Privacy issues	(Shrestha et al., 2019; Saad et al., 2021;	Issues of privacy can be resolved by Proxy re-encryption and Homomorphic encryption techniques. Blockchain in association with Federated learning allows privacy-preserving computation.

In this article, recent state-of-the-art developments in blockchain for IoT with its challenges and future prospects are covered as it is gained a lot of interest and attraction from researchers. Moreover, we tried to present the research gap and possible solutions found by several researchers. As blockchain works in a decentralized fashion, all the participating nodes need to broadcast the blocks and synchronization is another issue in the context of validation. IoT devices face the challenges of bandwidth limitation (Dai et al.,2019). To mitigate this bandwidth constraint recently Edge devices are augmented and Patient Centric Agent (Iqbal et al.,2018) is used where instead of direct transmission of each transaction blocks are created with a certain number of transactions. In this article, several limitations in blockchain-associated IoT technology are acknowledged and how the technologies are being recognized is conveyed. The existing blockchain-associated IoT articles are analyzed based on several attributes for indicating their pros and cons.

CONCLUSION

Blockchain and IoT together can address security and privacy concerns, but resource limitations in IoT devices pose challenges. Ongoing research aims to mitigate threats like DoS and 51% attacks, establishing trust in a distributed environment. Despite limitations, integrating blockchain technology holds promise for various industries, demanding collaboration for scalability, energy efficiency, and regulatory compliance. Harmonious convergence of solutions will shape a secure and connected IoT future.

This study on blockchain-associated IoT and its benefits and challenges can help various stakeholders in multiple ways:

- Decision-Makers: Gain insights into blockchain's potential advantages for IoT and assess alignment with organizational goals.
- IoT Developers: Understand technical aspects of integrating blockchain, including security features and consensus mechanisms.
- Security Experts: Explore how blockchain can enhance IoT data security and develop robust measures.
- Regulatory Bodies: Learn about regulatory challenges and create policies for blockchain in IoT.
- Academic Researchers: Use this study as a foundation for further research and propose innovative solutions.
- Industry Adoption: Encourage industries to adopt blockchain in IoT for efficiency, transparency, and security.
- Privacy Advocates: Raise awareness of privacy implications and advocate for responsible data handling.
- Public Awareness: Educate consumers about blockchain-associated IoT benefits and challenges for informed decisions.

Overall, this study serves as a knowledge resource for various stakeholders, enabling them to make informed decisions, drive innovation, and address the complexities of integrating blockchain with IoT. It fosters a deeper understanding of this evolving technological landscape and its potential impact on various industries and our daily lives.

REFERENCES

Abawajy, J. (2013). SQLIA detection and prevention approach for RFIDsystems. *Journal of Systems and Software*, *86*(3), 751–758. doi:10.1016/j.jss.2012.11.022

Abawajy, J., & Fernando, H. (2015). Policy-based SQLIA detection and prevention approach for RFID systems. *Computer Standards & Interfaces*, *38*, 64–71. doi:10.1016/j.csi.2014.08.005

Abbasi, A. G., & Khan, Z. (2017). Veidblock: verifiable identity using blockchain and ledger in a software defined network. In: *Companion Proceedings of the10th International Conference on Utility and Cloud Computing,* (pp. 173–179). IEEE. 10.1145/3147234.3148088

Adapa, S., Fazal-e-Hasan, S. M., Makam, S. B., Azeem, M. M., & Mortimer, G. (2020). Examining the antecedents and consequences of perceived shopping value through smart retail technology. *Journal of Retailing and Consumer Services*, *52*, 101901. doi:10.1016/j.jretconser.2019.101901

Alfandi, O., Khanji, S., Ahmad, L., & Khattak, A. (2020). A survey on boosting IoT security and privacy through blockchain Exploration, requirements, and open issues.*Cluster Computing*; *Springer Science+Business Media*, LLC, part of Springer Nature 2020.

Anu, P., & Vimala, S. (2017), A survey on sniffing attacks on computer networks, *International Conference on Intelligent Computing and Control (I2C2)*. IEEE. 10.1109/I2C2.2017.8321914

Arif, S., Khan, M. A., Rehman, S. U., Kabir, M. A., & Imran, M. (2020). Investigating smart home security: Is blockchain the answer? *IEEE Access : Practical Innovations, Open Solutions*, *8*(June), 117802–117816. doi:10.1109/ACCESS.2020.3004662

Ashraf Uddin, M. (2018). Andrew Stranieri, Iqbal Gondal, Venki Balasubramanian (2018), Continuous patient monitoring with a patient centric agent: A block architecture. *IEEE Access : Practical Innovations, Open Solutions*, *6*, 32700–32726. doi:10.1109/ACCESS.2018.2846779

Ateniese, G., Goodrich, M. T., Lekakis, V., Papamanthou, C., Paraskevas, E., & Tamassia, R. (2014). Accountable Storage. IACR Cryptology ePrint Archive.

Atzori, L., Iera, A., & Morabito, G. (2017). Understanding the Internet of Things: Definition, potentials, and societal role of a fast evolving paradigm. *Ad Hoc Networks*, *56*, 122–140. doi:10.1016/j.adhoc.2016.12.004

Axon, L. (2015). Privacy-awareness in Blockchain-based PKI. University of Oxford. https://goo.gl/3Nv2oK

Baker, S. B., Xiang, W., & Atkinson, I. (2017). Internet of Things for Smart Healthcare: Technologies, Challenges, and Opportunities. *IEEE Access : Practical Innovations, Open Solutions*, *5*, 26521–26544. doi:10.1109/ACCESS.2017.2775180

Barber, S., Boyen, X., Shi, E., & Uzun, E. (2012). *Bitter to Better - How to Make Bitcoin a Better Currency, Financial Cryptography, ser* (Vol. 7397). Lecture Notes in Computer Science. Springer.

Bartoletti, M., Gessa, D., & Podda, A. S. (2017). *Idea: a general framework for decentralized applications based on the Bitcoin blockchain.*

Bharathi, M. V., Tanguturi, R. C., Jayakumar, C., & Selvamani, K. (2013). Node capture attack in Wireless Sensor Network: A survey. *In Proceedings of the 2012 IEEE International Conference on Computational Intelligence & Computing Research (ICCIC)*. IEEE.

Bissias, G. D., Ozisik, A. P., Levine, B. N., & Liberatore, M. (2014). *Sybil Resistant Mixing for Bitcoin, WPES*. ACM.

Bocovich, C., Doucette, J., & Goldberg, I. (2015). *Lavinia: An audit payment protocol for censorship-resistant storage*. Center for Applied Cryptographic Research.

Bylica, P., Glen, L., Janiuk, P., Skrzypcaz, A., & Zawlocki, A. (2015). *A Probabilistic Nanopayment Scheme for Golem*. Golem Project. https://golemproject.net/doc/GolemNanopayments.pdf

Calvaresi, D., Dubovitskaya, A., & Calbimonte, J. P. (2018), Multi-agent systems and blockchain: results from a systematic literature review. *International Conference on Practical Applications of Agents and Multi-Agent Systems.* Springer. 10.1007/978-3-319-94580-4_9

Chen, H., & Wang, Y. (2019). Sschain: A full sharding protocol for public blockchain without data migration overhead. *Pervasive and Mobile Computing*, *59*, 101055. doi:10.1016/j.pmcj.2019.101055

Dai, H. N., Zheng, Z., & Zhang, Y. (2019). Blockchain for internet of things: A survey. *IEEE Internet of Things Journal*, *6*(5), 8076–8094. doi:10.1109/JIOT.2019.2920987

Dev, J. A. (2014). *Bitcoin mining acceleration and performance quantification, CCECE.* IEEE.

Dorri, A., Kanhere, S. S., & Jurdak, R. (2019). A memory optimized and flexible blockchain for large scale networks. *Future Generation Computer Systems*, *92*, 357–373. doi:10.1016/j.future.2018.10.002

Eckhoff, D., & Wagner, I. (2018). Privacy in the Smart City - Applications, Technologies, Challenges, and Solutions. *IEEE Communications Surveys and Tutorials*, *20*(1), 489–516. doi:10.1109/COMST.2017.2748998

Eyal, I., & Sirer, E. G. (2013). Majority is not Enough: Bitcoin Mining is Vulnerable. CoRR.

Fakhri, D., & Mutijarsa, K. (2018). Secure IoT communication using blockchain technology. *International Symposium on Electronics and Smart Devices (ISESD)*, (pp. 1–6). IEEE.

Feld, S., Schonfeld, M., & Werner, M. (2014). Analyzing the Deployment of Bitcoin's P2P Network under an AS-level Perspective. ANT/SEIT, ser. Procedia Computer Science. Elsevier.

Feng, Y., Huang, W., Wang, S., Zhang, Y., & Jiang, S. (2021). Detection of RFID cloning attacks: A spatiotemporal trajectory data stream-based practical approach. *Computer Networks*, *189*.

Fromknecth, C., Velicanu, D., & Yakoubov, S. (2014). CertCoin: A Name Coin Based Decentralized Authentication System. CSail. https://courses.csail.mit.edu/6.857/2014/files/ 19-fromknecht-velicann-yakoubov-certcoin.pdf

Fromknecth, C., Velicanu, D., & Yakoubov, S. (2014). *CertCoin: A NameCoin Based Decentralized Authentication System.* CSail. https://courses.csail.mit.edu/6.857/2014/files/ 19-fromknecht-velicann-yakoubov-certcoin.pdf

Gao, J., Agyekum, K. O. B. O., Sifah, E. B., Acheampong, K. N., Xia, Q., Du, X., & Xia, H. (2019). A blockchain-SDN-enabled Internet of vehicles environment for fog computing and 5G networks. *IEEE Internet of Things Journal*, *7*(5), 4278–4291. doi:10.1109/JIOT.2019.2956241

M. Georgescu, and D, Popescul. (2015). Security, privacy and trust in internet of things: A straight road? *International Business Information Management Association, IBIMA*. IEEE.

Dittman, G. (2019). A blockchain proxy for lightweight IoT devices. In: *Crypto Valley Conference on Blockchain Technology (CVCBT).* IEEE.

Gharaibeh, A., Salahuddin, M. A., Hussini, S. J., Khreishah, A., Khalil, I., Guizani, M., & Al-Fuqaha, A. (2017). Smart Cities: A Survey on Data Management, Security, and Enabling Technologies. *IEEE Communications Surveys and Tutorials*, *19*(4), 2456–2501. doi:10.1109/COMST.2017.2736886

Gipp, B., Meuschke, N., & Gernandt, A. (2015). Decentralized Trusted Timestamping using the Crypto Currency Bitcoin. CoRR.

Gochhayat, S. P., Bandara, E., Shetty, S., & Foytik, P. (2019). Yugala: Blockchain based Encrypted Cloud Storage for IoT Data. *2019 IEEE International Conference on Blockchain (Blockchain)*. IEEE. 10.1109/Blockchain.2019.00073

Hasan, M. (2022, May 18). State of IoT 2022: Number of connected IoT devices growing 18% to 14.4 billion globally. *IOT Analytics*. https://iot-analytics.com/number-connected-iot-devices/

Herbert, J., & Litchfield, A. (2015). *A Novel Method for Decentralised Peer-to-Peer Software License Validation Using Cryptocurrency Blockchain Technology, ACSC, ser. CRPIT* (Vol. 159). Australian Computer Society.

Herrera-Joancomart, J. (2014). *Research and Challenges on Bitcoin Anonymity, DPM/SETOP/QASA, ser* (Vol. 8872). Lecture Notes in Computer Science. Springer.

Huang, J., Kong, L., Chen, G., Wu, M.-Y., Liu, X., & Zeng, P. (2019). Towards Secure Industrial IoT: Blockchain System With Credit-Based Consensus Mechanism. *IEEE Transactions on Industrial Informatics Volume*, *15*(6), 3680–3689. doi:10.1109/TII.2019.2903342

Huang, J., Kong, L., Chen, G., Wu, M.-Y., & Peng Zeng, X. L. (2019). Towards Secure Industrial IoT: Blockchain System With Credit-Based Consensus Mechanism. *IEEE Transactions on Industrial Informatics Volume*, *15*(6), 3680–3689. doi:10.1109/TII.2019.2903342

Hummen, R., Hiller, J., Wirtz, H., Henze, M., Shafagh, H., & Wehrle, K. (2013). 6LoWPAN fragmentation attacks and mitigation mechanisms. *WiSec 2013 - Proceedings of the 6th ACM Conference on Security and Privacy in Wireless and Mobile Networks*, (pp. 55–66). ACM.

Huszti, A., Kovács, S., & Oláh, N. (2022). SzabolcsKovács, Norbert Oláh (2022). Scalable, password-based and threshold authentication for smart homes. *International Journal of Information Security*, *21*(4), 707–723. doi:10.100710207-022-00578-7

Karafiloski, E., & Mishev, A. (2017). Blockchain solutions for big data challenges: a literature review. *IEEE EUROCON 2017—17th International Conference on Smart Technologies*. IEEE.

Khan, L. U., Saad, W., Han, Z., Hossain, E., & Hong, C. S. (2021). Federated Learning for Internet of Things: Recent Advances, Taxonomy, and Open Challenges. *IEEE Communications Surveys and Tutorials*, *23*(3), 1759–1799. doi:10.1109/COMST.2021.3090430

Khedr, W. I. (2013). SRFID. A Hash-Based Security Scheme For Low Cost RFID Systems. *Egyptian Informatics Journal*, *14*(1), 89–98. doi:10.1016/j.eij.2013.02.001

Kozlov, D., Veijalainen, J., & Ali, Y. (2012). Security and privacy threats in IoT architectures. *In Proceedings of the 7th International Conference on Body Area Networks*. ICST (Institute for Computer Sciences, Social-Informatics and Telecommunications Engineering).

Kravitz, D.W., & Cooper, J. (2017) Securing user identity and transactions symbiotically: Iot meets blockchain. *2017 Global Internet of Things Summit (GIoTS)*. IEEE.

Kumar, R., Jain, S., Kumawat, S., & Jangir, S. K. (2011). An analysis of security and privacy issues,Challenges with possible solution in cloud computing. *IRACST-International Journal of Computer Science and Information Technology & Security (IJCSITS), 1*(2)

Kyle. (2018). Blockchain issues: #1: Data storage. *Medium.* https://medium.com/@Kyle.May/blockchain-issues-1-data-storage

Lehtonen, M., Ostojic, D., Ilic, A., & Michahelles, F. (2009), *Securing RFID systems by detecting tag cloning.* Conference: Pervasive Computing, 7th International Conference, Pervasive 2009, Nara, Japan.

Leian, L., & Shengli, L. (2006). ALOHA-based anti-collision algorithms used in RFID system. 2006 *International Conference on Wireless Communications, Networking and Mobile Computing*, WiCOM.

Vailshery, L. (2022). *Number of IoT connected devices worldwide 2019-2021, with forecasts to 2030.* Statista. https://www.statista.com/statistics/1183457/iot-connected-devices-worldwide/

Sahay, R., Geethakumari, G., & Mitra, B. (2022). A holistic framework for prediction of routing attacks in IoT. *The Journal of Supercomputing, 78*(1), 1409–1433. doi:10.100711227-021-03922-1

Lu, N., Cheng, N., Zhang, N., Shen, X., & Mark, J. W. (2014). Connected Vehicles: Solutions and Challenges. *IEEE Internet of Things, 1*(4), 289–299. doi:10.1109/JIOT.2014.2327587

Luo, F. J., Zhao, Y. D., & Liang, G. (2018). A distributed electricity trading system in active distribution networks based on multiagent coalition and blockchain. *IEEE Transactions on Power Systems, 34*(5), 4097–4108. doi:10.1109/TPWRS.2018.2876612

McEwen, A., & Cassimally, H. (2013). *Designing the internet of things.*

Meiklejohn, S., & Orlandi, C. (2015). *Privacy-Enhancing Overlays in Bitcoin, Financial Cryptography Workshops, ser* (Vol. 8976). Lecture Notes in Computer Science. Springer.

Mitrokotsa, A., Rieback, M. R., & Tanenbaum, A. S. (2010). Classifying RFID Attacks and Defense. *Information Systems Frontiers, 12*(5), 491–505. doi:10.100710796-009-9210-z

Moser, M., Bohme, R., & Breuker, D. An Inquiry into Money Laundering Tools in the Bitcoin Ecosystem. *E-Crime Researchers' Summit.* IEEE. https://maltemoeser.de/paper/money-laundering.pdf

Norta, A., Othman, A. B., & Taveter, K. (2015). Conflict-resolution lifecycles for governed decentralized autonomous organization collaboration. *2015 2nd International Conference on Electronic Governance and Open Society: Challenges in Eurasia.* ACM.

Noura, M., Atiquzzaman, M., & Gaedke, M. (2019). Interoperability in Internet of Things: Taxonomies and Open Challenges. *Mobile Networks and Applications, 24*(3), 796–809. doi:10.100711036-018-1089-9

Otte, P., de Vos, M., & Pouwelse, J. (2017). TrustChain: A Sybil-resistant scalable blockchain. *Future Generation Computer Systems, 107*, 770–780. doi:10.1016/j.future.2017.08.048

Özyılmaz, K. R., & Yurdakul, A. (2017), Work-in-progress: integrating low-power IoT devices to a blockchain-based infrastructure, *International Conference on Embedded Software.* IEEE.

Panarello, A., Tapas, N., Merlino, G., Longo, F., & Puliafito, A. (2018). Blockchain and IoT integration: A systematic survey. *Sensors (Basel)*, *18*(8), 2575. doi:10.339018082575 PMID:30082633

Park, S., Pietrzak, K., Kwon, A., Alwen, J., Fuchsbauer, G., & Gazi, P. (2015), Spacemint: A Cryptocurrency Based on Proofs of Space. IACR Cryptology.

Pongle, P., & Chavan, G. (2015). *A Survey: Attacks on RPL and 6LoWPAN in IoT.* Conference: ICPC, Pune.

Puthal, D., Nepal, S., Ranjan, R., & Chen, J. (2016). Threats to networking cloud and edge data centers in the Internet of Things. *IEEE Cloud Computing*, *2016*(3), 64–71. doi:10.1109/MCC.2016.63

Qayumi, K. (2015), Multi-agent based intelligence generation from very large datasets, *International Conference on Cloud Engineering.* IEEE. 10.1109/IC2E.2015.96

Rathee, G., Garg, S., Kaddoum, G., & Choi, B. J. (2021). Decision-Making Model for Securing IoT Devices in Smart Industries. *IEEE Transactions on Industrial Informatics*, *17*(6), 4270–4278. doi:10.1109/TII.2020.3005252

Renuka, K., Kumari, S., Zhao, D., & Li, A. L. (2019). Design of a Secure Password-Based Authentication Scheme for M2M Networks in IoT Enabled Cyber-Physical Systems. *IEEE Access : Practical Innovations, Open Solutions*, *7*, 2169–3536. doi:10.1109/ACCESS.2019.2908499

Salman, T., Zolanvari, M., Erbad, A., Jain, R., & Samaka, M. (2019). Security services using blockchains: A state of the art survey. *IEEE Communications Surveys and Tutorials*, *21*(1), 850–880. doi:10.1109/COMST.2018.2863956

Shrestha, R., & Kim, S. (2019). Integration of IoT with blockchain and homomorphic encryption: Challenging issues and opportunities. *Advances in Computers*, *115*, 293–331. doi:10.1016/bs.adcom.2019.06.002

Si, H., Sun, C., Li, Y., Qiao, H., & Shi, L. (2019). IoT information sharing security mechanism based on blockchain technology. *Future Generation Computer Systems*, *101*, 1028–1040. doi:10.1016/j.future.2019.07.036

Nils Siegfried, N., Rosenthal T., & Benlian, A. (2018). Blockchain and the Industrial Internet of Things A requirement taxonomy and systematic fit analysis. *Journal of Enterprise Information Management.*

Singh, A., Click, K., Parizi, R. M., Zhang, Q., Dehghantanha, A., & Choo, K.-K. R. (2020). Sidechain technologies in blockchain networks: An examination and state-of-the-art review. *Journal of Network and Computer Applications*, *149*, 102471. doi:10.1016/j.jnca.2019.102471

Spagnuolo, M., Maggi, F., & Zanero, S. (2014). *BitIodine: Extracting Intelligence from the Bitcoin Network, Financial Cryptography, ser* (Vol. 8437). Lecture Notes in Computer Science. Springer.

Suo, H., Wan, J., Zou, C., & Liu, J. (2012). Security in the internet of things: A review. *265 Proceedings - 2012 International Conference on Computer Science and Electronics Engineering.* IEEE.

Thorat, N. B., & Sreevardhan, C. (2014). Survey On Security Threats And Solutions For Near Field Communication. *International Journal of Research in Engineering and Technology*, *3*(12).

Tom, R. J., Sankaranarayanan, S., & Rodrigues, J. J. (2020). Agent negotiation in an IoT-fog based power distribution system for demand reduction. *Sustainable Energy Technologies and Assessments*, *38*, 100653. doi:10.1016/j.seta.2020.100653

Tomescu, A., & Devadas, S. (2017). Efficient non-equivocation via bitcoin. *38th IEEE Symposium on Security and Privacy (SP)*, (pp. 393–409). IEEE. (2017).

Tomescu, A., & Devadas, S. (2017). Catena: Efficient non-equivocation via bitcoin. *38th IEEE Symposium on Security and Privacy*. IEEE.

Uddin, M. A., Stranieri, A., Gondal, I., & Balasubramanian, V. (2020). Dynamically recommending repositories for health data: a machine learning model. *Australasian Computer Science Week Multiconference*. ACM.

Uddin, M. A., Stranieri, A., Gondal, I., & Balasubramanian, V. (2020). Blockchain leveraged decentralized IoT ehealth framework. *Internet of Things*, *9*, 100159. doi:10.1016/j.iot.2020.100159

Uddin, M. A., Stranieri, A., Gondal, I., & Balasubramanian, V. (2021, June). A survey on the adoption of blockchain in IoT: Challenges and solutions. *Blockchain: Research and Applications*, *2*(2), 100006.

Valenta, L., & Rowan, B. (2015). *Blindcoin: Blinded, Accountable Mixes for Bitcoin, Financial Cryptography Workshops, ser* (Vol. 8976). Lecture Notes in Computer Science. Springer.

Vandervort, D. (2014). Challenges and Opportunities Associated with a BitcoinBased Transaction Rating System. In. Lecture Notes in Computer Science: Vol. 8438. *Financial Cryptography Workshops, ser* (pp. 33–42). Springer. doi:10.1007/978-3-662-44774-1_3

Vidgren, N., Haataja, K., Pati, L., & Jos, J. (2013). Security Threats in ZigBee-Enabled Systems: Vulnerability Evaluation, Practical Experiments, Countermeasures, and Lessons Learned. *46th Hawaii International Conference on System Sciences*. IEEE. 10.1109/HICSS.2013.475

Wallgren, L., Raza, S., & Voigt, T. (2013). Routing attacks and countermeasures in the RPL based internet of things. *International Journal of Distributed Sensor Networks*, *2013*(II), 794326. doi:10.1155/2013/794326

Weekly, K., & Pister, K. (2012) Evaluating Sinkhole Defense Techniques In RPL Networks. *IEEE International Conference on Network Protocols*. IEEE. 10.1109/ICNP.2012.6459948

Wilkinson, S. (2018). *Storj A Peer-to-Peer Cloud Storage Network*. Storj Labs. https://storj.io/storj.pdf

Wilson, D., & Ateniese, G. (2015). *From Pretty Good To Great: Enhancing PGP using Bitcoin and the Blockchain*. CoRR.

Winter, T., Thubert, P., Brandt, A., Hui, J., Kelsey, R., Levis, P., Pister, K., Struik, R., Vasseur, J., & Alexander, R. (2012). RPL: IPv6 Routing Protocol for Low-Power and Lossy Networks. *Network Architectures and Services*.

Worner, D., & von Bomhard, T. (2014). When your sensor earns money: ¨ exchanging data for cash with Bitcoin. In *UbiComp Adjunct* (pp. 295–298). ACM. doi:10.1145/2638728.2638786

Xu, X. (2013). Study on security problems and key technologies of the internet of things. *Proceedings - 2013 International Conference on Computational and Information Sciences*. IEEE.

Yu, T. X., Wang, X. B., & Zhu, Y. X. (2019). *Blockchain technology for the 5G—enabled internet of things systems: principle, applications and challenges, 5G—Enabled Internet of Things*. CRC Press.

Zhang, Y., & Wen, J. (2015). An IoT electric business model based on the protocol of bitcoin. In *ICIN* (pp. 184–191). IEEE. doi:10.1109/ICIN.2015.7073830

Zyskind, G., Nathan, O., & Pentland, A. (2015). Decentralizing Privacy: Using Blockchain to Protect Personal Data. *IEEE Symposium on Security and Privacy Workshops*. IEEE. 10.1109/SPW.2015.27

Chapter 18
Blockchain for Social Impact:
Enhancing Traceability and Economic Fairness in the Coffee Supply Chain

SzuTung Chen
University of Glasgow, UK

ABSTRACT

As customer demand and regulations drive the coffee industry towards greater traceability and sustainability, coffee farmers in producing countries continue to face challenges in capturing the intangible value-added in their products. This chapter examines the implementation of blockchain technology to address economic and social challenges faced by producers in the coffee industry. The findings demonstrate that blockchain implementation holds promise in reducing information asymmetry in the supply chain, establishing stronger customer-farmer connections, and generating various economic and social benefits for coffee farmers. However, blockchain-enabled third-party verification remains relatively uncommon in current practice. Several challenges must be effectively addressed to realize the full potential of blockchain and foster a more transparent, equitable, and sustainable coffee supply chain.

1. INTRODUCTION

Coffee is the first thing many people reach for in the morning, providing a jolt of caffeine to help kick-start their day. The world drinks approximately 3 billion cups of coffee every day (International Trade Centre [ITC], 2021, p.xxii), making it the most consumed hot drink globally (Food and Agriculture Organization of the United Nations [FAO], 2023). The coffee market is expected to grow annually by 4.47%, reaching global revenues of $540.8 billion by 2025 (Statista, 2023). The worldwide coffee demand has been steadily increasing since the 2000s, due in part to the increasing consumption in emerging economies and the increasing demand for specialty coffee in developed countries (FAO, 2023).

DOI: 10.4018/978-1-6684-9919-1.ch018

Copyright © 2023, IGI Global. Copying or distributing in print or electronic forms without written permission of IGI Global is prohibited.

However, as we enjoy coffee's invigorating aroma and taste, we rarely think about how the coffee beans come from farms to our cups. Behind the aromatic beverage, there are 25 million farmers and families whose lives depend on this plant (International Coffee Organization [ICO], 2019), with smallholder farmers accounting for 95% of the coffee-producing population (Voora et al., 2022, p.2). The escalating costs of coffee production also cast severe social and economic consequences on local coffee producers (Fiocco et al., 2023). Among the smallholder farmers worldwide, at least 5.5 million farmers live below the international poverty line of $3.20 a day (ITC, 2021, p.3).

The coffee industry has been moving towards sustainability, differentiation, and traceability, and customers are willing to pay more for specialty coffee, but the benefits from the expansion of the coffee industry are not trickling down to the poorest coffee producers (Daviron & Ponte, 2005). The industry has been facing the Coffee Paradox (Daviron & Ponte, 2005), and there has been an asymmetric income distribution among stakeholders along the coffee supply chain. Coffee roasters in the consuming countries that are closer to the final customers capture the highest margin as they concentrate on marketing and branding, benefitting from the intangible and symbolic quality attributes of the coffee (Daviron & Ponte, 2005; ITC, 2021; Lewin et al., 2004). Higher margins have been created along the entire coffee supply chain, but not on an equal basis. Value in the coffee supply chain is disproportionately concentrated in developed countries' marketing stage. According to Miatton and Amado (2020, p.3), in the Colombian coffee supply chain, coffee producers represent the largest segment, but they receive the lowest profit margin (See **Table 1**).

Table 1. Share of population and captured value of stakeholders in the Colombian coffee supply chain

Stakeholders in the value chain	Share of captured value	Share of value chain population
Producers	5%	89%
Mills/Processors	2%	5%
Exporters	9%	1%
Transporters/Shippers	7%	1%
Importers	32%	1%
Roasters	45%	3%

The Fairtrade movements, which started to gain popularity in the late 1980s, are meant to address this power inequality by guaranteeing a minimum income for coffee farmers, but the initiatives face several challenges. The biggest problem of the Fairtrade certification is the lack of power control of FairTrade International and TransFair USA over maintaining the integrity of Fairtrade principles as profit-oriented corporations increasingly acquire the Fairtrade label for their products (Jaffee, 2014). The lack of transparency further hinders public verification of Fairtrade information and the possibility to hold institutions accountable. Jaffee (2014) identified this problem as "the danger of reducing the qualifications of products to simple signs" (p.216). Addressing these externalities, as suggested by Weber et al. (2020), is crucial to enhancing the sustainability of the coffee supply chain.

To solve the Coffee Paradox and the information asymmetry inherent in the coffee supply chain, Daviron and Ponte (2005) asserted that it is essential to promote consumer knowledge of the coffee and the places of production, rather than brand recognition by itself, while increasing transparency and consumer-producer connectivity of the whole coffee supply chain. On the other hand, a two-way flow of information should also be established to allow farmers to gain insights into the current coffee market and trends to gain negotiating power.

In agricultural markets, power imbalances arise from the superior bargaining power of contracting partners (Daskalova, 2020), and the information asymmetry is leading to the occurrence of unfair trade practices (Arpášová & Rajčániová, 2022). Addressing these challenges involves challenging the status quo and potentially threatening vested interests in existing systems. Intermediaries in the coffee supply chain may lack sufficient incentives to ensure fair compensation for farmers (Chaudhuri et al., 2021) while roasters prefer to concentrate on marketing and branding without vertical integration upstream (Daviron & Ponte, 2005). As a result, in current practice, trust is established through governance mechanisms or standards, while end customers rely on brand recognition or third-party certifications to assess coffee quality and sustainability.

Amidst a shifting social paradigm, interest in blockchain technology for verified supply chain information and enhanced transparency is rising to address traceability and trust challenges. Blockchain utilizes cryptographic techniques, distributed consensus protocols, and peer-to-peer transactions to establish transparent and tamper-resistant records within distrustful networks. This research evaluates blockchain's potential in fostering social sustainability and addressing economic fairness in the coffee supply chain. Through case studies and interviews, this research explores the current state of blockchain implementation in the industry and identifies challenges, strategies, and future steps for advancement. The findings aim to offer valuable insights to professionals involved in coffee supply chain management seeking to enhance sustainability through technological innovation.

This study contends that blockchain technology facilitates transparent traceability in the coffee supply chain. By leveraging blockchain, verifiable evidence of quality attributes and coffee origins can be provided, meeting the demand for premium specialty coffee and regulatory traceability requirements. The enhanced traceability and premium pricing foster collaboration among stakeholders, despite misalignment of interests, benefiting all parties involved, particularly coffee farmers, who can now capture more of the coffee's intangible value.

2. LITERATURE REVIEW

2.1 Introduction of Blockchain Technology

A blockchain is a digital append-only ledger that is shared across a distributed network of independent computer nodes. Once the data is verified and added to the ledger, it is updated across all participating nodes and is protected by cryptographic protocols that make it practically impossible to tamper with (Casey & Vigna, 2018). Blockchain's consensus algorithm eliminates the need for intermediaries. People can trust that the information recorded on the distributed ledger will not be unilaterally modified or removed, and there will be a publicly visible record that can be verified at any given moment and is not controlled by centralized entities. Trust, as Domjan et al. (2021) argued, is "in the code that underlies the system" (p.15).

What blockchain technology enables is the ability to 1) reduce the costs of trust in a system full of strangers or actors that do not have incentives to trust and cooperate, and 2) increase the costs of betrayal or conducting malicious actions that might harm the collective good, for any unilateral corruption will be easily detected by all actors across the network. This is the fundamental feature that unleashes infinite possibilities to reimagine how to improve the current systems that we are living in.

Casey and Vigna (2018) argued that blockchain is fundamentally a social technology that can aid in the reconstruction of trust and social capital. Blockchain has been given various names by different authors, including the Confidence Machine (De Filippi et al., 2020), the Truth Machine (Casey & Vigna, 2018), and the Trust Machine (The Economist, 2015). Beyond financial applications and cryptocurrencies, the true value of blockchain technology envisions a more democratic, inclusive, and equitable world.

2.2 Rationale for Blockchain Adoption in Coffee

Blockchain technology has far-reaching implications beyond finance due to the elimination of intermediaries and increased trust among networks. Even though the majority of blockchain research tends to study the technical characteristics of blockchain, efficiency gains, or profits that the technology brings for profit-oriented companies, there has been a shift of narratives from focusing on commercial and consumer benefits to socially and environmentally beneficial applications (Kewell et al., 2017).

A growing number of blockchain-based systems aim to revolutionize, or at least improve, great swaths of industries, with supply chain management being a prominent area of exploration. Among all agricultural commodities, coffee is one of the most interesting products for blockchain applications. The characteristics of the coffee supply chain and the current industry trends make it an excellent commodity for the implementation of blockchain technology.

The flow chart adopted from Wüst and Gervais (2018, p.47) demonstrates that blockchain technology is well-suited for complicated global coffee supply chains (See **Figure 1**). Within the coffee industry, it is necessary to store the state of the network to increase transparency and enable various stakeholders to access shared information. In addition, there are trust issues among coffee supply chain stakeholders, stemming from dispersed participants across various countries, different jurisdictions, and their profit-maximization mindset (Bager, Düdder, et al., 2022).

The rising popularity of origin coffee underscores the importance of traceable and detailed information. Nevertheless, such attributes entail higher costs and raise concerns about intermediaries potentially trading non-origin products as if they were genuine (Bettín-Díaz et al., 2022), which makes public verification essential for fraudulent claims. Therefore, considering the presented flow, the adoption of a public blockchain seems justifiable for the coffee industry.

2.3 Blockchain Implementation in the Coffee Supply Chain

In the conventional approach (refer to the upper diagram in **Figure 2**), each participant within the coffee supply chain maintains their data independently, through respective digitized systems or software (Bager, Singh, et al., 2022). As articulated by Bager, Düdder, et al. (2022), even though the coffee supply chain operates in a decentralized manner without a dominant controlling entity, certain agents such as processors/exporters hold more information than others.

The coffee supply chain exhibits information asymmetry, with coffee buyers like importers and roasters having visibility limited to the freight-on-board (FOB) price, which is the price paid to the exporter for the coffee ready to ship. Farmers also lack visibility of downstream prices in the supply chain (Chaudhuri et al., 2021). One Colombian coffee producer shared in an interview that many of them were unaware of the current market price for coffee, and they only found out about the price fluctuations when selling

Figure 1. Flow chart explaining why blockchain technology makes sense in the coffee supply chain

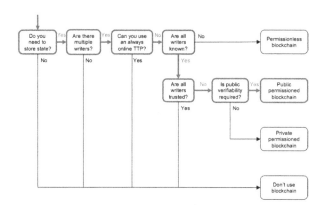

their harvested coffee cherries to cooperatives (iFinca, 2019). End customers also often lack complete comprehension of the characteristics and essential details of the coffee they purchase (Bettín-Díaz et al., 2022; Verhoeven et al., 2018).

By leveraging blockchain technology, all stakeholders within the coffee supply chain contribute their data to a streamlined ledger, ensuring transparency and accessibility for all (depicted in the lower diagram of **Figure 2**). Köhler and Pizzol (2020) indicated that the traceability and verifiable information offered by blockchain technology provides actors with an overview of their supply chains while fostering trust among stakeholders. Chaudhuri et al. (2021) argued that the information asymmetry in the coffee supply chain is significantly reduced after the blockchain implementation. This decentralized approach ensures equal access to information among participants, with no single entity holding privileged access. Additionally, the implementation of a consensus algorithm enhances data integrity, safeguarding the traceability and transparency of the data.

2.4 Benefits for Blockchain Implementation in Coffee Supply Chains

Various researchers have studied the practicability, benefits, and challenges of blockchain implementation in the agri-food supply chain. The primary focus is to increase transparency and traceability with the addition of blockchain technology. According to Sunny et al. (2020), traceability in the supply chain entails both *tracking* the product's journey from its origin to its endpoint and *tracing* its path from the endpoint back to its origin, which ensures transparency in the supply chain.

Coffee farmers have strong incentives to embrace blockchain technology and participate in a more transparent supply chain due to market volatility, information asymmetry, and vulnerabilities (Chaudhuri et al., 2021). Köhler and Pizzol (2020) stated that blockchain facilitates direct consumer-producer communication, enabling additional financial support like tips or microloans. Blockchain is also proposed as a potential solution for economic fairness issues in coffee, fostering equitable models that recognize quality and diligence (Miatton & Amado, 2020).

Furthermore, diverse stakeholders stand to benefit from blockchain integration in the coffee supply chain. Bager, Singh, et al. (2022) learned from their pilot test that transparent information enables roasters to access detailed information about coffee, allowing them to experiment with roasting profiles and improve quality. Roasters can also leverage the fair price paid to farmers and coffee information for

Figure 2. Illustration of the coffee supply chain before and after blockchain implementation

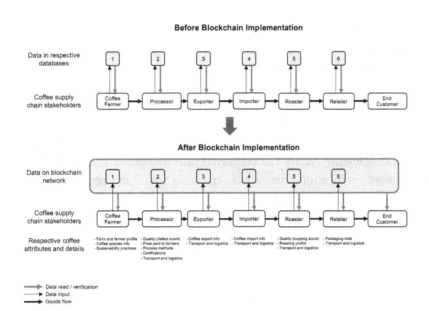

effective marketing, while exporters may experience an increase in overall trade volume (Chaudhuri et al., 2021). Blockchain-enabled traceability enhances quality assurance, while improved collaboration and efficiency contribute to overall quality enhancement (Alamsyah et al., 2023). Within the context of the specialty coffee trend prioritizing quality for premium pricing, this translates to improved coffee prices, benefiting all supply chain stakeholders.

Enhanced traceability and transparency also accrue benefits to end customers. Casey and Vigna (2018) contended that customers can obtain comprehensive information concerning the safety and ethical aspects of products. Empirical evidence by Damoska Sekuloska and Erceg (2022) and Alazab et al. (2021) indicated that blockchain's transparency and traceability enhance customer confidence. Pavlić Skender and Zaninović (2020) underscored that blockchain technology augments consumer security and trust through improved product visibility and provenance. The availability of product-specific information also empowers customers to make informed purchasing decisions (Chaudhuri et al., 2021; Köhler & Pizzol, 2020).

Another notable contribution of blockchain technology to the coffee industry is its influence on the auditing and verification process. Over at least the last two decades, the adoption of voluntary sustainability standards (VSS) is the main governance mechanism in agri-food sustainability, such as Fairtrade and Rainforest Alliance (Köhler et al., 2022). Daviron and Ponte (2005) stated that many firms market sustainable coffee without independent certification or verification (p.166). End customers cannot verify whether the claimed statement of being ethical and sustainable is true despite the efforts from coffee buyers and roasters to match the market trend and gain the trust from the young generation (Voora et al., 2022).

This leads coffee buyers to rely on well-established corporations, reputable brands, or certifications due to the absence of reliable verification mechanisms. This reliance on trust may enable malicious actors to exploit the situation and benefit from false marketing claims (Harper, 2020). Roberts (2018) also emphasized the importance of implementing a robust verification method so that the transparency movement will not be limited to relying on trust and the good intentions of those who voluntarily disclose information.

A salient distinction between blockchain solutions and conventional practices lies in the verifiability of the presented information. Public blockchains offer third-party accessibility to the distributed ledger, enabling the verification of data displayed on websites or applications to match the information recorded on the blockchain network.

To illustrate, when end customers scan the QR codes on the coffee bean package, they are directed to established platforms with access to publicly available information about the coffee supply chain (depicted in Step 1 in **Figure 3**). However, unlike private databases, public blockchains permit end customers or any third party to independently verify the displayed information on the blockchain network, thereby facilitating a transparent verification process (illustrated in Step 2 in **Figure 3**). Blockchain diminishes the necessity to rely on any individual actor for trust while maximizing the degree of confidence in the system (De Filippi et al., 2020). Domjan et al. (2021) argued that blockchain itself becomes the trusted intermediary, supplanting traditional third-party institutions with technology (p.8).

Figure 3. Illustration of end customer's interaction with supply chain data and blockchain network

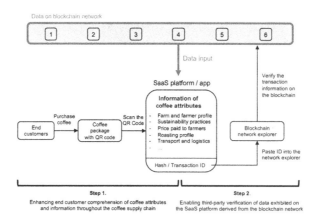

According to Düring and Fisbeck (2017) and Tröster (2020), the highest level of trust is attained when end customers can form their own opinions about a product's quality or compliance with specific criteria through acquired knowledge and personal control while being able to follow the product along the entire value chain (See **Figure 4**). The authors argued that blockchain technology facilitates a new form of trust, in which trust is not only created because customers have complete transparency but also because they are empowered to have that transparency at any time.

The auditing process in the coffee industry may shift from the "take my word for it" approach and placing trust in individual companies or certifications to continuous third-party verification. The implementation does not necessarily entail customers scanning QR codes and verifying transactions on the blockchain network every time they purchase coffee; instead, the key is that any third party will always have the option and power to double-check, verify, and hold the operating company accountable.

Figure 4. Visualization of the level of trust building

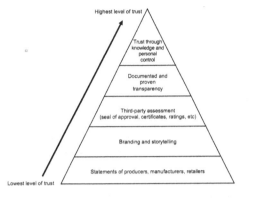

Note: The figure is adopted from Düring and Fisbeck (2017, p.452) and the English translation is adopted from Tröster (2020, p.7).

3. METHODOLOGY

The literature review identifies significant research gaps concerning the examination of social sustainability aspects and ongoing case studies in the context of blockchain-traced coffee supply chains, beyond initial pilot projects (Bager, Düdder, et al., 2022). Moreover, most benefits of blockchain for the coffee industry remain theoretical due to the lack of empirical studies (Singh et al., 2022). Existing practical studies predominantly focus on technology modeling rather than investigating real-world implementation cases (Rogerson & Parry, 2020).

This paper investigates ongoing company cases to understand the practical implications of blockchain technology in the coffee supply chain. It aims to explore how blockchain integration translates theoretical potential into tangible outcomes and examines its social impact on promoting economic fairness in the coffee industry.

To achieve these objectives and address existing research gaps, a qualitative research method is employed, combining multiple case studies and interviews. This approach allows for the identification of common patterns and enriches the findings through insights from key industry individuals.

Ten blockchain-based Software-as-a-Service (SaaS) companies focusing on enhancing traceability in the coffee supply chain were identified. Contact was established with relevant employees responsible for coffee supply chain projects or sustainability in these companies. Three blockchain implementation companies (Dimitra, Bext360, and iFinca) were successfully selected for interviews, while attempts to interview others were unsuccessful. However, an interview with the blockchain provider Topl Blockchain, responsible for FairFood's coffee supply chain, was scheduled.

To ensure a diverse range of perspectives, interviews were also conducted with industry experts from organizations such as the Specialty Coffee Association (SCA), Colombian Coffee Growers Federation (FNC), NewCoffee (Aldi's independent coffee subsidiary), and Colombian specialty coffee producer La Palma & El Tucán (See **Table 2**).

Table 2. Details of the conducted interviews

Company	Category	Designation of the interviewee	Duration of the interview
Dimitra	SaaS platform	CEO	27 mins
Bext360	SaaS platform	Sustainability Director	45 mins
iFinca / CoffeeChain	SaaS platform	CEO	37 mins
Topl Blockchain	Blockchain provider	Growth Associate	50 mins
NewCoffee (ALDi)	Coffee retailer	Lead of Procurement	36 mins
Specialty Coffee Association	NGO in the coffee industry	Sustainability Director	53 mins
Colombian Coffee Growers Federation	NGO in the coffee industry	Sustainable Commercial Coordinator	27 mins
La Palma & El Tucán	Colombian specialty coffee producer	Co-Founder & CEO	30 mins

4. KEY HIGHLIGHTS OF THE COFFEE INDUSTRY

4.1 Overview of the Coffee Supply Chain

The global coffee supply chain encompasses a complex network of stakeholders and processing stages. Coffee beans traverse various phases before reaching the final consumers, as depicted in **Figure 5**. Ranging from farming practices, coffee species, and processing methods at the farm level to the roasting profile at the roasters' end, each stage significantly influences the ultimate flavor of the coffee (ITC, 2021). Given the consequential impact of these particulars on coffee quality and subsequent pricing, comprehensive documentation becomes imperative. However, this process is intricate and susceptible to human errors.

Figure 5. Simplified Colombian coffee supply chain flow

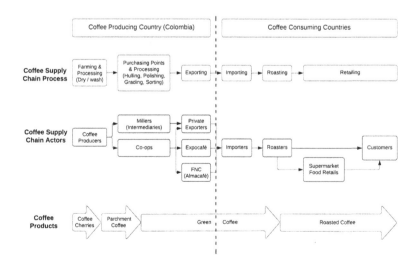

Note: The flow chart is created by the author. The coffee supply chain flow is adopted from Borrella et al. (2015, p.30), and the process from purchasing points to exporters is adopted from Giovannucci et al. (2002, p.41).

The coffee supply chain begins with the labor-intensive harvesting of coffee cherries, predominantly carried out through manual picking methods in most countries. Subsequently, the coffee cherries undergo processing to transform into *parchment coffee*, which is further subjected to hulling, grading, and sorting procedures. The resulting milled beans, termed *green coffee*, are then prepared for export. Finally, *green coffee* undergoes roasting, typically performed in importing countries to preserve freshness for end consumers.

Tracking and tracing coffee beans in the supply chain is a complex and challenging process, as emphasized by the Sustainability Director of SCA. The risk of losing traceability is prevalent within warehouses at purchasing points as the lack of segregation often leads to blending coffee beans. This observation aligns with the findings of Bager, Düdder, et al. (2022). The supply chain involves multiple stakeholders, including financial institutions, and can span a considerable time frame. The interviewee stated that cooperatives typically pay only 60% of the coffee price upfront to farmers upon purchase, as the exportation process and receipt of payment from roasters take 4 to 6 months. Additional risks arise when coffee is damaged, found defective, or rejected at the port post-purchase. Therefore, meticulously documenting every process in the coffee supply chain presents a significant challenge.

Let me give you an example with numbers. A full container of coffee, it's around 40,000 pounds. Let's say that you buy that coffee at a good price of 3.5 dollars. That means you need 140,000 dollars to purchase that coffee from your farmers. 140K is a lot of money, and usually, cooperatives don't have that much… you need to ask a bank to give you the money so that you can pay the farmer or at least cover half. – Sustainability Director of SCA.

Under current practice, achieving full traceability demands substantial administrative efforts. The Sustainability Coordinator of the FNC noted that each cooperative manages its invoice and farmer data using Excel spreadsheets which are subsequently uploaded to the FNC's data system. When coffee companies demand full traceability for a specific supply chain, the FNC staff manually download the files from their system and upload them to the corresponding platforms utilized by the companies, which introduces inefficiencies and potential human errors.

4.2 Market Trends of the Coffee Industry

The Third Wave of coffee, which emerged in the late 1990s and early 2000s, brought about a significant shift in the coffee industry. Coffee is sought after by bourgeois consumers who value quality, uniqueness, artisanal authenticity, and a link to the origin of production (Fischer, 2022). Customers are also willing to pay a premium for the distinctive flavor and aroma characteristics (Bettín-Díaz et al., 2022). Under this trend, the traceability of coffee information or the "narratives" of the coffee from farm to cup, has gained increasing significance and value.

As the coffee industry moves towards differentiation and traceability, there is also increasing attention on sustainability, which refers to "economic viability for farmers," "environmental conservation," and "social responsibility" (Daviron & Ponte, 2005, p.164). Specialty coffee enthusiasts have been paying more attention to the social dimension of sustainability, such as inequalities (Pendergrast, 2010), fair wages, labor rights, and social responsibility (Burroughes et al., 2023).

ITC (2021) identified a fairer, more ethical, and sustainable supply chain as a global priority, which significantly influences consumers' consuming behaviors. End customers demonstrate a willingness to pay a premium for ethically and sustainably sourced products (Pavlić Skender & Zaninović, 2020). Dionysis et al. (2022) discovered that 75.6% of their research participants expressed their willingness to pay a minimum of 5% extra for blockchain-traced coffee, with the majority indicating a price premium ranging from 5% to 30% above the base price.

The increased market demand for ethical and sustainable supply chains has been identified by the interviewees in this research as well.

As education and understanding on ESG sustainability practices and ethical labor is increasing and people are becoming more aware of where their goods come from, there's like an increase in demand from these points. – Growth Associate of Topl.

I think there's also the driver of transparency... a fair treatment, a fair remuneration, a fair condition to everyone who is involved in the supply chain. So, it's not just a business where the traders and the industry can make money, but also a business where the producers, the farmers themselves can also make a decent living. – Lead of Procurement of NewCoffee.

Data collected from the elite interviews and secondary sources further demonstrated that the young customers' demand and regulations are two main driving reasons for this ongoing trend, which paves the way for the increasing integration of blockchain technology into the coffee supply chain.

According to ITC (2021), millennials, adults born between 1981 and 1996, care more about global social and economic inequities. Meanwhile, transparency also stands as a defining characteristic of GenZ, young adults who were born between 1997 and 2012 (Petrock, 2021). Interviewees from Topl and iFinca also attributed this market trend to GenZ.

If you're looking at people of our age group, like GenZ and Millennials... when given a choice between two products that are almost equal, but one is more sustainably sourced than the other, they're going to pick the sustainably sourced one. – Growth Associate of Topl.

Another reason that agricultural supply chains are moving towards increased traceability and sustainability is due to regulations. As articulated in McKinsey's report (Fiocco et al., 2023), regulatory frameworks are poised to have a growing impact on driving the expansion of specific submarkets within agricultural technology.

The leading example is the coming European Union Deforestation Regulation (EUDR). The new regulation will impose stringent measures to prevent the inclusion of deforestation-linked products in the EU market. Operators and major traders are required to provide auditable evidence of origin, including geospatial coordinates, to verify the deforestation-free status of the product. Compliance with the regulation will be mandatory for companies by the end of 2024.

Representatives from Dimitra and Bext360 mentioned the significance of traceability as the EU is pushing deforestation regulations in the interviews. The Sustainable Coordinator of FNC also mentioned that the coming European regulations, such as the German Supply Chain Due Diligence Act (LkSG), are demanding full traceability for imported coffee.

5. BLOCKCHAIN IMPLEMENTATION AND IMPACT IN THE COFFEE SUPPLY CHAIN

This section provides an overview of the blockchain implementation in four case study companies and outlines their economic and social impact on coffee producers. The key findings emphasize the current limitations of third-party verification in blockchain implementation, which holds significant potential for enhancing social sustainability in coffee supply chains.

5.1 Blockchain Implementation

Dimitra

Blockchain is utilized to track coffee beans from farms to exporters via the Connected Coffee app, starting with farmers establishing a Geofence and documenting essential farm details (Cointelegraph, 2023). According to the CEO of Dimitra in the interview, advanced technologies like satellites, AI, IoT, sensors, and drones are employed to assess and optimize farming practices. The data is selected and regularly uploaded to Ethereum or Polygon by the Dimitra team. Staff at the purchasing stations register the farmers, assess the coffee quality based on predefined indicators, apply unique barcodes to individual bags, and document the corresponding price per kilo. Workers from the subsequent processes can scan the barcodes to associate the coffee with the recorded data as the coffee moves down the supply chain.

The main goal of Dimitra is to provide farmers with access to smart farming and technologies (Dimitra, 2021). The CEO stated that companies may not disclose the identities of individual farmers due to privacy considerations while contractual agreements may restrict stakeholders from obtaining specific price details.

iFinca and CoffeeChain

iFinca develops a mobile app and online platform that digitalizes the coffee supply chain and discloses the farmgate price, which is the actual price received by coffee farmers (iFinca, 2023). The platform captures 160 data points along the supply chain. This data is made accessible to stakeholders through CoffeeChain QR codes, and the encrypted nature of these codes ensures that only relevant supply chain participants can access the associated information (Chaudhuri et al., 2021).

In addition, the Meet the Farmer QR codes enable end customers to access farmer profiles, establishing a direct connection between coffee producers and consumers. In the interview, the CEO mentioned that customers can also engage with farmers by posting messages through the iFinca mobile app, offering a means for customers to independently verify the information and "check the checker."

However, the company now utilizes Amazon Web Services (AWS), instead of a blockchain network, to document all the data. As the company positions itself as an independent third-party verification entity, separate from the selling and buying of coffee beans, the CEO argued that the company's goal is to accurately disclose the real-time farmgate price and track the journey of the coffee supply chain.

Bext360

With blockchain technology, Bext360 aims to solve unfair treatment and increase social sustainability by developing a complete chain of information (Verhoeven et al., 2018). Through the use of RFID technology, coffee is tracked and recorded at each stage of the supply chain (Bext360, 2019). The farmers' unique IDs are tied to each product bundle, enabling traceability throughout its entire journey and premium rewards to go back to the farmers (Bext360, 2022). Platform participants can decide which information they want to disclose to other stakeholders in the supply chain while confidential information is protected with hashes. Meanwhile, Bext360 provides end customers with access to the BlockchainCoffeeBeans website, where they can view detailed information about the annual harvest of specific farmers and the coffee supply chain flow.

To increase the authenticity and credibility of the recorded data, digital files from stakeholders, such as geolocated and timestamped product photos, receipts, and scale results, are stored on the platform for verification purposes. Additionally, farmers also need to verify payments that the purchasing points upload to the blockchain network to ensure the authenticity of received payments.

Topl Blockchain and FairFood

The main goal of Topl is to build a blockchain network focusing on sustainability and social impact (Topl, 2023a). The blockchain plans to become decentralized by the end of 2023 (Topl, 2023b). Topl has been cooperating with FairFood to provide traceability in the coffee supply chain. From the FairFood TRACE platform, the public can track the coffee journey from farmers to importers. Transaction details, including transaction IDs or hashes, are provided for verification through the Annulus network explorer.

Table 3. Summary of blockchain implementation and impact of the studied cases

Company	Main Objective	Technical Infrastructure	Economic Impact	Social Impact	Third-party Verification
Dimitra	Reduce digital divide and empower farmers to improve farming practices	Hyperledger, Polygon, Ethereum	Increased income for farmers Documentation for loans, compliance, or certifications Blockchain-facilitated lending platform (planning)	Technological assistance	No
iFinca	Reduce information asymmetry in coffee supply chain and empower farmers to have more negotiating power	CoffeeChain (not blockchain)	Increased income for farmers Documentation for loans, compliance, or certifications	Foster customer-farmer connection Disclose farmgate price to farmers Technological assistance	Partially (via chat)
Bext360	Facilitate supply chain transparency and connect customers with producers	Stellar	Increased income for farmers "Third payment" mechanism for extra income Documentation for loans, compliance, or certifications	Foster customer-farmer connection Disclose supply chain information to farmers Technological assistance	No
Topl Blockchain (FairFood)	Empower customers to know whether their coffee meets ethical practices and fair wage standards	Topl	Increased income for farmers Carbon credits cooperation for extra income Documentation for loans, compliance, or certifications	Foster customer-farmer connection Disclose supply chain information to farmers Technological assistance	Yes (via blockchain)

According to the Growth Associate, to increase the authenticity and credibility of the recorded data, farmers should be the ones uploading transactions into the blockchain, but if not, they will receive a confirmation text to verify the transaction uploaded by the purchasing stations. Due to the publicly displayed information and immutability of the blockchain, she highlighted the potential reputational risks for a stakeholder with malicious intentions. Topl also allows their clients to choose what information they are disclosing, taking the safety and privacy of all stakeholders in their supply chain into account.

5.2 Economic Impact on Coffee Farmers

The growing consumer awareness of sustainability and ethical sourcing correlates positively with transparency and traceability, leading to increased sales of coffee products. The perceived value of verifiable transparency drives end customers to pay a premium for blockchain-traced coffee, ultimately benefiting coffee farmers and other stakeholders in the supply chain.

The current integration of blockchain technology in the coffee supply chain is in its experimental phase. Demonstrating the practical economic benefits that blockchain can bring to the coffee industry is challenging, given the significant variation in coffee prices attributable to both extrinsic and intrinsic factors. However, some positive economic impact on coffee farmers is identified by companies that are implementing blockchain technology.

As articulated by the CEO of Dimitra in the interview, from what they observed over the past few years, having the traceability documents allows farmers to sell to more premium customers:

To sell premium coffee, you need to collect all this data right from the farm, all the way through all of the processes. And if you have that data to substantiate that your coffee is premium, that you have a history, you can earn more dollars per kilo… that's one of the benefits that it allows the farmer to receive a higher price, the cooperative to receive a higher price, and the coffee company to make sure that they're getting a good quality of coffee. – CEO of Dimitra.

A four-year study conducted by a partner roaster of Bext360 revealed that blockchain-tracked coffee exhibited a 50% shorter sales cycle compared to non-tracked coffee. The interviewee explained:

There could be other factors that influence that, but I think a lot of it is the consumers, like the story behind the blockchain-traced coffee. They like having the QR codes where they can read more about the product itself and know that the producer is being treated fairly. – Sustainability Director of Bext360.

The second economic impact on coffee farmers is the development of additional income mechanisms facilitated by blockchain technology's security and immutability. The transparency and traceability offered by blockchain networks safeguard the authenticity of transactions, enabling the development of new income mechanisms for farmers. According to the Sustainability Director of Bext360, the company is committed to its "Third Payment" mechanism, where a dollar is sent back to the coffee producer for every bag sold at retail sites, increasing the coffee farmers' revenue by 25% to 30% during the harvest season. One Honduran farmer, for instance, received a total of $1000 extra from the mechanism in 2022, which was about a 28% increase in revenue (Career Illustrated, 2023).

The third observed economic impact of blockchain-recorded data is the provision of documentation and proof for rural farmers to access funding and participate in financial markets. According to the Lead of Procurement of NewCoffee, due to the absence of financial institutions, rural farmers rely on coffee buyers or intermediaries to get agricultural tools, supplies, and loans. This unequal power relationship has kept coffee farmers vulnerable and exploited as they are often compelled to sell their products at a disadvantageous price due to loan commitments.

Topl Blockchain, for example, offers secure infrastructure for farmers to record and share verifiable documentation with financial institutions, enabling access to loans (Supply Chain Innovators, 2022), which fosters financial inclusion for unbanked populations (Domjan et al., 2021, p.84). By leveraging collective data from the coffee farming community, farmers can secure larger loans to optimize practices, expand businesses, and increase profits. Additionally, Topl collaborates with carbon credit protocols, encouraging farmers to adopt blockchain technology and gain additional economic opportunities (Supply Chain Innovators, 2022).

5.3 Social Impact on Coffee Farmers

To achieve higher prices and equitable value distribution in coffee chains, Daviron and Ponte (2005) emphasized the need for trade networks to foster reciprocal information flow between producers and consumers. Blockchain technology and increased transparency in the coffee supply chain have a significant social impact by empowering farmers with knowledge and understanding of the coffee market and downstream supply chain dynamics.

The primary contribution of blockchain technology to the coffee supply chain is the reduction of information asymmetry and the establishment of stronger farmer-producer connectivity. Bext360, iFinca, and FairFood's platforms display vivid photos, farmer profiles, and prices paid to the farmers, helping customers to understand more about how the coffee beans travel from farms to cups.

Another social impact of blockchain implementation in the coffee supply chain is providing technological assistance to coffee farming communities. McKinsey's report (Fiocco et al., 2023, p.3) revealed farmers' openness to technological innovation. As Köhler and Pizzol (2020) highlighted, blockchain technology is not a stand-alone technology in the supply chain. In practice, blockchain is often integrated with other emerging technologies, such as AI, IoT, machine learning, satellites, and drones, which enables coffee farmers to adopt new technologies and improve their farming techniques.

Dimitra, for example, develops the free-of-charge Connected Coffee platform, a multi-stakeholder app that enables coffee farmers and traders to efficiently manage the coffee supply chain. The app provides farmers with access to sophisticated technologies, enabling them to monitor financial aspects, crop management, weather forecasts, and regulatory compliance (Dimitra Technology, 2023). The Sustainability Director of Bext360 also mentioned that the aggregated and structured data is utilized by farmers to adopt regenerative farming methods. Bext360's collaboration with satellite companies enables monitoring of land and crop rotation, providing significant on-farm benefits to coffee farmers.

Furthermore, Bager, Singh, et al. (2022) expected that the adoption of blockchain technology among smallholder farmers has the potential to foster a sense of community through peer learning and generate interest among the next generation of coffee growers. Moreover, it could strengthen their connections to the cooperative, which plays a crucial role in promoting sustainable farming practices.

5.4 Key Insights

The economic impact of blockchain implementation in the coffee supply chain hinges on end customers' willingness to pay a premium for high-quality, ethical, and sustainable coffee. Achieving this shift from trusting individual companies or certifications to continuous third-party verification is crucial. Third parties' ability to verify sustainable and ethical claims is essential, as immutability alone lacks significance without third-party verification. Merely offering a traceability solution does not suffice as a compliance tool.

In the current practice, blockchain-enabled third-party verification is relatively uncommon among the four studied companies. Only FairFood and its blockchain provider Topl offer on-chain data verification to end customers, while a leap of faith is still required in other cases. End customers still need to trust the companies to a certain extent. Similarly, Köhler et al. (2022) found out in their study that none of the 16 examined companies had publicly accessible blockchain data that could serve as indirect, external auditing for traceability verification.

Among the case studies, CoffeeChain, the infrastructure of iFinca, presents an interesting case. The company discontinued the use of blockchain technology and relied on AWS for storing and monitoring the coffee supply chain and disclosing the Farmgate price of coffee. The CEO highlighted that the immutability of on-chain data does not align effectively with their mission to reveal farmers' prices, and he emphasized that the notion of blockchain inherently guaranteeing transparency and traceability is an oversimplification.

Blockchain doesn't provide transparency; it protects transparency. It doesn't provide traceability; it protects traceability. – CEO of iFinca/CoffeeChain.

Positioning itself as a third-party verification entity, the company's CEO asserted that data security provided by blockchain technology is not critical for their goals. In this scenario, the company operates comparably to other existing verification institutions, like FairTrade International or Rainforest Alliance. The company necessitates a traceability tool, not a compliance tool, making blockchain unnecessary for their purposes. However, this paper underscores that blockchain's primary potential lies in creating a compliance tool that enables third-party verification and auditing, which can shift industry norms from relying solely on individual companies to embracing public auditing and verification.

6. CHALLENGES FOR BLOCKCHAIN IMPLEMENTATION

The introduction of public blockchain in the coffee supply chain offers numerous advantages and significant impacts for farmers and stakeholders. However, the literature review and case studies reveal several challenges that must be addressed to fully realize the potential of blockchain in enhancing traceability, transparency, and third-party verification in the coffee industry.

6.1 Guarantee for Authentic Data Input

A prominent concern regarding blockchain technology is the "garbage in, garbage out" issue, wherein the immutability of the network does not ensure the integrity of data uploaded onto the blockchain. Two main challenges that Bager, Singh, et al. (2022) encountered during their pilot test were to link digital records to physical assets along the supply chain and ensure the recorded data is authentic and uncorrupted. Blockchains provide tamper-proof information storage, but cannot guarantee the quality, accuracy, and trustworthiness of the stored information (Bager, Singh, et al., 2022; Bettín-Díaz et al., 2022; Köhler & Pizzol, 2020; Pavlić Skender & Zaninović, 2020). Wüst and Gervais (2018) drew attention to potential challenges at the intersection of the physical and digital realms.

In the interview, the Sustainability Director of SCA also identified this challenge from their blockchain experiment in 2015. The interviewee recalled one of the biggest challenges that the team encountered is to guarantee uncorrupted data being recorded onto the blockchain. During the project, due to the lack of automated systems, the team visited the farms and recorded farm information on paper or Excel spreadsheets before uploading the data onto the blockchain. In his opinion, there were spaces for human errors or corruption during the data collection before the information was even recorded on the blockchain.

Yes, the blockchain solves the transparency issue, but if your processes for introducing information in the blockchain are "conventional", you will have the same problems with or without blockchain. – Sustainability Director of SCA.

The interviewee emphasized that blockchain implementation involves "many things beyond the blockchain." This interestingly matches the observation of Bager, Düdder, et al. (2022), who argued from their pilot test that real-world implementation of blockchain presents several challenges that pertain to the characteristics of the supply chain and not necessarily the blockchain model.

The studied blockchain companies utilized different methods to reduce human errors and data corruption. First, different technologies are implemented to increase the automaticity of the data input. Representatives from Dimitra and Bext360 mentioned leveraging different technologies such as drones, satellites, or AI to automate data input on the farm levels and during supply chain transportation.

Additionally, data input undergoes different verification methods. According to the Sustainability Director of Bext360, stakeholders have to upload photos of payment receipts or products on the scale as proof along with the uploaded transaction onto the blockchain. The geolocation and timestamp that come with the photos can serve as proof to ensure data authenticity. Representatives from Bext360 and Topl mentioned that farmers also get to verify the payment via the app or SMS when the cooperatives upload the transaction to make sure that the producers receive the payment.

Last, to ensure the authenticity of the data input, the key still lies in providing appropriate incentives to motivate stakeholders towards collective interests and social responsibility. Implementing blockchain-based technologies requires participation and collaboration among numerous, if not all, stakeholders in the supply chain (Köhler & Pizzol, 2020). Interviewees of Bext360 and Topl emphasized that collective actions and alliances are requisite for fostering systemic change. They highlighted the necessity of effectively communicating the economic benefits, such as additional payments to farmers and the ability to command premium prices for blockchain-traced coffee. This approach enhances stakeholders' willingness to actively participate in the process.

6.2 The Costs of Traceability and Sustainability

Ensuring that coffee farmers benefit from blockchain-traced coffee hinges upon end customers' willingness to pay for such products, incentivizing companies to adopt blockchain solutions. While increased traceability offers associated benefits, the key question remains, as articulated by the representative of FNC, who bears the cost of the technology? He explained that currently only 25-30% of Colombian coffee is fully traced, with companies such as Starbucks (through its C.A.F.E. standards), Nespresso (through its AAA program), and Nestlé (through the Nescafé Plan) covering the associated costs. However, the majority of Colombian coffee lacks traceability, and additional expenses will be required to achieve that.

The studied companies aim to empower coffee farmers, and as a result, they do not burden farmers with blockchain technology costs. In Topl's case, last-mile stakeholders, such as final retailers, wholesalers, or importers, pay for the technology and the transaction fees. Bext360 charges the importers, exporters, and roasters to cover the cost of the technology on a per-pound basis. Consideration of cost implications and revenue generation is imperative for stakeholders investing in these solutions.

La Palma & El Tucán, for instance, decided to defer integrating blockchain into their supply chain due to substantial initial costs. The CEO cited the considerable investment of $40,000 for technology and consultancy, along with ongoing monthly fees and the need for specialized personnel, as challenges for smaller coffee enterprises like theirs.

We're offering traceability now by being completely honest, with the visits, the reviews, the social media posts telling our stories. I would love to move on to a blockchain platform, but at the moment we haven't found an option that's really reasonable for what the market is willing to pay. – CEO of La Palma & El Tucán.

Moreover, the target customer base of the coffee companies also plays a crucial role. The Commercial Coordinator at FNC indicated that while sustainability is highly valued in Europe, its significance may differ in the US or Asia. The varying levels of sustainability awareness and support among end customers in different regions could pose challenges to companies.

6.3 Scalability for Blockchain Implementation

Another interesting finding from this research is that current blockchain implementation in the coffee supply is of a smaller scale. This matches the insights from the literature review. Bager, Singh, et al. (2022) suggested that blockchain is currently suitable for niche markets characterized by smaller trade volumes and collaboration with fewer farmers. However, for bulk-traded coffee, the challenges of product mixing, processing, and linking digital and physical assets make blockchain less viable. Sunny et al. (2020) and Rogerson and Parry (2020) shared the same opinion, emphasizing that high-value product customers are more likely to embrace and invest in traceability solutions enabled by blockchain technology.

The case studies and interviews indicated that blockchain-based companies tracked a significantly smaller number of coffee farmers compared to bulk coffee. For instance, Bext360 traced coffee from only 4 farmers in Honduras during their 2022 harvest, while FairFood and Topl tracked 278 farmers in Ethiopia. However, it is important to consider that coffee beans are typically traded in large quantities. The Sustainability Director of SCA mentioned that one export container typically contains 40,000 pounds of coffee, and according to the Sustainability Coordinator of FNC, coffee beans in a container can come from 300 to 800 coffee farmers in Colombia, as smallholder farmers often sell small amounts of coffee each time.

The challenge of scaling blockchain implementation was acknowledged by the CEO of Dimitra during the interview. To facilitate farmers in adopting new technologies, Dimitra has introduced an expert program to provide continuous guidance. The CEO emphasized that scaling the platform entails not only a successful launch and attracting a large user base but also ensuring that a considerable number of farmers fully comprehend its features and functionalities.

In scaling, you know, you can get these apps out in the world and get a million people to sign up. But it would take a long time for us to get a million farmers in Indonesia to understand how to use the app. – CEO of Dimitra.

6.4 Regulatory Challenges

To address the Coffee Paradox, Daviron and Ponte (2005) emphasized the necessity of enhancing transparency and fostering consumer-producer connectivity. This involves transparency of prices, quality attributes, and identification of all actors involved in the coffee supply chain. However, the industry's endeavor toward sustainability and information disclosure may face obstacles due to existing antitrust laws.

According to Dreher and Held (2022), the conflict lies in balancing rigorous enforcement to protect competition and the need for a more flexible approach to achieve real sustainability impact through industry collaboration and consolidation. Companies that utilize blockchain technology to disclose coffee information along the supply chain should be cautious to avoid violating antitrust laws. D. Martino et al. (2022) also stated that sharing commercially sensitive details like prices, costs, production levels, business plans, or employee wages can raise antitrust concerns. As noted by Daskalova (2020), existing EU competition laws, primarily focused on maintaining open markets, have not adequately addressed issues related to unfair trading practices.

7. NEXT STEPS TO ADVANCE BLOCKCHAIN ADOPTION

The effectiveness of blockchain in promoting social sustainability and economic fairness depends on market dynamics, particularly whether end customers prioritize verifiable transparency and traceability over relying solely on individual companies and brands. To foster this shift, collaborative effort among companies, governments, and end customers is necessary to drive industry-wide transformation.

7.1 Governmental Efforts

As discussed in the previous chapter, companies employing blockchain technology to disclose coffee information within the supply chain have to ensure compliance with existing antitrust laws in the EU. Nevertheless, it is worth noting that the EU is currently reviewing its regulations with a focus on sustainability considerations.

Under the European Green Deal approved in 2020, the European Commission (EC) advocates for a transition towards a sustainable food system. The Farm to Fork Strategy, a core framework within the Green Deal, aims to foster fair distribution of economic gains along the supply chain (EC, 2020b).

In addition to the EUDR, various European countries, including the UK, Netherlands, France, and Germany, are enforcing laws to enhance supply chain due diligence, imposing stringent obligations on supply chain management (Dreher & Held, 2022). Governmental policies like the Digital Product Passport (DPP) further drive supply chains toward sustainability and traceability by enabling consumers to comprehend and monitor the environmental impacts associated with their purchases.

Furthermore, the EU's competition enforcement demonstrates a growing consideration for non-economic objectives (Ünekbas, 2022). The EC's proposal for a Corporate Due Diligence Directive aims to encourage businesses to respect human rights and environmental standards in their value chains (EC, 2022). To support companies in establishing sustainable supply chains, the EC introduced new Horizontal Block Exemption Regulations and Horizontal Guidelines in June 2023. A notable aspect of these guidelines is a chapter affirming that antitrust laws do not obstruct agreements between competitors seeking sustainability objectives (EC, 2023). Although the Guidelines have been recently published, the EC's proactive approach in addressing conflicts between sustainability and competition laws might be a step in the right direction to address the information asymmetry in the coffee supply chain.

7.2 Corporate Efforts

Despite having stronger incentives for a more transparent and inclusive supply chain, coffee producers encounter greater challenges in adopting new technology compared to coffee companies and brands. Dimitra and Bext360 interviewees stated that onboarding farmers unfamiliar with new technology was the primary challenge in implementing blockchain into the supply chain. This challenge was also highlighted by Bager, Singh, et al. (2022).

As articulated by the CEO of Dimitra, the technological components are easy, and the challenges lie in the adoption of technology and the varying levels of digital literacy among farmers. To address these challenges, Dimitra has developed an expert program aimed at assisting farmers in adopting the Connected Farmer app and providing them with guidance throughout the process.

We ran a program in Colombia a couple of weeks ago. We had 20 people in a classroom... 10 of them really struggled... just to download the app from the Google Play Store and get it set up. It takes some coaching, and it takes some time. – CEO of Dimitra.

The Sustainability Director of Bext360 also emphasized the difficulty to guide local farmers that may not be familiar with new technology or even illiterate to understand the platform and keep using the app after the coaching team leaves. Additionally, since many farmers in Latin America are indigenous, farmers only speak their local language which is a spoken language that cannot be written down, which makes the technological adoption even more challenging. The team develops an easy-to-use and intuitive platform for adoption while using more icons instead of text to help simplify the process for farmers.

On the other hand, it is also critical to make the onboarding process simple. The widespread adoption of agriculture technology faces significant challenges, including industry fragmentation, the absence of standardized data architecture, and limited cross-platform interoperability (Fiocco et al., 2023). Both Topl and Bext360 offer application programming interface (API) integration with the database of the collection points, washing and drying stations when data has always been collected. The data will automatically be uploaded from the existing system to the blockchain, saving the workers from having to upload the data manually to the network. The interoperability facilitates enhanced operational efficiency and empowers stakeholders to leverage the capabilities of the blockchain-based solutions within their existing infrastructure.

7.3 Customer Efforts

Apart from the technical support and incentives for supply chain stakeholders, customer demand is identified as an essential drive for sustainability and traceability in the coffee supply chain. As more and more customers recognize the value of traceability and sustainability in the supply chain, it will force companies to adopt technologies that can further provide traceability.

The Sustainability Director of Bext360 stated that it is challenging to ask end customers to verify and double-check all the brands and products they buy every time they go to the supermarket, but she encouraged people to start with the products that they purchase every week and try to understand more about the story behind the products (Career Illustrated, 2023). The EC also plans to launch a sustainable food labeling framework to empower consumers to make sustainable food choices in Q4 2023 (EC, 2020a). Curiosity fosters knowledge and comprehension, enhancing individuals' ability to interpret displayed data, which plays a crucial role in combating deceptive practices such as greenwashing. Acquiring the knowledge necessary to interpret information empowers end customers to discern and assess the claims made by corporations regarding their products.

8. CONCLUSION

The coffee industry is moving toward traceability and sustainability, with the narrative of coffee's supply chain journey assuming paramount importance in demonstrating quality and sustainability values. Social sustainability and equality also receive more and more attention from the coffee drinkers. This research explores the implementation of blockchain technology as a potential solution to address economic and social challenges faced by coffee producers. The findings suggest that blockchain technology can contribute to reducing information asymmetry in the supply chain, fostering stronger customer-farmer connections, and bringing about various economic and social benefits for coffee producers.

The current practice reveals limited progress in blockchain-enabled third-party verification, hindering its full potential for decentralization and public transparency. Identified challenges include regulatory considerations, cost dynamics, scalability issues, and the intricate task of bridging the digital-physical worlds while preserving data authenticity. However, by aligning the efforts of governments, corporations, and customers, the coffee industry can harness the potential of blockchain technology to create a more transparent, equitable, and sustainable coffee supply chain.

9. REFERENCES

Alamsyah, A., Widiyanesti, S., Wulansari, P., Nurhazizah, E., Dewi, A. S., Rahadian, D., Ramadhani, D. P., Hakim, M. N., & Tyasamesi, P. (2023). Blockchain traceability model in the coffee industry. *Journal of Open Innovation*, 9(1), 100008. doi:10.1016/j.joitmc.2023.100008

Alazab, M., Alhyari, S., Awajan, A., & Abdallah, A. B. (2021). Blockchain technology in supply chain management: An empirical study of the factors affecting user adoption/acceptance. *Cluster Computing*, *24*(1), 83–101. doi:10.100710586-020-03200-4

Arpášová, M., & Rajčániová, M. (2022). Legal Regulation of Unfair Trade Practices in Food Supply Chain. *EU Agrarian Law*, *11*(1), 1–8. doi:10.2478/eual-2022-0001

Bager, S. L., Düdder, B., Henglein, F., Hébert, J. M., & Wu, H. (2022). Event-Based Supply Chain Network Modeling: Blockchain for Good Coffee. *Frontiers in Blockchain*, *5*, 846783. doi:10.3389/fbloc.2022.846783

Bager, S. L., Singh, C., & Persson, U. M. (2022). Blockchain is not a silver bullet for agro-food supply chain sustainability: Insights from a coffee case study. *Current Research in Environmental Sustainability*, *4*, 100163. doi:10.1016/j.crsust.2022.100163

Bettín-Díaz, R., Rojas, A. E., & Mejía-Moncayo, C. (2022). Colombian Origin Coffee Supply Chain Traceability by a Blockchain Implementation. *Operations Research Forum, 3*(4), 64. 10.100743069-022-00174-4

Bext360 (Director). (2019, April 1). *Bext360 Journey*. [Video]. Youtube. https://www.youtube.com/watch?v=HYmIBRHLcjo

Bext360 (Director). (2022, September 3). *Bext360 Capabilities*. [Video]. Youtube. https://www.youtube.com/watch?v=gs0xr7Ie4vo

Borrella, I., Mataix, C., & Carrasco-Gallego, R. (2015). Smallholder Farmers in the Speciality Coffee Industry: Opportunities, Constraints and the Businesses that are Making it Possible. *IDS Bulletin*, *46*(3), 29–44. doi:10.1111/1759-5436.12142

Burroughes, E., Rys, J., & Wüllenweber, J. (2023, June 8). *Prioritizing socially responsible sourcing*. *McKinsey*. https://www.mckinsey.com/capabilities/operations/our-insights/enabling-socially-responsible-sourcing-throughout-the-supply-chain

Career Illustrated. (2023). *E5—Niki Lewis, Sustainability Director @ Bext360: Green is the New Green*. Career Illustrated - Podcast. https://music.amazon.com/es-us/podcasts/bb314ba5-dcc7-42b9-b546-706fc009387f/episodes/0eaabd5d-001c-4cfd-a499-500c92d20955/career-illustrated-e5---niki-lewis-sustainability-director-a-bext360-green-is-the-new-green

Casey, M., & Vigna, P. (2018). *The truth machine: The blockchain and the future of everything* (1st ed.). St. Martin's Press.

Chaudhuri, A., Bhatia, M. S., Kayikci, Y., Fernandes, K. J., & Fosso-Wamba, S. (2021). Improving social sustainability and reducing supply chain risks through blockchain implementation: Role of outcome and behavioural mechanisms. *Annals of Operations Research*. doi:10.100710479-021-04307-6

Cointelegraph (Director). (2023, March 22). *Farming Revolution: Blockchain and Tech Solutions by Dimitra*. [Video]. Youtube. https://www.youtube.com/watch?v=xutrxP29PO8

Damoska Sekuloska, J., & Erceg, A. (2022). Blockchain Technology toward Creating a Smart Local Food Supply Chain. *Computers*, *11*(6), 95. doi:10.3390/computers11060095

Daskalova, V. (2020). Regulating Unfair Trading Practices in the EU Agri-food Supply Chain: A Case of Counterproductive Regulation? *Yearbook of Antitrust and Regulatory Studies, 12*(21), 7–53. doi:10.7172/1689-9024.YARS.2020.13.21.1

Daviron, B., & Ponte, S. (2005). *The coffee paradox: Global markets, commodity trade, and the elusive promise of development.* Zed Books.

De Filippi, P., Mannan, M., & Reijers, W. (2020). Blockchain as a confidence machine: The problem of trust & challenges of governance. *Technology in Society, 62*, 101284. doi:10.1016/j.techsoc.2020.101284

Dimitra. (2021). *Dimitra Token Whitepaper Version1.3.* Dimitra.io. https://dimitra.io/wp-content/uploads/2023/02/Dimitra-Whitepaper-1.3-Revised.pdf

Dimitra Technology. (2023, March 28). Dimitra's Commitment to Advancing SDGs: Reduce Inequality. *Medium.* https://dimitratech.medium.com/dimitras-commitment-to-advancing-sdgs-reduce-inequality-79a686372739

Dionysis, S., Chesney, T., & McAuley, D. (2022). Examining the influential factors of consumer purchase intentions for blockchain traceable coffee using the theory of planned behaviour. *British Food Journal, 124*(12), 4304–4322. doi:10.1108/BFJ-05-2021-0541

Domjan, P., Serkin, G., Thomas, B., & Toshack, J. (2021). *Chain Reaction: How Blockchain Will Transform the Developing World.* Springer International Publishing., doi:10.1007/978-3-030-51784-7

Dreher, M., & Held, T.-E. (2022). ESG & supply chains: A practical outlook on opportunities and challenges under antitrust law. *European Competition Law Review, 9*, 417–424.

Düring, T., & Fisbeck, H. (2017). Einsatz der Blockchain-Technologie für eine transparente Wertschöpfungskette. In A. Hildebrandt & W. Landhäußer (Eds.), *CSR und Digitalisierung* (pp. 449–464). Springer Berlin Heidelberg. doi:10.1007/978-3-662-53202-7_33

European Commission. (2020a). *Timeline of Farm to Fork actions.* European Commission. https://food.ec.europa.eu/system/files/2022-04/f2f_timeline-actions_en.pdf

European Commission. (2020b). *Farm to Fork Strategy.* European Commission. https://food.ec.europa.eu/horizontal-topics/farm-fork-strategy_en

European Commission. (2022). *Proposal for a DIRECTIVE OF THE EUROPEAN PARLIAMENT AND OF THE COUNCIL on Corporate Sustainability Due Diligence and amending Directive (EU) 2019/1937.* European Commission. https://eur-lex.europa.eu/legal-content/EN/TXT/?uri=CELEX%3A52022PC0071

European Commission. (2023, June). *Antitrust: Commission adopts new Horizontal Block Exemption Regulations and Horizontal Guidelines* [Text]. European Commission - European Commission. https://ec.europa.eu/commission/presscorner/detail/en/IP_23_2990

Fiocco, D., Ganesan, V., Garcia de la Serrana Lozano, M., & Sharif, H. (2023). *Agtech: Breaking down the farmer adoption dilemma | McKinsey.* McKinsey & Company. https://www.mckinsey.com/industries/agriculture/our-insights/agtech-breaking-down-the-farmer-adoption-dilemma#/

Fischer, E. F. (2022). *Making Better Coffee: How Maya Farmers and Third Wave Tastemakers Create Value*. University of California Press.

Food and Agriculture Organization of the United Nations [FAO]. (2023). *FAO Publications Catalogue 2022—Markets and Trade: Coffee*. Food and Agriculture Organization of the United Nations. doi:10.4060/cc2323en

Giovannucci, D., Leibovich, J., Pizano, D., Paredes, G., Montenegro, S., Arévalo, H., & Varangis, P. (2002). *Colombia Coffee Sector Study* (SSRN Scholarly Paper 996138). https://papers.ssrn.com/abstract=996138

Harper, J. (2020, February 12). *Blockchain & Coffee: Separating The Marketing From The Reality*. Perfect Daily Grind. https://perfectdailygrind.com/2020/02/blockchain-coffee-separating-the-marketing-from-the-reality/

iFinca. (2023). *iFinca—The Key*. IFinca. https://www.ifinca.co/solutions

iFinca (Director). (2019, January 24). *iFinca.co Coffee Chain—Connecting Farmers*. [Video]. Youtube. https://www.youtube.com/watch?v=SlIZ2guZWUE

International Trade Centre [ITC]. (2021). *The Coffee Guide: Fourth Edition* (4; pp. 1–327). International Trade Centre. https://intracen.org/resources/publications/the-coffee-guide-fourth-edition

Jaffee, D. (2014). Brewing justice: Fair trade coffee, sustainability, and survival (Updated edition). University of California press.

Kewell, B., Adams, R., & Parry, G. (2017). Blockchain for good? *Strategic Change*, *26*(5), 429–437. doi:10.1002/jsc.2143

Köhler, S., Bager, S., & Pizzol, M. (2022). Sustainability standards and blockchain in agro-food supply chains: Synergies and conflicts. *Technological Forecasting and Social Change*, *185*, 122094. doi:10.1016/j.techfore.2022.122094

Köhler, S., & Pizzol, M. (2020). Technology assessment of blockchain-based technologies in the food supply chain. *Journal of Cleaner Production*, *269*, 122193. doi:10.1016/j.jclepro.2020.122193

Lewin, B., Giovannucci, D., & Varangis, P. (2004). Coffee Markets: New Paradigms in Global Supply and Demand. SSRN *Electronic Journal*. doi:10.2139/ssrn.996111

Martino, D. J., van Duyn, A., & Flores, N. (2022, December 7). *Antitrust, ESG, and Supply Chain: Risks and Tips*. Baker McKenzie - Global Supply Chain Compliance. https://supplychaincompliance.bakermckenzie.com/2022/12/07/antitrust-esg-and-supply-chain-risks-and-tips/

Miatton, F., & Amado, L. (2020). Fairness, Transparency and Traceability in the Coffee Value Chain through Blockchain Innovation. *2020 International Conference on Technology and Entrepreneurship - Virtual (ICTE-V)*, (pp. 1–6). IEEE. 10.1109/ICTE-V50708.2020.9113785

Pavlić Skender, H., & Zaninović, P. A. (2020). Perspectives of Blockchain Technology for Sustainable Supply Chains. In A. Kolinski, D. Dujak, & P. Golinska-Dawson (Eds.), *Integration of Information Flow for Greening Supply Chain Management* (pp. 77–92). Springer International Publishing. doi:10.1007/978-3-030-24355-5_5

Pendergrast, M. (2010). *Uncommon grounds: The history of coffee and how it transformed our world* (Rev. ed). Basic Books.

Petrock, V. (2021). *US Generation Z Demographic and Psychographic Overview: What Makes the Most Racially, Ethnically, and Sexually Diverse Generation in History Tick*. Insider Intelligence. https://www. insiderintelligence.com/content/us-generation-z-demographic-psychographic-overview

Roberts, P. (2018, April 18). *Green Coffee Pricing Transparency Is Critical (And Complicated)*. Perfect Daily Grind. https://perfectdailygrind.com/2018/04/green-coffee-pricing-transparency-is-critical-and-complicated/

Rogerson, M., & Parry, G. C. (2020). Blockchain: Case studies in food supply chain visibility. *Supply Chain Management*, *25*(5), 601–614. doi:10.1108/SCM-08-2019-0300

Singh, C., Wojewska, A. N., Persson, U. M., & Bager, S. L. (2022). Coffee producers' perspectives of blockchain technology in the context of sustainable global value chains. *Frontiers in Blockchain*, *5*, 955463. doi:10.3389/fbloc.2022.955463

Statista. (2023). *Coffee—Worldwide*. Statista. https://www.statista.com/outlook/cmo/hot-drinks/coffee/worldwide

Sunny, J., Undralla, N., & Madhusudanan Pillai, V. (2020). Supply chain transparency through blockchain-based traceability: An overview with demonstration. *Computers & Industrial Engineering*, *150*, 106895. doi:10.1016/j.cie.2020.106895

Supply Chain Innovators. (2022, October 21). *How Topl Uses Blockchain to Create a More Transparent Supply Chain*. https://www.supplychaininnovators.io/post/how-blockchain-can-improve-supplychain

The Economist. (2015). *The trust machine: The technology behind bitcoin could transform how the economy works*. The Economist. https://www.economist.com/leaders/2015/10/31/the-trust-machine

Topl. (2023a). Dual Innovation: How Topl's technology unlocks a new impact economy. *Topl*. https://topl.co/manifesto/

Topl. (2023b). *Topl: Unlocking the economic potential of positive impact*. Topl. https://topl.co/

Tröster, B. (2020). *Blockchain technologies for commodity value chains: The solution for more sustainability?* (Research Report 27). ÖFSE Briefing Paper. https://www.econstor.eu/handle/10419/224986

Ünekbas, S. (2022, July 4). *Diligence is Due Indeed: Competition Law as a Barrier to Sustainable Supply Chains?* Kluwer Competition Law Blog. https://competitionlawblog.kluwercompetitionlaw.com/2022/07/04/diligence-is-due-indeed-competition-law-as-a-barrier-to-sustainable-supply-chains/

Verhoeven, P., Sinn, F., & Herden, T. (2018). Examples from Blockchain Implementations in Logistics and Supply Chain Management: Exploring the Mindful Use of a New Technology. *Logistics*, *2*(3), 20. doi:10.3390/logistics2030020

Voora, V., Bermúdez, S., & Larrea, C. (2022). *Global Market Report: Coffee* (Sustainable Commodities Marketplace Series, pp. 1–34) [Standards and Value Chains]. International Institute for Sustainable Development (IISD). https://www.iisd.org/system/files/publications/ssi-global-market-report-coffee.pdf

Weber, H., Wiek, A., & Lang, D. J. (2020). Sustainability entrepreneurship to address large distances in international food supply. *BUSINESS STRATEGY & DEVELOPMENT, 3*(3), 318–331. doi:10.1002/bsd2.97

Wüst, K., & Gervais, A. (2018). Do you Need a Blockchain? *2018 Crypto Valley Conference on Blockchain Technology (CVCBT)*, (pp. 45–54). IEEE. 10.1109/CVCBT.2018.00011

Chapter 19
Web 3.0:
Unleashing the Innovative Potential and Its Future Implications in the Education Sector

Ratnakar Mann

https://orcid.org/0009-0003-6861-4914

University Canada West, Canada

ABSTRACT

Web 3.0 has revolutionized the internet with its salient features of decentralization, trustful and permissionless, artificial intelligence and machine learning, connectivity, and ubiquity. Although the idea of Web 3.0 gained much popularity in 2021, the term was coined in 2014 by Gavin Wood. The advent of Web 3.0 has ushered in a new era of blockchain technology, and this chapter is an attempt to unleash the tremendous potential of this technology with a prime focus in the education sector. Although the fields in which this technology has contributed are wide and diverse, the innovative potential of Web 3.0 in the education field is explored in this chapter and its future implications are assessed and analyzed. There has been a profound impact of Web 3.0 in education services and the amalgamation of Web 3.0 technologies has altogether transformed the education sector and its contribution to society is undeniably important. In adherence to this, this chapter unravels the transformations caused by Web 3.0 in the teaching-learning process.

INTRODUCTION

Education plays a crucial role in facilitating societal transformation. The absence of education hinders progress and development. Competent individuals are required to manage the system effectively. In the past, education was confined to the classroom, where teachers interacted with students. However, at present, education has transcended geographical boundaries. With the advent of online teaching, students are no longer solely reliant on their school teachers for learning. This has led to a more open and flexible learning experience. From the comfort of their homes, students can now acquire knowledge on a wide range of subjects using technology. Technology has revolutionized education by providing an engaging, creative, and immersive learning environment for learners (Benito et al., 2013).

DOI: 10.4018/978-1-6684-9919-1.ch019

Copyright © 2023, IGI Global. Copying or distributing in print or electronic forms without written permission of IGI Global is prohibited.

The introduction of Web 3.0 technology as the "future of the Internet" is poised to bring about a revolution in the field of education (Hew et al., 2013). The COVID-19 crisis forced us to retreat indoors and severed our ties with society. Attending school in a traditional setup was no longer viable due to the new norm of social distancing. Consequently, we transitioned from in-person teaching and learning to online methods (Robin, 2011).

Web 3, a cutting-edge technology, embraces this transition and promotes a fresh teaching and learning experience for all (Dominic et al., 2014). Web 3.0 envisions a decentralized Internet built on blockchain technology. This concept has gained widespread attention in recent years, with companies like Microsoft and Meta investing heavily to gain a competitive edge in the field.

Currently, the education system primarily relies on traditional pedagogical techniques that are largely teacher-centric. However, Web 3 development aims to disrupt this approach and enhance educational outcomes. The technology holds significant potential for empowering the education industry, offering student-friendly, experiential learning and goal-oriented teaching (Firat, 2020).

Often referred to as the "semantic web," "spatial web," or "the 3D web of the future," Web 3 represents a user-centric version of the Internet that revolutionizes the way we create, interact with, and exchange digital content. Web 3 is a decentralized Internet powered by blockchain technology, offering advanced security, transparency, and immutability. Given its early stage of development, Web 3 lacks a single, definitive definition. Nonetheless, experts view it as the next generation of the Internet, encompassing various concepts such as blockchain, cloud computing, artificial intelligence, Metaverse technology, spatial technology, 5G, cryptocurrencies, and more (Miranda et al.,2014).

By leveraging Web 3 technology as a resource, we gain access to decentralized clusters and digital tools. In a Web 3.0 ecosystem, a network of interconnected computers functions as validators, verifying data without relying on central authorities like banks or government regulators. A Web 3 expert designs projects that fulfill user requirements to the best of their ability (Giannakos & Lapatas, 2010).

Within the semantic web realm, information proactively reaches users instead of users actively searching for it (Allison et al., 2015). The decentralized interface analyzes user activities and interests to determine how data should be delivered to them. It also considers the format in which users prefer their data and facilitates its display through their chosen channels.

Web 3 has had a direct or indirect impact on the fundamental infrastructure of various industries, ranging from finance and banking to art, hospitality, medicine, and more. This technology has prompted a paradigm shift towards decentralized systems that are owned by creators and users. The education sector is gradually embracing this trend and following a similar path (Hew et al., 2013).

This transition can be explained as follows:

In Web 1.0, education primarily took place within educational institutions, where knowledge was transferred between teachers and students.

In Web 2.0, the focus shifted to centralized online education portals.

Now, in Web 3.0, the educational infrastructure relies on the decentralization of data and resources. It enables learners to gather skills from numerous sources (Chisega, 2013).

The knowledge acquired is then verified and stored on the blockchain network, ensuring access to a tamper-proof system. This technology introduces concepts like "Proof of Skill," which has the potential to unlock significant opportunities within the field of education.

INSIGHT INTO SALIENT FEATURES OF WEB 3.0 AND APPLICATIONS

Web 3.0 stands apart from its predecessors by introducing significant structural changes and exhibiting various distinctive features. These include the semantic web, enhanced connectivity, artificial intelligence, immersive 3D graphics, decentralization, and ubiquitous presence. However, it is the key attributes of Web 3 that truly set it apart as a powerful and influential force in shaping the future of the internet. Web 3.0 holds the potential to fulfill what Web 2.0 cannot by granting content creators autonomy to monetize their data using blockchain, decentralization, user data ownership, and private keys (Lal, 2011). The most remarkable characteristics of Web 3 have been highlighted below that emphasize its significance and potential impact.

Semantic Web

The semantic web, often referred to as a "human-understandable web," aims to enhance online technologies by providing additional functionalities. It enables users to generate, distribute, and connect content through advanced search and analysis capabilities. With the advent of web 3.0, these search and analysis features prioritize comprehending the true essence and contextual significance of words (Miranda et al.,2014). The semantic web represents a substantial advancement beyond interpreting data solely based on numerical values or keywords, offering a more meaningful and nuanced interpretation of information (Ohler, 2008).

Redefined Data Ownership

According to Litan, in the Web 2.0 era, major digital corporations and service providers possess customer data, which they exploit for financial gains. Consumers willingly trade their personal information in exchange for access to platforms like Facebook. However, in Web 3.0, content is separated from Web 2.0 services. Users have ownership over their own data and can generate revenue from it, receiving direct payments that are facilitated by blockchain transaction validators (Ohei et al., 2019).

Trustless and Permission-Less Controls and Environments

Web 3.0 aspires to create a "trustless" ecosystem where decentralized data network protocols incorporate inherent safeguards. For instance, blockchain technology is renowned for being trustless and permissionless since it operates without a centralized authority overseeing ownership. However, it is essential to understand that "trustless" does not imply complete automation. In blockchain, individuals are responsible for validating transactions, which are then recorded in a transparent public ledger visible to all.

Artificial Intelligence

The discussion on the features of Web 3 would undoubtedly highlight the role of artificial intelligence (AI). AI has the capability to enable computers and devices to comprehend information in a manner akin to human beings, yielding faster and more efficient outcomes. When integrated into Web 3.0, AI features exhibit substantial advancements over human-driven unethical practices, such as data manipulation or biased product reviews. Moreover, Web 3 leverages user feedback as a valuable resource to foster the provision of reliable information on the internet. The incorporation of AI functionalities empowers the web to discern between counterfeit and authentic data, thereby enhancing its ability to deliver accurate and trustworthy content (Pentland, 2022).

3D Graphics

Another significant characteristic among the essential features of Web 3 is spatial computing and 3D graphics. Referred to as the spatial web by many experts, Web 3 holds the promise of bridging the gap between the physical and virtual realms. It presents an opportunity to revolutionize graphic technologies and enable seamless interactions with three-dimensional virtual worlds, including the metaverse.

Three-dimensional design takes center stage in Web 3 applications, services, and websites. The integration of 3D graphics empowers Web 3 to construct immersive environments that extend beyond gaming, finding applications in vital sectors such as healthcare, ecommerce, and real estate. This enables transformative experiences and opens up new possibilities for various industries.

Connectivity and Ubiquity

The discussion on important features within Web 3.0 also brings attention to connectivity and ubiquity. Web 3.0 aims to establish seamless connections between users and devices within its ecosystem, ensuring constant availability (Noskova et al., 2016). The notion of the "Web 3 never sleeps" holds true, serving as a crucial differentiating factor between Web 3 and Web 2.

The features of Web 3 capitalize on semantic metadata, setting new standards for connectivity. Additionally, the association of Web 3 with IoT sensors on a large scale is noteworthy. As a result, Web 3 guarantees internet access to individuals regardless of their location or the time of day. Moreover, there are no limitations based on the type of device used, ensuring unrestricted internet accessibility.

Blockchain and Decentralization

Blockchain technologies play a significant role among the prominent features of Web 3, primarily due to their capacity to enable decentralization. This capability empowers Web 3 applications and systems to offer cryptographic security for user data. Importantly, the assurance provided by blockchain, and decentralization facilitates seamless communication between software and browser plugins. Web 3 harnesses blockchain technologies to enhance transparency within the ecosystem, thereby creating opportunities for improved auditing and security measures.

INADEQUACIES IN EDUCATION SECTOR AND LEVERAGING WEB 3.0 TO PROVIDE SOLUTIONS

The incorporation of Web 3.0, the next iteration of the internet, in the field of education has the potential to revolutionize the educational landscape for both students and teachers.

Inadequacies of Present Education System

Limited accessibility: The existing education system typically relies on in-person setups where students and teachers interact within the confines of educational institutions. This setup often leads to disparities and exclusion. In schools and colleges, classes are conducted according to a fixed schedule, which makes it challenging for individuals who cannot commit to the entire semester. Moreover, these courses are structured around semesters, offering little flexibility for participants. The physical location of these institutions can also pose challenges for certain students, affecting their ease of access.

Substantial Financial Burden: Educational institutions impose exorbitant fees for their services, leading to a significant increase in the overall cost of a child's education, from school to university. This exponential rise in expenses has created a significant obstacle for prospective students who lack sufficient financial support. Their talent often goes untapped simply because they are unable to afford the college fees. In some cases, parents are forced to take out education loans at excessively high-interest rates for their children, further burdening their already complex lives.

Inadequate Skill Development: One significant drawback of the current education system is its failure to foster practical skills among learners. The majority of academic years are focused on achieving high grades rather than acquiring practical knowledge. The scores recorded on our transcripts are often seen as a measure of intelligence. The teaching methods employed by schools and colleges tend to be outdated and unprogressive. There is less emphasis on skill acquisition and more emphasis on rote memorization of concepts. As a result, students may gain an understanding of principles but remain disconnected from their real-life application. Skills evolve over time, but the education system fails to keep pace with these changes. Consequently, by the time students complete their degrees, many of the skills taught to them during the four-year period have become obsolete.

ROLE OF WEB 3.0 IN ACCELERATING EDUCATION

Transformed Teaching-Learning Methods: Web 3.0 technology aims to revolutionize the methods of teaching and learning. It offers the potential to enhance the educational process by harnessing the power of technology (Hussain, 2012).

With tools like AI, Metaverse blockchain, and IoT, Web 3 will facilitate access to a vast pool of knowledge for individuals worldwide, regardless of their location. These technologies will enable teachers to create engaging assignments using innovative resources (Jiang, 2014).

Rather than being passive recipients, learners will actively participate in content creation. Advanced forms of online teaching will foster the development of creative, analytical, and practical skills in students. Through the use of Metaverse technology, teachers can transport students to virtual spaces while teaching concepts. IoT and Artificial Intelligence will contribute to a more immersive and interactive learning experience. Features such as holoportation, holographic sharing, and immersive visual experiences will provide a rich online teaching experience. To expand their knowledge in the field, individuals can enroll in training programs to learn about Metaverse blockchain and Metaverse wallets.

TEACHING-LEARNING PROCESS

Through the integration of Web 3.0, students are no longer restricted to passive listening as it facilitates the design of collaborative lessons in education. This transformation leads to a two-way learning process involving active engagement from both students and teachers. Web 3.0 empowers educators to create more intricate assignments and sessions, utilizing diverse resources. Consequently, students gain greater independence, allowing teachers to focus on smaller groups.

With the assistance of AI technology, Web 3.0 aims to organize the vast body of knowledge while encouraging students to generate content that leverages their analytical and creative capabilities. Additionally, Web 3.0 enables teachers to transport students to virtual environments, fostering interactive and immersive learning experiences. Furthermore, Web 3.0 streamlines the data gathering process for students, freeing up their time and granting them the flexibility to learn at their own pace and from any location.

TIME SAVER

Smart searches in Web 3.0 will revolutionize personalized searching, delivering tailored information to users based on their specific search queries. This feature effectively prevents wastage of time and energy. In general, technology alleviates the workload for both students and teachers. For students, modern technology eliminates the need for manual data collection and organization, allowing them to obtain desired results promptly. Smart searches significantly reduce the time students spend on gathering information.

For teachers, Web 3.0 brings data integration capabilities that automate the assessment process and facilitate the creation of engaging study materials. It also enables the generation of comprehensive performance reports for students over an extended period. Consequently, Web 3.0 empowers teachers to streamline their workflow and enhance their ability to monitor student progress effectively.

EDUCATIONAL ADMINISTRATION

Web 3.0 facilitates expedited delivery of degrees and certificates to students as physical exchanges are eliminated. This accelerates the transfer of credits and certificates, benefiting institutions and schools by streamlining administrative procedures. Additionally, with proper permission, this digital process allows for the reuse of credentials, further enhancing efficiency and accessibility.

DECENTRALIZED SHARING

Web 3.0 expands sharing capabilities beyond central servers, enabling data to be distributed across multiple servers while benefiting from the protection of blockchain technology. This advancement allows students to leverage these capabilities by creating comprehensive portfolios encompassing their internships, research papers, and awards. These portfolios can then be easily shared with administrative authorities. The implementation of blockchain technology ensures the preservation and security of these portfolios, safeguarding the integrity of the information they contain.

DIGITAL SKILLS

Education using Web 3.0 empowers students by equipping them with a competitive edge in digital skills (Allison et al., 2012). It enables them to develop proficiencies relevant to IT-enabled industries, enhancing their overall efficiency and effectiveness. Consequently, this enhanced skill set not only makes them more employable but also prepares them to excel in a global competitive landscape.

INFORMED DECISION MAKING

Web 3.0 facilitates seamless career planning and goal setting for students. Through its smart search capabilities, Web 3.0 can provide personalized recommendations of relevant and applicable information to students, empowering them to make informed decisions regarding their future paths.

ALTERNATIVE TO REGULAR SCHOOLING

The cost of education, spanning from school to university, has witnessed a significant surge over time. This, coupled with the impact of the pandemic, has prompted many individuals to explore homeschooling or micro-schooling alternatives for their children. These options often offer freedom from traditional school tests and curricula. Web 3.0 plays a pivotal role in establishing an interconnected relationship among parents, teachers, and students, fostering active participation from all parties (Shaltout et al., 2013). With the advent of Web 3.0, students gain the ability to access their lectures and educational resources from any location, unlocking greater flexibility in their learning journey.

CONTRIBUTION OF WEB 3.0 IN EDUCATION AND RESEARCH

Learning in Web 2.0 encourages active participation and social interaction among internet users through various social network tools and software, such as blogs, wikis, social bookmarking, and social networking platforms. In contrast, Web 3.0 technologies introduce a more open approach to learning, emphasizing the integration of high-powered graphics (like Scalable Vector Graphics or SVG) and semantic data. There are ongoing discussions about the potential integration of 3D social networking systems and immersive environments within the internet, combining the strengths of virtual worlds like Second Life and gaming environments with the web (Poore, 2014).

Regarding the impact of Web 3.0 on learning, Tony Bingham, President and CEO of ASTD, expressed that in the Semantic Web, content will proactively reach the learner based on their activities and interests (Shaltout et al., 2013). It will be delivered in the preferred format and channel of the individual. Bingham highlights the immense potential of the Semantic Web in facilitating learning. We are currently at the early stages of a transformative revolution in information management and sharing. This revolution will make a vast amount of content accessible to humans.

Some of the useful Web 3.0 tools and services for education and research include 3D-Wikis and virtual 3D encyclopedias. Wikis are collaborative platforms where individuals can create and edit interconnected web pages, facilitating content creation, publishing, editing, and collaboration for knowledge building.

Wikis are commonly utilized for maintaining repositories of content and materials, enabling students to collaborate and share extensive information. The user-friendly nature of wiki software allows editors, such as faculty members, to easily modify or delete content.

With the advancement of 3D web technology, researchers and technocrats have been working on projects that enhance the capabilities of Wikis and encyclopedias by incorporating a new dimension. An example of this is the Copernicus-3D Wikipedia software, which introduces a unique experience. For instance, if a learner searches for information about a specific geographical region, the camera in the 3D environment will navigate to the relevant location on a spinning globe and present audio/video information related to that place. This immersive approach enhances the learning experience by providing rich multimedia content and animations through 3D Wikis.

Immersive Learning Experience With Web 3.0

The advent of Web 3.0 has transformed the educational landscape, providing students with an immersive and revolutionary learning atmosphere (Chisega, 2012). By leveraging advanced technologies and interactive elements, Web 3.0 has ushered in a new era of immersive learning. Through the utilization of virtual reality (VR) and augmented reality (AR) applications, students can immerse themselves in lifelike simulations, engaging with educational content in a practical and hands-on manner. They have the opportunity to interact with three-dimensional models, manipulate objects, and actively participate in virtual experiments, resulting in a dynamic and captivating learning experience. Moreover, Web 3.0 facilitates personalized learning by utilizing intelligent algorithms that adapt to individual students' requirements, offering tailored content and feedback. Collaborative tools and platforms foster peer-to-peer learning, allowing students to connect and collaborate with their peers worldwide, thereby enhancing their cultural awareness and broadening their perspectives. With the integration of blockchain technology, Web 3.0 ensures the security and authenticity of educational records, enabling lifelong learning while establishing a transparent and verifiable system (Atabekova et al., 2015). In this immersive learning environment, students are empowered to actively engage in their education, fostering their curiosity, creativity, and critical thinking abilities. Web 3.0 has opened up a realm of new possibilities, transforming education into a more engaging, inclusive, and impactful endeavor than ever before.

Learning With 3D Virtual Worlds and Avatars

A 3D virtual world combines elements of 3D gaming technology, augmented reality, and simulated environments powered by Internet technology. In these virtual worlds, users interact through movable avatars, creating and residing in their own digital representations. Virtual worlds offer a new era of e-learning, providing learners with opportunities for role-play, 3D modeling, simulations, creativity, and active engagement (Amarin, 2015). There is immense potential for conducting research on the pedagogical benefits of teaching and learning in 3D virtual worlds.

Several web-based 3D virtual worlds, such as Second Life, IMVU, Active Worlds, and Red Light Center, have gained popularity among students and teachers worldwide for educational purposes (Samarawickrema & Stacey, 2007).

Educators can conduct classes in various settings within a 3D virtual world, allowing for real-like interactions in a classroom environment. Collaborative sessions can be conducted by educators and learners from geographically dispersed locations in a shared virtual 3D space. These virtual worlds enable educators and learners to conduct meetings, seminars, presentations, and digital exhibitions, providing an immersive and interactive learning experience similar to real-life interactions.

The available and upcoming 3D virtual worlds have extensive applications across diverse disciplines, including education, medicine, business, commerce, science, communication, media, art, architecture, design, law, computer science, language learning, history, geography, and more (Blaum et al., 2013).

Intelligent Search Engines

In recent years, advancements in web technology have significantly impacted learning processes. The widespread accessibility of the web has facilitated the introduction of flexible educational approaches, enabling easier access to learning resources. Nowadays, the internet has become the primary and powerful source of information. To effectively navigate the vast amount of web information, sophisticated search engines have been developed, capable of retrieving relevant multimedia content for users (Demartini & Benussi, 2017).

Traditional web search engines primarily focus on identifying web pages containing specific keywords but lack the ability to interpret the context of search queries. In contrast, the emergence of Web 3.0 introduces agent-based search engines that not only identify keywords but also comprehend the context of user requests. These advanced search engines can provide relevant search results while suggesting related content. Experts anticipate that Web 3.0 will enhance user experiences, tailoring browsing experiences based on each individual's unique internet profile, which is formed from their browsing history.

Web 3.0 also brings the concept of knowledge construction powered by the Semantic Web. Agent-based search engines, operating within this framework, can provide multimedia reports instead of a simple list of search results. These intelligent agents can retrieve local lectures, relevant blogs, books, and television programs related to a particular topic, personalized to the learner's needs. Ontologies establish connections between the learner's requirements and characteristics, enabling personalized agents to search for learning materials that align with individual needs. Learners can apply similar search possibilities to other media objects such as images, audio, and video.

Notable examples of such technologies include Ojos Riya, a photo-sharing tool that automatically tags images using face recognition, and Like.com, which allows users to search for products based on similar images.

WEB 3.0 TOOLS FACILITATING EDUCATION SECTOR

Online 3-D Virtual Labs / Educational labs / Simulations or 3D Web

3D immersive graphical user interfaces will serve as a robust platform, enabling users to actively engage in collaborative activities, share outcomes, and exchange media information in a more organic manner. These interfaces have the potential to transform education by offering interactive and realistic experiences.

Virtual exploration of inaccessible locations offers numerous benefits to learners. It allows students to virtually visit ancient sites and landmarks, such as the Taj Mahal, Red Fort, Rome, Egyptian pyramids, or even an Egyptian village. Through immersive experiences in virtual worlds, students can interact with the environment, engage with fellow students, and have their teacher serve as a guide. This approach provides a safe, cost-effective, and convenient way for students to experience and learn about different cultures, historical places, and diverse environments that would otherwise be challenging to access.

To foster student collaboration, students can gather and interact in virtual environments in diverse and engaging ways. They have the opportunity to collaborate on shared projects, engaging in discussions, connecting, and chatting with both fellow students and educators. Moreover, in the 3D virtual world, they can freely navigate, manipulate objects, and even work simultaneously in multiple 3D environments, enhancing their collaborative experiences.

To facilitate assessment through Project-Based Learning, students can engage in research and construct a virtual village representing a historical era like the Roman Empire. Notably, a globally distributed group of students participating in a distance learning course can collaboratively develop this virtual environment. By working together on such projects, students can gain valuable experience and explore the unique opportunities offered by distance learning.

To create immersive scenarios and simulations, advanced graphics and feature-rich 3D internet applications can be utilized. These technologies enable the development of web-based simulation environments or labs where learners can engage in learning activities and even conduct experiments. These virtual labs, often referred to as dry labs, offer significant benefits for online learners. For instance, students can explore an immersive virtual science lab to conduct simulated experiments. Following the simulation, they can transition to a physical science lab offline to perform the actual experiment and witness its practical application. This approach allows for high-level scientific experiments and expert technical training that may not be feasible within the constraints of a traditional university or school setting. For example, learners can simulate activities such as splitting atoms, performing surgical procedures, piloting an aircraft, or exploring inhospitable environments.

IMPACT OF INCLUSION OF WEB 3.0 FROM STUDENT'S LEARNING PERSPECTIVE

The inclusion of Web 3.0 technologies in the learning process has a profound impact from the student's perspective. Firstly, it promotes personalized and interactive learning experiences. With Web 3.0, students have access to a wealth of resources and tools tailored to their individual needs and preferences. They can engage in self-directed learning, exploring topics at their own pace and in ways that suit their learning style. The interactive nature of Web 3.0 fosters active participation, enabling students to collaborate with peers, interact with instructors, and engage in hands-on activities through simulations, virtual labs, and immersive environments. This level of personalization and interactivity empowers students, making learning more engaging, meaningful, and effective.

Secondly, Web 3.0 expands the boundaries of learning beyond the traditional classroom. Students are no longer limited by physical constraints or geographical boundaries. They can access educational resources, connect with experts, and collaborate with peers from around the world. Web 3.0 technologies enable virtual field trips, allowing students to explore diverse cultures, historical sites, and inaccessible locations through immersive experiences. This global connectivity and exposure to diverse perspectives enhance students' understanding of the world and cultivate a sense of global citizenship. Moreover, the inclusivity of Web 3.0 ensures that students with different learning abilities, backgrounds, and access to resources can equally benefit from the opportunities it offers, fostering a more inclusive and equitable learning environment.

Overall, the inclusion of Web 3.0 from the student's learning perspective revolutionizes education by providing personalized, interactive, and globally connected learning experiences. It empowers students to take ownership of their learning journey, promotes collaboration, and enables access to a wealth of educational resources. Web 3.0 facilitates inclusive learning environments that cater to diverse needs and backgrounds, ensuring equal opportunities for all students to thrive and succeed in their educational pursuits.

FUTURE POTENTIAL OF WEB 3.0

The future potential of Web 3.0 is incredibly promising, with transformative implications for various aspects of our lives. In terms of education, Web 3.0 holds the potential to revolutionize learning experiences by offering enhanced interactivity, personalization, and collaboration. As technology continues to advance, we can expect even more immersive virtual environments, augmented reality applications, and intelligent agents that cater to individual learning styles and preferences. This could enable students to engage in realistic simulations, virtual laboratories, and interactive educational games, providing hands-on experiences that enhance understanding and retention of complex concepts.

Furthermore, Web 3.0 has the capacity to create a more interconnected and decentralized internet ecosystem. Blockchain technology, which underpins many Web 3.0 applications, offers increased security, transparency, and ownership of data. This has significant implications for various industries, including education, where it can facilitate trusted and verified credentials, promote lifelong learning pathways, and enable secure peer-to-peer transactions. With Web 3.0, we may witness the emergence of new educational models, such as decentralized learning platforms, peer-to-peer knowledge exchange networks, and personalized learning ecosystems that adapt to the needs of individual learners.

The future potential of Web 3.0 extends beyond education, as it has the ability to reshape industries such as healthcare, finance, entertainment, and governance. With the integration of artificial intelligence, Internet of Things, and big data analytics, Web 3.0 can create a seamless and intelligent digital ecosystem that empowers individuals, promotes innovation, and drives economic growth. However, as with any technological advancement, ethical considerations, privacy concerns, and the need for digital literacy and inclusivity should be addressed to ensure that the future potential of Web 3.0 is harnessed responsibly and for the benefit of all.

CHALLENGES FACED BY WEB 3.0 IN EDUCATION

Similar to any technology, Web 3.0 has its own drawbacks to consider. It can potentially impact students' learning capacity by diverting their focus towards content curation and analytical skills, resulting in less time dedicated to actual learning. This overreliance on technology may have implications for their learning abilities.

The Smart Search feature in Web 3.0, designed to simplify and expedite the educational process, presents its own set of challenges. It relies on assigning keyword terms, or tagging, to information for easy accessibility. However, the vast amount of data available on the web poses difficulties in effectively tagging this information, requiring significant time and resources. Additionally, even minor adjustments to the tagging information can hinder users from accessing essential information.

While Web 3.0 holds immense potential for revolutionizing the education industry by integrating technological resources into traditional systems, it is crucial to understand its pros and cons. This knowledge allows individuals to utilize it to their advantage, safeguarding against the risks associated with Web 3.0 and fostering a more interactive and enriching learning and teaching experience.

CASE STUDIES

The integration of Web 3.0 technologies has ushered in a new era of innovation and transformation in various sectors, and education is no exception. As mentioned above, Web 3.0 offers great potential to enhance the learning experience. In lieu of that, several case studies which highlight the role of Web 3.0, specifically blockchain technology, in revolutionizing the education sector are presented next.

Knowledge Token (KNW): The Knowledge Token project epitomizes the potential of blockchain technology in the education domain. By leveraging blockchain's decentralized nature and smart contracts, Knowledge Token empowers educators to tokenize their expertise and offer courses directly to students, eliminating the need for traditional intermediaries (Song et al., 2021). Students, in turn, gain access to a diverse range of courses and are rewarded with KNW tokens upon course completion and active participation within the learning community. This decentralized and incentivized education ecosystem not only ensures equitable access to education but also enhances the transparency and traceability of learning achievements.

ODEM (On-Demand Education Marketplace): ODEM exemplifies the seamless integration of blockchain into education by creating a direct link between educators and students. Utilizing blockchain's inherent security features, ODEM enables educators to design and deliver tailor-made courses, while students can explore and enroll in courses of their choice using either cryptocurrencies or traditional fiat payments (Demchenko et al., 2017). The use of blockchain ensures the integrity of credentials and certificates, offering a robust solution for verifying educational achievements.

University of Nicosia: The University of Nicosia's pioneering adoption of blockchain technology in education positions it as a trailblazer in the field. By offering specialized programs such as a Master's degree in Digital Currency and a Blockchain Technologies program, the university not only imparts knowledge but also equips students with skills relevant to the emerging digital economy (Themistocleous et al., 2023). This early integration of blockchain education demonstrates the potential for universities to embrace decentralized technologies and prepare students for the future workforce.

Centrality: Centrality exemplifies the transformative impact of blockchain on education's administrative aspects. By utilizing blockchain for managing student records, certifications, and micro-credentials, Centrality offers a transparent and immutable system for verifying qualifications. This approach not only reduces the risk of fraud but also enhances the credibility and portability of educational achievements, ultimately benefiting both students and employers (Fitzgerald et al., 2020).

Gitcoin Grants: Gitcoin Grants showcases the community-driven potential of Web 3.0 in supporting educational initiatives. By utilizing blockchain's crowdfunding capabilities, Gitcoin Grants enables educators and educational projects to secure funding from a global community (Disruption, 2021). The integration of cryptocurrencies facilitates borderless contributions, fostering collaboration and innovation in the education sector.

Decentraland: While primarily a virtual reality platform, Decentraland demonstrates the creative fusion of blockchain and education. By offering virtual spaces for educational activities such as lectures, workshops, and events, Decentraland expands the boundaries of traditional learning environments (Yasar, 2022). This immersive approach leverages blockchain's capabilities to enhance engagement and interactivity in education.

Edublock: Edublock underscores the importance of secure and tamper-proof record-keeping in education. By leveraging blockchain's decentralized infrastructure, Edublock ensures the permanence and integrity of educational records and achievements (Haveri et al., 2020). This innovative solution addresses concerns related to data manipulation and counterfeit credentials, offering a trustworthy system for verifying students' accomplishments.

All in all, these case studies illuminate the diverse applications of Web 3.0 technologies, particularly blockchain, in the education sector. From decentralized course offerings to secure record-keeping and innovative virtual learning environments, these examples underscore the transformative potential of Web 3.0 in shaping the future of education. As these initiatives continue to evolve and gain traction, they pave the way for a more accessible, transparent, and effective educational landscape.

LIMITATIONS OF THE STUDY

While this research paper provides valuable insights into the role of Web 3.0 in the education sector, it is important to acknowledge certain limitations that may impact the scope and generalizability of the findings. These limitations highlight areas where further research and exploration are warranted:

1. **Emerging Nature of Web 3.0**: The concept of Web 3.0 and its applications in education are still evolving, and as such, this paper may not capture the entirety of its potential impact. Ongoing developments and innovations in the field could introduce new perspectives and use cases that were not addressed in this study.
2. **Limited Adoption and Availability**: While the case studies presented offer promising examples, it is important to note that the adoption of Web 3.0 technologies in education may be limited to specific regions, institutions, or demographic groups. As a result, the findings may not accurately represent the broader educational landscape.
3. **Technical Barriers**: The successful implementation of Web 3.0 technologies often requires a certain level of technical expertise and infrastructure. Not all educational institutions or individuals may have the resources or capabilities to effectively integrate and utilize these technologies, potentially leading to unequal access and participation.
4. **Regulatory and Legal Challenges**: The integration of blockchain and cryptocurrency-based systems in education may raise regulatory and legal concerns in different jurisdictions. The paper does not delve deeply into the legal implications that could arise from the adoption of these technologies, which warrants further investigation.
5. **Educational Pedagogy and Effectiveness**: While Web 3.0 technologies offer innovative approaches to education, their actual impact on teaching and learning outcomes may require more extensive study. The paper does not extensively address the pedagogical implications and the effectiveness of these technologies in enhancing student engagement, knowledge retention, and skill development.

6. **Privacy and Data Security**: The use of blockchain and other decentralized technologies may introduce privacy and data security concerns, particularly in handling sensitive student information. This paper does not thoroughly explore the potential risks and mitigation strategies associated with data protection in Web 3.0-enabled educational environments.

7. **Economic and Socioeconomic Factors**: The adoption of Web 3.0 technologies in education may involve economic costs, ranging from infrastructure investment to cryptocurrency transactions. Additionally, socioeconomic disparities could influence the accessibility and equitable distribution of the benefits offered by these technologies.

Despite these limitations, this research paper provides a comprehensive exploration of the potential impact of Web 3.0 in the education sector, offering valuable insights and a foundation for future studies to delve deeper into specific aspects and implications of this transformative trend.

CONTRIBUTIONS OF THE STUDY

This research paper makes significant contributions to the understanding of the role of Web 3.0 in the education sector, shedding light on its potential implications and opportunities for educators, students, institutions, and the broader educational ecosystem. The following contributions highlight the value and significance of this study:

1. **Comprehensive Exploration of Web 3.0 in Education**: This paper provides an in-depth exploration of how Web 3.0 technologies, particularly blockchain, are being integrated into the education sector. By examining a range of case studies, the study offers a comprehensive overview of the diverse applications and benefits that these technologies bring to education.

2. **Identification of Innovative Use Cases**: The paper identifies and analyzes innovative use cases of Web 3.0 technologies in education, such as decentralized course offerings, secure record-keeping, virtual learning environments, and community-driven funding. These use cases showcase the potential for transforming traditional educational paradigms and fostering new approaches to teaching and learning.

3. **Insights into Decentralization and Disintermediation**: Through the presented case studies, the paper highlights how Web 3.0 technologies enable decentralization and disintermediation in education. This has the potential to empower educators and students, reduce reliance on traditional intermediaries, and create more equitable and accessible learning opportunities.

4. **Envisioning Future Educational Ecosystems**: The study contributes to envisioning future educational ecosystems that leverage Web 3.0 technologies. By showcasing decentralized education platforms, secure credential verification, and immersive virtual learning spaces, the paper stimulates discussions on how education could evolve in the digital age.

5. **Awareness of Technological and Pedagogical Trends**: This paper raises awareness of the technological and pedagogical trends that are shaping the future of education. It highlights the importance of staying attuned to emerging technologies and innovative approaches, emphasizing their potential to enhance educational experiences and outcomes.

6. **Foundation for Further Research**: The research presented in this paper serves as a foundation for further exploration and investigation. It offers a starting point for researchers, educators, policymakers, and industry stakeholders to delve deeper into specific aspects of Web 3.0 in education, such as pedagogical methodologies, legal considerations, privacy concerns, and socioeconomic impacts.

7. **Inspiration for Educational Innovation**: The case studies and insights provided in the paper can inspire educators and educational institutions to innovate and experiment with Web 3.0 technologies. By showcasing successful implementations, the paper encourages educators to consider new ways of designing and delivering educational content.

8. **Transdisciplinary Dialogue**: The study facilitates a transdisciplinary dialogue by bringing together concepts from education, technology, economics, and blockchain. It encourages collaboration and knowledge exchange between professionals from different fields, fostering a holistic understanding of the potential implications of Web 3.0 in education.

9. **Contributing to Educational Transformation**: Ultimately, this paper contributes to the ongoing transformation of education by highlighting the potential of Web 3.0 technologies to reshape traditional educational practices. By advocating for a decentralized, transparent, and learner-centric approach, the study aligns with broader efforts to create more inclusive and effective learning environments.

Therefore, this research paper's contributions serve to deepen the understanding of the role of Web 3.0 in the education sector, providing valuable insights and inspiration for future endeavors aimed at harnessing the transformative power of emerging technologies to enhance education for learners worldwide.

CONCLUSION

Web 3.0 transcends being merely a collection of innovative technologies and services. It encompasses a range of services that can truly transform online classrooms into a reality. Due to its inherent nature, Web 3.0 services have a positive impact on teaching and learning. These technologies provide numerous advantages, including 3D-wikis, 3D Labs, intelligent agent-based search engines, virtual environments like avatars, and semantic digital libraries. In vision of Web 3.0, we anticipate a future where these ubiquitous technologies converge real and virtual environments, enabling seamless interaction between users, whether through virtual means or in the physical world. These benefits align directly with existing best practices in online education, fostering an authenticated and effective educational environment.

In conclusion, the future growth potential and impact of Web 3.0 in the field of education are immense. With its innovative technologies and services, Web 3.0 offers transformative opportunities for students, teachers, and institutions alike. From personalized learning experiences and enhanced collaboration to immersive virtual environments and intelligent search capabilities, Web 3.0 opens up new frontiers in education. It empowers learners to access information and resources with greater ease and efficiency, while enabling educators to design more engaging and tailored instructional approaches. As Web 3.0 continues to evolve, it holds the promise of revolutionizing the education landscape, creating a more inclusive, interactive, and effective learning environment for learners across the globe. The potential for Web 3.0 to shape the future of education is truly exciting, and its impact will be felt for years to come.

REFERENCES

Acikgul Firat, E., & Firat, S. (2020). Web 3.0 in learning environments: A systematic review. *Turkish Online Journal of Distance Education*, *22*(1), 148–169. doi:10.17718/tojde.849898

Allison, C., Miller, A., Oliver, I., Michaelson, R., & Tiropanis, T. (2012). The Web in education. *Computer Networks*, *56*(18), 3811–3824. doi:10.1016/j.comnet.2012.09.017

Allison, M., & Kendrick, L. M. (2015). Toward education 3.0: Pedagogical affordances and implications of social software and the semantic web. *New Directions for Teaching and Learning*, *144*(144), 109–119. doi:10.1002/tl.20167

Amarin, N. Z. (2015). Web 3.0 and its reflections on the future of e-learning. *Academic Journal Of Science*, *4*(02), 115–122.

Atabekova, A., Belousov, A., & Shoustikova, T. (2015). Web 3.0-based non-formal learning to meet the third millennium education requirements: University Students' perceptions. *Procedia: Social and Behavioral Sciences*, *214*, 511–519. doi:10.1016/j.sbspro.2015.11.754

Benito-Osorio, D., Peris-Ortiz, M., Armengot, C. R., & Colino, A. (2013). Web 5.0: The future of emotional competences in higher education. *Global Business Perspectives*, *1*(3), 274–287. doi:10.100740196-013-0016-5

Blaum, W. E., Jarczweski, A., Balzer, F., Stötzner, P., & Ahlers, O. (2013). Towards Web 3.0: Taxonomies and ontologies for medical education-a systematic review. *GMS Zeitschrift für Medizinische Ausbildung*, *30*(1). PMID:23467484

Chisega-Negrilă, A. M. (2012). WEB 3.0 in education. In *Conference proceedings of» eLearning and Software for Education «(eLSE)* (Vol. 8, No. 01, pp. 455-460). Carol I National Defence University Publishing House. 10.12753/2066-026X-12-073

Chisega-Negrilă, A. M. (2013). Education in web 3.0. *JADLET Journal of Advanced Distributed Learning Technology*, *1*(1), 50–59.

Demartini, C., & Benussi, L. (2017). Do web 4.0 and industry 4.0 imply education X. 0? *IT Professional*, *19*(3), 4–7. doi:10.1109/MITP.2017.47

Demchenko, Y., Belloum, A., de Laat, C., Loomis, C., Wiktorski, T., & Spekschoor, E. (2017, December). Customisable data science educational environment: From competences management and curriculum design to virtual labs on-demand. In *2017 IEEE International Conference on Cloud Computing Technology and Science (CloudCom)* (pp. 363-368). IEEE. 10.1109/CloudCom.2017.59

Disruption, J. (2021). *Token Engineering Open Program: A Multidisciplinary Study of Gitcoin Grants.* Gitcoin. Published.

Dominic, M., Francis, S., & Pilomenraj, A. (2014). E-learning in web 3.0. *International Journal of Modern Education and Computer Science*, *6*(2), 8–14. doi:10.5815/ijmecs.2014.02.02

Fitzgerald, H. E., Karen, B., Sonka, S. T., Furco, A., & Swanson, L. (2020). The centrality of engagement in higher education. In *Building the Field of Higher Education Engagement* (pp. 201–219). Routledge.

Giannakos, M. N., & Lapatas, V. (2010, July). Towards Web 3.0 concept for collaborative e-learning. In *International Conference on Technology-Enhanced Learning* (Vol. 2, pp. 147-151). SCITEPRESS.

Haveri, P., Rashmi, U. B., Narayan, D. G., Nagaratna, K., & Shivaraj, K. (2020, July). Edublock: Securing educational documents using blockchain technology. In *2020 11th International Conference on Computing, Communication and Networking Technologies (ICCCNT)* (pp. 1-7). IEEE.

Hew, K. F., & Cheung, W. S. (2013). Use of Web 2.0 technologies in K-12 and higher education: The search for evidence-based practice. *Educational Research Review*, *9*, 47–64. doi:10.1016/j.edurev.2012.08.001

Hussain, F. (2012). *E-Learning 3.0= E-Learning 2.0+ Web 3.0?* International Association for Development of the Information Society.

Jiang, D. (2014). What will web 3.0 bring to education? *World Journal on Educational Technology: Current Issues*, *6*(2), 126–131.

Lal, M. (2011). Web 3.0 in Education & Research. *BVICAM's International. Journal of Information Technology*, *3*(2).

Miranda, P., Isaias, P., & Costa, C. J. (2014). E-Learning and web generations: Towards Web 3.0 and E-Learning 3.0. *International Proceedings of Economics Development and Research*, *81*, 92.

Miranda, P., Isaias, P., & Costa, C. J. (2014). The impact of Web 3.0 technologies in e-Learning: Emergence of e-Learning 3.0. In *EDULEARN14 Proceedings* (pp. 4139-4149). IATED.

Noskova, T., Pavlova, T., & Iakovleva, O. (2016). Web 3.0 technologies and transformation of pedagogical activities. In Mobile Computing and Wireless Networks: Concepts, Methodologies, Tools, and Applications (pp. 728-748). IGI Global.

Ohei, K. N., & Brink, R. (2019). Web 3.0 and web 2.0 technologies in higher educational institute: Methodological concept towards a framework development for adoption. *International journal for Infonomics (IJI), 12*(1), 1841-1853.

Ohler, J. (2008). The semantic web in education. *EDUCAUSE Quarterly*, *31*(4), 7–9.

Pentland, A. (2022). Building a New Economy: Data, AI, and Web 3: How distributed technologies could return more control to users. *Communications of the ACM, 65*(12), 27–29. https://doi-org.ezproxy.myucwest.ca/10.1145/3547659. doi:10.1145/3547659

Poore, M. (2014). The Next G Web. Discernment, meaning-making, and the implications of Web 3.0 for education. *Technology, Pedagogy and Education, 23*(2), 167–180. doi:10.1080/1475939X.2013.802992

Morris, R. (2011). *Web 3.0: Implications for online learning.*

Samarawickrema, G., & Stacey, E. (2007). Adopting Web-Based Learning and Teaching: A case study in higher education. *Distance Education, 28*(3), 313–333. doi:10.1080/01587910701611344

Shaltout, M. S. A. F., & Salamah, A. I. B. (2013, May). The impact of Web 3.0 on E-Learning. In *2013 Fourth International Conference on e-Learning" Best Practices in Management, Design and Development of e-Courses: Standards of Excellence and Creativity"* (pp. 227-232). IEEE. 10.1109/ECONF.2013.70

Song, L., Ju, X., Zhu, Z., & Li, M. (2021). An access control model for the Internet of Things based on zero-knowledge token and blockchain. *EURASIP Journal on Wireless Communications and Networking*, *2021*(1), 1–20. doi:10.118613638-021-01986-4

Themistocleous, M., Christodoulou, K., & Iosif, E. (2023). Academic certificates issued on blockchain: the case of the University of Nicosia and Block. co. In *Supporting Higher Education 4.0 with Blockchain* (pp. 166–178). Routledge. doi:10.4324/9781003318736-8

Yaşar, Ş. (2022). Reflection Of Virtual Reality On Accounting Education: Transformation Of University To Metaversity. *Journal of Business in The Digital Age*, *5*(2), 95–104.

Chapter 20
Decentralized Identity in Web 3:
Transforming Marketing and Consumer Engagement

Himanshu Sisodia

https://orcid.org/0009-0003-1550-0884

SSBM Geneva, Switzerland

ABSTRACT

Web 3, or the decentralized web, uses blockchain technology and decentralised principles to revolutionize online interactions and commercial practises. It gives people authority, builds trust, and allows for peer-to-peer interactions. Blockchain is a decentralized and secure database that ensures transparent transactions without the need of middlemen. Web 3 is reshaping the financial, healthcare, supply chain, and entertainment industries. Cryptocurrencies provide safe and borderless transactions. It improves supply chain management, assures ethical sourcing, and gives content producers more influence. Decentralised identification systems overcome the problems associated with centralized identity. Scalability, interoperability, and performance are all difficult issues. The importance of interoperability and standardization cannot be overstated. Regulatory and legal problems must be consistent with the ideas of decentralized identity. Decentralized identification systems provide personalised and transparent experiences that foster trust and consumer loyalty.

1. INTRODUCTION

1.1. Web 3 and Its Influence on Industries

Web 3, also known as the decentralized web, signifies a significant change in the manner in which we interact with the internet and conduct commerce. The term was coined to characterise the next iteration of the internet, which will be based on blockchain technology and decentralized principles (Potts & Rennie, 2019). Web 3 seeks to empower individuals, promote trust, and facilitate peer-to-peer interactions, as opposed to its antecedent Web 2, which extensively relied on centralized platforms and intermedi-

DOI: 10.4018/978-1-6684-9919-1.ch020

Copyright © 2023, IGI Global. Copying or distributing in print or electronic forms without written permission of IGI Global is prohibited.

aries. Web 3 has an impact on numerous industries, including finance, healthcare, supply chain, and entertainment, among others. Blockchain-based cryptocurrencies have emerged as a viable alternative to traditional centralized financial systems in the financial sector. The capacity of cryptocurrencies to conduct secure, transparent, and transnational transactions has the potential to disrupt traditional banking and remittance systems. Decentralized finance (DeFi) applications built on blockchain technology allow individuals to access financial services such as lending, borrowing, and asset management without the need for intermediaries such as banks (Potts & Rennie, 2019). Web 3 offers possibilities for secure and interoperable health records in the healthcare industry. Decentralized identity solutions allow patients to maintain control over their health data while sharing it securely with healthcare providers. This can help to streamline medical processes, improve patient outcomes, and increase patient privacy (Holbl et al., 2018). Web 3 has the potential to transform supply chain management by enhancing transparency and traceability. Companies can monitor the movement of products and verify their authenticity at each stage of the supply chain using blockchain-based systems. This decreases the likelihood of counterfeiting, increases efficiency, and ensures ethical sourcing (Potts & Rennie, 2019). Web 3 will also benefit the entertainment and media industries. Using blockchain-based platforms, artists and content creators can distribute their work directly to consumers, eliminating the need for intermediaries and reducing costs. (Potts & Rennie, 2019) Smart contracts enable transparent and equitable revenue sharing, ensuring that creators receive their reasonable share of profits.

Blockchain technology, which functions as a decentralized and immutable ledger for documenting transactions and preserving data, is one of the fundamental components of Web 3. The distributed nature of blockchain ensures that no single entity controls the network, thereby enhancing security and removing the need for intermediaries in numerous industries (Nakamoto, 2008). This technology has garnered significant attention due to its potential to revolutionise industries outside of cryptocurrencies.

By introducing decentralisation, transparency, and trust, Web 3 has immense potential to reshape numerous industries. Integrating blockchain technology and decentralized principles has the potential to revolutionise finance, healthcare, supply chain, and other industries. By utilising Web 3's advantages, businesses can expedite operations, enhance security, cultivate trust, and create new opportunities for individuals to participate in the digital economy.

1.2. The Significance of Decentralized Identity

Decentralized Identity is concerned with the application of decentralisation concepts to the complex realm of identity. Decentralisation has provided the technology industry with cryptocurrencies and blockchains in which there is a high level of trust between unknown entities. When trust is discussed in this context, it does not refer to getting to know someone, forming a relationship, and then developing trust; it refers to cryptographic trust between two entities that could be acting completely anonymously. In the context of Web 3, decentralized identity is crucial for addressing identity management, privacy, and security challenges. Traditional identity systems have relied on centralized authorities to verify and authenticate individuals, leading to concerns regarding data breaches, identity theft, and a lack of control over personal information. Decentralized identity, on the other hand, offers a paradigm transition by restoring individual control and proprietorship of identity data. Individuals with decentralized identity are able to securely manage and control their personal information. Individuals can store their identity credentials on a blockchain or distributed ledger to ensure immutability and tamper-resistance instead of relying on centralized entities (Dib & Toumi, 2020). These credentials can be selectively shared with third parties, allowing for granular control over the disclosure of personally identifiable information. This enhanced control over identity data addresses privacy concerns, as individuals can choose which attributes are shared and with whom, thereby reducing the likelihood that personal information will be exploited.

Decentralized identity systems cultivate confidence and allow for seamless interactions in Web 3 environments. The use of cryptography and consensus mechanisms to establish trust enables relying parties to verify the authenticity and integrity of identity credentials (Gupta et al., 2023). This eliminates the need for intermediaries or reliable third parties to verify the identity of an individual. Decentralized identity streamlines the identity verification process by removing intermediaries, thereby reducing friction and facilitating quicker enrollment for various services and platforms. Decentralized identity also addresses the issue of system and platform interoperability. Traditional identity systems require individuals to create and administer multiple accounts with various providers, resulting in identity data that is fragmented and stored in silos. Individuals can have a singular, portable identity that can be used across multiple services and platforms with decentralized identity, reducing the burden of administering multiple accounts and streamlining user experiences (Gupta et al., 2023).

In addition, decentralized identity has the potential to encourage innovation and generate new business models. By granting individuals control over their personal information, businesses are able to provide personalised and customised experiences while respecting customers' privacy preferences. Moreover, decentralized identity can enable new forms of digital trust and reputation systems, in which individuals' past interactions and transactions can be verified and used to establish their trustworthiness in various contexts (Dib & Toumi, 2020).

2. COMPREHENSION OF DECENTRALIZED IDENTITY

2.1. Definition and Fundamental Concepts of Decentralized Identity

Decentralized identity is a new approach to identity management that uses blockchain technology and decentralized principles to give individuals control and ownership over their personal data. It seeks to resolve the limitations of traditional identity systems by transferring the power dynamic away from centralized authorities and towards individuals. Self-sovereign identity (SSI), which emphasises the individual's ability to administer their identity attributes, credentials, and confidential data without relying on centralized entities, is the foundation of decentralized identity. Individuals can store their identity credentials on a blockchain or distributed ledger in this context, ensuring immutability and tamper-resistance (Dib & Toumi, 2020). These credentials are cryptographically protected, ensuring their authenticity and integrity.

Privacy by design is one of the fundamental principles of decentralized identity. Individuals have the freedom to choose which identity characteristics or personal information to disclose. Individuals can selectively disclose only the pertinent information required for a particular transaction or interaction as opposed to providing superfluous and excessive personal data (Gupta et al., 2023). This principle addresses the developing concerns regarding privacy and data vulnerabilities in centralized systems, as individuals retain control over sensitive data.

The concepts of verifiability and trustworthiness are also significant. Cryptographic techniques are utilised by decentralized identity systems to establish trust and validate the authenticity of identity credentials. Using public-private key pairs, digital signatures, and decentralized consensus mechanisms, relying parties can independently verify the integrity and provenance of identity data (Dib & Toumi, 2020). This principle enables direct trust between individuals and service providers, eliminating the need for intermediaries and reducing the risk of identity deception.

The fundamental principle of decentralized identity is interoperability. Traditional identity systems are frequently plagued by fragmentation and data silos, requiring individuals to manage multiple accounts with various providers. Decentralized identity endeavours to facilitate portability and interoperability by permitting individuals to possess a singular, portable identity that can be used across multiple services and platforms (Gupta et al., 2023). This principle simplifies identity verification, improves user experiences, and eliminates the need for redundant identity data.

Decentralized identity is a paradigm transition in identity management because it gives individuals control, privacy, and trust over their personal information. Decentralized identity systems rest on the principles of self-sovereign identity, privacy by design, verifiability, and interoperability. Decentralized identity offers a plausible solution to the problems of centralized identity systems and sets the foundation for a more secure, privacy-preserving, and user-centric approach to administering digital identities by adhering to these principles.

2.2. Conventional Centralized Identity Systems

Decentralized identity systems contrast sharply with traditional centralized identity systems in a number of significant ways. Traditional centralized identity systems, such as government agencies or corporations, rely on a centralized authority to validate, store, and manage identity information (Dunphy & Petitcolas, 2018). Decentralized identity systems, on the other hand, utilise blockchain technology and distributed ledger technology to eradicate the need for a central point of control and disseminate identity data across a network of participants. The possession and control of identity information is a significant distinction between decentralized and centralized identity systems. Individuals typically cede control of their confidential information to a centralized authority in centralized systems. This central authority becomes the custodian of individuals' identity information, which raises concerns regarding data breaches, misuse, and lack of transparency (Dhamija et al., 2020). Decentralized identity systems, on the other hand, grant individuals ownership and control over their identity data. Individuals can store their identity attributes and credentials securely on a blockchain or distributed ledger, ensuring that they retain control over their personal data (Dunphy & Petitcolas, 2018).

Decentralized identity systems are superior to centralized systems in terms of privacy. In conventional systems, individuals are frequently required to disclose superfluous personal information that is not directly relevant to the transaction or interaction at hand. This practise raises privacy concerns and exposes individuals to potential data breaches and misappropriation of their sensitive information. (Gupta et al., 2023) Decentralized identity systems allow individuals to selectively disclose only the necessary identity attributes for specific transactions, thereby minimising the exposure of personal data and preserving privacy. Decentralized identity systems are more resilient and secure than centralized systems. A singular point of control becomes a target for malicious actors and hackers in centralized systems. (Dunphy & Petitcolas, 2018) A breech of the central authority's security can result in enormous data breaches and identity theft incidents. On the other hand, decentralized identity systems distribute identity data across a network of nodes, making it more difficult for adversaries to compromise the entire system. In decentralized systems, the use of cryptographic techniques and consensus mechanisms increases security and reduces reliance on single points of failure.

Decentralized identity systems have the potential to provide smoother and more seamless interactions in terms of user experience. Traditional centralized systems frequently necessitate the creation and management of multiple accounts with various service providers. This fragmented strategy makes the user experience cumbersome and increases the risk of password fatigue and security vulnerabilities. (Gupta et al., 2023) Decentralized identity systems enable individuals to have a singular, portable identity that can be used across multiple services and platforms, thereby facilitating the user experience and reducing the need for redundant identity data.

2.3. Benefits of Decentralized Identity for Enterprises and Individuals

In the digital landscape, decentralized identity offers numerous benefits to both individuals and enterprises. By transferring control and custody of identity data to individuals, decentralized identity systems grant users greater privacy, security, and autonomy over their personal data (Dib & Touma, 2020). Moreover, businesses can leverage the benefits of decentralized identity to improve customer experiences, streamline operations, and cultivate trust in customer interactions.

Enhanced privacy is one of the primary advantages of decentralized identity for individuals. Traditional centralized identity systems often require individuals to share an excessive amount of personal information, exposing them to potential privacy risks and data intrusions. (Avellanedaet al., 2019) Decentralized identity systems enable individuals to selectively disclose only the required identity attributes, preserving their privacy and reducing the risk of personal information being exploited. Individuals can maintain control over their personal data and determine who has access to specific pieces of information with decentralized identity. Decentralized identity provides greater security than centralized systems. Centralized identity systems are susceptible to single points of failure, where a violation or compromise of the central authority can result in significant data breaches and identity theft. Decentralized identity systems, on the other hand, distribute identity information across a network of nodes, making it more difficult for malicious actors to compromise the entire system (Dib & Toumi, 2020). In decentralized systems, the use of cryptographic techniques and consensus mechanisms increases security and reduces the risk of unauthorised access or manipulation.

Decentralized identity can provide numerous advantages for businesses. First, decentralized identity systems enable businesses to establish trustworthy customer relationships. Businesses can establish a foundation of trust and openness by granting individuals control over their identity information and respecting their privacy preferences. This can strengthen brand reputation and increase customer loyalty (Sorokinet, 2021). Decentralized identity simplifies user interactions and reduces friction in digital interactions. Traditional identity systems frequently require users to create and administer multiple accounts with various service providers, resulting in fragmented user experiences and password fatigue. Users' registration and authentication processes are streamlined by decentralized identity systems (Dib & Touma, 2020). Decentralized identity can enable new opportunities and business models. By leveraging decentralized identity systems, businesses are able to provide consumers with personalised and customised experiences while respecting their privacy preferences. The ability to selectively and securely share identity attributes enables businesses to provide personalised recommendations, targeted advertising, and customised services, resulting in increased consumer satisfaction and engagement (Dib & Touma, 2020).

Decentralized identity has numerous advantages for individuals and businesses. It offers individuals enhanced privacy, control, and security over their personal data. Businesses can utilise decentralized identity to improve consumer experiences, nurture trust, and uncover new avenues for personalised services. Individuals and enterprises can navigate the digital landscape with greater autonomy, privacy, and security if they adopt decentralized identity.

2.4. Concept of Self-Sovereign Identity (SSI)

Self-sovereign identity (SSI) is the fundamental concept of decentralized identity systems. Individuals can manage their identity attributes and credentials without relying on centralized authorities or intermediaries (Preukschat & Reed, 2021). It positions individuals at the centre of their digital identities, allowing them to assert their identity and share pertinent data as necessary.

An important principle of self-sovereign identity is the capacity of the individual to administer their own identity attributes and credentials. In a conventional centralized identity system, individuals have limited control over their confidential information because it is stored and managed by centralized authorities. SSI alters the balance of power by enabling individuals to retain control over their identity data and determine when and how to disclose particular characteristics (Preukschat & Reed, 2021). This control over confidential information confers greater privacy and autonomy on individuals.

Use of decentralized and distributed technologies, such as blockchain or distributed ledger technology, is another fundamental aspect of self-sovereign identity. These technologies enable individuals to preserve their identity attributes and credentials in an unalterable and tamper-resistant manner. SSI ensures that the authenticity and integrity of identity data can be verified without relying on a centralized authority by leveraging cryptographic techniques and decentralized consensus mechanisms (Preukschat & Reed, 2021). This feature increases the security and reliability of identity information.

Self-sovereign identity facilitates interoperability and portability. Traditional identity systems are frequently fragmented, requiring individuals to manage multiple accounts and identities with various service providers. SSI enables individuals to have a portable identity that can be utilised across multiple platforms and services (Preukschat & Reed, 2021). This portability makes interactions seamless and reduces the burden of managing multiple identities.

Self-sovereign identity incorporates the principles of minimal disclosure and selective attribute sharing. Individuals can divulge only the identity attributes or credentials required for a specific transaction or interaction, without disclosing superfluous personal data (Deret al., 2017). This principle increases privacy and decreases the likelihood that personal data will be mishandled or exploited.

Moreover, self-sovereign identity highlights the significance of user consent and control. Individuals have the right to give informed consent and make decisions regarding the use and sharing of their identity data. SSI systems allow users to govern consent settings, giving them granular control over the disclosure and use of their identity attributes (Der et al., 2017). This aspect assures individuals' control over their digital identities.

The concept of self-sovereign identity is fundamental to decentralized identity systems. It positions individuals in charge of their own identity information, allowing them to manage and share their identity attributes and credentials as necessary. SSI improves privacy, security, interoperability, and user control through the use of decentralized technologies. Decentralized identity systems empower individuals and pave the way for a more user-centric, privacy-preserving, and secure approach to identity management in the digital age by embracing self-sovereign identity.

3. MARKETING'S USE OF DECENTRALIZED IDENTITY

3.1. Increasing Trust and Transparency in Marketing Relationships

Decentralized identity plays a significant function in enhancing marketing relationships' trust and transparency. In conventional marketing, credibility and repute of businesses or centralized intermediaries are frequently used to establish trust. However, decentralized identity systems introduce a new paradigm in which trust is established directly between individuals and businesses, eliminating the need for middlemen.

Providing individuals with control over their confidential information is one way decentralized identity increases trust. In traditional marketing practises, individuals typically have limited control over the collection, storage, and utilisation of their data. This lack of control can erode confidence and contribute to privacy and data abuse concerns. Individuals can manage their identity attributes and selectively disclose information to businesses using decentralized identity systems (Fukami et al., 2021). Decentralized identity fosters a sense of trust and transparency in marketing relationships by granting individuals the ability to determine which information is shared and with whom.

Another crucial aspect that decentralized identity provides to marketing is transparency. In traditional marketing practises, individuals typically have limited visibility into how their data is used and shared. Individuals with decentralized identity systems have access to their identity transaction history, which is maintained on a blockchain or distributed ledger (Fukami et al., 2020). This visibility into the usage and movement of personal data inspires trust in individuals and enables them to confirm that their information is being handled appropriately.

Additionally, decentralized identity can facilitate transparent and authorised data sharing. In conventional marketing, companies frequently rely on data brokers or centralized databases to access consumer data. This procedure can be opaque and lack clarity. Businesses can request specific identity attributes directly from individuals in a transparent and consent-driven manner with decentralized identity (Fukami et al., 2021). This ensures that individuals are aware of and can provide informed consent for the use of their data, fostering a relationship of trust in marketing.

Decentralized identity can facilitate reputation systems based on verified credentials and interactions. Reputation plays a crucial role in marketing, as consumers frequently base their purchasing decisions on the reputation of businesses and products. (Fukami et al., 2020) Decentralized identity systems can utilise verified credentials stored on a blockchain to establish and maintain reputation scores. These reputation scores may be derived from verifiable interactions, such as past purchases or user feedback. By providing transparent and verifiable reputation systems, decentralized identity increases consumer confidence and facilitates well-informed choices.

By empowering individuals with control over their personal information, providing visibility into data usage, facilitating transparent data sharing, and enabling reputation systems, decentralized identity brings trust and transparency to marketing relationships. By embracing decentralized identity, businesses can create stronger and more trustworthy relationships with customers, nurturing loyalty and enhancing the marketing experience as a whole.

3.2. Decentralized Identity for Customization and Tailored Experiences

Decentralized identity creates new opportunities for personalization and customization in marketing and consumer engagement. Traditional approaches to personalization frequently rely on centralized databases and third-party data aggregators, which can result in privacy concerns and restricted access to personal data. Decentralized identity systems, on the other hand, allow individuals to manage their own identity attributes and selectively share them with businesses, paving the way for more personalised and tailored experiences.

Businesses can gain access to verified and authenticated identity attributes directly from individuals by leveraging decentralized identity (Razec et al., 2022). This allows for a greater comprehension of the preferences, interests, and behaviours of consumers, enabling businesses to deliver highly targeted and pertinent experiences. Businesses can access specific identity attributes such as demographic information, purchase history, and product preferences, which can be used to personalise marketing messages, recommendations, and offers, with the consent of individuals. Decentralized identity enables a more granular and nuanced approach to personalization. Individuals are able to disclose only the identity attributes required for a specific interaction or transaction (Razec et al., 2022). This means that businesses can receive only the information they require, without superfluous or unnecessary information. The outcome is a more efficient and targeted personalization strategy that respects the privacy preferences of individuals. Decentralized identity permits cross-platform customization. In conventional systems, personalization efforts are frequently restricted to particular platforms or service providers, resulting in fragmented user experiences. Decentralized identity enables the construction of a portable identity that is usable across multiple services and platforms (Razec et al., 2022). This portability allows businesses to provide seamless personalised experiences regardless of the platform or channel through which the interaction occurs. For instance, a customer's preferences and purchase history can be used to provide personalised recommendations on both an e-commerce website and a mobile application.

Individuals are also empowered by decentralized identity to actively shape their own personalised experiences. Individuals can directly update and manage their preferences, interests, and demographic information when they have control over their identify data. This enables dynamic personalization, in which consumers can change their preferences over time, affecting the nature and type of personalised experiences they receive (Razec et al., 2022).

Decentralized identity offers significant potential for marketing and consumer engagement personalization and customization. By granting individuals control over their identity attributes and facilitating selective sharing, businesses can gain access to verified and pertinent consumer information. In turn, this enables more precise and targeted personalization strategies, enhancing consumer experiences and engagement.

3.3. Credential Verification for Targeted Advertising

Utilising verifiable credentials within the context of decentralized identity can considerably improve the efficacy of targeted advertising. Traditional approaches to targeted advertising frequently rely on third-party data brokers and centralized databases, which can raise privacy concerns and limit precision. With decentralized identity, however, businesses can access verified and authenticated identity attributes directly from individuals, allowing for more precise and targeted advertising campaigns.

Verified credentials stored on a blockchain or distributed ledger can provide businesses with accurate and current information about demographic data, interests, and preferences of individuals (Bertocci et al., 2007). These authenticated credentials can be used to construct in-depth user profiles, allowing businesses to better comprehend their target audience and modify their advertising messages accordingly.

By gaining access to authenticated credentials, businesses can ensure that the data used for targeting is trustworthy and reliable.

Decentralized identity permits fine-grained targeting based on particular identity attributes. Individuals who have control over their own identity data can grant businesses access to specific characteristics, such as age, location, and interests. This method guarantees that businesses receive the necessary information for targeting without jeopardising the privacy of individuals or disclosing superfluous personal information (Bertocci et al., 2007). The ability to target advertisements based on verified and agreed-upon characteristics results in more accurate and relevant advertising messages.

Using verified credentials permits precise ad targeting across multiple platforms and channels. With a portable identity, businesses can seamlessly deliver targeted advertisements regardless of the individual's platform or device. (Bertocci et al., 2007) This cross-platform targeting provides a consistent and personalised advertising experience, enhancing the efficacy of the campaigns. For instance, a user's verified credentials can be used to deliver personalised advertisements on a website, mobile app, or social media platform, ensuring a cohesive and targeted advertising strategy. Decentralized identity enables targeted advertising that protects privacy. Unlike conventional advertising models that rely on extensive data collection and monitoring, decentralized identity enables businesses to target advertisements without violating the privacy of individuals. Businesses can respect privacy preferences and minimise the collection of sensitive personal data by accessing only the necessary identity attributes for targeting (Ermolaev et al., 2023). This method fosters consumer confidence and addresses privacy concerns associated with conventional targeted advertising.

Utilising verifiable credentials through decentralized identity has significant advantages for targeted advertising. Businesses are able to construct accurate user profiles and deliver personalised advertisements by gaining access to verifiable and authenticated identity attributes directly from individuals. Targeting on a granular level, cross-platform capabilities, and protection of privacy are significant benefits of this method. By adopting decentralized identity, businesses can increase the efficacy of their advertising campaigns, provide consumers with more pertinent content, and cultivate a positive and personalised advertising experience.

3.4. Decentralized Identity to Mitigate Data Breaches and Privacy Concerns

Decentralized identity has significant potential for mitigating data intrusions and addressing privacy concerns associated with conventional centralized identity systems. Hackers attempting to exploit personal information are increasingly targeting centralized databases, which have become lucrative targets (Ermolaev et al., 2023). Built on the principles of self-sovereign identity and distributed ledger technology, decentralized identity introduces a more secure and privacy-preserving identity management system.

Elimination of a single point of failure is a critical benefit of decentralized identity for preventing data intrusions. In centralized systems, a violation of the central authority can compromise a vast quantity of personally identifiable information. Distributing identity data across a network of nodes, decentralized identity systems make it more difficult for malicious actors to compromise the entire system (Maram et al., 2021). The use of cryptographic techniques and consensus mechanisms ensures the security and integrity of identity data, thereby decreasing the likelihood of data breaches. Decentralized identity systems are designed with privacy in mind. In traditional centralized systems, individuals have limited control over their personal information, resulting in privacy concerns and the possibility of abuse. (Maram et al., 2021) Decentralized identity empowers individuals with control and proprietorship over their identity attributes and credentials. Selective attribute disclosure enables individuals to share only the information required for particular interactions, minimising the exposure of personal data and the associated privacy risks.

Decentralized identity reduces reliance on third-party data brokers. Businesses rely on intermediaries to collect and provide access to consumer data in conventional systems. This practise raises data quality, security, and privacy concerns. (Maram et al., 2021). This direct interaction reduces the risks associated with data brokers and increases the credibility of the data used for a variety of purposes. Decentralized identity enables data sharing based on consent. Personal information is frequently collected and shared without the explicit consent of individuals in traditional systems. (Maram et al., 2021) Decentralized identity systems emphasise individual consent and control over data exchange. Individuals have the ability to grant or deny access to their identity attributes, ensuring that data sharing is based on voluntary, informed consent. This strategy increases transparency, empowers individuals, and reduces the probability of data misuse.

Decentralized identity is a promising solution for mitigating data intrusions and addressing the privacy concerns of centralized identity systems. By eradicating single points of failure, prioritising privacy, decreasing reliance on intermediaries, and emphasising consent-driven data sharing, decentralized identity systems improve security, safeguard personal data, and give individuals greater control over their identities. Decentralized identity provides a path towards a more secure and privacy-preserving identity management strategy, as data intrusions continue to pose significant risks.

4. CONSUMER ENGAGEMENT AND DECENTRALIZED IDENTITIES

4.1. Consumers Dominion Over Their Personal Data and Identity

Decentralized identity systems give consumers control over their data and identity, altering the balance of power away from centralized authorities and towards individuals. Individuals have limited control and visibility over how their data is collected, utilised, and shared in traditional systems. (Zhao et al., 2008) Decentralized identity establishes the concept of self-sovereign identity, in which individuals have proprietorship and control over their own identity attributes and credentials. This empowerment provides numerous benefits for consumers.

Decentralized identity provides individuals with the ability to control the sharing and disclosure of their personal information. In conventional systems, personal information is frequently collected and utilised without the explicit consent or knowledge of individuals. (Zhao et al., 2008) Decentralized identity permits individuals to selectively share specific identity attributes or credentials, ensuring that only necessary and pertinent information is disclosed for a specific transaction or interaction. This control over data sharing increases privacy and reduces the likelihood that personal information will be misappropriated or exploited.

Moreover, decentralized identity systems provide individuals with visibility and transparency into the usage and mobility of their identity data. Individuals have limited insight into how their data is processed and shared with traditional systems. Built on the principles of blockchain or distributed ledger technology, decentralized identity provides a transparent and auditable journal of identity transactions (Baars et al., 2016). This transparency enables individuals to confirm the accuracy of their data, monitor its usage, and ensure compliance with privacy policies and regulations.

Decentralized identity promotes individual autonomy and selection. In conventional systems, individuals frequently have few options for administering their identity and data. (Baars et al., 2016) Decentralized identity systems enable individuals to control their own identity attributes, update them as necessary, and select the platforms and services they interact with. This independence permits individuals to shape their digital identities in accordance with their preferences, requirements, and values.

Decentralized identity permits individuals to partake in the digital economy on their own terms. Individuals are frequently regarded as passive data subjects with limited control or influence over the use of their data under traditional systems. Individuals can actively partake in the administration and monetization of their data via decentralized identity systems. Individuals can, for instance, choose to share their data in exchange for personalised services or incentives (Zhao et al., 2008). This transition towards consumer autonomy promotes a more equitable and equitable digital ecosystem.

4.2. Seamless Authentication and Authorization to Enhance the User Experience

Decentralized identity systems have the potential to enhance the user experience through seamless authentication and authorization procedures. Traditional systems frequently rely on username-password combinations or fragmented authentication processes across multiple platforms, resulting in a difficult user experience and password fatigue. Decentralized identity introduces a more streamlined, user-centric strategy, thereby enhancing both convenience and security.

Single sign-on (SSO), which is facilitated by decentralized identity, is a crucial aspect of enhancing the user experience. Individuals must frequently establish and administer multiple accounts across multiple platforms and services when using conventional systems. This disjointed method can be time-consuming and aggravating. (Crumlish et al., 2009) Decentralized identity allows for a portable and unified identity, allowing individuals to authenticate themselves across multiple services with a single set of credentials. This seamless authentication process streamlines the user experience by eliminating the need for duplicate account creation and logon stages.

Self-sovereign identity attributes confer greater control and convenience to individuals within decentralized identity systems. In conventional systems, individuals are frequently required to provide their personal information or credentials to multiple service providers, which can be laborious and time-consuming. Individuals can securely manage and maintain their identity attributes on a blockchain or distributed ledger, and selectively share them as necessary (Crumlish et al., 2009). This selective attribute sharing eliminates the need for duplicate data entry and verification, saving users time and effort.

Decentralized identity also improves the user experience by reducing password usage. There are security vulnerabilities associated with password-based authentication, such as insecure passwords and password reuse. For authentication and authorization, decentralized identity systems employ cryptographic techniques, such as public-private key pairs (Crumlish et al., 2009). This eliminates the need for traditional passwords and makes authentication more secure and user-friendly. Users can access their accounts and authorise transactions in a secure manner without having to recollect intricate passwords.

User-centric consent management is supported by decentralized identity. Individuals frequently encounter situations in which their personal information is collected and disseminated without their explicit consent or knowledge in traditional systems. Decentralized identity systems prioritise individual consent by allowing users to control the sharing of their identity attributes and administer their consent settings

(Crumlish et al., 2009). This user-centric approach increases transparency, fosters trust, and ensures that individuals have control over how their personal information is used.

Decentralized identity systems provide substantial enhancements to the user experience via seamless authentication and authorization procedures. Decentralized identity improves the convenience, security, and privacy of users by facilitating single sign-on, providing self-sovereign identity attributes, decreasing reliance on passwords, and supporting user-centric consent management. This user-centric approach to identity management facilitates a more streamlined, productive, and user-friendly digital experience.

4.3. Enabling Secure and Frictionless E-Commerce Transactions

By facilitating secure and frictionless transactions, decentralized identity systems have the potential to revolutionise e-commerce. Traditional e-commerce transactions frequently require individuals to disclose personal and financial information to various platforms and merchants, which can raise data security and privacy concerns. Decentralized identity introduces a more secure and efficient method, thereby enhancing confidence and facilitating transactions.

The enhanced security provided by decentralized identity in e-commerce is a significant advantage. Traditional systems frequently store and manage sensitive consumer data using centralized databases. These centralized repositories are prime hacker targets and can lead to data breaches. Using cryptographic techniques and distributed ledger technology, decentralized identity systems ensure that personal and financial information is securely stored and shared (Rodimataylor et al., 2019). Using public-private key pairs and decentralized consensus mechanisms improves the security and integrity of transactions, thereby reducing the risk of fraud and unauthorised access.

Decentralized identity eliminates the need for individuals to repeatedly provide their personal and financial information for every transaction. In conventional e-commerce, users are frequently required to establish separate accounts and input their information for each platform or merchant they interact with. This fragmented procedure can be tedious and time-consuming for users. (Rodimataylor et al., 2019) With decentralized identity, individuals have a portable and verifiable identity that can be used across multiple platforms. This streamlines the transaction process, reduces the need for duplicate data input and verification, and improves the user experience overall.

In addition, decentralized identity facilitates trust and openness in e-commerce transactions. Individuals require assurance that their personal information and funds will be handled securely in order to engage in online transactions. (Rodimataylor et al., 2019) Decentralized identity systems allow for the verification of identity attributes and credentials, ensuring that individuals are interacting with legitimate entities. This verification process fosters a more secure and dependable e-commerce environment by nurturing trust between consumers and merchants.

The implementation of smart contracts and automated transactions is also facilitated by decentralized identity. Smart contracts are agreements that execute themselves and are stored on a blockchain or distributed ledger. This eliminates the need for intermediaries and reduces transaction costs (Rodimataylor et al., 2019). Decentralized identity plays a crucial role in facilitating the authentication and authorization processes required for the execution of smart contracts. By leveraging decentralized identity, e-commerce platforms can offer more efficient and transparent transactions, thereby augmenting the user experience as a whole.

4.4. Developing Faith and Loyalty Via Decentralized Reputation Systems

In numerous domains, including e-commerce, peer-to-peer transactions, and online communities, decentralized reputation systems play an essential role in cultivating trust and loyalty. Trust is essential for establishing successful relationships, and reputation systems based on decentralized identity provide a robust method for evaluating the trustworthiness and dependability of individuals and organisations.

The transparency and immutability of decentralized reputation systems is a significant advantage. Traditional reputation systems frequently rely on centralized authorities or platforms for the collection and management of reputation data. Concerns regarding bias, manipulation, and lack of transparency are raised by this centralized method. Decentralized reputation systems utilise the immutability and transparency of blockchain or distributed ledger technology to record and verify reputation data (Walsh & Sirer, 2006). This ensures that reputation scores and feedback are not susceptible to tampering and can be audited by all participants, thereby enhancing trustworthiness.

Decentralized reputation systems also allow individuals to establish a reputation based on interactions and feedback that have been verified. In conventional systems, individuals frequently have limited opportunities to develop and exhibit their reputation outside of particular platforms or communities. (Walsh & Sirer, 2006) Decentralized reputation systems allow individuals to accumulate reputation scores based on verified interactions, such as successful transactions, dependable contributions, and participant feedback. This reputation can then be used across multiple platforms and communities, providing a portable and reliable measure of a person's dependability and trustworthiness.

Decentralized reputation systems encourage accountability and encourage positive behaviour. In traditional systems, there may be a lack of consequences or incentives for responsible and ethical behaviour. Decentralized reputation systems introduce the concept of tokenized incentives and penalties, in which an individual's reputation score can affect his or her access to services, rewards, or privileges (Walsh & Sirer, 2006). Individuals are motivated to maintain a positive reputation and engage in trustworthy behaviour, nurturing a culture of responsibility and accountability, when reputation is linked to tangible incentives. Decentralized reputation systems empower users by enabling them to make informed decisions based on dependable reputation data. When assessing the veracity of others in conventional systems, individuals frequently must rely on limited or biassed information. Decentralized reputation systems allow users to access and evaluate reputation scores and feedback from a wider variety of sources (Walsh & Sirer, 2006). This broader perspective improves the capacity for decision-making, decreases information asymmetry, and increases confidence in transactions and interactions.

Decentralized reputation systems offer substantial benefits for nurturing trust and promoting loyalty. By leveraging the transparency, immutability, and portability of decentralized identity, reputation systems provide trustworthy and verifiable information regarding a person's dependability and trustworthiness. These systems encourage accountability, incentivize positive behaviour, empower users, and facilitate well-informed decisions. Decentralized reputation systems play a crucial role in establishing trust and loyalty across multiple domains, thereby contributing to a more trustworthy and secure digital ecosystem.

4.5. Blockchain-Based Loyalty Programmes and Consumer Engagement at Venmo

This case study examines Venmo, a well-known peer-to-peer mobile payment platform, and its use of blockchain technology to enhance loyalty programmes and customer engagement. In the competitive digital payment landscape, PayPal-owned Venmo has acknowledged the significance of consumer engagement and loyalty. To differentiate itself and provide additional value to its users, Venmo has implemented blockchain technology within its loyalty programmes.

The purpose of Venmo's blockchain initiative is to establish a transparent and secure loyalty programme that increases customer engagement, incentivizes usage, and nurtures long-term customer loyalty. By integrating blockchain technology, Venmo intends to provide its users with a seamless and rewarding experience.

Venmo uses distributed ledger technology to monitor and verify customer transactions, allowing for real-time rewards and incentives, when implementing blockchain-based loyalty programmes. By preserving transactional data on a distributed ledger, Venmo ensures transparency and immutability, thereby reducing the likelihood of fraud or manipulation.

Transparency is a crucial aspect of Venmo's blockchain-based loyalty programme. Venmo provides users with complete visibility into their loyalty programme rewards, transactions, and redemption options using blockchain technology. As users have a clear view of their loyalty programme activities, this transparency fosters confidence and strengthens the customer-brand bond.

The provision of real-time rewards and incentives is also a key feature. Venmo can offer immediate rewards and incentives based on user transactions by utilising blockchain technology. Users can receive immediate advantages, such as compensation or loyalty points, as transactions are recorded and verified on the blockchain. This real-time feature improves the user experience and encourages continued platform usage.

Incorporating blockchain technology into Venmo's loyalty programmes ensures transactions are secure and immutable. The inherent security and immutability of blockchain improve the loyalty program's integrity. Users can have confidence that their transactional data and rewards are stored securely and cannot be modified, fostering a sense of security and dependability.

The benefits of Venmo's exploration of blockchain-based loyalty programmes are numerous. Initially, it improves consumer engagement by offering customised and real-time rewards. Users feel acknowledged and valued, resulting in increased loyalty and sustained platform usage.

Second, blockchain technology improves transparency and trust. The users have a plain view of their loyalty programme activities, removing any uncertainty regarding concealed terms and conditions. This transparency fosters confidence between Venmo and its users, thereby strengthening their loyalty.

Moreover, blockchain technology facilitates the seamless redemption and adaptability of rewards. Users can readily access their rewards and redeem them for a variety of products and services, or convert them into digital assets. This adaptability improves the overall customer experience and enables customers to maximise the value of their loyalty reward. Blockchain-based loyalty programmes aid in fraud prevention and security. With transactional data stored on a distributed ledger, the likelihood of manipulation or unauthorised access is greatly diminished, ensuring the safety of customer rewards and data.

In conclusion, Venmo's investigation of blockchain-based loyalty programmes demonstrates its dedication to improving consumer engagement and loyalty. By utilising blockchain's transparency, real-time rewards, and secure transactions, Venmo intends to provide its users with a seamless and rewarding experience. Incorporating blockchain technology into the financial technology sector has the potential to increase trust, enhance transparency, and strengthen consumer loyalty. As blockchain technology continues to evolve, Venmo's initiative serves as a notable example for other industry actors to consider integrating blockchain-based solutions to increase consumer engagement and cultivate long-term loyalty.

5. DIFFICULTIES AND FUTURE COURSE

5.1. Scalability and Efficacy in Decentralized Identity Systems

In the design and implementation of decentralized identity systems, scalability and performance are crucial considerations. As these systems become more prevalent, the ability to efficiently manage a large number of users and transactions becomes crucial to ensuring their viability. Decentralized identity systems, attaining scalability without compromising security and privacy is a significant obstacle. Traditional centralized systems frequently rely on robust infrastructure and centralized databases to manage a high transaction volume. Decentralized identity systems, on the other hand, operate on distributed networks in which the processing and storage of identity data are distributed across multiple nodes (Vukoli, 2006). As the network expands and the number of transactions rises, this distribution may present scalability challenges. It becomes essential to design scalable protocols and algorithms capable of meeting the system's expanding demands while maintaining security and privacy guarantees.

In decentralized identity systems, numerous approaches have been proposed to resolve scalability concerns. Off-chain solutions, in which certain operations are performed outside the blockchain or distributed ledger to reduce network burden, is one such approach (Xie et al., 2019). Off-chain solutions can enhance scalability by enabling quicker transaction processing and reducing the network's computational burden. These solutions frequently utilise techniques such as state channels or sidechains to achieve scalability while preserving the security guarantees of the decentralized infrastructure underpinning them.

Interoperability and incorporation of decentralized identity systems with existing infrastructure and platforms is another consideration for scalability. As decentralized identity systems evolve, seamless integration with diverse services, applications, and ecosystems becomes crucial (Xie et al., 2019). Interoperability facilitates the widespread adoption of decentralized identity by allowing users to utilise their decentralized identities across multiple platforms and services. In the decentralized identity landscape, interoperability and scalability rely heavily on standardisation efforts and open protocols.

Another crucial aspect of decentralized identity systems is performance. Users anticipate quick response times and efficient transaction processing, particularly in authentication and authorization scenarios that necessitate real-time interaction. Considerations regarding performance include transaction latency, throughput, and system responsiveness. The key to obtaining excellent performance in decentralized identity systems (Xie et al., 2019) is to design effective consensus mechanisms and optimise cryptographic operations. Utilising techniques such as sharding or parallel processing can increase throughput and decrease latency. In addition, the expansion and adoption of decentralized identity systems necessitate a robust infrastructure able to meet the increased demands. Effective performance requires scalable and distributed storage solutions, efficient network communication protocols, and optimised computational resources (Ray et al., 2023). To ensure the scalability and efficacy of decentralized identity systems as they evolve and expand, it is vital to perpetually investigate and employ innovative technologies and optimisation strategies.

5.2. Regulatory and Legal Obstacles to Decentralized Identity Adoption

Adoption of decentralized identity systems presents a number of regulatory and legal challenges that must be addressed to assure compliance, safeguard user rights, and promote widespread adoption of these systems. The regulatory landscape encircling identity management and data protection is a significant obstacle. Existing regulations and legal frameworks may not adequately account for the unique qualities and complexities of decentralized identity systems. Traditional identity management practises frequently entail the acquisition, storage, and processing of personal data by centralized entities, which is subject to numerous data protection and privacy regulations (Ray et al., 2023). In contrast, decentralized identity systems distribute data across a network, making it difficult to discern the duties and responsibilities of the numerous entities involved. To address these regulatory challenges, new frameworks and standards must be developed that can accommodate the decentralized character of identity systems while protecting user data. In addition, decentralized identity systems introduce novel concepts, such as self-sovereign identity and selective attribute disclosure, that may conflict with existing legal requirements. For instance, anti-money laundering or Know Your Customer (KYC) regulations mandate the collection and retention of specific identity information for various purposes. Respecting these requirements while adhering to the principles of self-sovereign identity and selective attribute disclosure may prove difficult due to the decentralized nature of identity systems. To achieve a balance between these legal obligations and the principles of decentralized identity, regulatory bodies, legal experts, and technology developers must examine and collaborate carefully.

The global character of decentralized identity systems presents a further difficulty. Identity systems frequently operate across international borders, and local regulations can vary substantially. Achieving interoperability and compliance with diverse legal frameworks is crucial to facilitate the seamless use of decentralized identity across different regions and guarantee international cooperation (Avellaneda et al., 2019). Harmonising legal requirements and nurturing cross-jurisdictional collaboration are essential for addressing regulatory challenges and promoting the global adoption of decentralized identity systems.

Decentralized identity systems may pose liability and accountability concerns. In conventional systems, security and preservation of user data are often the responsibility of centralized entities. In decentralized systems, the distribution of data and lack of a central authority can complicate the assignment of liability in the event of data breaches or misuse. Determining the legal and regulatory frameworks that regulate liability and accountability in decentralized identity systems requires careful consideration to ensure that users' rights are protected and suitable mechanisms are in place to address potential problems.

Adoption of decentralized identity systems presents substantial regulatory and legal difficulties. To overcome these obstacles, new frameworks and standards must be developed that address the unique characteristics of decentralized identity while assuring compliance with data protection and privacy regulations. Harmonising legal requirements across jurisdictions, addressing liability and accountability issues, and fostering international cooperation are essential measures for promoting the global adoption of decentralized identity. Collaboration between regulatory bodies, legal experts, and technology developers is essential for overcoming these obstacles and establishing an environment that supports the secure, privacy-enhancing, and legally compliant use of decentralized identity systems.

5.3. Standardisation and Interoperability Efforts for Decentralized Identity

Interoperability and standardisation initiatives are crucial to the development and implementation of decentralized identity systems. As the prevalence of these systems increases, it becomes imperative to establish common protocols, formats, and data structures that enable seamless interoperability across various platforms, services, and ecosystems.

The fragmentation of identity systems and the absence of interoperability between them is a significant obstacle for decentralized identity. In conventional systems, identities are frequently compartmentalised within particular platforms or organisations, restricting their applicability and impeding the development of a unified identity ecosystem. Interoperability efforts aim to address this difficulty by designating common standards and protocols that permit diverse decentralized identity systems to communicate and interchange information efficiently (Avellaneda et al., 2019). These standards permit the seamless incorporation of decentralized identity across multiple domains, thereby fostering identity portability and pervasive adoption.

The primary objective of standardisation is to define common data formats and protocols that facilitate interoperability. Decentralized Identifiers (DIDs) and Verifiable Credentials (VCs) provide a common framework for representing and exchanging identity attributes and credentials in a decentralized manner (Kubach et al., 2020). These standards ensure that identity data is consistently structured and encoded, allowing various systems to interpret and verify the information accurately. In addition, protocols such as the DID Communication protocols and DID Auth protocols define standard methods for authentication, authorization, and secure communication between various decentralized identity systems.

The development of interoperability standards necessitates collaboration between multiple parties, including technology developers, industry consortia, standards authorities, and regulatory agencies. These parties collaborate to define and refine standards that address the technical, legal, and regulatory challenges of decentralized identity systems. The objective is to establish open, consensus-based, interoperable, transparent, and inclusive standards.

In decentralized identity systems, efforts to standardise also seek to protect privacy and security. The standards incorporate privacy-enhancing technologies and protocols to safeguard sensitive information and prevent unauthorised access. For instance, zero-knowledge proofs and other cryptographic techniques can be used to verify the authenticity of identity attributes without disclosing the actual data (Kubach et al., 2020). These privacy-protecting mechanisms are indispensable for maintaining user confidence and promoting the widespread adoption of decentralized identity.

In addition, interoperability and standardisation initiatives extend beyond technical specifications. In addition, they include models of governance, legal frameworks, and policy considerations. To ensure the long-term viability and evolution of decentralized identity ecosystems, it is crucial to establish governance models that encourage collaboration, openness, and inclusivity. Moreover, legal and regulatory frameworks must be aligned with the principles and requirements of decentralized identity in order to resolve potential conflicts and provide legal certainty for consumers and service providers (Kubach et al., 2020).

Interoperability and standardisation initiatives are crucial to the development and implementation of decentralized identity systems. These initiatives promote the portability and usability of identities across platforms and services by allowing diverse systems to effectively communicate and exchange information. Interoperability and standardisation enhance the privacy, security, and trustworthiness of decentralized identity systems by establishing common protocols, data formats, and governance models. To define open, consensus-based standards that drive the evolution and extensive adoption of decentralized identity ecosystems, collaboration among stakeholders is essential.

5.4. Future Trends and Potential for Decentralized Identity in Marketing and Consumer Engagement

Decentralized identity has the potential to revolutionise marketing and consumer engagement, and a number of emergent trends and future possibilities will shape the landscape in the coming years.

Integration of decentralized identity with emergent technologies such as artificial intelligence (AI) and machine learning is an important development. Decentralized identity systems can analyse enormous quantities of data and generate valuable insights about consumer preferences, behaviours, and requirements by leveraging the power of artificial intelligence (Blau & Vikram, 2022). These insights can inform personalised marketing strategies, allowing businesses to provide customised consumer experiences and targeted communications. The combination of decentralized identity and AI creates new hyper-personalization opportunities, enabling marketers to engage with consumers on a deeper and more meaningful level.

Decentralized identity for seamless and secure cross-platform experiences is an additional trend. Traditional marketing frequently involves fragmented interactions across multiple channels and platforms, which results in inconsistent user experiences. Individuals can maintain a unified and verified identity across multiple platforms with decentralized identity, allowing for seamless and consistent experiences (Blau & Vikram, 2022). Individuals can, for instance, authenticate themselves on one platform and then access personalised content or services on another platform without the need for duplicate logins or data re-entry. This unified and frictionless experience increases user satisfaction and engagement.

Additionally, decentralized identity has the potential to promote trust and openness in influencer marketing and user-generated content. In the current environment, it can be difficult to determine the authenticity and dependability of influencers and user-generated content. Decentralized identity systems can facilitate the verification and substantiation of influencers' identities and the veracity of user-generated content (Blau & Vikram, 2022). This transparency enhances the credibility and efficacy of influencer marketing campaigns and user-generated content strategies by fostering trust between brands, influencers, and consumers.

The future of decentralized identity in marketing and consumer engagement presents opportunities for the development of novel business models and revenue streams. With individuals having ownership and control over their data, businesses can investigate innovative data monetization strategies with consumer consent. In exchange for personalised offers, incentives, or rewards, consumers can choose to share their data with reputable entities (Blau & Vikram, 2022). This transition from traditional data collection to a value exchange model can facilitate more meaningful and mutually beneficial interactions between businesses and customers.

Decentralized identity can facilitate new forms of community-driven marketing and engagement. Online communities based on decentralized identity systems can facilitate trustworthy interactions, peer recommendations, and collective decision making. These communities can provide businesses with valuable insights, enabling them to comprehend consumer preferences, co-create products, and strengthen customer loyalty (Blau & Vikram, 2022). By delving into the collective intelligence of these communities, businesses are able to develop interactive and participatory consumer experiences that align with their values and aspirations.

The emerging trends and future possibilities presented by decentralized identity have the potential to revolutionise marketing and consumer engagement. The integration of decentralized identity with AI, the emphasis on seamless cross-platform experiences, the improvement of trust in influencer marketing and user-generated content, the exploration of new business models, and the development of community-driven marketing approaches all present businesses and consumers with exciting opportunities. As decentralized identity continues to evolve, it is imperative that marketers and industry stakeholders remain apprised of these trends and embrace the opportunities to create more personalised, transparent, and engaging consumer experiences.

6. CONCLUSION

6.1. Influence of the Decentralized Identity

Decentralized identity has the potential to revolutionise the future of marketing, bringing about significant effects and altering the manner in which businesses interact with customers. The following points describe the prospective effects of decentralized identity on future marketing:

- Enhanced Personalization: Decentralized identity enables the construction of rich and accurate consumer profiles based on verified and authorised data. This plethora of data enables businesses to provide consumers with highly personalised and customised experiences (Sorokin, 2022). By understanding consumer preferences, behaviours, and requirements, marketers can create targeted messaging, product recommendations, and offers that have a more profound effect on individual consumers. Consequently, consumer relationships are strengthened and engagement is increased.

- Trust and Transparency: Trust is a crucial aspect of marketing, and decentralized identity can substantially improve trust and transparency in the relationship between businesses and customers. Through decentralized identity systems, consumers have greater control over their data, ensuring that it is stored securely and shared with only trusted parties (Sorokin, 2021). This transparency fosters confidence because consumers are aware of how their data is being used and have the ability to manage their consent and permissions. Businesses can increase consumer loyalty and engagement by demonstrating a commitment to data protection and privacy.

- Targeted and Relevant Advertising: Decentralized identity enables businesses to utilise verified identity attributes and credentials to provide targeted and relevant advertising. Businesses can ensure that their advertising efforts reach the most relevant audience if they can verify user attributes and qualifications (Sorokin, 2022). This targeted approach reduces advertising expenditure waste and increases the efficacy of campaigns. In addition, decentralized identity enables consumers to selectively disclose particular attributes to advertisers, ensuring that they receive advertisements that align with their interests and preferences, resulting in a more positive and personalised advertising experience.

- Data Security and Privacy Data breaches and privacy concerns have become significant obstacles in the marketing environment. These dangers can be mitigated by the robust security and privacy mechanisms provided by decentralized identity systems. Decentralized identity reduces the appeal of single points of failure for cyberattacks by eradicating the need for centralized data repositories. In addition, the use of cryptographic techniques assures the privacy and confidentiality of personal data, allowing users to retain control over their data (Sorokin, 2021). This improved data security and privacy protection fosters consumer trust and confidence, making them more receptive to engaging with businesses and sharing data.

- Customer Empowerment: Decentralized identity gives consumers ownership and control over their data and identity, empowering them. Consumers can control and share their identity attributes and credentials as they see appropriate, enhancing their privacy (Sorokin, 2021). As consumers actively partake in their digital identities, this empowerment promotes a sense of ownership and engagement. Businesses that embrace decentralized identity can capitalise on this sense of empowerment by offering consumers personalised services and experiences that align with their preferences and aspirations.

Identity decentralisation has the potential to transform the future of marketing. Through enhanced personalization, increased trust and transparency, targeted advertising, improved data security and privacy, and customer empowerment, decentralized identity provides businesses with new opportunities to engage with consumers in a more meaningful and customised manner. By adopting decentralized identity systems, businesses can strengthen their relationships with their target demographic, increase consumer loyalty, and establish a more efficient and effective marketing ecosystem.

6.2. Organisational Approach Towards Decentralized Identity Solutions

The advent of decentralized identity presents businesses with a thrilling opportunity to reimagine their identity management and consumer engagement strategies. This call to action describes why businesses should investigate decentralized identity solutions and adopt this transformative technology.

First, decentralized identity offers businesses the opportunity to increase customer trust and strengthen customer relationships. Businesses can demonstrate their commitment to privacy, data security, and transparency by employing decentralized identity systems (Avellaneda et al., 2019). This commitment can inspire confidence among consumers, who are growingly concerned about the security of their personal data. By granting individuals greater control over their data and allowing them to selectively share verified attributes, businesses can establish trust and lay the groundwork for long-term consumer relationships.

Second, decentralized identity solutions enable businesses to provide customised and personalised consumer experiences. By utilising the rich and verifiable identity attributes made available by decentralized identity systems, businesses can acquire a deeper understanding of consumer preferences and behaviours (Avellaneda et al., 2019). This information enables the customization of products, services, and marketing messages to satisfy the requirements of specific individuals. Personalization has been shown to be a significant factor in consumer satisfaction, loyalty, and engagement. By embracing decentralized identity, businesses can tap into this potential and deliver consumer experiences with profound resonance.

Moreover, decentralized identity solutions allow businesses to optimise their marketing and advertising expenditures. Businesses can ensure that their communications reach the most relevant and receptive audience using targeted advertising based on verified identity attributes (Avellaneda et al., 2019). Businesses can maximise their return on investment and improve the efficacy of their campaigns by reducing the dispersion of their marketing efforts and focusing on consumers who are genuinely interested in their offerings. The ability to selectively disclose attributes enables businesses to deliver advertisements that are tailored to consumer preferences, resulting in a more positive and engaging advertising experience.

Decentralized identity also enables businesses to anticipate evolving data protection and privacy regulations and legal requirements. As governments and regulatory bodies continue to implement stricter rules, businesses that employ decentralized identity solutions proactively position themselves as compliance leaders (Avellaneda et al., 2019). By adopting the principles of decentralized identity, businesses can demonstrate their commitment to data privacy and security, ensuring that they are well-equipped to navigate the evolving regulatory environment.

Businesses are encouraged to investigate decentralized identity solutions to take advantage of their numerous benefits. Decentralized identity has the potential to transform how businesses interact with their consumers in a variety of ways, such as by enhancing trust and fostering stronger customer relationships, providing personalised experiences, and optimising marketing efforts. By embracing decentralized identity proactively, businesses can differentiate themselves on the market, increase consumer loyalty, and future-proof their operations in an increasingly privacy-conscious and digitally-driven environment.

REFERENCES

Avellaneda, O., Bachmann, A., Barbir, A., Brenan, J., Dingle, P., Duffy, K. H., Maler, E., Reed, D., & Sporny, M. (2019). Decentralized identity: Where did it come from and where is it going? *IEEE Communications Standards Magazine*, *3*(4), 10–13. doi:10.1109/MCOMSTD.2019.9031542

Baars, D. S. (2016). *Towards self-sovereign identity using blockchain technology* [Master's thesis, University of Twente].

Bertocci, V., Serack, G., & Baker, C. (2007). *Understanding windows cardspace: an introduction to the concepts and challenges of digital identities*. Pearson Education.

BlauB.VikramS. (2022). Entering a new era of decentralized customer experience (dcx) web3 unlocks the new market category of decentralized customer experience with unforeseen value across industries. *Available at* SSRN 4219848. doi:10.2139/ssrn.4219848

Crumlish, C., & Malone, E. (2009). *Designing social interfaces: Principles, patterns, and practices for improving the user experience*. O'Reilly Media, Inc.

Der, U., Jähnichen, S., & Sürmeli, J. (2017). Self-sovereign identity $-$ opportunities and challenges for the digital revolution. arXiv preprint arXiv:1712.01767.

Dib, O., & Toumi, K. (2020). Decentralized identity systems: Architecture, challenges, solutions and future directions. *Annals of Emerging Technologies in Computing (AETiC)*.

Dunphy, P., & Petitcolas, F. A. (2018). A first look at identity management schemes on the blockchain. *IEEE Security and Privacy*, *16*(4), 20–29. doi:10.1109/MSP.2018.3111247

Ermolaev, E., Abellán Álvarez, I., Sedlmeir, J., & Fridgen, G. (2023, May). z-Commerce: Designing a Data-Minimizing One-Click Checkout Solution. In *International Conference on Design Science Research in Information Systems and Technology* (pp. 3-17). Cham: Springer Nature Switzerland. 10.1007/978-3-031-32808-4_1

Fukami, Y., Shimizu, T., & Matsushima, H. (2021, December). The impact of decentralized identity architecture on data exchange. In *2021 IEEE International Conference on Big Data (Big Data)* (pp. 3461-3465). IEEE. 10.1109/BigData52589.2021.9671674

Gupta, S., Bairwa, A. K., Kushwaha, S. S., & Joshi, S. (2023, January). Decentralized Identity Management System using the amalgamation of Blockchain Technology. In *2023 3rd International Conference on Intelligent Communication and Computational Techniques (ICCT)* (pp. 1-6). IEEE. 10.1109/ICCT56969.2023.10076117

Hölbl, M., Kompara, M., Kamišalić, A., & Nemec Zlatolas, L. (2018). A systematic review of the use of blockchain in healthcare. *Symmetry*, *10*(10), 470. doi:10.3390ym10100470

Kubach, M., Schunck, C. H., Sellung, R., & Roßnagel, H. (2020). Self-sovereign and Decentralized identity as the future of identity management?. *Open Identity Summit 2020*.

Maram, D., Malvai, H., Zhang, F., Jean-Louis, N., Frolov, A., Kell, T., & Miller, A. (2021, May). Candid: Can-do decentralized identity with legacy compatibility, sybil-resistance, and accountability. In *2021 IEEE Symposium on Security and Privacy (SP)* (pp. 1348-1366). IEEE. 10.1109/SP40001.2021.00038

Moran, T. (2020). *An Exploration of Decentralised Identity: A COVID-19 Vaccine Passport*.

Nakamoto, S. (2008). Bitcoin: A peer-to-peer electronic cash system. *Decentralized business review*.

Potts, J., & Rennie, E. (2019). Web3 and the creative industries: how blockchains are reshaping business models. *A research agenda for creative industries*, 93-111.

Preukschat, A., & Reed, D. (2021). *Self-sovereign identity*. Manning Publications.

Ray, P. P. (2023). Web3: A comprehensive review on background, technologies, applications, zero-trust architectures, challenges and future directions. *Internet of Things and Cyber-Physical Systems*.

Razec, I. (2022). The Complex Ramifications of Digital Identity. *International Journal of Cross-Cultural Studies and Environmental Communication*, *11*(1), 52–60.

Rodima-Taylor, D., & Grimes, W. W. (2019). Virtualizing diaspora: New digital technologies in the emerging transnational space. *Global Networks*, *19*(3), 349–370. doi:10.1111/glob.12221

Sorokin, L. (2022). A Peek into the Future of Decentralized Identity (v2). *IDPro Body of Knowledge, 1*(7).

Vukolić, M. (2016). The quest for scalable blockchain fabric: Proof-of-work vs. BFT replication. In *Open Problems in Network Security: IFIP WG 11.4 International Workshop, iNetSec 2015, Zurich, Switzerland, October 29, 2015, Revised Selected Papers* (pp. 112-125). Springer International Publishing.

Walsh, K., & Sirer, E. G. (2006, May). Experience with an Object Reputation System for Peer-to-Peer Filesharing. In NSDI (Vol. 6, pp. 1-1).

Xie, J., Yu, F. R., Huang, T., Xie, R., Liu, J., & Liu, Y. (2019). A survey on the scalability of blockchain systems. *IEEE Network*, *33*(5), 166–173. doi:10.1109/MNET.001.1800290

Zhao, S., Grasmuck, S., & Martin, J. (2008). Identity construction on Facebook: Digital empowerment in anchored relationships. *Computers in Human Behavior*, *24*(5), 1816–1836. doi:10.1016/j.chb.2008.02.012

Chapter 21
Past Impact and Future Implications of the World Wide Web on the Accounting Industry

Jaspal Singh

University Canada West, Canada

ABSTRACT

With the initial development of Web 1.0 in 1989, the groundwork was laid out for radical and rapid transformation of an accounting industry which had been slowly evolving over thousands of years. In the late 1990s, with Web 2.0, simple websites and email were eclipsed by innovative accounting software and collaborative online tools. Accountants have taken advantage of these features as many of the lower-level functions are now replaced by value-adding analytics and ongoing communication. The newest version of the World Wide Web, Web 3.0, strives to progress business further with decentralized, blockchain-based applications. Distributed ledger technology, securely storing data in multiple locations with immutable transaction records, is increasing reliability of accounting functions. With smart contracts, business agreements can be executed via blockchain, adding another layer of security. However, the accounting industry is not without challenges as technology advances- it must stand with its ethical principles as the business world around it evolves with Web 3.0.

INTRODUCTION

Ever since the introduction of computers into the accounting world, technological advancement has occurred at what can only be described as a torrid pace (Fahmi et al. 2023). Computer technology was initially used to produce and organize accounting data in a better format than paper-based ledgers. Then came a great leap forward with specialized software that automated some accounting and bookkeeping functions (Kee 1993). However, humans still had to input data into the system to get the computer to update the firm's books.

DOI: 10.4018/978-1-6684-9919-1.ch021

Copyright © 2023, IGI Global. Copying or distributing in print or electronic forms without written permission of IGI Global is prohibited.

Things have progressed further with better technology. For the most part, the efficiency, accuracy, and security of accounting systems have been significantly improved (Minan et al 2023). Data-entry functions have become progressively automated, allowing accountants to focus on higher-level, value-adding tasks to better serve their clients. Accountants are now expected to help businesses streamline their operations, engage in sound financial planning, and provide other important insight via regular communications (Samanthi & Gooneratne 2023, Tillema et al. 2022).

Businesses themselves have evolved with web technology. With Web 1.0, they were able to create simple websites with branding, product images and features, and contact information (physical addresses, phone numbers, and emails). They also took advantage of a new way to maintain communications with the customers- emails were undoubtedly more efficient and cost effective compared to mass-mailing flyers or letters.

With Web 2.0, businesses have been able to increase meaningful online interactions with their customers (Mabic et al. 2019; Nath et al. 2010)- there is now online chat, online shopping, even customizable website features which engaged internet surfers can spend hours on. Consumer data has become valuable and e-advertising can now be tailored to the specific needs/preferences of the individual shopper. Of course, this targeting capability has triggered new arguments on ethical usage of user data.

As businesses have evolved, so have their accountants. In addition to providing better services, accounting firms are now able to use technology to deliver higher quality audit, review, and tax preparation outcomes to their clients. The traditional accounting work is not only quicker (and cheaper) but also more accurate. With transition to increased machine use, the impact of human error can be minimized and final documentation can be entrusted at a higher level, resulting in more confident and possibly better business decision-making.

This chapter will take a detailed look at how the accounting industry has evolved alongside the World Wide Web, from Web 1.0 to Web 2.0. There will also be a forward look at Web 3.0 and specific features or products which may significantly impact the modern business world and especially the accounting industry. The potential benefits and risks will be analyzed and some best practices will be suggested.

Literature Review

A significant body of publications have looked into the impact of earlier versions of the World Wide Web, Web 1.0 and Web 2.0, so the findings of a few relevant works will be summarized. Predictably, the number of publications focused on the impact of newer technologies, such as blockchain and Web 3.0, on the accounting industry is considerably smaller- likely due to the relatively short time passing since emergence. However, that is not to say there is not already some quality research available for the accounting industry to utilize and build on going forward.

In an article in The CPA Journal, Cong and Du (2007) described Web 2.0 in a rather creative manner:

"Compared to "Web 1.0." Web 2.0 fills the gap between a web browser and desktop applications, it brings together documents and data scattered over local computers and the Internet, and facilitates collaboration and sharing."

Cong and Du went on to discuss how webpages were evolving into wikis and emailed files were being replaced by collaborative online tools. They cautioned, rightfully, that corporate information systems were combining data from a variety of internal and external sources, making auditing increasingly challenging. However, the two authors also encouraged accounting professionals to "use new Web 2.0 technologies to exchange ideas, share information, and communicate with clients and colleagues."

Looking at more recent research after the transition to Web 2.0 had become more complete, Mihai (2014) also discussed ways in which independent accounting professionals can employ the Web 2.0 technology. She provided specifics for improving communication and collaboration with clients and within the firm, transmitting and receiving information in novel ways, and maintaining higher professional development standards.

In his academic research which stretched to pre-introduction of Web 1.0, Quinto II (2022) pointed out some of the limitations of technological advancements in the past. Although calculators and computers facilitated the math side of accounting, the fact remained that accountants needed to manually enter transactions until data could be imported. Similar to Mehai (2014), Quinto II went on to praise some benefits the newer technology was bringing to the accounting industry. However, he did caution about some risks, particularly the issues which would arise in the event of a power outage, security breach, or system crash.

A recent study by Alkafaji, B.K.A., Dashtbayaz, M.L., & Salehi M. (2023) focused on recent technology's impact on accounting. The authors discovered that "blockchain technology has positively and significantly impacted the quality of accounting information". The study found that both listed and unlisted Iraqi businesses who have embraced blockchain technology have been able to report better information to users of financial statements.

Along the same lines, Wang, J. (2022) found that even in a country with "low audit quality" such as China, blockchain technology was capable of enhancing the security of audit information and improving audit quality by up to 20%. The financial impact of better technology in accounting firms has also been explored (Kolisnyk et al. 2023). With fewer accounting errors and quicker detection and fixing of errors can reduce the financial penalties resulting from accounting mistakes.

Current and past research have covered well the impact of the World Wide Web on the accounting industry. This chapter will aim to summarize these perspectives meaningfully to paint a picture of how things have evolved over the past three decades and then provide an outlook of how Web 3.0 will impact the accounting industry going forward.

HISTORICAL IMPACT OF THE WORLD WIDE WEB ON THE ACCOUNTING INDUSTRY

Web 1.0's Impact

Let's start with Web 1.0's impact on the accounting industry. Web 1.0 was developed in the late 1980's and was the initial phase of the World Wide Web. At its core, it was a Content Delivery Network (CDN) that permitted websites to display information. It is important to note that with Web 1.0, users could not interact with websites they visited; they could only view the content (Richter 2022).

While we would be dismissive of such capabilities in the modern day- perhaps rightfully so, Web 1.0 was a revolutionary step forward for the accounting industry. Embracing of the new technology resulted in advances in several areas, discussed below (Dehinbo 2010, Rebecca 2022).

1.   Improved information availability

With the ability to look up information online, accountants were able to improve their performance due to several Web 1.0 benefits. First, they were able to better educate themselves on industry trends. In some cases, accountants were performing services for a diverse clientele, and it can be difficult to stay informed about each industry. So, with the world wide web, they could quickly access specific information about the industry in question, such as how sales might be trending recently.

And so, the research process became much quicker and saved time and money for many. Clients may get frustrated by accountants who are constantly interrupting valuable work time, as it can hinder productivity. Since asking others about file specifics can breach confidentiality (CPABC 2021), accountants may have no choice but to wait for frustrated responses from clients. By using the internet, accountants ended up with fewer questions that absolutely had to be answered by busy clients. Accountants could simply visit trustworthy websites to acquire information which they previously relied on industry experts for.

It is easy to see why quick independent verification had value in an accounting function such as an audit. Using the internet, accountants were able to reduce risk and bias in the audit. In essence, they were no longer relying heavily on the client to fill in their knowledge gaps. Instead, the accountants were able to easily seek information from a wide breadth of independent sources. The client's ability to mislead them had been significantly diminished.

In addition to acquainting themselves with industry norms, accountants were able to research specific news pertaining to businesses. Often, major companies are covered in the news. As news is generally public information, there was little concern with use of undisclosed information when an accountant was searching for company news or other details online. Hence, searching for the latest news offered upside and no real downside.

Finally, accountants could better familiarize themselves with the latest regulatory changes were now published online. A problem with printed media, be it books, newspapers, or others, is that it can not be altered after the fact. So, outdated information and even errors were something accountants had to deal with. With the World Wide Web, up-to-date information was always available, such as recent policy changes impacting tax laws or generally accepted accounting practices. This naturally led to quicker adoption of new policies and, consequently, better accounting practices.

2.   Electronic Reporting

Society's reliance on paper is not a new idea- financial statements of various forms have been used for a variety of purposes for centuries (Lauwers & Willekens 1994). Even today, paper statements can be used to verify if an individual can be trusted with an equity investment or loan to start/expand a business. Income verification can be used as proof of sustainable employment which would logically imply a prospective renter (Morrison 2020) or homebuyer (Lucas 2023) can afford to make monthly payments for the foreseeable future.

The accounting industry is no different in its heavy usage of paper documents- bank statements, expense receipts, contractual agreements, etcetera. For seemingly forever, accountants have relied on information from banks to report and analyze financial information in a reliable and efficient manner. However, working with paper documents has always been a tedious process. To this day, accounting work is synonymous with meticulous data-entry and the tracking of numbers into T-accounts and financial statements.

While electronification of data may not have done enough to change the reputation of the accounting industry, it did help automate data-entry (Gunnoo 2023). With access to software which facilitated bookkeeping, tax preparation, and audit functions, accountants were able step away from data-entry and embrace higher value-adding tasks such as business analysis and regular communication with clients. This was a valuable step in getting accountants, at least some of them, away from a state of endless number-crunching upwards to business management.

Another way accountants could obtain electronic data was through email. While financial information could be communicated in person, over phone call, or even via mail, the World Wide Web brought in an incredibly useful option of communication with email. Accountants could now receive financial data directly from clients almost instantly. An example of this could be a scanned receipt or, to take things a step further, a digital receipt that was emailed to the client. In the case of the latter, the client could just forward the email to his/her accountant. Of course, there are now better and more secure options of sharing sensitive data, as email can expose the client or firm to data leakage risk (CPA Canada 2019).

While manual access to data was important, the true benefit of electronic data was realized in conjunctional use with accounting software (Autymate 2022). Data could now be imported into the file instead of being manually entered. This not only sped things up, but saved accounting firms time and money partly due elimination of "middle men" functions. The savings could either be passed down to clients or accountants could use the time to add value in other ways. As an added bonus, machines tend to be more reliable than humans with numerical accuracy, so clients were often getting work of higher quality while paying less for it.

Table 1, below, exhibits four popular examples of accounting software which emerged between the late 1990's and early 2000's were (Exilir Business Solution Private Limited 2023; CAL Business Solutions 2020; WikiWand 2023):

Table 1. Examples of accounting software

Software	Description
Intuit QuickBooks (desktop version)	QuickBooks was one of the leading accounting software options during the Web 1.0 period. It provided small and medium-sized businesses with bookkeeping capabilities and included invoicing, payroll management, and financial reporting functions. QuickBooks is still a popular accounting solution today, with both desktop and online versions.
Peachtree Accounting	Peachtree Accounting was another widely used accounting software during the Web 1.0 era. It catered to small businesses and offered features such as general ledger management, accounts payable and receivable, inventory tracking, and financial reporting. Later on, Peachtree Accounting evolved into Sage 50.
Great Plains Accounting	Great Plains Accounting was a robust accounting software option during Web 1.0, particularly for mid-sized businesses. It offered functionalities such as general ledger management, accounts payable and receivable, inventory management, and financial reporting. It eventually evolved into Microsoft Dynamics GP.
CaseWare Working Papers	This software, first released in 1989, provided accountants and auditors with a digital platform to organize, manage, and collaborate on financial statements, working papers, and audit files. This software significantly improved efficiency and accuracy in the accounting and auditing fields.

Web 2.0's Impact

Web 2.0 is best described as the World Wide Web we know and use today (Allen 2012). This version of the internet emerged in the late 1990s. Via the use of rich web technology, users could self-generate content to be included, shared, and interacted with on websites. Innovative corporations such as Facebook, Google, Amazon, and Twitter captured this user-generated content in their centralized databases. Users, happy to enjoy free access to applications, were generally permissive of allowing their data to be owned and monetized upon by the aforementioned companies (Sadowski 2016).

With Web 2.0, the accounting industry took another step forward. As they had done with Web 1.0, accountants welcomed change and took advantage of the new technology. Over the past two decades, the improved World Wide Web enhanced the accounting profession in several ways (The Answer Company 2023; Carbonell 2022; Lazanis 2022):

1. Cloud-based Accounting Software

This is typically the first major change which comes to mind when one thinks of how technology has shaped the accounting world, and rightfully so. Web 2.0 not only changed what accountants needed to do, it shifted the career, and the necessary skillset, significantly.

With cloud-based software, user options grew, and once-daunting tasks became less challenging. There are now an array of bookkeeping/accounting software out there (Xero, QuickBooks Online, FreshBooks, Sage Online to name a few) and savvy small business owners can handle most of them on their own, at least for bookkeeping functions. Even with tax preparation, we have low-fee or even free personal tax filing options available in Canada (UFile, TurboTax, Wealthsimple Tax, etc) and most other developed countries. With basic returns, the process is simple enough that most experienced computer users can figure things out with a bit of experimentation.

So, accountants had to evolve to stay afloat. Business and communication skills eclipsed keying and memorization capabilities. While technical skills were still important, they were elevated to higher analytical levels.

Accountants now had fully online (cloud-based) software which they could use for major functions such as bookkeeping and tax preparation. As a result of cloud-based technology which could be accessed from any computer, bookkeepers no longer had to visit their client's workplaces to enter data- it could be done remotely.

As mentioned earlier, data entry functions could be bypassed completely by importing spreadsheets into the software. This process became even easier with cloud accounting technology. Real-time feeds could be set up to get bank or credit card transactions right into the software. Furthermore, with better artificial intelligence, the software could "learn" what a transaction could be classified/bookkept as. Now, the bookkeeper now only needed to confirm transactions with a mouse click!

Table 2, below, exhibits a few examples of innovative software used by accountants today (Adams 2023; Craig-Bourdin 2019):

Smartphones have also been integrated into the accounting process. In fact, many accounting software producers now have desktop versions, online versions, and cell phone apps. Cell phones have proven extremely handy for bookkeeping paper receipts. All the user (often the client) has to do is snap a photo into the app and the software "reads" the photos and sets up the transaction. On the accounting side of things, the classified transaction just needs to be confirmed/posted then it can be included in the client's books.

While we have dissected things largely from a public practice perspective, the advances of cloud technology can, of course, be extended to industry. Some small and medium-sized firms have also adopted cloud accounting systems to make things more efficient and cost-effective. With larger firms, there tends to be reliance on bigger systems, namely Enterprise Resource Planning (ERP) systems so the transition to new, leaner systems can be slower.

Table 2. Examples of innovative software

Software	Description
Intuit QuickBooks Online	QuickBooks Online, released 2001, can be described as the web-based version of QuickBooks Desktop. It can be used effectively for collaboration between client and accountant, or between two accounting professionals. With QuickBooks Online, small and medium-sized businesses can track income and expenses, send invoices, accept payments, etc. Other traditional developers of accounting software have similarly created online versions such as Sage Online.
Xero	Xero, released in 2006, is a new emergent in the accounting software space. Like other online accounting platforms, it offers convenient features like integration with banking services to the bookkeeping system. This facilitates easy bookkeeping and accounting processes and reduces costs.
UFile	UFile is an online tax preparation solution used by over one million Canadians each year. It is one of several online tax preparation options available for filing taxes at significantly lower costs than hiring an accountant.
CaseWare Cloud	Like online solutions for bookkeeping and tax preparation, CaseWare Cloud strives to securely move audit functions online and allow for easy collaboration between accountants and clients in separate physical locations.

2. Collaboration

As a convenient supplement to cloud-based accounting software, we have cloud-based storage solutions. Accounting firms can securely store data online where it is less likely to disappear. An added advantage of using cloud storage is that it makes collaboration with team members and clients much easier. As an example, a client can store her data online and share it with an accounting firm. A contract bookkeeper who works from home can be assigned to the file. Then, an accountant at the office can take a look at her work and call the client for more information. Everything can now be without the files or people being at the same location, and the collaboration element is still prevalent.

Going beyond sheerly storage, collaborative online tools have undoubtedly boosted productivity. People on opposite sides of the planet can collaborate in real-time on projects. Even in a local workspace, the headache of managing multiple versions of a file as it is emailed back and forth is no longer a real problem. Cloud technology, such as Microsoft Office online or Google Docs/Sheets has enabled smoother, unconflicted collaboration between colleagues. Like most other office workers, accountants working in public practice as well as industry have taken advantage of these innovative tools.

As the business world grows ever competitive, entrepreneurs and employees alike are seeking an edge. Accountants are now expected to communicate clearly and provide value-adding advice. Due to time saved as a result of automation and reduced need to travel, they meet clients over coffee, lunch, or even Zoom to discuss business ventures, tax-avoidance strategy, and the like. If accountants are not willing to engage in such conversations, they will likely lose business to those who are. Technological advances have pushed the accounting career into a more social direction.

3.   Social media

Another element on communication which accountants need to be wary of is social media. As mentioned earlier, Web 2.0 permits internet users to post their own content on the World Wide Web. This is a valuable feature that accountants, along with everyone else, can use to their benefit.

By using social media strategically, accountants can grow their business. As with any other business, advertising has evolved from being expensive with limited choices to potentially free with many viable options. Traditional media, such as TV, radio, and billboards, has faced competition from social media. Even top brands like Tesla have figured out that they don't need to spend a lot to make a splash.

For accounting firms, it is possible to have effective social media ads which promote certain services to target audiences, personal tax filing service to adults during tax season, for example. However, promotion of other services might prove more challenging, such as audits for large clients. In those cases, accounting firms might be better off just promoting more broadly, essentially spreading brand awareness. Of course, the firm should weigh the benefits and costs of such marketing strategy. Is it really helping the firm substantially?

Finally, businesses need to make sure that marketing is tasteful and ethical. Often, the most memorable ads are edgy, even borderline obscene. Firms should follow the guidance of industry peers, regulatory bodies, and the community to ensure their marketing isn't famous for the wrong reasons.

Web 3.0's Upcoming Impact on the Accounting Industry

With any emerging technology, projecting growth, societal benefit, and other elements can be difficult. However, with the accounting industry, there is a long track record of professionals and businesses using technology in innovative ways. Hence, some reasonable expectations can be formed taking into account the awesome capabilities of the Web 3.0 technology and the current nature of the accounting industry.

There are several notable ways in which the accounting industry can be impacted by Web 3.0 technology. The U.S. Bureau of Labour Statistics (2022) reported that accountants and auditors held about 1.4 million jobs in 2021.

Table 3, below, shows the largest employers of accountants and auditors at the time:

Table 3. Largest employers of accountants and auditors

Accounting, tax preparation, bookkeeping, and payroll services	24%
Finance and insurance	8%
Government	8%
Management of companies and enterprises	7%
Self-employed workers	4%

Hence, it is reasonable to assume about a quarter of accountants work in public practice. After a brief introduction of Web 3.0, the technology's most significant potential impacts on the accounting industry, particularly tax and audit, can be analyzed.

What is Web 3.0?

Entrepreneurs' Organization (2022) describes Web 3.0 as follows:

"Web 3.0 (also referred to as Web3) refers to the evolution of decentralized, blockchain-based applications that bring trade and commerce to a new level. Blockchain, simply put, is a distributed ledger technology that provides an immutable record of transactions between parties. Once a transaction is cryptographically recorded to a blockchain, the transaction cannot be altered, modified, or removed. Copies of the ledger are stored among many computers across the world, enhancing trust and providing transparency to the transactions on the ledger.

Web 3.0 decentralizes information storage but also allows peer-to-peer transactions through programming of "smart" contracts, which can transfer money, rights, and property between parties very efficiently. The evolution of smart contracts eliminates many of the middlemen--like banks--that facilitate transactions between parties. As a result, an entire financial system exists outside of the current traditional banking system. In this blockchain-based ecosystem, individuals and businesses are transacting among themselves, buying, borrowing, lending, and investing without needing to use a bank."

From an accounting perspective, there is much to digest here. Some of the elements mentioned, as well as a few others, are expected to significantly impact the accounting industry in coming years (Gudelci 2022). Of course, there will be some challenges with adoption- there is some documented hesitancy with some accounting firms implementing new technology (Lala et al. 2021).

1.   Distributed Ledger Technology (DLT)

Web 3.0 relies on DLT, which includes blockchain technology (Bhagat 2023). An important feature of blockchain is it permits secure, transparent, and tamper-proof recording and verification of transactions (Zhang et al. 2021). Of course, this feature can be of immense value to the accounting industry. By utilising DLT, accountants will boost the efficiency and accuracy of accounting processes by providing a decentralized and immutable ledger.

In particular, auditing and review functions will be made easier and more reliable as there will be real-time access to transactional data. If accountants are certain that transactions have not been manipulated, the process of reconciling accounts will be straightforward and airtight. This, in turn, will save accounting firms and their clients time and money (Fischer 2022).

Perhaps most importantly, auditors will also be held to higher standards. In recent history, there have been a few infamous examples of audit failures, including Enron and Bernie Madoff (University of Nevada, Reno 2023). With DLT making it harder to miss glaring issues or creatively adjust records, the public can be ever more certain that the audit or review process is trustworthy.

Recently, the European Union announced an incoming withholding tax system which will use DLT to seamlessly transfer tax data between countries (Mehboob 2022). Partly as a result of long, inefficient processing times for paper documents and even lost information, withholding tax refunds are complicated and slow.

Additionally, a growing number of central banks are exploring the viability of a central bank digital currency (CDBC) and are conducting relevant DLT proof-of-concept experiments and pilot programs (Caglayan et al. 2023). These are real-world examples of DLT speeding tasks up and reducing errors via automation.

2.   Smart Contracts

The concept of smart contracts was introduced in the mid-1990s, long before blockchain's rise to prominence (Smart Contracts Alliance 2016, Agrawal et al 2023). Smart contracts are agreements which can be fully enforced and executed by blockchain technology. They do not contain legal language, terms, or agreements. Instead, they are simply code which executes when specific conditions are met. Giancaspro (2017) describes smart contracts as "a computer program which verifies and executes its terms upon the occurrence of predetermined events."

There are a number of advantages to using smart contracts (Fandl 2020, Giancaspro 2017):

- *Increased efficiency:* Since certain "middle-men" functions can cost money, blockchain's ability to bypass some of those functions can make settlement of contracts quicker and cheaper.
- *Higher levels of trust in contract agreements:* When two parties engage in business for the first time, there can be a lack of confidence/trust in the other party. Since smart contracts can be self-executing, the business partners can be more certain about fair and timely settlement.
- *Transparency:* Since distributed ledger technology is visible to all and involved parties do not need to rely on a central authority or other intermediary to verify things, there can be better transparency through the process.
- *Improved privacy:* In addition to the previous point, central authorities and designated intermediaries no longer need to be entrusted with sensitive information to make the transaction(s) happen.

In the business world, smart contracts have the potential to serve many purposes. A practical and common way is to confirm a purchase agreement occurs between two parties. As an example, a manufacturer needing raw materials can set up payments using smart contracts, and the supplier can set up shipments. Then, following the agreement between the two businesses, the funds could be transferred automatically to the supplier upon shipment or delivery of goods. Some other ways smart contracts could be implemented could be for real estate transactions, stock and commodity trading, lending, corporate governance, supply chain, dispute resolution, and healthcare (Frankenfield 2023).

Automation generally results in fewer mistakes and increased overall reliability (Post 2023), so these creative setups, assuming no coding errors, would once again ease verification in an audit or review engagement. Going back to the automated purchase agreement function, accountants would be able to easily reconcile the blockchain-triggered actions with the corresponding flow of cash and goods. The reliance on physical documentation, which can be lost or even manipulated would be greatly reduced.

Accountants can also benefit directly from smart contract implementation (Taherdoost 2023). Smart contracts have the potential to automate various accounting functions such as invoicing, payments, and financial reporting. This automation can reduce manual errors, enhance transparency, and improve the efficiency of financial processes. With accountants not having to focus on certain stresses in running their own businesses, they can pay better attention to their clients' needs.

3.   Integration of Data

Technological advances could create better financial reporting directly resulting from enhanced interoperability between various systems and applications. A relatively new phrase, Internet of Things (IoT), describes the idea of networks of physical objects, or things, being "embedded with sensors, software, and other technologies for the purpose of connecting and exchanging data with other devices and systems over the internet" (Oracle 2023). These types of networks could allow seamless integration of data from different sources.

To view this through the eyes of an accountant, such a high level of interoperability could streamline data flows between accounting systems, banking systems, and other platforms. Accountants would be able to access relevant financial information from different sources in real time, improving data accuracy and decision-making. This could even revolutionize financial reporting as we know it. With strong artificial and communication networks, there could be a shift to continuous financial reporting, as opposed to the periodic financial reporting which we currently have. Of course, a radical shift of this nature would heavily depend on the network being reliable and secure.

4.   Tokenization of Assets

In layman terms, a "token" represents the ownership or access rights to some asset which can be traded on a decentralized platform (K. 2023). Web 3.0 can allow for the tokenization of certain assets, such as financial instruments, real estate, and intellectual property. Of course, modern-day accountants may be asked to provide some investment insight for their clients. In such cases, accountants should probably err on the side of caution as we have already seen some disastrous outcomes with "new-wave" investments such as non-fungible tokens and specifically FTX (Reguerra 2022).

Even more importantly, the accounting industry will be leaned on to develop appropriate accounting standards and frameworks for valuation, recognition, and disclosure of assets which the business world isn't quite familiar with yet (Ferris & Rehm 2022). This poses a definite challenge to accountants as errors here could significantly impact all kinds of business decisions including financing through share or debt sale.

Limitations of this Study

As this work attempts to include a diverse sample of research articles and other sources from around the world, it strives to fairly analyze the historical influence of the World Wide Web on the accounting industry. Furthermore, this chapter predicts the impact of Web 3.0 on the accounting industry and the reader gets an opportunity to develop some familiarity with the staples of blockchain technology and the potential impact on the business and accounting worlds.

However, it is important to note some of this work's limitations. First, since we merely attempt to provide a background on the Web 1.0 and Web 2.0 phases, the evolutionary progress of businesses and accounting firms is not depicted in a complete form. It is simply an overview to set the stage for better understanding of the chapter's core topic. By the time Web 3.0 and its link to the future of accounting is discussed, the reader has an understanding of current trends and origins of the World Wide Web-accounting industry relationship.

Also, since business and firm impact is discussed in a general sense, this work does not target specific industries well, nor specific accounting firms or even functions. Hence, for specific impacts on accounting services for businesses in a particular industry, other works can be consulted, or new research can be conducted. Along the same lines, for specific impacts on accounting functions such as audit and tax preparation, more focused studies can be consulted or conducted.

Finally, the study has focused on the major elements of Web 3.0, namely Distributed Ledger Technology Smart Contracts, Internet of Things, and tokenized assets, and their potential impacts on accounting firms. There are certainly other factors and technologies at play, but generally those which are currently expected to be less impactful. This study can be built upon to include other, perhaps more specific, technologies to analyze things at a more microscopic level- the potential uses and impacts of Ethereum in the accounting industry, for instance.

Contributions of this Study

This chapter provides a quick background of how the accounting industry has evolved over the past few decades as the World Wide Web has developed from a basic connectivity tool to a powerful global network capable of self-fulfilling complex business agreements. The reader can obtain a basic understanding of what Web 1.0 and Web 2.0 are, and how the accounting industry has been impacted by them. Since this work contains a number of non-academic sources such as news articles, the reader can potentially benefit from learning about new upcoming technologies such as DLT and Smart Contracts. An industry practitioner, specifically someone involved in the management of an accounting firm, can take steps to provide better services to businesses and also strengthen processes internally.

From an academic standpoint, this work can, in some ways, be viewed as a bridge between academia and the accounting profession- there are both academic and non-academic citations in this chapter. Hence, it can help academics understand the practical benefits that the World Wide Web has provided to the accounting industry, and can perhaps continue contributing in an even broader capacity with Web 3.0. Furthermore, this work can encourage more targeted research on specific technologies as outlined in the prior section.

Ultimately, the work is well positioned in this book which is focused on Web 3 technology and how it may shape various industries/sectors. By reading about the accounting industry along with other sectors, the reader of the book can obtain a holistic understanding of Web 3.

CONCLUSION

We have just looked at how the accounting industry's slow, steady evolution over thousands of years was suddenly disrupted by the emergence of the World Wide Web. With Web 1.0 introduced in the late 1980's, the accounting industry's accelerated growth began. This first offering of world-altering new technology in the form of the internet fueled further rapid innovation. With access to the latest information and some software options, accountants were able to do better work at a lower cost.

Then came Web 2.0, which accelerated evolution of the industry further. Relatively quickly, accountants were able to escape from the grind of data-entry. The time-consuming, basic accounting tasks became increasingly automated, and accountants were able to add more value with analytical skills and increased emphasis on regular communication with their clients. They were able to take advantage of customizable web functions to boost marketing, collaboration, and an array of other business functions.

Now, the accounting industry is on the verge of being disrupted yet again, this time with Web 3.0. We have covered some potential industry-altering components of the latest version of the World Wide Web, including ultra-reliable transaction records due to Distributed Ledger Technology and smart contracts which can securely automate business and accounting functions.

So, what does all of this mean for professionals in the accounting industry? First, there is certainly opportunity. As discussed, accountants have capitalized well on the World Wide Web over the past thirty-some years. The first step to thriving with Web 3.0 is to keep informed about the emerging technology. How is it disrupting the business world? What about the accounting industry specifically? Are there policy changes that one should be aware of?

Then, it is up to professionals to innovate themselves. With creative steps at the right time, accountants can partake in the change that is occurring and benefit from it. With initiative, they can even change and develop new technologies and policies which will shape the future. And so, those who react quickly with the right move would stand to gain considerably.

That is not to say that Web 3.0 will not bring its share of challenges- there is some documented hesitancy with accounting firms. One major challenge for accountants will be to try to act ethically as possible in uncertain situations. There will be unpredictability, even pain, as there seemingly always is with ground-breaking new technology. As mentioned, there will be opportunity to capitalize by acting quickly, so there will undoubtedly be temptation. Accountants should stand true to their ethical principles of integrity, objectivity, confidentiality, and competence.

Recognition

I would like to thank Dr. Pooja Lekhi for giving me this valuable opportunity to contribute to her book. I appreciate her guidance and support along the way.

REFERENCES

Adams, M. (2023). Comparing QuickBooks Online and QuickBooks Desktop. *Fourlane.* https://www.fourlane.com/blog/comparing-quickbooks-online-and-quickbooks-desktop/

Agrawal, T. K., Angelis, J., Khilji, W. A., Kalaiarasan, R., & Wiktorsson, M. (2023). Demonstration of a blockchain-based framework using smart contracts for supply chain collaboration. *International Journal of Production Research*, *61*(5), 1497–1516. https://doi-org.ezproxy.myucwest.ca/10.1080/00207543.2022.2039413. doi:10.1080/00207543.2022.2039413

Alkafaji, B. K. A., Dashtbayaz, M. L., & Salehi, M. (2023). The Impact of Blockchain on the Quality of Accounting Information: An Iraqi Case Study. *Risks*, *11*(3), 58. doi:10.3390/risks11030058

Allen, M. (2012). What was Web 2.0? Versions as the dominant mode of internet history. *Sage (Atlanta, Ga.)*, *15*(2), 2. doi:10.1177/1461444812451567

Ancajima Miñán, V. Á., Plasencia Latour, J. E., Rubio Cabrera, W. F., Torres Santillan, L. J., & Montaño Barbuda, J. J. (2023). Analysis Of The Impact Of Information And Communication Technologies On Accounting Systems. *Journal of Pharmaceutical Negative Results*, *14*(3), 3369–3379. https://doi-org. ezproxy.myucwest.ca/10.47750/pnr.2023.14.03.420

Bhagat, V. (2023). Web 3.0: how this new era of internet will change the world? *PixelCrayons*. https:// www.pixelcrayons.com/blog/web-3-0/

Business Solutions, C. A. L. (2020). A brief history of ERP software including Dynamics GP and Acumatica. *ERP Software Blog*. https://www.erpsoftwareblog.com/2020/04/a-brief-history-of-erp-software-including-dynamics-gp-and-acumatica/

Çağlayan, G., Öz, B. K., Özer, A., & Şener, E. (2023). Distributed ledger technology experiments in retail payments: Evidence from Turkey. *Journal of Payments Strategy & Systems*, *17*(2), 151–164.

Carbonell, J. (2022). Collaborative accounting: what is it and what does it consist of? *Tas Consultoria*. https://www.tas-consultoria.com/blog-en/collaborative-accounting-consist/

Cong, Y., & Du, H. (2007). Welcome to the World of Web 2.0. *The CPA Journal*, *77*(5), 6–10.

CPABC. (2021). *Maintaining confidentiality and public confidence*. CPABC. https://www.bccpa.ca/news-events/latest-news/2021/november/maintaining-confidentiality-and-public-confidence/

Craig-Bourdin, M. (2019). *How Xero is shaking up the accounting software landscape. CPA* Canada. https://www.cpacanada.ca/en/news/atwork/2019-11-26-xero-accounting-software

Dehinbo, J. (2010). Contributions of traditional Web 1.0 tools e.g. email and Web 2.0 tools e.g. Weblog towards knowledge management. *Information Systems Education, 8, 15*. https://files.eric.ed.gov/fulltext/EJ1146926.pdf

Elixir Business Solution Private Limited. (2023). The rise of technology in accounting: how it changed the game. *LinkedIn*. https://www.linkedin.com/pulse/rise-technology-accounting-how-changed/

Entrepreneurs' Organization. (2022). 3 ways Web3 may impact accounting (and how to prepare). *Inc*. https://www.inc.com/entrepreneurs-organization/3-ways-web3-may-impact-accounting-and-how-to-prepare.html

Fahmi, M., Muda, I., & Kesuma, S. A. (2023). Digitization Technologies and Contributions to Companies towards Accounting and Auditing Practices. [IJSSR]. *International Journal of Social Service & Research*, *3*(3), 639–643. https://doi-org.ezproxy.myucwest.ca/10.46799/ijssr.v3i3.298. doi:10.46799/ijssr.v3i3.298

Ferris, S., & Rehm, P. (2022). What CPAs need to know about NFTs. *Journal of Accountancy*. https://www.journalofaccountancy.com/issues/2022/oct/what-cpas-need-to-know-about-nfts.html

Fischer, D. (2022). Ethical and Professional Implications of Blockchain Accounting Ledgers. *Proceedings of the Northeast Business & Economics Association*, 27–30.

Frankenfield. (2023). What are smart contracts on the blockchain and how they work. *Investopedia*. https://www.investopedia.com/terms/s/smart-contracts.asp

Giancaspro, M. (2017). Is a 'smart contract' really a smart idea? Insights from a legal perspective. *Computer Law & Security Review*, *33*(6), 825–835. https://doi-org.ezproxy.myucwest.ca/10.1016/j.clsr.2017.05.007. doi:10.1016/j.clsr.2017.05.007

Güdelci, Ü. E. N. (2022). New Era in Blockchain Technology and Better Accounting Information. *Muhasebe ve Vergi Uygulamalari Dergisi (MUVU)* [JATS]. *Journal of Accounting & Taxation Studies*, *15*(2), 437–461.

Gunnoo, N. (2023). Data entry automation in 2023. *Parseur*. https://parseur.com/blog/data-entry-automation

K., D. (2023). What is Tokenization? *ND Labs*. https://ndlabs.dev/what-is-tokenization

Kee, R. (1993, December 1). Data processing technology and accounting: A historical perspective. *The Accounting Historians Journal*, *20*(2), 187–216. doi:10.2308/0148-4184.20.2.187

Kolisnyk, O., Hurina, N., Druzhynska, N., Holovchak, H., & Fomina, T. (2023). Innovative Technologies in Accounting and Auditing: The Use of Blockchain Technology. *Financial & Credit Activity: Problems of Theory & Practice*, *3*(50), 24–41. https://doi-org.ezproxy.myucwest.ca/10.55643/fcaptp.3.50.2023.4082

Lala, Z., Poole, V. B., & Kimmel, S. B. (2021). Adapting to New Technology in the Accounting Industry. *Business Education Innovation Journal*, *13*(2), 37–42.

Lauwers, L., & Willekens, M. (1994). 500 years of bookkeeping a portrait of Luca Pacioli. *Tijdschrift voor Economie en Management, XXXIX, 3*. https://lirias.kuleuven.be/bitstream/123456789/119065/1/TEM1994-3_289-304p.pdf

Lazanis, R. (2022). Social Media for Accountants: 7 Reasons Why + 11 Tips How. *Future Firm*. https://futurefirm.co/social-media-for-accountants/

Mabić, M., Lasić, M., & Zovko, J. (2019). Web 2.0 Technologies in Business: Why Not? *Interdisciplinary Description of Complex Systems*, *17*(2–B), 304–314. https://doi-org.ezproxy.myucwest.ca/10.7906/indecs.17.2.7

Mehboob, D. (2022). EU moves to blockchain for withholding tax data sharing. *International Tax Review*. https://www.internationaltaxreview.com/article/2a6abcbtm7tszx7breg3k/eu-moves-to-blockchain-for-withholding-tax-data-sharing

Mihai, G. (2014). Some Aspects of using Web 2.0/Enterprise 2.0 Technologies in Accounting. *Annals of the University Dunarea de Jos of Galati: Fascicle: I, Economics & Applied Informatics, 20*(1).

Morrison, R. (2020). *What do landlords in Canada look for in your bank statements*? Strawhomes. https://www.strawhomes.com/what-do-landlords-look-for-in-your-bank-statements/

Nath, A. K., Singh, R., Iyer, L. S., & Ganesh, J. (2010). Web 2.0: Capabilities, Business Value and Strategic Practice. *Journal of Information Science & Technology*, *7*(1), 22–39.

Oracle. (2023). *What is IoT?* Oracle. https://www.oracle.com/ca-en/internet-of-things/what-is-iot/

Perdue, B. (2022). History of automation in the accounting industry. *Autymate*. https://www.autymate.com/blog/history-of-automation-in-the-accounting-industry

Post, H. (2023). How automation helps reduce human error and improves data quality. *Trade Safe*. https://trdsf.com/blogs/news/how-automation-helps-reduce-human-error-and-improves-data-quality

Rebecca. (2022). What is Web 1.0? Everything you need to know. *History-Computer*. https://history-computer.com/web-1-0/

Reguerra, E. (2022). NFTs minted on FTX break, highlighting Web2 hosting flaws. *Cointelegraph*. https://cointelegraph.com/news/nfts-minted-on-ftx-break-highlighting-web2-hosting-flaws

Richter, J. (2022). History & definition of Web 1.0, 2.0, and 3.0- a comprehensive review. *Viral Solutions*. https://viralsolutions.net/definition-of-web-1-0-2-0-and-3-0/

Rotberg, E. (2019). Keep your emails between you and your client. *CPA Canada*. https://www.cpacanada.ca/en/news/atwork/2019-06-14-client-email-risk

Sadowski, J. (2016). Companies are making money from our personal data – but at what cost? *The Guardian*. https://www.theguardian.com/technology/2016/aug/31/personal-data-corporate-use-google-amazon

Samanthi, D., & Gooneratne, T. (2023). Bean counter to value-adding business partner: The changing role of the accountant and situated rationality in a multinational firm. *Journal of Accounting & Organizational Change*, *19*(3), 513–535. https://doi-org.ezproxy.myucwest.ca/10.1108/JAOC-04-2022-0063. doi:10.1108/JAOC-04-2022-0063

Smart Contracts Alliance. (2016). Smart contracts: 12 use cases for business & beyond. Chamber of Digital Commerce. Washington D.C.

Taherdoost, H. (2023). Smart Contracts in Blockchain Technology: A Critical Review. *Information (Basel)*, *14*(2), 117. doi:10.3390/info14020117

Tillema, S., Trapp, R., & van Veen, D. P. (2022). Business Partnering in Risk Management: A Resilience Perspective on Management Accountants' Responses to a Role Change. *Contemporary Accounting Research*, *39*(3), 2058–2089. https://doi-org.ezproxy.myucwest.ca/10.1111/1911-3846.12774. doi:10.1111/1911-3846.12774

University of Nevada. (2023). *7 worst accounting scandals in U.S. history*. University of Nevada. https://onlinedegrees.unr.edu/blog/worst-accounting-scandals/

U.S. Bureau of Labour Statistics. (2022). *Accountants and Auditors*. BLS. https://www.bls.gov/ooh/business-and-financial/accountants-and-auditors.htm#tab-3

Wang, J. (2022). Research on the construction of accounting information audit quality control system based on blockchain. *Security and Privacy*, *6*(2), e227. doi:10.1002py2.227

WikiWand. (2023). *CaseWare International*. WikiWand. https://www.wikiwand.com/en/CaseWare_International

Zhang, Y., Pourroostaei Ardakani, S., & Han, W. (2021). Smart ledger: The blockchain-based accounting information recording protocol. *Journal of Corporate Accounting & Finance (Wiley)*, *32*(4), 147–157. https://doi-org.ezproxy.myucwest.ca/10.1002/jcaf.22515. doi:10.1002/jcaf.22515

Chapter 22

Understanding the Impact of CBDCs on Financial Stability:
The Shift Towards a User-Centric Financial Ecosystem

Guneet Kaur
University of Stirling, UK

ABSTRACT

The development of digital banking and the introduction of cryptocurrencies have drawn considerable attention to central bank digital currencies (CBDCs) in the global financial system. Policymakers, economists, and business experts are debating the deployment of CBDCs and their effects on financial stability as central banks examine their potential. In order to investigate the possible risks and advantages of CBDCs for financial stability, this study presents a thorough narrative literature review that critically evaluates a wide range of academic publications, reports, and research studies. This study also highlights the necessity of a user-centric financial ecosystem that incorporates Web 3 concepts. It also explores the significance of carefully constructed CBDC frameworks by looking at the potential impacts of CBDC adoption on monetary policy, systemic risks, and banking intermediation.

1. INTRODUCTION

Central Bank Digital Currencies (CBDCs) have become a significant subject of debate and investigation in the international financial system. The idea of establishing CBDCs is a result of how the world of digital finance is changing and the popularity of cryptocurrencies like Bitcoin (BTC) and Ether (ETH). As a result, central banks have realized the need to investigate the possibilities of digital currencies they issue and regulate as technology advances continue to disrupt the financial sector (Coulter, 2023).

Policymakers, economists, and business professionals are all very interested in and debating the prospective implementation of CBDCs. Advocates claim that CBDCs can increase financial inclusion, simplify payment processes, lower transaction costs, and boost the efficacy of monetary policy (El Attar

DOI: 10.4018/978-1-6684-9919-1.ch022

Copyright © 2023, IGI Global. Copying or distributing in print or electronic forms without written permission of IGI Global is prohibited.

& Chaloui, 2023). Given the complex interactions between digital currencies and the larger financial ecosystem, worries and uncertainty about the possible impact of CBDCs on financial stability still exist.

The purpose of this paper is to conduct a narrative literature review on how CBDCs affect financial stability. This research aims to offer insights into the potential risks and benefits connected with the use of CBDCs by critically analyzing and synthesizing a wide range of academic publications, reports, and research studies. For regulators and market actors to successfully manage the emerging world of digital currencies, it is critical that they have a thorough understanding of the implications of CBDCs for financial stability.

This narrative literature review aims to conduct a comprehensive analysis of the existing knowledge on central bank digital currencies. Additionally, it will assess the degree of agreement or disagreement among academics and point out any research holes that need to be filled. The review's conclusions will add to the continuing debates over CBDCs and their possible effects on financial stability. The findings offered by this review will be useful to policymakers, central banks, academics, and business experts who are attempting to evaluate the risks and advantages of CBDC adoption.

In the sections that follow, the researcher will examine the body of research on CBDCs, describe the review, present findings and analysis, talk about how CBDCs affect financial stability, and conclude with suggestions for future research.

2. LITERATURE REVIEW

Various significant variables have influenced the consideration of CBDCs, including technological innovation, a changing payment landscape, financial inclusion, greater control and visibility over monetary policy and financial stability, consumer protection, and the need to streamline cross-border transactions.

The emergence of distributed ledger systems and blockchain technology has demonstrated the promise of safe and effective digital transactions. To improve their monetary systems, central banks are eager to take advantage of these technological advancements (Gupta et al., 2023). Traditional payment methods have undergone substantial changes as a result of the emergence of digital payments, mobile banking, and fintech developments. CBDCs are viewed as a solution to update payment methods and provide customers with quicker, more secure, and more economical transactions.

By offering comprehensive and accessible digital payment alternatives, CBDCs have the ability to address concerns about financial exclusion. Making sure that everyone has access to a central bank-issued digital currency can promote financial inclusion (Ozili, 2023), regardless of their socioeconomic status or location. Furthermore, CBDCs give central banks more oversight and control over money flows, enhancing the efficiency of monetary policy. Real-time transaction tracking enables more accurate economic monitoring, assisting efforts to preserve financial stability and reduce risks.

Central banks could introduce CBDCs as a dependable and governed replacement for decentralized cryptocurrencies. Consumers can be safeguarded from potential risks associated with unregulated digital assets by providing secure and trustworthy digital money. Also, CBDCs have the ability to streamline and simplify cross-border transactions. With fewer middlemen and lower transaction costs, the use of digital currencies issued by central banks can promote quicker and more effective international transfers.

2.1 Definition and Features of CBDCs

The Bank for International Settlements claims that the word "CBDC" is vague and incorporates a number of concepts (Ward & Rochemont, 2019). However, it is typically recognized as a novel form of central bank money. It functions as both a medium of exchange and a store of value and is a liability of the central bank, denominated in an existing unit of account. According to Lee et al. (2021), CBDC is the next step in the evolution process from metal currency to metal-backed banknotes and then to fiat money. The International Monetary Fund (IMF) provided one of the classifications that is most frequently used, which categorizes CBDC as a type of digital legal money (Kiff et al., 2020).

According to Bindseil (2019), a CBDC is a type of currency or legal tender that the central bank issues, is available in digital form, and is the central bank's liability. According to Sanchez-Roger and Puyol-Antón (2021), many CBDCs are built to enable the conversion of CBDC deposits into bank deposits and vice versa. According to Bindseil (2019), this movement of money from a bank account to a CBDC account is referred to as bank disintermediation since it lessens the amount of bank deposits that may be used for financial intermediation. Additionally, Bacchetta and Perazzi (2021) coined the term "deposit substitution" to describe the transfer of deposits from banks to the central bank and vice versa.

Banks and certain financial or public entities have historically had limited access to account-based systems (balances in reserve accounts) and other digital forms of central bank money (Bech & Garratt, 2017). Contrarily, the general population has had easy access to physical central bank money, or cash. This strategy has been used for a number of reasons and has typically been successful in preserving the stability of the financial and monetary systems. Therefore, any modifications to the current structure would need to be carefully thought out and strongly justified.

According to Bech & Garratt (2017), central bank digital currencies can be broadly divided into two categories: wholesale CBDCs (WCBDCs) and retail CBDCs (RCBDCs). Wholesale CBDC is a type of digital currency that is only used for financial transactions between the central bank, commercial banks, and other financial institutions. According to Simran & Adam (2023), this kind of CBDC is often developed using distributed ledger technology, such as blockchain. The use of wholesale CBDC in interbank settlements has the potential to increase the speed and security of monetary exchanges inside the banking system.

Retail CBDC, on the other hand, is a type of CBDC that is available to the general public. It is intended for use in daily transactions by both individuals and companies. According to Bech & Garratt (2017), accessibility is the main factor separating wholesale from retail CBDC. According to the Committee on Payments and Market Infrastructures (2018), the Bank for International Settlements distinguishes two categories of retail CBDC: those based on central bank accounts and those based on digital tokens. While token-based retail CBDC would involve the issuance of digital tokens that may be used as a form of payment, central bank account-based retail CBDC would require people and businesses to hold accounts directly with the central bank.

Additionally, Auer & Boehme (2020) discussed three different architectural models—direct issuance, two-tiered issuance, and hybrid models—that can be used to design CBDCs. These models establish the responsibilities and connections between the central bank and commercial banks in managing the CBDC. Here is a quick explanation of each design type:

- **Direct issue:** The central bank is essential and crucial to the direct issue paradigm. Because of its centralized architecture, fewer institutions are involved. The central bank oversees retail payments, tracks all transactions, and directly issues CBDC to end users. According to this paradigm, the central bank owns all claims, just like banknotes.

- **Two-Tier issuance:** Both the central bank and the commercial banks actively participate in the two-tier issuance framework. The central bank is responsible for issuing the CBDC, and commercial banks are in charge of overseeing daily interactions with retail customers. On behalf of the central bank, commercial banks function as intermediaries, offering services and facilitating transactions.

- **Hybrid model:** The combined key elements of the direct issuance and two-tiered issuance structures make up the hybrid approach. The central bank issues the CBDC, keeps a complete record of all transactions, and acts as a backstop for the payment system, much like the direct architecture. Additionally, similar to the two-tiered issuance concept, additional private financial institutions, such as commercial banks, are involved in supporting the operational facets of the CBDC system.

However, it is crucial to remember that each central bank has its own preferences, objectives, and strategies, which affect the architectural structure that will be used to implement the CBDC. The choice of a particular model dictates the allocation of duties and the degree of participation of various players in the management of the CBDC system.

As digital versions of national currencies are produced and governed by central banks, CBDCs have drawn a lot of attention. The following are some of the essential traits of CBDCs:

- **Digital representation:** CBDCs are represented digitally, enabling people to interact with them and conduct business with them online. They can be linked to a user's account or kept in digital wallets.

- **Central bank issues:** Central banks issue and oversee CBDCs, making the central bank directly responsible for them. This sets them apart from other kinds of digital money, such as cryptocurrencies, which lack centralized support and are decentralized.

- **Legal tender:** CBDCs frequently pass muster as legitimate currency, giving them the same status as central bank-issued money. Like conventional fiat currencies, they can be used for a variety of transactions, including payments for products and services.

- **Controlled supply:** CBDCs are subject to control by central banks, which gives them the ability to limit the quantity in circulation. As a result, central banks can control monetary policy and maintain price stability.

- **Programmable money:** CBDCs can have characteristics that are programmable, making it possible to construct smart contracts and automate processes. This programmability can enable the creation of creative financial apps as well as more efficient and safe transactions.

- **Greater transparency and traceability:** When compared to conventional cash transactions, CBDC transactions can provide greater transparency and traceability. Since central banks can see the movement of CBDCs in real time, they can more effectively monitor the economy and perhaps even curtail illegal activity.

- **Potential privacy features:** While CBDCs can provide openness, including privacy features is becoming more important. Central banks deploy protections to protect user data and transaction privacy in an effort to strike a balance between privacy and anti-money laundering procedures.

- **Interoperability:** CBDCs may be able to work with different platforms and payment systems. This interoperability enables frictionless transfers and cross-border transactions, improving financial inclusion and lowering costs.

2.2 Theoretical Perspectives on CBDCs and Financial Stability

In the history of money and banking, the introduction of CBDC marks a crucial turning point. CBDCs allow central banks to engage in substantial intermediation by putting up a fight with private financial intermediaries for deposits, which may eliminate the need for actual cash. This might entail the central bank utilizing those deposits for lending purposes. In essence, a CBDC gives customers the choice to open a bank account with the country's central bank. This section will look at various theoretical perspectives on CBDCs and financial stability.

2.2.1 The Impact of CBDC on Equilibrium Allocation and the Price System

In a study by Brunnermeier and Niepelt (2019), the circumstances under which a swap between private and public money has no effect on the equilibrium allocation and price system are examined. By tracing the origins of seigniorage rents and liquidity bubbles, the study derives the necessary conditions for equivalence. In the study, these requirements are applied to a variety of situations, such as the "Chicago Plan," cryptocurrencies, the Indian demonetization experiment, and CBDC. According to the findings, the implementation of CBDC with pass-through funding from the central bank does not always result in a credit shortage or threaten financial stability.

2.2.2 Impact of CBDCs on Central Bank Stability

The effects of implementing a CBDC on the stability of bank deposits and the asset side of the central bank were examined by Schilling et al. in 2020. A stylized version of the Diamond-Dybvig (1983) model was used in their analysis, and they discovered that the central bank might engage in maturity transformation if it so wished. Price stability, economic effectiveness, and financial stability were taken into consideration as the central bank's three goals in the study. The research showed that the central bank could only accomplish a maximum of two of the three goals due to the CBDC Trilemma. Notably, a commitment to price stability could result in a run on the bank, while a commitment to inflation is necessary to achieve the socially optimal allocation.

2.2.2.3 Impact of CBDCs on Open-Economy Dynamics

Ferrari et al. (2020) used a conventional two-country dynamic stochastic general equilibrium (DSGE) model with financial frictions to explore the implications of adding a CBDC in an open economy. They examined the influence of the CBDC's design on welfare, optimal monetary policy, and the transmission of monetary policy and technological shocks internationally. The study discovered that the presence of CBDC increased international links by amplifying shock spillovers between nations. However, certain CBDC design elements might considerably reduce the spillovers and affect how large these effects would be. Additionally, the domestic issue of CBDC undermined the independence of monetary policy in other nations, leading to imbalances in the global monetary system.

2.2.2.4 Impact of CBDC On Credit Supply and Financial Stability

In their research, Kim and Kwon (2022) used a monetary general equilibrium model to analyze the effect of CBDC on credit supply and financial stability. They discovered that when deposits were made into CBDC accounts, the availability of bank credit decreased. Because of this reduction in loan availability, the nominal interest rate rose and banks' reserve-deposit ratio decreased. As a result, the probability of a bank panic marked by the depletion of cash reserves increased. However, the researchers found that financial stability could be improved if the central bank had the authority to lend banks all of the deposits held in CBDC accounts. This was accomplished by increasing the amount of CBDC, which did not necessitate that banks maintain reserves. This increased the availability of credit and decreased the nominal interest rate.

2.2.2.5 Impacts of CBDCs On Welfare and Equilibrium Allocations

Keister & Sanches (2023) examined the effects of establishing a central bank digital currency (CBDC) on welfare and equilibrium allocations in an economy where transactions can be carried out using both cash and bank deposits. The authors drew attention to a significant trade-off that policymakers must make in this situation. The introduction of a digital currency may improve exchange rates, but it also has the potential to reduce investment, displace bank deposits, and raise funding costs for banks. They lay forth the prerequisites for targeted digital currencies, which only compete with fiat money or bank savings, to raise standards of living. When issuing targeted currencies is not practical, they investigated the trade-offs in terms of policy that come with releasing a single, global digital currency.

Their analysis shows that when there is a substantial incentive for financial inclusion, a digital currency that resembles cash is desirable. On the other hand, where there are modest financial frictions and a limited supply of productive projects compared to the need for deposits from transactions, a digital currency that resembles bank deposits is typically preferred. When a global digital currency is used, the same patterns still exist but interact in ways that could result in a larger or narrower circulation than what would be possible with specific digital currencies.

2.2.2.6 Impact of CBDCs On Balance Sheets of Commercial Banks

Samuele & Rosa (2023) applied the endogenous money theory to understand CBDCs and their impact. Their analysis explains the logical progression of connections that starts with bank loans granted by commercial banks and leads to deposits that can finally be converted into CBDC. The balance sheets of commercial banks would undergo major changes if deposits were fully converted and transmigrated into CBDC. These changes would include a reduction in size and a change in composition, as well as an expansion and a change in the makeup of the central bank's balance sheet. This point is also emphasized in the European Central Bank study, which comes from central bankers who are worried that CBDC could disintermediate deposits either fundamentally or cyclically. However, the adoption of CBDC does not necessarily imply a restricted banking model where commercial banks lose their capacity to issue currency.

2.2.2.7 Impact of CBDC Remuneration on Bank Fragility

Hoffmann et al. (2023) used global games to investigate a financial intermediation model that accounts for the likelihood of a bank run. Customers in this model have the choice to store their wealth in compensated CBDC as opposed to conventional bank deposits. The researchers discovered that when the central bank rewards CBDC with larger compensation, it increases consumer incentives to remove money from banks, increasing bank instability. However, the study also showed that banks provide better deposit rates in response to this increased competition in order to maintain financing, which ultimately lessens instability. As a result, there is a U-shaped pattern in the link between CBDC compensation and bank fragility. It is crucial to remember that any adjustments to deposit rates will directly affect bank stability. In particular, more CBDC compensation raises deposit rates while also raising bank instability.

2.2.2.8 The Macroeconomic Impact of a Foreign CBDC

A DSGE model is used by Moro and Landi (2023) to analyze the macroeconomic effects of a foreign CBDCS that is usable by citizens of a small open economy. Their research shows that a steady rise in domestic households' demand for overseas CBDC, particularly when it closely mimics domestic deposits, has a recessionary effect. However, interventions like capital flow management, macroprudential policy changes, or selling off foreign reserves might lessen the effects of a recession. In addition, compared to CPI targeting or exchange rate pegging, a Taylor rule that targets producer price index (PPI) inflation is more successful in reducing recession. The study also shows that, if the CBDC is not compensated, an economy with a sizable stock of overseas CBDC is less susceptible to shocks in the foreign interest rate.

3. SYSTEMIC RISK AND CONTAGION

It is critical to evaluate the potential risks connected with the adoption of CBDCs as they attract more attention globally. Three main risks are examined in this paper: operational risks, cyber risks, and contagion impacts on the larger financial system. Policymakers and central banks can create strong frameworks to prevent potential vulnerabilities by identifying these risks.

3.1 Operational Risks

The execution of the CBDC entails intricate operational procedures, which raise a number of operational hazards, such as:

- **System failures:** Technical issues or system outages in CBDC infrastructure could interfere with financial transactions and payment systems, causing disruptions in the economy and a decline in trust in the currency.
- **Scalability Issues:** CBDCs must effectively manage huge transaction volumes (Homoliak et al., 2023). Lack of scalability could cause delays, traffic congestion, and possible operational breakdowns.

- **User support and education:** Effective user assistance and education must be provided in order for CBDCs to be adopted and run efficiently. A lack of user education and inadequate support could result in mistakes, fraud, or financial losses.

3.2 Cyber Risks

Due to their digital character, CBDCs pose new cyber risks that may have an influence on the stability of the economy. These risks consist of:

- **Cyberattacks:** The CBDC systems could be the subject of sophisticated cyberattacks, such as data breaches, hacking attempts, and ransomware assaults (Tian et al., 2023). The integrity, confidentiality, and availability of the CBDC system could be jeopardized by such attacks.
- **Fraud and counterfeiting:** CBDCs may be targets of fraud and forgery attempts, necessitating strong security measures to stop unauthorized manufacture or replication of digital currency units.
- **Privacy concerns:** Concerns related to privacy and data protection are brought up by CBDCs' digital nature (Jabbar et al., 2023). To maintain the public's trust, it is crucial to protect user identities and transactional data and prevent illegal access (Takaragi & Kubota, 2023).

3.3 Contagion Effects on the Financial System

Contagion Effects on the Financial System: Financial stability may be negatively impacted by the widespread adoption and integration of CBDCs into the financial system.

- **Disintermediation risks:** The risks of disintermediation include the possibility of a destabilizing change in the funding structure of commercial banks as a result of the availability of CBDCs as a direct liability of the central bank (Wilmer, 2023).
- **Risks associated with liquidity and funding:** CBDCs may have an effect on the dynamics of funding and liquidity in the financial system. The liquidity environment could be strained by abrupt changes in CBDC holdings and their withdrawal patterns, thereby compromising the stability of financial institutions.
- **Cross-border effects:** The implementation of CBDCs in one country may have cross-border effects on capital flows, foreign exchange markets, and international monetary relations. Global frameworks and regulations that are coordinated may be necessary to facilitate the successful implementation and operation of CBDCs.

4. REGULATORY AND LEGAL CHALLENGES

In order to ensure financial stability, CBDCs face considerable regulatory and legal obstacles. Regarding challenges, privacy issues are a major one. Strong laws must be established to safeguard people's right to privacy because CBDCs acquire and store personal and transactional data. In order to manage and process user information securely and in accordance with applicable privacy regulations, this involves putting in place rigorous data protection procedures. Maintaining the public's confidence in CBDCs also depends on finding a balance between regulatory monitoring and protecting financial privacy.

The security of CBDC systems is a significant obstacle. CBDCs are vulnerable to a variety of cybersecurity concerns because of their digital nature, including hacking, data breaches, and fraudulent operations. Strong cybersecurity measures must be adopted to solve these issues. This entails adding encryption and authentication features, performing frequent security audits, and using cutting-edge technologies to thwart attempts at counterfeiting. By putting these controls in place, the legitimacy and integrity of CBDC transactions may be preserved, protecting the economy's stability.

Another crucial component of regulating CBDCs is compliance with anti-money laundering (AML) and know-your-customer (KYC) regulations (Wang, 2023). There is a need to create strong AML and KYC regulations since CBDCs make it possible for transactions to be seamless and anonymous. This is necessary to stop illegal activities like money laundering and the financing of terrorism. Risks associated with financial crimes can be reduced by putting in place strict identification and verification procedures, transaction monitoring systems, and reporting methods.

For CBDCs to be implemented successfully, these regulatory and legal issues must be resolved. Policymakers may sustain public confidence in CBDCs as a safe and dependable form of digital money by ensuring privacy protection, increasing cybersecurity safeguards, and enforcing AML and KYC regulations.

5. CROSS-BORDER IMPLICATIONS

The advent of CBDCs brings up crucial questions about international trade and how it affects the stability of the financial system. Due to their ability to provide quicker, less expensive, and more effective transactions, CBDCs have the potential to revolutionize cross-border payments (Kurian, 2023). Cross-border CBDC projects include the following:

5.1 Infrastructure Compatibility

Ensuring infrastructure compatibility and interoperability between various CBDC systems in various nations is a significant task. The efficiency of cross-border transactions can be increased by harmonizing technical standards and procedures. To create common norms and standards for CBDC interoperability, cooperation between central banks and international organizations is crucial.

5.2 Regulatory Coordination

Coordination of the regulatory environment is necessary to solve issues like AML, KYC, and counter-terrorism financing in cross-border transactions involving CBDCs. Cross-border transactions can be made more secure and compliant by harmonizing regulatory frameworks and developing efficient information sharing channels.

5.3 Foreign Exchange Implications

The cross-border use of CBDCs raises questions regarding the stability of exchange rates. Changes in CBDC exchange rates could have an effect on international business transactions and increase the possibility of currency valuation errors. Maintaining stability in cross-border transactions involving CBDCs requires close coordination between central banks and transparent communication of exchange rate policy.

5.4 Currency Substitution

People and businesses may opt to keep and conduct transactions with CBDCs rather than conventional fiat currencies as a result of their availability. The value of national currencies may be impacted by this substitution effect, which may have an impact on exchange rates.

5.5 Capital Flows

CBDCs may have an impact on international capital flows, which in turn may have an effect on exchange rates. Capital flows into or out of a country's CBDC may result in exchange rate swings depending on variables including interest rate differentials and investor preferences (Linden & Łasak, 2023).

5.6 Impact On Monetary Policy

CBDCs can influence monetary policy (Kaur & Vishwakarma, 2023), which indirectly affects exchange rates. To preserve stability in the face of shifting dynamics, central banks may need to take into account the effects of CBDCs on their monetary policy frameworks and exchange rate targeting tactics (Lukonga, 2023).

6. THE INTEGRATION OF CBDCS WITH WEB 3 PRINCIPLES AND TECHNOLOGIES

The future of finance may be reshaped by the incorporation of CBDCs with Web 3 concepts and technologies. The decentralized web's basic concepts and technologies aim to revolutionize how people interact with the internet and digital services. They center on concepts like user ownership of data, decentralization, transparency, and the usage of blockchain and cryptographic technologies. The following are some crucial concepts and Web 3-related technologies:

6.1 Decentralization

Web 3 encourages a decentralized approach in which authority is diffused among a network of participants rather than being held by a single entity. By eliminating single points of failure and decreasing reliance on intermediaries, decentralization makes it possible to promote trust, transparency, and resilience (Kaur & KrishnaKumar, 2023).

6.2 Blockchain Technology

By offering a safe, open, and impenetrable distributed ledger, blockchain serves as the foundation of Web 3. Decentralized data storage and verification are made possible, guaranteeing transparency, immutability, and consensus among network participants (Wan et al., 2023).

6.3 Smart Contracts

Smart contracts are self-executing digital contracts that, when certain conditions are satisfied, autonomously enforce predetermined conditions and actions (Taherdoost, 2023). They do away with the need for middlemen and make it possible to create decentralized applications (dApps) that operate on blockchain platforms, promoting efficient and trustworthy interactions.

6.4 Cryptocurrencies

Using cryptographic methods to safeguard transactions and regulate the generation of new units, cryptocurrencies are digital assets (Kaur & KrishnaKumar, 2023). Within Web 3 ecosystems, they act as a means of exchange and make it possible to transfer value without the use of conventional financial intermediaries.

6.5 Interoperability

The seamless exchange of information and interaction between various blockchain networks and decentralized applications (dApps) is referred to as interoperability. The flow of resources and information between distinct decentralized platforms is made possible through interoperability standards and protocols, which improve connectivity and enable complicated, cross-chain transactions (Ren et al., 2023).

6.6 Self-Sovereign Identity

Web 3 stresses the idea of a person having complete control over their personal information and digital identities (Ahmed et al., 2023). It improves privacy, security, and user autonomy by enabling users to manage and validate their own identities without relying on centralized identity providers.

6.7 Web 3 Wallets

Web 3 wallets are digital wallets that let users engage with and securely store digital assets like non-fungible tokens (NFTs) and cryptocurrencies (Wan et al., 2023). Users can participate in a variety of Web 3 activities with these wallets because they frequently offer seamless connections with dApps and blockchain networks.

6.8 Governance Mechanisms

With the introduction of new governance models by Web 3, decentralized decision-making is made possible within blockchain networks and decentralized communities. With the help of these methods, protocols and decentralized applications will be managed and developed in a fair, transparent, and consistent manner (Liu et al., 2023).

6.9 Web 3 Browsers

Specialized web browsers known as Web 3 browsers offer native support for engaging with decentralized applications, blockchain networks, and Web 3 technologies (Wan et al., 2023). They enable users to observe blockchain transactions, manage their Web 3 identities, and engage with dApps.

7. WEB 3 TECHNOLOGIES: TOWARDS A USER-CENTRIC FINANCIAL ECOSYSTEM

A financial ecosystem that puts users' wants, preferences, and control first is known as a "user-centric financial ecosystem." Individuals have more agency, ownership, and control over their financial activities and data in this ecosystem. The emphasis is on empowering users so they can take charge of their personal information, make informed decisions, and have access to a variety of financial services.

Transparency, confidence, and inclusivity are prioritized in a user-centric financial ecosystem. It strives to give people easy access to financial services, individualized experiences, and the capacity to effectively manage their money. The ability to select from a range of financial products and services, customize them to meet their unique needs, and quickly move between providers is available to users. They have complete control over how their information is used and shared because their financial data and privacy are safeguarded.

The development of a financial ecosystem that is focused on users is greatly assisted by Web 3 concepts and technologies, as discussed above. Users' transactions and data are secured thanks to these technologies' transparency, security, and immutability. Web 3 also places a strong emphasis on self-sovereign identification, which gives users total control over their online personas and data. In this context, CBDCs can transform established financial institutions by utilizing Web 3's decentralized architecture, programmability, interoperability, self-sovereign identity, and emphasis on financial inclusion. Web 3 and CBDCs together have the potential to democratize finance by giving people more control over their financial data and transactions.

CBDCs can be created to run on distributed ledgers, enabling transparent and immutable transactions by utilizing blockchain technology. This promotes financial inclusion and lessens dependency on intermediaries by ensuring that financial operations are not regulated by a central authority but rather are governed by a network of participants.

Smart contracts and programmable money can automate and simplify financial procedures, decreasing the need for middlemen and increasing effectiveness. Additionally, features that promote interoperability allow for smooth cross-border transactions, increasing global trade and liquidity. Additionally, the focus on privacy and self-sovereign identity in Web 3 can protect user information and advance financial inclusion. An inclusive, transparent, and effective financial ecosystem is presented through the integration of CBDCs with Web 3 concepts and technologies.

A study by Han et al. (2021) explored the idea of Cos-CBDC, a CBDC running on the Cosmos blockchain. It emphasizes how the Inter-Blockchain Communication (IBC) protocol is used to guarantee interoperability between various blockchains. The examination of Cos-CBDC's requirements and its implementation using Cosmos-SDK are covered in detail in the review. It also includes a method for group key management within Cos-CBDC that places a focus on giving users access to privileges and privacy-preserving tools while keys are being generated. This evaluation offers insightful information on the developments and possibilities of Cos-CBDC in the fields of blockchain technology and digital currency.

Similarly, Moiso & Minerva (2012) proposed a user-centric strategy for managing personal data. The model presents the idea of a "Bank of Individuals' Data" (BID), which gives people authority over how their data is gathered, managed, and shared. BID manages personal data in a manner similar to how banks manage money, establishing a new ecosystem that enables people to take advantage of their own data. Ray (2023) examined that by providing an open and user-centric environment, decentralized web infrastructure can improve the internet. Individuals and groups can benefit from a more open and empowering internet with enhanced control over digital assets and online interactions. The decentralized infrastructure of Web 3 encourages creativity, teamwork, and user empowerment, laying the foundation for a safe, connected, and fair digital ecosystem.

The blockchain-based system that Han et al. (2019) proposed, which consists of three interdependent layers called regulatory, network, and user, presents a structured approach to CBDCs. The regulatory layer distinguishes CBDCs from decentralized cryptocurrencies as a distinctive feature. This layer, which consists of the central bank, a fundamental Public Key Infrastructure (PKI) for identity verification, and regulatory organizations, makes sure that CBDC activities are meticulously supervised in both the technical and policy senses. Comprehensive monitoring is enforced by cooperation among regulatory organizations within a largely decentralized system. Between top-level regulators and common people, the network layer serves as a link. Contrary to decentralized cryptocurrencies, this layer uses two network architectures for CBDCs. A hierarchical tree structure that blends in with the current financial institutions encircles the central bank and regulatory organizations. On the other hand, a decentralized system involving commercial banks and outside operators uses blockchain to overcome scalability issues and broaden the range of accepted payment methods. Utilizing two networks improves security and usefulness.

End-users and transactions are included in the user layer, which is essential to the framework. This layer supports the verification and processing within the network layer and serves as the focus of regulatory examination and data generation. Cash transfers, CBDC deposits, withdrawals, and a variety of payment transactions are all included in this layer's activities (Han et al., 2019). By encasing intricate procedures and rules in the top layers, user experiences are streamlined. In essence, the framework integrates user, network, and regulatory components holistically, opening the door for efficient CBDC deployment and administration in the modern financial environment.

7.1 Need for a Balance Between User-Centricity, Legal Compliance, and Technological Innovation

The aforementioned analysis discusses the user-centric financial ecosystem concept, its alignment with Web 3 technologies, and the integration of CBDCs. While it emphasizes advantages like user empowerment and the promise of blockchain for financial inclusion and cross-border transactions, it's critical to solve legislative barriers, technical viability, user education, security, and interdisciplinary collaboration. The focus on user privacy is consistent with the discussion that is now taking place around data protection, and the potential for CBDCs to run on distributed ledgers is consistent with blockchain's role in financial inclusion. However, in order for implementation to be successful, legislative hurdles and technical difficulties must be resolved, along with user awareness. It will be crucial to strike a balance between user-centricity, legal compliance, and technological innovation in order to build a revolutionary financial ecosystem.

8. KEY FINDINGS AND RESEARCH GAP

According to the literature, the implementation of CBDC does not inevitably result in a credit crunch or a serious risk to the stability of the financial system. Potential risks related to the deployment of CBDC can be reduced with the right design decisions and policy initiatives. According to research, CBDC design elements are key in defining the scope of global spillovers and their effect on monetary policy autonomy in other economies. Future research should focus on figuring out the ideal design elements that strike a compromise between the advantages of CBDC and the stability of the financial system.

Multiple goals can be accomplished at once, but there are trade-offs and difficulties involved. When adopting CBDC, authorities must emphasize price stability, economic efficiency, and financial stability, as shown by the CBDC Trilemma. One important field of research involves investigating the best trade-offs and policy options to accomplish desired goals while minimizing negative consequences for financial stability.

However, there are still research gaps that need to be filled, even though the evaluated papers offer insightful information about how CBDC affects financial stability. To fully comprehend the unique CBDC design components that guarantee financial stability in both domestic and international contexts, more research is required. Additionally, investigating the best course of action, potential risks, and mitigation strategies while using CBDC would help close the current research gap.

Moreover, the subject of financial stability is given a fresh perspective by the incorporation of Web 3 principles and technology into CBDCs. It is possible to develop CBDC systems that prioritize stability while utilizing the benefits of Web 3 by fusing the decentralization, transparency, and user ownership of data concepts from Web 3 with the potential advantages of CBDCs. According to the literature, sensible design choices and policy measures can reduce the hazards of CBDC adoption.

9. CONCLUSION

Theoretical viewpoints on central bank digital currencies (CBDCs) and their effects on financial stability offer insightful information on the potential effects of CBDC adoption. By enabling central banks to engage in major intermediation and deposit competition with private financial intermediaries, the advent of CBDCs represents a crucial turning point in the history of money and banking. However, how CBDCs are developed and implemented will greatly influence how they affect financial stability.

According to the examination of how CBDC deployment affects equilibrium credit allocation and the price system, neither a credit crunch nor a threat to financial stability are certain to result from the use of CBDCs. Design choices and policy actions that are effective can reduce risks and guarantee a seamless transition.

Studies have shown the CBDC Trilemma, which underlines the difficulties and trade-offs central banks must make while implementing CBDCs. It takes careful thought and prioritization to achieve numerous objectives, such as maintaining price stability, economic effectiveness, and financial stability. To guarantee the general stability of the financial system, policymakers must carefully balance these goals.

Another important factor to take into account is how CBDCs may affect other countries. Implementing the CBDC may strengthen international ties and enhance cross-national shock waves. The characteristics of CBDCs' designs are key in deciding the scope of these effects and how they will affect the world's monetary system. Therefore, to successfully manage CBDCs and preserve stability in the global financial system, international coordination and collaboration are crucial.

Additionally, it is important to carefully evaluate how CBDCs may affect the availability of credit and financial stability. The adoption of the CBDC may result in less readily available bank lending, a rise in nominal interest rates, and possibly increased bank panic. However, financial stability can be preserved while enhancing loan availability and lowering interest rates with the proper power and processes in place, such as the central bank's ability to lend banks all CBDC deposits.

The consequences of CBDCs for welfare and equilibrium allocation were also clarified by the theoretical viewpoints. Financial inclusion, the relocation of bank deposits, and bank funding costs are trade-offs that policymakers must balance. CBDCs should be designed with specific goals in mind, taking into account elements like financial frictions and the need for productive projects.

In conclusion, despite the literature's insightful descriptions of how CBDCs affect financial stability, there are still unresolved research questions. Future studies should concentrate on determining the ideal structural components and policy alternatives that strike a compromise between CBDCs' benefits and the stability of the financial system. Additionally, addressing the current research gap and ensuring a seamless and stable transition to a financial environment powered by CBDCs will benefit from research into the optimum course of action, potential risks, and mitigation techniques while employing CBDCs.

Furthermore, future research can focus on how CBDCs can be made to adhere to the principles of Web 3 by embracing Web 3 ideas like decentralization, transparency, and user-centric control over data. By encouraging a more robust, open, and user-driven financial ecosystem, the adoption of Web 3 concepts in CBDC design and implementation can influence the financial industry. To achieve the desired results, it is essential to carefully weigh the trade-offs and difficulties associated with integrating Web 3 with CBDCs.

REFERENCES

Ahmed, K. A., Saraya, S. F., Wanis, J. F., & Ali-Eldin, A. M. (2023). A Blockchain Self-Sovereign Identity for Open Banking Secured by the Customer's Banking Cards. *Future Internet*, *15*(6), 208. doi:10.3390/fi15060208

Auer, R., & Boehme, R. (2020). The technology of retail central bank digital currency. *BIS Quarterly Review*. https://www.bis.org/publ/qtrpdf/r_qt2003j.htm

Bacchetta, P., & Perazzi, E. (2021). CBDC as Imperfect Substitute for Bank Deposits: A Macroeconomic Perspective. *Swiss Finance Institute Research Paper*, (21-81).

Bindseil, U. (2019). Central bank digital currency: Financial system implications and control. *International Journal of Political Economy*, *48*(4), 303–335. doi:10.1080/08911916.2019.1693160

Brunnermeier, M. K., & Niepelt, D. (2019). On the equivalence of private and public money. *Journal of Monetary Economics*, *106*, 27–41. doi:10.1016/j.jmoneco.2019.07.004

Committee on Payments and Market Infrastructures. (2018, March). *Central bank digital currencies. Bank for International Settlements*. BIS. https://www.bis.org/cpmi/publ/d174.pdf

Coulter, K. A. (2023). A Review of the Proposed Bank of England's "Retail" Central Bank Digital Currency (CBDC) as a Cryptocurrency Competitor. *Fintech, Pandemic, and the Financial System: Challenges and Opportunities*, 201-221.

El Attar, A., & ChaIoui, C. (2023). Central Bank Digital Money (CBDC): A Literature Review. *Dossiers de Recherches en Économie et Gestion, 11*(01), 133–147.

Fernández-Villaverde, J., Sanches, D., Schilling, L., & Uhlig, H. (2020). Central Bank Digital Currency: Central Banking For All? (*Working Paper No. 26753*). National Bureau of Economic Research. doi:10.3386/w26753

Ferrari, M. M., Mehl, A., & Stracca, L. (2020). Central bank digital currency in an open economy. European Central Bank (*Working Paper Series No. 2505*). https://www.ecb.europa.eu/pub/pdf/scpwps/ecb.wp2488~fede33ca65.en.pdf

Gupta, S., Pandey, D. K., El Ammari, A., & Sahu, G. P. (2023). Do perceived risks and benefits impact trust and willingness to adopt CBDCs? *Research in International Business and Finance, 66*, 101993. doi:10.1016/j.ribaf.2023.101993

Han, J., Kim, J., Youn, A., Lee, J., Chun, Y., Woo, J., & Hong, J. W. K. (2021, September). Cos-CBDC: Design and Implementation of CBDC on Cosmos Blockchain. In *2021 22nd Asia-Pacific Network Operations and Management Symposium (APNOMS)* (pp. 303-308). IEEE.

Han, X., Yuan, Y., & Wang, F. Y. (2019, November). A blockchain-based framework for central bank digital currency. In *2019 IEEE International conference on service operations and logistics, and informatics (SOLI)* (pp. 263-268). IEEE. 10.1109/SOLI48380.2019.8955032

Homoliak, I., Perešíni, M., Holop, P., Handzuš, J., & Casino, F. (2023). CBDC-AquaSphere: Interoperable Central Bank Digital Currency Built on Trusted Computing and Blockchain. arXiv preprint arXiv:2305.16893.

Jabbar, A., Geebren, A., Hussain, Z., Dani, S., & Ul-Durar, S. (2023). Investigating individual privacy within CBDC: A privacy calculus perspective. *Research in International Business and Finance, 64*, 101826. doi:10.1016/j.ribaf.2022.101826

Kaur, G., & KrishnaKumar, A. (2023). Technologies Behind Crypto-Based Decentralized Finance. In *Building Secure Business Models Through Blockchain Technology: Tactics, Methods, Limitations, and Performance* (pp. 149-166). IGI Global.

Kaur, G., & Vishwakarma, D. K. (2023). Digital, Programmable Euro: From Paper to Programmable Money. In Exploring the Dark Side of FinTech and Implications of Monetary Policy (pp. 187-206). IGI Global.

Keister, T., & Sanches, D. (2023). Should central banks issue digital currency? *The Review of Economic Studies, 90*(1), 404–431. doi:10.1093/restud/rdac017

Kiff, M. J., Alwazir, J., Davidovic, S., Farias, A., Khan, M. A., Khiaonarong, M. T., & Zhou, P. (2020). *A survey of research on retail central bank digital currency.*

Kim, Y. S., & Kwon, O. (2023). Central bank digital currency, credit supply, and financial stability. *Journal of Money, Credit and Banking*, *55*(1), 297–321. doi:10.1111/jmcb.12913

Kurian, A. (2023). *The Case for Harmonising Central Bank Digital Currencies for Cross-Border Transactions.*

Lee, D. K. C., Yan, L., & Wang, Y. (2021). A global perspective on central bank digital currency. *China Economic Journal*, *14*(1), 52–66. doi:10.1080/17538963.2020.1870279

Liu, Y., Lu, Q., Zhu, L., Paik, H. Y., & Staples, M. (2023). A systematic literature review on blockchain governance. *Journal of Systems and Software*, *197*, 111576. doi:10.1016/j.jss.2022.111576

Lukonga, I. (2023). *Monetary Policy Implications Central Bank Digital Currencies: Perspectives on Jurisdictions with Conventional and Islamic Banking Systems.*

Moiso, C., & Minerva, R. (2012, October). Towards a user-centric personal data ecosystem the role of the bank of individuals' data. In *2012 16th International conference on intelligence in next generation networks* (pp. 202-209). IEEE.

Ozili, P. K. (2023). eNaira central bank digital currency (CBDC) for financial inclusion in Nigeria. In Digital Economy, Energy and Sustainability: Opportunities and Challenges (pp. 41-54). Cham: Springer International Publishing.

Ray, P. P. (2023). Web3: A comprehensive review on background, technologies, applications, zero-trust architectures, challenges and future directions. *Internet of Things and Cyber-Physical Systems.*

Ren, K., Ho, N. M., Loghin, D., Nguyen, T. T., Ooi, B. C., Ta, Q. T., & Zhu, F. (2023). Interoperability in Blockchain: A Survey. *IEEE Transactions on Knowledge and Data Engineering*, 1–20. doi:10.1109/TKDE.2023.3275220

Samuele, B., & Rosa, C. (2023). The Interpretation of CBDC Within An Endogenous Money Framework. *Research in International Business and Finance*, *65*, 101970. doi:10.1016/j.ribaf.2023.101970

Sanchez-Roger, M., & Puyol-Antón, E. (2021). Digital bank runs: A deep neural network approach. *Sustainability*, *13*(3), 1513. doi:10.3390u13031513

Schilling, L., Fernández-Villaverde, J., & Uhlig, H. (2020). Central Bank Digital Currency: When Price and Bank Stability Collide. (*NBER Working Paper No. 202*). https://www.sas.upenn.edu/~jesusfv/CBDC_Nominal.pdf

Simran, S., & Adam, R. (2023). Legal Analysis Of Cbdc's Role As A Digital Payment Instrument Regulatory System In Indonesia. *Asian Journal of Management. Entrepreneurship and Social Science*, *3*(03), 270–286.

Taherdoost, H. (2023). Smart Contracts in Blockchain Technology: A Critical Review. *Information (Basel)*, *14*(2), 117. doi:10.3390/info14020117

Takaragi, K., & Kubota, T. (2023). A Proposal for Enhancing the Security and Privacy of Digital Currencies. In Government Response to Disruptive Innovation: Perspectives and Examinations (pp. 183-211). IGI Global. doi:10.4018/978-1-6684-6429-8.ch010

Tian, S., Zhao, B., & Olivares, R. O. (2023). Cybersecurity risks and central banks' sentiment on central bank digital currency: Evidence from global cyberattacks. *Finance Research Letters*, *53*, 103609. doi:10.1016/j.frl.2022.103609

van der Linden, R. W., & Łasak, P. (2023). The Digitalization of Cross-Border Payment Systems and the Introduction of the CBDC. In *Financial Interdependence, Digitalization and Technological Rivalries: Perspectives on Future Cooperation and Integration in Sino-American Financial Systems* (pp. 75–92). Springer Nature Switzerland. doi:10.1007/978-3-031-27845-7_7

Wan, S., Lin, H., Gan, W., Chen, J., & Yu, P. S. (2023). Web 3: The Next Internet Revolution. arXiv preprint arXiv:2304.06111.

Wang, Z. (2023). Money Laundering and the Privacy Design of Central Bank Digital Currency. *Review of Economic Dynamics*. doi:10.1016/j.red.2023.06.004

Ward, O., & Rochemont, S. (2019). Understanding central bank digital currencies (CBDC). *Institute and Faculty of Actuaries*, 1-52.

Wilmer, W. (2023). Different designs of CBDC, the likelihood of bank disintermediation and the impact on monetary policy: a literary review.

Chapter 23
Web 3 Challenges:
A Systemic Analysis

Alexandra Overgaag
Thrilld Labs, Italy

ABSTRACT

This chapter highlights the need for a systemic, multi-disciplinary approach to understanding Web3's development. By disaggregating Web3 into interrelated networks of actors that hold distinct interests and beliefs, this chapter aims to describe and map Web3 to advance a more systemic understanding of its order and functioning. While presenting Web3 as a black box, the work underscores the importance of considering both the inherent nature of the technology itself and the broader societal context in which it operates and interacts with. Employing a Science, Technology, and Society lens, the work combines industry insights with a holistic approach to conceptualize the values, interests, and risks associated with Web3. The research holds that systemic challenges flow from Web3's inherent socio-technical and early-stage nature, and that its development is neither solely technologically determined nor entirely reliant on social actors. Instead, Web3's trajectory results from a complex interplay of its technological nature, societal values, stakeholder interests, and external (f)actors.

INTRODUCTION

We are witnessing the *coming into being* of Web 3, both in the technological realm and far beyond. Web 3 establishes a distributed network using blockchain and cryptocurrencies (Wan, et al., 2023), hereby representing a paradigm shift (Sadowski & Beegle, 2023) in the trust properties of technology, relationships, and societies at large by shifting power away from centralized intermediaries towards decentralized networks. Blockchain technology is able to fundamentally transform wealth transmission and the boundaries of organizations (Freeman et al., 2020), and states, hereby challenging existing power structures by actively questioning their future role and reason for existence. Moreover, the ongoing shift that Web 3 brings about will profoundly transform the relationships among users and platforms, of forces and relations of production, and of the global economy as a whole (Wan et al., 2023). Indeed,

DOI: 10.4018/978-1-6684-9919-1.ch023

Copyright © 2023, IGI Global. Copying or distributing in print or electronic forms without written permission of IGI Global is prohibited.

developers and early adopters argue that Web3 has the potential to reorganize and democratize how value is distributed to bring about a fairer world (Adams et al., 2020). In contrast, skeptics argue that Web 3 is characterized by mythology and hype which clouds judgment and that the sector ultimately relies on idealized values embedded in its cultural and technical architecture (Chohan, 2022). Surely, Web 3 is actively shaped by various social actors and networks that bring about their own interests and beliefs. Therefore, it is necessary to technically, practically, and more broadly take an overview of the actors and forces shaping Web 3.

In this chapter, it is argued that understanding the trajectory of Web 3 is crucial for grasping its opportunities and challenges. Hereto, the work proposes a systemic, multi-disciplinary approach to grasp Web 3's development. By dissecting Web 3 into interconnected networks, the work aims to map its functioning and order, fostering a holistic understanding. Acknowledging Web 3's paradoxical nature as a black box, the work argues that analyzing Web 3's inherent nature and the broader societal context are both key to fostering an understanding of the trajectory of the space. Employing a Science, Technology, and Society (STS) lens, the work combines industry insights with a comprehensive analysis to conceptualize Web 3's values, interests, and risks to ultimately highlight various challenges flowing from external sources, as well as inherent challenges arising from Web 3's socio-technical and early-stage nature. The ambition of this work is not to advance the theory of socio-technical systems or to provide a conclusive discussion on the nature of Web 3, blockchain, and their various underlying assets. Nor is it a goal to provide an exhaustive discussion on the various (systemic) challenges Web 3 is coping with. Instead, the work is meant to help provide new insights into Web 3 as an emerging socio-technical construct and may allow researchers and (aspiring) industry professionals to better understand the Web 3 ecosystem and its very development.

This chapter's analysis is based on a comprehensive study of Web 3, aiming to delve beyond its surface and uncover its underlying foundation. This approach is motivated by a noticeable gap in the academic literature. As posed by Nabben (Nabben, 2023), few analytical frameworks exist to address the complex nature of Web 3, leading to deficiencies in our understanding of Web 3 as a bound-breaking ecosystem. To fill this gap, this chapter adopts the theoretical lens of STS to provide an analytical framework for understanding the emerging field of Web 3. Indeed, one of the challenges in comprehending Web3 lies in the need for more clarity regarding the distinctions between various technologies, their interrelationships, their alignment with societal visions and the beliefs of various actors, and their role within the ever-evolving ecosystem that is fundamentally characterized by a range of diverging interests. Indeed, it is not always clear how Web 3, blockchain, and cryptocurrency assets are different, what they mean, how they relate to each other, and how they plug into tightly held social visions (Sadowski & Beegle, 2023) expressed and kept by different industry stakeholders. Besides, still in its nascent stage, this ecosystem seems to sometimes overlook the systemic risks and challenges that hinder mass adoption. The misalignment between ambitions and outcomes arguably contributes to skepticism towards Web 3 from external actors. A sense of uncertainty, characterized by the diffusion of Web 3, presents a critical juncture for comprehending how the space navigates its aspirations and apprehensions regarding the future.

This work seeks to go beyond the surface of Web 3 in order to gain a systemic understanding of the ecosystem's underlying foundation. The methodology and observations stem from independent research on Web 3, from experience working within a Web 3 company (which has not endorsed or supported this article), and from founding a company that by its nature seeks to serve key stakeholders in the Web 3 ecosystem with regard to their business and funding efforts. It must be noted that this chapter does not advocate for any specific legal framework or any policy guideline whatsoever. Instead, it merely aims to express the notion that achieving widespread adoption of Web 3 may necessitate addressing the systemic challenges mentioned in this work, which is nonetheless a non-exhaustive discussion. It must be reckoned that the ultimate approach taken to tackle systemic challenges will inevitably depend on numerous variables and the interests and normative assumptions of the diverse stakeholders involved. While the theoretical framework serves as a foundation for understanding the development of Web 3, it explicitly does not encompass all aspects of Web 3 as an ecosystem. Future research could expand upon the notions presented in this work by integrating insights from other relevant theories or perspectives. As Web 3 continues to develop, it is evident that a complex merge of technological advancements, societal responses, economic incentives, regulatory interventions, and new systemic challenges will continue to shape and interact with Web 3's very trajectory. Finally, in the context of this chapter the words 'ecosystem' and 'system' will be used interchangeably, whilst 'blockchain' may be read as falling within the scope of the chapters' definition of Web 3 (unless indicated otherwise). The word 'construct' in this chapter indicates a more narrow, internal, vision of Web3 as a socio-technical system that is argued lies in the Web3 ecosystem's inner core.

Related Work

To date, scholarly investigations of the Web 3 ecosystem have often adopted either a social or technical standpoint (Brennecke et al., 2022), with limited attention given to comprehensive examinations of the broader Web 3 ecosystem encompassing blockchain technology and digital assets. Moreover, studies have often approached these subjects from isolated disciplinary perspectives or as case studies. Some have considered systemic risks flowing from the cryptocurrency markets (Fracassi & Di Maggio, 2022) and have regarded the implications of black swan event, including the fall of FTX (a centralized cryptocurrency exchange) and that of Terra/LUNA (an algorithmic stablecoin protocol) (Jalan & Matkovskyy, 2023). Other notable contributions to the field include work by Brennecke et al. (Brennecke, et al., 2022) providing a holistic ecosystem perspective diving into the intricate human-machine interactions within the Ethereum ecosystem and hereby providing a comprehensive analysis of said ecosystem. Similarly, Chow-White et al. have taken a social constructivist approach (Chow-White, et al., 2020), examining various technological controversies surrounding blockchain to identify the discourses, beliefs, and persuasive arguments that shape its interpretation and potential applications. Specifically exploring blockchain adoption through the lens of actor-network theory (ANT), Zein and Twinomurinzi (Zein & Twinomurinzi, 2022) have highlighted the complex socio-technical dynamics at play in introducing blockchain networks in government. A distinct perspective was presented in the work by Sadowski and Beegle (Sadowski & Beegle, 2023) who argued that Web 3, with its defining concepts, conflicts, and interests, should be regarded as a case study of innovation within the dominant model of Silicon Valley venture capitalism. For those further interested in the narrative of blockchain as a response to undemocratic forces, the analysis conducted by Bodo and Giannopoulou (Bodo & Giannopoulou, 2020) offers valuable insights. They argue that the genesis of blockchain technology cannot be solely attributed to the global financial crisis of 2008. Rather, the crisis of governance within Web 2 also played a role in popularizing blockchain technologies. This latter perspective highlights the multifaceted factors contributing to the mainstreaming of blockchain, and to an extent, Web 3 as an overarching umbrella definition. The works mentioned above collectively contribute to a deeper understanding of Web 3 as a complex and evolving phenomenon.

Web 3 as a Black Box

Web 3 exists as a nascent and emerging field of technological and institutional innovation. While Web 3 sounds like a buzzword (Wan et al., 2023) and arguably can be defined in various ways, the dominant narrative and contemporary literature appear to have readily decided upon its nature. Sadowski & Beegle, 2023 have described a rather common evolutionary view of Web 3, noting the often repeated origin story — Web as an *'algebraic sum of Web1 and Web2'*. In this evolutionary view, Web 3 is the next phase of the internet in which users generate content, and said content only belongs to the user himself or herself (Wan et al., 2023). Taking a more systemic approach, Web 3 may also serve as an umbrella term bringing together a decentralized ecosystem of technology infrastructures based on blockchain networks that are interoperable, that work alongside digital assets, and that are free of traditionally trusted third parties such as businesses, governmental institutions, and financial intermediaries (Wan et al., 2023). If this view turns out accurate, Web 3 may prove to be able to organize society in the broadest possible way. Looking more in detail, Web 3 can indeed be considered as bringing together multiple layers of technological applications, infrastructural protocols, competing stakeholders, and ideological commitments. At the surface level, Web 3 comprises various applications such as cryptocurrencies, non-fungible tokens (NFTs), and front-end interfaces. Supporting these applications are protocols encompassing blockchain architectures alongside smart contracts, which can differ in nature and their application (Dempsey et al., 2022). Simply put, a blockchain is a distributed digital ledger of cryptographically signed transactions that are grouped into blocks (Yaga et al., 2018) which records transactions and is open for everyone to see. Arguably, *the* blockchain does not exist since there are several different types of blockchains (Noto La Diega & Stacey, 2020), whilst supplementary and complementary technologies and solutions are launched on a constant basis. Smart contracts are self-enforcing agreements on-chain whose execution enforces the terms of the contract (Tonelli et al., 2023).

It is crucial to stress that the technical and institutional models of Web 3 are still being conceptualized and developed (Nabben, 2023). In that state of diffusion, the world of Web 3 is both untouchable and real since it relies not only on code, software, and hardware, but also invokes deep emotional resonance in its stakeholders (Chohan, 2022). The commitments to heartfelt values are arguably fundamental to Web 3, with decentralization as the core ideology that manifests (Bodo and Giannopoulou, 2019) in the various dynamics of the system. It has been argued that Web 3 originates from anti-establishment ideals and aims to provide the prefigurative means to build new structures for decentralized self-governance from within the prevailing power structures of society (Nabben, 2023) through cryptographically verifiable ownership in digital domains and beyond, indicating a global ambition. Indeed, the rise of Web 3 and the adoption of cryptocurrencies have increased dramatically (Wan et al., 2023) over the last few years, whilst Web 3's core narratives acquired a somewhat mainstream area of notoriety, with ever-increasing institutional interests, wide-ranging media coverage (Chohan, 2022), and comprehensive (legal) debates on Web 3's nature and its underlying assets' taxonomy[1]. This short discussion clearly indicates that Web 3's definition, development, and diffusion are all still solidifying (Adams et al., 2020) and with Web 3 still in its early stages (Wan et al., 2023), entrepreneurs, investors, community members, regulators, and other groups all play substantial roles in determining its course.

For this chapter, 'Web 3' can be considered a collection of technologies, applications, and protocols that go alongside normative concepts and contestations of various stakeholders, actors, and networks that carry their own interests and preferred operations. More simply, Web 3 can be considered an ecosystem formed through its technological nature, societal values, stakeholder interests, and other interactions with external (f)actors. For this chapter, the term 'ecosystem' refers to the interconnected network of technologies, platforms, applications, and stakeholders that collectively form, and are involved with, Web 3. As such, the ecosystem encompasses a wider network of parties that influence how value is created and captured (Freeman et al., 2020). Technocratic solutions often omit the complexity of human society and obfuscate the role of people in building and maintaining digital infrastructure rather than acknowledging the social inputs that shape and maintain technological interventions (Nabben, 2023). In Web 3, the social element is generally acknowledged, but less is known about the practical functioning of the ecosystem (Nabben, 2023) even though an increasing number of actors and organizations throughout entire economies and societies get into contact with Web 3. Indeed, not only did Web 3 capture the imagination of a diverse group of social actors ranging from crypto-anarchist software geeks, via investors, to governments (Bodó and Giannopoulou, 2019), Web 3 also presents a new market for existing big tech companies (Nabben, 2023) and VC (venture capital) and other commercial entities that seek to capture new value. The growing collaboration amongst companies, users, investors, and other actors is evolving into a multilateral network (Brennecke et al., 2022) between all the parties engaged with Web 3. This is one reason why one may argue that to truly understand Web 3, it is necessary to uncover the human interactions within the ecosystem.

However, especially for outsiders the Web 3 ecosystem can appear to be a black box. A black box refers to a complex system or process whose internal workings are unknown or not transparent to the observer (Bijker et al., 2012). It is characterized by a focus on the inputs and outputs of the system, without understanding the internal mechanisms or logic. Black boxes are not necessarily restricted to physical artifacts or technologies; instead, black boxes consist of knowledge that is accepted and used regularly as a matter of fact (Besel, 2011). Crucially for the nature of Web 3, creating a black box does not require consensus (Zein & Twinomurinzi, 2022). If Web 3 is considered a black box, this indicates a contrast with the very ideology and features of Web 3 and blockchain, respectively, particularly as regards the notion of trust, transparency, and consensus embodied in the stack's underlying ideology. The 'microstruggles' discussed later in this chapter will seek to highlight that there is arguably a tension between the nature of decentralization, as prescribed by Web 3's ideology, and the practical forms in which the centralisation of power manifests itself in and around the Web 3 ecosystem. This chapter argues that said ambiguity may result in systemic challenges that undermine the potential for the sustainable long-term trajectory of the sector.

To start investigating the complex interplay between Web 3 and society, the tradition of Science and Technology Studies (STS) offers[2] a source of appropriate concepts and frameworks with which to understand Web 3. The following section will explore and apply several branches from the field of STS, ultimately seeking to offer a new lens via which systemic challenges Web 3 faces may be regarded.

Theoretical Framework

The perspectives offered by STS provide a valuable lens for investigating technology, including Web 3, thanks to its inherent interdisciplinary and holistic nature (Pinch & Bijker, 1984). STS acknowledges that technology is not a standalone entity but is deeply intertwined with social, cultural, political, and economic contexts (Pinch & Bijker, 1984). STS has splintered into various approaches (Redshaw, 2018), all focusing on how different actors are involved in constructing new technologies. The STS lens recognizes that technology does not solely determine societal outcomes, but rather, its development and impact are shaped by complex interactions between different actors and broader social structures and networks. Such constructive processes, STS posits, are not confined to engineers, yet rather involve a variety of actors (Redshaw, 2018).

Simply put, actors influence the meanings attached to technology and how it is designed and developed. More specifically, the approach (Pinch & Bijker, 1987; Mackenzie & Wajcman, 1999) highlights that humans (and sometimes non-human actors) significantly influence the design, development, and social meanings of innovation as technologies are linked directly to culture, values, and socially accepted practices (Adams et al., 2020). Interestingly, these meanings are not static. Instead, the technologies diffuse and solidify over time. The ends pursued by technology are thus constructed through and by the interactions that different social groups develop around new technologies (Feenberg, 1992; Lane, 2016), and these interactions generate different and diverging interpretations of the meaning of a technology (Chow-White et al., 2020), ultimately influencing its very development. It is worth looking more in detail at several different branches of STS because that allows for a more holistic understanding of the complex relationships between technology and society and enables one to draw a more systemic analysis of the nature of Web 3 hereafter.

The Social Construction of Technology (SCOT) branch of STS goes beyond discussing how social conditions influence technology by emphasizing how the interactions around technology influence social systems (Pinch & Bijker, 1984). More profoundly, the branch provides a valuable means of interpreting the role played by the interests and beliefs of different social groups that all have a stake in technology development and thus determine the directions in which technologies are developed (Redshaw, 2018). Simply put, the interactions and negotiations amongst relevant social groups thus influence the design, features, and direction of technological development. In this way, technology and society continuously shape one another (Pinch & Bijker, 1984). Bijker held that the advancement of technology is largely influenced by challenges that arise from existing technologies and the decision-making process involved in finding solutions to these challenges. Crucially, this observation emphasizes that the identification of problems and corresponding solutions is not solely within the domain of engineers, but involves diverse social groups who contribute their own interpretations and meanings to a given technology (Redshaw, 2018; Bijker et al., 2012).

Interestingly, the concept of 'interpretative flexibility' (Pinch & Bijker, 1984) accounts for the range of meanings that social groups attach to technologies, implying that different social groups, stakeholders, or users may perceive and understand a technology differently based on their own values, interests, and experiences. These interpretations then shape the trajectory of technological development and subsequently influence how technology is implemented and used. Crucially, SCOT accounts for the existence of many variants of a new technology that emerge and co-exist, implying that the interpretations associated with the technology and its perceived significance may inherently vary among different individuals or groups at a specific moment in time. Yet over time, the interpretative flexibility of technology diminishes. Indeed, SCOT recognizes that technologies go through phases of 'closure' and 'stabilization' during the development process. At some point, a consensus among the different relevant social groups about the dominant meaning of technology emerges and the technology's 'pluralism' decreases, after which the technology becomes standardized and established within society (Bijker, 1995).

While SCOT is highly descriptive and focuses on analyzing social processes and interpretative flexibility in the construction and consolidation of technology in order to understand how technology evolves through social negotiations and interpretations, the critical constructivist model (Feenberg 1999; 2002) builds upon SCOT whilst introducing a narrative of ideology. Indeed, Feenberg critically examines the ideological assumptions and power dynamics deeply ingrained in technology. It has been noted that not all social groups possess the ability to exert influence over the design process. This capacity is typically limited to those who can mobilize substantial resources, and their impact on technological advancements frequently reinforces the conditions that uphold their authoritative position (Redshaw, 2018). Within the context of capitalist systems, it is argued that a specific set of norms pertaining to technology have emerged, prioritizing imperatives of control and efficiency in the process of technical development (Feenberg, 1999). The capacity for technology to structure human action thus affords considerable power to those that govern its design and development, guiding technological development to reproduce structures of capitalism and hereby arguably perpetuating existing power asymmetries. Interestingly, Feenberg (Feenberg, 1999) argues that technology has the potential to undergo a process of 'democratization' through the active involvement of social groups, allowing for the inclusion of marginalized voices, ultimately fostering social deliberation. Significantly, democratic intervention goes alongside different phenomena including the emergence of 'controversies'. These controversies ignite debates and, in certain instances, lead to collective action and public engagement in the design process, enabling dialogue between technology developers and communities. Such controversies allow social groups to challenge dominant ideologies, reshape technological systems, and influence technological development. Ultimately, the interventions in a technology's design could lead to the effective resistance of said groups against priorly dominating groups towards the final establishment of a technology framework in which social and ethical considerations, rather than capitalist imperatives (Feenberg, 1999), inform the dominant narrative and underlying technical nature. Hence, adapting technologies to serve new purposes and rationales that represent the interests of newly mobilized groups thus challenges priorly dominant narratives. Consequently, power dynamics shift between human actors, hereby impacting technological development.

Another perspective on social power within STS focuses on the activities of a broader range of actors constantly trying to expand their networks. Fundamentally, this branch treats the technical and the social as inseparable by offering an extensive theoretical framework. Indeed, actor-network theory (ANT) allows for the renegotiation of the boundaries between the technical and the social, and between the human and the non-human, hereby ultimately merging society and technology (Latour, 1992; 1999; 2005). Highlighting that human and non-human actors engage in activities that maintain and expand networks, the theory emphasizes the role of said non-human actors — often technology itself — in reproducing narratives of power (Redshaw, 2018). While it is not the intention of this work to exhaustively discuss ANT, in the context of this chapter it is crucial to expand on the significance of human and non-human actors, such as machines, in shaping technical development. In the realm of digital technologies, actors thus include people, organizations, software, computers, communications hardware, and infrastructure standards (Zein & Twinomurinzi, 2022). According to the concept of 'delegation' (Latour, 1992) which is inherent to ANT, actors can delegate actions or decision-making authority to other actors or non-human actors, such as technologies. This delegation allows for the distribution of agency and responsibility. In this context, non-human actors are entrusted with carrying out specific actions. According to ANT, technologies then structure human action by executing 'predefined programs' (Latour, 2005) that dictate specific values, responsibilities, and behavioral patterns. Whilst these programs are delegated to technologies through prior interactions, the notion does imply a recalibration of the rationales behind the behavior and functioning of the technology. Moreover, since ANT does not distinguish between micro (e.g., individuals) and macro actors (e.g., organizations) but rather acknowledges the inherently unstable nature of actors, ANT allows for a flexible consideration of a socio-technical *network* as a single actor or as a group of individual actors (Zein & Twinomurinzi, 2022). Actors within the network form connections, establish relationships and engage in various practices to maintain and transform the network, allowing for a hyper-adaptable framework of human and non-human actors. Such notion will turn out to be an interesting perspective for the examination of Web 3 as an ecosystem hereafter.

By applying an STS lens to Web 3 that borrows concepts from all the three branches of STS discussed above, one can more accurately analyze the intricate relationships between Web 3, its development, and the societal contexts in which it operates. This systemic perspective reveals how social and technical systems mutually shape and influence one another within the Web 3 ecosystem. By critically and constructively opening the 'black box' of Web 3, the actors, power dynamics, governance structures, networks, and interests that shape the functioning and outcomes of Web 3 technologies may be uncovered. Importantly, the systemic approach developed in this chapter considers both human and non-human entities as active actors within networks (ANT), which enables a nuanced understanding of how various social groups shape Web 3 (SCOT) and thus provides insights as to how Web 3 potentially reflects social values and power structures (critical constructivism). Ultimately, the aim is to shed light on the systemic challenges that arise from within the ecosystem and unveil the contradictions inherent in Web 3's aspirations and operational realities.

Web 3 as a Socio-Technological Construct

Before providing an in-depth analysis of Web 3 via the lens of STS and describing the technical and social systems that comprise the core of Web 3, it is imperative to establish a definition of Web 3 as employed in this particular chapter. This chapter poses that Web 3 as a concept is still open to interpretative flexibility. This is particularly crucial due to the contention that Web 3 remains susceptible to varying interpretations, thereby necessitating a more flexible approach. As highlighted in Figure 1, it can be argued that at its core, Web 3 is a socio-technical construct. In this notion, social and technical systems influence one another alongside the general lines as set out in the next sections.

Beyond the core construct, Web 3 also serves as an umbrella term in this chapter, bringing blockchain, digital assets[3], cryptocurrencies, and (decentralized) applications under its wings[4]. To grasp the nature of Web 3 and open up its black box, it is preliminary to comprehend the underpinnings of blockchain, so often mentioned as the underlying technological foundation of Web 3. 'Blockchain' — also a broad signifier without a standard definition — can be considered as decentralized technology, which smart contracts may underpin (Chow-White et al., 2020). Blockchain started surfacing in the academic and public discourse in mid-2014 (Yli-Huumo et al., 2016), whilst the term 'distributed ledger technologies' (yet another umbrella term encompassing technologies including public and private blockchain systems) has been used since 2009 with the emergence of Bitcoin. With blockchain technology, value is replicated in a network using protocols that validate, confirm, and control transactions through the network. These protocols offer a peer-to-peer transfer of value using algorithmic trust compared with the classical typology of trust between human agents (Zein & Twinomurinzi, 2022). An essential characteristic of blockchain is its distributed governance, where no single entity has complete control over the network. Instead, a consensus between the different groups has to be reached using, indeed, consensus algorithms. Consensus is what enables the nodes in a distributed peer-to-peer network to work together without having to know or trust each other (Noto La Diega & Stacey, 2020). Consequently, blockchain-based services are maintained not by a central authority but by a community of stakeholders, such as miners, developers, and other community members (Islam & Mäntymäki, 2019). It may be argued that

Figure 1. The Web 3 ecosystem

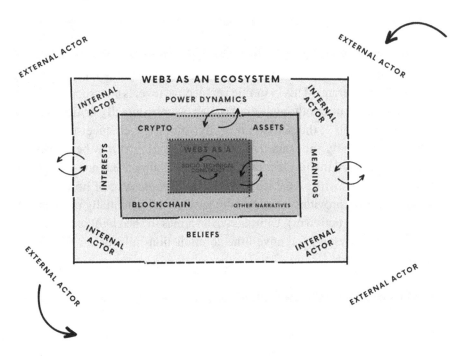

blockchain technology is an example of a *social technology,* which indicates technological ways to communicate, cooperate, compromise, and make consensus with other people (Flink, 2021). Looking at Web 3 as a socio-technological construct that incorporates blockchain technology, this section poses that the *technical system* of Web 3 is comprised of a physical and digital dimension, which consists mainly of the underlying (technical) infrastructure, with software, hardware and other blockchain-related concepts such as mining nodes and computational processes, front-end and back-end interactions, consensus mechanisms and smart contracts. On the other hand, the *social system* of Web 3's core construct comprises an internal group of participants that work on the actual development of Web 3, such as engineers, validators, and Web 3 founders. Fundamentally, both systems - the social and the technical - seek to be organized in a decentralized manner. While the social system is governed and developed by individual people and non-human actors such as organizations and foundations, the technical system consists of physical infrastructure and code that not only functions in a decentralized way but also inherently breathes the spirit of trustlessness and immutability[5]. These notions reflect the ideology of Web 3. It is important to note that the social and technical domains influence one another *and* overlap in practice. For instance, as developers are researchers, researchers propose new technological solutions which may impact the very functioning and the needs and wants of the social system. Moreover, as mentioned below, the lines between founders and investors are also often blurred. The merging of relevant social actors and networks makes the social and technical domains form an ongoing symbiosis, much in line with ANT.

Crucially, decentralized technologies aim to facilitate self-governance (Nabben, 2023) to configure social relations in a decentralized manner (Miscione & Kavanagh, 2015; Reijers & Coeckelbergh, 2018). Thus, if Web 3 is about re-ordering society[6] then Web 3, at its core, is the ultimate configuration of this premise. However, it is still 'not completely clear what society is being prefigured towards' (Nabben,

2023). Hence, to uncover Web 3's trajectory a more comprehensive discussion on the ecosystem is imperative. Mapping Web 3's workings and predicting its current and future systemic challenges require a more in-depth examination of which actors and power dynamics influence Web 3.

Actors, Networks, and Power

Web 3 can thus be seen as an ecosystem consisting of various actors with differing interests and power dynamics. The expansion of Web 3 is intrinsically linked to the simultaneous emergence of actors that, alone or with others, form networks. These actors actively contribute to constructing Web 3 ecosystems as they run nodes, interact with the front-end components of Web 3, and foster vibrant communities for interaction, and such networks even encompass semi-external actors that invest in or participate in regulatory activities associated with Web 3. Identifying various actors within the Web 3 ecosystem and precisely delineating their roles and interests poses other inherent challenges. While certain ecosystem actors can be easily identified, the identification of some external parties necessitates extensive research, privileged information, or insider insights (Brennecke et al., 2022). Consequently, the following discussion can only provide a limited overview, which may however suffice for the scope of this chapter.

The Web 3 ecosystem encompasses diverse actors who actively participate in its development and operation. This section discusses a range of actors in a non-exhaustive manner, moving from more internal to more external actors. Developers are arguably the backbone of the Web 3 ecosystem. They contribute their technical expertise to build and enhance the infrastructure, protocols, and applications that form the foundation of Web 3. Developers create smart contracts, decentralized applications (dApps), and innovative solutions that leverage blockchain technology to enable decentralization and new functionalities. Moreover, various operational entities — such as infrastructure providers, oracles, centralized and decentralized exchanges (CEX and DEX), and custodians — contribute to Web 3's functioning. Their collective efforts contribute to the operational infrastructure that supports Web 3 applications. Ultimately, the value that individuals derive from the ecosystem much depends on how operational entities use the resources provided to them (Brennecke et al., 2022). The Web 3 community also comprises other individuals and organizations. As a decentralized and open-source ecosystem, the active participation of community members plays a crucial role in the overall value creation of the Web 3 network. Community members contribute to the governance of decentralized platforms, provide feedback on projects, and foster collaboration within the ecosystem. Hence, the active participation of community members in the system is an essential contribution to the value creation of the overall network (Brennecke et al., 2022). Crucially, the founders and early staff of Web 3 projects drive innovation and play a vital role in bringing new ideas, products, and services to the Web 3 ecosystem and beyond. Yet oftentimes they need external capital to flourish and build. Indeed, investors such as venture capital (VC) funds, private equity (PE) funds, family offices, decentralized autonomous organization (DAO) investment funds, and launchpads provide (financial) support, de facto playing a highly significant role in the funding of projects and thus in the very development of the Web 3 ecosystem. It must be mentioned that a range of individuals and other actors also provide valuable financial and non-financial support, such as angel investors, grant programs, accelerators, and incubators. Moreover, there are other actors that can be labeled as 'Web 3 service providers' that contribute their expertise to the ecosystem, such as freelancers, marketing professionals, key opinion leaders, and other stakeholders who provide services – and sometimes corresponding products – to the Web 3 ecosystem.

Given its focus on networks, ANT is specifically beneficial when mapping the different stakeholders in Web 3. For instance, ANT's emphasis on the dynamic and relational aspects is a valuable lens for studying non-linear changes in roles assigned to different actors (Zein & Twinomurinzi, 2022). Indeed, while the complexity and vastness of Web 3 imply that it is almost impossible to map all the actors and their various roles (Brennecke et al., 2022), it is crucial to note that many people wear different hats that can rapidly be interchanged. For instance, many Web 3 founders are active as angel investors, and some founders and investors de facto serve as key opinion leaders and advisors to other actors in the ecosystem and beyond. Contributors, builders, and funders can thus be the same, which at times may result in conflicts of interest. Moreover, as the Web 3 ecosystem rapidly evolves, an expanding array of actors and organizations engage with the technology (Hays et al., 2023), leading to a dynamic and interconnected network. This network comprises various stakeholders beyond those mentioned above, including companies, customers, suppliers, and other actors, who all collaboratively shape the Web 3 landscape through their beliefs and interests and their needs and wants. Looking more at the technological side whilst taking an ANT perspective, one may also point out that several non-human actors, including smart contracts, are essential for the functioning of the Web 3 ecosystem. Interestingly, smart contracts have been described as a type of dialogue, as 'an algorithmic, collective encounter that generates a proven record' (Patrickson, 2020). In that way, smart contracts can indeed be considered non-human actors key in the Web 3 ecosystem as they serve as a nexus between two or more on-chain users. Moreover, partnerships and strategic collaborations, also seen as non-human actors, are essential in Web 3 and enable intricate networks and relationships within the ecosystem and beyond. Since the networks in Web 3 are not static but dynamic, it is critical to note external actors in their relation to Web 3. Such may include academics, who contribute to the advancement of knowledge in the Web 3 field, and regulators and political institutions who seek to shape the legal and regulatory frameworks that govern Web 3 activities or the tech stack itself.

It has been argued that 'what binds the diverse intersection of characters exploring all corners of Web 3 is the desire to build their own information infrastructures to enable new economic models of organization' (Nabben, 2023). This notion may be challenged. It is reasonable to argue that all the actors as described above actively engage in what has been called 'micropolitics' to influence interpretative flexibility and establish a specific technological frame for what Web 3 represents. According to SCOT, social groups engage in micropolitics (Bijker, 1995) as they seek to extend their understanding of technology to other actors, and through strategies, certain relevant social groups can expand their technological frame (Redshaw, 2018). One sees this play out in Web 3, with developers, entrepreneurs, and investors celebrating Web 3 as a paradigm shift that empowers individuals and fosters economic inclusivity alongside ever-increasing innovation. On the contrary, regulators may emphasize the need for governance frameworks and regulatory measures to mitigate Web 3's potential risks. Actors may also influence the interpretative flexibility of Web 3 through strategic communication, lobbying (Sadowski & Beegle, 2023), advocacy, and collaboration, ultimately shaping Web 3's technological frame in ways that align with actors' objectives. These efforts involve promoting specific narratives, highlighting certain features or use cases, financial investments (Sadowski & Beegle, 2023), and participating in debates and discussions to advance their agendas. Web 3's technological and semantic flexibility is also reflected in the proliferation of discourses used by different media outlets to describe this technology's potential (Chow-White et al., 2020), albeit the evolutionary discourse of Web 3 as a successor to Web 2 seems prevalent. Following the critical constructivist approach discussed above, it is worth considering discourses of power and counter-power that prevail in Web 3's discourses. First, one may frame Web 3 as a counter-hegemonic attempt against the old institutions of Web 2 that are characterized by centralized control and data monopolization practices. The most ardent supporters of Web 3 indeed frame it as a techno political coup focused on toppling the old giants of technology and finance, grabbing power away from them, and building a new order (Sadowski & Beegle, 2023). Similarly, Web 3 can be seen as a counter-tyranny (Bodo & Giannopoulou, 2019) move against traditional finance and legacy political institutions characterized by centralized authorities, such as banks and government institutions. Regardless of the chosen narrative, it might also be argued that Web 3, despite its counter-hegemonic ambitions, might be falling prey to similar hegemonic rationalities it sought to challenge. As the next section will point out, a number of contradictions, or challenges, derive from Web 3's inherent socio-technical nature and from external social groups trying to impose their strategies to impact Web 3's trajectory. If acknowledged, said challenges might be considered sore when deeming Web 3's ideological nature as built on beliefs and ideals of decentralization, trustlessness, and immutability. Therefore, those posed to spur Web 3's long-term trajectory must consider said challenges.

Systemic Challenges in Web 3

Having described Web 3 as a social-technical construct and ecosystem and having mapped key Web 3 actors via an STS lens, it is worth considering more holistically which systemic *challenges* derive from Web 3's inherently socio-technological nature and from external (f)actors. For this chapter, 'challenges' are considered notions, practices, and interests that may be considered counterintuitive to the ideological nature of Web 3 or may directly go against it. Again, it must be noted that 'the' Web 3 ideology does not exist since Web 3 is arguably still open to flexible interpretation. However, observative assumptions can be derived from the vital importance Web 3 gives to 'decentralization', 'immutability', and 'trustlessness', concepts elaborated upon below.

As a preliminary note, it is important to differentiate between systemic risks and systemic challenges. Systemic *risks* refer to the risk that a negative shock can propagate through linkages within a system and lead to the collapse of an entire system (Fracassi & Di Maggio, 2022). Systemic risks in Web 3 tend to be highly interconnected, with one factor potentially influencing or exacerbating others. Consider, for instance, a straightforward example of the failure of a smart contract on a particular blockchain. A bug could lead to a loss of funds, which could shake confidence in the platform, resulting in reduced usage and lower transaction fees for miners. This could potentially make the blockchain more vulnerable to a hostile 51% attack (Gervais et al., 2016), exemplifying the cascading, systemic nature of these risks. Other (systemic) risks may include environmental considerations, cryptocurrency's supposed complicity in criminal activity, regulatory and accountability gaps, and CBDCs (Chohan, 2022). Systemic *challenges*, in the context of this chapter, are defined as broad and complex characteristics that flow from Web 3's inherent socio-technological nature and that have or may have a pervasive impact on an entire system. These challenges are characterized by interconnected components, structures, and processes, deeply embedded within the Web 3 system. Systemic risks and challenges can be interconnected. Take, for instance, the collapse of FTX (Jalan & Matkovskyy, 2023). FTX's downfall led to heavy market volatility and liquidity issues, impacting the market more broadly due to FTX's connection to other major industry players and funding channels. The collapse had a cascading effect on the broader Web 3 ecosystem. Nonetheless, the collapse of FTX can also be viewed as a systemic challenge because it highlights inherent vulnerabilities and shortcomings within the system, exposing reliance on centralized intermediaries, excessive trust in key figures[7], and an ultimate reliance on legacy institutions to clean up the leftovers once the party went south. The same argumentation may go for interest hikes imposed by the United States Federal Reserve, uncovering not only the impacts of cheap money on cryptocurrency markets, but also the potential risks of increased institutionalization.

It is also important to note that differentiating between systemic risks and challenges requires distinguishing between external and internal factors and actors. From the ANT perspective, it is challenging to differentiate between internal and external factors because Web 3 operates as an ecosystem comprising constantly expanding and shrinking networks. In this perspective, the boundaries between internal and external actors and influences are blurred, and the distinction between internal and external is actually less meaningful. Indeed, the 'internal' Web 3 actors such as founders, Web 3 native entities, and other key entities are constantly interacting with more 'external' actors, such as regulators and people newly onboarding the space. Having said that, attempting to uncover systemic challenges that derive from Web 3's inherent socio-technical nature is essential because it allows for self-reflection, potentially even impacting Web 3's long-term trajectory.

Uncovering systemic challenges requires an in-depth analysis of today's practices in Web 3 as a technology that is still open to the politics of relevant social groups. A useful concept may be that of micro-struggles. Micro-struggles, as conceptualized under critical constructivism, are the everyday conflicts and tensions occurring within technology and its use. Micro-struggles highlight how inherent values and power relations manifest in the interactions and practices surrounding technology. Looking at Web 3, micro-struggles emerge since actors and networks are prone to social, political, and technical contingencies (Chow-White et al., 2020) and navigate the complexities and trade-offs inherent to the development of Web 3. Micro-struggles can arise from differing perspectives, conflicting interests, and the need to reconcile competing values of different actors.

Micro-struggle I: the Concentration of Power

Web 3 might be considered a socio-technical construct that leverages blockchain and related technologies to enable the decentralized coordination of data and digital assets (Nabben, 2023) instead of relying on central intermediaries. However, Web 3 pushes beyond solely the democratization of data ownership by creating entirely new kinds of assets, infrastructures, markets, organizations, and social relations, with decentralization at their core, which will replace their non-decentralized versions (Sadowski & Beegle, 2023). The term 'decentralization' enjoys an almost mythical status in the discourses around Web 3 (Bodo & Giannopoulou, 2019), whilst it appears conceptually impossible to disentangle Web 3 and decentralization. However, what that tangle looks like in practice is still debatable. While they may all share a commitment to decentralization, increasingly, there are differences between visions of what Web 3 should be that are in direct opposition to its decentralized nature (Sadowski & Beegle, 2023). For instance, it is worth considering the increasingly contradictory deployment of hosting services across the spectrum of Web 3 projects (Overgaag, 2022). Alongside, one may argue that it is worth examining Web 3's financial aspirations[8], especially where consolidation is reoccurring through established financial intermediaries (Allen, 2022). While the ecosystem and the various applications are accumulating power, and are building commercial value alongside more traditional technology and business branches, Web 3 is thus not a self-sustainable ecosystem. Instead, it must secure inputs from a wide variety of markets (Bodo & Giannopoulou, 2019): financial resources such as investment; human resources such as software development; technical resources such as the capacities required to mine or run a full node; or infrastructural resources such as access to specialized hardware, energy, on-ramping services, or cloud services. The reliance on external resources or intermediaries, be they financial, human, or technical, introduces potential avenues where power can concentrate. Consider, for instance, substantial reliance on traditional hyperscalers (Overgaag, 2022), a relative small group of core developers (Electric Capital, 2023), and powerful mining device manufacturers (Magas, 2018), to name a few. It is also worthwhile to briefly consider the vital role of venture capital in shaping the political economy of Web 3 and of the very development of the sector indeed. An emerging narrative is that VC funds become the gatekeepers (Lerner & Nanda, 2020) of innovation, their investment decisions significantly shaping the technologies that gain legitimacy and traction. A cycle emerges where the momentum of capital becomes the primary force propelling Web 3, setting a path dependent on the VC's needs and wants rather than the foundational ethos of decentralization. The consequent power dynamic is one where innovation and progress become synonymous with what VCs will fund (Lerner & Nanda, 2020).

It might be argued that Web 3 has been gradually shifting from idealism towards enlightened pragmatism. This pragmatism leaves space for deliberation, politics, and interpretations implying that the meanings and practices of power and counter-power in Web 3 will continue to prevail in the near future. Whilst decentralization is certainly not composed of static endpoints (Sadowski & Beegle, 2023) that can ever be finally secured once and for all, the notion of decentralization does require constant agility to prevent the concentration of power in third-party actors. Arguably, decentralized infrastructure cannot be (co-)governed by centralized bureaucracies (Nabben, 2023), funders, or traditional infrastructures, at least not in the long term.

Micro-struggle II: Recentralization via External Actors

The concept of immutability, another cornerstone of Web 3, presents its own complexities. Transactions on a blockchain are, in essence, deterministic and immutable due to their validation across the network (Chohan, 2022), thus diminishing the potential for malicious alterations. This level of transparency grants participants visibility into each other's network state, limiting possibilities for unnoticed illicit activities. As noted, smart contracts, instrumental in a decentralized framework, are designed deterministically, reinforcing consensus and contributing to the network's overall security. In that regard, Web 3 could indeed be considered inherently deterministic. Technological determinism, in its more challenging expression, shakes the constitutional foundation and legitimacy as a societal regulator (Flink, 2021). In that regard, external actors may argue that Web 3 poses a threat to the social order by removing the legislative power from the public authorities to technologists via the creation of an autonomous self-regulating system that acts through the concept of delegation as discussed earlier. Fundamentally, the emergence of intermediaries and operational entities supporting and contributing to Web 3 as an ecosystem brings Web 3 indirectly under the purview of regulation, even as Web 3 is meant to be detached from legal constraints. Indeed, one of the major forces that impact the development of Web 3 globally is regulation (Chow-White et al., 2020). Since each regulatory context has its own laws and governance, many intermediaries and Web 3 actors seek to carefully navigate these waters. Crucially for the context of this section on the recentralisation of power is that the governance mechanisms embedded in Web 3 are formed, in part, through the negotiation between internal and external Web 3 actors. For example, Know Your Customer[9] (KYC) requirements as set by legacy institutions serve as an attempt to reintroduce elements of recentralization within the Web 3 ecosystem, de facto translating to barriers to entry. Moreover, looking more specifically at cryptocurrencies, it appears that they receive a range of regulatory acceptance (Gil-Cordero et al., 2020), but as disruptive tools, they do pose a threat to traditional financial systems in the eyes of some authorities (Chohan, 2022). Indeed, certain jurisdictions have deployed an outright ban on cryptocurrency or their mining, hereby impacting Web 3 at its very base. When looking beyond cryptocurrencies to other regulations, it must be noted that the level at which Web 3 is regulated is paramount. Horizontal regulation, which involves regulating the platform, application level, and ecosystem, could be the regulator's chosen approach (Flink, 2021). As accurately noted by Bodo and Giannopoulou, with the introduction of smart contracts, the logic of decentralization reached the level of blockchain governance itself (Bodo & Giannopoulou, 2019). Smart contracts clearly provide a new avenue for regulating blockchain technology. Specifically, smart contracts may include suicide functions designed to allow specific third parties to activate them, rendering smart contracts unresponsive (Schrepel, 2021). A kill switch introduces a centralizing element into an otherwise immutable system, directly going against the notion of decentralization.

In sum, a range of legal strategies as introduced by external actors alongside newly introduced rights and obligations create a pathway towards the recentralisation of Web 3.

Micro-struggle III: Web 3, Business, and Trust

As famously put by Wood, the overarching goal of Web 3 is 'less trust and more truth' (Wood, 2014). Less reliance on third parties and intermediaries embodies a fundamental shift in transactional trust from traditional institutions towards technology, that is, moving trust from people and institutions to technology (Brennecke et al., 2022). Web 3 suggests a 'trustless' system, with trust vested in the blockchain's systemic integrity rather than its human participants. On the surface, blockchain replaces trust with a novel architecture wherein nodes function independently, each requiring proof of transaction. However, this does not entirely negate the existence or requirement of trust; rather, it signifies a redistribution of trust among network actors who collectively uphold the system's trustworthiness through mutually beneficial cooperation based on economic incentives (Sandbeck et al., 2020). Even as Web 3's technological mechanics do not necessitate interpersonal trust, it is often erroneously construed as eliminating the need for trust altogether, a sure misinterpretation (Chohan, 2022). Beyond the technological layer, trust remains key to much of the economic and social interactions within Web 3. Especially its role in Web 3's business landscape cannot be understated nor disregarded in any discussion about trust in Web 3. For instance, exchanges, Web 3 companies, and investors largely depend on establishing and maintaining trust for the successful growth and operation of their projects, companies and services. These entities usually engage in business interactions across borders, in a global marketplace where value propositions can be championed or defeated, and capital can be garnered or erased in seconds. For instance, the credibility of founders, the soundness of their vision, and their vocally expressed commitment to growth and success highly influence investors' financial decisions. Similarly, when Web 3 projects, companies, and other key social groups enter into partnerships or strategic collaborations with one another based on Memoranda of Understanding (MoUs) or verbal agreements, it is trust, more than anything else, that underpins these relationships. Moreover, the social structures surrounding and permeating the Web 3 space – communities, key opinion leaders, and the like – play a significant role in establishing and maintaining trust. Due to trust, relationships are fostered, referrals and warm introductions are made, token-based or equity-based investments are ultimately transferred, and business is conducted. All these business practices, which for the purpose of this chapter cannot be exhaustively discussed, highlight the integral role of trust in shaping Web 3's development and, indeed, its very adoption.

The crucial role of trust in Web 3's social system can be considered contrary to the technical nature of Web 3 as a supposedly trustless environment. This paradox of trust does not only reflect the ongoing struggle about how precisely trust is embedded into the socio-technical system that is Web 3, but it also highlights the persistent influence of societal norms and values deeply rooted in the practical development of Web 3 and hereby simultaneously impacting it's very trajectory.

Limitations and Future Research

While the work offers valuable insights into the systemic challenges of Web 3, it is paramount to acknowledge and address several limitations of the analysis. Firstly, the framework should recognize that the values and motivations of individual actors, networks, and stakeholders within the Web 3 ecosystem cannot be fully summarized under a singular ideology or under a one-dimensional narrative. Despite certain dominant financial drivers and cultural narratives that influence the socio-technical ecosystem that is Web 3, it must be stressed that rationales and interests differ from person to person and from actor to actor. Moreover, the complexity and vastness of actors and networks present in Web 3 make it challenging to map all interests, beliefs, strategies, micro-struggles, and meanings. At the same *token*, it must be realized that the work mentions different blockchain systems and types of digital assets in broad manner, which will continue to be challenging in comprehensive research approaches due to said systems' and assets' inherent variations and complexities. In that light, another similar consideration is the rapidly evolving nature of the ecosystem in its broadest sense, making it almost impossible for any researcher or industry professional to provide a concise review of the space that does justice to the multifaceted sophistication that Web 3 has achieved. In that regard, it must also be noted that industry professionals and researchers, as actors with differing knowledge in relation to the Web 3 ecosystem, will consequently hold differing perspectives on the status quo of the field. Moreover, significant legal, political, and technological changes remain constantly underway, which could easily render any comprehensive discussion, provided by either a researcher or industry professional, quickly outdated. As such, this paper aimed to shed light on critical areas that require ongoing and *systemic* analysis, whilst acknowledging the need for continuous exploration and adaptation in this ample field of research. Further work is required to refine and specify the conceptual frameworks noted in this chapter and to develop measurable tools for identifying the human role within blockchain ecosystems alongside a more quantified rather than conceptual approach.

Finally, the exploration of systemic risks which can potentially impact Web 3 has been intrinsically incomplete, hereby underscoring the need for further investigation in order to comprehensively grasp the interplay of social, technological, and external (f)actors that together shape systemic challenges in and beyond the Web 3 ecosystem.

CONCLUSION

This chapter underscored the importance of a systemic and multi-disciplinary approach to understanding the nature and trajectory of Web 3. Web 3, as a concept still open for interpretation, can be many things. It is a black box housing a technical system that provides a substrate to support a range of disruptive developments. It is a technical system inherently intertwined with a social system that includes an array of internal stakeholders that hold differing beliefs, interests, and views. Web 3 as an ecosystem is ultimately also influenced by the interests derived from a range of external actors that seek to tap into and influence Web 3's supposed socio-technical nature. The totality of all these notions arguably translates Web 3 into a *sui generis*.

Web 3's inherent flexible, nascent and unique nature also gives rise to systemic challenges that may jeopardize or at least influence the future trajectory of the sector. This chapter aimed to expose such challenges by considering Web 3 as a black box whilst conducting a systemic analysis. The work has also recognized that Web 3's ambition for societal improvement is marked by a tension between aspirations and the ecosystem's practical realities. Development in Web 3 goes alongside varying meanings, interests, and a complex network of interacting actors. The ecosystem's inherent socio-technological nature poses the risk of shaping an alternative institutional system with its own power imbalances instead of sustainably challenging today's legacy institutions. Such a holistic yet realistic understanding is crucial when seeking to analyze how the conditions and growth opportunities within Web 3 are (to be) cultivated.

As such, it can be argued that the ecosystem necessitates a systemic self-reflection ideally grounded in daily practices to ensure that its long-term trajectory aligns with its ideological promises. Drawing from the three branches of STS, this chapter provided a lens to elucidate the controversies and complexities arising from the multifaceted interactions within Web 3. It underscores that the diverse motivations and ideals shaping Web 3's development lead to different trajectories, which may challenge its foundational ideology. The chapter aimed to highlight the intertwined networks that compose Web 3, contributing to a more comprehensive understanding of its structure and operation. The chapter emphasized the need for a systemic analysis to recognize and understand the more extensive network and the prominent 'nodes' within Web 3 that interact with one another. Whilst not ignoring the technical nature of Web 3's decentralized architecture, the chapter introduced specific micro-struggles in order to illuminate the dynamics of power, external actors, and internal relationships that yield Web 3, highlighting the need for a critical examination of how these elements are wielded and how they may prove to bring about systemic challenges for the long-term development of Web 3.

It can be concluded that Web 3's trajectory is not purely technologically determined nor entirely reliant on social actors. Instead, it is a product of complex interactions among its technological nature, societal values, stakeholder interests, and external (f)actors. Comprehending its complexities is indispensable for those operating within Web 3 and those seeking to spur its long-term trajectory in order to successfully shape societal transformation at large.

The author of this publication declares there are no competing interests. This research received no specific grant from any funding agency in the public, commercial, or not-for-profit sectors. Funding for this research was covered by the author of the article

REFERENCES

Adams, P. R., Frizzo-Barker, J., Ackah, B. B., & Chow-White, P. A. (2020). Making space for women on the blockchain. In M. Ragnedda & G. Destefanis (Eds.), *Blockchain and Web 3.0: Social, Economic, and Technological Challenges* (pp. 48–61). Routledge.

AllenH. J. (2023). DeFi: Shadow Banking 2.0? 64 Wm. & Mary L. Rev. 919. Available at SSRN: https://ssrn.com/abstract=4038788

Besel, R. D. (2011). Opening the 'black box' of climate change science: Actor-network theory and rhetorical practice in scientific controversies. *The Southern Communication Journal, 76*(2), 120–136. doi:10.1080/10417941003642403

Bijker, W. E. (1995). *Of Bicycles, Bakelites, and Bulbs*. MIT Press.

Bijker, W. E., Hughes, T. P., & Pinch, T. J. (Eds.). (2012). *The Social Construction of Technological Systems: New Directions in the Sociology and History of Technology*. MIT Press.

Bijker, W. E., Hughes, T. P., & Pinch, T. J. (Eds.). (2012). *The social construction of technological systems: New directions in the sociology and history of technology*. MIT Press.

Bodo, B., & Giannopoulou, A. (2020). The logics of technology decentralization – the case of distributed ledger technologies. In M. Ragnedda & G. Destefanis (Eds.), *Blockchain and Web 3.0: Social, Economic, and Technological Challenges* (pp. 114–129). Routledge.

Brennecke, M., Guggenberger, T., Sachs, A., & Schellinger, B. (2022). The Human Factor in Blockchain Ecosystems: A Sociotechnical Framework. In *Wirtschaftsinformatik 2022 Proceedings (Vol. 3)*. AISEL. https://aisel.aisnet.org/wi2022/finance_and_blockchain/finance_and_blockchain/3

Casey, M. J. (2022). *Crypto's Very Human Fatal Flaw: Hero Worship*. Coindesk. https://www.coindesk.com/layer2/2022/11/18/cryptos-very-human-fatal-flaw-hero-worship/

Chohan, U. W. (2022). *Cryptocurrencies: A Brief Thematic Review*. SSRN. https://ssrn.com/abstract=3024330 or doi:10.2139/ssrn.3024330

Chow-White, P., Lusoli, A., Phan, V. T. A., & Green, S. Jr. (2020). 'Blockchain Good, Bitcoin Bad': The Social Construction Of Blockchain In Mainstream And Specialized Media. *Journal of Digital Social Research, 2*(2), 1–27. doi:10.33621/jdsr.v2i2.34

Chow-White, P., Lusoli, A., Phan, V. T. A., & Green, S. Jr. (2020). 'Blockchain Good, Bitcoin Bad': The Social Construction Of Blockchain In Mainstream And Specialized Media. *Journal of Digital Social Research, 2*(2), 1–27. doi:10.33621/jdsr.v2i2.34

Dempsey, C., Wang, A., & Mart, J. (2022). A simple guide to the Web3 stack. *Coinbase Blog*. https://blog.coinbase.com/a-simple-guide-to-the-Web3-stack-785240e557f0

Feenberg, A. (1999). *Questioning Technology*. Routledge.

Feenberg, A. (2002). *Transforming Technology*. University.

Feenberg, A. (2002). *Transforming Technology: A Critical Theory Revisited* (2nd ed.). Oxford University Press.

Flink, M. (2021). *International blockchain regulation: Regulation by code – outlaws or new conceptions of law?* UTU Pub. https://www.utupub.fi/bitstream/handle/10024/151678/Flink_Mona_opinnayte.pdf?sequence=1

Fracassi, C., & Di Maggio, M. (2022). *Coinbase Institute: Evaluation of systemic risk in crypto*. CTFAssets. https://assets.ctfassets.net/c5bd0wqjc7v0/2KwhyMnQvPbhbGWtSEaEaZ81acc71cafa40a8d090a0eb5f4ed4e4b/CBI-Systemic_Risk_Newsletter.pdf

Freeman, S., Beveridge, I., & Angelis, J. (2019). Drivers of digital trust in the crypto industry. In M. Ragnedda & G. Destefanis (Eds.), *Blockchain and Web 3.0: Social, Economic, and Technological Challenges* (pp. 62–77). Routledge. doi:10.4324/9780429029530-5

Gervais, A., Karame, G. O., & Capkun, S. (2016). *On the security and performance of proof of work blockchains*. IACR Cryptology ePrint Archive. https://eprint.iacr.org/2016/555.pdf

Gil-Cordero, E., Cabrera-Sánchez, J. P., & Arrás-Cortés, M. J. (2020). Cryptocurrencies as a financial tool: Acceptance factors. *Mathematics, 8*(11), 1974. doi:10.3390/math8111974

Hays, D., & Tabone, M. (2023). *Blockchain Use Cases and Adoption Report*. Cointelegraph Research. https://research-backend.cointelegraph.com/uploads/attachments/clgav9x5o6yvqzyqng1kmb32g-blockchain-use-cases-and-adoption-report-3.pdf

Islam, N., Mäntymäki, M., & Turunen, M. (2019). Understanding the role of actor heterogeneity in blockchain splits: An actor-network perspective of bitcoin forks. In *Proceedings of the 52nd Hawaii International Conference on System Sciences* (pp. 4595-4604). Scholar Space. 10.24251/HICSS.2019.556

JalanA.MatkovskyyR. (2023). Systemic Risks in the Cryptocurrency Market: Evidence from the FTX Collapse. SSRN. https://ssrn.com/abstract=4364121 or doi:10.2139/ssrn.4364121

Kline, R., & Pinch, T. (1999). The social construction of technology. In D. MacKenzie & J. Wajcman (Eds.), *The Social Shaping of Technology*. Open University Press.

Lane, D. A. (2016). Innovation cascades: Artefacts, organization and attributions. Philosophical Transactions of the Royal Society B. *Biological Sciences, 371*(1690), 20150194. doi:10.1098/rstb.2015.0194

Latour, B. (1992). Where Are the Missing Masses? The Sociology of a Few Mundane Artifacts. In W. Bijker & J. Law (Eds.), *Shaping Technology/Building Society: Studies in Sociotechnical Change* (pp. 225–258). MIT Press.

Latour, B. (1999). A Collective of Humans and Nonhumans. In Kaplan (Ed.), Readings in the Philosophy of Technology (pp. 174-215). Oxford: Rowman and Littlefield.

Latour, B. (2005). *Reassembling the Social: An Introduction to Actor-Network Theory*. Oxford University Press.

Lerner, J., & Nanda, R. (2020). Venture capital's role in financing innovation: What we know and how much we still need to learn. *The Journal of Economic Perspectives, 34*(3), 237–261. doi:10.1257/jep.34.3.237

Miscione, G., & Kavanagh, D. (2015). Bitcoin and the Blockchain: A Coup D'État through Digital Heterotopia? *Humanistic Management Network, Research Paper Series (23/15),* 1–26.

Nabben, K. (2023). Web3 as 'self-infrastructuring': The challenge is how. *Big Data & Society, 10*(1). doi:10.1177/20539517231159002

Noto La Diega, G., & Stacey, J. (2019). Can permissionless blockchains be regulated and resolve some of the problems of copyright law? In M. Ragnedda & G. Destefanis (Eds.), *Blockchain and Web 3.0: Social, Economic, and Technological Challenges* (pp. 30–47). Routledge. doi:10.4324/9780429029530-3

Patrickson, B. (2020). Lightbulb concrete. In M. Ragnedda & G. Destefanis (Eds.), *Blockchain and Web 3.0: Social, Economic, and Technological Challenges* (pp. 78–93). Routledge.

Pinch, T., & Bijker, W. E. (1984). The social construction of facts and artifacts: Or how the sociology of science and the sociology of technology might benefit each other. *Social Studies of Science*, *14*(3), 399–441. doi:10.1177/030631284014003004

Ragnedda, M., & Destefanis, G. (2019). Blockchain: A disruptive technology. In M. Ragnedda & G. Destefanis (Eds.), *Blockchain and Web 3.0: Social, Economic, and Technological Challenges* (pp. 1–11). Routledge. doi:10.4324/9780429029530-1

Redshaw, T. (2018). *Of Bitcoins and Blockchains: The Social Construction of Crypto-Currencies.*

Reijers, W., & Coeckelbergh, M. (2018). The blockchain as a narrative technology: Investigating the social ontology and normative configurations of cryptocurrencies. *Philosophy & Technology*, *31*(1), 103–130. doi:10.100713347-016-0239-x

Sadowski, J., & Beegle, K. (2023). Expansive and extractive networks of Web3. *Big Data & Society*, *10*(1). doi:10.1177/20539517231159629

Sandbeck, S., Kingsmith, A. T., & von Bargen, J. (2019). The block is hot: A commons-based approach to the development and deployment of blockchains. In M. Ragnedda & G. Destefanis (Eds.), *Blockchain and Web 3.0: Social, Economic, and Technological Challenges* (pp. 15–29). Routledge. doi:10.4324/9780429029530-2

SchrepelT. (2021). Smart Contracts and the Digital Single Market Through the Lens of a 'Law + Technology' Approach. European Commission. SSRN. https://ssrn.com/abstract=3947174

Tonelli, R., Pierro, G., Ortu, M., & Destefanis, G. (2023). Smart Contracts Software Metrics: A First Study. *PLoS One*, *18*(4), e0281043. doi:10.1371/journal.pone.0281043 PMID:37043512

Wan, S., Lin, H., Gan, W., Chen, J., & Yu, P. S. (2023). Web3: The Next Internet Revolution. ArXiv. Retrieved from https://arxiv.org/abs/2304.06111

Wood, G. (2014). *ÐApps: What Web 3.0 Looks Like*. Gavwood. https://gavwood.com/dappsweb3.html

Yaga, D., Mell, P., Roby, N., & Scarfone, K. (2018). *Blockchain Technology Overview*. NIST. doi:10.6028/NIST.IR.8202

Zein, R., & Twinomurinzi, H. (2022). Perspective Chapter: Actor-Network Theory as an Organising Structure for Blockchain Adoption in Government. In *IntechOpen*.

ENDNOTES

[1] Each regulatory context, such as the nation-state or supranational institutions such as the European Union, has its own laws and governance with regard to the regulation of digital assets, blockchain, and DLT (distributed ledger technologies). See for instance: Overgaag, A. (2023). An overview of cryptocurrency regulations in Portugal. Cointelegraph. Retrieved from https://cointelegraph.com/learn/an-overview-of-cryptocurrency-regulations-in-portugal; Overgaag, A. (2023). An overview of cryptocurrency regulations in South Korea Cointelegraph. Retrieved from https://cointelegraph.com/learn/crypto-regulations-in-south-korea; and Overgaag, A. (2022). Cryptocurrency regulation in the UAE and the Dubai Virtual Assets Law Cointelegraph. Retrieved from https://cointelegraph.com/learn/cryptocurrency-regulation-in-the-uae-and-the-dubai-virtual-assets-law

[2] Redshaw readily acknowledged in 2018 that STS stands out as a theoretical lens via which to analyze social interactions surrounding Bitcoin. The author's article stands as a testament to their exceptional scholarly accomplishment, characterized by profound theoretical insights that transcend the boundaries of the original topic.See Redshaw, T. (2018,). Of Bitcoins and Blockchains: The Social Construction of Crypto-Currencies.

[3] Digital assets encompass a broad array of digital content and representations of value that can be electronically stored, transferred, or accessed. They include cryptocurrencies, tokens, digital collectibles, digital certificates, virtual currencies, and more. The interpretation of cryptocurrencies, in particular, remains open to flexibility, as various stakeholders such as states, regulators, and investors strive to establish their classification as an asset, commodity, currency, or collectible. At noted by Chohan (Chohan, 2022), cryptocurrencies are primarily built upon two functions: production (mining) and transaction (exchange), yet the author would argue that the utility function of cryptocurrencies is often overlooked. 'Utility' refers to the practical applications and functionalities that cryptocurrencies offer beyond mere transactions, highlighting the key role of cryptocurrencies in decentralised applications and blockchain ecosystems.

[4] This comprehensive definition presented diverges somewhat from the prevailing evolutionary discourse as previously examined in this chapter, which appears to exert dominance in the literature. However, it is important to note that the author maintains that Web 3, as a socio-technological concept, remains subject to interpretive flexibility. Indeed, the primary objective of this very chapter is to contribute to the analysis of Web 3, with the ultimate aim of mapping the systemic challenges that the broader ecosystem is currently confronting or may encounter in the future.

[5] These concepts will be elaborated upon whilst discussing the various 'micro-struggles', below.

[6] Via concepts including *decentralization*, *trustlessness*, and *immutability*, which will be discussed below.

[7] Misplaced admiration in key leadership figures in Web 3 is a paradox yet very human tendency, as argued by Casey (Casey 2022).

[8] A promise of Web 3 lies in its potential to foster financial inclusion and mitigate economic inequalities by making decentralized technologies accessible to anyone. Such narratives may be contested by the realization that the nature of inequality in Web 3 is in fact not too different from that of traditional forms of capital. Chohan (2022) noted that whilst the ownership of certain Web 3 assets is highly concentrated in a small number of wallets, this does not automatically implies that financial inclusion cannot be realised. A remark to stipulate is to recognize that Web 3 is not a panacea for all societal challenges and remains an ecosystem in progress. Indeed, the issue of digital

infrastructure accessibility persists, with many individuals still lacking the necessary resources and connectivity to engage fully in Web 3. Addressing this digital divide and other access barriers that characterize Web 3 is crucial for achieving broader inclusivity within the Web 3 ecosystem towards more diverse demographics, different genders, age groups, and proficiency levels.

[9] KYC regulations, often imposed at Web 3 operational entities such as centralized exchanges, are designed to verify the identities of individuals or entities participating in financial transactions or accessing certain services.

Chapter 24
Regulatory Challenges and Opportunities in Web 3:
Navigating the Decentralized Landscape

Lisa-Marie Ross

ⓘ https://orcid.org/0000-0002-5073-4251

National University of Singapore, Singapore

ABSTRACT

The novel use of distributed ledger technology (DLT) in the financial sector poses considerable regulatory challenges, such as anonymity, technology neutrality, interconnectedness within the market of virtual assets, as well as with the traditional financial system and new legal risks to regulators around the globe. At the same time, the novelty of DLT for financial uses embodies also significant potential benefits to the financial sector, like innovation, inclusion, and competition. This chapter analyses these challenges and opportunities in detail and subsequently reviews possible regulatory responses at the current stage of virtual asset revolution and financial services innovation. Given the ongoing rapid development in the DLT financial services sphere, the analysis identifies the risk-based regulatory approach as potentially the most universal approach for national/regional regulators with advantages of high flexibility and resource efficiency.

INTRODUCTION

Since at least the mid-2010s, the development of web 3 and various virtual assets has been on the rise and in the eye of the public. Public attention was very much focused on the novelty of the new distributed ledger technology (DLT) that virtual assets are based on (Arner, et al., 2020). The use of this new DLT enables faster, cheaper, and safer transactions through its encrypted, decentralized network. The potential elimination of intermediaries provides many more advantages, such as financial inclusion, crowdsourcing, new business models and more.

DOI: 10.4018/978-1-6684-9919-1.ch024

Copyright © 2023, IGI Global. Copying or distributing in print or electronic forms without written permission of IGI Global is prohibited.

However, one decade forward, it turns out that despite the decentralized origin, in practice, many applications are indeed involving intermediaries (Haentjens, et al., 2022; Anker-Sørensen & Zetzsche, 2021), resulting in familiar financial regulatory approaches like for conventional payments or financial products (Blandin, et. al., 2019). At the same time, virtual assets and transactions raise new questions of ownership and possession that challenge traditional legal understandings and impact regulatory practice and oversight.

Furthermore, the borderless nature of web 3 and global interconnections pose additional challenges of jurisdiction and applicable law to regulators and courts, making enforcement of rights and titles increasingly difficult. Consequently, leading to prevailing uncertainty among market participants.

Especially the past two years have been dominated by negative headlines, largely about stablecoins and failures of crypto exchanges. While Bitcoin and Ethereum are said to be the first generation of virtual tokens, stablecoins were often considered as the even better versions, being pegged to fiat money or algorithms, and hence uniting the novel technology with trusted and familiar elements. However, the crash of TerraUSD and its sister currency Luna has revealed that the underlying collateral, structures, and algorithms are not necessarily subject to comprehensive supervision. Instead, inadequate disclosure rules and a lack of mandatory audits for stablecoins pose potential risks of a run (Adams & Ibert, 2022), as well as to consumer protection and financial stability. Consequently, the Terra Luna crash and the failures of lending giants like Celsius Network and Voyager, as well as the collapse of the FTX group, led to concerns voiced by the public about the lack of regulatory supervision, investor protection and clear legal guidance; leading to an escalation of public calls for regulation (Burroughes, 2022). As such, there appears to be a momentum to implement and improve regulation in the virtual asset infrastructure globally.

Due to the high speed of technological developments, regulation and governance might be outdated once they enter into force. This rapidity reinforces the need to regulate technology neutrally. Accordingly, regulators globally are faced with the task of accelerating the regulatory process and incorporate innovative and flexible tools to address the risks involved in the web 3 market through functional approaches.

This chapter features opportunities and challenges faced by regulators domestically, regionally, and internationally and reviews new developments in global principles and standards. These include, on the one hand, opportunities, such as:

- Enabling innovation
- Improving inclusion
- Enhancing competition

As well as, on the other hand, challenges, such as:

- Anonymity
- Technology neutrality
- Interconnectedness
- Legal risks.

Furthermore, this chapter aims to combine the theoretical findings with practice examples of virtual asset regulation in Singapore, Switzerland, the European Union, and the United States. Accordingly, the chapter includes a display of regulatory approaches such as risk-based regulation, agile regulation, and regulation by enforcement. While strategic approaches and regulation vary in many aspects in the regions of the world, the regulatory authorities pursue similar objectives, e.g., ensuring that money laundering and terrorism financing risks are adequately addressed while supporting the growth of digital products and services in web 3. This discussion of different regulatory approaches offers valuable insights on the success and developments of these regulatory paths and highlights remaining common challenges for regulators: the blind spot of decentralized finance (DeFi).

For the context of this book chapter and considering that definitions differ significantly across jurisdictions, the terms virtual asset and virtual asset service providers will be, in line with international standards set by the Financial Action Task Force (FATF) (2023a), defined as follows: "A virtual asset is a digital representation of value that can be digitally traded, or transferred, and can be used for payment or investment purposes"; "Virtual asset service provider means any natural or legal person who is…as a business conduct[ing] one or more of the following activities or operations for or on behalf of another natural or legal person: exchange between virtual assets and fiat currencies; exchange between one or more forms of virtual assets; transfer of virtual assets; safekeeping and/or administration of virtual assets or instruments enabling control over virtual assets; and participation in and provision of financial services related to an issuer's offer and/or sale of a virtual asset" (p. 135).

RELATED WORK AND LIMITATIONS

This chapter sets its focus on the DLT-based transfer of value as financial services and its corresponding regulation. As intermediaries for the trade, storage and control of virtual assets, the regulation of virtual asset service providers will be closely examined. This includes more broadly the analysis of challenges and chances of virtual assets as well as the examination of different regulatory approaches at the national/regional level. While regulators face common challenges regarding virtual asset service providers, the regulatory approaches vary globally. To address these differences, academics, renowned institutes and committees around the globe initiated research studies to support legal common ground and to help understand the implications of the novel technology as well as to share various policy recommendations.

The European Systemic Risk Board (ESRB) (2023) voiced in their May 2023 report in particular future financial stability concerns in case of a continued fast-growing prevalence of virtual assets paired with high volatility of virtual assets in case of increased interconnectedness with the traditional financial sector.

Arner et al. (2023b) introduced in that regard the term "financialization of crypto" to describe the partial mirroring of crypto to traditional finance in its today's evolution and duplication of institutions, services, and products. Therewith, highlighting its vulnerability to well-known problems of traditional finance like information asymmetries, conflicts of interests, monopolization of transaction power and more (Arner, et al., 2023a). The authors argue that the failures of crypto exchanges and lending giants have demonstrated that the crypto sector has evolved away from its origin idea of peer-to-peer transactions and is nowadays instead characterized by frequent usage of intermediaries, which are prone to problems of the traditional financial sector. A supervisory regime which bases oversight on the original notion of decentralization and peer-to-peer exchanges, with market trust deriving from technology, seems insufficient given the turbulent market events of the past years. Consequently, the increasing alienation from decentralization and the trend towards centralized intermediaries create regulatory lacunas where liquidity and solvency crises are possible to occur. Considering that on the one hand a financialization of crypto has already taken place, and on the other hand a partial decentralization in the form of

DLT-based transfers poses substantial complexities of cross-border coordination, they argue in favor of a bespoke regulation and supervision regime for virtual assets. The bespoke virtual assets regime is proposed to consist of clear licensing, disclosure requirements and other financial regulation elements like segregation and custody rules, market abuse and restructuring and resolution legislation, as well as significantly enhanced levels of cross-border coordination through Multilateral Memorandum of Understanding (MMoU) (Arner, et al., 2023a).

Most recently, the World Economic Forum (WEF) (2023) highlighted in its May 2023 report the need to develop a coordinated global approach to achieve an effective and consistent framework for virtual assets. To support this development, the WEF proposes prioritized pathways for international bodies, regional/national regulators, and the industry, aiming to enable enhanced levels of cross-border coordination through responsible regulatory evolution. These prioritized pathways contain three recommendations each. For international organizations, WEF (2023) recommends to "promote a harmonized understanding of taxonomy/classification of crypto-assets and activities; set out best practices and baseline regulatory standards for achieving the desired regulatory outcomes; encourage passportability of entities and data sharing" (p. 25). For regional/national regulatory authorities, WEF (2023) recommends "cross-sector coordination; regulatory certainty; using technology for regulation by design" (p. 26). As recommendation for the industry, WEF states "standard setting; sharing best practices; responsible technology innovation" (p. 27).

In the same vein, the Financial Stability Board (FSB) (2022) proposed in October 2022 and the International Monetary Fund (IMF) (2023) in February 2023 respectively, a set of nine recommendations specifically addressing national/regional regulators with a focus on financial stability concerns to avoid spillovers to the traditional financial system.

The proposed FSB recommendations include: regulatory powers and tools; general regulatory framework; cross-border cooperation, coordination, and information-sharing; governance; risk management; data collection, recording and reporting; disclosures; addressing financial stability risks arising from interconnections and interdependencies; comprehensive regulation of crypto asset service providers with multiple functions (FSB 2022).

The IMF recommends to "safeguard monetary sovereignty and stability by strengthening monetary policy frameworks and do not grant crypto assets official currency or legal tender status; guard against excessive capital flow volatility and maintain effectiveness of capital flow management measures; analyze and disclose fiscal risks and adopt unambiguous tax treatment of crypto assets; establish legal certainty of crypto assets and address legal risks; develop and enforce prudential, conduct, and oversight requirements to all crypto market actors; establish a joint monitoring framework across different domestic agencies and authorities; establish international collaborative arrangements to enhance supervision and enforcement of crypto asset regulations; monitor the impact of crypto assets on the stability of the international monetary system; strengthen global cooperation to develop digital infrastructures and alternative solutions for cross-border payments and finance" (IMF, 2023, p. 1).

Overall, there is significant overlap of the WEF (2023), FSB (2022) and IMF (2023) recommendations, all of them aiming to strengthen cross-border coordination and supporting the development of a framework that promotes consistency and comprehensiveness in the international regulation of virtual asset activities.

In sum, the regulation of DLT-based transfer of value as financial services has high priority at the national/regional level as well as internationally. Considering the imminent threat of use of virtual assets for money laundering and terrorism finance purposes based on the anonymity of DLT-based transfers of value, it seems justified to prioritize financial regulation of virtual assets as a focus topic. Virtual assets constitute present-day challenges and chances to regulators around the globe, seeking to find balance between prudential regulation and the establishment of the respective jurisdiction as an innovative virtual assets hub that welcomes new businesses and services.

At the same time, virtual assets pose challenges in many more areas of law. They raise novel issues in private law in traditional fields like property and contract law, criminal law, tax law, insolvency law and more. Furthermore, privacy concerns are being voiced with regard to the proposed data collection and data sharing as well as the aimed exchange of data between jurisdictions. Nevertheless, the focus of this chapter is limited to financial regulation.

REGULATORY CHALLENGES AND OPPORTUNITIES IN WEB 3

Challenges

The novel use of DLT in the financial sector poses considerable challenges, such as anonymity, technology neutrality, interconnectedness within the market of virtual assets as well as with the traditional financial system, and new legal risks to regulators around the globe.

Anonymity

Most commonly, anonymity is used when referring to the DLT-based transfer of value, which allows transacting without the personal information of the user. This leads to concerns of use for criminal activity and illicit financing. Instead of using personal information, the transfer is executed through the wallet addresses of the counterparties of the executed trade, which are unique codes. Therefore, the transaction should not be referred to as anonymous but pseudonymous. Although 'pseudonymity' is the more precise description of this challenge, this chapter uses the term 'anonymity' because such transactions are mostly referred to as anonym forms of transfer. The FATF is the main international authority and global standard-setter in the area of Anti-Money Laundering (AML), Combating the Financing of Terrorism (CFT) and Combatting Proliferation Financing (CPF) (FATF, 2019). AML, CFT and CPF form the baseline of all financial regulation, in other words, they constitute the minimum reason for enacted regulation even before consumer protection and financial stability concerns. The FATF Recommendations (2023a) set out the international standard for AML/CFT/CPF. Considering the anonymity of a DLT-based transfer of value, virtual assets and virtual assets service providers are explicitly covered in Recommendation 15. The FATF recommends in respect to virtual assets and virtual assets service providers "to manage and mitigate the risks emerging from virtual assets, countries should ensure that virtual asset service providers are regulated for AML/CFT purposes, and licensed or registered and subject to effective systems for monitoring and ensuring compliance with the relevant measures called for in the FATF Recommendations" (p. 17). In the interpretative note to Recommendation 15, the FATF elaborates further with regard to specific regulatory measures to be taken by countries. At first, FATF Recommendations (2023a) equal virtual assets to "property", "proceeds", "funds", "funds or other assets" to ensure application of the international standard (p. 76). Overall, the FATF recommends a risk-based regulatory approach to virtual assets and virtual asset providers. The corresponding recommended measures include licensing/ registration requirements, supervision and monitoring by a competent authority to ensure compliance with national AML/CFT rules, providing a range of sanctions and international information sharing. Furthermore, FATF Recommendation 16 explicitly applies to virtual assets and virtual asset providers, which contains the 'travel rule'. The travel rule requires obtaining, holding, and transmitting originator and beneficiary information relating to virtual assets transactions (FATF, 2023b).

Consequently, the FATF Recommendations apply to the DLT-based transfer of value just like for traditional transactions and virtual asset service providers are subject to the same preventive measures as financial institutions. In other words, the principle 'same activity, same risk, same regulation' applies to virtual assets and virtual asset service providers. However, it is important to keep in mind that while the FATF Recommendations are indeed setting the international standard for AML/CFT/CPF, they are not binding jurisdictions and regulatory implementation of the FATF Recommendations at the national/regional level is required.

In June 2023, the FATF published a report on the implementation progress for virtual assets and virtual asset service providers based on conducted surveys and evaluations (FATF, 2023b). The report identifies considerable gaps and deficits in the implementation at the national/regional level. Especially the elements of supervision and enforcement are insufficiently observed and compliance with FATF's Recommendations are behind most other financial sectors with three quarters of jurisdictions being only partly or non-compliant (FATF, 2023b, p. 2). Also, the travel rule provides opportunities for improvement as only less than half of the participating jurisdictions (62 of 151) have started the implementation process in the context of virtual assets with additional 54 non-responding jurisdictions to the surveys (FATF, 2023b, p. 2). In summary, implementation of the FATF Recommendations is still improvable in many jurisdictions.

Technology Neutrality

The WEF (2023) describes DLT as "transformational technology with the ability to disrupt the way people record transactions, enhance transparency and governance, exchange value and coordinate and collaborate across geographies and industries" (p. 6). The speed of technology development is seeing no slowing down and the industry keeps introducing new products, services and applications relating to virtual assets regularly. As such, the novelty of DLT in virtual assets for financial uses embodies significant potential benefits to the traditional financial sector, like innovation, inclusion, and competition. However, this novel use of DLT in the financial sector poses also considerable challenges to regulators around the globe. While the standard configuration of laws and regulations is to regulate technology neutrally, which means that regulation is neither favoring nor discriminating against technology, it becomes more difficult than ever with the new arising technology-based products, services, and applications. Furthermore, it can be especially difficult to assign jurisdictions to intermediaries that engage in the DLT sphere, given a lack of defined headquarters or business practice. Regulatory gaps and resulting regulatory arbitrage have occurred in the virtual space, which constitute a threat to the market, its participants, and potentially to financial stability as well as the trust in law and enforcement. Concurrently, it becomes even more important to regulate technology neutral as regulation that targets specific technologies is similarly vulnerable to becoming outdated; in a worst case, becoming outdated even before legislative processes are completed. Arguably, technology innovation is faster than its regulatory responses. Practically, an enhanced level of cross-border coordination is required to address regulatory lacunas and tackle regulatory arbitrage. This issue is also addressed by the FATF Recommendations regarding virtual asset service providers. Namely, the FATF has included the requirement of licensing or registration in the jurisdictions of their creation as a minimum requirement, with the additional opening to further licensing or registration requirements depending on the business conducted in other jurisdictions (FATF, 2023a). National/regional regulators are consequently urged to enhance licensing policies. For instance, Singapore implemented the extended recommendation through the Financial Services and Markets Act 2022 (FSM Act), which now subjects every virtual asset service provider based in Singapore to obtain a license in Singapore, even if they conduct their business exclusively outside of Singapore.

Interconnectedness

The interconnectedness of virtual assets is threefold. On the one hand, an interconnectedness within the market of virtual assets exists. On the other hand, interconnectedness with the traditional financial system is also of concern. The latter comprises of the above-described partial mirroring of virtual assets to traditional finance in its today's evolution and duplication of institutions, services, and products (Arner, et al., 2023b). Further, it also includes financial stability concerns arising from traditional financial institutions' exposure to virtual assets (FSB, 2022).

The interconnectedness within the market of virtual assets could be observed in practice during the past failures of crypto exchanges, lending giants and crash of tokens and stablecoins (FSB, 2022). These market turbulences led to market stress as well as rapid contagion and resulted in prices to tumble across the sector. The FSB (2022) stresses in this context regulatory gaps and arbitrage regarding co-ownership, affiliations as well as bailout agreements, which are mitigated in the traditional financial sector through regulation.

While the level of interconnectedness in relation to the traditional financial system in both alternatives is widely described to be low as of now, the risk of financial stability resonates and the interconnectedness with the traditional financial system could pose a future challenge.

Legal Risks

Virtual assets and therewith the tokenization of assets come with new challenges to legal understandings that are relevant to regulation, businesses, investors, and courts. These include questions of applicable jurisdictions and law as well as questions to custodial relationship, ownership, and possession (Lehmann, 2019). These legal issues are traditionally separate from financial regulation and therefore, as described above, not part of this chapter. However, traditional understandings of legal issues are challenged by virtual assets and services in a matter that also influence regulatory practice and supervision. Specifically, legal risks that can accrue from these new legal issues of virtual assets and virtual asset service providers, have regulatory effects.

For instance, the legal issue of custodial relationship relates to the question of whether virtual tokens qualify as species that are capable of being held on trust, which keeps academia and courts to date engaged. It has also led to differing judgments within and across jurisdictions, like in Singapore with B2C2 Ltd v Quoine Pte Ltd, [2019] SGHC(I) 03, in which the court affirmed the property status and subsequently the creation of a trust between the parties. However, this decision was reversed in Quoine Pte Ltd v B2C2 Ltd [2020] SGCA(I) 02, where the court held that there was no certainty of intention to create a trust. In addition, it is a regular practice for virtual asset service providers and exchange platforms to frequently change their terms and conditions as well as website wordings. This practice further adds to uncertainties and leads to varying results. Regarding the private law issues, the International Institute for the Unification of Private Law (UNIDROIT) is currently working on the development of model laws to support compatibility and harmonization internationally. On the regulatory side, regulators have started to address these legal risks. Singapore has for example announced to implement measures to require virtual asset service providers to "segregate customers' assets from their own assets, and to hold these customers' assets on trust for the benefit of the customer" (MAS, 2023, p. 5). This measure mirrors extensive experience in regulating capital market service providers and signifies enhanced regulatory intervention addressing the increased risk in the sphere of virtual asset service providers.

Opportunities

At the same time, the novelty of DLT in virtual assets for financial uses also embodies significant potential benefits to the financial sector, like innovation, inclusion, and competition.

Innovation

As quoted above, DLT holds transformational potential in respect to financial services (WEF, 2023). DLT innovations of payment systems facilitate improved efficiency in form of faster, safer, and cheaper transactions, locally and cross-border (Zetzsche, et al., 2022). Cross-border payments are especially, until today, expensive, slow, and not always reliable.

In detail, innovation includes the recording of transactions, enhancing of transparency, enhancing of accessibility and greater independence from intermediaries using DLT (Lee & L'heureux, 2020). Virtual assets constitute value that is free of external political impacts, devaluation by inflation, and independent of one's location and residency. Further, the on-chain, record-keeping, and open-source data could potentially facilitate eased tracing of illicit activities through automated triggers as well as simplify analysis to understand demands and customize products and services.

Inclusion

Virtual assets have the potential to enhance inclusion in several areas. Firstly, virtual assets provide financial access to those who do not have access to accounts with financial institutions. Secondly, the DLT-based transfer of value allows for the transfer of small values in an economic viable usage at lower prices and fees, without being subject to minimum fees that pose disproportionate costs in proportion to small values. Thirdly, DLT-based financial services support maintaining an open and competitive payment services market through the inclusion of new entities in traditional regimes. Virtual asset service providers originated the need to introduce new licenses in several jurisdictions, which was also accompanied by designation power to regulatory authorities by some jurisdictions. For example, in the EU and Singapore, regulators have the authority to force designated payment systems into compliance with certain technical standards to ensure inter-operability between payment systems.

Competition

To date, the gross market capitalization of all virtual assets taken together amounts to approximately more than US$ 1 trillion, according to the WEF (WEF, 2023). While it does by far not match the aggregated size of the traditional financial sector, it constitutes a new ecosystem of significance, which is still growing (WEF, 2023). Despite the negative headlines surrounding the virtual assets sphere during the past two years, the industry is still booming (Jeng, 2023). Furthermore, international, and national/regional efforts to establish regulation aiming to create clearer regulatory and legal certainty, set the precondition to attract even more web 3 companies, reduce interconnectedness within the market of virtual assets, and consequently support a more robust virtual asset environment (Jeng, 2023). Competition within the market of virtual assets and especially with the traditional financial sector promotes innovation and better quality of assets and services.

REGULATORY RESPONSES

This chapter has reviewed above international concepts and ideas on how to best regulate virtual assets, considering the significant cross-border dimension it entails. Simultaneously, this chapter aims to further provide examples of the regulatory status quo of virtual assets and related activities to assess how far theory and practice are apart. How are the challenges and opportunities in web 3 currently addressed in different jurisdictions? Which regulatory approaches may be used?

Regulatory responses range from existing rules and regulations that have been adapted to include virtual assets and virtual asset service providers (Singapore), to newly enacted frameworks (Switzerland, EU) to regulation by enforcement (US).

Regulatory Approaches: Examples

Adaption of the Old, Risk-Based Regulation in Singapore

A risk-based approach based on the adaption of existing regulation to new technologies allows fast responses and provides certainty for market participants. The existing regulation is already implemented and subject to supervision and enforcement actions. The embedding of virtual assets regulation into existing frameworks reduces the number of open questions that go together with newly introduced regulation, even though the adoption of existing regulation does not avoid interpretation uncertainties completely. Further, risk-based regulation allows for flexible regulatory responses, which are resource-efficient. On the one hand, entities are regulated based on their level of risk. If they perform high-risk activities, the intervention of the regulator is higher; if they perform low-risk activities, the regulation is streamlined (WEF, 2023). Also, the entity's size, complexity and systemic importance can be taken into consideration applying a risk-based approach (FSB, 2022). Especially for virtual asset service providers, this approach could signify regulatory easing as opposed to uniform application of benchmarks and risk management standards in the banking sector. To promote innovation, virtual asset service providers are thereby enabled to launch their business despite being less experienced and offering a limited range of services. In case the entities become relevant to financial stability and concern consumer protection, regulatory intervention increases, and these entities become subject to additional rules, requirements, and supervision. On the other hand, this approach enables regulatory authorities to use their limited capacities efficiently and focus these on high-risk activities.

Exemplarily, Singapore applies a risk-based approach to virtual assets and virtual asset service providers. Virtual assets are assigned into different categories of tokens, depending on their function, with payment and security tokens being the most relevant ones for their current regulatory activities.

Security tokens are subject to Singapore's Securities and Futures Act (SFA) and subject to the requirements that apply to capital market products. Consequently, the activities of offering security tokens and offering services related to security tokens constitute regulated activities in Singapore. Payment tokens are covered by Singapore's Payment Services Act (PS Act) and currently subject to limited regulatory intervention, focused on the prevention of illegal conduct to support the growth of digital products and services. Singapore's PS Act does not regulate the issuance or creation of payment tokens but addresses transactions and activities that facilitate the transfer of the payment tokens. In line with Singapore's general approach to financial services, it requires a license from the Monetary Authority of Singapore (MAS) as a pre-condition for any virtual asset service provider to start operating. Hence, any service provided in relation to payment tokens is an activity that triggers the license requirement under the PS Act. While the Act is currently primarily focused on AML/CFT and the risks resulting from new payment technologies, several new amendments consider the turbulences on the virtual asset markets and the incidents at the intermediary level. These amendments include new provisions that empower MAS to address consumer protection and financial stability concerns in a relatively wide and open manner. These were introduced as anticipatory amendments to consult as and when needed. Furthermore, MAS announced in July 2023 the implementation of enhanced measures for virtual asset service providers, such as measures relating to the segregation and custody of consumers' assets (as described above under legal risks) as well as prohibiting measures in respect to lending and staking of customers' assets by virtual asset service providers (MAS, 2023). These amendments epitomize exemplary the above-described evaluation of virtual assets. Starting with very limited regulatory intervention with trust deriving from technology and developing to enhanced regulatory intervention because of increased intermediaries, emerging regulatory lacunas as well as consumer protection and financial stability concerns.

Enacting New Regulation, Agile, and Risk-Based Regulation in Switzerland and the EU

Only a few jurisdictions chose the path of creating and enacting a new and dedicated framework for virtual assets. Switzerland and the European Union (EU) are two such role models: Switzerland's framework as an early pioneering example, and the EU due to its framework's scope of application. Both frameworks constitute a mixture of regulatory approaches, namely the agile and risk-based approach. In addition to the above-described risk-based approach, the agile approach entails a flexible, proactive, and iterative approach. This includes testing of new types of solutions and multistakeholder involvement, exemplarily through regulatory sandboxes, classifications, and guidance (instead of rules) by the regulator (WEF, 2023). However, it is important to mention that the agile approach is not universal but builds on market maturity and ecosystem development in the respective jurisdictions (WEF, 2023).

One of the first newly enacted frameworks to regulate virtual assets and virtual asset service providers was Switzerland's Federal Act on the Adoption of Federal Law to Developments in DLT (Swiss Blockchain Act), which entered into force on 1 August 2021. With the aim to become a global hub for the fintech and DLT ecosystem, Switzerland's goal succeeded insofar as regulatory clarity attracted world-renowned entities like the Ethereum Foundation or the Solana Foundation to Switzerland. Potentially, Switzerland's success with its mixture of regulatory approaches initiated the enaction of similar composed regulatory elements in the EU, also utilizing a combination of agile and risk-based regulation. 20 months and several rounds of draft proposals later, the EU Parliament approved on 20 April 2023 the Regulation on Markets in Crypto-Assets (MiCA) by the European Commission. MiCa marks a monumental day for the virtual assets' ecosystem with the introduction of the first comprehensive pan-European virtual assets framework. Concurrently, the EU Parliament has passed legislation to implement the travel rule (see above under anonymity) with the Regulation on Information Accompanying Transfers of Funds and Certain Crypto-Assets. Like the regulation in Singapore and Switzerland, MiCA defines and assigns virtual assets and virtual asset service providers. Security tokens are not covered by MiCA since they are already covered by the Markets in Financial Instruments Directive II (MiFID II). Further, MiCA introduces regulatory measures for all virtual assets and virtual asset service providers to avoid regulatory lacunas and arbitrage within the EU member states. These measures comprise of FATF compliant AML/CFT regulation, consumer protection and financial stability regulatory measures, such as white paper publications, disclosure requirements, minimum capital requirements, and measures for preventing market abuse and market manipulation. Further, MiCA sets out a license requirement for virtual asset service providers to conduct business in the EU. A significant advantage of the MiCA license constitutes the passporting system within the EU member states. Once an entity has received the MiCA license, it is authorized to conduct business in all EU member states.

The downside of creating and enacting a new and dedicated framework is the remaining uncertainty regarding implementation standards and enforcement practices. For now, the technical implementation standards still pose risks of burdening businesses with high levels of complexity and intervention.

Regulation by Enforcement in the United States

In stark contrast to the two previous regulatory approaches stands the United States' (US) approach of virtual asset regulation by enforcement. Regulation by enforcement means the "use of enforcement actions for making rules" (WEF, 2023, p. 22). Regulators facilitating this approach abstain from creating a dedicated framework for virtual assets and virtual asset service providers and from the adaptation of existing regulation to new technologies. Instead, regulatory authorities reference existing regulatory frameworks like security or AML/CFT regulation to bring enforcement actions against virtual asset entities. This approach is accompanied by uncertainties for businesses since the rule formulation occurs at a stage where they could find themselves already accused of having violated regulatory frameworks (WEF, 2023). Exemplarily, the US Securities and Exchange Commission (SEC) brought lawsuits against virtual assets entities Binance and Coinbase as well as against related individuals, like Binance Founder Changpeng Zhao (SEC, 2023). According to SEC (2023a), charges against Binance include "operating unregistered exchanges, broker-dealers, and clearing agencies; misrepresenting trading controls and oversight on the Binance.US platform; and the unregistered offer and sale of securities". Coinbase was similarly charged for "operating as an unregistered securities exchange, broker and clearing agency" (SEC, 2023b). SEC initiated both lawsuits very recently in June 2023, therefore the outcome is still unclear. However, an outflow of virtual assets entities in the past years could be observed in the US (Jeng, 2023; Gonzalez, 2022).

Reflection Regulatory Approaches

WEF (2023) conducted a noteworthy analysis of regulatory approaches based on "qualitative multistakeholder consultations with regulators, industry and civil society", in which they have rated regulatory approaches against perceived outcomes (WEF, 2023). While such an analysis has many limitations and can only provide a broad indication, the results might nevertheless serve as reflection of the general atmosphere on virtual assets regulation. The categories of assessment are "providing certainty for businesses, addressing data gaps, enforcement effectiveness and promoting innovation" (p. 22). The best scoring regulatory approach is risk-based regulation. Interestingly, risk-based regulation scores equivalently to regulation by enforcement in the category of enforcement effectiveness. Regulation by enforcement is apart from this, and was the least scoring regulatory approach in the analysis.

Overall, the analysis has shown that academics, renowned institutes and committees around the globe identify and declare their support to develop a coordinated global approach to achieve an effective and consistent framework for virtual assets that promotes consistency and comprehensiveness in virtual asset regulation. This equals regulatory certainty. WEF (2023) explicitly recommends regulatory certainty as one of their three recommendations tailored for national/regional regulators (p. 26). The FATF, as global standard setter for AML/CFT/CPF, recommends in its FATF Recommendations (2023) the application of a risk-based approach to virtual assets and virtual asset service providers. The recommendation is limited to AML/CFT/CPF and it does therefore not cover new regulatory developments like in Singapore that aim to include consumer protection and financial stability concerns going forward, however, it declares nevertheless their support for regulatory certainty.

After all, the risk-based regulatory approach potentially provides the most universal approach for national/regional regulators with advantages of high flexibility and resource efficiency. The agile approach allows for flexibility and innovative solutions but is limited in its applicability since it builds on market maturity and ecosystem development in the respective jurisdiction. The regulation by enforcement approach, as aforementioned, lacks regulatory certainty and predictability.

Importantly, the regulatory approaches are not exclusive, and jurisdictions can refer to more than one approach as seen above in the cases of Switzerland and the EU. In respect to the use of existing rules and regulation that have been adapted to include virtual assets (Singapore) or the use of newly enacted frameworks (Switzerland, EU), it depends on individual capacities, preferences, and adoptability of the existing regulation for jurisdictions.

FUTURE WORK

As the DLT ecosystem evolves further, a development in the direction of DeFi with lesser involvement of intermediaries and financial institutions – in line with its genesis – is possible and would once again fundamentally transform financial services as they exist today. This development would pose significant unaddressed regulatory and practical challenges, such as identifying responsible parties in DeFi arrangements and overseeing opaque governance structures (FSM, 2022). For now, the analyzed regulatory responses do not address DeFi. However, the FATF (2023a, 2023b) reported increased activity on decentralized exchanges and applications in response to headlines about the failure and collapses of centralized exchanges. Also, the report highlights concerns expressed by jurisdictions to assess DeFi risks due to lack of data and experience (FATF, 2023b). If the risks are not clear, regulatory responses are for the moment not in prospect, but should be on the agenda for the future.

CONCLUSION

A global approach to virtual assets is required to correspond to the borderless nature of the underlying technology. However, measures implemented within jurisdictions remain center pieces for the overall success of the desired global approach. As mirrored in the WEF recommendations for the respective addressees, the recommendations at the international level concern baseline regulatory standards, such as technology-neutral principles, characterization, and classification as well as promoting clarity, interoperability, and data-sharing. At the same time, the global approach builds on the implementation through regulatory authorities at the national/regional level. Therefore, it is important to not seek an optimum but unattainable goal of responsible global regulatory evolution but be aware of deviations between theory and practice, for example in the form of gaps of implementation and capacity constraints in different jurisdictions. At the national/regional level, much regulatory activity is seen, utilizing various regulatory approaches, and adjusting regulatory intervention over time, according to new and increased risks occurring. Given the ongoing rapid development in the DLT financial services sphere, the risk-based regulatory approach is identified as potentially the most universal approach for national/regional regulators with the significant advantages of high flexibility and resource efficiency.

However, as also identified in this chapter, regulations at the current stage of virtual asset revolution are mainly implemented for identified centralized intermediaries, utilizing requirements and rules from financial regulation. Therefore, much work lies ahead of regulatory authorities, to address the distinct features and decentralized applications of virtual assets.

REFERENCES

Adams, A., & Ibert, M. (2022). *Runs on Algorithmic Stablecoins: Evidence from Iron, Titan, and Steel. FEDS Notes.* Board of Governors of the Federal Reserve System. https://www.federalreserve.gov/econres/notes/feds-notes/runs-on-algorithmic-stablecoins-evidence-from-iron-titan-and-steel-20220602.html

Anker-SørensenL.ZetzscheD. A. (2021). From Centralized to Decentralized Finance: The Issue of `Fake-DeFi´. SSRN. https://papers.ssrn.com/sol3/papers.cfm?abstract_id=3978815 doi:10.2139/ssrn.3978815

Arner, D. W., Auer, R., & Frost, J. (2020). *Stablecoins: Risks, potential and regulation.* BIS Working Papers No 905.

Arner, D. W., Zetzsche, D. A., Buckley, R. P., & Kirkwood, J. M. (2023a). How Crypto Has Become Vulnerable to Problems of Traditional Finance. *The CLS Blue Sky Blog.* https://clsbluesky.law.columbia.edu/2023/05/30/the-financialization-of-crypto/

Arner, D. W., Zetzsche, D. A., Buckley, R. P., & Kirkwood, J. M. (2023b). *The Financialization of Crypto: Lessons from FTX and the Crypto Winter of 2022-2023.* University of Hong Kong Faculty of Law Research Paper No. 2023/19.

Blandin, A., Cloots, A. S., Hussain, H., Rauchs, M., Saleuddin, R., Allen, J. G., Zhang, Z. B., & Cloud, K. (2019). *Global Cryptoasset Regulatory Landscape Study.* Cambridge Centre for Alternative Finance, Cambridge Judge Business School, University of Cambridge. https://www.jbs.cam.ac.uk/wp-content/uploads/2020/08/2019-04-ccaf-global-cryptoasset-regulatory-landscape-study.pdf

Burroughes, T. (2023). *FTX Collapse May Prompt Big Regulatory Crackdown – Lawyer.* Wealth Briefing. https://www.wealthbriefing.com/html/article.php?id=196248

European Systemic Risk Board. (2023). *Crypto-assets and decentralized finance May 2023.* https://www.esrb.europa.eu/pub/pdf/reports/esrb.cryptoassetsanddecentralisedfinance202305~9792140acd.en.pdf

Financial Action Task Force. (2019). *Mandate.* https://www.fatf-gafi.org/en/the-fatf/mandate-of-the-fatf.html

Financial Action Task Force 2023. (2023a) *International Standards on Combating Money Laundering and the Financing of Terrorism & Proliferation: The FATF Recommendations.* https://www.fatf-gafi.org/content/dam/fatf-gafi/recommendations/FATF%20Recommendations%202012.pdf.coredownload.inline.pdf

Financial Action Task Force 2023. (2023b) *Targeted Update on Implementation of the FATF Standards on Virtual Assets and Virtual Asset Service Providers.* https://www.fatf-gafi.org/content/fatf-gafi/en/publications/Fatfrecommendations/targeted-update-virtual-assets-vasps-2023.html

Financial Stability Board. (2022). *Regulation, Supervision and Oversight of Crypto-Asset Activities and Markets: Consultative Document.* https://www.fsb.org/wp-content/uploads/P111022-3.pdf

Gonzalez, N. E. (2022). Does Cryptocurrency Staking Fall Under SEC Jurisdiction? *Fordham Journal of Corporate & Financial Law, 27*(2), 521–561.

Haentjens, M., De Graaf, T., & Kokorin, I. (2020). The Failed Hopes of Disintermediation: Crypto-custodian Insolvency, Legal Risks and How to Avoid Them, *Singapore Journal of Legal Studies,* 526-63.

International Monetary Fund. (2023). *IMF Policy Paper Elements of Effective Policies for Crypto Assets.* https://www.imf.org/en/Publications/Policy-Papers/Issues/2023/02/23/Elements-of-Effective-Policies-for-Crypto-Assets-530092

Jeng, L. (2023). Crypto Migration: European And Asian Regulators Welcome Crypto Innovation While U.S. Cracks Down. *Forbes.* https://www.forbes.com/sites/digital-assets/2023/04/07/crypto-migration-european-and-asian-regulators-welcome-crypto-innovation-while-us-cracks-down/?sh=2777e18d481c

Lee, J., & L'heureux, F. (2020). A Regulatory Framework for Cryptocurrency. *European Business Law Review, 31*(3), 423–446. doi:10.54648/EULR2020018

Lehmann, M. (2019). Who Owns Bitcoin? Private Law Facing the Blockchain. *Minnesota Journal of Law, Science & Technology, 21*(1), 95–135. doi:10.2139srn.3402678

Monetary Authority of Singapore. (2023). *Response to Public Consultation on Proposed Regulatory Measures for Digital Payment Token Services (Part 1).* https://www.mas.gov.sg/-/media/mas/news-and-publications/consultation-papers/2022-proposed-regulatory-measures-for-dpt-services/response-to-public-consultation-on-proposed-regulatory-measures-for-dpt-services-part-1.pdf

U.S. Securities and Exchange Commission. (2023a). *Press Release SEC Files 13 Charges Against Binance Entities and Founder Changpeng Zhao.* https://www.sec.gov/news/press-release/2023-101

U.S. Securities and Exchange Commission. (2023b). *Press Release SEC Charges Coinbase for Operating as an Unregistered Securities Exchange, Broker, and Clearing Agency.* https://www.sec.gov/news/press-release/2023-102

World Economic Forum. (2023). *Pathways to the Regulation of Crypto-Assets: A Global Approach May 2023.* https://www3.weforum.org/docs/WEF_Pathways_to_the_Regulation_of_Crypto_Assets_2023.pdf

Zetzsche, D. A., Anker-Sørensen, L., Passador, M. L., & Wehrli, A. (2022). *DLT-Based Enhancement of Cross-Border Payment Efficiency – a Legal and Regulatory Perspective.* BIS Working Papers No 1015.

KEY TERMS AND DEFINITIONS

Multilateral Memorandum of Understanding: Multilateral Memorandum of Understanding (MMoU) represents a common understanding and conduct among signatories, pursuing the same aim.

Payment Tokens: Payment tokes are defined by Singapore's PS Act (Section 2) as "any digital representation of value…that: is expressed in a unit, is not denominated in any currency and not pegged by its issuer to any currency, is, or is intended to be, a medium of exchange accepted by the public or a section of the public, as payment for goods or services or for the discharge of a debt, and can be transferred, stored or traded electronically."

Security Tokens: Virtual tokens that serve the same functions as a conventional capital markets products.

Chapter 25
The Future of Web 3:
A Roadmap for the Decentralized Web

Azadeh Eskandarzadeh
University Canada West, Canada

ABSTRACT

This article examines the ways in which Web 3.0 technologies can be advanced through research and innovation across disciplines. To completely benefit from the semantic web, efforts must be made to establish semantic standards and compensate data providers. To ensure ethical AI in the Web 3.0 era, researchers in the field must fixate on creating systems that are both reliable and readily explicable. Enhanced scalability, usability, and governance models are among the objectives of developing decentralized technologies like blockchain. When decentralized and AI-enabled systems become the norm, security, privacy, and accountability research will become increasingly crucial. Multi Stakeholder engagement will be required to resolve governance concerns in order to maximize the benefits of Web 3.0 while minimizing the risks.

INTRODUCTION

Web 3 and Web 3.0

This leads us to the subsequent stage of the internet, wherein numerous individuals aspire to regain authority from the dominant entities that have established hegemony over it. The terms web 3 and Web 3.0 are frequently utilized interchangeably, although they represent distinct concepts.

web 3 represents the paradigm shift towards a decentralized internet infrastructure constructed upon blockchain technology. The concept of Web 3.0 can be traced back to the initial vision of Tim Berners-Lee for the internet, wherein he envisioned a network of interconnected websites operating at the data level. The current internet infrastructure can be characterized as a vast collection of documents. Computational systems demonstrate the capability to retrieve information in response to human instructions. However, they are limited in their capacity to comprehend the inherent significance or deeper meaning embedded within our queries.

DOI: 10.4018/978-1-6684-9919-1.ch025

Copyright © 2023, IGI Global. Copying or distributing in print or electronic forms without written permission of IGI Global is prohibited.

WEB 3.0

Berners-Lee, Hendler, and Lassila came up with the concept of the Semantic Web in the year 2001. In certain areas, the Semantic Web is also referred to as Web 3.0. They were of the view that this forward-thinking method had the potential to totally revolutionize the manner in which we engage with the World Wide Web. If we were to integrate characteristics such as content that is machine-readable and artificial intelligence (AI), it has been hypothesized that the Semantic Web may completely alter the manner in which we interact with websites. This is something that has been suggested. According to O'Reilly (2007), the modern web, also known as Web 2.0, makes it feasible for users to easily share the content that they have created on the website. This ability to easily share content is made possible by Web 2.0. However, it is difficult for robots to read and comprehend the information, which is one of the areas in which it falls short. This is one of the areas in which it falls short. Ontologies and semantic labeling, according to Shadbolt, Berners-Lee, and Hall's (2006) interpretation, will be included into Web 3.0 as a solution to this problem, which they claim will be resolved. Robots will be able to acquire a deeper knowledge of the content found on the internet as a direct result of the development of these technologies. Berners-Lee and colleagues (2001) argue that the building of the Semantic Web makes use of a variety of distinct technologies. These technologies include the Resource Description Framework (RDF), Web Ontology Language (OWL), and Simplified Knowledge Organisation System (SKOS). According to Shadbolt et al. (2006), the combination of many different technological systems leads to the development of a worldwide "semantic graph." The data in the graph are connected in some way, and it is possible that AI systems will make use of this information. Berners-Lee and colleagues (2001) postulated that Web 3.0 will bring forth a multitude of advantages, one of which would be enhanced search capabilities that are both easier to use and understand. In order to deliver tailored ideas and automatic responses, the technology that our organization offers takes use of semantic query responding and reasoning over the network of data. The introduction of Web 3.0 is just around the horizon, and it has the potential to bring about a fundamental shift in the manner in which we take in information when interacting with websites online. The effective utilization of nonrenewable resources, the reduction of waste and pollution, the development of social and economic benefits for local communities, and the cultivation of a sustainable ethos within the organization are some of the important considerations that need to be taken into account. Other important considerations include the cultivation of a sustainable ethos within the organization. In addition, the United Nations Global Compact (2015) states that the implementation of sustainable innovation has the potential to facilitate the reduction of costs, the enhancement of competitiveness, and the provision of new opportunities within the market. As a consequence of this, it is extremely required to recognise that it plays an essential part in establishing a sustainable future and in resolving the grave concerns posed by climate change and social inequality. Consequently, it is absolutely necessary to acknowledge that it plays an essential role in reaching a sustainable future. This is a prerequisite that cannot be ignored under any circumstances.

The Evolution of the Web

As stated by Hearn (2009), the advent of Web 1.0 facilitated the creation of web pages that possessed a static nature, limiting their functionality to mere reading capabilities. In 2005, O'Reilly provided a description of Web 2.0 as a period characterized by the emergence of user-generated content and the prominence of social networking. In the year 1890, Warren and Brandeis made an observation regarding the advent of Web 2.0, noting the emergence of concerns pertaining to data silos and privacy risks. The individuals involved were endeavoring to address particular challenges associated with these matters. Nguyen (2020) posits that the primary objective of web 3 is to achieve decentralization of the internet by leveraging cutting-edge technologies.

The Advantages of Decentralization

One fundamental principle of WEB 3 is to gradually dismantle the existing hierarchical structure by establishing a decentralized internet. This is achieved through the utilization of Blockchain technology, which operates on a peer-to-peer network. Instead of relying on a centralized server system for data transmission, Blockchain Technology employs a network of devices known as nodes to collectively store and share files. This decentralized approach eliminates the need for central administration or control, ensuring that each node possesses equal power and performs the same tasks. Consequently, no single entity can assert dominance over the data, resulting in a digital democracy where every connected device contributes to the platform's strength. Peer-to-peer and blockchain technologies are currently prevalent in various domains, particularly in the realm of cryptocurrency. These technologies have revolutionized the financial industry by offering a decentralized approach to investment and banking. Decentralization has the potential to significantly alter the manner in which the internet is utilized, particularly in the context of Web 3.

Is web 3 Already in Existence?

The complete attainment of a fully decentralized online architecture, as envisioned by advocates of web 3, has not yet been fully realized. Nevertheless, several attributes and functionalities frequently linked with web 3 are already evident within the existing online environment. Several enterprises operating in the field of cryptocurrency, non-fungible tokens (NFTs), decentralized finance (DeFi), and other web 3 technologies have obtained significant financial support from private venture capital firms. A wide range of cryptocurrencies and non-fungible tokens (NFTs) are available, exhibiting diverse levels of trading activity. Currently, there are several decentralized autonomous organizations (DAOs) and decentralized applications (dApps) that are in operation, such as Decentraland, Axie Infinity, and OpenSea. However, a considerable proportion of these applications and services demonstrate a level of centralization in their decision-making processes regarding platform selection, thus restricting their availability solely to web browsers. Due to the fluid and dynamic nature of the web 3 concept as a decentralized web, it is plausible that prevailing attributes, applications, and enterprises presently affiliated with it may not hold substantial prominence within a more developed web 3 framework.

Moreover, it is worth noting that some applications, which are deemed essential elements of web 3, can be developed by companies that operate within the Web 2.0 framework. These applications may also function in collaboration with Web 2.0 services or be adopted and integrated into Web 2.0 platforms.

Approval of web 3

web 3 has emerged as a reactionary solution to address the apprehensions associated with centralized technological platforms. The development of this technology has occurred concurrently, with a primary emphasis on resolving concerns pertaining to user privacy, data ownership, and data security. Advocates of web 3 applications and services hold the perspective that these platforms will not be subject to monopolistic control by any singular corporate entity or governing body. Conversely, the ownership will reside within the control of the users themselves. Individuals will be afforded the chance to acquire ownership tokens through active engagement in the advancement and maintenance of said services. Individuals are afforded the chance to generate income through their online engagements by receiving cryptocurrencies and other tokens as a means of remuneration for their contributions, such as posting, sharing, or composing reviews pertaining to diverse products and services. These tokens have the potential to grant individuals membership to decentralized autonomous organizations (DAOs), facilitate access to decentralized applications (dApps), or confer voting rights on the decisions made by web 3 companies. Proponents of this framework assert that it possesses the capacity to democratize ownership of data and diminish the sway of centralized Web 2.0 corporations.

Technologies Driving web 3

Drescher (2017) argues that blockchains offer several advantages, including the promotion of decentralization, transparency, and immutability. Szabo (1997) explains that smart contracts enable the establishment of rules that can be programmed without the need for a central authority. Benet (2014) explains that IPFS offers a decentralized storage solution. Narayanan et al. (2016) argue that cryptocurrencies and tokens have the ability to generate economic incentives. Chaum (1981) proposed that anonymity networks have the potential to enhance privacy, while Diffie and Hellman (1976) argued that encryption plays a crucial role in safeguarding data security.

Barriers to the Implementation of Web 3

Zervas, Proserpio, and Byers (2017) highlight that a notable obstacle within the web 3 ecosystem revolves around the lack of established governance norms. According to Cuozzo (2020), the issue of scalability in blockchains presents an additional challenge that needs to be taken into account. According to Chander (2014), one of the prominent obstacles encountered by web 3 pertains to the problem of inequitable accessibility. An additional obstacle, as highlighted by Wu (2003), pertains to the potential hazards that pose a threat to the principle of network neutrality. Moreover, Sundararajan (2016) highlights that a notable obstacle within the web 3 framework pertains to the lack of essential competencies.

LITERATURE REVIEW

Holowczak and Wargo (2020) as well as Popescu (2019) have underscored the importance of the web 3 concept. The underlying premise of this concept entails envisioning an internet ecosystem that operates in a decentralized manner, devoid of central authority control. The proposed system would exhibit transparency and openness, allowing for unrestricted access and dissemination of information. The realization of this vision is facilitated by the advancements in technologies, notably blockchain. In order to fully realize the capabilities of web 3, it is imperative to confront a number of obstacles that have been identified by Zervas et al. (2017), Cuozzo (2020), and Chander (2014). The primary objective of this literature review is to examine the existing body of research pertaining to the significant technologies, obstacles, and prospective advancements associated with web 3. Drescher (2017) and Schwartz et al. (2019)

posit that the incorporation of blockchain and distributed ledger technologies represents a substantial transformation, facilitating the decentralization of web 3.Emerging technologies such as the Internet of Things (IoT) and blockchain have the potential to revolutionize a variety of different business sectors. When combined, they have the potential to provide answers to problems relating to the decentralization, traceability, and security of data. Blockchain technology has the potential to solve some of the trust and security problems that are inherent in IoT networks.

According to Gubbi et al. (2013), the Internet of Things (IoT) is a network that consists of physical devices, automobiles, household appliances, and other things that are integrated with electronics, software, sensors, actuators, and connections to allow the objects to communicate with one another and share data. According to Al-Fuqaha et al. (2015), an Internet of Things (IoT) system will usually include cloud-based platforms for data storage and analysis, sensors for the collection of data, and network connection for the transmission of data.

According to Narayanan et al. (2016), blockchain is a decentralized ledger system that enables the exchange of data over a network of nodes in a way that is both safe and transparent. According to Zhao et al. (2019), the most important characteristics of blockchain technology for Internet of Things applications are decentralization, transparency, auditability, security, and traceability.

The utilization of blockchain technology enables the creation of applications such as smart contracts, as indicated by Szabo (1997) and Baumann et al. (2020). The functionality of these applications is achieved through decentralization, eliminating the requirement for centralized control. Benet (2014) asserts that the integration of decentralized storage solutions, such as IPFS, is of paramount importance for the progress of web 3 infrastructure. Narayanan et al. (2016) posits that cryptocurrencies and tokens are perceived as mechanisms to incentivize individuals to engage in decentralized systems.

Numerous scholars, such as Zervas et al. (2017), Cuozzo (2020), Chander (2014), and Sundararajan (2016), have undertaken investigations aimed at identifying the barriers that could hinder the complete realization of web 3's capabilities, notwithstanding its remarkable technological progress. The challenges encountered encompass concerns pertaining to governance, scalability, disparities in access, and deficiencies in skills. Antonopoulos (2015) and Yujnovsky (2019) posit that the advancement of web 3 necessitates the incorporation of established norms, protocols, and policies to augment governance. According to a study conducted by d'Anjou (2019), the incorporation of artificial intelligence (AI) and machine learning (ML) has the potential to significantly augment the cognitive capabilities of decentralized applications in the web 3 era. The utilization and commercial frameworks of the aforementioned technology have been investigated by scholars Shi and Li (2020) as well as Ceballos et al. (2020) in their respective studies

Nevertheless, the successful implementation of this technology is contingent upon surmounting the existing challenges. Throughout the years, researchers have conducted comprehensive investigations into the impacts of technology on various facets of human existence. These encompass various domains such as security, privacy, economy, and society. Several significant contributions have been made in this particular domain, such as the scholarly investigations carried out by Warren and Brandeis in 1890, Hearn in 2009, and Wu in 2003. The author posits that there is a rapid advancement in the development of technologies that facilitate the implementation of web 3. Nevertheless, the author highlights a number of obstacles that necessitate resolution in order for web 3 to effectively disrupt and transform the internet. Several challenges that are encountered are associated with governance, scalability, access, and skills. The author posits that the resolution of these challenges holds significant importance in the pursuit of decentralization within the context of web 3. Alternatively, its scope will continue to be confined to a restricted segment of the centralized internet.

METHODOLOGY

In order to explore the current as well as potential developments relating to Web 3.0, a methodical search of databases was carried out to locate relevant academic work produced between the years of 2010 and 2022. This was done so that the topic could be investigated. The following databases were searched as part of the investigation:

Materials and Procedure

A comprehensive search was performed across five prominent academic databases, specifically IEEE Xplore, ACM Digital Library, Web of Science, Scopus, and Google Scholar. In the present study, a variety of search terms were employed to investigate the subject matter. The aforementioned terms encompassed within the discourse are "Web 3.0," "semantic web," "machine readable web," "decentralized web," "peer to peer web," and "future of the web."

The studies included in the analysis were required to satisfy the following criteria: In order to satisfy the established criteria, it is imperative that the articles conform to the prescribed categories: The publications should have encompassed the period from 2010 to 2022. (b) The articles and proceedings should possess the characteristic of having undergone a rigorous process of peer review. The articles should consist of either original research findings or comprehensive review articles. The analysis did not encompass opinion pieces, editorials, book chapters, and studies that specifically examined trends prior to the advent of Web 3.0.A two-step selection process was employed. Initially, the titles and abstracts were scrutinized to evaluate their preliminary pertinence in accordance with the inclusion criteria. Subsequently, we acquired the complete texts and conducted a comprehensive examination of them in order to arrive at our ultimate choices for selection.

Planning and Evaluation

(Braun & Clarke, 2006) conducted a thematic analysis of the Web 3.0 literature to identify key themes surrounding emerging technologies and their potential applications. This analysis is based on the studies identified through the search process outlined in the Materials and Methods section. These aspects of each study were evaluated:

- Technologies and applications of Web 3.0 are discussed.
- Future trends for Web 3.0 technologies and architectures have been identified.
- Obstacles and obstacles to the adoption of Web 3.0 are highlighted.
- Discussion of Web 3.0's potential effects and implications.

The relevant concepts, findings, and insights from each study were synthesized and organized by the researchers into initial themes. After undergoing multiple iterations of refinement, we successfully discerned the primary subjects that pertain to the realm of contemporary and forthcoming Web 3.0

technologies. This paper aims to conduct a comprehensive analysis of the existing literature on Web 3.0. The primary emphasis of our study will revolve around the fundamental technologies that are driving the concept of a decentralized web, the diverse range of applications that can derive advantages from this notion, and the challenges that necessitate resolution. According to Braun and Clarke (2006), This analysis provides a comprehensive examination of the technologies, opportunities, challenges, and potential future advancements associated with Web 3.0 over the course of the next decade.

Where is web 3.0 at the moment?

The concept of years, as elucidated by Berners-Lee et al. in their seminal work published in 2001. Nevertheless, scholars specializing in the domain of technology concur that the advancement of Web 3.0 is currently in its nascent phase (Clarke, 2018; Sundararajan, 2016). Technologies such as blockchain, decentralized storage, and peer-to-peer networks have demonstrated notable advancements and are increasingly reaching a state of maturity (Narayanan et al., 2016; Benet, 2014; Szabo, 1997).Scholars have undertaken efforts to develop and deploy decentralized applications across various domains, including finance, supply chains, governance, and identity management (Ceballos et al., 2020; Shi & Li, 2020).The field of Web 3.0 is experiencing rapid growth in research, as evidenced by the scholarly contributions made by Yli-Huumo et al. (2016).However, Web 3.0 continues to face several challenges pertaining to governance, scalability, access, and skills. The aforementioned challenges have been identified in prior research conducted by Zervas et al. (2017), Cuozzo (2020), Chander (2014), and Sundararajan (2016). As stated by d'Anjou (2019), there is a deficiency in the current integration and interoperability of Web 3.0 technologies and applications.

The future of the Web

According to Berners-Lee et al. (2001), the introduction of the World Wide Web caused a substantial paradigm change in the ways in which people access information, participate in communication, and carry out economic operations. The current architecture of the web is susceptible to a number of restrictions, which has resulted in the development of a conceptual framework sometimes referred to as "Web 3.0." According to Shadbolt et al.'s 2019 research, the framework that is now under development intends to combine semantic capabilities, intelligent features, and a decentralized structure. The purpose of this study is to conduct an analysis of the key trends that are affecting the development of the internet towards the goal.

The Machine-Readable data and the Semantic web

The primary objective of the semantic web is to enhance the machine-readability of web-based information by employing semantic standards and ontologies (Berners-Lee et al., 2001). The aforementioned feature facilitates the seamless sharing and integration of data across various applications (Shadbolt et al., 2019). The World Wide Web Consortium (W3C) has formulated a set of recommendations, namely RDF, OWL, and SPARQL, with the aim of providing support for the semantic web (W3C, 2004). In order to fully actualize the potential of the semantic web, it is imperative that semantic technologies be more extensively embraced (Shadbolt et al., 2019).

The process of organizing web content in a manner that enables machines to interpret and analyze it is a fundamental prerequisite for the realization of the "Web 3.0" concept, as proposed by Shadbolt et al. (2019). The objective of initiatives such as schema.org is to apply machine-readable metadata to web content to facilitate the functioning of intelligent applications (Guha et al., 2016). When integrated with semantic technologies, the "machine readable web" has the potential to unleash novel functionalities. The proposal for the Semantic Web emerged as a strategy to augment the functionalities of the World Wide Web, allowing machines to effectively search and analyze web content by considering the semantic significance of the information. The identification and comprehension of relationships between various elements of web content are facilitated by the application of inference rules and organizational tools (Dominic, Francis, & Philomena, 2014). The introduction of the Semantic Web brings forth a novel dimension by facilitating the personalization of content based on individual user preferences. The internet search function offers more than a comprehensive compilation of websites that users must manually sift through to locate the desired information. In contrast, the platform provides a multimedia file that has undergone translation, personalization, and customization to cater to the unique requirements of each user. The concept of the Semantic Web involves the advancement of virtual personal assistants or agents that assist users in effectively finding relevant information within a specified time frame (Maria & Negrila, 2012).

Points from Hitzler et al. (2014)

First they claimed semantic web has the potential to describe knowledge by using a format that machines can understand. This format allows for data about documents and how they are connected to be easily processed. The process is achieved by using several tools and languages, including Resource Description Framework (RDF), RDF Schema (RDFS), Web Ontology Language (OWL), query language for RDF (SPARQL), and Simple Knowledge Organization System (SKOS). Use logical reasoning to draw important conclusions.

Second, to facilitate the exchange of information, we use TCP/IP protocols and file formats like RSS. The study conducted by Rubens, Kaplan, and Okamoto (2011) found that... Can you give me more examples of how e-learning can be used in different situations? The term "3.0 technologies" encompasses the most recent advancements and innovations in the world of technology. Artificial intelligence (AI) has the potential to revolutionize e-Learning by allowing us to focus more on modeling tasks instead of getting bogged down by the tedious process of implementing countless rules. Moreover, using a data-driven approach in this context will lead to reduced costs for maintenance and adaptation. The reason for this is that the model has the ability to adapt well to new users, content, and possible changes. Web 2.0 tools are a collection of online applications and platforms that allow users to interact, collaborate, and share information with each other. In addition, people often use collaborative tools in a casual and independent way. This helps them better understand how to work together, even outside of traditional classrooms and formal educational settings. In the past, this task was quite difficult or even impossible to achieve.

Decentralized technologies and applications

The utilization of decentralized technologies, such as blockchain, peer-to-peer networks, and IPFS, facilitates the emergence of a novel paradigm for distributed data storage and applications (Benet, 2014;

Larimer et al., 2014; Sinnathamby et al., 2019). Although these technologies are currently in the early stages of development, they possess the capacity to enhance the democratic, resilient, and open nature of the internet by diminishing centralized control (Morris, 2019; Wood, 2014). There persist certain challenges pertaining to scalability, governance, and security that have the potential to impede the extensive adoption of the technology (Crosby et al., 2016).

The rise of Artificial Intelligence

Learning and natural language processing has facilitated the development of novel intelligent applications. According to Shadbolt et al. (2019), the integration of AI with the semantic web has the potential to facilitate the development of highly intelligent services on the internet. Nevertheless, it is imperative to acknowledge and tackle concerns pertaining to data privacy, ethics, and fairness to ensure responsible development and advancement of AI (Agrawal et al., 2018; Jobin et al., 2019).

In summary, it is anticipated that the future of the web will be influenced by the prevailing patterns of semantic intelligence, decentralization, and artificial intelligence. The manner in which these technologies strike a harmonious equilibrium between openness, privacy, and control will ultimately shape the future landscape of "Web 3.0 and beyond." The successful navigation of future challenges and opportunities will necessitate collaboration among technologists, businesses, and policymakers.

Challenges Encountered in The Adoption of Web 3.0

Despite the fact that technologies based on Web 3.0 have a number of desirable features, there are still obstacles that prevent their broad use. The difficulties encompass a variety of aspects such as the lack of established criteria and compatibility, apprehensions regarding the security, governance, and scalability of decentralized technologies, difficulties in ensuring the reliability and explain ability of AI, and obstacles in the adoption of Semantic Web technology (Shadbolt et al., 2019; Crosby et al., 2016; Jobin et al., 2019). Maria and Negrila (2012), Hussain (2012), and Rubens, Kaplan, and Okamoto (2011) have all discussed additional challenges, including the following: The confidentiality of data in the MashUps of the linked globe that will occur in the hyperspace may be compromised due to varying privacy regulations across different countries. There are various hazards that pose a threat to safety: Based on the research conducted by Weippl and Ebner (Hussain, 2012), it has been identified that an organization may be vulnerable to security threats due to the absence of server-side checks and the presence of excessive access. The attainment of accessibility to online content for individuals with special needs is anticipated to present greater challenges, similar to the provision of web-based applications for individuals with special needs. Insufficient standards are impeding the unrestricted dissemination of information and content among diverse computer systems. Existing standards, including the Shareable Course Object Reference Model (SCORM), the IEEE Learning Technology Standards Committee (LTSC), and the Instructional Management Systems project (IMS), among others, will require enhancements to effectively support the forthcoming iteration of the World Wide Web. The proliferation of e-Learning management systems has given rise to a notable surge in ethical dilemmas, prompting proponents to propose an expansion of the existing "Three Ps" pedagogical model to encompass the "P3E" model. The model encompasses various dimensions, namely personalization, participation, productivity, lecturer's ethics, learner's ethics, and organizational ethics. Silva, Costa, Prior, and Rogerson were cited in the study conducted by Rubens, Kaplan, and Okamoto (2011). The utilization of the internet across multiple languages: Currently, there is a lack of practical means to translate information due to the absence of interoperable and standardized models. This poses challenges for users who prefer straightforward and unchanging software, as it hinders their ability to effectively utilize such models. Furthermore, it is currently not possible to find a suitable rendition of the provided data. The dynamic nature of language as a living entity contributes to the obsolescence of translations over time, particularly when software lacks the ability to adapt and evolve.

Potential implications of Web 3.0

Web 3.0, once it becomes available, has the potential to bring about positive social changes. It can do this by making it easier to share and reuse data, encouraging the creation of more open and strong networks, and speeding up the development of intelligent apps. However, it is important to acknowledge that there is a potential for unintended consequences when it comes to matters like data privacy, algorithmic bias, and the centralized control of artificial intelligence (AI) systems (Agrawal et al., 2018). This topic necessitates thoughtful deliberation. Having prudent governance will be crucial in order to maximize benefits and minimize potential harm.

CONCLUSION AND FUTURE WORK

The aim of Web 3.0 is to make the Internet more accessible, adaptable, and useful for users of all different backgrounds and skills. This will be accomplished by the adoption of an architecture that is semantic, decentralized, and intelligent. According to Sahoo et al. (2022) and Crosby et al. (2016), there is still a large lot of work to be done in the areas of standardization, security, governance, and ethical use of AI. Both of these studies were conducted in the year 2022. If we want to be successful in solving these challenges, we will need to make major investments in research and actively encourage innovation at the confluence of semantic technologies, distributed ledgers, and artificial intelligence. According to the findings of a study that was conducted by Jain and colleagues in the year 2020, the goals of these activities are to enhance interoperability, make it simpler to reuse data across apps, and provide scalability so that the Web may continue to expand to handle its massiveness. According to Zhang et al. (2021), doing study into the reasons data publishers employ semantic technology might potentially help to the progress of this industry. It is difficult to lay enough attention on the relevance of growing funds for research into artificial intelligence, especially in the context of the creation of trustworthy and intelligible systems. This is because it is impossible to place enough emphasis on the significance of developing artificial intelligence. According to Amodei et al. (2016) and Kaur et al. (2010), adversarial training and the use of causal and counterfactual explanations are two other methods that might potentially be of aid in reaching this purpose. This strategy, if it is successful, might result in a better understanding of the need of creating artificial intelligence in an ethical manner in order for it to be employed in the age of Web 3.0. According to Biswas et al. (2021), if there is to be an increase in scalability, efficiency, and utility, then there has to be improvements made to blockchain technology, peer-to-peer networks, distributed ledgers, and other related technologies. According to Greiner and Ahmad (2021), there is a need for more research to be conducted on the governance and administration procedures of decentralized Web 3.0 infrastructure. As decentralized systems and systems that are enabled by AI become more prevalent, there will be a rise in the amount of privacy and security issues. As a consequence of this, doing research on preventative methods, accountability systems, and mitigation strategies is very important in order to solve these challenges. (Laubheimer, 2021; Lu et al., 2022) is an example that illustrates this point. There is a direct link between decentralization, artificial intelligence, and semantic technologies; all three will play a part in the role that plays a role in the development of the Web in the next several years. They are all working together to further the development of the Internet and contribute to its extension. According to Heeks and Renken (2018), the most effective method for addressing governance issues is often to enable a number of stakeholders to work together on the discovery of solutions. With this technique, the development of Web 3.0 will go forward at a faster pace, and it will also optimize Web 3.0's potential advantages while simultaneously reducing its possible negatives.

In conclusion, the combination of blockchain technology with the internet of things carries with it a number of potential benefits; yet, it is not without some disadvantages, the resolution of which will need more research. There will continue to be roadblocks in the way of standardization, security, governance, and ethical AI use as decentralized and AI-enabled systems grow more pervasive. Semantic technology, artificial intelligence, and decentralization are going to be the defining characteristics of Web 3.0, provided that stakeholders can collaborate to address governance challenges.

REFERENCES

Agrawal, A., Gans, J., & Goldfarb, A. (2018). Prediction, judgment, and artificial intelligence. In *Economics of artificial intelligence* (pp. 33–41). University of Chicago Press.

Antonopoulos, A. M. (2015). *Mastering Bitcoin: Unlocking Digital Cryptocurrencies*. O'Reilly Media, Inc.

Benet, J. (2014, November 5). *IPFS (InterPlanetary File System) is a content-addressed, versioned, peer-to-peer file system*. Retrieved from https://ipfs.io/

Berners-Lee, T., Hendler, J., & Lassila, O. (2001). The Semantic Web. Scientific American, 284(5), 34-43. The Semantic Web. *Scientific American*, *284*(5), 34–43. doi:10.1038cientificamerican0501-34 PMID:11681174

Biswas, K., Muthukkumarasamy, V., & Tan, W. L. (2021). Blockchain Technology: A Review from Theory to Applications. *IEEE Access : Practical Innovations, Open Solutions*, *9*, 79520–79548.

Bonneau, J., Miller, A., Clark, J., Narayanan, A., Kroll, J. A., & Felten, E. W. (2015). SoK: Research perspectives and challenges for Bitcoin and cryptocurrencies. In *IEEE Symposium on Security and Privacy (SP)* (pp. 104-121). IEEE. 10.1109/SP.2015.14

Bygrave, L. A. (2017). *Internet censorship*. Elgar Encyclopedia of Law and Technology.

Catalini, C., & Gans, J. S. (2020). Some simple economics of the blockchain. In *Economics of Blockchain* (pp. 13–25). University of Chicago Press.

Ceballos, K., Nikou, S., Giovanidis, T., & Hosking, J. (2020). A systematic mapping study on business models and monetization strategies for decentralized applications. *Journal of Software: Evolution and Process*, *32*(10), e2242.

Chander, A. (2014). The Racist Algorithm? *Michigan Law Review*, *115*(5), 1023–1046.

Clarke, R. (2018). What is Web 3.0? Transforming the Internet into a decentralised information market-place. *Computer Fraud & Security*, *2018*(12), 8–12.

Crosby, M., Pattanayak, P., Verma, S., & Kalyanaraman, V. (2016). BlockChain technology: Beyond bitcoin. *Applied Innovation*, *2*(6-10), 71.

Cuozzo, A. (2020). Blockchain Scalability: An Overview of Challenges and Proposals. In Handbook of Blockchain, Digital Finance, and Inclusion (Vol. 1, pp. 201-214). Academic Press.

Danjou, K. (Ed.). (2019). *The Decentralized Web Manifesto: Principles for a New Decentralized Web Architecture*. Internet Archive Book Images.

Dinh, T. T. A., Wang, J., Chen, G., Liu, R., Ooi, B. C., & Tan, K. L. (2018). BLOCKBENCH: A Framework for Analyzing Private Blockchains. In *Proceedings of the 2018 International Conference on Management of Data* (pp. 1085-1100). Academic Press.

Greiner, M., & Ahmad, I. (2021). Decentralized Governance for Decentralized Autonomous Organizations. *IEEE Access : Practical Innovations, Open Solutions*, *9*, 5229–5243.

Heeks, R., & Renken, J. (2018). Crafting rigorous action design research: Lessons from the applied collaborative design approach. *Information Technology for Development*, *24*(3), 632–651.

Holowczak, R., & Wargo, C. (2020). Cryptocurrencies as an Investment Vehicle: Analysis of Blockchain networks, Decentralization and Security Implications. *Technology Innovation Management Review*, *10*(9).

Johnston, A., Brown, C., & McSherry, C. (2020). *Roundup of cryptography and censorship research 2020*. Cryptography, Surveillance, and Privacy. Electronic Frontier Foundation.

Kaur, H., Nori, H., Jenkins, S., Caruana, R., Wallach, H., & Wortman Vaughan, J. (2020). Interpreting interpretability: Understanding data scientists' use of interpretability tools for machine learning. In Proceedings of the 2020 CHI conference on human factors in computing systems (pp. 1-14).ACM.

Li, F., Huh, E. N., Kwon, D., & Miller, E. L. (2020). Decentralized consensus protocols in blockchain networks: A survey. *ACM Computing Surveys*, *53*(3), 1–38.

Lu, J., Li, C., Zhu, H., Cao, Z., Du, X., Guizani, M., & Chen, H. H. (2022). Security and privacy in 6G: Fundamentals, applications, and solutions. *IEEE Wireless Communications*, *29*(1), 82–89.

Maria, A., & Negrila, C. (2012). Web 3.0 in Education. *eLearning and Software for Education (eLSE)*, *1*, 455-460.

Morris, D. Z. (2019). Blockchain could give us a peer-to-peer internet. *Fortune, 1*.

Narayanan, A., Bonneau, J., Felten, E., Miller, A., & Goldfeder, S. (2016). *Bitcoin and cryptocurrency technologies: a comprehensive introduction*. Princeton University Press.

Popescu, B. (2019). Web 3.0 and its impact on business models. *Expert Journal of Economics.*, *7*(2), 51–59.

Sahoo, S. S., Singh, B., Mohapatra, D. P., & Barik, R. K. (2022). *Web 3.0: Challenges, applications, and research issues*. Internet Technology Letters.

Schweizer, A. (2019). Commons-based peer production and open innovation. *Journal of Open Innovation, 5*(3), 52.

Shadbolt, N., Berners-Lee, T., & Hall, W. (2019). The semantic web revisited. *IEEE Intelligent Systems, 21*(3).

W3C. (2004). *W3C semantic web activity.* https://www.w3.org/2001/sw/

Wood, G. (2014). Ethereum: A secure decentralized generalized transaction ledger. *Ethereum Project Yellow Paper, 151*(2014), 1-32.

Wu, T. (2003). Network neutrality, broadband discrimination. *Journal on Telecommunications & High Technology Law, 2,* 141.

Yli-Huumo, J., Ko, D., Choi, S., Park, S., & Smolander, K. (2016). Where is current research on blockchain technology? a systematic review. *PLoS One, 11*(10), e0163477. doi:10.1371/journal.pone.0163477 PMID:27695049

Zervas, G., Proserpio, D., & Byers, J. W. (2017). The rise of the sharing economy: Estimating the impact of Airbnb on the hotel industry. *JMR, Journal of Marketing Research, 54*(5), 687–705. doi:10.1509/jmr.15.0204

Zhang, K., Liang, L., & Jin, H. (2021). Semantic web application promotion–challenges and countermeasures. *Semantic Web, 12*(6), 931–945.

Compilation of References

Abawajy, J. (2013). SQLIA detection and prevention approach for RFIDsystems. *Journal of Systems and Software, 86*(3), 751–758. doi:10.1016/j.jss.2012.11.022

Abawajy, J., & Fernando, H. (2015). Policy-based SQLIA detection and prevention approach for RFID systems. *Computer Standards & Interfaces, 38*, 64–71. doi:10.1016/j.csi.2014.08.005

Abbasi, A. G., & Khan, Z. (2017). Veidblock: verifiable identity using blockchain and ledger in a software defined network. In: *Companion Proceedings of the 10th International Conference on Utility and Cloud Computing*, (pp. 173–179). IEEE. 10.1145/3147234.3148088

Abdalla, R., & Esmail, M. (2019). Immersive Environments for Disaster and Emergency Management. In *Advances in Science*. Technology and Innovation. doi:10.1007/978-3-030-03828-1_8

Abrol, A. (2022). *Decentraland Metaverse: A Complete Guide*. Blockchain Council. Available at: https://www.blockchain-council.org/metaverse/decentraland-metaverse/

Accenture. (2021). Banking on AI: Unlocking Value. *Accenture*. https://www.accenture.com/_acnmedia/PDF-56/Accenture-Banking-on-AI-Unlocking-Value.pdf

Acikgul Firat, E., & Firat, S. (2020). Web 3.0 in learning environments: A systematic review. *Turkish Online Journal of Distance Education, 22*(1), 148–169. doi:10.17718/tojde.849898

Adams, A., & Ibert, M. (2022). *Runs on Algorithmic Stablecoins: Evidence from Iron, Titan, and Steel. FEDS Notes*. Board of Governors of the Federal Reserve System. https://www.federalreserve.gov/econres/notes/feds-notes/runs-on-algorithmic-stablecoins-evidence-from-iron-titan-and-steel-20220602.html

Adams, M. (2023). Comparing QuickBooks Online and QuickBooks Desktop. *Fourlane*. https://www.fourlane.com/blog/comparing-quickbooks-online-and-quickbooks-desktop/

Adams, P. R., Frizzo-Barker, J., Ackah, B. B., & Chow-White, P. A. (2020). Making space for women on the blockchain. In M. Ragnedda & G. Destefanis (Eds.), *Blockchain and Web 3.0: Social, Economic, and Technological Challenges* (pp. 48–61). Routledge.

Adams, R. J., & Hannaford, B. (1999). Stable haptic interaction with virtual environments. *IEEE Transactions on Robotics and Automation, 15*(3), 465–474. doi:10.1109/70.768179

Adapa, S., Fazal-e-Hasan, S. M., Makam, S. B., Azeem, M. M., & Mortimer, G. (2020). Examining the antecedents and consequences of perceived shopping value through smart retail technology. *Journal of Retailing and Consumer Services, 52*, 101901. doi:10.1016/j.jretconser.2019.101901

Adel, A. (2022). Future of industry 5.0 in society: Human-centric solutions, challenges and prospective research areas. *J Cloud Comp*, *11*(1), 40. doi:10.118613677-022-00314-5

Agarwal, S., & Zhang, J. (2020). FinTech, lending and payment innovation: A review. *Asia-Pacific Journal of Financial Studies*, *49*(3), 353–367. doi:10.1111/ajfs.12294

Agrawal, A., Gans, J., & Goldfarb, A. (2018). Prediction, judgment, and artificial intelligence. In *Economics of artificial intelligence* (pp. 33–41). University of Chicago Press.

Agrawal, T. K., Angelis, J., Khilji, W. A., Kalaiarasan, R., & Wiktorsson, M. (2023). Demonstration of a blockchain-based framework using smart contracts for supply chain collaboration. *International Journal of Production Research*, *61*(5), 1497–1516. https://doi-org.ezproxy.myucwest.ca/10.1080/00207543.2022.2039413. doi:10.1080/00207543.2022.2039413

Ahluwalia, A., Mahto, R. V., & Guerrero, M. (2020). Blockchain technology and startup financing: A transaction cost economics perspective. *Technological Forecasting and Social Change*, *151*, 119854. Advance online publication. doi:10.1016/j.techfore.2019.119854

Ahmad, M., Ali, A., & Khiyal, M. S. H. (2023). Fog Computing for Spatial Data Infrastructure: Challenges and Opportunities (pp. 152–178). doi:10.4018/978-1-6684-4466-5.ch008

Ahmad, M., Khayal, M. S. H., & Tahir, A. (2022). Analysis of Factors Affecting Adoption of Volunteered Geographic Information in the Context of National Spatial Data Infrastructure. *ISPRS International Journal of Geo-Information*, *11*(2), 120. doi:10.3390/ijgi11020120

Ahmed, K. A., Saraya, S. F., Wanis, J. F., & Ali-Eldin, A. M. (2023). A Blockchain Self-Sovereign Identity for Open Banking Secured by the Customer's Banking Cards. *Future Internet*, *15*(6), 208. doi:10.3390/fi15060208

Ahn, D., & Shin, D.-H. (2013). Is the social use of media for seeking connectedness or for avoiding social isolation? Mechanisms underlying media use and subjective well-being. *Computers in Human Behavior*, *29*(6), 2453–2462. doi:10.1016/j.chb.2012.12.022

Ahram, T., Sargolzaei, A., Sargolzaei, S., Daniels, J., & Amaba, B. (2017, June). Blockchain technology innovations. In 2017 IEEE technology & engineering management conference (TEMSCON) (pp. 137-141). IEEE. doi:10.1109/TEMSCON.2017.7998367

Aichner, T., Grünfelder, M., Maurer, O., & Jegeni, D. (2021). Twenty-Five Years of Social Media: A Review of Social Media Applications and Definitions from 1994 to 2019. *Cyberpsychology, Behavior, and Social Networking*, *24*(4), 215–222. doi:10.1089/cyber.2020.0134 PMID:33847527

Aiello, L. M., & Ruffo, G. (2012). Lotusnet: Tunable privacy for distributed online social network services. *Computer Communications*, *35*(1), 75–88. doi:10.1016/j.comcom.2010.12.006

Alaeddin, O., & Altounjy, R. (2018). Trust, Technology Awareness and Satisfaction Effect into the Intention to Use Cryptocurrency among Generation Z in Malaysia. *International Journal of Engineering and Technology*, *7*(4.29), 8–10. doi:. doi:10.14419/ijet.v7i4.29.21588

AlAhmad, M. A., & Alshaikhli, I. F. (2013). Broad View of Cryptographic Hash Functions - ProQuest. [IJCSI]. *International Journal of Computer Science Issues*, *10*(4). https://www.proquest.com/openview/848b6a4f46a36abf1c97cf30c78acd2f/1?pq-origsite=gscholar&cbl=55228

Alam, S. S., Susmit, S., Lin, C. Y., Masukujjaman, M., & Ho, Y. H. (2021). Factors affecting augmented reality adoption in the retail industry. *Journal of Open Innovation*, *7*(2), 142. doi:10.3390/joitmc7020142

Alamsyah, A., Widiyanesti, S., Wulansari, P., Nurhazizah, E., Dewi, A. S., Rahadian, D., Ramadhani, D. P., Hakim, M. N., & Tyasamesi, P. (2023). Blockchain traceability model in the coffee industry. *Journal of Open Innovation*, *9*(1), 100008. doi:10.1016/j.joitmc.2023.100008

Alazab, M., Alhyari, S., Awajan, A., & Abdallah, A. B. (2021). Blockchain technology in supply chain management: An empirical study of the factors affecting user adoption/acceptance. *Cluster Computing*, *24*(1), 83–101. doi:10.100710586-020-03200-4

Al-Bassam, M., Sonnino, A., & Bano, S. (2019). Fraud Proofs: Maximising Light Client Security and Scaling Blockchains with Dishonest Majorities. arXiv preprint arXiv:1809.09044.

Albayati, H., Kim, S. K., & Rho, J. J. (2020). Acceptance of financial transactions using blockchain technology and cryptocurrency: A customer perspective approach. *Technology in Society*, *62*, 101320. doi:10.1016/j.techsoc.2020.101320

Alcañiz, M., Bigné, E., & Guixeres, J. (2019). Virtual reality in marketing: A framework, review, and research agenda. *Frontiers in Psychology*, *10*, 1530. doi:10.3389/fpsyg.2019.01530 PMID:31333548

Alfandi, O., Khanji, S., Ahmad, L., & Khattak, A. (2020). A survey on boosting IoT security and privacy through block-chain Exploration, requirements, and open issues. *Cluster Computing*; *Springer Science+Business Media*, LLC, part of Springer Nature 2020.

Al-Gnbri M. (2022). Accounting and auditing in the metaverse world from a virtual reality perspective: A future research. *Journal of Metaverse*, *2*(1), 2941.

Alharby, M., & Van Moorsel, A. (2017). Blockchain-based smart contracts: A systematic mapping study. arXiv preprint arXiv:1710.06372. doi:10.5121/csit.2017.71011

Ali, A., & Ahmad, M. (2013). *Geospatial Data Sharing in Pakistan: Possibilities and Problems*. Spatial Enablement in Support of Economic Development and Poverty Reduction.

Ali, A., & Imran, M. (2020). The Evolution of National Spatial Data Infrastructure in Pakistan-Implementation Challenges and the Way Forward. *International Journal of Spatial Data Infrastructures Research*, *15*(0).

Ali, A., Imran, M., Jabeen, M., Ali, Z., & Mahmood, S. A. (2021). Factors influencing integrated information management: Spatial data infrastructure in Pakistan. *Information Development*. doi:10.1177/02666669211048483

Ali, M., & Bagui, S. (2021). Introduction to NFTs: The future of digital collectibles. *International Journal of Advanced Computer Science and Applications*, *12*(10), 50–56. doi:10.14569/IJACSA.2021.0121007

Ali, O., Momin, M., Shrestha, A., Das, R., Alhajj, F., & Dwivedi, Y. K. (2023). A review of the key challenges of non-fungible tokens. *Technological Forecasting and Social Change*, *187*, 122248. doi:10.1016/j.techfore.2022.122248

Alkafaji, B. K. A., Dashtbayaz, M. L., & Salehi, M. (2023). The Impact of Blockchain on the Quality of Accounting Information: An Iraqi Case Study. *Risks*, *11*(3), 58. doi:10.3390/risks11030058

Allam, Z. (2018). On smart contracts and organisational performance: A review of smart contracts through the blockchain technology. *Review of Economic and Business Studies*, *11*(2), 137–156. doi:10.1515/rebs-2018-0079

Allen, J. (2021). Bodies without Organs: Law, Economics, and Decentralised Governance. *Stanford Journal of Blockchain Law & Policy*. https://stanford-jblp.pubpub.org/pub/law-econ-decentralised-governance

Allen, D. W., & Potts, J. (2023). Web3 toolkits: A user innovation theory of crypto development. *Journal of Open Innovation*, *9*(2), 100050. doi:10.1016/j.joitmc.2023.100050

AllenH. J. (2023). DeFi: Shadow Banking 2.0? 64 Wm. & Mary L. Rev. 919. Available at SSRN: https://ssrn.com/abstract=4038788

Allen, M. (2012). What was Web 2.0? Versions as the dominant mode of internet history. *Sage (Atlanta, Ga.)*, *15*(2), 2. doi:10.1177/1461444812451567

Allison, C., Miller, A., Oliver, I., Michaelson, R., & Tiropanis, T. (2012). The Web in education. *Computer Networks*, *56*(18), 3811–3824. doi:10.1016/j.comnet.2012.09.017

Allison, M., & Kendrick, L. M. (2015). Toward education 3.0: Pedagogical affordances and implications of social software and the semantic web. *New Directions for Teaching and Learning*, *144*(144), 109–119. doi:10.1002/tl.20167

Allombert, V., Bourgoin, M., & Tesson, J. (2019, July). Introduction to the tezos blockchain. In *2019 International Conference on High Performance Computing & Simulation (HPCS)* (pp. 1-10). IEEE.

Amarin, N. Z. (2015). Web 3.0 and its reflections on the future of e-learning. *Academic Journal Of Science*, *4*(02), 115–122.

Amir Latif, R. M., Hussain, K., Jhanjhi, N. Z., Nayyar, A., & Rizwan, O. (2020). A remix IDE: Smart contract-based framework for the healthcare sector by using Blockchain technology. *Multimedia Tools and Applications*, 1–24.

Amsden, R., & Schweizer, D. (2021). Are blockchain crowdfunds the future of finance? Initial coin offerings (ICOs) as an alternative financing method. *European Journal of Finance*, 1–25.

Ana C., Junior, E., & Gewehr, B. B. (2020). Prospects for using gamification in Industry 4.0. *Thematic Section - Present and Future of Production*, 30.

Ananya Babu, M. U., & Mohan, P. (2022). Impact of the Metaverse on the Digital Future: People's Perspective. IEEExplore. doi:10.1109/ICCES54183.2022.9835951

Ancajima Miñán, V. Á., Plasencia Latour, J. E., Rubio Cabrera, W. F., Torres Santillan, L. J., & Montaño Barbuda, J. J. (2023). Analysis Of The Impact Of Information And Communication Technologies On Accounting Systems. *Journal of Pharmaceutical Negative Results*, *14*(3), 3369–3379. https://doi-org.ezproxy.myucwest.ca/10.47750/pnr.2023.14.03.420

Anderson, P. (2022). Of cypherpunks and sousveillance. *Surveillance & Society*, *20*(1), 1–17. doi:10.24908s.v20i1.14322

Andringa, C. (2022). *Property of the future-A research into factors influencing the value of virtual land* [Doctoral dissertation, Groningen University].

Anker-SørensenL.ZetzscheD. A. (2021). From Centralized to Decentralized Finance: The Issue of `Fake-DeFi´. SSRN. https://papers.ssrn.com/sol3/papers.cfm?abstract_id=3978815 doi:10.2139/ssrn.3978815

Ante, L. (2022). Non-fungible token (NFT) markets on the Ethereum blockchain: Temporal development, cointegration and interrelations. *Economics of Innovation and New Technology*, 1–19. doi:10.1080/10438599.2022.2119564

Anthony, B. Jnr. (2022). Investigating the Decentralized Governance of Distributed Ledger Infrastructure Implementation in Extended Enterprises. *Journal of the Knowledge Economy*. doi:10.100713132-022-01079-7

Antier. (2021). *An In-depth Insight into ERC-721 and Other NFT Standards*. Antier Solutions. https://www.antiersolutions.com/an-in-depth-insight-into-erc-721-and-other-nft-standards/#:~:text=ERC-721%20is%20an%20Ethereum%20standard%20used%20in%20non

Antonopoulos, A. M. (2015). *Mastering Bitcoin: Unlocking Digital Cryptocurrencies*. O'Reilly Media, Inc.

Antonopoulos, A. M., & Wood, G. (2018). *Mastering ethereum: building smart contracts and dapps*. O'reilly Media.

Anu, P., & Vimala, S. (2017), A survey on sniffing attacks on computer networks, *International Conference on Intelligent Computing and Control (I2C2)*. IEEE. 10.1109/I2C2.2017.8321914

Apostu, S. A., Panait, M., Vasa, L., Mihaescu, C., & Dobrowolski, Z. (2022). NFTs and Cryptocurrencies—The Metamorphosis of the Economy under the Sign of Blockchain: A Time Series Approach. *Mathematics*, *10*(17), 3218. doi:10.3390/math10173218

AquilinaM.FrostJ.SchrimpfA. (2023). Decentralised finance (DeFi): a functional approach. Available at SSRN 4325095.

Aria, R., Archer, N., Khanlari, M., & Shah, B. (2023). Influential factors in the design and development of a sustainable web3/metaverse and its applications. *Future Internet*, *15*(4), 131. doi:10.3390/fi15040131

Arif, S., Khan, M. A., Rehman, S. U., Kabir, M. A., & Imran, M. (2020). Investigating smart home security: Is blockchain the answer? *IEEE Access : Practical Innovations, Open Solutions*, *8*(June), 117802–117816. doi:10.1109/ACCESS.2020.3004662

Arner, D. W., Auer, R., & Frost, J. (2020). *Stablecoins: Risks, potential and regulation.* BIS Working Papers No 905.

Arner, D. W., Zetzsche, D. A., Buckley, R. P., & Kirkwood, J. M. (2023a). How Crypto Has Become Vulnerable to Problems of Traditional Finance. *The CLS Blue Sky Blog.* https://clsbluesky.law.columbia.edu/2023/05/30/the-financialization-of-crypto/

Arner, D. W., Zetzsche, D. A., Buckley, R. P., & Kirkwood, J. M. (2023b). *The Financialization of Crypto: Lessons from FTX and the Crypto Winter of 2022-2023.* University of Hong Kong Faculty of Law Research Paper No. 2023/19.

Arpášová, M., & Rajčániová, M. (2022). Legal Regulation of Unfair Trade Practices in Food Supply Chain. *EU Agrarian Law*, *11*(1), 1–8. doi:10.2478/eual-2022-0001

Ashraf Uddin, M. (2018). Andrew Stranieri, Iqbal Gondal, Venki Balasubramanian (2018), Continuous patient monitoring with a patient centric agent: A block architecture. *IEEE Access : Practical Innovations, Open Solutions*, *6*, 32700–32726. doi:10.1109/ACCESS.2018.2846779

Asthana, H., & Cox, I. J. (2013) A framework for peer-to-peer micro-blogging. In: *5th International workshop on peer-to-peer systems and online social networks, (HotPOST 2013).* IEEE. 10.1109/ICDCSW.2013.63

Atabekova, A., Belousov, A., & Shoustikova, T. (2015). Web 3.0-based non-formal learning to meet the third millennium education requirements: University Students' perceptions. *Procedia: Social and Behavioral Sciences*, *214*, 511–519. doi:10.1016/j.sbspro.2015.11.754

Ateniese, G., Goodrich, M. T., Lekakis, V., Papamanthou, C., Paraskevas, E., & Tamassia, R. (2014). Accountable Storage. IACR Cryptology ePrint Archive.

Atherton, J., Bratanova, A., & Markey-Towler, B. (2020). Who is the Blockchain employee? Exploring skills in demand using observations from the Australian labour market and Behavioural Institutional Cryptoeconomics. *The Journal of the British Blockchain Association*, *3*(2), 1–12. doi:10.31585/jbba-3-2-(4)2020

Atzei, N., Bartoletti, M., & Cimoli, T. (2017). A survey of attacks on ethereum smart contracts (sok). *Principles of Security and Trust: 6th International Conference, POST 2017, Held as Part of the European Joint Conferences on Theory and Practice of Software, ETAPS 2017, Uppsala, Sweden, April 22-29, 2017 Proceedings*, *6*, 164–186.

Atzei, N., Bartoletti, M., & Cimoli, T. (2017, April). A survey of attacks on ethereum smart contracts (sok). In *International conference on principles of security and trust* (pp. 164-186). Springer, Berlin, Heidelberg. 10.1007/978-3-662-54455-6_8

Atzori, M. (2015). Blockchain Technology and Decentralized Governance: Is the State Still Necessary? SSRN *Electronic Journal*. doi:10.2139/ssrn.2709713

Atzori, L., Iera, A., & Morabito, G. (2017). Understanding the Internet of Things: Definition, potentials, and societal role of a fast evolving paradigm. *Ad Hoc Networks*, *56*, 122–140. doi:10.1016/j.adhoc.2016.12.004

Atzori, M. (2017). Blockchain technology and decentralized governance: Is the state still necessary? *Journal of Government & Regulation*, *6*(1), 45–62. doi:10.22495/jgr_v6_i1_p5

Auer, R., & Boehme, R. (2020). The technology of retail central bank digital currency. *BIS Quarterly Review*. https://www.bis.org/publ/qtrpdf/r_qt2003j.htm

Avellaneda, O., Bachmann, A., Barbir, A., Brenan, J., Dingle, P., Duffy, K. H., & Sporny, M. (2019). Decentralized identity: Where did it come from and where is it going? *IEEE Communications Standards Magazine*, *3*(4), 10–13. doi:10.1109/MCOMSTD.2019.9031542

Axelsen, H., Jensen, J. R., & Ross, O. (2022). When is a DAO Decentralized? *Complex Systems Informatics and Modeling Quarterly*, *31*(31), 51–75. doi:10.7250/csimq.2022-31.04

Axford, S., Keltie, G., & Wallis, C. (2007). Virtual reality in urban planning and design. *Multimedia Cartography*, 283–294.

Axon, L. (2015). Privacy-awareness in Blockchain-based PKI. University of Oxford. https://goo.gl/3Nv2oK

Aydar, M., Cetin, S. C., Ayvaz, S., & Aygun, B. (2020). Private key encryption and recovery in blockchain. ArXiv:1907.04156 [Cs]. https://arxiv.org/abs/1907.04156

Aydinli, K. (2019). Performance Assessment of Cardano. *Independent Study–Communication Systems Group*, 1-39.

Azouvi, S., Maller, M., & Meiklejohn, S. (2020). Egalitarian Society or Benevolent Dictatorship: The State of Cryptocurrency Governance. In *International Conference on Financial Cryptography and Data Security* (pp. 127-146). Springer, Cham.

Aztori, M. (2015). Blockchain technology and decentralized governance: Is the state still necessary? SSRN Electronic Journal.

Azuma, R. T. (1997). A survey of augmented reality. *Presence (Cambridge, Mass.)*, *6*(4), 355–385. doi:10.1162/pres.1997.6.4.355

Baars, D. S. (2016). *Towards self-sovereign identity using blockchain technology* [Master's thesis, University of Twente].

Ba, C., Zignani, M., & Gaito, S. (2022). The role of cryptocurrency in the dynamics of blockchain-based social networks: The case of Steemit. *PLoS One*, *17*(6), e0267612. doi:10.1371/journal.pone.0267612 PMID:35709197

Bacchetta, P., & Perazzi, E. (2021). CBDC as Imperfect Substitute for Bank Deposits: A Macroeconomic Perspective. *Swiss Finance Institute Research Paper*, (21-81).

Baden, Randy & Bender, Adam & Spring, Neil & Bhattacharjee, Bobby & Starin, Daniel. (2009). Persona: An Online Social Network with User-Defined Privacy. *Computer Communication Review – CCR*, *39*, 135-146.. doi:10.1145/1594977.1592585

Bager, S. L., Düdder, B., Henglein, F., Hébert, J. M., & Wu, H. (2022). Event-Based Supply Chain Network Modeling: Blockchain for Good Coffee. *Frontiers in Blockchain*, *5*, 846783. doi:10.3389/fbloc.2022.846783

Bager, S. L., Singh, C., & Persson, U. M. (2022). Blockchain is not a silver bullet for agro-food supply chain sustainability: Insights from a coffee case study. *Current Research in Environmental Sustainability*, *4*, 100163. doi:10.1016/j.crsust.2022.100163

Bagrecha, N. R., Polishwala, I. M., Mehrotra, P. A., Sharma, R., & Thakare, B. S. (2020). Decentralised blockchain technology: Application in banking sector. In *2020 International Conference for Emerging Technology (INCET)*. IEEE. 10.1109/INCET49848.2020.9154115

Bailenson, J. (2018). *Experience on demand: What virtual reality is, how it works, and what it can do.* WW Norton & Company.

Baker, S. B., Xiang, W., & Atkinson, I. (2017). Internet of Things for Smart Healthcare: Technologies, Challenges, and Opportunities. *IEEE Access: Practical Innovations, Open Solutions, 5,* 26521–26544. doi:10.1109/ACCESS.2017.2775180

Baliga, A., Subhod, I., Kamat, P., & Chatterjee, S. (2018). Performance evaluation of the quorum blockchain platform. arXiv preprint arXiv:1809.03421.

Ball, M., 2020. The Metaverse: What It Is. *Where to Find It, Who Will Build It, and Fortnite, 13.*

Barber, S., Boyen, X., Shi, E., & Uzun, E. (2012). *Bitter to Better - How to Make Bitcoin a Better Currency, Financial Cryptography, ser* (Vol. 7397). Lecture Notes in Computer Science. Springer.

Bartoletti, M., & Pompianu, L. (2017). An empirical analysis of smart contracts: platforms, applications, and design patterns. In Financial Cryptography and Data Security: FC 2017 International Workshops, WAHC, BITCOIN, VOT-ING, WTSC, and TA, Sliema, Malta, April 7, 2017, Revised Selected Papers 21 (pp. 494-509). Springer International Publishing. doi:10.1007/978-3-319-70278-0_31

Bartoletti, M., Gessa, D., & Podda, A. S. (2017). *Idea: a general framework for decentralized applications based on the Bitcoin blockchain.*

Basel Committee on Banking Supervision. (2010). *Basel III: A global regulatory framework for more resilient banks and banking systems.* Bank for International Settlements.

Batty, M., Axhausen, K. W., Giannotti, F., Pozdnoukhov, A., Bazzani, A., Wachowicz, M., Ouzounis, G., & Portugali, Y. (2012). Smart cities of the future. *The European Physical Journal. Special Topics, 214*(1), 481–518. doi:10.1140/epjst/e2012-01703-3

Beck, R., Czepluch, J. S., Lollike, N., & Malone, S. (2016). Blockchain-the gateway to trust-free cryptographic transactions. In ECIS.

Beck, A. R., Avital, M., Rossi, M., & Thatcher, J. B. (2017). Blockchain technology in business and information systems research. *Business & Information Systems Engineering, 59*(6), 381–384. doi:10.100712599-017-0505-1

Belchior, R., Vasconcelos, A., Guerreiro, S., & Correia, M. (2021). A survey on blockchain interoperability: Past, present, and future trends. [CSUR]. *ACM Computing Surveys, 54*(8), 1–41. doi:10.1145/3471140

Bellavitis, C., Fisch, C., & Momtaz, P. P. (2022). The rise of decentralized autonomous organizations (DAOs): A first empirical glimpse. *Venture Capital,* 1–17.

Benet, J. (2014). *IPFS - Content Addressed, Versioned, P2P File System.* ArXiv. /abs/1407.3561.

Benet, J. (2014, November 5). *IPFS (InterPlanetary File System) is a content-addressed, versioned, peer-to-peer file system.* Retrieved from https://ipfs.io/

Beniiche, A., Rostami, S., & Maier, M. (2022). Society 5.0: Internet as if people mattered. *IEEE Wireless Communications, 29*(6), 160–168. doi:10.1109/MWC.009.2100570

Benito-Osorio, D., Peris-Ortiz, M., Armengot, C. R., & Colino, A. (2013). Web 5.0: The future of emotional competences in higher education. *Global Business Perspectives, 1*(3), 274–287. doi:10.100740196-013-0016-5

Benji, M., & Sindhu, M. (2019). A study on the Corda and Ripple blockchain platforms. In *Advances in Big Data and Cloud Computing: Proceedings of ICBDCC18* (pp. 179-187). Springer Singapore. 10.1007/978-981-13-1882-5_16

Benson, V., Saridakis, G., & Tennakoon, H. (2015). Information disclosure of social media users: Does control over personal information, user awareness and security notices matter? *Information Technology & People*, 28(3), 426–441. doi:10.1108/ITP-10-2014-0232

Berg, C., Davidson, S., & Potts, J. (2019). *Understanding the blockchain economy: An introduction to institutional cryptoeconomics*. Edward Elgar. doi:10.4337/9781788975001

Berger, A. N. (2003). The economic effects of technological progress: Evidence from the banking industry. *Journal of Money, Credit and Banking*, 35(2), 141–176. doi:10.1353/mcb.2003.0009

Berners-Lee, T., Cailliau, R., Groff, J. F., & Pollermann, B. (2010). World-wide web: The information universe. *Internet Research*, 20(4), 461–471. doi:10.1108/10662241011059471

Berners-Lee, T., Cailliau, R., Groff, J.-F., & Pollermann, B. (1992). World-Wide Web: The Information Universe. *Electron. Netw. Res. Appl. Policy.*, 2(1), 52–58. doi:10.1108/eb047254

Berners-Lee, T., Hendler, J., & Lassila, O. (2001). The Semantic Web. Scientific American, 284(5), 34-43. The Semantic Web. *Scientific American*, 284(5), 34–43. doi:10.1038cientificamerican0501-34 PMID:11681174

Bertocci, V., Serack, G., & Baker, C. (2007). *Understanding windows cardspace: an introduction to the concepts and challenges of digital identities*. Pearson Education.

Besel, R. D. (2011). Opening the 'black box' of climate change science: Actor-network theory and rhetorical practice in scientific controversies. *The Southern Communication Journal*, 76(2), 120–136. doi:10.1080/10417941003642403

Bettín-Díaz, R., Rojas, A. E., & Mejía-Moncayo, C. (2022). Colombian Origin Coffee Supply Chain Traceability by a Blockchain Implementation. *Operations Research Forum, 3*(4), 64. 10.100743069-022-00174-4

Beuscart, J. S., & Mellet, K. (2008). Business models of the web 2.0: Advertising or the tale of two stories. [special issue]. *Communications & Stratégies*.

Bext360 (Director). (2019, April 1). *Bext360 Journey*. [Video]. Youtube. https://www.youtube.com/watch?v=HYmIBRHLcjo

Bext360 (Director). (2022, September 3). *Bext360 Capabilities*. [Video]. Youtube. https://www.youtube.com/watch?v=gs0xr7Ie4vo

Bez, M., Fornari, G., & Vardanega, T. (2019, April). The scalability challenge of ethereum: An initial quantitative analysis. In *2019 IEEE International Conference on Service-Oriented System Engineering (SOSE)* (pp. 167-176). IEEE. 10.1109/SOSE.2019.00031

Bhagat, V. (2023). Web 3.0: how this new era of internet will change the world? *PixelCrayons*. https://www.pixelcrayons.com/blog/web-3-0/

Bharathi, M. V., Tanguturi, R. C., Jayakumar, C., & Selvamani, K. (2013). Node capture attack in Wireless Sensor Network: A survey. *In Proceedings of the 2012 IEEE International Conference on Computational Intelligence & Computing Research (ICCIC)*. IEEE.

Bhargavan, K., Delignat-Lavaud, A., Fournet, C., Gollamudi, A., Gonthier, G., Kobeissi, N., & Zanella-Béguelin, S. (2016, October). Formal verification of smart contracts: Short paper. In *Proceedings of the 2016 ACM workshop on programming languages and analysis for security* (pp. 91-96). ACM. 10.1145/2993600.2993611

Bhattacharya, R., White, M., & Beloff, N. (2021). An Exploration of Blockchain in Social Networking Applications. In K. Arai (Ed.), *Intelligent Computing. Lecture Notes in Networks and Systems* (Vol. 284). Springer. doi:10.1007/978-3-030-80126-7_60

Bhushan, B., Sinha, P., Sagayam, K. M., & J, A. (2020). Untangling blockchain technology: A survey on state of the art, security threats, privacy services, applications and future research directions. *Computers & Electrical Engineering, 90,* 106897. doi:10.1016/j.compeleceng.2020.106897

Bielenberg, A., Helm, L., Gentilucci, A., Stefanescu, D., & Zhang, H. (2012). *The growth of Diaspora - A decentralized online social network in the wild.* In 2012 Proceedings IEEE INFOCOM Workshops (pp. 13-18). Orlando, FL. 10.1109/INFCOMW.2012.6193476

Bigi, G., Bracciali, A., Meacci, G., & Tuosto, E. (2015). Validation of decentralised smart contracts through game theory and formal methods. *Programming Languages with Applications to Biology and Security: Essays Dedicated to Pierpaolo Degano on the Occasion of His 65th Birthday,* 142-161.

Bijker, W. E. (1995). *Of Bicycles, Bakelites, and Bulbs.* MIT Press.

Bijker, W. E., Hughes, T. P., & Pinch, T. J. (Eds.). (2012). *The social construction of technological systems: New directions in the sociology and history of technology.* MIT Press.

Bijker, W. E., Hughes, T. P., & Pinch, T. J. (Eds.). (2012). *The Social Construction of Technological Systems: New Directions in the Sociology and History of Technology.* MIT Press.

Bindseil, U. (2019). Central bank digital currency: Financial system implications and control. *International Journal of Political Economy, 48*(4), 303–335. doi:10.1080/08911916.2019.1693160

Birrer, T.K., Amstutz, D., & Wenger, P. (2023). Decentralized Finance: From Core Concepts to DeFi Protocols for Financial Transactions (*Vol. 1,* pp. 39). *Financial Innovation and Technology* (FIT). Springer Wiesbaden.

Bissias, G. D., Ozisik, A. P., Levine, B. N., & Liberatore, M. (2014). *Sybil Resistant Mixing for Bitcoin,WPES.* ACM.

Biswas, K., Muthukkumarasamy, V., & Tan, W. L. (2021). Blockchain Technology: A Review from Theory to Applications. *IEEE Access : Practical Innovations, Open Solutions, 9,* 79520–79548.

Bizer, C., Heath, T., & Berners-Lee, T. (2011). Linked data: The story so far. In *Semantic services, interoperability and web applications: emerging concepts* (pp. 205–227). IGI global. doi:10.4018/978-1-60960-593-3.ch008

Blanchard, J., Koshal, S., Morley, S., & McGurk, M. (2022). The use of mixed reality in dentistry. *British Dental Journal, 233*(4), 261–265. doi:10.103841415-022-4451-z PMID:36028682

Blandin, A., Cloots, A. S., Hussain, H., Rauchs, M., Saleuddin, R., Allen, J. G., Zhang, Z. B., & Cloud, K. (2019). *Global Cryptoasset Regulatory Landscape Study.* Cambridge Centre for Alternative Finance, Cambridge Judge Business School, University of Cambridge. https://www.jbs.cam.ac.uk/wp-content/uploads/2020/08/2019-04-ccaf-global-cryptoasset-regulatory-landscape-study.pdf

BlauB.VikramS. (2022). Entering a new era of decentralized customer experience (dcx) web3 unlocks the new market category of decentralized customer experience with unforeseen value across industries. *Available at* SSRN 4219848. doi:10.2139/ssrn.4219848

Blaum, W. E., Jarczweski, A., Balzer, F., Stötzner, P., & Ahlers, O. (2013). Towards Web 3.0: Taxonomies and ontologies for medical education-a systematic review. *GMS Zeitschrift für Medizinische Ausbildung, 30*(1). PMID:23467484

Bloomberg. (2021, February 10). DeFi Faces Regulatory Crackdown in European Union's Latest Crypto Proposal. *Bloomberg.* https://www.bloomberg.com/news/articles/2021-02-10/defi-faces-regulatory-crackdown-in-european-unions-latest-crypto-proposal

Bobrowsky, M., & Needleman, S. E. (2022). *What Is the Metaverse? The Future Vision for the Internet.* WSJ. https://www.wsj.com/story/what-is-the-metaverse-the-future-vision-for-the-internet-ca97bd98

Bocovich, C., Doucette, J., & Goldberg, I. (2015). *Lavinia: An audit payment protocol for censorship-resistant storage.* Center for Applied Cryptographic Research.

Bodo, B., & Giannopoulou, A. (2020). The logics of technology decentralization – the case of distributed ledger technologies. In M. Ragnedda & G. Destefanis (Eds.), *Blockchain and Web 3.0: Social, Economic, and Technological Challenges* (pp. 114–129). Routledge.

Bodriagov, O., & Buchegger, S. (2013). Encryption for peer-to-peer social networks. In *Security and privacy in social networks* (pp. 47–65). Springer. doi:10.1007/978-1-4614-4139-7_4

Böhme, R., Christin, N., Edelman, B., & Moore, T. (2015). Bitcoin: Economics, technology, and governance. *The Journal of Economic Perspectives*, *29*(2), 213–238. doi:10.1257/jep.29.2.213

Boll, K. (2021). Decentraland: A virtual world powered by Ethereum. *Decentraland.* https://decentraland.org/

Boll, K. (2021). OpenSea: The world's largest NFT marketplace. *Opensea.* https://opensea.io/

Bonneau, J., Miller, A., Clark, J., Narayanan, A., Kroll, J. A., & Felten, E. W. (2015). SoK: Research perspectives and challenges for Bitcoin and cryptocurrencies. In *IEEE Symposium on Security and Privacy (SP)* (pp. 104-121). IEEE. 10.1109/SP.2015.14

Borrella, I., Mataix, C., & Carrasco-Gallego, R. (2015). Smallholder Farmers in the Speciality Coffee Industry: Opportunities, Constraints and the Businesses that are Making it Possible. *IDS Bulletin*, *46*(3), 29–44. doi:10.1111/1759-5436.12142

Borzacchiello, M. T., Torrieri, V., & Nijkamp, P. (2009). An operational information systems architecture for assessing sustainable transportation planning: Principles and design. *Evaluation and Program Planning*, *32*(4), 381–389. doi:10.1016/j.evalprogplan.2009.06.012 PMID:19631382

Bousba, Y., & Arya, V. (2022). Let's Connect in Metaverse. Brand's New Destination to Increase Consumer's Affective Brand Engagement & their Satisfaction and Advocacy. *Journal of Content. Community & Communication*, *15*(8), 276–293. doi:10.31620/JCCC.06.22/19

Bowman, D. A., & McMahan, R. P. (2007). Virtual reality: How much immersion is enough? *Computer*, *40*(7), 36–43. doi:10.1109/MC.2007.257

Boyd, D. M., & Ellison, N. B. (2007). Social Network Sites: Definition, History, and Scholarship. *Journal of Computer-Mediated Communication*, *13*(1), 210–230. doi:10.1111/j.1083-6101.2007.00393.x

Bozic, N., Pujolle, G., & Secci, S. (2016). A tutorial on blockchain and applications to secure network control-planes. *2016 3rd Smart Cloud Networks & Systems (SCNS)*, 1-8.

Bradshaw, S., & Howard, P. N. (2019). *The Global Disinformation Order: 2019 Global Inventory of Organised Social Media Manipulation.* University of Nebraska - Lincoln. https://digitalcommons.unl.edu/scholcom/207

Brennecke, M., Guggenberger, T., Sachs, A., & Schellinger, B. (2022). The Human Factor in Blockchain Ecosystems: A Sociotechnical Framework. In *Wirtschaftsinformatik 2022 Proceedings (Vol. 3)*. AISEL. https://aisel.aisnet.org/wi2022/finance_and_blockchain/finance_and_blockchain/3

Breunig, M., Bradley, P. E., Jahn, M., Kuper, P., Mazroob, N., Rösch, N., Al-Doori, M., Stefanakis, E., & Jadidi, M. (2020). Geospatial data management research: Progress and future directions. *ISPRS International Journal of Geo-Information, 9*(2), 95. doi:10.3390/ijgi9020095

Brewster, C., Dowling, P., & Holland, P. (2022). HRM and the smart and dark side of technology. *Asia Pacific Journal of Human Resources, 60*(1), 62–78. doi:10.1111/1744-7941.12319

Bridgesmith, L., ElMessiry, A., & Marei, M. (2022). Legal Service Delivery and Support for the DAO Ecosystem. *Springer, Blockchain – ICBC 2022.* 18-28.

Bridgesmith, L., Elmessiry, A., & Marei, M. (2022). Legal service delivery and support for the DAO ecosystem. In S. Chen, R. K. Shyamasundar, & L. J. Zhang (Eds.), Lecture Notes in Computer Science: Vol. 13733. *Blockchain – ICBC 2022* (pp. 18–28). Springer. doi:10.1007/978-3-031-23495-8_2

Browne, R. (2021). *Forget Bitcoin–Fintech Is the "Real Covid-19 Story.* Jpmorgan Says.

BrummerC. J.SeiraR. (2022). Legal Wrappers and DAOs. Available at SSRN: doi:10.2139/ssrn.4123737

Brunnermeier, M. K., & Niepelt, D. (2019). On the equivalence of private and public money. *Journal of Monetary Economics, 106,* 27–41. doi:10.1016/j.jmoneco.2019.07.004

Buccafurri, L. N. (2023). Blockchain-based Metaverses: Challenges and Opportunities. *Frontiers in Blockchain.*

Buchegger, S., Schïoberg D, Vu L-H, Datta A (2009) Peerson: P2Psocial networking: early experiences and insights. In: Proceedings of the second ACM EuroSys workshop on social network systems, SNS '09, (pp. 46–52). ACM. 10.1145/1578002.1578010

Buhalis, D., Leung, D., & Lin, M. (2023). Metaverse as a disruptive technology revolutionising tourism management and marketing. In Tourism Management (Vol. 97). doi:10.1016/j.tourman.2023.104724

Buhalis, D., Lin, M. S., & Leung, D. (2023). Metaverse as a driver for customer experience and value co-creation: Implications for hospitality and tourism management and marketing. *International Journal of Contemporary Hospitality Management, 35*(2), 701–716. Advance online publication. doi:10.1108/IJCHM-05-2022-0631

Bult, T. (2022). The implications of non-fungible tokens in video games from the perspective of the stakeholder capitalism theory. *USA Today.*

Burda, M., Locca, M., & Staykova, K. (2022, February 28). *Decision rights decentralization in DeFi platforms.* Wrap. warwick.ac.uk

Burroughes, E., Rys, J., & Wüllenweber, J. (2023, June 8). *Prioritizing socially responsible sourcing. McKinsey.* https://www.mckinsey.com/capabilities/operations/our-insights/enabling-socially-responsible-sourcing-throughout-the-supply-chain

Burroughes, T. (2023). *FTX Collapse May Prompt Big Regulatory Crackdown – Lawyer.* Wealth Briefing. https://www.wealthbriefing.com/html/article.php?id=196248

Bushell, C. (2022). The Impact of Metaverse on Branding and Marketing - A Study of How Individuals and Celebrities Use Metaverse as a Brand Extension, and the Implications for Marketing. SSRN *Electronic Journal.* doi:10.2139/ssrn.4144688

Business Solutions, C. A. L. (2020). A brief history of ERP software including Dynamics GP and Acumatica. *ERP Software Blog.* https://www.erpsoftwareblog.com/2020/04/a-brief-history-of-erp-software-including-dynamics-gp-and-acumatica/

Buterin, V. (2013). *A Next Generation Smart Contract & Decentralized Application Platform.* Ethereum White Paper.

Buterin, V. (2014). A Next-Generation Smart Contract and Decentralized Application Platform. *Ethereum.* https://ethereum.org/en/whitepaper/

Buterin, V. (2014). A next-generation smart contract and decentralized application platform. *white paper, 3*(37), 2-1.

Buterin, V. (2014). DAOs, DACs, DAs and More: An Incomplete Terminology Guide. *Ethereum Blog.* Vitalik. https://vitalik.ca/general/2019/04/03/collusion.html

Buterin, V. (2014). *Ethereum: A next-generation smart contract and decentralized application platform [White paper].* Ethereum. https://ethereum.org/669c9e2e2027310b6b3cdce6e1c52962/EthereumWhitepaper_-_Buterin_2014.pdf

Buterin, V. (2014a). Ethereum: A Next-Generation Smart Contract and Decentralized Application Platform. *Ethereum (blog).* https://ethereum.org/669c9e2e2027310b6b3cdce6e1c52962/Ethereum_Whitepaper_-_Buterin_2014.pdf

Buterin, V. (2014b) DAOs, DACs, DAs and More: An Incomplete Terminology Guide. *Ethereum (blog).* https://blog.ethereum.org/2014/05/06/daos-dacs-das-and-more-an-incomplete-terminology-guide/

Buterin, V. (2015). Ethereum: A Next-Generation Smart Contract and Decentralized Application Platform. *Ethereum.* https://ethereum.org/whitepaper/

Buterin, V. (2016) DAOs as a concept existed long before Ethereum. *Medium (blog).* https://medium.com/@VitalikButerin/i-invented-the-term-in-2013-and-daniel-larimer-came-up-with-dacs-s-organization-corporation-a-ef86db1524d5

Buterin, V., & Griffith, V. (2017). Casper the Friendly Finality Gadget.

Buterin, V., Hitzig, Z., & Weyl, E. G. (2019). A flexible design for funding public goods. *Management Science, 65*(11), 4951–5448. doi:10.1287/mnsc.2019.3337

Bygrave, L. A. (2017). *Internet censorship.* Elgar Encyclopedia of Law and Technology.

Bylica, P., Glen, L., Janiuk, P., Skrzypcaz, A., & Zawlocki, A. (2015). *A Probabilistic Nanopayment Scheme for Golem.* Golem Project. https://golemproject.net/doc/GolemNanopayments.pdf

Cachin, C. (2016, July). Architecture of the hyperledger blockchain fabric. In *Workshop on distributed cryptocurrencies and consensus ledgers* (Vol. 310, No. 4, pp. 1-4).

Çağlayan, G., Öz, B. K., Özer, A., & Şener, E. (2023). Distributed ledger technology experiments in retail payments: Evidence from Turkey. *Journal of Payments Strategy & Systems, 17*(2), 151–164.

Calvaresi, D., Dubovitskaya, A., & Calbimonte, J. P. (2018), Multi-agent systems and blockchain: results from a systematic literature review. *International Conference on Practical Applications of Agents and Multi-Agent Systems.* Springer. 10.1007/978-3-319-94580-4_9

Cao, L. (2022). Decentralized ai: Edge intelligence and smart blockchain, metaverse, web3, and desci. *IEEE Intelligent Systems, 37*(3), 6–19. doi:10.1109/MIS.2022.3181504

Carayannis, E. G., & Morawska-Jancelewicz, J. (2022). The futures of Europe: Society 5.0 and Industry 5.0 as driving forces of future universities. *Journal of the Knowledge Economy, 13*(4), 1–27. doi:10.100713132-021-00854-2

Carbonell, J. (2022). Collaborative accounting: what is it and what does it consist of? *Tas Consultoria.* https://www.tas-consultoria.com/blog-en/collaborative-accounting-consist/

Career Illustrated. (2023). *E5—Niki Lewis, Sustainability Director @ Bext360: Green is the New Green.* Career Illustrated - Podcast. https://music.amazon.com/es-us/podcasts/bb314ba5-dcc7-42b9-b546-706fc009387f/episodes/0eaabd5d-001c-4cfd-a499-500c92d20955/career-illustrated-e5---niki-lewis-sustainability-director-a-bext360-green-is-the-new-green

Casey, M. J. (2022). *Crypto's Very Human Fatal Flaw: Hero Worship*. Coindesk. https://www.coindesk.com/layer2/2022/11/18/cryptos-very-human-fatal-flaw-hero-worship/

Casey, M., & Vigna, P. (2018). *The truth machine: The blockchain and the future of everything* (1st ed.). St. Martin's Press.

Castronova, E. (2019). *Synthetic worlds: The business and culture of online games*. University of Chicago press.

Catalini, C., & Gans, J. S. (2020). Some simple economics of the blockchain. In *Economics of Blockchain* (pp. 13–25). University of Chicago Press.

Catalini, C., & Gans, J. S. (2021). The Tokenization of Assets and Blockchain Technology. *The University of Chicago Law Review. University of Chicago. Law School*, *88*(4), 1569–1604.

Ceballos, K., Nikou, S., Giovanidis, T., & Hosking, J. (2020). A systematic mapping study on business models and monetization strategies for decentralized applications. *Journal of Software: Evolution and Process*, *32*(10), e2242.

Ceccato, V. (2013). Integrating geographical information into urban safety research and planning. In *Proceedings of the Institution of Civil Engineers: Urban Design and Planning* (Vol. *166*, Issue 1). 10.1680/udap.11.00038

Cedeno Jimenez, J. R., Zhao, P., Mansourian, A., & Brovelli, M. A. (2022). Geospatial Blockchain: Review of decentralized geospatial data sharing systems. *AGILE: GIScience Series*, *3*, 1–6. doi:10.5194/agile-giss-3-29-2022

Centobelli, P., Cerchione, R., Vecchio, P. D., Oropallo, E., & Secundo, G. (2022). Blockchain technology for bridging trust, traceability and transparency in circular supply chain. *Information & Management*, *59*(7), 103508. doi:10.1016/j.im.2021.103508

CFDC vs. Ooki DAO, U.S. District Court for the Northern District of California, June 9th 2023. https://storage.courtlistener.com/recap/gov.uscourts.cand.400807/gov.uscourts.cand.400807.76.0.pdf

Chainlink. (2020). *What is the Oracle Problem?* Chainlink. https://chain.link/blog/what-is-the-oracle-problem.

Chalmers, D., Fisch, C., Matthews, R., Quinn, W., & Recker, J. (2022). Beyond the bubble: Will NFTs and digital proof of ownership empower creative industry entrepreneurs? *Journal of Business Venturing Insights*, *17*, e00309. doi:10.1016/j.jbvi.2022.e00309

Chander, A. (2014). The Racist Algorithm? *Michigan Law Review*, *115*(5), 1023–1046.

Chandra, Y. (2022). Non-fungible token-enabled entrepreneurship: A conceptual framework. *Journal of Business Venturing Insights*, *18*, e00323. doi:10.1016/j.jbvi.2022.e00323

Changelly. (n.d.). What is a Decentralized Exchange (DEX)? *Changelly*. https://changelly.com/blog/what-is-decentralized-exchange-dex/

Chang, S. E., Chen, Y. C., & Lu, M. F. (2019). Supply chain re-engineering using blockchain technology: A case of smart contract based tracking process. *Technological Forecasting and Social Change*, *144*, 1–11. doi:10.1016/j.techfore.2019.03.015

Chao, C. H., Ting, I. H., Tseng, Y. J., Wang, B. W., Wang, S. H., Wang, Y. Q., & Chen, M. C. (2022). The Study of Decentralized Autonomous Organization (DAO) in Social Network. In *Proceedings of the 9th Multidisciplinary International Social Networks Conference* (pp. 59-65). 10.1145/3561278.3561293

Chaturvedi, K., Matheus, A., Nguyen, S. H., & Kolbe, T. H. (2019). Securing Spatial Data Infrastructures for Distributed Smart City applications and services. *Future Generation Computer Systems*, *101*, 723–736. doi:10.1016/j.future.2019.07.002

Chaudhuri, A., Bhatia, M. S., Kayikci, Y., Fernandes, K. J., & Fosso-Wamba, S. (2021). Improving social sustainability and reducing supply chain risks through blockchain implementation: Role of outcome and behavioural mechanisms. *Annals of Operations Research*. doi:10.100710479-021-04307-6

Chauhan, A., Malviya, O. P., Verma, M., & Mor, T. S. (2018). *Blockchain and Scalability*. In 2018 IEEE International Conference on Software Quality, Reliability and Security Companion (QRS-C) (pp. 122-128). Lisbon, Portugal. 10.1109/QRS-C.2018.00034

Chen, X., Miraz, M.H., Gazi, A.I., Rahaman, A., Habib, M. & Hossain, A.I. (2022). Factors affecting cryptocurrency adoption in digital business transactions: The mediating role of customer satisfaction. *Technology in Society, 70*. . doi:10.1016/j.techsoc.2022.102059

Chen, C., Zhang, L., Li, Y., Liao, T., Zhao, S., Zheng, Z., & Wu, J. (2022). *When digital economy meets web 3.0: Applications and challenges*. IEEE Open Journal of the Computer Society.

Chengoden, R., Victor, N., Huynh-The, T., Yenduri, G., Jhaveri, R. H., Alazab, M., Bhattacharya, S., Hegde, P., Maddikunta, P. K. R., & Gadekallu, T. R. (2023). Metaverse for Healthcare: A Survey on Potential Applications, Challenges and Future Directions. *IEEE Access: Practical Innovations, Open Solutions, 11*, 12765–12795. doi:10.1109/ACCESS.2023.3241628

Chen, H., & Wang, Y. (2019). Sschain: A full sharding protocol for public blockchain without data migration overhead. *Pervasive and Mobile Computing, 59*, 101055. doi:10.1016/j.pmcj.2019.101055

Chen, Y. 2022, November. Research on the Communication of Sports Events in the Context of Metaverse. In *2022 International Conference on Sport Science, Education and Social Development (SSESD 2022)* (pp. 369-383). Atlantis Press.

Chen, Z., Chen, R., & Chen, S. (2021). Intelligent management information system of urban planning based on GIS. *Journal of Intelligent & Fuzzy Systems, 40*(4), 6007–6016. doi:10.3233/JIFS-189440

Chen, Z., Xu, Y., & Lim, E. T. (2018). Towards decentralised governance: Blockchain and the question of technology-based power. *Information Systems Frontiers, 22*(3), 501–515.

Chisega-Negrilă, A. M. (2012). WEB 3.0 in education. In *Conference proceedings of» eLearning and Software for Education «(eLSE)* (Vol. 8, No. 01, pp. 455-460). Carol I National Defence University Publishing House. 10.12753/2066-026X-12-073

Chisega-Negrilă, A. M. (2013). Education in web 3.0. *JADLET Journal of Advanced Distributed Learning Technology, 1*(1), 50–59.

Chohan, U. W. (2022). *Cryptocurrencies: A Brief Thematic Review*. SSRN. https://ssrn.com/abstract=3024330 or doi:10.2139/ssrn.3024330

Chorley, M. J., Whitaker, R. M., & Allen, S. M. (2015). Personality and location-based social networks. *Computers in Human Behavior, 46*, 45–56. doi:10.1016/j.chb.2014.12.038

Chowdhury, S. R., Roy, A. R., Shaikh, M., & Daudjee, K. (2015). A taxonomy of decentralized online social networks. *Peer-to-Peer Networking and Applications, 8*(3), 367–383. doi:10.100712083-014-0258-2

Chow-White, P., Lusoli, A., Phan, V. T. A., & Green, S. Jr. (2020). 'Blockchain Good, Bitcoin Bad': The Social Construction Of Blockchain In Mainstream And Specialized Media. *Journal of Digital Social Research, 2*(2), 1–27. doi:10.33621/jdsr.v2i2.34

Christian, R., Luois Cenisius, V., Darmawan, M., Ferrero, J., & Yansen, E. (2022). Impact of User-Generated Content on Intentions to Invest in NFTs. *Budapest International Research and Critics Institute (BIRCI-Journal). Humanities (Washington), 5*(2). doi:10.33258/birci.v5i2.5642

Christidis, K., & Devetsikiotis, M. (2016). Blockchains and Smart Contracts for the Internet of Things. *IEEE Access : Practical Innovations, Open Solutions, 4,* 2292–2303. doi:10.1109/ACCESS.2016.2566339

Christodoulou, K., Katelaris, L., Themistocleous, M., Christodoulou, P., & Iosif, E. (2022). NFTs and the metaverse revolution: Research perspectives and open challenges. *Blockchains and the Token Economy. Theory into Practice,* 139–178.

Chu, J., Chan, S., & Zhang, Y. (2023). An analysis of the return–volume relationship in decentralised finance (DeFi). *International Review of Economics & Finance, 85,* 236–254. doi:10.1016/j.iref.2023.01.006

Chu, J., Labonte, K., & Levine, B. N. (2002). Availability and locality measurements of peer-to-peer file systems. In Proceedings of ITCom.

Ciriello, R., Beck, R., & Thatcher, J. (2018). The Paradoxical Effects of Blockchain Technology on Social Networking Practices. *Conference: International Conference on Information Systems (ICIS 2018).* 10.2139srn.3920002

Clack, C. D., Bakshi, V. A., & Braine, L. (2016). Smart contract templates: foundations, design landscape and research directions. arXiv preprint arXiv:1608.00771.

Claessens, S., Glaessner, T., & Klingebiel, D. (2002). Electronic finance: Reshaping the financial landscape around the world. *Journal of Financial Services Research, 22*(1/2), 29–61. doi:10.1023/A:1016023528211

Clarke, R. (2018). What is Web 3.0? Transforming the Internet into a decentralised information marketplace. *Computer Fraud & Security, 2018*(12), 8–12.

Clegg, N. (2022). *Making the Metaverse: What it is, how it will be built, and why it matters.* Medium.

Clifford, T. (2021). *Paypal Cfo Says Company Is Unlikely to Invest Cash in Cryptocurrencies.* CNBC. https://www.cnbc.com/2021/02/11/paypal-cfo-says-company-is-unlikely-to-investcash-in-cryptocurrencies.html?__source5google%7Ceditorspicks%7C&par5google

CNBC. (2021). *DeFi has a money laundering problem, but experts say it can be fixed.* CNBC. https://www.cnbc.com/2021/08/31/defi-has-a-money-laundering-problem-but-experts-say-it-can-be-fixed.html

Coase, R. (1937). The nature of the firm. *Economica, 2*(1), 386–405. doi:10.1111/j.1468-0335.1937.tb00002.x

Coindesk. (2021, August 10). Poly Network Hack: $600M in Stolen Crypto Has Been Returned So Far. *Coindesk.* https://www.coindesk.com/poly-network-hack-600m-in-stolen-crypto-returned-so-far

CoinDesk. (2022). Scalability. *Coindesk.* https://www.coindesk.com/scalability

CoinMarketCap. (2019). *Global Charts | CoinMarketCap.* CoinMarketCap. https://coinmarketcap.com/charts/

Cointelegraph (Director). (2023, March 22). *Farming Revolution: Blockchain and Tech Solutions by Dimitra.* [Video]. Youtube. https://www.youtube.com/watch?v=xutrxP29PO8

Cointelegraph Research. (2022, October). *DAO: The evolution of organization.* Cointelegraph Research. https://research.cointelegraph.com/reports/detail/dao-the-evolution-of-organization

Cointelegraph. (2021, May 15). Ethereum's DeFi ecosystem faces its biggest challenge so far. *Cointelegraph.* https://cointelegraph.com/news/ethereum-s-defi-ecosystem-faces-its-biggest-challenge-so-far

Committee on Payments and Market Infrastructures. (2018, March). *Central bank digital currencies. Bank for International Settlements.* BIS. https://www.bis.org/cpmi/publ/d174.pdf

Cong, L. W., & He, Z. (2019). Blockchain disruption and smart contracts. *Review of Financial Studies, 32*(5), 1754–1797. doi:10.1093/rfs/hhz007

Cong, L. W., Li, Y., & Wang, N. (2020). Tokenomics: Dynamic Adoption and Valuation. *Review of Financial Studies*, *34*(5), 2258–2300.

Cong, Y., & Du, H. (2007). Welcome to the World of Web 2.0. *The CPA Journal*, *77*(5), 6–10.

Consensys. (2022). Decentralized Finance (DeFi). *Consensys*. https://consensys.net/decentralized-finance-defi/

Cornforth, C. (2004). The governance of cooperatives and mutual associations: A paradox perspective. *Annals of Public and Cooperative Economics*, *75*(1), 11–32. doi:10.1111/j.1467-8292.2004.00241.x

Coulter, K. A. (2023). A Review of the Proposed Bank of England's "Retail" Central Bank Digital Currency (CBDC) as a Cryptocurrency Competitor. *Fintech, Pandemic, and the Financial System: Challenges and Opportunities*, 201-221.

CPABC. (2021). *Maintaining confidentiality and public confidence.* CPABC. https://www.bccpa.ca/news-events/latest-news/2021/november/maintaining-confidentiality-and-public-confidence/

Craig-Bourdin, M. (2019). *How Xero is shaking up the accounting software landscape.* CPA Canada. https://www.cpacanada.ca/en/news/atwork/2019-11-26-xero-accounting-software

Croman, K., Decker, C., Eyal, I., Gencer, A. E., Juels, A., Kosba, A., & Wattenhofer, R. (2016). On scaling decentralized blockchains. In *International Conference on Financial Cryptography and Data Security* (pp. 106-125). Springer, Berlin, Heidelberg.

Crosby, M., Pattanayak, P., Verma, S., & Kalyanaraman, V. (2016). BlockChain technology: Beyond bitcoin. *Applied Innovation*, *2*(6-10), 71.

Crumlish, C., & Malone, E. (2009). *Designing social interfaces: Principles, patterns, and practices for improving the user experience.* O'Reilly Media, Inc.

Cryptopedia Staff. (2021, December 1). *What Is a DAO's Role in Decentralized Governance?* Gemini. https://www.gemini.com/cryptopedia/dao-crypto-decentralized-governance-blockchain-governance#section-what-is-a-dao

Cuffe, P. (2018). *The role of the erc-20 token standard in a financial revolution: the case of initial coin offerings.*

Cuozzo, A. (2020). Blockchain Scalability: An Overview of Challenges and Proposals. In Handbook of Blockchain, Digital Finance, and Inclusion (Vol. 1, pp. 201-214). Academic Press.

Cutillo, L., Molva, R., & Strufe, T. (2009). Safebook: A privacy-preserving online social network leveraging on real-life trust. *Commun Mag IEEE*, *47*(12), 94–101. doi:10.1109/MCOM.2009.5350374

Cyberpunk manifesto. (n.d.). Nakamoto Institute. https://nakamotoinstitute.org/static/docs/cypherpunk-manifesto.txt

D'Amato, C., Bernstein, A., & Tresp, V. (2011). *Induction on the Semantic Web1.*

Dai, C. (2020). DEX: A DApp for the decentralized marketplace. *Blockchain and Crypt Currency*, 95.

Daian, P., Goldfeder, S., Kell, T., Li, Y., Zhao, X., Bentov, I., Breidenbach, L., & Juels, A. (2020). Flash Boys 2.0: Frontrunning, Transaction Reordering, and Consensus Instability in Decentralized Exchanges. *IEEE Symposium on Security and Privacy.* IEEE.

Dai, H. N., Zheng, Z., & Zhang, Y. (2019). Blockchain for internet of things: A survey. *IEEE Internet of Things Journal*, *6*(5), 8076–8094. doi:10.1109/JIOT.2019.2920987

Damoska Sekuloska, J., & Erceg, A. (2022). Blockchain Technology toward Creating a Smart Local Food Supply Chain. *Computers*, *11*(6), 95. doi:10.3390/computers11060095

Danjou, K. (Ed.). (2019). *The Decentralized Web Manifesto: Principles for a New Decentralized Web Architecture.* Internet Archive Book Images.

DappRadar. (2023). *All Dapp rankings.* Dappar Radar. https://dappradar.com/rankings

Daryaei, M., Jassbi, J., Radfar, R., & Khamseh, A. (2020). Bitcoin Adoption as a New Technology for Payment Mechanism in a Tourism Collaborative Network. Boosting Collaborative Networks 4.0, 167–176. doi:10.1007/978-3-030-62412-5_14

Das, M., Tao, X., & Cheng, J. C. P. (2020). A Secure and Distributed Construction Document Management System Using Blockchain. *Lecture Notes in Civil Engineering*, 850–862. doi:10.1007/978-3-030-51295-8_59

Dasgupta, D., Roy, A., & Nag, A. (2017). Multi-Factor Authentication. *Infosys Science Foundation Series*, 185–233. doi:10.1007/978-3-319-58808-7_5

Daskalova, V. (2020). Regulating Unfair Trading Practices in the EU Agri-food Supply Chain: A Case of Counterproductive Regulation? *Yearbook of Antitrust and Regulatory Studies*, *12*(21), 7–53. doi:10.7172/1689-9024.YARS.2020.13.21.1

Datta, A., Buchegger, S., Vu, L.-H., Strufe, T., & Rzadca, K. (2010). Decentralized online social networks. In *Handbook of Social Network Technologies and Applications* (pp. 349–378). Springer. doi:10.1007/978-1-4419-7142-5_17

Davila, J. (2021, May 27). Decentralisation at work: Cooperatives on the blockchain. *General format.* https://www.dgen.org/blog/decentralisation-at-work-cooperatives-on-blockchain

Daviron, B., & Ponte, S. (2005). *The coffee paradox: Global markets, commodity trade, and the elusive promise of development.* Zed Books.

Davis, A., Murphy, J., Owens, D., Khazanchi, D., & Zigurs, I. (2009). Avatars, people, and virtual worlds: Foundations for research in metaverses. *Journal of the Association for Information Systems*, *10*(2), 90–117. doi:10.17705/1jais.00183

de Best, R. (2021). *Topic: Cryptocurrency adoption among businesses.* Statista. https://www.statista.com/topics/7712/cryptocurrency-adoption-among-businesses/#topicHeader__wrapper

de Best, R. (2022a). *Cryptocurrencies - statistics & facts.* Statista. https://www.statista.com/topics/4495/cryptocurrencies/#topicHeader__wrapper

de Best, R. (2022b). *NFT - statistics & facts.* Statista. https://www.statista.com/topics/8513/nft/#topicHeader__wrapper

De Filippi, P., & Mauro, R. (2014). Ethereum: the decentralised platform that might displace today's institutions. *Internet Policy Review, 25*(08).

De Filippi, L. (2016). *The invisible politics of Bitcoin: governance crisis of a decentralized infrastructure.* Internet Policy Review.

De Filippi, P., Mannan, M., & Reijers, W. (2020). Blockchain as a confidence machine: The problem of trust & challenges of governance. *Technology in Society*, *62*, 101284. doi:10.1016/j.techsoc.2020.101284

De Filippi, W. (2018). *Blockchain and the Law: The Rule of Code.* Harvard University Press.

de Haro, I. D. (2022). *How NFTs Are Driving the Latest Evolution of Art from Physical to Digital in a Pandemic Age.* Proquest. https://www.proquest.com/openview/7d11aa8708c36a3081171854dea8cab8/1?cbl=18750&diss=y&parentS essionId=HU7qElwYw9pMEjgn5sfhiRy82ePOolb69cXoyHpVJNQ%3D&pq-origsite=gscholar&parentSessionId=GT dHpKNqLM%2FmmU065Eipn82vv%2F6AtczufDrsmsAHYck%3D

De Jesus, B. Jr, Lopes, M., Moinnereau, M.-A., Gougeh, R. A., Rosanne, O. M., Schubert, W., & Falk, T. H. (2022). Quantifying multisensory immersive experiences using wearables: Is (stimulating) more (senses) always merrier? In *Proceedings of the 2nd workshop on multisensory experiences-sensoryx'22*. 10.5753ensoryx.2022.20001

De Salve, A., Mori, P., & Ricci, L. (2018). A survey on privacy in decentralized online social networks. *Computer Science Review*, 27, 154–176. doi:10.1016/j.cosrev.2018.01.001

De Salve, A., Mori, P., Ricci, L., & Di Pietro, R. (2023). Content privacy enforcement models in decentralized online social networks: State of play, solutions, limitations, and future directions. *Computer Communications*, 203, 199–225. doi:10.1016/j.comcom.2023.02.023

Decrypt. (2021, May 21). DeFi's UX Problem: Why Decentralization Is Not User-Friendly. *Decrypt*. https://decrypt.com/72033/defis-ux-problem-why-decentralization-is-not-user-friendly

Dede, C. (2009). Immersive interfaces for engagement and learning. *Science, 323*(5910), 66-69.

DeFi Pulse. (2023). Home. *DeFi Pulse*. https://defipulse.com/

DeFi Pulse. (2023). *Total Value Locked in DeFi*. DeFi Pulse. https://defipulse.com/

DeFi Pulse. (n.d.). Decentralized Finance (DeFi) - Total Value Locked (TVL) in USD. *DeFi Pulse*. https://defipulse.com/

Dehinbo, J. (2010). Contributions of traditional Web 1.0 tools e.g. email and Web 2.0 tools e.g. Weblog towards knowledge management. *Information Systems Education, 8, 15*. https://files.eric.ed.gov/fulltext/EJ1146926.pdf

Deller, S., Hoyt, A., Hueth, B., & Sundaram-Stukel, R. (2009). *Research on the economic impact of cooperatives*. University of Wisconsin Center for Cooperatives Projecthttps://resources.uwcc.wisc.edu/Research/REIC_FINAL.pdf

Deloitte. (2022). *Real estate prediction 2022*. Deloitte. https://www2.deloitte.com/content/dam/Deloitte/nl/Documents/real-estate/deloitte-nl-fsi-real-estate-predictions-2022.pdf

Delphi Labs. (2023). Assimilating the BORG: A New Framework for CryptoLaw Entities. *Medium*. https://delphilabs.medium.com/assimilating-the-borg-a-new-cryptolegal-framework-for-dao-adjacent-entities-569e54a43f83

Demartini, C., & Benussi, L. (2017). Do web 4.0 and industry 4.0 imply education X. 0? *IT Professional, 19*(3), 4–7. doi:10.1109/MITP.2017.47

Demchenko, Y., Belloum, A., de Laat, C., Loomis, C., Wiktorski, T., & Spekschoor, E. (2017, December). Customisable data science educational environment: From competences management and curriculum design to virtual labs on-demand. In *2017 IEEE International Conference on Cloud Computing Technology and Science (CloudCom)* (pp. 363-368). IEEE. 10.1109/CloudCom.2017.59

Dempsey, C., Wang, A., & Mart, J. (2022). A simple guide to the Web3 stack. *Coinbase Blog*. https://blog.coinbase.com/a-simple-guide-to-the-Web3-stack-785240e557f0

Der, U., Jähnichen, S., & Sürmeli, J. (2017). Self-sovereign identity $-$ opportunities and challenges for the digital revolution. arXiv preprint arXiv:1712.01767.

Dev, J. A. (2014). *Bitcoin mining acceleration and performance quantification, CCECE*. IEEE.

Dhawan, S., Hegelich, S., Sindermann, C., & Montag, C. (2022). Re-start social media, but how? *Telematics and Informatics Reports, 8*, 100017. doi:10.1016/j.teler.2022.100017

Di Angelo, M., & Salzer, G. (2019, April). A survey of tools for analyzing ethereum smart contracts. In *2019 IEEE International Conference on Decentralized Applications and Infrastructures (DAPPCON)* (pp. 69-78). IEEE. 10.1109/DAPPCON.2019.00018

Di Domenico, G., Sit, A., & Ishizaka, D. (2021). Fake news, social media and marketing: A systematic review. *Journa-media, Business Research, 124,* 329-341. ISSN 0148-2963. doi:10.1016/j.jbusres.2020.11.037

Díaz, R. L. S., Ruiz, G. R., Bouzouita, M., & Coninx, K. (2022). Building blocks for creating enjoyable games—A systematic literature review. *International Journal of Human-Computer Studies, 159,* 102758. doi:10.1016/j.ijhcs.2021.102758

Dib, O., & Toumi, K. (2020). Decentralized identity systems: Architecture, challenges, solutions and future directions. *Annals of Emerging Technologies in Computing (AETiC).*

Dimitra Technology. (2023, March 28). Dimitra's Commitment to Advancing SDGs: Reduce Inequality. *Medium.* https://dimitratech.medium.com/dimitras-commitment-to-advancing-sdgs-reduce-inequality-79a686372739

Dimitra. (2021). *Dimitra Token Whitepaper Version1.3.* Dimitra.io. https://dimitra.io/wp-content/uploads/2023/02/Dimitra-Whitepaper-1.3-Revised.pdf

Dinh, T. T. A., Wang, J., Chen, G., Liu, R., Ooi, B. C., & Tan, K. L. (2018). BLOCKBENCH: A Framework for Analyzing Private Blockchains. In *Proceedings of the 2018 International Conference on Management of Data* (pp. 1085-1100). Academic Press.

DiNucci, D. (1999). *Fragmented Future., 53*(4), 32.

Dionisio, J.D.N., III, W.G.B. & Gilbert, R. (2013). 3D virtual worlds and the metaverse: Current status and future possibilities. *ACM Computing Surveys (CSUR), 45*(3), 1-38.

Dionysis, S., Chesney, T., & McAuley, D. (2022). Examining the influential factors of consumer purchase intentions for blockchain traceable coffee using the theory of planned behaviour. *British Food Journal, 124*(12), 4304–4322. doi:10.1108/BFJ-05-2021-0541

Disruption, J. (2021). *Token Engineering Open Program: A Multidisciplinary Study of Gitcoin Grants.* Gitcoin. Published.

Dittman, G. (2019). A blockchain proxy for lightweight IoT devices. In: *Crypto Valley Conference on Blockchain Technology (CVCBT).* IEEE.

Dixon, S. (2022). Average daily time spent on social media worldwide 2012-2022. Statista. Retrieved June 18, 2023, from.

Dixon, S. (2023). *Daily time spent on social networking by internet users worldwide from 2012 to 2022.* Statista.

Dominic, M., Francis, S., & Pilomenraj, A. (2014). E-learning in web 3.0. *International Journal of Modern Education and Computer Science, 6*(2), 8–14. doi:10.5815/ijmecs.2014.02.02

Domjan, P., Serkin, G., Thomas, B., & Toshack, J. (2021). *Chain Reaction: How Blockchain Will Transform the Developing World.* Springer International Publishing., doi:10.1007/978-3-030-51784-7

Donnermann, M., Lein, M., Messingschlager, T., Riedmann, A., Schaper, P., Steinhaeusser, S., & Lugrin, B, (2021). Social robots and gamification for technology supported learning: An empirical study on engagement and motivation. *Computers in Human Behavior, 121,* 106792. doi:10.1016/j.chb.2021.106792

Dorri, A., Kanhere, S. S., & Jurdak, R. (2019). A memory optimized and flexible blockchain for large scale networks. *Future Generation Computer Systems, 92,* 357–373. doi:10.1016/j.future.2018.10.002

Douceur, J. R., & Wattenhofer, R. P. (2001). Large-scale simulation of replica placement algorithms for a serverless distributed file system. In *Proceedings of MASCOTS*. IEEE. 10.1109/MASCOT.2001.948882

Dreher, M., & Held, T.-E. (2022). ESG & supply chains: A practical outlook on opportunities and challenges under antitrust law. *European Competition Law Review, 9*, 417–424.

Du, L., Kim, M., & Lee, J. (2022). The Art NFTs and Their Marketplaces. arXiv preprint arXiv:2210.14942

Dubey, S., Subramanian, G., Shukla, V., Dwivedi, A., Puri, K., & Kamath, S. S. (2022). Blockchain technology: A solution to address the challenges faced by the international travellers. *OPSEARCH, 59*(4), 1471–1488. doi:10.100712597-022-00597-x

Dubnevych, N. (2023). Three key functions of a DAO foundation. *Legal nodes.* https://legalnodes.com/article/dao-foundation-functions

Ducheneaut, N., Yee, N., Nickell, E., & Moore, R. J. 2006, April. " Alone together?" Exploring the social dynamics of massively multiplayer online games. In *Proceedings of the SIGCHI conference on Human Factors in computing systems* (pp. 407-416). ACM. 10.1145/1124772.1124834

Ducheneaut, N., Yee, N., Nickell, E., & Moore, R. J. 2007, April. The life and death of online gaming communities: a look at guilds in world of warcraft. In *Proceedings of the SIGCHI conference on Human factors in computing systems* (pp. 839-848). ACM. 10.1145/1240624.1240750

Dunphy, P., & Petitcolas, F. A. (2018). A first look at identity management schemes on the blockchain. *IEEE Security and Privacy, 16*(4), 20–29. doi:10.1109/MSP.2018.3111247

DuPont, Q. (2017). Experiments in algorithmic governance: A history and ethnography of "The DAO," a failed Decentralized Autonomous Organization. In Bitcoin and Beyond (pp. 157-177). Routledge.

DuPont, Q. (2017). Experiments in algorithmic governance: a history and ethnography of the DAO, a failed decentralized autonomous organization. In M. Campbell-Verduyn (Ed.), *Bitcoin and Beyond: Cryptocurrencies, Blockchains and Global Governance* (pp. 157–177). Routledge. doi:10.4324/9781315211909-8

Düring, T., & Fisbeck, H. (2017). Einsatz der Blockchain-Technologie für eine transparente Wertschöpfungskette. In A. Hildebrandt & W. Landhäußer (Eds.), *CSR und Digitalisierung* (pp. 449–464). Springer Berlin Heidelberg. doi:10.1007/978-3-662-53202-7_33

Dwivedi, Y. K., Hughes, L., Baabdullah, A. M., Ribeiro-Navarrete, S., Giannakis, M., Al-Debei, M. M., Dennehy, D., Metri, B., Buhalis, D., Cheung, C. M. K., Conboy, K., Doyle, R., Dubey, R., Dutot, V., Felix, R., Goyal, D. P., Gustafsson, A., Hinsch, C., Jebabli, I., & Wamba, S. F. (2022). Metaverse beyond the hype: Multidisciplinary perspectives on emerging challenges, opportunities, and agenda for research, practice and policy. *International Journal of Information Management, 66*, 102542. doi:10.1016/j.ijinfomgt.2022.102542

Dwivedi, Y. K., Hughes, L., Wang, Y., Alalwan, A. A., Ahn, S. J., Balakrishnan, J., Barta, S., Belk, R., Buhalis, D., Dutot, V., & ... (2022). How metaverse will change the future of marketing: Implications for research and practice. *Psychology and Marketing.*

Eckhoff, D., & Wagner, I. (2018). Privacy in the Smart City - Applications, Technologies, Challenges, and Solutions. *IEEE Communications Surveys and Tutorials, 20*(1), 489–516. doi:10.1109/COMST.2017.2748998

Egan, M. (2020). *This Startup Is Taking on Big Banks. And It's Working.* CNN. https:// www.cnn.com/2020/10/05/business/chime-bank-startup/index.html

El Attar, A., & Chaloui, C. (2023). Central Bank Digital Money (CBDC): A Literature Review. *Dossiers de Recherches en Économie et Gestion, 11*(01), 133–147.

Elixir Business Solution Private Limited. (2023). The rise of technology in accounting: how it changed the game. *LinkedIn*. https://www.linkedin.com/pulse/rise-technology-accounting-how-changed/

Elliptic. (2020). *The Importance of Oracles in DeFi*. Elliptic. https://www.elliptic.co/blog/the-importance-of-oracles-in-defi

Elliptic. (2020). *The Oracle Problem: How Can Smart Contracts Reach Out to the Real World?* Elliptic. https://www.elliptic.co/blog/the-oracle-problem-how-can-smart-contracts-reach-out-to-the-real-world

EllulJ. (2021). Blockchain is dead! Long live Blockchain! *The Journal of The British Blockchain Association*. SSRN. https://ssrn.com/abstract=3813872

Elmasry, T. K., Hazan, E., Khan, H., Kelly, G., Srivastava, S., Yee, L., & Zemmel, R. W. (2022). *Value creation in the metaverse: The real business of the virtual world*. McKinsey & Company.

Eltuhami, M., Abdullah, M., & Talip, B. A. (2022, November). Identity Verification and Document Traceability in Digital Identity Systems using Non-Transferable Non-Fungible Tokens. In *2022 International Visualization, Informatics and Technology Conference (IVIT)* (pp. 136-142). IEEE. 10.1109/IVIT55443.2022.10033362

Entrepreneurs' Organization. (2022). 3 ways Web3 may impact accounting (and how to prepare). *Inc*. https://www.inc.com/entrepreneurs-organization/3-ways-web3-may-impact-accounting-and-how-to-prepare.html

Ermolaev, E., Abellán Álvarez, I., Sedlmeir, J., & Fridgen, G. (2023, May). z-Commerce: Designing a Data-Minimizing One-Click Checkout Solution. In *International Conference on Design Science Research in Information Systems and Technology* (pp. 3-17). Cham: Springer Nature Switzerland. 10.1007/978-3-031-32808-4_1

Ethereum Foundation. (2020). *Ethereum 2.0 Overview*. Ethereum Foundation.

European Commission. (2020a). *Timeline of Farm to Fork actions*. European Commission. https://food.ec.europa.eu/system/files/2022-04/f2f_timeline-actions_en.pdf

European Commission. (2020b). *Farm to Fork Strategy*. European Commission. https://food.ec.europa.eu/horizontal-topics/farm-fork-strategy_en

European Commission. (2022). *Proposal for a DIRECTIVE OF THE EUROPEAN PARLIAMENT AND OF THE COUNCIL on Corporate Sustainability Due Diligence and amending Directive (EU) 2019/1937*. European Commission. https://eur-lex.europa.eu/legal-content/EN/TXT/?uri=CELEX%3A52022PC0071

European Commission. (2023, June). *Antitrust: Commission adopts new Horizontal Block Exemption Regulations and Horizontal Guidelines* [Text]. European Commission - European Commission. https://ec.europa.eu/commission/press-corner/detail/en/IP_23_2990

European Systemic Risk Board. (2023). *Crypto-assets and decentralized finance May 2023*. https://www.esrb.europa.eu/pub/pdf/reports/esrb.cryptoassetsanddecentralisedfinance202305~9792140acd.en.pdf

Eve, S., & Graham, S. (2020). Spatial Data Visualisation and Beyond. In Archaeological Spatial Analysis. doi:10.4324/9781351243858-24

Eyal, I., & Sirer, E. G. (2013). Majority is not Enough: Bitcoin Mining is Vulnerable. CoRR.

Fahmi, M., Muda, I., & Kesuma, S. A. (2023). Digitization Technologies and Contributions to Companies towards Accounting and Auditing Practices. [IJSSR]. *International Journal of Social Service & Research, 3*(3), 639–643. https://doi-org.ezproxy.myucwest.ca/10.46799/ijssr.v3i3.298. doi:10.46799/ijssr.v3i3.298

Fakhri, D., & Mutijarsa, K. (2018). Secure IoT communication using blockchain technology. *International Symposium on Electronics and Smart Devices (ISESD)*, (pp. 1–6). IEEE.

Famulari, A., & Hecker, A. (2013). Mantle: a novel dosn leveraging free storage and local software. In *Advanced Infocomm Technology* (pp. 213–224). Springer. doi:10.1007/978-3-642-38227-7_24

Fang, X., Wang, H., Liu, G., Tian, X., Ding, G., & Zhang, H. (2022). Industry application of digital twin: From concept to implementation. *International Journal of Advanced Manufacturing Technology*, *121*(7-8), 4289–4312. doi:10.100700170-022-09632-z

Faqir-Rhazoui, Y. Arroyo, & J., Hassan, S. (Eds). (2021). A scalable voting system: Validation of holographic consensus in DAOstack. In *Proceedings of the 54th Hawaii International Conference on System Sciences.* Scholar Space. http://hdl.handle.net/10125/71296

Faqir-Rhazoui, Y., Arroyo, J., & Hassan, S. (2020). An overview of decentralized autonomous organizations on the blockchain. pp. 1-8. *Proceedings of the 16th International Symposium on Open Collaboration.* UCM. https://eprints.ucm.es/id/eprint/62273/1/os20-paper-a11-el-faqir.pdf

Faqir-Rhazoui, Y., Arroyo, J., & Hassan, S. (2021). A Comparative Analysis of the Adoption of Decentralized Governance in the Blockchain Through DAOs. doi:10.21203/rs.3.rs-166470/v1

Fat, J., & Candra, H. (2020, December). Blockchain Application in Internet of Things for Securing Transaction in Ethereum TestNet. *IOP Conference Series. Materials Science and Engineering*, *1007*(1), 012194. doi:10.1088/1757-899X/1007/1/012194

Fauziah, Z., Latifah, H., Omar, X., Khoirunisa, A., & Millah, S. (2020). Application of blockchain technology in smart contracts: A systematic literature review. *Aptisi Transactions on Technopreneurship*, *2*(2), 160–166. doi:10.34306/att.v2i2.97

Feenberg, A. (1999). *Questioning Technology.* Routledge.

Feenberg, A. (2002). *Transforming Technology.* University.

Feenberg, A. (2002). *Transforming Technology: A Critical Theory Revisited* (2nd ed.). Oxford University Press.

Feichtinger, R., Fritsch, R., Vonlanthen, V., & Wattenhofer, R. (2023). *The hidden shortcomings of (D)AOs—An empirical study of on-chain governance.* doi:10.48550/arXiv.2302.12125

Fekete, D. L., & Kiss, A. (2023). Toward Building Smart Contract-Based Higher Education Systems Using Zero-Knowledge Ethereum Virtual Machine. *Electronics (Basel)*, *12*(3), 664. doi:10.3390/electronics12030664

Feld, S., Schonfeld, M., & Werner, M. (2014). Analyzing the Deployment of Bitcoin's P2P Network under an AS-level Perspective. ANT/SEIT, ser. Procedia Computer Science. Elsevier.

Feng, Y., Huang, W., Wang, S., Zhang, Y., & Jiang, S. (2021). Detection of RFID cloning attacks: A spatiotemporal trajectory data stream-based practical approach. *Computer Networks*, *189*.

Fennel, A. (2022). Gig economy statistics UK. *Standout CV.* https://standout-cv.com/gig-economy-statistics-uk

Fernandes, D. L. S. (2023). *Designing player agency experiences for environmental awareness gameplay* [PhD diss.]. UMA.

Fernández-Villaverde, J., Sanches, D., Schilling, L., & Uhlig, H. (2020). Central Bank Digital Currency: Central Banking For All? (*Working Paper No. 26753*). National Bureau of Economic Research. doi:10.3386/w26753

Ferrari, M. M., Mehl, A., & Stracca, L. (2020). Central bank digital currency in an open economy. European Central Bank (*Working Paper Series No. 2505*). https://www.ecb.europa.eu/pub/pdf/scpwps/ecb.wp2488~fede33ca65.en.pdf

Ferreira, J. F., Cruz, P., Durieux, T., & Abreu, R. (2020, December). Smartbugs: A framework to analyze solidity smart contracts. In *Proceedings of the 35th IEEE/ACM International Conference on Automated Software Engineering* (pp. 1349-1352). IEEE. 10.1145/3324884.3415298

Ferris, S., & Rehm, P. (2022). What CPAs need to know about NFTs. *Journal of Accountancy.* https://www.journalofaccountancy.com/issues/2022/oct/what-cpas-need-to-know-about-nfts.html

Figueira, Á., & Oliveira, L. (2017). The current state of fake news: Challenges and opportunities. *Procedia Computer Science*, *121*, 817–825. doi:10.1016/j.procs.2017.11.106

Filipčić, S. (2022). Web 3 & DAOs: an overview of the development and possibilities for the implementation in research and education. *45th Jubilee International Convention on Information, Communication and Electronic Technology (MIPRO)*, Croatia. 10.23919/MIPRO55190.2022.9803324

Financial Action Task Force 2023. (2023a) *International Standards on Combating Money Laundering and the Financing of Terrorism & Proliferation: The FATF Recommendations.* https://www.fatf-gafi.org/content/dam/fatf-gafi/recommendations/FATF%20Recommendations%202012.pdf.coredownload.inline.pdf

Financial Action Task Force 2023. (2023b) *Targeted Update on Implementation of the FATF Standards on Virtual Assets and Virtual Asset Service Providers.* https://www.fatf-gafi.org/content/fatf-gafi/en/publications/Fatfrecommendations/targeted-update-virtual-assets-vasps-2023.html

Financial Action Task Force. (2019). *Mandate.* https://www.fatf-gafi.org/en/the-fatf/mandate-of-the-fatf.html

Financial Stability Board. (2022). *Regulation, Supervision and Oversight of Crypto-Asset Activities and Markets: Consultative Document.* https://www.fsb.org/wp-content/uploads/P111022-3.pdf

Fiocco, D., Ganesan, V., Garcia de la Serrana Lozano, M., & Sharif, H. (2023). *Agtech: Breaking down the farmer adoption dilemma | McKinsey.* McKinsey & Company. https://www.mckinsey.com/industries/agriculture/our-insights/agtech-breaking-down-the-farmer-adoption-dilemma#/

Fischer, D. (2022). Ethical and Professional Implications of Blockchain Accounting Ledgers. *Proceedings of the Northeast Business & Economics Association*, 27–30.

Fischer, E. F. (2022). *Making Better Coffee: How Maya Farmers and Third Wave Tastemakers Create Value.* University of California Press.

Fitzgerald, H. E., Karen, B., Sonka, S. T., Furco, A., & Swanson, L. (2020). The centrality of engagement in higher education. In *Building the Field of Higher Education Engagement* (pp. 201–219). Routledge.

Flavi'an, C., Ib'an˜ez-S'anchez, S., & Oru's, C. (2021). Impacts of technological embodiment through virtual reality on potential guests' emotions and engagement. *Journal of Hospitality Marketing & Management*, *30*(1), 1–20. doi:10.1080/19368623.2020.1770146

Flink, M. (2021). *International blockchain regulation: Regulation by code – outlaws or new conceptions of law?* UTU Pub. https://www.utupub.fi/bitstream/handle/10024/151678/Flink_Mona_opinnayte.pdf?sequence=1

Food and Agriculture Organization of the United Nations [FAO]. (2023). *FAO Publications Catalogue 2022—Markets and Trade: Coffee.* Food and Agriculture Organization of the United Nations. doi:10.4060/cc2323en

Foody, G. M. (2002). Status of land cover classification accuracy assessment. In Remote Sensing of Environment (Vol. 80, Issue 1). doi:10.1016/S0034-4257(01)00295-4

Forra. (2018). *Methods and ways to obtain cryptocurrency.* Forra. https://forra.io/obtaining-cryptocurrency/

Forsyth, S., & Daudjee, K. (2013). Update management in decentralized online social networks. In *5th International workshop on peer-to-peer systems and online social networks (HotPOST 2013)22*.

Fracassi, C., & Di Maggio, M. (2022). *Coinbase Institute: Evaluation of systemic risk in crypto*. CTFAssets. https://assets.ctfassets.net/c5bd0wqjc7v0/2KwhyMnQvPbhbGWtSEaEaZ81acc71cafa40a8d090a0eb5f4ed4e4b/CBI-Systemic_Risk_Newsletter.pdf

Franco, A. (2021). *How Blockchain Technology Can Help Rearchitect Social Networks: An Analysis of Desmos Network*. Università Ca' Foscari Venezia. http://dspace.unive.it/handle/10579/19800

Frank, A. U. (2014). Sharing Geographic Data: How to Update Distributed or Replicated Data. *REAL CORP 2014–PLAN IT SMART! Clever Solutions for Smart Cities. Proceedings of 19th International Conference on Urban Planning, Regional Development and Information Society*, (pp. 959–966). ACM.

Frankenfield. (2023). What are smart contracts on the blockchain and how they work. *Investopedia*. https://www.investopedia.com/terms/s/smart-contracts.asp

Freeman, S., Beveridge, I., & Angelis, J. (2019). Drivers of digital trust in the crypto industry. In M. Ragnedda & G. Destefanis (Eds.), *Blockchain and Web 3.0: Social, Economic, and Technological Challenges* (pp. 62–77). Routledge. doi:10.4324/9780429029530-5

Friedrich, M. (2020). *Square Valuation Model: Cash App's Potential*. ARK Invgaurgaestment. https://ark-invest.com/articles/analyst-research/square-valuation/

Fromknecth, C., Velicanu, D., & Yakoubov, S. (2014). CertCoin: A Name Coin Based Decentralized Authentication System. CSail. https://courses.csail.mit.edu/6.857/2014/files/ 19-fromknecht-velicann-yakoubov-certcoin.pdf

Fromknecth, C., Velicanu, D., & Yakoubov, S. (2014). *CertCoin: A NameCoin Based Decentralized Authentication System*. CSail. https://courses.csail.mit.edu/6.857/2014/files/ 19-fromknecht-velicann-yakoubov-certcoin.pdf

Fukami, Y., Shimizu, T., & Matsushima, H. (2021, December). The impact of decentralized identity architecture on data exchange. In *2021 IEEE International Conference on Big Data (Big Data)* (pp. 3461-3465). IEEE. 10.1109/BigData52589.2021.9671674

Gajek, S. (2018). Knowledge extractable voting for blockchain & distributed governance. *Hacker Noon*. https://hackernoon.com/knowledge-extractable-voting-for-blockchain-distributed-governance-radically-new-mechanisms-ed2ca47f065f

Ganado, M., & Tendon, S. (2018). Malta: Legal personality for Blockchains, DAOs and Smart Contracts. *MonDaq.*. https://www.mondaq.com/fin-tech/707696/legal-personality-for-blockchains-daos-and-smart-contracts

Gangwal, A., Gangavalli, H. R., & Thirupathi, A. (2023). A survey of Layer-two blockchain protocols. *Journal of Network and Computer Applications*, *209*, 103539. doi:10.1016/j.jnca.2022.103539

Gao, J., Agyekum, K. O. B. O., Sifah, E. B., Acheampong, K. N., Xia, Q., Du, X., & Xia, H. (2019). A blockchain-SDN-enabled Internet of vehicles environment for fog computing and 5G networks. *IEEE Internet of Things Journal*, *7*(5), 4278–4291. doi:10.1109/JIOT.2019.2956241

Gartner. (2022). *Emerging Technology Analysis: Virtual Worlds*. Gartner. [www.gartner.com/en/information-technology]

Gee, J.P. (2013). *Digital media and learning: A prospective retrospective*. ACM.

German Federal Government. (2020). Blockchain Strategy of the German Federal Government.

Gervais, A., Karame, G. O., & Capkun, S. (2016). *On the security and performance of proof of work blockchains*. IACR Cryptology ePrint Archive. https://eprint.iacr.org/2016/555.pdf

Gharaibeh, A., Salahuddin, M. A., Hussini, S. J., Khreishah, A., Khalil, I., Guizani, M., & Al-Fuqaha, A. (2017). Smart Cities: A Survey on Data Management, Security, and Enabling Technologies. *IEEE Communications Surveys and Tutorials*, *19*(4), 2456–2501. doi:10.1109/COMST.2017.2736886

Giancaspro, M. (2017). Is a 'smart contract' really a smart idea? Insights from a legal perspective. *Computer Law & Security Review*, *33*(6), 825–835. https://doi-org.ezproxy.myucwest.ca/10.1016/j.clsr.2017.05.007. doi:10.1016/j.clsr.2017.05.007

Giang Barrera, K., & Shah, D. (2023). Marketing in the Metaverse: Conceptual understanding, framework, and research agenda. *Journal of Business Research*, *155*, 113420. doi:10.1016/j.jbusres.2022.113420

Giannakos, M. N., & Lapatas, V. (2010, July). Towards Web 3.0 concept for collaborative e-learning. In *International Conference on Technology-Enhanced Learning* (Vol. 2, pp. 147-151). SCITEPRESS.

Gil-Aciron, L. A. (2022). The gamer psychology: A psychological perspective on game design and gamification. *Interactive Learning Environments*, 1–25. doi:10.1080/10494820.2022.2082489

Gilbert, S. (2022). *Crypto, web3, and the Metaverse. Bennett Institute for Public Policy*. Policy Brief.

Gil-Cordero, E., Cabrera-Sánchez, J. P., & Arrás-Cortés, M. J. (2020). Cryptocurrencies as a financial tool: Acceptance factors. *Mathematics*, *8*(11), 1974. doi:10.3390/math8111974

Gillpatrick, T., Boǧa, S., & Aldanmaz, O. (2022). How Can Blockchain Contribute to Developing Country Economies? A Literature Review on Application Areas. *ECONOMICS*, *10*(1), 105–128. doi:10.2478/eoik-2022-0009

Giordani, M., Polese, M., Mezzavilla, M., Rangan, S., & Zorzi, M. (2020). Toward 6G networks: Use cases and technologies. *IEEE Communications Magazine*, *58*(3), 55–61. doi:10.1109/MCOM.001.1900411

Giovannucci, D., Leibovich, J., Pizano, D., Paredes, G., Montenegro, S., Arévalo, H., & Varangis, P. (2002). *Colombia Coffee Sector Study* (SSRN Scholarly Paper 996138). https://papers.ssrn.com/abstract=996138

Gipp, B., Meuschke, N., & Gernandt, A. (2015). Decentralized Trusted Timestamping using the Crypto Currency Bitcoin. CoRR.

Glarer, A., Linder, T., Müller, L., & Mesero, S. D. (2020, May 4). Decentralized Autonomous Assotiation (DAA). *MME*. https://www.mme.ch/en/magazine/articles/decentralized-autonomous-association-daa

Glatz, F. (2023). DAOs are Dead! Long live DAOs! *Hecker Hut*. https://heckerhut.medium.com/daos-are-dead-long-live-daos-50de94e8ee1e

Global Social Media Statistics. (2023). DataReportal – Global Digital Insights. GSMS.

GlobalData. (2022). *Bitcoin's Market Capitalization History (May 1, 2013 – September 4, 2022, $ Billion)*. GlobalData. https://www.globaldata.com/data-insights/cards-amp-payments/bitcoins-market-capitalization-history/

Gochhayat, S. P., Bandara, E., Shetty, S., & Foytik, P. (2019). Yugala: Blockchain based Encrypted Cloud Storage for IoT Data. *2019 IEEE International Conference on Blockchain (Blockchain)*. IEEE. 10.1109/Blockchain.2019.00073

Gonzalez, N. E. (2022). Does Cryptocurrency Staking Fall Under SEC Jurisdiction? *Fordham Journal of Corporate & Financial Law*, *27*(2), 521–561.

Goodchild, M. F. (2007). Citizens as sensors: The world of volunteered geography. In GeoJournal. doi:10.100710708-007-9111-y

Graffi, K., Gross, C., Stingl, D., Hartung, D., Kovacevic, A., & Steinmetz, R. (2011). *LifeSocial. KOM: A Secure and P2P-based Solution for Online Social Networks*. IEEE. . doi:10.1109/CCNC.2011.5766541

Green, D., McCann, J., Vu, T., Lopez, N., & Ouattara, S. (2018). Gig economy and the future of work. A Fiverr.com case study. *Management and Economics Research Journal*, *4*(2), 281–288. doi:10.18639/MERJ.2018.04.734348

Greiner, M., & Ahmad, I. (2021). Decentralized Governance for Decentralized Autonomous Organizations. *IEEE Access : Practical Innovations, Open Solutions*, *9*, 5229–5243.

Groos, J. (2020). *Crypto Politics: Notes on Sociotechnical Imaginaries of Governance in Blockchain Based Technologies.* Semantic Scholar. https://pdfs.semanticscholar.org/4809/ea5ae690a4b332dad0660a5834e2706182eb.pdf

Gu, B., Jiang, W., & Tan, C. W. (2016). Theme: Embracing the Internet of Things to drive data-driven decisions. *Journal of Management Analytics*, *3*(1), 112–113. doi:10.1080/23270012.2016.1140597

Guberović, E., Lipić, T., & Čavrak, I. (2021). Dew intelligence: Federated learning perspective. In *2021 IEEE 45th Annual Computers, Software, and Applications Conference (COMPSAC)*, (pp. 1819-1824). IEEE. 10.1109/COMPSAC51774.2021.00274

Güdelci, Ü. E. N. (2022). New Era in Blockchain Technology and Better Accounting Information. *Muhasebe ve Vergi Uygulamalari Dergisi (MUVU)* [JATS]. *Journal of Accounting & Taxation Studies*, *15*(2), 437–461.

Guegan, D. (2017). *Public blockchain versus private blockchain.* Academic Press.

Guegan, D. (2017). Public Blockchain versus Private blockhain. *Shs.hal.science*. https://shs.hal.science/halshs-01524440

Guides, C. (2021). *Why was Cryptocurrency Created, was there a reason?* Crypto Set Go. https://cryptosetgo.com/why-was-cryptocurrency-created-was-there-a-reason/ .

Guidi, B. (2020). When Blockchain meets Online Social Networks. *Pervasive and Mobile Computing*, *62*, 101131. doi:10.1016/j.pmcj.2020.101131

Guidi, B. (2021). An Overview of Blockchain Online Social Media from the Technical Point of View. *Applied Sciences (Basel, Switzerland)*, *11*(21), 9880. doi:10.3390/app11219880

Guidi, B., Michienzi, A., & Ricci, L. (2020). Steem Blockchain: Mining the Inner Structure of the Graph. *IEEE Access : Practical Innovations, Open Solutions*, *8*, 210251–210266. doi:10.1109/ACCESS.2020.3038550

Gunitsky, S. (2015). Corrupting the Cyber-Commons: Social Media as a Tool of Autocratic Stability. *Perspectives on Politics*, *13*(1), 42–54. doi:10.1017/S1537592714003120

Gunnoo, N. (2023). Data entry automation in 2023. *Parseur*. https://parseur.com/blog/data-entry-automation

Gupta, S., Bairwa, A. K., Kushwaha, S. S., & Joshi, S. (2023, January). Decentralized Identity Management System using the amalgamation of Blockchain Technology. In *2023 3rd International Conference on Intelligent Communication and Computational Techniques (ICCT)* (pp. 1-6). IEEE. 10.1109/ICCT56969.2023.10076117

Gupta, S., Pandey, D. K., El Ammari, A., & Sahu, G. P. (2023). Do perceived risks and benefits impact trust and willingness to adopt CBDCs? *Research in International Business and Finance*, *66*, 101993. doi:10.1016/j.ribaf.2023.101993

Gurkov, A. (2022). Alignment of a traditional cooperative identity to the design of Decentralised Autonomous Organisations. In *Nottingham Insolvency and Business Law E-Journal, 10* (9). http://hdl.handle.net/10138/351666

Guych, N., Anastasia, S., & Jennet, A. (2018). *Munich Personal RePEc Archive Factors influencing the intention to use cryptocurrency payments: An examination of blockchain economy.* MPRA. https://mpra.ub.uni-muenchen.de/99159/1/MPRA_paper_99159.pdf

Guzdial, M., Snodgrass, S., & Summerville, A. J. (2022). *Procedural content generation via machine learning: An overview*. Springer. doi:10.1007/978-3-031-16719-5

Haar, R. (2021). The Future of Cryptocurrency: 5 Experts' Predictions After a 'Breakthrough' 2021. *Time*. https://time.com/nextadvisor/investing/cryptocurrency/future-of-cryptocurrency/

Hacker. (2018). *Smart contracts: A smart way to automate performance*. Georgia Law Review.

Hackl, C., Lueth, D., & Di Bartolo, T. (2022). *Navigating the metaverse: A guide to limitless possibilities in a Web 3.0 world*. John Wiley & Sons.

Haentjens, M., De Graaf, T., & Kokorin, I. (2020). The Failed Hopes of Disintermediation: Crypto-custodian Insolvency, Legal Risks and How to Avoid Them, *Singapore Journal of Legal Studies*, 526-63.

Hagerty, J. R. (2021, March 11). Non-Fungible Tokens 101: A Primer On NFTs For Brands And Business Professionals. *Forbes*. https://www.forbes.com/sites/jonathanhagerty/2021/03/11/non-fungible-tokens-101-a-primer-on-nfts-for-brands-and-business-professionals/

Haileyesus, S. (2022). How to Make Money with Cryptocurrency. *Small Business Trends*. https://smallbiztrends.com/2022/06/how-to-make-money-with-cryptocurrency.html#:~:text=There%20are%20three%20ways%20to%20acquire%20cryptocurrency%3A%20you

Hakak, S., Nurul, F. M. N., Ayub, M. N., Affal, H., Hussin, N., & Imran, M. (2019). Cloud-assisted gamification for education and learning–Recent advances and challenges. *Computers & Electrical Engineering*, *74*, 22–34. doi:10.1016/j.compeleceng.2019.01.002

Haklay, M. (2010). How good is volunteered geographical information? A comparative study of OpenStreetMap and ordnance survey datasets. *Environment and Planning. B, Planning & Design*, *37*(4), 682–703. doi:10.1068/b35097

Haklay, M., Antoniou, V., Basiouka, S., Soden, R., & Mooney, P. (2014). *Crowdsourced geographic information use in government*. World Bank Publications.

Hamilton, M. (2020). Blockchain distributed ledger technology: An introduction and focus on smart contracts. *Journal of Corporate Accounting & Finance*, *31*(2), 7–12. doi:10.1002/jcaf.22421

Han, J., Kim, J., Youn, A., Lee, J., Chun, Y., Woo, J., & Hong, J. W. K. (2021, September). Cos-CBDC: Design and Implementation of CBDC on Cosmos Blockchain. In *2021 22nd Asia-Pacific Network Operations and Management Symposium (APNOMS)* (pp. 303-308). IEEE.

Han, L., Nath, B., Iftode, L., & Muthukrishnan, S. (2011). Social butterfly: social caches for distributed social networks. In: Proceedings ofSocialCom/PASSAT, (pp. 81–8623). PASSAT. doi:10.1109/PASSAT/SocialCom.2011.105

HanJ.LeeJ.LiT. (2023). *DAO governance*. SSRN. doi:10.2139/ssrn.4346581

Han, L., Punceva, M., Nath, B., Muthukrishnan, S. M., & Iftode, L. (2012) SocialCDN: caching techniques for distributed social networks. In: *2012 IEEE International conference on peer-to-peer computing*. IEEE. 10.1109/P2P.2012.6335799

Han, R., Foutris, N., & Kotselidis, C. (2019). Demystifying Crypto-Mining: Analysis and Optimizations of Memory-Hard PoW Algorithms. In *2019 IEEE International Symposium on Performance Analysis of Systems and Software (ISPASS)*. IEEE. 10.1109/ISPASS.2019.00011

Han, X., Yuan, Y., & Wang, F. Y. (2019, November). A blockchain-based framework for central bank digital currency. In *2019 IEEE International conference on service operations and logistics, and informatics (SOLI)* (pp. 263-268). IEEE. 10.1109/SOLI48380.2019.8955032

Hardin, G. (1968). The Tragedy of the Commons. *Science, 162*(3859), 1243–1248. https://pages.mtu.edu/~asmayer/rural_sustain/governance/Hardin%201968.pdf. doi:10.1126cience.162.3859.1243 PMID:5699198

Harper, J. (2020, February 12). *Blockchain & Coffee: Separating The Marketing From The Reality*. Perfect Daily Grind. https://perfectdailygrind.com/2020/02/blockchain-coffee-separating-the-marketing-from-the-reality/

Harvey, C. R., Ramachandran, A., & Santoro, J. (2021). *DeFi and the Future of Finance*. John Wiley & Sons.

Harz, D., Gudgeon, L., Gervais, A., & Knottenbelt, W. (2020). Balance: Dynamic Adjustment of Cryptocurrency Deposits. *Workshop on Trusted Smart Contracts*.

Hasan, M. (2022, May 18). State of IoT 2022: Number of connected IoT devices growing 18% to 14.4 billion globally. *IOT Analytics*. https://iot-analytics.com/number-connected-iot-devices/

Hassan, S., & De Filippi, P. (2021). Decentralized autonomous organization. *Internet Policy Review: Journal on Internet Regulation, 10*(2), 1–10. doi:10.14763/2021.2.1556

Haveri, P., Rashmi, U. B., Narayan, D. G., Nagaratna, K., & Shivaraj, K. (2020, July). Edublock: Securing educational documents using blockchain technology. In *2020 11th International Conference on Computing, Communication and Networking Technologies (ICCCNT)* (pp. 1-7). IEEE.

Hays, D., & Tabone, M. (2023). *Blockchain Use Cases and Adoption Report*. Cointelegraph Research. https://research-backend.cointelegraph.com/uploads/attachments/clgav9x5o6yvqzyqng1kmb32g-blockchain-use-cases-and-adoption-report-3.pdf

Heeks, R., & Renken, J. (2018). Crafting rigorous action design research: Lessons from the applied collaborative design approach. *Information Technology for Development, 24*(3), 632–651.

Hellström, E. (2022). *Fair Voting System for Permissionless Decentralized Autonomous Organizations*. [(UPTEC IT, ISSN 1401-5749; 22005) [Independent thesis, Uppsala University]. https://uu.diva-portal.org/smash/record.jsf?pid=diva2%3A1671220&dswid=-508

Hendaoui, A., Limayem, M., & Thompson, C. W. (2008). 3D social virtual worlds: Research issues and challenges. *IEEE Internet Computing, 12*(1), 88–92. doi:10.1109/MIC.2008.1

Herbert, J., & Litchfield, A. (2015). *A Novel Method for Decentralised Peer-to-Peer Software License Validation Using Cryptocurrency Blockchain Technology, ACSC, ser. CRPIT* (Vol. 159). Australian Computer Society.

Herrera-Joancomart, J. (2014). *Research and Challenges on Bitcoin Anonymity, DPM/SETOP/QASA, ser* (Vol. 8872). Lecture Notes in Computer Science. Springer.

Herrington, J. (2006). Authentic e-learning in higher education: Design principles for authentic learning environments and tasks. In *E-Learn: World Conference on E-Learning in Corporate, Government, Healthcare, and Higher Education* (pp. 3164-3173). Association for the Advancement of Computing in Education (AACE).

Hewa, T. M., Hu, Y., Liyanage, M., Kanhare, S. S., & Ylianttila, M. (2021). Survey on blockchain-based smart contracts: Technical aspects and future research. *IEEE Access : Practical Innovations, Open Solutions, 9*, 87643–87662. doi:10.1109/ACCESS.2021.3068178

Hewa, T., Ylianttila, M., & Liyanage, M. (2021). Survey on blockchain based smart contracts: Applications, opportunities and challenges. *Journal of Network and Computer Applications, 177*, 102857. doi:10.1016/j.jnca.2020.102857

Hew, K. F., & Cheung, W. S. (2013). Use of Web 2.0 technologies in K-12 and higher education: The search for evidence-based practice. *Educational Research Review, 9*, 47–64. doi:10.1016/j.edurev.2012.08.001

Hiremath, B. K., & Kenchakkanavar, A. Y. (2016). An alteration of the Web 1.0, Web 2.0 and Web 3.0: A comparative study. Imperial Journal of Interdisciplinary Research, 2(4), 705–710. https://www.academia.edu/download/51816194/327-660-1-SM.pdf

Hirsh-Pasek, K., Zosh, J. M., Hadani, H. S., Golinkoff, R. M., Clark, K., Donohue, C., & Wartella, E. (2022). A whole new world: Education meets the metaverse. *Center for Universal Education, February.*

Hodgson, G. M. (2002). The legal nature of the firm and the myth of the firm-market hybrid. *International Journal of the Economics of Business*, 9(1), 37–60. doi:10.1080/13571510110102967

Hofmann, S. B. (2019). Digital supply chain management agenda for the automotive supplier industry. *Journal of Business Logistics.*

Hölbl, M., Kompara, M., Kamišalić, A., & Nemec Zlatolas, L. (2018). A systematic review of the use of blockchain in healthcare. *Symmetry*, 10(10), 470. doi:10.3390ym10100470

Hollensen, S., Kotler, P., & Opresnik, M. O. (2022). Metaverse – the new marketing universe. *The Journal of Business Strategy.* doi:10.1108/JBS-01-2022-0014

Holmstrom, B. (1999). Future of cooperatives: A corporate perspective. *Liiketaloudellinen aikakauskirja LTA - The Finnish Journal of Business Economics, (*4), 404–417.

Holowczak, R., & Wargo, C. (2020). Cryptocurrencies as an Investment Vehicle: Analysis of Blockchain networks, Decentralization and Security Implications. *Technology Innovation Management Review*, 10(9).

Homoliak, I., Perešíni, M., Holop, P., Handzuš, J., & Casino, F. (2023). CBDC-AquaSphere: Interoperable Central Bank Digital Currency Built on Trusted Computing and Blockchain. arXiv preprint arXiv:2305.16893.

Hopkins, E. (2022). Virtual Commerce in a Decentralized Blockchain-based Metaverse: Immersive Technologies, Computer Vision Algorithms, and Retail Business Analytics. *Linguistic and Philosophical Investigations*, (21), 203–218.

Hrenyak, A. (2022). *Implications of Non-Fungible Tokens for the Online Artist* [Theses within Digital Humanities, Uppsala University]. Digitala Vetenskapliga Arkivet. https://www.diva-portal.org/smash/record.jsf?pid=diva2%3A1675820&dswid=-1340

Hsiao, J., Chung, T. M., & Liang, C. (2021). On design issues and architectural styles for blockchain-driven IoT services. *Computers & Electrical Engineering*, 87, 106781.

Huang, J., Kong, L., Chen, G., Wu, M.-Y., Liu, X., & Zeng, P. (2019). Towards Secure Industrial IoT: Blockchain System With Credit-Based Consensus Mechanism. *IEEE Transactions on Industrial Informatics Volume*, 15(6), 3680–3689. doi:10.1109/TII.2019.2903342

Huckle, S., Bhattacharya, R., White, M., & Beloff, N. (2016). Internet of things, blockchain and shared economy applications. *Procedia Computer Science*, 98, 461–466. doi:10.1016/j.procs.2016.09.074

Hummen, R., Hiller, J., Wirtz, H., Henze, M., Shafagh, H., & Wehrle, K. (2013). 6LoWPAN fragmentation attacks and mitigation mechanisms. *WiSec 2013 - Proceedings of the 6th ACM Conference on Security and Privacy in Wireless and Mobile Networks*, (pp. 55–66). ACM.

Hurst, W., Spyrou, O., Tekinerdogan, B., & Krampe, C. (2023). Digital Art and the Metaverse: Benefits and Challenges. *Future Internet*, 15(6), 188. doi:10.3390/fi15060188

Hussain, F. (2012). *E-Learning 3.0= E-Learning 2.0+ Web 3.0?* International Association for Development of the Information Society.

Huszti, A., Kovács, S., & Oláh, N. (2022). SzabolcsKovács, Norbert Oláh (2022). Scalable, password-based and threshold authentication for smart homes. *International Journal of Information Security, 21*(4), 707–723. doi:10.100710207-022-00578-7

Hwang, H., & Kim, O. (2015). Social media as a tool for social movements: The effect of social media use and social capital on intention to participate in social movements. *International Journal of Consumer Studies, 39*(5), 478–488. doi:10.1111/ijcs.12221

IBM.com. (2020). *What are smart contracts on blockchain?* IBM. https://www.ibm.com/topics/smart-contracts#:~:text=Smart%20contracts%20are%20simply%20programs,intermediary's%20involvement%20or%20time%20loss

Ibrahim, I. S., & Kenwright, B. (2022). Smart education: Higher education instruction and the internet of things (iot). arXiv preprint arXiv:2207.02585.

Idelberger, F., & Mezei, P. (2022). Non-fungible tokens. *Internet Policy Review, 11*(2).

iFinca (Director). (2019, January 24). *iFinca.co Coffee Chain—Connecting Farmers.* [Video]. Youtube. https://www.youtube.com/watch?v=SlIZ2guZWUE

iFinca. (2023). *iFinca—The Key.* IFinca. https://www.ifinca.co/solutions

Ilul, J., & Pace, G. J. (2020). The Blockchain 2.0 Factor in The Internet of Things. *IEEE Consumer Electronics Magazine, 9*(4), 35–40.

Ilyushina, N., & MacDonald, T. (2022). Decentralised Autonomous Organisations: A New Research Agenda for Labour Economics. *The Journal of the British Blockchain Association, 1*(5), 50–53.

Imteaj, A., Amini, M. H., Pardalos, P. M., Imteaj, A., Hadi Amini, M., & Pardalos, P. M. (2021). Toward smart contract and consensus mechanisms of Blockchain. *Foundations of Blockchain: Theory and Applications,* 15-28.

International Monetary Fund. (2023). *IMF Policy Paper Elements of Effective Policies for Crypto Assets.* https://www.imf.org/en/Publications/Policy-Papers/Issues/2023/02/23/Elements-of-Effective-Policies-for-Crypto-Assets-530092

International Trade Centre [ITC]. (2021). *The Coffee Guide: Fourth Edition* (4; pp. 1–327). International Trade Centre. https://intracen.org/resources/publications/the-coffee-guide-fourth-edition

Irresberger, F., John, K., Mueller, P., & Saleh, F. (2021). *The public blockchain ecosystem: An empirical analysis.* NYU Stern School of Business.

Isaak, J., & Hanna, M. J. (2018). User data privacy: Facebook, Cambridge Analytica, and privacy protection. *Computer, 51*(8), 56–59. doi:10.1109/MC.2018.3191268

Islam, N., Mäntymäki, M., & Turunen, M. (2019). Understanding the role of actor heterogeneity in blockchain splits: An actor-network perspective of bitcoin forks. In *Proceedings of the 52nd Hawaii International Conference on System Sciences* (pp. 4595-4604). Scholar Space. 10.24251/HICSS.2019.556

Jabbar, A., Geebren, A., Hussain, Z., Dani, S., & Ul-Durar, S. (2023). Investigating individual privacy within CBDC: A privacy calculus perspective. *Research in International Business and Finance, 64,* 101826. doi:10.1016/j.ribaf.2022.101826

Jacksi, K., & Abass, S. M. (2019). Development history of the world wide web. *Int. J. Sci. Technol. Res, 8*(9), 75–79.

Jaffee, D. (2014). Brewing justice: Fair trade coffee, sustainability, and survival (Updated edition). University of California press.

Jahid, S., Nilizadeh, S., Mittal, P., Borisov, N., & Kapadia, A. (2012). Decent: A decentralized architecture for enforcing privacy in online social networks. In *Pervasive Computing and Communications Workshops, 2012 IEEE International Conference on* (pp. 326-332). IEEE. 10.1109/PerComW.2012.6197504

Jain, A. K., Sahoo, S. R., & Kaubiyal, J. (2021). Online social networks security and privacy: Comprehensive review and analysis. *Complex Intell. Syst.*, 7(5), 2157–2177. doi:10.100740747-021-00409-7

JalanA.MatkovskyyR. (2023). Systemic Risks in the Cryptocurrency Market: Evidence from the FTX Collapse. SSRN. https://ssrn.com/abstract=4364121 or doi:10.2139/ssrn.4364121

Jemielniak, D. (2020). Researching Social Networks: Opportunities and Challenges. *Frontiers in Human Dynamics*, 2, 528336. doi:10.3389/fhumd.2020.00001

Jeng, L. (2023). Crypto Migration: European And Asian Regulators Welcome Crypto Innovation While U.S. Cracks Down. *Forbes*. https://www.forbes.com/sites/digital-assets/2023/04/07/crypto-migration-european-and-asian-regulators-welcome-crypto-innovation-while-us-cracks-down/?sh=2777e18d481c

Jennings, M., & Kerr, D. (2022). How to pick a DAO legal entity. *A16ZCrypto*. https://a16zcrypto.com/posts/article/dao-legal-entity-how-to-pick/

Jeon, S., Liu, H., & Ostrovsky, Y. (2022). Measuring the gig economy in Canada using administrative data. *The Canadian Journal of Economics. Revue Canadienne d'Economique.*

Jesuthasan, R., & Zarkadis, G. (2022). How will Web 3 impact the future of work? World Economic Forum. https://www.weforum.org/agenda/2022/07/web-3-change-the-future-of-work-decentralized-autonomous-organizations/

Jiang, D. (2014). What will web 3.0 bring to education? *World Journal on Educational Technology: Current Issues*, 6(2), 126–131.

Jiang, L., & Zhang, X. (2019). Bcosn: A blockchain-based decentralized online social network. *IEEE Transactions on Computational Social Systems*, 6(6), 1454–1466. doi:10.1109/TCSS.2019.2941650

Jing, T. W., & Murugesan, R. K. (2019). A theoretical framework to build trust and prevent fake news in social media using blockchain. In *Recent trends in data science and soft computing: Proceedings of the 3rd international conference of reliable information and communication technology (IRICT 2018)* (pp. 955-962). Springer International Publishing. 10.1007/978-3-319-99007-1_88

Jin, L., & Parrott, K. (2021). *The web3 renaissance: A golden age for content*. Online Communication Article.

Johnson, M., & Rubery, J. (2019). HRM in crisis. In D. Collings & G. Wood (Eds.), *Human Resource Management: A Critical Approach* (pp. 396–411). Routledge. doi:10.4324/9781315299556-20

Johnston, A., Brown, C., & McSherry, C. (2020). *Roundup of cryptography and censorship research 2020*. Cryptography, Surveillance, and Privacy. Electronic Frontier Foundation.

Jonker, N. (2019). What drives the adoption of crypto-payments by online retailers? *Electronic Commerce Research and Applications*, 35, 100848. doi:10.1016/j.elerap.2019.100848

Joy, M. (2017). An investigation into gamification as a tool for enhancing recruitment process. *Ideal Research An International Multidisciplinary e -Journal*, 3(1).

Junejo, A., Hashmani, M., Alabdulatif, A., Memon, M. M., Jaffari, S. R., & Abdullah, M. Z. (2022). RZee: Cryptographic and statistical model for adversary detection and filtration to preserve blockchain privacy. *Journal of King Saud University - Computer and Information Sciences, 34*(10), 7885–7910. doi:10.1016/j.jksuci.2022.07.007

Jung, T., tom Dieck, M. C., & Rauschnabel, P. A. (Eds.). (2020). *Augmented reality and virtual reality: Changing realities in a dynamic world.* Springer. doi:10.1007/978-3-030-37869-1

K., D. (2023). What is Tokenization? *ND Labs.* https://ndlabs.dev/what-is-tokenization

Kadry, A. (2022). The Metaverse Revolution and Its Impact on the Future of Advertising Industry. *Journal of Design Sciences and Applied Arts*, *3*(2), 347–358. doi:10.21608/jdsaa.2022.129876.1171

KakavandH.Kost De SevresN.ChiltonB. (2017, January 1). *The Blockchain Revolution: An Analysis of Regulation and Technology Related to Distributed Ledger Technologies.* SSRN. https://papers.ssrn.com/sol3/papers.cfm?abstract_id=2849251 doi:10.2139/ssrn.2849251

Kanellopoulos, I. F., Gutt, D., & Li, T. (2021). Do Non-Fungible Tokens (Nfts) Affect Prices of Physical Products? Evidence from Trading Card Collectibles. SSRN *Electronic Journal.* [online] doi:10.2139/ssrn.3918256

Kappert, N., Karger, E., & Kureljusic, M. (2021, June 24). *Quantum Computing - The Impending End for the Blockchain?* Social Science Research Network. https://papers.ssrn.com/sol3/papers.cfm?abstract_id=4075591

Karafiloski, E., & Mishev, A. (2017). Blockchain solutions for big data challenges: a literature review. *IEEE EUROCON 2017—17th International Conference on Smart Technologies.* IEEE.

KarjalainenR. (2020, May 21). *Governance in Decentralized Networks.* Papers.ssrn.com. https://papers.ssrn.com/sol3/papers.cfm?abstract_id=3551099 doi:10.2139/ssrn.3551099

Kashyap, S., & Jeyasekar, A. (2020, September 1). *A Competent and Accurate BlockChain based E-Voting System on Liquid Democracy.* IEEE Xplore. doi:10.1109/BRAINS49436.2020.9223308

Kasiyanto, S., & Kilinc, M. R. (2022). The legal conundrums of the metaverse. *Journal of Central Banking Law and Institutions*, *1*(2), 299–322. doi:10.21098/jcli.v1i2.25

Kaspersky. (2019). *What is Cryptocurrency? Cryptocurrency Security: 4 Tips to Safely Invest in Cryptocurrency.* Kasperksy. https://www.kaspersky.com/resource-center/definitions/what-is-cryptocurrency

Katatikarn, J. (2023). *NFT Statistics 2023: Market Size and Trends.* Academy of Animated Art. https://academyofanimatedart.com/nft-statistics/

Kauffman, R. J., Liu, J., & Ma, D. (2015). Innovations in financial IS and technology ecosystems: High-frequency trading in the equity market. *Technological Forecasting and Social Change*, *99*, 339–354. doi:10.1016/j.techfore.2014.12.001

Kaur, G., & KrishnaKumar, A. (2023). Technologies Behind Crypto-Based Decentralized Finance. In *Building Secure Business Models Through Blockchain Technology: Tactics, Methods, Limitations, and Performance* (pp. 149-166). IGI Global.

Kaur, G., & Vishwakarma, D. K. (2023). Digital, Programmable Euro: From Paper to Programmable Money. In Exploring the Dark Side of FinTech and Implications of Monetary Policy (pp. 187-206). IGI Global.

Kaur, H., Nori, H., Jenkins, S., Caruana, R., Wallach, H., & Wortman Vaughan, J. (2020). Interpreting interpretability: Understanding data scientists' use of interpretability tools for machine learning. In Proceedings of the 2020 CHI conference on human factors in computing systems (pp. 1-14).ACM.

Kaur, J., & Dabas, D. (2023). *Literature Review of Smart Contracts Using Blockchain Technology.* New Approaches for Multidimensional Signal Processing. doi:10.1007/978-981-19-7842-5_16

Kee, R. (1993, December 1). Data processing technology and accounting: A historical perspective. *The Accounting Historians Journal*, *20*(2), 187–216. doi:10.2308/0148-4184.20.2.187

Keister, T., & Sanches, D. (2023). Should central banks issue digital currency? *The Review of Economic Studies*, *90*(1), 404–431. doi:10.1093/restud/rdac017

Kenney, M., & Zysman, J. (2019). Work and value creation in the platform economy. In *Work and labor in the digital age* (Vol. 33, pp. 13–41). Emerald Publishing Limited.

Kenwright, B. (2021). Introduction to webxr. In Acm special interest group on computer graphics and interactive techniques conference 2021.

Kenwright, B. (2022a). Introduction to computer graphics and ray-tracing using the webgpu api. In *15th acm siggraph conference and exhibition on computer graphics and interactive techniques in asia 2022.* ACM.

Kenwright, B. (2022b). Introduction to the webgpu api. In Acm siggraph 2022 courses (pp. 1–184). ACM. doi:10.1145/3532720.3535625

Kenwright, B. (2023). Impact of xr on mental health: Are we playing with fire? arXiv preprint arXiv:2304.01648.

Kenwright, B. (2018). Virtual reality: Ethical challenges and dangers. *IEEE Technology and Society Magazine*, *37*(4), 20–25. doi:10.1109/MTS.2018.2876104

Kenwright, B. (2019). *Virtual reality: Where have we been? where are we now? and where are we going? Kenwright, B. (2020a). The future of extended reality (xr).* Communication Article. January.

Kenwright, B. (2020b). There's more to sound than meets the ear: Sound in interactive environments. *IEEE Computer Graphics and Applications*, *40*(4), 62–70. doi:10.1109/MCG.2020.2996371 PMID:32540788

Kewell, B., Adams, R., & Parry, G. (2017). Blockchain for good? *Strategic Change*, *26*(5), 429–437. doi:10.1002/jsc.2143

Khan, L. U., Saad, W., Han, Z., Hossain, E., & Hong, C. S. (2021). Federated Learning for Internet of Things: Recent Advances, Taxonomy, and Open Challenges. *IEEE Communications Surveys and Tutorials*, *23*(3), 1759–1799. doi:10.1109/COMST.2021.3090430

Khan, S. N., Loukil, F., Ghedira-Guegan, C., Benkhelifa, E., & Bani-Hani, A. (2021). Blockchain smart contracts: Applications, challenges, and future trends. *Peer-to-Peer Networking and Applications*, *14*(5), 2901–2925. doi:10.100712083-021-01127-0 PMID:33897937

Khatoon, A. (2020). A blockchain-based smart contract system for healthcare management. *Electronics (Basel)*, *9*(1), 94. doi:10.3390/electronics9010094

Khedr, W. I. (2013). SRFID. A Hash-Based Security Scheme For Low Cost RFID Systems. *Egyptian Informatics Journal*, *14*(1), 89–98. doi:10.1016/j.eij.2013.02.001

Kidd, D., & McIntosh, K. (2016). Social Media and Social Movements. *Sociology Compass*, *10*(9), 785–794. doi:10.1111oc4.12399

Kiff, M. J., Alwazir, J., Davidovic, S., Farias, A., Khan, M. A., Khiaonarong, M. T., & Zhou, P. (2020). *A survey of research on retail central bank digital currency.*

Kim, C. (2009). Spatial Data Mining, Geovisualization. In International Encyclopedia of Human Geography. doi:10.1016/B978-008044910-4.00526-5

KimH. M.TanaS.LaskowskiM.ZhongC.JainA. (2022). Overcoming the Balkanization of Blockchain Research: Web3 is about Tokens AND Protocols AND Online Communities. *Available at* SSRN 4248958. doi:10.2139/ssrn.4248958

Kim, Y. S., & Kwon, O. (2023). Central bank digital currency, credit supply, and financial stability. *Journal of Money, Credit and Banking*, *55*(1), 297–321. doi:10.1111/jmcb.12913

Kirjavainen, E. (2022). *The future of luxury fashion brands through NFTs*. Aaltodoc. https://aaltodoc.aalto.fi/handle/123456789/114089

Kiwelekar, A. W., Mahamunkar, G. S., Netak, L. D., & Nikam, V. B. (2020). *Deep Learning Techniques for Geospatial Data Analysis*. doi:10.1007/978-3-030-49724-8_3

Kline, R., & Pinch, T. (1999). The social construction of technology. In D. MacKenzie & J. Wajcman (Eds.), *The Social Shaping of Technology*. Open University Press.

Knottenbelt, Z. & [Second Author Needed]. (2019). XCLAIM: Trustless, Interoperable Cryptocurrency-Backed Assets. *IEEE Symposium on Security and Privacy*. IEEE.

Köhler, S., Bager, S., & Pizzol, M. (2022). Sustainability standards and blockchain in agro-food supply chains: Synergies and conflicts. *Technological Forecasting and Social Change*, *185*, 122094. doi:10.1016/j.techfore.2022.122094

Köhler, S., & Pizzol, M. (2020). Technology assessment of blockchain-based technologies in the food supply chain. *Journal of Cleaner Production*, *269*, 122193. doi:10.1016/j.jclepro.2020.122193

Kohli, A., Lekhi, P., & Hafez, G. A. A. (2023). Blockchain Tech-Enabled Supply Chain Traceability: A Meta-Synthesis. In *Financial Technologies and DeFi: A Revisit to the Digital Finance Revolution* (pp. 99–107). Springer International Publishing. doi:10.1007/978-3-031-17998-3_7

Koivisto, J., & Hamari, J. (2019). The rise of motivational information systems: A review of gamification research. *International Journal of Information Management*, *45*, 191–210. doi:10.1016/j.ijinfomgt.2018.10.013

Kolisnyk, O., Hurina, N., Druzhynska, N., Holovchak, H., & Fomina, T. (2023). Innovative Technologies in Accounting and Auditing: The Use of Blockchain Technology. *Financial & Credit Activity: Problems of Theory & Practice, 3*(50), 24–41. https://doi-org.ezproxy.myucwest.ca/10.55643/fcaptp.3.50.2023.4082

Koosel, S. M. (2013). *Exploring digital identity: Beyond the private public paradox. The digital turn: Users' practices and cultural transformations*. Peter Lang.

Korkut, E. H., & Surer, E. (2023). Visualization in virtual reality: A systematic review. *Virtual Reality (Waltham Cross)*, *27*(2), 1–34. doi:10.100710055-023-00753-8

Kosba, A., Miller, A., Shi, E., Wen, Z., & Papamanthou, C. (2016, May). Hawk: The blockchain model of cryptography and privacy-preserving smart contracts. In 2016 IEEE symposium on security and privacy (SP) (pp. 839-858). IEEE.

Kozinets, R. V. (2023). Immersive netnography: A novel method for service experience research in virtual reality, augmented reality and metaverse contexts. *Journal of Service Management*, *34*(1), 100–125. doi:10.1108/JOSM-12-2021-0481

Kozlov, D., Veijalainen, J., & Ali, Y. (2012). Security and privacy threats in IoT architectures. *In Proceedings of the 7th International Conference on Body Area Networks*. ICST (Institute for Computer Sciences, Social-Informatics and Telecommunications Engineering).

Kravitz, D.W., & Cooper, J. (2017) Securing user identity and transactions symbiotically: Iot meets blockchain. *2017 Global Internet of Things Summit (GIoTS)*. IEEE.

Kshetri, N. (2022). Policy, ethical, social, and environmental considerations of web3 and the metaverse. *IT Professional*, *24*(3), 4–8. doi:10.1109/MITP.2022.3178509

Kubach, M., Schunck, C. H., Sellung, R., & Roßnagel, H. (2020). Self-sovereign and Decentralized identity as the future of identity management?. *Open Identity Summit 2020.*

Kuem, J., Ray, S., Siponen, M., & Kim, S. S. (2017). What leads to prosocial behaviors on social networking services: A tripartite model. *Journal of Management Information Systems, 34*(1), 40–70. doi:10.1080/07421222.2017.1296744

Kuhn, K., & Galloway, T. (2019). Expanding perspectives on gig work and gig workers. *Journal of Managerial Psychology, 34*(4), 186–191. doi:10.1108/JMP-05-2019-507

Kumar, M., Nikhil, N., & Singh, R. (2020). Decentralising finance using decentralised blockchain oracles. In *2020 International Conference for Emerging Technology (INCET) IEEE*, (pp. 1-4). IEEE. 10.1109/INCET49848.2020.9154123

Kumar, R., Jain, S., Kumawat, S., & Jangir, S. K. (2011). An analysis of security and privacy issues,Challenges with possible solution in cloud computing. *IRACST-International Journal of Computer Science and Information Technology & Security (IJCSITS), 1*(2)

Kumar, S., Lim, W. M., Sivarajah, U., & Kaur, J. (2022). Artificial Intelligence and Blockchain Integration in Business: Trends from a Bibliometric-Content Analysis. *Information Systems Frontiers.* doi:10.100710796-022-10279-0 PMID:35431617

Kuo, T. T., Kim, H. E., & Ohno-Machado, L. (2017). Blockchain distributed ledger technologies for biomedical and health care applications. *Journal of the American Medical Informatics Association : JAMIA, 24*(6), 1211–1220. doi:10.1093/jamia/ocx068 PMID:29016974

Kurian, A. (2023). *The Case for Harmonising Central Bank Digital Currencies for Cross-Border Transactions.*

Kye, B., Han, N., Kim, E., Park, Y., & Jo, S. (2021). Educational applications of metaverse: Possibilities and limitations. In Journal of Educational Evaluation for Health Professions (Vol. 18). doi:10.3352/jeehp.2021.18.32

Kyle. (2018). Blockchain issues: #1: Data storage. *Medium.* https://medium.com/@Kyle.May/blockchain-issues-1-data-storage

La Cava, L., Greco, S., & Tagarelli, A. (2021). Understanding the growth of the Fediverse through the lens of Mastodon. *Applied Network Science, 6*(1), 1–35. doi:10.100741109-021-00392-5

Laato, S., Mäntymäki, M., Islam, A., Hyrynsalmi, S., & Birkstedt, T. (2022). Trends and Trajectories in the Software Industry: Implications for the future of work. *Information Systems Frontiers, 25*, 929–944. doi:10.100710796-022-10267-4

Lafourcade, P., & Lombard-Platet, M. (2020). About blockchain interoperability. *Information Processing Letters, 161*, 105976. doi:10.1016/j.ipl.2020.105976

Lala, Z., Poole, V. B., & Kimmel, S. B. (2021). Adapting to New Technology in the Accounting Industry. *Business Education Innovation Journal, 13*(2), 37–42.

Lal, M. (2011). Web 3.0 in Education & Research. *BVICAM's International. Journal of Information Technology, 3*(2).

Lane, D. A. (2016). Innovation cascades: Artefacts, organization and attributions. Philosophical Transactions of the Royal Society B. *Biological Sciences, 371*(1690), 20150194. doi:10.1098/rstb.2015.0194

Langley, K. (2021a). Distributed Autonomous Organizations, A primer. *Insight.* https://insight.openexo.com/distributed-autonomous-organizations-daos-getting-started/

Langley, K. (2021b). DAO's are novel but not new. *Insight.* https://insight.openexo.com/daos-are-novel-but-not-new/

Lanier, J. (2011). *You are not a gadget: A manifesto.* Vintage.

Lanier, J. (2017). *Dawn of the new everything: Encounters with reality and virtual reality.* Henry Holt and Company.

Lara, R., Cantador, I., & Castells, P. (2007). Semantic web technologies for the financial domain. In *The Semantic Web: Real-World Applications from Industry* (pp. 41–74). Springer US. doi:10.1007/978-0-387-48531-7_3

Larimer, S. (2013). Bitcoin and the three laws of robotics. *Insight.* https://steemit.com/bitshares/@stan/bitcoin-and-the-three-laws-of-robotics

Lashkari, B., & Musilek, P. (2021). A comprehensive review of blockchain consensus mechanisms. *IEEE Access : Practical Innovations, Open Solutions*, 9, 43620–43652. doi:10.1109/ACCESS.2021.3065880

Latour, B. (1999). A Collective of Humans and Nonhumans. In Kaplan (Ed.), Readings in the Philosophy of Technology (pp. 174-215). Oxford: Rowman and Littlefield.

Latour, B. (1992). Where Are the Missing Masses? The Sociology of a Few Mundane Artifacts. In W. Bijker & J. Law (Eds.), *Shaping Technology/Building Society: Studies in Sociotechnical Change* (pp. 225–258). MIT Press.

Latour, B. (2005). *Reassembling the Social: An Introduction to Actor-Network Theory.* Oxford University Press.

Lauwers, L., & Willekens, M. (1994). 500 years of bookkeeping a portrait of Luca Pacioli. *Tijdschrift voor Economie en Management, XXXIX*, 3. https://lirias.kuleuven.be/bitstream/123456789/119065/1/TEM1994-3_289-304p.pdf

Lazanis, R. (2022). Social Media for Accountants: 7 Reasons Why + 11 Tips How. *Future Firm.* https://futurefirm.co/social-media-for-accountants/

Le Brocq, S., Hughes, E., & Donnelly, R. (2023). Sharing in the gig economy: From equitable work relations to exploitative HRM. *Personnel Review*, 52(3), 454–469. doi:10.1108/PR-04-2019-0219

Lee, C. (2011). Litecoin whitepaper. *Litecoin White Paper.*

Lee, C. W. (2022). Application of Metaverse Service to Healthcare Industry: A Strategic Perspective. *International Journal of Environmental Research and Public Health*, 19(20), 13038. doi:10.3390/ijerph192013038 PMID:36293609

Lee, D. K. C., Yan, L., & Wang, Y. (2021). A global perspective on central bank digital currency. *China Economic Journal*, 14(1), 52–66. doi:10.1080/17538963.2020.1870279

Lee, J., & L'heureux, F. (2020). A Regulatory Framework for Cryptocurrency. *European Business Law Review*, 31(3), 423–446. doi:10.54648/EULR2020018

Lehmann, M. (2019). Who Owns Bitcoin? Private Law Facing the Blockchain. *Minnesota Journal of Law, Science & Technology*, 21(1), 95–135. doi:10.2139srn.3402678

Lehtonen, M., Ostojic, D., Ilic, A., & Michahelles, F. (2009), *Securing RFID systems by detecting tag cloning.* Conference: Pervasive Computing, 7th International Conference, Pervasive 2009, Nara, Japan.

Leian, L., & Shengli, L. (2006). ALOHA-based anti-collision algorithms used in RFID system. 2006 *International Conference on Wireless Communications, Networking and Mobile Computing*, WiCOM.

Lekhi, P. (2023). Currency and Payment Tech: Cryptocurrencies Transforming the Face of Finance. In *Financial Technologies and DeFi: A Revisit to the Digital Finance Revolution* (pp. 57–66). Springer International Publishing. doi:10.1007/978-3-031-17998-3_4

Leng, J., Sha, W., Wang, B., Zheng, P., Zhuang, C., Liu, Q., Wuest, T., Mourtzis, D., & Wang, L. (2022). Industry 5.0: Prospect and retrospect. *Journal of Manufacturing Systems*, 65, 279–295. doi:10.1016/j.jmsy.2022.09.017

Lerner, J., & Nanda, R. (2020). Venture capital's role in financing innovation: What we know and how much we still need to learn. *The Journal of Economic Perspectives*, *34*(3), 237–261. doi:10.1257/jep.34.3.237

Lerner, J., & Tufano, P. (2011). The consequences of financial innovation: A counterfactual research agenda. *Annual Review of Financial Economics*, *3*(1), 41–85. doi:10.1146/annurev.financial.050808.114326

Lessig, L. (1999). *Code and Other Laws of Cyberspace*. Basic Books.

Leung, D., & Dickinger, A. (2017). Use of Bitcoin in Online Travel Product Shopping: The European Perspective. *Information and Communication Technologies in Tourism*, *2017*, 741–754. doi:10.1007/978-3-319-51168-9_53

Levi, A. (2019). Reputation vs Tokens. *Medium*. https://medium.com/daostack/reputation-vs-tokens-6d7642c7a538

Levi, S., Fisch, E., Drylewski, A., Skadden, A., Slate, M., & Flom, L. L. P. (2021). *Legal considerations in the minting, marketing and selling of NFTs*. Global Legal Insights.

Levy, A. (2022). *Digital Collectibles: What They Are and How to Get Started*. The Motley Fool. https://www.fool.com/investing/stock-market/market-sectors/financials/non-fungible-tokens/digital-collectibles/

Lewin, B., Giovannucci, D., & Varangis, P. (2004). Coffee Markets: New Paradigms in Global Supply and Demand. SSRN *Electronic Journal*. doi:10.2139/ssrn.996111

Li, C., Palanisamy, B., & Xu, R. (2019, April). Scalable and privacy-preserving design of on/off-chain smart contracts. In *2019 IEEE 35th International Conference on Data Engineering Workshops (ICDEW)* (pp. 7-12). IEEE.

Liao, C. F., Cheng, C. J., Chen, K., Lai, C. H., Chiu, T., & Wu-Lee, C. (2017, November). Toward a service platform for developing smart contracts on blockchain in bdd and tdd styles. In *2017 IEEE 10th Conference on Service-Oriented Computing and Applications (SOCA)* (pp. 133-140). IEEE. 10.1109/SOCA.2017.26

Li, F., Huh, E. N., Kwon, D., & Miller, E. L. (2020). Decentralized consensus protocols in blockchain networks: A survey. *ACM Computing Surveys*, *53*(3), 1–38.

Lin, L., Duan, H., & Cai, W. (2023). Web3dp: A crowdsourcing platform for 3d models based on web3 infrastructure. In *Proceedings of the 14th conference on acm multimedia systems* (pp. 397–402). ACM. 10.1145/3587819.3592549

Liu, C., & Wang, H. (2019). Crypto tokens and token offerings: an introduction. *Cryptofinance and mechanisms of exchange: The making of virtual currency*, 125-144.

Liu, H., Li, X., Xu, K., & Jiang, F. (2021). NFT and Its Application in Virtual Asset Economy. In *2021 IEEE International Conference on Blockchains and Cryptocurrencies (IEEE ICBC)* (pp. 141-148). IEEE.

Liu, L., Zhou, S., Huang, H., & Zheng, Z. (2021). From technology to society: An Overview of blockchain-based DAO. *IEEE Open Journal of the Computer Society*, *2*, 204–215. doi:10.1109/OJCS.2021.3072661

Liu, N., & Ye, Z. (2021). Empirical research on the blockchain adoption – based on TAM. *Applied Economics*, *53*(37), 4263–4275. doi:10.1080/00036846.2021.1898535

Liu, Y., Lu, Q., Zhu, L., Paik, H. Y., & Staples, M. (2023). A systematic literature review on blockchain governance. *Journal of Systems and Software*, *197*, 111576. doi:10.1016/j.jss.2022.111576

Liu, Z., Li, Y., Min, Q., & Chang, M. (2022). User incentive mechanism in blockchain-based online community: An empirical study of Steemit. *Information & Management*, *59*(7), 103596. doi:10.1016/j.im.2022.103596

Li, X., Lv, Z., Wang, W., Zhang, B., Hu, J., Yin, L., & Feng, S. (2016). WebVRGIS based traffic analysis and visualization system. *Advances in Engineering Software*, *93*, 1–8. doi:10.1016/j.advengsoft.2015.11.003

Li, Y., Li, Y., Yan, Q., & Deng, R. H. (2015). Privacy leakage analysis in online social networks. *Computers & Security*, *49*, 239–254. doi:10.1016/j.cose.2014.10.012

Ljungberg, J. (2000). Open source movements as a model for organising. *European Journal of Information Systems*, *9*(4), 208–216. doi:10.1057/palgrave.ejis.3000373

Long, Y., & Liu, L. (2016). Transformations of urban studies and planning in the big/open data era: a review. In International Journal of Image and Data Fusion, 7(4). doi:10.1080/19479832.2016.1215355

Long, C. (2021). *Wyoming's DAO law: What it means and how it came to be*. CoinDesk.

Longley, P. (2005). *Geographic information systems and science*. John Wiley & Sons.

Lucking, L. (2020). *Decentraland: A virtual world owned by its users*. TechCrunch.

Lu, J., Li, C., Zhu, H., Cao, Z., Du, X., Guizani, M., & Chen, H. H. (2022). Security and privacy in 6G: Fundamentals, applications, and solutions. *IEEE Wireless Communications*, *29*(1), 82–89.

Lukonga, I. (2023). *Monetary Policy Implications Central Bank Digital Currencies: Perspectives on Jurisdictions with Conventional and Islamic Banking Systems*.

Lu, N., Cheng, N., Zhang, N., Shen, X., & Mark, J. W. (2014). Connected Vehicles: Solutions and Challenges. *IEEE Internet of Things*, *1*(4), 289–299. doi:10.1109/JIOT.2014.2327587

Luo, F. J., Zhao, Y. D., & Liang, G. (2018). A distributed electricity trading system in active distribution networks based on multiagent coalition and blockchain. *IEEE Transactions on Power Systems*, *34*(5), 4097–4108. doi:10.1109/TPWRS.2018.2876612

Luu, L., Chu, D. H., Olickel, H., Saxena, P., & Hobor, A. (2016). Making smart contracts smarter. In *Proceedings of the 2016 ACM SIGSAC Conference on Computer and Communications Security* (pp. 254-269). ACM. 10.1145/2976749.2978309

Lu, Y., & Liu, Y. (2012). Pervasive location acquisition technologies: Opportunities and challenges for geospatial studies. *Computers, Environment and Urban Systems*, *36*(2), 105–108. doi:10.1016/j.compenvurbsys.2012.02.002

Lyytinen, K., & Rose, G. M. (2003). The disruptive nature of information technology innovations: The case of internet computing in systems development organizations. *Management Information Systems Quarterly*, *27*(4), 557–596. doi:10.2307/30036549

M. Georgescu, and D, Popescul. (2015). Security, privacy and trust in internet of things: A straight road? *International Business Information Management Association, IBIMA*. IEEE.

Mabić, M., Lasić, M., & Zovko, J. (2019). Web 2.0 Technologies in Business: Why Not? *Interdisciplinary Description of Complex Systems*, *17*(2–B), 304–314. https://doi-org.ezproxy.myucwest.ca/10.7906/indecs.17.2.7

Macdonald, M., Liu-Thorrold, L., & Julien, R. (2017). The blockchain: A comparison of platforms and their uses beyond bitcoin. *Work. Pap*, 1–18.

Macedo, C. R., Miro, D. A., & Hart, T. (2022). The Metaverse: From Science Fiction to Commercial Reality—Protecting Intellectual Property in the Virtual Landscape. *NYSBA Bright Ideas*, *31*(1), 216.

Macrinici, D., Cartofeanu, C., & Gao, S. (2018). Smart contract applications within blockchain technology: A systematic mapping study. *Telematics and Informatics*, *35*(8), 2337–2354. doi:10.1016/j.tele.2018.10.004

Maddikunta, P. K. R., Pham, Q.-V., B, P., Deepa, N., Dev, K., Gadekallu, T. R., Ruby, R., & Liyanage, M. (2022). Industry 5.0: A survey on enabling technologies and potential applications. *Journal of Industrial Information Integration*, *26*, 100257. doi:10.1016/j.jii.2021.100257

Madhavan, N. (2007, July 6). India gets more Net Cool. *Hindustan Times*. http://www.hindustantimes.com/StoryPage/StoryPage.aspx?id=f2565bb8-663e-48c1-94ee-d99567577bdd

Madhwal, R., & Pouwelse, J. (2023). The Universal Trust Machine: A survey on the web 3 path towards enabling long term digital cooperation through decentralised trust. ArXiv:2301.06938 [Cs]. https://arxiv.org/abs/2301.06938

Maesa, D. D. F., Mori, P., & Ricci, L. (2017). Blockchain-based access control. In *IFIP International Conference on Distributed Applications and Interoperable Systems* (pp. 206-220). Springer.

Magazzeni, D., McBurney, P., & Nash, W. (2017). Validation and verification of smart contracts: A research agenda. *Computer*, *50*(9), 50–57. doi:10.1109/MC.2017.3571045

Maharg, P., & Owen, M. (2007). Simulations, learning and the metaverse: changing cultures in legal education. *Journal of Information, Law and Technology, 1*(May 2014).

Majer, A. (2022). *The Carbon Footprint of NFTs*. The Linux Foundation.

Mannell, K., & Smith, E. T. (2022). Alternative Social Media and the Complexities of a More Participatory Culture: A View From Scuttlebutt. *Social Media + Society*, *8*(3). Advance online publication. doi:10.1177/20563051221122448

Maram, D., Malvai, H., Zhang, F., Jean-Louis, N., Frolov, A., Kell, T., & Miller, A. (2021, May). Candid: Can-do decentralized identity with legacy compatibility, sybil-resistance, and accountability. In *2021 IEEE Symposium on Security and Privacy (SP)* (pp. 1348-1366). IEEE. 10.1109/SP40001.2021.00038

Marcon, M., Viswanath, B., Cha, M., & Gummadi, K. P. (2011). Sharing social content from home: A measurement-driven feasibility study. In *Proceedings of NOSSDAV '11* (pp. 45-50). ACM. 10.1145/1989240.1989253

Marco, V., Cinzia, D. A., Rosario, F., & Elmo, G. C. (2020). *About on Organizational Impact on the Adoption of New Technologies in Tourism*. Cultural and Tourism Innovation in the Digital Era. doi:10.1007/978-3-030-36342-0_20

Maria, A., & Negrila, C. (2012). Web 3.0 in Education. *eLearning and Software for Education (eLSE), 1*, 455-460.

Mark Graham. (2015). The hidden biases of Geodata. *The Guardian*. https://www.theguardian.com/news/datablog/2015/apr/28/the-hidden-biases-of-geodata

Marr, B. (2022). The 10 Best Examples Of The Metaverse Everyone Should Know About. *Forbes*. https://www.forbes.com/sites/bernardmarr/2022/05/16/the-10-best-examples-of-the-metaverse-everyone-should-know-about/?sh=6afa4a3a3f5f

Martino, D. J., van Duyn, A., & Flores, N. (2022, December 7). *Antitrust, ESG, and Supply Chain: Risks and Tips*. Baker McKenzie - Global Supply Chain Compliance. https://supplychaincompliance.bakermckenzie.com/2022/12/07/antitrust-esg-and-supply-chain-risks-and-tips/

Martino, P. (2019). Blockchain technology: Challenges and opportunities for banks. *International Journal of Financial Innovation in Banking*, *2*(4), 314–333. doi:10.1504/IJFIB.2019.104535

Marx, D., & Chli, M. (2018). *On the Security of Oracles for Smart Contracts*. In *UK Workshop on Cyber Security (UKWCS)*. UK.

Mathis, T. (2016). Blockchain: A Guide To Blockchain, The Technology Behind Bitcoin, Ethereum And Other Cryptocurrency. Level Up Lifestyle Limited.

Maulani, G., Gunawan, Leli, Nabila, E., & Sari, W. (2021). Digital Certificate Authority with Blockchain Cybersecurity in Education. *International Journal of Cyber and IT Service Management, 1*, 5.

McEwen, A., & Cassimally, H. (2013). *Designing the internet of things.*

McHatton, J., & Ghazinour, K. (2023) Mitigating Social Media Privacy Concerns - A Comprehensive Study. In *Proceedings of the 9th ACM International Workshop on Security and Privacy Analytics (IWSPA '23)*. Association for Computing Machinery, New York, NY, USA. 10.1145/3579987.3586565

Meegan, X., & Koens, T. (2021). *Lessons learned from decentralised finance (DeFi)*. ING. https://new. ingwb. com/ binaries/content/assets/insights/themes/distributed-ledger-technology/defi_white_paper_v2. 0. pdf.

Mehboob, D. (2022). EU moves to blockchain for withholding tax data sharing. *International Tax Review.* https://www. internationaltaxreview.com/article/2a6abcbtm7tszx7breg3k/eu-moves-to-blockchain-for-withholding-tax-data-sharing

Mehdi, I., Sbai, M., Mazlin, M., & Azghiou, K. (2022). Data Centric DAO: When blockchain reigns over the Cloud. *IEEE International IOT, Electronics and Mechatronics Conference (IEMTRONICS)*, (pp. 1-7). IEEE. 10.1109/IEMTRONICS55184.2022.9795753

Meiklejohn, S., & Orlandi, C. (2015). *Privacy-Enhancing Overlays in Bitcoin, Financial Cryptography Workshops, ser* (Vol. 8976). Lecture Notes in Computer Science. Springer.

Melnikovas, A. (2018). Towards an Explicit Research Methodology: Adapting Research Onion Model for Futures Studies. *Journal of Futures Studies.* Advance online publication. doi:10.6531/JFS.201812_23(2).0003

Ménard, C. (2004). The economics of hybrid organizations. *Journal of Institutional and Theoretical Economics, 160*(3), 345–376. doi:10.1628/0932456041960605

Ménard, C. (2007). Cooperatives: Hierarchies or hybrids? In K. Kostas & N. Jerker (Eds.), *Vertical Markets and Cooperative Hierarchies* (pp. 1–18). Springer. doi:10.1007/1-4020-5543-0_1

Ménard, C. (2018). Research frontiers of new institutional economics. *RAUSP Management Journal, 53*(1), 3–10. doi:10.1016/j.rauspm.2017.12.002

Ménard, C. (2021). Hybrids: Where are we? *Journal of Institutional Economics, 18*(2), 297–312. doi:10.1017/S1744137421000230

Mendoza-Tello, J. C., Mora, H., Pujol-Lopez, F. A., & Lytras, M. D. (2018). Social Commerce as a Driver to Enhance Trust and Intention to Use Cryptocurrencies for Electronic Payments. IEEE Access, 50737–50751. doi:10.1109/ACCESS.2018.2869359

Messari. (2021). *Non-fungible tokens (NFTs)*. Messari. https://messari.io/resource/non-fungible-tokens

MeunierS.Zhao-MeunierD. (2019). Bitcoin, Distributed Ledgers and the Theory of the Firm. doi:10.2139/ssrn.3327971

Miatton, F., & Amado, L. (2020). Fairness, Transparency and Traceability in the Coffee Value Chain through Blockchain Innovation. *2020 International Conference on Technology and Entrepreneurship - Virtual (ICTE-V)*, (pp. 1–6). IEEE. 10.1109/ICTE-V50708.2020.9113785

MiCA. (2023). *Regulation of The European Parliament and of The Council on Markets in Crypto-assets, and amending Directive (EU) 2019/1937*. European Commission.

Michalopoulos, S., Leaven, L., & Levine, R. (2009). Financial Innovation and Endogenous Growth. National Bureau of Economic Research. (*Working Paper 15356*). Cambridge.

Mienert, B. (2021). How can a decentralized autonomous organization (DAO) be legally structured? *E-zeitschrift für Wirtschaftsrecht und Digitalisierung, 336.* https://www.lrz.legal/2021Rn336

MienertB. (2021). How Can a Decentralized Autonomous Organization (DAO) Be Legally Structured? *Legal Revolutionary Journal LRZ 2021.* SSRN. doi:10.2139/ssrn.3992329

Mienert, B. (2022). Dezentrale autonome Organisationen (DAOs) als alternative Organisationsstruktur der Zukunft. *Rethinking Law., 04,* 2022.

Mihai, G. (2014). Some Aspects of using Web 2.0/Enterprise 2.0 Technologies in Accounting. *Annals of the University Dunarea de Jos of Galati: Fascicle: I, Economics & Applied Informatics, 20*(1).

Milgram, P., Takemura, H., Utsumi, A., & Kishino, F. 1995, December. Augmented reality: A class of displays on the reality-virtuality continuum. In Telemanipulator and telepresence technologies (Vol. 2351, pp. 282-292).

Milgram, P., & Kishino, F. (1994). A taxonomy of mixed reality visual displays. *IEICE Transactions on Information and Systems, 77*(12), 1321–1329.

Milinković, A., Ristić, K., & Tucikešić, S. (2014). Modern technologies of collecting and presenting of geospatial data. *Geonauka, 02*(02), 19–27. doi:10.14438/gn.2014.12

Minocha, S., & Roberts, D. (2008). Laying the groundwork for socialisation and knowledge construction within 3D virtual worlds. *ALT-J, 16*(3), 181–196. doi:10.3402/rlt.v16i3.10897

Miranda, P., Isaias, P., & Costa, C. J. (2014). The impact of Web 3.0 technologies in e-Learning: Emergence of e-Learning 3.0. In *EDULEARN14 Proceedings* (pp. 4139-4149). IATED.

Miranda, P., Isaias, P., & Costa, C. J. (2014). E-Learning and web generations: Towards Web 3.0 and E-Learning 3.0. *International Proceedings of Economics Development and Research, 81,* 92.

Miscione, G., & Kavanagh, D. (2015). Bitcoin and the Blockchain: A Coup D'État through Digital Heterotopia? *Humanistic Management Network, Research Paper Series (23/15),* 1–26.

Mishkin, F. S. (2007). *The economics of money, banking, and financial markets.* Pearson education.

Mitic, I. (2022). *30 Cryptocurrency Statistics for 2022: A Modern-Day Gold Rush.* Fortunly | Statistics. https://fortunly.com/statistics/cryptocurrency-statistics/#:~:text=Here%20are%20the%20top%2010%20statistics%20on%20the

Mitrokotsa, A., Rieback, M. R., & Tanenbaum, A. S. (2010). Classifying RFID Attacks and Defense. *Information Systems Frontiers, 12*(5), 491–505. doi:10.100710796-009-9210-z

Modi, N. (2023). Comparative Analysis of Different Blockchain Technology to Improve the Security in Social Network. In V. E. Balas, V. B. Semwal, & A. Khandare (Eds.), *Intelligent Computing and Networking. Lecture Notes in Networks and Systems* (Vol. 632). Springer. doi:10.1007/978-981-99-0071-8_7

Mohanta, B. K., Panda, S. S., & Jena, D. (2018, July). An overview of smart contract and use cases in blockchain technology. In *2018 9th international conference on computing, communication and networking technologies (ICCCNT)* (pp. 1-4). IEEE. 10.1109/ICCCNT.2018.8494045

Moiso, C., & Minerva, R. (2012, October). Towards a user-centric personal data ecosystem the role of the bank of individuals' data. In *2012 16th International conference on intelligence in next generation networks* (pp. 202-209). IEEE.

Mollet, N., Chellali, R., & Brayda, L. (2009). Virtual and augmented reality tools for teleoperation: improving distant immersion and perception. Transactions on edutainment II, 135-159.

Momtaz, P. (2022). Some Very Simple Economics of Web3 and the Metaverse. FinTech. *MDPI AG, 1*(3), 225–234. doi:10.3390/fintech1030018

Monetary Authority of Singapore. (2023). *Response to Public Consultation on Proposed Regulatory Measures for Digital Payment Token Services (Part 1)*. https://www.mas.gov.sg/-/media/mas/news-and-publications/consultation-papers/2022-proposed-regulatory-measures-for-dpt-services/response-to-public-consultation-on-proposed-regulatory-measures-for-dpt-services-part-1.pdf

Monte, G. D., Pennino, D., & Pizzonia, M. (2020, September). Scaling blockchains without giving up decentralization and security: A solution to the blockchain scalability trilemma. In *Proceedings of the 3rd Workshop on Cryptocurrencies and Blockchains for Distributed Systems* (pp. 71-76). ACM. 10.1145/3410699.3413800

Moran, T. (2020). *An Exploration of Decentralised Identity: A COVID-19 Vaccine Passport.*

Morimoto, T., Kobayashi, T., Hirata, H., Otani, K., Sugimoto, M., Tsukamoto, M., Yoshihara, T., Ueno, M., & Mawatari, M. (2022). Xr (extended reality: virtual reality, augmented reality, mixed reality) technology in spine medicine: status quo and quo vadis. *Journal of Clinical Medicine, 11*(2), 470. doi:10.3390/jcm11020470 PMID:35054164

Moro-Visconti, R. (2022). The Valuation of Digital Platforms and Virtual Marketplaces. In *The Valuation of Digital Intangibles: Technology, Marketing, and the Metaverse* (pp. 591–612). Springer International Publishing. doi:10.1007/978-3-031-09237-4_20

Morris, D. Z. (2019). Blockchain could give us a peer-to-peer internet. *Fortune, 1.*

Morris, R. (2011). *Web 3.0: Implications for online learning.*

Morrison, R. (2020). *What do landlords in Canada look for in your bank statements?* Strawhomes. https://www.strawhomes.com/what-do-landlords-look-for-in-your-bank-statements/

Moser, M., Bohme, R., & Breuker, D. An Inquiry into Money Laundering Tools in the Bitcoin Ecosystem. *E-Crime Researchers' Summit.* IEEE. https://maltemoeser.de/paper/money-laundering.pdf

Mougayar, W. (2016). *The Business Blockchain: Promise, Practice, and Application of the Next Internet Technology.* John Wiley & Sons.

Mukhopadhyay, M. (2018). *Ethereum Smart Contract Development: Build blockchain-based decentralized applications using solidity.* Packt Publishing Ltd.

Muldoon, J., & Raekstad, P. (2022). Algorithmic Domination in the Gig Economy. *European Journal of Political Theory, 0*(0), 1–21. doi:10.1177/14748851221082078

Murray, A., Kim, D., & Combs, J. (2023). The promise of a decentralized internet: What is Web3 and how can firms prepare? *Business Horizons, 66*(2), 191–202. doi:10.1016/j.bushor.2022.06.002

Musiał, K., & Kazienko, P. (2013). Social networks on the Internet. *World Wide Web (Bussum), 16*(1), 31–72. doi:10.100711280-011-0155-z

Nabben, K. (2022). The Ethnography of a 'Decentralized Autonomous Organization' (DAO): De-mystifying Algorithmic Systems. *EPIC, (1), 74–97.

Nabben, K. (2023). "Governance by Algorithms, Governance of Algorithms: Human-Machine Politics in Decentralised Autonomous Organisations (DAOs)", *puntOorg. International Journal (Toronto, Ont.), 8*(1), 36–54. doi:10.19245/25.05. pij.8.1.3

Nabben, K. (2023). Web3 as 'self-infrastructuring': The challenge is how. *Big Data & Society*, *10*(1). doi:10.1177/20539517231159002

NabbenK.PuspasariN.KelleherM.SanjayS. (2021). Grounding Decentralised Technologies in Cooperative Principles: What Can 'Decentralised Autonomous Organisations' (DAOs) and Platform Cooperatives Learn from Each Other? doi:10.2139/ssrn.3979223

Nahavandi, S. (2019). *Industry 5.0—A Human-Centric Solution*. Institute for Intelligent Systems Research and Innovation. doi:10.3390u11164371

Nair, M. M., Tyagi, A. K., & Sreenath, N. (2021). The future with industry 4.0 at the core of society 5.0: Open issues, future opportunities and challenges. In 2021 international conference on computer communication and informatics (ICCCI), (pp. 1-7). IEEE. doi:10.1109/ICCCI50826.2021.9402498

Nakamoto, S. (2008). *Bitcoin: A Peer-to-Peer Electronic Cash System*.

Nakamoto, S. (2008). *Bitcoin: A Peer-to-Peer Electronic Cash System*. Bitcoin. https://bitcoin.org/bitcoin.pdf

Nakamoto, S. (2008). Bitcoin: A peer-to-peer electronic cash system. *Decentralized business review*.

Nakamoto, S. (2008). Re: Bitcoin P2P e-cash paper. *The Cryptography Mailing List*, 1-2.

Nakavachara, V., & Saengchote, K. (2022). Is Metaverse LAND a good investment? It depends on your unit of account! SSRN *Electronic Journal*. doi:10.2139/ssrn.4028587

Nambiampurath, R. (2022). What is a DAO? *The Defiant*. https://thedefiant.io/what-are-daos

Nam, K., Dutt, C. S., Chathoth, P., & Khan, M. S. (2019). Blockchain technology for smart city and smart tourism: Latest trends and challenges. *Asia Pacific Journal of Tourism Research*, 1–15. doi:10.1080/10941665.2019.1585376

Narang, S., Bhardwaj, G., & Srivastava, A. P. (2022). Gamification in HRM: An Overview. *ECS Transactions*, *107*(1), 3573–3580. doi:10.1149/10701.3573ecst

Narayanan, A., Bonneau, J., Felten, E., Miller, A., & Goldfeder, S. (2016). *Bitcoin and cryptocurrency technologies: a comprehensive introduction*. Princeton University Press.

Nasim, R., & Buchegger, S. (2014). Xacml-based access control for decentralized online social networks. In *2014 IEEE/ACM 7th International Conference on Utility and Cloud Computing* (pp. 671-676). IEEE. 10.1109/UCC.2014.108

Nath, K. (2022). *Evolution of the internet from web 1.0 to metaverse: The good, the bad and the ugly*.

Nath, A. K., Singh, R., Iyer, L. S., & Ganesh, J. (2010). Web 2.0: Capabilities, Business Value and Strategic Practice. *Journal of Information Science & Technology*, *7*(1), 22–39.

Nath, K., Dhar, S., & Basishtha, S. (2014, February). Web 1.0 to Web 3.0-Evolution of the Web and its various challenges. In *2014 International Conference on Reliability Optimization and Information Technology (ICROIT)* (pp. 86-89). IEEE. 10.1109/ICROIT.2014.6798297

Naughtin, C., Hajkowicz, S., Schleiger, E., Bratanova, A., Cameron, A., Zamin, T., & Dutta, A. (2022). *Our Future World: Global megatrends impacting the way we live over coming decades*. MPRA.

Nepali, R. & Wang, Y. (2013). SONET: A SOcial NETwork model for privacy monitoring and ranking, (pp. 162-166). IEEE. . doi:10.1109/ICDCSW.2013.49

NFTs Street. (2021). *History Of NFT or Non-Fungible-Tokens | How NFTs came into Existence?* NFT Street. https://www. nftsstreet.com/history-of-nft/#:~:text=NFT%20or%20Non-fungible-token%20was%20first%20created%20by%20Kevin

Ngak, C. (2011) Then and now: a history of social networking sites. *CBS news.*

Nieradka, P. (2019). Using virtual reality technologies in the real estate sector. *Annales Universitatis Mariae Curie-Skłodowska, Sectio H – Oeconomia, 53*(2), 45. doi:10.17951/h.2019.53.2.45-53

Nilizadeh, S., Jahid, S., Mittal, P., Borisov, N., & Kapadia, A. (2012). Cachet: A decentralized architecture for privacy preserving social networking with caching. In *Proceedings of the 8th CoNEXT* (pp. 337-348). ACM. 10.1145/2413176.2413215

Nils Siegfried, N., Rosenthal T., & Benlian, A. (2018). Blockchain and the Industrial Internet of Things A requirement taxonomy and systematic fit analysis. *Journal of Enterprise Information Management.*

Non-Fungible Tokens (NFTs) Market Size Worth $2.7 Billion by 2027 | CAGR: 48.4%: Grand View Research, Inc. (2021, September 1). PR Newswire. https://www.prnewswire.com/news-releases/non-fungible-tokens-nfts-market-size-worth-2-7-billion-by-2027--cagr-48-4-grand-view-research-inc-301367259.html

NonFungible.com. (2021). *NFT Market Report Q1 2021.* NonFungible. https://nonfungible.com/blog/nft-market-report-q1-2021

NonFungible.com. (2021). *NFT Market Report Q2 2021.* NonFungible. https://nonfungible.com/blog/nft-market-report-q2-2021

NonFungible.com. (2021). *NFT Market Report Q3 2021.* NonFungible. https://nonfungible.com/blog/nft-market-report-q3-2021

Norta, A., Othman, A. B., & Taveter, K. (2015). Conflict-resolution lifecycles for governed decentralized autonomous organization collaboration. *2015 2nd International Conference on Electronic Governance and Open Society: Challenges in Eurasia.* ACM.

Norta, A. (2015). Creation of smart-contracting collaborations for decentralized autonomous organizations. In *International Conference on Business Informatics Research* (pp. 3-17). Springer, Cham. 10.1007/978-3-319-21915-8_1

Noskova, T., Pavlova, T., & Iakovleva, O. (2016). Web 3.0 technologies and transformation of pedagogical activities. In Mobile Computing and Wireless Networks: Concepts, Methodologies, Tools, and Applications (pp. 728-748). IGI Global.

Noto La Diega, G., & Stacey, J. (2019). Can permissionless blockchains be regulated and resolve some of the problems of copyright law? In M. Ragnedda & G. Destefanis (Eds.), *Blockchain and Web 3.0: Social, Economic, and Technological Challenges* (pp. 30–47). Routledge. doi:10.4324/9780429029530-3

Noura, M., Atiquzzaman, M., & Gaedke, M. (2019). Interoperability in Internet of Things: Taxonomies and Open Challenges. *Mobile Networks and Applications, 24*(3), 796–809. doi:10.100711036-018-1089-9

O'Dwyer, R. (2017). The Revolution Will (Not) Be Decentralized: Blockchains. In *Proceedings of the 8th International Conference on Social Media & Society* (pp. 1-5). ACM.

Ohei, K. N., & Brink, R. (2019). Web 3.0 and web 2.0 technologies in higher educational institute: Methodological concept towards a framework development for adoption. *International journal for Infonomics (IJI), 12*(1), 1841-1853.

Ohler, J. (2008). The semantic web in education. *EDUCAUSE Quarterly, 31*(4), 7–9.

Oláh, J., & Nica, E. (2022). Biometric Sensor Technologies, Virtual Marketplace Dynamics Data, and Computer Vision and Deep Learning Algorithms in the Metaverse Interactive Environment *Journal of Self-Governance & Management Economics, 10*(3).

Onwukwe A. Adeniran I. (2022, December 31). *Proposing Policy Formulation for Web 3.0.* Papers.ssrn.com. https://papers.ssrn.com/sol3/papers.cfm?abstract_id=4315626 doi:10.2139/ssrn.4315626

Oracle. (2023). *What is IoT?* Oracle. https://www.oracle.com/ca-en/internet-of-things/what-is-iot/

ØstbyeP. (2022). Exploring The Role of Law in The Governance of Cryptocurrency Systems and Why Limited Liability DAOs might be a Bad Idea. doi:10.2139/ssrn.4007547

Ostrom, E. (1990). *Governing the Commons: The Evolution of Institutions for Collective Action.* Cambridge University Press. doi:10.1017/CBO9780511807763

Othman, A. (2020). The Application of Decentralized Autonomous Organizations for Sustainable Management and Operations: A Case Study Approach. *International Journal of Advanced Computer Science and Applications, 11*(5).

Otte, P., de Vos, M., & Pouwelse, J. (2017). TrustChain: A Sybil-resistant scalable blockchain. *Future Generation Computer Systems, 107*, 770–780. doi:10.1016/j.future.2017.08.048

Ozili, P. K. (2023). eNaira central bank digital currency (CBDC) for financial inclusion in Nigeria. In Digital Economy, Energy and Sustainability: Opportunities and Challenges (pp. 41-54). Cham: Springer International Publishing.

Ozili, P. K. (2023). Digital finance research and developments around the World: A literature review. *International Journal of Business Forecasting and Marketing Intelligence, 8*(1), 35–51. doi:10.1504/IJBFMI.2023.127698

Özyılmaz, K. R., & Yurdakul, A. (2017), Work-in-progress: integrating low-power IoT devices to a blockchain-based infrastructure, *International Conference on Embedded Software*. IEEE.

Panarello, A., Tapas, N., Merlino, G., Longo, F., & Puliafito, A. (2018). Blockchain and IoT integration: A systematic survey. *Sensors (Basel), 18*(8), 2575. doi:10.339018082575 PMID:30082633

Parizi, R. M., Dehghantanha, A., Choo, K. K. R., & Singh, A. (2018). Empirical vulnerability analysis of automated smart contracts security testing on blockchains. arXiv preprint arXiv:1809.02702.

Parizi, R. M., & Dehghantanha, A. (2018). Smart contract programming languages on blockchains: An empirical evaluation of usability and security. *Blockchain–ICBC 2018: First International Conference, Held as Part of the Services Conference Federation, SCF 2018, Seattle, WA, USA, June 25-30, 2018 Proceedings, 1*, 75–91.

Park, S., Pietrzak, K., Kwon, A., Alwen, J., Fuchsbauer, G., & Gazi, P. (2015), Spacemint: A Cryptocurrency Based on Proofs of Space. IACR Cryptology.

Park, A., Wilson, M., Robson, K., Demetis, D., & Kietzmann, J. (2023). Interoperability: Our exciting and terrifying Web3 future. *Business Horizons, Volume, 4*(66), 529–541. doi:10.1016/j.bushor.2022.10.005

Park, S. M., & Kim, Y. G. (2022). A Metaverse: Taxonomy, Components, Applications, and Open Challenges. *IEEE Access : Practical Innovations, Open Solutions, 10*, 4209–4251. doi:10.1109/ACCESS.2021.3140175

Pastrana, S., & Suarez-Tangil, G. (2019). A First Look at the Crypto-Mining Malware Ecosystem. In *Proceedings of the Internet Measurement Conference.* ACM. 10.1145/3355369.3355576

Patel ThompsonA.WinnE.OatesG.EsberJ.JinL.KanterM.MannanM.PouxP.HubbardS.MooreS.DeleveauxS.ScholzT. R.HumQ. Z. (2022, December 14). *Toward A More Cooperative web 3.* https://papers.ssrn.com/sol3/papers.cfm?abstract_id=4302681 doi:10.2139/ssrn.4302681

PatilA.ShindeA.PanigrahiA.AroraA.RavirajaD. S.BabuR. 2022. The role of blockchain technology in decentralized real estate marketplace: recent findings. *Available at* SSRN 4096395. doi:10.2139/ssrn.4096395

Patrickson, B. (2020). Lightbulb concrete. In M. Ragnedda & G. Destefanis (Eds.), *Blockchain and Web 3.0: Social, Economic, and Technological Challenges* (pp. 78–93). Routledge.

Patrickson, B. (2021). What do blockchain technologies imply for digital creative industries? *Creativity and Innovation Management, 30*(3), 585–595. doi:10.1111/caim.12456

Paul, T., Famulari, A., & Strufe, T. (2014). A survey on decentralized Online Social Networks. *Computer Networks, 75*, 437–452. doi:10.1016/j.comnet.2014.10.005

Pavlić Skender, H., & Zaninović, P. A. (2020). Perspectives of Blockchain Technology for Sustainable Supply Chains. In A. Kolinski, D. Dujak, & P. Golinska-Dawson (Eds.), *Integration of Information Flow for Greening Supply Chain Management* (pp. 77–92). Springer International Publishing. doi:10.1007/978-3-030-24355-5_5

Peachey, A., & Childs, M. (Eds.). (2011). *Reinventing ourselves: Contemporary concepts of identity in virtual worlds.* Springer Science & Business Media. doi:10.1007/978-0-85729-361-9

Pendergrast, M. (2010). *Uncommon grounds: The history of coffee and how it transformed our world* (Rev. ed). Basic Books.

Pennycook, G., McPhetres, J., Zhang, Y., Lu, J. G., & Rand, D. G. (2020). Fighting COVID-19 misinformation on social media: Experimental evidence for a scalable accuracy-nudge intervention. *Psychological Science, 31*(7), 770–780. doi:10.1177/0956797620939054 PMID:32603243

Pentland, A. (2022). Building a New Economy: Data, AI, and Web 3: How distributed technologies could return more control to users. *Communications of the ACM, 65*(12), 27–29. https://doi-org.ezproxy.myucwest.ca/10.1145/3547659. doi:10.1145/3547659

Perdue, B. (2022). History of automation in the accounting industry. *Autymate.* https://www.autymate.com/blog/history-of-automation-in-the-accounting-industry

Pereira, J. R. (2016). Producer Cooperatives: A Transaction Cost Economic Approach. In F. Taisch, A. Jungmeister, & H. Gernet (Eds.), *Cooperative Identity and Growth: Conference Proceedings of ICCS 2016 in Lucerne* (pp. 528–536). Verlag Raiffeisen Schweiz.

Pérez-Juárez, M. A., Aguiar-Pérez, J. M., Alonso-Felipe, M., Del-Pozo-Velázquez, J., Rozada-Raneros, S., & Barrio-Conde, M. (2022). Exploring the Possibilities of Artificial Intelligence and Big Data Techniques to Enhance Gamified Financial Services. In Next-Generation Applications and Implementations of Gamification Systems, (pp. 187-204). IGI Global. doi:10.4018/978-1-7998-8089-9.ch010

Pestunov, A. I. (2020). Cryptocurrencies and Blockchain: Potential Applications in Government and Business. *Problems of Economic Transition, 62*(4-6), 286–297. doi:10.1080/10611991.2020.1968751

Peters, G. W., & Panayi, E. (2016). Understanding Modern Banking Ledgers Through Blockchain Technologies: Future of Transaction Processing and Smart Contracts on the Internet of Money. In Banking Beyond Banks and Money (pp. 239–278). doi:10.1007/978-3-319-42448-4_13

Petrock, V. (2021). *US Generation Z Demographic and Psychographic Overview: What Makes the Most Racially, Ethnically, and Sexually Diverse Generation in History Tick.* Insider Intelligence. https://www.insiderintelligence.com/content/us-generation-z-demographic-psychographic-overview

Pfeiffer, A., Kriglstein, S., Wernbacher, T., & Bezzina, S. (2020). Blockchain technologies and social media: A snapshot. In *ECSM 2020 8th European Conference on Social Media* (p. 196). Academic Conferences and publishing limited.

Pham, H. L., Tran, T. H., & Nakashima, Y. (2018, December). A secure remote healthcare system for hospital using blockchain smart contract. In 2018 IEEE globecom workshops (GC Wkshps) (pp. 1-6). IEEE. doi:10.1109/GLOCOMW.2018.8644164

Pinch, T., & Bijker, W. E. (1984). The social construction of facts and artifacts: Or how the sociology of science and the sociology of technology might benefit each other. *Social Studies of Science, 14*(3), 399–441. doi:10.1177/030631284014003004

Politou, E., Casino, F., Alepis, E., & Patsakis, C. (2019). Blockchain mutability: Challenges and proposed solutions. *IEEE Transactions on Emerging Topics in Computing, 9*(4), 1972–1986. doi:10.1109/TETC.2019.2949510

Pongle, P., & Chavan, G. (2015). *A Survey: Attacks on RPL and 6LoWPAN in IoT.* Conference: ICPC, Pune.

Pongnumkul, S., Siripanpornchana, C., & Thajchayapong, S. (2017, July). Performance analysis of private blockchain platforms in varying workloads. In *2017 26th International Conference on Computer Communication and Networks (ICCCN)* (pp. 1-6). IEEE. 10.1109/ICCCN.2017.8038517

Poon, J., & Buterin, V. (2017). Plasma: Scalable autonomous smart contracts. *White paper*, 1-47.

Poore, M. (2014). The Next G Web. Discernment, meaning-making, and the implications of Web 3.0 for education. *Technology, Pedagogy and Education, 23*(2), 167–180. doi:10.1080/1475939X.2013.802992

Popescu, B. (2019). Web 3.0 and its impact on business models. *Expert Journal of Economics., 7*(2), 51–59.

Popov, S. (2016). *The Tangle.* IOTA Whitepaper. https://assets.ctfassets.net/r1dr6vzfxhev/2t4uxvsIqk0EUau6g2sw0g/45eae33637ca92f85dd9f4a3a218e1ec/iota1_4_3.pdf

Poskitt, Z. (2019). Annotated bibliography: Decentralized autonomous organization. SSRN Electronic Journal.

Post, H. (2023). How automation helps reduce human error and improves data quality. *Trade Safe.* https://trdsf.com/blogs/news/how-automation-helps-reduce-human-error-and-improves-data-quality

Potts, J., & Rennie, E. (2019). Web3 and the creative industries: how blockchains are reshaping business models. *A research agenda for creative industries*, 93-111.

Pouwelse, J. A., Garbacki, P., Wang, J., Bakker, A., Yang, J., Iosup, A., Epema, D. H., Reinders, M., Van Steen, M. R., & Sips, H. J. (2008). Tri-bler: A social-based peer-to-peer system. *Concurr Comput PractExperience, 20*(2), 127–138. doi:10.1002/cpe.1189

Pouwels, J. L., Keijsers, L., & Odgers, C. (2022). Who benefits most from using social media, the socially rich or the socially poor? *Current Opinion in Psychology, 47*, 101351. doi:10.1016/j.copsyc.2022.101351 PMID:35662060

Powell, J., & Clarke, A. (2002). The WWW of the World Wide Web: Who, what, and why? *Journal of Medical Internet Research, 4*(1), e4. doi:10.2196/jmir.4.1.e4 PMID:11956036

Preukschat, A., & Reed, D. (2021). *Self-sovereign identity.* Manning Publications.

Pries, J., & Quakernack, N. (2023). Decentralized Autonomous Organization. *Organisationsentwicklung*, (2), 81–83.

Purcarea, I. M. (2022). Digital twins, web3, metaverse, value innovation and e-commerce retail. *Romanian Distribution Committee Magazine, 13*(3), 41–47.

Purdy, M. (2022). *How the Metaverse Could Change Work.* Harvard Business Review. https://hbr.org/2022/04/how-the-metaverse-could-change-work

Puthal, D., Nepal, S., Ranjan, R., & Chen, J. (2016). Threats to networking cloud and edge data centers in the Internet of Things. *IEEE Cloud Computing, 2016*(3), 64–71. doi:10.1109/MCC.2016.63

PVH. (2022). *Tommy Hilfiger Joins the First-Ever Decentraland Metaverse Fashion Week.* PVH. https://www.pvh.com/news/tommy-hilfiger-metaverse-fashion-week-2022

Qamar, M., Malik, M., Batool, S., Mehmood, S., Malik, A. W., & Rahman, A. (2016). Centralized to decentralized social networks: Factors that matter (pp. 37-54).

Qayumi, K. (2015), Multi-agent based intelligence generation from very large datasets, *International Conference on Cloud Engineering*. IEEE. 10.1109/IC2E.2015.96

Qin, R., Ding, W., Li, J., Guan, S., Wang, G., Ren, Y., & Qu, Z. (2022). web 3-Based Decentralized Autonomous Organizations and Operations: Architectures, Models, and Mechanisms. *IEEE Transactions on Systems, Man, and Cybernetics*, *53*(4), 2073–2082. doi:10.1109/TSMC.2022.3228530

Quasim, M. T., Khan, M. A., Algarni, F., Alharthy, A., & Alshmrani, G. M. M. (2020). Blockchain frameworks. *Decentralised Internet of Things: A Blockchain Perspective*, 75-89.

Ragnedda, M., & Destefanis, G. (2019). Blockchain: A disruptive technology. In M. Ragnedda & G. Destefanis (Eds.), *Blockchain and Web 3.0: Social, Economic, and Technological Challenges* (pp. 1–11). Routledge. doi:10.4324/9780429029530-1

Raja, G., Manaswini, Y., Vivekanandan, G. D., Sampath, H., Dev, K., & Bashir, A. K. (2020, July). AI-powered blockchain-a decentralized secure multiparty computation protocol for IoV. In *IEEE INFOCOM 2020-IEEE Conference on Computer Communications Workshops (INFOCOM WKSHPS)* (pp. 865-870). IEEE. 10.1109/INFOCOMWKSHPS50562.2020.9162866

Rajabifard, A., Binns, A., Masser, I., & Williamson, I. (2006). The role of sub-national government and the private sector in future spatial data infrastructures. *International Journal of Geographical Information Science*, *20*(7), 727–741. doi:10.1080/13658810500432224

Ramiro, A., & de Queiroz, R. (2022). Cypherpunk. *Internet Policy Review*, *11*(2). doi:10.14763/2022.2.1664

Ranttila, K. (2020). *Social Media and Monopoly. Ohio NUL Rev.*, *46*, 161.

Raskin, M. (2017). The Law and Legality of Smart Contracts. *Georgetown Law Technology Review, 1*(2).

Rathee, G., Garg, S., Kaddoum, G., & Choi, B. J. (2021). Decision-Making Model for Securing IoT Devices in Smart Industries. *IEEE Transactions on Industrial Informatics*, *17*(6), 4270–4278. doi:10.1109/TII.2020.3005252

Rathore, S., Sharma, P. K., Loia, V., Jeong, Y., & Park, J. H. (2017). Social network security: Issues, challenges, threats, and solutions. *Information Sciences*, *421*, 43–69. doi:10.1016/j.ins.2017.08.063

Ravichandran, K., & Ilango, S. K. (2023). A preliminary analysis of the quality of the content produced by ai bots using ai in content generation. *International Journal of Intelligent Systems and Applications in Engineering*, *11*(5s), 585–590.

Ray, P. P. (2023). Web3: A comprehensive review on background, technologies, applications, zero-trust architectures, challenges and future directions. *Internet of Things and Cyber-Physical Systems*.

Raybourn, E. M., Stubblefield, W. A., Trumbo, M., Jones, A., Whetzel, J., & Fabian, N. (2019). *Information design for xr immersive environments: Challenges and opportunities*. In Virtual, augmented and mixed reality. multimodal interaction. Orlando, Florida.

Ray, P. P. (2023). web 3: A comprehensive review on background, technologies, applications, zero-trust architectures, challenges and future directions. *Internet of Things and Cyber-Physical Systems*, *3*, 213–248. Advance online publication. doi:10.1016/j.iotcps.2023.05.003

Razec, I. (2022). The Complex Ramifications of Digital Identity. *International Journal of Cross-Cultural Studies and Environmental Communication*, *11*(1), 52–60.

Rebecca. (2022). What is Web 1.0? Everything you need to know. *History-Computer*. https://history-computer.com/web-1-0/

Redshaw, T. (2018). *Of Bitcoins and Blockchains: The Social Construction of Crypto-Currencies*.

Reguerra, E. (2022). NFTs minted on FTX break, highlighting Web2 hosting flaws. *Cointelegraph*. https://cointelegraph.com/news/nfts-minted-on-ftx-break-highlighting-web2-hosting-flaws

Reijers, W., & Coeckelbergh, M. (2018). The blockchain as a narrative technology: Investigating the social ontology and normative configurations of cryptocurrencies. *Philosophy & Technology*, *31*(1), 103–130. doi:10.100713347-016-0239-x

Ren, K., Ho, N. M., Loghin, D., Nguyen, T. T., Ooi, B. C., Ta, Q. T., & Zhu, F. (2023). Interoperability in Blockchain: A Survey. *IEEE Transactions on Knowledge and Data Engineering*, 1–20. doi:10.1109/TKDE.2023.3275220

Renuka, K., Kumari, S., Zhao, D., & Li, A. L. (2019). Design of a Secure Password-Based Authentication Scheme for M2M Networks in IoT Enabled Cyber-Physical Systems. *IEEE Access : Practical Innovations, Open Solutions*, *7*, 2169–3536. doi:10.1109/ACCESS.2019.2908499

ResearchAndMarkets. (2020). *Global virtual and augmented reality market - Growth, trends, and forecast*. Research and Markets.

Resnik, F., & Bellmore, A. (2021). Is Peer Victimization Associated With Adolescents' Social Media Use, Engagement, Behavior, and Content? *Merrill-Palmer Quarterly*, *67*(2), 175–202. doi:10.13110/merrpalmquar1982.67.2.0175

Rhee, E. (2023). Employment contract and wage payment using blockchain and smart contract. *International Journal of Internet Technology and Secured Transactions*, *13*(1), 1–10. doi:10.1504/IJITST.2023.127387

Richter, J. (2022). History & definition of Web 1.0, 2.0, and 3.0- a comprehensive review. *Viral Solutions*. https://viral-solutions.net/definition-of-web-1-0-2-0-and-3-0/

Rikken, O., Janssen, M., Kwee, Z. (2023). The ins and outs of decentralized autonomous organizations (DAOs) unraveling the definitions, characteristics, and emerging developments of DAOs. *Blockchain: Research and Applications* . doi:10.1016/j.bcra.2023.100143

Rikken, O., van Heukelom-Verhage, S., Naves, J., & Terpoorten, H. (2018). *Smart Contracts as Specific Application of Blockchain Technology*. Dutch Blockchain Coalition. https://dutchdigitaldelta.nl/uploads/pdf/Smart-Contracts-ENG-report.pdf

Riva, S. (2020). Decentralized Autonomous Organizations (Daos) In the swiss legal order. In A. Bonomi & G. P. Romano (Eds.), *Yearbook of Private International Law, 21,* 601-638. Verlag Dr. Otto Schmidt & Swiss Institute of Comparative Law, Germany. https://www.unine.ch/files/live/sites/florence.guillaume/files/Publications/Riva%20DAO%20in%20Swiss%20legal%20order.pdf

Roberts, P. (2018, April 18). *Green Coffee Pricing Transparency Is Critical (And Complicated)*. Perfect Daily Grind. https://perfectdailygrind.com/2018/04/green-coffee-pricing-transparency-is-critical-and-complicated/

Rocas-Royo, M. (2019). Decentralization as a new framework for the sharing economy. Handbook of the Sharing Economy, pp. 218-228.

Rodima-Taylor, D., & Grimes, W. W. (2019). Virtualizing diaspora: New digital technologies in the emerging transnational space. *Global Networks*, *19*(3), 349–370. doi:10.1111/glob.12221

Rodrigues, L. F., Oliveira, A., & Rodrigues, H. (2019). Main gamification concepts: A systematic mapping study. *Heliyon*, *5*(7), e01993. doi:10.1016/j.heliyon.2019.e01993 PMID:31360779

Rogerson, M., & Parry, G. C. (2020). Blockchain: Case studies in food supply chain visibility. *Supply Chain Management*, *25*(5), 601–614. doi:10.1108/SCM-08-2019-0300

Rojas, N., Carolina, G. A. A. P., Diego, F. L. B., & Carlos, A. T. R. (2021). Society 5.0: A Japanese concept for a super-intelligent society. *Sustainability*, *13*(12), 6567. doi:10.3390u13126567

Romansky, R. P., & Noninska, I. S. (2020). Challenges of the digital age for privacy and personal data protection. *Mathematical Biosciences and Engineering*, *17*(5). doi:10.3934/mbe.2020286 PMID:33120553

Rosenberg, A. (2022). Getting down with DAOs: Decentralized autonomous organizations in bankruptcy. *American Bankruptcy Institute. Journal Issue*, *41*(7), 12–51.

Rosenberg, L. (2022, March). Regulation of the Metaverse: A Roadmap: The risks and regulatory solutions for largescale consumer platforms. In *Proceedings of the 6th international conference on virtual and augmented reality simulations* (pp. 21-26). ACM. 10.1145/3546607.3546611

Rossi, S., Guedes, A., & Toni, L. (2023). Streaming and user behavior in omnidirectional videos. In *Immersive Video Technologies* (pp. 49–83). Academic Press. doi:10.1016/B978-0-32-391755-1.00009-2

RossO.JensenJ. R.AsheimT. 2019. Assets under Tokenization. *Available at* SSRN 3488344.

Rotberg, E. (2019). Keep your emails between you and your client. *CPA Canada*. https://www.cpacanada.ca/en/news/atwork/2019-06-14-client-email-risk

Rozas, D., Tenorio Fornés, A., Díaz Molina, S., & Hassan, S. (2021). When Ostrom meets Blockchain: Exploring the potentials of blockchain for commons governance. *SAGE Open*, *11*(1), 1–14. doi:10.1177/21582440211002526

Ruane, Y., & McAfee, A. (2022, May 10). What a DAO Can—and Can't—Do. *Harvard Business Review*. https://hbr.org/2022/05/what-a-dao-can-and-cant-do

Rupa, C., Midhunchakkaravarthy, D., Hasan, M. K., Alhumyani, H., & Saeed, R. A. (2021). Industry 5.0: Ethereum blockchain technology based DApp smart contract. *Mathematical Biosciences and Engineering*, *18*(5), 7010–7027. doi:10.3934/mbe.2021349 PMID:34517569

Rutskiy, V., Allam, S., Elkin, S., Beknazarov, Z., Semina, E., Ikonnikov, O., & Tsarev, R. (2022). Non-fungible Tokens: Value for Digital Arts and Pricing Factors. In *Proceedings of the Computational Methods in Systems and Software* (pp. 805-816). Cham: Springer International Publishing.

Sadowski, J. (2016). Companies are making money from our personal data – but at what cost? *The Guardian*. https://www.theguardian.com/technology/2016/aug/31/personal-data-corporate-use-google-amazon

Sadowski, J., & Beegle, K. (2023). Expansive and extractive networks of Web3. *Big Data & Society*, *10*(1). doi:10.1177/20539517231159629

Sahani, A. R. (2022). The Potential Applications and Implications of Decentralized Finance. *NOLEGEIN-Journal of Information Technology & Management*, *5*(2), 22–28.

Sahay, R., Geethakumari, G., & Mitra, B. (2022). A holistic framework for prediction of routing attacks in IoT. *The Journal of Supercomputing*, *78*(1), 1409–1433. doi:10.100711227-021-03922-1

Sahni, S. (2022). How are NFTs affecting the art market? *International Journal of Mechanical Engineering*, *7*(5).

Sahoo, S. S., Singh, B., Mohapatra, D. P., & Barik, R. K. (2022). *Web 3.0: Challenges, applications, and research issues*. Internet Technology Letters.

Sailer, M., Hense, J. U., Mayr, S. K., & Mandl, H. (2017). How gamification motivates: An experimental study of the effects of specific game design elements on psychological need satisfaction. *Computers in Human Behavior*, *69*, 371–380. doi:10.1016/j.chb.2016.12.033

Saingre, D., Ledoux, T., & Menaud, J. M. (2020, November). BCTMark: a framework for benchmarking blockchain technologies. In *2020 IEEE/ACS 17th International Conference on Computer Systems and Applications (AICCSA)* (pp. 1-8). IEEE. 10.1109/AICCSA50499.2020.9316536

Saito, Y., & Rose, J. A. (2022). Reputation-based Decentralized Autonomous Organization for the non-profit sector: Leveraging blockchain to enhance good governance. *Frontiers in Blockchain*, 5(1083647), 1083647. doi:10.3389/fbloc.2022.1083647

Salah, O. H., & Alzaghal, Q. K. (2021). A Conceptual Model for Implementing Gamification in Education and Its Impact on Academic Performance. In *Innovation of Businesses, and Digitalization during Covid-19 Pandemic: Proceedings of The International Conference on Business and Technology (ICBT 2021)*, (pp. 765-775). Cham: Springer International Publishing.

Salman, T., Zolanvari, M., Erbad, A., Jain, R., & Samaka, M. (2019). Security services using blockchains: A state of the art survey. *IEEE Communications Surveys and Tutorials*, 21(1), 850–880. doi:10.1109/COMST.2018.2863956

Samanthi, D., & Gooneratne, T. (2023). Bean counter to value-adding business partner: The changing role of the accountant and situated rationality in a multinational firm. *Journal of Accounting & Organizational Change*, 19(3), 513–535. https://doi-org.ezproxy.myucwest.ca/10.1108/JAOC-04-2022-0063. doi:10.1108/JAOC-04-2022-0063

Samarawickrema, G., & Stacey, E. (2007). Adopting Web-Based Learning and Teaching: A case study in higher education. *Distance Education*, 28(3), 313–333. doi:10.1080/01587910701611344

Samudra, A. (2022). Non-Fungible Tokens (NFTs): New Renaissance for the Artists. SSRN *Electronic Journal*. doi:10.2139/ssrn.4112932

Samuele, B., & Rosa, C. (2023). The Interpretation of CBDC Within An Endogenous Money Framework. *Research in International Business and Finance*, 65, 101970. doi:10.1016/j.ribaf.2023.101970

Sanchez-Roger, M., & Puyol-Antón, E. (2021). Digital bank runs: A deep neural network approach. *Sustainability*, 13(3), 1513. doi:10.3390u13031513

Sandbeck, S., Kingsmith, A. T., & von Bargen, J. (2019). The block is hot: A commons-based approach to the development and deployment of blockchains. In M. Ragnedda & G. Destefanis (Eds.), *Blockchain and Web 3.0: Social, Economic, and Technological Challenges* (pp. 15–29). Routledge. doi:10.4324/9780429029530-2

Santana, C., & Albareda, L. (2022). Blockchain and the emergence of Decentralized Autonomous Organizations (DAOs): An integrative model and research agenda. *Technological Forecasting and Social Change*, 182, 121806. Advance online publication. doi:10.1016/j.techfore.2022.121806

Saraf, C., & Sabadra, S. (2018, May). Blockchain platforms: A compendium. In *2018 IEEE International Conference on Innovative Research and Development (ICIRD)* (pp. 1-6). IEEE.

Saunders, M. N. K., Lewis, P., & Thornhill, A. (2016). *Research Methods For Business Students*. Pearson Education Limited.

Saurabh, K., Rani, N., & Upadhyay, P. (2023). Towards blockchain led decentralized autonomous organization (DAO) business model innovations. *International Journal (Toronto, Ont.)*, 30(2), 475–502. doi:10.1108/BIJ-10-2021-0606

Schär, F. (2021). Decentralized Finance: On Blockchain-and Smart Contract-Based Financial Markets. *Review - Federal Reserve Bank of St. Louis*, 103(1), 153–176.

Schecter, B. (2021). The Future of Work is Not Corporate — It's DAOs and Crypto Networks. *A16ZCrypto*. https://a16zcrypto.com/posts/article/the-future-of-work-daos-crypto-networks/#section--3

Schilling, L., Fernández-Villaverde, J., & Uhlig, H. (2020). Central Bank Digital Currency: When Price and Bank Stability Collide. (*NBER Working Paper No. 202*). https://www.sas.upenn.edu/~jesusfv/CBDC_Nominal.pdf

Schmid, J. J., & Amsler, T. (2021). The Emergence of Local Government Blockchain Applications: A Swiss Case Study. In *Handbook of Blockchain and Sustainable Finance* (pp. 267–280). Springer.

Scholz, T. (2016). *Platform cooperativism. Challenging the corporate sharing economy. Rosa Luxemburg Stiftung*. New York Office.

Schrader-Rank, A. (2021). *How NFTs Influence Society: A Look at Scarcity Mindset*. Generational Gaps in Education, and the Impact on the Environment.

Schrepel, T. (2023). The Complex Relationship between Web2 Giants and web 3 Projects. *Amsterdam Law & Technology Institute Working Paper*, 1-2023.

SchrepelT. (2021). Smart Contracts and the Digital Single Market Through the Lens of a 'Law + Technology' Approach. European Commission. SSRN. https://ssrn.com/abstract=3947174

Schuemie, M. J., Van Der Straaten, P., Krijn, M., & Van Der Mast, C. A. (2001). Research on presence in virtual reality: A survey. *Cyberpsychology & Behavior*, *4*(2), 183–201. doi:10.1089/109493101300117884 PMID:11710246

Schuppli, B., & Jafari, G. A., (2023). Piercing the Digital Veil: A Case Study for a DAO legal framework under Swiss Law. *Journal of Intellectual Property, Information Technology and E-Commerce Law* (JIPITEC), *12* (331).

Schutte, N. S., & Stilinovi'c, E. J. (2017). Facilitating empathy through virtual reality. *Motivation and Emotion*, *41*(6), 708–712. doi:10.100711031-017-9641-7

Schwab, K. (2016) The Fourth Industrial Revolution: What It Means, How to Respond. *World Economic Forum*. https://www.weforum.org/agenda/2016/01/the-fourth-industrialrevolution-what-it-means-and-how-to-respond

Schweizer, A. (2019). Commons-based peer production and open innovation. *Journal of Open Innovation*, *5*(3), 52.

Schweizer, D., Amsden, R., & Morkunas, V. J. (2021). A Blockchain Perspective on Process Inefficiencies in the Life Cycle of a Corporate Bond. *Journal of Alternative Investments*, *23*(4), 9–24.

Schwittmann, L., Wander, M., Boelmann, C., & Weis, T. (2014). Privacy Preservation in Decentralized Online Social Networks. *IEEE Internet Computing*, *18*(2), 16–23. doi:10.1109/MIC.2013.131

Scott, B., Loonam, J., & Kumar, V. (2017). Exploring the rise of blockchain technology: Towards distributed collaborative organizations. *Strategic Change*, *26*(5), 423–428. doi:10.1002/jsc.2142

Senthil Kumar, N., Saravanakumar, K., & Deepa, K. (2016). On Privacy and Security in Social Media – A Comprehensive Study. *Procedia Computer Science*, *78*, 114–119. doi:10.1016/j.procs.2016.02.019

Seong, S.-W., Seo, J., Nasielski, M., Sengupta, D., Hangal, S., Teh, S. K., Chu, R., Dodson, B., & Lam, M. S. (2010). Prpl: A decentralized social networking infrastructure. In *Proceedings of the 1st ACM Workshop on Mobile Cloud Computing & Services: Social Networks and Beyond* (pp. 8:1-8:8). ACM.

Sergey, I., Kumar, A., & Hobor, A. (2018). Scilla: a smart contract intermediate-level language. arXiv preprint arXiv:1801.00687.

Sermet, Y., & Demir, I. (2022). GeospatialVR: A web-based virtual reality framework for collaborative environmental simulations. *Computers & Geosciences*, *159*, 105010. doi:10.1016/j.cageo.2021.105010

Seth, D., Gupta, M., & Singh, B. J. (2022). *A Study to Analyse the Impact of Using the Metaverse in the Banking Industry to Augment Performance in a Competitive Environment.* Advances in Marketing, Customer Relationship Management, and E-Services. doi:10.4018/978-1-6684-6133-4.ch002

Shadbolt, N., Berners-Lee, T., & Hall, W. (2019). The semantic web revisited. *IEEE Intelligent Systems*, *21*(3).

Shahriar, N., Chowdhury, S. R., Sharmin, M., Ahmed, R., Boutaba, R., & Mathieu, B. (2013) Ensuring β-Availability in P2P Social Networks. In: *5th International workshop on peer-to-peer systems and online social networks (HotPOST 2013).* IEEE. 10.1109/ICDCSW.2013.91

Shahriar, N., Sharmin, M., Ahmed, R., Rahman, M., Boutaba, R., & Mathieu, B. (2012). Diurnal availability for peer-to-peer systems. In *Proceedings of CCNC*, Las Vegas, Nevada, USA.

Shakimov, A., Lim, H., Caceres, R., Cox, L. P., Li, K. A., Liu, D., & Varshavsky, A. (2011). Vis-`a-vis: privacy-preserving online social networking via virtual individual servers. In: *Proceedings of COMSNETS*, (pp. pp 1–10). IEEE.

Shalender, K., Singla, B., & Sharma, S. (2023). *Emerging Technologies and Their Game-Changing Potential: Lessons from Corporate World.* Contemporary Studies of Risks in Emerging Technology.

Shaltout, M. S. A. F., & Salamah, A. I. B. (2013, May). The impact of Web 3.0 on E-Learning. In *2013 Fourth International Conference on e-Learning" Best Practices in Management, Design and Development of e-Courses: Standards of Excellence and Creativity"* (pp. 227-232). IEEE. 10.1109/ECONF.2013.70

Sharifi, S., Parvizimosaed, A., Amyot, D., Logrippo, L., & Mylopoulos, J. (2020, August). Symboleo: Towards a specification language for legal contracts. In *2020 IEEE 28th international requirements engineering conference (RE)* (pp. 364-369). IEEE.

Sharma, R. (2021a). *Non-Fungible Token Definition: Understanding NFTs.* Investopedia. https://www.investopedia.com/non-fungible-tokens-nft-5115211

Sharma, R., & Datta, A. (2012) Supernova: super-peers based architecture for decentralized online social networks. In: Proceedings ofCOMSNETS, (pp. 1–10). IEEE. doi:10.1109/COMSNETS.2012.6151349

Sharma, T., Zhou, Z., Huang, Y., & Wang, Y. (2022). *'It's A Blessing and A Curse': Unpacking Creators' Practices with Non-Fungible Tokens (NFTs) and Their Communities.* doi:10.48550/arXiv.2201.13233

Sharma, V. (2021b). *What is the Metaverse? Beginner's Guide.* Quytech Blog. https://www.quytech.com/blog/what-is-metaverse/

Sharma, V., & Halevi, T. (2022). A Survey on Research Directions in Blockchain Applications Usability. In *Proceedings of Seventh International Congress on Information and Communication Technology* (pp.727–738). Springer. 10.1007/978-981-19-1610-6_64

Sharma, A., Tomar, R., Chilamkurti, N., & Kim, B. G. (2020). Blockchain based smart contracts for internet of medical things in e-healthcare. *Electronics (Basel)*, *9*(10), 1609. doi:10.3390/electronics9101609

Sheridan, D., Harris, J., Wear, F., Cowell, J., Jr., Wong, E., & Yazdinejad, A. (2022). Web3 challenges and opportunities for the market. arXiv preprint arXiv:2209.02446.

Shilina, S. (2022). *A comprehensive study on Non-Fungible Tokens (NFTs): Use cases, ecosystem, benefits & challenges.* Research Gate. . doi:10.13140/RG.2.2.15324.67206

Shivalingaiah, D., & Naik, U. (2008). *Comparative study of web 1.0, web 2.0 and web 3.0.*

Shrestha, R., & Kim, S. (2019). Integration of IoT with blockchain and homomorphic encryption: Challenging issues and opportunities. *Advances in Computers*, *115*, 293–331. doi:10.1016/bs.adcom.2019.06.002

Shu, K., Bhattacharjee, A., Alatawi, F., Nazer, T. H., Ding, K., Karami, M., & Liu, H. (2020). Combating disinformation in a social media age. *Wiley Interdisciplinary Reviews. Data Mining and Knowledge Discovery*, *10*(6), e1385. doi:10.1002/widm.1385

Siegel, D. (2016). *Understanding The DAO Attack*. CoinDesk.

Si, H., Sun, C., Li, Y., Qiao, H., & Shi, L. (2019). IoT information sharing security mechanism based on blockchain technology. *Future Generation Computer Systems*, *101*, 1028–1040. doi:10.1016/j.future.2019.07.036

Simran, S., & Adam, R. (2023). Legal Analysis Of Cbdc's Role As A Digital Payment Instrument Regulatory System In Indonesia. *Asian Journal of Management. Entrepreneurship and Social Science*, *3*(03), 270–286.

Sims, A. (2019). *Blockchain and decentralised autonomous organisations (DAOs): the evolution of companies?*

SimsA. (2021). Decentralised Autonomous Organisations: Governance, Dispute Resolution and Regulation. SSRN. doi:10.2139/ssrn.3971228

Singh, S. (2023, April 14). What are cross-border payments, and how do they work? *Cointelegraph*. https://cointelegraph.com/explained/what-are-cross-border-payments-and-how-do-they-work

Singh, A., Click, K., Parizi, R. M., Zhang, Q., Dehghantanha, A., & Choo, K.-K. R. (2020). Sidechain technologies in blockchain networks: An examination and state-of-the-art review. *Journal of Network and Computer Applications*, *149*, 102471. doi:10.1016/j.jnca.2019.102471

Singh, A., Parizi, R. M., Zhang, Q., Choo, K. K. R., & Dehghantanha, A. (2020). Blockchain smart contracts formalization: Approaches and challenges to address vulnerabilities. *Computers & Security*, *88*, 101654. doi:10.1016/j.cose.2019.101654

Singh, C., Wojewska, A. N., Persson, U. M., & Bager, S. L. (2022). Coffee producers' perspectives of blockchain technology in the context of sustainable global value chains. *Frontiers in Blockchain*, *5*, 955463. doi:10.3389/fbloc.2022.955463

Siripipatthanakul, S., & Siripipattanakul, S. (2023). Gamification and Edutainment in 21st Century Learning. Multidisciplinary Approaches to Research, 2, 210-219.

Slater, M. (2009). Place illusion and plausibility can lead to realistic behaviour in immersive virtual environments. *Philosophical Transactions of the Royal Society of London. Series B, Biological Sciences*, *364*(1535), 3549–3557. doi:10.1098/rstb.2009.0138 PMID:19884149

Slocum, T. A., McMaster, R. M., Kessler, F. C., Howard, H. H., & Mc Master, R. B. (2008). *Thematic cartography and geographic visualization.*

Smart Contracts Alliance. (2016). Smart contracts: 12 use cases for business & beyond. Chamber of Digital Commerce. Washington D.C.

Smith, M., Szongott, C., Henne, B., & von Voigt, G. (2012). Big data privacy issues in public social media. In *2012 6th IEEE International Conference on Digital Ecosystems and Technologies (DEST)* (pp. 1-6). Campione d'Italia, Italy. 10.1109/DEST.2012.6227909

Smith, R. (2022). NPD with the Metaverse, NFTs, and Crypto. *Research Technology Management*, *65*(5), 54–56. doi:10.1080/08956308.2022.2090182

Sobral, T., Galvão, T., & Borges, J. (2019). Visualization of urban mobility data from intelligent transportation systems. In Sensors (Switzerland), 19(2). doi:10.339019020332

Solouki, M., & Bamakan, S. M. H. (2022). An in-depth insight at digital ownership through dynamic NFTs. *Procedia Computer Science*, *214*, 875–882. doi:10.1016/j.procs.2022.11.254

Song, L., Ju, X., Zhu, Z., & Li, M. (2021). An access control model for the Internet of Things based on zero-knowledge token and blockchain. *EURASIP Journal on Wireless Communications and Networking*, *2021*(1), 1–20. doi:10.118613638-021-01986-4

Sookhak, M., Jabbarpour, M. R., Safa, N. S., & Yu, F. R. (2021). Blockchain and smart contract for access control in healthcare: A survey, issues and challenges, and open issues. *Journal of Network and Computer Applications*, *178*, 102950. doi:10.1016/j.jnca.2020.102950

Sorokin, L. (2022). A Peek into the Future of Decentralized Identity (v2). *IDPro Body of Knowledge, 1*(7).

Spagnuolo, M., Maggi, F., & Zanero, S. (2014). *BitIodine: Extracting Intelligence from the Bitcoin Network, Financial Cryptography, ser* (Vol. 8437). Lecture Notes in Computer Science. Springer.

Spathoulas, G., Negka, L., Pandey, P., & Katsikas, S. (2021). Can Blockchain Technology Enhance Security and Privacy in the Internet of Things? Advances in Core Computer Science-Based Technologies: Papers in Honor of Professor Nikolaos Alexandris.

Statista. (2022). Total Value of Blockchain Transactions Worldwide from 2017 to 2021. Statista. https://www.statista.com/statistics/647231/worldwide-blockchain-transactions/

Statista. (2023). *Coffee—Worldwide*. Statista. https://www.statista.com/outlook/cmo/hot-drinks/coffee/worldwide

Steinkuehler, C. A., & Williams, D. (2006). Where everybody knows your (screen) name: Online games as "third places". *Journal of Computer-Mediated Communication*, *11*(4), 885–909. doi:10.1111/j.1083-6101.2006.00300.x

Stephenson, N. (1992). *Snow Crash*. Bantam Books.

Stephenson, N. (2003). *Snow crash: A novel*. Spectra.

Steuer, J. (1995). Defining Virtual Reality: Dimensions Determining Telepresence. *Journal of Communication*, *42*(4), 73–93. doi:10.1111/j.1460-2466.1992.tb00812.x

Storublevtcev, N. (2019). Cryptography in blockchain. In *Computational Science and Its Applications–ICCSA 2019: 19th International Conference, Saint Petersburg, Russia, July 1–4, 2019 Proceedings, 19*(Part II), 495–508.

Stroh, J. (2023). *DAOs, Web 3, Decentralization, Governance. Blockchance 2023 Hamburg*. Conference Keynote.

Stutzbach, D., & Rejaie, R. (2006). Understanding churn in peer-to-peer networks. In *Proceedings of IMC* (pp. 189-202). ACM. 10.1145/1177080.1177105

Suanpang, P., Niamsorn, C., Pothipassa, P., Chunhapataragul, T., Netwong, T., & Jermsittiparsert, K. (2022). Extensible Metaverse Implication for a Smart Tourism City. *Sustainability (Switzerland)*, *14*(21), 14027. Advance online publication. doi:10.3390u142114027

Sulkowski, A. (2019). Industry 4.0 Industry 4.0 era technology (AI, big data, blockchain, DAO): Why the law needs new memes. *Kan. JL & Pub. Pol'y*, *29*, 1.

Sundararajan, A. (2016). *The Sharing Economy: The End of Employment and the Rise of Crowd-Based Capitalism*. MIT Press.

Sung, Y., Moon, J., & Lin, J. S. (2011). Actual self vs. avatar self: The effect of online social situation on self-expression. *Journal of Virtual Worlds Research*, *4*(1). doi:10.4101/jvwr.v4i1.1927

Sunny, J., Undralla, N., & Madhusudanan Pillai, V. (2020). Supply chain transparency through blockchain-based traceability: An overview with demonstration. *Computers & Industrial Engineering, 150*, 106895. doi:10.1016/j.cie.2020.106895

Suo, H., Wan, J., Zou, C., & Liu, J. (2012). Security in the internet of things: A review. *265 Proceedings - 2012 International Conference on Computer Science and Electronics Engineering.* IEEE.

Supply Chain Innovators. (2022, October 21). *How Topl Uses Blockchain to Create a More Transparent Supply Chain.* https://www.supplychaininnovators.io/post/how-blockchain-can-improve-supplychain

Suryono, R. R., Budi, I., & Purwandari, B. (2020). Challenges and trends of financial technology (Fintech): A systematic literature review. *Information (Basel), 11*(12), 590. doi:10.3390/info11120590

Swan, M. (2021). *What is Decentralized Finance (DeFi)?* CoinMarketCap. https://coinmarketcap.com/alexandria/article/what-is-decentralized-finance-defi

Swan, M. (2015). *Blockchain: Blueprint for a New Economy.* O'Reilly Media, Inc.

Swathi, E., Vivek, G., & Rani, G. S. (2016). Role of Hash Function in Cryptography. *International Journal of Advanced Engineering Research and Science.* doi:10.22161/ijaers/si.3

Szabo, N. (1996). Smart contracts: Building blocks for digital markets. EXTROPY. *The Journal of Transhumanist Thought, 16*, 18–26.

Szabo, N. (1997). Formalizing and securing relationships on public networks. *First Monday, 2*(9). doi:10.5210/fm.v2i9.548

Szczepanska, T., Antosz, P., Berndt, J. O., Borit, M., Chattoe-Brown, E., Mehryar, S., Meyer, R., Onggo, S., & Verhagen, H. (2022). GAM on! Six ways to explore social complexity by combining games and agent-based models. *International Journal of Social Research Methodology, 25*(4), 541–555. doi:10.1080/13645579.2022.2050119

Taherdoost, H. (2023). Smart Contracts in Blockchain Technology: A Critical Review. *Information (Basel), 14*(2), 117. doi:10.3390/info14020117

Takaragi, K., & Kubota, T. (2023). A Proposal for Enhancing the Security and Privacy of Digital Currencies. In Government Response to Disruptive Innovation: Perspectives and Examinations (pp. 183-211). IGI Global. doi:10.4018/978-1-6684-6429-8.ch010

Tanaka, K., Nakamura, S., Ohshima, H., Yamamoto, Y., Yanbe, Y., & Kato, M. P. (2010). Improving Search and Information Credibility Analysis from Interaction between Web1. 0 and Web2. 0 Content. *Journal of Software, 5*(2), 154–159. doi:10.4304/jsw.5.2.154-159

Tapscott, [First Name Needed]. (2020). Financial services: Building blockchain one block at a time. *Financial Times.*

Tapscott, D., & Tapscott, A. (2016). *Blockchain revolution: how the technology behind bitcoin is changing money, business, and the world.* Penguin.

Tassi, P. (2020). Fortnite's Travis Scott Concert Was a Stunning Spectacle and a Glimpse at the Metaverse. *Forbes.* https://www.forbes.com/sites/paultassi/2020/04/23/fortnites-travis-scott-concert-was-a-stunning-spectacle-and-a-glimpse-at-the-metaverse/?sh=b07798a2e1f5

Tatavarti, S. (2022). How the metaverse can be a force for good in an uncertain world. *World Economic Forum.*

Teutsch, J., & Masmej, A. (2021). *Oracles: The State of the Art and Future Directions.* Chainlink. Retrieved from https://research.chain.link/whitepaper-v2.pdf.

Tham, A., & Sigala, M. (2020). Road block(chain): bit(coin)s for tourism sustainable development goals? *Journal of Hospitality and Tourism Technology.* . doi:10.1108/JHTT-05-2019-0069

The Economist. (2015). *The trust machine: The technology behind bitcoin could transform how the economy works.* The Economist. https://www.economist.com/leaders/2015/10/31/the-trust-machine

Themistocleous, M., Christodoulou, K., & Iosif, E. (2023). Academic certificates issued on blockchain: the case of the University of Nicosia and Block. co. In *Supporting Higher Education 4.0 with Blockchain* (pp. 166–178). Routledge. doi:10.4324/9781003318736-8

Thompson, S. (2017). The preservation of digital signatures on the blockchain. *See Also, 3*. doi:10.14288a.v0i3.188841

Thorat, N. B., & Sreevardhan, C. (2014). Survey On Security Threats And Solutions For Near Field Communication. *International Journal of Research in Engineering and Technology, 3*(12).

Tian, S., Zhao, B., & Olivares, R. O. (2023). Cybersecurity risks and central banks' sentiment on central bank digital currency: Evidence from global cyberattacks. *Finance Research Letters, 53*, 103609. doi:10.1016/j.frl.2022.103609

Tian, Y., Wang, Z., Xiong, J., & Ma, J. (2020). A Blockchain-Based Secure Key Management Scheme With Trustworthiness in DWSNs. *IEEE Transactions on Industrial Informatics, 16*(9), 6193–6202. doi:10.1109/TII.2020.2965975

Tillema, S., Trapp, R., & van Veen, D. P. (2022). Business Partnering in Risk Management: A Resilience Perspective on Management Accountants' Responses to a Role Change. *Contemporary Accounting Research, 39*(3), 2058–2089. https://doi-org.ezproxy.myucwest.ca/10.1111/1911-3846.12774. doi:10.1111/1911-3846.12774

Tlili, A., Huang, R., & Kinshuk, X. (2023). Metaverse for climbing the ladder toward 'Industry 5.0' and 'Society 5.0'? *Service Industries Journal, 43*(3-4), 1–28. doi:10.1080/02642069.2023.2178644

Tomescu, A., & Devadas, S. (2017). Catena: Efficient non-equivocation via bitcoin. *38th IEEE Symposium on Security and Privacy.* IEEE.

Tomescu, A., & Devadas, S. (2017). Efficient non-equivocation via bitcoin. *38th IEEE Symposium on Security and Privacy (SP),* (pp. 393–409). IEEE. (2017).

Tomlinson, R. F. (1969). A Geographic Information System for Regional Planning. [Chigaku Zasshi]. *The Journal of Geography, 78*(1), 45–48. doi:10.5026/jgeography.78.45

Tom, R. J., Sankaranarayanan, S., & Rodrigues, J. J. (2020). Agent negotiation in an IoT-fog based power distribution system for demand reduction. *Sustainable Energy Technologies and Assessments, 38*, 100653. doi:10.1016/j.seta.2020.100653

Tonelli, R., Pierro, G., Ortu, M., & Destefanis, G. (2023). Smart Contracts Software Metrics: A First Study. *PLoS One, 18*(4), e0281043. doi:10.1371/journal.pone.0281043 PMID:37043512

Topl. (2023a). Dual Innovation: How Topl's technology unlocks a new impact economy. *Topl.* https://topl.co/manifesto/

Topl. (2023b). *Topl: Unlocking the economic potential of positive impact.* Topl. https://topl.co/

Treiblmaier, H., Leung, D., Kwok, A. O. J., & Tham, A. (2020). Cryptocurrency adoption in travel and tourism – an exploratory study of Asia Pacific travellers. *Current Issues in Tourism,* 1–17. doi:10.1080/13683500.2020.1863928

Treleaven, P., Brown, R. G., & Yang, D. (2017). Blockchain technology in finance. *Computer, 50*(9), 14–17. doi:10.1109/MC.2017.3571047

Trepte, S. (2021). The Social Media Privacy Model: Privacy and Communication in the Light of Social Media Affordances. *Communication Theory, 31*(4), 549–570. doi:10.1093/ct/qtz035

Triantafyllou, S. A., & Georgiadis, C. K. (2022). Gamification Design Patterns for User Engagement. *Informatics in Education*, *21*(4), 655–674. doi:10.15388/infedu.2022.27

Trivedi, S., Mehta, K., & Sharma, R. (2021). Systematic literature review on application of blockchain technology in E-finance and financial services. *Journal of Technology Management & Innovation*, *16*(3), 89–102. doi:10.4067/S0718-27242021000300089

Tröster, B. (2020). *Blockchain technologies for commodity value chains: The solution for more sustainability?* (Research Report 27). ÖFSE Briefing Paper. https://www.econstor.eu/handle/10419/224986

Tsai, W.-T., Blower, R., Zhu, Y., & Yu, L. (2016, March 1). *A System View of Financial Blockchains*. IEEE Xplore. doi:10.1109/SOSE.2016.66

Turk, A. (2021). Decentraland: A virtual world powered by Ethereum. *Decentraland*. https://decentraland.org/

Tussyadiah, I. P., & Pesonen, J. (2016). Impacts of peer-to-peer accommodation use on travel patterns. *Journal of Travel Research*, *55*(8), 1022–1040. doi:10.1177/0047287515608505

U.S. Bureau of Labour Statistics. (2022). *Accountants and Auditors*. BLS. https://www.bls.gov/ooh/business-and-financial/accountants-and-auditors.htm#tab-3

U.S. Securities and Exchange Commission. (2023a). *Press Release SEC Files 13 Charges Against Binance Entities and Founder Changpeng Zhao*. https://www.sec.gov/news/press-release/2023-101

U.S. Securities and Exchange Commission. (2023b). *Press Release SEC Charges Coinbase for Operating as an Unregistered Securities Exchange, Broker, and Clearing Agency*. https://www.sec.gov/news/press-release/2023-102

Uddin, M. A., Stranieri, A., Gondal, I., & Balasubramanian, V. (2020). Dynamically recommending repositories for health data: a machine learning model. *Australasian Computer Science Week Multiconference*. ACM.

Uddin, M. A., Stranieri, A., Gondal, I., & Balasubramanian, V. (2020). Blockchain leveraged decentralized IoT ehealth framework. *Internet of Things*, *9*, 100159. doi:10.1016/j.iot.2020.100159

Uddin, M. A., Stranieri, A., Gondal, I., & Balasubramanian, V. (2021, June). A survey on the adoption of blockchain in IoT: Challenges and solutions. *Blockchain: Research and Applications*, *2*(2), 100006.

Ukpere, C. L., Slabbert, A. D., & Ukpere, W. (2014). A relationship between social media platforms and the financial success of modern African entrepreneurs. *Mediterranean Journal of Social Sciences*, *5*(4), 479. doi:10.5901/mjss.2014.v5n4p479

Ünekbas, S. (2022, July 4). *Diligence is Due Indeed: Competition Law as a Barrier to Sustainable Supply Chains?* Kluwer Competition Law Blog. https://competitionlawblog.kluwercompetitionlaw.com/2022/07/04/diligence-is-due-indeed-competition-law-as-a-barrier-to-sustainable-supply-chains/

University of Nevada. (2023). *7 worst accounting scandals in U.S. history*. University of Nevada. https://onlinedegrees.unr.edu/blog/worst-accounting-scandals/

Ur. Rahman, M., Guidi, B., & Baiardi, F. (2020). Blockchain-based access control management for Decentralized Online Social Networks. *Journal of Parallel and Distributed Computing*, *144*, 41–54. doi:10.1016/j.jpdc.2020.05.011

Usman, M., & Qamar, U. (2020). Secure electronic medical records storage and sharing using blockchain technology. *Procedia Computer Science*, *174*, 321–327. doi:10.1016/j.procs.2020.06.093

Vailshery, L. (2022). *Number of IoT connected devices worldwide 2019-2021, with forecasts to 2030*. Statista. https://www.statista.com/statistics/1183457/iot-connected-devices-worldwide/

Valaskova, K., Machova, V., & Lewis, E. (2022). Virtual Marketplace Dynamics Data, Spatial Analytics, and Customer Engagement Tools in a Real-Time Interoperable Decentralized Metaverse. *Linguistic and Philosophical Investigations*, *21*(0), 105–120. doi:10.22381/lpi2120227

Valenta, L., & Rowan, B. (2015). *Blindcoin: Blinded, Accountable Mixes for Bitcoin, Financial Cryptography Workshops, ser* (Vol. 8976). Lecture Notes in Computer Science. Springer.

Van der Heijden, B. I. J. M., Burgers, M. J., Kaan, A. M., Lamberts, B. F., & Koen Migchelbrink, R. C. P. M. (2020). Van den Ouweland, and T. Meijer. "Gamification in dutch businesses: An explorative case study. *SAGE Open*, *10*(4), 2158244020972371. doi:10.1177/2158244020972371

van der Linden, R. W., & Łasak, P. (2023). The Digitalization of Cross-Border Payment Systems and the Introduction of the CBDC. In *Financial Interdependence, Digitalization and Technological Rivalries: Perspectives on Future Cooperation and Integration in Sino-American Financial Systems* (pp. 75–92). Springer Nature Switzerland. doi:10.1007/978-3-031-27845-7_7

van Dijck, J. (2013). *The Culture of Connectivity: A Critical History of Social Media*. Oxford University Press. doi:10.1093/acprof:oso/9780199970773.001.0001

van Meerten, M., Ozkan, B. K., & Panichella, A. (2023, May). Evolutionary Approach for Concurrency Testing of Ripple Blockchain Consensus Algorithm. *In 2023 IEEE/ACM 45th International Conference on Software Engineering: Software Engineering in Practice (ICSE-SEIP)* (pp. 36-47). IEEE.

Van VulpenP.JansenS. (2023). Decentralized Autonomous Organization Design for the Commons and the Common Good. doi:10.2139/ssrn.4418782

Vandervort, D. (2014). Challenges and Opportunities Associated with a BitcoinBased Transaction Rating System. In. Lecture Notes in Computer Science: Vol. 8438. *Financial Cryptography Workshops, ser* (pp. 33–42). Springer. doi:10.1007/978-3-662-44774-1_3

Vardhini, B., Dass, S. N., Sahana, R., & Chinnaiyan, R. (2021, January). A blockchain based electronic medical health records framework using smart contracts. In *2021 International Conference on Computer Communication and Informatics (ICCCI)* (pp. 1-4). IEEE.

Venugopal, J. P., Subramanian, A. A. V., & Peatchimuthu, J. (2023). The realm of metaverse: A survey. *Computer Animation and Virtual Worlds*, e2150. doi:10.1002/cav.2150

Verhoeven, P., Sinn, F., & Herden, T. (2018). Examples from Blockchain Implementations in Logistics and Supply Chain Management: Exploring the Mindful Use of a New Technology. *Logistics*, *2*(3), 20. doi:10.3390/logistics2030020

Vi, C. T., Ablart, D., Gatti, E., Velasco, C., & Obrist, M. (2017). Not just seeing, but also feeling art: Mid-air haptic experiences integrated in a multisensory art exhibition. *International Journal of Human-Computer Studies*, *108*, 1–14. doi:10.1016/j.ijhcs.2017.06.004

Vidgren, N., Haataja, K., Pati, L., & Jos, J. (2013). Security Threats in ZigBee-Enabled Systems: Vulnerability Evaluation, Practical Experiments, Countermeasures, and Lessons Learned. *46th Hawaii International Conference on System Sciences*. IEEE. 10.1109/HICSS.2013.475

Vijayan, V., Connolly, J. P., Condell, J., McKelvey, N., & Gardiner, P. (2021). Review of wearable devices and data collection considerations for connected health. *Sensors (Basel)*, *21*(16), 5589. doi:10.339021165589 PMID:34451032

Voon Kiong, L. (2022). *Web3 Made Easy: A Comprehensive Guide to Web3: Everything you need to know about Web3, Blockchain, DeFi, Metaverse, NFT and GameFi*. Xiang Xiang Liew.

Voora, V., Bermúdez, S., & Larrea, C. (2022). *Global Market Report: Coffee* (Sustainable Commodities Marketplace Series, pp. 1–34) [Standards and Value Chains]. International Institute for Sustainable Development (IISD). https://www.iisd.org/system/files/publications/ssi-global-market-report-coffee.pdf

Voshmgir, S. (2020). Token Economy: How the web 3 reinvents the Internet. *Token Kitchen.* https://books.google.com.pk/books?hl=en&lr=&id=vWo-EAAAQBAJ&oi=fnd&pg=PT6&dq=Unlike+Web2+ecosystems

Voshmgir, S. (2020). *Token Economy: How the Web3 reinvents the Internet* (Vol. 2). Token Kitchen.

Vosoughi, S., Roy, D., & Aral, S. (2018). The spread of true and false news online. *Science, 359*(6380), 1146–1151. doi:10.1126cience.aap9559 PMID:29590045

Vučinić, M. (2020). Fintech and financial stability potential influence of FinTech on financial stability, risks and benefits. *Journal of Central Banking Theory and Practice, 9*(2), 43–66. doi:10.2478/jcbtp-2020-0013

Vujičić, D., Jagodić, D., & Ranđić, S. (2018, March). Blockchain technology, bitcoin, and Ethereum: A brief overview. In *2018 17th international symposium infoteh-jahorina (infoteh)* (pp. 1-6). IEEE. 10.1109/INFOTEH.2018.8345547

Vukolić, M. (2016). The quest for scalable blockchain fabric: Proof-of-work vs. BFT replication. In *Open Problems in Network Security: IFIP WG 11.4 International Workshop, iNetSec 2015, Zurich, Switzerland, October 29, 2015, Revised Selected Papers* (pp. 112-125). Springer International Publishing.

W3C. (2004). *W3C semantic web activity.* https://www.w3.org/2001/sw/

Wallgren, L., Raza, S., & Voigt, T. (2013). Routing attacks and countermeasures in the RPLbased internet of things. *International Journal of Distributed Sensor Networks, 2013*(II), 794326. doi:10.1155/2013/794326

Walsh, K., & Sirer, E. G. (2006, May). Experience with an Object Reputation System for Peer-to-Peer Filesharing. In NSDI (Vol. 6, pp. 1-1).

Wan, S., Lin, H., Gan, W., Chen, J., & Yu, P. S. (2023). Web 3: The Next Internet Revolution. arXiv preprint arXiv:2304.06111.

Wan, S., Lin, H., Gan, W., Chen, J., & Yu, P. S. (2023). Web3: The Next Internet Revolution. arXiv preprint arXiv:2304.06111.

Wan, S., Lin, H., Gan, W., Chen, J., & Yu, P. S. (2023). Web3: The Next Internet Revolution. ArXiv. Retrieved from https://arxiv.org/abs/2304.06111

Wang, Q., Li, R., Wang, Q., & Chen, S. (2021). Non-fungible token (NFT): Overview, evaluation, opportunities and challenges. arXiv preprint arXiv:2105.07447.

Wang, J. (2022). Research on the construction of accounting information audit quality control system based on blockchain. *Security and Privacy, 6*(2), e227. doi:10.1002py2.227

Wang, P., Zhu, J., & Ma, Q. (2023). Private Data Protection in Social Networks Based on Blockchain. *International Journal of Advanced Networking and Applications., 14*(04), 5549–5555. doi:10.35444/IJANA.2023.14407

Wang, R., & Chan-Olmsted, S. (2020). Content marketing strategy of branded YouTube channels. *Journal of Media Business Studies, 17*(3-4), 294–316. doi:10.1080/16522354.2020.1783130

Wang, S., Ding, W., Li, Y., Ouyang, L., & Wang, F. (2019). Decentralized autonomous organizations: Concept, model, and applications. *Institute of Electrical and Electronics Engineers (IEEE). Transactions on Computational Social Systems, 6*(5), 870–878. doi:10.1109/TCSS.2019.2938190

Wang, S., Ouyang, L., Yuan, Y., Ni, X., Han, X., & Wang, F. Y. (2019). Blockchain-enabled smart contracts: Architecture, applications, and future trends. *IEEE Transactions on Systems, Man, and Cybernetics. Systems*, *49*(11), 2266–2277. doi:10.1109/TSMC.2019.2895123

Wang, W., Gan, H., Wang, X., Lu, H., & Huang, Y. (2022). Initiatives and challenges in using gamification in transportation: A systematic mapping. *European Transport Research Review*, *14*(1), 1–19. doi:10.118612544-022-00567-w

Wang, Y., Song, W., Tao, W., Liotta, A., Yang, D., Li, X., Gao, S., Sun, Y., Ge, W., Zhang, W., & Zhang, W. (2022). A systematic review on affective computing: Emotion models, databases, and recent advances. *Information Fusion*, *83-84*, 19–52. doi:10.1016/j.inffus.2022.03.009

Wang, Z. (2023). Money Laundering and the Privacy Design of Central Bank Digital Currency. *Review of Economic Dynamics*. doi:10.1016/j.red.2023.06.004

Ward, O., & Rochemont, S. (2019). Understanding central bank digital currencies (CBDC). *Institute and Faculty of Actuaries*, 1-52.

Watanabe, H., Fujimura, S., Nakadaira, A., Miyazaki, Y., Akutsu, A., & Kishigami, J. (2016, January). Blockchain contract: Securing a blockchain applied to smart contracts. In 2016 IEEE international conference on consumer electronics (ICCE) (pp. 467-468). IEEE.

Weber, H., Wiek, A., & Lang, D. J. (2020). Sustainability entrepreneurship to address large distances in international food supply. *BUSINESS STRATEGY & DEVELOPMENT*, *3*(3), 318–331. doi:10.1002/bsd2.97

Weekly, K., & Pister, K. (2012) Evaluating Sinkhole Defense Techniques In RPL Networks. *IEEE International Conference on Network Protocols*. IEEE. 10.1109/ICNP.2012.6459948

Wei, Y., Di, L., Liao, G., Zhao, B., Chen, A., & Bai, Y. (2009). Sharing of distributed geospatial data through grid technology. In Handbook of Research on Geoinformatics. doi:10.4018/978-1-59140-995-3.ch028

Weinberger, M. (2022). What Is Metaverse?—A Definition Based on Qualitative Meta-Synthesis. *Future Internet*, *14*(11), 310. doi:10.3390/fi14110310

Wellman, B., Salaff, J., Dimitrova, D., Garton, L., Gulia, M., & Haythornthwaite, C. (1996). Computer networks as social networks: Collaborative work, telework, and virtual community. *Annual Review of Sociology*, *293*(1), 2031–2034. doi:10.1146/annurev.soc.22.1.213

Werbach, K. (2018). *The Blockchain and the New Architecture of Trust*. MIT Press. doi:10.7551/mitpress/11449.001.0001

Werbach, K., & Cornell, N. (2017). Contracts Ex Machina. *Duke Law Journal*, *67*(2), 313–382.

White, B., Mahanti, A., & Passi, K. (2022, April). Characterizing the OpenSea NFT marketplace. In *Companion Proceedings of the Web Conference 2022* (pp. 488-496). 10.1145/3487553.3524629

Wiki. (2023). *Metaverse*. https://en.wikipedia.org/wiki/Metaverse

WikiWand. (2023). *CaseWare International*. WikiWand. https://www.wikiwand.com/en/CaseWare_International

Wilkinson, S. (2018). *Storj A Peer-to-Peer Cloud Storage Network*. Storj Labs. https://storj.io/storj.pdf

WilliamsonO. E. (1975). Markets and hierarchies: Analysis and antitrust implications: A study in the economics of internal organisation. SSRN https://ssrn.com/abstract=1496220

Williamson, O. E. (1991). Comparative economic organization: The Analysis of discrete structural alternatives. *Administrative Science Quarterly*, *36*(2), 269–296. doi:10.2307/2393356

Wilmer, W. (2023). Different designs of CBDC, the likelihood of bank disintermediation and the impact on monetary policy: a literary review.

Wilson, D., & Ateniese, G. (2015). *From Pretty Good To Great: Enhancing PGP using Bitcoin and the Blockchain.* CoRR.

Wilson, K. B., Karg, A., & Ghaderi, H. (2021). Prospecting non-fungible tokens in the digital economy: Stakeholders and ecosystem, risk and opportunity. *Business Horizons.* doi:10.1016/j.bushor.2021.10.007

Winter, T., Thubert, P., Brandt, A., Hui, J., Kelsey, R., Levis, P., Pister, K., Struik, R., Vasseur, J., & Alexander, R. (2012). RPL: IPv6 Routing Protocol for Low-Power and Lossy Networks. *Network Architectures and Services.*

Wood, G. (2014). *ÐApps: What Web 3.0 Looks Like.* Gavwood. https://gavwood.com/dappsweb3.html

Wood, G. (2014). Ethereum: A secure decentralised generalised transaction ledger. *Ethereum project yellow paper, 151*(2014), 1-32.

Wood, G. (2014). Ethereum: A secure decentralised generalised transaction ledger. *Ethereum project yellow paper*, 151, 1-32.

Wood, G. (2014). Ethereum: A secure decentralized generalized transaction ledger. *Ethereum Project Yellow Paper, 151*(2014), 1-32.

Wood, G. (2016). Polkadot: Vision for a heterogeneous multi-chain framework. *White paper, 21*(2327), 4662.

World Economic Forum. (2022). *Decentralized Autonomous Organizations: Beyond the Hype.* White paper, pp. 1-24. https://www3.weforum.org/docs/WEF_Decentralized_Autonomous_Organizations_Beyond_the_Hype_2022.pdf

World Economic Forum. (2023). *Pathways to the Regulation of Crypto-Assets: A Global Approach May 2023.* https://www3.weforum.org/docs/WEF_Pathways_to_the_Regulation_of_Crypto_Assets_2023.pdf

Worner, D., & von Bomhard, T. (2014). When your sensor earns money: ¨ exchanging data for cash with Bitcoin. In *UbiComp Adjunct* (pp. 295–298). ACM. doi:10.1145/2638728.2638786

Wright, A. (2021). The Rise of Decentralized Autonomous Organizations: Opportunities and Challenges. *Stanford Journal of Blockchain Law & Policy.* https://stanford-jblp.pubpub.org/pub/rise-of-daos

Wright, A. (2021). The Rise of Decentralized Autonomous Organizations: Opportunities and Challenges. *Stanford Journal of Blockchain Law & Policy.* https://stanford-jblp.pubpub.org/pub/rise-of-daos/release/1

Wright, A. (2023). DAOs & ADSs. IEEE 15th International Symposium on Autonomous Decentralized System (ISADS), (pp. 1-6). IEEE. 10.1109/ISADS56919.2023.10091973

WrightA.De FilippiP. (2015). Decentralized Blockchain Technology and the Rise of Lex Cryptographia. Available at SSRN 2580664. doi:10.2139/ssrn.2580664

Wu, H., Zheng, W., Chiesa, A., & Popa, R. (2018). *DIZK: A Distributed Zero Knowledge Proof System Open access to the Proceedings of the 27th USENIX Security Symposium.* USENIX. . https://www.usenix.org/system/files/conference/usenixsecurity18/sec18-wu.pdf

Wu, T. C., & Ho, C. T. B. (2023). A scoping review of metaverse in emergency medicine. In Australasian Emergency Care (Vol. 26, Issue 1). doi:10.1016/j.auec.2022.08.002

Wu, R., Ishfaq, K., Hussain, S., Asmi, F., Siddiquei, A. N., & Anwar, M. A. (2022). Investigating e-Retailers' Intentions to Adopt Cryptocurrency Considering the Mediation of Technostress and Technology Involvement. *Sustainability, 14*(2), 641. doi:10.3390u14020641

Wüst, K., & Gervais, A. (2018). Do you Need a Blockchain? *2018 Crypto Valley Conference on Blockchain Technology (CVCBT)*, (pp. 45–54). IEEE. 10.1109/CVCBT.2018.00011

Wu, T. (2003). Network neutrality, broadband discrimination. *Journal on Telecommunications & High Technology Law*, 2, 141.

Xie, J., Yu, F. R., Huang, T., Xie, R., Liu, J., & Liu, Y. (2019). A Survey on the Scalability of Blockchain Systems. *IEEE Network*, *33*(5), 166–173. doi:10.1109/MNET.001.1800290

Xie, R., Wang, Y., Tan, M., Zhu, W., Yang, Z., Wu, J., & Jeon, G. (2020). Ethereum-blockchain-based technology of decentralized smart contract certificate system. *IEEE Internet of Things Magazine*, *3*(2), 44–50. doi:10.1109/IOTM.0001.1900094

Xiong, W., & Xiong, L. (2019). Smart contract based data trading mode using blockchain and machine learning. *IEEE Access : Practical Innovations, Open Solutions*, *7*, 102331–102344. doi:10.1109/ACCESS.2019.2928325

Xu, X. (2013). Study on security problems and key technologies of the internet of things. *Proceedings - 2013 International Conference on Computational and Information Sciences*. IEEE.

Xu, L., Shi, H., Shen, M., Ni, Y., Zhang, X., Pang, Y., Yu, T., Lian, X., Yu, T., Yang, X., & Li, F. (2022). The effects of mHealth-based gamification interventions on participation in physical activity: Systematic review. *JMIR mHealth and uHealth*, *10*(2), e27794. doi:10.2196/27794 PMID:35113034

Xu, Z., & Chen, L. (2022). L2chain: Towards High-performance, Confidential and Secure Layer-2 Blockchain Solution for Decentralized Applications. *Proceedings of the VLDB Endowment International Conference on Very Large Data Bases*, *16*(4), 986–999. doi:10.14778/3574245.3574278

Yadav, S. P., Agrawal, K. K., Bhati, B. S., Al-Turjman, F., & Mostarda, L. (2022). Blockchain-Based Cryptocurrency Regulation: An Overview. *Computational Economics*, *59*(4), 1659–1675. doi:10.100710614-020-10050-0

Yaga, D., Mell, P., Roby, N., & Scarfone, K. (2019). Blockchain technology overview. arXiv preprint arXiv:1906.11078.

Yaga, D., Mell, P., Roby, N., & Scarfone, K. (2018). *Blockchain Technology Overview*. NIST. doi:10.6028/NIST.IR.8202

Yang, J., Wen, J., Jiang, B., & Wang, H. (2020). Blockchain-based sharing and tamper-proof framework of big data networking. *IEEE Network*, *34*(4), 62–67. doi:10.1109/MNET.011.1900374

Yang, L., Su, G., & Yuan, H. (2012). Design principles of integrated information platform for emergency responses: The case of 2008 Beijing Olympic Games. *Information Systems Research*, *23*(3 PART 1), 761–786. doi:10.1287/isre.1110.0387

Yaşar, Ş. (2022). Reflection Of Virtual Reality On Accounting Education: Transformation Of University To Metaversity. *Journal of Business in The Digital Age*, *5*(2), 95–104.

Yavin, O., & Reardon, A. J. (2021). What digital banks can learn from decentralised finance. *Journal of Digital Banking*, *5*(3), 255–263.

Yen, N. Y., Zhang, C., Waluyo, A. B., & Park, J. J. (2015). Social Media Services and Technologies Towards Web 3.0. *Multimedia Tools and Applications*, *74*(14), 5007–5013. doi:10.100711042-015-2461-4

Yeoh, P. (2017). Regulatory issues in blockchain technology. *Journal of Financial Regulation and Compliance*, *25*(2), 196–208. doi:10.1108/JFRC-08-2016-0068

Yeung, C., Liccardi, I., Lu, K., Seneviratne, O., & Berners-Lee, T. (2011). Decentralization: The Future of Online Social Networking (2nd ed.). Research Gate.

Yli-Huumo, J., Ko, D., Choi, S., Park, S., & Smolander, K. (2016). Where is current research on blockchain technology? a systematic review. *PLoS One*, *11*(10), e0163477. doi:10.1371/journal.pone.0163477 PMID:27695049

Yoo, J., Jung, Y., Shin, D., Bae, M., & Jee, E. (2019, February). Formal modeling and verification of a federated byzantine agreement algorithm for blockchain platforms. In *2019 IEEE International Workshop on Blockchain Oriented Software Engineering (IWBOSE)* (pp. 11-21). IEEE. 10.1109/IWBOSE.2019.8666514

Yousaf, I., & Yarovaya, L. (2022). Static and dynamic connectedness between NFTs, Defi and other assets: Portfolio implication. *Global Finance Journal*, *53*, 100719. doi:10.1016/j.gfj.2022.100719

Yu, G., Wang, X., Wang, Q., Bi, T., Dong, Y., Liu, R. P., & Reeves, A. (2022). Towards web 3 applications: Easing the access and transition. arXiv preprint arXiv:2210.05903.

Yu, G., Wang, X., Wang, Q., Bi, T., Dong, Y., Liu, R. P., & Reeves, A. (2022). Towards web3 applications: Easing the access and transition. arXiv preprint arXiv:2210.05903.

Yu, H., Guo, J., Cheng, Y., & Lou, Q. (2013). Techniques and Methods of Spatial Data Fusion. *Applied Mechanics and Materials*, *263–266*(PART 1), 3274–3278. doi:10.4028/WWW.SCIENTIFIC.NET/AMM.263-266.3274

Yuniartik, Y. (2023). Bitcoin Cryptocurrency Practices Sharia Maqashid Perspective. *International Journal of Humanities, Social Sciences And Business*, *2*(1), 1–10.

Yurder, Y., & Akdol, B. (2020). Social Media as a Communication Channel. In A. Özbebek Tunç & P. Aslan (Eds.), *Business Management and Communication Perspectives in Industry 4.0* (pp. 115–131). IGI Global. doi:10.4018/978-1-5225-9416-1.ch007

Yu, T. X., Wang, X. B., & Zhu, Y. X. (2019). *Blockchain technology for the 5G—enabled internet of things systems: principle, applications and challenges, 5G—Enabled Internet of Things*. CRC Press.

Zamani, M., Movahedi, M., & Raykova, M. (2018, October). Rapidchain: Scaling blockchain via full sharding. In *Proceedings of the 2018 ACM SIGSAC conference on computer and communications security* (pp. 931-948). ACM. 10.1145/3243734.3243853

Zamfir, V., Rush, A., & Asgaonkar, A. (2020). *Ethereum 2.0: A Complete Guide [Complete Source Needed]*. Ethereum.

Zamyatin, A., Harz, D., Lind, J., Panayiotou, P., Gervais, A., & Knottenbelt, W. J. (2019). XCLAIM: Trustless, *Interoperable Cryptocurrency-Backed Assets. IEEE Symposium on Security and Privacy (SP)*, (pp. 193-210). IEEE.

Zein, R., & Twinomurinzi, H. (2022). Perspective Chapter: Actor-Network Theory as an Organising Structure for Blockchain Adoption in Government. In *IntechOpen*.

Zervas, G., Proserpio, D., & Byers, J. W. (2017). The rise of the sharing economy: Estimating the impact of Airbnb on the hotel industry. *JMR, Journal of Marketing Research*, *54*(5), 687–705. doi:10.1509/jmr.15.0204

Zetzsche, B. A. (2018). The ICO Gold Rush: It's a Scam, It's a Bubble, It's a Super Challenge for Regulators. *University of Luxembourg Law Working Paper*.

Zetzsche, D. A., Anker-Sørensen, L., Passador, M. L., & Wehrli, A. (2022). *DLT-Based Enhancement of Cross-Border Payment Efficiency – a Legal and Regulatory Perspective*. BIS Working Papers No 1015.

Zetzsche, D. A., Buckley, R. P., Arner, D. W., & Föhr, L. (2018). The ICO Gold Rush: It's a Scam, It's a Bubble, It's a Super Challenge for Regulators. *University of Luxembourg Law Working Paper No. 11/2017*.

Zhang, K., & Poskitt, C. J. (2019). Annotated bibliography: Decentralized autonomous organization. SSRN Electronic Journal.

Zhang, D., Huang, T., & Duan, L. (2020). Emerging self-emissive technologies for flexible displays. *Advanced Materials*, *32*(15), 1902391. doi:10.1002/adma.201902391 PMID:31595613

Zhang, K., Liang, L., & Jin, H. (2021). Semantic web application promotion–challenges and countermeasures. *Semantic Web*, *12*(6), 931–945.

Zhang, L., Xu, H., & Hu, H. (2009, December). Design and Implementation of Web2. 0-Based XCU2. 0. In *2009 International Conference on Computational Intelligence and Software Engineering* (pp. 1-4). IEEE.

Zhang, X., Yang, D., Yow, C. H., Huang, L., Wu, X., Huang, X., Guo, J., Zhou, S., & Cai, Y. (2022). Metaverse for Cultural Heritages. *Electronics (Switzerland)*, *11*(22), 3730. doi:10.3390/electronics11223730

Zhang, Y., Pourroostaei Ardakani, S., & Han, W. (2021). Smart ledger: The blockchain-based accounting information recording protocol. *Journal of Corporate Accounting & Finance (Wiley)*, *32*(4), 147–157. https://doi-org.ezproxy.myucwest.ca/10.1002/jcaf.22515. doi:10.1002/jcaf.22515

Zhang, Y., & Wen, J. (2015). An IoT electric business model based on the protocol of bitcoin. In *ICIN* (pp. 184–191). IEEE. doi:10.1109/ICIN.2015.7073830

Zhang, Y., Wen, J., & Qian, Y. (2020). DeFi: Blockchain and the rise of decentralized financial market. *Frontiers of Computer Science*, *15*, 1–24.

Zhao, Q., Li, Y., & Xue, J. (2016). *Research on influence factors of the internet financial product consumption based on innovation diffusion theory*. CORE.

Zhao, S., Grasmuck, S., & Martin, J. (2008). Identity construction on Facebook: Digital empowerment in anchored relationships. *Computers in Human Behavior*, *24*(5), 1816–1836. doi:10.1016/j.chb.2008.02.012

Zheng, Z., Xie, S., Dai, H., Chen, X., & Wang, H. (2018). An overview of blockchain technology: Architecture, consensus, and future trends. In *2018 IEEE International Congress on Big Data (BigData Congress)* (pp. 557-564). IEEE.

Zheng, Z., Xie, S., Dai, H. N., Chen, W., Chen, X., Weng, J., & Imran, M. (2020). An overview on smart contracts: Challenges, advances and platforms. *Future Generation Computer Systems*, *105*, 475–491. doi:10.1016/j.future.2019.12.019

Zheng, Z., Xie, S., Dai, H. N., Chen, X., & Wang, H. (2018). Blockchain challenges and opportunities: A survey. *International Journal of Web and Grid Services*, *14*(4), 352–375. doi:10.1504/IJWGS.2018.095647

Zhou, Q., Huang, H., Zheng, Z., & Bian, J. (2020). Solutions to Scalability of Blockchain: A Survey. *IEEE Access : Practical Innovations, Open Solutions*, *8*, 16440–16455. doi:10.1109/ACCESS.2020.2967218

Zhou, Z. M. (2013). The role of the integrated management of spatial data in urban management. *Applied Mechanics and Materials*, *241*, 3063–3066.

Ziegler, C., & Welpe, I. (2022). A Taxonomy of Decentralized Autonomous Organizations. In *ICIS 2022 Proceedings*, 1, AISeL. https://aisel.aisnet.org/icis2022/blockchain/blockchain/1/

Zignani, M., Gaito, S., & Rossi, G. P. (2018). Follow the "Mastodon": Structure and Evolution of a Decentralized Online Social Network. *Proceedings of the International AAAI Conference on Web and Social Media, 12*(1), 541-550. 10.1609/icwsm.v12i1.14988

Zlatanova, S. (2010). Geospatial Information Technology for Emergency Response. *Disaster Prevention and Management: An International Journal*, *19*(2), 275–276. doi:10.1108/dpm.2010.19.2.275.4

Zou, T., Li, W., Liu, P., Su, X., Huang, H., Han, Y., & Guo, X. (2018). An Overview of Geospatial Information Visualization. *Proceedings of the 2018 IEEE International Conference on Progress in Informatics and Computing, PIC 2018.* IEEE. 10.1109/PIC.2018.8706332

Zou, W., Lo, D., Kochhar, P. S., Le, X. B. D., Xia, X., Feng, Y., Chen, Z., & Xu, B. (2019). Smart contract development: Challenges and opportunities. *IEEE Transactions on Software Engineering, 47*(10), 2084–2106. doi:10.1109/TSE.2019.2942301

Zubir, D., Aishah, D. N., Ali, D. A., Mokhlis, D. S., & Sulong, D. F. (2020). Doing Business using Cryptocurrency in Malaysia. *International Journal of Management and Humanities, 4*(9), 148–157. doi:10.35940/ijmh.I0899.054920

Zulli, D., Liu, M., & Gehl, R. (2020). Rethinking the "social" in "social media": Insights into topology, abstraction, and scale on the Mastodon social network. *New Media & Society, 22*(7), 1188–1205. doi:10.1177/1461444820912533

Zupan, M. (2020). *Moloch DAO: a new era of collaboration.* Cryptonews.

Zyskind, G., Nathan, O., & Pentland, A. 'Sandy'. (2015). Decentralizing Privacy: Using Blockchain to Protect Personal Data. *2015 IEEE Security and Privacy Workshops.* doi:10.1109/SPW.2015.27

About the Contributors

Pooja Lekhi (Ph.D.) is a proficient professional with over nine years of experience in teaching and research within the business administration field, specializing in finance. She currently holds the positions of Vice Chair in the Department of Quantitative Studies and finance professor at University Canada West. Backed by a strong academic foundation and a comprehensive grasp of effective pedagogical and assessment methodologies, she adeptly communicates intricate technical and financial concepts with clarity. Her instructional responsibilities embrace both management and finance courses. She possesses a Ph.D. in business administration (finance) and a master's in business administration (finance) from Punjab Technical University in India. Her contributions numerous published research articles, magazine pieces, and book reviews. Moreover, she's frequently cited in various international media outlets, including Express.co.uk, capital.com, and currency.com. Her research interests span analyzing asset quality management practices in banks, evaluating banks' loan and investment portfolios, along with exploring cryptocurrencies and financial technologies.

Guneet Kaur a distinguished professional, brings a wealth of expertise from academia and industry. As the FinTech editor for Cointelegraph's Cryptopedia Section, she thrives in the blockchain, crypto, and fintech landscape, with over 5 years of experience. Presently pursuing a professional doctorate in data science at the prestigious University of Stirling, Guneet's research delves into the pressing topic of privacy concerns associated with CBDCs. Guneet's notable accomplishments include securing distinction in her MSc in Financial Technology (Fintech) from the University of Stirling, Scotland along with holding a gold medalist MBA in Finance & Marketing from Guru Nanak Dev University, India. During her tenure at an IT company, which she joined after completing MBA, Guneet not only honed her skills but also excelled as a Global Client Partner and Business Manager for the APAC region, all while securing a funded scholarship for a Singapore training trip in 2016. Additionally, Guneet has co-edited books, authored book chapters published by IGI Global. Moreover, she has also served as an assessor for blockchain courses by The Economist, and as head coach for blockchain and crypto-related courses by the Institute for Management Development, Switzerland. She is a sought-after speaker and has presented at conferences and events worldwide. Her research interests encompass digital finance, blockchain, Central Bank Digital Currencies (CBDCs), cryptocurrencies, monetary policy, and financial technologies.

* * *

Debora Dhanya A. has been working as Assistant Professor at CHRIST (Deemed to be University), Bengaluru, India. Her core area of research is in consumer behaviour, Digital and social media marketing, Online advertising consumer engagement, and online marketing. She has attended various seminars and workshops at national level and presented research papers in various national & international Conferences. She has to her credit several research papers published in refereed national & international journals.

Munir Ahmad is a Ph.D. in Computer Science with over 23 years of extensive experience in spatial data development, management, processing, visualization, and quality control. He has dedicated expertise in open data, crowdsourced data, volunteered geographic information, and spatial data infrastructure. A seasoned professional with extensive knowledge in the field, he has served as a trainer for the latest spatial technologies. With a passion for research and over 25 publications in the same field, he obtained his Ph.D. degree in Computer Science from Preston University Pakistan, in 2022. He is committed to advancing the industry and sharing knowledge through his expertise and experience. #SpatialData #GIS #GeoTech.

Asmat Ali is PhD in Remote Sensing & GIS. He is Director of Cartography and GIS at Survey of Pakistan. In, 1998 he earned Professional Master Degree in Geoinformatics with specialization in Cartography from Faculty of Geo-Information Science and Earth Observation (ITC), University of Twente, Enschede The Netherlands. Later on, he got MSc Degree in Geo-information Science and Earth Observation, with specialization in Geo-Information Management from the same university. In 2022, he got PhD degree in Remote Sensing and GIS from PMAS-Arid Agriculture University Rawalpindi, Pakistan. He has 34 years of experience in geospatial information production and management discipline as practitioner, trainer and educator. He has served on a number of operational, administrative and instructional appointments. He was in-charge of the team which started GIS mapping and digital cartography at Survey of Pakistan in 1999. His more than 25 research papers including two book chapters and articles on Spatial Data Infrastructure (SDI), GIS, Remote Sensing, E-governance, as well as Land Administration have been published in various international conferences and renowned journals. In 2008, SDI Asia-Pacific identified him as focal point for SDI development in Pakistan. GSDI in 2016, acknowledged and awarded him as SDI implementer from Pakistan. He is on the visiting faculty of Bahria University Islamabad and PMAS- Arid Agriculture University Rawalpindi, Pakistan.

Senthil Kumar Arumugam is an Associate Professor of the Professional Studies department, CHRIST (Deemed to be University), Bangalore. His areas of specialisation are Accounting, Human Resource Management, E-Commerce, and Finance. He secured a PhD degree in Commerce from Bharathiar University, India, in 2014. He also qualified for UGC-NET in 2012. He completed his M.Phil in Commerce from Madurai Kamaraj University in 2003 and his M.Phil in Computer Science from Periyar University in 2007. He has 23 years of teaching, research, and admin experience in the Commerce and Computer Application fields. He is the author of 60 research articles, including one edited book and six book chapters. He is an Executive editorial member in six peer-reviewed journals. He has guided more than 100 students' research projects in UG/PG/M.Phil Programmes and currently guiding four PhD research scholars.

Margherita Bandirali is a jurist with an international background. After completing a five-year degree with a focus on civil law at the University of Parma, she moved to Germany to study German law at the University of Goettingen as part of the Magister Juris program, designed for foreign students. She later completed an international apprenticeship as a lawyer and successfully passed her bar exam in Bologna. Subsequently, she relocated to Switzerland to delve deeply into Swiss Law, attending several courses at the University of Insubria. She specializes in blockchain law and works at Lexify SA in Lugano, supporting blockchain projects as a legal consultant. She is also a PhD student at the University of Freiburg, studying Comparative Law. Driven by her interest in blockchain from an associative standpoint, she became a member of DAO Suisse.

Eleonóra Bassi earned her Ph.D. in Sociology from the Budapest Corvinus University, focusing her university research on the relationship between education and the labor market. She delved deeper into applied research through a project centered on youth community organization, which sparked her interest in DAOs. As a senior analyst at a public research firm, she also gained insights into multiple business sectors. Currently, she serves as a researcher at the Zurich University of Applied Sciences, with a primary focus on the societal impacts of Web 3, especially its influence on organizations. An active member and mentor in several Web 3-related professional bodies, she is also a founding member of DAO Suisse.

Szu Tung Chen is a highly motivated professional with extensive international academic and working experiences across Europe and Taiwan. Currently pursuing her master's degree in sustainable business development, she has developed a strong passion for blockchain technology and its potential to drive innovation and empower local enterprises and NGOs. Holding certification as a blockchain specialist from the European Tech School, SzuTung actively contributes to the field through the development of educational content and the provision of valuable insights into the transformative capabilities of blockchain. Her ongoing research focuses on the social impact of blockchain in the Colombian coffee supply chain, aiming to enhance social and economic sustainability while integrating ReFi/DeFi protocols to provide additional income and environmental benefits.

Azadeh Eskandarzadeh has two notable Master's degrees that have significantly influenced her level of competence and perspective. Her scholastic trajectory demonstrates a steadfast pursuit of greatness and a resolute determination to comprehend the intricacies inherent in the contemporary global landscape. She acquired her first MBA with a project management specialization to traverse the ever-changing project execution environment. She also has an MSc in Global Technology. This programme opened her eyes to the complex relationship between technology, society, and culture worldwide.

Pratibha Giri is working as Associate Professor in School of Business and Management at Christ(Deemed to be University),Delhi-NCR. She is having more than 13 years of experience in academics. She has obtained her MBA degree from Faculty of Management Studies, BHU, Varanasi. She has also qualified UGCNET. She holds a doctorate in the area of International Business. She has attended various seminars and workshops at national level and presented research papers in various national & international Conferences. She has to her credit more than 18 research papers published in refereed national & international journals and her research articles are spanning over various streams of Management ranging from Marketing, Human Resources, Entrepreneurship to International Trade.

Babita Jha is an Associate Professor at Christ (Deemed to be University), Delhi NCR. She has 15+ years of teaching experience in the field of Finance and Accounting. She has worked with institutes like Jaipuria Institute of Management, Jaipur, TAPMI School of Business, Manipal University, Centurion Institute of Professional Studies etc. In her previous organization, Dr Babita Jha was awarded with the 'Best Faculty Award' for the two consecutive years. She has done her Doctorate in the area of Finance from University of Rajasthan, Jaipur. She believes in constant learning. She has published several research papers in the area of Finance and Banking in the reputed journals including ABDC, Scopus and Web of Science indexed Journals. She has participated and presented her papers in different International and National Conferences. She is an active member of the Institute of Global Professionals. She has taken international sessions related to Finance and Accounting. Dr Jha has conducted several corporate training and has taken several MDPs at national and International level including MDPs conducted for the Bhutanese executive (Finance for Non Finance Executives).

Deepak Jha is an Assistant Professor in the School of Business and Management at Christ (Deemed to be University),Delhi,NCR. He is having more than 20 years of experience in corporate and academics. He has attended various seminars and workshops at national level and presented research papers in various national & international Conferences. He has to his credit several research papers published in refereed national & international journals and his research articles are spanning over various streams of Management.

Przemysław Kępczyński, LLM, is a graduate of the Łódź University of Technology, specializing in software engineering, where he researched stock price forecasting using artificial neural networks. Furthering his academic pursuits, he completed postgraduate studies at the Warsaw School of Economics, where he wrote his thesis on the valuation of capital companies using exotic options. Kępczyński began his professional journey in investment finance, playing a key role in the formation of the trading department at XTB. He later contributed to the establishment of the Alior Trader and efx platforms at Alior Bank. In 2013, he pivoted to the rapidly evolving blockchain industry, collaborating with investors on projects related to cryptocurrency exchanges and token issuance. A significant aspect of Kępczyński's research concentrates on the intricate interplay between game theory and consensus mechanisms in decentralized protocols and organizations, particularly DAOs (Decentralized Autonomous Organizations). Through this, he explores how game-theoretical models can be leveraged to ensure honesty, fairness, and efficiency in decentralized systems, ensuring that participants act in the best interests of the network. Such studies are pivotal in understanding the sustainability and security of emerging decentralized structures, as they operate based on mutual trust and collaboration among anonymous entities. Besides this, Kępczyński is the esteemed author of a publication that delves into the application of game theory in mediation, published by the Institute of Justice. His current academic venture involves comprehensive research for his doctoral thesis, focusing on the legal implications and status of smart contracts in Polish private law.

Risha Khandelwal has expertise in finance and global business as an academician and researcher. She has been teaching and conducting research for more than six years. She has held positions at JECRC University in Jaipur and GL A University in Mathura. She received the UGC fellowship after passing the NET-JRF. She has written case studies, book chapters, and research papers that have been indexed by Google Scholar and SCOPUS. She is proficient in utilising econometrics to analyse secondary data. She is currently a freelancer, helping academics with their research projects.

Ratnakar Mann is a passionate educator and researcher with over 10 + years of teaching experience in Department of Computer Science & IT, LKC and intending to create positive impact and contribute meaningfully to world of academia.

Aneta Napieralska stands as a beacon in the legal realm, especially in financial law and the intricacies of emerging technologies. A proud alumnus of the renowned Jagiellonian University, she not only earned her law degree but also delved deep into a dissertation topic that explored the "Private Foundation as an Alternative to Polish Inheritance Law." Since 2017, the world of blockchain has been privileged to have her expertise. Napieralska has been at the forefront of investment projects, significantly in real estate tokenization and ICO token issuance. Her collaboration with Swiss legal firms has expanded her horizons, offering her invaluable experience in investment projects, AML procedures, and addressing cryptocurrency thefts. While many know her as an advocate and an industry expert, she's also a distinguished author. One of her notable contributions is a publication on cross-border mediation for the Ministry of Justice in Poland, shedding light on economic matters surrounding new technologies. Currently on her journey towards a doctorate, Napieralska's academic pursuits focus on investment agreements in the burgeoning blockchain sector. Her research delves deep into tokenization, financial instruments, and the intersections of intellectual property rights in new technologies and AI. An active voice in the fintech conversation, she has graced numerous industry conferences, leaving an indelible mark with her insights.

Alexandra Overgaag is the founder and CEO of Thrilld Labs, a Web2.5 company that has built a free and open-access business solution for Web3 projects, professional investors, developers, and Web3 service providers. She also is an independent researcher, has written for the Cointelegraph, provides open-access workshops, and is a mentor to various educational Web3 initiatives. She also is a regular speaker at industry conferences. Alexandra obtained a law degree from the University of Amsterdam (Hons.), holds a dual Master's in International Relations and European Studies from the Unversity of Florence (summa cum laude) and has a Master in Politics and Digital Technologies from the LUISS Guido Carli University in Rome, for which she received a full scholarship. Prior to joining Web3, Alexandra worked as an entrepreneur in the hospitality sector in the Netherlands and Italy alongside her studies.

Lisa-Marie Ross is a full time Researcher at the Centre for Asian Legal Studies (CALS) at the National University of Singapore, Faculty of Law. She received her first law degree from the University of Kiel specializing in Banking and Finance Law and her Master of Laws degree in International and Comparative Law from the National University of Singapore. Lisa's research interests are comparative studies between Asia and Europe with a focus on comparative commercial law, as well as comparative international law. Currently, she is working on projects on crypto assets regulation, international commercial arbitration, and climate change litigation. Lisa is a regular speaker at international academic and industry conferences and has published her research in leading international and local journals and books. Further, she is contributing to the Digital Euro Association and the International Token Standardization Association as an expert and working group member. Prior to joining CALS, Lisa worked for six years as a Research Associate at the Goethe-University Frankfurt. Furthermore, Lisa is a trained banker and has worked in several banking and lecturing positions. Therefore, she is particularly interested in responses to legal challenges resulting from the transformation of financial markets by the fast-moving digital ledger technology.

S M Nazmuz Sakib was born in Dinajpur, Bangladesh on the 16th of April in 2001. He achieved his Primary School Certificate (PSC) from Cotton Research Station School, Sreepur, Gazipur and after several months of studying Class 6 in Alhaz Dhanai Bepari Memorial High School, Sreepur, Gazipur, he relocated to Jashore. He accomplished his Junior School Certificate (JSC) from Jagodishpur Mirzapur Ismail Secondary School, Jagodishour, Chaowgacha, Jashore and his Secondary School Certificate (SSC) from A. K. High School And College, Dhania, Dhaka-1236. He obtained his Higher Secondary Certificate (HSC) from Chowgacha Government College, Chowgacha, Jashore. He received a BSc in Business Studies, earning a CGPA of 4 out of 4 (1st class 1st) with 97.06% marks from School of Business and Trade, an online business school situated in Switzerland. He completed an MBA in Human Resources from International MBA Institute, an online business institute in Switzerland. He studied Bachelor of Laws (Hon's) or LLB(Hon's) at Dhaka International University, Dhaka, Bangladesh. He has accomplished CPD verified advanced diploma and diploma programs i.e. Advanced Diploma in Tissue Engineering, Advanced Diploma in Genetic Engineering - Theory and Application, Diploma in Fashion Design, Diploma in Nutrition, Therapeutics and Health, Diploma in Biology, Diploma in Pharmacy Technician, Software Test Engineer Diploma (Advanced), Advanced Diploma in Soil Science and Technology, Diploma in Energy Economics, Energy Systems and Environmental Impact, Advanced Diploma in Political Ideologies, Diploma in Community Psychology, Diploma in Training of Trainers, Advance Diploma in Principles of Industrial Engineering, Advanced Diploma in Production & Operation Management, Advanced Diploma in Modelling and Analytics for Supply Chain Management, Business Administration Diploma (Foundation), Diploma in Effective Human Resource Administration, Diploma in Audio System Engineering, Diploma in ISO Standards - Integrated Management System (IMS), Diploma in Lean Manufacturing - Productive Management with Fundamental Tools, Advanced Diploma in Tourism and Hospitality Management, Diploma in Web Design, Diploma in Human Resources, and Diploma in Basic English Grammar, Diploma in River Engineering and has obtained certifications such as TESOL from Arizona State University, TEFL from Teacher Record, Scrum Master Professional Certificate (SMPC®), EF SET Certificate (C2 Level), Google IT Support Professional Certificate, Google Data Analytics Professional Certificate, Google Project Management Professional Certificate, Google Business Intelligence Professional Certificate, Google Digital Marketing & E-commerce Professional Certificate and IBM New Collar: Customer Engagement Specialist credential etc. As a multidisciplinary researcher, he has published several articles in the Asian Pacific Journal of Environment and Cancer, Simulacra, Journal of Innovation Information Technology and Application (JINITA), Waste Technology, and The IUP Journal of Electrical and Electronics Engineering. Several of his articles are published by Cambridge Open Engage, a publication of Cambridge University Press. Some of the titles of his published research works include "The Impact of Oil and Gas Development on the Landscape and Surface in Nigeria," "Assessing the Impact of Arctic Melting in the Predominantly Multilateral World System," "LiDAR Technology - An Overview," "Exploring the Intersection of Software Engineering and Mobile Technology from 2010 to 2021: A Review of Recent Research" "Comparing the sociology of culture in Bangladesh and India: Similarities and differences in Bangladeshi and Indian cultures" "Electrochemical Waste Water Treatment.". Published chapters i.e. "Chapter 3: Artificial Intelligence Model for Analyzing the Buying Patterns of Customers" and "Chapter 11: Restaurant Sales Prediction Using Machine Learning" of the book titled "Handbook of Research on AI and Machine Learning Applications in Customer Support and Analytics", "Chapter 15: The Role of Innovation in Driving the Bioeconomy: The Challenges and Opportunities (pages 288-311)" of the book, "Handbook of Research on Bioeconomy and Economic Ecosystems". Authored a chapter in the book "Advancement in Business

Analytics Tools for Higher Financial Performance" also. The concept of Sakibphobia is invented by him and several researches are ongoing on this topic. In a last research works published by more than 100 scientists were "S M Nazmuz Sakibs Toxic Comparative Theorys Psychiatrys Perspectives on the Sociological Analysis of Sakibphobia using Structural Functionalism, Symbolic Interactionism, and Conflict Perspective" and "S M Nazmuz Sakibs Toxic Comparative Theory, Sakibphobia with Structural Functionalism, Symbolic Interactionism, and Conflict Perspective, A Sociological Analysis". There are many researches are ongoing in this topic. According to various sources, Sakibphobia is a term coined by S M Nazmuz Sakib, a Bangladeshi researcher and author, to describe the phenomenon of fear, hatred, or discrimination towards those who are perceived as being more successful or accomplished than oneself. Sakibphobia is based on Sakib's toxic comparative theory (TCT), which suggests that individuals may develop negative emotions and behaviors when they compare themselves unfavorably with others who have achieved higher levels of success in various domains of life, such as education, career, wealth, fame, or social status. According to Sakib, Sakibphobia can manifest in various ways, such as envy, jealousy, resentment, anger, hostility, insecurity, inferiority, anxiety, depression, or isolation. Sakibphobia can also lead to irrational or harmful actions, such as sabotage, slander, violence, discrimination, or self-harm. Sakib argues that Sakibphobia is a widespread and serious problem that affects individuals and society at large. He claims that Sakibphobia can undermine personal well-being, interpersonal relationships, social harmony, and global peace. Sakibphobia is a novel concept that has attracted attention from various fields of study, such as psychology, sociology, economics, politics, education, media, etc. Sakib's toxic comparative theory has been applied to analyze various phenomena and issues related to social comparison and inequality in different contexts. Sakibphobia is a concept that has sparked debate and discussion among various stakeholders and audiences. It has raised awareness and interest about the phenomenon of social comparison and its consequences for individuals and society. It has also challenged and provoked people to rethink their views and values about success and happiness. Whether one agrees or disagrees with Sakibphobia, it is undeniable that it is a concept that deserves attention and exploration. Environmental Scientist, S M Nazmuz Sakib's hypotheses and theories on environmental science and climate studies are highly used and reused in latest papers.

Kalyani Satone is a distinguished educator, researcher, and software expert, whose journey in the realm of Computer Science and Engineering has been nothing short of remarkable. With a Bachelor's (B.E.) and Master's (M.E.) degree in Computer Science and Engineering from Govt. Engineering College Amravati, she laid the foundation for a flourishing career filled with accomplishments and contributions to the field. Currently pursuing her Ph.D. from Amravati University, Kalyani's insatiable thirst for knowledge and passion for innovation continue to drive her forward. Her academic journey has been one of relentless pursuit, and she has been recognized for her exceptional academic achievements and dedication to her craft.

Airi Helen Schnauder is an economic lawyer with 15 years of expertise in pharma, banking, intellectual property, data protection, IT security, as well as extensive knowledge of the token economy, smart contracts and blockchain technology. She has published on intellectual property rights and smart contracts. With the rise of technology and data-driven economies, she broadened her focus to encompass data protection and cybersecurity matters. Interested in the intersection between innovation and regulation she has gained proficiency in compliance matters in harmony with evolving legal frameworks.

Sasha Shilina is a Ph.D. graduate from Lomonosov Moscow State University interested in all practices rooted in modern science, technology, culture, and the synergetic relationship between them. She is the Managing Partner and Chief Research Officer of Paradigm Research Institute, a Researcher at Humanode crypto-biometric blockchain network, a distributed technology analyst with 5+ years of experience, a creator of the 'Defi in Ether' info platform, and an Ethereum Foundation scholar.

Shailey Singh is a dynamic force in the realm of web 3 marketing, content, and growth strategy. With a decade of experience spanning across web 3, healthcare, education, and lifestyle sectors, she stands as an expert at the intersection of innovative technology and compelling storytelling. Shailey has actively worked in strategic roles with various web 3 and NFT projects - content director for Fancy Studios (GameFi), head of growth & content BUK technology (tokenized bookings), CCO at NFT marketplace & web 3 launchpad, consultant for stealth blockchain and Gen AI projects, and has authored numerous articles and research publications. Her marketing acumen, creative flair, and commitment to authentic communication makes her an invaluable asset in the ever-evolving landscape of web 3. Shailey obtained her MBA in marketing and international business from SIU, India and further pursued executive education in digital marketing from IIT-Bombay. As a seasoned professional with extensive knowledge in the field, she also serves as guest professor for India's top-ranked B-schools and media & communications colleges. Her dedication paves way to pushing the limits, reshaping conventions, and carving the path for brands to flourish in the constantly evolving virtual and technology terrain.

Jaspal Singh is a Chartered Professional Accountant with a Master of Science in Finance degree from Simon Fraser University. He has been working simultaneously in public practice and academia for the past nine years. Since 2020, Jaspal has held the position of Assistant Professor at University Canada West. Jaspal's teaching and research focus has been in the accounting and finance fields. However, he also holds adult teaching qualifications and has been heavily involved in workshop, course, and graduate program development. He has also worked with other educators to help them achieve better active learning outcomes.

Himanshu Sisodia is a dynamic and results-driven marketing professional, recognized for his expertise in digital strategy, SEO consultancy, and Web 3 research. With an unwavering commitment to fostering organic growth and amplifying online prominence for diverse businesses, Himanshu stands as a true trailblazer in the realm of digital marketing. Armed with an MBA from the esteemed University of Stirling in the United Kingdom, Himanshu laid the cornerstone for a thriving career in Digital Marketing. Currently embarking on a remarkable Doctorate journey, Himanshu is pursuing his Doctorate degree from SSBM Geneva. His focus centres on pioneering research within the fascinating realm of Metaverse Marketing Frameworks. As an ardent researcher, he delves into the intricate art of tracking digital footprints, an essential endeavour to empower brands in crafting compelling customer engagement experiences within the Metaverse. His journey exemplifies a commitment to pushing boundaries, redefining norms, and illuminating the path for brands to thrive in the ever-evolving digital landscape.

Tanuj Surve stands at the forefront of blockchain innovation, merging his deep expertise in research and product management to drive transformative solutions in the digital space. With a keen focus on creating products that connect producers and consumers, he has consistently demonstrated success in developing and scaling blockchain-based applications. A true believer in thinking big yet executing diligently, Tanuj's iterative approach to product development is grounded in meticulous research and data-driven insights. His prowess in competitive strategy and real-time user experiences sets him apart, making him a sought-after voice in intelligent UX design within the blockchain domain. Beyond technical expertise, Tanuj champions a collaborative ethos, understanding that the synergy of diverse minds leads to unparalleled problem-solving. His commitment to empathy research, design thinking, and visionary storytelling not only informs his investment choices but also ensures a lasting and loyal customer base. As the blockchain landscape continues to evolve, Tanuj remains dedicated to exploring its vast potential and fostering connections that drive global impact..

Amit Kumar Tyagi is working as Assistant Professor, at National Institute of Fashion Technology, 110016, New Delhi, India. Previously he has worked as Assistant Professor (Senior Grade 2), and Senior Researcher at Vellore Institute of Technology (VIT), Chennai Campus, 600127, Chennai, Tamilandu, India for the period of 2019-2022. He received his Ph.D. Degree (Full-Time) in 2018 from Pondicherry Central University, 605014, Puducherry, India. About his academic experience, he joined the Lord Krishna College of Engineering, Ghaziabad (LKCE) for the periods of 2009-2010, and 2012-2013. He was an Assistant Professor and Head- Research, Lingaya's Vidyapeeth (formerly known as Lingaya's University), Faridabad, Haryana, India for the period of 2018-2019. His supervision experience includes more than 10 Masters' dissertations and one PhD thesis. He has contributed to several projects such as "AARIN" and "P3- Block" to address some of the open issues related to the privacy breaches in Vehicular Applications (such as Parking) and Medical Cyber Physical Systems (MCPS). He has published over 100 papers in refereed high impact journals, conferences and books, and some of his articles awarded best paper awards. Also, he has filed more than 20 patents (Nationally and Internationally) in the area of Deep Learning, Internet of Things, Cyber Physical Systems and Computer Vision. He has edited more than 20 books for IET, Elsevier, Springer, CRC Press, etc. Also, he has authored 3 Books on Internet of Things, Intelligent Transportation Systems, Vehicular Ad-hoc Network with BPB Publication, Springer and IET publisher. He is a Winner of Faculty Research Award for the Year of 2020, 2021 and 2022 (consecutive three years) given by Vellore Institute of Technology, Chennai, India. Recently, he has been awarded the best paper award for a paper titled "A Novel Feature Extractor Based on the Modified Approach of Histogram of Oriented Gradient", in ICCSA 2020, Italy (Europe). His current research focuses on Next Generation Machine Based Communications, Blockchain Technology, Smart and Secure Computing and Privacy. He is a regular member of the ACM, IEEE, MIRLabs, Ramanujan Mathematical Society, Cryptology Research Society, and Universal Scientific Education and Research Network, CSI and ISTE.

Index

A

Accounting 290, 375, 440-452

Agreement 7, 107, 118, 133-134, 141, 144, 147, 290, 354, 449, 457

AI 104-105, 115, 155, 214, 251, 284, 307, 318-319, 333, 365, 385, 388, 390, 402-405, 435, 511-512, 515, 518-521

Algorithms 4, 27-28, 47, 49, 52-55, 57, 59-61, 63, 81, 104-105, 116, 160, 167, 177, 180, 214, 253, 263, 279, 291, 301, 318, 333, 407, 432, 481, 497

Anonymity 47-49, 57, 61, 109, 201, 261, 356, 364, 496, 499-500, 506, 514

Anti-Money Laundering (AML) 132, 464, 500

Art 5, 12, 18, 24, 26, 64-66, 79-81, 84-85, 101, 111, 122, 162, 203-204, 208, 211-212, 217, 223-224, 229-230, 242-243, 401, 408

Artwork 12, 25, 66, 204, 207-208, 217, 224-225, 228

Asymmetric Encryption 61, 63

Augmented Reality 17, 65, 198-201, 207, 213, 217, 223, 257-258, 261, 271-272, 274, 276-277, 318, 407, 410

Authentication 51, 54-57, 59, 61, 63, 225, 230-231, 294, 331, 346, 356, 359, 363, 422, 428-429, 432, 434, 464

Avatar 232

B

Bitcoin 9-12, 17, 48, 54-56, 64-66, 72-74, 76-77, 95, 110, 132, 178, 185-186, 222, 294, 296-297, 299, 318-319, 330, 456, 481, 497

Blockchain Governance 488

Blockchain Technology 1, 3, 5-10, 14-19, 23-24, 26-30, 34, 47-53, 55, 57-61, 63-64, 78-79, 91-92, 94, 99-100, 104, 109, 117, 119, 131-133, 136-139, 141, 143-144, 149, 158, 161-162, 165-167, 173, 177-178, 180, 183-184, 189, 207-208, 216-217, 222-226, 228-229, 231, 234-236, 239-240, 245,

254, 273, 278, 290, 293, 298, 301, 319, 330, 333, 358, 364-366, 374, 376-381, 384, 386-389, 391-392, 394, 400-402, 405, 407, 410-411, 418-421, 430-431, 442, 448-450, 457, 465, 467-468, 474, 476, 481-483, 488, 511, 513, 515, 520-521

C

CBDCs 456-465, 467-470, 485

Censorship Resistance 109, 172, 178, 189

Central Bank Digital Currencies 456-458, 469

Coffee 374-394, 446

Collective Action 117-120, 122, 144-145, 157, 480

Consensus Mechanism 107, 116, 132, 241, 294, 297-298, 300

Contract Enforcement 56-57, 63

Conventional Finance 33, 36

Cooperatives 112, 116-117, 120-123, 137, 378, 383, 390

Cross-Border 11, 27-28, 165, 457, 464-465, 467-468, 499, 501, 503-504

Cryptocurrency 7, 28-30, 41, 48, 55-56, 64-68, 71-75, 77, 83-85, 95, 98-99, 111, 137, 140, 163, 180, 183-185, 187-188, 295-298, 475-476, 485-486, 488, 513

Cryptography 48-61, 63, 109, 293, 318, 346, 359, 420

Customer Experience 76, 82, 431

D

DAOs 1, 7, 15-16, 18-19, 91, 95, 100-102, 105, 108-124, 130-131, 137-149, 155-167, 179, 181-182, 513-514

Decentraland 16, 65, 199, 204, 208, 254, 257, 412, 513

Decentralized Governance 11-12, 16, 18-19, 42, 91-96, 99-100, 102-105, 107-108, 110, 143, 166-167

Decentralized Social Networks 101, 172-173, 175, 177-180, 187-189

Decentralized web 3, 23, 34, 331, 418, 465, 468, 511, 513, 516-517, 520

Recommended Reference Books

IGI Global's reference books are available in three unique pricing formats:
Print Only, E-Book Only, or Print + E-Book.

Order direct through IGI Global's Online Bookstore at
www.igi-global.com or through your preferred provider.

Premier Reference Source

Biomedical and Business Applications Using Artificial Neural Networks and Machine Learning

ISBN: 9781799884552
EISBN: 9781799884576
© 2022; 394 pp.
List Price: US$ 270

Premier Reference Source

Advances in Deep Learning Applications for Smart Cities

ISBN: 9781799897101
EISBN: 9781799897125
© 2022; 335 pp.
List Price: US$ 250

Premier Reference Source

3D Modeling Using Autodesk 3ds Max With Rendering View

ISBN: 9781668441398
EISBN: 9781668441411
© 2022; 291 pp.
List Price: US$ 270

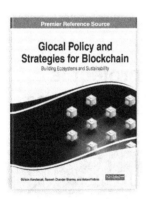

Premier Reference Source

Glocal Policy and Strategies for Blockchain
Building Ecosystems and Sustainability

ISBN: 9781668441534
EISBN: 9781668441558
© 2023; 335 pp.
List Price: US$ 270

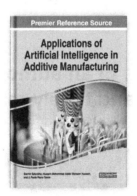

Premier Reference Source

Applications of Artificial Intelligence in Additive Manufacturing

ISBN: 9781799885160
EISBN: 9781799885184
© 2022; 240 pp.
List Price: US$ 270

Premier Reference Source

Unmanned Aerial Vehicles and Multidisciplinary Applications Using AI Techniques

ISBN: 9781799887638
EISBN: 9781799887652
© 2022; 306 pp.
List Price: US$ 270

Do you want to stay current on the latest research trends, product announcements, news, and special offers?
Join IGI Global's mailing list to receive customized recommendations, exclusive discounts, and more.
Sign up at: **www.igi-global.com/newsletters**.

Publisher of Timely, Peer-Reviewed Inclusive Research Since 1988

www.igi-global.com   Sign up at www.igi-global.com/newsletters   facebook.com/igiglobal   twitter.com/igiglobal   linkedin.com/igiglobal

Ensure Quality Research is Introduced to the Academic Community

Become an Evaluator for IGI Global Authored Book Projects

Premier Reference Source

Tax Audit and Taxation in the Paradigm of Sustainable Development

Premier Reference Source

Controlling Epidemics With Mathematical and Machine Learning Models

Premier Reference Source

School-Museum Relationships and Teaching Social Sciences in Formal Education

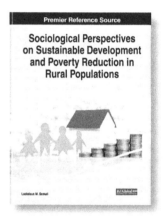
Premier Reference Source

Sociological Perspectives on Sustainable Development and Poverty Reduction in Rural Populations

The overall success of an authored book project is dependent on quality and timely manuscript evaluations.

Applications and Inquiries may be sent to:
development@igi-global.com

Applicants must have a doctorate (or equivalent degree) as well as publishing, research, and reviewing experience. Authored Book Evaluators are appointed for one-year terms and are expected to complete at least three evaluations per term. Upon successful completion of this term, evaluators can be considered for an additional term.

If you have a colleague that may be interested in this opportunity, we encourage you to share this information with them.

Easily Identify, Acquire, and Utilize Published
Peer-Reviewed Findings in Support of Your Current Research

IGI Global OnDemand

Purchase Individual IGI Global OnDemand Book Chapters and Journal Articles

For More Information:

www.igi-global.com/e-resources/ondemand/

Browse through 150,000+ Articles and Chapters!

Find specific research related to your current studies and projects that have been contributed by international researchers from prestigious institutions, including:

- Accurate and Advanced Search

- Affordably Acquire Research

- Instantly Access Your Content

- Benefit from the InfoSci Platform Features

It really provides **an excellent entry into the research literature of the field.** *It presents a manageable number of* **highly relevant sources** *on topics of interest to a wide range of researchers. The sources are* **scholarly, but also accessible** *to 'practitioners'.*

- Ms. Lisa Stimatz, MLS, University of North Carolina at Chapel Hill, USA

Interested in Additional Savings?

Subscribe to

IGI Global OnDemand *Plus*

Learn More

Acquire content from over 128,000+ research-focused book chapters and 33,000+ scholarly journal articles for as low as US$ 5 per article/chapter (original retail price for an article/chapter: US$ 37.50).

7,300+ E-BOOKS.
ADVANCED RESEARCH.
INCLUSIVE & AFFORDABLE.

IGI Global
PUBLISHER of TIMELY KNOWLEDGE

IGI Global e-Book Collection

- **Flexible Purchasing Options** (Perpetual, Subscription, EBA, etc.)
- Multi-Year Agreements with **No Price Increases** Guaranteed
- **No Additional Charge** for Multi-User Licensing
- No Maintenance, Hosting, or Archiving Fees
- Continually Enhanced & Innovated **Accessibility Compliance Features** (WCAG)

Handbook of Research on Digital Transformation, Industry Use Cases, and the Impact of Disruptive Technologies
ISBN: 9781799877127
EISBN: 9781799877141

Handbook of Research on New Investigations in Artificial Life, AI, and Machine Learning
ISBN: 9781799886860
EISBN: 9781799886877

Handbook of Research on Future of Work and Education
ISBN: 9781799882756
EISBN: 9781799882770

Research Anthology on Physical and Intellectual Disabilities in an Inclusive Society (4 Vols.)
ISBN: 9781668435427
EISBN: 9781668435434

Innovative Economic, Social, and Environmental Practices for Progressing Future Sustainability
ISBN: 9781799895909
EISBN: 9781799895923

Applied Guide for Event Study Research in Supply Chain Management
ISBN: 9781799889694
EISBN: 9781799889717

Mental Health and Wellness in Healthcare Workers
ISBN: 9781799888130
EISBN: 9781799888147

Clean Technologies and Sustainable Development in Civil Engineering
ISBN: 9781799898108
EISBN: 9781799898122

Request More Information, or Recommend the IGI Global e-Book Collection to Your Institution's Librarian

For More Information or to Request a Free Trial, Contact IGI Global's e-Collections Team: eresources@igi-global.com | 1-866-342-6657 ext. 100 | 717-533-8845 ext. 100

Are You Ready to
Publish Your Research

IGI Global PUBLISHER of TIMELY KNOWLEDGE

IGI Global offers book authorship and editorship opportunities across 11 subject areas, including business, computer science, education, science and engineering, social sciences, and more!

Benefits of Publishing with IGI Global:

- Free one-on-one editorial and promotional support.

- Expedited publishing timelines that can take your book from start to finish in less than one (1) year.

- Choose from a variety of formats, including Edited and Authored References, Handbooks of Research, Encyclopedias, and Research Insights.

- Utilize IGI Global's eEditorial Discovery® submission system in support of conducting the submission and double-blind peer review process.

- IGI Global maintains a strict adherence to ethical practices due in part to our full membership with the Committee on Publication Ethics (COPE).

- Indexing potential in prestigious indices such as Scopus®, Web of Science™, PsycINFO®, and ERIC – Education Resources Information Center.

- Ability to connect your ORCID iD to your IGI Global publications.

- Earn honorariums and royalties on your full book publications as well as complimentary content and exclusive discounts.

Join Your Colleagues from Prestigious Institutions, Including:

Australian National University

MIT — Massachusetts Institute of Technology

JOHNS HOPKINS UNIVERSITY

HARVARD UNIVERSITY

TSINGHUA UNIVERSITY

COLUMBIA UNIVERSITY IN THE CITY OF NEW YORK

Learn More at: www.igi-global.com/publish

or Contact IGI Global's Aquisitions Team at: acquisition@igi-global.com

Individual Article & Chapter Downloads
US$ 29.50/each

Easily Identify, Acquire, and Utilize Published Peer-Reviewed Findings in Support of Your Current Research

- Browse Over *170,000+ Articles & Chapters*

- *Accurate & Advanced* Search

- Affordably Acquire *International Research*

- *Instantly Access* Your Content

- Benefit from the *InfoSci® Platform Features*

THE UNIVERSITY
of NORTH CAROLINA
at CHAPEL HILL

" *It really provides* **an excellent entry into the research literature of the field.** *It presents a manageable number of* **highly relevant sources** *on topics of interest to a wide range of researchers. The sources are* **scholarly, but also accessible** *to 'practitioners'.* "

- Ms. Lisa Stimatz, MLS, University of North Carolina at Chapel Hill, USA

Interested in Additional Savings?

Subscribe to

IGI Global OnDemand *Plus*

Learn More

Acquire content from over 137,000+ research-focused book chapters and 33,000+ scholarly journal articles for as low as US$ 5 per article/chapter (original retail price for an article/chapter: US$ 29.50).

IGI Global Proudly Partners with

International

Editorial Services

Providing you with High-Quality, Affordable, and Expeditious
Editorial Support from Manuscript Development to Publication

Copy Editing & Proofreading

Perfect your research paper before publication.
Our expert editors will correct faulty spelling,
grammar, punctuation, and word usage.

Scientific & Scholarly Editing

Increase your chances of being published. Our
expert editors will aid in strengthening the quality
of your research before submission.

Figure, Table, Chart & Equation Conversions

Enhance the visual elements of your research. Let
our professional designers produce or correct your
figures before final submission.

Journal Recommendation

Save time and money when you rely on our
expert journal selectors to provide you with a
comprehensive journal recommendation report.

Order now to receive an automatic
10% Academic Discount on all your editorial needs.

Scan the QR Code to Learn More

Upload Your Manuscript, Select Your Desired Editorial Service, and Receive a Free Instant Quote

Email: customerservice@econtentpro.com

econtentpro.com

Printed in the United States
by Baker & Taylor Publisher Services